Adolescence

Thirteenth Edition

Adolescence

Laurence Steinberg

Temple University

ADOLESCENCE

Published by McGraw Hill LLC, 1325 Avenue of the Americas, New York, NY 10019. Copyright ©2023 by McGraw Hill LLC. All rights reserved. Printed in the United States of America. No part of this publication may be reproduced or distributed in any form or by any means, or stored in a database or retrieval system, without the prior written consent of McGraw Hill LLC, including, but not limited to, in any network or other electronic storage or transmission, or broadcast for distance learning.

Some ancillaries, including electronic and print components, may not be available to customers outside the United States.

This book is printed on acid-free paper.

1 2 3 4 5 6 7 8 9 LWI 27 26 25 24 23 22

ISBN 978-1-265-19728-5
MHID 1-265-19728-8

Cover Image: *Pollyana Ventura/Getty Images*

mheducation.com/highered

For Henry, at the beginning of life's journey.

About the Author

Laurence Steinberg

LAURENCE STEINBERG, Ph.D., is the Distinguished University Professor and Laura H. Carnell Professor of Psychology at Temple University. He graduated from Vassar College in 1974 and from Cornell University in 1977, where he received his Ph.D. in human development and family studies. He is a Fellow of the American Psychological Association, the Association for Psychological Science, and the American Academy of Arts and Sciences, and former President of the Society for Research on Adolescence and the Division of Developmental Psychology of the American Psychological Association. Dr. Steinberg has been on the editorial boards of many major journals, including *Developmental Psychology* and *Child Development,* where he served as Associate Editor. He chaired the National Academies' Committee on the Science of Adolescence and has been a frequent consultant to state and federal agencies and lawmakers on child labor, secondary education, and juvenile justice policy. His work was cited numerous times by the U.S. Supreme Court in its landmark decisions that abolished the juvenile death penalty and mandatory sentences of life without parole for juveniles.

Dr. Steinberg is one of the most highly cited scholars in the field of developmental psychology. His own research has focused on a range of topics in the study of contemporary adolescence, including parent–adolescent relationships, risk taking and decision making, mental health, adolescent brain development, school-year employment, academic achievement, and juvenile crime and justice. He has been the recipient of numerous honors, including the John P. Hill Award for Outstanding Contributions to the Study of Adolescence, given by the Society for Research on Adolescence; the Society for Adolescent Medicine's Gallagher Lectureship; and, from the American Psychological Association, the Urie Bronfenbrenner Award for Lifetime Contribution to Developmental Psychology in the Service of Science and Society, the Award for Distinguished Contributions to Research in Public Policy, and the APA Presidential Citation. In 2009, he was named as the first recipient of the Klaus J. Jacobs Research Prize for Productive Youth Development.

Dr. Steinberg also has been recognized for excellence in research and teaching by the University of California, the University of Wisconsin, and Temple University, where he was honored in 1994 as one of that university's Great Teachers. He has taught undergraduate and graduate courses in adolescence for more than 45 years and has served as the primary advisor to more than 40 graduate students, many of whom have gone on to become influential scholars in their own right in the field of adolescence. In 2013, he received the Elizabeth Hurlock Beckman Award, a national prize given to college professors who have "inspired their former students to achieve greatness."

In addition to *Adolescence,* Dr. Steinberg is the author or co-author of approximately 500 scholarly articles on growth and development during the teenage years, as well as the books *You and Your Adolescent: The Essential Guide for Ages 10-25*; *When Teenagers Work: The Psychological and Social Costs of Adolescent Employment* (with Ellen Greenberger); *Crossing Paths: How Your Child's Adolescence Triggers Your Own Crisis* (with Wendy Steinberg); *Beyond the Classroom: Why School Reform Has Failed and What Parents Need to Do* (with B. Bradford Brown and Sanford Dornbusch); *The 10 Basic Principles of Good Parenting* (which has been published in 11 languages); *Rethinking Juvenile Justice* (with Elizabeth Scott); and *Age of Opportunity: Lessons From the New Science of Adolescence.* He is co-editor of *Studying Minority Adolescents: Conceptual, Methodological, and Theoretical Issues* (with Vonnie McLoyd) and the *Handbook of Adolescent Psychology* (with Richard Lerner).

Brief Contents

About the Author   vi
A Note from the Author   xx
Preface   xxi

Introduction The Study of Adolescent Development   1

PART 1

The Fundamental Changes of Adolescence   13
  1   Biological Transitions   13
  2   Cognitive Transitions   40
  3   Social Transitions   68

PART 2

The Contexts of Adolescence   94
  4   Families   94
  5   Peer Groups   121
  6   Schools   152
  7   Work, Leisure, and Media   179

PART 3

Psychosocial Development During Adolescence   208
  8   Identity   208
  9   Autonomy   236
  10   Intimacy   262
  11   Sexuality   293
  12   Achievement   322
  13   Psychosocial Problems in Adolescence   348

 McGraw Hill Education Psychology's APA Documentation Style Guide

Glossary   G-1
References   R-1
Name Index   I-1
Subject Index   I-37

Contents

About the Author   vi
A Note from the Author   xx
Preface   xxi

Introduction
The Study of Adolescent Development   1

The Boundaries of Adolescence   2
Early, Middle, and Late Adolescence   3

A Framework for Studying Adolescent Development   4
The Fundamental Changes of Adolescence   4
The Contexts of Adolescence   5
Psychosocial Development in Adolescence   7

Theoretical Perspectives on Adolescence   8
Biosocial Theories   8
Organismic Theories   9
Learning Theories   10
Sociological Theories   10
Historical and Anthropological Perspectives   11

Stereotypes Versus Scientific Study   11

PART 1
The Fundamental Changes of Adolescence   13

Chapter 1
Biological Transitions   13

Puberty: An Overview   14
The Endocrine System   14
What Triggers Puberty?   16
How Hormones Influence Adolescent Development   16

Somatic Development   17
The Adolescent Growth Spurt   17
Sexual Maturation   19

The Timing and Tempo of Puberty   22
Variations in the Timing and Tempo of Puberty   22

Genetic and Environmental Influences on Pubertal Timing   22

The Psychological and Social Impact of Puberty   25
The Immediate Impact of Puberty   25
The Impact of Specific Pubertal Events   29
The Impact of Early or Late Maturation   30

Obesity and Eating Disorders   33
Obesity   34
Anorexia Nervosa, Bulimia, and Binge Eating Disorder   35

Chapter 2
Cognitive Transitions   40

Changes in Cognition   41
Thinking About Possibilities   41
Thinking About Abstract Concepts   42
Thinking About Thinking   42
Thinking in Multiple Dimensions   43
Adolescent Relativism   44

Theoretical Perspectives on Adolescent Thinking   44
The Piagetian View of Adolescent Thinking   44
The Information-Processing View of Adolescent Thinking   45

The Adolescent Brain   47
How Your Brain Works   48
The Age of Opportunity   50
What Changes in Adolescence?   51
Implications for Adolescent Behavior   57

Individual Differences in Intelligence in Adolescence   57
The Measurement of IQ   58
Culture and Intelligence   58

Adolescent Thinking in Context   59
Social Cognition in Adolescence   59
Adolescent Risk Taking   62

Chapter 3
Social Transitions 68

Social Redefinition and Psychosocial Development 69

The Elongation of Adolescence 70

Adolescence as a Social Invention 71

The "Invention" of Adolescence 71

Emerging Adulthood: A New Stage of Life or a Luxury of the Middle Class? 73

Changes in Status During Adolescence 76

Drawing a Legal Boundary 76

Inconsistencies in Adolescents' Legal Status 77

The Process of Social Redefinition 78

Common Practices in the Process of Social Redefinition 79

Variations in Social Transitions 80

Variations in Clarity 80

Variations in Continuity 83

The Transition into Adulthood in Contemporary Society 86

Special Transitional Problems of Poor, Minority, and Immigrant Youth 86

The Effects of Poverty on the Transition into Adulthood 87

What Can Be Done to Ease the Transition? 88

The Influence of Neighborhood Conditions on Adolescent Development 89

Processes of Neighborhood Influences 91

PART 2
The Contexts of Adolescence 94

Chapter 4
Families 94

Changes in Family Relationships at Adolescence 95

What Do Adolescents and Parents Usually Fight About? 95

The Adolescent's Parents at Midlife 98

Changes in Family Needs and Functions 99

Special Concerns of Immigrant Families 99

Transformations in Family Relations 100

Sex Differences in Family Relationships 102

Family Relationships and Adolescent Development 103

Parenting Styles and Their Effects 104

Adolescents' Relationships with Siblings 107

Genetic Influences on Adolescent Development 108

Genetic and Environmental Influences on Adolescent Development 108

Why Are Siblings Often So Different? 110

The Adolescent's Family in a Changing Society 111

Adolescents and Divorce 113

The Specific Impact of Marital Conflict 114

The Longer-Term Effects of Divorce 115

Custody, Contact, and Conflict Following Divorce 115

Remarriage 116

Economic Stress and Poverty 117

Special Family Forms 118

The Importance of the Family in Adolescent Development 120

Chapter 5
Peer Groups 121

The Origins of Adolescent Peer Groups in Contemporary Society 122

Changes in the Size of the Youth Population 122

Why Peer Groups Are Necessary in Today's World 123

The Nature of Adolescent Peer Groups 126

Cliques and Crowds 127

Changes in Clique and Crowd Structure Over Time 129

Adolescents and Their Crowds 131

The Social Map of Adolescence 131

Crowds as Reference Groups 131

Adolescents and Their Cliques 133

Similarity Among Clique Members 133

Common Interests Among Friends 135

Similarity Between Friends: Selection or Socialization? 137

Popularity, Rejection, and Bullying 139

Determinants of Popularity and Rejection 139

Relational Aggression   143

Bullies and Victims   145

Cyberbullying   149

The Peer Group and Psychosocial Development   151

**Chapter 6
Schools   152**

The Broader Context of U.S. Secondary Education   153

The Origins of Secondary Education   153

School Reform: Past and Present   154

What Should Schools Teach?   156

Education in the Inner Cities   157

The Social Organization of Schools   158

School Size and Class Size   158

Age Grouping and School Transitions   159

Tracking   161

Ethnic Composition   165

Alternatives to Public Schools   166

Classroom Climate   167

The Best Classroom Climate for Adolescents   167

Teacher Expectations and Student Performance   168

The Importance of Student Engagement   170

School Violence   173

Beyond High School   175

The College-Bound   175

The Non-College-Bound   176

Schools and Adolescent Development   177

Characteristics of Good Schools   177

The Effects of School on Adolescent Development   178

**Chapter 7
Work, Leisure, and Media   179**

Adolescents' Free Time in Contemporary Society   180

Adolescents and Work   181

The Rise and Fall of the Student Worker   181

The Adolescent Workplace Today   182

Employment and Adolescent Development   182

Adolescents and Leisure   185

Adolescents' Free Time and Their Moods   185

Structured Leisure Activities   186

Unstructured Leisure Time   188

Promoting Positive Youth Development   190

Adolescents and Screen Time   191

Theories of Media Influence and Use   195

Exposure to Controversial Media Content   196

Adolescents and Social Media   201

Social Media and Socializing   202

Problematic Social Media Use   204

Free Time and Adolescent Development   206

**PART 3
Psychosocial Development During Adolescence   208**

**Chapter 8
Identity   208**

Identity as an Adolescent Issue   209

Puberty and Identity Development   209

Cognitive Change and Identity Development   209

Social Roles and Identity Development   210

Changes in Self-Conceptions   210

Changes in the Content and Structure of Self-Conceptions   210

Dimensions of Personality in Adolescence   212

Changes in Self-Esteem   213

Stability and Changes in Self-Esteem   213

Group Differences in Self-Esteem   215

Antecedents and Consequences of High Self-Esteem   217

The Adolescent Identity Crisis   218

Erikson's Theoretical Framework   218

The Social Context of Identity Development   218

Problems in Identity Development   220

Research on Identity Development   221

Determining an Adolescent's Identity Status   221

Studying Identity Development Over Time   222

Identity and Ethnicity   224

The Development of Ethnic Identity   224

Discrimination and Its Effects   227

Multiethnic Adolescents   228

Identity and Gender   229

Gender-Role Development   231

Gender-Role Socialization During Adolescence   232

Masculinity and Femininity   233

Chapter 9
Autonomy   236

Autonomy as an Adolescent Issue   237

Puberty and the Development of Autonomy   238

Cognitive Change and the Development of Autonomy   238

Social Roles and the Development of Autonomy   238

The Development of Emotional Autonomy   239

Emotional Autonomy: Detachment or Individuation?   239

Research on Emotional Autonomy   240

Parenting and Emotional Autonomy   241

The Development of Behavioral Autonomy   244

Changes in Decision-Making Abilities   244

When Do Adolescents Make Decisions as Well as Adults?   245

Changes in Susceptibility to Influence   246

Ethnic and Cultural Differences in Expectations for Autonomy   249

The Development of Cognitive Autonomy   250

Moral Development During Adolescence   250

Prosocial Reasoning, Prosocial Behavior, and Volunteerism   253

Political Thinking During Adolescence   256

Religious Beliefs During Adolescence   258

Chapter 10
Intimacy   262

Intimacy as an Adolescent Issue   263

Puberty and the Development of Intimacy   263

Cognitive Change and the Development of Intimacy   264

Changes in Social Roles and the Development of Intimacy   264

Theoretical Perspectives on Adolescent Intimacy   264

Sullivan's Theory of Interpersonal Development   264

Interpersonal Development During Adolescence   265

Attachment Theory   266

The Development of Intimacy in Adolescence   269

Changes in the Nature of Friendship   269

Changes in the Display of Intimacy   270

Does Using Social Media Hurt the Development of Intimacy?   271

Sex Differences in Intimacy   272

Changes in the Targets of Intimacy   274

Friendships with the Other Sex   278

Dating and Romantic Relationships   279

Dating and the Development of Intimacy   281

The Development of Dating Relationships   283

The Impact of Dating on Adolescent Development   287

Intimacy and Psychosocial Development   291

Chapter 11
Sexuality   293

Sexuality as an Adolescent Issue   294

Puberty and Adolescent Sexuality   294

Cognitive Change and Adolescent Sexuality   294

Social Roles and Adolescent Sexuality   295

Sexual Activity During Adolescence   295

Stages of Sexual Activity   295

Sexual Intercourse During Adolescence   296

The Sexually Active Adolescent   299

Sexual Activity and Psychological Development   299

Causation or Correlation?   300

Hormonal and Contextual Influences on Sexual Activity   301

Parental and Peer Influences on Sexual Activity   302

Sex Differences in the Meaning of Sex   305

Sexual Orientation   308

Sexual Harassment, Rape, and Sexual Abuse During Adolescence   309

Risky Sex and Its Prevention   311

Adolescents' Reasons for Not Using Contraception   313

Improving Contraceptive Behavior   313

AIDS and Other Sexually Transmitted Diseases   314

Teen Pregnancy   314

Sex Education   320

Chapter 12
Achievement   322

Achievement as an Adolescent Issue   323

Puberty and Achievement   324

Cognitive Change and Achievement   324

Social Roles and Achievement   324

The Importance of Noncognitive Factors   324

Achievement Motivation   325

Beliefs About Success and Failure   326

Environmental Influences on Achievement   331

The Influence of the Home Environment   331

The Influence of Friends   334

Educational Achievement   336

The Importance of Socioeconomic Status   336

Ethnic Differences in Educational Achievement   337

Changes in Educational Achievement over Time   339

Dropping Out of High School   341

Occupational Achievement   344

The Development of Occupational Plans   344

Influences on Occupational Choices   345

Chapter 13
Psychosocial Problems in Adolescence   348

Some General Principles About Problems in Adolescence   349

Most Problems Reflect Transitory Experimentation   349

Not All Problems Begin in Adolescence   349

Most Problems Do Not Persist into Adulthood   350

Problems During Adolescence Are Not Caused by Adolescence   350

Psychosocial Problems: Their Nature and Covariation   351

Comorbidity of Externalizing Problems   351

Comorbidity of Internalizing Problems   353

Substance Use and Abuse   353

Prevalence of Substance Use and Abuse   354

Causes and Consequences of Substance Use and Abuse   358

Drugs and the Adolescent Brain   361

Prevention and Treatment of Substance Use and Abuse   363

Externalizing Problems   364

Categories of Externalizing Problems   364

Developmental Progression of Antisocial Behavior   366

Changes in Juvenile Offending over Time   367

Causes of Antisocial Behavior   370

Prevention and Treatment of Externalizing Problems   374

Internalizing Problems   375

The Nature and Prevalence of Depression   375

Sex Differences in Depression   377

Suicide and Non-Suicidal Self-Injury   378

Causes of Depression and Internalizing Disorders   381

Treatment and Prevention of Internalizing Problems   382

Stress and Coping   383

 McGraw Hill Education

Psychology's APA Documentation Style Guide

Glossary   G-1

References   R-1

Name Index   I-1

Subject Index   I-37

Guide to Diversity, Equity, and Inclusion

The Thirteenth Edition of *Adolescence* has been fully revised and updated with topics related to diversity, equity, and inclusion in mind. In addition to the chapter-specific revisions, this edition has undergone global changes, including an updated photo program to enhance diversity and inclusion. This edition also includes new citations of studies and researchers who represent diverse and international samples and topics.

Introduction: The Study of Adolescent Development

- "Making the Cultural Connection" box asking students to consider ceremonies and informal events that signify the transition to adulthood
- Adolescence in developing countries, including anthropological perspectives of adolescence in developing and developed countries
- Stereotypes about adolescents and teenagers, including cross-cultural studies related to the connection between how adolescents behave and how they are perceived, including research by Qu et al. (2020).

Chapter 1: Biological Transitions

- Geographic and environmental factors that influence puberty
- Body image and body dissatisfaction, including influences related to gender, ethnicity, and culture, citing research from BeLue, Francis, & Colaco (2009), Skinner et al. (2018), Huh et al. (2012), and Qualter et al. (2018)
- Pubertal maturation, including cross-cultural and familial trends and influences, citing research from Nagata et al. (2018)
- Sex changes resulting from prenatal hormone exposure, citing research from Sisk & Romeo (2019)
- Obesity and its prevalence in both industrialized and developing countries, citing research from Lewis-Smith et al. (2020), Neumark-Sztainer et al. (2006), and Jackson & Chen (2014)
- Eating disorders, including cross-cultural research and sociocultural factors, citing research from Bodell et al. (2018), Lee et al. (2013), and Olvera et al. (2015)

Chapter 2: Cognitive Transitions

- Brain structure and function, including similarities and differences related to sex
- Intelligence, cross-cultural contexts and environmental influences, citing research from Ramsden et al. (2011), van den Bos, Crone, & Güroğlu (2012), and others

- "Making the Cultural Connection" box asking students to consider why, globally, rates of risky adolescent behavior varies, despite the universality of adolescent brain development
- Exemplifies how school-based tests alone may not accurately reflect intelligence as it is applied in the real world, citing research from Uncapher et al. (2016), Ahmed et al. (2019), and others
- Adolescents questioning of parental authority, including research from Chen-Gaddini, Liu, & Nucci (2020), Cheah, Leung, & Özemir (2018), and Thomas et al. (2020)

Chapter 3: Social Transitions

- Adolescence, adulthood, and cross-cultural rites of passage
- Ethnic, religious, and cross-cultural processes of social redefinition
- Adolescents' views of themselves, including criterial in both developing and developed countries
- Passage to adulthood in both contemporary industrialized and traditional cultures, including cross-cultural research from Arnett & Padilla-Walker (2015), Markstrom (2011), and others
- "Making the Cultural Connection" box asking readers to consider how globalization affects adolescence across various cultures in an international society
- Updated cross cultural data from the United Nations on the international adolescent population
- Discussion of cross-cultural problems faced by poor, underrepresented, and immigrant youth, including updated information from the U.S. Census Bureau and research from Ananat et al. (2017), Motti-Stefanidi (2019), Torres et al. (2018), Stevens et al. (2020), Bayram Özdemir et al. (2018), and Miklikowska, Bohrman, & Titzmann (2019)
- Effects of poverty on adolescent development and transition to adulthood, including difficulties faced by poor rural and urban communities, including research from Brieant et al. (2020), Ellwood-Lowe et al. (2018), Coley, O'Brien & Spielvogel (2019), Uy et al. (2019)
- Subjective social status and its effects, citing Du, Chi & King (2019), Rahal et al. (2020), Rivenbark et al. (2019), Russell & Odgers (2020), and Raposa et al. (2019)
- Neighborhood conditions and their effects on adolescent development, including the effects of relocation on striving adolescents, citing Burnside & Gaylord-Harden (2019), Kan et al. (2020), Xiao, Romanelli, Vélez-Grau,

& Lindsay (2020), Orihuela et al. (2020), Wang, Choi, & Shin (2020), DaViera et al. (2020), and Evans et al. (2020)

Chapter 4: Families

- Concerns between adolescents and parents in immigrant families and across ethnic groups, citing Cruz et al. (2018), Stein et al. (2020), Motti-Stefandi (2018), Toyokawa & Toyokawa (2019), and Sun, Geeraert, & Simpson (2020)
- Ethnic differences and cross-cultural influences in parenting styles and practices, citing Anguiano (2018), De Los Reyes, Ohannessian, & Racz (2019), Hou et al. (2020), Qu, Pomerantz & Deng (2016), Luebbe, Tu, & Fredrick (2018), and Li et al. (2019)
- Family patterns and composition, including cross-cultural and ethnic trends, citing Wang-Schweig & Miller (2019), Nair, Roche, & White (2018), Yuen et al. (2018), and Van der Cruijsen et al. (2019)
- Poverty and its effect on families of adolescents, including ethnic and cross-cultural disparities, citing Fisher et al. (2015) and Maas, Bray, & Noll (2018)
- Financial strain and its effects on families and adolescents, citing Deater-Deckard et al. (2019), Herd, King-Casas, & Kim-Spoon (2020), Simons & Steele (2020), Kotchick, Whitsett, & Sherman (2020), and Di Giunta et al. (2020)
- Homelessness and its connection to ethnic and LGBTQ youth, citing data from the National Runaway Safeline (2018), Gerwitz, O'Brien et al. (2020), and Tyler, Schmitz, & Ray (2018)
- Special family forms, including adolescents raised by same-sex parents, citing Farr (2017) and McConnachie et al. (2021)

Chapter 5: Peer Groups

- Updated global population data to show changing demographics
- Anthropological approach to postfigurative, cofigurative, and prefigurative cultures, including the significance of the American cofigurative society, citing Silva et al (2016) and Van Hoorn, Van Dijk, Güroglu, & Crone (2016)
- The role of sex segregation, gender roles, and sexual identity in adolescent peer groups
- Ethnicity and adolescent membership in particular crowds, including the role of ethnicity and identity in students at multiethnic schools, citing Wölfer & Hewstone (2018), Mali et al. (2019), Kelleghan et al. (2019), and Rastogi & Juvonen (2019)
- Ethnicity and discrimination in adolescent cliques, including the role of parental discrimination and cross-ethnic friendships, citing Umaña-Taylor et al. (2020) and Motti-Stefandini, Paclopoulos, & Asendorpf (2018)

- The benefits of cross-ethnic friendships and ethnic diversity within classrooms, citing Lessard, Kogachi, & Juvonen (2019)
- Cross-ethnic differences in bullying and peer victimization, including global research from Koyanagi et al. (2019)

Chapter 6: Schools

- Global U.N. data about school enrollment around the world
- The effects of No Child Left Behind on students of different ethnic backgrounds
- "Making the Cultural Connection" box prompting students to consider the benefits and drawbacks of global prevalence of national graduation examinations and why this practice is not popular in the United States
- Racial and ethnic data related to inner-city education, including disparities in proficiency in key subjects that result from the achievement gap
- Updated data from the Centers for Disease Control and Prevention (2020) and NCES (2019 and 2020) illustrating the correlation between school violence, bullying, attendance, achievement, and job opportunities in inner-city communities
- School transitions and the challenges faced by boys, underrepresented ethnic students, and adolescents from disadvantaged families, citing Benner, Boykle, & Bakhtiari (2017), Kiuru et al. (2020), and Nelemans et al. (2018)
- The effects of school tracking on poor and underrepresented ethnic students due to discrimination
- The issues faced by neurodiverse adolescents, including ADHD, citing Murray et al. (2019) and Humphreys et al. (2019)
- The effects of ethnic diversity and desegregation in schools and classrooms, including the role of stereotypes and private schools and the experiences of students from ethnic and socioeconomic groups, citing DuPont-Reyes & Villatoro (2019) among others
- The cross-cultural issues related to how an adolescent's ethnic and socioeconomic background influences teacher expectations and behavior, and, in turn, student engagement, citing Alm et al. (2019), Burns (2020), and Engels et al. (2020), Houston, Pearman, & McGee (2020)
- Two new figures about beneficial classroom climate based on Piccolo et al. (2019) and Amemiya, Fine, & Wang (2020)
- School climate and bullying, including effects of gay-straight alliances and LGBTQ-focused policies, citing Day et al. (2020)
- Cross-cultural disparities in school victimization and violence, including the racial gap in school discipline and the disproportionate negative impact of zero-tolerance policies on Black students, which mirrors racial inequities in arrests, citing Jacobsen (2020), Rosenbaum (2020), and Wiley et al. (2020)

- Updated cross-cultural data about college enrollment, including among immigrants and racial and ethnic populations from the NCES (2019 and 2020)

Chapter 7: Work, Leisure, and Media

- Student employment trends based on socioeconomic background and the effects of working on academic achievement, citing Twenge & Park (2019), Hwang & Domina (2017), and Staff et al. (2020)
- Disparities in the negative effects of social media and texting on adolescent girls versus boys, citing Perrino et al. (2019), Lee et al. (2020), Stockdale & Coyne (2020), and Twenge & Martin (2020)

Chapter 8: Identity

- Cross-cultural differences in adolescent self-conception, comparing the United States and China as an example (Setoh et al., 2015)
- Disparities in self-esteem among adolescents of different ethnicities and socioeconomic groups, including the effects on students in schools or communities where they are members of an underrepresented ethnic group, citing White, Zeiders, & Safa (2018), Huey et al. (2020), and Krauss, Orth, & Robins (2020)
- "Making the Cultural Connection" box asking students to reflect on how political changes in the Arab world may affect adolescent identity development
- The role of ethnic identity in an adolescent's overall sense of personal identity, including the trends related to race, religion, and immigration status, citing Abo-Zena (2019), Kiang & Witkow (2018), and Chan, Kiang & Witkow (2020)
- Factors and effects related to the process of ethnic identity development in adolescents, including the benefits of strong ethnic identity and ethnic pride on mental health and academic achievement, citing Hughes, Del Toro, & Way (2017), Cross et al. (2018), Meca et al. (2019), and Spiegler, Wölfer, & Hewstone (2019)
- The effects of mainstream culture on underrepresented ethnic youth, including an awareness of racism and discrimination and a mistrust of others, citing White et al. (2018), Cross et al. (2020), and Anderson et al. (2019)
- The importance of ethnic socialization, including the role of parents in teaching children about dealing with racism, valuing one's culture, and success in the mainstream culture, citing Svensson & Shannon (2020)
- Trends and consequences of altercations between law enforcement and Black adolescents, including research identifying conversation topics between Black parents and teenagers following the shooting of Michael Brown in Ferguson, Missouri: the extent of racism in America, the special dangers faced by Black boys, the effects of violent and nonviolent protests,

and fighting discrimination by succeeding in school, citing Dunbar et al. (2017) and Threlfall (2018)
- Research about the special situation faced by underrepresented ethnic youth who are recent immigrants, foreign-born adolescents from underrepresented ethnic groups, and first-generation underrepresented ethnic youth, citing Filion, Fenelon, & Boudreaux (2018) and Svensson & Shannon (2020)
- The adverse effects of discrimination on the identity development of underrepresented adolescents, including citations and examples of Latinx, Black, immigrant, Iranian, and Native American adolescents, citing Wang & Yip (2020), Benner et al. (2018), and Del Toro, Hughes, & Way (2020)
- Discrimination's negative effects on adolescents' physiology (e.g., poor sleep, inflammatory response), mental health (e.g., substance abuse, depression), behavior, and achievement, citing Bennett et al. (2020), Zapolski et al. (2020), Martin et al. (2019), and Yip et al. (2020)
- Updated discussion of research related to the specific effects of discrimination on Black teenagers, citing Seaton & Tyson (2019)
- Updated discussion of the complicated impact of having race as a central part of one's identity, which can make adolescents more sensitive to discrimination and also make them better able to cope with it, citing Seaton & Iida (2019), Meca et al. (2020), and Thomann & Suyemoto (2017)
- Updated discussion of the particular challenges of identity faced by multiethnic youth, citing Nishina & Witkow (2020) and Rozek & Gaither (2020)
- Expanded discussion of terminology related to sex and gender, including a new figure illustrating the variability of sexual orientation among different gender identity groups based on research from Watson, Wheldon, & Puhl (2020)
- The adverse effects of discrimination and societal ignorance faced by LBGTQ youth, including potential hostility from parents, citing Mills-Koonce et al. (2018), Robinson (2018), and others
- Discussion of the prevalence of mental-health challenges among transgender adolescents, citing Paceley et al. (2020), Diamond (2020), and others
- The negative effects of stigmatization and discrimination within their communities, including excerpts from interviews with transgender youth living in a conservative, rural Midwestern community, including interview excerpts from Paceley et al. (2020)
- Updated discussion of the fluidity of gender-role behavior rather than absolute categories
- Gender-role socialization, including the role of beliefs and pressures to conform on behavior and attitudes, including a new figure based on research from Looze et al. (2018)

Chapter 9: Autonomy

- Cross-cultural discussion of the parents' role in adolescent individuation and the effects of parental support of autonomy
- Ethnic and cultural differences in expectations for autonomy, including racial trends within different countries and how immigration affects perceptions of parents and their adolescents, citing Kiang & Bhattacharjee (2019), Nalipay, King, & Cai (2020), Tran & Rafaeli (2020), Yu et al. (2019), Cheah et al. (2019), and Rogers et al. (2020), among others
- Trends in peer influence related to sex, ethnicity, immigration background, and family structure
- Differences in socioeconomic status as it relates to changes in adolescent political thinking and views of American society
- New research on the political and civil engagement of underrepresented adolescents, including excerpts of interviews from Roy et al. (2019) and the link between political engagement and victimization
- Discussion about adolescent attitudes related to social justice, race relations, and financial insecurity, including the potential effects of Black Lives Matter, COVID-19, and concerns about climate change, including citations from Sanson, Van Hoorn, & Burke (2019) and Oosterhoff et al. (2019), and a new figure based on Metzger et al. (2020)
- Cross-cultural data related to religious beliefs during adolescence, including data related to religious participation in the United States and a figure illustrating differences across countries, citing Vasilenko & Espinosa-Hernández (2019) and a new figure based on Hardy et al. (2020)
- "Making the Cultural Connection" box exploring cultural variability around the world as it relates to the role of religion in adolescents' lives
- Discussion of how religiosity and spirituality change over the course of adolescence and how religious involvement affects adolescent development, including new research from Lee & Neblett (2019) on the impact on Black youth living in urban communities of low socioeconomic status

Chapter 10: Intimacy

- Critique of Sullivan's theory of interpersonal development (1953) to address the transition from nonromantic to romantic relationships as opposed to the same-sex and other-sex relationships described by Sullivan
- Sex differences in intimacy, including greater levels of intimacy among girls than boys and the advantages and disadvantages of male and female intimacy, plus a discussion of similarities between male and female intimacy, citing Benner, Hou, & Jackson (2019), Bastin et al. (2018), and others

- Examination of the origins of sex differences in intimacy, including the effects of social pressure, trends among some ethnic groups, and discrimination against gay teenagers, citing Savickaitė et al. (2019)
- Discussion of factors related to the "sex cleavage" and friendships across sexes, including the transition to mixed-sex friendships, curiosity about sexual feelings, and the advantages and disadvantages of platonic friendships, citing Savickaitė et al. (2019), among others
- Differences in the capacity for intimacy among boys and girls during adolescence, including addressing stereotypes about sex differences in romantic relationships
- Cross-cultural nuances in how Latinx and Black adolescents approach dating and their attitudes about gendered roles in relationships
- Challenges, prejudices, and harassment faced by LGBTQ youth when freely expressing their romantic interests and sexual identity, including the increased risks of dating violence on LGBTQ youth, as illustrated in a new figure based on Költő et al. (2018)
- The adverse effects of early dating, sexual harassment, sexual coercion, and date rape on high-school girls, including updated research on the prevalence and effects of dating violence in romantic relationships, citing Cava et al., 2020, Rothman et al. (2020), and Centers for Disease Control and Prevention (2020) data, among others

Chapter 11: Sexuality

- Updated CDC research reporting ethnic differences in the age of sexual initiation, which are greater between boys than girls
- Data correlating sexual activity with immigration and socioeconomic status
- The impact of social factors that influence involvement in sexual activity, including the larger effect of social attitudes on girls than boys
- Factors and trends that lead to significant differences in how boys and girls interpret the meaning of sex, including expectations and social disapproval, including excerpts from interviews from Garceau & Ronis (2019) and a figure based on that research
- Discussion of the social and scientific history that has impacted LGBTQ individuals, with a focus on contemporary research that sexual orientation is primarily determined by hormonal and genetic factors, citing Stewart et al. (2019) and Zhang, Solazzo, & Gorman (2020).
- Updated data about the prevalence of gender fluidity and sexual orientation among adolescents and young people, including a new figure illustrating teen participation in both same-sex and other-sex activities, citing Li & Davis (2020), including a new figure based on their research

- Discussion of the importance of parental support when LGBTQ individuals come out, including coverage of peer harassment and discrimination, especially of younger teenagers, citing Hequembourg, Livingston, & Wang (2020), Kaufman, Baams, & Veenstra (2020), and others
- Trends related to sexual harassment and date rape, including the negative effects of sexual coercion and the link between sexual harassment and general bullying, citing Katz et al. (2019), Duncan, Zimmer-Gembeck, & Furman (2019), and others
- Updated discussion of the harassment of LGBTQ adolescents, the negative consequences of discrimination and hostility, the increased rates of depression and suicide among LGBTQ youth, and the importance of school- and community-based programs designed to promote tolerance and provide resources, citing la Roi et al. (2020), Ioverno & Russell (2020), Watson, Wheldon, & Puhl (2020), Eisenberg et al. (2020), Zhang et al. (2020), and Raifman et al, (2020), among others
- Risk factors related to adolescent rape and reasons why rape and sexual abuse are likely far more common that reported studies reveal
- Updated data of contraception use among adolescents, including the challenges of planning, access, and knowledge about sex, contraception, and pregnancy, citing Centers for Disease Control and Prevention (2020)
- "Making the Cultural Connection" box encouraging students to consider why rates of STDs and teen pregnancy are higher in the United States, despite similar rates of sexual activity to other countries
- Cross-cultural data related to U.S. rates of teen pregnancy by ethnicity, including discussion of the correlation of income inequality and school attendance with teenage childbearing, citing Sedgh et al. (2015)
- Effects of abortion of unplanned pregnancy on both adolescent girls and boys, and the disproportionate impact of policies limiting abortion access on ethnic youth, including figures based on Jalanko et al. (2020) and Everett et al. (2020), and data from the ACLU (2021)
- The risks and negative effects of teenage motherhood and marriage, and how they can be offset by moving in with their own family, a practice that is more common in Black families than in white or Latinx families

Chapter 12: Achievement

- Self-handicapping strategies, including sex differences and the impact of prejudice and discrimination on underrepresented ethnic youth
- Updated discussion of stereotype threat, including its impact on students of different ethnic backgrounds and sexes, citing McKellar et al. (2019), among others
- Discussion of how school environments and classroom atmosphere influence achievement, including how a lack resources negatively affects opportunity, especially for poor and underrepresented students
- Updated discussion of mixed results related to parental involvement in different ethnic households, including studies of Black, Latinx, Mexican American, Asian, and white students, citing Aceves, Bámaca-Colbert, & Robins (2020) and Day & Dotterer (2018), among others
- Effects of quality of home life, cultural capital, social capital, and Internet access on adolescent achievement, including how inadequate housing, economic and social stress, and poverty can undermine academic achievement and parental support
- Cross-cultural discussion of trends related to the connection between peer influence and student grades, citing Laninga-Wijnen et al. (2018), Shin (2020), Zhang et al. (2019), and Chen, Saafir, & Graham (2020)
- Socioeconomic gaps in school achievement across all ethnic groups and in different countries, including the effects of affluence on brain development and disadvantages in standardized testing, citing (NCES) 2020
- The effects of socioeconomic level, family background, and environmental factors on students, including the effects of neighborhoods
- Ethnic differences in educational achievement, including the success of immigrants of different backgrounds, citing Peguero, Bondy, & Hong (2017), among others
- Discussion of the similarity of educational aspirations and attitudes across ethnic backgrounds, but the gap in academic performance, especially for Black and Latinx students
- Theories of false optimism among Black and Latinx adolescents with high aspirations and positive beliefs about school, including the role of prejudice and discrimination by classmates and teachers on achievement
- Effects of academic performance on Asian teenagers, including increased time spent studying and the benefits of engagement and motivation
- "Making the Cultural Connection" box prompting students to consider the factors that drive immigrant achievement, even when immigrant students are unfamiliar with the English language or American culture
- Updated NCES (2020) and U.S. Census Bureau (2020) research about trends in the achievement gap between white and nonwhite individuals, including an increase in educational attainment
- Global data on U.S. proficiency scores in core subjects, which are mediocre in comparison with other industrialized countries, citing OECD (2020) data
- Cross-cultural, socioeconomic, and ethnic trends related to U.S. high school graduation rates, including the correlates and risk factors of dropping out of school, citing National Center for Education Statistics, 2020 data

- Socioeconomic influences on occupational choice, including social class, status, and educational attainment as determinants of what people look for in jobs, citing Afia et al. (2019), Gubbels, van der Put, & Assink (2019), and Samuel & Burger (2020)

Chapter 13: Psychosocial Problems in Adolescence

- Differences in drug use among adolescents of different sexes, ethnicities, and immigration status, including updated research and explanation that sex, socioeconomic status, and ethnicity respond to risk factors in much the same way, citing Johnston et al. (2020), Alamilla et al. (2018), and others
- Differences in alcohol, tobacco, and drug use between American and European adolescents, citing Miech et al. (2020) and ESPAD (2019)
- The role of environment and social context as it influences adolescent substance use and abuse, including availability of drugs, community norms, drug-law enforcement, and mass media portrayal, citing Meisel & Colder (2020), Wesche, Kreager, & Lefkowitz (2019), Griesler et al. (2019), and Parra et al. (2020)
- Discussion of protective factors related to substance abuse and how they operate similarly across ethnic groups, citing Su et al. (2019), Quach et al. (2020), and others
- Discussion of successful substance-abuse treatments, which are not as available to underrepresented ethnic groups due to financial or insurance reasons
- Sex differences in aggression, including social factors that influence its stability, and the overall gender gap in violent offending, which has closed over time, citing data from the National Center for Juvenile Justice (2020)

- Trends in victimization and shootings by race and ethnicity, including those related to school shootings and inner-city communities, citing Wylie & Rufino (2018) and Yu et al. (2018)
- Trends related to underreporting and selective reporting of rates of juvenile offending, including higher reporting levels among poor and underrepresented adolescents and racial bias and stereotypes that are most likely to impact Black individuals and influence the processing of minor crimes, citing data from the Federal Bureau of Investigation (2020), the Office of Juvenile Justice and Delinquency Prevention (2020), and the National Center for Juvenile Justice (2020)
- Discussion of the fact that ethnic differences in the prevalence of self-reported offending are smaller than those in official records, citing Singer (2017)
- Gender roles as a driver of sex differences in depression, including correlated pressures on young women to behave in sex-stereotyped ways, a tendency to respond to stress by turning feelings inward, and greater orientation toward interpersonal relations, citing Kwong et al. (2019), LeMoult et al. (2019), and Owens et al. (2019)
- Ethnic and sex differences in attempted suicide and sex differences in non-suicidal self-injury, citing Centers for Disease Control and Prevention (2020) data and research from Zhu, Chen, & Su (2020), Hamza & Willoughby (2019), and Schwartz-Mette & Lawrence (2019)
- Cross-cultural similarities in the connection between stress and psychosocial problems

A Note from the Author

Two psychopathic killers persuaded me to abandon my dreams to someday become a comedy writer and study psychology instead. I did not enter college intending to become either a psychologist or a professor. I majored in English, hoping to study creative writing. I became interested in psychology during the second semester of my freshman year because of an introductory course in personality theory. My professor had assigned the book *In Cold Blood,* and our task was to analyze the personalities of Dick and Perry, the two murderers. I was hooked. I followed this interest in personality development to graduate school in developmental psychology, where I learned that if you really wanted to understand how we develop into the people we ultimately become, you have got to know something about adolescence. That was nearly 50 years ago, and I'm still as passionate about studying this period of life as I was then.

I hope that this book gets you more excited about adolescence, too.

One reason I like teaching and writing about adolescence is that most students find it inherently interesting, in part because pretty much everyone has such vivid recollections of what it was like to be a teenager. In fact, researchers have discovered that people actually remember events from adolescence more intensely than events from other times, something that has been referred to as the "reminiscence bump."

The reminiscence bump makes teaching adolescence both fun and frustrating. Fun, because it isn't hard to get students interested in the topic. Frustrating, though, because it's a challenge to get students to look at adolescence from a scientific, as well as personal, perspective. That, above all, is my goal for this book. I don't want you to forget or set aside your own experience as an adolescent. (I couldn't make that happen, anyway.) But what I hope I can do is to help you understand adolescence—your own adolescence as well as the adolescence that is experienced by others around the world—more deeply and more intelligently by introducing you to the latest science on the subject. I still maintain a very active program of research of my own, and that necessitates staying on top of the field's most recent and important developments. There is a lot of exciting work being done on adolescence these days (one of my interests is the adolescent brain), and I want to share this excitement with you. Who knows, maybe you'll become hooked, too.

I've tried to do my best at covering the most important topics and writing about them in a way that is not only informative but fun and interesting to read. If there's something I could have done better, please let me know.

Laurence Steinberg
Temple University
laurence.steinberg@temple.edu
www.laurencesteinberg.com

Preface

Cutting-Edge Science, Personalized for Today's Students

As a well-respected researcher, Laurence Steinberg connects current research with real-world application, helping students see the similarities and differences in adolescent development across different social, economic, and cultural backgrounds.

Paired with McGraw Hill **Connect™**, a digital assignment and assessment platform that strengthens the link between faculty, students, and course work, instructors and students accomplish more in less time and improve their performance.

Apply Concepts and Theories in an Experiential Learning Environment

An engaging and innovative learning game, **Quest: Journey Through the Lifespan®** provides students with opportunities to apply content from their human development curriculum to real-life scenarios. Students play unique characters who range in age and make decisions that apply key concepts and theories for each age as they negotiate events in an array of authentic environments. Additionally, as students analyze real-world behaviors and contexts, they are exposed to different cultures and intersecting biological, cognitive, and socioemotional processes. Each quest has layered replayability, allowing students to make new choices each time they play—or offering different students in the same class different experiences. Fresh possibilities and outcomes shine light on the complexity of and variations in real human development. This experiential learning game includes follow-up questions, assignable in Connect and auto-graded, to reach a high level of critical thinking.

A Personalized Experience that Leads to Improved Learning and Results

How many students think they know everything about adolescent psychology but struggle on the first exam? Students study more effectively with Connect and SmartBook. ▤ SMARTBOOK˙

- Connect's assignments help students contextualize what they've learned through application, so they can better understand the material and think critically.
- Connect reports deliver information regarding performance, study behavior, and effort so instructors can quickly identify students who are having issues or focus on material that the class hasn't mastered.
- SmartBook helps students study more efficiently by highlighting what to focus on in the chapter, asking review questions, and directing them to resources until they understand.
- SmartBook creates a personalized study path customized to individual student needs.

SmartBook is now optimized for mobile and tablet and is accessible for students with disabilities. Content-wise, it has been enhanced with improved learning objectives that are measurable and observable to improve student outcomes. SmartBook personalizes learning to individual student needs, continually adapting to pinpoint knowledge gaps and focus learning on topics

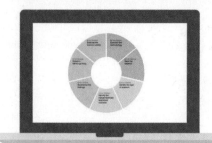

Power of Process for

PSYCHOLOGY

that need the most attention. Study time is more productive and, as a result, students are better prepared for class and coursework. For instructors, SmartBook tracks student progress and provides insights that can help guide teaching strategies.

Preparing Students for Higher-Level Thinking

At the higher end of Bloom's taxonomy, **Power of Process** helps students improve critical-thinking skills and allows instructors to assess these skills efficiently and effectively in an online environment. Available through Connect, preloaded journal articles are available for instructors to assign. Using a scaffolded framework such as understanding, synthesizing, and analyzing, Power of Process moves students toward higher-level thinking and analysis.

Writing Assignment

New to this edition and found in Connect, Writing Assignments offer faculty the ability to assign a full range of writing projects to students with just-in-time feedback.

You may set up manually scored assignments in a way that students can:

- automatically receive grammar and high-level feedback to improve their writing before they submit a project to you;
- run originality checks and receive feedback on "exact matches" and "possibly altered text" that includes guidance about how to properly paraphrase, quote, and cite sources to improve the academic integrity of their writing before they submit their work to you.

The new Writing Assignments will also have features that allow you to assign milestone drafts (optional), easily re-use your text and audio comments, build/score with your rubric, and view your own originality report of student's final submission.

Real People, Real World, Real Life

McGraw Hill Education's Milestones is a powerful video-based learning tool that allows students to experience life as it unfolds, from infancy through emerging adulthood. New to this edition, Milestones are available in a more engaging, WCAG-compliant format. Ask your McGraw Hill representative about this new upgrade.

Inform and Engage on Psychological Concepts

Located in Connect, **NewsFlash** is a multimedia assignment tool that ties current news stories, TedTalks, blogs, and podcasts to key psychological principles and learning objectives. Students interact with relevant news stories and are assessed on their ability to connect the content to the research findings and course material. NewsFlash is updated twice a year and uses expert sources to cover a wide range of topics including: emotion, personality, stress, drugs, COVID-19, disability, social justice, stigma, bias, inclusion, gender, LGBTQIA+, and many more.

Chapter-by-Chapter Changes

The thirteenth edition of *Adolescence* features updated and expanded coverage of key issues in development in every chapter. This revision is reflected primarily in Chapters 3, 4, 8, and 12.

Below is a complete list of changes in each chapter:

Chapter 1

- Thorough update of all content (more than 70 new citations)
- Four new figures in total
- Added discussion of changes in brain physiology during adolescence
- Refocused discussion of adrenarche
- Updated discussion of the timing of puberty and additions related to the concept of "precocious" puberty
- Updated discussion of genetic and environmental influences on pubertal timing
- New subsection on the connection between puberty and stress
- New "Making the Scientific Connection" box about the complicated relationship between puberty, psychological functioning, and other significant events.
- Expanded discussion on sleep patterns and the related effects of academic and extracurricular demands
- New figure about the correlation between early-maturing boys and delinquent behavior
- Revised section on obesity, including two new figures and consideration of the potential related effects of COVID-19 on adolescent activity levels

Chapter 2

- Thorough update of all content (more than 60 new citations)
- Five new figures in total
- Refined discussion of adolescent reasoning abilities and metacognition
- Two new figures illustrate patterns of neural connectivity, white matter, and gray matter
- New figure illustrates the brain regions responsible for social cognition, cognitive control, and reward processing
- New figure illustrates the maturity gap
- Updated discussion of IQ and intelligence tests.
- Added discussion of social conventions and laws in the context of the COVID-19 pandemic
- Updated discussion of adolescent risk taking, including a new figure and descriptions of recent research

Chapter 3

- Thorough update of all content (more than 80 new citations)
- Four new figures and two new tables in total
- Updated discussion about the elongation of adolescence
- New discussion and figure about perceptions in the importance of traditional markers of adulthood
- Expanded discussion of the concept of "emerging adulthood," including the factors and experiences that are related to it
- Revised discussion of social redefinition of adolescents in contemporary society
- Updated data on number of young adults living at home and leaving home during the COVID-19 pandemic, including a new figure
- Updated discussion of transitional problems of poor, minority, and immigrant youth
- Updated discussion of the effects of chronic stress, poverty, and income inequality on adolescents, including a new figure
- Updated discussion of the impact of mentoring programs
- Fully revised discussion of the impact of poverty on adolescent development, including a new figure
- New discussion and table showing the effects of violence and stress on behavioral, emotional, and physical health

Chapter 4

- Thorough update of all content (more than 100 new citations)
- Four new figures in total

- Expanded discussion of changing family relationships during adolescence
- New figure showing what parents are likely to lie to their children about
- Updated discussion about relationships between parents and adolescents in immigrant families
- New figure illustrating the differences in adolescent relationships with their mothers versus fathers
- New figure showing the correlation between an adolescent's impulsivity and aggression in rejecting parenting
- Updated and refined discussion of attachment, parenting style, and adolescent autonomy
- Updated discussion of household composition based on 2020 census data
- Updated discussion of the effects of stress and poverty, including the economic downturn related to the COVID-19 pandemic
- Updated data related to homelessness among the LGBTQ, Black, and Latinx adolescents

Chapter 5

- Thorough update of all content (more than 80 new citations)
- Four new figures in total
- Population trend data updated to reflect the 2020 census
- Updated "Making the Cultural Connection" box about values in different parts of the world
- New figure showing correlation between popularity and peer satisfaction
- New discussion of victimization and depression
- Updated discussion of bullying and victimization, including a new figure showing global trends in adolescent suicide
- New figure showing the different ways adolescents deal with cyberbullying

Chapter 6

- Thorough update of all content (more than 30 new citations)
- Four new and two revised figures in total
- Population trend data updated to reflect the 2020 census
- Updated "Making the Cultural Connection" box about values in different parts of the world
- New content about the impact of remote schooling during the COVID-19 pandemic
- New content about the effects of the shift in focus to standardized testing in schools
- Updated data about the achievement gap among students of different ethnic backgrounds
- New content about school inequality and school size
- Updated content about ADHD, including a figure illustrating gender differences in diagnoses
- Updated research about the connection between school diversity on mental health
- Updated research about school climate, cognitive performance, and striving students, including a new figure
- New figure about school discipline and student trust and engagement
- Updated content about the prevalence of the bullying of LGBTQ teenagers
- New figure illustrating the prevalence of boredom in school

Chapter 7

- Thorough update of all content (more than 80 new citations)
- Five new figures in total
- Updated content about adolescent free time
- New "Making the Cultural Connection" box about student employment
- New figure about participation in extracurricular activities
- Updated discussion of media saturation and sources
- New figure about the topics teenagers text about
- Updated discussion of media exposure
- New figure illustrating the connection between screen time and adolescent depression
- Updated data on the impact of violent video games and adolescent aggression
- Updated discussion of social media's impact and use among adolescents
- Revised subsection on Internet addiction

- New figure about sexting among contemporary teenagers
- New figure about victimization on social media

Chapter 8

- Thorough update of all content (more than 100 new citations)
- Four new figures in total
- Updated discussion of self-concept
- Expanded discussion of dimensions of personality in adolescence, including a new figure
- Updated discussion of self-esteem in adolescence
- Updated discussion of the social context of identity development
- Expanded discussion of ethnic identity, including a new figure and text on multiethnic adolescents
- Revised discussion of discrimination
- New discussion of gender identity, including a section on terminology and a new figure about gender identity and sexual orientation
- Expanded section on transgender adolescents
- Revised discussion of gender-role socialization, including a new figure

Chapter 9

- Thorough update of all content (more than 80 new citations)
- Six new figures in total
- Revised discussion of parenting and emotional autonomy, including a new figure
- Updated discussion of parental and peer influence, including a new figure
- New research on the role of peer influence on adolescent compliance with social-distancing guidelines during the COVID-19 pandemic, including a new figure
- Updated discussion of prosocial reasoning and behavior
- New figure about relationship between socioeconomic status and adolescent views of American society
- Expanded discussion of adolescent political thinking, including a new figure
- Expanded discussion of adolescent religious involvement, including two new figures

Chapter 10

- Thorough update of all content (more than 30 new citations)
- Three new and one revised figure in total
- Updated discussion of changes in the nature of friendship
- Updated discussion of loneliness in adolescence, including a new figure
- Updated discussion of targets of intimacy, low-income youth, and youth programs
- Revised discussion of the role of context in intimacy
- Updated discussion of LGBTQ intimate relationships, including a new figure
- Updated discussion of violence in romantic relationships, including a new figure

Chapter 11

- Thorough update of all content (more than 60 new citations)
- Four new and two revised figures in total
- Updated data related to sexual intercourse, based on 2020 CDC research
- Revised discussion of changes in sexual activity over time, using updated CDC data as a foundation
- Updated discussion of the relationship between sex and drugs
- Revised discussion of parent-adolescent communication
- Expanded discussion of the influence of peers on sexual activity
- Updated discussion of the meaning of sex, including a new figure
- Expanded and heavily revised discussion of same-sex attraction, including a new figure
- Updated discussion of the harassment of sexual minority youth
- Updated discussion of AIDS and other sexually transmitted diseases
- Updated discussion of teenage pregnancy and abortion, including two new figures
- Expanded and updated discussion of teenage pregnancy and motherhood

Chapter 12

- Thorough update of all content (more than 30 new citations)
- One new and two new revised figures and one new table in total
- Updated discussion of fear of failure and the Yerkes-Dodson law, including a new figure
- Revised discussion of stereotype threat
- Updated discussion of the transition to high school
- Updated discussion of environmental influences on achievement
- Updated discussion of socioeconomic status on educational achievement
- Revised and updated discussion of ethnicity and achievement
- Updated discussion in educational achievement changes and discrepancies, including across races and ethnicities
- Updated discussion of the correlates of dropping out of high school

Chapter 13

- Thorough update of all content (more than 90 new citations)
- Six new figures in total
- Updated discussion of substance abuse and a new figure
- Updated discussion of ethnic trends and risk factors of drug use
- Updated data related to crime rates and juvenile offenders, including a new figure
- Revised and updated discussion of changes in juvenile offending over time, including trends in gender differences
- Updated discussion of antisocial adolescents
- Revised and expanded discussion of internalizing problems, including a new figure
- New figure illustrating rates of depression among American adolescents
- New figure illustrating sex differences in rates of depression that emerges in adolescence and disappears in early adulthood
- Updated discussion of risk factors for suicide, including a new figure illustrating the connection between suicide and the menstrual cycle
- Updated discussion about suicide contagion

Online Instructor Resources

The resources listed here accompany the Thirteenth Edition of *Adolescence.* Please contact your McGraw Hill representative for details concerning the availability of these and other valuable materials that can help you design and enhance your course.

Instructor's Manual Broken down by chapter, the Instructor's Manual includes chapter outlines, suggested lecture topics, classroom activities and demonstrations, suggested student research projects, essay questions, and critical thinking questions.

Test Bank and Test Builder Organized by chapter, the questions are designed to test factual, conceptual, and applied understanding; all test questions are available within Test Builder. Available within Connect, Test Builder is a cloud-based tool that enables instructors to format tests that can be printed, administered within a learning management system, or exported as a Word document of the test bank. Test Builder offers a modern, streamlined interface for easy content configuration that matches course needs, without requiring a download.

Test Builder allows you to:

- access all test bank content from a particular title.
- easily pinpoint the most relevant content through robust filtering options.
- manipulate the order of questions or scramble questions and/or answers.
- pin questions to a specific location within a test.
- determine your preferred treatment of algorithmic questions.
- choose the layout and spacing.
- add instructions and configure default settings.

Test Builder provides a secure interface for better protection of content and allows for just-in-time updates to flow directly into assessments.

PowerPoint Presentations The PowerPoint presentations, available in both dynamic, lecture-ready and accessible, WCAG-compliant versions, highlight the key points of the chapter and include supporting visuals. All of the slides can be modified to meet individual needs.

Remote Proctoring and Browser-Locking Capabilities Remote proctoring and browser-locking capabilities, hosted by Proctorio within Connect, provide control of the assessment environment by enabling security options and verifying the identity of the student. Seamlessly integrated within Connect, these services allow instructors to control students' assessment experience by restricting browser activity, recording students' activity, and verifying students are doing their own work. Instant and detailed reporting gives instructors an at-a-glance view of potential academic integrity concerns, thereby avoiding personal bias and supporting evidence-based claims.

Acknowledgments

Revising *Adolescence* at a time when so much new information is available is a challenge that requires much assistance. For this new edition, McGraw Hill Education commissioned a broad survey of the course, and I am grateful to the more than 150 instructors who provided feedback on trends in the field and challenges in the classroom. I'm especially grateful to Colleen Brown and Emily Kan for their assistance in identifying new research that informed this revision.

The following instructors provided invaluable guidance for the Thirteenth Edition of *Adolescence*:

Myra Bundy, *Eastern Kentucky University*
Stephen Burgess, *Southwestern Oklahoma State University*
Juan F. Casas, *University of Nebraska Omaha*
Maria-Carla Chiarella, *University of North Carolina at Charlotte*
Jaelyn Farris, *Youngstown State University*
Richelle Frabotta, *Miami University*
Beverly George, *Old Dominion University*
Tawanna Hall, *Buena Vista University*
Michael Langlais, *Florida State University*
Sarah Lupis, *Brandeis University*
Margaret Maghan, *Ocean County College*
Alan Meca, *The University of Texas at San Antonio*
Rachel Miller-Slough, *East Tennessee State University*
Francesca Penner, *University of Houston*
Elayne Thompson, *Harper College*
Gary W. Tirrell, *Holyoke Community College*
Osman Umarji, *University of California Irvine*
Alexander T. Vazsonyi, *University of Kentucky*

In addition, I am grateful to the many colleagues and students across the country who took the time during the past 40 years to send me comments and suggestions based on their firsthand experiences using *Adolescence* in the classroom. They have improved the text with each edition.

The Study of Adolescent Development

The Boundaries of Adolescence
Early, Middle, and Late Adolescence

A Framework for Studying Adolescent Development
The Fundamental Changes of Adolescence
The Contexts of Adolescence
Psychosocial Development of Adolescence

Theoretical Perspectives on Adolescence
Biosocial Theories
Organismic Theories
Learning Theories
Sociological Theories
Historical and Anthropological Perspectives

Stereotypes Versus Scientific Study

Troy Aossey/Getty Images

1

During the early months of 2020, the rapid and frightening spread of the virus that causes COVID-19 created one of the most serious public health and economic crises the world has ever seen. One of the most difficult challenges faced by countries with a high incidence of infection, such as the United States, was how to safely provide education to millions of elementary, secondary, and college students. Experts worried about the spread of the virus not only among students but also between students and others with whom they come into contact—teachers, parents, and other adults in the community.

As an expert on adolescent development, I was asked frequently about the potential impact of the pandemic on adolescents. There were so many issues to contemplate: whether it was safe to return to school, whether students could learn just as effectively through remote instruction as in in-person classes, whether college undergraduates who returned to campus were capable of adhering to their schools' guidelines for safe behavior, whether the increased use of social media was likely to hurt teenagers' social development, and, of course, how to help adolescents protect their mental health during this difficult time.

Fortunately, today's scientists can do much more than make educated guesses. Over the past three decades, there's been enormous growth in the science of adolescence, so when experts are asked these sorts of questions, we have plenty of research to draw on—research on adolescent decision making, on the impact of social media on teenagers' psychological development, on instructional technology, on factors that make some young people more vulnerable to depression than others.

Research on adolescent risk taking has been especially relevant to discussions about whether it was safe for campuses to reopen. Personally, I was pessimistic about many of the plans colleges and universities had proposed. In an op-ed I published in *The New York Times*, I wrote that students might be able to comply with social distancing guidelines for awhile, but not for more than two weeks or so, and that once they started socializing with each other, the virus would spread rapidly (Steinberg, 2020).

In the early months of the COVID-19 pandemic, many college undergraduates ignored public health experts who cautioned against large group gatherings. Mike Stocker/Sun Sentinel/Tribune News Service/Getty Images

It turned out that my two-week estimate was overly optimistic. As soon as colleges reopened, students started partying. Within one week of reopening, universities all over the country began reversing course, closing dorms, sending students home, resuming online instruction, and disrupting the plans of thousands of students. By late August, before very many students had returned to campus, there already were more than 25,000 confirmed cases of COVID-19 on college and university campuses across the United States. By late October, there were nearly 220,000 (New York Times, 2020).

No one familiar with research on adolescent risk taking would have been surprised by this. Dozens of studies have shown that risk taking is more common during the late teens and early 20s than at any other age, not just in the United States, but around the world (Duell et al., 2018). Had university administrators looked to the science of adolescence for guidance, they might have decided to do things differently.

The Boundaries of Adolescence

The word *adolescence* is derived from the Latin *adolescere,* which means "to grow into adulthood" (Lerner & Steinberg, 2009). In all societies, adolescence is a time of growing up, of moving from the immaturity of childhood into the maturity of adulthood, of preparation for the future (Larson, Wilson, & Rickman, 2009; Schlegel, 2009). **Adolescence** is a period of transitions: biological, psychological, social, economic. During adolescence, individuals become interested in sex and biologically capable of having children. They become wiser, more sophisticated, and better able to make their own decisions. They become more self-aware, more independent, and more concerned about what the future holds. Think for a moment about how much you changed between when you finished elementary school and when you graduated from high school. I'm sure you'll agree that the changes you went through were remarkable.

making the practical connection

Studies of adolescent brain development have revealed that the brain continues to mature well into the mid-20s. This research was used in several U.S. Supreme Court cases in which the court ruled that adolescents should not be punished as severely as adults, even when they have been convicted of the same crimes. But some advocates for youth have worried that this same research can be used to limit what teenagers are allowed to do, such as drive or seek an abortion without their parents' knowledge. How would you respond to someone who, on the basis of this research, says that if adolescents are too young to be punished like adults, they are too young to be treated like adults in other ways as well?

As you can see in Table I.1, there are a variety of boundaries we might draw between childhood and adolescence, and between adolescence and adulthood. A biologist would place a great deal of emphasis on the attainment and completion of puberty, but an attorney would look instead at important age breaks designated by law, and an educator might draw attention to differences between students enrolled in different grades in school. Is a biologically mature fifth-grader an adolescent or a child? Is a 20-year-old college student who lives at home an adolescent or an adult? There are no right or wrong answers to these questions. Determining the beginning and ending of adolescence is more a matter of opinion than of absolute fact.

We can think of development during adolescence as involving a *series* of transitions from immaturity into maturity (Howard & Galambos, 2011; Trejos-Castillo & Vazsonyi, 2011). Some of these passages are long and some are short; some are smooth and others are rough. And not all of them occur at the same time. Consequently, it is quite possible—even likely—that an individual will mature in some respects before she matures in others. The various aspects of adolescence have different beginnings and different endings for every individual. An individual can be a child in some ways, an adolescent in other ways, and an adult in still others.

For the purposes of this book, we'll define adolescence as beginning with puberty and ending when individuals make the transition into adult roles, roughly from age 10 until the early 20s. Although at one time "adolescence" may have been synonymous with the teenage years (from ages 13 to 19), the adolescent period has lengthened considerably in the past 100 years, both because physical maturation occurs earlier and because so many individuals delay entering into work and marriage until their mid-20s (Steinberg, 2014a).

Early, Middle, and Late Adolescence

Today, most social scientists and practitioners view adolescence as composed of a series of phases rather than one single stage (Samela-Aro, 2011). The 11-year-old

Table I.1   The boundaries of adolescence. Here are some examples of the ways in which adolescence has been distinguished from childhood and adulthood that we examine in this book. Which boundaries make the most sense to you?

Perspective	When Adolescence Begins	When Adolescence Ends
Biological	Onset of puberty	Becoming capable of sexual reproduction
Emotional	Beginning of detachment from parents	Attaining a separate sense of identity
Cognitive	Emergence of more advanced reasoning abilities	Consolidation of advanced reasoning abilities
Interpersonal	Beginning of shift in interest from parental to peer relations	Development of the capacity for mature intimacy with peers
Social	Beginning of training for adult work, family, and citizen roles	Full attainment of adult status and privileges
Educational	Entrance into junior high school	Completion of formal schooling
Legal	Attainment of juvenile status	Attainment of majority status
Chronological	Attainment of designated age of adolescence (e.g., 10 years)	Attainment of designated age of adulthood (e.g., 21 years)
Cultural	Entrance into period of training for ceremonial rite of passage	Completion of ceremonial rite of passage

early adolescence
The period spanning roughly ages 10 to 13, corresponding roughly to the junior high or middle school years.

middle adolescence
The period spanning roughly ages 14 to 17, corresponding to the high school years.

late adolescence
The period spanning roughly ages 18 to 21, corresponding approximately to the college years.

emerging adulthood
The period spanning roughly ages 18 to 25, during which individuals make the transition from adolescence to adulthood.

puberty
The biological changes of adolescence.

whose time and energy is wrapped up in hip-hop, Tik-Tok, and basketball, for example, has little in common with the 21-year-old who is involved in a serious romance, worried about pressures at work, and looking for an affordable apartment. Social scientists who study adolescence differentiate among **early adolescence** (about ages 10 to 13), **middle adolescence** (about ages 14 to 17), and **late adolescence** (about ages 18 to 21).

Some writers also have suggested that a new phase of life, called **emerging adulthood** (Arnett, 2004), characterizes the early and mid-20s. However, despite the popularity of this idea in the mass media, there is little evidence that "emerging adulthood" is a universal stage or that the majority of young people in their mid-20s are in some sort of psychological or social limbo (Côté & Bynner, 2008; Kloep & Hendry, 2014). Indeed, what is most striking about the transition from adolescence to adulthood today is just how many different pathways there are. Some individuals spend their 20s single, dependent on their parents, and bouncing from job to job, while others leave adolescence and go straight into marriage, full-time employment, and economic independence (Osgood et al., 2005).

One study of rural American youth, in which high school juniors were asked about their expectations for the future, found three distinct groups: "early starters," "employment focused," and "education focused." "Early starters" expected to finish their schooling, enter the labor force, and live on their own immediately after high school; they thought they would start a family before they were 22. The "employment-focused" group expected to finish school, start regular employment, and live on their own before turning 21 but did not expect to start a family until several years later. The "education-focused" group did not expect to finish their schooling until they were 22 and did not expect to start a family until age 24 or 25 (Beal, Crockett, & Peugh, 2016) (see Figure I.1). Clearly, there are multiple pathways from adolescence into adulthood.

A Framework for Studying Adolescent Development

This book uses a framework for studying adolescence that is based on a model originally suggested by John Hill (1983). The model has three basic components: (1) the fundamental changes of adolescence, (2) the contexts of adolescence, and (3) the psychosocial developments of adolescence.

The Fundamental Changes of Adolescence

What, if anything, is distinctive about adolescence as a period in development? This is the first component of Hill's framework of study, the *fundamental changes of adolescence*, which encompasses biological, cognitive, and social dimensions. According to Hill, three features of adolescent development give the period its special flavor and significance: (1) the onset of puberty (biological), (2) the emergence of more advanced thinking abilities (cognitive), and (3) the transition into new roles in society (social). Importantly, these three sets of changes are universal; virtually without exception, all adolescents in every society go through them.

Biological Transitions   The chief elements of the biological changes of adolescence—which collectively are referred to as **puberty**—involve changes in the young person's physical appearance (including breast development in girls, the growth of facial hair in boys, and a dramatic

Figure I.1   In one study of expectations for the future among rural high school juniors, three groups were found: "early starters," "employment focused," and "education focused." (Beal, Crockett, & Peugh, 2016)

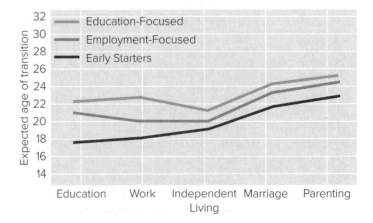

increase in height for both sexes) and the development of the ability to conceive children (Worthman, Dockray, & Marceau, 2019). We'll look at the biological changes that occur in early adolescence and examine how puberty affects the adolescent's psychological development and social relationships.

Cognitive Transitions The word *cognitive* refers to the processes that underlie how people think. Changes in cognitive abilities make up the second of the three fundamental changes of adolescence. Compared with children, adolescents are much better able to think about hypothetical situations (that is, things that have not yet happened but might or things that may not happen but could) and about abstract concepts, such as friendship, democracy, or morality (Keating, 2011). As you'll read, groundbreaking research on brain development is beginning to shed light on the ways in which these and other changes in thinking during adolescence result from the maturation of various brain regions and systems (Spear & Silveri, 2016).

making the cultural connection

In contemporary industrialized society, we do not have formal ceremonies that designate when a person has become an "adult." Do we have more informal ways to let individuals know when they have made the transition? What were the most important events in your life that signaled your entrance into adulthood?

Social Transitions All societies distinguish between individuals who are viewed as children and those who are seen as ready to become adults. Our society, for example, distinguishes between people who are "underage," or minors, and people who have reached the age of majority. Not until adolescence are individuals permitted to drive, marry, and vote. Such changes in rights, privileges, and responsibilities constitute the third set of fundamental changes that occur at adolescence: social changes. In some cultures, the social changes of adolescence are marked by a formal ceremony—a **rite of passage**. In most contemporary industrialized societies, the transition is less clearly marked, but a change in social status is a universal feature of adolescence (Markstrom, 2011).

The Contexts of Adolescence

Although all adolescents experience the biological, cognitive, and social transitions of the period, the *effects* of these changes are not uniform for all young people. Puberty makes some adolescents feel attractive and self-assured, but it makes others feel ugly and self-conscious. Being able to think in hypothetical terms

The implications of the cognitive changes of adolescence are far-reaching. Getty Images

makes some teenagers thankful that they grew up with the parents they have, but it prompts others to run away from home. Reaching 18 prompts some teenagers to enlist in the military or apply for a marriage license, but for others, becoming an adult is something they'd like to delay as long as possible.

If the fundamental changes of adolescence are universal, why are their effects so varied? Why isn't everyone affected in the same ways by puberty, by advanced thinking abilities, and by changes in legal status? The answer is that the psychological impact of the biological, cognitive, and social changes of adolescence is shaped by the environment in which the changes take place. In other words, psychological development during adolescence is a product of the interplay between a set of three very basic, universal changes and the context in which these changes are experienced.

Consider, for example, two 14-year-old girls growing up in neighboring communities. When Mariana went through puberty, around age 13, her parents' first reaction was to restrict her social life. They were afraid she would become too involved with boys and neglect her schoolwork. Mariana thought her parents were being ridiculous. She rarely had a chance to meet anyone she wanted to date because all the older boys went to the high school across town. Even though she was in the eighth grade, she was still going to school with fifth-graders. Mariana reacted by pulling away from parents she felt were overprotective.

Kayla's adolescence was very different. When she had her first period, her parents did not panic about her developing sexuality. Instead, they took her aside and discussed sex and

rite of passage
A ceremony or ritual marking an individual's transition from one social status to another, especially marking the young person's transition to adulthood.

pregnancy with her. They explained how different contraceptives worked and made an appointment for Kayla to see a gynecologist in case she ever needed to discuss something with a doctor. This made perfect sense. Although she was still only 14, Kayla would probably begin dating soon because in her community, the junior and senior high schools had been combined into one large school, and the older boys frequently showed interest in the younger girls. Puberty brought Kayla closer to her parents, not more distant.

Two teenage girls. Each goes through puberty, each grows intellectually, and each moves closer in age to adulthood. Yet each grows up under very different circumstances: in different families, in different schools, with different groups of peers, and in different communities. Both are adolescents, but their adolescent experiences are markedly different. And, as a result, each girl's psychological development will follow a different course.

Imagine how different your adolescence would have been if you had grown up a century ago and, instead of going to high school, had been expected to work full-time from the age of 15. Imagine how different it might be to grow up 100 years from today. And imagine how different adolescence is for a teenager from a very poor family than for one whose family is wealthy. It is impossible to generalize about the nature of adolescence without taking into account the surroundings and circumstances in which young people grow up.

For this reason, the second component of our framework is the *context* of adolescence. According to the **ecological perspective on human development**, whose main proponent was Urie Bronfenbrenner (1979), we cannot understand development without examining the environment in which it occurs. In modern societies, there are four main contexts in which young people spend time: families, peer groups, schools, and work and leisure settings.

Of course, these settings themselves are located within neighborhoods, which influence how they are structured and what takes place in them. It would be naive, for example, to discuss the impact that "school" has on adolescent development without recognizing that a school in an affluent suburb is likely very different from one in the inner city or in a remote rural area. And the community in which these settings are located is itself embedded in a broader context that is shaped by culture, geography, economics, and history.

In this book, we'll be especially interested in the contexts of adolescence in contemporary industrialized society and the ways in which they affect young people's development. Key contexts include the following:

ecological perspective on human development
A perspective on development that emphasizes the broader context in which development occurs.

Families   Adolescence is a time of dramatic change in family relationships (Cox, Wang, & Gustafsson, 2011; Martin, Bascoe, & Davies, 2011). In addition, many changes in what constitutes a "family" have taken place over the past several decades, leading to tremendous diversity in family forms and household composition in modern society. It's important to understand how changes within the family, and in the broader context of family life, affect young people's psychological development.

Peer Groups   Over the past 100 years, the peer group has come to play an increasingly important role in the socialization and development of teenagers (Dijkstra & Veenstra, 2011). But has the rise of peer groups in contemporary society been a positive or negative influence on young people's development? This is one of the many questions that has interested researchers who study the nature and function of adolescent peer groups and their effects on teenagers' psychological development.

Schools   Contemporary society depends on schools to occupy, socialize, and educate adolescents. But how good a job are schools doing? What should schools do to help prepare adolescents for adulthood? And how should schools for adolescents be structured (Cortina & Arel, 2011)?

Work, Leisure, and the Mass Media   Some of the most important influences on adolescent development are found outside of home and school: part-time jobs (Neyt et al., 2017), extracurricular activities (Farb & Matjasko, 2012), and the mass media (Brown & Bobkowski, 2011a), including social media, which have become increasingly important in teenagers' lives (Twenge et al., 2018). To what extent do these forces influence adolescents' attitudes, beliefs, and behavior?

One of the most important contexts for adolescent development is the peer group. SW Productions/Getty Images

Psychosocial Development in Adolescence

The third, and final, component of our framework concerns the major *psychosocial developments* of adolescence—identity, autonomy, intimacy, sexuality, and achievement—as well as certain psychosocial problems that may arise at this age. Social scientists use the word **psychosocial** to describe aspects of development that are both psychological and social in nature. Sexuality, for instance, is a psychosocial issue because it involves both psychological change (that is, changes in the individual's emotions, motivations, and behavior) and changes in the individual's relationships.

Of course, it is not only during the adolescent years that concerns: identity, autonomy, intimacy, sexuality, and achievement arise, and psychological or social problems can and do occur during all periods of life. They represent basic developmental challenges that we face as we grow and change: (1) discovering and understanding who we are as individuals—**identity;** (2) establishing a healthy sense of independence—**autonomy;** (3) forming close and caring relationships with others—**intimacy;** (4) expressing sexual feelings and enjoying physical contact with others—**sexuality;** and (5) being successful and competent members of society—**achievement.**

Although these concerns are not unique to adolescence, development in each of these areas takes a special turn during this stage. Understanding how and why such psychosocial developments take place during adolescence is a major interest of scientists who study this age period. We know that individuals form close relationships before adolescence, for example, but why is it that romantic relationships first develop during adolescence? We know that toddlers struggle with learning how to be independent, but why during adolescence do individuals need to be more on their own and make some decisions apart from their parents? We know that children fantasize about what they will be when they grow up, but why don't these fantasies become serious concerns until adolescence?

Identity In adolescence, a variety of important changes in the realm of identity occur (Harter, 2011; Thomaes, Poorthuis, & Nelemans, 2011). The adolescent may wonder, "Who am I, and what kind of life will I have?" Coming to terms with these questions may involve a period of experimentation—a time of trying on different personalities in an attempt to discover one's true self. The adolescent's quest for identity is not only a quest for a personal sense of self but also for recognition from others that he or she is a special, unique individual. Some of the most important changes of adolescence take place in the realms of identity, self-esteem, and self-conceptions.

Autonomy Adolescents' struggle to establish themselves as independent, self-governing individuals—in their own eyes and in the eyes of others—is a long and occasionally difficult process, not only for young people but also for those around them, especially their parents (Zimmer-Gembeck, Ducat, & Collins, 2011). Three aspects of autonomy are of special importance during adolescence: becoming less emotionally dependent on parents (McElhaney et al., 2009), learning to function independently (Steinberg, 2014), and establishing a personal code of values and morals (Morris, Eisenberg, & Houltberg, 2011).

Intimacy During adolescence, important changes take place in the individual's capacity to be intimate with others, especially with peers. During adolescence, friendships emerge that involve openness, honesty, loyalty, and exchange of confidences, rather than simply a sharing of activities and interests (Brown & Larson, 2009). Dating takes on increased importance, and as a consequence, so does the capacity to form romantic relationships that are trusting and loving (Shulman, Connolly, & McIssac, 2011).

Sexuality Sexual activity usually begins during adolescence (Diamond & Savin-Williams, 2011). Becoming

psychosocial
Referring to aspects of development that are both psychological and social in nature, such as developing a sense of identity or sexuality.

identity
The domain of psychosocial development involving self-conceptions, self-esteem, and the sense of who one is.

autonomy
The psychosocial domain concerning the development and expression of independence.

intimacy
The psychosocial domain concerning the formation, maintenance, and termination of close relationships.

sexuality
The psychosocial domain concerning the development and expression of sexual feelings.

achievement
The psychosocial domain concerning behaviors and feelings in evaluative situations.

Sexuality is a central psychosocial issue of adolescence. Maria Teijeiro/Getty Images

biosocial theories
Theories of adolescence that emphasize the biological changes of the period.

sexual is an important aspect of development at this age—not only because it transforms relationships between adolescents and their peers but also because it raises many difficult questions for the young person. These concerns include incorporating sexuality into a still-developing sense of self, understanding one's sexual orientation, resolving questions about sexual values and morals, and coming to terms with the sorts of relationships the adolescent is prepared—or not prepared—to enter.

Achievement   Adolescence is a time of important changes in individuals' educational and vocational behavior and plans. Crucial decisions—many with long-term consequences—about schooling and careers are made during adolescence. Many of these decisions depend on adolescents' achievement in school, on their evaluations of their own competencies and capabilities, on their aspirations and expectations for the future, and on the direction and advice they receive from parents, teachers, and friends (Wigfield, Ho, & Mason-Singh, 2011).

Psychosocial Problems   Although most adolescents move through the period without experiencing major psychological upheaval, this stage of life is the most common time for the first appearance of serious psychological difficulties (Kessler et al., 2005; Olfson, Druss, & Marcus, 2015). Three sets of problems are often associated with adolescence: drug and alcohol use and abuse (Chassin, Hussong, & Beltran, 2009), delinquency and other "externalizing problems" (Farrington, 2009), and depression and other "internalizing problems" (Graber & Sontag, 2009). In each case, we examine the prevalence of the problem, the factors believed to contribute to its development, and approaches to prevention and intervention.

Theoretical Perspectives on Adolescence

The study of adolescence is based not just on empirical research but also on theories of development (Newman & Newman, 2011). You will read more about different theories of adolescence throughout this book, but, for now, let's look briefly at the major ones.

It's useful to organize theoretical perspectives on adolescence around a question that has long dominated discussions of human development more generally: How much is due to "nature," or biology, and how much is due to "nurture," or the environment? Some theories of adolescence emphasize biology, others emphasize the environment, and still others fall somewhere between the two extremes (see Figure I.2). We'll begin with a look at the most extreme biological perspectives and work our way across a continuum toward the other extreme—perspectives that stress the role of the environment.

Biosocial Theories

The fact that biological change during adolescence is noteworthy is not a matter of dispute—how could it be, when puberty is such an obvious part of adolescence? But experts on adolescence disagree about just how important this biological change is in defining the psychosocial issues of the period. Theorists who have taken a biological or, more accurately, "biosocial," view of adolescence stress the hormonal and physical changes of puberty as driving forces. This places **biosocial theories** far at the biological end of the theoretical-perspective continuum. The most important biosocial theorist was G. Stanley Hall (1904), considered the "father" of the scientific study of adolescence.

Hall's Theory of Recapitulation   G. Stanley Hall, who was very much influenced by Charles Darwin, the author of the theory of evolution, believed that the development of the individual paralleled the development of the human species. Infancy, in his view, was equivalent to the time during our evolution when we were more like animals than humans. Adolescence, in contrast, was seen as a transitional and turbulent time that paralleled the evolution of our species from primitive "savages" into civilized adults. For Hall, the development of the individual through these stages was determined primarily by instinct—by biological and genetic forces within the person—and hardly influenced by the environment.

The most important legacy of Hall's view of adolescence is the belief that the adolescence is inevitably a period of "storm and stress." He believed that the hormonal changes of puberty cause upheaval, both for the individual and for those around him or her. Because this

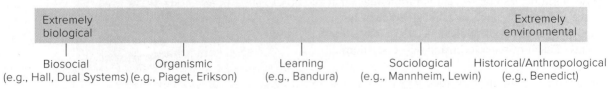

Figure I.2   Theories of adolescence range from the extremely biological, such as that of G. Stanley Hall, to the extremely environmental, such as that of Ruth Benedict.

turbulence is biologically determined, it is unavoidable. The best that society can do is to find ways of managing the young person whose "raging hormones" invariably cause difficulties.

Although scientists no longer believe that adolescence is inherently problematic or that pubertal hormones themselves cause emotional problems, much contemporary work continues to emphasize the role that biological factors play in shaping the adolescent experience. More than 100 years ago, in fact, Hall speculated about brain maturation, hormonal influences on behavior, and changes in patterns of sleep during adolescence—all very hot topics in the study of adolescence today (Dahl & Hariri, 2005). Current work in the biosocial tradition, influenced by Hall and his followers as well, also explores the genetic bases of individual differences in adolescence and the evolutionary bases of adolescent behavior (Hollenstein & Lougheed, 2013). Support for the biosocial perspective is also found in many studies of "adolescence" in other species, which have revealed striking similarities between juvenile animals and their human counterparts (Sisk & Romeo, 2019).

Dual Systems Theories Recent advances in brain science have given rise to an alternative biosocial account of adolescent development, one that stresses changes in the anatomy and activity of the brain. Among the most prominent of these theories are so-called "dual systems" or "maturational imbalance" theories, which stress the simultaneous development of two different brain systems—one that governs the ways in which the brain processes rewards, punishments, and social and emotional information, and another that regulates self-control and advanced thinking abilities, such as planning or logical reasoning (Shulman et al., 2016). The arousal of this first system takes place early in adolescence, while the second system is still maturing. This creates a maturational imbalance (Casey, Jones, & Somerville, 2011), which has been compared to starting a car without having a good braking system in place. The main challenge of adolescence, according to this view, is to develop better self-regulation, so that this imbalance doesn't create problems (Steinberg, 2014a).

Organismic Theories

Our next stop on the continuum is what are called *organismic* theorists. Like biosocial theorists, organismic theorists recognize the importance of the biological changes of adolescence. But unlike their biosocial counterparts, **organismic theories** also take into account the ways in which contextual forces interact with and modify these biological forces. For example, all adolescents experience the biological changes of puberty, but how they are affected by them can be influenced by how their parents and peers respond.

If you have had previous coursework in developmental psychology, you have undoubtedly encountered the major organismic theorists. Three of these theorists, in particular, have had a great influence on the study of adolescence: Sigmund Freud (1938), Erik Erikson (1968), and Jean Piaget (Inhelder & Piaget, 1958). Although these theorists share in common an organismic orientation, the theories they developed emphasize different aspects of individual growth and development.

Freudian Theory For Freud, development was best understood in terms of the psychosexual conflicts that arise at different points in development. Like Hall, Freud saw adolescence as a time of upheaval. According to Freud, puberty temporarily throws the adolescent into a period of psychological crisis by reviving old conflicts over uncomfortable sexual urges that had been buried in the unconscious (including feelings toward one's parents).

Freud actually had very little to say specifically about adolescence. But his daughter, Anna Freud (1958), extended much of her father's thinking to the study of development during the second decade of life, emphasizing the need for adolescents to break away, or "detach," from their parents in order to develop normally.

Eriksonian Theory Erik Erikson, whose work built on Freud's, also believed that internal, biological developments moved the individual from one developmental stage to the next. But unlike Freud, Erikson stressed the psychosocial, rather than the psychosexual, conflicts faced by the individual at each point in time. Erikson proposed eight stages in psychosocial development, each characterized by a specific "crisis" that arises at that point in development because of the interplay between the internal forces of biology and the demands of society. In Erikson's theory, development in adolescence revolves around the identity crisis. According to Erikson, the challenge of adolescence is to resolve the identity crisis and to emerge with a coherent sense of who one is and where one is headed.

Piagetian Theory For Jean Piaget, development was best understood by examining changes in the nature of thinking. Piaget believed that, as children mature, they pass through distinct stages of cognitive development.

In Piaget's theory, adolescence marks the transition from concrete to abstract thought. Adolescence is the period in which individuals become capable of thinking in hypothetical terms, a development that permits a broad expansion of logical capabilities. The development of abstract thinking in adolescence is influenced both by the

organismic theories
Theories of adolescence that emphasize the interaction between the biological changes of the period and the contexts in which they take place.

learning theories
Theories of adolescence that emphasize the ways in which patterns of behavior are acquired through reinforcement and punishment or through observation and imitation.

sociological theories
Theories of adolescence that emphasize the ways in which adolescents, as a group, are treated by society.

internal biological changes of the developmental period and by changes in the intellectual environment encountered by the individual.

Learning Theories

At the center of the theoretical continuum, between the extreme biological views and extreme environmental ones, are **learning theories.** Whereas organismic theorists emphasize the interaction between biological change and environmental demands, learning theorists stress the context in which behavior takes place. The capacity of the individual to learn from experience is assumed to be a biological given—one that is in place long before adolescence. Learning theorists who study adolescence are interested in the content of what is learned.

Learning theorists have little to say specifically about adolescence as a developmental period because they assume that the basic processes of human behavior are the same during adolescence as during other periods of the life span. But learning theorists have been extremely influential in the study of adolescent development because they have helped us understand how the specific environment in which an adolescent lives shapes his or her behavior. There are two general categories of learning theorists: *behaviorists* and *social learning theorists.*

Behaviorism   Behaviorists emphasize the processes of reinforcement and punishment as the main influences on adolescent behavior. The main proponent of this view was B. F. Skinner (1953), whose theory of operant conditioning has had a tremendous impact on the entire field of psychology. Within this framework, reinforcement is the process through which a behavior is made more likely to occur again, whereas punishment is the process through which a behavior is made less likely to occur again. Adolescents' behavior is nothing more or less than the product of the various reinforcements and punishments they've been exposed to. An adolescent who strives to do well in school, for example, does so because in the past she or he has been reinforced for this behavior or has been punished for not behaving this way. Similarly, a teenager who continues to experiment with risky behavior is being reinforced for this sort of activity or punished for being especially cautious.

Social Learning Theory   Social learning theorists, such as Albert Bandura (Bandura & Walters, 1959), also emphasize the ways in which adolescents learn how to behave, but they place more weight on the processes of observational learning and imitation. According to these theorists, adolescents learn how to behave not simply by being reinforced and punished by forces in the environment but also by watching and modeling those around them. Social learning approaches to adolescence have been very influential in explaining how adolescents learn by watching the behavior of others, especially parents, peers, and figures in the mass media, such as celebrities. From this vantage point, an adolescent who strives to do well in school or who takes a lot of risks is probably imitating family members, friends, or celebrities portrayed in the mass media.

Sociological Theories

The emphasis of biosocial, organismic, and learning theories is mainly on forces within an individual, or within that individual's environment, that shape development and behavior. In contrast, **sociological theories** of adolescence attempt to understand how adolescents, *as a group,* come of age in society. Instead of emphasizing differences among individuals in their biological makeups or their experiences in the world, sociological theorists focus on the factors that all adolescents or groups of adolescents have in common by virtue of their age. Two themes have dominated these discussions: adolescent marginality and intergenerational conflict.

Adolescent Marginality   There is a vast difference in power between the adult and the adolescent generations, which may leave young people feeling marginalized, or insignificant. Two important thinkers in this vein are Kurt Lewin (1951) and Edgar Friedenberg (1959). Contemporary applications of this viewpoint stress the fact that because adolescents are often prohibited from occupying meaningful roles in society, young people often become frustrated and restless. Some writers have claimed that many of the problems we associate with adolescence have been created, in part, by the way in which we have structured the adolescent experience, treating adolescents as if they are more immature than they actually are and isolating them from adults (Epstein, 2007).

Intergenerational Conflict   The other theme in sociological theories of adolescence concerns conflict between the generations. Theorists such as Karl Mannheim (1952) and James Coleman (1961) stressed the fact that adolescents and adults grow up under different social circumstances and therefore develop different sets of attitudes, values, and beliefs. As a consequence, there is inevitable tension between the adolescent and the adult generations. For example, adults often criticize Millennials (people born between 1982 and 2004) for being spoiled and lazy, and for taking too long to become adults. But many Millennials are taking longer to become adults simply because they face many more financial challenges than their parents' generation did. As the title of one article put it, "Millennials Are Screwed" (Hobbes, 2017).

Historical and Anthropological Perspectives

Historians and anthropologists who study adolescence share with sociologists an interest in the broader context in which young people come of age. Historical perspectives, such as those offered by Glen Elder (1980), Joseph Kett (1977), and Thomas Hine (1999), stress that adolescence as a developmental period has varied considerably from one historical era to another. As a consequence, it is impossible to generalize about such issues as the degree to which adolescence is stressful, the developmental tasks of the period, or the nature of intergenerational relations. Historians would say that these issues all depend on the social, political, and economic forces present at a given time. Even something as basic to our view of adolescence as the "identity crisis," they say, is a social invention that arose because of industrialization and the prolongation of schooling. Prior to the Industrial Revolution, when most adolescents followed in their parents' occupation, people didn't have "crises" over who they were or what they were going to do in life.

Adolescence as an Invention   One group of theorists has taken this viewpoint to its extreme, arguing that adolescence is *entirely* a social invention (Bakan, 1972). They believe that the way in which we divide the life cycle into stages—drawing a boundary between childhood and adolescence, for example—is nothing more than a reflection of the political, economic, and social circumstances in which we live. They point out that, although puberty has always been a feature of adolescent development, it was not until the rise of compulsory education that we began treating young people as a special and distinct group. In other words, social conditions, not biological givens, define the nature of adolescent development. We noted earlier that contemporary writers debate whether a new phase of life, "emerging adulthood," actually exists. Writers who believe that different stages of life are social inventions would say that if emerging adulthood has become a stage in development, it only has because society has made it so, not because people have really changed in any fundamental way.

Anthropological Perspectives
A similar theme is echoed by anthropologists who study adolescence, the most important of whom were Ruth Benedict (1934) and Margaret Mead (1928/1978). Benedict and Mead pointed out that societies vary considerably in the ways in which they view and structure adolescence. As a consequence, these thinkers viewed adolescence as a culturally defined experience—stressful and difficult in societies that saw it this way, but calm and peaceful in societies that had an alternative vision. Benedict, in particular, drew a distinction between nonindustrialized societies, where the transition from adolescence to adulthood is generally gradual and peaceful, and modern industrialized societies, where transition to adulthood is abrupt and difficult.

making the scientific connection

Some writers have argued that the stage of life we call adolescence is a social invention. What do they mean by this? Could you say this about other periods of development? Is infancy a social invention? Is middle age? What about "emerging adulthood"?

Stereotypes Versus Scientific Study

One of the oldest debates in the study of adolescence is whether adolescence is an inherently stressful time for individuals. As we noted earlier, G. Stanley Hall, who is generally acknowledged as the father of the modern study of adolescence, likened adolescence to the turbulent, transitional period in the evolution of the human species from savagery into civilization.

This portrayal of teenagers as passionate, troubled, and unpredictable persists today. One 12-year-old girl I was counseling told me that her mother had been telling her that she would go through a difficult time when she turned 14—as if some magical, internal alarm clock was set to trigger storm and stress on schedule.

The girl's mother wasn't alone in her view of adolescence. Sometime this week, pay attention to how teenagers are depicted in popular media. If they are not portrayed as troublemakers—the usual role in which they

One response to adolescents' feelings of marginalization is political protest. LeoPatrizi/Getty Images

are cast—adolescents are sex-crazed idiots (if they are male), giggling fools or "mean girls" (if they are female), or tormented lost souls, searching for their place in a strange, cruel world (if they aren't delinquent, sex-crazed, giggling, or gossiping). It's not only fictionalized portrayals of teenagers that are stereotyped. Scholars, too, have been influenced by this viewpoint; a disproportionate number of scientific studies of adolescents have focused on young people's problems rather than their normative development (Steinberg, 2014a).

Stereotypes of adolescents as troubling and troubled have important implications for how teenagers are treated by parents, teachers, and other adults. Parent–teenager relations, especially, are influenced by the expectations they have about each other. For example, one study found that when mothers believed that their teenagers were likely to use alcohol, this actually led to increases in their child's drinking (Madon et al., 2006). Similarly, snooping on teenagers leads them to become more secretive, which is likely to prompt parents to snoop even more (Hawk et al., 2013). Teenagers themselves are affected by the stereotypes they hold about the period; middle school students who believe that adolescence is a time of irresponsibility actually engage in more risk taking in high school than their peers (Qu et al., 2018). One study of Chinese seventh-graders found that those who believed that adolescents were emotional and impulsive were more likely to develop problems in self-control 1 year later (Qu et al., 2020),

Fortunately, the tremendous growth of the scientific literature on adolescence over the past four decades has led to more accurate views of normal adolescence among practitioners who work with young people, although a trip to the "Parenting" section of your local bookstore will quickly reveal that the storm-and-stress stereotype is still alive and well, where most books are "survival guides" (Steinberg, 2014a). Today, most experts do not dismiss the storm-and-stress viewpoint as entirely incorrect but

see the difficulties that some adolescents have as due largely to the context within which they grow up.

making the personal connection

If someone were to make generalizations about the nature of adolescence by analyzing *your* experiences as a teenager, how would the period be portrayed?

Adolescence, like any other developmental stage, has both positive and negative elements (Siegel & Scovill, 2000). Young people's willingness to challenge authority, for instance, is both refreshing (when we agree with them) and annoying (when we do not). Their propensity to take risks is both admirable and frightening. Their energy and exuberance is both exciting and unsettling.

One of the goals of this book is to provide you with a more realistic understanding of adolescent development in contemporary society—an understanding that reflects the best and most up-to-date scientific research. As you read the material, think about your personal experiences as an adolescent, but try to look beyond them and be willing to question the "truths" about teenagers that you have grown accustomed to over the years. This does not mean that your experiences weren't valid or that your recollections inaccurate. (In fact, studies show that we remember things that happen during adolescence more vividly than any other time [Steinberg, 2014a].) But remember that your experiences as a teenager were the product of a unique set of forces that have made you who you are today. The person who sits next to you in class—or the person who right now, in some distant region of the world, is thinking back to his or her adolescence—was probably exposed to different forces than you were and probably had a different set of adolescent experiences as a consequence.

Biological Transitions

Puberty: An Overview

The Endocrine System

What Triggers Puberty?

How Hormones Influence Adolescent
Development

Somatic Development

The Adolescent Growth Spurt

Sexual Maturation

The Timing and Tempo of Puberty

Variations in the Timing and Tempo of Puberty

Genetic and Environmental Influences on
Pubertal Timing

**The Psychological and Social Impact
of Puberty**

The Immediate Impact of Puberty

The Impact of Specific Pubertal Events

The Impact of Early or Late Maturation

Obesity and Eating Disorders

Obesity

Anorexia Nervosa, Bulimia, and Binge
Eating Disorder

PhotoAlto/Sandro Di Carlo Darsa/Getty Images

Not all adolescents experience identity crises, rebel against their parents, or fall madly in love, but virtually all go through puberty, the biological changes that change our appearance and ultimately make us capable of sexual reproduction.

Physical development is influenced by a host of environmental factors, and the timing and rate of pubertal growth vary across regions of the world, socioeconomic classes, ethnic groups, and historical eras. Today, in contemporary America, the average girl has her first period at about age 12. At the turn of the 20th century, she was around 14½.

Physical and sexual maturation profoundly affect the ways in which adolescents view themselves and are viewed and treated by others. But the social environment exerts a tremendous impact on the psychological and social consequences of going through puberty (Worthman, Dockray, & Marceau, 2019). In some traditional societies, pubertal maturation brings with it a series of public initiation rites that mark the passage of the young person into adulthood, socially as well as physically.

In other societies, recognition of the physical transformation from child into adult takes more subtle forms. Parents may merely remark, "Our little boy has become a man," when they discover that he needs to shave, or "Our little girl has grown up," when they learn that she has gotten her first period. Early or late maturation may be cause for celebration or cause for concern, depending on what is admired or made fun of in a given peer group at a given point in time. The fifth-grader who is developing breasts might be embarrassed, but the ninth-grader who has not developed breasts might be equally self-conscious.

In sum, even the most universal aspect of adolescence—puberty—is hardly universal in its impact on the young person. In this chapter, we examine just how and why the environment in which adolescents develop exerts its influence even on something as fundamental as puberty. As you will learn, the adolescent's social environment even affects the age at which puberty begins.

Puberty: An Overview

Technically, puberty refers to the period during which an individual becomes capable of sexual reproduction. More broadly, however, puberty encompasses all the physical changes that occur in adolescents as they pass from childhood into adulthood (Worthman, Dockray, & Marceau, 2019).

Puberty has four chief physical manifestations:

1. A rapid acceleration in growth, resulting in dramatic increases in height and weight.

2. The development of primary sex characteristics, including the further development of the gonads (sex glands), which results in a series of hormonal changes.

3. The development of secondary sex characteristics, including changes in the genitals and breasts, and the growth of pubic, facial, and body hair.

4. Changes in the brain's anatomy and activity as a result of hormonal influences.

Each of these sets of changes is the result of developments in the endocrine and central nervous systems, many of which

begin years before the signs of puberty are evident—some actually occur at conception (Dorn et al., 2019). No new hormones are produced at puberty. Rather, the levels of some hormones that have been present since before birth increase, whereas others decline.

The Endocrine System

The **endocrine system** produces, circulates, and regulates levels of hormones. **Hormones** are highly specialized substances that are secreted by one or more endocrine glands and then enter the bloodstream and travel throughout the body. **Glands** are organs that stimulate particular parts of the body to respond in specific ways. Many of the hormones that play important roles at puberty carry their instructions by activating certain brain cells, called **gonadotropin-releasing hormone (GnRH) neurons** (Sisk & Romeo, 2019).

The Hormonal Feedback Loop   The endocrine system receives its instructions to increase or decrease circulating levels of particular hormones from the central nervous system, mainly through the firing of GnRH neurons (Aylwin et al., 2019). The system works like a thermostat. Hormonal levels are "set" at a certain point, which may differ depending on the stage of development, just as you might set a thermostat at a certain temperature (and use different settings during different seasons or different times of the day). By setting your room's heating thermostat at 60°F, you are instructing your heating system to go into action when the room becomes colder than that. Similarly, when a

endocrine system
The system of the body that produces, circulates, and regulates hormones.

hormones
Highly specialized substances secreted by one or more endocrine glands.

glands
Organs that stimulate particular parts of the body to respond in specific ways to particular hormones.

gonadotropin-releasing hormone (GnRH) neurons
Specialized neurons that are activated by certain pubertal hormones.

particular hormonal level in your body dips below the endocrine system's **set point** for that hormone, secretion of the hormone increases; when the level reaches the set point, secretion temporarily stops. And, as is the case with a thermostat, the setting level, or set point, for a particular hormone can be adjusted up or down, depending on environmental or internal bodily conditions.

Such a **feedback loop**—the HPG axis (for hypothalamus, pituitary, gonads)—becomes increasingly important at the onset of puberty. Long before adolescence—in fact, before birth—the HPG axis develops involving three structures: the **pituitary gland** (which controls hormone levels in general), the **hypothalamus** (the part of the brain that controls the pituitary gland and where there is a concentration of GnRH neurons), and the **gonads** (in males, the **testes**; in females, the **ovaries**), which release the "sex" hormones—**androgens** and **estrogens** (see Figure 1.1).

Your HPG axis is set to maintain certain levels of androgens and estrogens. When these hormone levels fall below their set points, the hypothalamus stops inhibiting the pituitary, permitting it to stimulate the release of sex hormones by the gonads. When hormone levels reach the set point, the hypothalamus responds by once again inhibiting the pituitary gland. Just as you might change the setting on your heating thermostat automatically every November 1, or when your utility bill has become too expensive, your brain is constantly monitoring a variety of signals and adjusting your hormonal set points in response. Puberty begins when several different signals—genetic as well as environmental—instruct the brain to change the set point (Sisk & Romeo, 2019).

Adrenarche Do you remember the first time you felt sexually attracted to someone? Most people report that their first sexual attraction took place *before* they went through puberty. These early sexual feelings may be stimulated by maturation of the adrenal glands, called **adrenarche** (Herdt & McClintock, 2000), which also contributes to the development of body odor, which is a way of signaling the beginning of sexual maturation to others (Campbell, 2011).

Changes at puberty in the brain system that regulates the adrenal gland are also important because this is the brain system that controls how we respond to stress (Kircanski et al., 2019; Lucas-Thompson, McKernan, & Henry, 2018). One reason adolescence is a period of great vulnerability for the onset of many serious mental disorders is that the hormonal changes of puberty make us more responsive to stress (Burke et al., 2017; Monahan et al., 2016; Sisk & Romeo, 2019). This leads to excessive secretion of the stress hormone **cortisol**, a substance that at high and chronic levels can cause brain cells to die (Carrion & Wong, 2012). Keep in mind, though, that there is a difference between saying that adolescence is an inherently stressful time (which it is not) and saying that adolescence is a time of heightened vulnerability to stress (which it is).

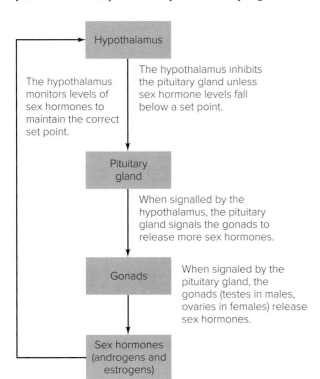

Figure 1.1 Levels of sex hormones are regulated by a feedback system (the HPG axis) composed of the hypothalamus, pituitary gland, and gonads. (Grumbach et al., 1974)

The hypothalamus monitors levels of sex hormones to maintain the correct set point.

Hypothalamus

The hypothalamus inhibits the pituitary gland unless sex hormone levels fall below a set point.

Pituitary gland

When signalled by the hypothalamus, the pituitary gland signals the gonads to release more sex hormones.

Gonads

When signaled by the pituitary gland, the gonads (testes in males, ovaries in females) release sex hormones.

Sex hormones (androgens and estrogens)

set point
A physiological level or setting (e.g., of a specific hormone) that the body attempts to maintain through a self-regulating system.

feedback loop
A cycle through which two or more bodily functions respond to and regulate each other, such as that formed by the hypothalamus, the pituitary gland, and the gonads.

pituitary gland
One of the chief glands responsible for regulating levels of hormones in the body.

hypothalamus
A part of the brain that controls the functioning of the pituitary gland.

gonads
The glands that secrete sex hormones: in males, the testes; in females, the ovaries.

testes
The male gonads.

ovaries
The female gonads.

androgens
A class of sex hormones secreted by the gonads, found in both sexes but in higher levels among males than females following puberty.

estrogens
A class of sex hormones secreted by the gonads, found in both sexes but in higher levels among females than males following puberty.

adrenarche
The maturation of the adrenal glands that takes place during adolescence.

cortisol
A hormone produced when a person is exposed to stress.

making the personal connection

Do you remember your first feelings of sexual attraction for someone? How old were you?

What Triggers Puberty?

Although the HPG axis is active before birth, it is relatively quiet during childhood. During middle childhood, the HPG axis is reawakened and signals that the body is ready for puberty. Some of this is caused by an internal clock whose "puberty alarm" is set very early in life by information coded in our genes (the age at which someone goes through puberty is largely inherited). But some of the reawakening of the HPG axis at puberty is due to multiple signals that tell the brain it is time to start preparing for childbearing. These signals indicate whether there are sexually mature mating partners in the environment, whether there are sufficient nutritional resources to support a pregnancy, and whether the individual is physically mature and healthy enough to begin reproducing.

The onset of puberty is stimulated by an increase in a brain chemical called **kisspeptin** (Aylwin et al., 2019) (so named because it was discovered in Hershey, Pennsylvania, the birthplace of chocolate kisses). The production of kisspeptin in the brain is affected by other chemicals, most importantly **leptin**, which stimulates it, and **melatonin**, which suppresses it. Leptin is a protein produced by fat cells and exists in our body in levels proportionate to our amount of body fat. It plays a critical role in the regulation of hunger and appetite by suppressing our desire to eat when we're full. In some senses, leptin serves to signal the brain not just that we are full enough but that we are "fat enough." Melatonin is a hormone whose levels rise and fall as a function of how light or dark it is, which helps regulate the sleep cycle (we'll discuss this later in this chapter). Our melatonin levels are lower when it is light and higher when it is dark.

Your genes predispose you to go through puberty around a particular age (Horvath, Knopik, & Marceau, 2020), but the more fat cells you have, and the more light to which you have been exposed during childhood, the more likely it is that you will go through puberty on the early side of your inherited propensity. Someone with the same genes but who is thin and doesn't get as much light exposure will go through puberty later (Aylwin et al., 2019). This is why puberty starts earlier among overweight children and among children who grow up closer to the equator (Lee et al., 2016). Obese children have more body fat and therefore produce a lot more leptin, which stimulates kisspeptin production. Children who live near the equator are exposed to relatively more sunlight each year, and they have lower melatonin levels as a result, so their kisspeptin production is not suppressed as

Early feelings of sexual attraction to others are stimulated by adrenarche, the maturation of the adrenal glands, which takes place before the outward signs of puberty are evident. Glow Images

much as it is among children who live closer to the poles. Exposure to artificial light, especially the kind of light emitted from electronic gadgets, can also suppress melatonin levels and hasten puberty (Greenspan & Deardorff, 2014). Children who spend a lot of time in front of electronic screens may be inadvertently speeding up the onset of puberty.

The reason that body fat and light exposure affect the timing of puberty is found in our evolutionary history. Humans evolved when resources were scarce, and it was adaptive to conceive and bear as many offspring as possible since not all of them would survive. If the ultimate goal is to bear as many healthy children as possible, once someone has developed enough fat and senses that the season is right for gathering food, it is time to start maturing physically. Our genes don't know that we no longer live in a resource-scarce world and can store food in our cupboards and refrigerators so that we have plenty to eat in the dark of winter. Although conditions have changed, our brains evolve much more slowly, and the timing of puberty is still affected by how much fat we have accumulated and how much light we've been exposed to.

How Hormones Influence Adolescent Development

Most people understandably think that changes in behavior at puberty result from changes in hormones at that time. But this is only partially correct.

Long before adolescence—in fact, before birth—hormones organize the brain in ways that may not be manifested in behavior until childhood or even adolescence (Sisk & Romeo, 2019). Generally, until about eight

kisspeptin
A brain chemical believed to trigger the onset of puberty.

leptin
A protein produced by the fat cells that may play a role in the onset of puberty through its impact on kisspeptin.

melatonin
A hormone secreted by the brain that contributes to sleepiness and that triggers the onset of puberty through its impact on kisspeptin.

Even though our dog, Benson, was neutered soon after he was born, he still displayed stereotypic "humping" behavior when he reached adolescence as a result of the impact of prenatal testosterone on his brain. He is pictured here with his favorite romantic partner, Lambie. Wendy Steinberg

weeks after conception, the human brain is "feminine" unless and until it is exposed to certain "masculinizing" hormones, such as testosterone. Because levels of testosterone are higher among males than females while the brain is developing, males usually end up with a more "masculinized" brain than females. This sex difference in brain organization predetermines certain patterns of behavior, many of which may not actually appear until much later (Sisk & Romeo, 2019). Studies of sex differences in aggression, for example, show that even though some of these differences may not appear until adolescence, they likely result from the impact of prenatal hormones, rather than from hormonal changes at puberty.

For instance, our dog, Benson, a male who was neutered shortly after birth and therefore didn't have testicles when he reached "adolescence" (which in dogs begins sometime between 6 months and 1 year, with smaller dogs maturing earlier than larger ones), still displayed stereotypical male "humping" behavior when he reached this age. This was likely due to the way his brain was programmed by sex hormones before he was born.

In other words, the presence or absence of certain hormones early in life "program" the brain and the central nervous system to develop in certain ways and according to a certain timetable (Sisk & Romeo, 2019). Because we may not see the resulting changes in behavior until adolescence, it is easy to mistakenly conclude that the behaviors result from hormonal changes that take place at the time of puberty. In reality, however, exposure to certain hormones before birth may set a sort of alarm clock that does not go off until adolescence. Just because the alarm clock rings at the same time that puberty begins does not mean that puberty *caused* the alarm to go off.

Many changes in behavior at adolescence do occur because of changes in hormone levels at puberty, however (Schulz & Sisk, 2016). For instance, the increase in certain hormones at puberty is thought to stimulate the development of secondary sex characteristics, such as the growth of pubic hair. There is also growing evidence that puberty affects the brain in ways that increase adolescents' emotional arousal and desire for highly rewarding, exciting activities, which may make teenagers who are especially sensitive to rewards more prone to emotional and behavioral problems (Goddings et al., 2019; Icenogle et al., 2017).

Other changes during puberty are likely caused by an interaction between prenatal and pubertal hormones. Hormones that are present prenatally may organize a certain set of behaviors (e.g., our brains may be set up to have us later engage in sexual behavior), but certain changes in those hormones at puberty may be needed to activate the pattern; that is, individuals may not become motivated to engage in sex until puberty.

Somatic Development

The effects of the hormonal changes of puberty on the adolescent's body are remarkable. The individual enters puberty looking like a child but within 4 years or so has the physical appearance of a young adult. During this relatively brief period, the average individual grows about 10 inches taller, matures sexually, and develops an adult-proportioned body. Along with many other organs, the brain changes in size, structure, and function at puberty, a series of developments we'll discuss in Chapter 2.

The Adolescent Growth Spurt

The simultaneous release of growth hormones, thyroid hormones, and androgens stimulates rapid acceleration in height and weight. This dramatic increase in stature is called the **adolescent growth spurt**. What is most incredible about the adolescent growth spurt is not so much the absolute gain of height and weight that typically occurs but the speed with which the increases take place.

adolescent growth spurt
The dramatic increase in height and weight that occurs during puberty.

epiphysis
The closing of the ends of the bones, which terminates growth after the adolescent growth spurt has been completed.

Think for a moment of how quickly very young children grow. At the time when the adolescent is growing most rapidly, he or she is growing at the same rate as a toddler, about 4 inches (10.3 centimeters) per year for boys and about 3.5 inches (9.0 centimeters) per year for girls. One marker of the conclusion of puberty is the closing of the ends of the long bones in the body, a process called **epiphysis**, which terminates growth in height. Puberty is also a time of significant increase in weight—nearly half of one's adult body weight is gained during adolescence (Susman & Dorn, 2009).

Figure 1.2 shows just how remarkable the growth spurt is with respect to height. The graph on the left shows changes in absolute height and indicates, as you would expect, that the average individual grows throughout infancy, childhood, and adolescence. As you can see, there is little gain in height after age 18. But look now at the right-hand graph, which shows the average increase in height per year (i.e., the *rate* of change) over the same age span. Here you can see the acceleration in height at the time of peak height velocity.

Figure 1.2 also indicates that the growth spurt occurs, on average, about 2 years earlier among girls than boys. As you can see, boys tend to be somewhat taller than girls before age 11, girls tend to be taller than boys between ages 11 and 13, and boys tend to be taller than girls from about age 14 on. Sex differences in height can be a concern for many young adolescents when they begin socializing with members of the opposite sex, especially if they are tall, early-maturing girls or short, late-maturing boys.

The sequence in which various parts of the body grow is fairly regular. Extremities—the head, hands, and feet—are the first to accelerate in growth. Accelerated growth occurs next in the arms and legs, followed by the torso and shoulders.

Because different parts of the body do not all grow at the same rate or at the same time during puberty, young adolescents often appear to be out of proportion physically—as though their nose or legs were growing faster than the rest of them (which may actually be the case). This is why young adolescents often look clumsy or gawky. It is probably little consolation for someone going through the awkward phase of puberty to be told that an attractive balance probably will be restored within a few years, but, fortunately, this is what usually happens.

Body Dissatisfaction Among Adolescent Girls. Sex Differences in Muscle and Fat   The spurt in height during adolescence is accompanied by a gain in weight that results from an increase in both muscle and fat, but there are important sex differences in adolescent body composition. Before puberty, there are relatively few sex differences in muscle development and only slight sex differences in body fat. In both sexes, muscular development is rapid during puberty, but muscle tissue grows faster in boys than girls (Bogin, 2011). In contrast, body fat increases for both sexes during puberty, but more so for females than for males, especially during the years just before puberty. (For boys, there is actually a slight decline in body fat just before puberty.)

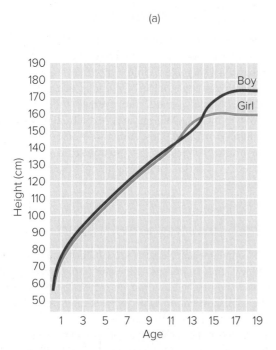

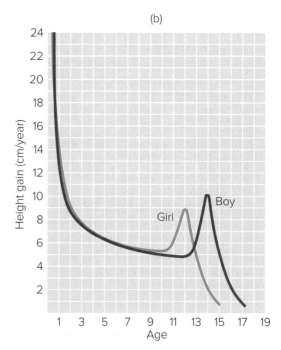

Figure 1.2   (a) Height (in centimeters) at different ages for the average male and female youngster. (b) Gain in height per year (in centimeters) for the average male and female youngster. Note the adolescent growth spurt. (Adapted from Marshall, 1978)

The end result of these sex differences is that boys finish adolescence with a muscle-to-fat ratio of about 3 to 1, but the comparable ratio for girls is approximately 5 to 4. This has important implications for understanding why sex differences in strength and athletic ability often appear for the first time during adolescence. According to one estimate, about half of the sex difference in athletic performance during early adolescence results simply from the difference in body fat (Smoll & Schutz, 1990).

The rapid increase in body fat among females in early adolescence frequently prompts girls to become overly concerned about their weight—even when their weight is within the normal range for their height and age (Calzo et al., 2012). As you will read later in this chapter, adolescence is the period of greatest risk for the development of eating disorders such as anorexia, bulimia, and binge eating disorder. One study of college undergraduates found that women who recalled being unprepared for and disliking going through puberty were at relatively greater risk for developing an eating disorder many years later (Moore, McKone, & Mendle, 2016).

Although the majority of girls diet unnecessarily during this time in response to the increase in body fat, the girls who are most susceptible to feelings of dissatisfaction with their bodies during this phase of development are those who mature early and begin dating early (Smolak, Levine, & Gralen, 1993). Girls who spend a lot of time talking about their looks with their friends, who are teased about their weight (especially by boys), or who are pressured to be thin are especially vulnerable to feelings of body dissatisfaction (Webb & Zimmer-Gembeck, 2014). Girls' body dissatisfaction is often blamed on the impact of the mass media's excessively positive portrayal of thinness, but studies show that it is comparing themselves with their friends, and not just being exposed to media imagery, that leads to unhappiness about their appearance (Ferguson et al., 2014). Adolescent girls' conversations about their looks are affected by the media images they are exposed to in a way that leads them to reinforce each other, however (Rousseau & Eggermont, 2017; Trekels & Eggermont, 2017), in part because girls who are especially weight-conscious often hang around with peers who share the same concerns (O'Connor et al., 2016).

There are also important ethnic and cross-cultural differences in the ways in which adolescent girls feel about their changing bodies. In many parts of the world, including North and South America, Europe, and Asia, there is strong pressure on girls to be thin (Jones & Smolak, 2011). Black adolescents seem less vulnerable to these feelings of body dissatisfaction than other girls (Ali, Rizzo, & Heiland, 2013; Jung & Forbes, 2013), and consequently, they are less likely to diet, in part because of ethnic differences in conceptions of the ideal body type (Granberg, Simons, & Simons, 2009).

Sexual Maturation

Puberty brings with it a series of developments associated with sexual maturation. In both boys and girls, the development of **secondary sex characteristics** is typically divided into five stages, often called **Tanner stages**, after the British pediatrician who devised the categorization system.

Sexual Maturation in Boys

The sequence of developments in secondary sex characteristics among boys is fairly orderly (see Table 1.1). Generally, the first stages of puberty involve

secondary sex characteristics
The manifestations of sexual maturity at puberty, including the development of breasts, the growth of facial and body hair, and changes in the voice.

Tanner stages
A widely used system that describes the five stages of pubertal development.

Table 1.1 The sequence of physical changes at puberty

Girls		Boys	
Age of First Appearance (Years)	**Characteristic**	**Age of First Appearance (Years)**	**Characteristic**
1. 7–13	Growth of breasts	1. 10–13½	Growth of testes, scrotal sac
2. 7–14	Growth of pubic hair	2. 10–15	Growth of pubic hair
3. 9½–14½	Body growth	3. 10½–16	Body growth
4. 10–16½	Menarche	4. 11–14½	Growth of penis
5. About 2 years after pubic hair	Underarm hair	5. About the same time as penis growth	Change in voice (growth of larynx)
6. About same time as underarm hair	Oil- and sweat-producing glands	6. About 2 years after pubic hair appears	Facial and underarm hair
		7. About same time as underarm hair	Oil- and sweat-producing glands, acne

Source: Goldstein, B. (1976).

growth of the testes and scrotum, accompanied by the first appearance of pubic hair. Approximately 1 year later, the growth spurt in height begins, accompanied by growth of the penis and further development of pubic hair—now coarser and darker. The five Tanner stages of penis and pubic hair growth in boys are shown in Figure 1.3.

The emergence of facial and body hair are relatively late developments. The same is true for the deepening of the voice, which is gradual and generally does not occur until very late adolescence. During puberty, boys' skin becomes rougher, especially around their upper arms and thighs, and there is increased development of the sweat glands, which often gives rise to acne, pimples, and increased oiliness of the skin.

Other, internal changes that permit ejaculation occur that are important elements of sexual maturation. At the time that the penis develops, the seminal vesicles, the prostate, and the bulbourethral glands also enlarge and develop. The first ejaculation of semen generally occurs about 1 year after the beginning of accelerated penis growth, although this is often determined culturally rather than biologically since for many boys, their first ejaculation occurs as a result of masturbation (J. Tanner, 1972). One interesting observation about the timing and

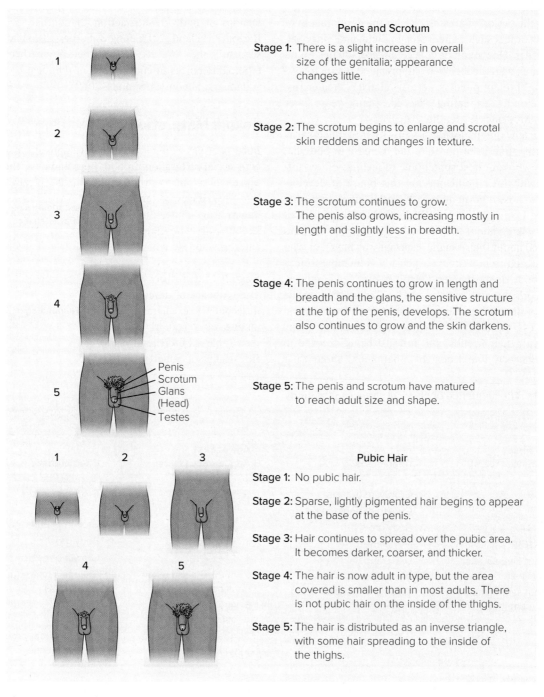

Penis and Scrotum

Stage 1: There is a slight increase in overall size of the genitalia; appearance changes little.

Stage 2: The scrotum begins to enlarge and scrotal skin reddens and changes in texture.

Stage 3: The scrotum continues to grow. The penis also grows, increasing mostly in length and slightly less in breadth.

Stage 4: The penis continues to grow in length and breadth and the glans, the sensitive structure at the tip of the penis, develops. The scrotum also continues to grow and the skin darkens.

Stage 5: The penis and scrotum have matured to reach adult size and shape.

Penis
Scrotum
Glans (Head)
Testes

Pubic Hair

Stage 1: No pubic hair.

Stage 2: Sparse, lightly pigmented hair begins to appear at the base of the penis.

Stage 3: Hair continues to spread over the pubic area. It becomes darker, coarser, and thicker.

Stage 4: The hair is now adult in type, but the area covered is smaller than in most adults. There is not pubic hair on the inside of the thighs.

Stage 5: The hair is distributed as an inverse triangle, with some hair spreading to the inside of the thighs.

Figure 1.3 **The five pubertal stages for penile and pubic hair growth.** (From Morris & Udry, 1980)

sequence of pubertal changes in boys is that boys usually are fertile (i.e., capable of fathering a child) before they have developed an adultlike appearance (Bogin, 2011). As you will read in the next section, the opposite is true for girls.

Sexual Maturation in Girls The sequence of development of secondary sex characteristics among girls (shown in Table 1.1) is less regular than it is among boys. Usually, the first sign of sexual maturation in girls is the elevation of the breast—the emergence of the "breast bud." In about one-third of all adolescent girls, however, the appearance

of pubic hair precedes breast development. The development of pubic hair in females follows a sequence similar to that in males—generally, from sparse, downy, light-colored hair to denser, curlier, coarser, darker hair. Breast development often occurs concurrently with the growth of pubic hair and generally proceeds through several stages during which the shape and definition of the nipple and areola change. The female breast undergoes these changes at puberty regardless of changes in breast size (which is why breast size alone is a poor indicator of pubertal maturation). The five Tanner stages of breast and pubic hair growth in girls are shown in Figure 1.4.

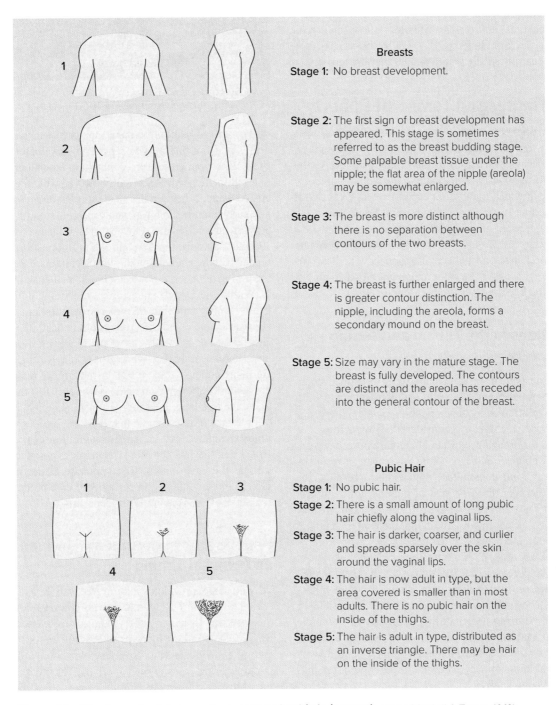

Breasts

Stage 1: No breast development.

Stage 2: The first sign of breast development has appeared. This stage is sometimes referred to as the breast budding stage. Some palpable breast tissue under the nipple; the flat area of the nipple (areola) may be somewhat enlarged.

Stage 3: The breast is more distinct although there is no separation between contours of the two breasts.

Stage 4: The breast is further enlarged and there is greater contour distinction. The nipple, including the areola, forms a secondary mound on the breast.

Stage 5: Size may vary in the mature stage. The breast is fully developed. The contours are distinct and the areola has receded into the general contour of the breast.

Pubic Hair

Stage 1: No pubic hair.

Stage 2: There is a small amount of long pubic hair chiefly along the vaginal lips.

Stage 3: The hair is darker, coarser, and curlier and spreads sparsely over the skin around the vaginal lips.

Stage 4: The hair is now adult in type, but the area covered is smaller than in most adults. There is no pubic hair on the inside of the thighs.

Stage 5: The hair is adult in type, distributed as an inverse triangle. There may be hair on the inside of the thighs.

Figure 1.4 **The five pubertal stages for breast and pubic hair growth.** (From Marshall & Tanner, 1969)

menarche
The time of first menstruation, one of the most important changes to occur among females during puberty.

As is the case for boys, puberty brings important internal changes for adolescent girls that are associated with the development of reproductive capacity. In girls, these changes involve development and growth of the uterus, vagina, and other aspects of the reproductive system. In addition, there is enlargement of the labia and clitoris.

As is apparent in Table 1.1, the growth spurt is likely to occur during the early and middle stages of breast and pubic hair development. **Menarche**, the beginning of menstruation, is a relatively late development. Generally, full reproductive function does not occur until several years after menarche, and regular ovulation follows menarche by about 2 years (Bogin, 2011). Unlike boys, girls typically appear physically mature before they are fertile.

The Timing and Tempo of Puberty

Thus far, no mention has been made of the "normal" ages at which various pubertal changes are likely to take place. This is because variations in the timing of puberty (the age at which puberty begins) and in the tempo of puberty (the rate at which maturation occurs) are so great that it is misleading to talk even about average ages. As you'll read, differences among adolescents in when and how quickly they go through puberty, how synchronized the different changes on puberty are, and how adolescents perceive their own pace of development all have important mental health implications (Mendle, 2014).

Variations in the Timing and Tempo of Puberty

Today, the typical onset of puberty in developed countries is between 8 and 13 in girls and between 9 and 14 in boys. (Children who begin puberty outside these age ranges are technically considered "precocious" or "delayed," although a substantial increase in recent years of girls who begin puberty before 8 is causing a reconsideration of what constitutes "precocious.") In girls, the interval between the first sign of puberty and complete physical maturation can be as short as a year and a half or as long as 6 years. In boys, the comparable interval ranges from about 2 to 5 years (J. Tanner, 1972).

Think about it: Within a totally normal population of young adolescents, some individuals will have completed the entire sequence of pubertal changes before others have even begun. In more concrete terms, it is possible for an early-maturing, fast-maturing youngster to complete pubertal maturation by age 10—3 years before a late-maturing youngster has even begun puberty and 8 years before a late-maturing, slow-maturing youngster has matured completely!

Individuals vary considerably in when puberty begins and the rate at which it progresses. Peathegee Inc/Getty Images

There is no relation between the age at which puberty begins and the rate at which pubertal development proceeds. The timing of puberty may have a small effect on one's ultimate height or weight, however, with late maturers, on average, being taller than early maturers as adults and early maturers, on average, being somewhat heavier—at least among females (St. George, Williams, & Silva, 1994). Adult height and weight are far more strongly correlated with height and weight during childhood than with the timing of puberty, however (Pietiläinen et al., 2001).

Within the United States, there are ethnic differences in the timing and rate of pubertal maturation. Several large-scale studies of U.S. youngsters indicate that Black girls mature significantly earlier than Latinx girls, who, in turn, mature earlier than white girls (Chumlea et al., 2003; Herman-Giddens et al., 1997). Although the reasons for these ethnic differences are not known, they do not appear to be due to ethnic differences in income, weight, or area of residence (Anderson, Dallal, & Must, 2003). One possible explanation for the earlier maturation of non-white girls is that they may be more frequently exposed to chemicals in the environment that stimulate earlier puberty, such as those contained in certain hair care products and cosmetics (Greenspan & Deardorff, 2014).

Genetic and Environmental Influences on Pubertal Timing

Why do some individuals mature relatively early and others relatively late? Researchers who study variability in the onset and timing of puberty approach the issue in two ways. One strategy involves the study of differences among individuals (i.e., studying why one individual matures earlier or faster than another). The other involves the study of differences among groups of adolescents (i.e., studying why puberty occurs earlier or more rapidly in certain populations than in others). Both sets of studies point to both genetic and environmental factors (Geet al., 2007).

Individual Differences in Pubertal Maturation The timing and tempo of pubertal maturation are largely inherited (Mustanski et al., 2004). A specific region on chromosome 6 has been identified as one of the markers for pubertal timing in both boys and girls (Bogin, 2011).

Despite this powerful influence of genetic factors, the environment plays an important role. In all likelihood, every individual inherits a predisposition to develop at a certain rate and to begin pubertal maturation at a certain time. But this predisposition is best thought of as an upper and lower age limit, not a fixed absolute. Whether the genetic predisposition that each person has to mature around a given age is actually realized and when within the predisposed age boundaries she or he actually goes through puberty are influenced by many external factors. In other words, the timing and tempo of pubertal maturation are the product of an interaction between nature and nurture.

The two most important environmental influences on pubertal maturation are nutrition and health. Puberty occurs earlier among individuals who are better nourished and grow more throughout their prenatal, infant, and childhood years, whereas delayed puberty is more likely to occur among individuals with a history of protein and/or caloric deficiency (Terry et al., 2009). Chronic illness during childhood and adolescence is also associated with delayed puberty, as is excessive exercise. Generally, then, after genetic factors, the most important determinant of the timing of puberty is the overall physical well-being of the individual from conception through preadolescence (Susman & Dorn, 2009).

Familial Influences on Pubertal Timing A number of studies have shown that social factors in the home environment also influence the onset of maturation, especially in girls. Puberty occurs somewhat earlier among girls who grew up in father-absent families, in less cohesive or more conflict-ridden households, or with a stepfather (Joos et al., 2018); early puberty is also more common among girls who were sexually abused during childhood (Mendle, Ryan, & McKone, 2016; Negriff, Blankson, & Trickett, 2015). Although it may seem surprising that something as biological as puberty can be influenced by factors in the social environment, scientists have long known that our social relationships affect our biological functioning.

One explanation for the finding that family conflict may accelerate pubertal maturation is that tension in the family may induce stress, which, in turn, may affect hormonal secretions in the adolescent (Belsky et al., 2015; Saxbe et al., 2015), especially among girls who are genetically susceptible to this influence (Ellis et al., 2011; Hartman, Widaman, & Belsky, 2015). (Other types of stress,

such as economic stress, hasten the onset of puberty, too; Sun et al., 2017.) In addition, the presence of a stepfather may expose the adolescent girl to **pheromones** (a class of chemicals secreted by animals that stimulate certain behaviors in other members of the species) that stimulate pubertal maturation. In general, among humans and other mammals, living in proximity to one's close biological relatives appears to slow the process of pubertal maturation, whereas exposure to unrelated members of the other sex may accelerate it.

Group Differences in Pubertal Maturation Unlike differences among adolescents growing up in the same environment, which are mainly due to genetics, differences among countries in the average rate and timing of puberty are more likely to reflect differences in their environments (Bogin, 2011).

The influence of the broader environment on the timing and tempo of puberty can be seen in more concrete terms by looking at two sets of findings: (1) comparisons of the average age of menarche across countries and (2) changes in the average age of menarche over time. Although menarche does not signal the onset of puberty, researchers often use the average age of menarche when comparing the timing of puberty across different groups or historical eras because it can be measured more reliably than other indicators. And while the age of menarche doesn't directly reflect when males in that same group are going through puberty, it does so indirectly because in places where girls mature early, boys mature early, too (Steinberg, 2014a).

Given the importance of nutrition and health as influences on pubertal timing, it comes as no surprise that menarche generally is earlier in countries where individuals are less likely to be malnourished or to suffer from chronic disease (Bogin, 2011). For example, in Western Europe and in the United States, the median age of menarche ranges from about 12 to 13½ years. In Africa, however, the median age ranges from about 14 to 17 years. The range is much wider across Africa because of the greater variation in environmental conditions there.

The Secular Trend We can also examine environmental influences on the timing of puberty by looking at changes in the average age of menarche over the past two centuries. Because nutritional conditions have improved during the past 150 years, we would expect to find a decline in the average age at menarche over time. This is indeed the case, as can be seen in Figure 1.5. This pattern, known as the **secular trend**, is attributable not only to improved nutrition but also to

pheromones
A class of chemicals secreted by animals that stimulate certain behaviors in other members of the species.

secular trend
The tendency, over the past two centuries, for individuals to be larger in stature and to reach puberty earlier, primarily because of improvements in health and nutrition.

Figure 1.5   **The age at menarche has declined considerably over the past 150 years. This decline is known as the secular trend.** (Adapted from Eveleth & Tanner, 1990)

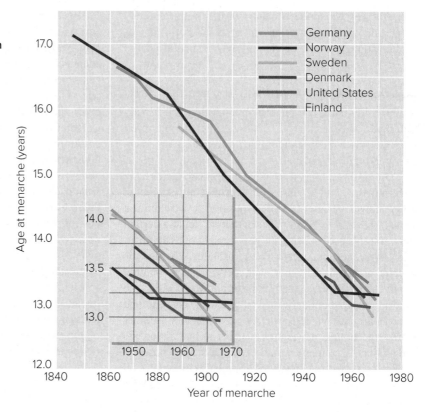

better sanitation and better control of infectious diseases. In most European countries, maturation has become earlier by about 3 to 4 months per decade. For example, in Norway 175 years ago, the average age of menarche may have been about 17 years. Today, it is between 12 and 13 years. A study of Danish adolescents found that five times the number of girls were diagnosed with clinically significant "precocious puberty" in 2017 than 20 years earlier (Brauner et al., 2020). Similar declines have been observed over the same period in other industrialized nations and, more recently, in developing countries as well. In China, for example, the average age of menarche dropped by nearly 2 years between 1991 and 2011 (Meng et al., 2017).

The secular trend is less well documented among boys, in part because there is no easily measured marker of puberty like menarche. One unusual factoid that is consistent with the decline in the age of puberty among boys over many centuries, though, is the observation that the average age at which boys experience their voice breaking (a sign of male pubertal development), based on reports from European children's choirs, dropped from about 18 in the mid-1700s to around 10 today (Mendle & Ferrero, 2012). The drop in the age of male puberty appears to be continuing and has fallen during the past three decades (Herman-Giddens et al., 2012). Interestingly, although puberty is starting earlier, there is some evidence that it is taking longer to complete, meaning that children are

spending more time in the midst of puberty than ever before (Mendle, 2014).

The average age of puberty among American adolescents has continued to decline, most probably because of increased rates of obesity, which affects leptin levels (Currie et al., 2012); exposure to certain human-made chemicals in cosmetics, food, and the environment that affect development by mimicking actual pubertal hormones; and increased exposure to artificial light, which affects melatonin secretion (Greenspan & Deardorff, 2014).

One reason scientists have expressed concern about the continuing decline in the age when puberty begins is that pubertal hormones affect the developing brain in ways that make adolescents more inclined to engage in sensation seeking (Steinberg, 2014a). Brain systems that govern self-regulation are less influenced by puberty, so the secular trend has not greatly affected the age at which the maturation of impulse control takes place. If the increase in sensation seeking is taking place before children are able to regulate urges to do exciting things, it may lead to increases in risky and reckless behavior, especially when the risk taking is impulsive (Khurana et al., 2012). The end result is that, as the age of puberty has dropped, the amount of time elapsed between the arousal of sensation seeking and the maturation of self-control has grown, creating a larger window of vulnerability to risky behavior (Steinberg, 2014). Consistent with this, as the age of puberty has fallen, rates of adolescent mortality have risen (Mendle, 2014).

Scientists have expressed concern about the continuing decline in the age when puberty begins because pubertal hormones affect the developing brain in ways that increase sensation seeking. Mike Powell/Getty Images

making the scientific connection

Some studies indicate that the secular trend has been more dramatic among females than males. Why might this be the case?

The Psychological and Social Impact of Puberty

Puberty can affect the adolescent's behavior and psychological functioning in a number of ways (Lougheed, Hollenstein, & Lewis, 2016). First, the biological changes of puberty can have a direct effect on behavior through its impact on the structure and functioning of the brain (Boivin et al., 2018). For example, increases in levels of sex hormones at puberty heighten activity in brain regions that control our experience of reward, our basic emotions, and our reactions to social stimuli, such as how we interpret our interactions with and the behavior of others (Goddings et al., 2019).

Second, the biological changes of puberty may change the adolescent's self-image, which, in turn, may affect how he or she behaves (Kwon & Park, 2018). For example, a boy who has recently gone through puberty may feel more grown up as a result of his more adultlike appearance. This, in turn, may make him seek more independence from his parents. He may ask for a later curfew, a larger allowance, or the right to make decisions about

things that previously were decided by his parents. As we will see later in this chapter, the physical changes of puberty often spark conflict between teenagers and their parents, in part because of the ways in which puberty affects the adolescent's desire for autonomy.

Finally, biological change at puberty transforms the adolescent's appearance, which, in turn, may elicit changes in how *others* react to the teenager. One recent international study found that puberty leads parents to become less warm and less strict (Lansford et al., 2021). These changes in reactions may also provoke changes in the adolescent's peer relationships. An adolescent girl who has recently matured physically may find herself suddenly receiving the attention of older boys who had not previously noticed her. She may feel nervous about all the extra attention and confused about how she should respond to it. Moreover, she must now make decisions about how much time she wishes to devote to dating and how she should behave when out with someone who is sexually interested in her.

Researchers have generally taken two approaches to studying the psychological and social consequences of puberty. One approach is to look at individuals who are at various stages of puberty, either in a **cross-sectional study** (in which groups of individuals are compared at different stages of puberty) or in a **longitudinal study** (in which the same individuals are tracked over time as they mature through the different stages of puberty). Studies of this sort examine the impact of puberty on young people's psychological development and social relations. Researchers might ask, for example, whether youngsters' self-esteem is higher or lower during puberty than before or after.

A second approach compares the psychological development of early and late maturers. Because there is large variation in pubertal timing, individuals of the same chronological age and who are in the same grade in school may be at very different stages of puberty. How does being early or late to mature affect the adolescent's psychological development? Here, a typical question might be whether early maturers are more popular in the peer group than are late maturers.

cross-sectional study A study that compares two or more groups of individuals at one point in time.

longitudinal study A study that follows the same group of individuals over time.

The Immediate Impact of Puberty

Studies of the psychological and social impacts of puberty indicate that physical maturation, regardless of whether it occurs early or late, affects the adolescent's self-image, mood, and relationships with parents.

Is Puberty Stressful? The connection between puberty and stress is complicated. Although it had long been thought that puberty is a stressful experience, it

Contrary to widespread belief, there is little evidence that the hormonal changes of puberty contribute in a dramatic way to adolescent moodiness. Sladic/Getty Images

looks like stress is more likely to be a cause, rather than a consequence, of pubertal maturation. There is evidence that a modest, but not overwhelming, amount of stress early in life speeds the onset of puberty (Belsky, 2019). Some theorists have proposed that going through puberty at a younger age is an evolved adaptation to chronic early adversity. Being raised under stressful conditions creates uncertainty about the future and actually may stimulate the body to mature faster in order to be able to have children sooner, rather than later.

Whether going through puberty *creates* stress is a different matter. Here, the research indicates that the timing of puberty is key: Maturing early may be stressful, especially for girls, but going through puberty "on time" is generally not; research on whether late maturation is stressful is inconclusive (Joos et al., 2018). As you will read, girls who mature early are more likely to develop emotional and behavioral problems, such as depression and delinquency. It is not clear, however, if the higher incidence of problems among early-maturing girls is actually caused by early maturation or, instead, by the stress that led to early puberty; the problematic outcomes associated with early maturation are also associated with exposure to stress, independent of pubertal timing.

An additional complicating factor is that, as noted earlier in this chapter, puberty affects the brain in ways that make people more *vulnerable* to stress (Dorn et al., 2019). As a consequence, the same stressors have a more adverse impact on mental health when they occur in adolescence than when they occur in childhood or adulthood (Andersen, 2021). Not surprisingly, a wide range of mental health problems, including mood disorders, substance abuse, and eating disorders, are more likely

plasticity
The capacity of the brain to change in response to experience.

to have their onset during adolescence than at any other time (Paus, Keshavan, & Giedd, 2008).

Heightened susceptibility to stress in adolescence is a specific example of the fact that puberty makes the brain more malleable, or "plastic" (Goddings et al., 2019). This makes adolescence both a time of risk (because the brain's **plasticity** increases the chances that exposure to a stressful experience will cause harm) but also a window of opportunity for advancing adolescents' health and well-being (because the same brain plasticity makes adolescence a time when interventions to improve mental health may be more effective).

Puberty and Adolescent Moodiness Although an adolescent's self-image can be expected to change during a time of dramatic physical development, self-esteem or self-image is reasonably stable over time, with long and sturdy roots reaching back to childhood. For this reason, some researchers have turned their attention to the impact of puberty on more transient states, such as mood. One reason for this focus is that adolescents are thought to be moodier, on average, than either children or adults.

Averages can be deceiving, however. Research that has monitored changes in adolescents' daily emotions by having them keep diaries about their activities and feelings has found that the majority of teenagers do not report large ups and downs in their moods. Moreover, teenagers become less moody as they get older (Maciejewski et al., 2015), although those who do not follow this trajectory are more likely to report psychological problems (Maciejewski et al., 2019).

Many people assume that adolescent moodiness is directly related to the hormonal changes of puberty. However, according to several comprehensive reviews of research on hormones and adolescent mood and behavior, the direct connection between hormones and mood is weak (Duke, Balzer, & Steinbeck, 2014).

When studies do find a connection between hormonal changes at puberty and adolescent mood or behavior, the effects are strongest early in puberty, when the process is being "turned on" and when hormonal levels are more likely to fluctuate. For example, *rapid* increases in many of the hormones associated with puberty—such as testosterone, estrogen, and various adrenal androgens—may be associated with increased irritability, impulsivity, aggression (in boys) and depression (in girls), especially when the increases take place very early in adolescence. One interpretation of these findings is that it is not so much the absolute increases in these hormones during puberty but their rapid fluctuation early in puberty that may affect adolescents' moods. Once the hormone levels stabilize at higher levels, later in puberty, their negative effects wane (Buchanan, Eccles, & Becker, 1992).

Although rapid increases in hormones early in puberty are associated with depressed mood in girls, it turns out that stressful life events, such as problems in the family, in school, or with friends, play a far greater role in the development of depression and negative moods than do hormonal changes (Brooks-Gunn, Graber, & Paikoff, 1994; Santiago et al., 2017). Similarly, while high levels of testosterone have been associated with impulsivity and aggression and low levels with depression, these associations are weaker among adolescents who have positive family relationships or strong self-control (Chen, Raine, & Granger, 2018). However, pubertal hormones affect brain systems responsible for emotional arousal in ways that make adolescents more responsive to what is going on around them socially (Forbes et al., 2011; Motta-Mena & Scherf, 2017; Op de Macks et al., 2017). If an adolescent's interpersonal world is stressful, the hormonal changes of puberty may intensify the impact of these social stressors.

In other words, there is little evidence that adolescents' moodiness results exclusively from the "storm and stress" of raging hormones. Over the course of a day, a teenager may shift from elation to boredom, back to happiness, and then to anger. But these shifts in mood appear to have more to do with shifts in activities—elated when seeing a girlfriend, bored during biology, happy when having lunch with friends, and angry when assigned extra chores around the house—than with internal, biological changes (Schneiders et al., 2006). Not surprisingly, adolescents' moods fluctuate over the course of the school year, too, with teenagers reporting the highest levels of anxiety and stress at the end of the school year (Verma et al., 2017).

making the scientific connection

One challenge facing researchers interested in the impact of puberty on psychological functioning is that puberty often coincides with other events that themselves may have significant consequences, such as starting middle school. This makes it difficult to know if an observed change in adolescent behavior or mood during early adolescence is due to puberty, changing schools, or both (or something else entirely). Can you think of ways in which this problem might be addressed through the design of research studies?

Puberty and Changes in Patterns of Sleep Many parents complain that their teenagers go to bed too late in the evening and sleep in too late in the morning, a pattern that begins to emerge in early adolescence (see Figure 1.6). It now appears that the emergence of this pattern—called a **delayed phase preference**—is driven by the biological changes of puberty, and it is seen not only in humans but in other mammals as well (Crowley et al., 2018). Changes in the way the brain regulates sleep—referred to as "sleep architecture"—are more dramatic in adolescence than any other stage of life (Galván, 2020).

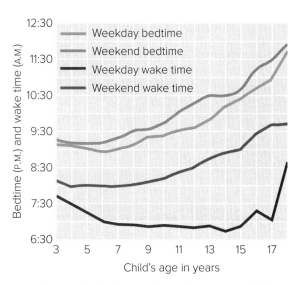

Figure 1.6 **Children's weekday and weekend bedtimes and wake times, by age.** (Adapted from Snell, Adam, & Duncan, 2007)

Falling asleep is caused by a combination of biological and environmental factors. One of the most important is the secretion of melatonin, which, as you know, plays a role in triggering puberty. Melatonin levels change naturally over the course of the 24-hour day, mainly in response to the amount of light in the environment. Feelings of sleepiness increase and decrease with melatonin levels—as melatonin rises, we feel sleepier, and as it falls, we feel more awake. Over the course of the day, we follow a sleep–wake cycle that is calibrated to changes in light and regulated by melatonin secretion.

During puberty, the time of night at which melatonin levels begin to rise changes, becoming later and later as individuals mature physically. In fact, the nighttime increase in melatonin starts about 2 hours later among adolescents who have completed puberty than among those who have not yet begun (Carskadon & Acebo, 2002). As a result of this shift, individuals become able to stay up later before feeling sleepy (Hummer & Lee, 2016). In fact, when allowed to regulate their own sleep schedules (as on weekends), most teenagers will stay up until around 1:00 A.M. and sleep until about 10:00 A.M. Because the whole cycle of melatonin secretion is shifted later at puberty, this also means that once adolescents have gone through puberty, they are more sleepy early in the morning than they had been before puberty.

Falling asleep is affected by the environment as well— it's much easier to fall asleep when a room is dark than when it's bright. When preadolescents get into bed at night, they tend to fall asleep very quickly—even if there is something that they want to stay up for—because their melatonin levels are already high. After going through puberty, though, because

delayed phase preference
A pattern of sleep characterized by later sleep and wake times, which usually emerges during puberty.

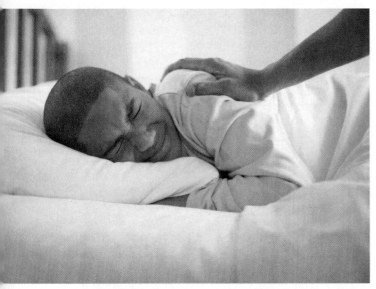

Important changes in the sleep cycle take place after puberty. This "delayed phase preference" causes adolescents to want to stay up later at night and makes them feel more tired in the early morning hours. Randy Faris/Corbis/age fotostock

of the delayed timing of the increase in melatonin, it is easier for individuals to stay up later, so that if there is something more exciting to do—watch a couple of Tik-Tok videos, play a video game, text a friend—it is not difficult to remain awake (Hamilton, et al., 2020; Scott & Woods, 2018).

Thus, the tendency for adolescents to stay up late is due to the interaction of biology (which delays the onset of sleepiness) and the environment (which provides a reason to stay up). This shift in sleep preferences, to a later bedtime and a later wake time, begins to reverse around age 20, at a slightly earlier age among females than males (Fischer et al., 2017). The end result is that there is a marked decline in the amount of sleep people get each night during adolescence followed by an increase during the early 20s (Maslowsky & Ozer, 2014).

If getting up early the next day were not an issue, staying up late would not be a problem. Unfortunately, most teenagers need to get up early on school days, and the combination of staying up late and getting up early leads to sleep deprivation and daytime sleepiness (Tarokh, Saletin, & Carskadon, 2016). The shift in the timing of the melatonin cycle contributes to this; when teenagers get out of bed early in the morning, their melatonin levels are relatively higher than they are at the same time of day for preadolescents. Ironically, adolescents are least alert between the hours of 8:00 and 9:00 A.M. (when most schools start) and most alert after 3.00 P.M., when the school day is usually over. Because of early school start times, adolescents get 2 fewer hours of sleep per night when the school year begins than they did during the preceding summer months (Hansen et al., 2005). This has prompted many experts to call for communities to delay their school starting times (Crowley et al., 2018).

The tendency for individuals to go to bed later as they become teenagers has become stronger over the past 30 years (Keyes et al., 2015), perhaps because the availability of television, the Internet, and other electronic media during late-night and early-morning hours has increased (Adolescent Sleep Working Group, 2014; Mazzer et al., 2018). This suggests that the late-night hours kept by many adolescents are voluntary but made easier by the changes in the sleep centers of the brain. There is also evidence that exposure to light depresses melatonin secretion, so that staying up late with the lights on or staring at a computer, smartphone, tablet, or TV screen will delay the rise in melatonin even more; wearing glasses that block the blue-wavelength light emitted by these screens can help reduce the adverse effects of screen light on sleep (van der Lely et al., 2015). It has also been suggested that the demands of school and extracurricular activities are taking their toll on adolescents' sleep by keeping them busy into the late hours (Gaarde et al., 2020) (see Figure 1.7).

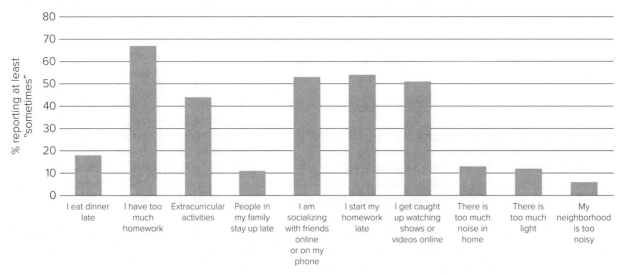

Figure 1.7 **The demands of school and extracurricular activities are taking their toll on adolescents' sleep by keeping them busy into the late hours.** Source: Gaarde, Hoyt, Ozer, Maslowsky, Deardorff, & Kyauk. (2020).

Whatever the reason, because teenagers' wake time has not changed, but their bedtime has gotten later, today's teenagers get significantly less sleep than their counterparts did several decades ago. In the early 1990s, one-third of American 15-year-olds reported getting adequate sleep most nights; today fewer than 25% do (Keyes et al., 2015). More than 40 percent of U.S. adolescents report daytime sleepiness (Kolla et al., 2019).

Although individuals' preferred bedtime gets later as they move from childhood into adolescence, the amount of sleep they need each night remains constant, at around 9 hours (Crowley et al., 2018). There is now a consensus among scientists that most teenagers are not getting enough sleep and that inadequate sleep in adolescence leads to all sorts of problems, including depression (Kuhlman et al., 2020); alcohol, tobacco, and illicit drug use (Pasch et al., 2012); obesity (Turel , Romashkin, & Morrison, 2016); worse relationships (Tavernier & Willoughby, 2015); cognitive impairment and poor school performance (Crowley et al., 2018); behavior problems (Fuligni et al., 2018); and greater reactivity to stress (Chue et al., 2018). Many of the negative consequences of sleep deprivation are due to its adverse impact on self-control (Galván, 2020).

The good news is that getting just one additional hour of sleep each night has been shown to significantly improve adolescents' well-being (Winsler et al., 2015). This may be especially beneficial for teenagers from poor families, who are more likely than those from more advantaged homes to get sufficient sleep (Doane et al., 2019) and whose mental health is especially harmed by sleep problems (El-Sheikh et al., 2020).

Despite many adolescents' belief that catching up on sleep on weekends will make up for sleep deprivation during the week, having markedly different bedtimes on weekends versus weekdays actually contributes to further sleep-related problems (Wolfson & Carskadon, 1998). The best thing teenagers can do to avoid problems waking up on school days is to force themselves to get up at the same time on the weekend as on school days, regardless of how late they have stayed up.

Puberty and Family Relationships Research into the impact of puberty on family relationships has found that puberty appears to increase conflict and distance between parents and children, although the "distancing" effect of puberty on adolescent-parent relationships is not as consistently observed in ethnic minority families (Sagrestano et al., 1999). In white families, however, as youngsters mature from childhood toward the middle of puberty, emotional distance between them and their parents increases, and conflict intensifies, especially between adolescents and mothers (Laursen, Coy, & Collins, 1998). The change that takes place is reflected in an increase in "negatives" (e.g., conflict, complaining, anger) and, to a lesser extent, a decrease in "positives"

(e.g., support, smiling, laughter) (Flannery, Torquati, & Lindemeier 1994).

Although negative interchanges may diminish after midpuberty, adolescents and their parents do not immediately regain the closeness they had previously. Interestingly, puberty also increases distance between children and their parents in most species of monkeys and apes, and some writers have suggested that the pattern seen in human adolescents may have some evolutionary basis: It helps ensure that once they mature sexually, adolescents will leave home and mate outside the family (Steinberg & Belsky, 1996).

This connection between pubertal maturation and parent-child distance is not affected by the age at which the adolescent goes through puberty; the pattern is seen among early as well as late maturers. To date, we do not know whether this effect results from the hormonal changes of puberty (which may make young adolescents more testy), from changes in the adolescent's physical appearance (which may change the way parents treat their adolescent), or from changes in other aspects of adolescents' psychological functioning that are affected by puberty and, in turn, affect family relationships (such as a newfound interest in dating).

The Impact of Specific Pubertal Events

Several studies have focused specifically on adolescents' attitudes toward and reactions to particular events at puberty, such as girls' reactions to menarche or breast development and boys' reactions to their first ejaculation.

In general, most adolescents react positively to the bodily changes associated with puberty, especially those associated with the development of secondary sex characteristics. Girls' attitudes toward menarche are less negative today than they were in the past (J. Lee, 2008), a change that may be attributable to the increase in information about menstruation provided in schools and in the media (Merskin, 1999). Nevertheless, many young women have developed a negative image of menstruation before reaching adolescence, and they enter puberty with a mixture of excitement and fear (S. Moore, 1995). Girls whose mothers are helpful and matter-of-fact in their response to their daughter's menarche report the most positive memories of the experience (J. Lee, 2008).

Menstrual symptoms are reported to be more severe among women who expect menstruation to be uncomfortable, among girls whose mothers lead them to believe that menstruation will be unpleasant or uncomfortable, and in cultures that label menstruation as an important event. In Mexico and China, for example, where attitudes toward menarche are especially ambivalent, menarche may have an adverse effect on girls' mental health, an effect not generally observed in the United States (Benjet & Hernandez-Guzman, 2002; Tang, Yeung, & Lee, 2003). In addition, girls who experience menarche early and who are unprepared for puberty report more negative reactions to the event (Koff & Rierdan, 1996; Tang, Yeung, & Lee, 2004).

Far less is known about boys' reactions to their first ejaculation, an experience that is analogous to menarche in girls. Although most boys are not very well prepared for this event by their parents or other adults, first ejaculation does not appear to cause undue anxiety, embarrassment, or fear. In contrast to girls, who generally tell their mothers shortly after they have begun menstruating and tell their friends soon thereafter, boys, at least in the United States, usually do not discuss their first ejaculation with either parents or friends. Cultural differences in boys' responses to their first ejaculation are likely related to differences in how cultures view masturbation. As is the case with girls and menarche, boys' reactions to their first ejaculation are more positive when they have been prepared for the event (Stein & Reiser, 1994).

The Impact of Early or Late Maturation

Teenagers who mature relatively early or relatively late may elicit different sorts of reactions and expectations from those around them. Adolescents often are all too aware of whether they are early or late relative to their classmates, and their feelings about themselves are likely to be influenced by their comparisons. One study found that early-maturing adolescents were more likely to be "pseudomature"—wishing they were older, hanging around with older peers, less involved in school, and more oriented toward their peers (Galambos, Barker, & Tilton-Weaver, 2003).

Indeed, adolescents' *perceptions* of whether they are an early or a late maturer are often more strongly related to how they feel about and are affected by puberty than whether they actually are early or late (Kretsch, Mendle, & Harden, 2016; Moore, Harden, & Mendle, 2014). Further, adolescents' behavior is related to how old they feel, not simply to how physically mature they are (Galambos et al., 1999). Nevertheless, early and late maturers are often treated differently by others and view themselves

differently, and as a result, they may behave differently. As we shall see, early and late maturation have different consequences during puberty than in the long run, different consequences in different contexts, and, most important, different consequences for boys and girls.

Early Versus Late Maturation Among Boys

Research on boys' pubertal timing has found that early-maturing boys feel better about themselves (Carter, Seaton, & Blazek, 2020) and are more popular than their late-maturing peers, although a few studies have found higher rates of depression and anxiety among early-maturing boys than their on-time peers (Mendle & Ferrero, 2012; Negriff & Susman, 2011) and among boys who go through puberty especially rapidly (Mendle et al., 2010). And, while they are in the midst of puberty, early maturers lose their temper more often and more intensely than late maturers (Ge et al., 2003). Interestingly, although all adolescents are adversely affected by being bullied by their peers, the impact of victimization is greater for early maturers, perhaps because being picked on when one is larger than average is all the more embarrassing (Nadeem & Graham, 2005). As young adults, later-maturing boys are more susceptible to depression, primarily because they perceive themselves as less masculine (Beltz, 2018).

Although the emotional effects of early maturation on boys are generally positive, early-maturing boys are more likely than their peers to get involved in antisocial or deviant activities, including truancy, minor delinquency, and school misbehavior (Beltz et al., 2019). They are also more likely to use drugs and alcohol and engage in other risky activities (Baams et al., 2015; Kogan et al., 2015), even as young adults (Biehl, Natsuaki, & Ge, 2007). One explanation for this is that boys who are more physically mature are less closely supervised by adults and spend more time hanging out with antisocial peers in settings in which delinquent behavior is more likely to occur, such as parts of neighborhoods where there are few adults around (Bucci & Staff, 2020; Klopack et al., 2020; Stepanyan et al., 2020) (see Figure 1.8). It is also likely

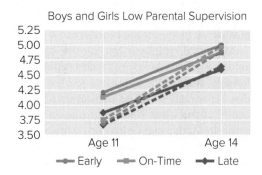
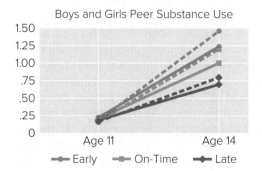

Figure 1.8 Boys who are more physically mature are less closely supervised by adults and spend more time hanging out with antisocial peers in settings in which delinquent behavior is more likely to occur. Source: Bucci & Staff. (2020). Pubertal timing and adolescent delinquency. *Criminology, 58,* Figure 1, p. 552.

Early-maturing boys are more likely to be involved in problem behavior than adolescents who are the same age but slower to mature. Alexandra Dudkina/EyeEm/Getty Images

that older-looking boys develop friendships with older peers, who lead them into activities that are problematic for the younger boys (Negriff, Ji, & Trickett, 2011a). Once they are involved with these older peer groups, the higher rates of delinquency and substance use of early maturers increase over time.

Early-maturing boys enjoy some psychological advantages over late maturers with respect to self-esteem and admiration from peers during early adolescence, when some boys have matured physically but others have not. But what about later during adolescence, when the late maturers have caught up? It turns out that there may be some interesting advantages for late-maturing boys, despite their initially lower popularity. Although early and late maturers exhibit similar psychological profiles before adolescence, late maturers ultimately score higher on measures of intellectual curiosity and social initiative. Having to deal with the challenges of being a late maturer may help boys develop better coping skills.

Early Versus Late Maturation in Girls In contrast to the generally positive impact that early maturation has on the emotional well-being of boys, it is well established that early-maturing girls have more emotional difficulties than their peers, including poorer self-image and higher rates of depression, anxiety, eating disorders, and panic attacks (Copeland et al., 2019; Greenspan & Deardorff, 2014). There is also evidence that early maturation in girls is associated with higher emotional arousal (Graber, Brooks-Gunn, & Warren, 2006). Several studies have found the effects of early maturation on girls' emotional well-being persist into adulthood (Mendle, Ryan, & McKone, 2018), as do the effects of late maturation on depression (Beltz, 2018).

The psychological difficulties experienced by early maturing girls are related to the ways in which looking different from their peers affects girls' feelings about their appearance and their relationships with other adolescents (Mendle, Turkheimer, & Emery, 2007). For example, depression among early-maturing girls is more highly correlated with their breast development (which is more likely to be visible to others) than their pubic hair development (which is not) (Lewis et al., 2018). And the impact of early maturation is worse on girls who are heavier than their peers (Tanner-Smith, 2010).

Given the role of social factors in linking early maturation and girls' psychological distress, it's no surprise that the ultimate impact of early maturation on the young girl's feelings about herself depends on the broader context in which maturation takes place. Studies of American girls generally find that early-maturing girls have lower self-esteem and a poorer self-image because of the culture's preference for thinness and ambivalence about adolescent sexuality. The negative effects of early maturation on girls' mental health vary across ethnic groups, however, with more adverse consequences seen among white and Asian-American girls than in other ethnic groups, presumably because puberty is less likely to lead to body dissatisfaction among Black and Latinx girls (Negriff & Susman, 2011).

Girls who are prone to ruminate or cope poorly when they have problems seem especially vulnerable to the stress of maturing early (Hamilton et al., 2014; Stumper et al., 2019). Context matters, though: One study of both boys and girls found that the adverse consequences of early puberty were limited to adolescents who came from high-risk households, consistent with the idea that puberty itself isn't inherently stressful but can intensify the effects of other stressors, such as transitioning to middle school (Lynne-Landsman, Graber, & Andrews, 2010b; Morales-Chicas & Graham, 2015).

Although some early-maturing girls have self-image difficulties, their popularity with peers is not necessarily jeopardized. Early maturers are more popular than other girls, especially, as you would expect, when the index of popularity includes popularity with boys (Simmons, Blyth, & McKinney, 1983). However, although early-maturing girls are often more popular with boys, they are frequent victims of rumors, gossip, and social exclusion (Carter, Halawah, & Trinh, 2018; Reynolds & Juvonen, 2011) and are more likely to suffer from social anxiety (Blumenthal et al., 2011).

Ironically, then, it may be in part because the early maturer is more popular with boys that she reports more emotional upset: Early pressure to date and, perhaps, to be involved in a sexual relationship may take its toll on girls' mental health. Consistent with this, research indicates that early-maturing girls are more vulnerable to emotional distress when they have relatively more friendships with boys (Ge et al., 1996) and when they are in

Although they are often more popular than their peers, early-maturing girls are at greater risk for a wide range of emotional and behavioral problems. JGI/Jamie Grill/Getty Images

schools with older peers (e.g., sixth-graders who are in a school that has seventh- and eighth-graders, too) (Blyth, Simmons, & Zakin, 1985). Perhaps the problem isn't early maturation as much as it is the way that older boys react to it; the link between early maturation and depression is due in part to the fact that early-maturing girls are more likely to be sexually harassed, bullied, and abused by their boyfriends (Chen, Rothman, & Jaffee, 2017; Skoog, Ozdemir, & Stattin, 2016; Su et al., 2018) (see Figure 1.9).

There are several theories explaining why early maturation is harder on girls than boys (Negriff & Susman, 2011; Rudolph et al., 2020). One explanation is the "maturational deviance" hypothesis. Simply put, youngsters

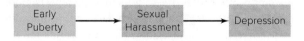

Figure 1.9 **One reason for the elevated rates of depression among early-maturing girls is that they are more likely than their peers to be sexually harassed.** (Based on Skoog, Ozdemir, & Stattin, 2016)

who stand far apart from their peers—in physical appearance, for instance—may experience more psychological distress than adolescents who blend in more easily. Because girls on average mature earlier than boys, early-maturing girls mature earlier than both their male and female peers. This makes them really stand out at a time when they would rather fit in and, as a result, may make them more vulnerable to emotional distress. This explanation would also account for the lower self-esteem of late-maturing boys, who deviate toward the other extreme.

A second explanation for the sex difference in the impact of early maturation concerns "developmental readiness." If puberty is a challenge that requires psychological adaptation by the adolescent, perhaps younger adolescents are less ready to cope with the challenge than older ones. Because puberty occurs quite early among early-maturing girls, it may tax their psychological resources. Early maturation among boys, because it occurs at a later age, would pose less of a problem. This also helps to explain why late-maturing boys seem better able than early maturers to control their temper and their impulses when they are going through puberty: They are relatively older and psychologically more mature. If the developmental readiness hypothesis is true, both girls and boys should experience more difficulty if they are early maturers than if they are on time or late, but the difficulty should be temporary. This appears to be the case among boys (for whom the negative effects of early puberty occur during puberty itself but then fade) but not for girls (for whom the negative effects of early puberty persist) (Ge et al., 2003).

A final explanation for the relatively greater disadvantage of early maturation for girls concerns the cultural desirability of different body types (Petersen, 1988). Early maturation for girls means leaving behind the culturally admired state of thinness. We've already noted that many girls are distressed when they mature because they gain weight. Early maturers experience this weight gain at a time when most of their peers are still girlishly thin. One interesting study showed that in ballet companies—where thinness is even more important than in the culture at large—late maturers, who can retain the "ideal" shape for dancers much longer than earlier maturers, have fewer psychological problems than even on-time girls (Brooks-Gunn & Warren, 1985).

In contrast, at puberty, boys move from a culturally undesirable state for males (short and scrawny) to a culturally admired one (tall and muscular). Early maturers enjoy the advantage of being tall and muscular before their peers—a special benefit in a society that values males' athletic prowess—and therefore are more likely to react well to puberty. The fact that the effects of early maturation on girls' self-esteem vary across cultures suggests that contextual factors need to be taken into account in explaining this pattern of sex differences.

Whatever the explanation, it's important for parents and school counselors to bear in mind that early-maturing girls are at heightened risk for psychological problems. Unfortunately, as long as our culture overvalues thinness and encourages the view that females should be judged on the basis of their physical appearance rather than their abilities, values, or personality, the risks of early puberty will probably endure. Adults can help by being supportive, by helping the early-maturing girl recognize her strengths and positive features—physical and non-physical alike—and by preparing her for puberty before it takes place.

Like their male counterparts, early-maturing girls are also more likely to become involved in problem behavior, including delinquency, drinking, and drug use; to have school problems; and to experience early sexual intercourse (Beltz et al., 2020; Verhoef et al., 2014). This is true in Europe and the United States (Silbereisen et al., 1989) and across ethnic groups within the United States (Baams et al., 2015; Deardorff et al., 2005).

These problems appear to arise because early-maturing girls, like early-maturing boys, are more likely to spend time unsupervised (Kretschmer, Oliver, & Maughan, 2014), hanging out with older adolescents, especially older adolescent boys, who initiate them into activities that might otherwise be delayed (Negriff, Susman, & Trickett, 2011b; Savolainen et al., 2015); early-maturers whose parents are not very knowledgeable about their daughter's activities are especially likely to get into trouble (Marceau, Abar, & Jackson, 2015). This situation is worsened by the fact that, as early maturers start to get involved in more problem behavior, they start to lose their friends who aren't interested in these activities (Franken et al., 2016). Other explanations for the link between early maturation and girls' problem behavior have also been proposed: Some research suggests that the association may be partly due to common genetic influences (i.e., some of the genes that influence the timing of puberty also influence involvement in delinquency) (Harden & Mendle, 2012; Vaughan et al., 2015). Another found that early maturation leads to early sexual activity, which in turn leads to delinquency (Negriff, Susman, & Trickett, 2011b).

Again, however, it is important to consider the role of context in interaction with pubertal change. Although early-maturing girls are more likely to engage in delinquent behavior than late maturers, this is true only for girls who attend coeducational high schools (Caspi et al., 1993). Early-maturing girls in all-female schools are no more likely than late maturers to be involved in delinquent activities, presumably because there are far fewer opportunities for delinquency in same-sex schools. Thus, while early puberty may predispose girls toward more frequent and earlier deviance, this predisposition may be realized only in an environment that permits the behavior—such as a school or out-of-school setting that

places early-maturing girls in close contact with older boys (Stattin, Kerr, & Skoog, 2011). Similarly, among both boys and girls, the impact of early maturation on problem behavior or depression is accentuated when adolescents have many stressful life events, have harsh and inconsistent parents, or live in disadvantaged urban neighborhoods (Benoit, Lacourse, & Claes, 2013; Deardorff et al., 2013; Obeidallah et al., 2004). This helps explain why the impact of early maturation on problem behavior is relatively greater among minority adolescents, who are more likely to live in poor communities (Negriff & Susman, 2011); early maturation does not have especially adverse effects on Black girls who don't live in poor neighborhoods (Carter et al., 2011; DeRose et al., 2011).

The earlier involvement of early-maturing girls in problem behavior may adversely affect their long-term educational achievement and mental health. In one study of Swedish girls, the school problems of early-maturing girls persisted over time, leading to the development of negative attitudes toward school and lower educational aspirations. In young adulthood, there were marked differences between early- and late-maturing girls' educational attainment; late-maturing girls were twice as likely as early maturers to continue beyond the compulsory minimum number of years of high school (Magnusson, Stattin, & Allen, 1986). In a different study, of American girls, researchers found that women who had been early maturers reported higher levels of psychological distress and were more likely than others to have experienced a serious mental disorder at some point in adolescence or young adulthood (Graber et al.,2004). Early-maturing girls are also more likely to experience poorer physical health in adulthood (Belsky & Shalev, 2016).

making the cultural connection

Consider the research on the psychological consequences of early versus late maturation in males and females. Most of this research has been done in the United States. Are the effects of being early, on time, or late likely to be similar in different parts of the world?

Obesity and Eating Disorders

Although a variety of nutritional and behavioral factors can lead to weight gain during adolescence, weight gain sometimes results directly from the physical changes of puberty. Not only does the ratio of body fat to muscle increase markedly during puberty (especially in girls) but the body's **basal metabolism rate**—the minimal amount of energy used when resting—also

> **basal metabolism rate**
> The minimal amount of energy used by the body during a resting state.

body mass index (BMI)
A measure of an individual's body fat, the ratio of weight to height; used to gauge overweight and obesity.

drops about 15%. (A person's weight is partly dependent on this rate.) In light of the tremendous emphasis that contemporary society places on being thin, the normal weight gain and change in body composition that accompany puberty lead many adolescents, especially girls, to become extremely concerned about their weight.

Obesity

Many adolescents, of course, have legitimate concerns about being overweight. The easiest way to determine whether someone is overweight is to calculate his or her **body mass index (BMI).** Individuals are considered obese if their BMI is at or above the 95th percentile for people of the same age and gender, at great risk for obesity if their BMI is at or above the 90th percentile, and overweight if their BMI is at or above the 85th percentile (Zametkin et al., 2004). (Charts showing the BMI cutoffs for males and females of different ages can be found at www.cdc.gov/growthcharts.) Using this definition, about 20% of adolescents in the United States are obese and another 20% are overweight, rates that increased dramatically between 1970 and 2000 and have continued to climb since then (Skinner et al., 2018) (see Figure 1.10). Alarmingly, nearly *half* of all 16- to 19-year-old females in the United States are overweight or obese. Obesity is the single most serious public health problem afflicting American teenagers. The adolescent obesity epidemic is by no means limited to the United States, however, and has been documented in many other industrialized and developing nations (Braithwaite et al., 2013).

Correlates and Consequences of Obesity Obesity is the result of the interplay of genetic and environmental factors (Zametkin et al., 2004). Recent neuroimaging studies find that individuals at risk for obesity show relatively greater activation of the brain's reward centers in general, heightened responses to images of food, and poorer impulse control (Lavagnino et al., 2016; Rapuano et al., 2016). Obesity is especially prevalent among poor youth and among Black, Latinx, and Native American adolescents (Burdette & Needham, 2012; Huh et al., 2012; Skinner et al.,2018). There is also worrisome evidence that, with each successive generation born in the United States, Latinx youth show increasingly poorer nutrition (M. L. Allen et al., 2007).

Research on the psychological consequences of obesity has not led to consistent conclusions, in part because the psychological correlates of being overweight vary across ethnic groups, with more adverse correlates seen among white and Latinx than Black adolescents (BeLue, Francis, & Colaco, 2009). While some studies show higher levels of psychological distress among obese individuals (such as depression and low self-esteem), many studies show no such effect, and some research indicates that psychological problems can both cause and result in weight gains (Qualter et al., 2018; Zametkin et al., 2004). To complicate things even further, the impact of obesity on mental health depends on the adolescent's school: Heavier adolescents report more problems in schools in which there is a lot of "weight-policing" (Juvonen et al., 2019). The long-term psychological consequences of obesity in adolescence appear to be greater for females than males, perhaps because overweight girls are teased more than overweight boys (Lampard et al., 2014).

Because nearly 80% of obese adolescents will become obese adults, obesity during adolescence places the individual at much higher risk for other health problems, including hypertension (high blood pressure), high cholesterol levels, diabetes, and premature death (Ma et al., 2011). The good news is that the long-term health

Figure 1.10 **The percentage of adolescents who are overweight or obese has increased significantly.** Source: Skinner, Ravanbakht, Skelton, Perrin, & Armstrong. (2018). Prevalence of obesity and severe obesity in US Children, 1999–2016, Table 2. *Pediatrics, 141,* e20173459

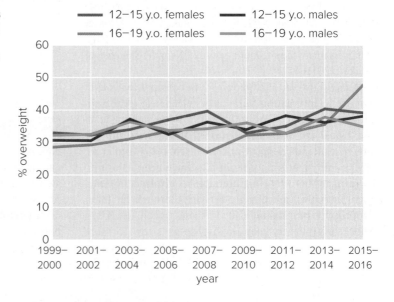

consequences of adolescent obesity disappear among individuals who are not obese as adults (Juonala, Magnussen, & Berenson, 2011). Increasing one's physical activity in adolescence is also associated with improved academic performance (Bezold et al., 2014; Srikanth et al., 2015) and diminished risk for depression (McPhie & Rawana, 2015).

Genetic factors are important contributors to obesity, but the condition also has strong environmental causes. Although rates of adolescent obesity differ from country to country, the factors that contribute to it are similar in different parts of the world (Braithwaite et al., 2013). It's not rocket science: Too many adolescents eat too much high-calorie, low-fiber food (drinking far too many sugary soft drinks and consuming too much junk food), and too few are physically active, spending excessive amounts of time with television, video games, and electronic media, and not enough time exercising or playing sports (Bai et al., 2016; Suchert, Hanewinkel, & Isensee, 2016).

There is a pronounced increase in sedentary behavior between childhood and adolescence, which continues as adolescence progresses, especially among girls (Beal et al., 2016; Ortega et al., 2013). In one study of American adolescents, only one-fourth reported a lifestyle characterized by high levels of physical activity and diets high in fruits and vegetables; another quarter reported lots of time watching TV or on the computer and diets high in sweets, soft drinks, and chips; and the remaining half fell somewhere in between these extremes (Iannotti & Wang, 2013). It is likely that this situation worsened during the COVID-19 pandemic because many young people were not able to go to school, which impacted their participation in physical education classes and extracurricular sports.

In addition, as noted earlier, inadequate sleep also contributes to weight gain, and there has been an increase in the proportion of adolescents who are sleep-deprived. The combination of poor nutrition, insufficient exercise, and inadequate sleep is a recipe for obesity (Spruijt-Metz, 2011). And because adolescents tend to affiliate with peers who share their tastes and interests (including, literally, tastes in food), obese teenagers are relatively more likely to have obese friends, which may reinforce bad habits (de la Haye et al., 2013; Simpkins et al., 2013); in contrast, physically active teens are more likely to have physically active friends (Marks et al., 2015). Attending a high school where a large proportion of juniors and seniors are obese significantly increases the likelihood that the freshmen and sophomores will be obese, too (Leatherdale & Papadakis, 2011). Finally, numerous studies have shown that exposure to adversity early in life is associated with obesity in adolescence, perhaps because stress exposure can undermine the subsequent development of self control (Bae, Wickrama, & O'Neal, 2014; Hanson et al., 2013).

Preventing and Treating Obesity Much recent attention has focused on the availability of unhealthy foods and beverages in and near American schools (Hoyt et al., 2014). Manufacturers of high-calorie and high-fat foods have been criticized for marketing these products to younger children because food preferences are known to develop largely during early childhood (IOM and NRC, 2006). Of course, although schools and advertisers undoubtedly influence what children and adolescents eat and drink, the bulk of what children and adolescents put into their mouths comes from their own homes. Obesity is less likely to develop among adolescents who have good relationships with their parents, probably because they are more likely to share family meals at which healthy food is served (Berge et al., 2010; Hammons & Fiese, 2011). In addition, the availability of parks and recreational facilities is linked to lower rates of obesity, as is parental encouragement of exercise (Nesbit et al., 2014; Spruijt-Metz, 2011). Taken together, these studies indicate that preventing obesity will require multifaceted efforts involving parents, the mass media, food and beverage manufacturers, restaurants, schools, and communities.

Research has also evaluated a variety of approaches to individual weight loss, including behavioral therapy designed to gradually alter patterns of diet and exercise and medications designed to promote weight loss. Adolescents can be taught to successfully regulate their cravings for food (Silvers et al., 2014). Several evaluations indicate that the combination of behavior modification and weight-loss medication is more effective than either component by itself (Kirschenbaum & Gierut, 2013). Although some weight-loss programs have been shown to work, there is wide variability in success rates, depending on the nature of the program (Sarwer & Dilks, 2012; Stice, Shaw, & Marti, 2006). One thing is certain, though: Radical approaches to weight control—fad diets and the like—actually increase, rather than decrease, obesity (Neumark-Sztainer et al., 2012; Stice et al., 2005; Zhang et al., 2011). Ironically, adolescents who mistakenly believe that they are overweight often engage in unhealthy dieting behavior, which actually increases the likelihood that they will become obese (Sutin & Terracciano, 2015).

Anorexia Nervosa, Bulimia, and Binge Eating Disorder

Health-care professionals are concerned not only about adolescents who are obese but also about adolescents who have unhealthy attitudes toward eating and toward their body image. Only about one-fourth of American adolescents are highly satisfied with their body (A. Kelly et al., 2005). More than half of all adolescent girls consider themselves overweight and have attempted to diet (Fisher et al., 1995).

Disordered Eating Experts today think about **disordered eating** on a continuum, ranging

disordered eating
Mild, moderate, or severe disturbance in eating habits and attitudes.

anorexia nervosa
An eating disorder found chiefly among young women, characterized by dramatic and severe self-induced weight loss.

bulimia
An eating disorder found primarily among young women, characterized by a pattern of binge eating and extreme weight-loss measures, including self-induced vomiting.

binge eating disorder
An eating disorder characterized by a pattern of binge eating that is not accompanied by drastic attempts to lose weight.

from dieting that may be unnecessary but not unhealthy, to disordered eating that is unhealthy but not at a level requiring treatment, to full-blown clinical disorders (Tyrka, Graber, & Brooks-Gunn, 2000). Disordered eating is associated with a range of stress-related psychological problems, including poor body image, depression, alcohol and tobacco use, and poor interpersonal relationships (Eichen et al., 2012; Neumark-Sztainer et al., 1998). It is not clear, however, whether these problems precede or follow from the eating disorder (Leon et al., 1999).

Studies of magazines aimed at women and adolescent girls reveal clear and consistent messages implying that women cannot be beautiful without being slim and promoting a range of weight loss products (Davison & McCabe, 2011). Exposure to commercials containing images of females with idealized thin bodies increases girls' dissatisfaction with their own bodies (Rodgers, McLean, & Paxton, 2015). Interestingly, among Latinx girls in the United States, those who are more Americanized are significantly more likely to develop disordered eating than those who are less acculturated (Gowen et al., 1999). Girls whose mothers have body image problems are especially likely to engage in extreme weight loss behaviors (Ogle & Damhorst, 2003), as are those who report more negative relationships with their parents (Archibald, Graber, & Brooks-Gunn, 1999).

Body dissatisfaction during adolescence can lead to disordered eating. GlobalStock/Getty Images

Some young women become so concerned about gaining weight that they take drastic—and dangerous—measures to remain thin. In the more severe cases, young women who suffer from an eating disorder called **anorexia nervosa** actually starve themselves in an effort to keep their weight down. Others go on eating binges and then force themselves to vomit or take laxatives to avoid gaining weight, a pattern associated with an eating disorder called **bulimia**. A related disorder is **binge eating disorder** (Tanofsky-Kraff, Schvey, & Grilo, 2020). Individuals with binge eating disorder frequently report loss of control while eating, during which they consume large quantities of food in a short period of time and feel distressed about doing so but do not try to compensate for their binges through extreme weight-loss measures, such as purging. As a consequence, individuals with binge eating disorder are at high risk for obesity.

Adolescents with these sorts of eating disorders have an extremely disturbed body image: They may see themselves as overweight when they are actually underweight, or they simply may be excessively unhappy with their appearance. Some anorexic youngsters may lose between 25% and 50% of their body weight. As you might expect, bulimia and anorexia, if untreated, lead to a variety of serious physical problems. Nearly 20% of anorexic teenagers inadvertently starve themselves to death.

Anorexia and bulimia each began to receive a great deal of popular attention during the 1980s because of their dramatic nature and their frequent association in the mass media with celebrities. Perhaps because of this attention, initial reports characterized these eating disorders as being of epidemic proportion. Although unhealthy eating and unnecessary dieting are prevalent among teenagers, the combined incidence of clinically defined anorexia, bulimia, and binge eating disorder among adolescents is substantially lower, about 4.5% (Flament et al., 2015). About 1% of women will develop anorexia in their lifetime, about 1.5% will develop bulimia, and about 3.5% will develop binge eating disorder (Hudson et al., 2007). Rates among females are substantially higher than among males: Anorexia and bulimia are three times more prevalent among females than males, and binge eating disorder is about twice as prevalent among females.

Although it is widely believed that eating disorders are especially common among affluent, suburban, white, and Asian American girls, systematic studies do not support this contention. Disordered eating and body dissatisfaction have been reported among poor as well as affluent teenagers and among Black and Latinx as well as Asian and white youngsters. Generally speaking, eating disorders decline between childhood and early adolescence but increase between mid-adolescence and young adulthood, although the are ethnic differences in the age of onset and progression, with more Black females reporting more dieting and disordered eating than white females as preteens but less as young adults, which likely reflects the

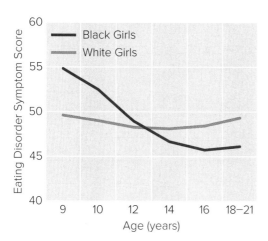

Figure 1.11 **Black females report more dieting and disordered eating than white females as preteens but less as young adults.** Source: Bodell, Wildes, Cheng, Goldschmidt, Keenan, Hipwell, & Stepp. (2018).

fact that Black girls on average begin puberty at a younger age (see Figure 1.11) (Bodell et al., 2018; Lee et al., 2013; Olvera et al., 2015).

Body Dissatisfaction Although the incidence of clinical eating disorders is small, the proportion of adolescents who are unhappy with their body shape or weight is not. In one study, more than a third of girls whose weight was considered normal by medical and health standards believed that they were overweight—including 5% who actually were *underweight* by medical criteria. (In contrast, fewer than 7% of normal-weight boys and no underweight boys described themselves as being overweight.) More than 70% of the girls reported that they would like to be thinner than they are (as opposed to one-third of the boys), and more than 80% said that being thinner would make them happier, more successful, and more popular (Paxton et al., 1991).

Dissatisfaction with body shape and weight is likely to lead to the development of eating problems (Francisco et al., 2015; Rodgers et al., 2016), depression (Stice & Bearman, 2001; Stice et al., 2000), and the initiation of smoking and drinking (Andrew, Tiggemann, & Clark, 2016). More than half of high school girls have engaged in some form of unhealthy behavior (e.g., fasting, smoking, vomiting after eating, using diet pills) in order to lose weight (Croll et al., 2002), although there is evidence that this practice has waned somewhat in recent years (Park et al., 2014).

Unfortunately, many girls gain weight during puberty, and for early adolescent girls, being overweight is highly correlated with being seen as unattractive by others (Rosenblum & Lewis, 1999). Despite adults' wishes that girls not place so much emphasis on being thin, the widespread belief among adolescent girls that being slim will increase their popularity, especially with boys, is in fact based in reality (Halpern et al., 1999). That is, the

pressure girls feel to be thin in order to attract boys does not just come from television, movies, and magazines; it comes from their actual experience. One analysis found that each 1-point increase in a young woman's **BMI** was associated with a 6% decrease in the probability of her being in a romantic relationship (Halpern et al., 2005). In that study, a 5-foot 3-inch tall girl who weighed 110 pounds was twice as likely to date as a girl of the same height and level of pubertal maturity who weighed 126 pounds.

Fewer studies have examined body dissatisfaction among adolescent boys, although it is clear that there is an idealized, muscular, male body type that many boys aspire to; according to one study, 40% of normal-weight boys and one-fourth of overweight or obese boys report trying to gain weight (Nagata et al., 2019). As is the case with girls, boys who do not fit this image report more body dissatisfaction, but the relation between appearance and body dissatisfaction among males is more complicated than it is among females. Whereas being heavy is the main source of dissatisfaction among girls, being heavy *or* being thin are both sources of dissatisfaction among boys (Calzo et al., 2012) (see Figure 1.12). As is the case among girls, being teased by peers about one's body is a significant source of distress for boys (Lawler & Nixon, 2011).

Contributing Factors Historical and cross-cultural trends in the prevalence of anorexia and bulimia point to important differences between the two disorders (Keel & Klump, 2003). Whereas anorexia has been observed all over the world, bulimia has been reported mainly in Western cultures or in cultures exposed to strong Western influences. (Because binge eating disorder is a relatively new diagnosis, we do not yet have good cross-cultural data on its prevalence, but it appears to have more in common with bulimia than anorexia.) And whereas anorexia has increased in prevalence steadily over time, the prevalence of bulimia increased significantly between 1970 and 1990 but has declined somewhat since then, despite the fact that individuals' BMI has continued to increase (Cash et al., 2004). This suggests that bulimia is a much more culturally determined disorder than is anorexia. Consistent with this, the degree to which anorexia is an inherited disorder is far more comparable from one culture to another than is the case for bulimia.

Today, experts view eating disorders as part of a more general syndrome of psychological distress. Many studies have found links between eating disorders and other serious mental health problems, such as depression, obsessive-compulsive disorder, or substance abuse; many adolescents with eating disorders display such psychological problems (Lee & Vaillancourt, 2018; Sharpe et al., 2018; Verschuren et al., 2020), and depression sometimes precedes the development of an eating disorder, rather than the reverse (Ferreiro et al., 2014). These studies suggest

Figure 1.12 Body dissatisfaction by BMI classification for girls and boys. (Lawler & Nixon, 2011)

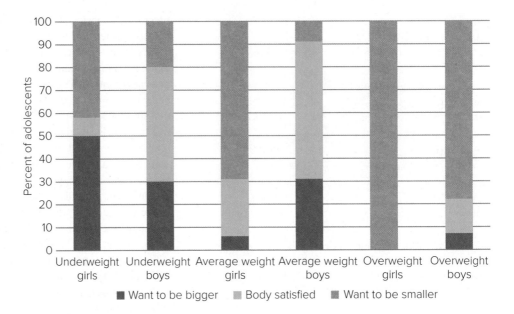

that eating disorders may be best understood as particular manifestations of a more general underlying psychological problem—called "internalized distress"—that can be displayed in a variety of ways (Juarascio et al., 2016). In support of this view, some evidence suggests that the same medications that are successful in treating depression and obsessive-compulsive disorder are useful in treating bulimia (but not anorexia) (Walsh et al., 2006). Eating disorders that are accompanied by other psychological problems, such as depression, are more likely to persist into adulthood (Goldschmidt et al., 2016).

Given that anorexia and bulimia are far more common in females than males, broader social forces are probably a main factor in the development of these eating disorders (Keel & Klump, 2003). Research indicates that girls who are early maturers are likely to report greater dissatisfaction with their body and to be at greater risk for disordered eating (Greenspan & Deardorff, 2014); that girls who perceive that they are under pressure to be thin or who have accepted thinness as an ideal toward which to strive are more susceptible to eating disorders (Fairweather-Schmidt & Wade, 2016; Stice & Van Ryzin, 2019); and that girls who turn to popular magazines for information about dieting and appearance are more likely to have a high drive for thinness, low body satisfaction, and disturbed patterns of eating (Jones, Vigfusdottir, & Lee, 2004). Some adolescents seem to pay special attention to information and imagery about physical appearance, which makes them especially vulnerable to feelings of body dissatisfaction (Saunders & Frazier, 2017; Verschuren et al., 2020).

Adolescents' beliefs about ideal body types are also shaped by the people they spend time with. Girls' attitudes toward eating and dieting are influenced by the attitudes of their parents (especially their mothers) and friends (Rodgers et al., 2016; Salafia & Gondoli, 2011;

Simone, Long, & Lockhart, 2018), as well as frequent use of social media (De vries et al., 2016). Being teased about one's weight is especially likely to lead to disordered eating, as well as symptoms of depression (Zimmer-Gelbeck et al., 2020).

Just because cultural factors contribute to the development of disordered eating doesn't mean that individual characteristics do not play a role as well. Cultural conditions may predispose females more than males toward disordered eating, and girls and young women who have certain genetic vulnerabilities (eating disorders are partly heritable), psychological traits (such as proneness to depression or low self-esteem), physical characteristics (such as early pubertal maturation), familial characteristics (such as strained relations with parents), or social concerns (such as a strong interest in dating) may be more likely to develop problems (Nagata et al., 2018). One study found that the likelihood of a 9th-grader developing disordered eating, such as binge eating or purging, could be predicted from the adolescent's proneness toward negative affect in fifth grade, before there were any signs of disordered eating (Pearson & Smith, 2015). The onset of eating disorders, like so many aspects of adolescent development, is likely the product of a complex interaction between individual and contextual factors.

Less is known about the causes and consequences of body dissatisfaction among adolescent males than among females, but many contemporary adolescent boys feel pressure to be especially muscular, and some engage in unhealthy behaviors, such as anabolic steroid use, "driven" exercise, and fasting in order to develop an appearance that is more similar to the idealized male body type (Davis, Guller, & Smith, 2016; Ricciardelli & McCabe, 2004). Moreover, body dissatisfaction is predictive of dieting, unhealthy weight control behaviors, and binge eating among males as well as females, regardless of whether they are actually overweight (Lewis-Smith et al., 2020; Neumark-Sztainer et al., 2006). Studies of male adolescents in China have found similar patterns (Jackson & Chen, 2014).

A variety of therapeutic approaches have been employed successfully in the treatment of eating disorders, including individual psychotherapy and cognitive behavioral therapy, group therapy, family therapy, and antidepressant medications (Stice, Shaw, & Ochner, 2011). The treatment of anorexia often requires hospitalization initially in order to ensure that starvation does not progress to fatal or near-fatal levels. The treatment of bulimia and binge eating disorder, especially with cognitive behavioral therapy, has proven far more successful than the treatment of anorexia.

making the practical connection

What might be done to counter the impact of cultural pressures that encourage the development of eating disorders among young women? Is the spread of Western media around the world likely to contribute to rising rates of eating disorders in other countries?

2

Cognitive Transitions

Changes in Cognition

Thinking About Possibilities

Thinking About Abstract Concepts

Thinking About Thinking

Thinking in Multiple Dimensions

Adolescent Relativism

Theoretical Perspectives on Adolescent Thinking

The Piagetian View of Adolescent Thinking

The Information-Processing View of Adolescent Thinking

The Adolescent Brain

How Your Brain Works

The Age of Opportunity

What Changes in Adolescence?

Implications for Adolescent Behavior

Individual Differences in Intelligence in Adolescence

The Measurement of IQ

Culture and Intelligence

Adolescent Thinking in Context

Social Cognition in Adolescence

Adolescent Risk Taking

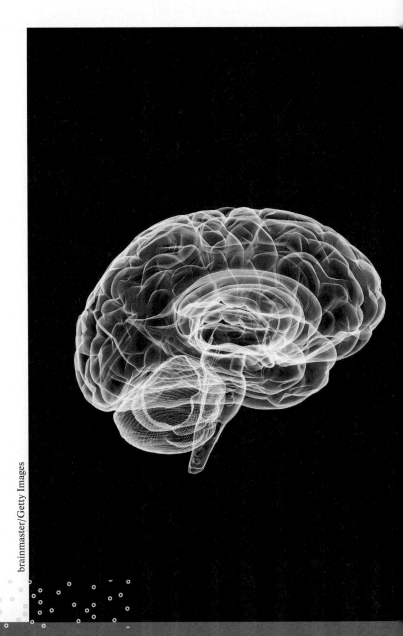

brainmaster/Getty Images

Changes in cognition, or thinking, represent the second of three fundamental changes that occur during adolescence—in addition to puberty and the transition into new social roles. Like developments in the other two domains, the cognitive transitions of adolescence have far-reaching implications for the young person's psychological development and social relations. Indeed, the expansion of thought during adolescence represents as significant an event and as important an influence on the adolescent's development and behavior as puberty.

During the last two decades, scientists have made tremendous gains in understanding brain maturation during adolescence through the use of imaging techniques that permit us to look inside the adolescent brain, just as an X-ray permits physicians to look directly at bones. We now have a good idea of how the brain's structure and patterns of activity change during adolescence and the implications of these changes for behavioral, emotional, and, of course, cognitive development. Later in this chapter, we'll look at brain maturation in adolescence in detail. But let's begin by simply describing how adolescents think and, more importantly, how their thinking differs from that of children and adults.

Changes in Cognition

Most people would agree that adolescents are "smarter" than children. Teenagers clearly *know* more than children—after all, the longer we live, the more opportunities we have to acquire new information. But adolescents also *think* in ways that are more advanced, more efficient, and generally more effective than children (Keating, 2011; Kuhn, 2009). Compared to children:

- Adolescents are better at thinking about what is possible, instead of limiting their thinking to what is real.
- Adolescents are better at thinking about abstract things.
- Adolescents think more often about the process of thinking itself.
- Adolescents' thinking is more often multidimensional, rather than limited to a single issue.
- Adolescents are more likely to see things as relative, rather than as absolute.

Let's look at each of these advantages—and some of their implications for adolescents' behavior—in greater detail.

Thinking About Possibilities

Children's thinking is oriented to the here and now—to things and events that they can observe directly. But adolescents are able to consider what they observe against a backdrop of what is possible. Put another way, for the child, what is possible is what is real; for the adolescent, what is real is just a subset of what is possible. This allows adolescents to think "counterfactually"—to think not only about how things actually are but also to think about what might have been (Beck & Riggs, 2014).

Consider how individuals think about themselves. Children don't wonder, the way adolescents often do, about how their personalities might change in the future or how they might have been different had they grown up under different circumstances. When you are a child, you simply are who you are. In adolescence, though, who you are is just one possibility of who you could be.

This does not mean that children are incapable of imagination or fantasy. Nor does it mean that children are unable to conceive of things being different from what they observe. But adolescents are able to move easily between the actual and the possible, to generate alternative possibilities and explanations systematically, and to compare the ways things are with the way they might be under different circumstances.

The adolescent's ability to reason systematically in terms of what is possible comes in handy when learning math and science. The study of mathematics in junior and senior high school (algebra, geometry, and trigonometry) often requires that you begin with an abstract or theoretical formulation; for example, "the square of a right triangle's hypotenuse is equal to the sum of the squares of the other two sides" (the Pythagorean theorem). This theorem is a proposition about all *possible* right triangles, not just triangles that you might actually observe. In mathematics, you learn how to apply these theorems to concrete examples (that is, real triangles). You understand that the theorem still holds true even for right triangles you have never seen. Scientific experimentation also involves the ability to generate possibilities systematically. In a chemistry experiment in which you are trying to identify an unknown substance by performing various tests, you must first be able to imagine alternative possibilities for the substance's identity in order to know what tests to conduct.

The adolescent's use of this sort of thinking is not limited to mathematical or scientific problem solving. We see it in the types of arguments adolescents employ, in which they are better able than children to envision and anticipate the possible responses of an opponent and to have one or more counterarguments handy.

Although many parents believe that their children become more argumentative during adolescence, what is more likely going on is that the cognitive changes of the period enable them to be better arguers. Tetra Images/Getty Images

making the practical connection

In what ways did your high school classes take advantage of the advanced thinking abilities that develop in adolescence? In what ways were opportunities to do this missed? What might teachers do to stimulate more advanced thinking?

Related to the development of reasoning abilities is the emergence of hypothetical, or "if-then," thinking. In order to think hypothetically, you need to see beyond what is directly observable and apply logical reasoning to anticipate what might be possible. Being able to plan ahead, to see the future consequences of an action, and to provide alternative explanations of events all require being able to think hypothetically.

Hypothetical thinking has important implications for the adolescent's social behavior. Taking the perspective of others enables the adolescent to think through what someone else might be thinking or feeling ("If I were in her situation, I'd be pretty angry"). This helps in formulating and arguing a viewpoint because it allows adolescents to think a step ahead of the opposition—a cognitive tool that can come in handy when dealing with parents ("If they come back with 'You have to stay home and clean up the garage,' then I'll remind them about the time they let my sister go out when *she* had chores to do").

Many parents believe that their children become more argumentative during adolescence. What probably happens, though,

metacognition
The process of thinking about thinking itself.

is that their children become *better arguers* (Steinberg, 2011). Adolescents don't accept other people's points of view unquestioningly—including their parents' viewpoints. They evaluate them against other theoretically possible beliefs. This improvement in the adolescent's intellectual ability likely contributes to the bickering and squabbling that often occur between teenagers and their parents (Smetana, 1989).

Thinking About Abstract Concepts

The appearance of more systematic, abstract thinking is a second notable aspect of cognitive development during adolescence. We noted earlier that children's thinking is more concrete and more bound to observable events and objects than is that of adolescents. This difference is clear when we consider the ability to deal with abstract concepts—things that cannot be experienced directly through the senses.

Abstract thinking is clearly seen in adolescents' ability to think in more advanced ways about interpersonal relationships, politics, philosophy, religion, and morality—topics that involve such abstract concepts as friendship, faith, democracy, fairness, and honesty. The growth of social thinking during adolescence is directly related to the young person's improving ability to think abstractly. Later in this chapter, we'll examine the ways in which social thinking—generally referred to as "social cognition"—improves in adolescence.

Thinking About Thinking

A third gain in cognitive ability during adolescence involves thinking about thinking itself, a process sometimes referred to as **metacognition.** Metacognition often involves monitoring your own cognitive activity during the thinking process; for example, when you consciously use a strategy for remembering something (such as the mnemonic device *Every Good Boy Deserves Fun* to recall that the notes of the treble clef are E-G-B-D-F) or when you make sure you've understood something you're reading before going on to the next paragraph.

Because adolescents are better at thinking about their own thoughts, they are much better at monitoring their own learning (Crone et al., 2006; Kuhn, 2009). While studying, adolescents are able to step back and assess how well they are learning the material. Doing this enables them to pace their studying accordingly—to speed up and skim the material if they feel that they are learning it easily or to slow down and repeat a section if they are having a hard time. Brain systems that are active when individuals are monitoring their own performance continue to mature throughout adolescence and early adulthood, which may help the development of metacognition (Ladouceur, Dahl, & Carter, 2007).

Thinking about thinking also leads to increased introspection and self-consciousness. When we are introspective, we are thinking about our own emotions. When we are self-conscious, we are thinking about how others think about us. These processes permit the sorts of self-examination and exploration that are important tools for establishing a coherent sense of identity.

Adolescent Egocentrism The ability to think about thinking sometimes results in problems for young adolescents before they adjust to having such powerful cognitive tools. Being able to introspect, for instance, may lead to periods of extreme self-absorption—referred to as "adolescent egocentrism" (Elkind, 1967). **Adolescent egocentrism** results in two distinct problems in thinking that help to explain some of the seemingly odd beliefs and behaviors of teenagers (Goossens, Seiffge-Krenke, & Marcoen, 1992).

The first, the **imaginary audience,** comes from having such a heightened sense of self-consciousness that you imagine that your behavior is the focus of everyone else's attention. For example, a teenager who is going to a concert with 10,000 other people may worry about dressing the right way because "everybody will notice." Given the cognitive limitations of adolescent egocentrism, it is hard to persuade young adolescents that the "audience" is not all that concerned with their behavior or appearance. We now know that the parts of the brain that process social information—such as perceptions of what others are thinking—undergo significant change during early adolescence, just when self-consciousness is increasing (Mills et al., 2014b; Pfeifer et al., 2013; Somerville et al., 2013).

A second problem resulting from adolescent egocentrism is called the **personal fable.** The personal fable revolves around the adolescent's egocentric (and erroneous) belief that his or her experiences are unique. For instance, an adolescent teenager whose relationship with a girlfriend has just ended might tell his sympathetic mother that she could not possibly understand what it feels like to break up with someone—even though breaking up is something that most people experience plenty of times in life. Maintaining a personal fable of uniqueness has some benefits, in that it enhances adolescents' self-esteem and feelings of self-importance. But holding on to a personal fable also can be dangerous: think about a sexually active adolescent who believes that pregnancy simply won't happen to her or a reckless driver who believes that he will defy the laws of nature by taking hairpin turns at breakneck speed.

making the personal connection

Think back to your own adolescence. Can you recall times when you experienced an imaginary audience? How about more recently? Do you think this happened more when you were younger than it does now?

Thinking in Multiple Dimensions

A fourth way in which thinking changes during adolescence involves the ability to think about things in multiple dimensions (Kuhn, 2009). Whereas children tend to think about things one aspect at a time, adolescents can see things through more complicated lenses. For instance, when a certain batter comes up to the plate in a baseball game, a preadolescent who knows that the player has a good home-run record might exclaim that the batter will hit the ball out of the stadium. An adolescent, however, would consider the hitter's record in relation to the specific pitcher on the mound and would weigh both factors before making a prediction (perhaps this player often hits homers against left-handed pitchers but frequently strikes out against righties).

The ability to think in multidimensional terms is evident in a variety of situations. Adolescents can give much more complicated answers than children to questions such as "Why did the Civil War begin?" or "How did Jane Austen's novels reflect the changing position of women in European society?" Thorough answers to these sorts of questions require thinking about several dimensions simultaneously because many factors led to the Civil War, just as many factors affected the way in which people reacted to Austen's work.

As is the case with other gains in cognitive ability, the ability of individuals to think in multiple dimensions also has consequences outside of school. Adolescents describe themselves and others in more complicated terms ("I'm shy with strangers but extroverted with people once I've met them") and find it easier to look at problems from multiple perspectives ("I know that's the way you see it, but try to look at it from her point of view"). Understanding that people's personalities are not one-sided or that social situations can have different interpretations permits the adolescent to have far more sophisticated—and far more complicated—self-conceptions and relationships.

Sarcasm and *South Park* Adolescents' ability to look at things in multiple dimensions also enables their understanding of sarcasm. As an adult, you know that the meaning of a speaker's statement is communicated by a combination of what is said, how it is said, and the context in which it is said. If I turned to you during a boring lecture, rolled my eyes, and said, in an exaggeratedly earnest tone, "This is the most interesting lecture I've ever heard," you'd know that I actually meant just the opposite. But you'd know this only if you paid attention to my inflection and to the context, as well as the

adolescent egocentrism
Extreme self-absorption, often a consequence of too much "thinking about thinking."

imaginary audience
The belief, often brought on by the heightened self-consciousness of early adolescence, that everyone is watching and evaluating one's behavior.

personal fable
An adolescent's belief that he or she is unique and therefore not subject to the rules that govern other people's behavior.

The development of advanced thinking abilities allows adolescents to appreciate sarcasm, irony, and satire, such as that used in shows such as South Park. Hulton Archive/Getty Images

content, of my statement. Only by attending simultaneously to multiple dimensions of speech can we distinguish between the sincere and the sarcastic. It's no surprise that our ability to use and detect sarcasm and irony improves during preadolescence and adolescence (Glenwright & Pexman, 2010).

Why do young adolescents laugh hysterically when characters in movies aimed at their age group say things like "He said 'erector set'"? Adolescents' ability to think in multiple dimensions also permits them to appreciate satire, metaphor, and the ways in which language can be used to convey multiple messages. Teenagers' ability to use and appreciate sarcasm, irony, and satire helps to explain why shows such as *The Simpsons, South Park,* and *Rick and Morty* have always had such strong appeal in this age group. (Not to mention that they are often pretty funny to adults, too. Our son's school once summoned his class's parents to watch an "offensive" episode of *South Park* to show us how our children were being harmed by television; the demonstration ended prematurely, though, because we parents were laughing too hard.)

Adolescent Relativism

A final aspect of cognition that changes during adolescence concerns a shift from seeing things in absolute terms—in black and white—to seeing things as relative. Compared to children, adolescents are more likely to question others' assertions and less likely to accept "facts" as absolute truths.

This increase in relativism can be exasperating to parents, who may feel as though their teenagers question everything just for the sake of argument. Difficulties often arise, for example, when adolescents begin seeing parents' values that they had previously considered absolutely correct ("Moral people do not have sex before they are married") as completely relative ("Welcome to the twenty-first century, Dad").

Theoretical Perspectives on Adolescent Thinking

Although it's clear that adolescents' thinking is more advanced than children's, researchers disagree about the processes underlying this advantage. Part of the lack of agreement stems from the fact that no one single factor distinguishes thinking during adolescence from thinking during childhood (Keating, 2011). And part stems from the different points of view that theorists have taken toward cognitive development in general. Because researchers working from different theoretical perspectives have posed different research questions, used different tasks to measure thinking, and emphasized different aspects of cognitive activity, their studies provide different, but nevertheless compatible, pictures of mental development during adolescence.

Two theoretical viewpoints that have been especially important are the Piagetian perspective and the information-processing perspective. Although these two views of adolescent thinking begin from different assumptions about the nature of cognitive development in general, they each provide valuable insight into why thinking changes during adolescence (Kuhn, 2009).

The Piagetian View of Adolescent Thinking

Theorists who adopt a Piagetian perspective take a **cognitive-developmental view** of intellectual development. They argue that cognitive development proceeds through a fixed sequence of qualitatively distinct stages, that adolescent thinking is fundamentally different from the type of thinking employed by children, and that during adolescence, individuals develop a special type of thinking that they use across a variety of situations.

According to Piaget, cognitive development proceeds through four stages: (1) the **sensorimotor period** (from birth until about age 2), (2) the **preoperational period** (from about age 2 until about age 5), (3) the period of **concrete operations** (from about age 6 until early adolescence), and (4) the period of **formal operations** (from adolescence through

cognitive-developmental view
A perspective on development, based on the work of Piaget, that takes a qualitative, stage-theory approach.

sensorimotor period
The first stage of cognitive development, according to Piaget, spanning the period roughly between birth and age 2.

preoperational period
The second stage of cognitive development, according to Piaget, spanning roughly ages 2 to 5.

concrete operations
The third stage of cognitive development, according to Piaget, spanning the period roughly between age 6 and early adolescence.

formal operations
The fourth stage of cognitive development, according to Piaget, spanning the period from early adolescence through adulthood.

adulthood). Each stage is characterized by a particular type of thinking, with earlier stages of thinking being incorporated into new, more advanced, and more adaptive forms of reasoning. Piagetian theorists believe that abstract logical reasoning is the chief feature that differentiates adolescent thinking from that of children (Keating, 2011).

We noted that adolescents' thinking can be distinguished from the thinking of children in several respects—among them, being able to think hypothetically, multidimensionally, and abstractly. The connection between these skills and the development of formal operations is clear: In order to think about alternatives to what really exists, to think in multidimensional terms, and to systematically think about concepts that aren't directly observable, you need a system of reasoning that works just as well in hypothetical situations as it does in actual ones.

There is a difference, of course, between what adolescents are capable of doing and what they actually do. Gaps between people's reasoning abilities and how logically they think in everyday situations are huge, and everyday decision making is fraught with logical errors that cannot be explained by cognitive incompetence (Kahneman, 2011). This is true for adults as well as adolescents. For example, if asked whether they would rather try to pull a lucky lottery ticket from an envelope of 10 tickets, of which only 1 is lucky, versus an envelope of 100 tickets, of which 10 are lucky, most people select the second option—even if they know that the mathematical odds of pulling a lucky ticket are identical in the two scenarios.

The Piagetian perspective on cognitive development during adolescence has stimulated a great deal of research on how young people think, although not all of the perspective's predictions have held up (Keating, 2011). Actually, very little research supports the idea that cognitive development proceeds in a stage-like fashion and that there is a qualitatively unique stage of thinking that is characteristic of adolescence (Keating, 2011; Kuhn, 2009). Rather, advanced reasoning capabilities develop gradually and continuously from childhood through adolescence and beyond, in more of a steady fashion than was proposed by Piaget (that is, more like a ramp than like a staircase). Rather than talking about a distinct stage of cognitive activity characteristic of adolescence, it is more accurate to depict these advanced reasoning capabilities as skills that are employed by older children more often than by younger ones, by some adolescents more often than by others, and by individuals when they are in certain situations (especially familiar ones) more often than when they are in other ones (Kuhn, 2009).

The Information-Processing View of Adolescent Thinking

Piaget attempted to describe adolescent thinking in broad terms and to use one overarching concept—formal operations—to characterize the period. Other scientists have tried to identify the specific abilities that improve as individuals move from childhood into adolescence and beyond. This question has been the focus of researchers working from the **information-processing perspective.**

Studies of changes in specific components of information processing have focused on four areas in which improvement occurs during adolescence: attention, memory, processing speed, and organization. All of these skills improve as individuals move from childhood through adolescence, mainly during the first half of the adolescent decade (Keating, 2004).

information-processing perspective
A perspective on cognition that derives from the study of artificial intelligence and attempts to explain cognitive development in terms of the growth of specific components of the thinking process (such as memory).

selective attention
The process by which we focus on one stimulus while tuning out another.

divided attention
The process of paying attention to two or more stimuli at the same time.

Attention During adolescence, we become better at paying attention (Thillay et al., 2015). Improvements take place both in **selective attention,** in which adolescents must focus on one thing (a reading assignment) and tune out another (the electronic beeping of a younger brother's video game), and in **divided attention,** in which adolescents must pay attention to two different things at the same time (such as studying while texting with a friend) (Memmert, 2014; Mizuno et al., 2011). Improvements in attention mean that adolescents are better able than children to concentrate and stay focused on complicated tasks, such as reading and comprehending difficult material. There also is considerable evidence that the ability to inhibit an unwanted response (for instance, stopping

Improvements in selective attention and divided attention enable adolescents to tune out interference and focus on the task at hand. Dougal Waters/Getty Images

yourself from looking up at a commercial that suddenly appears on the television in the corner of the room while you are reading) improves during early and middle adolescence (Kuhn, 2009). This improvement is likely linked to maturation of brain systems that govern impulse control (Casey & Caudle, 2013; Church et al., 2017). As we'll discuss in the chapter on "Work, Leisure, and Media," one concern that has been raised in recent years is the possible adverse impact that media multitasking has on adolescents' ability to sustain attention on information they need to focus on (Rothbart & Posner, 2015; Uncapher, Thieu, & Wagner, 2016).

Memory   Second, memory abilities improve during adolescence. This is reflected both in **working memory,** which involves the ability to remember something for a brief period of time, such as 30 seconds, and in **long-term memory,** which involves being able to recall something from a long time ago (Keating, 2004). Studies of adolescents' ability to remember personally meaningful events from earlier in life, an aspect of long-term memory called **autobiographical memory,** find that our earliest memories, some of which we lose during childhood, stabilize sometime during early adolescence, when most people can remember back to when they were about two and a half years old, but not much earlier than this (Reese, Jack, & White, 2010).

Adults generally remember details about the people, places, and events they encountered during adolescence better than those from other years, a phenomenon called the **reminiscence bump** (Rubin et al., 1986). The reminiscence bump does not appear to result from better memory because basic memory abilities remain strong until midlife. Nor is it due to the fact that so many important events happen for the first time during adolescence (e.g., first love, first job, first time living away from parents). Even mundane events that took place during adolescence are recalled better than those that happened at other ages. Moreover, we tend to remember other, less personal things from adolescence better, too—things such as movies, books, music, and current events (Janssen, Chessa, & Murre, 2007).

Something is different about how everyday experiences are encoded during adolescence, as if the brain's "recording device" is calibrated to be hypersensitive at this age. When certain chemicals in the brain are released at the same time an event is experienced, the event is more easily remembered than when levels of these chemicals are not as high. These chemicals are released when we experience something that elicits strong negative or positive feelings. As we'll see, brain regions responsible for strong emotions are especially sensitive during adolescence. As a result, the adolescent brain is chemically primed to encode memories more deeply (Knutson & Adcock, 2005). As you'll read later in this chapter, brain systems that govern emotion undergo dramatic change in adolescence. The reminiscence bump doesn't exist because more emotional events take place in adolescence but because ordinary events trigger stronger emotions.

When we think of the importance of memory in problem solving, we typically think of having to retrieve facts that we deliberately have memorized—one aspect of long-term memory. But working memory may be even more important than long-term memory for the sort of problem solving likely encountered in adolescence (Ahmed et al., 2019; Amso et al., 2014). For example, in order to answer multiple-choice questions, you need to be able to remember each option long enough to compare it with the other choices as you read them. Think for a moment of how frustrating it would be to try to solve a multiple-choice problem if, by the time you had read the final potential answer, you had forgotten the first one!

Working memory skills increase between childhood and adolescence and over the course of adolescence (Carriedo et al., 2016). Improvements in working memory coincide with the continued maturation of brain regions during adolescence that are responsible for this aspect of cognition (Hanson et al., 2012; Jolles et al., 2011). More specifically, advances in working memory during adolescence are linked to the ways in which these areas of the brain are organized and connected, which permits more efficient and powerful information processing (Wendelken et al., 2016; Sole-Padulles et al., 2016). And because these brain regions are still developing in early adolescence, it is possible to improve individuals' basic cognitive abilities through training (Schmiedek, Lovden, & Lindenberger, 2014). As is the case with media multitasking and attention, though, concerns have been raised about the impact of multitasking on memory; adolescents who are frequent multitaskers perform worse on tests of both working memory and long-term memory (Uncapher et al., 2016).

Speed   A third component of information processing related to improvements in thinking in adolescence is an increase in the sheer speed of information processing (Kail & Ferrer, 2007). Regardless of the task employed, older adolescents process the information necessary to solve the problem faster than early adolescents, who, in turn, process information faster than preadolescents. This increase in the speed of information processing occurs mainly in early adolescence; the difference in speed between a 9-year-old and a 12-year-old is greater than that between a 12-year-old and a 15-year-old, which, in turn, is greater than that between a 15-year-old and an

working memory
That aspect of memory in which information is held for a short time while a problem is being solved.

long-term memory
The ability to recall something from a long time ago.

autobiographical memory
The recall of personally meaningful past events.

reminiscence bump
The fact that experiences from adolescence are generally recalled more than experiences from other stages of life.

18-year-old (Kail & Ferrer, 2007). Processing speed does not change very much between middle adolescence and young adulthood (Church et al., 2017).

Organization A fourth information-processing gain in adolescence involves improvements in organizational strategies (Siegler, 2006). Adolescents are more planful than children; they are more likely to approach a problem with an appropriate strategy in mind and are more flexible in their ability to use different strategies in different situations (Albert & Steinberg, 2011a). The use of mnemonic devices (such as using HOMES to remember the names of the Great Lakes—Huron, Ontario, Michigan, Erie, and Superior) and other organizational strategies helps to account for differences in the performance of older and younger children on academic tasks requiring memory (Siegler, 2006).

For instance, think for a moment about how you approach learning the information in a new textbook chapter. After years of studying, you are probably well aware of particular strategies that work well for you (underlining, highlighting, taking notes, writing in the margins), and you begin a reading assignment with these strategies in mind. Because children are not as planful as adolescents, their learning is not as efficient.

Developmental differences in levels of planning during childhood and adolescence can be seen quite readily by comparing individuals' approaches to the guessing game 20 Questions. With age, individuals' strategies become increasingly more efficient; when guessing the name of a person, an adolescent might begin by asking whether the person is dead or alive, then male or female, and so forth, whereas a young child might just start randomly throwing out the names of specific people (Drumm & Jackson, 1996).

Is Cognitive Development Complete by Age 15?
By the time they have turned 15, adolescents are just as proficient as adults in basic cognitive abilities (Icenogle et al., 2019). Working memory, attention, and logical reasoning abilities increase throughout childhood and early adolescence and then level off around this age (Gathercole et al., 2004; Luciana et al., 2005). However, at this age people are still developing more sophisticated cognitive skills, such as thinking creatively, planning ahead, or judging the relative costs and benefits of a risky decision (Kleibeuker et al., 2013; Albert & Steinberg, 2011b), and in the coordination of cognition and emotion, when feelings might interfere with logical reasoning (e.g., when you have to make a decision when you are angry or facing peer pressure) (Albert, Chein, & Steinberg, 2013). Much of what we have learned about brain maturation in adolescence—the subject of the next section—helps explain why basic information-processing skills may mature by age 15 but the development of more advanced abilities may not be complete until individuals reach their mid-20s.

The Adolescent Brain

In the past 25 years, there has been an explosion in research on adolescent brain development, and the speed with which our understanding of adolescent brain development has grown has been absolutely breathtaking (Blakemore, 2018; Dahl, 2016; Spear & Silveri, 2016).

Improvements in the methods used to study brain maturation—including studies of brain growth and development in other animals (because all mammals go through puberty, it is possible to study "adolescent" brain development in other species), studies of changes in brain chemistry, and postmortem studies of brain anatomy—have advanced the field in important ways (Doremus-Fitzwater, & Spear, 2016; Mychasiuk & Metz, 2016). But the major contribution to our understanding of what takes place in the brain during adolescence has come from studies using various imaging techniques, especially **functional magnetic resonance imaging (fMRI)** and **diffusion tensor imaging (DTI).** These techniques allow researchers to take pictures of individuals' brains and compare their anatomy and activity. Some aspects of brain development in adolescence are reflected in changes in **brain structure** (for instance, certain parts of the brain are relatively smaller in childhood than adolescence, while others are relatively larger), whereas others are reflected not so much in the brain's structure but in changes in **brain function** (for instance, adolescents may use different parts of the brain than children when performing the same task) (e.g., Dosenbach et al., 2010; O'Hare et al., 2008; Wang, Huettel, & De Bellis, 2008).

Using DTI, scientists are able to see the ways in which various regions of the brain are connected and compare patterns of interconnections among people at different ages (e.g., Klingberg, 2006). This allows us to better understand how "communication" patterns linking different regions of the brain change with development. Researchers use fMRI to examine patterns of activity in various regions of the brain while individuals are performing different tasks (e.g., recalling a list of words, viewing photos of friends, or listening to music).

Participants in an fMRI study are asked to perform tasks on a computer while they are lying inside a brain scanner. With this setup, it is possible to study both how patterns of brain activity differ during different tasks (e.g., when we are actively reading versus being read to) and whether people of different ages show different patterns of brain activity while performing the same task. In

functional magnetic resonance imaging (fMRI) A technique used to produce images of the brain, often while the subject is performing some sort of mental task.

diffusion tensor imaging (DTI) A technique used to produce images of the brain that shows connections among different regions.

brain structure The physical form and organization of the brain.

brain function Patterns of brain activity.

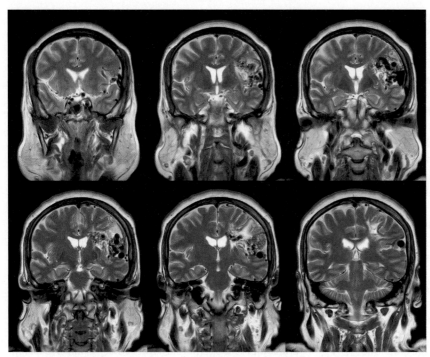

Advances in brain-imaging technology have contributed to our understanding of how the brain changes at adolescence. These images are created through a process known as functional magnetic resonance imaging, or fMRI. AkeSak/Shutterstock

between pubertal hormones and brain development, since male and female brains are exposed to different levels of testosterone and estrogen both prenatally and during puberty (Boivin et al., 2018; Bramen et al., 2012; Herting et al., 2012). It is clear that the structure of the brain is changed by exposure to sex hormones, but the ways in which the brains of adolescent boys and girls differ as a result of sex hormones is enormously complicated (Cédric et al., 2014). Some studies also show different patterns of connections between brain regions in males and females (Lopez-Larson et al., 2011; Satterthwaite et al., 2015; Tomasi & Volkow, 2012), although the importance of these changes for understanding sex differences in behavior or cognition is not known.

By and large, however, the similarities between males and females in brain structure and function—before, during, and after adolescence—are far more striking than the differences (Gur & Gur, 2016). Most experts agree that differences between how males and females think are too small to be of practical significance and do not justify educational curricula or teaching techniques that have been specially geared for boys or girls (Miller & Halpern, 2014). There may be other reasons to prefer single-sex schools over coeducational ones, but sex differences in brain development isn't one of them.

our lab, for instance, my collaborators and I study how patterns of brain activity vary when individuals perform tasks either alone or with their friends watching them and whether the ways in which the impact of an audience of peers on brain activity differs between teenagers and adults (e.g., Smith et al., 2015).

Are Male and Female Brains Different?   Many popular books claim that there are important differences between the brains of adolescent boys and girls (and, for that matter, adult men and women). Research indicates, however, that differences between the genders in brain structure and function are very small and unlikely to explain differences between males and females in the way they behave or think. In general, male brains are about 10% larger than female brains (even accounting for the fact that male bodies, on average, are bigger than females'), but because there is no relation between brain size and intellectual functioning, it is unlikely that this small difference in size has any practical significance. In addition, there are few consistent sex differences in the size of specific brain regions or structures; some parts of the brain are slightly larger among females, and some are slightly larger among males (Goddings et al., 2019). There is some evidence, however, that there is more variability in the ways in which the structure of the brain changes during adolescence among males than females (Wierenga et al., 2018). Several studies have looked specifically for connections

neurons
Nerve cells.

How Your Brain Works

The brain functions by transmitting electrical signals across circuits that are composed of interconnected cells, called **neurons.** Each neuron has three parts: a cell body; a longish projection called an axon, which terminates in many small tips; and thousands of tiny, antennae-like branches, called dendrites, which themselves split off into smaller and smaller spines, like a plant's root system. In the adult brain, each neuron has about 10,000 connections. Collectively, neurons and the projections that connect them are called "gray matter."

When electrical impulses travel along a neural circuit, they leave one neuron through its axon and enter the next one through one of the receiving neuron's dendrites. The transmission of current from one neuron to another can be thought of as the passage of information along that particular pathway, like runners on a track team passing a baton during a relay race. Everything we think, perceive, feel, or do depends on the flow of electrical impulses across the brain's circuits.

The axon of one neuron is not actually connected to the dendrites of another, the way an electrical wire in your home is connected to a light switch or the way the prongs of an appliance plug touch the active contacts inside an outlet. There is a tiny gap, called a **synapse,** between the tip of one neuron's axon and another neuron's dendrite. In order for an impulse to be relayed to a neighboring neuron, the electrical charge has to "jump" across this gap. How does this happen?

The transfer of current across the synapse when a neuron fires is enabled by the release of chemicals called **neurotransmitters.** You've probably heard of some of the most important neurotransmitters, such as dopamine or serotonin. Many of the most widely prescribed antidepressants work, for instance, by altering the amount of serotonin in brain circuits that control mood.

When neurotransmitters are released from the "sending" neuron and come into contact with the receptors on the dendrites of the "receiving" neuron, a chemical reaction occurs on the other side of the synapse that triggers a new electrical impulse, which travels on its way to the next neuron in the circuit, jumping across the next synapse with the help of neurotransmitters. This process is repeated whenever information travels through the brain's elaborate circuitry.

Each neurotransmitter has a specific molecular structure that fits into a receptor for which it is precisely designed, the way a key fits into a lock. An impulse that stimulates a neuron to release dopamine will trigger a response in other neurons that have dopamine receptors but not in ones that only have receptors for a different neurotransmitter. This enables the brain to stay organized; if any time a neuron fired it activated every other neuron in the neighborhood, all helter-skelter, it would be impossible to maintain well-defined brain circuits—an enormous challenge in an organ that packs 100 billion neurons, each with 10,000 connections, into the space inside your skull. This way, when a neuron that is part of a circuit that regulates mood fires, it affects how you feel, not whether you move your big toe.

A key process in early brain development is the development of billions and billions of synapses—the connections between neurons. The formation of some of these synapses is genetically programmed, but others are formed through experience. The rate of synapse formation peaks at about age 1 and slows down in early childhood, but the development of new synapses continues throughout life as we learn new skills, build memories, acquire knowledge, and adapt to changing circumstances. The more a synapse is used, the stronger its electrical pathway becomes.

Gray Matter Initially the brain produces many more connections among cells than it will use. At 1 year of age, the number of synapses in the infant brain is about *twice* the number in the adult brain (Couperus & Nelson, 2006). However, soon after birth unused and unnecessary synapses start to be eliminated, a process called **synaptic pruning.**

As a general rule, we tend to assume that "more is better," but that's not the case with the number of synapses in the brain. Imagine a meadow between two patches of forest. Hundreds of lightly trodden paths connect one side to the other (the unpruned brain). Over time, people discover that one path is more direct than others. More people begin using this path more often, so it becomes wider and deeper. Because the other paths are no longer used, the grass grows back and those paths disappear. That's what synaptic pruning is like: The "paths" we use repeatedly become more and more ingrained, whereas those we do not use disappear. Synaptic pruning results in a decrease in the amount of gray matter in the brain, which is often manifested in a thinning of the areas that have been pruned (Tamnes et al., 2017).

Synaptic pruning continues through adolescence and is normal and necessary to healthy brain development. Just as pruning a rose bush—cutting off weak and misshapen branches—produces a healthier plant with larger flowers, so synaptic pruning enhances the brain's functioning. Synaptic pruning makes the brain more efficient by transforming an unwieldy network of small pathways into a better organized system of "superhighways."

Generally, the development of synapses is characterized by a period of growth (when more and more synapses

synapse
The gap in space between neurons, across which neurotransmitters carry electrical impulses.

neurotransmitters
Specialized chemicals that carry electrical impulses between neurons.

synaptic pruning
The process through which unnecessary connections between neurons are eliminated, improving the efficiency of information processing.

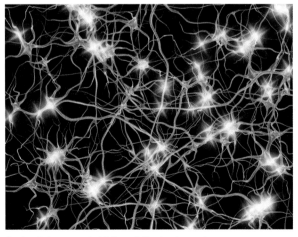

During infancy and childhood, the brain produces more connections between neurons, called synapses, than is necessary. Adolescence is a time when many of these unnecessary synapses are eliminated, a process called "pruning." Science Photo Library - Pasieka/Getty Images

myelination
The process through which brain circuits are insulated with myelin, which improves the efficiency of information processing.

plasticity
The capacity of the brain to change in response to experience.

developmental plasticity
Extensive remodeling of the brain's circuitry in response to experiences during childhood and adolescence, while the brain is still maturing.

adult plasticity
Relatively minor changes in brain circuits as a result of experiences during adulthood, after the brain has matured.

are created) followed by a period of decline (when more and more synapses are pruned). When we plot the density of synapses over time, we see a ∩-shaped curve—or, more accurately, a series of ∩-shaped curves that peak at different ages, depending on the specific region of the brain, because different regions are pruned at different ages (Tanaka et al., 2012). As a rule, the brain regions in which pruning is taking place at a particular point in development are the regions associated with the greatest changes in cognitive functioning during that stage because as a particular pathway of neural transmission becomes more efficient, the specific cognitive process it supports improves. For example, synaptic pruning in the brain's visual system is most dramatic early in infancy, when our visual abilities are improving the most.

White Matter   Cells other than neurons also play a role in transmitting electrical impulses along brain circuits. These cells, known as "white matter," provide support and protection for neurons and compose a fatty substance, called myelin, that surrounds the axons of certain neurons, like the plastic sheath around electrical wires. Myelin insulates brain circuits, keeping the impulses flowing along their intended pathways rather than leaking out. Circuits that are coated in myelin carry impulses about a hundred times faster than circuits that are not myelinated, making them much more efficient, especially if the circuits cover a large distance.

The growth of myelin, called **myelination,** occurs in waves, beginning before birth and continuing into young adulthood (Paus, 2009). Unlike synapses, with their ∩-shaped pattern of growth, white matter increases throughout childhood and adolescence, well into adulthood, although at different rates in different regions of the brain at different points in development (Brain Development Cooperative Group, 2012). As with synaptic pruning, examining *where* myelination is occurring most dramatically at a particular point in development provides clues about the aspects of cognitive functioning that are changing most at that stage.

The Age of Opportunity

One of the most exciting new discoveries in neuroscience is that some areas of the brain may be especially malleable, or "plastic," in adolescence; they are more easily shaped, for better or for worse, by experience during adolescence than at any time other than the first few years of life (Lillard & Erisir, 2011; Selemon, 2013; Zelazo & Carlson, 2012). That's why adolescence has been described as an "age of opportunity" (Steinberg, 2014).

Scientists have known for some time now that the brain is particularly malleable during the first 3 years after birth. But the discovery that adolescence is a second period of heightened brain **plasticity** is a relatively recent development and one that scientists have become increasingly interested in (Fuhrmann, Knoll, & Blakemore, 2015). There is increasing evidence that the increase in brain plasticity in adolescence is influenced by the hormonal changes of puberty (Laube, van den Bos, & Fandakova, 2020).

Plasticity refers to the capacity of the brain to change in response to experience. It's the process through which the outside world gets inside us and changes us. The brain's remarkable malleability in response to experience enables us to learn and strengthen abilities, from very basic ones (such as memory) to very advanced ones (such as planning ahead). This is at the heart of brain plasticity. It's not only "use it or lose it." It's also "use it and improve it." This is true at all ages, but it is much more easily and reliably accomplished before adulthood, when the brain is much more plastic.

Why It's Hard for Old Dogs to Learn New Tricks
There are two types of brain plasticity: developmental and adult. **Developmental plasticity** refers to the malleability of the brain during periods in which the brain is being built, when its anatomy is still changing in profound ways, as is the case in adolescence. Some of these changes involve the development or loss of brain cells, but the most important changes involve the brain's "wiring"—that is, how its 100 billion neurons are interconnected (Markovic, Kaess, & Tarokh, 2020).

The other type of plasticity is **adult plasticity.** Because every time we learn or remember something there must be some enduring biological change in the brain, the brain must possess a certain degree of plasticity at all ages. If this weren't true, it would be impossible to acquire new knowledge or abilities in adulthood. Because we can always learn new things, however, there is always some amount of plasticity in the brain, no matter how old we are. But the two kinds of plasticity differ significantly.

First, adult plasticity doesn't fundamentally alter the neural structure of the brain, whereas developmental plasticity does. Developmental plasticity involves the growth of new brain cells and the formation of new brain circuits. Adult plasticity mainly involves fairly minor modifications to existing circuits. It's like the difference between learning how to read (which is a life-altering change) and reading a new book (which usually is not).

Second, brain systems are far less malleable during periods of adult plasticity than they are during periods of developmental plasticity. In fact, the developing brain is chemically predisposed to be modified by experiences, like clay when it is still soft, whereas the adult brain is predisposed to resist modification, like that same clay once it has hardened (Spear, 2013a). This is the reason we don't become better at seeing or hearing after we have matured beyond infancy or why we have so much more trouble learning to ski or surf as adults than as children. By the time we are adults, the brain systems that regulate vision, hearing, and coordination have hardened. This is also why it is far easier to learn a foreign language before adolescence than after; brain systems responsible for language acquisition have lost a lot of their plasticity by then.

Finally, because the developing brain is so much more malleable, it can be influenced by a far wider range of experiences than can the mature brain. When the brain is developing, it is shaped by experiences that we aren't even aware of. Once the brain has matured, we need to pay attention to and give meaning to our experiences in order to be affected by them in an enduring way.

In other words, the developing brain is sculpted both by passive exposure and by active experience. That means that before our brain has fully matured, we can be affected, in potentially permanent ways, by *every* experience, whether it's positive or negative, whether we understand it or not—in fact, whether or not we're even aware of it.

Because plasticity is what allows us to learn from experience, it enables us to adapt to the environment. Without it, our ancestors couldn't have remembered which contexts were safe and desirable because they supplied food or water and which were to be avoided because they were dangerous. The malleability of our brains greatly benefits us because it allows us to acquire new information and abilities. Periods of heightened plasticity, such as infancy or adolescence, are therefore good times to intervene in order to promote positive development and ameliorate the negative effects of harmful experiences earlier in life (Graf, Biroli, & Belsky, 2021; Laube, van den Bos, & Fandakova, 2020).

But this malleability is a risk as well because during these times of heightened sensitivity, the brain is also more vulnerable to damage from physical harms, such as drugs or environmental toxins, or psychological ones, such as trauma and stress (Sisk & Romeo, 2019; Tottenham & Galván, 2016). As you will read later, the plasticity of the adolescent brain is why the adverse effects of using recreational drugs during adolescence (and during early adolescence, in particular) are more lasting than those associated with using the same drugs in adulthood (Giedd, 2015).

making the scientific connection

Advances in neuroscience have revealed that adolescence is a second period of heightened brain plasticity. Why might this be evolutionarily adaptive? What is it about adolescence that might make it an important time for the brain to be malleable?

What Changes in Adolescence?

The brain undergoes significant changes in both structure and function during adolescence. These changes alter the way adolescents think and process information, as well as how they interact with others.

Changes in Brain Structure During Adolescence

During adolescence, the brain is "remodeled" through synaptic pruning and myelination in particular brain regions (Spear, 2013a). One part of the brain that is pruned dramatically in adolescence is the **prefrontal cortex,** the region of the brain most important for sophisticated thinking abilities, such as planning, thinking ahead, weighing risks and rewards, and controlling impulses (Casey et al., 2005). Pruning also takes place in other parts of the cortex in adolescence (Blakemore, 2012).

There is also continued myelination of the cortex throughout adolescence, which also leads to many cognitive advances (Darki & Klingberg, 2015; Ferrer et al., 2013). Myelination is stimulated by puberty (Menzies et al., 2015) but also by experiences such as education (Noble et al., 2013) and exercise (Herting et al., 2014).

The increase in white matter during adolescence improves the efficiency of connections within and across brain regions (Khundrakpam et al., 2016; Stevens, 2016). Better connectivity between different parts of the cortex allows us to think faster and better (Wendelken et al., 2017). Better connectivity between the prefrontal cortex and the **limbic system,** an area of the brain involved in the processing of emotions, social information, and reward and punishment, leads to improvements in our ability to regulate our emotions and coordinate our thoughts and feelings (Gee et al., 2018; Larsen et al., 2018; Nelson et al., 2019; Silvers et al., 2017a) (see Figure 2.1).

As with many aspects of development, there is considerable variability among adolescents of the same chronological age in the timing and extent of brain maturation, which are likely due to both genetic and

prefrontal cortex
The region of the brain most important for sophisticated thinking abilities, such as planning, thinking ahead, weighing risks and rewards, and controlling impulses.

limbic system
An area of the brain that plays an important role in the processing of emotional experience, social information, and reward and punishment.

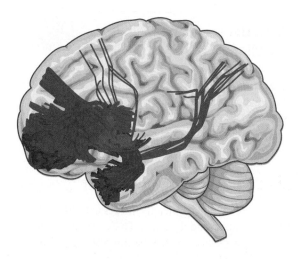
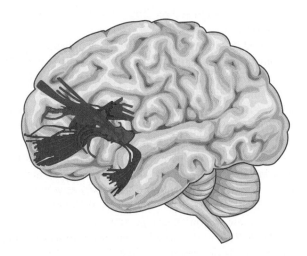

Figure 2.1   Neuroscientists are able to map patterns of connectivity between different brain regions and compare people of different ages by locating white-matter fiber tracts. These images show patterns of connectivity between limbic (red) and cortical (blue) regions. The purple region shows where these areas overlap. (Larsen et al., 2018)

environmental influences (Foulkes & Blakemore, 2018) (see Figure 2.2). One team of scientists has developed a "Neural Maturation Index" that combines measures of synaptic pruning and myelination to yield an overall measure of brain development during adolescence (Truelove-Hill et al., 2020). Although we can certainly identify average patterns of change over time in various brain regions and use these averages to describe adolescent brain development *in general*, it also true that not all individuals follow identical patterns, which can be linked to

response inhibition
The suppression of a behavior that is inappropriate or no longer required.

executive function
More advanced thinking abilities, enabled chiefly by the maturation of the prefrontal cortex, especially in early adolescence.

Improvements in connectivity between the prefrontal cortex and limbic system helps adolescents regulate emotions and navigate the social world. CREATISTA/Shutterstock

differences in how people behave. One recent study found that individuals high in prosocial behavior, such as helping others, evinced greater and faster thinning of the cortex during the transition from early to mid-adolescence, which has been associated more generally with psychological maturation (Ferschmann et al., 2019).

Changes in Brain Function During Adolescence

The two most important changes in brain function involving the prefrontal cortex in adolescence both lead to greater efficiency in information processing (Spear, 2010). First, patterns of activation *within* the prefrontal cortex generally become more focused. For instance, in experiments in which participants are presented with a rapid succession of images and asked to push a button when a certain image appears but refrain from pushing it when a different image appears (a process known as **response inhibition**), adolescents are less likely than children to activate prefrontal regions that are not relevant to performing the task well. As adolescents grow into adulthood and these brain systems further mature, self-control improves, as does performance on tests that measure other aspects of advanced thinking, often referred to as **executive function** (Crone & Steinbeis, 2017; Carriedo et al., 2016).

Second, over the course of adolescence individuals become more likely to use multiple parts of the brain simultaneously and coordinate activity *between* prefrontal regions and other areas, including other portions of the cortex and areas of the limbic system (Casey, Galván, & Somerville, 2016; Casey et al., 2019; Crone & Steinbeis, 2017). This is especially important on difficult tasks, where the task demands may overtax the prefrontal cortex working alone, and especially on tasks that require self-control, where it is necessary to coordinate thinking and feeling (Aite et al., 2017). In fact, when adolescents

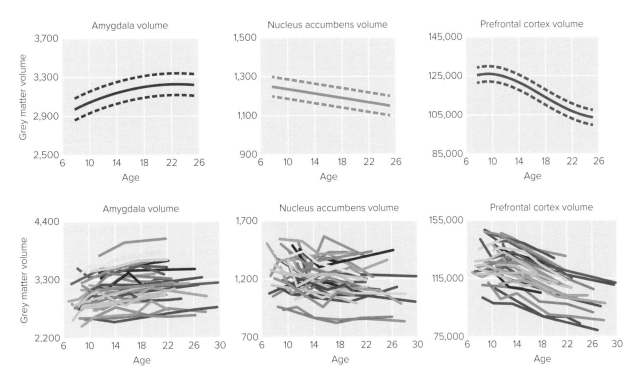

Figure 2.2 The three upper graphs in this figure show average patterns of change in gray matter volume during adolescence and early adulthood in three brain regions. The three lower graphs, which show individual patterns of change (each line represents one person), demonstrate that there is considerable variation around these average patterns. (Foulkes & Blakemore, 2018).

who are tested for self-control are told that they will be rewarded for controlling themselves, they perform better than when no such rewards are offered (Magis-Weinberg, Custers, & Dumontheil, 2019; Strang & Pollak, 2014; Teslovich et al., 2014).

This simultaneous recruitment of multiple brain regions working as a "team," referred to as **functional connectivity,** is made possible by the increase in physical connections between brain regions (Dosenbach, Petersen, & Schlaggar, 2013). Children's brains are characterized by a large number of relatively "local" connections (i.e., connections between nearby brain regions), but as individuals mature through adolescence and into adulthood, more distant regions become increasingly interconnected (Baker et al., 2015; Calabro et al., 2020; Sherman et al., 2014; Váša et al., 2018). This is seen even when individuals are lying still, just resting (Stevens, 2016). Interestingly, individuals with relatively weaker connectivity actually have worse sleep (Tashjian et al., 2018)! The maturation of functional connectivity is more or less complete by age 22 (see Figure 2.3).

Risk and Reward A different type of functional change results from changes, especially in the limbic system, in the ways in which the brain is affected by certain neurotransmitters, including **dopamine** (which plays an important role in our experience of reward) and **serotonin** (which plays an important role in the experience of different moods). These changes, which are partly caused by puberty, make adolescents more emotional, more responsive to stress, more sensitive to rewards (especially immediate rewards), and more likely to engage in sensation seeking than either children or adults (Anandakumar et al., 2018; Barkley-Levenson & Galván, 2017; Goddings et al., 2019). These changes are also thought to increase individuals' vulnerability to both substance abuse and binge eating because they seek higher levels of reward; to depression because of their increased vulnerability to stress; and to other mental health problems because of their easily aroused emotions, including anger, anxiety, and sadness (Bodell et al., 2018; Casement et al., 2015; Guyer, Silk, & Nelson, 2016).

One other negative consequence of this increase in emotional reactivity is an increase in adolescents' sensitivity to feeling threatened, which may prompt some adolescents to lash out at others or deliberately seek out experiences that are frightening (Dreyfuss et al., 2014; Spielberg et al., 2014). As adolescents mature toward adulthood, these trends begin to reverse, and individuals become less easily aroused by

functional connectivity
The extent to which multiple brain regions function at the same time, which improves during adolescence.

dopamine
A neurotransmitter especially important in the brain circuits that regulate the experience of reward.

serotonin
A neurotransmitter that is especially important for the experience of different moods.

Figure 2.3   The maturation of functional connectivity is more or less complete by age 22. (Dosenbach et al., 2010)

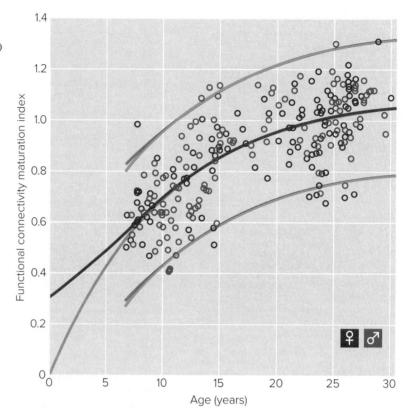

positive or negative stimuli and better able to regulate their emotions (Silvers et al., 2017b; Silvers et al., 2015).

These changes in the functioning of the limbic system occur relatively early in adolescence (Insel & Somerville, 2018), in contrast to developments in the prefrontal cortex, which are still ongoing in early adulthood (Luciana, 2013; Mills et al., 2014). Unlike the changes that occur in the limbic system, which have been directly linked to the impact of pubertal hormones on the brain, the development of cognitive control is more or less independent of puberty (Icenogle et al., 2017; Ordaz et al., 2017).

The relatively late maturation of the prefrontal cortex, particularly compared to the changes that take place in the limbic system at puberty, has been the subject of much discussion among those interested in risk taking and behavioral problems in adolescence because this gap in timing may help explain the dramatic increase in risky behavior that takes place between childhood and adolescence, as well as the decline in risk taking that occurs as individuals mature into adulthood (Casey, Jones, & Somerville, 2011; Steinberg, 2008). In essence, the brain changes in ways that may provoke individuals to seek novelty, reward, and stimulation several years before the complete maturation of the brain systems that regulate judgment, decision making, and impulse control (Galván, 2010; Padmanabhan et al., 2011; Van Leijenhorst et al., 2010). It's like a car with accelerator pressed to the floor

positive risk taking
Risk taking that promotes healthy psychological development

before a good braking system is in place. As the "braking system" improves, in part because of maturation of the prefrontal cortex and its connections to other brain regions, and as reward seeking declines, individuals become less likely to engage in risky behavior (Steinbeis et al., 2016; Peters et al., 2017).

Many writers have pointed out that adolescents' sensitivity to reward isn't always maladaptive, however (Telzer, 2016), and that some risk taking is not impulsive but planned (Do, Sharp, & Telzer, 2020; Maslowsky et al., 2019). Although sensation seeking may lead some teenagers to do dangerous things, it may lead others to explore the environment in ways that lead them to engage in prosocial behavior, learn new skills, be flexible, and increase their knowledge of the world (Duell & Steinberg, 2019; van Duijvenvoorde et al., 2016). This makes perfect sense, given that adolescence evolved as a stage during which individuals venture out on their own; to be successful, they must be both willing to take risks and able to learn from their experience. In contrast to sensation seeking, which is predictive of both positive and maladaptive risk taking, impulsivity is associated with maladaptive risk taking but not **positive risk taking** (Duell & Steinberg, 2020).

The Social Brain   Yet another important change in the brain in adolescence involves a network of regions referred to as the "social brain" (Braams & Crone, 2017; Kilford, Garrett, & Blakemore, 2016; McCormick et al., 2018). Figure 2.4 shows the main brain regions

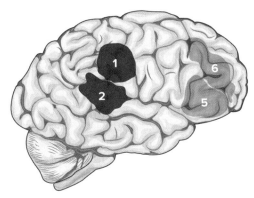

Social Cognition
(1) Temporal Parietal Junction (TPJ)
(2) Posterior Superior Temporal Sulcus (PSTS)

Cognitive Control
(5) Ventrolateral PFC (VLPFC)
(6) Dorsolateral PFC (DLPFC)

Figure 2.4 Primary brain regions that govern how we make sense of the social world, exercise self-control, and experience reward. (Telzer et al., 2017)

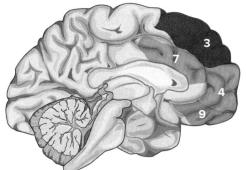

Social Cognition
(3) Dorsomedial PFC (DMPFC)

Cognitive Control
(4) Medial Prefeontal Cor tex
(7) Anterior Cingulate Cortex (ACC)

Reward Processing
(9) Orbitofrontal Cortex (OFE)/
    Ventromedial PFC (VMPFC)

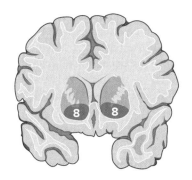

Reward Processing
(8) Ventral Striatum

responsible for social cognition, cognitive control, and reward processing (Telzer, Rogers, & Van Hoorn, 2017).

In most species of mammals, individuals become more social around the time of puberty, which makes perfect sense, given that adolescence evolved as a stage of development designed to prepare individuals for mating and reproduction (Goddings et al., 2019; Walker et al., 2017). Changes in the social brain in early adolescence, which increase the brain's sensitivity to social cues (Frankenhuis & Walasek, 2020), such as other people's facial expressions and behavior, intensify adolescents' sensitivity to social evaluation (van den Bos, van Duijvenvoorde, & Westenberg, 2016), which is why adolescents are more prone to feel embarrassed than either children or adults (see Figure 2.5) (Guyer et al., 2012; Silk et al., 2012; Somerville, 2013). This also may be why adolescents are so susceptible to social influence and, especially, peer pressure (Welborn et al., 2016). In one study that tested individuals' ability to exercise response

inhibition, adolescents had a harder time controlling themselves than either children or adults when responding to pictures showing peers having a good time (Perino, Miernicki, & Telzer, 2016). Another study found that being observed by a friend interfered with adolescents' cognitive performance but had no such effect on adults (Wolf et al., 2015).

Individuals' ability to recognize subtle changes in others' facial expressions improves during adolescence (Garcia & Scherf, 2015; Shaw et al., 2016). The increase in sex hormones at puberty appears to play a role in influencing this increase in sensitivity to others' facial expressions (Goddings et al., 2019; Motta-Mena & Scherf, 2017), which makes perfect sense, given the ultimate purpose of adolescence. If your goal is to find a willing sex partner, it helps to pay close attention to other peoples' facial expressions. One fascinating study found that, after going through puberty, individuals were more likely to remember the faces of people who were at the same level of

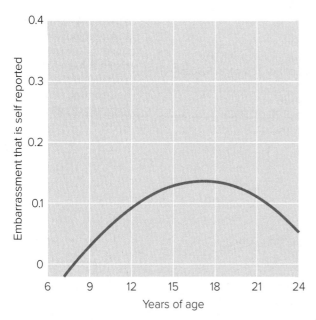

Figure 2.5 Changes in the social brain during adolescence have both costs and benefits. One downside is that people become more self-conscious. Adolescents report feeling embarrassed more often than either children or adults. (Somerville, 2013)

pubertal maturation than those who were either less or more physically advanced (Picci & Scherf, 2016).

Other research indicates that sensitivity to others' mental states increases during adolescence, a change that also is reflected in changes in patterns of brain activity when individuals observe others (Burnett et al., 2011;

Masten et al., 2013). Keep in mind, though, that adolescents vary in how sensitive they are to the influence of others; some are highly aware of the social world, whereas others are close to oblivious (Schriber & Guyer, 2016). Adolescents who are especially responsive to social rewards are more likely to engage in risky sexual behavior, perhaps because their increased sensitivity to such rewards leads them to downplay the costs of this type of risk taking (Ambrosia et al., 2018; Eckstrand et al., 2017). However, adolescents are able to ignore social feedback when they believe that the advice others are giving them will interfere with their goals (McCormick, Perino, & Telzer, 2018).

This increased attentiveness to other people's mental states likely has a number of benefits, such as encouraging the development of social skills or empathic (Rosen et al., 2018; Tamnes et al., 2018; van Hoorn, McCormick, & Telzer, 2018); it also makes adolescents more easily distracted by others' emotional expressions (Cohen-Gilbert & Thomas, 2013). An important implication of this for parents is that yelling at a teenager angrily may not be an effective means of getting the adolescent to listen because the teenager may end up paying more attention to the angry emotion than to the content of what is being said. Indeed, when adolescents listen to recordings of their mother being critical, this increases activity in emotional regions of the brain but dampens activity in regions that govern self-regulation and logical reasoning (K. Lee et al., 2014). These effects are lessened, however, when mothers' criticism is accompanied by warmth (Butterfield et al., 2020).

Changes in a region referred to as "the social brain" make adolescents more sensitive to other people's emotional states. I love images/city break/Alamy Stock Photo

making the cultural connection

New research shows that brain systems governing things such as impulse control, planning ahead, and balancing risk and reward are still maturing during late adolescence. Yet, rates of adolescents' risky behavior, such as experimentation with drugs or unprotected sex, vary considerably around the world. If these sorts of behaviors are more common in adolescence because of the way the brain is changing, shouldn't they be more universal?

Implications for Adolescent Behavior

Evidence of a correlation between changes in brain structure or function and changes in adolescent behavior does not necessarily mean that the first is necessarily causing the second (Kuhn, 2009; Paus, 2009). Adolescents' behavior affects their brain development, as well as the reverse.

An obvious illustration of this involves the impact of using alcohol and other drugs on the brain, but there are other, more subtle examples as well. As mentioned earlier, the process of synaptic pruning is influenced by experience: Repeated activation of a specific collection of neurons as a result of engaging in a particular behavior will actually result in structural changes that strengthen the connections among those neurons, which in turn will make them function more efficiently. For example, practicing the same task over and over again makes it easier and easier to perform the task each time. Scientists have grown increasingly interested in seeing whether different sorts of training programs or interventions can improve adolescents' self-control (Modecki, Zimmer-Gembeck, & Guerra, 2017) or reduce their tendencies toward sensation seeking (Romer et al., 2011), both of which may reduce risky behavior.

I'm often asked when adolescents start to think like adults or at what age the adolescent brain becomes the adult brain. As you now know, the answer depends on which aspects of thinking or brain development one is concerned about (Steinberg & Icenogle, 2019). When it comes to psychosocial maturity, as evidenced by thinking ahead, envisioning the future consequences of a decision, balancing risks and rewards, resisting peer pressure, or controlling impulses—all of which are governed mainly by the prefrontal cortex—research on brain maturation certainly suggests that these capabilities are still developing well after individuals enter their 20s. But when it comes to more basic cognitive abilities, such as those involving memory, attention, and logical reasoning, especially under optimal conditions, brain and behavioral studies indicate that the average 15-year-old performs no worse than the average adult (Icenogle et al., 2019). The different developmental trajectories of cognitive capability

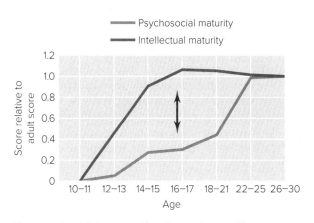

Figure 2.6 **Adolescents' intellectual capability reaches adult levels before they are emotionally and socially mature, creating what some psychologists have called a "maturity gap."** (Adapted from Icenogle et al., 2019)

and psychosocial maturity create a "maturity gap" (see Figure 2.6). This helps explain why many obviously bright teenagers sometimes act in ways that seem immature and reckless.

In addition, some young adults show patterns of brain activity that are significantly less mature than what one would predict based on their chronological age, whereas others demonstrate patterns of brain activity that are more mature than what one would expect. In one study, the young adults whose estimated "brain age" was lower than their chronological age were more likely than other people their age to report enjoying risk taking (Rudolph, Davis, & Monti, 2017). Moreover, patterns of age differences in brain activity depend on the circumstances under which individuals are tested; when 18- to 21-year-olds are emotionally aroused, their cognitive performance and brain activity resembles that of teenagers, but under more calming conditions, young adults look more like people in their mid-20s (Cohen et al., 2016). Where we draw the boundary between adolescence and adulthood—at least as far as cognitive development is concerned—should probably depend on why the boundary is being drawn and on what specific abilities are relevant to the behavior in question (Steinberg & Icenogle, 2019).

Individual Differences in Intelligence in Adolescence

For the most part, theorists who have studied adolescent cognitive development from either a Piagetian or an information-processing framework or through brain research have focused on the universals in adolescent intellectual growth. Other theorists have been more interested in studying individual differences in intellectual abilities. How large are individual differences in intelligence in adolescence? Why are some adolescents brighter than others?

The Measurement of IQ

To answer questions about the relative intelligence of individuals, psychologists have had to devise ways of assessing intelligence—no easy feat given the considerable disagreement over what "intelligence" really is. Today, the most widely used measures are intelligence tests, or IQ (for "intelligence quotient") tests. Among these tests are the Stanford-Binet, the Wechsler Intelligence Scale for Children (WISC-IV), and the Wechsler Adult Intelligence Scale (WAIS-III). An individual's IQ is computed by dividing his or her mental age by his or her chronological age and then multiplying the result by 100. A score of 100 is used to designate the midway point. An IQ score below 100 indicates a poorer test performance than the average person of the same age; a score above 100 indicates a better performance than average.

Changes in specific aspects of IQ performance during adolescence are correlated with synaptic pruning in brain regions known to play a role in those specific types of learning (Ramsden et al., 2011; van den Bos, Crone, & Güroğlu, 2012). And there is a link between intelligence and brain development. More intelligent adolescents have a more dramatic and longer period of production of synapses before adolescence and a more dramatic pruning of them after (P. Shaw et al., 2006), more connections between the prefrontal cortex and other brain regions (Cole et al., 2012), and a longer period of brain plasticity (van den Bos, Crone, & Güroğlu, 2012).

In one recent study, the researchers used brain imaging to construct a "Brain Development Index," which quantified how mature the brain's circuitry was. Not surprisingly, scores on the measure improved steadily between ages 8 and 22 (Erus et al., 2015). The researchers then identified individuals whose level of brain development was more advanced than would be expected based on their chronological age. Individuals with advanced brain development scores performed significantly faster (although not necessarily more accurately) on tests of cognitive ability, including various tests of attention, memory, and reasoning (see Figure 2.7).

Mental abilities assessed by conventional IQ tests increase dramatically through childhood and adolescence, reaching a plateau sometime in mid-to-late adolescence. (It is no coincidence that this plateau occurs at around the same age as that for information processing because IQ test performance depends a lot on information-processing abilities.) This argues strongly in favor of educational interventions prior to mid-adolescence; interventions in early childhood, especially, have been shown to improve intellectual performance during adolescence (Campbell et al., 2001). In addition, research shows that extended schooling during adolescence itself enhances individuals' performance on standardized tests of intelligence (Ceci & Williams, 1999). Whereas individuals who had dropped out of school early showed unchanging—and

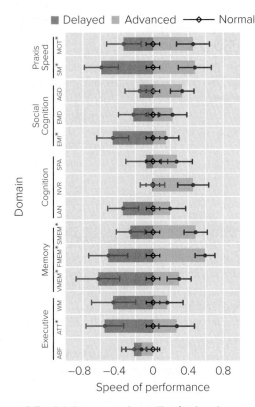

Figure 2.7   Adolescents whose "brain development index" is advanced relative to their chronological age perform tests of cognitive ability faster than those whose brain development index is average or delayed.
Source: Erus, Battapady, Satterthwaite, Hakonarson, Gur, Davatzikos, & Gur. (2015).

relatively lower—scores on intelligence tests during adolescence, students who remained in school, especially those in the more advanced tracks, showed impressive gains in verbal ability over time. Another study found that it is possible to facilitate the development of creative thinking in adolescence through training (Kleibeuker et al., 2017).

Culture and Intelligence

Much of our current thinking about the nature of intelligence has been influenced by the work of the Russian psychologist Lev Vygotsky (1930/1978), who emphasized the broader context in which intellectual development occurs. According to this view, it is essential that we understand the nature of the environment in which an adolescent develops in terms of its demands for intelligent behavior and its opportunities for learning. Individuals develop and use intellectual skills not simply as a function of their cognitive maturation but also in response to the everyday problems they are expected to solve. The very same children who perform poorly on school-based tests of knowledge may excel when faced with an equally challenging test of competence in the real world, such as figuring out the most efficient route between school and home through a dangerous neighborhood.

Vygotsky argued that children and adolescents learn best in everyday situations when they encounter tasks that are neither too simple nor too advanced but just slightly more challenging than their abilities permit them to solve on their own. Within this **zone of proximal development,** young people, through close collaboration with a more experienced instructor (whether an adult or another child), are stimulated to "reach" for the more advanced level of performance. The role of the instructor is to help structure the learning situation so that it is within the reach of the student, a process called **scaffolding.** If you watch good parents, teachers, or coaches at work, you will probably observe a great deal of scaffolding.

One fascinating discovery about how adolescents learn is that novelty and challenge are key to maintaining the brain's plasticity (Steinberg, 2014). By encouraging teenagers to learn new things and by challenging them to work harder, good teachers can use scaffolding to take advantage of the adolescent brain's exceptional malleability. In doing so, not only can teachers help adolescents learn at that time, but they can actually make future learning more likely by helping to keep the brain plastic. Some research suggests that learning certain skills may be easier in late adolescence than early adolescence, which suggests that the window of opportunity created by heightened brain plasticity may be open longer than one might think (Knoll et al., 2016).

Adolescent Thinking in Context

As our understanding of adolescent thinking has expanded, researchers have begun to look beyond laboratory experiments and standardized tests to examine how the cognitive changes of adolescence actually affect teenagers' day-to-day thoughts and actions. Do advances in hypothetical thinking or information-processing abilities make a difference in the real world? How do the brain changes that take place in adolescence play out in everyday experiences? To answer these questions, psychologists have studied the practical side of adolescent thinking with respect to how people think about social situations and how they think about risk.

Social Cognition in Adolescence

Social cognition involves such cognitive activities as thinking about people, social relationships, and social institutions (Smetana & Villalobos, 2009). Compared with those of children, adolescents' conceptions of interpersonal relationships, their understanding of human behavior, their ideas about social institutions and organizations, and their ability to figure out what other people are thinking are far more developed. Gains in the area of social cognition help account for many of the psychosocial advances typically associated with adolescence—advances in the realms of identity, autonomy, achievement, intimacy, and sexuality. Individual differences in social cognitive abilities also help explain why some adolescents have more social problems than others (Dodge, Coie, & Lynam, 2006; Fontaine et al., 2008).

Research on social cognition during adolescence includes many topics, but four of the most often studied concern (1) theory of mind; (2) thinking about social relationships; (3) understanding social conventions; and (4) conceptions of laws, civil liberties, and rights (Rote & Smetana, 2011; Smetana & Villalobos, 2009).

Theory of Mind During preadolescence and adolescence, individuals develop a more nuanced understanding of other people's personalities and psychological states, enabled in part by brain maturation in systems that support what is called **mentalizing**—the ability to understand someone else's mental state (Burnett et al., 2011; C. Harenski et al.,2012; Pfeifer & Peake, 2012). As they develop a more sophisticated **theory of mind,** the ability to understand that others have beliefs, intentions, and knowledge that may be different from one's own, adolescents are better able to interpret the feelings of others and to infer their motives and feelings, even when specific information of this sort is not directly observable (Choudhury, Blakemore, & Charman, 2006; Dumontheil, Apperly, & Blakemore, 2010). This can be especially helpful when evaluating an advertisement or some other attempt at persuasion, such as an Internet video designed to influence a purchasing decision (van Reijmersdal & van Dam, 2020). Adolescents also become better at lying as a result of these improvements in social cognition (Evans & Lee, 2011).

Not only are adolescents more capable of discerning another person's perspective on some issue or event, they are also better able to understand that person's perspective on their own point of view. They are especially able to take the perspective of someone the same age (Conson et al., 2017). Ultimately, adolescents' improvements in their ability to figure out what others are thinking lead to improvements in communication because they become more capable of formulating arguments in terms that are more likely to be understood by someone whose opinion is different.

zone of proximal development

In Vygotsky's theory, the level of challenge that is still within the individual's reach but that forces an individual to develop more advanced skills.

scaffolding

Structuring a learning situation so that it is just within the reach of the student.

social cognition

The aspect of cognition that concerns thinking about other people, about interpersonal relations, and about social institutions.

mentalizing

The ability to understand someone else's mental state.

theory of mind

The ability to understand that others have beliefs, intentions, and knowledge that may be different from one's own.

This gain in perspective taking may change the dynamics of adolescents' relationships with their parents—for better (because adolescents are able to see more things from their parents' point of view) and for worse (because adolescents may use these advanced social cognitive abilities to challenge their parents' authority or deceive them) (Gingo, Roded, & Turiel, 2017; Smetana & Villalobos, 2009).

Thinking About Social Relationships   Improvements in mentalizing lead to changes in the way that adolescents think about relationships with peers and parents. One topic that researchers have been especially interested in concerns adolescents' beliefs about peer exclusion (Leets & Sunwolf, 2005). All other things equal, children believe that it is wrong to exclude peers from social activities (e.g., whether to invite the whole class or just one's close friends to a birthday party). With age, however, as adolescents' understanding of group dynamics becomes more sophisticated, they begin to take into account other considerations, such as personality ("She's not open-minded . . . we all feel weird around her"), the activity context ("We thought he wasn't good enough to play basketball"), and the reason for excluding some individuals but not others ("[The party] was a team thing") (Recchia, Brehl, & Wainryb, 2012, p. 198). On the other hand, adolescents generally believe that social exclusion on the basis of gender orientation, nationality, race, or ethnicity is wrong (Brenick & Killen, 2014; Ruck et al., 2015).

Changes in adolescents' understanding of social relationships also transform their beliefs about authority, which has important implications for their relationships with parents and other adults (Smetana & Villalobos, 2009). With age, adolescents increasingly distinguish between moral issues (such as whether it is acceptable to steal from someone else) and conventional ones (such as whether one eats dessert before or after the main course) (Lahat, Helwig, & Zelazo, 2013). Although the stereotype of adolescents is that they invariably come to reject the authority of adults, research shows that what happens instead is that adolescents increasingly distinguish between issues that authority figures have the right to regulate and issues that are their own personal choices (Gingo et al., 2017). For example, adolescents by and large are in favor of laws that prohibit stealing and vandalism but are less accepting of laws concerning curfews and loitering (Oosterhoff & Metzger, 2017).

As adolescents begin to make these distinctions, they often question their parents' authority (Thomas et al., 2020). Issues that had been viewed as matters of right and wrong start to seem like matters of personal choice and, as such, beyond the bounds of parental authority (Cheah, Leung, & Özdemir, 2018; Van Petegem et al., 2017). Parents' rules about such things as the cleanliness of the adolescent's bedroom

social conventions
The norms that govern everyday behavior in social situations.

or bedtimes on school nights, which had been accepted as matters of right and wrong, start to seem like arbitrary conventions that are open to debate. Here's how one girl described it:

> In the beginning their word was law I guess. Whatever they decided together was what we would do regardless of what. . . . Now I will push back if I don't think it's fair. . . . I won't maybe give in as easily which can be good and bad. (Parkin & Kuczynski, 2012, p. 645).

One main source of conflict between adolescents and their parents involves which issues parents have legitimate authority over and which they do not (Chen-Gaddini, Liu, & Nucci, 2020). An adolescent boy explained how he handled it:

> I don't enjoy that they ask me questions all the time and nag me about going out and stuff. . . . I'll give them answers but they're discreet answers. I'll give them little parts of things just to make it sound good, I guess. (Parkin & Kuczynski, 2012, p. 649).

Similar changes occur in adolescents' beliefs about their teachers' authority (Smetana & Bitz, 1996) and the authority of groups to dictate how individuals should behave (Helwig et al., 2011). For instance, adolescents understand that teachers have the right to demand that students show up for class on time and sit quietly if asked, but they believe that students should be able to decide where they sit. It's also the case that juvenile offenders who believe they have been treated fairly by police officers and other adults they encounter fare better and are less cynical about the legal system than those who feel mistreated (Hofer, Womack, & Wilson, 2020; Slocum & Wiley, 2018).

Understanding Social Conventions   The realization that individuals' perspectives vary and that their opinions may differ as a result leads to changes in the ways that adolescents approach issues regarding social conventions (Smetana & Villalobos, 2009). During middle childhood, **social conventions**—the social norms that guide day-to-day behavior, such as waiting in line to buy movie tickets—are seen as arbitrary and changeable but adherence to them is not; compliance with such conventions is based on rules and on the dictates of authority. When you were 7 years old, you might not have understood why people had to wait in line to buy movie tickets, but when your parents told you to wait in line, you waited.

By early adolescence, however, conventions often are seen as arbitrary social expectations. As an adolescent, you begin to realize that people wait in line because they are expected to, not because they are forced to. Indeed, young adolescents often see social conventions as *nothing but* social expectations and, consequently, as insufficient reasons for compliance. You can probably imagine young teenagers saying something like this: "Why wait in a ticket line simply because other people are lined up? There isn't a *law* that forces you to wait in line, is there?"

Adolescence is a time of changes in the way we think abut social conventions, such as having to wait in a line to buy movie tickets. martinedoucet/Getty Images

Gradually, however, adolescents begin to see social conventions as the means by which society regulates people's behavior. Conventions may be arbitrary, but we follow them because we share an understanding of how people are expected to behave in various situations. We wait in line for theater tickets not because we want to comply with any rule but because it is something we are accustomed to doing.

Ultimately, individuals come to see that social conventions help to coordinate interactions among people. Social norms and expectations are derived from and maintained by individuals having a common perspective and agreeing that, in given situations, certain behaviors are more desirable than others because such behaviors help society and its institutions function more smoothly. Without the convention of waiting in line to buy movie tickets, the pushiest people would always get tickets first. Older adolescents can see that waiting in line not only benefits the theater by keeping order but also preserves everyone's right to a fair chance to buy tickets. In other words, we wait in line patiently because we all agree that it is better if tickets are distributed fairly.

Conceptions of Laws, Civil Liberties, and Rights

As is the case with individuals' developing understanding of relationships between people, over the course of adolescence individuals also become more nuanced in the way they think about the relationship between the individual and society.

Most research on adolescents' beliefs about rights and civil liberties comes from studies of Western, middle-class youth, and it is important to be cautious about generalizing the findings of these studies to young people from other cultures. Nevertheless, even in collectivist cultures that place less emphasis on the rights of the individual, adolescents become increasingly likely to believe that there are some freedoms—such as freedom of speech and freedom of religion—that should not be restricted (Smetana & Villalobos, 2009). That said, research also finds that, with age, teenagers come to believe that there are situations in which it may be legitimate to restrict individual rights to serve the benefit of the community.

The distinction that adolescents draw between laws and social conventions became perfectly clear during the COVID-19 pandemic. As you probably remember, during the summer prior to the 2020 fall semester, college administrators struggled to come up with ways of reopening campuses without jeopardizing the health of students, faculty, university personnel, and members of the surrounding community. Authorities made clear that these plans depended on students' willingness to voluntarily comply with social distancing guidelines, which urged people to avoid large indoor parties and social events.

Even before they returned to campus, though, students began gathering in bars, fraternity houses, and off-campus house parties, protesting that it was their "right" to socialize as they pleased. After all, some students said, these weren't laws but social conventions (like waiting in line for movie tickets). Perhaps it would have been wiser, at least from a public health perspective, for state and municipal governments to close these gathering spots, rather than depend on students' adherence to social conventions: Within the first few weeks of the semester, many universities saw such dramatic surges in coronavirus infections that they had to close their campuses and send students home.

Several themes cut across the research findings from studies of different aspects of social cognition—the way we think about people, relationships, conventions, and rights. First, as individuals move into and through adolescence, they become better able to step outside themselves and see things from other vantage points. Second, adolescents are better able to see that the social "rules" we follow (in the family, at school, and in broader society) are not absolute and are therefore subject to debate and questioning. Third, with age, adolescents develop a more differentiated, more nuanced understanding of social norms. Yes, individuals are entitled to certain rights, but there are some situations under which it might be appropriate to curtail them. Yes, it is generally wrong to exclude others, but sometimes social exclusion is justifiable (Killen et al., 2013).

These gains in social cognition help to account for gains in social competence during adolescence. Adolescents who have more sophisticated social cognitive abilities actually behave in more socially competent ways (Eisenberg et al., 2009). Although there is more to social competence than social cognition, being able to understand social relationships is an important component of social maturity.

Adolescent Risk Taking

A second practical application of research into adolescent thinking involves the study of adolescent risk taking. The main health problems of adolescence are the result of behaviors that can be prevented—behaviors such as substance abuse, reckless driving, and unprotected sex. In the real world (IOM and NRC, 2011) and on many laboratory tasks of risky decision making (Defoe et al., 2015; Rosenbaum et al., 2018; Shulman & Cauffman, 2014), adolescents take more risks than adults, not only in the United States, where much of this research has been conducted, but around the world (Duell et al., 2018). Although of course not all adolescents are risk takers, by and large, adults are more risk avoidant than teenagers are (van Duijvenvoorde et al., 2015).

behavioral decision theory
An approach to understanding adolescent risk taking, in which behaviors are seen as the outcome of systematic decision-making processes.

The Centers for Disease Control and Prevention, a federal agency that monitors the health of Americans, surveys American high school students annually and asks whether they had engaged in various behaviors during the previous 30 days (Centers for Disease Control and Prevention, 2020). Risk taking is common among adolescents. Nearly half of all sexually active students did not use a condom the last time they had intercourse. Close to 40% of teen drivers report having texted while driving. Nearly 15% have tried opiod medication that had been prescribed for someone else.

Behavioral Decision Theory   A number of writers have looked at adolescent risk taking from a perspective called **behavioral decision theory** (Kahneman, 2011). In this perspective, which draws heavily on economics, decision making is a rational process in which individuals calculate the costs and benefits of alternative courses of action and behave in ways that maximize the benefits and minimize the costs. According to this theory, all behaviors, including risky ones, can be analyzed as the outcome of a process involving five steps: (1) identifying alternative choices, (2) identifying the consequences that might follow from each choice, (3) evaluating the costs and benefits of each possible consequence, (4) assessing the likelihood of each possible consequence, and (5) combining all this information according to some decision rule (Beyth-Marom et al., 1993).

For example, an adolescent girl who is trying to decide whether to accept a ride home from a party with friends who have been drinking will (1) identify the choices (to accept the ride or not), (2) identify the consequences ("If I accept the ride and we get into an accident, I could be seriously hurt, but if I don't accept the ride, my friends will make fun of me for being a 'loser'"), (3) evaluate the desirability of each consequence ("Appearing like a 'loser' to my friends is bad, but being in an accident would be terrible"), (4) assess the likelihood of each consequence ("My friends probably won't really change their opinion of me just because I turn down the ride, and my friend who is driving is so drunk that he really might get into an accident"), and (5) combine all the information according to some decision rule ("All things considered, I think I won't take the ride").

From the perspective of behavioral decision theory, then, it is important to ask whether adolescents use different processes than adults in identifying, estimating, and evaluating behavioral options and consequences. If risky decisions are the result of faulty information processing—in attention or memory, for example—perhaps it would make sense to train adolescents in these basic cognitive abilities as a means of lessening their risk taking.

As we have seen, however, adolescents, at least by the time they are 15 or so, have the same basic cognitive abilities as adults (Steinberg & Icenogle, 2019). This is true even for issues as complicated as deciding whether to abort a pregnancy (Icenogle et al., 2019). The major gains in the cognitive skills that affect decision making appear to occur between childhood and adolescence, rather than between adolescence and adulthood. Thus, educating

Recent research on cognitive development in adolescence has been aimed at understanding the thinking behind adolescent risk taking. Photodisc/Getty Images

adolescents in how to make "better" decisions is not likely to reduce risk taking (Steinberg, 2015). There is no evidence, for example, that adolescents are worse at perceiving risks than adults are (Ivers et al., 2009; Van Leijenhorst, Westenberg, & Crone, 2008). However, research indicates that adolescents vary far more than adults in how they interpret words and phrases used to describe risk—words such as "probably," "likely," or "a very low chance"—suggesting that health educators and practitioners should not take for granted that an adolescent's understanding of a message about risk is what the educator thinks it is (Mills, Reyna, & Estrada, 2008). Similarly, just because an adolescent says that she knows that having "safe sex" can protect her against sexually transmitted diseases doesn't necessarily mean that she knows the specific behaviors that constitute safe sex (Reyna & Farley, 2006).

Age Differences in Values and Priorities If adolescents use the same decision-making processes as adults and if adolescents are no more likely than adults to think of themselves as invulnerable, why, then, are adolescents more likely to engage in risky behavior? One answer may involve the different values and priorities that adolescents and adults have (Do, Sharp, & Telzer, 2020). For example, an individual's decision to try cocaine at a party may involve evaluating a number of different consequences, including the legal and health risks, the pleasure the drug may induce, and the way in which he or she will be judged (both positively and negatively) by peers (Andrews et al., 2020). An adult and an adolescent may both consider all these consequences, but the adult may place relatively more weight on the health risks of trying the drug, while the adolescent may place relatively more weight on the social consequences of not trying it. (Young adolescents' risky decision making is especially influenced by the opinions of their peers; Knoll et al., 2015). Although an adult may see an adolescent's decision to value peer acceptance more than health as irrational, an adolescent may see the adult's decision as equally incomprehensible. Behavioral decision theory reminds us that many decisions—even risky ones—can be seen as rational once we understand how an individual estimates and evaluates the consequences of various courses of action.

One very important difference between adolescents and adults is that, when weighing the costs and benefits of engaging in a risky behavior, adolescents are more attuned to the potential rewards than are adults (Modecki, 2016). This difference is consistent with changes that are taking place in the limbic system around the time of puberty, which we discussed earlier in this chapter. Studies of juvenile offenders have found, for instance, that adolescents' criminal activity is more strongly related to their beliefs about the potential rewards of the activity (e.g., being seen as "cool") than to their perceptions of the activity's potential costs (e.g., the chances of being arrested) (Loughran et al., 2016; Shulman, Monahan, & Steinberg, 2017). As several writers have pointed out, this has important implications for the prevention of risky behavior among adolescents (Victor & Hariri, 2016). It may be more important to convince adolescents that the rewards of a risky activity are small (e.g., that few people will actually look up to someone for being violent) than to persuade them that the costs are large (e.g., that being incarcerated will be terrible).

In all likelihood, of course, neither adolescents' nor adults' decisions are always made in as straightforward or rational a way suggested by behavioral decision theory. Nevertheless, this approach has opened up a new way of thinking about adolescent risk taking. Instead of viewing risky activities as the result of irrational or faulty judgment, experts are now trying to understand where and how adolescents obtain the information they use in reaching their conclusions and how accurate the information is. If, for example, adolescents underestimate the likelihood of getting pregnant following unprotected sex, sex education efforts might focus on teaching teenagers the actual probability. (Of course, this presumes that adolescents' decisions about whether to have sex are made rationally, which may not be the case [Levine, 2001].)

Emotional and Contextual Influences on Risk Taking We should also keep in mind that emotional and contextual factors, as well as cognitive ones, contribute to adolescent risk taking (Dahl, 2008; Rivers, Reyna, & Mills, 2008; Steinberg, 2010). Several researchers have noted that adolescents may differ from adults in important ways that are not captured by measures of logical reasoning, such as susceptibility to peer pressure, impulsivity, orientation to the present rather than the future, or reward seeking (Cauffman et al., 2010; de Water, Cillessen, & Scheres, 2014; Steinberg & Icenogle, 2019). A number of studies have shown that adolescents' decision making is as good as adults' when individuals are tested under calm conditions but that the quality of adolescents' decision making declines more than adults' when they are emotionally aroused (Figner & Weber, 2011; van Duijvenvoorde et al., 2010) or fatigued (Silva et al., 2017).

With respect to emotional factors, for example, studies show that individuals who are high in reward seeking and **sensation seeking**—that is, who seek out novel and intense experiences—are more likely to engage in various types of risky behaviors, both positive and maladaptive, than their peers (Harden & Mann, 2015) and that both reward seeking and sensation seeking are higher during adolescence than childhood or adulthood (Duckworth & Steinberg, 2015). Similarly, adolescents who are especially impulsive are also more likely to engage in maladaptive risky behavior (Forrest et al., 2019; Kim-Spoon et al., 2017; Khurana et al., 2018).

sensation seeking
The pursuit of experiences that are novel or exciting.

Figure 2.8 Around the world, adolescence is a time of heightened sensation seeking and still developing self-regulation. The gray bars indicate the age at which there is a peak (sensation seeking) or plateau (self-regulation).
(Figure 1 from Steinberg et al., 2018)

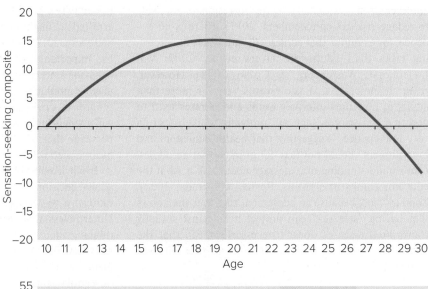

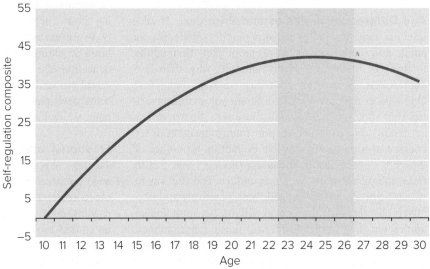

One reason that middle adolescence is a period of heightened risk taking is that it is a period characterized by a combination of high sensation seeking and high impulsivity (Harden & Tucker-Drob, 2011; Smith, Xiao, & Bechara, 2012), especially among boys (Shulman et al., 2014), most likely because of the impact of testosterone in particular on sensation seeking and impulsivity (Harden et al., 2018; Laube, Lorenz, & van den Bos, 2020). One study of more than 5,000 people from 11 countries found that, around the world, adolescence is a time of heightened reward seeking and immature self-control (Steinberg et al., 2018) (see Figure 2.8). At all ages, people who are high in sensation seeking and low in impulse control are more likely to be risk takers, both in the real world and in laboratory experiments (Duell et al., 2016; Lydon-Staley & Geier, 2018; Wasserman, Crockett, & Hoffman, 2017).

The context in which individuals spend time matters, too (Boyer, 2006). A good deal of adolescents' risk taking takes place in contexts in which they are emotionally aroused (either very positively or very negatively), unsupervised by adults, and with their peers (Kretsch & Harden, 2014). As noted earlier, individuals' susceptibility to peer pressure is higher during early and middle adolescence than later, suggesting that one reason for teenagers' greater risk taking is the fact that they spend so much time in the peer group (Steinberg & Monahan, 2007). Most adolescent risk taking, including delinquency, drinking, and reckless behavior, occurs when other teenagers are present (Steinberg, 2014a). But the ways in which adolescents are influenced by their friends also depend on what adolescents think their peers would do. In one experiment in which adolescents were asked to complete a risk-taking task, compared to participants who were not given information about other players' performance, adolescents were more likely to take risks when they were told that this is what other people their age had done, but they were more likely to play it safe if they were told that their peers had done so (Braams, Davidow, & Somerville, 2019) (see Figure 2.9).

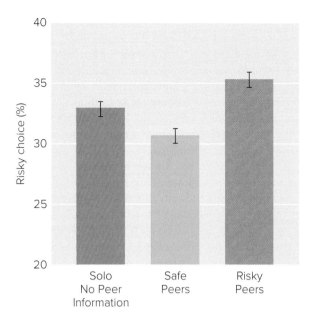

Figure 2.9 **When playing a risk-taking game, compared to participants who were not given information about other players' performance, teenagers were more likely to make risky decisions if they had been told that this is what other people their age had done but less likely to do so if they were told that their peers had made safe decisions.** (Braams et al., 2020)

Several studies of adolescent risk taking have looked at teenagers' decision making while driving. Although adolescent drivers, on average, take more chances than adults, how adolescents drive depends on who is in the car; adolescents drive much more safely when their parents are passengers than when they are driving alone or with their friends (Simons-Morton et al., 2011; Telzer, Ichien, & Qu, 2015). One study found that having their mother around actually increases activation in adolescents' reward centers when they are making safe decisions but decreases it when they are making risky ones (Guassi Moreira & Telzer, 2016). In other words, when

your mother is around, it may actually feel better to make prudent choices than dangerous ones! And, when faced with risky choices, teenagers who have relatively more positive relationships with their parents are less likely to take risks (Do, Guassi Moreira & Telzer, 2017) and less likely to show activation of the brain's reward centers (Qu et al., 2015).

The effect of peers on adolescent risk taking is clearly evident in studies of driving crashes. As Figure 2.10 shows, having multiple passengers in the car increases the risk of crashes dramatically among 16- and 17-year-old drivers, significantly among 18- and 19-year-old drivers, and not at all among adults. This is both because adolescent passengers can be distracting to new drivers and because adolescents are simply more likely to take risks in the presence of peers (Clentifanti et al., 2014; Foss & Goodwin, 2014; Pradhan et al., 2014).

Consistent with this, one experiment in which adolescents, college undergraduates, and adults who were either alone or in a room with their friends played a video driving game that permitted risky driving—for instance, driving through an intersection after a traffic light had turned yellow—found that the mere fact of having friends watching their performance increased risk taking among adolescents and undergraduates but not among adults (Gardner & Steinberg, 2005). In a subsequent study in which the researchers imaged the teens' brains while they played a similar video driving game, the results indicated that the brain regions associated with the experience of reward were much more likely to be activated when the teenagers were observed by their friends than when they were alone and that risky driving was correlated with heightened activity in the brain's reward areas. Thus, in the presence of their peers, adolescents may pay more attention to the potential rewards of a risky decision than they do when they are alone (O'Brien et al., 2011; Smith et al., 2015). This peer effect on adolescent risk taking is not seen, however, if a slightly older adult is present (Silva, Chein, & Steinberg, 2016) (see Figure 2.11).

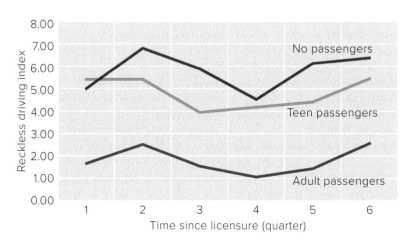

Figure 2.10 **Although adolescents on average are riskier drivers than adults, who is in the car makes a big difference. Teens drive more recklessly when they are alone or with peers than when they have adult passengers.** (Simons-Morton et al., 2011)

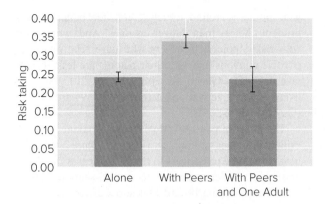

Figure 2.11 Adolescents make riskier decisions when they are with their peers, but the presence of a slightly older adult eliminates this peer effect on risk taking. (Figure 1 from Silva, Chein, & Steinberg, 2016)

Logic and Intuition More recently, several theorists have proposed models of adolescent risk taking that consider the ways in which two different thinking systems—one that is deliberative and logical, and one that is intuitive and gut-level—interact to influence behavior (Reyna et al., 2015; Romer, Reyna, & Satterthwaite, 2017). According to these perspectives, the heightened risk taking seen during adolescence and the drop in risk taking in adulthood can't be entirely due to deficiencies in logical reasoning because adults themselves do not always act logically. As the Nobel Prize-winning psychologist Daniel Kahneman has pointed out (2011), we all often behave in ways that defy logic.

For instance, suppose I describe someone to you as quiet, introspective, methodical, and nerdy, and ask you whether that person is more likely to be a mathematician or a waiter. Most people say "mathematician." But this is certainly not correct—since in the United States, there are over 7 million people who are waiters or waitresses and only 3,000 people employed as mathematicians! If you answered "mathematician," you were probably using your intuition, rather than logic. In this example, the gut-level choice happens to be wrong, but in many situations in life, our intuitions are correct. Being able to make some decisions intuitively takes advantage of experience and permits us to make decisions much more quickly than we would be able to do if we had to reason everything out. Although the development of logical thinking may differentiate adolescents from children, the main change to take place between adolescence and adulthood is not the further development of logical decision making (as you read earlier, this is pretty much completed by age 15 or so) but the continued development of intuitive decision making that is based on experience.

What stops adults from taking a lot of risks is not that they are good at systematically analyzing the probabilities of various outcomes but because they get a gut-level feeling that keeps them away from the risky act. If I am

standing on a cliff overlooking a dark body of water that I can't see into, the reason I don't jump is not that I've logically assessed my chances of getting hurt and decided that the odds are not in my favor. I don't jump because something inside me immediately tells me that it is a dumb thing to do. I don't even have to think about it. In one study in which adolescents and adults were asked while their brain was scanned whether some obviously risky things (e.g., "setting your hair on fire," "swimming with sharks") were bad things to do, the researchers found that the adolescents took longer to respond and were more likely than adults to activate brain regions that are involved in deliberative thinking; adults, in contrast, were more likely than adolescents to activate regions that reflect gut-level responding (Baird, Fugelsang, & Bennett, 2005). One other study has found that improvements in deliberative decision-making abilities are associated with more, not less, risk taking (Wolff & Crockett, 2011).

Reducing Adolescent Risk Taking Generally speaking, the most common approach to reducing adolescent risk taking is through classroom-based education programs designed to teach adolescents about the dangers of various activities (e.g., smoking, unprotected sex, drinking and driving), about making better decisions, and about resisting peer pressure to engage in risky activity. However, the evidence that these programs work is very shaky. For example, one evaluation of laws banning texting while driving found significant reductions in crash-related hospitalizations among adults but not among teenagers (Ferdinand et al., 2015). If, as we have seen, adolescents do not seem to be ignorant about the risks of these activities or deficient in the ways in which they make decisions, it does not seem likely that efforts to change their knowledge or decision making will result in very much risk reduction. Indeed, some writers have argued that enabling adolescents to make more accurate determinations of risk may inadvertently *increase* risky behavior because the actual probabilities of something bad happening after engaging in a risky act are actually very small (Reyna, Weldon, & McCormick, 2015). Plus, adolescents are more likely than adults to be swayed by their personal experiences than by information alone (Rosenbaum et al., 2018). And if recent research on brain maturation is pointing to reasons for the inherent vulnerability of adolescence—the combination of heightened sensation seeking and immature impulse control—perhaps it makes sense to rethink our approach to the problem (Reniers et al., 2016; Steinberg, 2015).

One alternative approach might focus on limiting adolescents' opportunities to put themselves in risky situations. For example, because we know that adolescents are more likely to have automobile accidents when they have teenage passengers in the car or drive at night, limiting the situations under which teenagers are permitted to drive, especially after they are newly licensed, would give adolescents the driver's license they so covet but limit risky driving. Many states have found that graduated driver licensing, which phases adolescent drivers into full unrestricted driving privileges over time, lowers the incidence of fatal crashes involving 16-year-old drivers, although it appears to increase the incidence of crashes among 18-year-olds (Masten, Foss, & Marshall, 2011).

It is also possible to reduce adolescent risk taking through economic policies. For example, although antitobacco education has met with only limited success, increases in the cost of cigarettes have dramatically reduced the rate of teen smoking. Thus, raising the price of tobacco or alcohol would likely diminish adolescents' use of these products because adolescents generally do not have a great deal of money and would therefore be sensitive to increases in the cost of smoking or drinking (Chaloupka, 2004). Another possibility would be to make risky things harder for adolescents to obtain by more strictly enforcing policies that prohibit stores from selling tobacco and alcohol to minors, limiting the supply of illegal drugs, or enforcing laws that limit adolescents' access to firearms (Rowland, Toumbourou, & Livingston, 2015). Yet a third possibility would be to make the penalties for engaging in certain risky behaviors, such as reckless or drunk driving, more severe and in so doing increase the salience of the potential costs of engaging in the risky behavior. Finally, to the extent that sensation seeking may be a normal part of adolescence, perhaps we can figure out how to provide safe outlets for this motivation. Not all risk taking is bad, after all, and many adolescents take risks in order to help others (Do et al., 2017). The challenge for parents, educators, and policy makers is to find ways to permit adolescents to take risks without putting themselves in situations in which they can hurt themselves.

Design Elements: (Brain): McGraw Hill Education; (Globe): Jupiterimages/Stockbyte/Getty Images; (Compass): Jacques Cornell/McGraw Hill Education; (Lightbulb): ansonsaw/Getty Images; (Girl with laptop): Africa Studio/Shutterstock.

3

Social Transitions

Social Redefinition and Psychosocial Development

The Elongation of Adolescence

Adolescence as a Social Invention

The "Invention" of Adolescence

Emerging Adulthood: A New Stage of Life or a Luxury of the Middle Class?

Changes in Status During Adolescence

Drawing a Legal Boundary

Inconsistencies in Adolescents' Legal Status

The Process of Social Redefinition

Common Practices in the Process of Social Redefinition

Variations in Social Transitions

Variations in Clarity

Variations in Continuity

The Transition into Adulthood in Contemporary Society

Special Transitional Problems of Poor, Minority, and Immigrant Youth

The Effects of Poverty on the Transition into Adulthood

What Can Be Done to Ease the Transition?

The Influence of Neighborhood Conditions on Adolescent Development

Processes of Neighborhood Influences

adamkaz/Getty Images

What events in your life told you—and others around you—that you were no longer a child and had finally become an adolescent? Was it when you turned 13? Finished elementary school? Went to your first boy–girl party? Were allowed to be at the mall without an adult?

And what signaled, or will signal, that you are an adult? Turning 18? Turning 21? No longer being financially dependent on your parents? Getting your first full-time job? Getting your driver's license? Graduating from college? Getting your first apartment? Getting married?

Each of these social transitions is not just an event. Each is also a source of information—to the adolescent and those in his or her life—about the person's stage of development. Parents may treat their children differently once they start high school, even if their appearance and behavior haven't changed. Neighbors might look at a child who has grown up next door differently once they see him or her driving. Adolescents may feel different about themselves once they have started working at a "real" job.

In all societies, adolescence is a period of social transition for the individual. Over the course of these years, people cease to be viewed by society as children and come to be recognized as adults.

This chapter is about the ways in which individuals are redefined during adolescence and the implications of this process for psychological development. Although the specific elements of this social passage from childhood into adulthood vary across time and place, the recognition that the individual's status has changed—a **social redefinition**

of the individual—is universal. In this chapter, we will look at a third fundamental feature of adolescence: changes in the way in which society defines who that person is and determines what rights and responsibilities she or he has as a consequence.

Along with the biological changes of puberty and changes in thinking abilities, changes in social roles and social status constitute yet another universal feature of development during adolescence. As you will read, some theorists have argued that the nature of adolescent development is far more influenced by the way in which society defines the economic and social roles of young people than by the biological or cognitive changes of the period.

The study of social transitions in adolescence provides an interesting vehicle through which to compare adolescence across different cultures and historical epochs. Puberty, after all, is pretty much the same everywhere (although its timing and meaning may vary from place to place). Abstract thinking and logical reasoning don't differ from one society to the next (although *what* people think and reason about certainly does). The social transitions of adolescence are not the same, however. Huge differences exist between the processes of social redefinition in different parts of the world, just as they have differed during different historical epochs. In examining some of these differences, you will come to understand better how the way in which society structures the transition of adolescents into adult roles influences the nature of psychosocial development during the period.

Social Redefinition and Psychosocial Development

Like the biological and cognitive transitions of adolescence, the social transitions have important consequences for the adolescent's psychosocial development. In the realm of identity, for example, attainment of adult status may transform a young woman's self-concept, causing her to feel more mature and to think more seriously about future work and family roles. Similarly, someone may feel older and more mature the first time he reports to work, goes into a bar, drives without an adult in the car, or votes. In turn, these new activities and opportunities may prompt self-evaluation and introspection.

Becoming an adult member of society, accompanied as it is by increases in responsibilities and freedom, also has an impact on the development of autonomy, or independence. In contrast to the child, the adolescent-turned-adult faces a wider range of decisions that may have serious long-term consequences (Cauffman et al., 2015). An

individual who has reached the drinking age, for example, must decide how to handle this new privilege. Should he go along with the crowd and drink every weekend night, follow his parents' example and abstain from drinking, or chart a middle ground? And in return for the privileges that come with adult status, the adolescent-turned-adult is expected to behave in a more responsible fashion. For example, receiving a driver's license carries with it the obligation of driving safely. The attainment of adult status provides chances for the young person to exercise autonomy and to develop a greater sense of independence.

Reaching adulthood often has important implications in the realm of achievement. In contemporary society, people can hold informal jobs, such as babysitting, when they are still young, but it is not until adult work status is attained (typically at age 15 or 16 in the United States) that young people can enter the labor force as full-time employees. And not until young people

social redefinition
The process through which an individual's position or status is redefined by society.

age of majority
The designated age at which an individual is recognized as an adult.

statutory rape
Sex between two individuals, even when it is consensual, when at least one of the persons is below the legal age of consent; in the United States, the specific age of consent varies from state to state.

have reached a designated age are they permitted to leave school of their own volition. In less industrialized societies, becoming an adult typically entails entrance into the productive activities of the community. Together, these shifts are likely to prompt changes in the young person's skills, aspirations, and expectations.

Changes in social definition often bring with them changes in relationships with others. Social redefinition at adolescence is therefore likely to raise new questions and concerns for the young person about intimacy—including such matters as dating and marriage. Many parents prohibit their children from dating until they have reached an "appropriate" age. Not until the **age of majority** (the legal age for adult status) are individuals allowed to marry without first gaining their parents' permission. In certain societies, young people may even be *required* to marry when they reach adulthood, entering into a marriage that may have been arranged while they were children (Schlegel, 2009).

Finally, changes in status at adolescence also may affect sexual development. In contemporary society, for example, laws governing sexual behavior (such as the definition of **statutory rape**) typically differentiate between individuals who have and have not attained adult status. One problem continuing to face contemporary society is whether sexually active individuals who are not yet legal adults should be able to make independent decisions about such matters as abortion and contraception (Cauffman et al., 2015).

The Elongation of Adolescence

Adolescence is longer today than it has ever been in human history.

Deciding how we define a stage of life—when it begins and when it ends—is inherently subjective. Experts use puberty to mark the beginning of adolescence because it's easy to measure, has obvious consequences (such as sexual maturation), and is universal. In societies that have formal rites of passage, puberty has long been used to indicate when people are no longer children. We may lack formal initiation ceremonies in contemporary society, but many people still think of puberty as marking the beginning of adolescence.

Getting consensus on when adolescence ends is harder. Although there are a few objective biological boundaries between adolescence and adulthood—for instance, the point at which people stop growing taller or when they are able to bear children—these somehow just

don't feel right. Some people finish their growth spurts when they're as young as 12 or 13, and some can even become parents at this age, but few of us, at least in today's world, feel comfortable labeling a 13-year-old as an "adult." That's why we tend to use some sort of social indicator to draw the line between adolescence and adulthood, such as attaining the age of legal majority, starting a full-time job, or moving out of one's parents' home. Reasonable people may disagree about *which* social indicator makes the most sense, but they would probably agree that a cultural marker of adulthood makes more sense than a biological one. This is why experts define adolescence as *beginning in biology and ending in culture.*

Of all the possible markers of the beginning and end of adolescence, menstruation and marriage are probably the best ones to use in order to see if adolescence actually has gotten longer. Both are widely experienced, and we can date both of them accurately. For most women, menarche is a memorable event and one whose date is regularly recorded in doctors' files. Scientists in the Western world have been keeping track of the average age of girls' first menstruation since about 1840, and we have a very good idea of how the advent of puberty has changed since then. There is no comparable pubertal event for boys that screams, "I am a man," but the ages at which males and females within the same society go through puberty are highly correlated. Even though girls typically go through puberty a year or two before boys, in societies in which puberty is early for girls, it comes early for boys, too.

The age at which people marry is even more reliably documented than the age of menarche. Government officials have long noted how old people are when they take their wedding vows, and as a consequence, we have accurate statistics about marriage that go back for centuries. This is not to say that one must be married in order to be an adult, only that changes in the average age of marriage are useful for tracking historical trends. Trends in the age at which people complete their schooling, begin their careers, or set up independent households would also be fine ways to measure historical changes in the transition into adulthood, but we haven't kept very good official records of these for nearly as long we've been recording marriages. And although getting married, leaving school, starting a career, or setting up a home do not all take place at the same age, they tend to move in lockstep from one generation to the next. When the average age for getting married rises over time, so do the others (Steinberg, 2014a).

In the middle of the nineteenth century, adolescence lasted around 5 years—that's how long it took girls to go from menarche to marriage in the mid-1800s. At the turn of the twentieth century, the average American woman got her first period between 14 and 15 and married when she was just under 22. In 1900, adolescence lasted a little less than 7 years.

The stage of adolescence has been lengthened by an increase in the age at which people make the transition into adult roles. The age of marriage has risen steadily over the past 50 years. (Left): Neustockimages/Getty Images; (Right): Kelvin Murray/Getty Images

During the first half of the twentieth century, people began getting married at a younger age, but the age of puberty continued to decline. This froze the length of adolescence at about 7 years. In 1950, for example, the average American female went through menarche at around 13½ and married at 20.

From 1950 on, though, things changed. The drop in the age of puberty continued, but people started marrying later and later. Each decade, the average age of menarche dropped by about 3 or 4 months, whereas the average age at marriage rose by about a year. By 2010, it took 15 years for the average girl to go from menarche to marriage (Steinberg, 2014a)—twice as long as it did in 1950.

Adolescence as a Social Invention

Many writers, often referred to as **inventionists,** have argued that adolescence is mainly a social invention (e.g., Fasick, 1994). They point out that although the biological and cognitive changes characteristic of the period are important in their own right, adolescence is defined primarily by the ways in which society recognizes (or does not recognize) the period as distinct from childhood or adulthood.

Our conception of adolescence as a separate stage of development is influenced by the fact that society draws lines between adolescence and childhood (for instance, the boundary between elementary and secondary school) and between adolescence and adulthood (for instance, the age at which someone can vote). Inventionists stress that it is only because we see adolescence as distinct that it exists as such. They point to other cultures and other historical periods in which adolescence has been viewed very differently.

Many of these theorists view the behaviors and problems characteristic of adolescence in contemporary society, such as delinquency, as a consequence of the way that adolescence is defined and young people are treated, rather than the result of the biological or cognitive givens of the period. As you know, this is an entirely different view from that espoused by writers such as G. Stanley Hall, who saw the psychological changes of adolescence as driven by puberty and, as a result, by biological destiny.

The "Invention" of Adolescence

Have there always been adolescents? Although this may seem like a simple question with an obvious answer, it is actually a very complicated issue. Naturally, there have always been individuals between the ages of 10 and 20, or who just passed through puberty, or whose frontal lobes were still maturing. But according to the inventionist view, adolescence as we know it in contemporary society did not really exist until the Industrial Revolution of the mid-nineteenth century (Fasick, 1994). In the agricultural world of the sixteenth and seventeenth centuries, children were treated primarily as miniature adults, and people did not make precise distinctions among children of different ages (*child* referred to anyone under the age of 18 or even 21). Children provided important labor to their families, and early in their development, they learned the roles they were expected to fill later in life. The main distinction between children and adults was based not on their age or their abilities but on whether they owned property (Modell & Goodman, 1990). As a consequence, there was little reason to label some youngsters as "children" and others as "adolescents"—in fact, the term *adolescent* was not widely used prior to the nineteenth century.

The Impact of Industrialization With industrialization came new patterns of work, education, and family life. Adolescents were among those most dramatically affected by these changes. First, because the economy was changing so rapidly, away from the simple and predictable life known in agrarian society, the connection between what individuals learned in

inventionists
Theorists who argue that the period of adolescence is mainly a social invention.

child protectionists
Individuals who argued, early in the twentieth century, that adolescents needed to be kept out of the labor force in order to protect them from the hazards of the workplace.

teenager
A term popularized about 50 years ago to refer to young people; it connoted a more frivolous and lighthearted image than did *adolescent*.

childhood and what they would need to know in adulthood became increasingly uncertain. Although a man may have been a farmer, his son would not necessarily follow in his footsteps.

One response to this uncertainty was that parents, especially in middle-class families, encouraged adolescents to spend time in school, preparing for adulthood. Instead of working side by side with their parents and other adults at home, as was the case before industrialization, adolescents became increasingly more likely to spend their days with peers, being educated or trained for the future. This led to the increased importance of peer groups and youth culture, two defining characteristics of modern adolescence that we take for granted today but that were not prominent until the early twentieth century.

Inventionists point out that the redefinition of adolescence as a time of preparation rather than participation also suited society's changing economic needs (Fasick, 1994). One initial outcome of industrialization was a shortage of job opportunities because machines were replacing workers. Although adolescents provided inexpensive labor, they were now competing with adults for a limited number of jobs. One way of protecting adults' jobs was to remove adolescents from the labor force by turning them into full-time students.

To accomplish this, society needed to begin discriminating between individuals who were "ready" for work and those who were not. Although there was little factual basis for the distinction, society began to view adolescents as less capable and more in need of guidance and training—legitimizing what was little more than age discrimination. Individuals who earlier in the twentieth century would have been working next to adults were now seen as too immature or too unskilled to carry out similar tasks—even though the individuals themselves hadn't changed in any meaningful way.

A less cynical view of the events of the late nineteenth century emphasizes the genuine motivation of some adults to protect adolescents from the dangers of the new workplace, rather than the selfish desire to protect adults' jobs from teenagers. Many factories were dangerous working environments, filled with new and unfamiliar machinery. Industrialization also brought with it worrisome changes in community life, especially in cities. The disruption of small farming communities and the growth of large urban areas was accompanied by increases in crime and "moral degeneracy." **Child protectionists** argued that young people needed to be kept away from the labor force for their own good. In addition to the rise of schools during this time, the early twentieth century saw the

growth of many organizations aimed at protecting young people, such as the Boy Scouts and other adult-supervised youth clubs (Modell & Goodman, 1990).

The Origins of Adolescence as We Know It Today

It was not until the late nineteenth century that adolescence came to be viewed as it is today: a lengthy period of preparation for adulthood in which young people, in need of guidance and supervision, remain economically dependent on their elders. This view started within the middle class—where parents had more to gain by keeping their children out of the labor force and educating them for a better adulthood—but it spread quickly throughout society. Because the workplace has continued to change in ways that make the future uncertain, the idea of adolescence as a distinctive period of preparation for adulthood has remained intact. Adolescence, as a transitional stage between childhood and adulthood, now exists in virtually all societies around the world (Larson, Wilson, & Rickman 2009).

Two other modifications of the definition of adolescence also gave rise to new terminology and ideas. The first of these is the introduction of the term **teenager,** which was not employed until about 75 years ago. In

Although adolescence was invented during the late nineteenth century, it was not until the middle of the twentieth century that our present-day image of the teenager was created. Making an important contribution to this image were the mass media—magazines such as Seventeen *cultivated a particular image of the modern teenager as a way of targeting advertisements toward an increasingly lucrative adolescent market.*
Retro AdArchives/Alamy Stock Photo

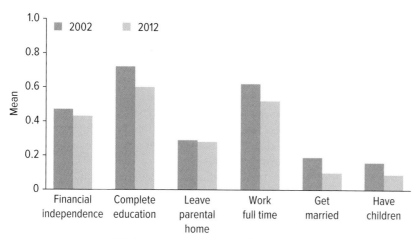

Figure 3.1 **As society changes, so do our ideas about what it means to be an adult. Between 2002 and 2012, there were significant declines in how important people thought completing one's education, working full time, marriage, and parenthood are as marking adulthood.** (Cepa & Furstenberg, 2020)

contrast to *adolescent, teenager* suggested a less serious age, during which individuals concern themselves with cars, clothes, and cosmetics. An important social change that led to the development of the concept of teenager was the increased affluence and economic freedom enjoyed by American adolescents during the late 1940s and early 1950s (Hine, 1999). Advertisers recognized that teenagers represented an important consumer group and, with the help of new publications such as *Seventeen* magazine, began cultivating the image of the happy-go-lucky teenager as a means of targeting ad campaigns toward the lucrative adolescent market (Osgerby, 2008; Palladino, 1996). Interestingly, although the image of the American teenager—fun-loving, irresponsible, and independent—now appears all over the world, in some societies it is viewed favorably (because it is evidence that the society has reached a level of affluence to be able to afford it), while in others it is held up as an example of what adults do *not* want their children to become (Larson, Wilson, & Rickman, 2009).

A second term whose acceptance grew as a result of social change is **youth,** which was used long before *adolescent.* But, prior to industrialization, youth had a vague, imprecise meaning and could refer to someone as young as 12 or as old as 24 (Modell & Goodman, 1990). Gradually, and especially during the 1960s, the growth of the college population and the rise in student activism focused attention on individuals who were somewhere between adolescence and young adulthood—those from 18 to 22. Many adults referred to the changes they saw in attitudes and values among college students as the "youth movement." One theorist went so far as to argue that youth is a separate stage in the life cycle, psychologically as well as chronologically distinct from both adolescence and adulthood (Keniston, 1970), an idea that is similar to the concept of "emerging adulthood," which we'll examine later in this chapter.

Many college students today are unsure about whether they are adolescents or adults, since they may feel mature in some respects (keeping up an apartment or being involved in a serious relationship) but immature in others (having to depend on parents for economic support or having to have an advisor approve class schedules). Although it may strike you as odd to think of 22-year-olds as adolescents, the lengthening of formal schooling in contemporary society has altered the way we define adolescence because the majority of young people continue their education past high school and are forced to delay their transition into many adult work and family roles (Cepa & Furstenberg, 2020) (see Figure 3.1). By this definition, many 22-year-olds (and some individuals who are even older) are still not yet adults—a situation that often perplexes parents as much as their adult children.

youth
Today, a term used to refer to individuals ages 18 to 22; it once referred to individuals ages 12 to 24.

making the personal connection

Think for a moment about how your parents' adolescence differed from yours. What changes have taken place in society since then that might have contributed to this?

Emerging Adulthood: A New Stage of Life or a Luxury of the Middle Class?

The transition to adulthood has become so delayed in many industrialized societies that some have argued that there is a new stage in life—emerging adulthood—that may last for some individuals until their mid-20s (Arnett, 2009). Proponents of this idea contend that the period from ages 18 to 25 is neither adolescence nor adulthood but a unique developmental period in its own right, characterized by five main features:

- the exploration of possible identities before making enduring choices;
- instability in work, romantic relationships, and living arrangements;
- a focus on oneself and, in particular, on functioning as an independent person;
- the feeling of being between adolescence and adulthood; and
- the sense that life holds many possibilities.

Is Emerging Adulthood Universal? This profile certainly describes many young people in contemporary society, particularly those whose parents can foot the bill while their "emerging adults" are figuring out what they want to do with their lives. As many writers have pointed out (e.g., Arnett, 2009), however, emerging adulthood does not exist in all cultures—in fact, it exists in very few (the United States, Canada, Australia, New Zealand, Japan, and the more affluent nations of Western Europe). And even within countries in which there are significant numbers of emerging adults, the majority of individuals cannot afford to delay the transition from adolescence into full-fledged adulthood for a half decade. As a result, there is a great deal of variability among people in their mid-20s in the nature of emerging adulthood (Beal, Crockett, & Peugh, 2016; Côté, 2014).

It is also important to note that the existence of emerging adulthood is not entirely an economic phenomenon. Many emerging adults live the way they do because the economy forces them to, but many simply do it by choice—they want to take some time before assuming full adult responsibilities. Expectations about the age at which one gets married appear to be especially important to this decision (Carroll et al., 2007). The existence of emerging adulthood may have a lot to do with values and priorities, and not just the economy.

Psychological Well-Being in Emerging Adulthood
Very little research has examined psychological development and functioning during emerging adulthood. The profile initially described by some writers suggests both a potentially difficult time, characterized by floundering and financial instability, and a time of carefree optimism and independence. There is evidence for both views. Several studies show that for the majority of people, emerging adulthood is generally one of positive and improving mental health (see Figure 3.2). At the same time, however, the period between 18 and 25 is a time during which a substantial number of people report serious mental health problems, such as depression or substance abuse. In any given year, nearly one-fifth of people this age suffer from some sort of mental illness, and despite the media attention given to teen suicide, the suicide rate among young adults is twice what it is among teenagers (Institute of Medicine, 2015). Not surprisingly, young adults whose family environments have been unsupportive and who have experienced economic hardship and discrimination report a steeper decline in life satisfaction than their peers (Willroth, Atherton, & Robbins, 2020).

One study of mental health during this age period followed a national sample of American youths from age 18 to their mid-20s. The researchers compared four groups: (1) those who reported positive well-being across the entire interval, (2) those who reported negative well-being across the entire interval, (3) those whose well-being started low but increased, and (4) those whose well-being started high but decreased (Schulenberg, Bryant, & O'Malley, 2004). (There also was a large group whose well-being was average to begin with and stayed that way.) They then looked to see whether these patterns of well-being over time were related to indicators of individual functioning by rating whether individuals had been succeeding, maintaining, or stalling as they moved into adulthood (see Table 3.1). Three main findings emerged.

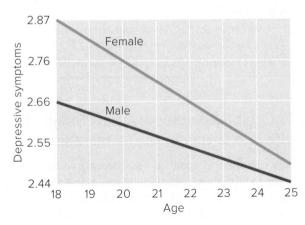

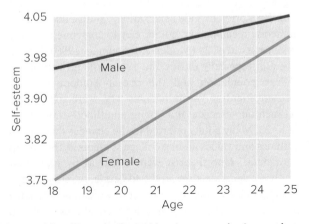

Figure 3.2 For some, early adulthood is a time of improved mental health, as indicated by decreases in depression and increases in self-esteem. (Galambos, Barker, & Krahn, 2006)

Table 3.1 Descriptions of developmental task domains

Domain	Succeeding	Maintaining	Stalling
Peer involvement	• Goes out two or more times a week for fun and recreation at age 22 and age 26	• Neither succeeding nor stalling	• Goes out one or fewer times a week for fun and recreation at age 22 and age 26
Education	• Graduated from 4-year college by age 26, or • Expected to graduate from 2-year college and received 2-year degree	• Expected to graduate from 4-year college and received 2-year degree, or • Did not expect 2- or 4-year degree and did not receive either degree, or • Expected 2-year degree and did not receive 2-year degree by age 26	• Expected 4-year college degree and did not receive either 2- or 4-year degree by age 26
Work	• No unemployment at age 22 or 26, and • Working 10+ months/year at full-time job by age 26, and • High job confidence at age 26	• Neither succeeding nor stalling (e.g., homemaker or otherwise not working and not looking for work outside home)	• Some unemployment at age 22 and/or 26, and • Low job confidence at age 26
Substance abuse avoidance (healthy coping/ lifestyle)	• No substance use at any age (18, 22, 26) [Four indicators of substance use: cigarettes (current use), binge drinking (in past 2 weeks), marijuana (current use), and other illicit drugs (in past 12 months)]	• Some substance use but less than stalling	• Use of two or more substances at all three ages (18, 22, 26), and/or • Use of three or more substances at age 26
Romantic involvement	• At age 26, married or engaged (with or without cohabitation), and • No divorce history	• At age 26, cohabiting, or • Dating more than once a month, and/or • Divorced but remarried	• At age 26, not married, not engaged, not cohabiting, and • Dating once a month or less
Citizenship	• Three indicators reported at age 22 and age 26: social conscience, charity, and awareness of social/ political events • Measures indicate at least one strong connection at age 22 and at least two strong connections at age 26	• Measures indicate some strong connections but not as frequent as at succeeding level	• Measures indicate no strong connections at age 26
Financial autonomy	• Self and/or spouse providing all resources at age 26	• Some resources come from other than self or spouse (and not stalling)	• At age 26, less than half of support is from self and/or spouse, and/or • Live with parents and receive some financial help (>20%) from them

(Schulenberg, Bryant, & O'Malley, 2004)

First, over 80% of the sample showed great stability in their well-being over the period, consistent with many other studies indicating that psychological functioning in childhood and adolescence is highly predictive of success later in life (e.g., Shanahan & Bauer, 2004). This is because success in one stage (doing well in high school) usually leads to success in the next stage (getting into a good college), and some basic "resources" predict success throughout the life span—as the old joke goes, if you want to succeed in life, make sure you have a high IQ, money, and

initiation ceremony
The formal induction of a young person into adulthood.

status offense
A violation of the law that pertains to minors but not adults.

juvenile justice system
A separate system of courts and related institutions developed to handle juvenile crime and delinquency.

criminal justice system
The system of courts and related institutions developed to handle adult crime.

good parents (e.g., Burt, Obradović, Long, & Masten, 2008).

Second, for more than a sixth of the sample, this period was one of substantial change in mental health: About 7% of the sample were well-functioning adolescents whose mental health declined, and another 10% were troubled adolescents who became "exemplary" young adults.

Finally, experiences in the domains of work, romance, and citizenship—but not in the domains of school or finances—were especially linked to changes in well-being. Other studies also have found that success in the worlds of work and romance are related to well-being during this time (Galambos, Barker, & Krahn, 2006).

So, what's the verdict on emerging adulthood? Has a new stage of life actually arisen? How widespread does a pattern of behavior have to be for us to conclude that a new stage of development has emerged? Does emerging adulthood exist if it is common in Boston or Berkeley but not in Biloxi, Baghdad, or Beijing?

It's hard to say. "Midlife" is a stage that we take for granted in contemporary America but that doesn't exist everywhere, or at least, not as we think of it (Schweder, 1998). Nevertheless, the notion that people go through a distinct and unique set of psychological transitions during middle age has become widely accepted, if perhaps less supported by hard evidence than in popular media portrayals.

Clearly, in some parts of the world and in some segments of society, the transition between adolescence and adulthood has been lengthened—that much is indisputable. More individuals attend college than in previous eras, which delays their entrance into the world of work, and more postpone getting married, which delays their settling into a more stable lifestyle. But whether this means that the psychological functioning of 23-year-olds who follow this pattern of a delayed and prolonged transition is significantly different from that of 23-year-olds who transition from college directly into full-time employment and marriage is anyone's guess because it hasn't been studied.

In other words, whether a *psychological* stage of emerging adulthood really exists has yet to be established (Côté, 2014). It is entirely possible that economic forces have delayed the transition into *social* adulthood (i.e., the roles that people occupy) but have not affected the transition into *psychological* adulthood. In fact, I have written that there may be some advantages of delaying adulthood, both psychologically and with regard to brain development (Steinberg, 2014b).

Changes in Status During Adolescence

The social transitions of adolescence typically involve two different sorts of changes in status. On the one hand, the adolescent is given certain privileges and rights that are typically reserved for the society's adult members. On the other hand, this increased power and freedom generally are accompanied by increased expectations for self-management, personal responsibility, and social participation.

Drawing a Legal Boundary

With the attainment of adult status, the young person is often permitted more extensive participation in the community's decision making. In many Native American groups, such as the Navajo or Apache, it is only after a formal **initiation ceremony** that adolescents are granted adult status (Markstrom, 2011a). In contemporary America, attaining the age of majority brings the right to vote.

But along with this increased power usually come new obligations. In most societies, young adults are expected to serve their communities in cases of emergency or need, and in many cultures, training for warfare is often demanded of young people once they attain adult status (Benedict, 1934). On the other hand, in most societies, it is not until adult status is attained that individuals are permitted to participate in certain activities that are reserved for adults. Gambling, purchasing alcoholic beverages or marijuana, and seeing X-rated films are but three of the many privileges we reserve in America for individuals who have reached the legal age of adulthood.

Once an adolescent is designated as an adult, she or he is also subject to a new set of laws. In some instances, attaining adult status brings with it greater leniency under the law, whereas in others, it is associated with harsher treatment. In the United States, for example, certain activities that are permissible among adults are violations of the law when they are committed by young people (Davis et al., 2013). (We use the term **status offense** to refer to a behavior that is problematic because of the young person's *status* as a juvenile.) As a college student, you cannot be legally punished for not showing up for class, as would have been the case if you didn't show up for high school. If you decide you don't want to return home when you are on a break, you don't have to, at least not as far as the law is concerned; in contrast, running away from home during adolescence is against the law in many jurisdictions. Certain crimes when committed by a minor are adjudicated in a separate **juvenile justice system,** which operates under different rules and principles than the **criminal justice system** that applies to adults. Although being tried in the juvenile justice system usually results in a less severe sanction than being found guilty of the

In the United States, there are many inconsistencies under the law with respect to the treatment of adolescents. Some Supreme Court rulings have viewed young people as having the same rights as adults, whereas others have not.
Cass Gilbert/Image Source

same crime in adult court, this is not always the case (Kurlychek & Johnson, 2010).

The legal regulation of adolescent behavior in the United States has been controversial in recent years. Part of the problem is that development during adolescence is so rapid and so variable between individuals that it is difficult to know at what chronological age a line should be drawn between legally viewing someone as an adult and viewing him or her as a child (Cauffman et al., 2015). This problem is compounded by the fact that we draw the boundary at different places for different purposes (e.g., driving at 16, voting at 18, buying alcohol at 21, and so on). This inconsistency makes it hard to point to any specific age and say with certainty that there is consensus about where the legal boundary should be drawn. One current controversy is whether new findings from studies of adolescent brain development should influence where we draw these legal lines (Cohen et al., 2016; Steinberg, 2014a). If the brain isn't totally mature by the time people are in their mid-twenties, should 20-year-olds be treated like adolescents under the law (Scott, Bonnie, & Steinberg, 2016)?

making the practical connection

At what age do you think we should draw the line between legal adolescence and legal adulthood? Should this age be the same for all activities, or should different activities have different age boundaries? Should the boundary be changed as we discover new things about brain development?

Adolescents as Criminal Defendants There is especially great disagreement about how we should view and treat young people who commit serious violent offenses (Scott & Steinberg, 2008). Are juveniles who commit crimes less blameworthy than adults because they are less able to foresee the consequences of their actions or resist the pressure of others to engage in antisocial activity? Or should we hold adolescents and adults to the same standards of criminal responsibility? If a youngster has committed a violent crime, should he or she be treated as a child (and processed by the legal system as a delinquent) or tried as an adult (and processed as a criminal)? Should young teenagers and adults who are convicted of the same crime receive the same penalties? In 2005, in a landmark case called *Roper v. Simmons,* the U.S. Supreme Court raised the age at which individuals can be exposed to the death penalty from 16 to 18, and several cases that were decided in the years after *Roper* have asked whether it is constitutional to sentence juveniles to life without parole (Steinberg, 2018).

One issue that arises in cases in which a juvenile might be tried as an adult is whether the adolescent is competent to stand trial and make other legal decisions. In the United States, it is not permissible to try someone in a criminal proceeding if the individual does not understand the charges, does not understand the nature of the trial, or is unable to make reasoned decisions about the case (e.g., whether to take the stand in his or her own defense). Historically, questions about a defendant's competence to stand trial have been raised only in cases in which the individual is mentally ill or intellectually disabled. Now that many juveniles are being tried as adults—some who are young teenagers—experts have asked whether some young defendants may be incompetent to stand trial simply because of cognitive or emotional immaturity (Viljoen et al., 2010). One study found that about one-third of those aged 13 and younger and one-fifth of 14- and 15-year-olds were as impaired in their abilities to serve as a competent defendant as were mentally ill adults who had been found not competent to stand trial (Grisso et al., 2003). Research also indicates that juveniles, even those who are relatively mature, are less likely than adults to understand their rights when being questioned by the police, more likely to confess to a crime than remain silent, less likely to consider the long-term consequences of making plea agreements, and less likely to discuss disagreements about their defense with their attorneys (Pimentel, Arndorfer, & Malloy, 2015; Redlich & Shteynberg, 2016; Zottoli & Dallary-Kapur, 2019).

Inconsistencies in Adolescents' Legal Status

Every so often, the U.S. Supreme Court hears a case that asks whether high school students have the right to free speech. In 2021, for example, the Court was presented with a case about that asked whether, and under what circumstances, schools can regulate what students post on social media (Liptak, 2021). In this case, *Mahanoy Area School District v. Levy,* Brandi Levy, a high school

cohort

A group of individuals born during the same general historical era.

freshman who had not made the varsity cheerleading squad (but who did make the junior varsity team), posted her candid opinion about her rejection on Snapchat: "Fuck school fuck softball fuck cheer fuck everything" (with an accompanying photo of her raising her middle finger). After one of her followers forwarded the snap and the school administrators found out about the posting, Levy was kicked off the junior varsity team as punishment. She and her parents sued the school. They argued that because the girl was not on school grounds when she posted the material, the school had no right to try to censor her off-campus speech, even if what she posted was going to be visible to classmates and teachers. The Court agreed with student, consistent with prior rulings that schools can regulate students' speech but only when it is potentially disruptive to what goes on at school or harmful to a member of the school community (e.g., if someone threatens a classmate or teacher online).

Students' right to free speech has not always been supported by the Supreme Court, however, and many other issues concerning the legal status of adolescents in the United States remain vague and confusing (Cauffman et al., 2015). For example, in one case, the Court ruled that a public high school can censor articles written by students for their school newspaper on the grounds that adolescents are so immature that they need the protection of wiser adults. Yet, in another case, the Court also ruled that students who wanted to form a Bible study group had the right to meet on campus because high school students are mature enough to understand that a school can permit the expression of ideas that it does not necessarily endorse. Students can wear black arm bands to school in peaceful protest, the Court has ruled, but they are prohibited from expressing speech that might be seen as advocating behavior that the school forbids, as the Court ruled in a case involving a student at a rally who carried a banner on which he had written, "Bong Hits for Jesus."

There are many other examples of this sort of inconsistency in where we draw the line between adolescents and adults. For example, courts have ruled that teenagers have the right to obtain contraceptives or purchase violent video games without their parents' approval. But they also have upheld laws forbidding adolescents access to cigarettes or to magazines that, although vulgar, are not considered so obscene that they are outlawed among adults (Cauffman et al., 2015). As you know, the age at which adolescents are permitted to engage in various adult behaviors—driving, voting, drinking, viewing R-rated movies, smoking—varies considerably from one domain to the next. Is there a pattern to this inconsistency? In general, legal decisions tend to set the age boundary high when the behavior in question is viewed as potentially damaging to the young person (e.g., buying alcohol) but low when the behavior is thought to have potential benefit (e.g., having access to contraceptives) (Scott & Steinberg, 2008).

The Process of Social Redefinition

Social redefinition during adolescence is not a single event. Like puberty or cognitive maturation, it is a series of events that often occur over a relatively long time. In contemporary America, the process of redefinition typically begins at age 15 or 16, when people are first permitted to drive and work in the formal labor force. But in most states, the social redefinition of the adolescent continues well into young adulthood. Some privileges of adulthood, such as voting, are not conferred until the age of 18, and others, such as purchasing alcoholic beverages, don't come until the age of 21, 5 or 6 years after the redefinition process begins.

Even in societies that mark the social redefinition of the young person with a dramatic and often complicated initiation ceremony, the social transformation from child into adult may span many years, and the initiation ceremony may represent just one element of the process (Markstrom, 2011b). In fact, the initiation ceremony usually marks the *beginning* of a long period of training and preparation for adulthood, not the adolescent's final passage into adult status.

In many cultures, the social redefinition of young people occurs in groups. The young people of a community are grouped with peers of approximately the same age—a **cohort**—and move through the series of status transitions together. One of the results of such age grouping is that

Formal rites of passage from adolescence to adulthood are rare in contemporary society. Certain cultural ceremonies—such as the quinceañera, a coming-of-age celebration for young women in some Latinx communities—are about as close as we come in today's society. Image Source/Getty Images

very strong bonds are formed among people who have shared certain rituals. In many American high schools, for example, attempts are made to create class spirit or class unity by fostering bonds among students who will graduate together. In many Latinx communities, adolescent girls participate together in an elaborate sort of "coming-out" celebration called the **quinceañera.** On college campuses, fraternities and sororities may conduct group initiations that involve difficult or unpleasant tasks, and special ties may be forged between "brothers" or "sisters" who have pledged together.

Common Practices in the Process of Social Redefinition

Although the specific ceremonies, signs, and timetables of social redefinition during adolescence vary from one culture to another, several general themes characterize the process in all societies.

Real or Symbolic Separation from Parents First, social redefinition usually entails the real or symbolic separation of young persons from their parents (Markstrom, 2011b). During late childhood, children in some societies are expected to begin sleeping in households other than their own. Youngsters may spend the day with their parents but spend the night with friends of the family, with relatives, or in a separate residence reserved for preadolescents. In America, during earlier times, it was customary for adolescents to leave home temporarily and live with other families in the community, either to learn specific occupational skills as apprentices or to work as domestic servants (Kett, 1977). In contemporary societies, the separation of adolescents from their parents takes somewhat different forms. They are sent to summer camps, boarding schools, or, as is more common, college.

Emphasizing Differences Between the Sexes A second aspect of social redefinition during adolescence entails the accentuation of physical and social differences between males and females (Schlegel & Barry, 1991). This accentuation of differences occurs partly because of the physical changes of puberty and partly because in many cultures adult work and family roles are often highly sex-differentiated. Many societies separate males and females during religious ceremonies, keep males and females apart during initiation ceremonies, and have individuals begin wearing sex-specific articles of clothing (rather than clothing permissible for either gender).

In many non-Western societies today, the privileges extended to males and females once they have reached puberty are so different that adolescence often is an entirely different phenomenon for boys and girls (Larson, Wilson, & Rickman, 2009). In many developing societies, girls' behavior generally is more subject to the control of

adults, whereas boys are given more freedom and autonomy (Markstrom, 2011b). Girls are expected to remain virgins until marriage, for example, whereas boys' premarital sexual activity is tolerated. Girls are expected to spend time preparing for domestic roles, whereas boys are expected to acquire vocational skills for employment outside the home. And formal schooling is far less available to girls than to boys, especially in rural societies.

The separation of males and females in adolescence is also seen in Western industrialized societies, if not always explicitly. In earlier times in America (and to a certain extent in many other industrialized societies today), during adolescence, males and females were separated in educational institutions, either by excluding adolescent girls from secondary and higher education, grouping males and females in different schools or different classrooms, or having males and females follow different curricula. In present-day America, many of these practices have been discontinued because of legal rulings prohibiting sex discrimination, but some elements of accentuated sex differentiation and sex segregation during adolescence still exist—for example, in clothing, athletic activities, and household chores. And many contemporary ceremonies designed to recognize the young person's passage into adulthood differentiate between males and females (e.g., the **Bar Mitzvah** and the **Bas Mitzvah** ceremonies for Jewish males and females, respectively).

Passing on Information from the Older Generation
A third aspect of social redefinition during adolescence typically entails passing on cultural, historical, and practical information from the adult generation to the newly inducted cohort of young people. This information may concern (1) matters thought to be important to adults but of limited utility to children (e.g., information about the performance of certain adult work tasks), (2) matters thought to be necessary for adults but unfit for children (e.g., information regarding sex), or (3) matters concerning the history or rituals of the family or community (e.g., how to perform certain ceremonies). In traditional societies, initiates are often sent to some sort of "school" in which they are instructed in the productive activities of the community (hunting, fishing, or farming). Following puberty, boys and girls receive instruction about sexual relations, moral behavior, and societal lore (Fried & Fried, 1980; Miller, 1928).

In contemporary society, too, adolescence is a time of instruction in preparation for adulthood. Elementary

There are very few formal rites of passage in modern society, although in many religions, there are ceremonies that signify coming of age, such as the Bar or Bas Mitzvah ceremony in Judaism. 3bugsmom/Getty Images

school students, for example, are generally not taught a great deal about sexuality, work, or financial matters; such coursework is typically reserved for high school students. We also restrict participation in certain "adult" activities (such as viewing sexually explicit movies) until adolescents are believed old enough to be exposed to them.

Because formal initiation ceremonies are neither very common nor very meaningful in modern society, it is easy to overlook important similarities between the processes of social redefinition in traditional and contemporary societies. Practices such as separating children from their parents or **scarification**—the intentional creation of scars on some part or parts of the body, often done as part of an initiation ceremony—may seem alien to us.

But if we look beneath the surface, at the meaning and significance of each culture's practices, we find many common threads. In contemporary society, for example, although we do not practice anything as "alien" as scarification, we do have our share of body rituals, many of which are not seen until adolescence and which might seem equally alien to someone unfamiliar with our society: punching of holes in earlobes or other parts of the body (piercing), scraping of hair from faces or legs (shaving), permanently decorating the skin (tattoos), and applying brightly colored paints to lips, eyes, and cheeks (makeup).

scarification
The intentional creation of scars on some part or parts of the body, often done as part of an initiation ceremony.

Variations in Social Transitions

Although the presence of social redefinition in a general sense is a universal feature of adolescent development, there is considerable diversity in the nature of the transition. Examining social redefinition from cross-cultural and historical perspectives provides a valuable means of contrasting the nature of adolescence in different social contexts. Two very important dimensions along which societies differ in the process of social redefinition are in the explicitness, or *clarity,* of the transition and in the smoothness, or *continuity,* of the passage.

Variations in Clarity

Because initiation ceremonies are in many ways religious ceremonies, they are most often found in societies in which a shared religious belief unites the community and structures individuals' daily experiences. Universal, formal initiation ceremonies therefore have never been prevalent in U.S. society, largely because of the cultural diversity of the population and the general separation of religious experience from everyday affairs.

There are, however, factors other than the presence of formal rites of passage that determine how clear the transition into adult status is to young people and society. One such factor concerns the extent to which various aspects of the transition to adulthood occur at about the same time for individuals and during the same general period for adolescents growing up together (Elder, 1980).

When transitions into adult work, family, and citizenship roles occur close in time and when most members of a cohort experience these transitions at about the same age, the passage into adulthood has greater clarity. If all young people were to graduate from high school, enter the labor force, and marry at the age of 18, this age would be an implicit boundary between adolescence and adulthood, even without a formal ceremony. When different aspects of the passage occur at different times, though, and when adolescents growing up in a similar environment experience these transitions in different order and along different schedules, the boundary between adolescence and adulthood is cloudier.

The Clarity of Social Redefinition in Contemporary Society   When did you become an adolescent? When did you (or when will you) become an adult? If you are like most individuals in contemporary society, your answers to these questions will not be clear-cut. In one study of Danish youth, for example, when asked if they felt like adults, most 17- to 24-year-olds and nearly half of 25- to 29-year-olds answered that they were adults in some ways but not in others (Arnett & Padilla-Walker, 2015).

In modern society, we have no formal ceremonies marking the transition from childhood into adolescence, nor do we formally mark the passage from adolescence into adulthood (of course, there are plenty of informal "ceremonies" that do this—perhaps you had a special party to celebrate turning 18 or 21). School graduation ceremonies perhaps come the closest to universal rites of passage in contemporary society, but school graduation doesn't bring with it many meaningful or universal changes in social status, responsibilities, or privileges.

As a result, social redefinition in contemporary society does not give adolescents any clear indication of when their responsibilities and privileges as an adult begin. As we noted earlier, laws governing the age at which individuals can and cannot do "adult" activities are inconsistent. In many states, for example, the age for starting employment is 15; for driving, 16; for attending restricted (R-rated) movies without parents, 17; for voting, 18; and for drinking, 21. In some states, the age at which someone can be tried as an adult for a serious violent crime is as low as 10 (Hartney, 2006).

In short, today we have few universal markers of adulthood—adolescents are treated as adults at different times by different people in different contexts. A young person may be legally old enough to drive, but his parents may feel that 16 is too early and may refuse to let him use the family car. Another may be treated like an adult at work, where she works side by side with people three times her age, but be treated like a child at home. A third may be viewed as an adult by her mother but as a child by her father. The same young person we send into combat is not permitted to buy beer (and in many states, not permitted to buy a gun), even though combat is far more dangerous than drinking. It is little wonder, in light of the mixed and sometimes contradictory expectations facing young people, that for many adolescents the transition into adult roles is sometimes a confusing passage. An attorney I know once received a request for assistance from one of his adolescent clients who was incarcerated in adult prison—because the prison said he was too young to smoke cigarettes!

Adolescents' Views of Themselves Because contemporary society does not send clear or consistent messages to young people about when adolescence ends and adulthood begins, young people living within the same society can have widely varying views of their own social status and beliefs about age-appropriate behavior. For this reason, it is instructive to ask people what they think defines the transition to adulthood, as a way of gauging the way in which adult status is conceptualized by the broader society. Studies of how people define adulthood in contemporary society indicate three interesting trends.

First, in modern society, adolescents place relatively less emphasis than they do in traditional societies on attaining specific roles (e.g., worker, spouse, parent) as defining characteristics of adulthood and relatively more on the development of various character traits indicative of self-reliance (e.g., being responsible, independent, or self-controlled) (Kenyon et al., 2007). Among contemporary American youths, for instance, "accepting responsibility for one's self" is the most frequently mentioned criterion for being an adult.

Second, there has been a striking decline over time in the importance of family roles—marriage and parenthood—as defining features of what it means to be an adult. In early American society, the role of head of household was an especially important indicator of adult status for males, and taking on the roles of wife and mother defined adulthood for females. Today, though, very few adolescents say that marriage or parenthood are necessary for an individual to be considered an adult.

Finally, the defining criteria of adulthood have become more or less the same for males and females in contemporary industrialized society, unlike the case in traditional societies or during previous eras. In nonindustrialized cultures, the requirements for male adulthood were to be able to "provide, protect, and procreate," whereas for females, the requirements for adulthood were to care for children and run a household (Markstrom, 2011b). Contemporary youth, in contrast, view the various indicators of adult status as equally important (or equally unimportant) for males and females.

Given the absence of clear criteria that define adult status in contemporary societies, it is not surprising that, among people of the same age, some may feel older than their peers, while others may feel younger. This may be important because how old an adolescent feels affects his or her behavior. Psychologists have studied when individuals make the transition from feeling older than they really are (as most teenagers do) to feeling younger than they really are (as most adults do) (Galambos et al., 2005). Studies of North American youth have found that this shift takes place around age 25, among both males and females.

The Clarity of Social Redefinition in Traditional Cultures Unlike the case in contemporary society, social redefinition during adolescence is very clear in most traditional cultures. Typically, the passage from childhood into adolescence is marked by a formal initiation ceremony, which publicly proclaims the young person's assumption of a new position in the community (Markstrom, 2011b). For boys, such ceremonies may take place at puberty, at a designated chronological age, or at a time when the community decides that the individual is ready for the status change. For girls, initiation is more often linked to puberty and, in particular, to the onset of menstruation.

In many initiation ceremonies, the adolescent's physical appearance is changed, so that other members of the community can easily distinguish between initiated and uninitiated young people. New types of clothing might be worn following initiation, or some sort of surgical operation or scarification might be performed to create a

baby boom
The period following World War II, during which the number of infants born was extremely large.

permanent means of marking the individual's adult status. Unlike the case in contemporary society, where we often can't tell who is a juvenile and who is an adult by physical appearance alone (and where adults are often upset by images of preadolescents that are too adultlike), in most traditional societies, there is no mistaking who are adults and who are still children. In most modern industrialized societies, we have grown accustomed to seeing teenagers who try to dress like adults and adults who try to dress like teenagers, but these practices would be highly uncommon in traditional cultures.

The Clarity of Social Redefinition in Previous Eras

What is the transition to adulthood like today? Well, compared to what?

We often use the **baby boom** generation—individuals who were adolescents in the late 1950s and 1960s—as an implicit point of comparison when characterizing today's young people, perhaps because the baby boom generation has provided the basis for so many of the images of modern family life that are deeply embedded in our cultural psyche. But the baby boomers' transition to adulthood was highly unusual in many respects. For purposes of illustration, let's compare life today with life in 1960:

- In 1960, the average age of marriage was 20 for women and 22 for men; today, it is 28 and 30, respectively (U.S. Census Bureau, 2020).

- In 1960, fewer than 30% of young adults between the ages of 18 and 29 lived with their parents, whereas in 2020, more than half half did. Some of the increase was due to the COVID-19 pandemic, when many college campuses closed their dorms, but the proportion was already 52% by February 2020 (U.S. Census Bureau, 2020).

- In 1960, a very high proportion of adolescents went directly from high school into full-time employment or the military, and only one-third of American high school graduates went directly to college; today, nearly 70 percent of high school graduates go to college soon after graduating (National Center for Education Statistics, 2019).

In other words, in 1960, three key elements of the transition to adulthood—getting married, moving out of the parents' home, and completing one's education—all occurred relatively early compared to today, and all took place within a fairly constricted time frame.

By that standard, today's transition to adulthood looks excessively long and vaguely defined. Indeed, one study of patterns of schooling, work, romance, and residence during emerging adulthood found that individuals frequently move back and forth between periods of independence and dependence. This suggests that the progression from adolescence to adulthood today not only is long but also occurs in fits and starts (Cohen et al., 2003). It's little wonder that the majority of people in their mid-20s today don't know whether they are adolescents or adults.

But the transition into adulthood was just as disorderly and prolonged during the nineteenth century as it is today (Kett, 1977). Many young people at that time moved back and forth between school, where they were viewed as children, and work, where they were viewed as adults. Moreover, timetables for the assumption of adult roles varied considerably from one individual to the next because they were highly dependent on family and household needs rather than on generally accepted age patterns of school, family, and work transitions. An adolescent might have been working and living away from home, but if his family needed him—because, let's say, someone became ill—he would leave his job and move back in with his parents. During the middle of the nineteenth century, in fact, many young people were neither enrolled in school nor working, occupying a halfway stage that was not quite childhood but not quite adulthood, either (Katz, 1975).

At the beginning of the twentieth century, the transition to adulthood was very drawn out. Age at first

Contrasts are often drawn between adolescence today and adolescence in the 1950s, as portrayed in shows such as Leave It to Beaver. *This is probably not the best point of comparison, though, because the 1950s was a very unusual time. The long passage into adulthood characteristic of adolescence today actually shares much in common with adolescence at the beginning of the twentieth century.* CBS Photo Archive/Archive Photos/Getty Images

marriage was just about the same among males at the turn of the twentieth century (26) as it is today (30), although age at first marriage among females is much older today (28) than it was a century ago (22) (U.S. Census Bureau, 2020). And the proportion of 25- to 34-year-olds living at home was much higher early in the twentieth century than it was during the 1950s (Parker, 2012).

The brief and clear transition into adulthood experienced by many American baby boomers in the mid–twentieth century was the exception, not the rule. It's important not to lose sight of that. Although the notion of "emerging adulthood" may ring true today, it is by no means a new phenomenon. The label didn't exist 150 years ago, but young people then shared a great deal in common with today's emerging adults.

Variations in Continuity

The process of social redefinition also varies in the extent to which the adolescent's transition into adulthood is gradual or abrupt. Gradual transitions, in which the adolescent assumes the roles and status of adulthood bit by bit, are referred to as **continuous transitions.**

Transitions that are not so smooth, in which the young person's entrance into adulthood is more sudden, are referred to as **discontinuous transitions.** For example, children who grow up working on the family farm and continue this work as adults have a continuous transition into adult work roles. In contrast, children who do not have any work experience while they are growing up and who enter the labor force for the first time when the graduate from college have a discontinuous transition into adult work roles.

The Continuity of the Adolescent Passage in Contemporary Society In contemporary society, we tend to exclude young people from the world of adults; we give them little direct training for adult life and then thrust them abruptly into total adult independence. Transitions into adulthood in contemporary society are more discontinuous than in other cultural or historical contexts. Consider, for example, three of the most important roles of adulthood that individuals are expected to carry out successfully: worker, parent, and citizen. Adolescents in contemporary society receive little prior preparation for any of these positions.

For instance, young people are segregated from the workplace throughout most of their childhood and early adolescent years, and they receive little direct training in school relevant to the work roles they will likely find themselves in as adults. The sorts of jobs available to teenagers today, such as working the counter of a fast-food restaurant, bear little resemblance to the jobs most of them will hold as adults. The transition into adult work roles, therefore, is discontinuous for most young people today.

The transition into adult family roles is even more abrupt. Before actually becoming parents, most young people have little training in child rearing or other related matters. Families are relatively small today, and youngsters are likely to be close in age to their siblings, if they even have siblings; as a result, few opportunities exist for participating in child care activities at home. Schools generally offer little, if any, instruction in family relationships and domestic activities.

continuous transitions Passages into adulthood in which adult roles and statuses are entered into gradually.

discontinuous transitions Passages into adulthood in which adult roles and statuses are entered into abruptly.

Passage into adult citizenship and decision-making roles is also highly discontinuous. Adolescents are permitted few opportunities for independence and autonomy in high school and are segregated from most of society's political institutions until they complete their formal education. Young people are permitted to vote once they turn 18, but they receive little preparation for participation in government and community roles prior to this time. In the United States, for example, we require foreigners who wish to become citizens to understand the workings of the American government, but no such familiarity is required of individuals in order to graduate from high school.

Instead of being gradually socialized into work, family, and citizenship roles, adolescents in modern society typically are segregated from activities in these arenas during most of their childhood and youth. Yet young people are expected to perform these roles capably when they become adults. With little experience in meaningful work, adolescents are expected to find, get, and keep a job immediately after completing their schooling. With essentially no training for marriage or parenting, they are expected to form their own families, manage their own households, and raise their own children soon after they reach adulthood. And without any previous involvement in community activities, once they have reached the age of majority, adolescents are expected to vote, file their taxes, and behave as responsible citizens.

The Continuity of the Adolescent Passage in Traditional Cultures The high level of discontinuity found in contemporary America has not been characteristic of adolescence in traditional societies, especially when hunting, fishing, and farming are the chief work activities. The emphasis in these societies is on informal education in context rather than on formal education in schools. Children are typically not isolated in separate educational institutions, and they accompany the adult members of their community in daily activities. Adolescents' preparation for adulthood, therefore, comes largely from observation and hands-on experience in the same tasks that they will carry out as adults. Typically, boys learn the tasks performed by adult men, and girls learn those performed by adult women. When work activities take adults out of the community, it is not uncommon for children to accompany their parents on these expeditions (Miller, 1928).

As several writers have pointed out, modernization and globalization have made the transition from adolescence to adulthood longer and increasingly more discontinuous all over the world (Larson, Wilson, & Rickman, 2009; Tomasik & Silbereisen, 2011). As successful participation in the workforce increasingly has come to require formal education, parents have become less able to provide their children with advice on how best to prepare for adulthood. School, rather than hands-on experience in the workplace, is how individuals all over the world are expected to prepare for adult work (National Research Council, 2005).

How these changes are affecting the psychological development of young people in developing countries is a question that researchers are only now beginning to examine. It is very likely, however, that many of the familiar psychological struggles that have up until now been characteristic of adolescence in modern, industrialized societies—developing a sense of identity, choosing among occupational alternatives, stressing out over getting into a good college, and renegotiating relationships with one's parents, to name just a few—are becoming more common among young people all over the world. Ironically, then, at the same time that cross-cultural research on adolescents has expanded dramatically, the nature of adolescence has become more and more similar around the world. In research my colleagues and I have been conducting in a diverse array of countries in Asia, Africa, Europe, and the Americas, we have been surprised at how similar patterns of development are across these very different cultural contexts (Steinberg et al., 2018).

making the cultural connection

Globalization is changing the face of adolescence all over the world, but many experts believe that it has been a mixed blessing for many developing countries. With respect to young people, what are some of the pros and cons of the increasing integration of various countries and cultures into a more global society?

The Continuity of the Adolescent Passage in Previous Eras   During earlier periods in American history, the transition into adult roles and responsibilities began at a younger age and proceeded along a more continuous path than it is today. This is especially true with regard to work. During the eighteenth and the early nineteenth centuries, when many families were engaged in farming, many adolescents were expected to work on the family farm and learn the skills necessary to carry on the enterprise

after their parents became elderly. Boys often accompanied their fathers on business trips, learning the nuances of salesmanship and commerce (Kett, 1977)—a pattern reminiscent of that found in many traditional societies.

Many other young people left home relatively early—some as early as age 12—to work for nonfamilial adults in the community or in nearby villages (Kett, 1977). In the mid-nineteenth century, young adolescents commonly worked as apprentices, learning skills and trades; others left home temporarily to work as servants or to learn domestic skills. The average nineteenth-century youngster in Europe or America left school well before the age of 15 (Chisholm & Hurrelmann, 1995; Modell, Furstenberg, & Hershberg, 1976).

Although adolescents of 100 years ago took on full-time employment earlier in life than they typically do today, they were likely to live under adult supervision for a longer period of time. Although the transition into work roles may have occurred at a younger age in the nineteenth century than in the twentieth, this transition was made in the context of semi-independence rather than complete emancipation (Katz, 1975; Kett, 1977; Modell & Goodman, 1990). This semi-independent period—which for many young people lasted from about 12 to 22 and often beyond—may have increased the degree of continuity of the passage into adulthood by providing a time during which young people could assume certain adult responsibilities gradually (Katz, 1975).

By 1900, though, the semi-independence characteristic of adolescence in the nineteenth century had largely disappeared (Modell & Goodman, 1990). Despite the complaints today of many social commentators (and many college graduates) about the prevalence of unpaid internships as a bridge between college and full-time paid employment (e.g., Kamenetz, 2006), this transitional pathway into the world of adult work today is actually pretty similar to what existed in the nineteenth century.

Socialization for family and citizenship roles may also have been more continuous in previous eras. Living at home during the late-adolescent and early-adult years, particularly in the larger families characteristic of households 100 years ago, contributed to the preparation of young people for future family life. It was common for the children in a family to span a wide age range, and remaining at home undoubtedly placed the older adolescent from time to time in child-rearing roles. Adolescents were also expected to assist their parents in maintaining the household (Modell, Furstenberg, & Hershberg, 1976), which no doubt benefited young people when they eventually established a home separate from their parents.

Current Trends in Home Leaving   Recent reports of trends in home leaving suggest that this aspect of the transition into adulthood is changing in many industrialized countries. Individuals are living with their parents longer

Changes in the economy have led many young adults to move back in with their parents. Matelly/Getty Images

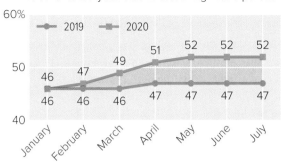

% of 18- to 29-year-olds in U.S. living with a parent

Note: "Living with a parent" refers to those who are residing with at least one parent in the household.

Figure 3.3 **During the first half of 2020, the economic downturn caused by the COVID-19 pandemic forced many young people to move in with their parents.** (Fry, Passel, & Cohn, 2020)

today than in recent years. By 2014, for the first time in more than a century, more Americans between the ages of 18 and 34 were living with their parents than in any other arrangement (and this doesn't even count the proportion who weren't living with their parents but depended on them for financial support) (Fry, 2016). Most experts attribute this change in living arrangements to the increased costs of housing and transportation, which make it difficult for individuals to move out of their parents' home (or give up their parents' financial support) and establish a separate residence, and to the increase in the proportion of high school graduates who attend college (and rely on their parents' support for this).

The proportion of young adults living with their parents remained steady between 2014 and 2019 but rose once again as a consequence of the COVID-19 pandemic, which forced many college students to return home and led to massive job losses among people between 18 and 24, the age group hit hardest by the economic downturn; unemployment in this age group *doubled* during the first half of 2020 (U.S. Census Bureau, 2021). Between February and May 2020, the proportion of 18- to 29-year-olds living with their parents rose from

47% to 52% (Fry, Passel, & Cohn, 2020) (see Figure 3.3). This is the first time since the Great Depression that the majority of Americans this age were living with one or both parents.

The news isn't all bad, though. One potentially positive consequence of the increase in young adults living at home is that the usual rise in alcohol and drug use seen when adolescents go off to college (Fromme, Corbin, & Kruse, 2008) is not nearly as great when individuals continue to live with their parents (White et al., 2008). The presence of parents tends to put a damper on partying.

How living with their parents in late adolescence affects psychological development and mental health likely depends on the extent to which this experience is seen as normative. But even in the United States, where a premium is placed on becoming independent from one's parents, about half of all young adults living at home report that it has not affected their relationships with their parents one way or the other, and one-quarter actually say that their relationship has improved (Parker, 2012). Other studies of the impact of continuing to live with one's parents or moving back in with them have found inconsistent effects (Sandberg-Thoma, Snyder, & Jang, 2015).

The impact of the economy on adolescents' home leaving reaffirms the importance of looking at the broader context in defining what "normal" adolescence is. In 1960, because it was uncommon for adolescents to live at home past high school, we tended to view individuals who did so as being less independent or less mature than their peers. Now that living at home has become the norm, we no longer view it as a sign of immaturity. Because adolescence is in part defined by society, its nature changes over time (Tomasik & Silbereisen, 2012). Historic events, such as the Great Recession in 2008, the #MeToo movement, natural disasters, or the COVID-19 pandemic, have affected the nature of the adolescent passage for many young people.

The Transition into Adulthood in Contemporary Society

We do not know for certain whether today's prolonged and discontinuous passage into adulthood impedes or enhances adolescents' psychosocial development. Much probably depends on whether the adolescent has access to the resources necessary for such a protracted transition, especially when jobs are scarce and the cost of housing is high. Indeed, many commentators have noted that there is not one transition into adulthood in contemporary America but three very different transitions: one for the "haves," one for the "have-nots," and one for those who are somewhere in between (Furstenberg, 2006). Growing income inequality, not only in the United States but around the world, is furthering this trend (Steinberg, 2014a).

As we look to the future, we can point to two specific societal trends that are reshaping the nature of the transition from adolescence to adulthood (Mortimer & Larson, 2002). First, as I have noted throughout this chapter, the length of the transitional period is increasing. As the labor force continues to shift toward jobs that demand more and more formal education, the amount of time individuals need to spend as economically dependent students will increase, which will delay their assumption of all sorts of adult roles, including family roles. One of the reasons that individuals are marrying at a later age today is that it takes longer to accumulate enough wealth to establish a separate residence or start a family. Another is that the progress made by young women in higher education and in the labor force has encouraged more of them to delay getting married to devote attention to their careers before starting a family. The continuing decline in the age of puberty is also lengthening adolescence. Today, the transition between childhood and adulthood takes longer than it did in the past century. Tomorrow, it will take even longer.

Second, as success in the labor force comes to be increasingly dependent on formal education, the division between the "haves"—those who have access to money, schools, and information technology—and "have-nots"—those who are poor, less well educated, and cut off from important resources—will grow. This division will be seen not only between wealthy and poor countries but also, increasingly, between the affluent and the poor within countries, because globalization, for all its many positive features, contributes to income inequality (Ananat et al., 2017). As the economies of developing countries improve, the importance of formal education increases, which then further separates the life conditions of the educated and the uneducated, a pattern seen vividly today in countries such as China and India.

One extremely important international trend concerns different birth rates in different parts of the world: Because the birth rate in poor and developing countries is so much higher than it is in wealthy nations, the distribution of the world's adolescents is changing dramatically. As we move further into the twenty-first century, relatively fewer and fewer of the world's teenagers will come from affluent parts of the world, and relatively more and more will live in impoverished countries (Larson, Wilson, & Rickman, 2009) (Figure 3.4).

Special Transitional Problems of Poor, Minority, and Immigrant Youth

No discussion of the transitional problems of young people in America today would be complete without noting that youngsters from some minority groups—Black, Latinx, and Native American youth, in particular—have more trouble negotiating the transition into adulthood than do their white and Asian counterparts. This is due to many factors, including poverty, discrimination, segregation, and disproportionate involvement with the justice system (Iselin et al., 2012; Neblett et al., 2011; McLoyd et al., 2009).

Youngsters from minority backgrounds make up a substantial and growing portion of the adolescent population in America. At the beginning of this century, about

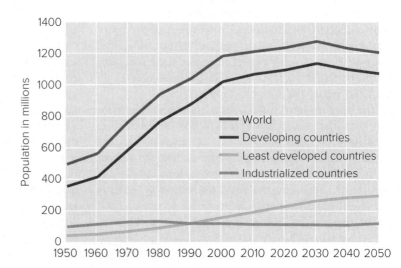

Figure 3.4 **The projected growth of the world's adolescent population will occur primarily in developing and in less developed nations.** (United Nations, Department of Economic and Social Affairs, Population Division, 2019)

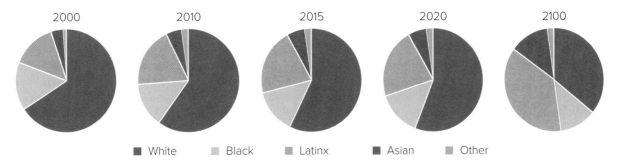

2000 2010 2015 2020 2100

■ White ■ Black ■ Latinx ■ Asian ■ Other

Figure 3.5 The ethnic composition of the United States will continue to change dramatically over the twenty-first century. (Federal Interagency Forum on Child and Family Statistics, 2005)

two-thirds of American adolescents were white. Today, about 24% of American adolescents are Hispanic, 14% Black, 5% Asian or Pacific Islanders, 4% biethnic youth, and 1% Native American and Native Alaskan youth (U.S. Census Bureau, 2019). In other words, about half of American adolescents are from ethnic minority groups. By the end of this century, the U.S. Census Bureau estimates that nearly two-thirds of American adolescents will be non-white and that Latinx adolescents will be the largest ethnic group in the country (see Figure 3.5).

Many American adolescents were not born in the United States, of course. One curiosity within studies of ethnic minority youth and the transition to adulthood concerns the better-than-expected mental health and school performance of immigrant adolescents in the United States. For reasons not entirely understood, foreign-born adolescent immigrants generally have better mental health, exhibit less problem behavior, and perform better in school than do adolescents from the same ethnic group who are native-born Americans (Fuligni, Hughes, & Way, 2009). Indeed, one of the most interesting findings to emerge from research on immigrant adolescents is that their "Americanization" appears to be associated with worse, not better, outcomes.

This may no longer be the case, though. Recent waves of immigrants, many of whom have not been welcomed into their receiving countries, don't necessarily show these patterns because having the support of schools and the acceptance of peers are important contributors to immigrant adolescents' well-being (Motti-Stefanidi, 2019). These transitional problems are exacerbated by immigration policies that create fear, mistrust, and economic disadvantage (Torres et al., 2018). A recent study of adolescents in multiple countries across the world found that immigrants are significantly more likely to be bullied than nonimmigrants from similar ethnic backgrounds (Stevens et al., 2020). This is especially the case in schools in which there is a strong anti-immigrant climate (Bayram Özdemir, et al., 2018). Parents play an important role in the development of adolescents' prejudicial attitudes, which ultimately affects the degree to which students are biased against their immigrant classmates (Miklikowska, Bohrman, & Titzmann, 2019).

The Effects of Poverty on the Transition into Adulthood

Of all the factors that may impair youngsters' ability to move easily from adolescence into adulthood, poverty is at the top of the list (Yoshikawa, Aber, & Beardslee, 2012). Growing up poor adversely affects adolescents' brain development, especially in regions that are important for higher-order cognitive abilities and self-control (Brieant et al., 2020; Ellwood-Lowe et al., 2018; Piccolo et al., 2016) (see Figure 3.6). Fortunately, adolescents from poor families show gains in brain function when their family's income increases (D. Weissman et al., 2018).

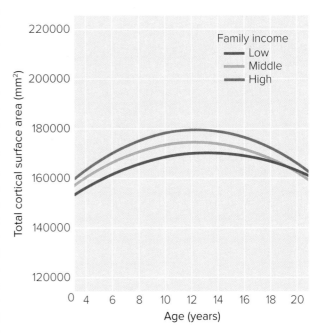

Figure 3.6 Recent research has demonstrated a link between socioeconomic status and the development of brain regions important for advanced thinking abilities. Cortical brain regions grow more rapidly during childhood and are pruned more extensively during adolescence among affluent adolescents than their less fortunate peers. (Figure 3 [left panel only] from Piccolo et al., 2016)

subjective social status
Where one believes he or she ranks socioeconomically (regardless of his or her actual socioeconomic class).

Not surprisingly, poverty is associated with failure in school, unemployment, delinquency, depression, and teen pregnancy, all of which contribute to transitional difficulties (McLoyd et al., 2009). Because minority youngsters are more likely than other teenagers to grow up in poverty, they are also more likely to encounter transitional problems during middle and late adolescence. Growing income inequality in the United States and much of the developed world will lead to even larger gaps in the well-being of young people from different social classes; for instance, as the gap in income between people from different social classes has grown, so have differences in rates of depression seen among adolescents from low and high socioeconomic status communities (Coley, O'Brien, & Spielvogel, 2019). Perceiving oneself as poorer than one's peers—what is referred to as **subjective social status**—is especially detrimental (Du, Chi, & King, 2019; Rahal et al., 2020; Rivenbark et al., 2019; Russell & Odgers, 2020).

Poverty is not limited to minority families, of course, but research on low-income, white families is relatively sparse. Although minority families are disproportionately likely to experience poverty, in sheer numbers, there are more poor white people in the United States than Black or Latinx people. Strong biases against rural, low-income white families, who are often the subjects of mockery and negative stereotypes on television shows such as *Here Comes Honey Boo Boo* (e.g., "white trash" who survive on "dumpster dives"), only compound the problems of social isolation, hopelessness, economic insecurity, and drug addiction that afflict many poor, rural communities. Some writers have noted that these circumstances may lead parents to socialize their teenagers to adopt a "live fast, die young" mentality, which may impair educational achievement and generate maladaptive patterns of behavior (Jones, Loiselle, & Highlander, 2018) (see Figure 3.7).

The negative impact of growing up in a poor home environment on brain development has an especially negative effect on adolescents' school achievement (Kendig, Mattingly, & Bianchi, 2014; Uy et al., 2019). Poverty impedes the transition to adulthood among all teenagers, regardless of race, of course, but because minority youth are more likely to grow up poor, they are also more likely to have transition problems. As you will see in later chapters, school dropout rates are much higher among Latinx and Native American teenagers than among other groups, and college enrollment is lower among Black, Latinx, and Native American youth. In addition, unemployment is much higher among Black, Latinx, and Native American teenagers; Black and Latinx youth are more likely to be victimized by crime and exposed to violence; and rates of out-of-wedlock births are higher among Black and Latinx teenagers than among white teenagers. All these factors disrupt the transition into adulthood by limiting individuals' economic and occupational success.

What Can Be Done to Ease the Transition?

A variety of suggestions have been offered for making the transition into adulthood smoother for all young people, including restructuring secondary education, expanding work and volunteer opportunities, and improving the quality of community life for adolescents and their parents. Some have suggested that adolescents be encouraged to spend time in voluntary, nonmilitary service activities—such as staffing day care centers, working with the elderly, or cleaning up the environment—for a few years after high school graduation so that they can learn responsibility and adult roles (Sherrod & Lauckhardt, 2009). Still others have pointed out that adolescents cannot come of age successfully without the help of adults and that programs are needed to strengthen families and communities and to bring adolescents into contact with adult mentors (Burt & Paysnick, 2012; Farruggia, Bullen, & Davidson, 2013). Overall, most experts agree that a comprehensive approach to the problem is needed and that such an approach must simultaneously address the educational, employment, interpersonal, and health needs of adolescents from all walks of life (Balsano, Theokas, & Bobek, 2009).

Mentoring   There has been growing interest in mentoring programs for at-risk adolescents, many of whom have few relationships with positive adult role models (Hurd, Varner, & Rowley, 2013; Rhodes, 2004). Adolescents who

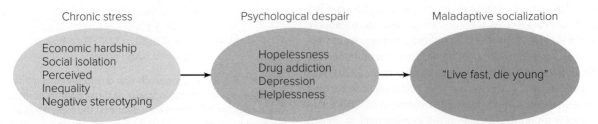

Figure 3.7   **Chronically stressful conditions in rural, low-income, white communities engender feelings of hopelessness and helplessness, which often leads parents to socialize their teenagers into a "live fast, die young" mentality.**

lack positive adult role models are more likely to have psychological and behavioral problems (Bryant & Zimmerman, 2003; Parker & Reckdenwald, 2008).

Mentoring programs seek to pair adults with young people through community or school-based efforts designed to facilitate positive youth development, improve academic achievement, and deter antisocial behavior. Evaluations of mentoring programs indicate that they have a small, positive effect on youth development (Raposa et al., 2019). Adolescents who have been mentored are less likely to have problems in school and at home, less likely to use drugs and alcohol, and less likely to get into trouble with the law (Hurd et al., 2012; Miranda-Chan et al., 2016; Timpe & Lunkenheimer, 2015).

Not surprisingly, the impact of mentoring varies as a function of characteristics of the mentor, the young person, and their relationship (Spencer et al., 2016). Mentoring appears to have the most beneficial effects on adolescents whose other relationships are good but not great (perhaps because the ones with great other relationships didn't need the mentoring as much and because the ones with poor ones did not have the social skills to profit from the mentoring) (Schwartz et al., 2011). In general, mentoring tends to be more successful when the mentor maintains a steady presence in the youth's life over an extended period (at least 2 years); has frequent contact with the youngster; and involves the adolescent in a wide range of recreational, social, and practical activities that are targeted toward the specific needs of the teenager (Austin et al., 2020; Christensen et al., 2020). It is important to note, however, that although mentoring may benefit adolescents, other influences in their lives are also important, and mentoring alone is not sufficient to meet the needs of at-risk youth (DuBois & Silverthorn, 2005). One potentially important influence, to which we now turn, is the neighborhood in which the adolescent lives.

The Influence of Neighborhood Conditions on Adolescent Development

One factor contributing to the especially worrisome situation of poor and minority youth in the United States is that poverty has become much more concentrated over the past 40 years, with greater and greater clustering of poor families into economically and racially segregated communities. In response to this, a number of researchers have studied the ways in which neighborhoods influence adolescent development (Leventhal, Dupéré, & Brooks-Gunn, 2009). Although other characteristics of neighborhoods in addition to poverty potentially can affect adolescents' development (e.g., the ethnic composition, crime rate, or availability of social service programs), far more is known about the effects of poverty than about any other factor. Exposure to neighborhood poverty is an

especially prevalent problem among nonwhite adolescents (Chauhan, Reppucci, & Turkheimer, 2009).

Studying neighborhood influences on adolescent development is tricky. We know that growing up in a very poor household increases adolescents' risks for all sorts of problems. But because poor families tend to live in poor neighborhoods, it is not always easy to separate the effects of *neighborhood* disadvantage from the effects of *family* disadvantage. To do this, researchers must compare adolescents whose family situations are similar but who live in very different types of neighborhoods. This is not always easy to do—as you can imagine, few affluent families live in poor neighborhoods, and few poor families live in affluent ones.

There is also the problem of cause and effect. If families in a good neighborhood seem to be functioning better than families in a poor one, it might simply reflect the fact that better-functioning families choose to live in better neighborhoods (rather than indicate that the neighborhood actually influenced family functioning) (Boyle et al., 2007). There have been a few experiments in which the researchers took this into account by randomly assigning families from poor neighborhoods who expressed interest in moving to either remain where they were or be relocated into more advantaged neighborhoods and then tracking the psychological development and behavior of adolescents in the two groups. These studies have found mixed effects of relocation, with some studies showing positive effects, others showing no effect, and some actually showing negative effects (Graif, 2015; Kling, Ludwig, & Katz, 2005; Leventhal, Fauth, & Brooks-Gunn, 2005; Osypuk et al., 2012).

To complicate things further, some of these experiments have found that moving to a more affluent neighborhood tends to have a more positive effect on girls than boys and among children than adolescents (Schmidt, Krohn, & Osypuk, 2018). Other studies have found similarly puzzling results. For example, one analysis of changes in the level of neighborhood poverty found that very poor adolescents whose neighborhoods improved in quality were *more* likely to show increases in problems than those whose neighborhoods did not improve but that the opposite pattern held for adolescents in moderate-poverty neighborhoods, where change for the better led to improvements in boys' well-being (Leventhal & Brooks-Gunn, 2011).

How can we account for the finding that relocating poor families to more affluent neighborhoods sometimes has negative effects on adolescents' behavior? There are several possible explanations (Fauth, Leventhal, & Brooks-Gunn, 2007). First, adolescents from poor families that moved may encounter more discrimination in the new neighborhoods than in their old ones. Second, although it is generally true that advantaged communities have more resources than disadvantaged ones, it is possible that poor families who moved to more affluent

A variety of psychological and social problems are more common among adolescents who grow up amidst poverty. DenisTangneyJr/Getty Images

neighborhoods actually may have less access to community resources than they did in their old neighborhoods. Third, adolescents who moved to more advantaged neighborhoods may end up feeling more disadvantaged than their peers who remained in poor communities because the adolescents who moved may compare their life circumstances to those of their more affluent peers; although their living circumstances improved, their *subjective social status* declined (Nieuwenhuis et al., 2017). This account is consistent with other research showing that income inequality has adverse effects on adolescents' mental health above and beyond the effects of poverty (Vilhjalmsdottir et al., 2016). Finally, there is some evidence that parents in poor neighborhoods may monitor their children relatively more vigilantly because they worry about crime and other dangers; adolescents who are more closely monitored tend to have fewer problems.

The Price of Privilege Although poverty has a wide range of adverse consequences for adolescents' development, there is accumulating evidence that growing up in an extremely affluent neighborhood may carry its own risks. Compared to teenagers in middle-class communities, adolescents in wealthy neighborhoods report higher levels of delinquency, substance abuse, anxiety, and depression (Lund, Dearing, & Zachrisson, 2017); there is some evidence that the higher rates of drug use seen among teenagers in affluent communities carry forward into college and beyond (Luthar, Small, & Ciciolla, 2018). This is consistent with several studies that have documented the surprisingly high prevalence of psychological and behavioral problems among teenagers in affluent suburban communities (Coley et al., 2018; Kleinepier & van Ham, 2018; Luthar, Barkin, & Crossman, 2013),

especially among teenagers whose personalities may make them prone to problem behavior (Jensen, Chassin, & Gonzales, 2017).

The higher incidence of problems among adolescents from wealthy communities appears to emerge in early adolescence, when teenagers begin experimenting with alcohol and illegal drugs, which may be fueled by pressure to excel in school and extracurricular activities and enabled by parents who are either too preoccupied to notice or simply choose to look the other way. Affluent adolescents' substance use, in turn, leads to all sorts of troubles, among them delinquency, depression, and precocious sex.

Impact of Poverty on Adolescent Development

Although there admittedly are problems associated with growing up amid wealth, growing up in a poor neighborhood has devastating effects on adolescent behavior, achievement, and mental health, and these effects are above and beyond those attributable to growing up in a poor family or attending a financially strapped school (Cambron et al., 2018; Foster & Brooks-Gunn, 2012; Leventhal, Dupéré, & Brooks-Gunn, 2009; Snedker & Herting, 2016). Most neighborhood research has focused on urban adolescents, but studies find that growing up in poor rural communities also places adolescents at risk (Jones, Loiselle, & Highlander, 2018).

Whether in inner-city neighborhoods or rural communities, adolescents who see nothing but poverty and unemployment around them have little reason to be hopeful about their own future, and they may feel that they have little to lose by using drugs, having a baby, dropping out of school, or becoming involved in criminal activity (Burnside & Gaylord-Harden, 2019; Kan et al., 2020; Schmidt, Pierce, & Stoddard, 2016; Xiao,

Growing up in extreme affluence may carry its own sort of risks to healthy development. RichLegg/Getty Images

Figure 3.8 Living amidst neighborhood disadvantage lowers how long adolescents expect to live, which in turn increases their drug use, crime, and risky sex. (Kan et al., 2020)

Romanelli, & Kindsay, 2020) (see Figure 3.8). Even among adolescents who have already become involved with the justice system, delinquents who have higher expectations for their future are less likely to reoffend and more likely to achieve in school (Mahler et al., 2018). Neighborhood poverty also has an impact on adolescents' sexual behavior and decisions about whether to abort a pregnancy, with those living in poor neighborhoods more likely to be sexually active at an early age and engage in risky sex (Orihuela et al., 2020). The impact of poverty on sexual behavior is especially strong in poor, rural neighborhoods (Warner, 2018).

Adolescents growing up in impoverished urban communities are more likely than their peers from equally poor households but better neighborhoods to bear children as teenagers, to become involved in criminal activity, and to achieve less in, or even drop out of, high school—factors that seriously interfere with the successful transition into adulthood (Carlson et al., 2014; E. Romero et al., 2015). Interestingly, it is the absence of affluent neighbors, rather than the presence of poor ones, that seems to place adolescents in impoverished communities at greatest risk (Leventhal & Brooks-Gunn, 2004).

Processes of Neighborhood Influences

Most of the effects of neighborhoods on adolescent development are indirect, transmitted through the impact of the neighborhood on the more immediate settings in which adolescents spend time (Dunn et al., 2015; Riina et al., 2013). For example, neighborhood disorder affects the way that parents behave, and this, in turn, affects

adolescents' development and mental health (Jensen, 2020). Neighborhoods influence individuals by transforming what takes place within the more immediate contexts that are embedded in them. Three different processes have been suggested (Leventhal et al., 2009) (see Figure 3.9).

collective efficacy
A community's social capital, derived from its members' common values and goals.

Collective Efficacy First, neighborhood conditions shape the norms that guide individuals' values and behaviors. Poverty in neighborhoods breeds social isolation and social disorganization, undermining a neighborhood's sense of **collective efficacy**—the extent to which neighbors trust each other, share common values, and count on each other to monitor the activities of youth in the community (Sampson, Raudenbusch, & Earls, 1997). As a consequence, it is easier for deviant peer groups to form and to influence the behavior of adolescents in these communities (Trucco et al., 2014). Rates of teen pregnancy, school failure, mental health problems, and antisocial behavior are all higher in neighborhoods that have low levels of collective efficacy (Elfassi et al., 2016; Liu et al., 2017; Wang, Choi, & Shin, 2020).

Living in a neighborhood high in collective efficacy—where adults monitor the behavior of all adolescents, not just their own—is especially important for adolescents whose parents are themselves not very vigilant (Booth & Shaw, 2020; Kirk, 2009). In addition, it appears that collective efficacy encourages adolescents to form a deeper emotional bond with their community, which in turn makes them feel safer and less lonely, a finding that has been replicated in

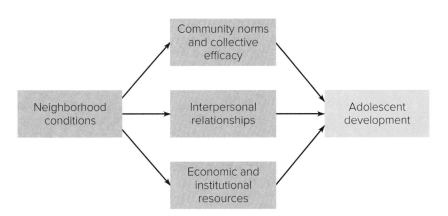

Figure 3.9 Neighborhood conditions influence adolescents' development by shaping the norms to which adolescents are exposed; by influencing the quality of the relationships they have with others, including their parents; and by facilitating or limiting adolescents' and families' access to economic and institutional resources.

many countries (Dallago et al., 2009; Matthews et al., 2019; Wang & Fowler, 2019). This connection also protects adolescents somewhat from the adverse effects of being exposed to neighborhood violence (Browning et al., 2014) and discrimination (Saleem, Busby, & Lambert, 2018).

Under conditions of low collective efficacy, social problems are contagious; they spread from one adolescent to another like a disease epidemic. To the extent that poverty increases behavior problems, for example, adolescents living in poor neighborhoods will come into contact with deviant peers more often (Gartstein, Seamon, & Dishion, 2014; Tompsett, Veits, & Amrhein, 2016; Vogel & Van Ham, 2018), and adolescents who associate with delinquent peers are more likely to be drawn into criminal and delinquent activity (Bond & Bushman, 2016). Similarly, adolescents who live in neighborhoods characterized by high rates of teenage parenthood grow up exposed to large numbers of peers who are relatively more tolerant of this behavior, which affects their own attitudes toward premarital childbearing (Baumer & South, 2001).

The Impact of Stress   Second, the stresses associated with poverty undermine the quality of people's relationships. Across all ethnic groups, poverty is associated with harsh, inconsistent, and punitive parenting, which, in turn, are linked to adolescent misbehavior (Deater-Deckard et al., 2019; Elliott et al., 2016). When parents are not effective in supervising and monitoring their teenagers and when teenagers have little social support from parents or other adults, the teenagers are more likely to associate with antisocial peers and get into trouble (Odgers et al., 2012; Wang, Choi, & Shin, 2020). Living in poor housing appears to have a particularly bad impact on girls' mental health, perhaps because girls are more likely than boys to spend their free time at home (Elliott et al., 2016).

The link between family poverty and delinquency is even stronger in poor neighborhoods (Hay et al., 2007). Consistent with this, the harmful effects of exposure to negligent or harsh parenting are even more pronounced in disadvantaged neighborhoods (Brody, et al., 2019; Roche, Ensminger, & Cherlin, 2007). Studies of whether the impact of good parenting is affected by neighborhood conditions have not yielded consistent results, however. Some studies show that positive family relationships are more effective in good neighborhoods (e.g., Cleveland, Feinberg, & Greenberg, 2010), while others show the reverse (e.g., Salzinger et al., 2011).

The impact of poverty on neighborhood violence is especially severe. Adolescents from poor neighborhoods are far more likely than other youth to be exposed to chronic community violence (DaViera et al., 2020) (see Table 3.2), and repeated exposure to violence and other types of stress increases the risk of behavioral, emotional, and physical health problems (Farrell et al., 2014; Heinze et al., 2017; Jaggers, Prattini, & Church, 2016; D. Schwartz et al., 2016). They also are more likely to interpret ambiguous situations as threatening, to have poor emotion regulation, to become desensitized to violence, and to show increases in blood pressure (Criss et al., 2016; Heleniak et al., 2018; Kennedy & Ceballo, 2016; Mrug, Madan, & Windle, 2016). There is even evidence that growing up in violence-ridden neighborhoods affects brain development in ways that interfere with the development of self-control, emotion regulation, delay of gratification, and empathy (Evans et al., 2020; Gonzalez, Allen, & Coan, 2016; Lambert et al., 2017; Saxbe et al., 2018; Weissman et al., 2018).

Adolescents who themselves have been exposed to violence are more likely to engage in violent behavior, think about killing themselves, attempt suicide, and report symptoms of depression, post-traumatic stress disorder (PTSD), hopelessness, callousness, precocious sex, and substance abuse (Deane, Richards, & Santiago, 2020; Farrell et al., 2020; Goldstick, 2019; White et al., 2019; Yildiz, Demirhan, & Gurbuz, 2019). The adverse effects of exposure to violence have been documented in hundreds of studies, not only of urban youth in the United States (where most of these studies have been conducted) but in other parts of the world as well, such as Colombia (Gaias et al., 2019) and the Middle East (Klodnick et al., 2014). Being the victim of violence has more consistent harmful effects than witnessing it, which, in turn, is more harmful than simply hearing about it (Fowler et al., 2010). Participating in youth-based community programs is associated with better mental health and less risky behavior (Camacho-Thompson & Vargas, 2018; Lardier et al., 2019).

Not all adolescents who are exposed to violence and other sorts of neighborhood stressors are equally affected, of course. Among the factors that help protect against their harmful effects are having strong self-control, positive family relationships, and supportive peer relationships, and being involved in structured extracurricular activities (Affrunti, Suárez, & Simpson, 2018; Hardaway et al., 2016; Taylor, Widaman, & Robins, 2018; Zimmerman & Farrell, 2017). One study found that mindfulness instruction may ameliorate some of the stress-related problems experienced by inner-city adolescents (Sibinga et al., 2016). In contrast, the impact of community disadvantage on adolescent violence is relatively greater among impulsive teenagers and those with poor emotion regulation (King & Mrug, 2016; Myers et al., 2018; Vogel & Van Ham, 2018).

making the scientific connection

Inner-city neighborhoods typically come to mind when we think of adolescents growing up in poverty, but many poor adolescents live in rural, not urban, areas. In what ways is poverty different for urban versus rural youth? How might this affect the nature of adolescence in each type of community?

Table 3.2 Examples of community violence or danger reported by Chicago adolescents.

Pseudonym	Experiences of Community Violence or Danger	Safety Strategies
Caleb (15BM)	Aware of gang activity in the neighborhood	Avoidance, hypervigilance
Elena (17LF)	Did not mention violence or danger	Avoidance, emotional management
Shantay (14BF)	Witnessed a shooting, aware of violence and fights in the neighborhood	Avoidance, hypervigilance, self-defense
Pierre (16BM)	Aware of shootings and gang activity in the neighborhood	Avoidance, emotional management, self-defense
Fillip (16WM)	Experienced threats from people in the neighborhood	Avoidance
Catalina (15LF)	Aware of gang activity in the neighborhood	Avoidance, self-defense
Labron (15BM)	Two friends died due to shooting	Avoidance, emotional management
Oscar (15LM)	Was robbed at gunpoint, aware of gang activity in the neighborhood	Avoidance, hypervigilance
Mackenzie (17BF)	Aware of violence, shootings, and gang activity in the neighborhood	Avoidance, self-defense
Deonte (17BM)	Was "jumped" in a park, friends have died due to shootings, aware of gang activity and shootings in the neighborhood	Avoidance, emotional management, hypervigilance
Jalen (16BM)	Witnessed someone shot and killed, was chased by "30 guys," knows people who have been killed due to shootings, aware of violence and gang activity in the neighborhood	Avoidance, emotional management, hypervigilance
Daniel (15BRM)	Mother was "chased" in car, mother's boyfriend was shot, father used to be in a gang, aware of violence and gang activity in the neighborhood	Avoidance, hypervigilance
Alejandra (17LF)	Feels in danger in the neighborhood, did not mention violence	Self-defense
Amelia (16BF)	Feels in danger in the neighborhood, did not mention violence	Avoidance
Karina (15BF)	Knows several people who have been killed, knows people currently in gangs, aware of violence, shootings, and gang activity in neighborhood	Avoidance, self-defense

Next to pseudonym in parentheses are age, ethnicity (B = Black, L = Latinx, W = white, BR = biracial), and gender (M = male, F = female).

(DaViera et al., 2020)

Limited Access to Resources Third, adolescents who grow up in poor neighborhoods have more limited access to resources than do those who grow up in more advantaged communities. In poor neighborhoods, for example, the quality of schools, health care, transportation, employment opportunities, and recreational services are all lower than they are in affluent neighborhoods (M. Gardner & Brooks-Gunn, 2009). As a result, adolescents in poor communities have fewer chances to engage in activities that facilitate positive development or to receive services when they are having difficulties (Lardier, et al., 2020; T. Leventhal & Brooks-Gunn, 2004).

On the other hand, adolescents who live in communities with relatively greater resources, such as higher-quality schools, are less likely to become involved in antisocial behavior (Molnar et al., 2008) and more likely to have positive peer relationships (Smith, Faulk, & Sizer, 2016). In neighborhoods with higher levels of resources and greater feelings of cohesion, adults' beliefs about teenagers tend to be more favorable, probably because the casual interactions that take place between adults and adolescents in these settings are more positive (Zeldin & Topitzes, 2002). The presence of institutional resources, then, often goes hand in hand with the presence of positive social relationships.

4 Families

Changes in Family Relationships at Adolescence

What Do Adolescents and Parents Usually Fight About?

The Adolescent's Parents at Midlife

Changes in Family Needs and Functions

Special Concerns of Immigrant Families

Transformations in Family Relations

Sex Differences in Family Relationships

Family Relationships and Adolescent Development

Parenting Styles and Their Effects

Adolescents' Relationships with Siblings

Genetic Influences on Adolescent Development

Genetic and Environmental Influences on Adolescent Development

Why Are Siblings Often So Different?

The Adolescent's Family in a Changing Society

Adolescents and Divorce

The Specific Impact of Marital Conflict

The Longer-Term Effects of Divorce

Custody, Contact, and Conflict Following Divorce

Remarriage

Economic Stress and Poverty

Special Family Forms

The Importance of the Family in Adolescent Development

Thinkstock/Alamy Stock Photo

The next time you are in a bookstore, take a look at the books in the section on parent–adolescent relationships. Judging from the number of "survival guides"—ones such as *Get Out of My Life, But First, Could You Drive Me and Cheryl to the Mall?; The Teenage Brain: A Neuroscientist's Survival Guide to Raising Adolescents and Young Adults; Your Defiant Teen; Yes, Your Teen Is Crazy;* and even *Yes, Your Parents Are Crazy*—you'd think that stress and strain between teenagers and parents is commonplace, even normal. Unlike advice books on infancy, which emphasize normative development, books for parents of teenagers tend to focus on problems (Steinberg, 2011). This is unfortunate, for two reasons.

First, the stereotype presented in these writings just isn't true. And second, the more parents believe in the stereotype of adolescents as difficult, the more they expect their own child to conform to it, and the worse their relationship with their teenager becomes (Jacobs, Chin, & Shaver, 2005; Martin, Sturge-Apple, Davies, & Romero, 2017). In other words, parents' beliefs that they are going to have a difficult time with their child once he or she enters adolescence can become what psychologists call a **self-fulfilling prophecy**—an expectation that is realized because we act in ways that make it happen.

In truth, scientific studies indicate that, on average, there is very little emotional distance between young people and their parents (Laursen & Collins, 2009). Although some families have serious problems, the overwhelming majority of adolescents feel close to their parents, respect their judgment, feel that they love and care about them, and have a lot of respect for them as individuals (Steinberg, 2001).

Sure, there are times when adolescents and parents have their problems. But there are times when younger children and their parents have problems and when adults and their parents do, too. Family problems are no more likely to occur during adolescence than at other times in the life span. Moreover, among teenagers and parents who report having problems, the great majority had troubled relations during childhood (Laursen & Collins, 2009), and declines in the quality of family relationships in adolescence are greatest in families where relationships were less close to begin with (Laursen, DeLay, & Adams, 2010). In other words, only a very small percentage of families who enjoy positive relations during childhood develop serious problems during adolescence.

In this chapter, we'll look at the family as a context for adolescent development with three broad questions in mind. First, how do family relationships change during adolescence—that is, what is the effect of adolescence on the family? Second, how are adolescents affected by their experiences in the family—in other words, what is the effect of the family on adolescents? And third, how have changes in family life over the past half century affected the adolescent experience?

Changes in Family Relationships at Adolescence

Whenever a family enters a new stage in their child's development, it takes them a while to figure out how best to deal with it. With time, they usually reach a comfortable place, a sort of equilibrium. According to **family systems theory,** relationships in families change most dramatically during times when individual family members or the family's circumstances are changing because it is during these times that the family's equilibrium often is upset. Not surprisingly, one period in which family relationships usually change a great deal is adolescence. One study of interactions between adolescent boys and their parents found that the peak time for dramatic changes in their relationships was around age 13 or 14; the researchers speculate that because some of this transformation may be driven by puberty, in families with girls (who mature earlier than boys), this "disequilibrium" is more likely to occur earlier, around age 11 or 12 (Granic et al., 2003).

As you read in earlier chapters, adolescence has long been portrayed as an painfully difficult time for parents and teenagers. Although this turns out to be the exception rather than the rule, adolescence is nevertheless a period of change and reorganization in family relationships and daily interactions (Branje, 2018). Occasionally, this reorganization temporarily strains family relationships. Not surprisingly, parent-adolescent conflict has received a great deal of attention from scientists who study this age period.

self-fulfilling prophecy The idea that individuals' behavior is influenced by others' expectations for them.

family systems theory A perspective on family functioning that emphasizes interconnections among different family relationships (such as marital, parent-child, sibling).

What Do Adolescents and Parents Usually Fight About?

Parents and teenagers typically don't argue over "big" issues, but they do have their share of disagreements. They squabble about such things as curfews, leisure time activities, clothing, and the cleanliness of bedrooms,

One source of conflict between parents and teenagers involves differences in the way they define issues. Making sure that the adolescent's bedroom is tidy is seen by parents as an area over which parents should have jurisdiction. Teenagers, however, tend to see their bedroom as their own private space and decisions about neatness as matters of personal choice.
B2M Productions/Digital Vision/Getty Images

which have been the major sources of disagreement in families with teenagers for at least as long as scientists have been studying the issue (Laursen & DeLay, 2011). And, although conflict between adolescents and parents over these mundane matters is generally less frequent in ethnic minority than in white families, the topics of disagreement are similar across ethnic groups and cultures (Smetana, Daddis, & Chuang, 2003). A study of adolescents in China and Hong Kong, for example, found that the most common sources of conflict between adolescents and parents were everyday issues, such as time spent on schoolwork, household chores, and choice of friends (Yau & Smetana, 2003).

Why do parents and teenagers argue over such mundane things? According to several studies, a major contributor to adolescent-parent bickering is the fact that teenagers and their parents define the issues of contention very differently—a finding that has been replicated across many cultural and ethnic groups (Chen-Gaddini, 2012; Smetana & Villalobos, 2009). Parents view many issues as matters of right and wrong—not necessarily in a moral sense, but as matters of custom or convention. Adolescents, in contrast, are likely to define these same issues as matters of personal choice (Martin, Bascoe, & Davies, 2011). A mother who disapproves of her daughter's clothing says, "People just don't dress that way to go to school." The daughter responds, "Maybe *you* wouldn't dress this way, but *I* do."

Rebels With a Cause Contrary to stereotype, though, adolescents rarely rebel against their parents just for the

sake of rebelling (Darling, Cumsille, & Martínez, 2007). In fact, they are willing to accept their parents' rules as legitimate when they agree that the issue is a moral one (whether it is permissible to cheat on a school test) or one involving safety (whether it is permissible to drink and drive), but they are less inclined to accept their parents' authority when they view the issue as personal (what clothes to wear to a party) (Cheah, Leung, & Bayram Özdemir, 2018; Smetana & Daddis, 2002).

In other words, rather than resisting all of their parents' attempts to make and enforce rules (the stereotype that many people have of teenagers), adolescents distinguish between rules they think their parents have a right to make (for instance, having to let their parents know what time they'll be home after going out) and rules that they think are out of bounds (e.g., having to keep their bedroom tidy), a distinction that in many ways is quite understandable (Kuhn, Phan, & Laird, 2014; Smetana & Villalobos, 2009) and one that parents share (Smetana & Rote, 2015). Of course, there are differences among adolescents in the extent to which they believe their parents have the authority to regulate various sorts of decisions, and adolescents who see parents as having more legitimate authority have fewer behavior problems (LaFleur et al., 2016; Pérez, Cumsille, & Martínez, 2016). Not surprisingly, adolescents who are less likely to believe that their parents have a right to know how they spend their time are more likely to conceal their activities from them (Keijsers & Laird, 2014; Rote & Smetana, 2015; Tilton-Weaver, 2014).

One reason that teenagers and their parents argue as much as they do is that as they mature cognitively, adolescents come to view many issues that they previously saw as legitimate for their parents to regulate (e.g., how late they can stay up on school nights) as matters of personal choice (Milnitsky-Sapiro, Turiel, & Nucci, 2006; Smetana, 2005). When parents attempt to regulate what adolescents believe are personal issues, teens are likely to describe their parents as being overly controlling (Chen-Gaddini, Liu, & Nucci, 2020).

Perhaps because of this, the effects of feeling psychologically controlled by their parents, which has a negative impact on adolescents' mental health, are very different from the effects of feeling that their parents simply want to know where they go and what they do, which has a positive impact (Loukas, 2009; Padilla-Walker, 2008). Adolescents who think their parents are overcontrolling are likely to become oppositional (Flamant et al., 2020). How parents get their information also matters: Snooping, as opposed to asking, is likely to lead to problems (Hawk, Becht, & Branje, 2016; Rote & Smetana, 2018), as is close parental monitoring in the absence of a warm parent–adolescent relationship (Lippold et al., 2014).

In other words, teenagers and their parents often clash more over the definition of the issue (e.g., whether something is a matter of safety rather than a matter of personal choice) than over the specific details. The struggle, then,

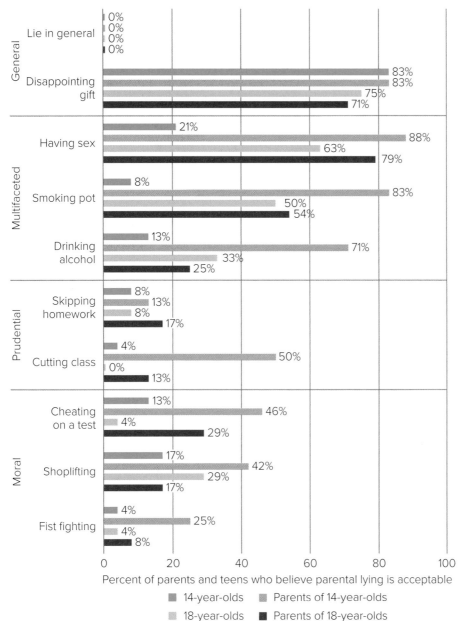

Figure 4.1 This chart shows the percent of parents who admit to lying to their teenager about their own adolescence. Parents are more likely to lie about their own adolescent years when their teenagers are younger and about activities they don't want their children to try, such as having sex or smoking marijuana. (Gingo, Roded, & Turiel, 2020)

is over who has the authority—and whose jurisdiction the issue falls into. Because early adolescence is a time when adolescents' reasoning abilities are changing, the ways that individuals understand family rules and regulations change as well (Cheah, Leung, & Bayram Özdemir, 2018). As a consequence of normal cognitive development, a 9-year-old child who is willing to accept his parents' views—who doesn't question his mother when she says, "We do not leave clothes on the floor"—grows into an adolescent who understands that some issues are matters of personal choice, rather than social convention ("It's my room, so why should it bother you?").

Adolescents' expectations for secrecy are much greater than parents' (Elsharnouby & Dost-Gözkan, 2020). There is an increase, with age, in adolescents' willingness to lie to their parents, especially about matters the adolescent thinks are personal (Rote & Smetana, 2015). Some families fall into a maladaptive cycle in which negative relationships between adolescents and their parents prompt teenagers to conceal things from their parents, which only makes their relationships more negative (Kapetanovic et al., 2020; Rote, Smetana, & Feliscar, 2020).

Of course, there are plenty of occasions when the tables are turned and parents lie to their adolescents, especially when they want to hide some of the more questionable activities they engaged in as teenagers (Gingo, Roded, & Turiel, 2020). Parents are more likely to lie to younger adolescents than older ones and more likely to lie about activities they wish their teens wouldn't do, such as having sex or smoking marijuana (see Figure 4.1).

The Adolescent's Parents at Midlife

The specific concerns and issues characteristic of families at adolescence arise not just because of the changing needs and concerns of the young person but also because of changes in the adolescent's parents and in the needs and functions of the family. You already have an understanding of the biological, cognitive, and social changes adolescents go through and can probably imagine how these may affect the family system. But to fully understand family relationships during the adolescent years, we need to take into account characteristics of the adolescent's parents and of families at this stage as well.

Because people typically have their first child around age 30, most parents are in their early 40s when the first child enters early adolescence. This age can be a potentially difficult time for many adults, whether they have children or not. Some theorists have gone so far as to describe it as a time of **midlife crisis** (Lachman, 2004).

Midlife Meets Adolescence   If we look at the nature of the midlife crises in some detail, we see that the developmental concerns of parents and adolescents are complementary (Steinberg & Steinberg, 1994). Consider the issue of biological change. At the same time that adolescents are entering into a period of rapid physical growth, sexual maturation, and, ultimately, the period of the life span that society has labeled one of the most physically attractive, their parents are beginning to feel increased concern about their own bodies, about their physical attractiveness, and about their sexual appeal (Banister, 1999). One mother of an early-adolescent girl once remarked, in an interview with my research staff, that it was jarring to realize that when she and her daughter walked down the street, men now looked at her daughter and not at her.

A second overlap of crises concerns perceptions of time and the future. At the same time that adolescents are developing the capability to think systematically about the future and do, in fact, start looking ahead, their parents are beginning to feel that possibilities for changing their own lives are limited. Interestingly, before midlife, individuals tend to measure time in terms of how long they have been alive; after midlife, they are more likely to see things in terms of how much longer they have to live (Lang & Carstensen, 2002). One reason for this shift may be that at midlife adults are reminded of their mortality because they see their own parents aging. Whatever the reason, the naïve optimism of adolescence may clash with the hardened pragmatism of middle age.

Finally, consider the issue of power, status, and entrance into the roles of adulthood. Adolescence is the time when individuals are on the threshold of

midlife crisis
A psychological crisis over identity believed to occur between the ages of 35 and 45, the age range of most adolescents' parents.

For many adults, their child's adolescence coincides with their own passage through midlife. Not all adults experience a "midlife crisis," but for many, this is a time of heightened introspection and self-doubt. The collision of adolescence and midlife may make the period an especially challenging one in some families. Uwe Umstaetter/Getty Images

gaining a great deal of status. Their careers and marriages lie ahead of them, and choices may seem limitless. For their parents, many choices have already been made—some successfully, others perhaps less so. Most adults reach their "occupational plateau"—the point at which they can tell how successful they are likely to be—during midlife, and many must deal with whatever gap exists between their early aspirations and their actual achievements (Lachman, 2004). In sum, for adolescents, this phase in the family life cycle is a time of boundless horizons; for their parents, it means coming to terms with choices made when they were younger.

This overlap of crises is likely to have an impact on family relationships. A father who isn't as limber as he once was may feel less enthusiastic about playing one-on-one basketball games with his growing son, as they had done for years when the boy was younger. An adolescent girl with big plans for the future may find it difficult to understand why her father seems so cautious and narrow-minded when she asks him for advice. An adolescent boy may find his mother's constant attention annoying; he doesn't see that, to her, his interest in privacy signifies the end of an important stage in her career as a parent. The adolescent's desire for independence appears to be especially stressful for parents (Steinberg & Steinberg, 1994).

This generalization about the collision of adolescence and midlife must be tempered, though. The average age at marriage has increased, and proportionately more couples today are delaying childbearing until they have become established in their careers (Gregory, 2007). How being an older parent affects relationships during adolescence hasn't been adequately studied.

The Mental Health of Parents In families with middle-aged adults, adjusting to adolescence may take more of a toll on the mental health of parents than their adolescents (Steinberg & Steinberg, 1994). Nearly two-thirds of mothers and fathers describe adolescence as the most difficult stage of parenting, and this period is the low point in parents' marital and life satisfaction (Gecas & Seff, 1990). Parents who are deeply involved in work outside the home or who have an especially happy marriage may be buffered against some of these negative consequences, however, whereas single mothers may be especially vulnerable to them (Silverberg, Marczak, & Gondoli, 1996). In fact, a strained relationship between a midlife parent and his or her adolescent child may drive the parent to devote relatively more time to work (Fortner, Crouter, & McHale, 2004). At the same time, studies show that parents' mental health problems negatively affect the way they interact with their adolescents, which in turn adversely affects the teenagers (Yap et al., 2010).

You may have heard that parents' mental health declines when their children leave home and they enter the "empty nest." Not so. Parents' mental health is worse when their teenage children are living at home than it is once they have moved out, and when children leave home, it is fathers, not mothers, who typically feel the greatest sense of loss (Steinberg & Steinberg, 1994). Many mothers are glad to be relieved of much of the household work they did when their teenager was living at home.

making the scientific connection

Many studies have found that marital satisfaction among parents is lower when their firstborn child is a teenager than at any other point in the marriage. Why do you think this might be?

Changes in Family Needs and Functions

It is not only individual family members who undergo change during the family's adolescent years. The family as a unit changes as well in its economic circumstances, its relationship to other social institutions, and its functions.

Family finances are often strained during adolescence. Children grow rapidly during puberty, and clothing for adolescents is expensive. Keeping up with the "must-haves" of the peer culture—designer clothes, the newest smartphone, and so forth, not to mention car expenses—may push a family budget to the limit. Many families also begin saving money for large anticipated expenditures, such as the adolescent's college education. And in some families, parents may find themselves having to help support their own parents when their children are still economically dependent. The financial demands placed on parents in the "sandwich generation" (that is, sandwiched

between their adolescent children and their aging parents) require considerable adjustment.

The adolescent's family also must cope with the increasing importance of the peer group (Laursen & DeLay, 2011). During elementary school, the child's social world is fairly narrow. The family is the central setting. During late childhood and early adolescence, however, the peer group becomes a setting in which close ties are forged, and parents and adolescents often argue about the teenager's reluctance to give up time with friends for family activities.

Special Concerns of Immigrant Families

How adolescents and parents adjust to this shift in orientation varies across ethnic groups, since certain cultures are more likely to stress family obligations—such as helping with household chores—than others (Hardway & Fuligni, 2006; Kiang et al., 2013). Many immigrant families place an especially high value on **familism,** an orientation toward life in which the needs of one's family take precedence over the needs of the individual (Tsai, Gonzales, & Fuligni, 2016). Adolescents who value familism and assist their families are more likely to develop prosocial values, less likely to get depressed, and less likely to get involved with antisocial peer groups, which lessens their chances of drinking or using illicit drugs (Cruz et al., 2018; Knight, Mazza, & Carlo, 2018; Stein et al., 2020; Wheeler et al., 2017). One study of Mexican-origin adolescents living in the United States found that parental effectiveness was greater in families in which the parents and their teenager preferred to speak the same language (Schofield et al., 2017).

Immigrant parents' ideas about family responsibilities sometimes clash with the more individualistic orientation characteristic of many mainstream American families. Adolescents who are assigned a lot of housework but who do not have strong familism values are more likely to do poorly at school, especially when they come from families with high socioeconomic status (Toyokawa & Toyokawa, 2019). Along similar lines, when adolescents are expected to spend a lot of time translating important paperwork such as bills or insurance forms for their parents, this can undermine parents' authority and lead to problems in family relationships and adolescent psychological well-being; similar effects are not seen, however, when the translating occurs during everyday situations (Anguiano, 2018; Roche et al., 2015).

Different expectations between immigrant parents and teenagers are a significant source of stress for adolescents and parents alike, especially when the adolescent has adopted values and expectations of the new country and the parents are less so, something known as **generational dissonance** (Motti-Stefandi,

familism
An orientation toward life in which the needs of one's family take precedence over the needs of the individual.

generational dissonance
Divergence of views between adolescents and parents that is common in families of immigrant parents and American-born adolescents.

Different expectations between immigrant parents and teenagers are a significant source of stress for adolescents and parents alike, especially when the adolescent is more Americanized and the parents are less so, a phenomenon known as "generational dissonance." CRS PHOTO/Shutterstock

2019; Wang-Schweig & Miller, 2019; Wu & Chao, 2011). Some studies conducted in the United States have found that stress and family conflict are higher in Latinx families with relatively more acculturated adolescents (Nair, Roche, & White, 2018; Schwartz et al., 2016), but not all studies have reached this conclusion (e.g., Telzer et al., 2016). In fact, one way for families to reduce generational dissonance is by having immigrant parents be more accepting of the new culture and adolescents be more accepting of the old one (Sun, Geeraert, & Simpson, 2020). However, in families where there is a lot of conflict, it actually may be better for teenagers to be less focused on their family (Yuen et al., 2018).

Transformations in Family Relations

Together, the biological, cognitive, and social transitions of adolescence; the changes experienced by adults at midlife; and the changes undergone by the family during this stage set in motion a series of transformations in family relationships. There is a movement away from patterns of influence and interaction in which parents have unchallenged authority toward ones in which parents and adolescents are on a more equal footing. Early adolescence—when this shift toward more egalitarian relationships first begins—is frequently a challenging time.

Changes in the Balance of Power   During early adolescence, young people begin to try to play a more forceful role in the family, but parents may not yet acknowledge adolescents' input. Young adolescents may interrupt their parents more often but have little impact. Between ages 12 and 16, adolescents increasingly try to assert their autonomy, and conflict with parents is common; brain imaging studies have found that an increase in adolescents' negative feelings about their mothers coincides with an increase in the extent to which teenagers are more focused on themselves (Van der Cruijsen et al., 2019). By middle adolescence, however, teenagers act and are treated much more like adults. They have more influence over family decisions, but they do not need to assert their opinions through interruptions and similarly immature behavior. Between ages 16 and 20, as adolescents begin to feel more independent, their relationships with their parents improve (Hadiwijaya et al., 2017) (see Figure 4.**2**).

To adapt to the changes triggered by the child's entrance into adolescence, family members must have some shared sense of what they are experiencing and how they are changing. Frequent communication between adolescents and parents over mobile devices can help strengthen their relationship and help teenagers deal with fears of missing out (FOMO) (Alt & Boniel-Nissim, 2018; Warren & Aloia, 2018). Yet parents and teenagers often live in "separate realities," perceiving their day-to-day experiences in very different ways (Abar et al., 2015; De Los Reyes, Ohannessian, & Racz, 2019).

Although adolescents' descriptions of their parents' behavior are correlated, the correlations are not large, and parents tend to describe their own parenting more positively than their teenagers do (Hou et al., 2020). A mother and son, for example, may have a conversation about schoolwork. She may experience the conversation as simply a serious discussion; he may perceive it as an argument. A parent may speak to an adolescent in a serious voice, but the adolescent may experience it as anger (Nelson et al., 2005). One interesting finding to emerge from research on brain maturation in adolescence is that young adolescents may be especially sensitive—and perhaps even overreact—to the emotional signals given off by others (Pfeifer & Blakemore, 2012), which may make more sensitive teenagers more likely to be adversely affected by fights with their parents (Van Lissa et al., 2017).

The Role of Puberty   The adolescent's biological and cognitive maturation likely plays a role in unbalancing the family system during early adolescence. Family relationships change during puberty, with adolescents and their parents bickering more frequently and feeling less close (De Goede, Branje, & Meeus, 2009; Marceau, Ram, & Susman, 2015).

Although puberty seems to distance adolescents from their parents, it is not associated with familial "storm and stress." Rates of outright conflict between parents and

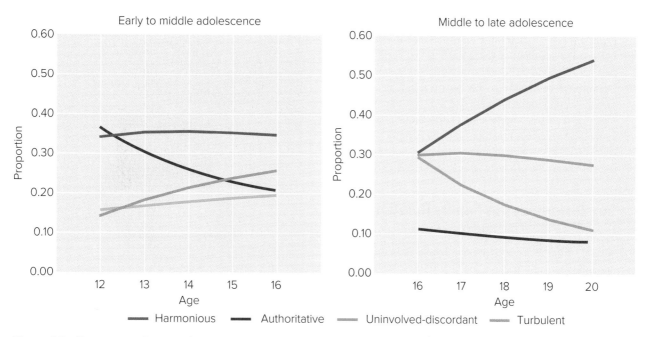

Early to middle adolescence

Middle to late adolescence

— Harmonious   — Authoritative   — Uninvolved-discordant   — Turbulent

Figure 4.2 Between early and mid-adolescence, there is an increase in the proportion of families in which parents and teenagers have a turbulent relationship, but between mid- and late adolescence, parent–adolescent relationships improve markedly. (Hadiwijaya et al., 2017)

children are not dramatically higher during adolescence than before or after (Laursen & DeLay, 2011). Rather, disputes between parents and teenagers are typical of the sorts of arguments people have when a more powerful person (the parent) is trying to get a less powerful one (the adolescent) to do something (Adams & Laursen, 2001). Similarly, the diminished closeness is more likely to be manifested in increased privacy on the part of the adolescent and less physical affection between teenagers and parents, rather than any serious loss of love or respect between them (Keijsers et al., 2010; Laursen & Collins, 2009).

The distancing that takes place between parents and teenagers in early and middle adolescence is temporary, however. Parent–child relationships tend to become less conflicted and more intimate during late adolescence and show no decline in closeness as the adolescent enters young adulthood. If anything, identifying with and feeling responsible for one's family increases during the early 20s (Tsai, Telzer, & Fuligni, 2013). Nevertheless, the frequent bickering can take a toll on parents' and teenagers' mental health (McCauley Ohannessian, Laird, & De Los Reyes, 2016). (A mother once told me that living with her teenager was like "being bitten to death by ducks.") In some families, adolescents and parents even disagree about what they argue about (Ehrlich et al., 2016)!

Some studies have found that individuals who reported more conflict with their parents during adolescence had more problems later in adolescence, during young adulthood, and at midlife (Berg et al., 2017; Klahr, McGue, Iacono, & Burt, 2011). Although it is certainly possible that adolescents who have problems are more likely to provoke conflict with their parents, studies that have been able to separate cause and effect have found that family conflict actually leads to the development of teenagers' mental health problems (Klahr, Rueter, et al., 2011) and emotional distress, regardless of ethnicity (Chung, Flook, & Fuligni, 2009). Frequent criticism by parents also can adversely affect adolescents' mood and elevate their cortisol levels, which can take its toll on physical health (Griffith et al., 2018; Lippold et al., 2016). Conflict at home can spill over into the adolescents' school life and relationships with friends, causing problems and emotional distress (Chung, Flook, & Fuligni, 2011; Timmons & Margolin, 2015).

The first half of adolescence may be an especially strained and distant time for the family, although this may be more true in the case of firstborns than in the case of

Conflict between parents and adolescents can play a very important and positive role in the adolescent's social and cognitive development, so long as family relationships are warm. Digitalskillet/E+/Getty Images

later-borns, perhaps because parents may learn from their experiences with their older child (Shanahan et al., 2007). Part of the problem is that conflicts between teenagers and parents tend to be resolved not through compromise but through one party giving in or walking away, neither of which enhances the quality of the relationship or contributes to anyone's well-being (Ferrar et al., 2020; Moed et al., 2015). As relationships between parents and adolescents become more egalitarian, they get better at resolving conflicts (Van Doorn, Branje, & Meeus, 2011).

Sex Differences in Family Relationships

You may be surprised to learn that, according to scientific studies, differences between the family relations of sons and daughters are minimal. Although there are occasional exceptions to the rule, sons and daughters report comparable degrees of closeness to their parents, amounts of conflict, types of rules (and disagreements about those rules), and patterns of activity (Buehler, 2020). Observational studies of interactions between parents and adolescents indicate that sons and daughters interact with their parents in remarkably similar ways (Steinberg & Silk, 2002). There is some evidence, though, that, compared to adolescent boys, adolescent girls are more affected by the quality of their relationship with their parents (Ohannessian & Vannucci, 2020).

Adolescents' relationships with their mothers and fathers are very different. Don Hammond/Design Pics

Teenagers relate very differently to mothers and fathers, though. Across many ethnic groups and cultures, adolescents tend to be closer to their mothers, to spend more time alone with their mothers, and to feel more comfortable talking to their mothers about problems and other emotional matters (Ebbert, Infurna, & Luthar, 2019) (see Figure 4.3). Fathers often rely on mothers for

Figure 4.3 Adolescents tend to be closer to their mothers, to spend more time alone with their mothers, and to feel more comfortable talking to their mothers about problems and other emotional matters. (Ebbert, Infurna, & Luthar, 2019)

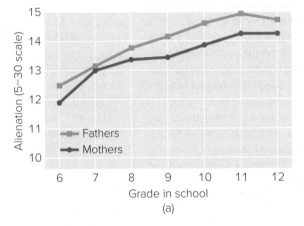

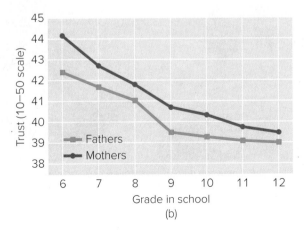

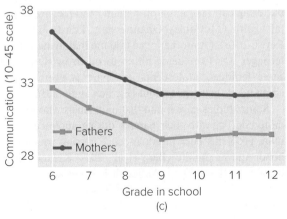

information about their adolescent's activities, but mothers rarely rely on fathers for this (Crouter et al., 2005; Waizenhofer, Buchanan, & Jackson-Newsom, 2004). Fathers are more likely to be perceived as relatively distant authority figures to be consulted for objective information (such as help with homework) but not for emotional support (such as help with problems with a boyfriend or girlfriend) (Crockett et al., 2007). Interestingly, adolescents also fight more often with their mothers than with their fathers and perceive mothers as more controlling, but this does not appear to jeopardize the closeness of the mother–adolescent relationship (Shek, 2007). Although adolescents spend about twice as much time with their mothers as with their fathers, time spent with fathers—perhaps because it is a relative rarity—is more predictive of adolescents' social competence and feelings of self-worth (Lam, McHale, & Crouter, 2014) (see Figure 4.3).

Family Relationships and Adolescent Development

Thus far, we have looked at the sorts of issues and concerns faced by most families during the adolescent years. We have not discussed how relationships differ from family to family and whether these differences have consequences for the adolescent. Some parents are stricter than others. Some adolescents are given a great deal of affection, while others are treated more distantly. In some households, decisions are made through open discussion and verbal give-and-take; in others, parents lay down the rules, and children are expected to follow them. Are some styles of parenting more likely to be associated with healthy development than others?

Before we try to answer these questions, several cautions are in order. Although we tend to see children's behavior as the result of their parents' behavior, socialization is a two-way street (Collins et al., 2000). Just as parents affect their adolescents' behavior, adolescents affect how their parents behave (Li et al., 2019; Hannigan et al.,

2017). Harsh discipline leads to increases in adolescent behavior problems, but when adolescents behave badly, parents respond by becoming more punitive, overcontrolling, or detached (Mastrotheodorus et al., 2020; Pinquart, 2017; Wang & Kenny, 2014). This interplay between parenting and adolescent development is so strong that it even contributes to the transmission of parenting styles across generations (Deater-Deckard, 2014). Parents who punish their children by hitting them may inadvertently make their children more aggressive, and when these children grow up and become parents, they may use the same sort of physical punishment their parents used on them.

making the cultural connection

Cultures vary in the extent to which physical punishment is used. In some countries, it is illegal for parents to hit their children. In others, however, physical punishment is common. Do you think that the effect of physical punishment on adolescent development would be different in countries where it is acceptable than in countries where it is outlawed?

In addition, various types of parenting affect different adolescents differently. For example, although adolescents whose parents are hostile or uninvolved are more likely to exhibit antisocial behavior (Milkie, Nomaguchi, & Denny, 2015), the link between negative parenting and adolescent problem behavior is stronger among teenagers who are temperamentally more impulsive; among adolescents who are more timid, the same sort of parenting leads to anxiety and depression (Guyer et al., 2015; Hentges, Shaw, & Wang, 2018) (see Figure 4.4). Furthermore, adolescents who have a greater genetic risk for developing problems (by virtue of their family history) are more likely to evoke from their parents the sort of behavior that has been shown to lead to the development of problems (O'Connor et al., 1998).

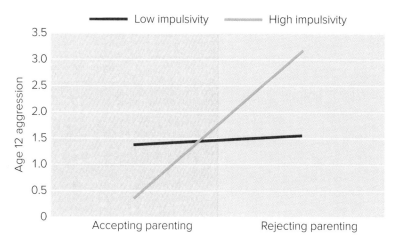

Figure 4.4 **Impulsive adolescents are significantly more likely than their nonimpulsive peers to become aggressive in responsive to rejecting parenting.** (Hentges, Shaw, & Wang, 2018)

parental responsiveness
One of the two important dimensions of parenting; responsiveness refers to the degree to which the parent responds to the child's needs in an accepting, supportive manner.

parental demandingness
One of two important dimensions of parenting; demandingness refers to the degree to which the parent expects and insists on mature, responsible behavior from the child.

authoritative parents
Parents who use warmth, firm control, and rational, issue-oriented discipline, in which emphasis is placed on the development of self-direction.

authoritarian parents
Parents who use punitive, absolute, and forceful discipline, and who place a premium on obedience and conformity.

indulgent parents
Parents who are characterized by responsiveness but low demandingness and who are mainly concerned with the child's happiness.

Parenting Styles and Their Effects

One of the most useful ways to characterize parents' behavior toward their children derives from the work of psychologist Diana Baumrind (1978). According to her, two aspects of the parent's behavior toward the adolescent are critical: parental responsiveness and parental "demandingness" (Maccoby & Martin, 1983). **Parental responsiveness** is the degree to which the parent responds to the child's needs in an accepting, supportive manner. **Parental demandingness** is the extent to which the parent expects and demands mature, responsible behavior.

Four Styles of Parenting
Because parental responsiveness and demandingness are more or less independent of each other—that is, it is possible for a parent to be demanding without being responsive, and vice versa—it is possible to look at various combinations of these two dimensions (see Figure 4.5).

Parents who are both responsive and demanding are authoritative. **Authoritative parents** are warm but firm. They set standards for the child's conduct but form expectations consistent with the child's needs and capabilities. They value the development of autonomy and self-direction but assume the ultimate responsibility for their child's behavior. Authoritative parents deal with their child in a rational, issue-oriented manner, frequently engaging in discussion over matters of discipline. Authoritative parents strive to raise a child who is self-reliant, with a strong sense of initiative.

Parents who are very demanding but not responsive are authoritarian. **Authoritarian parents** value obedience and conformity. They tend to favor more punitive, absolute, and forceful discipline. Verbal give-and-take is not common because authoritarian parents believe that children should accept their parents' rules and standards without question. They don't encourage independent behavior and, instead, place a good deal of importance on restricting the child's autonomy. Authoritarian parents place a premium on compliance.

A parent who is very responsive but not at all demanding is indulgent. **Indulgent parents** behave in an accepting, benign, and more passive way in matters of discipline. These parents demand very little, giving their children a high degree of freedom to act as they wish. Indulgent parents believe that control is an infringement on children's freedom that may interfere with healthy development. Instead of actively shaping their child's behavior, indulgent parents are more likely to view themselves as resources for the child. Indulgent parents are especially concerned with raising a happy child.

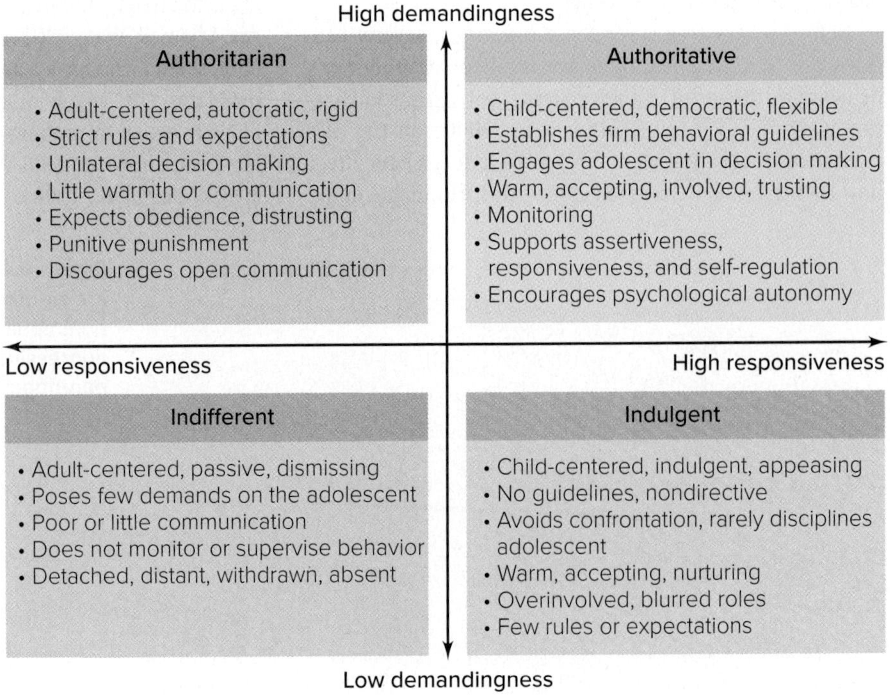

Figure 4.5   A typological conceptualization of parenting styles based on the dimensions of responsiveness and demandingness. (Adapted from Martin, Bascoe, & Davies, 2011)

High demandingness

Authoritarian
- Adult-centered, autocratic, rigid
- Strict rules and expectations
- Unilateral decision making
- Little warmth or communication
- Expects obedience, distrusting
- Punitive punishment
- Discourages open communication

Authoritative
- Child-centered, democratic, flexible
- Establishes firm behavioral guidelines
- Engages adolescent in decision making
- Warm, accepting, involved, trusting
- Monitoring
- Supports assertiveness, responsiveness, and self-regulation
- Encourages psychological autonomy

Low responsiveness — High responsiveness

Indifferent
- Adult-centered, passive, dismissing
- Poses few demands on the adolescent
- Poor or little communication
- Does not monitor or supervise behavior
- Detached, distant, withdrawn, absent

Indulgent
- Child-centered, indulgent, appeasing
- No guidelines, nondirective
- Avoids confrontation, rarely disciplines adolescent
- Warm, accepting, nurturing
- Overinvolved, blurred roles
- Few rules or expectations

Low demandingness

Parents who are neither demanding nor responsive are indifferent. **Indifferent parents** do whatever is necessary to minimize the time and energy they must devote to interacting with their child. They know little about their child's activities and whereabouts, show little interest in their child's experiences at school or with friends, rarely converse with their child, and rarely consider their child's opinion. Rather than raising their child according to a set of beliefs about what is good for the child's development (as do the other three parent types), indifferent parents structure their home life primarily around their own needs and interests.

making the personal connection

Where would you place your parents in the four-way model of parenting styles? Would your parents agree?

The Power of Authoritative Parenting Few areas of research in the field of adolescent development have received as much attention as the link between what parents do and how adolescents turn out, and the findings of this body of work are amazingly consistent (Collins & Steinberg, 2006). Young people who have been raised in authoritative households are more psychologically mature than those who have been raised in authoritarian, indulgent, or indifferent homes. Adolescents raised in authoritative homes are more responsible, self-assured, creative, curious, socially skilled, academically successful, and able to regulate their emotions and behavior. Adolescents raised in authoritarian homes, in contrast, are more dependent, more passive, less socially adept, less self-assured, and less curious. Adolescents raised in indulgent households are less mature, less responsible, and more conforming to their peers. Adolescents raised in indifferent homes are often impulsive and more likely to be involved in delinquent behavior and in precocious experimentation with sex, drugs, and alcohol. Although it generally is not a good thing for parents to disagree about how

Adolescents fare better when their parents are warm and firm, a style known as authoritative parenting. kali9/Getty Images

they raise their teenagers, studies show that it is better to have at least one authoritative parent than two nonauthoritative ones who share the same point of view (Simons & Conger, 2007; Smetana & Ahmad, 2018).

indifferent parents
Parents who are characterized by low levels of both responsiveness and demandingness.

Parenting that is neglectful, hostile, or abusive has harmful effects on adolescents' mental health and development, often leading to anxiety, depression and a variety of behavior problems (Mak, Fosco, & Feinberg, 2018; Thomas et al., 2018; Weymouth, Fosco, & Feinberg, 2019). Severe psychological abuse (excessive criticism, rejection, or emotional harshness) appears to have the most deleterious effects (Dickerson, Milojevich, & Quas, 2019). Unfortunately, maltreatment is all too common, especially among adolescents growing up in poverty, and teenagers who have been physically abused or neglected are also more likely to be exposed to violence, sexually abused, victimized by peers and siblings, and sexually victimized over the Internet (Fisher et al., 2015; Maas, Bray, & Noll, 2018).

The link between authoritative parenting and healthy adolescent development has been found in studies of a wide range of ethnicities, social classes, and family structures, not only within the United States but all over the world, across countries in Africa, Asia, Europe, the Middle East, and North and South America. In fact, the evidence favoring authoritative parenting is so strong that some experts have suggested that the question of which type of parenting benefits teenagers the most need not be studied anymore (see Table 4.1) (Steinberg, 2001). Educational programs designed to teach parents how to be

Table 4.1 The 10 basic principles of good parenting

Several years ago, after reviewing decades of research on parenting and child development, I came to the conclusion that we really did know what sort of parenting is most likely to help children and adolescents grow up in healthy ways. I summarized this evidence in a book titled *The 10 Basic Principles of Good Parenting*. Here's what all parents, regardless of their child's age, should keep in mind:

1. What you do matters.
2. You cannot be too loving.
3. Be involved in your child's life.
4. Adapt your parenting to fit your child.
5. Establish rules and set limits.
6. Help foster your child's independence.
7. Be consistent.
8. Avoid harsh discipline.
9. Explain your rules and decisions.
10. Treat your child with respect.

(Steinberg, 2005)

more responsive and more demanding have been shown to foster healthy adolescent development and behavior (e.g., Brody et al., 2006; Connell & Dishion, 2008).

Ethnic Differences in Parenting Practices   A number of researchers have asked whether parents from different ethnic groups vary in their child rearing and whether the relation between parenting styles and adolescent outcomes is the same across different ethnic groups. These are two different questions (Deater-Deckard et al., 2018). The first concerns average differences between groups in their approaches to parenting (e.g., whether Asian parents are stricter than white parents), whereas the second concerns the correlation between parenting practices and adolescent adjustment in different groups (e.g., whether the effect of strictness is the same in Latinx families as it is in Black families).

In general, authoritative parenting is less prevalent among Black, Asian, or Latinx families than among white families, no doubt because parenting practices are often linked to cultural values and beliefs (Qu, Pomerantz, & Deng, 2016). Ethnic minority parents are often more demanding than white parents (Chao & Otsuki-Clutter, 2011), sometimes employing an approach exemplified (some might say, caricatured) by a type of parent described as a "Tiger Mother" (Chua, 2011), an approach to parenting that may foster academic achievement but that may also increase adolescents' anxiety and distress (S. Kim et al., 2015; Luebbe, Tu, & Fredrick, 2018). Some ethnic minority families that appear authoritarian actually may not be, however. In many Asian and Asian American families, parents employ a style that might be mislabeled as authoritarian when it is actually better understood as protective or "strict-affectionate" (Zhang

Although parenting practices vary across cultures, the ways in which adolescents are affected by different types of parenting generally do not. Michael DeLeon/Getty Images

et al., 2017) and that does not have the same negative impact as authoritarian parenting. In addition, because ethnic minority families are more likely to live in dangerous communities, authoritarian parenting, with its emphasis on control, may not be as harmful as it is in safe communities and may even offer some benefits (Richman & Mandara, 2013; White et al., 2016).

Nevertheless, even though authoritative parenting is less common in ethnic minority families, its effects on adolescent adjustment are beneficial in all ethnic groups (Li et al., 2019; Simons, Simons, & Su, 2013). In other words, ethnic minority youngsters benefit from parenting that is responsive and demanding, just as their nonminority peers do.

How Authoritative Parenting Works   Why is authoritative parenting so consistently associated with healthy adolescent development? First, authoritative parents provide an appropriate balance between restrictiveness and autonomy, giving the adolescent opportunities to develop self-control while providing the standards, limits, and guidelines that teenagers still need (Li et al., 2019). Authoritative parents are more likely to give children more independence gradually as they get older, which helps children develop self-assurance. Because of this, authoritative parenting promotes the development of adolescents' competence and enhances their ability to withstand a variety of potentially negative influences, including stress (Hazel et al., 2014) and exposure to antisocial peers (Flamm & Grolnick, 2013; Tilton-Weaver et al., 2013).

Second, because authoritative parents are more likely to engage their children in verbal give-and-take, they are likely to promote the sort of intellectual development that provides an important foundation for the development of maturity (Smetana, Crean, & Daddis, 2002). Authoritative parents are less likely than other parents to assert their authority by turning adolescents' personal decisions (such as over what type of music they listen to) into moral issues (Smetana, 1995). Family discussions in which decisions, rules, and expectations are explained help the child understand social systems and social relationships. This understanding plays an important role in the development of reasoning abilities, perspective taking, moral judgment, and empathy (Eisenberg et al., 2009).

Third, because authoritative parenting is based on a warm parent-child relationship, adolescents are more likely to identify with, admire, and form strong attachments to their parents, which makes them more open to their parents' influence (Darling & Steinberg, 1993; Li et al., 2019). Adolescents who are raised by nonauthoritative parents often end up having friends their parents disapprove of, including those involved in problem behavior (Knoester, Haynie, & Stephens, 2006). And adolescents who are forced to spend time with parents they don't get along with do not benefit from joint activities (Offer, 2013).

Finally, the child's own behavior, temperament, and personality shape parenting practices (Lansford et al., 2018). Children who are responsible, self-directed, curious, and self-assured elicit warmth, flexible guidance, and verbal give-and-take (Li et al., 2019). Conversely, children who are irritable, aggressive, dependent, or immature may provoke behavior that is excessively harsh, passive, or distant (Harris, Vazsonyi, & Bolland, 2017; Rothenberg et al., 2020). Parents enjoy being around children who are responsible, independent, and willing to tell them about their activities and whereabouts, and they treat them more warmly as a result.

Although parental monitoring does deter adolescent problem behavior (Laird, Marrero, & Sentse, 2010), some of what often appears to be effective parental monitoring may actually be the end result of a warm parent-adolescent relationship in which the adolescent willingly discloses information (Dotterer & Day, 2019; Kerr, Stattin, & Özdemir, 2012; Liu, Chen, & Brown, 2020; Wertz et al., 2016). Indeed, just because parents try to monitor their children vigilantly doesn't guarantee that they will know everything their teenagers are up to. Parents are often unaware of their adolescents' online activities, for example (Symons et al., 2017). As it turns out, the combination of monitoring and being supportive of the teenager's autonomy is more effective that monitoring alone (Rodriguez-Meirinhos et al., 2020).

Adolescents' Relationships with Siblings

Sibling relationships during adolescence have characteristics that set them apart both from relationships with parents and relationships with friends (Campione-Barr & Killoren, 2019). Adolescents rate their sibling relationships similarly to those with their parents in companionship and importance, but more like friendships with respect to power, assistance, and their satisfaction with the relationship.

Because siblings live in close proximity to each other, they have added opportunities for both positive and negative interactions.
Jen Collins/EyeEm/Getty Images

Young adolescents often have emotionally charged relationships with siblings that are marked by conflict and rivalry but also by nurturance and support (Campione-Barr & Killoren, 2019). As children mature from childhood to early adolescence, sibling conflict increases, with adolescents reporting more negativity in their sibling relationships than in their relationships with peers and less effective conflict resolution than with their parents. Researchers have pointed to two common sources of sibling conflict: invasion of the personal (e.g., wearing a sibling's favorite sweater without asking permission) and disagreements over equity and fairness (e.g., arguing about whether a sibling is doing her fair share of chores) (Odudu, Williams, & Campione-Barr, 2020). Adolescents see aggression toward siblings as more acceptable than aggression toward friends, which sometimes leads to behavior between siblings that is absolutely ruthless. Consider this 16-year-old girl's account of her behavior toward her younger sister:

I'm kind of mean to her just 'cause she's my sister, you know? ... Sometimes I tell her like, "oh just because you don't have any friends, that doesn't mean you can come and hang out with my friends" because that's something that usually gets to her, so you tend to lean towards that, to make her go away. . . . One time . . . she kept on trying to play with me and my friend, and we were yelling at her . . . We hurt her a little bit and she started crying. . . . I wish it didn't happen. . . . We were really mad at her, and I don't know why, and she just really wanted someone to play with. (Recchia, Wainryb, & Pasupathi, 2013)

Over time, adolescents' relationships with siblings, and especially with younger siblings, become more egalitarian but also more distant and less emotionally intense (Tucker, Updegraff, & Baril, 2010; Whiteman, Solmeyer, & McHale, 2015), although patterns of change in sibling relationships differ between same-sex and mixed-sex dyads. In same-sex dyads, intimacy increases between preadolescence and middle adolescence, and then declines somewhat. In mixed-sex dyads, the pattern is the opposite: Intimacy drops between preadolescence and mid-adolescence, and then increases. In fact, by late adolescence, brothers and sisters are closer than are same-sex siblings, although both types of relationships become closer as individuals leave home and mature into young adulthood (Whiteman, McHale, & Crouter, 2011). Despite these changes, though, there is considerable stability in the quality of sibling relationships between childhood and adolescence.

A Network of Relationships The adolescent's interpersonal world is a web of interconnected relationships. The quality of the parent-adolescent relationship influences the quality of relations among brothers and sisters. Harmony and cohesiveness in the parent-adolescent relationship are associated with less sibling conflict and a more positive sibling relationship (East, 2009). In

behavioral genetics
The scientific study of genetic influences on behavior.

molecular genetics
The scientific study of the structure and function of genes.

alleles
Different versions of the same gene.

shared environmental influences
Nongenetic influences that make individuals living in the same family similar to each other.

contrast, adolescents who experience maternal rejection and negativity are more aggressive with siblings.

By the same token, children and adolescents learn much about social relationships from sibling interactions, and they bring this knowledge and experience to their friendships and romantic relationships (Doughty, McHale, & Feinberg, 2015; Harper, Padilla-Walker, & Jensen, 2016). In poorly functioning families, aggressive interchanges between unsupervised siblings often provide a training ground within which adolescents learn, practice, and perfect antisocial and aggressive behavior (Criss & Shaw, 2005; Snyder, Bank, & Burraston, 2005). The reverse is true as well: The quality of adolescents' relationships with their friends influences how they interact with their siblings (Kramer & Kowal, 2005).

The quality of the sibling relationship also affects adolescents' psychological well-being (Gallagher et al., 2018; Whiteman, Solmeyer, & McHale, 2015). Positive sibling relationships contribute to adolescents' academic competence, romantic competence, familism, sociability, health, autonomy, and self-worth (Rodríguez De Jesús et al., 2019; Doughty et al., 2015; Wang, Degol, & Amemiya, 2019). Having a close sibling relationship can partially ameliorate the negative effects of family stress (Waite et al., 2011) and of not having friends in school (East, 2009), and siblings can serve as role models as well as sources of advice and guidance (Rogers et al., 2018; Wheeler et al., 2016).

Of course, siblings can influence the development of problems, too (Bank, Burraston, & Snyder, 2004). For example, girls with adolescent older sisters are relatively more likely to engage in early sexual activity and to become pregnant during adolescence (East, Reyes, & Horn, 2007). Siblings also influence each other's drug use (Samek et al., 2018), antisocial behavior (Walters, 2019), risk taking (Rogers et al., 2020), feelings of anxiety (Serra Poirer et al., 2017), and thoughts about suicide (Tucker & Wiesen-Martin, 2015).

Genetic Influences on Adolescent Development

So far, we have discussed the ways in which interactions between parents and teenagers and between teenagers and their siblings shape adolescent development. But this is not the only way in which adolescents are affected by their families. Another way the family influences

adolescent development is transmitted through the genes they inherit from their parents. Recent advances in the study of **behavioral genetics** have provided new insights into this issue, as well as a host of others concerning the joint impact of genes and the environment on development.

Researchers examine genetic influences in three main ways: (1) studying adolescents who are twins, to see whether identical twins are more similar than fraternal twins (e.g., Dick, Adkins, & Kuo, 2016); (2) studying adolescents who have been adopted, to see whether adopted adolescents are more like their biological parents than like their adoptive parents (e.g., Beaver et al., 2015); and (3) studying adolescents and their siblings in stepfamilies, to see whether similarity between siblings varies with their biological relatedness (e.g., Neiderhiser et al., 2004). In addition to examining whether and how much given traits are genetically versus environmentally determined, researchers also ask how these two sets of factors interact (e.g., whether the same environment affects people with different genetic makeups in different ways or whether people with different genetic makeups evoke different reactions from others) (Collins et al., 2000).

In recent years, advances in **molecular genetics** have enabled scientists to identify specific genes (or, more accurately, different versions of a particular gene) that are associated with particular traits. Genetic markers for a wide range of traits and behavioral propensities such as aggression, depression, impulsivity, and sensation seeking, for instance, have been found. Different forms of the same gene, called **alleles**, arise because of genetic mutations and may guide development in different directions.

For instance, two genes determine the color of your eyes, but each gene has different versions, and your eye color is dependent on which combination of alleles you inherit from your parents. This applies to psychological development as well. There are different versions of a gene that influences a person's vulnerability to depression, one that is short and one that is long. We all inherit two of these genes (one from each parent). Whereas having the short version makes depression more likely, having the long one makes it less so (having one short and one long version puts someone at moderate risk). In the face of the same level of stress, individuals with two short alleles are much more likely to develop depression than those with two long versions (Caspi et al., 2003).

Genetic and Environmental Influences on Adolescent Development

In studies of genetic and environmental influences on adolescent development, researchers distinguish between two types of environmental influences. **Shared environmental influences** are factors in the environment that individuals, such as siblings, have in common and that make the individuals similar in personality and behavior. **Nonshared environmental influences** are factors in the environments of individuals that are not similar and that, as a consequence, make the them different from one another (Turkheimer & Waldron, 2000).

Both genetic and nonshared environmental influences, such as differential parental treatment, peer relations, and school experiences, are particularly strong in adolescence. In contrast, shared environmental factors, such as family socioeconomic status or the neighborhood in which two siblings live, are less influential (McGue, Sharma, & Benson, 1996; Pike et al., 1996). In studies of siblings, nonshared environmental influences can include factors within the family as well as outside of it. For example, if two siblings are treated very differently by their parents, this would be considered a nonshared environmental influence. This sort of nonshared environment— that is, the nonshared environment that results from people having different experiences within what would appear to be the same context—seems to be the most important (Turkheimer & Waldron, 2000).

Genetic factors strongly influence many qualities that previously had been assumed to be shaped mainly by the environment. Aggressive behavior is highly driven by genetics, although shared and nonshared environmental influences on adolescents' antisocial behavior, including aggression, also have been found (Burt et al., 2007; Laursen et al., 2017; Vitaro et al., 2015). Genetic factors also have been linked to various emotional and behavioral problems, such as risk for suicide and depression (Jacobson & Rowe, 1999) and alcohol dependence (Dick, 2011). Research also has found strong genetic influences on adolescent competence, self-image, and self-conceptions (McGuire et al., 1999).

Intelligence in adolescence (as indexed by IQ) is also under strong genetic control, with genetic influences compounding over time and ultimately becoming more influential than the quality of the family environment (Briley & Tucker-Drob, 2013; Tucker-Drob, Briley, & Harden, 2013). Over time, genetic control over the maturation of brain regions associated with complex reasoning also increases (Lenroot & Giedd, 2008). Genetic influences on school performance, in contrast to intelligence, are more modest (Loehlin, Neiderhiser, & Reiss, 2005).

Many studies have shown that adolescents with the same genetic predispositions (such as genes associated with risk for depression) develop differently if they grow up in different environments (e.g., Li, Berk, & Lee, 2013). For instance, genetic influences on antisocial behavior are stronger among adolescents who have delinquent peers (Vitaro et al., 2015) and weaker among those who do well in school (Johnson, McGue, & Iacono, 2009). Genetic influences on intelligence are stronger in families with highly educated parents because the influence of genes on intelligence is stronger in environments that provide more learning opportunities, allowing children to benefit

from their genetic advantages (Tucker-Drob & Harden, 2012). In other words, genes may shape *tendencies,* but whether these tendencies are actualized often depends on the environment. The inverse is also true. People who are exposed to the same environment may be affected differently as a consequence of their genes.

Differential Susceptibility to the Environment Psychologists have long been interested in whether some individuals are more prone to develop problems because they have inherited a vulnerability to particular disorders. This vulnerability, called a diathesis, makes some people more likely to develop depression, for example, in the face of stress than others who face the same stressors but do not develop the disorder. (A diathesis doesn't have to be genetic, but in many instances, it is.) In positive environments, neither individual will become depressed. But in negative ones, the person who has the diathesis toward depression will be more likely to be harmed by the stress, whereas the one without the diathesis will not (see Figure 4.6 on page 110).

This **diathesis-stress model** is how most experts understand depression: the product of an interaction between a predisposition (the diathesis) and an environmental trigger (the stress). Although this view has been most commonly used to explain the development of depression, the model can be applied to any psychological disorder that is the product of the interplay between a cause that is inside the individual, such as a genetic tendency, and a cause that is in the environment, such as an acute stressor.

Inherited tendencies to develop particular disorders is the reason that all sorts of mental illnesses run in families. This does not mean that every adolescent with an alcoholic parent is destined to develop alcoholism or that every adolescent with a depressed parent is doomed to develop depression, but it does mean that individuals whose parents suffer from a psychological disorder are more likely to develop it than individuals whose parents do not.

Not all people with a genetic tendency toward a particular problem develop the disorder, though, because most disorders are the product of an interaction between genetic and environmental factors. Someone who has inherited a diathesis toward substance abuse or depression but who grows up in a positive, protective environment is far less likely to develop behavioral problems such as substance abuse or delinquency than someone who has the same diathesis but grows up under highly stressful circumstances (Rioux et al., 2016) or with unsupportive parents (Chhangur et al., 2015; Little et al., 2019).

nonshared environmental influences
The nongenetic influences in individuals' lives that make them different from people they live with.

diathesis-stress model
A perspective on psychological disorder that posits that problems are the result of an interaction between a preexisting condition (the diathesis) and exposure to stress in the environment.

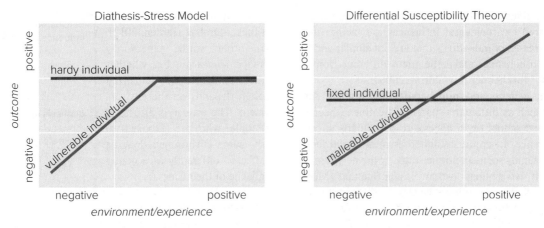

Figure 4.6 **The diathesis-stress model and the differential susceptibility theory.** (Belsky & Pluess, 2009)

Similar findings have been reported in studies of environmental influences on various types of psychopathology (Guyer, 2020).

Until recently, psychologists had not asked whether the same logic holds for positive as well as problematic development. Are some people genetically inclined to benefit from positive influences in their environment? Yes, they are. Two adolescents can be exposed to equally advantageous environments—homes with authoritative parents, for example—but may not be equally affected by this influence because one has inherited a stronger tendency than the other to profit from exposure to positive parenting.

Even more important, according to **differential susceptibility theory** (Belsky & Pluess, 2009), is that the very same genetic factors that make some people more susceptible to stress and other toxic environmental influences also make them more easily influenced by positive contexts (see Figure 4.6). This differential susceptibility has been found to affect the extent to which adolescents profit from authoritative parenting (Janssens et al., 2017; Rioux et al., 2016; Stocker et al., 2017), benefit from affiliating with positive peers (Trucco et al., 2016), or suffer as a result of peer rejection (Janssens et al., 2015) or negative parenting (Deane et al., 2020; Tung et al., 2019). Differential susceptibility also predicts which adolescents are more likely to benefit from interventions, such as programs designed to deter drug use (Brody, Yu, & Beach, 2015).

In other words, although some periods of development, such as adolescence, are times of heightened plasticity, or malleability, even among people of the same age, some are genetically more malleable than others. As a consequence, some people are "dandelions" (which grow pretty much the same way

differential susceptibility theory
The idea that the same genetic tendencies that make an individual especially susceptible to develop problems when exposed to adverse environmental influences also make him or her especially likely to thrive when exposed to positive environmental influences.

in any environment), but others are "orchids" (which thrive under good conditions but languish under bad ones) (Boyce, 2019). Researchers have now begun to identify the specific genetic factors that make some people more susceptible to the environment than others, and studies have found that the more of these factors one has, the more susceptible he or she is likely to be (Belsky & Pluess, 2013).

Why Are Siblings Often So Different?

If the family is an important influence on development, how can we explain the fact that siblings who grow up in the same family often turn out to be very different from one another? One answer is that, unless they are identical twins, two siblings may have inherited different genes from their parents, at least with respect to some traits. If a green-eyed mother and a brown-eyed father have children, it is entirely possible that some of them will have green eyes and others will have brown eyes. The same sort of pattern holds true for personality traits as well as physical ones.

A less obvious answer is that siblings actually may have very different family experiences. Even though we may assume that children growing up in the same family have shared the same environment, this is not necessarily the case. This can be because they have been treated differently by their parents, they perceive similar experiences in different ways, or they grew up in the same household at different times in the family's life (Darling & Tilton-Weaver, 2019; B. J. Ellis et al., 2012). One brother may describe his family as close-knit, while another may have experienced it as distant. One girl may describe her family life as plagued with argument and conflict, while her sister describes it as peaceful and agreeable. One child may have grown up during a financially secure phase in the family's life, whereas the family's finances may have been precarious during a sibling's formative years.

As you might expect, unequal treatment from mothers or fathers often creates conflict among siblings and is linked to a variety of problems, such as depression, antisocial behavior, and early pregnancy, especially among adolescents who are prone to comparing themselves with their brothers or sisters (Jensen & McHale, 2017; Jensen, Pond, & Padilla-Walker, 2015). Studies also show that differences in siblings' real and perceived family experiences are related to different patterns of development (Turney & Halpern-Meekin, 2020). Better-adjusted adolescents are more likely than their siblings to report that they had close relationships with their parents, that their relations with brothers or sisters were friendly, that they were involved in family decision making, and that they were given a high level of responsibility around the house (Shanahan et al., 2008). As they get older, adolescents appreciate the reasons for parents treating siblings differently. Sibling relationships are strained only when this differential treatment is perceived as unfair (Feinberg et al., 2000; Kowal & Kramer, 1997).

Treating siblings differently may actually be a good thing for parents to do, so long as each sibling is treated well. When siblings are treated differently by their parents, they get along better—presumably because this differential treatment makes them feel unique and lessens **sibling rivalry** (Feinberg et al., 2003). Perhaps you have a brother or sister whom you resemble more than you'd like—so much, in fact, that you've had a hard time establishing your own personality. When siblings feel this way, they often deliberately try to be different from each other. An adolescent whose brother or sister is a star athlete, for instance, may shun sports and focus on cultivating other types of talents, perhaps in academics or in the arts, in order to diminish feelings of competition. Similarly, although having an older sibling who is academically successful seems to promote younger adolescents' achievement, too much academic support from an older sibling may actually undermine a younger adolescent's success in school (Bouchey et al., 2010).

In addition to having different experiences inside the family, siblings also may have very different experiences outside the family—at school, with friends, in the neighborhood. These contexts provide yet another source of nonshared environmental influence. Because factors other than the family environment shape adolescent development and behavior, siblings may turn out very different if they have divergent experiences outside the home.

The Adolescent's Family in a Changing Society

In America and in many other industrialized countries, the family has undergone a series of profound changes during the past half century that have diversified its form and, as a result, adolescents' daily experiences (Pearce et al., 2018). High rates of divorce, cohabitation, and childbearing outside of marriage, as well as a changing international economy, have dramatically altered the world in which children and adolescents grow up. Although some of the most striking trends in family life slowed during the early 1990s, many did not reverse. The proportion of single-parent families, which increased during the 1970s and 1980s, stabilized at their historically high levels in the mid-1990s and has changed relatively little since then.

> **sibling rivalry**
> Competition between siblings, often for parental attention.

Divorce The U.S. divorce rate increased markedly beginning in the 1960s, rising steadily, and at times rapidly, until around 1980, when it peaked (Wolfers, 2014). This rate declined during the 1990s and by all accounts has continued declining, although it is difficult to compare today's statistics with those from past eras because the marriage rate also has declined and more couples are cohabiting (and when they split up, it is not recorded as a divorce). But based on the best data available, it appears that around one-third of people who married during the 2000s will have divorced within 20 years (Miller, 2014). More striking, perhaps, is that divorce has become far less common among college graduates than nongraduates; among today's college graduates, divorce is actually quite uncommon (Hurley, 2005). Because most divorces occur early in a marriage, adolescents are less likely than children to actually experience their parents' divorce at the time it is occurring.

Single Parenthood In addition to adolescents who live in a single-parent household as a consequence of their parents' divorce, a sizable percentage of youngsters will spend time in a single-parent household from birth; indeed, today, 60% of all children are born outside of

One reason adolescents with divorced parents are more likely to have problems than their peers is that divorce often exposes children to marital conflict, which adversely affects their mental health. Prasit photo/Getty Images

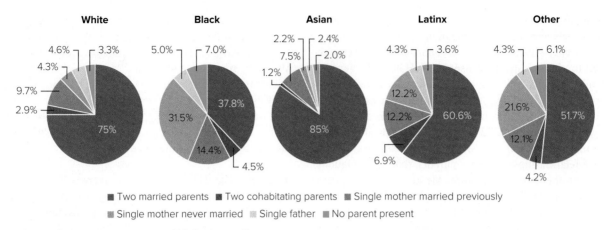

Figure 4.7   **Differences in the household composition of children and adolescents from different ethnic groups.** (U.S. Census Bureau, 2020)

marriage (Cherlin, Ribar, & Yasutake, 2016). Keep in mind, though, that a substantial number of adolescents who are classified as living in single-parent households actually live with more than one adult, often with the unmarried partner of the child's parent (Fields, 2003). When youngsters live with only one of their biological parents, either in single-parent or in two-parent households, it is usually with the mother; only about 15% of children who live with one parent live with their father (Pearce et al., 2018).

There are important racial and ethnic differences in these patterns of family life. Whereas 86% of all Asian children, 78% of all white children, and 68% of all Latinx children live with two parents, only 38% of Black children do (U.S. Census Bureau, 2020) (see Figure 4.7). Black youngsters are far more likely to be born outside of marriage and to experience parental divorce, but they are far less likely to experience their parents' remarriage. As a consequence, Black adolescents spend longer periods of time in single-parent households than do other teenagers.

Remarriage   Because two-thirds of divorced men and half of divorced women remarry (Livingston, 2014), the majority of youngsters whose parents separate also live in a stepfamily at some time. And, because the divorce rate is higher for second marriages than for first ones, the majority of youth whose parents remarry will experience a *second* divorce. If these changes in family relationships lead to frequent changes in living arrangements, this may cause problems, too; adolescents are adversely affected by having to move frequently (Anderson & Leventhal, 2017).

Poverty   Approximately 20% of all adolescents in the United States grow up in abject poverty, and an additional 20% grow up in low-income families (Jiang, Granja, &

Koball, 2017) (see Figure 4.8). Perhaps more important, the gap between the very poor and the very wealthy is at an all-time high (White, 2014). Poverty is much more likely to touch the lives of nonwhite adolescents; approximately 32% of Black, 27% of Latinx, and 27% of Native American children grow up in poverty (Jiang, Granja, & Koball, 2017). One reason for the large disparity in poverty rates between white and nonwhite children is the racial disparity in rates of single parenthood: Because nonwhite children are more likely to be raised in single-parent homes, they are more likely to be poor.

Before we turn to a discussion of how adolescents are affected by factors such as single parenthood or poverty, an important caution is in order. Because the conditions under which divorce, single parenthood, and remarriage take place vary tremendously from family to family, it is hard to generalize about their effects. (In contrast, it is relatively easy to generalize about the effects of poverty on adolescents, which are almost always negative.) For some young people, divorce may bring a welcome end to family conflict and tension; for others, it may be extremely disruptive. Some young people living with only their mother actually see their father more often than do their peers who live in homes where the father ostensibly is present (Hawkins, Amato, & King, 2006).

It is also the case that broad categories of family structures (e.g., "intact," "single-parent," etc.) often combine types of households that are very different in other respects (Pearce et al., 2018). Adolescents whose biological parents are cohabiting have a rate of antisocial behavior that is 40% higher than those whose biological parents are married and a rate of antisocial behavior that is about the same as adolescents who live in households with a biological mother and no other adult. Similarly, adolescents from "intact" families who live with both biological parents in families where one or both of the parents has a child from a prior marriage generally have a fairly high

Percent (%)

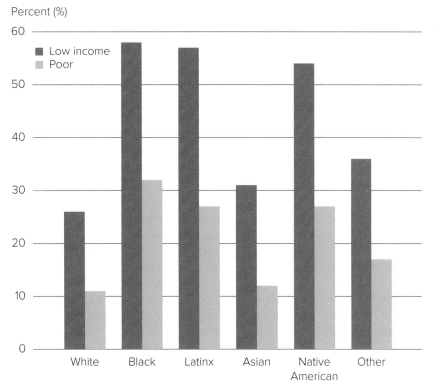

Figure 4.8   In the United States, there are substantial racial and ethnic differences in the percentage of adolescents who are classified as "low income" and, within that category, classified as "poor." (Jiang, Granja, & Koball, 2017)

rate of problems, despite their living with both biological parents (Halpern-Meekin & Tach, 2008).

Finally, hundreds of studies—perhaps even thousands—have shown that the same parenting practices that have been shown to be associated with healthy adolescent adjustment are effective across all family types (Buehler, 2020; King, Boyd, & Pragg, 2018). Just as authoritative parenting benefits teenagers in households with two biological parents, it benefits adolescents in single-parent homes and stepfamilies. Regardless of family structure, teenagers fare better when they have warm, supportive, and involved parents, and they fare worse when their parents are aloof, harsh, or uninvolved. In other words, variations *within* different family structures are more important than the differences among them. This is readily apparent when we look at how adolescents are affected by parental divorce.

Adolescents and Divorce

At one time, research on adolescents and divorce would likely have started with the assumption that living with one parent was not as good as living with two and that children whose parents divorced would be at a disadvantage relative to those whose parents remained married. Over time, researchers' ideas about divorce have changed dramatically, as new and better studies have challenged, clarified, and tempered the conclusions of past research. While most social scientists still agree that adolescents from divorced homes have more difficulties than those

from nondivorced homes, the explanation for this finding is far more complicated than the conventional wisdom that "Two parents are better than one" or "All children need a mother and a father." Five sets of findings have questioned these simple assertions.

The Effect of Divorce Is Small in Magnitude   First, although divorce clearly diminishes youngsters' well-being, the impact of divorce itself is small (Amato & Anthony, 2014). Although there are differences between children from divorced and nondivorced homes in school achievement, behavior problems, psychosocial adjustment, and family relations—all favoring individuals from nondivorced homes—the differences are seldom substantial. In general, the effects of divorce tend to be stronger among school-aged individuals than preschoolers or college students.

Quality Matters   Second, the quality of the relationships the young person has with the important adults in her or his life matters more than the number of parents present in the home (Arnold et al., 2017). Adolescents from stepfamilies have as many, if not more, problems than those from single-parent households, even though adolescents in stepfamilies live with two parents. In addition, youngsters from single-parent families that have not experienced divorce (e.g., youngsters who have lost a parent through death or youngsters with a single mother who never married) have fewer difficulties than their counterparts from divorced or remarried homes (Demo & Acock,

1996). Finally, adolescents in two-parent homes do not always have warm and close relationships with their parents. Indeed, adolescents living in father-absent homes have fewer problems than adolescents who live in two-parent homes with harsh or punitive fathers (Simmons et al., 2018).

Adaptation to Divorce Third, it is the process of going through a divorce, not the resulting family structure, that matters most for adolescents' mental health. The period of greatest difficulty for most adolescents is right around the time of the divorce (Jeynes, 2001). Although many young people show signs of difficulty immediately after their parents split up—problems in school, behavior problems, and increased anxiety—2 years later, the majority have adjusted to the change and behave comparably to teens whose biological parents have remained married (Hetherington, Bridges, & Insabella, 1998). Although adolescents whose parents have divorced have more problems than those whose parents remain married, the vast majority of individuals with divorced parents do not have significant problems.

Conflict and Stress Fourth, research has linked the adverse consequences of divorce to a number of factors not specifically due to having a single parent (Crosnoe & Cavanaugh, 2010). These include the exposure of the children to marital conflict (Amato & Cheadle, 2008), disorganized or disrupted parenting (Linver, Brooks-Gunn, & Kohen, 2002), and increased stress in the household (Daryanani et al., 2017), often due to loss of income (Pong & Ju, 2000). Adolescents living in two-parent families in which no divorce has occurred are also harmed by marital conflict, suboptimal parenting (especially parenting that is too lenient, too harsh, or inconsistent), and economic stress. In other words, the adverse, and usually temporary, effects of divorce or remarriage on adolescent well-being usually reflect the heightened conflict, disorganization, and stress surrounding the event, not the divorce or remarriage per se. The most important pathway through which divorce may adversely affect adolescent adjustment is via its disruptive impact on parenting (Daryanani et al., 2016; Markowitz & Ryan, 2016).

Genetic Influences Finally, although some of the apparent effects of parental divorce are the result of exposure to such stressors as marital conflict or disorganized parenting (S. A. Burt et al., 2008), genetic differences between adolescents whose parents have divorced and those whose parents have not may account for part of this. Adults who divorce are different from those who do not with respect to many traits that have strong genetic origins—such as predispositions to different sorts of emotional and behavioral problems, such as depression or substance abuse—and these traits are passed on from parents to children (D'Onofrio et al., 2006). One reason that adolescents from divorced homes have more problems than their peers is that they have inherited from their divorced parents some of the same traits that may have influenced their parents' decision to get divorced in the first place (O'Connor et al., 2000).

Individual Differences in the Effects of Divorce There are differences among children in how vulnerable they are to the short-term effects of divorce. In general, immediate problems are relatively more common among boys, younger children, children with difficult temperaments, children who do not have supportive relationships with adults outside the family, and youngsters whose parents divorce during the transition into adolescence (Saxbe et al., 2012). Because early adolescence is a time during which individuals seem to be especially sensitive to stress, parental divorce at this time may have a relatively stronger impact (Ivanova, Mills, & Veenstra, 2011).

Social support from others may be an especially important resource for inner-city children growing up in single-parent homes (Pallock & Lamborn, 2006). Support from kin appears to increase single parents' effectiveness in child rearing, and this, in turn, tends to limit adolescents' misbehavior. Studies of Black youngsters have found that children growing up in home environments that include a grandparent as well as a parent fare significantly better than those growing up in single-parent homes or in stepfamilies.

These studies, as well as others, remind us that relatives other than parents may play an extremely important role in adolescents' lives (Henderson et al., 2009; Richardson, 2009), especially within ethnic groups that historically have placed a great deal of importance on maintaining close ties to extended family members. This helps explain why the impact of divorce on adolescent adjustment is weaker among Black adolescents than among adolescents from other backgrounds (Heard, 2007; Kowaleski-Jones & Dunifon, 2006), although having excessively demanding extended family members can sometimes be a source of stress (Taylor, 2016).

The Specific Impact of Marital Conflict

Although divorce is generally associated with short-term difficulties for the adolescent, at least some of the differences between adolescents from divorced versus nondivorced homes were present before the parents divorced (Sun, 2001). One explanation for this is that children in the households that later divorced were exposed to higher levels of marital unhappiness and conflict, as well as strained parent-child relationships, both of which are known to disrupt parenting and increase children's difficulties (Amato & Booth, 1996). Children's maladjustment, in turn, adversely affects the quality of their parents' marriage, creating a vicious cycle (Cui, Donnellan, & Conger, 2007).

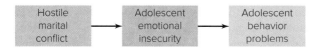

Figure 4.9 Hostile marital conflict makes adolescents feel insecure, which leads to behavior problems. (Based on Davies et al., 2016)

The recognition that exposure to marital conflict, apart from and in addition to divorce itself, has harmful effects on children's development has prompted many researchers to study how the quality of the adolescent's parents' marriage affects teenagers' mental health and behavior (Hou, Kim, & Wang, 2016; Davies et al., 2020a). Several conclusions have emerged from this research.

First, children are more adversely affected by marital conflict when they are aware of it than when it is hidden from them. Marital conflict is particularly harmful to children when it is especially hostile, physically violent, or frightening (Lucas-Thompson, Lunkenheimer, & Granger, 2017). Exposure to overt marital conflict and domestic violence has been linked to a wide range of adolescent problems, including depression, aggression, precocious sex, and dropping out of school (Adhia et al., 2019; Davies et al., 2020b; Wadman, Hiller, & St. Clair, 2020).

Second, children are more negatively affected when the marital conflict leads to feelings of insecurity or self-blame (Davies et al., 2016) (see Figure 4.9). Adolescents who blame themselves for their parents' conflict, whose feelings of security are challenged, or who are drawn into their parents' arguments are more likely to feel anxious, depressed, and distressed (Cheung et al., 2016; Cummings, Koss, & Davies, 2015).

Finally, marital conflict more adversely affects the adolescent when the conflict disrupts the quality of the parent-child relationship (Amato & Sobolewski, 2001). Adolescents are directly affected by exposure to their parents' conflict, to be sure, but several studies have found as well that tension between spouses spills over into the parent-child relationship, increasing family conflict and making parents more irritable and less effective (Cui & Conger, 2008; Rothenberg, Hussong, & Chassin, 2017). As you read earlier, adolescents who perceive their parents as hostile or uncaring are more likely to report a wide range of emotional and behavioral problems than are their peers.

making the practical connection

Based on the available research, what advice would you give to parents of teenagers who are considering divorce?

The Longer-Term Effects of Divorce

Individuals whose parents divorce during preadolescence and adolescence often demonstrate adjustment difficulties later, even after 2 or 3 years. Some research indicates that individuals whose parents divorced during childhood or adolescence continue to have adjustment problems well into their 30s (Cherlin, Chase-Lansdale, & McRae, 1998). These effects do not appear to be ameliorated by parental remarriage; adolescents from stepfamilies score similarly, or worse, on measures of longer-term adjustment, as do adolescents from single-parent, divorced homes.

Sleeper Effects To what can we attribute these "sleeper" effects—effects of divorce that may not be apparent until much later in the child's development? Two possible explanations come to mind. The first is that the ways in which adjustment difficulties might be expressed may not surface until adolescence. For example, social scientists believe that increased drug use and higher rates of early pregnancy are consequences of the lower level of parental monitoring in divorced homes (Moore & Chase-Lansdale, 2001). But because younger children are unlikely to use drugs or be sexually active, no matter what their parents' marital status is, the effect of the poor monitoring is not seen until adolescence, when individuals might begin using drugs and having sex.

A second explanation concerns the particular developmental challenges of adolescence. Adolescence is a time when individuals first begin experimenting with intimate sexual relationships. If having one's parents divorce or being exposed to marital conflict affects one's conceptions of relationships or views of romantic commitment and marriage (Shulman et al., 2012; Willoughby et al., 2020), it makes sense that some of the effects of early parental divorce will not be manifested until the adolescent begins dating and gets seriously involved in romantic relationships (Donahue et al., 2010).

Custody, Contact, and Conflict Following Divorce

After a divorce, do adolescents fare better or worse in different kinds of living arrangements? Does contact with the nonresidential parent contribute to the adolescent's well-being?

The nature of the relationship between the adolescent's divorced parents, and not which one he or she lives with, is the key factor (Booth, Scott, & King, 2010). In the years immediately following a divorce, children may fare a bit better in the custody of the parent of the same sex, but these effects don't last very long; over time, both male and female adolescents fare equally well either in dual custody or in sole custody (Buchanan, Maccoby, and Dornbusch, 1996), a finding that has been replicated in research on lesbian couples who have separated (Gartrell et al., 2011).

More important, especially for adolescents who have dual residences, are two factors: whether the ex-spouses continue to fight and place the child between them, and whether the adolescent's discipline is consistent across the two households. Adolescents whose parents have a congenial, cooperative relationship and who receive consistent and appropriate discipline from both homes report less emotional difficulty and fewer behavioral problems (Buchanan, Maccoby, & Dornbusch, 1996).

Adolescents whose parents have divorced also vary in the extent to which they have contact with the parent they no longer live with, typically their father. Contact between adolescents and their father following a divorce usually diminishes very quickly after the father moves out and continues to decline over time, especially among men who remarry or enter into a new romantic relationship (Stephens, 1996). Generally speaking, after their parents have divorced, adolescents who have regular contact with their father have fewer problems (Elam, Sandler et al., 2016; Gold, Edin, & Nelson, 2020), although not all studies have reached this conclusion; some have concluded that it is healthy adolescent functioning that influences fathers' involvement, rather than the reverse (Hawkins, Amato, & King, 2006).

More important than the father's involvement is the level of conflict between the divorced parents and the nature of the adolescent's relationship with the father before and after the divorce (Karre & Mounts, 2012). Adolescents benefit from contact with their nonresidential parent when conflict between their parents is minimal but suffer from such contact when parental conflict is intense (Elam, Sandler et al., 2016). Similarly, adolescents benefit when they have frequent contact with a nonresidential parent with whom they had a close relationship when their parents were married but suffer from contact with one with whom they didn't get along prior to the divorce. One consistent finding, though, is that financial support from fathers is associated with less problem behavior and higher academic achievement (Menning, 2002).

Remarriage

Adolescents growing up in stepfamilies—especially if the remarriage occurred during early adolescence rather than childhood—often have more problems than their peers, a finding that holds regardless of whether the stepparents are legally married or cohabiting (Harcourt et al., 2015; Steele et al., 2020). Youngsters growing up in single-parent homes are more likely than those in intact homes to be involved in delinquent activity, but adolescents in stepfamilies are even more at risk for this sort of problem behavior than are adolescents in single-parent families. This results, in part, because they are exposed to a "double dose" of marital conflict—normal, everyday conflict between the parent and stepparent and additional conflict between ex-spouses (Hanson, McLanahan, & Thomson, 1996)—and because they are exposed to a new set of

potentially difficult issues that arise from the blending of children from two different marriages, such as parents having different opinions about to how to raise children (Hetherington, Henderson, & Reiss, 1999).

Like the short-term effects of divorce, the short-term effects of remarriage vary among children, although not necessarily in the same ways. In general, girls have more difficulty in adjusting to remarriage than boys, and older children have more difficulty than younger ones (V. Lee et al., 1994). One explanation for this is that both boys and younger children have more to gain from their mother's remarriage than do girls or older children, who may have become accustomed to having a single mother. Over time, gender differences in adjustment to remarriage disappear, and in remarriages that last more than 5 years, the adjustment of male and female children is similar (Hetherington, Henderson, & Reiss, 1999).

Difficulties Adjusting to Parental Remarriage

Remarriage during the adolescent years is extremely stressful when families are unable to accommodate the new stepparent relationship. Many adolescents find it difficult to adjust to a new authority figure moving into the household, especially if that person has different ideas about rules and discipline, and particularly if the new authority figure is not legally married to the child's biological parent (Hetherington, Henderson, & Reiss, 1999). This is especially true when the adolescent is already vulnerable, either because of previous psychological problems or because of a recent divorce or other stressful event.

By the same token, many stepparents find it difficult to join a family and not be accepted immediately by the children as the new parent. Stepparents may wonder why love is not forthcoming from their stepchildren, who may be critical, resistant, and sulky. Although many stepparents and their adolescent stepchildren establish positive relationships, the lack of a biological connection between stepparent and stepchild—coupled with the stresses associated with divorce and remarriage—make this relationship especially vulnerable to problems. Adolescents in remarried households fare better when their stepparent can establish a consistent, supportive, authoritative style of discipline (Hetherington, Henderson, & Reiss, 1999).

Several studies indicate that children's adjustment declines somewhat each time they must cope with a change in their family's household composition (Fomby & Bosick, 2013; Zito, 2015), in part because parenting may become less effective during each family transition (Kurdek & Fine, 1993). Adolescents whose family situation is unstable are also more likely to be exposed to violence (S. E. Cavanagh et al., 2018). Given the fact that the benefits of authoritative parenting are just as strong in divorced and remarried families as they are in other homes, experts believe that clinicians who work with families that have undergone marital transitions should help parents learn and adopt this parenting style.

One factor that seems to make a big difference in the adjustment of children in stepfamilies is the nature of the relationship they have with their noncustodial parent—the biological parent with whom they no longer live. Children fare better when there is consistency in discipline between their custodial and noncustodial parents and when they have a good relationship with the noncustodial parent, especially in the years immediately following the remarriage. Having a close relationship with the noncustodial parent does not appear to undermine the relationship with the custodial parent (Buchanan, Maccoby, & Dornbusch, 1996), nor does it undermine the relationship between the adolescent and the stepparent (Yuan & Hamilton, 2006). Indeed, adolescents who feel close to *both* their father and stepfather generally have better outcomes than those who feel close to one but not the other (Risch, Jodl, & Eccles, 2004), although the most consistent predictor of adolescents' mental health is the quality of the relationships they have with the parents they live with (Amato, King, & Thorsen, 2016).

Economic Stress and Poverty

In light of the economic downturn that accompanied the COVID-19 pandemic, there has been an upsurge in interest in the ways in which adolescents' mental health is affected by changes in their family's financial situation and exposure to other sorts of stress. Studies of family income loss and adolescent adjustment suggest a number of parallels with the research on divorce and remarriage.

The Effects of Financial Strain   Like divorce, income loss is associated with disruptions in parenting, which, in turn, lead to increases in adolescent difficulties, including a diminished sense of mastery, increased emotional distress, academic and interpersonal problems, and delinquency. According to the Family Stress Model (Deater-Deckard et al., 2019; Herd, King-Casas, & Kim-Spoon, 2020; Simons & Steele, 2020), financial strain increases mothers' and fathers' feelings of depression and anxiety, worsens marriages, and causes conflicts between parents and adolescents (Kotchick, Whitsett, & Sherman, 2020; Ponnet et al., 2015; White et al., 2015). These consequences, in turn, make parents more irritable, which adversely affects the quality of their parenting and their teenagers' psychological development (see Figure 4.10). These patterns have been observed in countries around the world and have been found in studies of other types of stressors that can disrupt family functioning, such as living in a dangerous neighborhood (Deater-Deckard et al., 2019; Di Giunta et al., 2020).

In contrast, parents who are able to maintain a more positive outlook through the difficult time are more likely to protect their adolescents from the psychological harm associated with financial strain (Neppli et al., 2015), and adolescents who have stronger self-regulation are better able to cope with their family's difficulties (Taylor, Widaman, & Robins, 2018). Not surprisingly, the family climate created by economic strain, often characterized by high levels of anger and conflict in multiple relationships, puts adolescents at risk for a variety of problems (Bodner et al., 2018; Ponnet et al., 2016).

The Impact of Chronic Poverty   Researchers also have studied the impact on adolescents of growing up amid chronic economic disadvantage (Yoshikawa, Aber, & Beardslee, 2012). Persistent poverty, like temporary economic strain, undermines parental effectiveness, making mothers and fathers harsher, more depressed, less involved, less consistent, and more embroiled in conflict

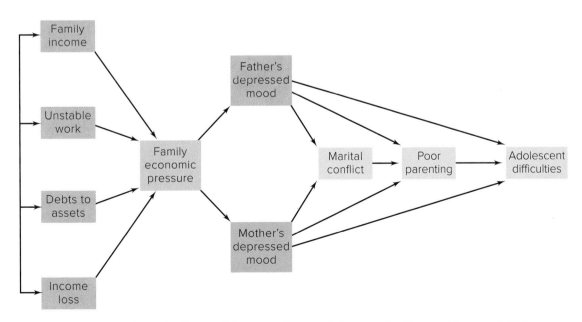

Figure 4.10   **Economic strain affects adolescent adjustment via several pathways.** (Conger et al. 1994)

(Camacho-Thompson et al., 2016). These consequences all have negative effects on adolescent adjustment, which are manifested in increases in anxiety and depression, more frequent conduct problems, diminished school performance, and less prosocial behavior (Carlo, Padilla-Walker, & Day, 2011; Lee, Wickrama, & Simons, 2013). Poor adolescents are more likely to be exposed to violence, to feel more alienated from school, and to be exposed to high levels of stress.

Studies of families living in poverty also tell us what parents living in poor neighborhoods can do to help protect their children from the adverse consequences of growing up in poor inner-city or rural neighborhoods (Brody, Stoneman, & Flor, 1996). Families fare better when they have adequate sources of social support (Taylor & Roberts, 1995) and when they have strong ties to religious institutions (Brody, Stoneman, & Flor, 1996). Two specific sets of family management strategies employed by parents in poor neighborhoods seem to work: those that attempt to strengthen the adolescent's competence through effective child rearing within the home environment or through involving the child in positive activities outside the home, and those that attempt to minimize the child's exposure to dangers in the neighborhood (Crosnoe, Mistry, & Elder, 2002). Although adolescents in poor neighborhoods benefit from consistent parental monitoring—perhaps even from monitoring that is more vigilant than that used by families in more advantaged communities—they do not thrive when their parents exercise excessive control (Rekker et al., 2017).

Homeless Adolescents According to the National Runaway Safeline (2018), in the United States on any given night, 1.3 million adolescents are living on the streets, often in abandoned buildings and frequently with strangers. Many runaway youth eventually return home, but a very large number do not. Teenagers are more likely to be homeless than any other age group.

Many teenagers become homeless because their families fall into financial ruin (due to unemployment, parental mental illness, or as a consequence of domestic violence) and lose their home. Other homeless adolescents have run away in order to escape family problems, including physical, emotional, and sexual abuse. And many teenagers became homeless after being released from foster care or incarceration without any provision for their postrelease living arrangements. Moving to a shelter is often not a possibility because many shelters do not accept unaccompanied teenagers (National Conference of State Legislatures, 2016).

Studies find that the population of runaway youth is 75% female (including many pregnant adolescents), most often between the ages of 12 and 17, and includes a large proportion of lesbian, gay, bisexual, transgender, and questioning (LGBTQ) teens—in some studies, as many as 40% of homeless youth have been sexual-minority

On any given night, more than a million American adolescents are living on the streets. SW Productions/Photodisc/Getty Images

adolescents. It is hard to generalize about the racial composition of the homeless adolescent population because this varies regionally as a function of the larger population. Nonetheless, it is estimated that about one-third of homeless adolescents nationally are Black, which is twice the proportion of Black youth in the general population; it is also estimated that Latinx adolescents are significantly less likely than other teenagers to be homeless. Homeless youth are more likely than other adolescents to engage in high-risk behaviors, including drug use, unprotected sex, and sex with multiple partners, and to suffer from a range of health problems, including depression, suicidal ideation, and poor nutrition (Gewirtz O'Brien et al., 2020; National Conference of State Legislatures, 2016; Tyler, Schmitz, & Ray, 2018).

Although many states have enacted policies to protect and support homeless teenagers, the extent of these services falls far short of the need for them. The consequences of homelessness can be dire. Rates of illness, poor nutrition, mental health problems, and substance abuse are significantly higher among homeless teenagers than in the general population. Disruptions in schooling are common, which makes it less likely that homeless adolescents will finish high school and become gainfully employed. Many homeless teenagers resort to dealing drugs or exchanging sex for food, clothing, or shelter. So-called "survival sex" is especially common among LGBTQ youth, who are more likely to be abused when they live in adult shelters and victimized when they are living on the street.

Special Family Forms

Diversity in family forms is also reflected in the sizable numbers of adolescents who are raised by adoptive parents, lesbian and gay parents, and foster parents. Although there isn't nearly as much research on teenagers growing up under these circumstances, it seems safe to conclude that there is plenty of variability in patterns of development among adolescents from these households, just as there is among those in more common home environments.

Adolescents and Adoption   Studies of the psychological development of adolescents who have been adopted have yielded mixed and often contradictory results. Adopted adolescents are as securely attached to their parents as nonadopted peers (Torres-Gomez, Alonso-Arbiol, & Gallarin, 2020). And although adopted individuals report relatively higher rates of psychological difficulties, poorer school performance, and fewer close friendships, the magnitude of the difference between adopted and nonadopted adolescents is small (Askeland et al., 2017; DeLuca, Claxton, & van Dulmen, 2018). One reason for the mixed results and relatively modest effects is that there is a good deal of variability among adopted adolescents in their feelings about being adopted. Adopted adolescents who are preoccupied with having been adopted are relatively more alienated from and mistrustful of their adoptive parents (Grotevant et al., 2017; Kohler, Grotevant, & McRoy, 2002).

Adolescents with Lesbian or Gay Parents   Although the right of same-sex couples to legally marry is now guaranteed under U.S. law, in many states a parent's sexual orientation may be a consideration in adoption, custody, and parental visitation decisions, in part because of concerns about the impact of living with a lesbian or gay parent. These concerns are unwarranted. There is no evidence whatsoever that children or adolescents with lesbian or gay parents are psychologically different from those with straight parents, a finding that has now been replicated numerous times, across many different domains of psychological development, including gender identity and sexual orientation (Farr, 2017; McConnachie et al., 2021). Importantly, the parenting practices that have been shown to predict adolescent adjustment in general have been shown to have similar beneficial effects in families in which adolescents had been adopted by gay or lesbian parents. In the words of one expert:

> *More than 25 years of research on the offspring of nonheterosexual parents has yielded results of remarkable clarity. Regardless of whether researchers have studied the offspring of divorced lesbian and gay parents or those born to lesbian and gay parents, their findings have been similar. Regardless of whether researchers have studied children or adolescents, they have reported similar results. Regardless of whether investigators have examined sexual identity, self-esteem, adjustment, or qualities of social relationships, the results have been remarkably consistent. In study after study, the offspring of lesbian and gay parents have been found to be at least as well adjusted overall as those of other parents.* (Patterson, 2009, p. 732)

There is no evidence that adolescents raised by gay or lesbian parents are psychologically any different from those raised by straight parents. Dragon Images/Shutterstock

Adolescents in Foster Care   According to recent estimates, about 175,000 American teenagers are in foster care. **Foster care** is a broad term that refers to a placement in a temporary living arrangement when the adolescent's parents are not able to provide care, nurturance, or safety (Pinderhughes et al., 2007). Such placements can be with members of the extended family, nonrelatives, or in group homes. Although we tend to think of foster homes as living arrangements for younger children, nearly one-third of young people in foster care enter into their foster home as adolescents. Moreover, because adolescents are less likely to be adopted than younger children, teenagers tend to remain in foster care longer.

Adolescents generally enter the foster care system for one of two reasons: parental maltreatment (when the adolescent's well-being or safety is endangered) or delinquency (when an adolescent's parents are unable to provide the supervision necessary to keep their teenager from violating the law). Adolescents who have spent time in foster care are at relatively greater risk for emotional and behavioral problems, some of which are the product of the abuse or neglect that necessitated their removal from their biological parents' home (maltreatment frequently causes psychological problems), some of which may have made it too difficult for their parents to adequately care for them (in which case the adolescent may be placed in a therapeutic environment designed for teenagers with psychological problems), and some of which may result from the foster care placement itself (e.g., placement in a group home increases the adolescent's risk for delinquency) (DeLuca, Claxton, & van Dulmen, 2018; Ryan et al., 2008).

foster care
A placement in a temporary living arrangement when a child's parents are not able to provide care, nurturance, or safety.

Many adolescents move in and out of different placements, back and forth between their parents' home and a foster care placement or between different foster care arrangements; frequent disruptions in living arrangements can lead to behavioral problems (Fisher et al., 2011). After a period of time in foster care, adolescents are either reunified with their biological parents or adopted by someone other than their parents or, if they are old enough, declared independent. As you can imagine, making the transition to independent adulthood—already a challenge for many youth who grew up in stable and supportive family environments—is even more difficult for adolescents whose lives have been so disrupted and who do not have parents on whom they can rely for support. Adolescents who have been in foster care are at higher risk for homelessness than other youth (Fowler, Toro, & Miles, 2009).

The Importance of the Family in Adolescent Development

As you have seen, there is considerable diversity among families with adolescents—diversity in background, in income, in parenting style, and in household composition. Yet no factor influences adolescent adjustment more than the quality of relationships at home. As one team of experts concluded on the basis of a comprehensive study of the lives, behavior, and health of 90,000 American teenagers:

> *Across all of the health outcomes examined, the results*
> *point to the importance of family and the home environment*
> *for protecting adolescents from harm. What emerges*
> *most consistently as protective is the teenager's feeling*
> *of connectedness with parents and family. Feeling loved*
> *and cared for by parents matters in a big way.*
> (Blum & Rinehart, 2000, p. 31)

Although this study was conducted more than 20 years ago, no research conducted since that time has challenged this conclusion. Study after study finds that adolescents who believe their parents or guardians are there for them—caring, involved, and accepting—are healthier, happier, and more competent than their peers, however health, happiness, or competence is assessed. This conclusion holds true regardless of the adolescent's age, sex, ethnicity, social class, or country and across all types of families, whether married or divorced, single-parent or two-parent, rich or poor (Murry & Lippold, 2018; Steinberg, 2001). This has led many psychologists, including myself, to call for widespread efforts to increase the quality of parenting that children and adolescents receive as a way of preventing emotional and behavioral problems and promoting healthy development (Kumpfer & Alvarado, 2003). As I have written elsewhere, we know what the basic principles of good parenting are (Steinberg, 2005). The challenge facing us is to figure out how best to disseminate this information to the people who need it most—parents.

Despite the tremendous growth and psychological development that take place as individuals leave childhood on the road toward adulthood, despite society's pressures on young people to grow up fast, despite all the technological and social innovations that have transformed family life, and contrary to claims that parents don't really make a difference (that by adolescence, parents' influence is overshadowed by the peer group or social media), adolescents continue to need the love, support, and guidance of adults who genuinely care about their development and well-being. Being raised in the presence of caring and committed adults is one of the most important advantages a young person can have in life. Having parents who provide the valuable combination of warmth and support for the development of autonomy even facilitates adolescents' departure from home and their successful transition into adulthood (Akin et al., 2020; Gillespie, 2020). Although parental love may be expressed in different ways in different parts of the world, its importance for healthy adolescent development is unquestionable, regardless of cultural context (Buehler, 2020).

5

Peer Groups

The Origins of Adolescent Peer Groups in Contemporary Society

Changes in the Size of the Youth Population

Why Peer Groups Are Necessary in Today's World

The Nature of Adolescent Peer Groups

Cliques and Crowds

Changes in Clique and Crowd Structure Over Time

Adolescents and Their Crowds

The Social Map of Adolescence

Crowds as Reference Groups

Adolescents and Their Cliques

Similarity Among Clique Members

Common Interests Among Friends

Similarity Between Friends: Selection or Socialization?

Popularity, Rejection, and Bullying

Determinants of Popularity and Rejection

Relational Aggression

Bullies and Victims

Cyberbullying

The Peer Group and Psychosocial Development

Flashpop/Getty Images

It is about 8:00 A.M. A group of teenagers congregates in the hallway in front of their first-period classroom, discussing their plans for the weekend. As the first-period bell sounds, they enter the classroom and take their seats. For the next 4 hours (until there is a break in their schedule for lunch), they will attend class in groups of about 25 adolescents to 1 adult.

At lunch, the group meets again to talk about the weekend. They have about 45 minutes until the first afternoon period begins. After lunch, they spend another 2 hours in class—again, in groups of about 25 adolescents and 1 adult. The school day ends, the group convenes yet again, and they go to someone's house to hang out for the rest of the day. Everyone's parents are working; they are on their own. At about 6:00 P.M., they disperse and head home for dinner. Some have plans to meet up later that night. Several will talk on the phone. Virtually all of them will text. And they will see one another first thing the next morning.

Adolescents in modern society spend a remarkable amount of time with people their own age. High school students in the United States and Europe spend twice as much of their time each week with peers as with parents or other adults—not even counting time in class (Dijkstra & Veenstra, 2011).

Time spent with peers increases steadily over the course of adolescence (Lam, McHale, & Crouter, 2014). It's easy to see why: Adolescents' moods are most positive when they are with their friends, time spent with friends becomes more rewarding over the course of adolescence, and teenagers' moods become more positive over the course of the week, as the weekend approaches (Larson & Richards, 1998).

American society is highly age segregated. From the time youngsters stop spending their full day at home—certainly by age 5, but for many of those in day care, as early as the first year of life—until they graduate from high school at age 18 or so, they are grouped with children their own age. Other than relatives, they have little extended contact with older or younger people. Age grouping carries over into after-school, weekend, and vacation activities. In contemporary society, **peer groups**—groups of people who are roughly the same age—are one of the most important contexts in which adolescents spend time. The significance of peer groups gives adolescence in contemporary society some of its most distinctive features.

The Origins of Adolescent Peer Groups in Contemporary Society

Contact between adolescents and their peers is found in all cultures, of course. But not all societies have peer groups that are as narrowly defined and age segregated as those in contemporary society (Brown, 2004).

The spread of compulsory education was a major factor in the development of peer groups as we know them today. Educators first developed the idea of free public education, with students grouped by age—a practice known as **age grading**—in the middle of the nineteenth century. In doing so, they established an arrangement that would encourage the development and maintenance of age-segregated peer groups. It was not until the second quarter of the twentieth century, however, that most adolescents were directly affected by educational age grouping. Attending elementary school was common before 1900, but until 1930 or so, high school was a luxury available only to the affluent. Adolescent peer groups based on friendships formed in school were not prevalent until well into the twentieth century.

peer groups
Groups of individuals of approximately the same age.

age grading
The process of grouping individuals within social institutions on the basis of age.

Changes in the Size of the Youth Population

Perhaps the most important factor influencing the rise of adolescent peer groups in contemporary society was the rapid growth of the teenage population between 1955

Contemporary society is very age-graded. Even when they are in activities outside school, adolescents tend to be with same-aged peers. Sergey Novikov/Shutterstock

and 1975. Following the end of World War II, many parents wanted to have children as soon as possible, creating the postwar **baby boom.** The products of this baby boom became adolescents during the 1960s and early 1970s, creating an "adolescent boom" for about 15 years. The size of the population ages 15–19 nearly doubled between 1955 and 1975.

This trend turned downward in 1975. But during the last decade of the twentieth century—when the products of the baby boom began raising adolescents of their own—the size of the teenage population began increasing once again. Today, approximately 13% of Americans (about 42 million people) are between ages 10 and 19 (U.S. Census Bureau, 2020a). Keep in mind, though, that patterns of change in the size of the adolescent population vary considerably around the world, mainly because of different birth rates (see Figure 5.1).

Social scientists track the size of the adolescent population for several reasons. First, changes in the number of adolescents may warrant changes in the allocation of funds for social services, educational programs, and health care, since adolescents' needs are not the same as those of children or adults.

Second, changes in the size of the adolescent population have implications for understanding the behavior of cohorts. A cohort is a group of individuals born during a particular period, such as the baby boomers (born in the late 1940s and early to mid-1950s), "Gen X" (born in the early 1970s), the "Millennials" (the children of the baby boomers, born in the 1980s and early 1990s, also known as "Generation Y"), or "Generation Z" (born between the mid-1990s and mid-2000s) (see Table 5.1).

Baby boomers, for example, were members of a very crowded cohort. During their adolescence, they encountered a lot of competition for places in college, jobs, and so on. The size of this cohort also meant that it could attract a great deal of public attention, from politicians to advertisers. In contrast, members of Gen X, who were adolescents in the late 1980s and early 1990s, were members of a much smaller cohort, with less competition among individuals but far less clout. Because the Gen Z cohort, today's teenagers, is considerably larger than Gen X, it will likely be much more influential.

Why Peer Groups Are Necessary in Today's World

In less industrialized societies, political, economic, and social institutions revolve around the family. Occupation, choice of spouse, place of residence, treatment under society's laws, and participation in governing the community are all tied to who one's relatives are. Individuals' family ties determine whom they can trade with and how much they pay for various commodities. In short, how adults are expected to behave depends on which family they come

Age grading in schools has been a major contributor to the rise of adolescent peer groups. LeoPatrizi/E+/Getty Images

from; people from different families are often expected to live by very different expectations and regulations.

In contemporary societies, things are quite different. Modernization has eroded much of the family's importance as a political, social, and economic unit. Generally speaking, in modern society, all individuals are expected to learn the same set of norms because the rules governing behavior apply equally to all members of the community.

Under these circumstances, it is not wise to limit the socialization of adolescents to the family because doing so does not ensure that all youngsters will learn the same set of norms. Teaching is better done in schools than left up to individual families. As the family has become a less important political and economic institution, this has required a change in the way in which adolescents are prepared for adulthood. Not only has modernization created age groups, it also has made them absolutely necessary. Without systematic age grouping in schools, it would be impossible to prepare young people for adulthood. And because age grouping in schools carries over into activities outside of school, the need for universal school-based education has created age-segregated peer groups.

Some theorists do not see this as a bad thing. They believe that as society has become more technologically advanced, adolescents have come to play a valuable role in preparing one another for adulthood. Moreover, recent studies have found that adolescents engage in more exploratory behavior, behave more prosocially, and learn faster when they are with their peers than when they are by themselves (Silva et al., 2016; Van Hoorn, Van Dijk, Güroglu, and Crone, 2016).

baby boom
The period following World War II, during which the number of infants born was extremely large.

YOUNG IN THE WORLD: CHANGING PROPORTIONS IN 1980, 2015, AND 2050

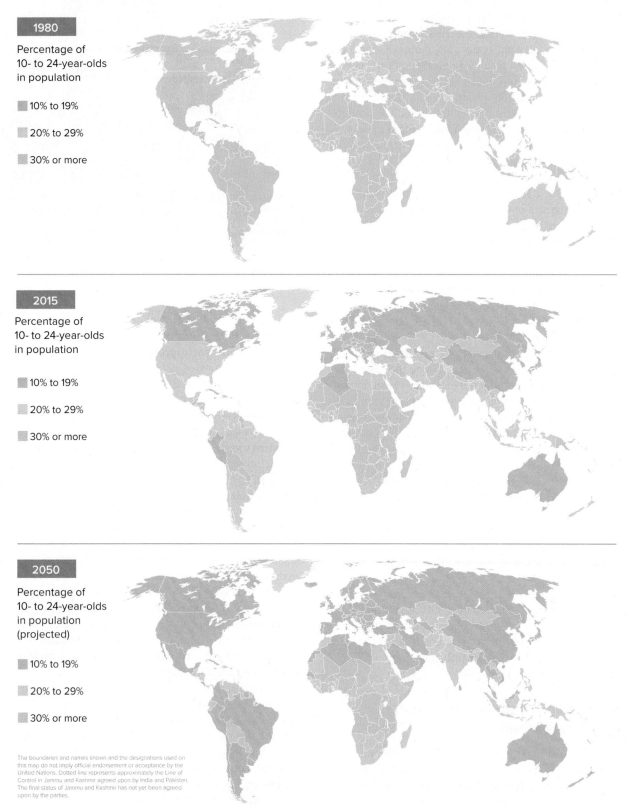

Figure 5.1   **The proportion of the population that is adolescent varies around the world: It is highest in developing countries, especially in Africa, and lowest in highly industrialized countries, such as Japan. This trend is expected to continue.** (United Nations, 2014)

Table 5.1 Cohorts, periods, and ages

Cohort Name	Became Young Adults (16–30)	Key Events at That Time	in Census Year											
			1900	1910	1920	1930	1940	1950	1960	1970	1980	1990	2000	2010
Generation Z	2002–2025	Internet explosion; "Great Recession"; COVID-19 pandemic												16–24
Millennials	1992–2015	Information era: economic growth and global politics											16–24	25–30
Gen X	1982–2005	Reagan era: economic polarization, political conservatism										16–24	25–30	
Late baby boomers	1972–1995	Watergate era: economic recession, employment restructuring									16–24	25–30		
Early baby boomers	1962–1985	Hippies: social movements, campus revolts								16–24	25–30			
Happy days generation	1952–1975	Family and conformity: baby boom and Cold War/McCarthy era							16–24	25–30				
Happy days/greatest generation	1942–1965	Family and conformity: baby boom and Cold War/McCarthy era						16–24	25–30					
Greatest generation/children of Great Depression	1932–1955	Hard times: economic depression and World War II					16–24	25–30						
Children of Great Depression	1922–1945	Hard times: economic depression and World War II				16–24	25–30							
Lost Generation	1912–1935	World War I and Roaring Twenties, Prohibition			16–24	25–30								
…	1902–1925	Age of invention and World War I		16–24	25–30									
…	1892–1915	Age of invention, urbanization	16–24	25–30										

postfigurative cultures
Cultures in which the socialization of young people is done primarily by adults.

cofigurative cultures
Cultures in which young people are socialized both by adults and by each other.

prefigurative cultures
Cultures in which society is changing so quickly that adults are frequently socialized by young people, rather than the reverse.

According to the anthropologist Margaret Mead (1978), the way in which young people are best socialized for adulthood depends on how fast their society is changing. In some cultures, cultural change is so slow that what a child needs to know to function as an adult changes very little over time. Mead called these **postfigurative cultures**; they socialize children almost exclusively through contact with the culture's elders because the way in which older generations have lived is almost identical to the way in which subsequent generations will live.

Imagine, for a moment, growing up in a world in which you had to know only what your grandparents knew in order to survive. In this age of smartphones, social media, and wireless Internet, growing up in a world in which very little changes over 50 years seems almost impossible to imagine. A little more than 50 years ago, color televisions had just become commonplace in American homes, a person had just walked on the moon for the first time, and the first automatic teller machine (ATM) was unveiled. Yet, strange as it may seem to us now, most societies until fairly recently have been postfigurative. In other words, until fairly recently, adolescents could learn exclusively from their elders what they needed to know to be successful adults.

During the past 100 years, contemporary societies have shifted away from being postfigurative cultures. They have become **cofigurative cultures**, in which socialization of young people is accomplished not merely through contact between children and their elders but also through contact between people of the same age. In cofigurative cultures, society changes so quickly that much of what parents are able to teach their children may be outdated by the time their children become adults. Today, we live in a cofigurative society. For adolescents in contemporary America, peers have become role models as important as parents and grandparents. As a result of such rapid change, adolescents increasingly need to turn to members of their own generation for advice, guidance, and information.

If you were a teenager living in a postfigurative culture, you might ask your grandparents for advice about how to hunt or prepare a meal in a hurry. But if you were a teenager in today's cofigurative culture, to whom would you turn for advice about how to post a video on TikTok or set up a virtual party on Zoom? Would you turn to your friends, who have grown up with the Internet, or to your grandparents, who probably are less experienced with the latest technologies than you are?

Mead believed that as cofigurative cultures changed even more rapidly, they would be replaced by **prefigurative**

In prefigurative cultures, society changes so quickly that young people often teach adults, rather than the reverse. Chaay_Tee/Shutterstock

cultures, in which young people would become adults' teachers. We already may be living in a prefigurative culture. Instead of parents asking, "Why can't Johnny read?" teenagers ask, "Why can't Mom and Dad figure out how to set up their new iPhones?"

Do these analyses mean that the adolescents of the future will cease to profit from having close relationships with adults? Of course not. Young people will always need the support, affection, and advice of their elders. But understanding how peer groups have been made necessary by modernization casts the issue of age segregation in a new light.

The Nature of Adolescent Peer Groups

When you look at a typical elementary school playground, it's clear that peer groups are an important feature of the social world of childhood. But even though peer groups exist well before adolescence, during the teenage years they change in significance and structure. Four specific developments stand out (Brown & Larson, 2009).

In What Ways Do Peer Groups Change? First, there is a sharp increase during adolescence in the sheer amount of time individuals spend with their peers and in the relative time they spend in the company of peers versus adults. If we count school as a setting in which adolescents are mainly with people their age, well over half of the typical American adolescent's waking hours are spent with peers, as opposed to only 15% with adults—including their parents (most of the remaining time is spent alone or

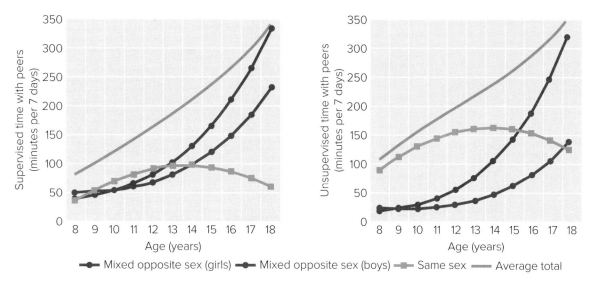

Figure 5.2 Both supervised (left) and unsupervised (right) time with peers increase during adolescence. The increase in the amount of time that girls spend with peers is especially steep. (Lam, McHale, & Crouter, 2014)

with a combination of adults and peers). Indeed, during the transition into adolescence, there is a dramatic drop in the amount of time adolescents spend with parents; for boys, this is mainly replaced by time spent alone, whereas for girls, it is replaced by time alone and time with friends (Dijkstra & Veenstra, 2011).

Second, during adolescence, peer groups function much more often without adult supervision than they do during childhood, partly because adolescents are more mobile and partly because they seek, and are granted, more independence (Dijkstra & Veenstra, 2011). As you can see from Figure 5.2, both supervised and unsupervised time with peers, and, especially, with opposite-sex peers, increase steadily throughout adolescence (Lam, McHale, & Crouter, 2014). Groups of younger children typically play in the presence of adults or in activities organized or supervised by adults (e.g., organized sports), whereas adolescents are granted far more independence.

Third, during adolescence, increasingly more contact with peers is between males and females (Lam, McHale, & Crouter, 2014). During childhood, peer groups are highly sex segregated. During adolescence, however, an increasingly larger proportion of a person's significant others are peers of the other sex (Dijkstra & Veenstra, 2011; Mehta & Strough, 2009). The shift from same-sex peer groups to mixed-sex groups tends to occur around the beginning of high school (Lam, McHale, & Crouter, 2014).

Finally, whereas children's peer relationships are limited mainly to relatively small groups—at most, three or four children at a time—adolescence marks the emergence of larger collectives of peers, called **crowds** (Brown & Larson, 2009). In junior high school cafeterias, for example, the "populars" sit in one section of the room, the "brains" in another, and the "jocks" in a third. These crowds typically develop their own minicultures, characterized by particular styles of dressing, talking, and behaving (Chen, 2012).

What Causes Peer Groups to Change? These changes in peer relations have their origins in the biological, cognitive, and social transitions of adolescence (Dijkstra & Veenstra, 2011). Puberty stimulates adolescents' interest in romantic relationships and distances them from their parents, which helps to explain why adolescents' social networks increasingly include more other-sex peers and fewer adults. The cognitive changes of adolescence permit a more sophisticated understanding of social relationships, which allows the sort of abstract categorization that leads to grouping individuals into crowds. And changes in social definition may stimulate changes in peer relations as a sort of adaptive response: The larger, more anonymous social setting of the secondary school forces adolescents to seek out individuals whom they perceive as having common interests and values, perhaps as a way of re-creating the smaller, more intimate groups of childhood (Brown, 2004). Instead of floundering in a large, impersonal high school cafeteria, someone who belongs to the cheerleader crowd, or even someone who is one of the "nerds," may head directly for a place at a familiar table.

cliques
Small, tightly knit groups of between 2 and 12 friends, generally of the same sex and age.

Cliques and Crowds

Adolescents' peer groups are organized around two related, but different, structures, called "cliques" and "crowds" (Brown & Larson, 2009). **Cliques** are small groups of between 2 and 12 individuals—the average is about 5 or 6—generally of the same sex and, of course, the same age. Cliques can be defined by common activities (e.g., the football players or a group of students who study together regularly) or simply by friendship (e.g., a group

Adolescents usually belong to at least one clique, a close group of about a half dozen friends, usually of the same age and sex. Shutterstock

of girls who have lunch together every day or a group of boys who have grown up together).

The clique provides the main social context in which adolescents interact with one another. It's the social setting in which adolescents hang out, talk to each other, and form close friendships. Some cliques are more closed to outsiders than others (that is, the members are more "cliquish"), but virtually all cliques are small enough that the members feel they know each other well and appreciate each other more than people outside the clique do (Brown & Larson, 2009).

Cliques are quite different in structure and purpose from crowds. **Crowds** are "reputation-based clusters of youths, whose function in part is to help solidify young people's social and personal identity" (Brown & Larson, 2009, p. 85). In contemporary American high schools, typical crowds include "jocks," "brains," "nerds," "populars," and "druggies." The labels for these crowds may vary from school to school ("nerds" versus "geeks," "populars" versus "preps"), but their generic presence is commonplace around the world, and you can probably recognize these different types of crowds from your own school experience (Delsing et al., 2007; Sim & Yeo, 2012). Unlike

crowds
Large, loosely organized groups of young people, composed of several cliques and typically organized around a common shared activity.

cliques, crowds are not settings for adolescents' intimate interactions or friendships but instead serve three broad purposes: to locate adolescents (to themselves and to others) within the social structure of the school, to channel adolescents toward some peers and away from others, and to provide contexts that reward certain lifestyles and disparage others (Brown & Larson, 2009).

The key point is that membership in a crowd is based mainly on reputation and stereotype, rather than on actual friendship or social interaction. This is very different from membership in a clique, which, by definition, hinges on shared activity and friendship. In concrete terms, and perhaps ironically, an adolescent does not have to actually have "brains" as friends or hang around with "brainy" students to be one of the "brains." If he dresses like a "brain," acts like a "brain," and takes AP courses, then he is a "brain" as far as his crowd membership goes.

The fact that crowd membership is based on reputation and stereotype has important implications. It can be very difficult for adolescents who—if they don't change their reputation early on in high school—may find themselves stuck, at least in the eyes of others, in a crowd they don't want to belong to or even see themselves as a part of (Brown, Von Bank, & Steinberg, 2008).

According to some estimates, close to half of high school students are associated with one crowd, about

Early adolescence is often marked by the transition from same-sex peer groups to mixed-sex peer groups. Pamela Moore/Getty Images

one-third are associated with two or more crowds, and about one-sixth do not clearly fit into any crowd (Brown, 2004). Although an adolescent's closest friends are almost always members of the same clique, some of them may belong to a different crowd, especially when one crowd is close in lifestyle to the other (Urberg et al., 1995). For example, a "brain" will have some friends who are also "brains" and some who are "nerds" but few, if any, who are "druggies" (Brown, Mory, & Kinney, 1994).

More importantly, crowds are not simply clusters of cliques; the two different structures serve entirely different purposes. Because the clique is based on activity and friendship, it is the peer setting in which adolescents learn social skills: how to be a good friend, how to communicate effectively, how to be a leader, how to enjoy someone else's company, or how to break off a friendship that is no longer satisfying. In contrast, because crowds are based more on reputation and stereotype than on interaction, they probably contribute more to the adolescent's sense of identity and self-conception—for better and for worse—than to his or her actual social development.

Changes in Clique and Crowd Structure Over Time

There are important changes in the structure of cliques and crowds during the adolescent years, driven in large measure by the increased importance of romantic relationships (Connolly, Furman, & Konarski, 2000; Kuttler & La Greca, 2004).

How Romance Changes the Peer Group During early adolescence, adolescents' activities revolve around

same-sex cliques. They are not yet involved in partying and typically spend their leisure time with a small group of friends, playing sports, talking, or simply hanging out.

Somewhat later, as adolescents become more interested in one another romantically—but before romantic relationships actually begin—boys' and girls' cliques come together. This is clearly a transitional stage. Boys and girls may go to parties or hang out, but the time they spend together mainly involves interaction with peers of the same sex. When young teenagers are still uncomfortable about dealing with members of the other sex, this context provides an opportunity in which they can learn more about peers of the other sex without having to be intimate or risk losing face. It is not unusual, for example, at young adolescents' first mixed-sex parties for groups of boys and girls to position themselves at other sides of a room, watching each other but seldom interacting.

As some adolescents become interested in romantic relationships, part of the group begins to split off into mixed-sex cliques, while other individuals remain in the group but in same-sex cliques. This shift is usually led by the clique leaders, with other clique members following along.

For instance, a clique of boys whose main activity is playing basketball may discover that one of the guys they look up to has become more interested in going to mixed-sex parties Saturday nights than in hanging out and playing video games with the group. Over time, they will begin to follow his lead, and their all-male activities will become more infrequent. A study of middle school dances over the course of the academic year found that the integration of boys' and girls' peer groups increased over time but that this occurred mainly among physically attractive adolescents (no surprise because being good-looking contributes to status in the peer group) (Pellegrini & Long, 2007).

During middle adolescence, mixed-sex and mixed-age cliques become more prevalent (Molloy et al., 2014), and in time, the peer group becomes composed entirely of mixed-sex cliques (Cooksey, Mott, & Neubauer, 2002). One clique might consist of the drama students—male and female students who know each other from school plays. Another might be composed of four girls and four boys who like to smoke weed. Preppies—male and female—might make up a third. Interestingly, the transition from same-sex groups to mixed-sex groups is associated with an increase in alcohol use among males and in both alcohol and drug use among females, most likely because the activities that draw males and females together often involve partying (Poulin, Denault, & Pedersen, 2011).

During late adolescence, peer crowds begin to disintegrate. The importance of the peer group starts to wane somewhat. As students approach their senior year and feel more secure about themselves, there is a decline in the extent to which they say they want to improve their social skills and the quality of their relationships (Makara & Madjar, 2015). Pairs of adolescents who see themselves as couples begin to split off from the activities of the

Peer crowds play an important role in defining the adolescent's place within the social hierarchy of the school. E+/Getty Images

larger group. The larger peer group is replaced by loosely associated sets of couples. Adolescents begin to shift some of their attention away from friends and toward romantic partners (Kuttler & La Greca, 2004). Groups of couples may go out together from time to time, but the feeling of being in a crowd has disappeared. This pattern—in which the couple becomes the focus of social activity—persists into adulthood.

The structure of the peer group changes during adolescence in a way that parallels the adolescent's development of intimacy: As the adolescent develops increasing facility in intimate relationships, the peer group moves from the familiarity of same-sex activities to contact with other-sex peers, but mainly in the safety of the larger group. It is only after adolescents have been slowly socialized into dating roles—primarily by modeling their higher-status peers—that the safety of numbers is no longer needed and adolescents begin pairing off.

Changes in Crowds   There also are changes in peer crowds during this time. Many of these changes reflect the growing cognitive sophistication of the adolescent. For example, as adolescents mature intellectually, they come to define crowds more in terms of abstract, global characteristics ("preppies," "nerds," "jocks") than in terms of concrete, behavioral features ("the ballet crowd," "the Fortnite crowd," "the kids who play basketball on 114th Street") (Dijkstra & Veenstra, 2011).

As you know, this shift from concrete to abstract is a general feature of cognitive development in adolescence. In addition, as adolescents become more cognitively capable, they become more consciously aware of the crowd structure of their school and their place in it (Brown, 2004). Over the course of adolescence, the crowd structure also becomes more differentiated, more permeable, and less hierarchical, which allows adolescents more freedom to change crowds and enhance their status (Brown, 2004; Horn, 2003). In early adolescence, a school may have only two broad crowds (e.g., "normals" and "losers"). By high school, there may be several different ways to be "normal" ("populars," "jocks," "average") and several different ways to be a "loser" ("brains," "nerds," "burnouts").

The Waxing and Waning of Crowds   As crowds become more salient influences on adolescents' view of their social world, they come to play an increasingly important role in structuring adolescents' social behavior (Brown & Larson, 2009). By ninth grade, there is nearly universal agreement among students about their school's crowd structure, and the strength of peer group influence is very high. Between ninth and 12th grades, however, the significance of the crowd structure begins to decline, and the salience of peer pressure wanes.

In one study, students were presented with several scenarios asking if it was all right to exclude someone from a school activity (cheerleading, basketball, student council) because the person was a member of a certain crowd ("jock," "gothic," "preppie") (Horn, 2003). They were also asked whether it was acceptable to deny individuals resources (e.g., a scholarship) on the basis of their crowd membership. Consistent with the decline in the salience of peer crowds between middle and late adolescence, 9th-graders were more likely than older students to say that excluding someone from an activity on the basis of his or her crowd was all right. Students of all ages agreed that it was less acceptable to deny students resources because of crowd membership (which virtually all students viewed as immoral) than to exclude them from an activity (which was less often seen as a moral issue).

Just as the changes in the structure of cliques play a role in the development of intimacy, changes in the salience of crowds play an important role in identity development. Adolescence is frequently a time for experimentation with different roles and identities. During the early adolescent years, before adolescents have "found" themselves, the crowd provides an important basis for self-definition (Newman & Newman, 2001). By locating themselves within the crowd structure of their school—through clothing, language, or choice of hangouts—adolescents wear "badges" that say "This is who I am." At a time when adolescents may not actually know just who they are, associating with a crowd provides them with a rudimentary sense of identity.

As adolescents become more secure in their identity as individuals, the need for affiliation with a crowd diminishes. By the time they have reached high school, older adolescents are likely to feel that remaining a part of a crowd stifles their sense of identity and self expression. The breakup of the larger peer group in late adolescence may both foreshadow and reflect the emergence of each adolescent's unique and coherent sense of self (Brown & Larson, 2009).

making the personal connection

Think back to your own high school experience. What were the major crowds in your school? What common characteristics did you share with the people who were in your clique?

Adolescents and Their Crowds
The Social Map of Adolescence

A helpful scheme for mapping the social world of adolescence classifies crowds along two dimensions: how involved they are in the institutions controlled by adults, such as school and extracurricular activities, and how

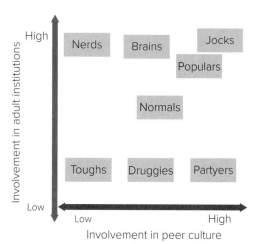

Figure 5.3 **A model for mapping the social world of adolescent peer groups.** (From Brown, 1990)

involved they are in the informal, peer culture (Brown, 1990) (see Figure 5.3).

"Jocks" and "populars," for example, are very involved in the peer culture, but they are also very involved in the institutions valued by adults (sports and school organizations, for example). "Brains" and "nerds," in contrast, are also involved in adult-controlled organizations (in their case, academics), but they tend to be less involved in the peer culture. "Partyers" are on the opposite side of the map from "nerds": These adolescents are very involved in the peer culture but are less so in adult institutions. "Burnouts" and adolescents who are members of delinquent gangs are not involved in either the peer culture or adult institutions. Other crowds, such as "normals" or "druggies," fall somewhere between these extremes.

making the cultural connection

In the United States, athletic ability, good looks, and money all contribute to popularity. Do you think the personal traits that adolescents value differ in different parts of the world, or are these likely to be important everywhere? If you have classmates who grew up somewhere other than the United States, ask them what made people popular in their high school.

Crowds as Reference Groups

Knowing where an adolescent fits into the social system of the school can tell us a lot about the person's behavior and values. This is because crowds contribute to the definition of norms and standards for such things as clothing, leisure, and tastes in music. Being a "jock" means more than simply being involved in athletics; it means wearing certain types of clothes, listening to certain types of

In multiethnic high schools, peer groups often divide along ethnic lines. Daniel M Ernst/Shutterstock

music, spending Saturday nights in certain spots, and using a particular slang.

Another way of putting this is that adolescents' crowds serve as **reference groups.** They provide their members with an identity in the eyes of others. Adolescents judge one another on the basis of the company they keep, and they become branded on the basis of the people they hang out with. Such labels as "jocks," "brains," "populars," "druggies," and "skaters" serve as shorthand notations—accurate or inaccurate—to describe what someone is like as a person, what he or she holds as important, and how he or she spends time. Individuals who are members of more unconventional crowds (e.g., "hip hoppers," "metalheads") engage in more problem behavior, whereas those who are in more conventional ones (e.g., "normals," "jocks") report less (Doornwaard et al., 2012).

Crowd Membership and Adolescent Identity

Crowd membership is important not only because crowds are used by adolescents when talking about one another but also because membership in a crowd is often the basis for an adolescent's own identity (Brown & Larson, 2009). A girl who hangs out with the "preppies" identifies herself as such by wearing their "uniform," shopping in their stores, and speaking their language. After a while, preppiness becomes part of her own self-concept. Or consider the boys whose clique is held together by a dislike of school. Since this attitude toward school is continuously reinforced by the clique, each boy's feelings about school become strengthened, and not liking school becomes part of each boy's identity. Even if something very positive happens at school, it

reference group

A group against which an individual compares him or herself.

becomes difficult for someone in the clique to admit that it makes him feel good about himself. Doing well on a test or receiving a compliment from a teacher is likely to be dismissed as unimportant.

Because the adolescent's peer group plays such an important role as a reference group and a source of identity, the nature of the crowd with which an adolescent affiliates is likely to have an important influence on his or her behavior, activities, and opinions about others (Brechwald & Prinstein, 2011; Pál et al., 2016). Although most adolescents feel pressure from their friends to behave in ways that are consistent with their crowd's values and goals, the specific pressure varies from one crowd to another. "Druggies" report much more pressure to misbehave, for example, than do "jocks" (Clasen & Brown, 1985).

Crowd membership can also affect the way adolescents feel about themselves. Adolescents' self-esteem is higher among students who are identified with peer groups that have relatively more status in their school (Brown, Von Bank, & Steinberg, 2008). Over the course of adolescence, symptoms of psychological distress decline among the "populars" and "jocks" but increase among the "brains" (Doornwaard et al., 2012; Prinstein & La Greca, 2002). Not surprisingly, adolescents whose peers identify them as members of low-status crowds fare better psychologically when they don't see themselves this way, but the opposite is true for adolescents whose peers label them as members of high-status crowds, where denying one's affiliation with the crowd is associated with worse mental health (Brown, Von Bank, & Steinberg, 2008).

Adolescents' behavior is affected by their crowd membership in several ways (Brechwald & Prinstein, 2011). First, adolescents often imitate the behavior of high-status peers—the crowd leaders. The socially popular girls, for example, may dress in a certain way, and the less popular ones (the "wannabes"), who want to be associated with them, follow suit. Popular students receive far more attention from others, especially from those who themselves are popular (Lansu, Cillessen, & Karremans, 2014).

Second, crowds establish social norms—values and expectations—that members strive to follow. That is, even lower-status members of a crowd influence each other by behaving in ways that identify them as members (e.g., using certain expressions when speaking), and other adolescents who want to be accepted by them conform to these standards. In potentially risky situations, teenagers are especially likely to conform to their peers when they are not sure just how to behave (Van Hoorn, Crone, & Van Leijenhorst, 2017).

Third, when crowd members behave in ways that are consistent with these norms, they are reinforced for doing so. An adolescent who dresses in a way that is consistent with a crowd's expectation may be complimented "Nice shoes, Sophie," whereas one who does not may be ignored or even made fun of with "I can't believe you're wearing those!"

Finally, when adolescents are reinforced for following a crowd's norms, they feel better about themselves and further incorporate their crowd membership into their identity. After being praised many times for her clothes by one of the popular crowd's members, for example, a girl will start to think of herself as a member of that crowd and begin to derive her identity in part from it.

Ethnicity and Crowd Membership Many of the basic distinctions among crowds that have been found in studies of predominantly white high schools (e.g., academically oriented crowds, partying crowds, deviant crowds, trendy crowds) also exist among adolescents from ethnic minority groups. There is evidence, however, that in multiethnic high schools, adolescents first divide across ethnic lines and then form into the more familiar adolescent crowds within ethnic groups. In a large multiethnic high school, there may be separate groups of Black "jocks" and white "jocks," of Latinx "populars" and Black "populars," and so on (Hardie & Tyson, 2013). In multiethnic schools, adolescents from one ethnic group are less likely to see crowd distinctions within other ethnic groups than they are within their own group. White students view their Asian classmates as members of the "Asian" crowd, whereas the Asian students see themselves as divided into "brains," "populars," and other groups.

The meaning associated with belonging to different crowds also may differ across ethnic and socioeconomic groups, although this varies considerably from school to school (Knifsend & Juvonen, 2014; Tyson, Darity, & Castellino, 2005). Although it is commonly believed that high-achieving Black students are ostracized for "acting white" (Fordham & Ogbu, 1986), many studies do not find this to be typical (e.g., Horvat & Lewis, 2003; Tyson, Darity, & Castillino, 2005). In fact, in many schools, *all* students who are highly committed to school, regardless of their ethnicity, are teased or excluded for being "nerds" or "brains," or simply for doing well in school (Schwartz, Kelly, & Duong, 2013). Similarly, in some schools, it may be admirable to be a "jock," while in others, it may be frowned upon. The values we associate with being in one crowd as opposed to another aren't the same across all school contexts.

Adolescents and Their Cliques

What draws adolescents into one clique and not another? Because cliques serve as a basis for adolescents' friendships and play an important role in their social development, many researchers have studied the determinants of clique composition.

Similarity Among Clique Members

The most important influence on the composition of cliques is similarity. Adolescents' cliques typically are composed of people who are of the same age, ethnicity, and—at least during early and middle adolescence—the same sex (Ennett & Bauman, 1996).

Age Segregation Although many adolescents have friends who are one school grade ahead or behind (Bowker & Spencer, 2010), age grouping in junior and senior high schools makes it unlikely that an individual will have friends who are substantially older or younger. A 10th-grader who is enrolled in 10th-grade English, 10th-grade math, 10th-grade history, and 10th-grade science simply does not have many opportunities to meet adolescents who are in different grades. Age segregation in adolescents' cliques appears to result mostly from the structure of schools. By way of comparison, adolescents' online friends are less similar in age than the friends they make in school (Mesch & Talmud, 2007).

Sex Segregation During early and middle adolescence, cliques also tend to be composed of adolescents of the same sex (Ennett & Bauman, 1996). This sex segregation begins in childhood and continues through most of adolescence, although it is stronger among white students than among Black students (Filardo, 1996), and it weakens later in adolescence (Mehta & Strough, 2009).

The causes of sex segregation in adolescents' cliques are more interesting than the causes of age segregation because schools seldom separate boys and girls into different classes. Why, then, do adolescent males and females separate themselves into different cliques? Social scientists who study gender and development have suggested several reasons (Maccoby, 1990).

First, cliques are formed largely on the basis of shared activities and interests. Preadolescent and early-adolescent boys and girls are interested in different things (Mehta & Strough, 2009). Not until adolescents begin dating do boys' cliques and girls' cliques mix, presumably because dating provides a basis for common activity. Consistent with this, one study of adolescents' social networks found that the proportion of other-sex friends more than doubles between sixth and 10th grades (Poulin & Pedersen, 2007). And, in keeping with the notion that this coincides with the onset of dating, the increase is especially notable among early-maturing girls, whose networks increasingly include somewhat older boys that they know outside of school. Even so, by 10th grade, most adolescents' networks are still dominated by same-sex friends, who make up about three-quarters of the average social network.

A second reason for sex segregation in adolescent peer groups concerns young adolescents' sensitivity about sex roles. Over the course of childhood, boys and girls become increasingly concerned about behaving in ways judged to be sex-appropriate. When little boys show an interest in dolls, they are often told either explicitly (by parents, friends, and teachers) or implicitly (by television, books, and other mass media), "Boys don't play with dolls. Those are for girls." And when girls start wrestling or roughhousing, they are often similarly reprimanded.

As a consequence of these continual reminders that there are boys' activities and girls' activities, early adolescents—who are trying to establish a sense of identity—are very concerned about acting in sex-appropriate ways, although this is more true of boys than girls (Galambos, Berenbaum, & McHale, 2009). This makes it very difficult for an adolescent boy to be a part of a girls' clique, in which activities revolve around clothing and talking about boys, or a girl to be part of a boys' clique, in which activities are often dominated by athletics and other physical pursuits (Mehta & Strough, 2009). Adolescents who go against prevailing sex-role norms by forming friendships with members of the other sex may be teased about being "fags" or may be ostracized by their peers because they are "girly" (Oransky & Marecek, 2009). (Interestingly, gay male adolescents typically have more other-sex friendships than same-sex friendships [Diamond & Dubé, 2002].) Ironically, once dating becomes the norm, adolescents who *don't* have relationships with peers of the other sex become the objects of equally strong suspicion and social rejection.

Ethnic Segregation Ethnicity is not a strong determinant of clique composition during childhood, but it becomes increasingly powerful as youngsters get older (Wölfer & Hewstone, 2018). By middle and late adolescence, adolescents' peer groups typically are ethnically segregated, with very few ethnically mixed cliques in most high schools (Ennett & Bauman, 1996).

Ethnicity is such a strong determinant of adolescents' cliques that teenagers are more likely to have friends of the same ethnicity who come from the opposite end of the socioeconomic spectrum than to have friends from the same social class but a different ethnic group. This appears to be the case, although somewhat less so, even within schools that have been deliberately desegregated. In fact, cross-ethnic friendships are less common in ethnically diverse schools and neighborhoods than in those where one ethnic group predominates (Munniksma et al., 2017; Quillian & Campbell, 2003). Same-ethnic and cross-ethnic friendships have different advantages: The former increase students' ethnic pride, but in ethnically diverse classrooms, the latter make students feel safer and less vulnerable (Graham, Munniksma, & Juvonen, 2014). They also have different effects on mental health, at least among boys: Unpopularity among teens from the same ethnic group adversely affects adolescents emotional well-being more than unpopularity among teens from a different background (Mali et al., 2019).

An analysis of data from a large, nationally representative sample of adolescents found that ethnicity continues to be an enormously powerful determinant of friendship patterns—far more powerful than socioeconomic status (Quillian & Campbell, 2003). The rift between Black students and students from all other ethnic groups, especially whites and Asians, is especially strong. Although Asian students report the highest degree of discrimination by peers, Black students' reports of being discriminated against by other students increase over time (Cooc & Gee, 2014; Greene, Way, & Pahl, 2006; Qin, Way, & Mukherjee, 2008).

Studies of found that immigrants are relatively less likely to have cross-ethnic friendships (Hamm, Brown, & Heck, 2005; Kiang, Peterson, & Thompson, 2011; Titzman, 2014) and more likely to have friendships with immigrants from the same background who have similar attitudes about the importance of maintaining their cultural identity (Umaña-Taylor et al., 2020). But even among ethnic minority youth whose families have been in the United States for generations, there is a strong preference for same-ethnicity friends (Quillian & Campbell, 2003).

This is unfortunate because having friends outside their cultural group facilitates immigrant adolescents' adaptation to the new culture and lessens discrimination against them (Motti-Stefandini, Paclopoulos, & Asendorpf, 2018). Parents appear to influence this preference, as indicated by a study of Mexican American adolescents that found that adolescents were more likely to have non-Mexican friends when their parents were themselves more strongly oriented toward Anglo culture (Updegraff et al., 2006). The social climate of the school likely matters as well: Feelings of discrimination often drive ethnic minority students into peer crowds that are defined by ethnicity (Brown et al., 2008).

It is difficult to know why such strong ethnic segregation persists in adolescents' friendship selection. Ethnic segregation in adolescents' cliques is only partly due to residential segregation (Mouw & Entwisle, 2006). One possibility is that some ethnic segregation in friendship patterns is due to differential levels of academic achievement of adolescents from different ethnic groups (Graham, Munniksma, & Juvonen, 2014). On average, white and Asian adolescents get significantly higher grades in school than Black or Latinx adolescents. As you'll read, friends usually have similar attitudes toward school, educational aspirations, and grades (Brown, 2004). Ethnic differences in school achievement therefore may lead to ethnic separation in adolescent peer groups (Hallinan & Williams, 1989). Cross-ethnic friendships are rarer in schools that frequently separate students into different academic tracks (Stearns, 2004).

A second reason for ethnically segregated peer groups—according to one study of adolescents in a school that had been recently desegregated—is attitudinal. In this school, the white adolescents perceived their Black peers as aggressive, threatening, and hostile. The Black students, in turn, saw the white students as conceited, prejudiced, and unwilling to be friends with them. These perceptions, which fed on each other, made the formation of interracial peer groups unlikely. The more the white students believed that the Black students were hostile, the more the white students acted distant and kept to themselves. But the more the white students acted this way, the more likely the Black students were to feel rejected and the more hostile they became.

In contrast, studies show that adolescents who have lasting friendships with peers from other ethnic backgrounds are more likely to have positive attitudes toward people from other backgrounds (Kelleghan et al., 2019; Rastogi & Juvonen, 2019). Contact with adolescents from other ethnic groups during adolescence is predictive of intergroup contact in adulthood (Wolfer et al., 2016). Although ethnic diversity within classrooms helps promote contact between students from different backgrounds, enduring cross-ethnic friendships are especially likely to develop when adolescents from different backgrounds have have opportunities to connect outside of school (Lessard, Kogachi, & Juvonen, 2019).

Parents' attitudes about the value of having friends from different ethnic groups also makes a difference (Smith, Maas, & van Tubergen, 2015). Whereas some parents actively encourage their teenagers to have friends from other ethnic groups, others discourage it, and still others are content to have their children make their own choices, although they may have mixed feelings about them.

Common Interests Among Friends

Thus far, we have seen that adolescents' cliques are usually composed of individuals who are the same age, in the same grade, and of the same ethnicity. But what about factors beyond these? Do adolescents who associate with one another also share certain interests and activities? Generally, they do. Three factors appear to be especially important in determining adolescent clique membership and friendship patterns: orientation toward school, orientation toward the teen culture, and involvement in antisocial activity (Crosnoe & Needham, 2004).

Orientation Toward School Adolescents and their friends tend to be similar in their attitudes toward school, their school achievement, their course selection, and their educational plans (Chow et al., 2018; Flashman, 2012; Kiuru, Salmela-Aro, et al., 2012). Adolescents who earn high grades, study a great deal, and plan to go on to college usually have friends who share these characteristics and aspirations. One reason for this is that how much time students devote to schoolwork affects their involvement in other activities. A second is that parents who stress achievement may insist that their teens only spend time with peers who do well in school (Zhao & Gao, 2014).

It's important to note that students' friendships are often drawn from the peers with whom they have classes,

Adolescents and their friends usually share common interests in everything from academics to antisocial behavior. Marie-Reine Mattera/Getty Images

and because schools assign students to tracks on the basis of their academic achievement, their friends will be more likely to have similar records of school performance (Crosnoe, 2002). Someone who is always studying will not have many friends who stay out late partying because the two activities conflict. By the same token, someone who wants to spend afternoons and evenings out having fun will find it difficult to remain friends with someone who prefers to stay home and study. When adolescents' academic performance changes (for better or for worse), they tend to change their friendships in the same direction (Flashman, 2012; Smirnov & Thurner, 2017).

Students also influence each other's academic performance (Gremmen et al., 2017; Shin & Ryan, 2014). For instance, girls' decisions about whether to take advanced math classes are significantly influenced by their friends' decisions about which classes to take (Frank et al., 2008). Friends exert a similar influence on grade point average (GPA): Given two students with similar records of past achievement, the student whose friends do better in school is likely to get better grades than the one whose friends do worse (Véronneau & Dishion, 2011). Indeed, of all the characteristics of friends that influence adolescents' behavior, their friends' school performance has the greatest impact, not only on their own academic achievement but also on their involvement in problem behavior and drug use (Cook, Deng, & Morgano, 2007). Perhaps not surprisingly, students whose friends tend to come from school have higher GPAs than those whose friends tend to come from other contexts, such as the neighborhood (Witkow & Fuligni, 2010).

gangs

Organized peer groups of antisocial individuals.

Involvement in Antisocial Activity A number of studies, involving both boys and girls from different ethnic groups, indicate that antisocial, aggressive adolescents often gravitate toward each other, forming deviant peer groups (Allen et al., 2019; Ragan, 2020). Contrary to the popular belief that antisocial adolescents do not have friends or that they are interpersonally inept, these youngsters do have friends, but their friends tend to be antisocial as well. Although adolescents with deviant friends show some of the same emotional problems as adolescents without friends, even those with deviant friends are less lonely than their friendless peers (Brendgen, Vitaro, & Bukowski, 2000). And cliques composed of antisocial boys exchange text messages about their antisocial activities, as well as more mundane matters (Ehrenreich et al., 2019).

As you might expect, adolescents with more antisocial friends are more likely to engage in antisocial activity (Criss, Sheffield Morris et al., 2016), but some adolescents have inherited traits, such as a proneness to sensation-seeking, that make them especially susceptible to the influence of antisocial peers (Schlomer et al., 2021; Mann et al., 2016; Samek et al., 2017). Adolescents are influenced by the antisocial behavior of their classmates, as well, even if the classmates are not actually friends (C. Müller et al., 2016). One study of more than 90,000 American students found that adolescents were 48% more likely to have been in a fight, 140% more likely to have pulled a weapon on someone, and 183% more likely to have badly hurt someone in the past year if a friend had engaged in the same behavior (Bond & Bushman, 2016). Peers appear even to influence the specific type of delinquency an adolescent engages in (e.g., theft versus violence) (Thomas, 2015).

Although we would not necessarily want to call all of these antisocial peer groups "delinquent," since they are not always involved in criminal activity, understanding the processes through which antisocial peer groups are formed provides some insight into the development of delinquent peer groups, or gangs (Gilman et al., 2014; Melde & Esbensen, 2011). **Gangs** are antisocial peer groups that can be identified by name (often denoting a neighborhood or part of the city) and common symbols ("colors," tattoos, hand signs, jewelry, etc.). Adolescents who belong to gangs are at greater risk for many types of problems in addition to antisocial behavior, including elevated levels of psychological distress, impulsivity, psychopathic tendencies, exposure to violence, and violent victimization (Dmitrieva et al., 2014; Gordon et al., 2014; Pyrooz, 2014). This is also true for female adolescents who hang around with male gangs, which increases their involvement in high-risk sexual behavior, drug use, and crime (Yarnell et al., 2014). Adolescents who are gang members also are more likely to have behavioral and mental health problems in adulthood (Augustyn, Thornberry, & Krohn, 2014; Gilman, Hill, & Hawkins, 2014).

Adolescent gangs both resemble and differ from other sorts of peer groups. On the one hand, gangs look much like other types of cliques and crowds, in that they are groups of adolescents who are similar in background and orientation, share common interests and activities, and use the group to derive a sense of identity. One study of Latinx youth in southern California found that it was especially important to differentiate between gangs, which were organized and had long histories of involvement in serious antisocial behavior, and "crews," which also engaged in fighting, tagging, and partying but which did not engage in serious violence (Lopez et al., 2006). This distinction has important legal ramifications, because antigang laws that mandate tougher penalties for crimes committed by gangs may be incorrectly applied to adolescents who commit delinquent acts with their friends (or crew) but who are not members of gangs.

The processes that lead adolescents to join gangs are not the same as those that lead to membership in crews and other sorts of peer groups, though. Gang members tend to be more isolated from their family, have more emotional and behavioral problems, and have poorer self-conceptions than other adolescents, including those who are involved in antisocial activity but who are not gang members (Garduno & Brancale, 2017). Many gang members have long histories of exposure to trauma and domestic violence, abuse and neglect, and family members who abused drugs, and many believe that joining a gang was necessary for survival in their neighborhood. As one 19-year-old male gang member explained:

> *Before I started hanging around the guys and shit, and being part of the gang, people say stuff like "you not from around here," "don't be around here," or "don't be surprised if something happen to you." Or you know, people try to rob me and other stuff that would make me feel like I want to show them I am tired of being afraid and I wanted to be around.* (Quinn et al., 2017, pp. 38–39)

Joining a gang often created its own set of problems, though. Here's how an 18-year-old female gang member explained this to an interviewer:

> *You can't really enjoy yourself. You got to always watch your back. You never know who you'll get into it with. It could not even be with you, but you never know who they [fellow gang members] into it with. So it is hard making new friends 'cause you're not sure like—so all that. You got to worry about your family 'cause people find out where you live. Then it's like—lots of worries.* (Quinn et al., 2017, p. 44)

The process of antisocial peer group formation in adolescence begins in the home, during childhood (Tolan, Gorman-Smith, & Henry, 2003). Problematic parent-child relationships—ones that are coercive and hostile—lead to the development of an antisocial disposition in the child, and this disposition contributes, in elementary school, to both school failure and rejection by classmates (Pardini, Loeber, & Stouthamer-Loeber, 2005). Rejected by the bulk of their classmates, aggressive boys "shop" for friends and are accepted only by other aggressive boys (Allen et al., 2019; Kornienko, Ha, & Dishion, 2020). Once these friendships are formed, the boys, like any other clique, reward each other for participating in a shared activity—in this case, antisocial behavior. Improvements in parenting during adolescence reduce teenagers' association with antisocial peers, which, in turn, reduces problem behavior (Forgatch et al., 2016).

The Role of Parents   Parents often "manage" their adolescent's friendships by monitoring the individuals their child spends time with, guiding their child toward peers they like, prohibiting contact with peers they dislike, and supporting friendships they approve of (Updegraff et al., 2010). Parents also act as "consultants," helping their teenagers work out problems with their friends (Mounts, 2011). Adolescents whose parents act as consultants in this way are less likely to be involved in drug use and delinquent activity and report more positive relationships with their friends (Mounts, 2004). On the other hand, excessive attempts to control an adolescent's choice of friends may backfire; when parents forbid adolescents from associating with peers the parents disapprove of, they may inadvertently drive adolescents to become closer to those peers, perhaps in defiance of these restrictions on their independence (Keijsers et al., 2012; Tilton-Weaver et al., 2013). Rather than viewing the family and peer contexts as separate worlds, it is important to keep in mind that what takes place in one setting often has an impact on what occurs in others.

The role of the family in friendship choice has also been described in studies of crowds (Brown et al., 1993). One of the factors that influences the crowd an adolescent belongs to is her or his upbringing. Parents play a role in socializing certain traits in their children, and these orientations, whether toward aggression or academic achievement, predispose adolescents toward choosing certain friends or crowds with which to affiliate. Once in these cliques or crowds, adolescents are rewarded for the traits that led them there in the first place, and these traits are strengthened.

Some accounts of adolescent development portray the peer group as more important than the family (e.g., J. Harris, 1998). One problem with this view is that it fails to take into account the fact that the family has a strong effect on adolescents' choice of peers. For example, a child who is raised to value academics will perform well in school and will likely select friends who share this orientation. Over time, these friends will reinforce the youngster's academic orientation and strengthen his or her school performance. By the same token, adolescents who have poor relationships at home are more likely to engage in antisocial behavior, are drawn to other antisocial peers, and become more antisocial over time as a result (Benson & Buehler, 2012; M. Li et al., 2015). Even when adolescents have relatively more antisocial friends, having better relationships at home and a stronger attachment to school will make them less susceptible to their friends' negative influence—even in the context of a gang (Trudeau et al., 2012).

> **iatrogenic effects**
> Unintended adverse consequences of a treatment or intervention.

The finding that adolescents become more antisocial when they spend time with antisocial peers has prompted some experts to question the wisdom of group-based interventions for adolescents with conduct problems (Dishion, McCord, & Poulin, 1999). Several studies of programs designed to reduce adolescents' delinquency or aggression, for example, have found that, instead of having the desired effect, the programs actually increase participants' problem behavior. They have what scientists call **iatrogenic effects** (Mahoney, Stattin, & Lord, 2004).

Iatrogenic effects are the undesirable consequences of well-intentioned treatments—for example, when the side effects of a medication are worse than the problem it's intended to treat. When antisocial adolescents spend time with like-minded peers, they frequently teach each other how to be "more effective" delinquents and reward each other for misbehavior. One observational study of adolescent friends talking to each other on camera (Piehler & Dishion, 2014) found that individuals who had a history of involvement in antisocial behavior engaged in more spontaneous conversation about antisocial activities and rewarded each other in the way they responded (e.g., "We were so wasted last Friday." "Oh, yeah, that was insane!" "Remember the time we stole that vodka?" "That was so awesome!"). Several writers have described this process as "deviancy training" (e.g., Forgatch et al., 2016). Knowing that group treatments for antisocial behavior have iatrogenic effects is obviously important for the design of programs for delinquent and aggressive youth.

Similarity Between Friends: Selection or Socialization?

Because antisocial activities are such a strong determinant of clique composition, many adults have expressed concern over the influence of peers in promoting delinquent activity and drug and alcohol use. Parents often feel that if their teenager runs with the wrong crowd, he or she will acquire undesirable interests and attitudes. They worry, for instance, when their child starts spending time with peers who seem to be less interested in school or more involved with drugs. But which comes first—joining a clique or being interested in a clique's activities? Do adolescents develop interests and attitudes because their friends influence them, or is it more that people with similar interests and tastes are likely to become friends?

This question has been examined in many studies that have tracked adolescents and their friendships over time. By tracing patterns of attitudinal and behavioral change and comparing these shifts with patterns of friendship formation and change, researchers can determine whether adolescents are attracted to one another because of their initial similarity (what social scientists refer to as *selection*), become similar because friends influence each other (referred to as *socialization*), or a combination of the two (Ellis & Zarbatany, 2017; Laursen, 2017).

In general, studies indicate that both selection and socialization are at work (see Figure 5.4) across a variety of attitudinal and behavioral domains, including school achievement, drug use, mental health, and delinquency (Chen & Chen, 2019; Gremmen et al., 2019; Scalco et al., 2015; Shin, 2017), and in romantic relationships as well as friendships (Simon, Aikins, & Prinstein, 2008). Adolescents who use alcohol, tobacco, or marijuana, for example, are more likely to select other users as friends (de la Haye et al., 2015; Leung et al., 2016). By the same token, spending time with friends who use these substances increases the adolescents' own use as well (Fujimoto, Unger, & Valente, 2012; Wesche, Kreager, & Lefkowitz, 2019).

The reverse also happens: when adolescents who smoke spend time with nonsmokers, the smokers are more likely to quit (Lakon et al., 2015). The more substance-using friends an adolescent has and the closer he or she feels to them, the more the adolescent is likely to use alcohol and drugs (McGloin, Sullivan, & Thomas, 2014). Even dating someone whose friends are substance users has similar effects (Haynie, Doogan, & Soller, 2014; Kreager & Haynie, 2011).

Similarly, adolescents who are bullies or who sexually harass others are more likely to have friends who behave similarly (Jewell, Brown, & Perry, 2015; Low, Polanin, & Espelage, 2013; Sijtsema et al., 2014). Conversely, antisocial adolescents who have few friends, and few aggressive friends in particular, are likely to become less antisocial over time (Adams, Bukowski, & Bagwell, 2005), whereas those with antisocial friends who become even more antisocial themselves become more delinquent (Monahan, Steinberg, & Cauffman, 2009; Weerman, 2011).

This process is not limited to antisocial behavior: Adolescents who report more depressive symptoms are likely to choose other depressed adolescents as friends, which,

in turn, negatively affects their own mood and that of their other friends (Kiuru, Burk et al., 2012; Veed, McGinley, & Crockett, 2019). Adolescents who are overweight are likely to have other overweight adolescents as friends, in part because they are rejected by their nonoverweight classmates (Schaefer & Simpkins, 2014) and in part because adolescents who are overweight, sedentary, glued to their electronic devices tend to have friends who have the same unhealthy lifestyle (Marks et al., 2015; Simone, Long, & Lockhart, 2018).

How much of adolescents' similarity to their friends is due to selection and how much is due to socialization? The answer depends on what behavior or attitude is being studied. Socialization is far stronger over day-to-day preferences in such things as clothing or music than over many of the behaviors that adults worry about, such as binge drinking or risky sex (Knecht et al., 2011), or even obesity (de la Haye et al., 2013). Although parents don't want to hear it, selection is a stronger factor than socialization when it comes to problem behavior (Fortuin, van Geel, & Vedder, 2015), smoking (DeLay et al., 2013), and drug use (de la Haye, Green et al., 2013; Franken et al., 2017). That is, adolescents who use drugs or engage in delinquency are more likely to select friends with these tastes than to be corrupted by them.

Stability of Adolescent Friendships   Adolescents' cliques show only moderate stability over the course of the school year—with some members staying in the clique, others leaving, and new ones joining—although cliques become more stable later in high school (Poulin & Chan, 2010). Although the actual composition of adolescents' cliques may shift over time, the defining characteristics of their cliques or their best friends do not (Hogue & Steinberg, 1995). That is, even though some members of an adolescent's clique may leave and be replaced by others, the new members are likely to have attitudes and values that are quite similar to the former members' (Brown, 2004). Over the course of high school, an academically oriented teenager may drift away from some of his friends, but these friends are probably going to be replaced by other academically oriented classmates, not by ones who aren't interested in school.

Even "best friendships" are likely to change during the school year. Only about one-third of students who name a best friend in the fall of a school year rename the same person as their best friend in the spring (that person was typically listed as a friend but not the best friend) (Değirmencioğlu et al., 1998). Instability is even the case in best friendships in which adolescents name each other as their best friend (Bowker, 2004).

Same-sex friendships tend to be more stable than opposite-sex friendships, and boys' friendships trend to be more stable than girls'. Generally speaking, friendship stability is higher among well-adjusted adolescents than among their more troubled peers, although it isn't clear whether

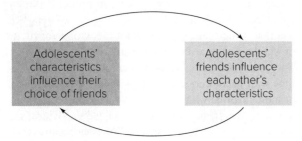

Figure 5.4   Adolescents' choice of friends both influences and is influenced by their traits and interests.

Table 5.2   Summary of broad categories of features that led to dislike

Category	Exemplar Quotes
Jealousy	"She stole my boyfriend and my closest friends. Then got angry when she found out I slept with him."
	"This person disliked my boyfriend/date I was going to bring to the prom, which led me to going to the prom with my boyfriend only. I felt that she had ruined my senior life in high school."
Incompatibility	"An argument started when my friend would just make really loud noises for no reason, and when I would ask her to stop, she would just continue."
	"This person was loud, annoying, and really had no point of talking because her argument made no sense."
	"We stopped talking and hanging out for no apparent reason. All of a sudden, it just ended."
Intimacy-rule violations	"We were best friends, but I couldn't trust her because she lied to me too many times."
	"In the beginning, she seemed like an awesome friend but then, after I started getting close to her, I saw her true colors revealed. She had a very evil way of trying to hurt people and put them down. She was also very untrustworthy."
Aggression	"She spread rumors about me because the guy she liked, liked me."
	"She was with a boy at our senior BBQ and was taking her time when we were in a rush. She and the boy went home with someone else instead of me and didn't tell me. The next day I confronted her, and we got into a fight and suspended from school. That's when she started spreading rumors."

this is because stability contributes to adjustment, because better-adjusted adolescents are better at maintaining friendships, or, most likely, a combination of both (Poulin & Chan, 2010). The most common causes of broken friendships are jealousy, incompatibility, betrayal, and aggression (Casper & Card, 2010) (see Table 5.2). Friendships are far more likely to end between seventh and eighth grade than at later ages, and mixed-sex friendships are especially vulnerable (Hartl, Laursen, & Cillessen, 2015) (see Figure 5.5).

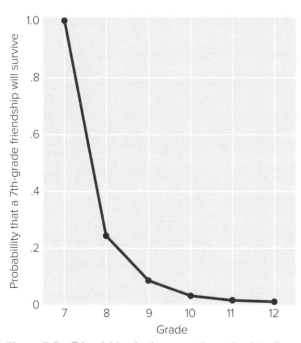

Figure 5.5   **Friendships in the seventh grade virtually never survive through the end of high school. Many friendships dissolve between seventh and eighth grades.** (Hartl, Laursen, & Cillessen, 2015)

Popularity, Rejection, and Bullying

Thus far, our discussion has focused on how and why crowds and cliques serve as the basis for adolescents' social activities and attitudes. But what about the internal structure of peer groups? Within a clique or a crowd, what determines which adolescents are popular and which are not? What factors influence bullying and victimization?

Determinants of Popularity and Rejection

In recent years, psychologists have changed their thinking about what it is that leads to popularity during adolescence. Although it is widely agreed that popular adolescents are generally more socially skilled than their unpopular peers, there is surprising variability among popular teenagers with respect to other characteristics.

One reason for this is that there are two forms of popularity, and they don't always go hand in hand (van den Berg, Lansu, & Cillessen, 2020). One form, **sociometric popularity,** refers to how well-liked someone is. The other form, **perceived popularity,** refers to how much status, or prestige, someone has (Litwack, Aikins, & Cillessen, 2012). So, for example, a leader of the "preppie" crowd who is snobby might be very high in perceived popularity but not in sociometric popularity. Conversely, a member of a crowd that has less prestige who happens to be a really nice person with a good sense of humor may be high in sociometric popularity but low in perceived popularity. By the time they are 14, adolescents

sociometric popularity
How well-liked an individual is.

perceived popularity
How much status or prestige an individual has.

understand the difference between the two (van den Berg, Burk, & Cillessen, 2015). If you think back to your own high school days, you can probably remember people of each type.

Sociometric popularity is determined mainly by social skills, friendliness, sense of humor, and so forth, which are valued by people of all ages and backgrounds. The determinants of perceived popularity are highly variable, though. Because the determinants of status can easily differ between schools, or even among groups within the same school, it is hard to predict which adolescents will be popular without knowing what is valued in that adolescent's social context (Jonkmann, Trautwein, & Lüdtke, 2009; Kreager, 2007a). For example, among white and Latinx teenagers, drinking is associated with status, but this is not the case among Black adolescents (Choukas-Bradley, Giletta, Neblett, & Prinstein, 2015a).

Although there is one main pathway to sociometric popularity (having good social skills), the determinants of perceived popularity are variable and ever-changing. For example, the importance of academic success for being perceived as "cool" declines as individuals move from fifth to sixth grade (North et al., 2019). Having a boyfriend or girlfriend may have little to do with perceived popularity in fifth grade but may be highly correlated with it in ninth grade. Within the same school, some adolescents are highly regarded by their peers because they are good-looking and athletic (the conventional image of the popular teenager), whereas others are equally admired because they are rebellious, delinquent, and aggressive (Becker & Luthar, 2007).

Moreover, whereas many of the things that *lead to* popularity also make adolescents more likable (e.g., athletic ability, physical attractiveness, social skills), some of the things that help to *maintain* popularity once it is established may actually make adolescents less likable (such as using gossip to control or manipulate others) (Dijkstra et al., 2010b; Lansu & Cillessen, 2011; Neal, 2010). In general, adolescents tend to affiliate with peers who have a similar level of popularity within their school (Dijkstra, Cillessen, & Borch, 2013; Logis et al., 2013), mainly because the more popular kids reject the less popular ones (Berger & Dikjstra, 2013).

Predicting perceived popularity is further complicated by the fact that peer norms change, and socially competent adolescents are skilled at figuring them out, adjusting their behavior in response to them, and even influencing them. If smoking marijuana becomes something that is valued by the peer group, popular adolescents will start getting high more regularly (Allen et al., 2005). And when popular adolescents start to engage in a particular behavior, that behavior often becomes more admired. Indeed, one of the reasons it is hard to persuade adolescents to "just say no" to drinking, smoking, and sex is that these activities are often associated with being popular (Balsa et al., 2011; Gommans et al., 2017).

Researchers distinguish between sociometric popularity—how well-liked someone is—and perceived popularity—how much prestige someone has. They don't always go hand in hand.
Tom Carter/Alamy Stock Photo

Even things such as fighting, bullying, or carrying a weapon, which most adolescents do not approve of, become more acceptable when popular adolescents start to do these things (Bellmore, Villarreal, & Ho, 2011; Laninga-Wijnen et al., 2017).

Adolescents are easily swayed by the opinions of high-status peers to behave prosocially (Choukas-Bradley, Giletta, Cohen, & Prinstein, 2015; Laninga-Wijnen et al., 2020) and, as well, to endorse activities that they might otherwise reject and to run the other way from activities endorsed by low-status peers, even if they secretly enjoy them (Cohen & Prinstein, 2006). Adolescents often behave in ways they believe popular students act, although these perceptions are not always accurate. For instance, popular kids are often thought to engage in more substance use than they actually do (Helms et al., 2014).

Popularity and Aggression Although psychologists used to believe that aggressive and antisocial adolescents are likely to be rejected by their classmates, it turns out that some of these teenagers are quite popular (Andrews, Hanish, & Santos, 2017; Lu et al., 2018; Malamut et al., 2020), although their popularity tends to wane as adolescents get older and antisocial behavior is no longer something that teenagers admire (Young, 2014). Nor do these traits continue to have the same effects on an individual's social life: One study, entitled "What Ever Happened to the 'Cool' Kids?" found that adolescents whose early popularity came from impressing their peers with delinquent and "pseudomature" behavior (such as precocious sex) had more interpersonal and behavioral problems as young adults (Allen et al., 2014; Simons et al., 2018).

Studies have identified two distinct types of popular boys (Rodkin et al., 2000). One group has characteristics typically identified in studies of popular youth: They are athletically and academically competent, friendly, and neither shy nor aggressive. A second group, however, is extremely aggressive, athletically competent, and average or below average in friendliness, academic competence, and shyness. Similarly, one study of girls found two distinctly different groups of popular adolescents: girls who were prosocial and good students, and girls who were antisocial and anti-academic, some of whom actually were even bullies (de Bruyn & Cillessen, 2006). Among both males and females, though, aggression tends to be a turn-off to potential romantic partners (Bower et al., 2015). Being prosocial is a weaker predictor of popularity in the United States than in China, though (Zhang et al., 2018).

How can we explain this? Wouldn't we expect adolescents who are antisocial or aggressive toward others to be *unpopular?* Evidently, it is not aggression alone but the combination of aggression and difficulty controlling emotions or a lack of social skills that leads to problems with peers (Pouwels et al., 2018; van den Berg, Burk, & Cillessen, 2019).

Consistent with this, aggressive adolescents who use their aggression strategically and selectively—what is referred to as **proactive aggression**—are much more popular than aggressive adolescents whose aggression is unplanned and frequent—what is referred to as **reactive aggression** (Ettekal & Ladd, 2015; Moore et al., 2019). It's also important to distinguish between aggression, which may increase adolescents' popularity, and delinquency, which tends to diminish it (Rulison, Kreager, & Osgood, 2014). Nevertheless, some adolescents engage in antisocial or aggressive behavior because they think it will increase their popularity (Kiefer & Wang, 2016; Laninga-Wijnen et al., 2019; van den Broek et al., 2016).

The Dynamics of Popularity Two ethnographies of early-adolescent girls provide insight into the dynamics of popularity. In a classic study, the researcher spent two years in a middle school observing interactions among early-adolescent girls in various extracurricular and informal settings (in the cafeteria, in the hallway, at school dances) (Eder, 1985). Although the study is more than 35 years old, many of the researcher's observations still ring true today.

In this school, the cheerleaders were considered the elite crowd, and girls who made the cheerleading squad were immediately accorded social status. Other girls then attempted to befriend the cheerleaders as a means of increasing their own perceived popularity. This, in turn, increased the cheerleaders' prestige within the school, as they became the most sought-after friends. Girls who were successful in cultivating friendships with the cheerleaders became a part of this high-status group and more popular. But because even popular

adolescents can only maintain a finite number of friendships, they ended up snubbing other classmates who wanted to be their friends. Ironically, this often leads to popular adolescents becoming disliked (Mayeux, Sandstrom, & Cillessen, 2008). Thus, adolescents who hang out with popular adolescents may themselves become perceived as more popular over time, but they may also become less well-liked and even victimized because they are seen as snobby status-seekers, especially by their less popular peers (Andrews et al., 2016; Dijkstra et al., 2010b; Lansu, Cillessen, & Karremans, 2012).

> **proactive aggression**
> Aggressive behavior that is deliberate and planned.
>
> **reactive aggression**
> Aggressive behavior that is unplanned and impulsive.

In another ethnography, the researcher spent time observing and interviewing a group described by teachers as the "dirty dozen" (Merten, 1997). This group of girls, "considered 'cool,' 'popular,' and 'mean,'" were "a combination of cute, talented, affluent, conceited, and powerful" (1997, p. 178). The researcher was interested in understanding "why a clique of girls that was popular and socially sophisticated was also renowned for its meanness" (1997, p. 188).

The answer, he discovered, was that meanness was one of the ways that the clique ensured that no one member became stuck-up as a result of her popularity in the eyes of her classmates. Thus, while it was important for clique members to maintain their popular image, if any clique member appeared to become too popular, the other members would turn on her, undermining her standing with other girls by gossiping, starting rumors, and deliberately attempting to disrupt her friendships. Although the study was conducted some 25 years ago, the following quote, from a girl whose friends turned on her, will sound all too familiar:

> *Gretchen was starting to get really mad at me. I talked to her about it and I asked her what was wrong. She just said, "Oh, I heard something you said about me." But I didn't say anything about her. Sara was mad at me. I don't know why. She started being mad at me and then she started making things up that [she said] I said. Sara told Brenda and Gretchen so that they would get mad at me, too. So now I guess Gretchen has made up something and told Wellesley. They are all mad at me and laughing and everything.* (Merten, 1997, p. 182)

Ironically, then, one of the potential costs of being popular in adolescence is that if you become too popular, you face the very real possibility of being the object of other classmates' meanness. The adage that it's important to seek "moderation in all things" applies to popularity as well: Students who are very high in popularity, as well as those who are very low, are less satisfied with their friendships and social life, and are more likely to be the victims of relational aggression than their peers who fall somewhere in between these extremes; as one study put

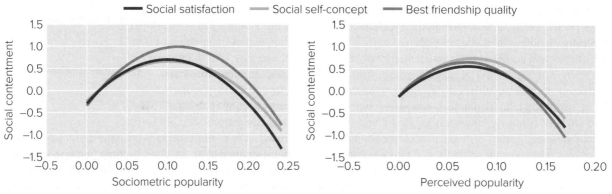

Figure 5.6   It's lonely at the top. Students who are very high in popularity, as well as those who are very low, are less satisfied with their friendships and social life than their peers who fall somewhere in between these extremes. (Ferguson & Ryan, 2019)

it, "It's lonely at the top" (Ferguson & Ryan, 2019; Malamut, Luo, & Schwartz, 2020; Yun & Graham, 2019) (see Figure 5.6).

Although popularity clearly has some costs, the advantages of being popular far outweigh the disadvantages. Being popular is not the same as having close and intimate friendships, but the two often go hand in hand (Asher, Parker, & Walker, 1996). Compared with their less popular peers, popular adolescents are more likely to have close and intimate friendships, have an active social life, take part in extracurricular activities, and receive more social recognition (such as being selected as leaders of school organizations) (Franzoi, Davis, & Vasquez-Suson, 1994). Perhaps you recall classmates who were not popular but who really wished they were—so-called "wannabes." These teenagers are especially likely to be rejected and the recipients of other students' meanness (Breslend et al., 2018).

Part of the overlap between popularity and friendship stems from the fact that many of the characteristics that make adolescents popular are the same ones that make them sought after as friends—chief among them, having good social skills. Actually, adolescents who describe themselves as well-liked and socially competent fare well psychologically over time, regardless of whether they are genuinely popular among their classmates (McElhaney, Antonishak, & Allen, 2008). Teenagers whose peers like them or who merely believe that their peers like them have higher self-esteem both as adolescents and as adults (Gruenenfelder-Steiger, Harris, & Fend, 2016).

Keep in mind that some adolescents who are not especially popular in school may have a well-developed network of friends outside of school. Because most research on adolescents' peer networks has been limited to school-based friendships, we know relatively little about the nature or effects of friendships from other sources. But we do know that many adolescents have a social life outside of school—at church, in the neighborhood, in nonschool extracurricular activities—that is

quite different from their life in school. Having friends outside school can buffer the harmful consequences of having few friends in school (Kiesner, Poulin, & Nicotra, 2003).

Rejected Adolescents   Just as there are different reasons for being popular, there are also different reasons for being rejected. It's important to distinguish among three types of disliked adolescents, though (Bierman & Wargo, 1995). One set of unpopular adolescents comprises teenagers who have trouble controlling their aggression. Withdrawn adolescents make up a second unpopular set; these adolescents are shy, anxious, and inhibited, and boys of this sort are frequently victims of bullying (Coplan et al., 2013; Erath, Flanagan, & Bierman, 2007). A third group is both aggressive *and* withdrawn. These adolescents have problems controlling their hostility, but like other withdrawn children, they tend to be nervous about initiating friendships with other adolescents.

The origins of peer rejection in adolescence can frequently be traced to earlier periods of development. Often, adolescents who are rejected by their peers were also spurned during middle childhood, and this rejection, in turn, was the consequence of behavioral and emotional difficulties apparent in early elementary school (Ettekal & Ladd, 2015a; Monahan & Booth-LaForce, 2016). Others are rejected in adolescence mainly because they've been rejected in the past (Ladd et al., 2014).

Regardless of its causes, rejection by peers is a significant source of stress for adolescents, who show greater brain activation to rejection than children do, as well as a stronger biological stress response to it (Bolling et al., 2011; Stroud et al., 2009). During adolescence, there are important changes in the brain that lead individuals to become more sensitive to the emotions, expressions, and opinions of others (Van Hoorn et al., 2016). The same reward centers as those activated by food, sex, and drugs are also activated when teenagers view Instagram photos that have received many "likes" (Sherman et al., 2016).

Relational Aggression

Most studies of the peer relations of aggressive children have focused on children who are overtly aggressive (either physically or verbally). This has led researchers to pay relatively more attention to the social relationships of aggressive boys than girls because boys exhibit more overt aggression (Card et al., 2008). Girls also act aggressively toward peers, but their aggression is often social, not physical (Crick, 1996). They often engage in **relational aggression**—aggression intended to harm other adolescents through deliberate manipulation of their social standing and relationships. Text messaging has provided added opportunities for adolescents to engage in this behavior (Vollet et al., 2020).

Individuals use relational aggression to hurt others by excluding them from social activities, damaging their reputations with others, or withdrawing attention and friendship. Different types of aggression follow similar developmental trajectories during adolescence, increasing during early adolescence and then declining from midadolescence on, and are correlated (individuals who are highly aggressive in one way are also aggressive in others, and individuals who are frequent victims of physical aggression are also frequent victims of relational aggression) (Card et al., 2008; Karriker-Jaffe et al., 2009). Boys who are academically successful and relatively less masculine are especially likely to be victims of both types of aggression (Lehman, 2020).

Researchers have found that some adolescents are especially prone to seek revenge when they have been excluded or insulted and are highly sensitive to signs of disrespect (McDonald & Asher, 2018). This may lead to relational aggression, especially among teenagers who are impulsive and who have difficulties with anger management (Espelage et al., 2018). Like physical aggression, the roots of relational aggression are often found in the family and peer group. Adolescents who use a lot of relational aggression frequently have parents who are harsh, controlling, or overly permissive, or antisocial peers (Aizpitarte et al., 2019; Kawabata et al., 2011).

"Mean Girls"   Although relational aggression was first noticed in observations of girls, studies show that boys also employ it (Juvonen, Wang, & Espinoza, 2013) but that girls are more aware of it, more distressed by it, and more often the victims of it (Card et al., 2008; Pronk & Zimmer-Gembeck, 2010). Although both girls and boys use physical and relational aggression, there are many more extremely physically aggressive boys than girls and many more extremely relationally aggressive girls (Ettekal & Ladd, 2015a).

Girls' use of relational aggression has attracted a great deal of popular attention, as reflected in the best-selling books *Odd Girl Out* (Simmons, 2003) and *Queen Bees and Wannabees* (Wiseman, 2003), which served as the basis for the movie *Mean Girls*. Perhaps in response, educators have expressed concerns about "meanness" in school environments, noting that teachers have devoted far more attention to preventing overt physical fighting than relational aggression—despite the fact that victims of relational aggression also suffer as a result (Chen et al., 2019; Desjardins & Leadbeater, 2011). Some have called for educational programs designed to help teachers understand, assess, prevent, and respond to the problem when it arises in their classroom, as well as schoolwide programs designed to teach tolerance and acceptance and encourage students to disapprove of relational aggression when they see it. In the opinion of most experts, middle schools ought to be the focus of such interventions (Yoon, Barton, & Taiarol, 2004).

> **relational aggression**
> Acts intended to harm another through the manipulation of his or her relationships with others, as in malicious gossip.

making the scientific connection

Is relational aggression something that is more common in adolescence than adulthood? If so, why might this be? If not, is it expressed differently among adults?

Preventing relational aggression is easier said than done. Adolescents who use relational aggression, especially if they don't overdo it, often are more popular than their peers (Casper, Card, & Barlow, 2020). Actually, this is hardly surprising because the whole *point* of using relational aggression is to maintain one's status and popularity and because the same social skills that make one popular (learning how to "read" other people, being able to adjust one's behavior to maintain one's status, having a good sense of humor, etc.) are useful when spreading rumors, gossiping, or trying to undermine someone else's reputation (Bowker & Etkin, 2014; Dumas, Davis, & Ellis, 2019). The reason some physically aggressive boys are often more popular than their peers is that physical aggression and relational aggression may go hand in hand, and it is their relational aggression, not their physical aggression, that contributes to their popularity.

Many programs designed to reduce relational aggression may be ineffective because adolescents are reluctant to stop doing something that maintains their popularity or even improves their friendships, even if it is at the expense of someone else (Banny et al., 2011; Rose & Swenson, 2009). Adolescents are less likely to react negatively toward their friends when they see them exclude others than when they witness unfamiliar peers doing the same thing (Spaans et al., 2019).

Consequences of Rejection   Being unpopular has negative consequences for adolescents' mental health

Although boys are more physically aggressive than girls, girls often engage in what has been called relational aggression—an attempt to harm someone by ruining his or her reputation or disrupting his or her friendships. stester/Shutterstock

and psychological development; peer rejection and friendlessness are associated with subsequent depression, behavior problems, alcohol use, interpersonal difficulties, and academic difficulties (Bellmore, 2011; Meisel et al., 2018; Schacter, Lessard,& Juvonen, 2019). But studies show that the specific consequences of peer rejection may differ for rejected youth who are aggressive versus those who are withdrawn.

Aggressive individuals who are rejected are at risk for conduct problems and involvement in antisocial activity as adolescents, not just as a direct result of their rejection but because the underlying causes of their aggression (for instance, poor self-control) also contribute to later conduct problems (Laird et al., 2005). In contrast, withdrawn children who are rejected are likely to feel lonely and are at risk for low self-esteem, depression, and diminished social competence—again, both as a result of being rejected and in part because the underlying causes of their timidity (for instance, high anxiety) also contribute to later emotional problems (Pedersen et al., 2007). Rejection is especially likely to lead to depression in adolescents who place a lot of importance on their standing in the peer group and who believe that they, rather than the peers who reject them, are at fault (Prinstein & Aikins, 2004). Adolescents who are both aggressive and withdrawn are at the greatest risk of all (Rubin, LeMare, & Lollis, 1990).

Many psychologists believe that unpopular youngsters lack some of the social skills and social understanding necessary to be popular with peers. Unpopular aggressive children

hostile attributional bias
The tendency to interpret ambiguous interactions with others as deliberately hostile.

are more likely than their peers to think that other children's behavior is deliberately hostile, even when it is not. When accidentally pushed while waiting in line, for instance, many unpopular aggressive children are likely to retaliate because they believe that the person who did the pushing did it on purpose. This so-called **hostile attributional bias** plays a central role in the aggressive behavior of rejected adolescents (Crick & Dodge, 1994). Adolescents who are prone to make hostile attributions tend to have friends who view the world through a similar lens (Halligan & Philips, 2010). Interventions aimed at changing the way aggressive adolescents view their peers have been successful in reducing rates of aggression (Dodge, Godwin, & Conduct Problems Prevention Group, 2013; Yeager, Miu et al., 2013).

What about unpopular withdrawn children? What are their social skills deficits? In general, unpopular withdrawn children are excessively anxious and uncertain around other children, often hovering around the group without knowing how to break into a conversation or activity. Their hesitancy, low self-esteem, and lack of confidence make other children feel uncomfortable, and their submissiveness makes them easy targets for bullying (Salmivalli, 1998). Many of these youngsters are especially sensitive to being rejected and show a heightened neural response to rejection, as well as increased susceptibility to depression as a consequence (Rudolph et al., 2016; Will et al., 2016). Rejection sensitivity increases in adolescence as brain regions that monitor social information become more easily aroused (Falk et al., 2014; Zimmer-Gembeck et al., 2014).

Some victimized adolescents are depressed, and their depression leads them to behave in ways that make them targets of harassment (people don't like to hang around with depressed individuals) (Saint-Georges & Vaillancourt, 2020). Adolescents who don't have friends at school are likely to view school as a threatening place, which often engenders feelings of depression (Lessard & Juvonen, 2018). Unfortunately, the more these children are teased, rejected, and bullied, the more anxious and hesitant they feel and the more they blame themselves for their victimization, which only compounds their problem—creating a cycle of victimization (see Figure 5.7) (Mathieson, Klimes-Dougan, & Crick, 2014; van Geel et al., 2018). Not all rejected students are bullied, though.

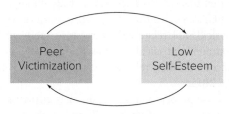

Figure 5.7 **Peer victimization diminishes adolescents' self-esteem, which often leads to more victimization.** (van Geel et al., 2018)

Children who are victimized but who have supportive friends are less likely to be caught in this vicious cycle than those who don't (Cuadros & Berger, 2016; Kochel et al., 2015; Liu et al., 2019).

Helping Unpopular Teens Psychologists have experimented with different sorts of interventions designed to improve the social skills of unpopular adolescents. These social-competence training programs have focused on three different strategies (Qualter et al., 2015). One type of program has been designed to teach social skills: self-expression, leadership, and how to converse. A second approach has been to have unpopular adolescents participate in group activities with popular ones under the supervision of psychologists. Finally, some social-competence programs focus on a combination of behavioral and cognitive abilities, including social problem solving.

Social-problem-solving programs, such as PATHS (Promoting Alternative Thinking Strategies), are designed to improve individuals' abilities to judge social situations and figure out acceptable ways of behaving. Adolescents are taught to calm down and think before they react, to decide what the problem is, to figure out what their goal is, and to think of positive approaches toward reaching that goal. Instead of lashing out at a classmate who grabbed the last basketball from a gym closet, for example, a hot-tempered boy who had been through this sort of program might calm himself down, tell himself that his goal is to play basketball rather than get into a fight, and approach another student to ask if he can get into a game. PATHS has been shown to effectively reduce behavioral problems among elementary school children (Conduct Problems Prevention Research Group, 1999).

Bullies and Victims

About one-third of students report having been physically bullied at some time during the past year, although in some studies, the percentage of students who report having been victimized has been considerably higher (Goldbach, Sterzing, & Stuart, 2018). One problem in coming up with accurate estimates of the prevalence of bullying or victimization is that researchers and survey respondents define them in so many different ways (Hymel & Swearer, 2015); in addition, rates of physical bullying and victimization vary across school grades, declining considerably as students move through middle school and into high school (Ladd, Ettekal, & Kochenderfer-Ladd, 2017). Sexual minority youth are especially likely to be bullied persistently and become depressed as a result (Kaufman, Baams, & Veenstra, 2020).

For example, Latinx and Black students are less likely than white students to report having been bullied, but they are just as likely as white students to report having been hit, robbed, stolen from, put down, and having their belongings damaged, which to most people qualifies as being bullied (Lai & Kao, 2018). Nevertheless, scholars differentiate bullying from other forms of aggression by its repetitive nature and by the imbalance of power that describes the bully and victim (Rodkin, Espelage, & Hanish, 2015). Rates of victimization vary considerably from country to country, although around the world, adolescents who come from less affluent families are more likely to be bullied (Analitis et al., 2009).

Interestingly, the prevalence of bullying is higher in schools and countries characterized by greater income inequality (Due et al., 2009; Menzer & Torney-Purta, 2012). For example, bullying is far less prevalent in Sweden, where the gap between rich and poor is very small, than in Russia, where income inequality is much greater (see Figure 5.8). Apparently, it is more acceptable for the strong to victimize the weak in countries where having a wide gap between the economically "strong" and economically "weak" is also more widely tolerated.

Although relationships between adolescents who dislike each other have not been studied extensively, such mutual antipathies are not uncommon. These relationships frequently involve bullies and victims, often with an antisocial adolescent repeatedly harassing a withdrawn classmate (Güroğlu et al., 2009). Although it may be difficult to understand why teenagers who have been repeatedly victimized by someone would maintain a friendship with the bully, victims may do so because they blame themselves, don't have other friends, or think that this is just the way things are. As one student put it (Bouchard, Smith, & Woods, 2021, p. 17):

> I know what friendship is supposed to be like and I wasn't feeling that anymore. But you see girls treating each other so badly everywhere in the media and movies and you see it every day at school so you start to change your mind.

Adolescents who are bullies are also likely to assist and reinforce other bullies and, like the bullies they support, are also more likely to have conduct problems, be callous and indifferent to the problems of others, and be "morally disengaged"—likely to justify unethical behavior as permissible (Van Noorden et al., 2015; Wang et al., 2017).

Bullying is something that students can be exposed to both directly (when they are the victims) or indirectly (when they witness harassment but aren't themselves victimized). These two different types of experience have both similar and dissimilar effects (Janosz et al., 2008; Nishina & Juvonen, 2005). Being victimized or witnessing the harassment of others makes students anxious, but, oddly enough, witnessing the harassment of others appears to buffer some of the harmful effects of being victimized (Yun & Juvonen, 2020). Adolescents who are victims of harassment but who do not see anyone else being victimized are more likely to feel humiliated and

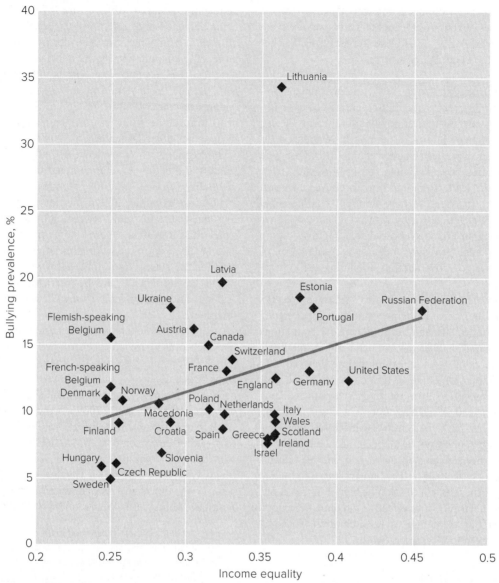

Figure 5.8 **Rates of bullying vary considerably from country to country. Bullying is more prevalent in countries with greater income inequality.** (Due et al., 2009)

angry than those who are both victims and witnesses. Presumably, being singled out for harassment feels worse than being just one of many who are picked on.

For this reason, some studies find that in ethnically diverse schools, victimized students whose ethnic group is in the minority are not as harmed psychologically as are victimized students whose ethnic group is in the majority (Echols & Graham, 2016), who are less able to attribute their victimization to their ethnicity and more likely to blame it on their own shortcomings (Graham et al., 2009). Other studies have found that the adverse effects of being bullied are pretty much the same regardless of a school's ethnic makeup, however (Mehari & Farrell, 2015).

making the practical connection

What can be done to reduce victimization in schools? If you were asked to design an intervention, what would it entail?

Victimization Students who are harassed by their classmates report a range of adjustment problems, including low self-esteem, depression, suicide, sleep difficulties, and academic difficulties, as well as loneliness, problems in social skills, and difficulties in controlling negative emotions, such as anger and aggression (Donoghue & Meltzer, 2018; Eastman et al., 2018; Farrell et al., 2018;

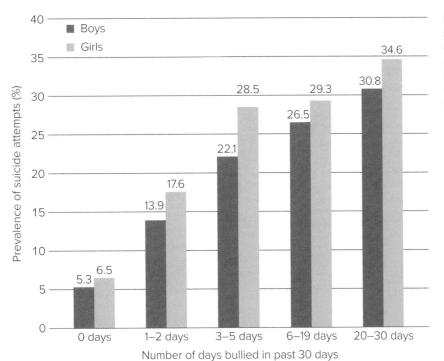

Figure 5.9 A comprehensive study of 12- to 15-year-olds from 48 countries found that adolescents' suicide attempts increase as a function of how frequently they are bullied. (Koyanagiu et al., 2019)

Koyanagi et al., 2019; Pan et al., 2020) (see Figure 5.9). Brain imaging studies also find that victimization increases adolescents' sensitivity to social cues, which may make them more susceptible to developing emotional and behavioral problems (Telzer et al., 2019) (see Figure 5.10).

In some studies, these psychological problems have been shown to be the causes of victimization, rather than the consequences (Krygsman & Vaillancourt, 2017; Marsh et al., 2016), whereas in others, there is clear evidence that victimization leads to subsequent problems, some of which may persist into adulthood (Adrian et al., 2019). Many researchers believe that both processes are at work: Victims are drawn into a downward spiral, where victimization leads to emotional problems, heightened sensitivity to rejection, and self-blame, which in turn prompt more victimization (Burke, Sticca, & Perren, 2017; Schacter & Juvonen, 2017; Zimmer-Gembeck, 2016).

Attributing one's victimization to one's own deficiencies (e.g., it's something about me that I can't change) is more common in schools where victimization is less common, but attributing it to bad decision making (e.g., I shouldn't have walked there by myself) is more common in schools where there is a lot of victimization (Schacter & Juvonen, 2015). In schools where bullying is common, victims who believe that people cannot change are especially likely to become depressed (Kaufman et al., 2020). Some adolescents who are victimized become alienated and disengaged from school and, ultimately, form bonds with antisocial peers, which draws the previously victimized teenagers into antisocial activity (Rudolph et al., 2020; Totura, Karver, & Gesten, 2014). Some end up in friendship groups with other victimized peers, not so much because they actively choose each other as friends but because they are avoided by other students and have few other choices (Turanovic & Young, 2016).

Although being bullied has adverse consequences regardless of whether other students witness it, public victimization, especially when other students watch but don't offer any assistance, is particularly humiliating (Nishina, 2012). Sadly, the effects of being harassed in middle school are still observed in high school (Rusby et al., 2005) and later in adulthood (Wolke et al., 2013). Adolescents who are the victims of physical victimization are also likely to be the victims of relational victimization, suggesting that some of the characteristics that prompt one type of bullying also prompt the other (Casper & Card, 2017).

One of the most pernicious effects of victimization is that it undermines academic performance, school attendance, school engagement, and feelings of academic competence, all of which has cascading effects well beyond adolescence; even after taking into account background factors, being bullied during adolescence is associated with lower educational attainment (Cornell et al., 2013), diminished earnings in adulthood (Moore et al., 2016; Steiner & Rasberry, 2015), and victimization in the workplace, likely as a consequence of depression (Brendgen & Poulin, 2018). Victimization can even harm cognitive development (Holmes, Kim-Spoon, & Deater-Deckard, 2016).

Many adolescents who report having been victimized also report bullying others. These adolescents have the greatest adjustment problems, just as children who are both aggressive and withdrawn are typically the most

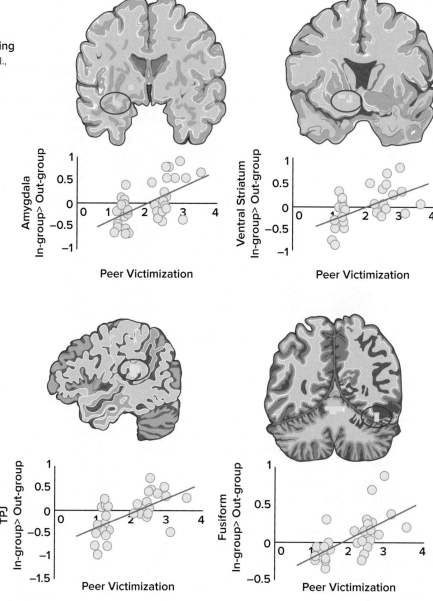

Figure 5.10 Adolescents who have been victimized show heightened activation of brain regions associated with monitoring the behavior of others. (Telzer et al., 2019)

disturbed (Daukantaitė, Lundh, & Wångby-Lundh, 2019; Stattin & Latina, 2018). One reason that bullying and victimization are often seen in the same children is that some adolescents react to victimization, especially those whose self-esteem is high, by becoming more aggressive and bullying other children (Choi & Park, 2018). (Victims are more likely to become bullies than the reverse [Haltigan & Vaillancourt, 2014].) Another may be that certain elements of the broader context—the climate of the school, for instance—may increase or decrease the likelihood of aggression between classmates (Diazgranados & Selman, 2014). Teachers and principals may be able to make changes in their school's climate in order to reduce aggression between students (Cornell, Shukla, & Konold, 2015; Veenstra et al., 2014).

Evaluations of school-based antibullying programs have shown small but significant effects when implemented during elementary school, but no effect whatsoever after seventh grade; in fact, during high school, antibullying interventions may actually lead to *more* bullying (Yeager, Fong, Lee, & Espelage, 2015) (see Figure 5.11). Whether older teenagers are just more resistant to such efforts or whether they need different sorts of programs than those used with younger students isn't known, but it is clear that much of the advice that bullying-prevention programs dispense just doesn't resonate with teenagers (Ybarra et al., 2019). In light of this evidence, school administrators would be well advised to seek the advice of teenagers when designing schoolwide antibullying programs.

What about students who see their classmates bullied? One study of bystanders found that onlookers were more likely to intervene and defend the victim in schools in which doing so was expected—not so much by teachers

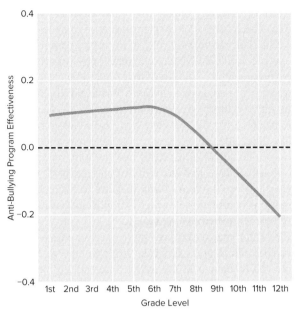

Figure 5.11 Evaluations of antibullying programs show they are moderately effective in elementary school but not in high school, where they may even have negative consequences. (Yeager et al., 2015)

but by other students (Banyard et al., 2020; Kollerováet al., 2018). This has important implications for intervention because it suggests that reducing the incidence of bullying in schools should focus on all students and not just the bullies or victims (Mulvey et al., 2019; Tu, Erath, & Flanagan, 2012).

Researchers are also studying the conditions under which students who witness someone being bullied will intervene to try to stop it, as well as the characteristics of students who are more likely to intervene (Meter & Card, 2015). Bystanders who intervene when someone is bullied are themselves more likely to have supportive relationships with teachers and friends, to be more religious, and to have a strong sense of ethnic identity (Evans & Smokowski, 2015; Jungert, Piroddi, & Thornberg, 2016). It is important to note, however, that a significant amount of bullying occurs outside of school; according to one national survey, in fact, more high school students reported being victimized *outside* school than at school (Turner et al., 2011).

Adolescents' responses to being bullied vary. One study found that there were four categories of victims: those who were mainly passive (e.g., ignoring the bully or walking away), those who were mainly aggressive (e.g., fighting back, either physically or verbally), those who were support-seeking (e.g., telling a parent), and those who did a little of everything. Support-seeking was reported by middle school students but was rarely seen in high school, perhaps because at this age, asking an adult for help in responding to a bully is seen as immature and weak, and may invite more victimization (Dirks et al., 2017)

Victims who used passive strategies reported fewer emotional or behavioral problems than those who fought back, sought help, or used a mixture of approaches (Waasdorp & Bradshaw, 2011), although feeling supported by parents or teachers (if not directly asking for their help) seems to have a protective effect against the adverse effects of victimization (Yeung Thompson & Leadbeater, 2013), as does having a stronger sense of self (Santo et al., 2018). Other studies find that victims who avoid blaming themselves for having been bullied and respond by behaving proactively (avoiding the bully), rather than retaliating, fare better (Singh & Bussey, 2011).

> **cyberbullying**
> Bullying that occurs over the Internet or via cell phones.

Cyberbullying

Rates of **cyberbullying** (e.g., bullying that occurs electronically) vary considerably from study to study, in part because researchers define cyberbullying in different ways (Patton et al., 2014). Physical bullying is more common; nearly 35% of students have been the victim of physical bullying, compared with about 15 to 20% who have been victims of electronic bullying (Modecki et al., 2014; Payne & Hutzell, 2017; Tsitsika et al., 2015). Even still, cyberbullying affects victims in ways that are similar to physical bullying (Bonanno & Hymel, 2013). Adolescents who are bullied frequently online report high levels of distress, anger, shame, aggression, sleep difficulties, and even physical symptoms (Espinoza, 2015; Holfeld & Mishna, 2019; Jose & Vierling, 2018; Tsitsika et al., 2015), although not to the same degree as reported by those who are victims of physical bullying (Espinoza, Schacter, & Juvonen, 2020; Kubiszewski et al., 2015; Wright, 2017).

Although cyberbullying receives a lot of media attention, it is only about half as common as face-to-face bullying. Andrey Shadrin/Getty Images

Unlike physical bullying, which declines over early–adolescence, cyberbullying becomes more common (Espinoza, Schacter, & Juvonen, 2020; Festl et al., 2017). In general, girls and boys use cyberbullying differently: Girls use it to spread gossip and rumors, whereas boys use it to directly insult others (Bradbury, Dubow, & Dornoff, 2018; Festl et al., 2017).

Many large-scale studies—including a review of 55 research reports that collectively included more than 250,000 American adolescents—find that being cyberbullied is associated with both emotional and behavioral problems (Fisher, Gardella, & Teurbe-Tolon, 2016). According to a study of more than 30,000 Canadian teenagers, males and females are affected differently by being cyberbullied: Girls are more likely to develop emotional problems (such as depression or anxiety), whereas boys are more likely to develop behavioral ones (such as fighting or delinquent activity) (Kim et al., 2018; Trompeter, Bussey, & Fitzpatrick, 2018). Either way, reading something negative about yourself online, being attacked by peers in social media, or discovering that you have been socially excluded can be very distressing (Cole et al., 2016; Landoll et al., 2015). Adolescents use a variety of strategies to deal with cyberbullying, with boys more likely than girls to retaliate and girls more likely than boys to distract themselves or seek the support of others (Bradbury, Dubow, & Dornoff, 2018) (see Figure 5.12).

Most adolescents who engage in traditional bullying also frequently engage in cyberbullying, and adolescents who are frequent victims of traditional bullying are also frequent victims of electronic harassment (Festl et al., 2017; Resnik & Bellmore, 2019; Waasdorp & Bradshaw, 2015). And, as is the case with physical bullying, adolescents who are both perpetrators and victims of cyberbullying have the most problematic histories (Buelga, Martinez-Ferrer, & Cava, 2017). Contrary to popular belief, most cyberbullying is not anonymous, and most victims of online bullying suspect a friend or someone else from their school (Juvonen & Gross, 2008; Waasdorp & Bradshaw, 2015).

Not surprisingly, bullies who "specialize" in cyberbullying, which takes a bit of planning, tend to be less reactive in their aggression and more instrumental, often using electronic bullying to enhance their own social status (Sontag et al., 2011), and they tend to be more popular and better adjusted than those who engage in physical bullying (Ranney & Troop-Gordon, 2020; Resett & Gámez-Guadix, 2017). They and their classmates are also less likely to view cyberbullying as wrong (Gámez-Guadix & Gini, 2016; Talwar, Gomez-Garibello, & Shariff, 2014), and the more often teenagers witness cyberbullying, the more likely they are to become more emotionally inured to it, which is important because perpetrators of cyberbullying tend to be less empathic over time, which may make them more likely to engage in the behavior (Brewer & Kerslake, 2015; Coelho & Marchante, 2018; Pabian et al., 2016). Interestingly, whereas conventional bullying tends to make adolescents less popular, cyberbullying tends to have the opposite effect (Wegge et al., 2014).

Adolescents are more likely to engage in cyberbullying if they believe that their friends are, too (Piccoli et al., 2020); if they have poor relationships with their parents (Boniel-Nissim & Sasson, 2018; Buelga, Martinez-Ferrer, & Cava, 2017); and if their parents are unaware of their online behavior, have few rules about Internet use, or overestimate the success of their rules regarding their child's Internet use (Barlett & Fennel, 2018; Lozano-Blasco, Cortés-Pascual, & Latorre-Martínez, 2020). Experts suggest that parents need to familiarize themselves with social media and talk with their teenagers about their online experiences (Underwood & Ehrenreich, 2017). Teenagers whose parents monitor their Internet activity are less likely to be harassed. Monitoring appears to be more effective than the imposition of restrictions on computer use, although limiting adolescents' Internet access in their bedroom appears to help (Khurana, Bleakley, Jordan, & Romer, 2015; Stockdale, Coyne, & Padilla-Walker, 2018). There also is evidence that making the school environment

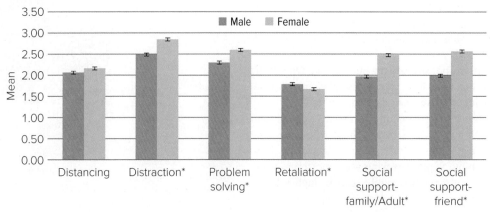

Figure 5.12 **Adolescent boys and girls deal with cyberbullying in different ways.** (Bradbury, Dubow, & Dornoff, 2018)

safer and more supportive may reduce cyberbullying (Holfeld & Leadbeater, 2017).

The Peer Group and Psychosocial Development

Regardless of the structure or norms of a particular peer group, peers play an extremely important role in the psychological development of adolescents. Problematic peer relationships are associated with a range of serious psychological and behavior problems during adolescence and adulthood. Individuals who are unpopular or who have poor peer relationships during adolescence are more likely than their socially accepted peers to be low achievers in school, drop out of high school, show higher rates of delinquent behavior, and suffer from an array of emotional and mental health problems as adults. Although it is likely that poorly adjusted individuals have difficulty making friends, psychological problems result from—as well as cause—problems with peers (Marion et al., 2013; Witvliet et al., 2010).

Adolescents consider the time they spend with their peers to be among the most enjoyable parts of the day. One reason is that activities with friends are typically organized around having a good time, in contrast to activities with parents, which are more likely to be organized around household chores or the enforcement of parental rules (Larson, 1983). Rather than being competing institutions, the family and peer group mainly provide contrasting opportunities for adolescent activities and behaviors. The family is organized around work and other tasks, and it is likely important in the socialization of responsibility and achievement. The peer group provides more frequent opportunities for interaction and leisure, which contribute to the development of intimacy and enhance the adolescent's mood and psychological well-being.

6

Schools

The Broader Context of U.S. Secondary Education

The Origins of Secondary Education

School Reform: Past and Present

What Should Schools Teach?

Education in the Inner Cities

The Social Organization of Schools

School Size and Class Size

Age Grouping and School Transitions

Tracking

Ethnic Composition

Alternatives to Public Schools

Classroom Climate

The Best Classroom Climate for Adolescents

Teacher Expectations and Student Performance

The Importance of Student Engagement

School Violence

Beyond High School

The College-Bound

The Non-College-Bound

Schools and Adolescent Development

Characteristics of Good Schools

The Effects of School on Adolescent Development

Rana Faure/Getty Images

Because of the important and multifaceted role it has come to play in modern society, our system of **secondary education**—middle schools, junior high schools, and high schools—has been the target of a remarkable amount of criticism, scrutiny, and research.

Secondary school touches the lives of all adolescents in industrialized societies, as well as an increasingly larger proportion of the population in the developing world. Virtually all American adolescents under the age of 17 and nearly all 17- and 18-year-olds are enrolled in school. In most developing countries, attending high school is much more common among children of the wealthy, often because poor families need their adolescents to work. But even in the poorest parts of the world—sub-Saharan Africa, for example—more than 60% of adolescents are enrolled in secondary school, although rates around the world vary considerably from country to country (United Nations, 2018).

Schooling is as time-consuming as it is pervasive. Between ages 11 and 18, the typical American student will spend about 8,000 hours in school—not even counting time on homework and school-related activities outside of school.

In this chapter, we examine the organization and workings of secondary schools at multiple levels of analysis. Perhaps your first inclination is to think about what takes place in the classroom. While this is important, a thorough understanding of schooling and its impact on adolescent development requires going beyond the classroom. What takes place in the classroom is influenced by the way in which the school is organized, and the way in which the school is organized, in turn, is influenced by the needs and demands of the community and of society. Unlike the family or peer group, whose structure is not under the direct or deliberate control of society, schools are environments created to serve specific purposes. In many respects, the schools we have today—for all their strengths and weaknesses—are the schools we designed. This is abundantly clear when we look at the history of secondary education in America.

> **secondary education**
> Middle schools, junior high schools, and high schools.

The Broader Context of U.S. Secondary Education

Today in the United States, virtually all young people ages 14 to 17 are enrolled in school. In 1930, only about half of this age group were students, and at the turn of the twentieth century, only 1 in 10 was (see Figure 6.1) (National Center for Education Statistics, 2019; D. Tanner, 1972)

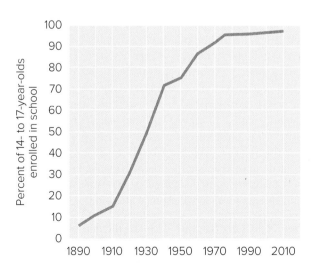

Figure 6.1 **The proportion of the 14- to 17-year-old population enrolled in school increased dramatically between 1910 and 1940, continued to increase until 1970, and then leveled off. Today, more than 95% of individuals this age are in school.** (National Center for Education Statistics, 2019; D. Tanner, 1972)

Not only are there considerably more youngsters enrolled in school today than 50 years ago, but today's students also spend more days per year in school. In 1920, for example, the average school term was 162 days, and the average student attended for only 121 days, or 75% of the term. By 1968, however, the school term had been lengthened to around 180 days, which remains the national average, and the typical student today attends more than 90% of the term (National Center for Education Statistics, 2019).

Adolescents also remain in school for more years now than they did in previous eras. In 1924, fewer than 33% of all youngsters entering the fifth grade eventually graduated from high school; today, more than 85% of all high school students graduate on time, and a substantial number of those who do not eventually get their diploma, either by completing high school at a later date or through equivalency programs or continuation schools (National Center for Education Statistics, 2019).

The Origins of Secondary Education

The rise of secondary education in America was the result of several historical and social trends that converged at the turn of the twentieth century. Most important were industrialization, urbanization, and immigration.

Following widespread industrialization during the late nineteenth century, the role of children and young adolescents in the workplace changed dramatically. As productivity became more dependent on workers' use of machines,

comprehensive high school An educational institution that evolved during the first half of the twentieth century, offering a varied curriculum and designed to meet the needs of a diverse population of adolescents.

employers recognized that they needed employees who were more skilled than youngsters ordinarily were. In addition, the few unskilled jobs that remained after industrialization required strength beyond the capacity of many youth (Church, 1976). Social reformers expressed concerns about the dangers children faced working in factories, and labor unions—an increasingly powerful force in the early 1900s—sought to protect not only the welfare of children but their own job security. New child labor laws narrowed and limited the employment of minors (Bakan, 1972). Together, these changes kept many youngsters out of the labor force.

Life in American cities was changing markedly. Industrialization brought with it urbanization and, along with several waves of immigrants, new problems. The effects of a rapidly expanding economy were seen in the tenements and slums of America's cities: poor housing, overcrowded neighborhoods, crime. Eager to improve living conditions for the masses, social reformers envisioned education as a means of improving the lives of the poor and working classes. Many also saw compulsory secondary education as a means of social control. High schools would take thousands of idle young people off the streets and place them in an environment where they could be supervised and kept out of trouble. By 1915, the idea of universal compulsory education for adolescents had gained widespread acceptance.

Prior to the early twentieth century, high schools were for the elite. In curriculum, staff, and student composition, they were similar to the colleges of the day, with the emphasis mainly on classical liberal arts instruction (Church, 1976; D. Tanner, 1972). By 1920, educators saw a need for curricular reform. Now that secondary education was aimed at the masses, schooling was not just a means of intellectual training but also a way of preparing youth for life in modern society. School reformers argued that education should be more practical and include preparation for work and citizenship. Anxious to see that foreign-born immigrants were well socialized into the American way of life, reformers presented universal secondary education as a necessary part of Americanization (Church, 1976; D. Tanner, 1972).

The 1920s marked the birth in the United States of what came to be known as the **comprehensive high school,** an educational institution that promised to meet the needs of a diverse and growing population of young people. Classes in general education, college preparation, and vocational education were all housed under one roof. New courses were added in music, art, family life, health, physical education, and other subjects designed to prepare adolescents for family and leisure as well as work.

By the middle of the twentieth century, the high school had come a long way from its exclusive focus at the turn of the century on the intellectual development of the elite. Its concern had broadened to include the social and intellectual development of all young people.

School Reform: Past and Present

Although we naturally think of schools as institutions whose primary goal is education, they are much more than this. During the COVID-19 pandemic, when many communities were unable to open schools and were forced to educate students remotely, maintaining the academic side of school was only one consideration. Schools provide breakfast and lunch to students from impoverished families. They offer extracurricular activities that keep students occupied and supervised during afternoon hours, when parents are at work. Schools are also potentially important tools of social intervention, such as public health campaigns to reduce smoking, unsafe sex, and bullying. And, of course, they provide the main setting in which adolescents socialize with their peers. One reason that schools today are asked to do so much more than educate adolescents is that new demands are placed on schools every time a different social problem involving adolescents receives widespread attention.

No Child Left Behind Toward the end of the 1990s, concerns grew that inner-city schools were not producing graduates who could compete for high-skills jobs. In response to a public increasingly interested in alternatives to conventional public education, such as charter schools or home schooling, schools were called upon to raise standards for all students (e.g., Ravitch, 2001). In January 2002, President George W. Bush signed into law the No

The proportion of American adolescents enrolled in high school grew dramatically between 1920 and 1940. Alpha Stock/Alamy Stock Photo

Child Left Behind Act, a sweeping and controversial piece of legislation mandating that states ensure that all students, regardless of their economic circumstances, achieve academic proficiency (U.S. Department of Education, 2006). No Child Left Behind (NCLB) required that schools create and enforce academic standards by annually testing all students and by reporting the results of students' performance to the public. Underperforming schools—schools in which students' test scores did not improve—would be given an opportunity to do a better job the following year by providing additional instruction, tutoring, or special services for students who needed them. But schools that continued to fail eventually would have funding taken away and might be forced to close.

On the face of it, NCLB sounds reasonable enough. Today, a huge proportion of American students do not meet even minimal standards for academic performance, and poor performance is disproportionately seen among disadvantaged, Black, Latinx, and Native American students. Many commentators had criticized the practice of **social promotion**—moving students from one grade to the next regardless of their academic performance—arguing that poor and ethnic minority youth especially were being cheated out of a good education and graduated without the skills necessary to succeed in college or the labor force (Steinberg, 1996). Forcing schools to regularly assess student progress and publicize how students were faring would give parents and the community the information they needed to put pressure on schools to do better.

Although NCLB sounded good in principle, it met with tremendous resistance from the start (Darling-Hammond, 2006). States complained that they did not have the resources to conduct the mandated

Assessing student achievement has been the focus of American education policy for the past two decades. Critics have complained that too much time is being spent testing students.
Klaus Vedfelt/Getty Images

assessments or to respond to failing students' poor performance. Teachers and parents complained that the focus on standardized testing adversely affects what takes place in the classroom: If a school's financial future depends only on test scores, why should teachers do anything other than teach to the test?

Many questions about NCLB were raised: What happens to subjects that will not appear on the test, such as current events, or to the teaching of skills that are impossible to assess through standardized exams, such as **critical thinking**? Who determines how tough the tests are or what level of achievement is acceptable? And, with millions of dollars at stake, what was to stop schools from manipulating their scores by encouraging poor-performing students to be absent on testing days or by helping students cheat on the tests, which some schools did (Levitt & Dubner, 2005)? Some critics of NCLB argued that it was having the opposite effect of what was intended, providing incentives for schools to push low-achieving students out (Darling-Hammond, 2006). Nevertheless, the movement toward performance-based accountability—holding teachers, schools, school districts, and states accountable for the achievement of their students—has been the most important change in the world of American education in the past 25 years (Elmore, 2009).

Some critics have worried that the shift in focus to standardized testing would discourage schools from using assignments that improve important capacities such as self-control, persistence, and determination—which are critical for success but more likely influenced through working on longer-term projects than studying for tests (Duckworth, Quinn, & Tsukayama, 2012). As research began to accumulate indicating that "noncognitive skills"—such as grit, empathy, and self-control—were just as significant influences on school success as intelligence or scholastic aptitude, experts began to call for schools to add "socioemotional learning" to their curriculum in order to stimulate the growth of social skills, self-reliance, and self-management (National Commission on Social, Emotional, and Academic Development, 2018).

No Child Left Behind remained in place after President Barack Obama took office in 2009, although his administration sought to fix many of the problems that had developed during the policy's early years: that schools were "gaming the system" by setting their standards especially low, so that they could report that a high proportion of their students were making passing grades; that teachers were teaching to the test in order to avoid being punished if their students tested poorly; and that school districts were reporting schoolwide average scores without revealing that there were huge achievement gaps between the low- and

social promotion
The practice of promoting students from one grade to the next automatically, regardless of their school performance.

critical thinking
Thinking that involves analyzing, evaluating, and interpreting information, rather than simply memorizing it.

standards-based reform
Policies designed to improve achievement by holding schools and students to a predetermined set of standards measured by achievement tests.

Common Core
A proposed set of standards in language arts and mathematics that all American schools would be expected to use.

charter schools
Public schools that have been given the autonomy to establish their own curricula and teaching practices.

high-performing students. President Obama's education secretary stressed the need to have high standards for all students and, just as important, a set of *common* standards across all 50 states (U.S. Department of Education, 2009).

The Obama administration also tried to build more flexibility into NCLB by encouraging schools to experiment with different approaches to raising student achievement through a competition called "Race to the Top." As new research began to demonstrate the importance of having high-quality teachers, schools were encouraged to develop better ways of evaluating their teachers, helping teachers improve their classroom skills, and replacing poor teachers with better ones. Unfortunately, "Race to the Top" didn't change high school student achievement any more than NCLB did (Steinberg, 2014a).

Debates about how to turn America's high schools around have continued. After President Donald Trump took office, he appointed a Secretary of Education whose main priority was expanding and strengthening parents' ability to choose their child's school. Although, like all education policy makers, her ultimate goal was to improve student achievement, she argued that the best way to do this is to encourage schools to improve by having them compete for students by letting parents use government-funded education vouchers across an array of conventional, charter, and private schools (including schools with religious affiliations). Critics of this approach argued that it would drain money from public school districts and create further gaps in quality between schools for children from affluent families (who would use their own resources to supplement the vouchers and withdraw their children from public schools) and poor ones.

During President Joseph Biden's first year, his administration's secondary education policy focused mainly on developing strategies for reopening the nation's middle schools and high schools, as the COVID-19 pandemic began to wane somewhat, mainly as a result of the massive push to vaccinate as many Americans as possible, including many secondary school students. Once schools reopen, the Biden's education team plans to turn their attention to undoing many of President Trump's education initiatives and, especially, reversing the flow of money that has been diverted to private schools through voucher programs and other mechanisms, so that public schools are better funded. One explicit goal of this plan is to close longstanding achievement gaps between students from different socioeconomic and ethnic backgrounds.

What Should Schools Teach?

Suppose you are asked to list the things you think young people need to know in order to be competent, responsible, satisfied adults. Which items on your list should be the responsibility of high schools? Should high school curricula be limited to traditional academic subjects, or should schools play a broader role in preparing young people for adulthood by providing instruction more directly relevant to work, family, leisure, and citizenship? Should students receive instruction only in English, mathematics, science, and social studies, or should they take courses as well in "general education"—in subjects such as art, home economics, health, sex education, driver education, and personal finance? Which courses should be required, and which should be left as electives?

Standards-Based Reform   The past five decades have been dominated by what is called **standards-based reform,** which focuses on policies designed to improve achievement by holding schools and students to a predetermined set of benchmarks measured by achievement tests. This gave rise to proposals that American schools adopt the **Common Core,** a set of standards in English language arts and mathematics that schools across the country would be expected to use to evaluate whether their students were learning what they ought to learn in each grade. Although states were given wide flexibility in how they would implement the standards—they would have control over the curriculum and instructional methods they would use—the Common Core continues to be controversial. Many states that signed on to the plan initially have since broken from it.

Like NCLB, standards-based reform sounds good in principle, but implementing this change has been more difficult than you might think. Educators haven't been able to agree on the body of knowledge and skills that comprise what high school graduates should know and be able to do. And, as states soon discovered, large numbers of their students did not fully acquire the knowledge and capabilities assessed on standardized graduation examinations. It sounds reasonable to require that all high school seniors pass a graduation test in order to earn a diploma, but what happens when one-third or one-half of a state's high school seniors fail the test, as was the case in many parts of the country when the new standards and tests were first implemented? The economic, social, and political costs of holding back such large numbers of students because they could not pass these "exit exams" was simply too great. This created a huge incentive for states to develop exams with very low requirements for passing, which, of course, defeats the whole purpose of standards-based reform.

Amid widespread disappointment over the state of public education in America, increasing numbers of parents began to look at other options—among them, **charter schools** (public schools that are given more freedom to set their own curricula), schools that are run by private corporations rather than local school boards, home schooling, and government-subsidized school **vouchers** (which can be used for private school tuition). Although all of these alternatives gained popularity during the late 1990s, research on their costs and benefits has been inconclusive (Steinberg, 2014a). There is considerable variability among charter, for-profit, and private schools, as well as homeschooling environments, just as there is among public schools. What takes place within a school is probably more important than the nature of its funding and oversight.

making the cultural connection

The United States is one of the only industrialized countries in the world that does not have national graduation examinations that are administered to all students, regardless of where they go to school. Do you think having national exams is a good or bad idea? Why do you think this practice is not as popular in the United States as it is elsewhere?

Education in the Inner Cities

The education crisis, and its implications for the future of the labor force, is especially urgent within inner-city public schools. Indeed, the achievement gap between white and nonwhite youngsters, which had been closing for some time, grew wider during the 1990s, especially in large urban school districts. It narrowed again toward the end of the twentieth century but has remained substantial since. Indeed, the race gap in achievement is nearly as large now as it was in the 1960s (Hanusshek, 2016).

Although there are occasional success stories, such as the Harlem Children's Zone (Tough, 2008) or KIPP (www.kipp.org), a system of charter schools that creates a culture of achievement, maintains high expectations for all students, and emphasizes character development as well as academics, inner-city schools in America continue to have tremendous problems. Just 10% of the high schools in the United States produce *half* of the country's dropouts, and one-third of Black and Latinx students attend one of these "dropout factories" (Sparks, 2015). And, although there have been modest improvements in some subjects at some grade levels, the gap in achievement between Black and Latinx students, on the one hand, and white and Asian students, on the other, remains very wide. Among 8th-graders, for example, 61% of Asian students and 43% of white students are proficient in math, compared to 19% of Latinx students and 13% of Black students. Huge gaps exist in reading as well, with 57% of Asian students and 42% of white students proficient, compared to 22% of Latinx students and 15% of

School reform has failed in many urban districts. Many commentators believe that it is necessary to change the community, not just the school. Don Tremain/Alamy Stock Photo

Black students (National Center for Education Statistics, 2020). In the nation's large inner-city public schools, fewer than 20% of students are judged proficient in science, a fact that has enormous implications for these adolescents' chances at success in an increasingly high-tech economy (National Center for Education Statistics, 2019a).

Why has school reform failed in so many urban schools? Experts point to several factors.

First, the concentration of poverty in many inner-city communities has produced a population of students with an array of personal problems—problems that few schools are equipped or able to address (Farrell et al., 2007). Recent surveys of American high school students indicate that so many are afraid of being victimized that nearly 10% of American high school students did not go to school during the month prior to the survey (Centers for Disease Control and Prevention, 2020). About 15% said that they had been threatened with a weapon, such as a gun or knife, and 20% said that they had been bullied during the past month. Many urban school districts are burdened by huge administrative

vouchers
Government-subsidized vouchers that can be used for private school tuition.

bureaucracies that impede reform and hinder educational innovation. Students in urban schools report less of a sense of "belonging" to their school, which leads to disengagement and poor achievement (Anderman, 2002). And the erosion of job opportunities in inner-city communities has left many students with little incentive to remain in school or to devote a great deal of effort to academic pursuits, a worry that likely increased during the COVID-19 pandemic. Many reformers now believe that to fix the problems of urban education, we must change the entire context in which inner-city children live, not merely what goes on in their schools (Tough, 2008).

The Social Organization of Schools

In addition to debating curricular issues, social scientists interested in school reform have discussed the ways in which secondary schools should be organized. Because the organization of a school affects students' day-to-day experiences, variations in school organization can have profound effects on adolescents' development and behavior. In this section, we examine the research on five key aspects of school organization: (1) school and classroom size, (2) different approaches to age grouping, (3) tracking, or the grouping of students in classes according to their academic abilities, (4) the ethnic composition of schools, and (5) public versus private schools.

School Size and Class Size

As the idea of the comprehensive high school gained widespread acceptance, educators attempted to deliver a wider range of courses and services under a single roof. As a consequence, schools became larger and larger over the course of the twentieth century. By the end of the 1990s, in many metropolitan areas, students attended enormous schools, with enrollments of several thousand students.

Is Bigger Better? One advantage enjoyed by larger schools is that they can offer a more varied curriculum; a large high school, for instance, may be able to offer many specialized courses that a small school is unable to staff. But is bigger necessarily better? Most research conducted over the past 40 years says no.

Evaluations of school reform efforts have found that student performance and interest in school improve when their schools are made less bureaucratic and more intimate. Numerous studies indicate that students achieve more when they attend schools that create a cohesive sense of

schools within schools Subdivisions of the student body within large schools created to foster feelings of belongingness.

community (Ready, Lee, & Welner, 2004). Students' attachment to school is weaker in larger schools, particularly when the number of students in a grade exceeds 400 (Holas & Huston, 2012; Weiss, Carolan, & Baker-Smith, 2010). Studies also find that there is more inequality in students' educational experiences in larger schools, where students may be sorted into tracks of differing quality. In small schools, in contrast, it is more likely that all students are exposed to the same curriculum, if only because the school cannot afford to offer more than one.

School size especially affects the participation of students whose grades are not very good. In large schools, academically marginal students often feel like outsiders and rarely get involved in school activities. In small schools, however, these students feel a sense of involvement and obligation equal to that of more academically successful students. The ideal size of a high school is between 600 and 900 students (Lee & Smith, 1997).

While school size may affect academic outcomes, it does not necessarily affect students' emotional attachment to the institution (Anderman, 2002) or their mental health (Watt, 2003). Contrary to widespread opinion, there is no evidence that rates of student victimization are higher in larger schools, although victimization is less likely in schools where the student-teacher ratio is lower, perhaps because it is easier for schools to establish and enforce norms about how to behave (Gottfredson & DiPietro, 2011; Klein & Cornell, 2010). In addition, many large schools are divided into **schools within schools.** Although few such transformations have been studied systematically, the existing research indicates both advantages and disadvantages to this approach. On the positive side, creating schools within schools leads to the development of a more positive social environment; on the negative side, though, if not done carefully, schools may inadvertently create "schools" within one school that vary considerably in their educational quality.

One potential advantage of larger schools is that they can support more athletic teams, after-school clubs, and student organizations. But because large schools also contain so many more students, actual rates of participation in different activities are only half as high in large schools as in smaller ones. As a result, in larger schools, students tend more often to be observers than participants in school activities. For instance, during the fall, a small school and a large school might each field teams in football, soccer, and cross-country running, together requiring a total of 100 students. An individual's chances of being 1 of those 100 students are greater in a school that has only 500 students than in a school with an enrollment of 4,000.

In a small school, chances are that most students eventually will find themselves on a team, in the student government, or in an extracurricular organization. Students in small schools also are more likely to be placed in positions of leadership and responsibility, and they more often report having done things that made them feel confident and diligent.

What About Class Size?   Encouraged by the results of research on smaller *schools,* many politicians have called for smaller *classes.* However, in contrast to studies of schools, studies of classrooms indicate that variations within the typical range of classroom sizes—from 20 to 40 students—do not affect students' scholastic achievement once they have reached adolescence. Small classes benefit young elementary school children (up until third grade), who may need more individualized instruction (Finn, Gerber, & Boyd-Zaharias, 2005), but adolescents in classes with 40 students learn just as much as those in classes with 20 (Mosteller, Light, & Sachs, 1996).

An important exception to this finding involves situations that call for highly individualized instruction or tutoring, where smaller classes are more effective even at the high school level. For example, in remedial classes, in which teachers must give a great deal of attention to each student, small classes are valuable. One implication of these findings is that it may be profitable for schools to increase the size of regular classes (e.g., from 25 students to 40) and reduce the number of classrooms in a school, which would allow the school to free up some teachers, add more classes for students who need specialized, small-group instruction, and keep these class sizes small.

Age Grouping and School Transitions

Early in the twentieth century, most school districts separated youngsters into an elementary school (which had either six or eight grades) and a secondary school (which had either four or six grades). Students changed schools once (after either sixth or eighth grade). However, many educators felt that the two-school system was unable to meet the special needs of young adolescents, whose intellectual and emotional maturity was greater than that expected in elementary school but not yet at the level necessary for high school. During the early years of compulsory secondary education, the establishment of separate schools for young adolescents began, and the **junior high school** (which contained the seventh, eighth, and sometimes ninth grades) was born (Hechinger, 1993). Toward the end of the twentieth century, the **middle school**—a three- or four-year school housing the seventh and eighth grades with one or more younger grades—gained in popularity, replacing the junior high school in many districts (Elmore, 2009).

In recent years, many school districts have moved away from housing young adolescents separately and are returning to a two-school model (usually kindergarten through eighth grade and ninth grade through 12th), in light of studies showing that students demonstrate higher achievement and fewer behavioral problems under this arrangement (Weiss & Baker-Smith, 2010). It is important to note, however, that the particular grade configuration of a school is less important than the school's educational climate and quality of instruction (Elmore, 2009; Holas & Huston, 2012).

> **junior high school**
> An educational institution designed during the early era of public secondary education in which young adolescents are schooled separately from older adolescents.
>
> **middle school**
> An educational institution housing 7th- and 8th-grade students along with adolescents who are 1 or 2 years younger.

Researchers have studied whether young adolescents fare better or worse in middle schools or junior high schools that separate them from children and older adolescents. Many districts are eliminating these schools and returning to a model that has just an elementary school and a high school. Maskot/Corbis

making the scientific connection

In light of what you know about development during early adolescence, what do you think of the idea of eliminating separate middle schools and dividing schools in a district into one serving grades kindergarten through eighth and the other serving grades ninth through 12th?

The Transition into Secondary School   Many studies find that students' academic motivation, school engagement, and school grades drop as they move from elementary into middle or junior high school (Castro-Schilo et al., 2016; Dotterer, McHale, & Crouter, 2009). Scores on standardized achievement tests don't decline during this same time, though, suggesting that the drop in grades may be more a reflection of changes in grading practices and student motivation than in students' knowledge (Eccles, 2004). There is some recovery of motivation and perseverance over the course of middle school, but, after increasing, these tend to plateau after the transition to high school (Shubert, Wray-Lake, & McKay, 2020).

Researchers also have examined how transitioning to a new school affects student achievement and behavior. In many of these studies, researchers compare school arrangements in which students remain in elementary school until eighth grade—that is, in which they change schools once—with arrangements in which they move from elementary school, to middle or junior high school, and then to high school—in which they change schools twice.

In general, school transitions, whenever they occur, temporarily disrupt the academic performance, behavior, and self-image of adolescents. More frequent school changes are associated with lower achievement as well as higher rates of emotional and behavioral problems (Herbers, Reynolds, & Chen, 2013). Over time, though, most youngsters adapt successfully to changing schools, especially when other aspects of their life—family and peer relations, for example—remain stable and supportive and when the new school environment is well suited for adolescents (Seidman et al., 2003).

Researchers do not agree about whether the drop in academic motivation and achievement that occurs after elementary school is due to the school transition itself (that is, whether it is simply because students suffer *whenever* they have to change schools) or to the nature of the difference between elementary school, on the one hand, and middle or junior high school, on the other. Some experts believe that the poor performance of middle and junior high schools is due primarily to their failure to meet the particular developmental needs of young adolescents (Booth & Gerard, 2014; Eccles & Roeser, 2009).

Between sixth and eighth grade, for example, students report declines in how supportive their teachers and classmates are, how much autonomy students have, and how clear and fair school rules are (Way, Reddy, & Rhodes, 2007). Because adolescence is a time during which relationships with peers and nonfamilial adults become more important, independence becomes more desirable, and rules and regulations are increasingly scrutinized, these changes in school climate create a mismatch between what adolescents need and what their schools provide. This leads many young adolescents to disengage from school (Hughes et al., 2015; Yu et al., 2016). Unfortunately, disengaging from school increases the risk of developing behavior problems, whereas remaining connected to school protects against some of the harmful effects of poor family relationships (Loukas, Roalson, & Herrera, 2010; Oelsner, Lippold, & Greenberg, 2011; Wang, Brinkworth, & Eccles, 2013).

How Secondary Schools Differ from Elementary Schools The classroom environment in the typical middle school or junior high school is usually very different from that in the typical elementary school (Eccles, Lord, & Roeser, 1996). Not only are junior high schools larger and less personal, but middle and junior high school teachers hold different beliefs about students than do elementary school teachers—even when they teach students of the same chronological age (Midgley, Berman, & Hicks, 1995), and they are less likely than other teachers to feel confident about their teaching ability (Eccles & Roeser, 2009).Teachers in junior high schools are less likely to trust their students and more likely to emphasize discipline, which creates a mismatch between what students at this age desire (more independence) and what their teachers want (more control). Teachers in junior high schools also tend to be more likely to believe that students' abilities are fixed and not easily modified through instruction—a belief that interferes with student achievement.

It is hardly surprising that students experience a drop in achievement motivation when they enter middle or junior high school, given the change in environments they experience and the mismatch between what adolescents need developmentally and what the typical school context offers. Although students' self-esteem drops during the transition into middle or junior high school, it increases during the early high school years, so changing schools in and of itself isn't the problem. Consistent with this, middle school students attending more personal, less departmentalized schools or schools where they are more involved do better than their peers in more rigid and more anonymous schools (Wang & Holcombe, 2010). Not surprisingly, changing schools is easier on students who move into small rather than large institutions.

Why do junior high school teachers differ from those who teach elementary school? The answer isn't clear-cut. People who choose to become junior high teachers do not differ all that much from those who choose to teach younger grades. Rather, it may be that the bureaucratic organization and anonymity of junior high schools have a negative effect on the teachers who work in them, which affects the way they interact with students. There is a lot of evidence that students are more engaged in school when their teachers are more engaged in their work (Louis & Smith, 1992).

Individual Differences in the Extent of Transitional Problems Although some aspects of the transition into secondary school may be difficult for students to negotiate, not all students experience the same degree of stress (Fenzel, 2001). Students who have more academic and psychosocial problems before making a school transition cope less successfully with it (Little & Garber, 2004; Murdock, Anderman, & Hodge, 2000). Often there are cascading effects, with academic and behavioral problems in elementary school leading to more problems during the transition into middle school (Moilanen, Shaw, & Maxwell, 2010).

Cascades can work in the opposite direction as well; students scoring high in social competence before the transition into a new school become even more competent over the course of the change. In the face of the challenges posed by changing schools, "the psychosocially rich become richer, while the psychologically poor become poorer" (Monahan & Steinberg, 2011, p. 576).

Factors other than students' prior record also influence their transition to middle or high school. Adolescents who have close friends before and during the transition adapt more successfully to the new school environment (Wentzel, Barry, & Caldwell, 2004), although the benefits of staying with their friends accrue only to students who had been doing well previously. Students who had been doing poorly actually adjust better if they enroll in a different school than their friends, perhaps because their friends were contributing to their poor performance (Schiller, 1999).

In short, the transition into secondary school does not have uniform effects on all students (Jackson & Schulenberg, 2013; Li & Lerner, 2011). More vulnerable adolescents, adolescents with fewer sources of social support, and adolescents moving into more impersonal schools are more susceptible to the adverse consequences of this transition than their peers are (Benner, Boyle, & Bakhtiari, 2017; Kiuru et al., 2020; Nelemans et al., 2018). Not surprisingly, studies of poor, inner-city youngsters, who often are coping with problems associated with economic stress and neighborhood disadvantage, find especially significant negative effects of the school transition on these students' self-esteem, achievement, perceptions of the school environment, reports of social support, and participation in extracurricular activities (Eccles, 2004).

Generally speaking, boys, ethnic minority students, and students from poor families are more likely to become disengaged from school during early adolescence (Li & Lerner, 2011). Among Black and Latinx students, transitioning to a school in which the proportion of students from the same ethnic background is lower than it had been at their previous school is associated with greater disengagement from school, lower grades, and more frequent absences (Benner & Graham, 2009).

Parental support and involvement also are associated with better adolescent adjustment during school transitions (Isakson & Jarvis, 1999). One study of low-income Black students found that students who fare best during the transition not only have parents who are involved in their education but supportive teachers as well (Gutman & Midgley, 2000). It is therefore possible to enhance low-income students' adjustment to middle school through interventions targeted at their parents.

Tracking

In some schools, students with different academic abilities and interests do not attend classes together. Some classes are designated as more challenging and more rigorous, and are reserved for students identified as especially capable. Other classes in the same subject area are designated as average classes and are taken by most students. Still others are designated as remedial classes and are reserved for students having academic difficulties. The process of separating students into different levels of classes within the same school is called ability grouping, or **tracking.** Not all high schools track students. In some schools, students with different abilities take all their classes together.

> **tracking**
> The practice of separating students into ability groups, so that they take classes with peers at the same skill level.

Pros and Cons of Tracking Educators have debated the pros and cons of tracking for years, but research provides no definitive answers about its overall effects (Eccles & Roeser, 2009). Proponents of tracking note that ability grouping allows teachers to design class lessons that are more finely tuned to students' abilities. Tracking may be especially useful in high school, where students must master certain basic skills before they can learn such specialized subjects as science, math, or foreign languages. Critics of tracking point out, however, that students in the remedial track receive not just a different education but one that's worse than that provided to those in more advanced tracks (Darling-Hammond, 1997). Moreover, the effects of tracking are not limited to academic outcomes. Schools play an important role in influencing adolescents' friendship choices. When students are tracked, they tend to socialize only with peers from the same academic group. Tracking can polarize the student body into different subcultures that are often hostile toward each other (Eccles & Roeser, 2009).

Critics of tracking also point out that decisions about track placements often discriminate against poor and ethnic minority students and may hinder rather than enhance their academic progress (Oakes, 1995). Some school counselors may assume that ethnic minority or poor youngsters are not capable of handling the work in advanced classes and may automatically assign them to average or remedial classes, where less material is covered and the work is less challenging. One analysis of national data found that Black students were especially likely to be enrolled in lower-track math classes in schools in which Blacks are in the minority, even after taking into account students' qualifications (Kelly, 2009).

Not all research indicates that track placements are biased. Other studies have found that students' ability has a stronger influence than their background on initial track placement (Dauber, Alexander, & Entwisle, 1996) but that middle-class and white students initially placed in lower tracks are more likely to be moved into higher ones, in part because their parents frequently succeed in "lobbying" their child's school for a higher track placement (Hallinan, 1996; Wells & Serna, 1996). Adolescents from well-off families more frequently consult with their parents about what courses to take than do less affluent adolescents, which leads more affluent students to take more (and more advanced) math and science classes (Crosnoe & Huston, 2007).

gifted students
Students who are unusually talented in some aspect of intellectual performance.

learning disability
A difficulty with academic tasks that cannot be traced to an emotional problem or sensory dysfunction.

On the Wrong Track   Early track placements set in motion an educational trajectory that is often difficult to change without the deliberate intervention of the student's parents (Dauber, Alexander, & Entwisle, 1996; Hallinan, 1996). And the ways in which students' schedules are arranged may lead students to be tracked in several different subject areas simply because they are tracked in one class, which makes the effects of tracking even more substantial (Heck, Price, & Thomas, 2004). If the only class period during which advanced math is offered is the same as the class period during which remedial English is taught, a student who is assigned to remedial English will not be able to take advanced math (Lucas & Berends, 2002).

Students in different tracks have markedly different opportunities to learn (Gamoran, 1996). Those in the more advanced tracks receive more challenging instruction and better teaching, and they are more likely to engage in classroom activities that emphasize critical thinking rather than rote memorization (Darling-Hammond, 1997). As a result, being placed in a more advanced track has a positive influence on school achievement (how much the student actually learns over time), on subsequent course selection (what curriculum the student is exposed to), and on ultimate educational attainment (how many years of schooling the student completes). To the extent that a student's family background influences his or her track placement, tracking has the effect of maintaining income inequality (Oakes, 2005).

Because students are assigned to different tracks on the basis of test scores and other indicators of aptitude

and because students in the lower tracks receive an inferior education (which leads to lower test scores), the net effect of tracking over time is to increase preexisting academic differences among students. Students who need the most help are assigned to the tracks in which the quality of instruction is the poorest; not surprisingly, studies find that students in lower tracks exert less effort, which also limits their learning (Callahan, 2005; Carbonaro, 2005). Although students in the lower tracks usually get the short end of the educational stick, there are some exceptions; for example, schools in which classes in the lower tracks are taught by strong teachers who insist on maintaining high standards (Hallinan, 1996).

The Effects of Tracking on Student Achievement
Hundreds of studies have looked at the impact of tracking on student achievement, but the answer is complicated (Hallinan, 1996). Some studies find that the effects are mixed and small in magnitude (Bygren, 2016). Others find that tracking has both positive and negative effects and, more important, different effects on students in different tracks. Generally, tracking has positive effects on the achievement of high-track students, negative effects on low-track students, and negligible effects on students in the middle (Hallinan, 1996). Because of this, decisions about whether to implement tracking in nontracked schools or to "detrack" schools that use tracking are often controversial. Understandably, parents of students in the higher tracks favor the practice, while parents of students in the lower tracks oppose it (Wells & Serna, 1996).

Even in schools that do not have formal tracking, teachers may group students within the same class into ability groups. In such an arrangement, students may have a wider range of peers with whom to compare themselves than they would in separate tracks, since their classes are more diverse in composition. The impact of this comparison on both students and teachers is quite interesting. For high-ability students, within-classroom ability grouping raises their expectations for achievement and raises their teachers' evaluations of them; for low-ability students, the opposite is true: They have lowered expectations and get worse grades from their teachers (Reuman, 1989). In classes with mixed ability groups, the high-ability students look better and the low-ability students look worse than they would in a conventionally tracked school or in a school in which ability grouping is not used (Marsh et al., 1995). As is the case with tracking, within-classroom ability grouping also exposes students in different groups to different levels of educational quality, with students in the high-ability groups receiving more challenging instruction and more engaging learning experiences.

Students at the Extremes   Related to the issue of tracking are questions concerning the placement of individuals who are considered **gifted students** and of those who have a **learning disability**. Adolescents who score 130

Research on tracking suggests that it has positive effects on the achievement of students in the more advanced tracks but negative effects on students in the lower tracks.
Pradeep Edussuriya/McGraw Hill

or higher on an intelligence test are considered gifted. Adolescents with a learning disability are those whose actual performance is significantly poorer than their expected performance (based on intelligence or aptitude tests, for example) and whose difficulty with academic tasks cannot be traced to an emotional problem, such as coping with a parental divorce, or a sensory dysfunction, such as a visual or hearing impairment.

Most learning disabilities are neurological in origin (Berninger & Miller, 2011). Common types of specific learning disabilities include **dyslexia** (impaired ability in reading or spelling), **dysgraphia** (impaired ability in handwriting), and **dyscalculia** (impaired ability in arithmetic). Learning disabilities are common: About one in five school-age children and youth is at risk for a learning disability, with rates of learning disabilities significantly more common among boys than girls (Berninger & Miller, 2011).

Educators have debated whether gifted students and those with learning disabilities are best served by instruction in separate classes (for example, in enriched classes for gifted students or in special education classes for students with a learning disability) or by **mainstreaming,** the integration of all students with special needs into regular classrooms. Pros and cons of each approach have been identified. On the one hand, separate special education programs can be tailored to meet the specific needs of students and can target educational and professional resources in a cost-effective way. On the other hand, segregating students on the basis of academic ability may foster social isolation and stigmatization—either for being "stupid" or for being a "brainiac."

Generally, educators favor mainstreaming over separate classrooms for adolescents with special needs. (In the case of adolescents with disabilities, mainstreaming, whenever possible, is required by law in the United States.) Proponents of mainstreaming argue that the psychological costs of separating adolescents with special academic needs from their peers outweigh the potential academic benefits. Studies of gifted youngsters have found, for example, that those who are integrated into regular classrooms have more positive academic self-conceptions than those assigned to special classes and that these effects persist even after graduating (Marsh et al., 2007).

One downside to being placed with students of high academic ability is that when students compare themselves to their high-achieving classmates, they don't feel as competent as they would if their point of comparison were students who were not so smart (Becker et al., 2014; Thijs, Verkuyten, & Helmond, 2010). This phenomenon, called the **big fish–little pond effect,** has been documented around the world (Marsh et al., 2015; Marsh & Hau, 2003). The effect seems to be limited to what goes on in students' regular schools; students who participate in summer programs for the academically talented don't seem to suffer psychologically as a consequence (Makel et al., 2012).

Being a big fish in a little pond is also helpful for admission to college. One study of some 45,000 applications to three elite universities found that applicants' chances of being accepted are greater when they come from high schools with a relatively lower proportion of other high-achieving students than when applicants with the same credentials come from high schools with many other high achievers (Espenshade, Hale, & Chung, 2005). In addition, high-ability students who attend schools in which the student body is more diverse also have higher career aspirations, in part because they feel better about themselves in comparison to their peers (Nagengast & Marsh, 2012). There's a catch, though: Although high-ability students who attend schools with peers who are less talented feel better about themselves, they actually may learn less (Wouters et al., 2012).

Whereas the big fish–little pond effect suggests that gifted students might not be better off psychologically in classes restricted to high-achieving students—and argues in favor of mainstreaming them—it poses a dilemma for those who favor mainstreaming students with learning disabilities. Low-achieving students, when mainstreamed, end up comparing themselves to students whose performance is better and may end up feeling worse about themselves than had they been separated into special classes with comparably achieving peers (Marsh & Hau, 2003). Perhaps because of this, even with mainstreaming, adolescents who have learning disabilities may suffer psychological consequences related to their problems in school. Compared with average-achieving students, adolescents with learning disabilities report more social and behavioral difficulties and more problems coping with school. They are also more likely than other adolescents to have poor peer relations, are less likely to participate in school-based extracurricular activities, and are more likely to drop out of school (Berninger & Miller, 2011). Given the tremendous importance society places on school success, it is not difficult to see why students who have difficulties learning would suffer psychological as well as scholastic problems.

Experts recommend that adolescents with learning disabilities receive extra instruction in study skills, time management, organization skills, note-taking, and proofreading. In addition, they may need help in increasing motivation, dealing with social and emotional difficulties resulting from problematic peer relationships, overcoming their reluctance to participate in class or seek assistance from teachers, and coping with fears that they are not as

dyslexia
Impaired ability in reading or spelling.

dysgraphia
Impaired ability in handwriting.

dyscalculia
Impaired ability in arithmetic.

mainstreaming
The integration of adolescents who have educational handicaps into regular classrooms.

big fish–little pond effect
The reason that individuals who attend high school with high-achieving peers feel worse about themselves than comparably successful individuals with lower-achieving peers.

intelligent as other students (which is not the case) or that they will be failures as adults (Berninger & Miller, 2011).

Attention Deficit/Hyperactivity Disorder Although it is not technically a learning disability, adolescents who have **attention deficit/hyperactivity disorder (ADHD)** frequently have academic difficulties that can be traced to this problem. ADHD is usually diagnosed during childhood, but the condition persists into adolescence in 50 to 70% of cases and into adulthood in about half of all children with the diagnosis (Antshel & Barkley, 2011). The estimated prevalence of ADHD in childhood and adolescence is approximately 7% (R. Thomas et al., 2015). One reason the prevalence of ADHD declines with age is that some individuals develop better attention and impulse control as they mature from childhood into adolescence and adulthood.

On average, ADHD is much more likely to be diagnosed in boys than girls, but one recent study indicates that this may simply be because boys show the signs at a younger age and in order for there to be a clinical diagnosis of the disorder, the symptoms have to have appeared prior to adolescence. Disproportionately more girls than boys first show the symptoms of ADHD after childhood, which technically disqualifies them from the formal diagnosis. This explains why, in childhood, many more boys than girls are diagnosed with ADHD, whereas the prevalence of the disorder among adults does not differ for men and women (Murray et al., 2019) (see Figure 6.2).

attention deficit/ hyperactivity disorder (ADHD)
A biologically based psychological disorder characterized by impulsivity, inattentiveness, and restlessness, often in school situations.

ADHD is defined by persistent and impairing symptoms of inattention, impulsivity, and/or hyperactivity, although the defining feature of ADHD in adolescence (as opposed to childhood) is generally inattention, rather than impulsivity or hyperactivity (Sibley et al., 2012). ADHD is a biological disorder with a very strong genetic component (Peng et al., 2016; Pingault et al., 2015; Chang et al., 2013). In addition, it can be caused by damage to the brain either prenatally (sometimes caused by maternal smoking or drinking during pregnancy) or shortly after birth (as the result of birth complications, low birth weight, or changes in the brain as a consequence of early childhood adversity) (Humphreys et al., 2019).

Adolescents with ADHD are classified into one of three subtypes: predominantly inattentive (about 30 to 40% of all cases), predominantly hyperactive/impulsive (fewer than 5% of all cases and rarely seen during adolescence), or combined (between 50 and 60% of all cases). In addition to being at risk for academic difficulties, individuals with ADHD are also at risk for a wide range of nonscholastic problems, including substance abuse, behavior problems, difficulties in delay of gratification, anxiety, problematic peer relations, obesity, and depression (Demurie et al., 2012; Khalife et al., 2014; Sayal, Washbrook, & Propper, 2015; Seymour et al., 2014; Tseng et al., 2014). ADHD also is present in many cases of serious juvenile delinquency.

Recent studies of brain development during adolescence point to delays or deficiencies in the development of regions that are known to be associated with self-regulation, such as the prefrontal cortex; synaptic pruning of this region occurs at a slower pace among individuals with ADHD than among those without the

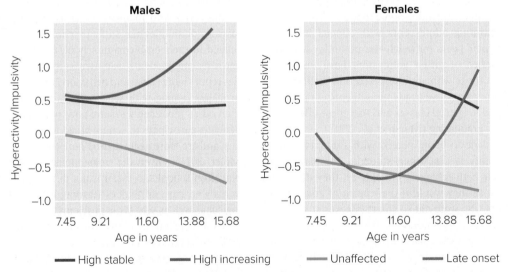

Figure 6.2 In early adolescence, there is a much steeper increase in hyperactivity and impulsivity among girls than boys. Adolescent boys with ADHD are much more likely to have exhibited the symptoms early in elementary school. Because many diagnostic guidelines for ADHD require the onset of symptoms prior to adolescence, many adolescent girls who have attention problems are never actually diagnosed with ADHD. (Murray et al., 2019)

disorder. Interestingly, individuals who do not have ADHD but who are more hyperactive and impulsive than their peers show patterns of brain development that are somewhere between those seen in adolescents with ADHD and adolescents who have very good impulse control, which suggests that ADHD may be an extreme point on a continuum rather than a qualitatively distinct category (Shaw et al., 2011). There is also evidence that adolescents with ADHD are more reward sensitive (Von Rhein et al., 2015), which may bias their decision making toward risk taking (Pollak et al., 2016).

ADHD is frequently treated with some sort of stimulant medication, such as methylphenidate (Ritalin) or a combination of amphetamines (e.g., Adderall). Stimulant medication is helpful in about 70% of cases. Certain types of antidepressants, such as bupropion (Wellbutrin), have also been shown to be effective, especially with adolescents who have both ADHD and some sort of mood disorder, such as anxiety or depression. Psychological therapies for ADHD also are widely used, often in conjunction with medication, although such therapies are more commonly used with children than adolescents (Antshel & Barkley, 2011).

One concern about the wide use of stimulant medication by adolescents with ADHD is that many individuals who receive such medication share it with their nonafflicted friends, who may use the medication recreationally or for help with studying (stimulant medication improves attention in most individuals, regardless of whether they have ADHD). In addition, students who attend high-pressure schools may use ADHD medication selectively to improve their test performance, going on medication during the school year but going off it during the summer,

a practice seen much more in affluent communities than in poorer ones (King, Jennings, & Fletcher, 2014).

Ethnic Composition

Following the landmark U.S. Supreme Court rulings in *Brown v. Board of Education of Topeka* (1954, 1955), in which the Court found that it was unconstitutional to maintain separate schools for children on the basis of race, many school districts adopted measures designed to make schools more diverse. They did this either by assigning students to schools in a way that would create ethnic diversity or by encouraging voluntary desegregation, through measures such as having "magnet" schools that would create diversity by drawing students from different neighborhoods (for instance, by having citywide schools specializing in the performing arts). Although the Supreme Court ruled in 2007 that school districts may no longer use race as a factor in deciding how to assign students to schools (R. Barnes, 2007), efforts to create ethnic and racial diversity through voluntary measures are still in use in many cities.

Effects of Desegregation Studies of the short-term effects of desegregation on high school students have been mixed. On the one hand, research indicates that desegregation has surprisingly little impact on the achievement levels of either minority or white youngsters (Entwisle, 1990). In addition, some evidence suggests that minority youngsters' self-esteem is higher when they attend schools in which they are in the majority. In general, students fare better psychologically when the cultural environment of their neighborhood is consonant with the cultural environment of their school (Seaton & Yip, 2009). In schools that mix students from low- and high-income neighborhoods, students from low-income neighborhoods actually do worse than they do when they attend schools that are less socioeconomically diverse, especially if they are Black or Latinx (Crosnoe, 2009; Owens, 2010).

Consistent with this, students who have been bused to school out of their neighborhood report weaker feelings of attachment to their school than do students whose schools draw directly from the local community (Anderman, 2002). Students feel more engaged, safer, less lonely, and less harassed in relatively more diverse multiethnic schools (i.e., where the proportions of students from different ethnic groups are similar) than in multiethnic schools that are less balanced (Juvonen, Nishina, & Graham, 2006; Morales-Chicas & Graham, 2017). In general, though, research suggests that being in the minority in one's school is hard on students; it undermines students' attachment to school, which leads to depression and substance use (see Figure 6.3) (Benner & Wang, 2015). Research shows that the impact of going to school with a large proportion of students from the same ethnic

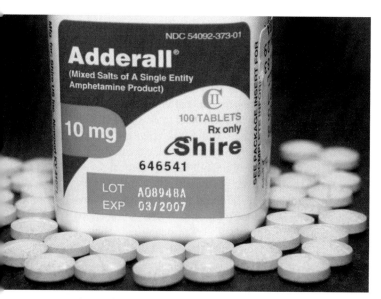

Adolescents with attention deficit/hyperactivity disorder (ADHD) are frequently prescribed stimulant medication, such as Ritalin or Adderall. These medicines are effective in about 70% of cases. Bloomberg/Getty Images

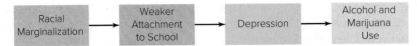

Figure 6.3 caption:

Figure 6.3 Students who are part of a very small racial minority in their school (less than 15% of the students) are less likely to feel attached to school, which increases depression and substance use. (Adapted from Benner & Graham, 2009)

background has more favorable consequences than attending a highly diverse school, which doesn't seem to affect students' mental health one way or the other (DuPont-Reyes & Villatoro, 2019).

Male and female students from ethnic minority groups often have different experiences with peers when they attend schools in which they are a small minority. Cross-ethnic friendships are more common among male than female students, in part because males are more likely to be involved in athletics, which provides opportunities for white and minority students to interact (Holland, 2012). In addition, in suburban schools to which inner-city students are bused, the view that Black boys are cool and tough leads them to be admired by white boys and included in social activities, whereas the stereotypes of Black girls as loud and assertive are off-putting to white girls, who aren't interested in socializing with them (Ispa-Landa, 2013).

Alternatives to Public Schools

Although the vast majority of students attending secondary school in America are enrolled in conventional public schools, a substantial minority attend private schools, either parochial (i.e., with a religious affiliation) or independent, or specially created public schools, such as charter schools or magnet schools. In the past, researchers cared little about studying differences between public schools and their alternatives. But during the late 1980s and 1990s, many policy makers suggested that one way to improve schools would be to give parents more choice in determining where their child was enrolled to force schools to compete for the best students. There is some evidence to support this: When information about school test scores is provided to parents, parents choose to send their children to higher-performing schools, which in turn increases the students' achievement (Hastings & Weinstein, 2008).

One concrete suggestion in this spirit, and one that was a centerpiece of education policy in the Trump administration, was that states provide parents with school vouchers that could be used to "purchase" education at a school of their choosing, private or public. Another suggestion was that states permit the development of charter schools—independent public schools that are freer to operate as they wish, without some of the constraints imposed by the state's education bureaucracy. In light of these suggestions, researchers became interested in whether some types of schools produced more high-achieving students than others.

making the practical connection

Providing parents with vouchers that they can use to send their children to private schools has been recommended as a way of improving the quality of schools by creating a "marketplace" in which schools must compete with each other. Critics of voucher programs argue that vouchers will encourage the families of the most talented students, with the most involved parents, to leave public schools and that public schools need good students and engaged parents to function effectively. Is there a way to resolve this conflict?

Are alternatives to public schools better than public schools? Although some studies have found that students' test scores are higher in private schools (especially Catholic schools), this appears to be due more to the characteristics of the students who attend them than to the private schools themselves (Hallinan & Kubitschek, 2012; Lubienski & Lubienski, 2006), although some studies have found genuine advantages for Catholic schools, especially for poor, inner-city, minority youth (Jeynes, 2002). Students who attend private school also may be encouraged (or required) to take more advanced courses than students in public schools, which contributes to their superior performance on achievement tests (Carbonaro & Covay, 2010).

There is less research on adolescents who are homeschooled, who account for about 3% of American adolescents, but it appears to be important to distinguish between homeschoolers who have strong religious ties and those who don't. Homeschooling for adolescents with strong religious ties doesn't seem to be a problem as far as achievement is concerned. But compared to teens with similar backgrounds who attend traditional schools, homeschooled adolescents with weak religious ties are three times more likely to be behind their expected grade level on achievement tests and only half as likely to participate in extracurricular activities (Green-Hennessy, 2014). In all likelihood, adolescents from religious families who are homeschooled are able to forge connections with other mentors and teenagers through their religious institutions, which may benefit them academically and with respect to extracurricular participation.

These studies, as well as a large body of research, indicate that students' family background is a far more powerful influence on their achievement than is the quality of the schools they attend. Similarly, evaluations of the impact of charter schools and voucher programs on student achievement, once students' background characteristics are taken into account, have not produced consistent results; at the very least, research indicates that these are not likely to be "silver bullets" in the effort to raise American student achievement (Loveless, 2002). This is also true in disadvantaged urban areas, where it had been hoped that charter schools might be the solution to the many problems that plague education in the inner city. One additional concern is that in urban areas, the availability of private schools contributes to racial segregation because many white students who would otherwise attend their neighborhood public school attend private school instead (Saporito & Sohoni, 2006).

Nevertheless, the climates of public and private schools, especially Catholic schools, are often very different. Many private schools are communities in which parents, teachers, and students all share similar values and attitudes. Strong communities, whether based in neighborhoods or schools, generate what has been called **social capital**—interpersonal resources that, like financial capital, give "richer" students advantages over "poorer" ones. Students profit from the social capital associated with attending a Catholic school because the lessons taught in school are reinforced at home, at church, and in the neighborhood and because the links between home and school are stronger (Teachman, Paasch, & Carver, 1996). In addition, private schools typically assign more homework and are more orderly and disciplined (an important element of the climate in good schools) (Coleman, Hoffer, & Kilgore, 1982). Students who attend private schools (Catholic or otherwise) are substantially less likely to report feeling unsafe, being exposed to gangs, or witnessing fighting between ethnic groups (Musu-Gillette, Zhang et al., 2017).

Although social scientists disagree over their interpretation, studies have shown that adolescents who attend parochial schools generally achieve at a higher rate than those attending public schools. The Washington Post/Getty Images

Classroom Climate

We have seen that certain elements of the school's social organization—size, age grouping, tracking, and so forth—can affect students' motivation, behavior, and achievement. But these factors have relatively modest effects on students, and they are important mainly because they influence what takes place in classrooms and in other school settings. Ultimately, the most important school-related influence on learning and psychosocial development during adolescence is what takes place in the classroom.

Various aspects of the school climate have important effects on youngsters' learning and achievement. How teachers interact with students, how classroom time is used, and what sorts of standards and expectations teachers hold for their students are all more important than the size of the school, its ethnic composition, its approach to ability grouping, or the way age groups are combined.

The Best Classroom Climate for Adolescents

What sort of climate brings out the best in students? Students achieve and are engaged more in school when they attend schools that are responsive and demanding. Moreover, academic functioning and psychological adjustment affect each other, so that a positive school climate—one in which relationships between students and teachers are positive and teachers are both supportive and demanding—enhances adolescents' psychological well-being, their beliefs about their future, their achievement, and their enrollment in higher education (Alm et al., 2019; Burns, 2020; Luengo Kanacri et al., 2017; Miklikowska, Thijs, & Hjerm, 2019; Minor & Benner, 2018), mainly by strengthening their engagement in class (Engels et al., 2020; Weyns et al., 2018) (see Figure 6.4). Attending a school with a positive climate even

social capital
The interpersonal resources available to an adolescent or family.

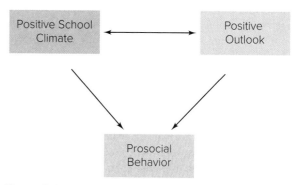

Figure 6.4 **A study of Colombian students found that a positive school climate contributes to, and results from, students' positive outlook on life and that both increase adolescents' prosocial behavior.** (Adapted from Luengo Kanacri et al., 2017)

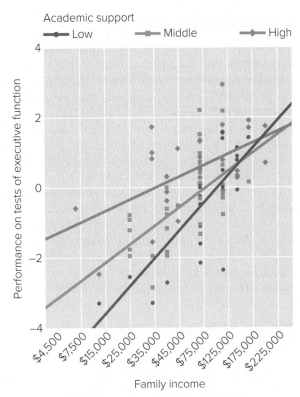

Figure 6.5 A supportive school climate has a much greater impact on cognitive performance among adolescents from disadvantaged families than on their peers from higher-income households. (Piccolo et al., 2019)

helps buffer the adverse consequences of exposure to violence in the community (Gaias et al., 2019) or poverty (Piccolo et al., 2019) (see Figure 6.5).

Students and teachers are more satisfied in classes that combine a moderate degree of structure with high student involvement and high teacher support, a finding that has emerged in studies of students from various socioeconomic backgrounds, ethnic groups, and countries (Jia et al., 2009; Way & Robinson, 2003). In these classes, teachers encourage students' participation but do not let class get out of control. Students do best when their teachers spend a high proportion of time on lessons (rather than on setting up equipment or dealing with discipline problems), begin and end lessons on time, provide clear feedback to students about what is expected of them, and give ample praise to students when they perform well (Eccles & Roeser, 2011). Students also demonstrate higher achievement when the classroom climate promotes cooperation between students, rather than competition (Roseth, Johnson, & Johnson, 2008).

One of the strongest influences on how much students enjoy going to school is the number of teachers they have positive relationships with (Martin & Collie, 2018). Students in schools in which teachers are supportive but firm and maintain high, well-defined standards for behavior and academic work have stronger bonds to their school and more positive achievement motives; these

beliefs and emotions, in turn, lead to fewer problems, even in the face of stress, as well as better attendance, stronger future orientation, lower rates of delinquency, more supportive friendships, less disruptive behavior, and higher test scores (Li & Lerner, 2011; Lindstrom Johnson, Pas, & Bradshaw, 2016; Shin & Ryan, 2017).

The pattern of classroom variables associated with positive student behavior and attitudes is similar to the authoritative family environment (Cornell & Huang, 2016; Pellerin, 2005). An overemphasis on control in the classroom in the absence of support is reminiscent of the authoritarian family, whereas a lack of clarity and organization is reminiscent of both the indulgent family and the indifferent family—and these styles in the classroom appear to affect adolescents detrimentally, just as they do at home. Schools that provide both structure and support have lower rates of suspension than other schools (Gregory, Cornell, & Fan, 2011). And when students trust their school and teachers, discipline is much more likely to improve student behavior (Amemiya & Wang, 2020) (see Figure 6.6).

School Climate and Bullying As awareness of the widespread problem of bullying has grown, researchers have asked whether certain school climates are more likely to produce bullying than others. Although we tend to think of bullying as a problem caused by callous and aggressive students, it is now well established that bullying is much more likely to occur in schools in which teachers are unsupportive and harsh, in which the school climate is disorderly, and in which students are not treated with respect (Banzon-Librojo, Garabiles, & Peña Alampay, 2017; Holfeld & Leadbeater, 2017; Shukla, Konold, & Cornell, 2016). Given the relatively higher prevalence of bullying of sexual minority teenagers, it is important that schools support the creation of gay-straight alliances and LGBTQ-focused policies (Day et al., 2020).

The recognition that a school's climate can contribute to the presence of bullying has raised a number of legal questions about whether schools are legally responsible for failing to take steps to prevent bullying; as of now, the law is unclear about this. But experts recommend that schools implement evidence-based antibullying programs, provide referrals for mental health services to both victims and bullies, provide training to school personnel in the identification and prevention of bullying, adopt and publicize policies that make it easier for students and parents to report bullying, and investigate reported or suspected bullying promptly (Cornell & Limber, 2015).

Teacher Expectations and Student Performance

There is a strong correlation between teacher expectations and student performance. This is both because teachers' expectations are often accurate reflections of

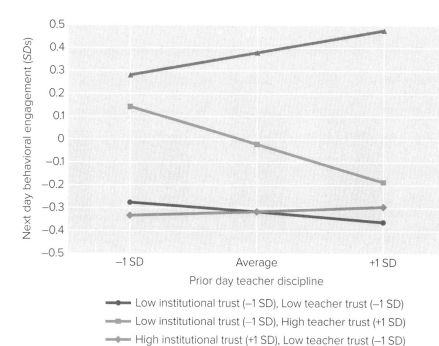

Figure 6.6 Students' engagement in school is likely to increase after they have been disciplined when they trust their school and their teacher. (Amemiya & Wang, 2020)

Student performance influences, and is influenced by, teacher expectations. SDI Productions/Getty Images

their students' ability and because teacher expectations actually create "**self-fulfilling prophecies**" that ultimately influence how their students behave (Jussim, Eccles & Madon, 1996). Teacher expectations have a cumulative long-term impact on student achievement, lowering the performance of students whose teachers perceive them as less capable than they actually are (de Boer, Bosker, & van der Werf, 2010). Children from poor families are particularly susceptible to the effects of teacher expectations, benefiting when expectations are high but suffering when they are low (Sorhagen, 2013).

Which pathway is more powerful: the impact of student performance on teacher expectations or the impact of teacher expectations on student performance? It appears that about 80% of the connection between teacher expectations and student achievement results from teachers having accurate perceptions, and about 20% is an effect of the self-fulfilling prophecy. Even though the self-fulfilling prophecy effect during any given school year is relatively small, it can be sizable when accumulated over years of schooling.

self-fulfilling prophecy The idea that individuals' behavior is influenced by others' expectations for them.

Because teachers' expectations influence students' performance, it is important to understand where these expectations come from. Unfortunately, teachers are likely to base their expectations in part on students' ethnic and socioeconomic background. In much the same way that these factors sometimes influence tracking decisions, they may consciously and unconsciously shape teachers' expectations. Teachers may call on poor or minority students less often than they call on affluent or white students—conveying a not-so-subtle message about whose responses the teacher believes are more worthy of class attention (Eccles & Roeser, 2011). Interestingly, teachers' expectations for minority student performance tend to be higher in schools in which there is more cross-ethnic interaction between students (Lewis et al., 2018).

Several studies report that Black and Latinx students perceive their teachers as having low expectations and holding stereotypes about their likelihood of misbehaving (Bottiani, Bradshaw, & Mendelson, 2016; Houston, Pearman, & McGee, 2020) and that when minority students attend

Figure 6.7 In one experiment, when asked to evaluate a second instance of student misbehavior, teachers were more likely to be troubled by it and to recommend harsh discipline when they were led to believe that the student was **Black.** (Okonofua & Eberhardt, 2015)

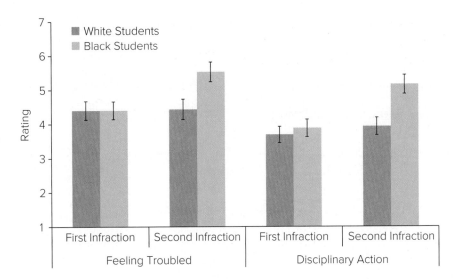

schools in which they perceive less discrimination, the students perform better and are more engaged (Baysu et al., 2016). Black students are perceived more negatively than their peers for the same misbehavior; in one experiment, the researchers presented teachers with scenarios about student misbehavior and used either stereotypically white or stereotypically Black names to describe the student. Teachers who were led to believe that the student was Black were more troubled by second infractions and more likely to recommend harsh discipline (see Figure 6.7) (Okonofua & Eberhardt, 2015). Not all minority students are perceived negatively by white teachers, however. Asian students are actually viewed more positively than white students, and white teachers' perceptions of Latinx students don't differ from their perceptions of white students (McGrady & Reynolds, 2013).

There is also evidence that teachers are more likely to give undeserved positive feedback to students who have done poor work when the students are Black or Latinx than when they are white, which undermines minority students' achievement by lowering the standards to which they are held (Harber et al., 2012). Teachers' biases against lower-class or minority adolescents may make it difficult for students from these groups to attain a level of academic accomplishment that permits upward mobility. In addition, biased treatment by teachers—having low expectations for some ethnic groups and high expectations for others—can increase student alienation and feelings of hostility between students from different ethnic groups (Debnam et al., 2014).

Parents also play an important role in the links between teacher expectations and student achievement. One study of Latinx students found that how involved a student's parents were in school directly influenced their high school children's achievement (adolescents whose parents are involved in school perform better than their peers) but also affected teachers' expectations for their child's achievement, which, in turn, led to better student performance (Kuperminc, Darnell, & Alvarez-Jiminez,

2008). Other research has found that one factor that helps protect low-income students against the impact of low teacher expectations is having high expectations for achievement from their parents (Benner & Mistry, 2007).

The Importance of Student Engagement

It is important to keep in mind that students, as well as teachers, influence the classroom climate. In much the same way that the relationship between parents and adolescents is reciprocal—parents influence how their teenagers develop, but teenagers influence what their parents do—so is the relationship between teachers and their students. Effective teachers can engage and excite their students, and engaged and excited students can motivate their teachers to be more effective. Students who are engaged in school profit more than just academically from it: It enhances their mental health and protects them against the harmful effects of family problems, stress, and victimization (Debnam et al., 2014; Tomasik, Napolitano, & Moser, 2019).

One reason so many teenagers complain of boredom in school is that few school hours are spent in activities that engage them intellectually or encourage critical thinking. Wavebreakmedia Ltd/ Getty Images

According to national surveys, levels of **student engagement** and excitement in American schools are low. Many students are just going through the motions when they are in school, and high school teachers often confront a roomful of students who are physically present but psychologically absent (Steinberg, 2014a). This is a shame because engaging students in school is also good for their overall mental health: Students who are disengaged from school are more likely to misbehave and engage in substance use, both because doing poorly in school leads to difficulties in self-regulation and problem behavior and because students who engage in problem behavior are evaluated more negatively by their teachers (Stefansson, et al., 2018; Zimmerman et al., 2013).

> **student engagement**
> The extent to which students are psychologically committed to learning and mastering the material rather than simply completing the assigned work.

Disengagement in school comes in different forms (see Table 6.1). Some disengaged students show their lack of interest in school through their behavior, by not

Table 6.1 Typology of engagement

Engagement type	Enjoy Affective	Put in effort Behavioral	See value Cognitive	Example
Purposefully engaged		√	√	A student studies hard for a calculus test because he knows that understanding the material and doing well on the test are important to achieving his future goals; he does not enjoy the studying, however.
Fully engaged	√	√	√	A student enjoys creating a documentary film project with her peers because she cares deeply about the topic and she sees the assignment as a worthwhile use of her time. She spends a lot of time and effort working on this project.
Rationally engaged			√	A student sees the importance of learning about global warming in Earth Science class, but he is not willing to exert effort required to concentrate and take notes because he finds the teacher's lecture to be excruciatingly boring.
Busily engaged		√		A student works hard to get her homework completed accurately, though she does not particularly care about the material or the questions. Nor does she see their relevance to her interests and aspirations. She finds the prefabricated worksheets she must complete to be boring and monotonous.
Pleasurably engaged	√			A student enjoys listening to his teacher relay stories about World War I; however, he does not value this topic or see it as relevant. He does not take notes, he does not concentrate on the details the teacher shares, and he allows his mind to wander occasionally.
Mentally engaged	√		√	A student enjoys working on her project in art class, and she cares about mastering the technique; however, it is the day before spring break and she is not putting a lot of thought or effort into her project. She is just trying to get it done quickly so the class can have a party.
Recreationally engaged	√	√		A student works hard to help his group-mates score more points than any other group during a game in class; he is thinking hard and reviewing his notes carefully to find the correct answers, and he is having fun with his peers, enjoying the game and the friendly competition; however, when asked if he values either the material the class is reviewing or the skills he may be developing by playing the game, he says, "No. They are not connected to my larger goals."

Figure 6.8 Only about one-sixth of students are highly engaged in high school. About one-third are disengaged either behaviorally, emotionally, or cognitively. (Wang & Peck, 2013)

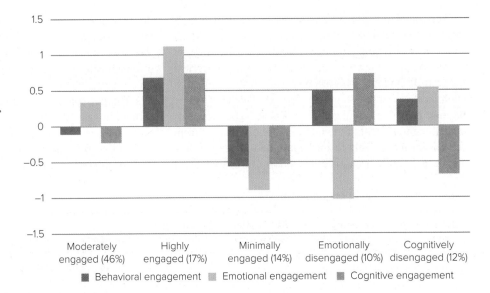

■ Behavioral engagement   ■ Emotional engagement   ■ Cognitive engagement

showing up regularly or failing to complete assignments. Others disengage emotionally, losing interest in school and feeling that school is depressing or an unsafe place. Still others disengage cognitively, checking out mentally when they are in class and devoting little effort to their schoolwork (Wang & Peck, 2013). In one study, about one-sixth of students were disengaged behaviorally, cognitively, and emotionally ("minimally engaged"), whereas an equal proportion were engaged in all three ways (see Figure 6.8).

Different forms of engagement feed on each other: Someone who starts to feel disconnected from school (emotional disengagement) is more likely to start skipping school (behavioral disengagement), which in turn increases the likelihood that he or she will lose interest (cognitive disengagement) (Wang & Fredericks, 2014). Not surprisingly, students who are only minimally engaged in school in ninth grade were more likely to drop out before graduating, less likely to enroll in college, and more likely to be depressed (although students who were just emotionally disengaged reported the highest rates of depression).

Boring Classes, Bored Students   In view of this, several writers have suggested that if we want to understand the impact of classroom climate on student achievement, we need to better understand how to enhance student engagement—the extent to which students are psychologically committed to learning and mastering the material rather than simply completing the assigned work (Steinberg, 2014a). Students frequently say they are bored while in school—especially high school students, who find school far more boring than do middle school students (Yeager, 2018) (see Figure 6.9). As you can see, students are bored for most of the time on weekdays between 8:00 A.M. and 3:00 P.M., and the improvement in their mood seems to have more to do with the school day ending than with any

Proportion of American students who "usually" feel bored in school

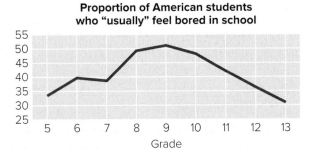

Figure 6.9 More than half of all American 9th-graders say they usually are bored in school. (Yeager, 2018)

special activity that takes place in the evening. The make-work, routinized, rigid structure of most classrooms, in which teachers lecture at students rather than engage them in discussion, alienates many adolescents from school and undermines their desire to achieve.

The notion that many students feel disengaged from school—unchallenged and bored—has been borne out in numerous studies of contemporary American students (Martz et al., 2018). Even in high-achieving schools, about two-thirds of students are not fully engaged; they work hard, but they don't enjoy their schoolwork or find it valuable. And this lack of engagement is associated with more frequent reports of school stress, cheating, and a variety of stress-related disorders, including depression, aggression, and psychosomatic problems, such as headaches and exhaustion (Conner & Pope, 2013).

Here's a sobering account from a researcher who spent more than 500 hours observing classes in 20 different high schools (Fine, 2014, p. 3):

Most of these schools were . . . fairly bleak places to spend time in. The tone of the teaching . . . seemed to reflect an uneasy truce between the adults and their charges. Most classrooms were places to passively sit and listen. Most work was comprised of tasks that asked students to recall or minimally apply what they had been told. At best, being in high school seemed to represent an investment in building an arsenal of facts and skills that might pave the way for interesting work in college and beyond; at worst, it was a way to wait out the four years before becoming a legal adult.

Think back to your own high school experience. What distinguished the good classes from the tedious ones? Students are engaged when teachers provide opportunities for students to genuinely display their competencies, when schools facilitate students' feelings of belonging to their school, and when students are assigned work that is "authentic"—challenging, fun, and relevant to the real world (Marks, 2000). There is nothing more alienating to students than being asked to perform tasks that are boring, uninteresting, and irrelevant. One evaluation of an intervention designed to help students make connections between their lives and what they were learning in science classes improved engagement and achievement among students who had low expectations about how well they would do (Hulleman & Harackiewicz, 2009).

Out-of-School Influences on Student Engagement

Teachers and school personnel, of course, are not the only influences on adolescents' behavior in school. The peer group's support, values, and norms also exert an important influence, especially in high school (Wang & Eccles, 2012b). Adolescents with friends who support academic achievement are more likely to feel connected to their school. Those with antisocial friends are more likely to feel alienated.

High schools vary a great deal in the extent to which the prevailing peer culture emphasizes academic success as a route toward status and popularity. In schools in which academic success is not valued, students are less likely to achieve grades that match their ability. A bright student who attends a school in which getting good grades is frowned upon by other students will actually get lower grades than he or she would in a school in which scholastic success is generally admired. Even within the same school, cliques and crowds differ enormously in the extent to which they encourage or discourage academic success. Some peer groups (for instance, the "brains") place a great deal of pressure on their members to succeed in school and may engage in behaviors (such as studying together) that promote academic success. Other groups, in contrast, may actively discourage scholastic efforts and disparage success.

Other researchers have focused on adolescents' experiences outside of school—at home, at work, and in extracurricular activities—and on the impact of those experiences on their school achievement and engagement (Dotterer, McHale, & Crouter, 2007; Mahoney et al., 2009). Students whose parents are involved in school activities (such as parent–teacher conferences and "back-to-school" nights), who encourage and emphasize academic success, and who use authoritative parenting practices do better in

secondary school than their peers (Harris et al., 2020; Hill & Tyson, 2009; Simons-Morton & Chen, 2009). After-school employment and extracurricular participation also affect school achievement. Generally speaking, involvement in school-based extracurricular activities strengthens students' attachment to school. In contrast, students who overextend themselves on the job may jeopardize their school performance (Mahoney et al., 2009; Staff, Messersmith, & Schulenberg, 2009). Students' engagement in school is also affected by their thinking about the economy and the job market (Hill et al., 2018).

School Violence

A sad fact of life in contemporary America is that many students attend schools in which serious disruption—even violence—is an all-too-prevalent feature of the school climate. According to a national survey of secondary school students in American public schools, 1 out of every 4 students has been a victim of violence in or around school, and 1 out of 6 is worried about being physically attacked or hurt there. Violence against teachers is also all too common. Each year, nearly 300,000 American teachers (about 1 out of every 12 teachers) are threatened, and in half of these incidents, the teachers have been physically attacked (Espelage et al., 2013).

These problems are especially common in middle schools (Nolle, Guerino, & Dinkes, 2007). One study found that nearly half of all middle schoolers had been threatened at school (Flannery, Weseter, & Singer, 2004). In another study, of 6th graders attending a multiethnic school in Los Angeles, half the students surveyed reported having been verbally harassed during the previous 2 weeks, and about one-fifth said they had been physically victimized (Nishina & Juvonen, 2005). Interestingly, white students are more likely to be victimized than Black students, especially when white students are in the minority, but Black students are more likely to be victimized in schools with a higher proportion of minority students (Fisher et al., 2015).

Interviews with students who live in communities in which violence is common illuminate the ways in which these youngsters manage their day-to-day activities to avoid exposing themselves to harm (Irwin, 2004). Some make sure that they steer clear of students who have reputations for violent behavior and go out of their way to act friendly if they can't avoid them. Others learn which parts of town to avoid. Still others befriend peers who can serve as protectors, as this 16-year-old Latina did after someone at her school threatened to kill her:

I got so scared. I didn't know what to do. I ran in the house and called my friend Daryl and I was really crying and [said] "I don't know what to do." And Daryl's all, "What's his number? What's his number?" And I gave it to him. Since that day, that same guy will leave me alone because Daryl went up to him and told him he better leave me alone or else something is going to happen to him and his family. (Irwin, 2004, pp. 467–468)

zero tolerance
A get-tough approach to adolescent misbehavior that responds seriously or excessively to the first infraction.

Experts disagree about how best to respond to violence in schools. Some educators have suggested that schools should refer aggressive students to law enforcement, and many schools have police officers on duty to deter assaults and arrest students who cause trouble. But some writers contend that the new, get-tough approach to violence prevention in schools—referred to as **zero tolerance**—has not helped. Suspending or expelling students from school *increases* their likelihood of getting into trouble at school, dropping out, not completing college, and getting arrested as adults (Jacobsen, 2020; Rosenbaum, 2020; Wiley et al., 2020). School violence is more effectively reduced through programs that attempt to create a more humane climate (Bushman et al., 2016).

One unintended consequence of zero-tolerance policies is that many students end up with arrest records and contact with the justice system for acts that in the past would have been treated by school officials as disciplinary infractions (Casella, 2003). This has a disproportionate impact on Black students, who are more likely than others to report that school rules are unfair and inconsistently enforced and to be suspended or expelled, even though they are no more likely to commit the sorts of acts that would warrant these responses. Closing the racial gap in school discipline would likely reduce racial inequities in arrests (Amemiya, Mortensen, & Wang, 2020; Barnes & Moltz, 2018).

Among the many recommendations offered by a task force of the American Psychological Association, after a careful review of the research evidence, are that schools define infractions carefully and train staff in how to respond appropriately, reserve suspension or expulsion for only the most serious disruptive behavior, require school police officers to have training in adolescent development, and implement preventive measures to improve school climate and increase students' attachment to school. Even students who are not the subject of exclusionary disciplinary practices are less engaged in school when these practices are used (Anyon, Zhang, & Hazel, 2016). And increasing visible security measures, such as metal detectors or security cameras, has no impact on academic performance; if anything, they can adversely affect student achievement (Tanner-Smith & Fisher, 2016). Students who are at risk for misbehavior in school are less likely to get into trouble in schools in which students generally feel more connected to school than in schools in which students are more alienated (Vogel & Barton, 2013).

Lethal School Violence   A series of widely publicized school shootings in the United States—such as those at Columbine High School, Sandy Hook Elementary School, and Marjory Stoneman Douglas High School—has drawn national attention to the problem of lethal school violence. As with many topics that generate a great deal of attention in the media, much of what was asserted about school shootings has turned out not to be the case (Moore

et al., 2003). Although violence in schools is indeed a significant problem, lethal school shootings are extremely rare events, especially when you consider the number of schools and students in the United States (there are about 50 million schoolchildren in the United States, and fewer than 20 students are killed in American schools each year) (National Center for Education Statistics, 2020a). In fact, the number of students killed in schools has decreased fourfold since the 1990s (Fox & Fridel, 2018).

Far more children and adolescents are killed at home or in the community than in or around school; schools are among the *safest* places for adolescents to be (Fox & Fridel, 2018). In addition, although the school shootings that have garnered public attention generally involved white youth, a disproportionate number of homicides in schools involve nonwhite youth, both as perpetrators and victims (Anderson et al., 2001).

Perhaps most important, it is virtually impossible to predict which students will commit acts of lethal violence (Mulvey & Cauffman, 2001). Boys; students with mental health problems, poor emotion regulation, and low empathy; and adolescents who have easy access to guns are more likely than others to be involved in school shootings (Estévez, Jiménez, & Segura, 2019; Moore et al., 2003), but identifying the specific students with these characteristics who will commit lethal crimes in school is a different matter. Most experts believe that, in the absence of a proven means of identifying in advance adolescents who will commit acts of lethal violence in school, the most effective policy involves limiting adolescents' access to guns and identifying and treating young people with mental health problems (Moore et al., 2003). It is also essential to create a school climate in which students feel responsible for one another and are willing to take action if they hear a peer talking about "doing something dangerous" (Flanagan & Stout, 2010; Syvertsen, Flanagan, & Stout, 2009).

Experts agree that the best way to prevent school shootings is to limit adolescents' access to firearms and provide services to young people with mental health problems. Sun Sentinel/Getty Images

Beyond High School

As the American economy has changed in ways that make it increasingly necessary to graduate from college in order to obtain a good job, the distinction between high school graduates who continue their schooling and those who do not has taken on new importance. Nevertheless, there are still a significant number of high school students who do not attend college. As we will see, deciding whether or not to go to college is a critical decision that can impact adolescents for the rest of their lives.

The College-Bound

The early twentieth century was an important time in the United States for the development not only of secondary schools but higher education as well. Although colleges and, to a lesser extent, universities, had existed for some time previously, not until the latter part of the nineteenth century did diversity in institutions of higher education begin to develop. Early postsecondary institutions were typically small, private, liberal arts academies, often with a strong theological emphasis. But during a relatively brief period bridging the nineteenth and twentieth centuries, these colleges were joined by a host of other types of institutions, including large private universities, technical colleges, professional schools, publicly financed state universities, land grant colleges, urban universities, and two-year community colleges (Brubacher & Rudy, 1976).

The Growth of College Enrollment   Although post-secondary educational institutions multiplied and became more varied during the early twentieth century, enrollment in college was still a privilege enjoyed by very few

young people until the 1960s. In 1900, only 4% of the 18- to 21-year-old population was enrolled in college, and by 1930, the proportion had grown only to 12%. During the first half of the twentieth century, then, colleges and universities were not prominent in the lives of most American youth. In 1950, fewer than 1 in 5 young people were enrolled in college (Church, 1976).

Postsecondary education grew dramatically between 1950 and 1970, paralleling the rise of secondary education between 1920 and 1940. By 1960, one-third of all young people were entering college directly from high school. Today, about 70% of high school graduates enroll in ether a two- or four-year college immediately after graduation (National Center for Education Statistics, 2020).

The increase in enrollments has been especially dramatic among women. In 1970, close to 70% of undergraduates were male; by the end of this decade, it is estimated that about 60% of all college students will be female (National Center for Education Statistics, 2012). Although there were large increases in the enrollment of minority youth in higher education during the 1970s, the proportion fell during the early 1980s, primarily because of reductions in the availability of financial aid (Baker & Velez, 1996). Today, among high school graduates, about 80% of Asian American students, 70% of white students, and about 60% of Latinx and Black students go directly from high school into college (National Center for Education Statistics, 2019) (see Figure 6.10). Despite the fact that their parents typically did not attend American colleges themselves, and despite often having to support their family financially, youth from immigrant families are just as likely to enroll in and succeed in college as are American-born youth (Fuligni & Witkow, 2004).

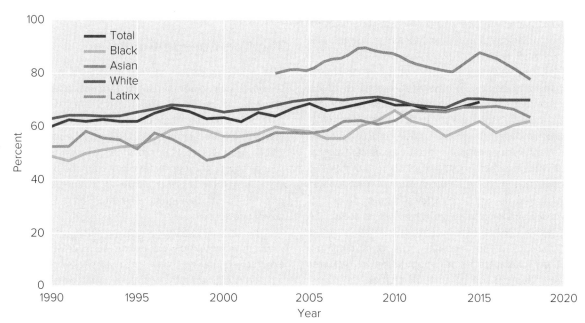

Figure 6.10   Rates of college enrollment immediately after high school have risen over time. (Data were not separated out for Asian American students prior to 2003.) (National Center for Education Statistics, 2019)

More than two-thirds of American high school graduates enroll in college immediately after graduation. Yellow Dog Productions/ Getty Images

American Postsecondary Education In countries other than the United States, postsecondary education is likely to be monopolized by monolithic public universities. Individuals are often separated into college and non-college-bound tracks early in adolescence, typically on the basis of standardized national examinations. In fact, rather than housing all high school students in comprehensive high schools such as those found in the United States, most other industrialized nations separate students during early or middle adolescence into schools for college-bound youngsters and schools designed to provide vocational and technical education. In the United States, the postsecondary education system is composed of a wide variety of public and private two- and four-year institutions, some emphasizing a liberal arts education and others focusing more on technical, vocational, and preprofessional training.

The goals of students attending college in the United States also vary greatly. The population of individuals enrolled in community college, which tends to be older than that attending four-year institutions, includes highly committed students who intend to transfer to a four-year college or are working toward a specific associate's degree or certificate (together, about half of all community college students). But it also includes students who are less committed and not sure why they are going to school (and whose attendance is sporadic), as well as some who are just taking a course here or there out of interest in the subject matter. Similar variability in commitment and goals likely characterizes the population of students enrolled in four-year colleges and universities.

The Transition from High School to College In some respects, the transition from high school to college parallels the transition from elementary to secondary school. For many students, going to college means entering an even larger, more formidable, and more impersonal environment. For some, the transition may coincide with other life changes, such as leaving home, breaking off or beginning an important romantic relationship, or having to manage their own residence or finances for the first time. Many Latinx students report that family obligations and financial responsibilities, in combination with commitments to school and work, can make the transition to college especially stressful, particularly for students whose parents are immigrants and may feel caught between the challenges of adapting to the university environment and the demands placed on them by their parents (Nuñez, 2009).

As a consequence of all these factors, although many more American adolescents enroll in college today than in previous years, a very large number do not graduate. The United States has one of the lowest college completion rates in the industrialized world (Steinberg, 2014a). Only about 60% of all students who enroll in a four-year college complete their degree there within 6 years; only about 25% of those who enroll in private, for-profit schools do (National Center for Education Statistics, 2020a). Perhaps as a consequence of increasing accessibility, poor matching, and a lack of "consumer" knowledge among college applicants, rates of college attrition are extremely high: More than one-third of students who enter a full-time, two-year college program drop out after just 1 year, as do about one-fifth of students who enter a four-year college (National Center for Education Statistics, 2020). And while many of the students who leave after 1 year eventually finish their degree program, if not necessarily at the same school they started in, one-third of all students who enroll in college never finish. In other words, although a great deal has been done to make college entrance more likely, rates of college graduation lag far behind rates of enrollment.

The Non-College-Bound

The problems associated with moving from high school to college pale in comparison to those associated with not going to college at all. College graduates earn substantially more income than do individuals who attend college but do not graduate (Bureau of Labor Statistics, 2019) (see Figure 6.11). Individuals who drop out of high school before graduation fare especially poorly economically and suffer a wide range of problems, including unemployment, delinquency, unintended pregnancy, and substance abuse.

One of the unfortunate by-products of our having made postsecondary education so accessible—and so expected—is that we have turned our backs on individuals who do not go directly to college, even though they compose *one-third* of the adolescent population. In most contemporary American high schools, counseling is geared toward helping college-bound students continue their education. Billions of dollars, in the form of financial aid

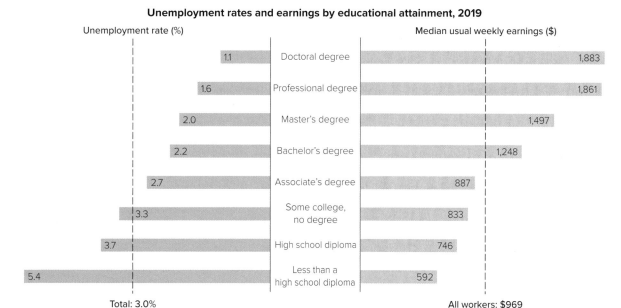

Unemployment rates and earnings by educational attainment, 2019

Unemployment rate (%)	Educational attainment	Median usual weekly earnings ($)
1.1	Doctoral degree	1,883
1.6	Professional degree	1,861
2.0	Master's degree	1,497
2.2	Bachelor's degree	1,248
2.7	Associate's degree	887
3.3	Some college, no degree	833
3.7	High school diploma	746
5.4	Less than a high school diploma	592

Total: 3.0% All workers: $969

Figure 6.11 Individuals with more years of education earn more and are more likely to be employed. One important change that has taken place in recent years is a decline in the value of going to college but not finishing. Completing a few years of college without getting a degree provides little advantage over just graduating from high school. (Bureau of Labor Statistics, 2019)

Note: Data are for persons age 25 and over. Earnings are for full-time wage and salary workers.

and subsidized public college tuition, are given to these students. Some critics have suggested that we should spend just as much time and money helping the other third of the adolescent population make their transition into adulthood as smooth as possible (Wald, 2005).

We noted earlier that opportunities for learning and for critical thinking are much greater in college-prep classes than in the general or vocational tracks. In addition, students who are not headed for college—some by choice, others by unavoidable circumstance—find that their high schools have not prepared them at all for the world of work. Even those who complete school and earn a diploma—who have done what they were supposed to do as adolescents—may have a hard time finding employment and a nearly impossible time finding a satisfying, well-paying job. As a consequence, many individuals who do not go to college spend their early adult years floundering between periods of part-time work, underemployment (working at a job that is less challenging than they would like or are qualified for), and unemployment.

Today, young adults without college experience often must try to make ends meet in minimum-wage jobs, which offer little in the way of promotion or advancement. The economic problems faced by non-college-bound youth have been compounded by the escalating costs of such essentials as housing and health care. It's not surprising that rates of depression are significantly higher among young adults who are not in school than among those who are, and they are especially high among individuals who are neither in school nor steadily employed (Aseltine & Gore, 2005).

Schools and Adolescent Development

The quality of secondary education has a significant impact on achievement and development. Good schools can have a number of positive effects, beyond increasing students' knowledge. And research has pointed to several factors that distinguish good schools from bad ones.

Characteristics of Good Schools

Despite all the debate about how secondary schools ought to be organized and reformed, there is a fair degree of consensus among experts about the characteristics of good schools for adolescents (Eccles & Roeser, 2011), at least as far as student achievement is concerned.

First and foremost, good schools emphasize intellectual activities (Ravitch, 2000). They create this atmosphere in different ways, depending on the nature and size of the student body, but in these good schools, a common purpose—quality education—is valued and shared by students, teachers, administrators, and parents (Lee, Smith, & Croninger, 1997). Learning is more important to students than athletics or extracurricular activities, and seeing that students learn is more important to teachers and administrators than seeing that they graduate. All students are expected to learn, and all students are taught by teachers who use proven instructional methods.

Second, good schools have teachers who are committed to their students and who are given freedom and autonomy by administrators in the way that they express this commitment in the classroom (Lee, Smith, & Croninger, 1997). In all schools, of course, teachers have curricular requirements that they must fulfill. But in good schools, teachers are given relatively more authority to decide how their lessons are planned and how their classes are conducted. When teachers are given a say in school governance, they find it easier to commit to the shared values of the institution.

Third, good schools are well integrated into the communities they serve (Eccles & Roeser, 2009). Active attempts are made to involve parents in education, which is an important influence on student achievement and a deterrent against dropping out (Rumberger & Palardy, 2005). Links are forged between the high school and local colleges and universities so that advanced students may take more challenging and more stimulating courses for high school credit. Bridges are built between the high school and local employers so that students begin to see the relevance of their high school education to their occupational futures.

Fourth, good schools are composed of good classrooms, where students are active participants in the process of education, not passive recipients of lecture material. The atmosphere is orderly but not oppressive. Innovative projects replace rote memorization as a way of encouraging learning. Students are challenged to think critically and to debate important issues, rather than being asked simply to regurgitate yesterday's lessons (Eccles & Roeser, 2011).

Finally, good schools for adolescents are staffed by teachers who are well-qualified and who have received specific training in teaching adolescents. Studies conducted in many different countries find that students who attend schools with a high proportion of teachers who are certified, who majored in the subject they are teaching, and who are experienced achieve more and are more likely to graduate than their peers in schools with less qualified teachers. Unfortunately, schools that serve the most needy students—from poor families or with limited language skills—are least likely to have qualified teachers (Eccles & Roeser, 2011).

making the personal connection

Based on the criteria of good schools discussed in this chapter, how would you rate the high school that you attended?

The Effects of School on Adolescent Development

Whatever the shortcomings of schools, staying in school is preferable to dropping out, not only in terms of future earnings but in terms of intellectual development as well. When Norway some years ago increased the number of years of schooling it required adolescents to complete, the average IQ of the young adult population increased significantly (Brinch & Galloway, 2012). In general, though, schooling affects adolescents' achievement test scores more than their performance on tests of cognitive skills, such as memory, suggesting that the impact of school may be primarily through students' acquisition of new information, rather than improved cognitive abilities (Finn et al., 2014).

Far less is known about the impact of schools on psychosocial development. Most schools are not structured to promote psychosocial development, given their excessive focus on conformity and obedience and their lack of encouragement for creativity, independence, and self-reliance (Friedenberg, 1967). This certainly comes through loud and clear when adolescents are asked about their classroom experiences. But there are many good schools in which students not only learn the academic material taught in classes but also learn about themselves, their relationships with others, and society. Attending a school that has a positive climate can even help protect against some of the adverse effects of exposure to the sort of family environment or peer group that increases the risk of alcohol and drug use (Mayberry, Espelage, & Koenig, 2009).

It is also important to recognize that despite adults' intentions and objectives, students do not view school solely in terms of its academic agenda. Adults may evaluate schools in terms of their contribution to adolescents' cognitive and career development, but for the typical adolescent, school is a primary setting for socializing. Students' happiness in school is most influenced by their relationships with their peers (Booth & Sheehan, 2008).

Studies also show that students' experiences within a school can vary widely according to their track, their peer group, and their extracurricular activities. Academically talented and economically advantaged students have a more positive experience in school than their less capable or less affluent counterparts—positive not only with respect to what they learn in class but also with respect to the impact of school on their feelings about themselves as individuals. They receive more attention from their teachers, are more likely to hold positions of leadership in extracurricular organizations, and are more likely to experience classes that are engaging and challenging. In other words, the structure of a school—its size, its tracking policy, its curricula—provides different intellectual and psychosocial opportunities for students who occupy different places within that structure. The best answer to the question "How do schools affect adolescent development?" is another question: "Which schools, which adolescents, and in what ways?"

Work, Leisure, and Media

Adolescents' Free Time in Contemporary Society

Adolescents and Work
The Rise and Fall of the Student Worker
The Adolescent Workplace Today
Employment and Adolescent Development

Adolescents and Leisure
Adolescents' Free Time and Their Moods
Structured Leisure Activities

Unstructured Leisure Time
Promoting Positive Youth Development

Adolescents and Screen Time
Theories of Media Influence and Use
Exposure to Controversial Media Content

Adolescents and Social Media
Social Media and Socializing
Problematic Social Media Use

Free Time and Adolescent Development

Igor Alecsander/Getty Images

One of the most important features of adolescence in contemporary society is the enormous amount of time they have to spend at their discretion. Many of today's teenagers spend more time in leisure activities than they do in school, more time alone than with members of their family, more time each week on a part-time job than on homework, and considerably more time online, texting with friends, using social media, or watching television than in the classroom (Roberts, Henricksen, & Foehr, 2009; Staff, Messersmith, & Schulenberg, 2009). In this chapter, we look at these other important contexts of adolescence—the contexts of work, leisure, and the mass media, including the Internet.

Adolescents' Free Time in Contemporary Society

The abundance of free time in the lives of today's teenagers has several origins. Ironically, one of the most important contributors was the development of compulsory schooling.

Prior to the early decades of the twentieth century, adolescents were expected to work full-time, and most maintained schedules comparable to those of adults, working long hours each week. With the spread of secondary schools, however, adolescents were more or less barred from the labor force: The part-time jobs held by teenagers that are familiar to us today—working behind fast-food counters or in supermarkets, for instance—did not exist in large numbers, making opportunities for after-school employment rare.

One indirect effect of compulsory high school, then, was to increase the amount of free time available to young people—time that previously would have been occupied by work. At the turn of the twentieth century, adults were so worried about the free time available to adolescents that they began to establish various youth clubs and activities, such as the Boy Scouts and organized sports, in order to occupy teenagers' "idle hands" (Hine, 1999). Organized leisure became an institutionalized part of adolescence as a supplement to school and a replacement for full-time employment.

A second influence on the rise of free time for adolescents in contemporary society was the increased affluence of Americans following World War II. The invention of the "teenager"—and, more important, the discovery of the teenager by advertisers and marketers—changed the nature of adolescence. As adolescents gained more autonomy, they became consumers with plenty of discretionary income (Osgerby, 2008). This week, notice the commercials and advertisements aimed at teenagers on television, in magazines, or online. You'll see that much of the advertising concerns leisure expenditures: music, movies, restaurants, electronics, cosmetics, sporting goods, and so on.

Over the past decade, there have been a few notable changes in how American teenagers spend their free time (Livingston, 2019). Surprisingly, they are spending more time sleeping and doing homework than their counterparts did a decade ago. And they are spending less time working in part-time jobs and socializing with friends. It probably will not surprise you that there are predictable sex differences in how adolescents spend their free time: boys spend more time than girls in front of screens and playing sports; girls spend more time than boys shopping, grooming, doing housework, and running household errands.

These studies show that adolescents' free time is not best thought of as a zero-sum phenomenon in which involvement in one activity automatically displaces involvement in another. Rather, there are well-rounded adolescents who have substantial time commitments across many different activities, adolescents who tend to focus on one type of activity (usually sports), and adolescents who don't do much of anything outside of school. Most studies find that a "mixed" extracurricular portfolio may be better for adolescents' development than one that only includes sports (Sharp et al., 2015; Viau & Poulin, 2015). Although it is the case that relatively busier adolescents are better adjusted and more accomplished than their classmates, whether their better adjustment is a cause or consequence of their busy schedules isn't clear (Nelson & Gastic, 2009).

One important feature of adolescence in contemporary society is the tremendous amount of time teenagers have for leisure activities. Thinkstock Images/Comstock Images/Getty Images

What is the effect of all this free time on adolescents' behavior and development? Are they learning about the real world from their part-time jobs? Are extracurricular activities beneficial? Are teenagers driven toward sex and violence by the mass media? Are they really affected by the music they listen to, videos on YouTube, or violent video games? Has the increase in time that they spend online adversely affected their ability to relate to others in person? Are concerns about adolescents' exposure to pornography on the Internet legitimate, or are they overstated? These are some of the questions we will address in this chapter. We begin by examining how teenagers are affected by after-school jobs.

Adolescents and Work

Many American high school students will have worked in an after-school job before graduating, although the proportion of teenagers who are employed during the school declined dramatically in the past two decades, as did the number of weekly hours employed teenagers devote to their jobs (Staff et al., 2020). Working while attending high school was especially common in the 1980s, but school-year employment became less common at the beginning of the twenty-first century. In fact, the proportion of high school students who work during the school year is now at its lowest level in recent history (Twenge & Park, 2017). Whereas over 75% of high school seniors worked during the school year in 1977, only 40% did in 2012 (Staff et al., 2020). The pattern of rise and fall in student employment tells an interesting story about the nature of adolescence in modern society.

The Rise and Fall of the Student Worker

Prior to 1925, teenagers from all but the most affluent families left school between the ages of 12 and 15 to become full-time workers (Horan & Hargis, 1991). Depending on their social class, adolescents were either students or workers but not both.

As secondary education became more widespread, more young people remained in school well into middle and late adolescence, and fewer dropped out to work. The employment of American teenagers declined steadily during the first four decades of the twentieth century. It's hard to imagine, given the presence of teenagers behind cash registers and fast-food counters today, but in 1940, only about 3% of high school students worked during the school year (U.S. Department of Commerce, 1940).

This state of affairs was transformed by the growth of the retail and service sectors of the economy during the last half of the twentieth century. Employers needed people who were willing to work part-time for low wages and short work shifts. Many businesses looked to teenagers to fill these jobs—and, in the mid-1970s, teenagers were plentiful. The proportion of American high school students holding part-time jobs rose dramatically during the 1970s. Working during the school year became a way of life.

Recent Trends in Adolescent Work   The trend of more and more students holding jobs during the school year began to reverse itself about 40 years ago for several reasons (Morisi, 2008). Policy makers began calling for tougher standards in high schools. Schools began requiring more from their students, and many implemented graduation requirements. As more and more students sought college admission, a higher proportion of them began taking Advanced Placement (AP) courses, which had homework requirements that placed demands on students when they were out of school. Eager to fill their college applications with lists of extracurricular activities, many high school students opted to join their schools' teams and clubs, and to volunteer in the community, rather than spend their time in after-school jobs.

Second, just as adolescent workers became increasingly in demand as the service economy expanded during the last half of the twentieth century, the retraction of the economy during the first decade of the twenty-first century increased competition for the same jobs that teenagers could have just for the asking a couple of decades before. As the recession worsened and many adults lost their jobs, stores and restaurants began hiring unemployed adults instead of high school students (a pattern reminiscent of the early twentieth century, when competition for factory jobs prevented many teenagers from working).

Immigration also brought to the United States many adults who were willing to take the part-time, minimum-wage jobs that had been the mainstays of the student employment. If you had walked into a fast-food restaurant in the 1980s, you would have been struck by the number of teenagers behind the counter. Today, many fast-food restaurants still employ a lot of adolescents, but they work side by side with people two, three, and even four times their age.

Finally, the growth of new technologies during the first part of the twenty-first century expanded leisure opportunities for many teenagers, many of whom preferred to spend their free time online rather than behind a cash register. Over the past three decades, there has been a significant increase in the proportion of adolescents who, when asked what they want out of a job, report that having time for leisure is important and a decline in the proportion who say they would work even if they had enough money (Wray-Lake et al., 2011).

During the recession, teenagers' hourly wages did not keep pace with increases in the price of the things they were interested in purchasing (Zick, 2010). As more and more attractive (and relatively inexpensive) leisure options became available online and as the economic benefits of working declined, teenagers saw less reason to take on after-school jobs. As Figure 7.1 shows, there were similar declines over this same time period in the proportion of teenagers who have a driver's license or go out on

Figure 7.1 There have been steady declines in the proportion of teenagers who work for pay, have a driver's license, or go out on dates. Researchers speculate that adolescents prefer to spend time at home, online, than out of the house. (Twenge & Park, 2019)

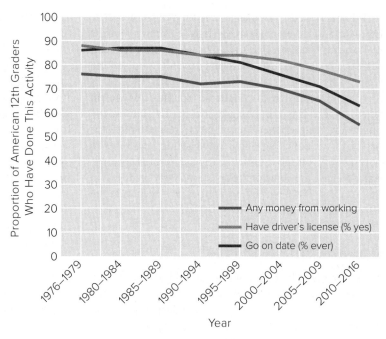

dates. Employment isn't the only activity that time spent online has likely displaced (Twenge & Park, 2019).

making the cultural connection

Student employment during the school year is far less common today that it was one or two generations ago. What might some of the positive and negative consequences of this be?

The Adolescent Workplace Today

Today, the majority of teenagers are employed in the retail and service industries. In general, older students are more likely to hold formal jobs (e.g., retail or restaurant work) than are younger students, who are more likely to hold informal jobs (e.g., baby-sitting or yard work) (Staff, Messersmith, & Schulenberg, 2009). As expected, working teenagers in rural areas are more likely to be employed in agricultural occupations than are their urban or suburban counterparts.

A small number of jobs accounts for a very large proportion of today's student workers. About 60% of employed 8th-graders work in just one of two jobs: babysitting or yard work. Job opportunities are nearly as restricted for older teenagers: Restaurant work (such as a counter worker in a fast-food restaurant) and retail sales work (such as a cashier in a clothing store) account for more than half of all working students' jobs. Very few teenagers are employed on farms or in factories anymore (Staff, Messersmith, & Schulenberg, 2009).

The Adolescent Work Environment Most teenagers' jobs are pretty dreary. With occasional exceptions, the work is repetitive, monotonous, and intellectually unchallenging. Some jobs are highly stressful, requiring that adolescents work under intense time pressure without much letup and exposing them to potential injury and accidents (National Research Council, 1998). Not all jobs are this tedious or dangerous, of course, and some researchers have argued that adolescents in better jobs, in which they can learn genuinely useful skills, benefit from employment (Mortimer et al., 1996). While this may be true in theory, only a small proportion of adolescents hold jobs in which there is ample opportunity to learn new or higher-level skills.

Teenagers themselves don't necessarily say that these jobs are tedious, however. The majority of adolescent workers describe their jobs favorably, saying that they learned things, liked the people with whom they worked, had opportunities to exercise responsibility, and were satisfied with their pay. Perhaps compared to school, where adolescents are frequently bored and seldom challenged, even menial jobs are comparatively satisfying. And perhaps there is something about earning money and having some responsibility, regardless of how modest, that makes adolescents feel better about themselves and translates into a positive description of their work experience. As you will see in a later section of this chapter, when adolescents are placed in positions of responsibility, they come to feel more responsible.

Employment and Adolescent Development

The impact of employment on the psychological development of adolescents has been the focus of numerous studies (Staff, Messersmith, & Schulenberg, 2009). Researchers have asked three broad questions: whether working helps adolescents develop a sense of responsibility; whether

Many adolescents hold part-time jobs during the school year. Research has questioned whether working is good or bad for adolescent development. Peter Mason/Photodisc/Getty Images

working interferes with other activities, such as school; and whether working promotes the development of undesirable behaviors, such as drug and alcohol use.

The Development of Responsibility Most people believe that working builds character, teaches adolescents about the real world, and helps them prepare for adulthood, but these assumptions are not generally supported by research. There is little evidence that holding a job makes adolescents more responsible (Monahan, Lee, & Steinberg, 2011). In fact, just the opposite may be true: Some research has found high rates of misconduct on the job among adolescent workers (e.g., stealing from employers, lying about the number of hours worked), especially those whose work is not closely supervised by adults (Staff, Messersmith, & Schulenberg, 2009).

People's recollections of what they learned from working as teenagers are far more positive than many studies of adolescent work indicate (Mortimer, 2003). Many adults say that their jobs as teenagers helped them learn such things as punctuality, ways to deal effectively with strangers, and even how to cope with work one didn't necessarily want to do. Here's how one adult put it, looking back on his job at a car wash:

> *It was a brainless job. . . . The hardest part was fighting off the boredom, and we would get creative about how to do this, usually while getting high. But it was an important*

experience—I saw what it was like to work, got more independent, and made some friends I still know. The money helped me get my first car and first real girlfriend. (Staff, Messersmith, & Schulenberg, 2009, p. 270)

One specific aspect of responsibility that working is believed to affect is money management. Because a high school senior who holds a minimum-wage job for 20 hours a week—a common pattern among high school seniors—earns close to $600 per month (and more than $1,000 per month in states where the minimum wage is much higher than the federal government requires), holding a job may provide many opportunities for learning how to budget, save, and spend money wisely. Few teenagers exercise a great deal of responsibility when it comes to managing their earnings, though. The majority of adolescent workers spend most of their earnings on personal expenses, such as clothes or cars. Fewer than 10% of adolescents who work save most of their income for future education, and even fewer use their earnings to help their families with household expenses (National Center for Education Statistics, 2005).

The most reasonable conclusion we can draw about the impact of working on psychological development is that it depends on the nature of the job, just as the impact of schooling depends on the nature of the school (Rauscher et al., 2013). In jobs in which adolescents are given genuine responsibility, make important decisions, and perform challenging tasks, they are more likely to come away feeling more mature, competent, and dependable. In jobs in which the work is repetitive, stressful, or unchallenging, they probably will gain very little from the experience. In other words, while it is *possible* for an adolescent to benefit psychologically from working, it is not *probable*. According to one analysis, the most common adolescent jobs—in fast-food restaurants or retail stores, for example—ranked highest in stress and in interference with other parts of life, and lowest in their likelihood of providing skills or leading to a career (Staff, Messersmith, & Schulenberg, 2009).

The Impact on Schooling A second question that has received a fair amount of research attention concerns the impact of working on adolescents' involvement in other activities, most notably, schooling. Here, studies indicate that the issue is not *whether* a teenager works but *how much* (Stone, 2011).

Youngsters who work long hours are absent from school more often, are less likely to participate in extracurricular activities, report enjoying school less, spend less time on their homework, and earn slightly lower grades. This appears to be true both because teenagers who are less interested in school choose to work longer hours and because working long hours leads to disengagement from school (Monahan & Steinberg, 2011; Nagengast et al., 2014). Working long hours takes an especially bad toll on achievement among white and Asian students from middle-class families (Bachman et al., 2013; Hwang & Domina, 2017).

Intensive involvement in a part-time job also increases the likelihood of dropping out of school (Staff et al., 2020). Students who spend a lot of time on the job have less ambitious plans for further education (Marsh & Kleitman, 2005), and they complete fewer years of college, in part because students with low aspirations for the future choose to work longer hours than their peers (Bachman et al., 2011). It is important to stress, however, that working fewer than 20 hours per week does not appear to have these adverse effects (Hwang & Domina, 2017). There is no evidence that summer employment, even for long hours, affects school performance, suggesting that the negative impact of working on school performance during the school year is probably due to the time demands of having a job while being a student (Oettinger, 1999).

The impact of working on students' actual grades and achievement test scores is small (Staff, Messersmith, & Schulenberg, 2009), but extensive employment during the school year may harm school performance in ways that are not revealed by looking only at grade point averages or test scores. Students who work a great deal pay less attention in class and exert less effort on their studies (Monahan, Lee, & Steinberg, 2011). When students work a great deal, they often develop strategies for protecting their grades. These strategies include taking easier courses, cutting corners on assignments, copying homework from friends, and cheating (Steinberg & Dornbusch, 1991).

Not surprisingly, teachers often express concern about the excessive involvement of students in after-school jobs (Bills, Helms, & Ozcan, 1995). Some teachers have responded by lowering classroom expectations, assigning less homework, and using class time for students to

Working long hours takes its toll on performance in school. Employed students often protect their grades by cutting corners, taking easier classes, and cheating. Antonio_Diaz/Getty Images

complete assignments that otherwise would be done outside of school. Thus, when large numbers of students in a school are employed, even those who don't have jobs can be affected indirectly. The fact that far fewer high school students are working today than in the past therefore is good news, at least for teachers.

The Promotion of Problem Behavior   Many people think that keeping teenagers busy with work keeps them out of trouble. Contrary to popular belief, however, employment during adolescence does not deter delinquent activity (Monahan, Steinberg, & Cauffman, 2013). Indeed, several studies suggest that working long hours may actually be associated with *increases* in aggression, school misconduct, minor delinquency, and precocious sexual activity (M. Lee et al., 2017; Staff et al., 2012). Many studies also have found that rates of smoking, drinking, and drug use are higher among teenage workers than nonworkers, especially among students who work long hours (Monahan, Lee, & Steinberg, 2011).

The extent to which working actually *causes* these problems isn't clear—as the saying goes, correlation is not causation. Working long hours clearly creates problems for some students. But the higher rate of delinquency among working adolescents is also because delinquent youth are simply more likely than their peers to choose to work long hours (Staff et al., 2010). Similarly, working long hours leads to increases in substance use, but students who smoke, drink, and use other drugs also are more likely to want to work long hours (Bachman et al., 2011; Monahan, Lee, & Steinberg, 2011).

The link between working and substance use probably reflects the fact that adolescents who work long hours have more discretionary income and, hence, greater opportunity to purchase cigarettes, alcohol, and other drugs. In addition, drug and alcohol use are more common among adolescents who work under conditions of high job stress than among their peers who work for comparable amounts of time and money but under less stressful conditions—and many adolescents work in stressful work settings (Staff, Messersmith, & Schulenberg, 2009). It may also be that working long hours disrupts adolescents' relationships with their parents, which, in turn, leads to problem behavior (Longest & Shanahan, 2007).

One point of debate among researchers who study adolescent employment concerns the differential impact of working on middle-class versus poor youth. Some researchers have found that working, even in the sorts of jobs available to teenagers, has special benefits for inner-city adolescents from single-parent families, from poor families, with poor school records, or with histories of delinquency (Monahan et al., 2013; Purtell & McLoyd, 2013). However, other researchers have found that working has similar detrimental effects for inner-city youth and middle-class teenagers (Staff et al., 2020).

In sum, studies of work and adolescent development point to a complicated pattern of cause and effect that unfolds over time. Adolescents who are less attached and committed to school and who are more involved in problem behavior are more likely to choose to work long hours. Working long hours, in turn, leads to more disengagement from school and increased problem behavior. In other words, intensive employment during the school year most threatens the school performance and psychological well-being of those students who can least afford to suffer the consequences of overcommitment to a job.

making the personal connection

Think back to your own work experiences as an adolescent, during either the summer or the school year. What were the best jobs you had? Which ones were the worst? Why?

Adolescents and Leisure

Adolescents in the United States and other Western countries spend nearly half their waking hours in leisure activities, such as socializing with friends, either in person, by phone, or electronically; watching television and listening to music; searching the Internet and playing video games; playing sports, practicing a musical instrument, or working on hobbies; and sometimes not doing anything at all (Mahoney et al., 2005).

One important difference between leisure and other activities is that adolescents choose their leisure activities, whereas their time at school and work is dictated by others. Perhaps as a consequence, and not surprisingly, adolescents report being in a better mood during leisure activities than during school or work. Leisure activities that are both structured and voluntary—such as sports, hobbies, artistic activities, and clubs—provide special psychological benefits (Larson, 2000).

Adolescents' Free Time and Their Moods

Researchers have been interested in how adolescents' moods change when they are involved in leisure activities, but studying adolescents' emotional states is tricky because individuals' emotions change during the day and a researcher's assessment at a specific point in time may not reflect their moods at other points in the day. Suppose a researcher wanted to know how adolescents' moods were affected by various activities—such as attending school, watching television, or having dinner with the family. Although it would be possible to interview respondents at some later point and ask them to recall their

moods at different points in the day, we can't be sure whether their recollections would be entirely accurate.

experience sampling method (ESM) A method of collecting data about adolescents' emotional states, in which individuals are signaled and asked to report on their mood and activity.

The Experience Sampling Method Using a technique called the **experience sampling method (ESM),** researchers are able to collect detailed information about adolescents' experiences over the course of the day. Adolescents carry electronic devices, such as smartphones, and, when they are signaled, report whom they are with, what they are doing, and how they are feeling. The ESM has been used to chart adolescents' moods, monitor their social relationships, and catalog their activities in far greater detail than would be possible through standard questionnaires.

In one of the first ESM studies (Larson & Richards, 1991), done long before there were smartphones, nearly 500 adolescents ages 9–15 carried pagers and booklets of self-report forms for one week and filled out a survey each time they were signaled. The form contained a series of questions about companionship ("Who were you with [or talking to on the phone]?"), location ("Where were you?"), activity ("What were you doing?"), and mood (the adolescents used a checklist to report their feelings). The adolescents were beeped seven times each day, once during every 2-hour block between 7:30 A.M. and 9:30 P.M. The researchers charted changes in activities, companionship, and mood over the course of the week.

According to this and other studies, adolescents' moods are most positive when they are with their friends and least positive when they are alone; their moods when with their family fall somewhere in between. Between grades 5 and 9, adolescents' moods while with friends become more positive, whereas their moods while with their family become more negative between elementary and middle school (between grades 5 and 7) and then rise between middle school and high school (between grades 8 and 9). This dip parallels findings from other research on family relations that point to early adolescence as a time of heightened strain in the parent–child relationship (Laursen & Collins, 2009).

When adolescents are in school, they report moderate levels of concentration but very low levels of motivation or interest in what they are doing. When they are with friends, teenagers report moderate levels of motivation and interest but low levels of concentration. But when adolescents are engaged in extracurricular activities, they usually report high levels of both concentration and interest.

One ESM study of after-school programs found that the combination of high motivation, concentration, and engagement was most commonly observed when young adolescents were involved in sports or some of the arts, such as playing a musical instrument or practicing ballet (Shernoff & Vandell, 2007). While adolescents are in

For many adolescents around the world, school-sponsored extracurricular activities provide the context for much of their leisure activity. John Flournoy/McGraw Hill

unstructured leisure activities, such as watching TV, they tend to show the same pattern as when they are socializing with friends: moderate interest but low concentration. Participation in structured extracurricular activities, such as hobbies or sports, has been shown to be the most valuable way for adolescents to spend free time, in terms of their current and future psychological development (McHale, Crouter, & Tucker, 2001). This argues against cutting back on extracurricular offerings and, instead, expanding them so that more students can reap their benefits.

Structured Leisure Activities

School-sponsored extracurricular activities provide the context for much of adolescents' leisure activity (Farb &

Matjasko, 2012). About 85% of American high school students participate in one or more extracurricular activities, a figure that has remained constant over recent decades. The most popular extracurricular activity in the United States is athletics, in which more half of all adolescents participate, either by itself or in combination with one or more nonsport activities; it is also the extracurricular activity that has been most extensively studied (Meier, Hartmann, & Larson, 2018) (see Figure 7.2). The other two main extracurricular activities are those related to music (about one-fifth of adolescents are members of a school band, chorus, orchestra, or glee club) and those related to academic or occupational interests (about one-fifth are members of clubs devoted to science, foreign languages, or certain careers).

Extracurricular participation is influenced by a number of factors (Lenzi et al., 2012; Mahoney et al., 2009; Meier, Hartmann, & Larson, 2018). It is more prevalent among adolescents from more affluent families, white students, students who earn better grades, and students from smaller schools and smaller, more rural communities, where school activities often play a relatively more central role in the lives of adults and adolescents alike (e.g., where an entire community may turn out for Friday night football).

Middle-class parents encourage their children to participate in extracurricular activities primarily as a means of self-improvement (often, with the child's future in mind), whereas working-class families are more likely to do so as a way of keeping their teens safe and out of trouble during after-school hours (Bennett, Lutz, & Jayaram, 2012; Lam & McHale, 2015). Adolescents whose parents are involved in the community or who reinforce their children's interests are also more likely to participate (Persson, Kerr, & Stattin, 2007). Extracurricular participation is stable over time: Students who are highly

Figure 7.2 About 85% of high school students participate in one or more extracurricular activities. The most common pattern is for students to participate in both athletic and nonathletic ones. (Meier, Hartmann, & Larson, 2018)

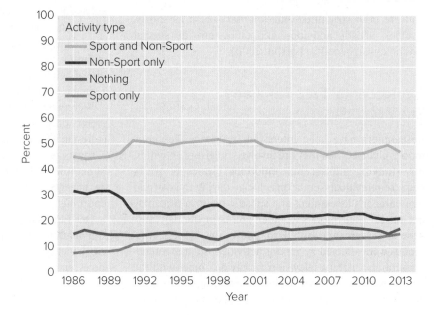

involved in these activities at the beginning of high school are likely to stay highly involved through graduation (Denault & Poulin, 2009).

The Impact of Extracurricular Participation on Development   Extracurricular participation has many benefits. It improves students' performance in school, increases the odds of college enrollment, and reduces the likelihood of dropping out (Shifrer et al., 2015; Van Boekel et al., 2016). It deters delinquency, drug use, and other types of risk taking (Eisman et al., 2018; McCabe, Modecki, & Barber, 2016). And it enhances students' psychological well-being and social status (Farb & Matjasko, 2012; Jewett et al., 2014). Participation in organized community-based activities also protects adolescents in disadvantaged neighborhoods from exposure to violence, by keeping them in safer settings after school (Gardner, Browning, & Brooks-Gunn, 2012). Despite concerns that overscheduling adolescents, especially in affluent communities, creates pressures that compromise their mental health (Mahoney & Vest, 2012), several studies have found no such effect (Luthar, Barkin, & Crossman, 2013; Randall, Bohnert, & Travers, 2015).

The one exception to this uniformly positive picture is involvement in team sports, which, while associated with many psychological benefits, such as better mental health, better sleep, and higher school achievement, is also associated with increased alcohol use and delinquency. This latter consequence is seen especially among boys who have a strong "jock" identity and who participate in school-sponsored, male-dominated sports, such as football (Mays & Thompson, 2009; Viau & Poulin, 2015).

Extracurricular participation in high school is correlated with participation in college and with community involvement in adulthood. Youngsters who are participants as 9th-graders are likely to be similarly busy throughout high school, and people who are "doers" during adolescence tend to remain so in young and middle adulthood. Along similar lines, individuals who participate in sports during adolescence are likely to continue athletic activities in adulthood (Agans, Johnson, & Lerner, 2017).

Studies have found benefits of participating in structured extracurricular activities as many as 8 years after high school graduation (Haghighat & Knifsend, 2019), especially among individuals whose extracurricular participation lasted at least 2 years and occupied a relatively high number of hours each week. These benefits were seen only among individuals whose activities were school-sponsored, however, perhaps because this helps strengthen students' attachment to school, which in turn contributes to their future educational success (Knifsend & Graham, 2012). This "spillover effect" is especially strong among adolescents who are less able students, among those who go to schools in poor communities, and among teenagers from immigrant families (Camacho &

Participation in school-sponsored extracurricular activities, such as athletics, leads to better school achievement.
HRAUN/Getty Images

Fuligini, 2015). There is some evidence, though, that whereas a reasonable amount of extracurricular participating contributes to earning a college degree on time, students who participate in many activities as high school students take longer to graduate from college, most likely because they continued their intense extracurricular participation in college, which may have slowed their academic progress (Gardner et al., 2020).

One study of a high school theater production also found that the experience contributed in important ways to adolescents' emotional development. Through the course of preparing for their performance, students learned how to better manage their emotions, better understand others' feelings, and how to deal more effectively with anger, frustration, and stress. The atmosphere cultivated by the activity's advisors appears to be crucial for making the experience a positive one (Gaudreau, Amiot, & Vallerand, 2009; Larson & Brown, 2007). The quality of relationships adolescents develop with the adults they encounter in extracurricular activities is an especially important influence on the overall impact of the experience (Oosterhoff et al., 2017).

Researchers speculate that extracurricular activities have positive effects because they increase students' contact with teachers and other school personnel who reinforce the value of school (as when a coach or advisor counsels a student about plans for college) and because participation itself may improve students' self-confidence and self-esteem (Denault & Guay, 2017; Guzmán-Rocha, McLeod, & Bohnert, 2017). Some educators believe that extracurricular participation also helps bond students to their school, perhaps by developing relationships with peers that make attending school more enjoyable (Knifsend et al., 2018; Oberle et al., 2019). This may be especially

routine activity theory
A perspective on adolescence that views unstructured, unsupervised time with peers as a main cause of misbehavior.

beneficial for those who are not achieving academically; for many of them, their extracurricular activity is what keeps them coming to school each day (Dotterer, McHale, & Crouter, 2007; J. Mahoney et al., 2009).

Adolescents who combine participation in sports with other sorts of extracurricular activities, and who therefore have multiple points of "attachment" to their school, fare better than those who are solely involved in athletics (Linver, Roth, & Brooks-Gunn, 2009; Zarrett et al., 2009). Extracurricular activities may also bring adolescents into contact with peers who influence them in beneficial ways (Schaefer et al., 2011; Viau, Denault, & Poulin, 2015), often among adolescents from different ethnic groups (Knifsend & Juvonen, 2017).

Participation in certain sports can increase adolescents' involvement in problem behavior, however (Crean, 2012). Studies of male football players have found that they were relatively more likely to get into serious fights (Beaver, Barnes, & Boutwell, 2016) and that violence was most common among football players whose friends also played football (Kreager, 2007b). Another found similar effects of sports participation on delinquency: Boys who participated in organized sports were more likely to spend their free time hanging out with their friends, and this led them to be involved in more antisocial (although not necessarily violent) behavior (Gardner & Brooks-Gunn, 2009). (As you will read in a moment, during adolescence, spending unstructured, unsupervised time with friends is a recipe for trouble.)

Several additional cautions have been raised about adolescents' participation in athletics (Steinberg, 2014c). As extracurricular sports have become more competitive, the number of young people injured during these activities has risen substantially. Each year, well over 1 million adolescent athletes are treated in emergency rooms. It is estimated that between 1 and 2 million children and teenagers in the United States experience a recreation- or sports-related concussion each year (Bryan et al., 2016). According to some estimates, more than half of all adolescents who play organized sports have played while injured. Half of all coaches say they've been aware that one of their players was playing with an injury, sometimes with a serious sprain or broken bones. One-third of all adolescent athletes say they've been deliberately injured by an opponent.

In addition, many adolescents feel anxious and tense within the competitive atmosphere that has come to dominate after-school sports in many communities. Nearly three-quarters of all student athletes have been screamed at by a coach, and 40% of these adolescents say they wanted to quit the team as a result. Many student-athletes report feeling so stressed that they experience academic burnout (Sorkkila et al., 2018, pp. 122–124):

> I don't know, it's pretty hard for me . . . umm . . . I didn't pass all the tests so it's pretty stressful 'cause I'm not passing the tests . . . after school I go straight to the rink, so I eat there are wait for practice to start . . . and after training I'm so tired, it's not good to start doing schoolwork then.

Thus, while competitive athletics are a source of considerable pleasure for some adolescents, they are a source of equally considerable stress for others (Larson, Hansen, & Moneta, 2006; Scanlan, Babkes, & Scanlan, 2005). This is why having a coach who understands and looks out for these potential problems is so important.

making the scientific connection

Why are the apparent effects of participation in extracurricular activities different from those associated with part-time employment? How might these two sets of experiences differ?

Unstructured Leisure Time

One important distinction is between structured and supervised leisure activities, such as school- or community-sponsored extracurricular activities, and unstructured leisure activities, such as hanging out with friends without any organized activity in mind. Participation in structured leisure activities tends to have positive effects on adolescent development. Time spent in unstructured leisure activities does the reverse (Siennick & Osgood, 2012).

Routine Activity Theory Several writers have argued that the combination of a lack of structure, socializing with peers, and the absence of adult supervision encourages delinquency and other problem behaviors. According to **routine activity theory,** "the less structured an activity, the more likely a person is to encounter opportunities for problem behavior in the simple sense that he or she is not occupied doing something else" (Osgood et al., 2005, p. 51). Because adolescence is a time of heightened peer pressure and heightened susceptibility to peer influence, and because one of the strongest deterrents against problem behavior is the presence of an adult, it is hardly surprising that unstructured peer activity without adult supervision is associated with all sorts of problems: depression, delinquency, drug and alcohol use, violence, and precocious sexual activity (O. Atherton et al., 2016; Frøyland, Bakken, & von Soest, 2020; Meldrum & Barnes, 2017).

Adolescents who spend five or more evenings out in an average week are at least four times more likely to be involved in antisocial activity than those who go out less

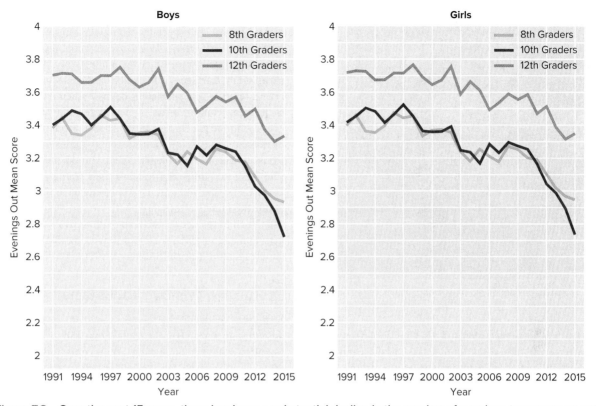

Figure 7.3 Over the past 15 years, there has been a substantial decline in the number of evenings teenagers go out each week. (Keyes et al., 2018)

than twice a week (Gage et al., 2005). As one team of writers wryly put it, "Whether you like or dislike your father, it will be more convenient to smoke marijuana when he isn't around" (Osgood et al., 1996, p. 640). Over the past two decades, however, the number of evenings adolescents spend out each week has dropped (see Figure 7.3) (Keyes et al., 2018).

Time After School A prime time for unstructured and unsupervised leisure is during the afternoon on school days—after school has let out but before parents have returned home from work. As Figure 7.4 indicates, for instance, delinquency is more common on weekday afternoons than at any other time (Osgood et al., 2005).

In 2019, about 75% of mothers with children between ages 6 and 17, and more than 90% of fathers with children this age, were employed. Both parents work in more than 65% of households with children this age (Bureau of Labor Statistics, 2020). While some youngsters whose parents are at work during the afternoon are involved in school- or community-based programs that provide adult supervision, others spend their after-school hours away from adults, in their homes, with friends, or simply hanging out in neighborhoods and shopping malls (Mahoney & Parente, 2009). Affluent, suburban, and white children are most likely to be home unsupervised, and poor, minority, and urban and rural children are least likely (Mahoney et al., 2009).

Figure 7.4 More arrests occur during school afternoons than at any other time, presumably because this is the time when adolescents are least likely to be supervised. (Osgood et al., 2005)

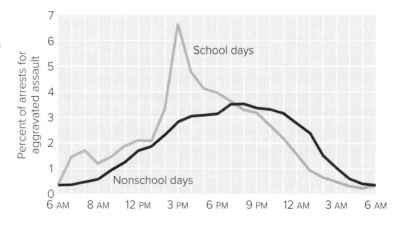

Many teenagers spend time after school unsupervised.
filadendron/Getty Images

Psychologists have debated whether adolescents who take care of themselves after school profit from these opportunities for self-management or are at greater risk for problems because they aren't supervised. Most studies show that children who are on their own after school do not differ from their peers when it comes to psychological development, school achievement, or self-conceptions (Mahoney et al., 2009). Self-care after school is associated with a wide range of adverse outcomes, however. Compared to young people who are supervised after school, those who aren't feel more socially isolated and depressed and are more likely to have school problems, use drugs and alcohol, be involved in antisocial behavior, and be sexually active at earlier ages (Mahoney & Parente, 2009; Lee et al., 2019; Shumow, Smith, & Smith, 2009).

One limitation of studies of youth in self-care is that they typically lump together all children who take care of themselves after school, even though there are important differences in their after-school arrangements (Mahoney et al., 2009). Spending time after school with friends in unsupervised settings is more problematic under some circumstances than others. Adolescents who go straight home after school are far less likely to engage in problem behavior than are those who go to a friend's house or who just hang out (Mahoney & Parente, 2009).

It's not simply spending unsupervised time with peers that increases an adolescent's likelihood of alcohol and drug use; it's the combination of lacking supervision, having friends who like to party and use drugs, and being especially susceptible to peer pressure (Caldwell & Darling, 1999). The harmful effects of low parental monitoring are especially bad in neighborhoods where other adults are unlikely to provide supervision if parents aren't around (Coley, Morris, & Hernandez, 2004). The negative

positive youth development The goal of programs designed to facilitate healthy psychosocial development and not simply to deter problematic development.

effects of low parental monitoring and unsupervised peer group activity are especially pronounced in unsafe neighborhoods (Pettit et al., 1999). Adolescents also differ in their susceptibility to the adverse effects of self-care; not surprisingly, teenagers with established behavior problems are more negatively affected by being on their own than are their peers (Coley, Morris, & Hernandez, 2004).

In summary, self-care after school probably doesn't hold great benefits for youngsters and, under some conditions, may cause problems. What should parents do if they have no choice but to leave their youngsters in self-care? Experts advise parents to provide clear instructions about the child's after-school activities and whereabouts, ask the child to check in with an adult as soon as the child gets home, and teach the child how to handle any emergencies that may arise (Steinberg, 2011).

Promoting Positive Youth Development

In light of evidence that certain types of extracurricular activities appear to benefit adolescents and in view of the potential dangers of leaving adolescents unsupervised after school, experts have called for better and more readily available after-school programming for adolescents. They argue that well-designed programs not only will deter problem behavior by providing adolescents with adult supervision but will also promote **positive youth development** (Seider, Jayawickreme, & Lerner, 2017; Tejada-Gallardo et al., 2020).

Although the label "positive youth development" is relatively new, the concept is not. Indeed, the goals espoused by proponents of positive youth development programs today bear a striking resemblance to the stated goals of youth programs that have been around for ages, such as the YMCA (founded in London in 1844 and transported to the United States in 1851), the Boys and Girls Clubs of America (founded in 1860), 4-H clubs (founded at the turn of the twentieth century), and scouting (founded in 1910). In 1866, the YMCA of New York City announced that its purpose was "the improvement of the spiritual, mental, social and physical condition of young men" (YMCA, 2006).

Experts' interest in helping young people develop strengths, rather than simply preventing them from getting into trouble, has burgeoned in recent decades (e.g., Lerner et al., 2010). There are many different models of positive youth development, but they all are very similar (Lerner et al., 2009; Mahoney et al., 2009). One of the most widely cited emphasizes the "Five C's" of positive youth development: Competence, Confidence, Connection, Character, and Caring/Compassion (see Table 7.1) (Bowers et al., 2014). Another model, the EPOCH model of positive adolescent psychology, stresses similar attributes: Engagement, Perseverance, Optimism, Connectedness, and Happiness (Kern et al., 2016).

These characteristics, in one form or another, are often the focus of contemporary community-based programming for youth, including programs emphasizing

Table 7.1 The Five C's of positive youth development

Competence	A positive view of one's actions in domain-specific areas, including social, academic, cognitive, and vocational. Social competence pertains to interpersonal skills (e.g., conflict resolution). Cognitive competence pertains to cognitive abilities (e.g., decision making). School grades, attendance, and test scores are part of academic competence. Vocational competence involves work habits and career choice explorations.
Confidence	An internal sense of overall positive self-worth and self-efficacy; one's global self-regard, as opposed to domain-specific beliefs.
Connection	Positive bonds with people and institutions that are reflected in bidirectional exchanges between the individual and peers, family, school, and community in which both parties contribute to the relationship.
Character	Respect for societal and cultural rules, possession of standards for correct behaviors, a sense of right and wrong (morality), and integrity.
Caring/compassion	A sense of sympathy and empathy for others.

(Lerner et al., 2005).

community service, volunteer activity, mentoring, and skill building. Evaluations of positive youth development programs have found small but significant effects on academic achievement and psychological adjustment but no impact on conduct problems, substance use, depression, or risky sex. Thus, while these programs may be helpful in promoting positive development, they do not seem to be effective in preventing problematic development (Ciocanel et al., 2017).

What makes a positive youth development program successful? Especially important are the extent to which participants volunteer their commitment, are placed in demanding roles, are encouraged to meet high expectations, are expected to take responsibility for their behavior, and are helped to understand the consequences of failing to fulfill their obligations (Dawes & Larson, 2011). Researchers have described a multistep process through which program participation contributes to the development of responsibility.

First, adolescents voluntarily take on new roles and obligations. As an adolescent stage manager in a theater company described it:

I'm the person that people are relying on to keep the show moving, like, I have to monitor the stage while the music is happening and if something goes wrong, it's my job to like, whatever it takes, ... like problem solving, but quickly to keep the show going. (Salusky et al., 2014, p. 422)

Second, adolescents must stick with their job, even in the face of challenges. Many volunteers experience frustration during the initial phases of their participation; sometimes the work is too hard, sometimes it was too boring; sometimes it is just overwhelming. It is important to hang in through difficult periods. One program leader explained how best to support program participants:

We hold a review session at the end so they can say, "Oh, that didn't really work." And we can go back to, "What was the decision to get to that and why didn't that work and how can we make it better the next time?" (Larson et al., 2016, p. 857)

Third, youth benefit most when they persevere and derive a sense of accomplishment and personal agency from their success (Hansen, Moore, & Jessop, 2018). Many attribute this to the expectations and support of the program leaders:

new media
Digital media typically accessed via computers, smartphones, or other Internet-based devices.

You feel that you owe it to them to do things right and to do them the way they are expected to be done ... not because necessarily they are always hounding you about it, but just because you want to do it. (Salusky et al., 2014, p. 423)

Ultimately, this leads to changes in adolescents' self-conceptions: They come to see themselves as more dependable and mature, which affects how they behave outside the program as well.

In other words, expecting adolescents to behave responsibly helps them develop a sense of responsibility (Coatsworth & Conroy, 2009; Hansen, Moore, & Jessop, 2018; Larson & Angus, 2011). This, in turn, often leads parents to see their teens as more self-reliant, which may increase parental autonomy-granting, further contributing to the development of independence (Larson et al., 2007). Parents frequently report that their teenagers had become more attentive and considerate after having been in a well-run program (Salusky et al., 2014).

Adolescents and Screen Time

Until the last 20 years or so, most research on the impact of the media on adolescent development focused on television, movies, and recorded music. During the past two decades, though, there has been an explosion in adolescents' use of **new media,** in part because access to electronic media has expanded so rapidly. Adolescents not only access music and video content through conventional sources, such as televisions, but on computers and, increasingly, on smartphones. The sheer amount of media content that is created and distributed today is incredibly vast.

Many of the questions adults have asked about new media focus on their assumed negative effects, just as with prior research on older media, when adults asked whether rock music promotes drug use, whether television viewing "rots your brain," whether video games encourage violence, and so on. It's an age-old inquiry: Consider the following passage, taken from a report of a U.S. Senate committee hearing on juvenile delinquency:

The child today in the process of growing up is constantly exposed to sights and sounds of a kind and quality undreamed of in previous generations. As these sights and sounds can be a powerful force for good, so too can they be a powerful [force for] evil. Their very quantity makes them a factor to be reckoned with in determining the total climate encountered by today's children during their formative years.

What media exposure do you think the committee was concerned about?

The Senate hearing, held in 1955, was about the contribution of *comic books* to adolescent crime (U.S. Senate Committee on the Judiciary, 1955, p. 1). If you find this surprising, consider this: in the late 1800s, adults voiced similar concerns about the corrupting influence of the "questionable" content contained in mass-market novels by Jane Austen, one of the most popular authors in contemporary society (Uhls, 2015)!

Research on new media and adolescent development is similarly slanted (Adachi & Willoughby, 2013a). Among the questions asked in the next two sections of this chapter are whether exposure to online sexual content encourages sexual activity, whether online gaming increases aggression, whether the growing use of electronic forms of communication is hampering the

development of social skills, and whether some adolescents have actually become addicted to the Internet. We'll take a look at these and other questions about the media's impact on adolescent development, but before we do, let's look at how widespread media use is among today's adolescents.

Media Saturation By any measure, the availability of media in young people's lives is remarkable; today's adolescents live in a world that is not simply "media-rich" but absolutely "media-saturated." Virtually all American households have at least one television (and three-quarters subscribe to premium channels or streaming services, such as Amazon Prime, Hulu, or Netflix) (Leichtman Research Group, 2020). Computers and Internet access are present in virtually all homes, regardless of family income. More than 93% of American teens go online daily, and nearly three-quarters use one or more social media sites (Lenhart et al., 2020). Given that 90% of 13- to 17-year-olds use one or more social media sites, it's not surprising that nearly half of people this age say they are on the Internet "constantly" (Jiang, 2018). The most popular social media sites among today's adolescents are YouTube, Instagram, and Snapchat (Auxier, 2020).

About three-fourths of all adolescents have their own smartphone or access to one (Lenhart et al., 2020), but they spend less time on their phones talking to other people than they do in other activities, such as texting or accessing social media. While it is certainly common throughout adolescence, texting increases between early and middle adolescence and then declines (Coyne, Padilla-Walher, & Holmgren, 2018). According to some surveys, the average teenager sends about 50 text messages each day (Rideout & Robb, 2019).

Although this seems like a lot of texting, an analysis of the content of teenagers' texts shows that the vast majority of texts are neither positive or negative but pretty mundane, regardless of whether the communication is with parents, friends, or romantic partners (Ehrenreich et al., 2020) (see Figure 7.5). (When parents ask me whether they should read their teenagers' texts, I say, "Probably not, but if you do, prepared to be very bored.") One problem that has received a great deal of attention is the high prevalence of texting while driving among teenagers—a dangerous practice that 40% of all American teenagers do monthly. Texting while driving now accounts for more auto fatalities than drunk driving (Centers for Disease Control and Prevention, 2019c).

Adolescents' total media exposure—the amount of time they spend each day using one of the mass media—is extremely high. There has been an enormous increase in the last decade in the amount of time adolescents spend on the Internet, in part because of easier access and in part because the Internet is now used to deliver content that had been delivered some other way in the past (e.g., watching television programs on Netflix rather than on a

Adults have worried about teenagers' exposure to mass media for centuries. Today it's the Internet. In the 1950s, it was comic books.
Ted Streshinsky Photographic Archive/Corbis Historical/Getty Images

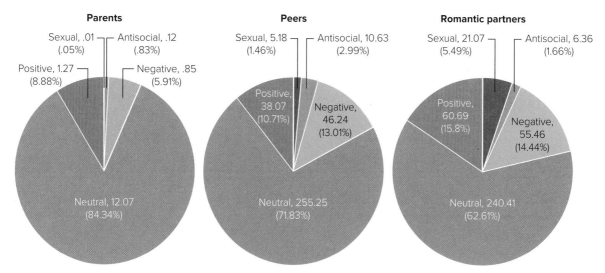

Figure 7.5 Teenagers' texts with parents, friends, and romantic partners are mainly about mundane topics.
(Ehrenreich et al., 2020)

conventional television network, playing video games online rather than with an Xbox or PlayStation).

The average adolescent spends nearly 9 hours each day using one or more media, and this includes time spent using different media simultaneously (that is, 1 hour watching TV while on the Internet and talking on a cell phone would be recorded as only 1 hour of media use, even though it technically is 3 hours of exposure). Although adolescents' time spent viewing television programs at their regularly scheduled times has declined, the availability of recorded programs and television content on other devices (such as smartphones or tablets) has led to an overall increase in time spent viewing video content. The only type of media use that has not increased in the past decade is reading. In 2019, adolescents spent only an average of 30 minutes a day reading (and more than half of that was on electronic devices) (Rideout & Robb, 2019).

It's Complicated Has adolescents' extensive use of the Internet affected their development and mental health? As the title of one book on the subject aptly conveys, *It's Complicated* (Boyd, 2014). Many unanswered questions remain, but it looks as if the effects of Internet use—whether positive or negative—are much smaller than its proponents or detractors have claimed (Jackson, 2008). In fact, a recent and very thorough analysis of data from more than 17,000 adolescents from Ireland, the United States, and the United Kingdom found little evidence that adolescent well-being is related to their screen time—either positively or negatively (Orben & Przybylski, 2019). Another paper by these authors compared the link between screen time and adolescent well-being with the association between well-being and other activities. It is clear from these analyses that parents should worry far more about their teenager being bullied, binge drinking, or using marijuana, all of which affect adolescent mental health much more than screen time (Orben & Przybylski, 2019).

Moreover, the relationship between screen time and adolescents' mental health depends on how much time is occupied in digital activity (Coyne et al., 2020; Salmela-Aro et al., 2017). One study of more than 120,000 English adolescents found that a moderate amount of screen time (depending on the activity and day of the week, between 1 and 3 hours a day) doesn't appear to have negative effects on mental health and may even have some positive ones (weekend use is less problematic than weekday use), although the average participant in this study clocked more screen time than was healthy (Przybylski & Weinstein, 2017) (see Figure 7.6). Similarly, whereas electronic gaming in excess of 3 hours a day is associated with more hyperactivity and conduct problems in school, gaming for less than 1 hour a day is associated with better functioning than no gaming at all, especially among adolescents who played single-player games (Przybylski & Mishkin, 2016).

Very few studies have looked at the impact of Internet use on cognitive development, despite hopes that adolescents will benefit from having increased access to a world of information and fears that the Internet will distract teenagers from more stimulating pursuits, such as reading (an odd fear, given the fact that even before computers were so widespread, reading outside of school had been pretty much been displaced by television). To date, though, research suggests that both the hopes and the fears about the impact of the Internet on teenagers' intellectual development are probably exaggerated (Hofferth & Moon, 2012).

According to a study of more than 190,000 students from 22 countries, there is no evidence that adolescents' school performance is either helped or harmed by playing video games (Drummond & Sauer, 2014). A few studies show that playing video games may enhance visual skills, reaction time, hand-eye coordination, information-processing skills, and problem-solving abilities (Adachi & Willoughby, 2013b; Buelow, Okdie, & Cooper, 2015). Not

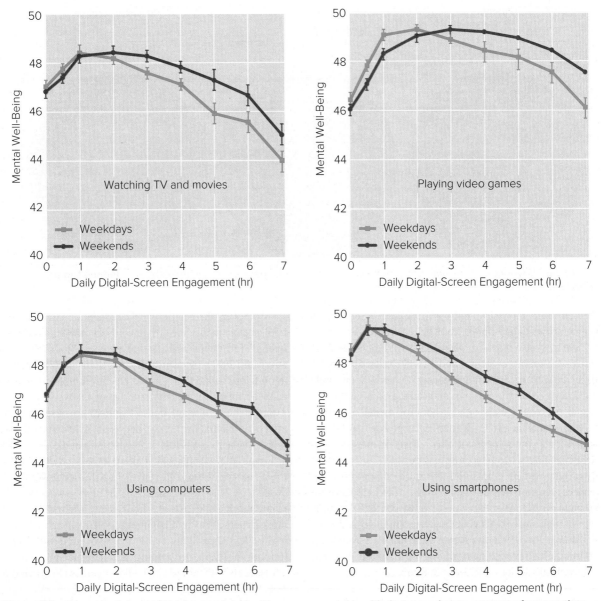

Figure 7.6 Excessive screen time is associated with poorer mental health, but a moderate amount of screen time may be better for adolescents than none at all. (Przybylski & Weinstein, 2017)

surprisingly, compulsive texting is associated with poorer school performance (Lister-Landman, Domoff, & Dubow, 2017), but this is the case with most nonacademic activities that are done to excess. And despite concerns about the impact of Internet use on brain development, credible scientific research on the topic is virtually nonexistent (Mills, 2014).

Compared to What? One of my favorite jokes involves two old friends who run into each other one day on the street. The first one asks, "How's your wife?" To which his friend answers, "Compared to what?"

Discussions of the impact of the Internet on adolescent development rarely ask, "Compared to what?" Indeed, one of the most important questions one might ask about adolescents' Internet use concerns the

activities that it is displacing. If using the Internet is taking time away from watching television, for example, it doesn't seem as worrisome as it would be if what was being displaced was studying, exercising, or spending time with friends. When parents ask me if they should worry about how much time their adolescent is spending online, the first question I ask is, "What is your teenager *not* doing because of it?"

We can safely assume that, to the extent that time on the Internet is taking time away from sleep and physical activity, it is having a detrimental impact on adolescents' mental health and achievement (Evers et al., 2020; Fomby et al., 2019; Vernon, Modecki, & Barber, 2018). Many adolescents suffer from sleep difficulties as a result of their social media use (Mac Cárthaigh, Griffin, & Perry, 2020), although there is some evidence that sleep difficulties may lead teenagers to use digital technology, rather than the reverse (Mazzer et al., 2018). And the amount of time adolescents spend in front of screens is inversely linked to the amount of time they spend in physical activity (Motl et al., 2006). On average, the typical American 15-year-old spends at least 9 hours each day sitting in front of one sort of screen or another but less than an hour in moderate physical activity (Nader et al., 2008; Rideout, Foeher, & Roberts, 2010).

Health experts are especially concerned that the vast amounts of time teenagers spend on the Internet are sedentary, because a chronic lack of sufficient activity is associated with obesity, high blood pressure, poor sleep, and other indicators of poor health (Mitchell et al., 2013; Rosen et al., 2014; Turel, Romashkin, & Morrison, 2016). Most experts believe that the high rate of obesity among American teenagers is due, in part, to the large amount of time—estimated to be more than 60 hours a week—young people spend in front of screens (Bai et al., 2016; Suchert, Hanewinkel, & Isensee, 2016). Keep in mind, though, that while some of the time adolescents spend on the Internet displaces physical activity, a fair amount simply replaces time that would have been spent in other sedentary activities, which is also correlated with obesity (Braithwaite et al., 2013).

Researchers have also asked whether adolescents use the Internet to acquire information that can improve their health or understanding of the world. To the extent that the Internet is used by adolescents to acquire accurate information, it can be a positive force. This may be especially true with respect to educating adolescents about healthy behavior, such as safe sex (Borzekowski, Fobil, & Asante, 2006). There also is some evidence that the Internet can be used successfully to promote mental health and help individuals deal with depression and anxiety, although research on the use of online psychological interventions is sparse (Clarke, Kuosmanen, & Barry, 2015).

Naturally, the ultimate value of the Internet as an educational tool depends on the quality and content of the information conveyed, as two studies of eating disorders illustrate. Whereas one study found that an Internet-based intervention was effective in reducing binge eating (M. Jones et al., 2008), another found that many adolescents with eating disorders visit websites that actually promote disordered eating (Wilson et al., 2006). Similarly, whereas some Internet sites devoted to self-injurious behavior, such as cutting, can provide valuable social support to adolescents who compulsively injure themselves, others encourage the behavior and actually provide instructions on various cutting techniques (Mitchell et al., 2014). Obviously, it is hard to generalize about the effects of spending time online without examining the content of the information that is exchanged. One study of race-related exchanges among adolescents on the Internet found plenty of examples of both hostile, racist comments and civil discussions of racial tolerance (Tynes, 2007).

Theories of Media Influence and Use

The impact of the media on teenagers' behavior and development has been the subject of much debate and disagreement (Brown & Bobkowski, 2011b; Strasburger et al., 2010). It is extremely difficult to disentangle cause and effect because adolescents choose which mass media they are exposed to and how much exposure they have (Roberts, Henriksen, & Foehr, 2009).

Although it has been speculated that TV violence images provoke aggression, for example, aggressive adolescents are more prone to choose to watch violent programs, whereas those who are more empathic are more likely to choose shows high in prosocial content (Padilla-Walker et al., 2016). Similarly, sexual behavior may be correlated with listening to "sexy" music or watching television programs with a lot of sexual content, but it is impossible to say which causes which (Steinberg & Monahan, 2011). And although several major studies of media use (Roberts, Foehr, & Rideout, 2005; Rideout, Foeher, & Roberts, 2010) have found that adolescents who report a lot of media use are significantly more troubled (bored, depressed, in trouble at home or school) than adolescents who use these media less often, it is not known whether large doses of mass media cause problems, whether adolescents with more problems spend more time online as a way of distracting themselves from their troubles or alleviating boredom, or both (Houghton et al., 2018) (see Figure 7.7). Little research has examined the impact of parents' media use on their adolescent children, but one recent study found that frequent parental "phubbing" (snubbing their teenager by looking at their cell phone while in the midst of a conversation with their child) can make some adolescents depressed (Wang et al., 2020).

It is important to keep in mind, too, that not all media exposure is the same and that not all exposure is bad. Some adolescents use the Internet to watch pornography; others use it to stay up on the news (Lin et al., 2010). Mass media have been used successfully to communicate accurate information about maintaining a healthy lifestyle, dissuade teenagers from using tobacco and illicit

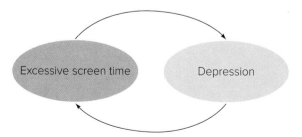

Figure 7.7 **The connection between screen time and adolescent depression is reciprocal. Too much screen time can lead to depression, but depression can lead to spending a lot of time using digital media.** (Based on Houghton et al., 2018)

cultivation theory
A perspective on media use that emphasizes the impact media exposure has on individuals.

uses and gratification approach
A perspective on media use that emphasizes the active role users play in selecting the media to which they are exposed.

media practice model
A perspective on media use that emphasizes the fact that adolescents not only choose what media they are exposed to but also interpret the media in ways that shape their impact.

correlation
The extent to which two things vary systematically with each other.

causation
The correlation between two things attributable to the effect one thing has on the other.

reverse causation
Relationship in which the correlation between two things is due not to the first thing causing the second but to the second causing the first.

spurious causation
Relationship in which the correlation between two things is due to the fact that each of them is correlated with some third factor.

drugs, and help chronically ill adolescents comply with their medication regimens (Brown & Bobkowski, 2011b; Strasburger, Jordan, & Donnerstein, 2010).

There are three basic schools of thought concerning the media's impact (or lack thereof) on adolescent development. One argues that adolescents' knowledge about the world, attitudes and values, and behavior are influenced by the content to which they are exposed. You've no doubt heard contentions like these hundreds of times: Playing violent video games makes adolescents aggressive, watching sexy movies makes adolescents horny, being exposed to Internet pornography affects the ways that adolescents think about gender roles, listening to rap lyrics encourages adolescents to engage in violence and crime, viewing beer commercials during the Super Bowl makes adolescents drink beer, and so on. According to this view, the media shape adolescents' interests, motives, and beliefs about the world—a view known as **cultivation theory** (Gerbner et al., 1994).

A second school of thought, called the **uses and gratifications approach** (Katz, Blumler, & Gurevitch, 1974), stresses that adolescents choose the media to which they are exposed. According to this view, any correlation between what adolescents are exposed to and what they do or think is due not to the influence of the media but to the fact that individuals with particular inclinations choose media that are consistent with their interests. Adolescents aren't randomly assigned to be exposed to various media, after all. They deliberately choose the media they use, either for entertainment, information, bonding with others, or developing a sense of identity. Aggressive adolescents are more likely to purchase violent video games because they enjoy being aggressive; teenagers who are interested in sex are more likely to look for pornography on the Internet because they want to masturbate or feel sexually aroused; and beer-drinking adolescents are more likely to watch football and to be exposed to beer commercials (which, after all, is why beer companies advertise during football games

and not on the Animal Planet network). According to this view, adolescents' preexisting interests and motives shape their media choices, rather than the other way around.

According to the third school of thought, adolescents' preferences and their media exposure affect each other. Moreover, adolescents not only choose what they are exposed to but also *interpret* the media in ways that shape their impact. This view is referred to as the **media practice model** (Steele & Brown, 1995). Imagine two adolescents who accidentally stumble onto a sexually explicit website on the Internet. One, a sexually experienced teenager who is curious about pornography, views the website with interest—perhaps it even makes him feel aroused. The other, who isn't interested in sex, sees the very same content and feels repulsed. Not only is the experience not arousing, but it also makes him even less interested in having sex than he was before landing on the site. One 13-year-old sees a beer commercial and thinks, "That's how I'm going to party when I'm old enough to drink." Another sees the exact same images and thinks, "What idiots those people are. Look how stupid beer makes you act." According to the media practice model, the ways in which media do (or do not) affect adolescents depend on the ways in which the media are experienced and interpreted.

These problems in distinguishing among **correlation** (when two things go hand in hand), **causation** (when one thing actually causes another), **reverse causation** (when the correlation between two things is due not to the first thing causing the second but to the reverse), and **spurious causation** (when the correlation between two things is due to the fact that each of them is correlated with some third factor) make it almost impossible to say for sure whether media exposure genuinely affects adolescent development (see Figure 7.8).

The only sure way to demonstrate cause and effect where media influence is concerned is to conduct an experiment in which people are randomly assigned to be (or not be) exposed to the medium to see how it affects them. But experiments of this kind are difficult to do well. Even the most ardent believers in the power of media influence acknowledge that a single exposure to a commercial, movie, song, or Internet site is unlikely to change someone's behavior. If the impact of media exposure is incremental and cumulative—perhaps taking years of exposure to have an effect—it may be quite powerful but impossible to demonstrate in a brief experiment. All of this is to say that you should view any claims about the presence—or absence—of media influence on adolescent development with caution.

Exposure to Controversial Media Content

These chicken-and-egg problems notwithstanding, a few generalizations about media usage and adolescent development have enough supporting evidence to generate

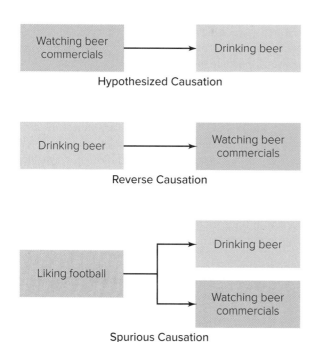

Hypothesized Causation

Reverse Causation

Spurious Causation

Figure 7.8 Two things can be correlated because the first causes the second (the hypothesized correlation), the second causes the first (reverse causation), or some third factor causes both of them (spurious causation). Research on media "effects" on adolescent development has a hard time separating the three.

some consensus among experts. The bulk of the research has focused on the three topics about which adults are most concerned (some might say obsessed): sex, violence, and drugs.

Sex   Sex is ubiquitous on television, with more than 70% of all shows containing explicit sexual content and with even more containing sexual content that is implied. Sexual content is found across virtually all television genres, so teenagers are exposed to sex on television whether their tastes run toward comedies, action shows, or dramas, although the context in which sex is depicted varies across different categories (Schooler et al., 2009). Most sexual content on prime-time TV does not contain graphic images of individuals having sex but instead is made up of humorous and suggestive comments. But as more and more television is viewed on cable and streaming channels, which are not as closely regulated as broadcast television networks, there has been a substantial increase in teenagers' exposure to sex on TV.

The most common sexual messages on television and in film involve men seeing women as sex objects, sex as a defining aspect of masculinity, sex as a competition, and sex as fun and exciting. The message that women are sex objects is one that teenagers seem especially susceptible to (Ward, Vandenbosch, & Eggermont, 2015). Similar messages are carried in many music videos, in which men are shown as aggressive and dominant, and women are seen as the subservient objects of men's sexual advances (Ward, 2016).

One issue that has concerned many sex educators is the relative absence of messages concerning the possible physical consequences of sex (e.g., pregnancy and STDs), although these messages have become more common now than in the past, in part because the entertainment industry has tried to respond more responsibly to concerns about the way sex has been portrayed (Kunkel et al., 2005). There are cross-cultural differences in the ways in which these messages are expressed, though: One study found that both losing one's virginity and becoming pregnant were depicted more positively in the Netherlands (where attitudes toward teen sex are more liberal) than in the United States (Joshi, Peter, & Valkenburg, 2014).

There is plenty of sexual content in new media as well, and the content is typically more explicit than that in older media. According to one survey of university students, virtually all young men had seen online pornography before they were 18, as had nearly two-thirds of all young women (Jones, 2018). A high proportion of teenagers believe that what pornography portrays is "realistic," and in one study of high school students, nearly three-fourths reported that it is their main source of information about sex. According to one sex educator, the problem with porn "is not just that it often shows misogynistic, unhealthy representations of relationships.... You can't learn relationship skills from porn, and if you are looking for pleasure and connection, porn can't teach you how to have those" (quoted in Jones, 2018, p. 49).

Whether and in what ways exposure to sexual media content affects adolescents' sexual development is controversial. Some studies have concluded that exposure to sex on television or online accelerates adolescents' sexual behavior, leading them to start having sex at an earlier age (O'Hara et al., 2012; Collins et al., 2011). Others have

Research on the impact of adolescents' exposure to sex on TV or in movies is controversial. Mondadori Portfolio/Getty Images

found that adolescents who are interested in sex choose to expose themselves to more sexual content but are not affected by it (Martyniuk & Štulhofer, 2018; Steinberg & Monahan, 2011). Still others find evidence for both (Bleakley et al., 2008) or different effects on different adolescents. For example, one study found that exposure to sexually explicit websites increased the likelihood of sexual activity among adolescents who had just entered puberty but decreased it among those who were sexually mature (Vandenbosch & Eggermont, 2013). Adults often express concerns about adolescents using the Internet to view pornography, but much of the pornographic material on the Internet to which adolescents are exposed is unwanted rather than actively sought. About 20% of all adolescents report receiving unwanted sexual material online, and 10% received online sexual solicitation; around one-fourth said that this distressed or frightened them (Madigan et al., 2018).

Although questions remain about whether exposure to sexual media content alters adolescents' sexual *behavior,* there is evidence that repeated exposure affects adolescents' attitudes, beliefs, and intentions, albeit modestly (Coyne et al., 2019; L'Engle, Brown, & Kenneavy, 2006; Roberts, Henriksen, & Foehr, 2009). For example, adolescents who are exposed to a lot of media in which women are objectified—presented as if their value is determined mainly by their sexual attractiveness—have more tolerant attitudes toward sexual harassment, more sex-stereotyped beliefs, and more sexist attitudes, although the impact of exposure appears to depend on how realistic the adolescent perceives the imagery to be (Baams et al., 2015).

Researchers have also asked whether exposure to certain media imagery affects adolescents' feelings about their bodies. Several commentators have raised concerns about the messages to which young women are exposed in magazines aimed at them, especially in light of widespread body dissatisfaction among adolescent girls (Ward, 2016). According to researchers, articles and advertisements in these magazines convey a clear message that attracting males by being physically beautiful is the road to true happiness for women (Trekels & Eggermont, 2017). Adolescent girls who frequently read fashion magazines are more dissatisfied with their bodies than are girls who do not, and controlled experiments have indicated that showing girls images of thin models increases their body dissatisfaction (Roberts, Henriksen, & Foehr, 2009). Adolescents who read these magazines also are more likely to try to appear sexy in the way they dress and style themselves (Trekels et al., 2018; Ward, 2016).

Moreover, frequently reading magazine articles about dieting or weight loss leads to increases in unhealthy weight control behaviors, such as intentional vomiting and inappropriate use of laxatives (van den Berg et al., 2007). There is also evidence that spending a lot of time on social media sites can increase girls' body image concerns (Tiggemann & Slater, 2014). This is consistent with other research suggesting that adolescents' body image concerns are more strongly influenced by comparing themselves with people they know than with celebrities (Chua & Chang, 2016; Ferguson et al., 2014). This is potentially problematic because body dissatisfaction may lead some girls to develop disordered eating (Espinoza et al., 2018).

Similar results are reported in studies of girls' responses to appearance-related commercials on television and websites, which, like ads in fashion magazines, typically feature attractive, thin models (Harrison & Hefner, 2008; Slater et al., 2012). Exposure to such imagery often prompts adolescent girls to discuss what they've seen with their friends, which, in turn, may make them even more concerned about their physical appearance

Many magazines marketed to teenage girls convey the message that, for women, being beautiful is the road to true happiness. John M. Heller/Getty Images

(Rousseau & Eggermont, 2017). Helping adolescents develop better media literacy skills may help counter this process (Ferguson et al., 2020; McClean, Paxton, & Wertheim, 2016).

Although very few studies have examined the media's impact on males' body image, boys also are more dissatisfied with their body after seeing music videos featuring exceptionally buff models or comparing themselves to others on social media (De vries et al., 2016; Mulgrew, Volcevski-Kostas, & Rendell, 2014; Rousseau, Eggermont, & Frison, 2017). Ironically, the same media that implicitly encourage adolescent girls to be thin and adolescent boys to be muscular devote considerable time and resources to encouraging adolescents to eat, and to eat unhealthy food at that! More than one-quarter of the television advertisements seen by American adolescents are for food, beverages, or restaurants, with ads for candy, snacks, cereals, and fast food among the most frequent (Brown & Bobkowski, 2011b).

making the practical connection

Politicians often argue that the mass media adversely affects adolescents' development and regularly propose legislation that would restrict adolescents' access to media content they believe is dangerous. What do you think about this? What policies, if any, do you support that would affect adolescents' access to mass media?

Violence Adolescents are also exposed to a great deal of violent imagery on television, in movies, in certain music genres, and in video games (Brown & Bobkowski, 2011a; D. Roberts, Henriksen, & Foehr, 2009). More than 60% of TV programming contains violence. Young people see about 10,000 acts of media violence each year, and more than one-fourth of all violent incidents on TV involve guns. By the age of 18, the typical adolescent will have seen about 200,000 violent acts just on television alone (Strasburger, Jordan, & Donnerstein, 2010). And the amount of violence in popular films has been on the rise (Bleakley, Jamieson, & Romer, 2012).

Precise estimates of the amount of violent imagery in the most popular video games or other visual media are not available, but frequent concerns have been raised over the impact of violent video games on young people (Strasburger, Jordan, & Donnerstein, 2010). Adolescents who spend a lot of time playing violent video games get into more fights and arguments than their peers (Krahé, Busching, & Möller, 2012), but it is difficult to know whether playing such games makes adolescents more hostile or impulsive, whether adolescents who are more aggressive and impulsive to begin with are simply more

likely to want to play violent games, or both (Adachi & Willoughby, 2013a; Gentile et al., 2012).

Some studies indicate that playing violent video games may not increase adolescents' violent behavior but may change their attitudes about the acceptability of aggression toward others (Coyne et al., 2018; Teng et al., 2019). Once researchers take into account factors that lead some adolescents to want to play violent video games (e.g., how aggressive they are), the actual effects of playing are small and often nonsignificant (Breuer et al., 2015; DeCamp & Ferguson, 2017; Ferguson & Colwell, 2018). And it may not be violent games but highly competitive ones that are problematic (Verheijen et al., 2019). Recent studies have found that playing competitive video games (although not violent ones) may make adolescents more aggressive and less prosocial (Adachi & Willoughby, 2016; Lobel et al., 2017).

The issue is further complicated by the fact that the impact of gaming on psychological development depends on the adolescent's motives for playing (playing for fun decreases negative consequences, whereas playing to escape increases them; Hellström et al., 2012) and personality (adolescents who are high in impulsivity and sensation seeking are more likely to develop problematic patterns of use; Li et al., 2016). The game's content matters, too: Playing prosocial games can lead to increases in empathy, which may increase adolescents' inclinations to help others (Prot et al., 2013), playing sports video games is associated with increased participation in sports (Adachi & Willoughby, 2015), and playing certain games can facilitate the development of problem-solving skills (Adachi & Willoughby, 2017).

Although most of the research on the impact of media violence is correlational, experimental research on the

Research has questioned the widespread belief that playing violent video games makes teenagers more aggressive. James Woodson/Digital Vision/Getty Images

effects of video games on adolescent behavior are inconclusive, with some studies finding small effects and others none at all (Ferguson et al., 2015), even among adolescents with mental health problems (Ferguson & Olson, 2014). Although controlled experiments have shown that exposure to the lyrics of violent songs increases individuals' aggressive thoughts (Anderson, Carnagey, & Eubanks, 2003; Coyne & Padilla-Walker, 2015), many experts doubt that playing violent video games or listening to music with violent lyrics causes adolescents to engage in the sorts of serious violent acts that alarmists have raised concerns about, such as lethal school shootings.

Actually, careful studies of the impact of playing violent video games find that they do not make adolescents more aggressive (Ferguson & Beresin, 2017). One expert estimates that it would take *27 hours of exposure a day* of exposure to violent video games to cause a clinically noticeable change in adolescent aggression (Ferguson & Wang, 2019). And, as some have noted, given the millions of copies of violent games that have been sold, if playing video games had a significant impact on real-world violence, we'd likely be in the midst of a violence epidemic—yet juvenile violence has declined substantially since peaking in the early 1990s, despite the proliferation of violent video games (see Figure 7.9). In fact, one analysis indicated that the proliferation of violent video games has led to a *drop* in violent crime (Markey, Markey, & French, 2015). Actually, there even is evidence that excessive gaming may make adolescents *depressed*, not aggressive, and that depression may lead adolescents to lose interest in gaming (Mikuška & Vazsonyi, 2017).

In contrast to studies of violent video games and music, numerous studies have shown that repeated exposure to violent imagery on television leads to aggressive behavior in children and youth, especially among those who have prior histories of aggression (Robertson, McAnally, & Hancox, 2013). It is now well established that exposure to TV violence in childhood is linked to aggressive behavior toward others in adolescence and adulthood, a heightened tolerance of violence, and greater desensitization to the effects of violence on others, although some of this effect is likely due to the tendency for people with aggressive tendencies to choose to watch violent programming (Roberts, Henriksen, & Foehr, 2009). Although studies have found differences in brain anatomy between adolescents who report frequent exposure to television or movie violence and those who do not, it is not clear whether exposure to media violence causes brain changes or whether individuals with certain patterns of brain structure or function are simply more drawn to certain types of stimulation (Strenziok et al., 2010). Although it has not been studied as extensively as physical violence, adolescents' exposure to relational aggression on television (for example, watching *Pretty Little Liars* or *Gossip Girl*) predicted their subsequent use of relational aggression (Coyne, 2016).

Drugs Alcohol, tobacco, or illicit drugs are present in nearly three-quarters of prime-time network dramatic programs, virtually all top-grossing movies, and half of all music videos. Nearly 10% of the commercials that young people see on TV are for beer or wine. For every public service announcement discouraging alcohol use, teenagers see 25 to 50 ads for alcoholic beverages. Plus, alcohol and tobacco companies have an increasing presence on the Internet (Strasburger, Jordan, & Donnerstein, 2010). Films popular among teenagers often depict actors smoking, a concern because teenagers are more likely to smoke if their favorite film star is a smoker (Roberts, Henriksen, & Foehr, 2009). Importantly, the

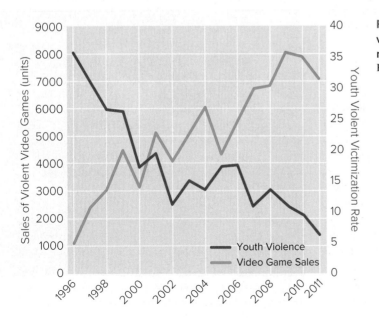

Figure 7.9 Contrary to popular wisdom, as violent video game consumption increased, rates of youth violence declined. (Ferguson & Beresin, 2017)

effects of seeing smoking in movies are strongest among adolescents who are initially less inclined to take up smoking, which argues against the notion that adolescents' desire to smoke leads to their exposure to smoking in movies and suggests instead that exposure to smoking in movies may actually influence adolescents to start smoking (Janssen et al., 2018).

Studies of exposure to ads for alcohol and tobacco, as well as antismoking commercial messages, have shown that they are effective in changing teenagers' attitudes about drinking and smoking, both positively and negatively (Roberts, Henriksen, & Foehr, 2009; Scull, Kupersmidt, & Erausquin, 2014). Exposure to ads for alcohol and tobacco can affect adolescents' beliefs about the degree to which using these substances is socially approved (Davis et al., 2019). Evaluations of media campaigns designed to reduce adolescent smoking, drinking, and drug use show that certain types of messaging may be more effective than others. Whereas emphasizing the questionable motives of the tobacco industry has proven to be effective, repeated exposure to other kinds of anti-drug messaging can lead adolescents to believe that drug use is more common than it actually is, inadvertently stimulating adolescents' interest in using drugs.

It is hard to know whether changing adolescents' exposure to messages about drinking and smoking actually changes their behavior. One problem in linking exposure to advertising and the use of alcohol or tobacco is that it is unethical to experimentally manipulate exposure in order to see whether increasing the number of ads adolescents see leads to an increase in their use of harmful substances. Although adolescents who report having seen ads for alcohol or tobacco are more likely to drink and smoke, this correlation could be due to the fact that people who use and enjoy a product are simply more likely to attend to and remember depictions of that product being used and are therefore more likely to report having seen the ad or movie scene. (For instance, if you are shopping for a car, you're probably more likely to pay attention to car commercials.) A few studies have tried to overcome this problem by looking at whether adolescents who live in media markets in which alcohol and tobacco advertising is more common drink and smoke more (they do), but it is hard to determine cause and effect, since it is likely that companies that sell these products spend more money advertising their brands in places where there are large numbers of people who buy their products.

Adolescents and Social Media

If I were to ask you what the impact of eating is on teenagers, you'd probably think this was a pretty dumb question. Obviously, it depends on what you eat, how you eat, when you eat, and so on. *Eating* is too nebulous a term to

draw any generalizations about its impact on our health and well-being. Binging on junk food in the middle of the night five times a week is very different than eating healthy and balanced meals three times a day.

Yet, many people ask the very same question about teens and social media. And, frankly, it's just as dumb a question. Like eating, the impact of social media on adolescents depends on the "what," "how," and "when" of it. Consider the following two examples of how a posting on Facebook might be used:

> . . . *you can request to be in a relationship with someone so you can change your drop down box to "in a relationship" and you type in their name and that sends a relationship request . . . So it's like that way you're telling the whole world, "We're connected, he's my boyfriend, she's my girlfriend"* (Howard, Debnam, & Strausser, 2017, p. 781)
>
> *One of my friends posted up a picture of our boy that had–rest in peace–that he died. And there was this one "Opp" that commented to disrespect. I know who he chilled with–just for him disrespecting my boy that he passed away–it was just me, my boys and two other guys–we knew where he was, and we knew what we could do. So we went after him. We were looking for him. And what we did: we just beat his ass.* (Patton et al., 2019, p. 763)

This is why it is hard to make sweeping generalizations about the impact of social media: Many adolescents use social media to get to know people better, but others use it to threaten rival gang members.

The next time you read or hear about a study concluding that social media are destroying a generation (e.g., Twenge et al., 2017), you should be cautious, perhaps even skeptical, about it. Although rates of social media use and severe depression among adolescents have both increased over time, there is no evidence the that increase in screen time has *caused* the rise in depression or that people who use social media a lot become depressed as a result (S. Coyne, Rogers et al., 2020; Ferguson, 2020).

If you wonder how this can be, consider the following: Both crime and ice cream sales follow similar patterns over the course of the year, increasing during the spring, peaking during the summer, and then declining over the fall. But this is not because eating ice cream causes people to commit crimes. It's because both increase when the weather gets warm and decline when it get chillier. You can eat as much ice cream as you like without worrying that doing so will turn you into a criminal! (Many similarly silly spurious correlations are complied in Vigen, 2015).

Today's concern about the harmful consequences of smartphones and social media on adolescent development is all too familiar. Similar worries were voiced about radio, television, computers, and the Internet when these technologies were introduced, and people who grew up under the influence of these "demons" all managed to grow into adulthood without brain damage or psychological maladjustment despite their putative dangers (Flora, 2018).

Social Media and Socializing

The increased availability of electronic communication undoubtedly has affected the way that adolescents socialize. According to recent estimates, close to 95% of teens who are online (and virtually all adolescents are online) use social media such as Instagram and Snapchat daily, often several times each day (Lenhart, 2015; Vannucci & Ohannessian, 2019). Close to 90% of teenagers with smartphones stay in touch with others through text messaging. Nearly one-fourth of teenagers say they are online constantly.

The impact of social media on adolescents' behavior and development is interesting, poorly understood, and controversial. Among the main concerns that have been raised are whether teenagers' extensive use of mobile technology is adversely affecting their physical and psychological health, social development, cognitive performance, and safety (George & Odgers, 2015). Some worry that electronic interactions have replaced face-to-face ones, to the detriment of the development of social skills. Still others worry that adolescents are forming relationships with strangers and that these may take time away from intimacy with "real" friends. And, of course, many simply worry that the sheer amount of time adolescents spend online is unhealthy because it has displaced other, more valuable activities.

Social communication on the Internet, like social communication face-to-face or over the phone, creates both positive and negative experiences (Szwedo, Mikami, & Allen, 2012). We hear a lot about things such as cyberbullying, but two-thirds of adolescents report that things have happened through social media that have made them feel *better* about themselves, and nearly 60% say that social media have made them feel closer to someone. On the other hand, 25% of adolescents report that something that happened online led to a face-to-face argument with someone, and nearly that percent reported that something online led to the end of a friendship. Almost all adolescents report having seen someone post something mean about someone, but 85% have said that they had told someone posting mean things to stop (Lenhart et al., 2011).

Many adults worry that adolescents' online friends will displace the friendships they maintain in person, but this fear appears to be unfounded (Valkenburg & Peter, 2011). Most adolescents use the Internet to communicate with people they also see in person (Underwood et al., 2013), which, for many, is an efficient way to stay in touch with friends (Reich, 2010). Studies find that more frequent online communication brings friends closer, perhaps because online communication facilitates self-disclosure (Manago et al., 2020). Social media use leads to improvements in empathy (Lozada & Tynes, 2017; Vossen & Valkenburg, 2016) and can facilitate adolescents' civic engagement (Lenzi et al., 2012). Communicating over the Internet with friends may be especially important for socially anxious adolescents, who may find it easier to interact online than in person (Dolev-Cohen & Barak, 2013; Forest & Wood, 2012).

Moreover, the impact of social media on adolescents' relationships with others depends on how social media are used. Using social media mainly to stay in touch with friends—which, after all, is an important part of being an adolescent—is not a threat to teenagers' mental health and may, in fact, improve adolescents' perspective-taking skills (Yau & Reich, 2019). This is not the case for all social media apps, though. Adolescents who spend a lot of time on Instagram or Snapchat, for example, report more support from friends than those who use social media a lot but do not use these particular apps very often. Teenagers who are constantly on other social media, using apps such as Twitter, Facebook, and different discussion boards, report relatively higher rates of anxiety and depression (Vannucci & Ohannessian, 2019), and using social media to view friends' postings of their own risky behavior is associated with greater risk-taking (Vannucci et al., 2020).

In other words, the Internet can help strengthen adolescents' close relationships and contribute to their well-being if it is used to communicate with one's existing friends (Rousseau, Frison, & Eggermont, 2019), but it has the potential to weaken friendships if it occupies the adolescent in activities that aren't shared or to cause adolescents to stress out if it leads friends to ruminate about their problems with each other (Murdock, Gorman, & Robbins, 2015). Girls seem especially susceptible to the negative effects of social media (Kosir et al., 2016; Perrino et al., 2019), which is not surprising, given that they are more sensitive than boys to social feedback in general (Flook, 2011).

The use of social media has similarly mixed effects in the context of romantic relationships (Van Ouytsel et al., 2016). On the plus side, adolescents find it easier to initiate conversations with crushes and potential romantic partners online than through face-to-face conversations, and they may find it easier to flirt on a social media site than in person. On the other hand, opportunities for misunderstanding the emotional context of a message are greater when people communicate online, which can create problems. And, of course, the public nature of many adolescents' postings can strengthen a relationship that is affirmed but can create jealousy and mistrust when unexpected images are encountered (such as seeing one's partner at a party with a romantic rival).

Not surprisingly, the impact of social media on adolescents' moods depends on what they learn when they check their accounts: When adolescents seek and find social support and positive feedback, they feel better; when they seek it but don't get it, they feel worse, especially if they have been subject to prior face-to-face victimization by peers (Lee et al., 2020; Valkenburg, Koutamanis, & Vossen, 2017) (see Figure 7.10).

Some teenagers become so addicted to maintaining their online relationships that they may develop what has

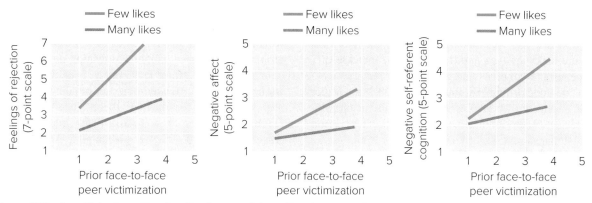

Figure 7.10 **Insufficient positive feedback on social media adversely affects teenagers' mental health, especially among those who had experienced prior victimization by peers.** (Lee et al., 2020)

been nicknamed "Facebook depression," which is thought to be the result of spending too much time obsessing about one's online relationships (O'Keefe, Clarke-Pearson, & Council on Communications and Media, 2011). Adolescents with high needs for popularity are more intensely concerned about what is posted online and report higher levels of **fear of missing out (FOMO)**, which can be upsetting (Underwood & Ehrenreich, 2017). Social media–induced FOMO can interfere with sleep, both by increasing late night social media use and by arousing emotions that interfere with falling asleep (Hamilton et al., 2020; Scott & Woods, 2018). One effective strategy for coping with feelings of exclusion generated by FOMO is to focus your thoughts on your positive offline relationships (Timeo, Riva, & Paladino, 2020).

Frequent messaging, especially with acquaintances who are not close friends, can become compulsive and lead to feelings of anxiety or depression, especially among adolescent girls and among teenagers who turn to social media to alleviate boredom (Stockdale & Coyne, 2020; Twenge & Martin, 2020; van den Eijnden et al., 2008). Of course, it is

not known whether these adolescents were especially prone to mental health problems or would have developed these feelings as a result of ruminating about their *offline* friendships, and there is some evidence that compulsive Internet users are more introverted, less agreeable, and less emotionally stable to begin with (van der Aa et al., 2009).

> **fear of missing out (FOMO)**
> Excessive worry that others are having rewarding experiences that don't include you.

The most reasonable interpretation of the scientific literature on social media and adolescent well-being is that social media sites are a context in which the socially rich get richer and the socially poor get poorer (Khan et al., 2016; Mikami et al., 2019). That is, the impact of social media use on adolescents' self-conceptions depends on the extent to which they have peer support at school; teenagers with a lot of friends benefit from frequent use of social media, whereas those with few friends suffer from it.

Rather than compensate for an absence of face-to-face friendships, social media make lonely adolescents feel even worse (see Figure 7.11). Adolescents who report

Figure 7.11 **Among adolescents with extensive peer support at school, social media use is associated with more positive self-conceptions, but among those without much peer support, social media use is associated with poorer self-conceptions.** (Khan et al., 2016)

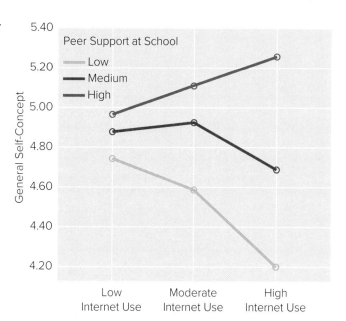

symptoms of depression are more likely to use social media to engage in social comparison (e.g., Is she more popular than me?) and feedback seeking (e.g., Does this picture make me look good?), which may increase their anxieties and concerns, just as these behaviors do when they are done offline (Fardouly et al., 2018; Nesi, Miller, & Prinstein, 2017). Depressed adolescents, in turn, are more likely to be victimized on social media sites (Frison, Subrahmanyam, & Eggermont, 2016).

Problematic Social Media Use

Even among those adolescents with both online and face-to-face friends, most maintain a balance of contact with each, and moderate use of social media does not appear to cause psychological problems (Coyne et al., 2019; Twigg, Duncan, & Weich, 2020). But for a small proportion of teenagers, things get out of hand, and they develop social media use problems (Boer et al., 2020; Ciarrochi et al., 2016), sometimes referred to as **Internet addiction** or **compulsive Internet use (CIU)** (Adiele & Olatokun, 2014; Smahel, Brown, & Blinka, 2012).

Internet Addiction   Internet addiction is defined by six symptoms: *salience* (being online is the most important thing in life), *mood change* (one's mood fluctuates as a function of Internet experiences), *tolerance* (needing more and more Internet time to feel satisfied), *withdrawal* (experiencing negative feelings when prevented from being online), *conflict* (the Internet has caused problems in one's relationships or some other aspect of life), and *relapse and reinstatement* (returning to addictive Internet behavior after getting it under control).

Although moderate use of social media appears to be harmless, problematic or excessive social media use is associated with a wide range of mental health problems, including depression, sleep difficulties, loneliness, procrastination, social anxiety, and ADHD (attention deficit hyperactivity disorder) (Boer et al., 2020; Brunborg & Burdzovic, 2019; Przepiorka & Blachnio, 2020; Wang et al., 2018). But the same limitations that plague studies of other sorts of media "effects" apply here: It is almost impossible to separate cause and effect.

In other words, it is not clear whether teenagers who are depressed or withdrawn turn to the Internet in order to feel better, whether excessive use of the Internet actually causes mental health problems, whether some third variable (such as poor family or peer relationships) causes both mental health problems and compulsive Internet

Internet addiction
A disorder in which an individual's use of the Internet is pathological, defined by six symptoms: salience, mood change, tolerance, withdrawal, conflict, and relapse and reinstatement.

compulsive Internet use (CIU)
Internet addiction.

sexting
Sending sexually explicit content, usually pictures, over the Internet.

use, or whether the cause is some combination of these (Lei et al., 2018; Sela et al., 2020). Some evidence suggests that adolescents with relatively more psychological problems and poorer family relationships are more likely than their peers to form close online relationships with strangers and post private information online, but we do not know whether having these sorts of online relationships leads to or follows from maladjustment (Blachnio et al., 2016; Szwedo, Mikami, & Allen, 2011).

Some scientists have drawn parallels between Internet addiction and other addictive disorders, noting similarities in brain structure and activity among individuals who cannot control their addiction to the Internet and those who have other types of behavioral addiction, such as compulsive gambling (Cerniglia et al., 2017; Wartberg, Kriston, & Thomasius, 2020). Receiving multiple "likes" for one's Instagram photos activates the same brain regions as other social (e.g., praise) and nonsocial (e.g., drugs) rewards (Sherman et al., 2016). It is not known, however, whether these brain features lead to Internet addiction or are the result of it. Nonetheless, the heightened plasticity of the adolescent brain has led many writers to raise concerns about the particular vulnerability of teenagers to this problem.

Sexting   Unfortunately, the Internet also has provided new opportunities for adolescents to engage in potentially risky activity, and none has received as much attention as sexting. The incidence of **sexting**—sending sexually explicit pictures over the Internet, usually by smartphone—is hard to estimate, in part because there is no single accepted definition of it. Researchers disagree as to whether a sext must include a picture or whether sexually suggestive language qualifies, and, if a picture, whether it must be completely nude or whether partial nudity counts. Estimates also vary greatly as a function of whether the data refer to senders or receivers of sexts (many more adolescents report sending than receiving them) and the age of the sample (young adults are more likely to sext than teenagers).

If the definition of sexting is limited to sending naked pictures of breasts, genitals, or buttocks and the data are limited to teenagers, it looks like approximately 20% of U.S. adolescents have sexted (Patchin & Hinduja, 2019; Rice et al., 2018). Studies of whether sexting is more common among males than females or in certain ethnic groups have not yielded consistent conclusions. As is the case with many behaviors whose prevalence is affected by perceptions of social norms, sexting is more common among teenagers whose peers also engage in sexting and who believe that this is what popular students do (Casas et al., 2019; Maheux et al., 2020; Rice et al., 2018). Fears that sexting will encourage sexual activity are unfounded (Doornwaard et al., 2015); if anything, it is sexual activity that leads to sexting, rather than the reverse (Van Oosten, Peter, & Boot, 2015).

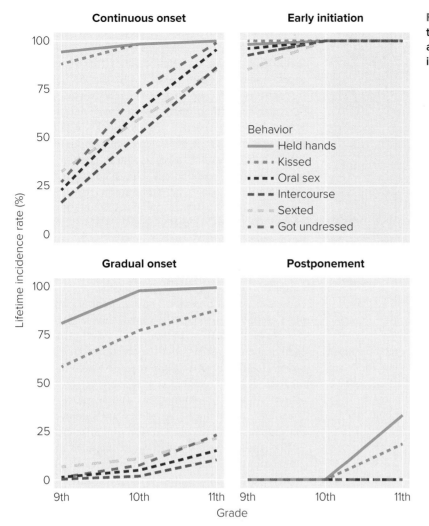

Continuous onset

Early initiation

Gradual onset

Postponement

Behavior
— Held hands
···· Kissed
▪▪▪ Oral sex
--- Intercourse
--- Sexted
-▪-▪ Got undressed

Lifetime incidence rate (%)

Grade

Figure 7.12 Among contemporary teenagers, sexting is a common activity once they begin having intercourse. (Steinberg et al., 2019)

Most sexting is flirtatious and consensual, and often done at the request of a romantic partner, although some adolescents report having been pressured by their partner to send nude pictures (Cooper et al., 2016). Sexting between romantic partners seems to be a harmless common activity among contemporary adolescents when they are in a sexual relationship (Choi et al., 2019; Van Ouytsel et al., 2018). As Figure 7.12 indicates, sexting tends to go hand in hand with having sexual intercourse; adolescents who become sexually active at a young age start sexting at a young age, too, whereas those who delay sexual intercourse delay sexting as well (Steinberg et al., 2019).

However, a small minority of adolescents have been the victims of nonconsensual sexting (where a picture they sent to a romantic partner is forwarded to others, usually to embarrass or humiliate someone, often as a way of retaliating after a breakup) or "sextortion" (where someone threatens to do something like this) (Wolak et al., 2018). As you might expect, victims of this form of cyberbullying have reported adverse consequences, such as depression and the receipt of online sexual solicitations

(Gámez-Guadix & Mateos-Pérez, 2019). Many commentators view sexting as another type of sexual harassment in which males are the usual perpetrators and females are the usual victims. Engaging in sexual harassment via social media is correlated with bullying more generally, both online and in person (Ojeda, Del Rey, & Hunter, 2019).

Rather than viewing sexting as having unique correlates, it makes more sense to view it as a specific instance of risk taking more generally. Consistent with this, teenagers who engage in unsolicited sexting are more prone to other sorts of risky activity, including risky sex (Delevi & Weisskirch, 2013; Görzig, 2016; Ybarra & Mitchell, 2014). The same personality traits—sensation seeking and impulsivity—that have been associated with a wide range of risky activities are correlated with sexting as well (Cooper et al., 2016).

Although adults have expressed concerns about the legal consequences of sexting (it is against the law in many states when minors are involved because technically it violates laws that prohibit the distribution of child pornography), law enforcement officials rarely arrest

Parents have become increasingly worried about the content of their teenagers' texting. Eric Audras/Getty Images

adolescents for sexting within consensual relationships. In most cases in which police take action, an adult has been involved (Wolak, Finkelhor, & Mitchell, 2012). Legal experts agree that consensual sexting between adolescents and their romantic partners should not be prosecuted (Holoyada et al., 2018).

Free Time and Adolescent Development

Adults have mixed feelings about adolescents' leisure activities. On the positive side, adults take pride in watching their children's sports teams and creative activities, and they believe that these productive uses of leisure time help build character and teach important skills, such as teamwork and perseverance. (Think about all the movies you have seen about the character-building benefits of team sports.) Similarly, most adults view holding a part-time job as a worthwhile activity that provides opportunities for learning and the development of responsibility.

On the other hand, adults view many adolescent leisure activities as wasted time or, worse, as preludes to trouble. They worry about groups of teenagers cruising the mall; they cringe at images of adolescents riveted to their smartphones; they worry about adolescents' exposure to sex and violence on television, in film, in music, and on the Internet. Although we might wish for the "good old days" before the advent of smartphones, Facebook, Instagram, and video streaming, those good old days are long gone. And keep in mind that even during those supposed good old days, adults worried about how adolescents spent their idle time and about the corrupting influence of such evils as rock 'n' roll, dime-store novels, television, and comic books.

This mixed view of adolescents' free time reflects an interesting paradox about the nature of adolescence in modern society. Because industrialized society has "given" adolescents a good deal of free time, adults expect them to use it productively. But by definition, free time is supposed to be time that can be used for purposes other than being productive. Some theorists believe that the existence of large blocks of uncommitted time is one feature of adolescence in modern society that has the potential to contribute in positive ways to young people's development. One potential benefit of participation in leisure activities is that it helps adolescents feel happier, more competent, and more connected to others (DesRoches & Willoughby, 2013; Leversen et al., 2012).

By valuing adolescents' free time only when it is used productively, adults may misunderstand the important functions that leisure time serves in the psychosocial development of young people. Free time plays an important role in helping young people develop a sense of themselves, explore their relationships with each other, and learn about the society around them. A moderate amount of solitude (during which daydreaming is a central activity) is positively related to high school students' psychological well-being, as long as spending time alone is the adolescent's choice, rather than the result of social exclusion (Thomas & Azmitia, 2019). And, for better or for worse, the mass media are globalizing adolescence, contributing to the development of a common culture that gives adolescents all over the world much to share.

Many misconceptions about the pros and cons of various uses of free time abound. Most adults view participation in structured extracurricular activities as a good thing, and this seems to be the case. But most people are equally sure that working is good for teenagers, even though studies show that the costs of intensive involvement in part-time work during the school year outweigh the benefits. And although adults believe that the mass media have a uniformly negative effect on adolescents' behavior, studies show that adolescents' interests affect their media use more than vice versa. Monitoring and discussing, rather than restricting, adolescents' media use appears to be the best strategy for parents to follow (Collier et al., 2016; Padilla-Walker, Coyne, & Collier, 2016; Shin & Kang, 2016). Unfortunately, research suggests that many parents are clueless about their teenagers' online activity (Symons et al., 2017).

The impact of the mass media on adolescent development has become especially controversial as the role of technology in adolescents' lives has expanded. Most adults, especially parents, are absolutely certain that nothing good comes from adolescents' exposure to video games, social media, and the Internet, and they often blame the mass media for a wide array of adolescents' problems—despite the fact that parents themselves exert a far greater influence on adolescent development than do any of the media about which they are often so alarmed. Moreover, because adolescents choose the media to which they are exposed, it is very difficult to demonstrate that adolescents are actually affected by what they see and hear.

This is not to say that the media have no impact on adolescents' behavior and well-being. But we should be careful not to confuse cause and effect or overstate the strength of the media's influence. It is also important to keep in mind that the mass media can be used to promote positive behavior and healthy development, to provide information about a rapidly changing world, and to facilitate communication with others. (Imagine how lonely and stressful adolescents' lives would have been like during the COVID-19 pandemic without social media.) Despite all of the hyperbolic claims that smartphones and social media are destroying the minds of a generation of young people, the scientific evidence indicates that the vast majority of teenagers use the Internet in ways that are not only benign but similar to those of their parents: to stay in touch with friends, to download and enjoy popular entertainment, and to keep up with the world around them.

8

Identity

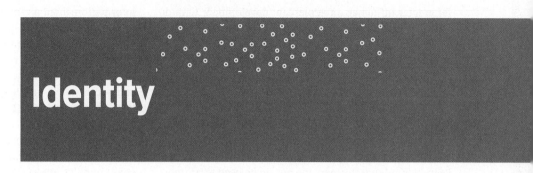

Identity as an Adolescent Issue
Puberty and Identity Development
Cognitive Change and Identity Development
Social Roles and Identity Development

Changes in Self-Conceptions
Changes in the Content and Structure of Self-Conceptions
Dimensions of Personality in Adolescence

Changes in Self-Esteem
Stability and Changes in Self-Esteem
Group Differences in Self-Esteem
Antecedents and Consequences of High Self-Esteem

The Adolescent Identity Crisis
Erikson's Theoretical Framework
The Social Context of Identity Development
Problems in Identity Development

Research on Identity Development
Determining an Adolescent's Identity Status
Studying Identity Development Over Time

Identity and Ethnicity
The Development of Ethnic Identity
Discrimination and Its Effects
Multiethnic Adolescents

Identity and Gender
Gender-Role Development
Gender-Role Socialization During Adolescence
Masculinity and Femininity

JGI/Jamie Grill/Getty Images

Because changes take place during adolescence in the ways people view and feel about themselves, the study of identity development has been a major focus of research and theory on adolescents (Harter, 2011). In this chapter, we examine why adolescence is a time of major changes in identity, why individuals differ in their patterns of identity development, and how the course of adolescent identity development is shaped by the nature of life in contemporary society.

Identity as an Adolescent Issue

Changes in the way we view and feel about ourselves occur throughout life. You've probably heard and read about the so-called midlife crisis, which is thought to occur during middle age. And certainly, important changes in our self-conceptions and in our self-image take place throughout childhood. When 4-year-olds and 10-year-olds are asked to describe themselves, the older children provide a far more complex self-portrait. Young children restrict their descriptions to lists of what they own or like to do. Older children are more likely to tell you about their personality as well.

Why have researchers who are interested in identity development paid so much more attention to adolescence than other stages? One reason is that the changes in identity that take place during adolescence involve the first substantial reorganization of the individual's sense of self at a time when people have the cognitive abilities to really appreciate just how significant the changes are. Compared to children, adolescents are far more self-conscious about these changes and feel them much more acutely.

Puberty and Identity Development

Another reason for the attention that researchers and theorists have given the study of identity development during adolescence concerns the fundamental biological, cognitive, and social changes characteristic of the period. It is not hard to see why puberty plays an important role in provoking identity development during adolescence. When you change the way you look—for example, when you have your hair colored or cut in a different way, lose a great deal of weight, or dramatically change how you dress—you sometimes feel as though your personality has changed, too. During puberty, when adolescents are changing so dramatically on the outside, they understandably have questions about changes that are taking place on the inside.

Cognitive Change and Identity Development

Just as the growth of intellectual capabilities during early adolescence provides new ways of thinking about problems, values, and interpersonal relationships, it also

permits adolescents to think about themselves in new ways. It is not until adolescence that people are able to think in systematic ways about hypothetical and future events. As a result, adolescents become much more able to imagine their **possible selves**—the various alternative identities that they may adopt (Markus & Nurius, 1986). This may stimulate heightened self-consciousness and experimentation with different identities. Brain-imaging studies find that patterns of brain activity during tasks in which individuals are asked to think about themselves differ significantly between adolescents and adults (Burnett et al., 2011; Pfeifer & Blakemore, 2012; Sebastian, Burnett, & Blakemore, 2008). In particular, there is evidence that adolescents exert more conscious, deliberate effort when asked to think about

possible selves
The various identities an adolescent might imagine for him- or herself.

Adolescence is often a time when individuals ask questions about who they are and where they are headed. Concerns with physical appearance often intensify. Image Source/Getty Images

future orientation
The extent to which an individual is able and inclined to think about the potential consequences of decisions and choices.

self-conceptions
The collection of traits and attributes that individuals use to describe or characterize themselves.

self-esteem
The degree to which individuals feel positively or negatively about themselves.

sense of identity
The extent to which individuals feel secure about who they are and who they are becoming.

themselves than adults do, who seem to do this more effortlessly (Blakemore, 2018). This may reflect the fact that adults already have a sturdy sense of identity, whereas teenagers are just beginning to develop one.

The development of a more advanced **future orientation**—the ability and tendency to consider the long-term consequences of one's decisions and imagine what one's life might be like in the years to come—is also important (Steinberg, Graham et al., 2009). It is not until adolescence that individuals typically begin to wonder, "Who will I become?" or "What am I really like?" Because the preadolescent child's thinking is concrete, it is difficult to think seriously about being a different person. But the changes in thinking that take place during adolescence open up a whole new world of alternatives. Adolescents who have a stronger future orientation report better mental health and less risky, delinquent, or impulsive behavior than their more short-sighted peers (Bromberg, Wiehler, & Peters, 2015; Chua, Milfont, & Jose, 2015; Lindstrom, Jones, & Cheng, 2015). In one experiment, high school students who were encouraged to think about their future self by receiving messages each day from an avatar whose face looked like an older version of their own reported less delinquency than a matched comparison group that received no such messages (Van Gelder et al., 2015).

Social Roles and Identity Development

Finally, changes in social roles at adolescence open up a new array of choices and decisions. In contemporary society, adolescence is a time of important decisions about school, work, relationships, and the future. Facing these decisions about their place in society does more than provoke adolescents to ask questions about who they are and where they are headed; it *necessitates* asking them. At this point in life, young people must make important choices about their education and their commitments to other people, and thinking about these questions prompts them to ask more questions about themselves: "What do I really want out of life?" "What things are important to me?" "What kind of person would I really like to be?" (Lawford & Ramey, 2015; Malin, Liauw, & Damon, 2017). Questions about the future, which inevitably arise as the adolescent prepares for adulthood, raise questions about identity (Côté, 2009).

Identity development is better understood as a series of interrelated developments—rather than one single

development—that involve changes in the way we view ourselves in relation to others and in relation to the broader society in which we live. Researchers and theorists have taken three different approaches to studying how people's sense of identity changes during adolescence.

The first approach emphasizes changes in **self-conceptions**—the traits and attributes individuals see in themselves. A second approach focuses on adolescents' **self-esteem,** or self-image—how positively or negatively they feel about themselves. Finally, a third approach emphasizes changes in one's **sense of identity**—who one is, where one has come from, and where one is going.

Changes in Self-Conceptions

As individuals mature intellectually and undergo the sorts of cognitive changes characteristic of adolescence, they start to conceive of themselves in much more sophisticated ways. Adolescents are far more capable than children of thinking about abstract concepts and considerably more proficient in processing large amounts of information. These intellectual capabilities affect the way in which individuals characterize themselves. Compared with children, who tend to describe themselves in relatively simple, concrete terms, adolescents are more likely to employ complex, abstract, and psychological self-characterizations (Harter, 2011). In addition, with development comes greater consistency between how individuals describe themselves and how they actually behave (Davis-Kean et al., 2008). There is also evidence that adolescents' ideas about the sort of person they would like to be (their "ideal self") become more stable over time (Zentner & Renaud, 2007).

Changes in the Content and Structure of Self-Conceptions

Self-conceptions change in structure and content during the transition from childhood into and through adolescence. They become more differentiated and better organized. Let's first consider the idea that self-conceptions become more differentiated.

Differentiation of the Self-Concept Imagine that you're at a party and someone you've just met says, "Tell me about yourself." What would you say?

Researchers have used this sort of question to see how self-conceptions change with age. Compared to children, adolescents are more likely to describe what they are like in different situations, rather than overall generalizations. A preadolescent might say something like "I'm nice" or "I'm friendly" but not specify when or under what conditions. An adolescent is more likely to say something like "I'm nice if I'm in a good mood" or "I'm friendly when I am with people I've met before." The realization that one's personality is expressed in different ways in different situations is an example of the increased differentiation that characterizes self-conceptions as adolescents mature toward adulthood.

There is another way in which self-conceptions become more differentiated at adolescence. Unlike characterizations provided by children, adolescents' self-descriptions take into account who is doing the describing (Harter, 2011). Neuroimaging studies show that adolescents' self-conceptions are particularly sensitive to the opinions of others (Pfeifer et al., 2009). Instead of saying "I'm shy" or "I'm outgoing," an adolescent might say something more complicated, such as "People don't think I'm shy, but I'm really nervous about meeting other kids for the first time." Adolescents also recognize that they may come across differently to different people; for example, "My parents think I'm quiet, but my friends know I really like to party a lot."

Organization and Integration of the Self-Concept

With this shift toward increased differentiation in self-conceptions comes better organization and integration (Harter, 2011). When children are asked to describe themselves, the attributes they list are often disorganized. Adolescents, in contrast, are likely to organize and integrate different aspects of their self-concept into a more logical, coherent whole. A younger child may list a sequence of several traits that appear to be contradictory ("I am friendly, I am shy"), but an adolescent will attempt to group what appear to be discrepant bits of information into more highly organized statements ("I am shy when I first meet people, but after I get to know them, I'm usually pretty friendly").

Self-conceptions continue to become more psychological well into the high school years, although this may be more characteristic of adolescents growing up in cultures like the United States, where teenagers tend to focus on their feelings and social life, than in cultures like China, where the focus is less on one's internal states and more on one's responsibilities and accomplishments (Setoh et al., 2015) (see Figure 8.1). The increased psychological complexity of self-conceptions may present some difficulties, though, when teenagers become able to recognize—but not yet quite understand or reconcile—inconsistencies and contradictions in their personality. The proportion of adolescents who give opposite traits in self-descriptions, who feel conflicts over such discrepancies, and who feel confused over such discrepancies increases markedly between seventh and ninth grades and then declines somewhat (Harter & Monsour, 1992).

Although the recognition that one's personality is multifaceted—even contradictory—may initially cause some distress, it has a number of advantages in the long run. Some psychologists think the development of a more complicated view of oneself is one way that individuals cope with the recognition of their faults and weaknesses,

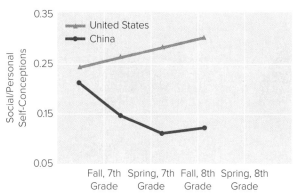

Figure 8.1 During early adolescence, American teenagers increasingly describe themselves with reference to their social and personal characteristics. In contrast, Chinese teenagers use these sorts of descriptions less and less. (Setoh et al., 2015)

a recognition that comes with increased self-awareness ("I'm not really a nasty person. I just act mean when people tease me"). Consistent with this, adolescents who have more complex and clearer self-conceptions are less likely to become depressed or anxious (Van Dijk et al., 2014) and report better relationships with their parents (Becht et al., 2017).

False-Self Behavior Another interesting consequence of adolescents' recognition that they are not always consistent in their personality concerns their ability to distinguish between their true and false selves (i.e., their authentic and inauthentic selves). Adolescents are most likely to behave inauthentically in romantic situations and with classmates, and they are least likely to put on a false front with close friends. **False-self behavior**—acting in a way one knows is inauthentic—occurs less often with parents than with acquaintances but more often with parents than with close friends (Harter, 2011). Although adolescents sometimes say that they dislike false-self behavior, they also say that sometimes it is acceptable, such as when trying to impress another person or hide an aspect of their personality that they know others don't like.

Adolescents differ in the degree to which they present false fronts and in their reasons for doing so. In general, adolescents who report less emotional support from parents and peers, who have low self-esteem, and who are relatively less satisfied with life are more likely to engage in false-self behavior (Thomaes et al., 2017). The connection between false-self behavior and low self-esteem runs in both directions; some adolescents engage in false-self behavior because they have low self-esteem, whereas others experience a drop in self-esteem because they knowingly put on a false front. Depression and hopelessness are highest among adolescents who engage in

false-self behavior
Behavior that intentionally presents a false impression to others.

Adolescence is a time during which individuals become more self-conscious. Fertnig/Getty Images

five-factor model
The theory that there are five basic dimensions to personality: extraversion, agreeableness, conscientiousness, neuroticism, and openness to experience.

false-self behavior because they genuinely devalue their true self, in contrast to those who put on a false front because they want to please others or because they are experimenting with different personalities (Harter et al., 1996).

making the personal connection

When was the last time you put on a false self? What people were you with? What was your motivation? How did you feel afterward?

Understanding how self-conceptions change during adolescence helps to explain why issues of identity begin to take on so much importance at this stage. You may recall having wondered as a teenager about your personality development, the influences that shaped your character, and how your personality had changed over time: "Am I more like my father or like my mother? Why do my sister and I seem so different? Will I always be so nervous?" Although these sorts of questions may seem commonplace to you now, in all likelihood, you did not think about these things until adolescence, when your own self-conceptions became more abstract and more sophisticated.

Dimensions of Personality in Adolescence

While many researchers have studied adolescent personality development by examining young people's self-conceptions, others have used standardized inventories designed to assess important aspects of personality. Most researchers who study personality use the **five-factor model** (McCrae & John, 1992). According to this model, there are five critical personality dimensions, often referred to as the "big five": *extraversion* (how outgoing and energetic someone is), *agreeableness* (how kind or sympathetic), *conscientiousness* (how responsible and organized), *neuroticism* (how anxious or tense), and *openness to experience* (how curious and imaginative).

Although the five-factor model was developed through research on adults, it has been successfully applied to adolescents, too (Caspi et al., 1997; McCrae et al., 2002). For example, delinquent adolescents are more likely than their peers to score high in extraversion and low in agreeableness and conscientiousness, whereas adolescents who are high achievers in school score high in conscientiousness and openness (John et al., 1994). Researchers have found that the five-factor model applies equally well across groups of adolescents from different ethnic backgrounds (Rowe, Vazsonyi, & Flannery, 1994).

There are both genetic and environmental influences on personality, although the environment becomes somewhat more important as people age (Kandler, 2012). Individuals may inherit temperamental predispositions (such as a high activity level or an inclination to be sociable), which are observable early in life, and these predispositions may "harden" and become organized into personality traits partially in response to the environment. For example, an active and sociable child who enjoys interacting with others may be rewarded for doing so and, over time, become extraverted. Both temperament and personality become increasingly stable as we grow older, in part because we tend to spend time in environments that reward and reinforce the traits that draw us to these settings (Mõttus et al., 2019; Wrzus, Wagner, & Reidiger, 2016). As a result, we become more like ourselves every day!

Between childhood and mid-adolescence, people become less extraverted, perhaps as they become more self-conscious, and less conscientious, perhaps as they begin to become more emotionally autonomous from their parents (Van den Akker et al., 2014). There is a temporary drop in maturity during early adolescence, "which appears to be the lifetime peak of meanness, laziness, and closed-mindedness" (Soto & Tackett, 2015, p. 360).

As they transition into young adulthood, individuals become less extraverted, but as they mature, they become more conscientious, more agreeable, more resilient, and more emotionally stable (Bleidorn, 2015; Hoff et al., 2020), which coincides with thinning of cortical brain regions associated with emotional regulation and cognitive control (Ferschmann et al., 2018). (In adolescence, thinning of the cortex is generally associated with brain maturation.) Girls mature earlier than boys emotionally (Zohar et al., 2019), but boys catch up over time, so that

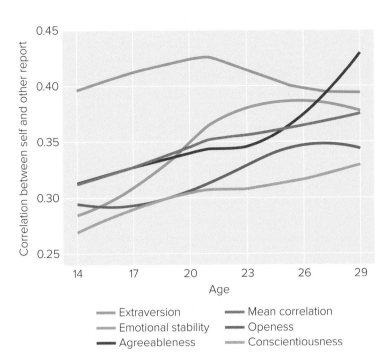

Figure 8.2   As we get older, we increasingly come to see ourselves as others see us. (Rohrer et al., 2018)

by the end of adolescence, there are few gender differences in maturity (De Bolle et al., 2015; Klimstra et al., 2009). The rate of change in personality begins to slow during the early 20s (Syed & Seiffge-Krenke, 2013).

In sum, many core personality traits, such as impulsivity or timidity, are stable between childhood and adolescence and between adolescence and young adulthood (Borghuis et al., 2017; Specht, Luhmann, & Geiser, 2014; Wangqvist et al., 2015). Although the external manifestations of these traits may change with age (e.g., anxiety may appear as bed-wetting in early childhood but as nervous talkativeness in adolescence), our basic, underlying traits turn out to be remarkably unchanging.

For example, individuals who displayed relatively more aggression in preadolescence, temper tantrums during childhood, or negative emotions during infancy, are more likely to behave aggressively as adolescents (Caspi et al., 1995; Hart et al., 1997). Similarly, individuals who had difficulty controlling their impulses as preschoolers are more likely to be rash, aggressive, and sensation seeking as adolescents and young adults, whereas individuals who were inhibited as young children tend to be relatively more timid, anxious, and shy. Not surprisingly, individuals who are well-adjusted in early and middle childhood tend to be resilient and competent in adolescence (Gest, 1997; Hart et al., 1997; Shiner, Masten, & Tellegen, 2002).

Despite popular stereotypes about adolescence as a time of "rebirth," then, research does not show that adolescence is a time of tumultuous upheaval in personality. Indeed, people's basic personality remains stable from high school all the way into their mid-60s, especially with respect to psychological maturity, aesthetic appreciation, tidiness, and social sensitivity (Damian et al, 2018). This stability of personality is observed regardless of whether the traits are measured by asking people to describe themselves or by asking people who know them well to provide the descriptions. Perhaps more important, the correlation between self-reports and the reports of others increases as people mature, consistent with the idea that part of growing up involves the ability to see yourself as others see you (Rohrer et al., 2018) (see Figure 8.2).

Changes in Self-Esteem

It's long been believed that the "storm and stress" of adolescence creates problems in self-esteem—how adolescents evaluate themselves. This turns out not to be true. But although there isn't a dramatic drop in self-esteem at this age, adolescents' feelings about themselves fluctuate from day to day, particularly during the early adolescent years. And, despite commentary in the popular press about the excessively high self-esteem characteristic of today's young people, careful statistical analyses show that there has been no appreciable increase in American adolescents' self-esteem during the past several decades (Steinberg, 2014a; Trzesniewski & Donnellan, 2009).

Stability and Changes in Self-Esteem

Self-esteem becomes increasingly more stable between childhood and early adulthood, as adolescents' feelings about themselves gradually consolidate and become less likely to fluctuate in response to different experiences (Erol & Orth, 2011; Trzesniewski, Donnellan, & Robins, 2003). Day-to-day fluctuations in mood tend to become smaller between early adolescence and late adolescence

self-consciousness
The degree to which an individual is preoccupied with his or her self-image.

self-image stability
The degree to which an individual's self-image changes from day to day.

(Larson et al., 2002). The fact that self-esteem is *stable* doesn't mean that self-esteem doesn't *change* over time. It simply means that people who enter adolescence with higher self-esteem than others leave adolescence with higher self-esteem than others, too. (If this seems confusing, think of it this way: Height is a very stable trait, in that relatively taller children, when they are adults, are also taller than other people their age. But this doesn't mean that people don't grow between childhood and adulthood.)

Studies of changes in self-esteem as individuals move through adolescence have not yielded consistent findings, partly because researchers have focused on different aspects of individuals' self-image. Some studies find that individuals' feelings about themselves become more negative over the course of adolescence (Jacobs et al., 2002), but others find that they become more positive (Orth & Robins, 2014).

In general, however, changes in self-perceptions (whether positive or negative) are greater during early adolescence than during middle or late adolescence (Liu & Xin, 2014). From middle adolescence through young adulthood, self-esteem either remains at about the same level or increases (Chung et al., 2014; Orth, Maes, & Schmitt, 2015; Von Soest, Wichstrom, & Lundin Kvalem, 2016). Although there is a general trend for individuals' average mood to become less positive over the course of adolescence (children are usually in a more positive mood than young adolescents, who are generally in a better mood than older adolescents), this trend begins to level off around age 16 (Larson et al., 2002). Teenagers who experience frequent fluctuations in mood also report higher levels of anxiety and depression (Maciejewski et al., 2014).

Volatility in Early Adolescents' Self-Evaluations

Although adolescence is not a time of storm and stress, problems in self-image may arise for a brief period during early adolescence. To fully understand why, it is necessary to distinguish among three aspects of adolescents' self-image: their self-esteem (how positively or negatively they feel about themselves), their **self-consciousness** (how much they worry about their self-image), and their **self-image stability** (how much their self-image changes from day to day) (Simmons, Rosenberg, & Rosenberg, 1973).

Fluctuations in adolescents' self-image are most likely to occur between the ages of 12 and 14. This is a time of major changes in brain systems that regulate how we think about ourselves and others (Pfeifer & Peake, 2012). Compared with preadolescents or older adolescents, early and middle adolescents have lower self-esteem, are more self-conscious, and have a more unstable self-image. Generally, the differences between preadolescents and

early or middle adolescents are greater than those between younger and older adolescents, which indicates that the most marked fluctuations in self-image occur during the transition into adolescence, rather than over the course of adolescence itself (Thomaes, Poorthuis, & Nelemans, 2011).

Does it seem to you that early and middle adolescents are a little obsessed with taking "selfies"? You may be right. In a recent experiment that looked at where people focused their gaze when looking at photos of themselves, friends, or strangers, focusing on one's own picture was more common during mid-adolescence than among younger or older individuals (Doi & Shinohara, 2018)!

The extent to which an individual's self-esteem is volatile is itself a stable trait. Young adolescents whose self-image fluctuates a lot from moment to moment are likely to develop into older adolescents who experience the same thing. Young adolescents with the most volatile self-image report the highest levels of anxiety, tension, and adjustment problems (Molloy, Ram, & Gest, 2011). This is especially likely among adolescents who have a great deal of stress in their day-to-day lives (Tevendale et al., 1997). Having a volatile self-image may make individuals especially vulnerable to the effects of stress. In contrast, believing that one has some control over one's personality and is capable of changing is an important asset that helps teenagers deal with interpersonal problems (Yeager, 2017).

Fluctuations in self-image during early adolescence probably are due to several interrelated factors. First, the sort of egocentrism that is common in early adolescence may make young adolescents painfully aware of others' reactions to their behavior. Second, as individuals become more socially active, they begin to learn that people play games when they interact, and they learn that it is not always possible to tell what others are thinking on the basis of how they act or what they say. This ambiguity may leave young adolescents puzzled and uncomfortable about how they are really viewed by others. Finally, because of the increased importance of peers, young adolescents are especially interested in their peers' opinions of them. For the first time, they may have to come to terms with contradictions between the messages they get from their parents ("That haircut you just got makes you even prettier—you look great with short hair") and the messages they get from their friends ("You'd better wear a hat until your hair grows back!"). Hearing contradictory messages can create uncertainty about oneself.

The Wrong Question?

Studies of age differences in self-esteem often hide substantial differences among people of the same age. Some adolescents have very stable self-esteem over time, whereas others do not (Birkeland et al., 2012; Morin et al., 2013). Not surprisingly, adolescents with better family and peer relationships are more likely than their peers to maintain positive self-esteem or develop enhanced self-esteem over time (Diehl, Vicary, & Deike, 1997). Similar variability in patterns of life satisfaction has also been reported (Tolan & Larsen, 2014). Interestingly, the brains of adolescents with relatively higher self-esteem tend to have stronger connections between areas of the brain that regulate how we think about ourselves and areas that control feelings of reward (Chavez & Heatherton, 2015).

Some critics of studies of the stability of self-esteem in adolescence also question the validity of examining self-esteem in such a general sense. Although most research on adolescent self-esteem has focused on teenagers' overall feelings about themselves, young people evaluate themselves both globally, which may be a good indicator of general psychological well-being, and along several distinct dimensions, such as academics, athletics, appearance, social relationships, and moral conduct (Côté, 2009; Esnaola et al., 2020). As a consequence, it is possible for an adolescent to have high self-esteem when it comes to academic abilities, low self-esteem when it comes to athletics, and moderate self-esteem when it comes to physical appearance, social relationships, or moral behavior.

Components of Self-Esteem   Even within broad domains of self-esteem (e.g., academics, athletics, or social relationships), adolescents often have quite differentiated views of themselves. For example, adolescents' evaluations of their social competence within the context of their relationships with their parents may be very different from the way they see themselves in their relationships with teachers, which in turn may differ from their evaluations of themselves in the peer group (Harter, Waters, & Whitesell, 1998). Within the realm of peer relationships, adolescents' social self-esteem may vary depending on whether they are thinking about their friendships or their romantic relationships; someone who is totally confident when he's around his friends may be nervous and insecure when talking to a crush. Therefore, it may be misleading to characterize an adolescent's "social self-esteem" as low or high without specifying the relationship being referred to. The same goes for academic self-esteem: Because students evaluate their abilities in specific subject areas both in comparison to other students ("I am terrible at math compared to everyone else in this class") and relative to their abilities in other subject areas ("I am so much better at math than I am at history"), making sweeping statements about an adolescent's overall academic self-image is often unwise (Arens et al., 2011; Marsh & Hau, 2004).

Do some aspects of self-esteem contribute more to an adolescent's overall self-image than others? Yes, they do. Adolescents' physical self-esteem—how they feel about their appearance—is the most important predictor of overall self-esteem, followed by self-esteem about relationships with peers (Vannucci & Ohannessian, 2018; Von

Soest, Wichstrom, & Lundin Kvalem, 2016). Less important are self-esteem about academic ability, athletic ability, or moral conduct.

Although researchers find that adolescents' physical self-esteem is the best predictor of their overall self-esteem, adolescents, when asked, say that their physical appearance is one of the least important contributors to how they feel about themselves. In other words, adolescents are often unaware of the degree to which their self-worth is based on their feelings about their appearance (DuBois et al., 2000). Physical self-esteem is a more important influence on overall self-esteem among girls than boys, although both genders' self-esteem is linked to how they feel about their appearance (Kistler et al., 2010; Thomaes, Poorthuis, & Nelemans, 2011; van den Berg et al., 2010). These findings help explain why girls are more likely than boys to experience self-image difficulties and depression.

Group Differences in Self-Esteem

Thus far, we've looked at how self-esteem changes on average during adolescence and at the factors that influence how teenagers feel about themselves. Psychologists also have asked whether some groups of adolescents have higher self-esteem than others.

Sex Differences   Early adolescent girls are more vulnerable to disturbances in their self-image than any other group of youngsters. Compared to early adolescent boys, early adolescent girls' self-esteem is lower, their degree of self-consciousness is higher, and their self-image is shakier. Girls also are more likely than boys to say negative things about themselves, to feel insecure about their abilities, and

Early adolescent girls' self-esteem is lower, their degree of self-consciousness is higher, and their self-image is shakier than is the case for boys. Paul/Getty Images

to worry whether other people like being with them. Some commentators worry that the increased prominence of social media in adolescent girls' daily experience is only making matters worse (Chua & Chang, 2016).

Sex differences in self-esteem are most pronounced among white adolescents. Similar patterns have been found among Latinx adolescents but not, for the most part, among Black adolescents (Erkut et al., 2000; van den Berg et al., 2010). Because Black girls do not feel as negatively about their appearance as white or Latinx girls, they have relatively higher overall self-esteem and show less of a decline in self-esteem over adolescence (Gray-Little & Hafdahl, 2000).

Why would girls have greater self-esteem problems during early adolescence than boys? The answer may be related to the special significance of physical appearance and acceptance by peers in determining self-esteem. Because young girls are more concerned than boys about physical attractiveness, dating, and peer acceptance, they may experience a greater number of self-image problems. Not surprisingly, girls who attend single-sex schools have higher self-esteem than those who go to coeducational ones (Cribb & Haase, 2016). Although sex differences in adolescent self-esteem, favoring males, are found all over the world, the gap is wider in wealthy, developed nations than in poor, developing ones, perhaps because more affluent societies place a greater emphasis on physical appearance (Bleidorn et al., 2016).

Ethnic Differences   Black adolescents on average have higher self-esteem than white adolescents, who, in turn, tend to have higher self-esteem than Latinx, Asian, or Native American youth (Biro et al., 2006; Twenge & Crocker, 2002). Several studies indicate that Asian American adolescents have particularly low self-esteem relative to their peers (e.g., Herman, 2004), a finding that some researchers have attributed to higher rates of peer rejection (Niwa, Way, & Hughes, 2014).

A number of researchers have asked why Black adolescents have such high self-esteem, given the prevalence of prejudice in American society and the generally disadvantaged position of Black individuals in the workplace and school, two institutions in which individuals' performance influences their self-image. There are two main explanations.

First, despite their encounters with racism and prejudice, Black teenagers often benefit from the support and positive feedback of adults in the Black community, especially in the family (Gaylord-Harden et al., 2007). This is not surprising, given the wealth of research showing that the approval of significant others is an especially powerful influence on adolescents' self-esteem—much more so than the opinion of the broader society (e.g., Gray-Little & Hafdahl, 2000; Whitesell et al., 2006).

Second, the very strong sense of ethnic identity that exists among Black adolescents enhances their overall

self-esteem (DuBois et al., 2002; Gaylord-Harden et al., 2007). Ethnic differences in self-esteem, favoring Black adolescents, have increased over the past 30 years (perhaps because ethnic identity has become a more relevant issue in society) and are greater during adolescence than childhood (perhaps because ethnic identity is a more salient issue during adolescence than before) (Twenge & Crocker, 2002).

Ethnic differences also exist in patterns of change in self-esteem during adolescence. In one study of Black, Latinx, and Asian urban adolescents, Black students and biracial students (mainly Black/Latinx) had relatively higher self-esteem in early adolescence, and their self-esteem remained high throughout the adolescent years. In contrast, Latinx students had relatively lower self-esteem early in adolescence but caught up with their Black peers by the end of high school. Asian students began with the lowest self-esteem, and it remained lower than that of other groups over time (see Figure 8.3). Similar patterns were found in a large national sample of American youth (Erol & Orth, 2011). In contrast to studies of white adolescents, there were no sex differences in levels or patterns of change in self-esteem in this sample of ethnic minority adolescents.

The ethnic diversity of the context in which adolescents develop has a substantial impact on their self-image. High school students who live in a social environment or go to a school in which their ethnic or socioeconomic group is in the minority are more likely to have self-image problems than those who are in the majority. This seems to be true with regard to religion, socioeconomic status, ethnicity, and household composition. Black teenagers, for example, have a higher opinion of themselves when they go to schools in which Black students are a majority

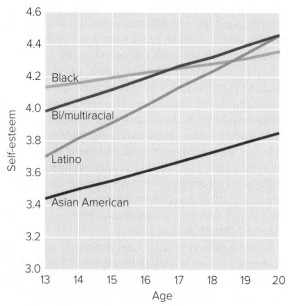

Figure 8.3   Ethnic differences in patterns of self-esteem over time. (Greene & Way, 2005)

Adolescents who attend schools in which they are in the ethnic minority may suffer greater self-esteem problems than their peers who attend schools in which they are in the majority. Although desegregation may have a positive impact on minority adolescents' academic achievement, this benefit may be counterbalanced by the apparently negative impact of desegregation on minority students' self-image. Thinkstock/Comstock Images/Getty Images

than when they attend predominantly white schools, where they may feel out of place and under pressure to play down their cultural heritage. By the same token, Jewish adolescents have higher self-esteem in schools in which there are many other Jewish students than in schools in which Jews compose a small minority of the student body. Similarly, levels of maladjustment are higher among Latinx youngsters when there is a lower concentration of Latinx families in their neighborhood (White, Zeiders, & Safa, 2018).

Antecedents and Consequences of High Self-Esteem

Several researchers have examined the link between self-esteem and adolescent behavior in an attempt to see whether certain sorts of experiences contribute—either positively or negatively—to adolescents' feelings about themselves. Others have posed the question in reverse: Does having high (or low) self-esteem lead adolescents to behave in particular ways?

Influences on Self-Esteem Even though there are ethnic differences in average levels of self-esteem, the correlates of self-esteem are similar in different ethnic groups and among immigrants and nonimmigrants alike. Self-esteem is enhanced by being raised by parents who are loving and supportive and by being accepted by one's peers (Birkeland, Bfreivik, & Wold, 2014; Huey et al.,

2020; Juang et al., 2018; Krauss & Orth, 2018). That said, although being close to one's parents and having good relations with one's peers are associated with higher self-esteem, it isn't clear which one leads to the other (Harris et al., 2015; van Geel et al., 2018). Similarly, although having high self-esteem is correlated with the use of social network sites, it appears that feeling positively about oneself leads teenagers to use social media, rather than the reverse (Valkenburg, Koutamanis, & Vossen, 2017).

Adolescents whose self-esteem is too wrapped up in the approval of others—especially the approval of peers—may be at risk for developing self-image problems, since peer acceptance may fluctuate over time as the values and expectations of the peer group change (Harter, Stocker, & Robinson, 1996). Adolescents who derive their self-esteem relatively more from peers than from teachers or parents show more behavioral problems and poorer school achievement (DuBois et al., 1999).

Consequences of High or Low Self-Esteem Although it once was believed that enhanced self-esteem leads to school success, there actually is little evidence for this, and a lot of evidence that the reverse is true (e.g., Schmidt & Padilla, 2003). Academic success leads to improvements in how adolescents feel about themselves, not the other way around. These findings cast doubt on the logic behind programs designed to raise teenagers' school performance by increasing their self-esteem. High self-esteem during adolescence does enhance adolescents' well-being, however, whereas low self-esteem may lead to mental health problems, both in the short run (Orth & Robins, 2013) and well into adulthood (Trzesniewski et al., 2006).

The relationship between low self-esteem and psychological problems is complicated (Gerard & Buehler, 2004). Low self-esteem is one of several symptoms of depression, but it appears that low self-esteem is more likely to lead to depression than result from it (Orth et al., 2014; Rieger et al., 2016). One reason that low self-esteem may lead to depression is that adolescents with negative feelings about themselves are less likely to seek positive feedback and social support from others (Marshall et al., 2014; Masselink, Van Roekel, & Oldehinkel, 2018). Perhaps as a consequence, they come to believe that other teenagers don't like them, which makes them feel lonely, further diminishing their self-esteem (Vanhalst et al., 2013) (see Figure 8.4).

The link between self-esteem and behavior problems (as opposed to emotional problems) is even less clear. Although low self-esteem initially may encourage some adolescents toward delinquency, involvement with delinquent peers actually may lead to an increase in self-esteem because involvement in delinquency earns teenagers approval from certain peers (Mason, 2001). Furthermore, adolescents with high self-esteem are more likely to

Figure 8.4   Low self-esteem often discourages adolescents from seeking out social support from others, which can lead to feelings of loneliness.

experiment with alcohol than are those with low self-esteem (Scheier et al., 2000), most probably because high self-esteem is associated with being in the more popular social crowds, in which drinking is more common.

The Adolescent Identity Crisis

If you were asked to write a novel about your own identity development, what would you mention? Perhaps you would talk about developing a sense of purpose, or clarifying long-term plans and values, or becoming more confident about who you really are and where you are headed (Hill, Burrow, & Summer, 2013). If these are the sorts of things that come to mind when you think about identity development in adolescence, you are thinking about an aspect of development that psychologists refer to as the sense of identity. The dominant view in the study of adolescent identity development emphasizes precisely these aspects of psychosocial development, and the theorist whose work has been most influential in this area is Erik Erikson.

Erikson's Theoretical Framework

Erikson's (1968) theory developed out of his clinical and cross-cultural observations of young people at various stages of development. He believed that development involved moving through a series of eight psychosocial crises over the course of the life span. Each crisis, although present in one form or another at all ages, takes on special significance at a given period of the life cycle because biological and social forces interact to make crisis especially salient. The establishment of a coherent sense of identity—what Erikson called the crisis of **identity versus identity diffusion**—is the chief psychosocial crisis of adolescence.

Achieving a balanced and coherent sense of identity is intellectually and emotionally taxing. Erikson believed that the key to resolving the crisis of identity versus identity diffusion lies in the adolescent's interactions with others. By responding to the reactions of people who matter, the adolescent selects and chooses from among the many elements that could conceivably become a part of his or her identity. The other people with whom the young person

identity versus identity diffusion

According to Erikson, the normative crisis characteristic of the fifth stage of psychosocial development, predominant during adolescence.

interacts serve as a mirror that reflects back information about who he or she is and ought to be.

As such, the responses of significant others shape the adolescent's developing sense of identity. Through others' reactions, adolescents learn whether they are competent or inept, attractive or ugly, socially adept or awkward. Perhaps more important—especially during periods when their sense of identity is still forming—adolescents learn from others what they do that they ought to keep doing and what they do that they ought to stop. Increasingly, adolescents use social media, such as Facebook, to accomplish this (Davis, 2013; Jordán-Conde, Mennecke, & Townsend, 2014).

The Social Context of Identity Development

The social context in which the adolescent attempts to establish a sense of identity exerts a tremendous impact on the nature and outcome of the process. If the adolescent's identity is forged out of a recognition on the part of society, society will play an important role in determining which sorts of identities are possible alternatives. And of those identities that are genuine options, society will influence which are desirable and which aren't.

As a consequence, the course of identity development varies over different historical eras, in different cultures, and among different subcultures within the same society (Kroger, 1993). For example, studies of identity development among contemporary youth in Japan have found increasing levels of uncertainty as Japanese society has become less collectivistic in recent decades. This uncertainty may be due to the fact that the older generations are less supportive of the individualized orientation that has become more common among Japanese young people (Sugimura, 2020).

The social context also influences whether the search for self-definition will be a full-blown crisis or a more manageable challenge. The rapid rate of social change in most of the world has raised new and more complex sets of questions for young people to consider—questions not only about occupational plans but also about values, lifestyles, and commitments to other people. Today, even in some countries where until recently individuals had little choice about the life they would lead, adolescents must ask themselves what sort of work they want to do; if they want to remain single, live with someone, or marry; and if

Role experimentation during adolescence often involves trying on different looks, images, and patterns of behavior. According to theorists such as Erik Erikson, having the time and freedom to experiment with different roles is an important prelude to establishing a coherent sense of identity. Beatriz Vera/ Shutterstock

and when they want to have children. The likelihood of going through a prolonged and difficult identity crisis is probably greater today, and more prevalent around the world, than it has ever been.

making the cultural connection

During the past 15 years, there have been dramatic political changes in much of the Arab world. Do you think that changes in these societies' "identity" will lead to changes in patterns of adolescent identity development?

The Psychosocial Moratorium   According to Erikson, the complications inherent in identity development in modern society have created the need for a **psychosocial moratorium**—a "time out" during adolescence from excessive responsibilities and obligations that might restrict the pursuit of self-discovery. Adolescents in contemporary America are given a moratorium of sorts by being encouraged to remain in school for a long time, where they can think seriously about their plans for the future without making irrevocable decisions. For adolescents who can tolerate not knowing where they are headed and who use this time to gather information and explore a variety of options, the moratorium can be an exhilarating experience. For others, though, the moratorium is a period of uncomfortable and anxious indecision (Becht et al., 2016.)

During the psychosocial moratorium, adolescents can experiment with different roles and identities in a context that permits and encourages exploration. The experimentation involves trying on different postures, personalities, and ways of behaving—sometimes to the consternation of the adolescent's parents, who may wonder why their child's personality seems so changeable.

> **psychosocial moratorium**
> A period during which individuals are free from excessive obligations and responsibilities and can therefore experiment with different roles and personalities.

One week, an adolescent girl will spend hours putting on makeup; the next week, she will insist to her parents that she is tired of caring so much about the way she looks. An adolescent boy will come home one day with a shaved head and piercings, and a few weeks later, he will discard this image for that of a preppie. Although many parents worry about their teenage children going through these sorts of phases, much of this behavior is normal experimentation.

Having the time to experiment with roles is an important prelude to establishing a coherent sense of identity. But role experimentation can take place only in an environment that allows and encourages it. Without a moratorium, a full and thorough exploration of the options and available alternatives cannot occur, and identity development will be impeded. According to Erikson, adolescents must grow into an adult identity, rather than be forced into one prematurely.

It is clear that the sort of moratorium Erikson described is an ideal. Some might even consider it to be a luxury of the affluent. Many young people—perhaps even most—do not have the economic freedom to enjoy a long delay before taking on the responsibilities of adult life. For many youngsters, alternatives do not exist in any realistic sense, and introspection only interferes with the more pressing task of survival. Does the 17-year-old who has to drop out of school to work a full-time job go through life without a sense of identity? Do youngsters who cannot afford a psychosocial moratorium fail to resolve the identity crisis?

Certainly not. But from Erikson's perspective, the absence of a psychosocial moratorium in some adolescents' lives—either because of restrictions they place on themselves, restrictions placed on them by others, or their life circumstances—is truly regrettable. The price these youngsters pay is not the failure to develop a sense of identity but lost potential. You may know people whose parents forced them into prematurely choosing a certain career or who had to drop out of college and take a job they really did not want because of financial pressures. Without a chance to explore, to experiment, and to choose among options for the future, these adolescents may not realize all that they are capable of becoming. It is easy to see how the broader context in which adolescents grow up affects this. Think, for example, of how individuals' plans for the future may have had to change during the COVID-19 pandemic.

identity diffusion
The incoherent, disjointed, incomplete sense of self characteristic of not having resolved the crisis of identity.

Resolving the Identity Crisis
Most writers on adolescence and youth believe that identity exploration continues well into young adulthood. But rather than thinking of adolescents as having a single identity crisis, it probably makes more sense to view the phenomenon as a series of crises that may concern different aspects of the young person's identity and that may surface—and resurface—at different points in time throughout the adolescent and young-adult years. During adolescence, the feeling of well-being associated with establishing a sense of identity is often fleeting, as individuals make commitments and plans, explore different identities, reconsider them, change commitments, and engage in more exploration (Crocetti, 2017; Wang, Douglass, & Yip, 2017) (see Figure 8.5). Ultimately, however, the identity crisis of adolescence, when successfully resolved, culminates in a series of basic life commitments: occupational, ideological, social, religious, ethical, and sexual (Côté, 2009).

Problems in Identity Development

Given the wide variations in developmental histories that individuals bring to adolescence and the substantial differences in the environments in which they develop, it is not surprising to find differences in the ways in which individuals approach and resolve the identity crisis. Problems in identity development can result when someone has not successfully resolved earlier crises or when the adolescent is in an environment that does not provide the necessary period of moratorium. Three sorts of problems received special attention from Erikson: identity diffusion, identity foreclosure, and negative identity.

Identity Diffusion   **Identity diffusion** is characterized by an incoherent, disjointed, incomplete sense of self. It can vary in degree from a mild state of not quite knowing who one is while in the midst of an identity crisis to a

more severe, clinical condition that persists beyond a normal period of exploration. Identity diffusion is marked by disruptions in the individual's sense of time (some things seem to happen much faster than they really do, while others seem to take forever); excessive self-consciousness, to the point that it is difficult to make decisions; problems in work and school; difficulties in forming intimate relationships with others; and concerns over sexuality. In other words, identity diffusion is reflected not only in problems of identity but also in the areas of autonomy, intimacy, sexuality, and achievement. Frequent fluctuation between temporary commitments and their reconsideration, without adequate exploration, is associated with behavioral problems (Mercer et al., 2017).

Identity Foreclosure   Some young people bypass—either willingly or unwillingly—the period of exploration and experimentation that precedes the establishment of a healthy sense of identity. Instead of considering a range of alternatives, these adolescents prematurely commit themselves to a role, or series of roles, and settle upon a certain identification as a final identity. In essence, these individuals are not given—or do not take advantage of—a psychosocial moratorium. A college freshman who made up her mind about becoming a doctor at the age of 13

Some adolescents fail to thoroughly engage in the process of identity exploration because their parents have selected an identity for them. Erikson called this "identity foreclosure."
JGI/Jamie Grill/Getty Images

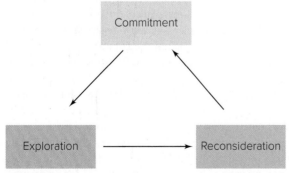

Figure 8.5   **The process of identity development is a cycle of making commitments, exploring them in depth, reconsidering them, and revising them.** (Adapted from Crocetti, 2017)

may enroll in a rigid premed curriculum without considering other career possibilities. The circumvention of the identity crisis is called **identity foreclosure.**

Typically, the roles adopted in the process of identity foreclosure revolve around the goals set for the young person by parents or other authority figures. The adolescent may be led into these roles directly or may be forced into them indirectly by being denied a true moratorium. Perhaps the parents of the would-be doctor have arranged their child's school schedule and summer vacations so that all of her spare time is spent taking extra science courses. No time is left for role experimentation or introspection. Individuals who have bypassed the identity crisis have made commitments, but they have not gone through a period of experimentation before making them. Identity foreclosure is an interruption of the identity development process, one that interferes with the individual's discovery of his or her full range of potentials.

Negative Identity Adolescents sometimes appear to select identities that are obviously undesirable to their parents and their community. The examples are familiar: the daughter of the local district attorney who repeatedly gets into trouble with the law, the son of prestigious and successful parents who refuses to go to college, the child of a devoutly religious family who insists that he or she is an atheist. Because the establishment of a healthy sense of identity is so intimately tied to the recognition of the adolescent by those who matter, the adoption of a so-called **negative identity** is a sign of problems in identity development. The adolescent who adopts a negative identity is recognized by those around him or her, but not in a way that fosters healthy development.

Selecting a negative identity usually represents an attempt to forge some sense of self-definition in an environment that has made it difficult to establish an acceptable identity. This appears to be especially likely when, after repeatedly trying and failing to receive positive recognition from those who are important in their lives, adolescents turn to a different, perhaps more successful, route to being noticed. Consider this example: The son of successful parents is a good student but not quite good enough to please his excessively demanding parents. He feels he is a nobody in his parents' eyes, so he drops out of school to join a band—something his parents vehemently oppose. But as Erikson wisely pointed out, most adolescents would rather be somebody "bad" than nobody at all.

making the practical connection

Are there any aspects of today's environment that might make the resolution of the identity crisis especially difficult? Can you think of anything that might be done to help facilitate healthy identity development?

Research on Identity Development

The term **identity status** refers to the point in the identity development process that characterizes an adolescent at a given time. In order to determine an individual's identity status, most researchers have used an approach that focuses on the processes of exploration (experimenting with different ideas about occupations, values, relationships, and so forth) and commitment (making choices among various alternatives) (Marcia, 1966). Some theorists (e.g., Negru-Subtiricia et al., 2016) also distinguish between exploration in "depth" (making a commitment to an identity and then exploring one's options) and exploration in "breadth" (exploring one's options and then making a further commitment). Others (e.g., Becht et al., 2017; Crocetti, 2017) see identity development as a more dynamic process, with individuals moving back and forth between commitment and exploration over time.

In all of these frameworks, the important point is that healthy identity involvement requires experimentation and exploration before finalizing one's choices about work, love, and lifestyle. Interestingly, brain imaging studies find that regions of the brain that are associated with motivation (e.g., the nucleus accumbens) are larger among adolescents who are engaged in the exploration process, whereas regions associated with cognitive control (e.g., the frontal cortex) are larger among those who are actively gathering information about their commitments and thinking about them (Becht et al., 2018).

Determining an Adolescent's Identity Status

In identity status research, based on their responses to an interview or questionnaire, individuals are assigned to one of four identity states (*state* is the right word because research shows that individuals move from state to state, and not necessarily in an orderly fashion): (1) identity achievement (the individual has established a coherent sense of identity—that is, has made commitments after a period of exploration), (2) moratorium (the individual is in the midst of a period of exploration), (3) identity foreclosure (the individual has made commitments but without a period of exploration), or (4) identity diffusion (the individual does not have firm commitments and is not currently trying to make them). Research employing this approach has

identity foreclosure
The premature establishment of a sense of identity, before sufficient role experimentation has occurred.

negative identity
The selection of an identity that is obviously undesirable in the eyes of significant others and the broader community.

identity status
The point in the identity development process that characterizes an adolescent at a given time.

supported many aspects of Erikson's theory (Meeus, 2011; Meeus et al., 2012). The strongest support comes from studies that show a pattern of correlations between various traits and the different identity states that are consistent with predictions based on Erikson's model.

For example, individuals who are in a state of identity achievement are psychologically healthier than others in a variety of ways: They score highest on measures of achievement motivation, moral reasoning, intimacy with peers, and career maturity. Individuals in the midst of a moratorium score highest on measures of anxiety, show the highest levels of conflict over issues of authority, and are themselves the least rigid and least authoritarian. Individuals classified as foreclosed have been shown to be the most authoritarian and most prejudiced and to have the highest need for social approval, the lowest level of autonomy, and the greatest closeness to their parents. Individuals in a state of identity diffusion display the highest level of psychological, behavioral, and interpersonal problems: They are the most socially withdrawn and most likely to engage in antisocial behavior and show the lowest level of intimacy with peers (Hatano & Sugimura, 2017; Meeus, 2011; Schwartz et al., 2015, 2017; Sznitman, Zimmerman, & Van Petegem, 2019).

Generally, individuals whose identity development is healthy are more likely to have grown up in authoritative homes characterized by warm, but not excessively constraining, relations (Beyers & Goossens, 2008; Dumas et al., 2009). People who grow up in these environments are encouraged to assert their individuality but remain connected to their families. Typically, the absence of parental warmth is associated with problems in making commitments—the most extreme case being identity diffusion—whereas the absence of parental encouragement of individuality is associated with difficulties in exploration (Côté, 2009).

One of the defining characteristics of individuals who have achieved a coherent sense of identity is that they approach life's decisions with a strong sense of **agency**: They take responsibility for themselves, feel in control of their decisions, and have confidence that they will be able to overcome obstacles along the way (Becht et al., 2018; Côté, 2000). A strong sense of personal agency is predictive of identity achievement across ethnic and socioeconomic groups (e.g., Schwartz, Côté, & Arnett, 2005).

Being in charge of one's life may be especially important in contemporary industrialized society, where the transition to adulthood is prolonged and individuals are faced with a tremendous number of identity-related decisions. Individuals in their late teens or early 20s who say they are not sure when asked whether they are adolescents or adults are less likely to have achieved a sense of identity than are those who are certain that they have reached adulthood (Nelson & Barry, 2005). It is not clear whether

agency
The sense that one has an impact on one's world.

Most research indicates that the chief period for identity development is in late adolescence, when many individuals are enrolled in college. Robert Daly/Caia Image/Glow Images

having a coherent sense of identity leads one to think of oneself as an adult or, instead, whether seeing oneself as an adult leads one to have a more coherent sense of identity. But it does seem that becoming an adult, at least in industrialized society, is as much a psychological transition as it is one defined by entering the formal roles of adulthood, such as beginning a career or setting up one's own household.

Studying Identity Development Over Time

In order to examine the development of a sense of identity, researchers have done both cross-sectional studies (comparing individuals of different ages) and longitudinal studies (following the same individuals over a period of time) (e.g., Bogaerts et al. 2019). Many of these studies have challenged some widely held beliefs about the nature of identity development in adolescence (Meeus, 2011).

First, studies show that a coherent sense of identity generally is not established before age 18, let alone earlier in adolescence, as originally theorized (Côté, 2009). This is especially true among boys, who tend to lag behind girls in identity development in early and middle adolescence but catch up by late adolescence (as is the case with emotional maturity more generally) (Klimstra et al., 2010). There is clearly a decline with age in the proportion of individuals who are in a state of moratorium or diffusion (Klimstra et al., 2010; Meeus et al., 2010). But the proportion of individuals who are in a state of identity achievement before late adolescence is low.

In general, when comparisons are made among groups of individuals of different ages over the span from 12 to 24, differences in identity status are most frequently observed between groups in the 18- to 21-year-old range. Few consistent differences emerge in comparisons of teenagers in the middle adolescent years. Although self-examination may take place throughout adolescence, the consolidation of a coherent sense of identity does not begin until very late in the period (Côté, 2009). The late teens and early 20s appear to be the critical times for a sense of identity to crystallize (Nurmi, 2004; Schwartz, Côté, & Arnett, 2005). Although individuals engage in more of this sophisticated self-reflection as they mature through adolescence, attempts to speed up this process, by training individuals to think more about how specific life events had played a role in their development, are not effective (Habermas & de Silveira, 2008).

Second, changes in identity status are less systematic than originally had been hypothesized. Although we might expect that individuals move from a state of diffusion to a state of foreclosure or moratorium and then either remain foreclosed or move to a state of identity achievement, not all individuals follow this pattern. In one study of Dutch youth, nearly 60% of the individuals classified as in a state of identity diffusion were no longer classified that way 4 years later, and nearly 75% of individuals who were in the midst of a moratorium at the beginning of the study were no longer in this category at the later assessment (Meeus, Iedema, & Vollebergh, 1999). But two-thirds of individuals who looked like they had foreclosed the identity development process were in the midst of an identity crisis 4 years later, suggesting that, for them, foreclosure may be a temporary stage rather than a permanent one.

Other studies have come to similar conclusions (Côté, 2009). Moreover, in these same studies, a large proportion of individuals who were at one point classified as "identity achieved" moved into a different state over the course of the study, indicating that "achievement," like "foreclosure," may be temporary (Meeus et al., 2010). In the Dutch study, for example, half of the adolescents who were classified as identity achieved at the first assessment were not classified this way 4 years later.

How could some individuals who at one point had apparently resolved their identity crisis actually not have resolved it—at least, not in any final sense? According to some writers, these sorts of regressions to a less mature identity status are part of the normal process of identity development (Kroger, 2003). The achievement of a sense of identity in adolescence is not a final state but a step on a long route toward the establishment of a mature sense of self.

Finally, many individuals who show signs of identity diffusion early on remain in this state, as do many individuals who spend time in a state of moratorium. In other words, there are some individuals who are perpetually confused (at least during adolescence and young adulthood) about who they are, and others who seem to be always exploring and experimenting with new identities (Meeus et al., 2010). Experiencing a moratorium in adolescence is beneficial; continuing to have one in young adulthood may not be (Hatano, Sugimura, & Crocetti, 2016). Individuals who are high in anxiety or prone to ruminate have an especially difficult time (Beyers & Luyckx, 2016; Crocetti et al., 2009).

Turning points in the development of a sense of identity appear to be provoked both by internal factors—discontent with one's life, for example—and by specific life events or changes in life circumstances, such as making the transition out of high school (Kalakoski & Nurmi, 1998; Kroger & Green, 1996). Individuals are able to make meaning out of these turning points, using the event to come to a better understanding of themselves (McLean, Breen, & Fournier, 2010; Tavernier & Willoughby, 2012). When adults look back on their life and attempt to tell a story that makes sense, they tend to put more weight on events that took place during adolescence and young adulthood, a phenomenon that has been described as a "reminiscence bump" (Thorne, 2000).

making the scientific connection

Adults tend to refer back to adolescence more than other periods when creating a narrative about their life. Do you think this is because events during adolescence *are* more important in shaping one's life, because events during adolescence are simply remembered more clearly, because adolescence is the first time that individuals begin creating a life story, or for some other reason?

Because college provides a psychosocial moratorium for many people, researchers have asked whether college attendance facilitates identity development (Côté, 2009). This has proven to be a difficult question to answer. While studies have found that the proportion of college students who are classified as identity achieved increases from around 20% during freshman year to as many as 40% by senior year, whether this development can be attributed to the college experience is hard to say, since this increase might have taken place just as a result of maturation (Pascarella & Terenzini, 2005). Although in theory one could test this by comparing identity development among college students with late adolescents who are not enrolled in college, in practice this is not easy to do. One problem (in addition to the difficulty researchers find in recruiting samples of noncollege individuals to participate in research studies) is that people are not randomly assigned to go to college or not. Thus, even if one were to find that college students showed relatively greater identity development than nonstudents, this could be due to factors that differentiate people who go to college from those who do not.

Identity and Ethnicity

For individuals who are not part of the majority culture, integrating a sense of **ethnic identity** into their overall sense of personal identity is often an important task of late adolescence, perhaps just as important as establishing a coherent occupational, ideological, or interpersonal identity (Chao & Otsuki-Clutter, 2011; Fuligni, Hughes, & Way, 2009; Seaton & Gilbert, 2011). An extensive literature has been amassed on the process through which ethnic identity develops and on the implications of having a strong versus weak sense of ethnic identity for adolescent adjustment and behavior. Ethnic identity has been studied in samples of Black, Latinx, Native American, Asian, and white youth (Fuligni, Hughes, & Way, 2009; Markstrom, 2011a). Less research has been conducted on adolescents whose identity is closely linked to their religion, as is the case for many Muslim youth (Abo-Zena, 2019).

In America, white youth generally have a weaker sense of ethnic identity than their nonwhite peers, but many white adolescents, especially those from more working-class backgrounds, identify strongly with a particular ethnic group (such as Irish, Italian, or Jewish) and derive part of their overall sense of self from this identification (Grossman & Charmaraman, 2009). Nevertheless, if given a list of labels to identify their own ethnic background, white adolescents in America are less likely than ethnic minority adolescents to choose labels based on their specific heritage (e.g., "German," "Russian," "Greek") and more likely to use generic labels (e.g., "white") or simply to identify themselves as "American" (Fuligni, Witkow, & Garcia, 2005). In the United States, white adolescents are less likely than Black, Latinx, or Asian adolescents to explore their ethnic identity or feel a strong commitment to it (Hughes, Del Toro, & Way, 2017).

Among immigrant adolescents, there is considerable vacillation between identifying oneself as a member of a broad ethnic category (e.g., Latinx, Asian) and identifying oneself as a member of a group defined by one's country of origin (e.g., Mexican, Chinese) (Fuligni et al., 2008; Kiang & Witkow, 2018), as well as variability in definitions of how best to maintain an identity that merges being a member of one's ethnic group and being a member of the country into which the family has immigrated (Ko & Perreira, 2010; Li, 2009; Nguyen & Brown, 2010; Qin, 2009). One study of Asian American adolescents found that having a strong ethnic identity was predictive of a strong preference for same-ethnic romantic partners, but encountering a high level of discrimination had the opposite effect, perhaps because dating someone from a different ethnic group helps to protect against further discrimination (Chan, Kiang, & Witkow, 2020).

ethnic identity
The aspect of individuals' sense of identity concerning ancestry or racial group membership.

Having a strong sense of ethnic pride is associated with a wide range of psychological benefits. Roberto Galan/Shutterstock

The Development of Ethnic Identity

The process of ethnic identity development is similar to the process of identity development more generally, with an unquestioning view of oneself often being displaced or upset by a crisis (Hughes, Del Toro, & Way, 2017; Yip, 2014). Often, but not always, the precipitating event involves an experience during which the individual encounters prejudice, becomes aware of his or her group's underrepresentation in some activity or setting, or suddenly feels different from adolescents from other backgrounds (Syed & Azmitia, 2008).

Following the crisis, individuals engage in a period of exploration, during which they may immerse themselves in learning about their ethnic heritage. (Increasingly, a good deal of this exploration occurs online, as is the case for identity exploration more generally; Davis, 2013). This process of exploration leads to increases in self-esteem (Corenblum, 2014; Umaña-Taylor, Gonzales-Backen, & Guimond, 2009), although exploration very early in adolescence can also lead to distress, perhaps because at an early age it is harder to make sense of everything one discovers (Gonzales-Backen, Bamaca-Colbert, & Allen, 2016). Eventually, as the value of having a strong ethnic identity becomes clear, the individual establishes a more coherent sense of personal identity that includes this ethnic identity (Seaton, Yip, & Sellers, 2009; Whitehead et al., 2009).

Adolescents' feelings about their own ethnic group become more positive during both early and middle adolescence (when ethnic identity first becomes salient and individuals become immersed in their own culture), although actual identity exploration does not really begin until middle adolescence (French et al., 2006). Between middle and late adolescence, exploration declines, as individuals begin to develop a more consolidated identity (Pahl & Way, 2006). Adolescents with a strong sense of ethnic identity have better mental health than those whose sense of ethnic identity is more diffuse (Gartner, Kiang, & Supple, 2014; Seaton, Scottham, & Sellers, 2006; Yip, Seaton, & Sellers, 2010). One reason for this is that a strong ethnic identity helps to foster a sense of meaning in life, which has been shown to be related to overall adjustment (Kiang & Fuligni, 2010).

Having a strong ethnic identity and a strong sense of ethnic pride is consistently associated with higher self-esteem, stronger self-efficacy, and better mental health (Cross et al., 2018); it is also associated with academic achievement (Miller-Cotto & Byrnes, 2016), and interventions designed to foster ethnic identity exploration and resolution have been shown to increase mental health and academic performance (Umaña-Taylor, Kornienko, Bayless, & Updegraff, 2018). Keep in mind that the relation between having a strong sense of identity and mental health works both ways; positive identity development leads to better mental health, and better mental health leads to more positive identity development (Meca et al., 2019).

The development of ethnic identity is profoundly affected by the context in which adolescents live (Tsai & Fuligni, 2012; Williams, Tolan, Durkee, Francois, & Anderson, 2012). For instance, patterns of ethnic identity development are affected by the ethnic composition of the adolescent's school, the adolescent's immediate peer group, and the extent to which the adolescent has contact with other teenagers from the same or different backgrounds (Douglass, Yip, & Shelton, 2014; Kiang et al., 2010; Nishina et al., 2010; Yip, Seaton, & Sellers, 2010).

Frequent contact with peers from the same ethnic group leads adolescents to develop stronger positive feelings about their ethnicity (Chen & Graham, 2017; Yip, Douglass, & Shelton, 2013), although this benefit is more likely to occur among adolescents who attend schools where they are part of a small ethnic minority (Douglass, Mirpuri, & Yip, 2017). But having positive attitudes about one's own ethnic group also is correlated with having positive attitudes about adolescents from other ethnic groups, suggesting that ethnic socialization may enhance, rather than upset, interracial relations (Phinney, Ferguson, & Tate, 1997). In fact, many adolescents with a strong ethnic identity are members of peer crowds for which ethnicity is *not* a defining feature (Brown et al., 2008).

The mental health of ethnic minority youth is also affected by their orientation to the mainstream culture. In general, positive mental health among ethnic minority adolescents is associated with biculturalism—having a strong, positive ethnic identity and a healthy awareness of the potential for discrimination, while maintaining involvement in the mainstream culture—a finding that has emerged in studies across a wide range of ethnic groups (Choi et al., 2018; Spiegler, Wölfer, & Hewstone, 2019; Umaña-Taylor et al., 2014).

This can be difficult for adolescents who live in neighborhoods and, as a consequence, attend schools in which there is a very high concentration of people from the same ethnic group. This situation fosters ethnic pride but undermines the development of an orientation toward the mainstream culture (White et al., 2017). Among ethnic minority youth, academic achievement is highest when adolescents feel connected to their ethnic group, are aware of racism, and believe that it is important to the people in their life to be academically successful within mainstream society (McGill et al., 2012). Being aware of potential racism and mistrusting others are not the same thing, however; awareness of racism is associated with positive outcomes, but mistrust is associated with negative ones (Kiang, Supple, & Stein, 2019).

> **ethnic socialization**
> The process through which individuals develop an understanding of their ethnic or racial background, also referred to as racial socialization.

Ethnic Socialization Moving through the early stages of ethnic identity development may be speeded up somewhat when parents take a more deliberate approach to the socialization of an ethnic identity (Hernandez et al., 2014; McHale et al., 2006; Umaña-Taylor et al., 2009). **Ethnic socialization** (sometimes referred to as "racial socialization") is the process parents use to attempt to teach their children about their ethnic or racial identity and about the special experiences they may encounter within the broader society as a result of their ethnic background (Evans et al., 2012). This may be especially important for the development of ethnic identity of adolescents living in neighborhoods in which there are relatively few people from their ethnic background (White et al., 2018).

Ethnic socialization in minority families typically focuses on at least three themes: understanding and valuing one's culture, dealing with racism, and succeeding in mainstream society (Moua & Lamborn, 2010; Varner & Mandara, 2013). These themes are especially salient in families of undocumented immigrants (Cross et al., 2020). As one mother of three teenagers explained:

> *I do tell them sometimes that it's not good to talk about what you think much in school, as far as the origin of countries. Like here, you see that racism is very high. I tell them, "When you hear that someone talks bad about Mexicans, it's not good to get involved in politics." Right now, you see with the president . . . you see that it's talked about a lot. And they said that they were asked a lot of questions. And I told them "Say that no, that it's all right. No problem." We cannot get involved . . . There are things we can talk about here, at home, and there is no problem.* (Cross et al., 2020, p. 1466)

Ethnic socialization by parents encourages adolescents to think positively about their ethnic heritage, which may lead to a stronger sense of ethnic identity (Butler-Barnes et al., 2018; Douglass & Umaña-Taylor, 2015, 2016; Knite et al., 2017). Although little research exists on the impact of racial socialization on outcomes other than identity development, experts believe that conversations between parents and teenagers about race should also deal with the ways in which race may affect the developing adolescent's autonomy, intimacy, sexuality, achievement, risk taking, and ability to cope with different types of stress (Anderson et al., 2019; McDermott, Umaña-Taylor, & Martinez-Fuentes, 2018; Stein et al., 2018). Ethnic socialization also occurs indirectly, for example, when parents stress the importance of family obligations (Kiang & Fuligni, 2009; Umaña-Taylor et al., 2009; Tsai et al., 2015).

The messages that parents convey also matter, however. When parents and other caregivers describe their own experiences of discrimination, this adversely affects their adolescents' mental health (Espinoza, Gonzales, & Fuligni, 2016; Ford et al., 2013). Occasional communication of highly positive messages in the context of a good parent–adolescent relationship may be the most effective approach for parents to take, and it is important that parents adjust their conversations to match the specific developmental needs of their children as they mature (Stein et al., 2018; Tang, McLoyd, & Hallman, 2016). Messages from peers about prejudice also can be important for the development of ethnic identity and can amplify the messages communicated at home (Nelson et al., 2018; Wang & Benner, 2016).

Recent events in the United States, in which altercations between law enforcement officers and Black adolescents have had tragic consequences, have motivated many parents to speak candidly with their teens about how to react in the face of bias and emotional arousal in tense situations (Dunbar et al., 2017). In one study in which parents and teenagers living in St. Louis were interviewed following the 2014 shooting of Michael Brown in the nearby city of Ferguson, the respondents identified four specific themes in these conversations: making sure their teenagers understood the extent of racism in America, describing the special dangers faced by Black boys, condemning the violent protests that followed the widely publicized shooting, and encouraging their teenagers to fight discrimination by succeeding in school (Threlfall, 2018).

Recent Immigrants   Several researchers have focused on the special situation of ethnic minority youth who are recent immigrants to a new culture (e.g., Fuligni, Hughes, & Way, 2009; Gonzales, 2011). Despite the fact that adolescents who are recent immigrants frequently report high levels of academic, familial, social, and economic stress (Cervantes & Cordova, 2011), foreign-born ethnic minority adolescents tend to express more positive feelings about mainstream American ideals than do their counterparts whose families have been in the United States longer. In addition, in the United States, foreign-born and first-generation ethnic minority youth (i.e., adolescents whose parents were born in a different country) perform better in school and are less likely to be involved in delinquent behavior or have physical, emotional, and behavioral problems than adolescents from the same ethnic group whose parents were born in America (Filion, Fenelon, & Boudreaux, 2018; Guarini et al., 2015; Hao & Woo, 2012), a phenomenon that is known as the **immigrant paradox** (Marks, Ejesi, & Garcia Coll, 2014). (The immigrant paradox is not always seen in countries outside the United States, however [Svensson & Shannon, 2020; Vaquera & Kao, 2012].)

One explanation for this is that ethnic minority immigrants arrive in the United States idealistic about their prospects, but the longer their family lives in the new context, the more likely they are to become both Americanized and disillusioned (Mroczkowski, Sánchez, & Carter, 2017; Tartakovsky, 2009). Studies of Mexican American youth have found that over the course of adolescence, there is a decline in teenagers' orientation to traditional Mexican family values, which is associated with increases in risky behavior and substance use (Cruz et al., 2017; Updegraff et al., 2012). Another explanation for the higher achievement and better mental health of immigrant adolescents is that newly arrived immigrant parents provide more effective supervision of their children (Chao & Otsuki-Clutter, 2011; Marsiglia et al., 2014; Schwartz et al., 2013).

Reports of altercations between police officers and Black teenagers have motivated many parents to speak candidly to their children about bias and discrimination in society.
Sean Rayford/Getty Images

Discrimination and Its Effects

Because identity development is profoundly influenced by the social context in which adolescents live, the development of minority adolescents must be understood in relation to the specific context that they face in contemporary society (Byrd & Chavous, 2011; Rivas-Drake et al., 2009). All too often, this context includes racial stereotypes, discrimination, and mixed messages about the costs and benefits of identifying too closely with the majority culture. Experiences with discrimination increase markedly during the transition from childhood to adolescence (Hughes et al., 2016) and again during the transition into high school, as the salience of peer crowds increases (Wang & Yip, 2020). Studies find that around 90% of Latinx and Black teenagers report having been the victim of discrimination (Umaña-Taylor, 2016).

The adverse effects of discrimination are especially intense among American ethnic minority youth with a strong attachment to the mainstream culture (Derlan et al., 2014) and for those whose parents were born in the United States (Sirin et al., 2015). Immigrant adolescents who speak with an accent are stereotyped as "perpetual foreigners," which can lead to discrimination and victimization (Kim et al., 2011; Bayram Özdemir & Stattin, 2014). One study of American adolescents of Iranian descent revealed that many of these teenagers identified themselves as Persian, rather than Iranian, because of the negative portrayals of Iranian individuals in the media (Daha, 2011). Similarly, it is impossible to fully understand the process of ethnic identity development among Native American adolescents without taking into account the particular history of Native Americans in the United States (Markstrom, 2011a).

It is well established that individuals—from any group—who report experiencing high levels of discrimination suffer psychologically as a result (Benner et al., 2018). The experience of feeling discriminated against adversely affects adolescents' mental health regardless of what they attribute the discrimination to (e.g., ethnicity, gender, physical appearance, etc.) (Seaton et al., 2010). One study of Black youth found that the combination of experiencing discrimination and growing up in a less supportive family environment actually affected adolescents' DNA and inflammatory responses in a way that is associated with faster aging (Brody et al., 2016, 2015).

Many studies of Asian, Black, and Latinx youth have found that feeling discriminated against in school, whether by teachers or peers, is predictive of subsequent conduct problems (I. Park et al., 2017), substance abuse (Martin et al., 2019; Zapolski et al., 2020), depression (Bennett et al., 2020), poor sleep (Majeno et al., 2018; Yip et al., 2020), and lower achievement (Banerjee, Byrd, & Rowley, 2018). Discrimination by adults outside school does not seem to have as negative impact as discrimination by peers, consistent with other research suggesting that the impact of discrimination by people the adolescent regularly interacts with is particularly toxic (Del Toro, Hughes, & Way, 2020). The adverse consequences of peer discrimination are less severe among adolescents who have some cross-ethnic friendships (Benner & Wang, 2017) and a strong sense of ethnic identity (A. Cavanaugh et al., 2018; Stein et al., 2016), though.

> **multidimensional model of racial identity**
> A perspective on ethnic identity that emphasizes three different phenomena: racial centrality (how important race is in defining individuals' identity), private regard (how individuals feel about being a member of their race), and public regard (how individuals think others feel about their race).

There are many reasons that feeling discriminated against may be harmful to one's mental health, but one important process concerns the effect of discrimination on adolescents' feelings of control: Adolescents who feel discriminated against in school report feeling less control over their academic achievement, which leads to feelings of depression (Smith-Bynum et al., 2014). Another possibility is that the experience of discrimination leads to depression and alienation, which, in turn, leads adolescents to affiliate with deviant peers, increasing the likelihood that they will engage in risky and antisocial behavior (Roberts et al., 2012). Individuals vary both in the extent to which they feel discriminated against and in the extent to which they are adversely affected by it (Martin-Storey & Benner, 2019), but having a strong ethnic identity is an especially important protective factor (Umaña-Taylor et al., 2015), as is having social support from parents, teachers, and friends (Wright & Wachs, 2019).

Although the general pattern of findings described in the previous two paragraphs generally holds true for both male and female adolescents, there are differences in the ways that discrimination is expressed toward adolescent boys and girls, especially among Black teenagers (Seaton & Tyson, 2019). As many writers have noted, and as recent events in which Black males have been shot by police officers have made all too clear, Black boys are treated with suspicion far more frequently than Black girls. However, Black girls face interpersonal prejudices that their male peers seldom do, but these forms of discrimination are far less visible. For example, their hair is often closely scrutinized and touched inappropriately by white peers and adults, and they are seen as less desirable romantic partners by white boys than Black boys are by white girls. As one 16-year-old Black girl noted in a study in which Black high school students were interviewed, "If I see a biracial couple it's a Black boy and a White girl. I don't usually see a Black girl and a White boy" (Seaton & Tyson, 2019, p. 66). In this study, several Black girls indicated that white boys view Black girls as objects, fine to have sex with but not appropriate to date.

Putting It All Together   The **multidimensional model of racial identity** has been used to help make sense out of a complex web of findings (Seaton et al., 2014; Sellers

multiethnic
Having two parents of different ethnic or racial backgrounds.

et al., 2006). According to this model, we need to take into account three different aspects of racial identity: racial centrality (how important race is in defining individuals' identity), private regard (how individuals feel about being a member of their race), and public regard (how individuals think others view their race).

Generally speaking, during adolescence racial centrality increases and private regard tends to remain stable, although private regard may drop temporarily during the transition into high school (Wang & Yip, 2020). Changes in public regard differ among adolescents from different backgrounds, however (Rivas-Drake & Witherspoon, 2013; Rogers, Scott, & Way, 2015). In one study of New York City middle school students, perceptions of public regard increased over time among Chinese American adolescents but declined among Black, Puerto Rican, and Dominican youth (Hughes, Way, & Rivas-Drake, 2011). One possible explanation for this is that Black and Latinx students report that their teachers have more negative attitudes toward them than toward Asian youth, whose teachers generally see them in a more favorable light.

Adolescents who have experienced discrimination firsthand are more likely to believe that the public has low regard for their ethnic group (Seaton, Yip, & Sellers, 2009). Having a strong ethnic identity appears to protect against this when the discrimination comes from adults, but when the discrimination comes from peers, whose opinions about race and ethnicity are especially salient during adolescence (Santos, Kornienko, & Rivas-Drake, 2017), even those with a strong ethnic identity come to believe that their ethnic group is viewed negatively (Douglass & Umaña-Taylor, 2017). However, individuals who believe that the public has low regard for their ethnic group are more sensitive to racial cues, which, in turn, may heighten their experience of discrimination. This is not to say that individuals with heightened sensitivity to discrimination are simply imagining it; rather, individuals with heightened sensitivity may be better at perceiving more subtle signs of racial bias. Regardless, believing that the public has low regard for one's race exacerbates the negative impact of discrimination on adolescents' mental health (Seaton & Iida, 2019).

How all of this works together to affect adolescents' mental health is complex. Having positive feelings about one's race is positively linked to psychological well-being and protects against the harmful effects of stress and discrimination (Jaramillo, Mello, & Worrell, 2016; Kogan, Yu et al., 2015; Williams et al., 2014). The combination of pride and working hard to prove discriminatory people wrong is the most effective way of coping with discrimination and is far more beneficial to mental health than either being passive or confrontational (McDermott, Umaña-Taylor, & Zeiders, 2019). Consistent with this, adolescents whose parents have emphasized

the positive aspects of ethnic socialization (e.g., being proud of one's ethnic group) and who have more positive family relationships fare better in the face of discrimination than those whose parents have emphasized the negative (e.g., the need to be wary about potential racism) (Berkel et al., 2009; Delgado et al., 2011; Juang & Alvarez, 2010). Having a strong ethnic identity is also protective against the harmful effects of online discrimination (Tynes et al., 2012).

However, the impact of having race as a central part of one's identity (which is not the same thing as having high private regard for one's ethnic group) is complicated: It makes adolescents more sensitive to discrimination (which hurts their mental health), but it may also make them more able to cope with it (which helps) (Brown et al., 2011; Gonzalez-Backen et al., 2018; Meca et al., 2020). Believing that the public has high regard for one's ethnic group lifts adolescents' school performance, but believing that the public has a positive view of one's race also intensifies the effects of discrimination— perhaps because people feel especially wounded when they don't expect to encounter it (Hughes, Way, & Rivas-Drake, 2011).

There appear to be differences in the effects of perceived discrimination by people in the adolescent's daily life, such as teachers and peers, and having an awareness of discrimination by society's institutions. Whereas the former is associated with negative effects on mental health, the latter may motivate adolescents to work harder in school, which leads to better grades as well as greater education attainment and occupational prestige in adulthood (Wheeler, Arora, & Delgado, 2020). As adolescents mature, they become more aware of institutional racism and more likely attribute racial gaps in achievement to it, especially when their parents have discussed it as a part of their racial socialization (Bañales et al., 2020). Of course, it's important that *all* parents discuss issues of institutional racism with their children, regardless of their ethnicity (Thomann & Suyemoto, 2017).

Multiethnic Adolescents

One understudied group of adolescents for whom developing a sense of ethnic identity may be especially challenging consists of **multiethnic** youth—adolescents whose parents are not from the same ethnic or racial group. (The terms *multiethnic* and *multiracial* are often used interchangeably, which can lead to different estimates of the size of this population. Because Latinx individuals can be from any racial group, researchers do not always agree on whether to classify children born to couples in which one parent is white and non-Latinx and the other is white and Latinx as multiracial, although they clearly are multiethnic). Understanding psychological development among multiethnic adolescents has taken on increased importance as their numbers have grown; in the United States, multiethnic

The growing share of multiracial and multiethnic babies in the U.S.

% of children younger than 1 who are multiracial or multiethnic, among those living with two parents

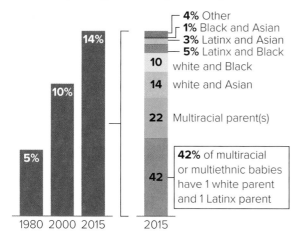

4% Other
1% Black and Asian
3% Latinx and Asian
5% Latinx and Black
10 white and Black
14 white and Asian
22 Multiracial parent(s)
42% of multiracial or multiethnic babies have 1 white parent and 1 Latinx parent

Note: Multiracial or multiethnic babies are those who have parents of different races, one Latinx and one non-Latinx parent, or at least one parent who is multiracial. Whites, blacks and Asians include only non-Latinxs. Latinxs are of any race. Asians include Pacific Islanders.

Figure 8.6 In 2015, 14% of all infants born in the United States, who will soon enter adolescence, had parents whose ethnicities were different. (Livingston, 2017)

individuals are the fastest growing demographic (Nishina & Witkow, 2020). In 2015, 14% of all infants born in the United States, who will soon enter adolescence, had parents whose ethnic or racial backgrounds were different (Livingston, 2017) (see Figure 8.6).

Developing a consistent ethnic identity is challenging for biracial adolescents, especially during early adolescence (Nishina & Witkow, 2020; Rozek & Gaither, 2020). Many biracial adolescents change their racial identity over time, switching during adolescence or young adulthood from being biracial to being "monoracial" (identifying oneself with just one ethnic group); in one study of Black, white, and biracial Black/white adolescents, nearly three-quarters of the biracial group changed their self-identification over a 4-year period, which may reflect the ways in which the cultural desirability of being seen as a member of one ethnic group or another fluctuates over time (Terry & Winston, 2010). Multiethnic teenagers are also more likely to have an ethnic identity that doesn't match their classmates' perception of their ethnicity, which is associated with distress and lower self-esteem (Nishina et al., 2018).

Identity and Gender

Identity and gender are linked in several different ways. **Gender identity** refers to one's sense of oneself as male,

female, or transgender, which refers to individuals whose gender identity does not match the sex they were designated at birth, usually based on their external sex organs. **Sexual orientation** refers to the extent to which someone is romantically and sexually attracted to members of the same sex (homosexual, which includes gay men and lesbians), members of the other sex (heterosexual, or "straight"), or both (i.e., bisexual). **Gender-role behavior** refers to the extent to which an individual behaves in traditionally "masculine" or "feminine" ways.

gender identity
One's sense of oneself as male, female, or transgender.

sexual orientation
Whether one is sexually attracted to individuals of the same sex, other sex, or both.

gender-role behavior
The extent to which an individual behaves in traditionally "masculine" or "feminine" ways.

Understanding the Terminology A great deal of confusion stems from the fact that these three concepts refer to completely different things. For example, there is not a strong connection between sexual orientation and sex-role behavior or gender identity. Individuals with strong, or even exclusive, same-sex attractions exhibit the same range of masculine and feminine behaviors that is seen among individuals with strong or exclusive heterosexual interests. In other words, exclusively gay men (like exclusively heterosexual men) may act in very masculine, very feminine, or both masculine and feminine ways. The same holds true for exclusively lesbian and exclusively heterosexual women, as well as bisexual men and women. Along similar lines, individuals with same-sex or bisexual preferences are generally not confused about their gender identity—or, at least, they are no more confused than are individuals with heterosexual preferences.

The complicated relationship between sexual orientation and gender identity is vividly illustrated in a study of a national sample of LGBTQ adolescents (i.e., categorized based on their *sexual orientation*), males and females who vary in their *gender identity* (either a gender identity that matches the sex they were assigned at birth, referred to as "cisgender"; a gender identity that is discordant from the sex they were assigned at birth, referred to as "transgender"; or neither ([nonbinary]) reported considerable variability in sexual orientation (Watson, Wheldon, & Puhl, 2020) (see Figure 8.7). For example, among transgender boys (i.e., individuals who were assigned a female gender at girth but who identify as male, shown in the third set of columns from the left), 17.7% describe their sexual orientation as gay or lesbian, 27.6% as bisexual (i.e., sexually attracted both to individuals who identity as male and to those who identity as female), 11.2% as heterosexual, and 24.3% as pansexual (i.e., being attracted to the people of all genders, including those who describe themselves as "nonbinary" or "fluid").

Several writers have described the process through which gay, lesbian, and bisexual individuals discover,

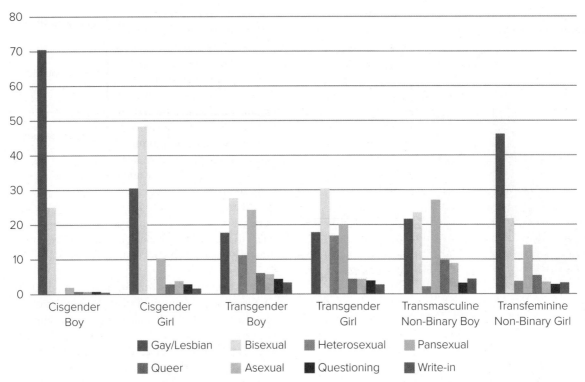

Figure 8.7 **Individuals from different gender identity groups vary considerably in their sexual orientation.**
(Watson, Wheldon, & Puhl, 2020)

transgender
Having a gender identity that differs from the sex one was assigned at birth.

come to terms with, and disclose their sexual orientation (Mills-Koonce, Rehder, & McCurdy, 2018). Although the traditional model of this progression—feeling different as a child, engaging in gender-atypical behavior, being attracted to members of the same sex and uninterested in those of the other sex, realizing one's sexual attraction to others of the same sex, and consciously questioning one's sexual orientation—describes the experience of many sexual-minority adolescents, it by no means is universal. Indeed, some writers have suggested that this may be more applicable to the development of white gay men than to lesbians, bisexual adolescents, or ethnic minority gay men (Diamond, 1998; Dubé & Savin-Williams, 1999). For example, there is evidence that females' sexual orientation may be more fluid than males', with many more bisexual or lesbian adolescents changing sexual orientation during young adulthood than heterosexual individuals or gay men (Diamond, 2008; Saewyc, 2011; Savin-Williams, Joyner, & Rieger, 2012).

Society's prejudice and ignorance about the gay community cause significant psychological distress for sexual-minority adolescents, especially if they encounter hostility from those around them, including their parents (Mills-Koonce et al., 2018; Robinson, 2018; Saewyc, 2011). Resolving concerns about identity, intimacy, and sexuality present formidable challenges for many

teenagers. But these challenges may be exacerbated for sexual-minority adolescents, who are forced to deal with these issues without the same degree of social support as their heterosexual peers (Mills-Koonce et al., 2018).

Gay, lesbian, and bisexual adolescents who believe that their sexual orientation is a burden to people in their lives are at greater risk for depression and suicidal thoughts (Baams, Grossman, & Russell, 2015). There is some evidence that using social networking sites to communicate about one's sexual orientation may be helpful to sexual-minority youth (Ceglarek & Ward, 2016).

Transgender Adolescents Although adolescents who describe themselves as **transgender** are often grouped for purposes of discussion with lesbian, gay, and bisexual youth, transgender individuals report the same variety of sexual orientations as do other individuals. Information on the size of the transgender population, either in adolescence or adulthood, is scant. According to some estimates, about 1 in 100,000 American adults is a transsexual woman (an individual who identifies herself as a woman but who was labeled male at birth) and 1 in 400,000 is a transsexual man (someone who identifies himself as a man but who was labeled female at birth) (IOM and NRC, 2011b).

There has not been a great deal of research to date on the psychological development and mental health of transgender adolescents, but the few studies that have been done find substantially higher rates of depression and anxiety in this group of adolescents (Reisner et al., 2016; Reisner et al., 2015). This is not surprising, given that transgender youth are more likely to be truant, to be victimized and bullied in school, and to describe their school climate in negative terms (Day, Perez-Brumer, & Russell, 2018). Assaults against transgender youth are higher in schools that have implemented restrictive policies regarding restrooms and locker rooms (Murchison et al., 2019).

One review concluded that transgender youth have higher rates of depression, suicidality, self-harm, and eating disorders than other teenagers (Connolly et al., 2016). Consistent with this, a recent large-scale study of California adolescents found that one-third of transgender teenagers reported suicidal ideation, a rate that is twice as high as that of their peers (Perez-Brumer et al., 2017), although a smaller-scale project found that rates of depression and anxiety among transgender adolescents who had transitioned socially (i.e., were now presenting themselves to others as a member of the other gender) were not any higher than those reported by a matched control group (Durwood, McLaughlin, & Olson, 2017).

Growing up in a conservative climate may exact an especially significant toll on transgender adolescents' psychological health for many reasons. In addition to being victimized, many transgender youth face frequent stigmatization and resistance. Consider these excerpts from interviews with transgender adolescents and young adults who lived in a rural Midwestern community (Paceley et al., 2020):

> *I have to pass by at least three groups of protesters when I go see my primary physician . . . when I first went in for my hormone appointment just to get the consultation for it all, I almost left instantly because of the amount of protestors. That sucks.* (p. 1869)
>
> *People have no problem calling a dog whatever the fucking name the dog's name is but have so much resistance calling someone by their name.* (p. 1870)
>
> *[T]hat's all everybody would talk about . . . My teachers would talk about . . . Everyone was debating whether or not trans people were dangerous . . . just kind of like a weird, sexual being that shouldn't be allowed to be in public spaces with other people.* (p. 1873)
>
> *I hear people saying at school all the time that's just making jokes about something that they probably don't fully understand, turning it into a caricature . . . They'll be like, "So you identify as a toaster" and stuff like that.* (p. 1874)

Many experts believe that we should view gender identity, sexual orientation, and gender-role behavior as fluid rather than fixed and as points along continua rather than absolute categories (Diamond, 2020; Savin-Williams & Vrangalova, 2013). A young man may go through a period during which he is sexually attracted to other men and wonder if he is gay, only to find at a later age that he is exclusively interested in women. Another may think of himself as "mostly heterosexual." An adolescent girl who expressed traditionally feminine interests as a child may

Researchers have only recently begun to study the psychological development of transgender youth. HEX/Getty Images

discover that she actually enjoys a mix of activities that include some stereotypically masculine ones and some stereotypically feminine ones. Someone who spent her childhood and adolescence identified as male may realize that she is more comfortable identifying as a woman.

Gender-Role Development

Popular books proclaim that men and women are fundamentally different; that men and women come from different "planets"; that males and females learn, speak, and navigate the world in different ways; and that adolescent boys and girls need to be schooled and raised in different ways. But the fact of the matter is that, apart from some obvious physical differences, adolescent males and females actually aren't all that different (Perry & Pauletti, 2011; Priess & Hyde, 2011). I'm sorry to disappoint you (if I have), but scientific studies of the sexes simply do not support the claims of those who argue that males and females have brains that are wired differently, have different perspectives on morality, or learn in fundamentally dissimilar ways.

Whether large sex differences in adolescent behavior had existed in the past but have disappeared (certainly a possibility, given the fact that men and women experienced different expectations and opportunities in past generations) or whether they were just assumed to be larger than they were isn't known. But differences *within* groups of males or females are far more substantial than differences between them. Throughout this book, I've noted when studies have found meaningful sex differences in the ways in which adolescents develop or function. If I haven't mentioned them, it's either because they weren't reported or weren't observed.

Apart from differences in physical strength, adolescent males and females do not differ in their abilities. Although

gender intensification hypothesis
The idea that pressures to behave in sex-appropriate ways intensify during adolescence.

girls are more "people-oriented" and boys are more "things-oriented," the magnitude of sex differences in interests and attitudes is smaller than most people think (Priess & Hyde, 2011). The most consistent sex differences are seen in the ways adolescent boys and girls express aggression (males are generally more physically aggressive than females, who tend to use social or verbal aggression) and intimacy (females are more likely to express intimacy verbally, whereas males express it mainly through shared activities), and in the extent to which males and females are prone to low self-esteem and depression (females are more prone to both). There are few, if any, sex differences in patterns of family relationships, in performance on achievement tests, or in the correlates of competence, popularity with peers, and healthy psychological development.

Gender-Role Socialization During Adolescence

Despite the fact that psychological differences between the sexes are trivial or nonexistent, many individuals continue to hold strong beliefs about what is "normal" for males and for females, and psychologists have been interested in the consequences of behaving or not behaving in

ways that are stereotypically masculine or feminine (Leaper & Brown, 2018). Some studies have found that pressures to behave in sex-stereotypic ways appear to increase temporarily during early adolescence, something referred to as the **gender intensification hypothesis** (Galambos, Berenbaum, & McHale, 2009).

Individuals' *beliefs* about gender roles become more flexible as they move through adolescence, largely as a result of the cognitive changes of the period, but social pressures may drive teenagers toward more gender-stereotypic *behavior;* indeed, the impact of environmental factors on gender-role behavior is much stronger than the impact of the hormonal changes of puberty (Galambos, Berenbaum, & McHale, 2009). The broader social context matters, too: Although there are some exceptions to the rule, adolescents who grow up in countries with relatively more gender equality report higher life satisfaction than their peers from countries in which women have less power and resources than men, a finding that is equally true for male and female youth (Looze et al., 2018) (see Figure 8.8). In fact, gender equality is a stronger predictor of adolescent well-being than income equality.

Adolescents tend to associate with peers who have similar attitudes about the importance of conforming to gender-role stereotypes, and there is pressure within some peer groups to act in ways that are consistent with gender-role expectations (Kornienko et al., 2016). Boys who

Many studies have found an increase in sex-stereotypic behavior during adolescence. Image Source/Getty Images

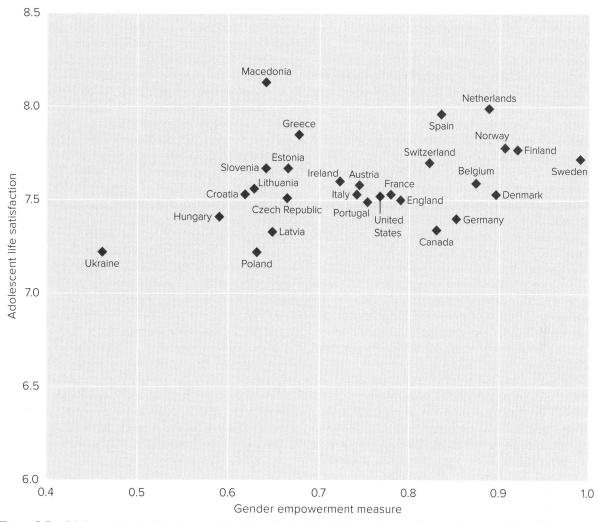

Figure 8.8 Adolescents who live in countries characterized by high gender equity report greater life satisfaction than their peers in less egalitarian countries. (Looze et al., 2018)

do not act masculine enough and girls who do not act feminine enough are more likely to be victimized than gender-typical teenagers and to report more mental health problems as a result (Sayre Smith & Juvonen, 2017). Adolescents are more intolerant about peers behaving in gender-atypical ways than they are about variations in sexual orientation (Bos & Sandfort, 2015; Toomey et al., 2010). The higher rates of mental health problems reported by gay and lesbian teenagers may be due to the higher likelihood of gender-role nonconformity found among sexual-minority youth; sexual-minority youth who behave in gender stereotypic ways (i.e., gay boys who are masculine and lesbians who are feminine) are far less likely to be harassed and victimized than those who behave in nonconforming ways (Martin-Storey, 2016).

Not all studies find an increase in gender-stereotyped behavior in adolescence (S. M. McHale et al., 2004) or in pressure to conform to traditional gender roles (Priess, Lindberg, & Hyde, 2009), however. One reason for discrepancies between studies is that the extent to which gender-stereotypic behavior becomes more pronounced or demanded in adolescence likely depends on the realm of behavior studied, the developmental history of the adolescent, and the broader context in which the adolescent lives (Daniels & Leaper, 2011; Galambos, Berenbaum, & McHale, 2009). For instance, over the past 30 years, there has been a significant increase in adolescents' support for gender equality in the workplace (e.g., whether women should have the same job opportunities as men), but adolescents' support for gender equality in the family (e.g., whether it is the woman's responsibility to take care of the home), which had been on the rise between 1975 and 1990, has declined (Pepin & Cotter, 2018).

Masculinity and Femininity

Individuals vary in their degrees of masculinity and femininity. Some are decidedly more masculine than feminine, and others are decidedly more feminine than masculine. And some people have a high degree of both masculinity and femininity; they might be both very assertive (a trait usually considered masculine) and very sensitive (a trait usually considered feminine).

Generally speaking, individuals' degree of masculinity or femininity is highly stable over time. In one study that tracked people from preschool through adolescence, girls who had been rated as relatively more masculine as preschoolers felt less similar to other girls when they were 13, were less content being girls, and had a stronger preference for traditionally male activities, whereas those who had been rated as more feminine had stronger preferences for traditionally female activities. Similarly, boys who had been rated as more feminine when they were preschoolers felt less similar to other boys when they were adolescents and were not especially drawn to traditionally male activities (Golombok, Rust, Zervoulis, Golding, & Hines, 2012).

If expectations to conform to traditional gender stereotypes intensify during adolescence, we would expect that boys who are especially masculine and girls who are especially feminine would fare better psychologically than their peers who behave in gender-atypical ways. Do more feminine girls and more masculine boys feel better about themselves?

The answer to this question differs for males and females (Galambos, Berenbaum, & McHale, 2009). Although boys and girls who behave in gender-typical ways are more accepted than their peers whose behavior does not conform with gender-role stereotypes (Kochel et al., 2012) and feel better about themselves as a result of this (Menon, 2011), the costs of being gender-atypical are greater for boys than girls (Smith et al., 2018). It is not surprising, therefore, to find that during adolescence boys are likely to cut back on the display of stereotypically feminine traits, such as being emotionally expressive, whereas neither boys nor girls reduce the display of traditionally masculine traits, such as instrumentality (McHale et al., 2009) (see Figure 8.9).

By the time they have reached early adolescence, teenagers understand that it is easier for girls to sometimes behave in masculine ways than it is for boys to occasionally act in feminine ways (Mulvey & Killen, 2015). Consistent with research on younger children, adolescent males who do not conform to traditionally masculine gender-role norms have lower self-esteem, are judged more deviant, and are more likely to be bullied than are females whose behavior or appearance departs from exclusively feminine roles (Gupta et al., 2013; Masters, Hixson, & Hayes, 2020; Roberts et al., 2013). Boys who have a more traditionally masculine orientation, while higher in self-acceptance than other boys, are more likely to be involved in various types of problem behavior—perhaps because part of being masculine in contemporary society involves being "man enough" to experiment with delinquency, drugs and alcohol, and unprotected sex (Kulis, Marsiglia, & Hurdle, 2003) or because boys who live in difficult environments, where problem behavior is prevalent, adopt a more "macho" posture to survive in the community (Cunningham, 1999).

Conversely, girls who have a more traditionally feminine gender-role orientation are more likely to develop more traditionally feminine sorts of psychological problems, such as disordered eating (McHale et al., 2001). Girls who believe that women's worth comes primarily from their sexual appeal earn lower grades and score worse on achievement tests than their peers. In one clever experiment in which adolescent girls were asked to prepare and videotape a mock newscast, ostensibly to measure their aptitude for journalism, the researchers found that girls who were more "sexualized" (i.e., who had internalized the idea that being attractive to men is an important part of one's identity) spent more time putting on makeup and less time going over the newscast script than girls who were less sexualized (McKenney & Bigler, 2014). Interestingly, girls who have highly sexualized Facebook photos are judged by other girls to be less competent—and less physically and socially attractive—than girls whose profiles are not as explicitly sexy (Daniels & Zurbriggen, 2016).

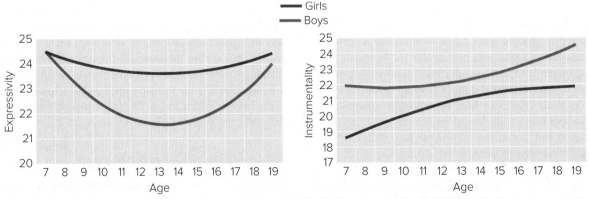

Figure 8.9 During adolescence, boys increasingly avoid displaying stereotypically feminine traits, but comparable pressure on girls to avoid stereotypically masculine traits is much milder. As a consequence, boys show a drop in emotional expressiveness, but girls do not show a similar decline in instrumentality. (McHale et al., 2009)

Given that pressures to conform with gender-role norms affect both girls and boys during adolescence, why is it that boys suffer greater self-image problems when they deviate from what is viewed as appropriate behavior for their sex? The answer is that although girls may be pressured to adopt (or maintain) certain feminine traits during adolescence, they are not necessarily pressured to relinquish all elements of masculinity (although girls who feel pressured to uphold masculine norms report more psychological problems than those who do not feel pressured in this way; Rogers et al., 2020). In contrast, boys are socialized from a very early age not to adopt feminine traits and are judged deviant if they show any signs of femininity. Boys are more likely to see themselves as "typical males" than girls are to see themselves as "typical females," more likely to be content to be male than girls are to be female, and more pressured to act in stereotypically male ways than girls are to act in stereotypically female ways (Hoffman et al., 2019).

In other words, girls can be highly pressured during adolescence to behave in feminine ways without necessarily being punished or labeled deviant for exhibiting some masculine traits; thus, for girls, having a mixture of masculine and feminine traits is a viable alternative to exclusive femininity. Girls may feel increasingly pressured to dress nicely and to wear makeup when they reach adolescence, but they are not pressured to give up typically masculine interests. Boys, however, from childhood on, are pressured not to behave in feminine ways. Their gender-role socialization does not intensify during adolescence as much as it does for girls because it is so intense to begin with.

9

Autonomy

Autonomy as an Adolescent Issue

Puberty and the Development of Autonomy

Cognitive Change and the Development of Autonomy

Social Roles and the Development of Autonomy

The Development of Emotional Autonomy

Emotional Autonomy: Detachment or Individuation?

Research on Emotional Autonomy

Parenting and Emotional Autonomy

The Development of Behavioral Autonomy

Changes in Decision-Making Abilities

When Do Adolescents Make Decisions as Well as Adults?

Changes in Susceptibility to Influence

Ethnic and Cultural Differences in Expectations for Autonomy

The Development of Cognitive Autonomy

Moral Development During Adolescence

Prosocial Reasoning, Prosocial Behavior, and Volunteerism

Political Thinking During Adolescence

Religious Beliefs During Adolescence

Maskot/Getty Images

For most adolescents, establishing a sense of autonomy is as important a part of becoming an adult as is establishing a sense of identity. Becoming an autonomous person—a self-governing person—is one of the fundamental developmental tasks of adolescence.

Although we often use the words *autonomy* and *independence* interchangeably, in the study of adolescence, they mean slightly different things. Independence refers to individuals' capacity to behave on their own. The growth of independence is surely a part of becoming autonomous during adolescence, but autonomy has emotional and cognitive as well as behavioral components. In other words, autonomy is not just about acting independently; it is also about feeling independent and thinking for oneself.

During adolescence, there is a movement away from the dependency typical of childhood and toward the autonomy typical of adulthood—not only among human adolescents but also among mammals more generally (all mammals go through puberty and therefore experience something analogous to human adolescence) (Casey, Duhoux, & Cohen, 2010). But the growth of autonomy during adolescence is frequently misunderstood. Autonomy is often confused with rebellion, and becoming an independent person is often equated with breaking away from the family.

Just as the view that adolescence is a period of storm and stress has been questioned repeatedly by scientific research, experts on adolescence have changed the way they think about the development of autonomy. Rather than viewing autonomy in adolescence as an abrupt rebellion against parental authority, researchers now see it as gradual, progressive, and—although important—relatively undramatic (McElhaney et al., 2009; Zimmer-Gembeck, Ducat, & Collins, 2011). Many writers have pointed to the adaptive nature of adolescents' desire for autonomy, arguing that the adolescents' need to distance themselves from their parents has an evolutionary basis, allowing an increase in novelty-seeking and exploration that facilitates reproduction outside of the family (Casey, Duhoux, & Cohen, 2010; Steinberg, 2010).

Because today's adolescents spend so much time away from the supervision of adults, either by themselves or with their peers, learning how to govern their own behavior in a responsible fashion is crucial. Given the large numbers of single-parent and two-career households in many industrialized countries, many young people are expected to care for themselves for a good part of the day. Many feel pressured—by parents, by friends, and by the media—to grow up quickly and to act like adults at an earlier age. Many adolescents who grow up in poverty feel a different sort of pressure to grow up: They are expected to take on adult responsibilities to assist their families during times of need (Burton, 2007).

There is a curious paradox in all of this, though. Although adolescents have been asked to become more autonomous psychologically and socially, they have become less autonomous economically. Because of the extension of schooling well into the 20s for most people and the difficulty many young adults have had finding satisfying employment during several recent recessions, financial independence may not come until long after psychological independence.

Many young people who are emotionally independent from their parents find it frustrating to have to abide by their rules as long as their parents are supporting them economically. They may believe that the ability to make their own decisions has nothing to do with financial dependence. An 18-year-old college freshman who has a part-time job, a full load of classes, and a serious relationship with his girlfriend may be independent in these respects, but he may still be living at home because he can't afford to do otherwise. His parents may feel that as long as their son lives in their home, they should decide how late he can stay out at night. But he may feel that his parents have no right to tell him when he can come and go. This sort of difference of opinion can be a source of problems and confusion for teenagers and their parents, particularly when they have difficulty agreeing on an appropriate level of independence for the adolescent (Steinberg, 2011). Disagreements over autonomy-related concerns are at the top of the list of things that provoke quarrels between adolescents and parents (Laursen & Collins, 2009).

Autonomy as an Adolescent Issue

Like identity, autonomy is a psychosocial concern that surfaces and resurfaces during the entire life cycle. Toddlers try to establish an initial sense of autonomy when they begin to explore their surroundings on their own and assert their desire to do as they please—a stage of development so frustrating to parents that it is often called "the terrible twos." The toddler who insists on saying "No!" and the young adolescent who insists on keeping her whereabouts secret are both demonstrating their growing sense of independence and autonomy. And just as psychologists see toddlers' oppositional behavior as normal, they also see adolescents' interest in privacy as normal, too—however frustrating that might be to parents (McElhaney et al., 2009).

Moreover, issues of autonomy are not resolved once and for all upon reaching young adulthood. Questions about being able to function independently arise whenever individuals find themselves in positions that demand a new degree of self-reliance. Following a divorce, someone who has depended on a spouse for economic support, guidance, or nurturance must find a way to function more independently. During late adulthood, autonomy may become a significant concern of someone who, after losing a spouse, suddenly finds it necessary to depend on others for assistance.

If establishing and maintaining a healthy sense of autonomy is a lifelong concern, why has it attracted so much attention among scholars interested in adolescence? When we look at the development of autonomy in relation to the biological, cognitive, and social changes of adolescence, it's easy to see why.

Puberty and the Development of Autonomy

Some theorists have suggested that puberty triggers changes in the young person's emotional relationships at home (Laursen & Collins, 2009; Zimmer-Gembeck, Ducat, & Collins, 2011). Adolescents' interest in turning away from parents and toward peers for emotional support—part of establishing adult independence—may be stimulated by their emerging interest in sexual relationships and concerns over dating and intimate friendships. From an evolutionary perspective, adolescent independence-seeking is a natural consequence of sexual and physical maturation, and "leaving the home" after puberty is something that is observed not just in humans but in other primates as well (Casey, Duhoux, & Cohen, 2010; Steinberg, 2014a). Puberty drives the

Leaving home and establishing independence at puberty is seen not just in humans but also in most primates and many other mammals. JeannetteKatzir/Getty Images

adolescent away from exclusive emotional dependence on the family. In addition, changes in stature and physical appearance at puberty may provoke changes in how much autonomy the young person is granted by parents and teachers. Children may be given more responsibility simply because they look older.

Cognitive Change and the Development of Autonomy

The cognitive changes of adolescence also play an important role in the development of autonomy (Albert & Steinberg, 2011a; Zimmer-Gembeck, Ducat, & Collins, 2011). Part of being autonomous involves being able to make independent decisions. When individuals turn to others for advice, they often receive conflicting opinions; if you are trying to decide between staying home to study for an exam and going to a party with your roommate, your professor and your friend may give you different advice. As an adult, you are able to see that each person's perspective influences his or her advice. The ability to see this, however, calls for a level of intellectual abstraction that is not available until adolescence. Being able to take other people's perspectives into account, to reason in more sophisticated ways, and to foresee the future consequences of alternative courses of action all help the adolescent weigh the opinions and suggestions of others more effectively and reach independent decisions. The cognitive changes of adolescence are important prerequisites to the development of a system of values based on one's own sense of right and wrong, not just on rules and regulations handed down by parents or other authority figures (Eisenberg et al., 2009; Morris, Eisenberg, & Houltberg, 2011; Smetana & Villalobos, 2009).

Social Roles and the Development of Autonomy

Finally, changes in social roles and activities during adolescence are bound to raise concerns related to independence, as the adolescent moves into new positions that demand increasing degrees of responsibility and self-reliance (Coatsworth & Conroy, 2009; Halpern-Felsher, 2011). Becoming involved in new roles and taking on new responsibilities, such as having a job or a driver's license, place the adolescent in situations that require and stimulate the development of independent decision making. A teenager might not really think much about the responsibilities associated with taking a job until she actually ends up in one (Wood, Larson, & Brown, 2009). Choosing whether to drink does not become an important question until the adolescent begins to approach the legal drinking age. And deciding what his political beliefs are becomes a more pressing concern when the young person realizes that he will soon have the right to vote.

Being able to drive greatly increases adolescents' autonomy from parental control. Rolf Bruderer/Getty Images

making the scientific connection

Many psychologists contend that the two periods of life during which autonomy is an especially salient issue are early adolescence and toddlerhood. What do these periods share in common that might account for the importance of autonomy during each?

Three Types of Autonomy Psychologists have described autonomy in three ways (McElhaney et al., 2009; Zimmer-Gembeck, Ducat, & Collins, 2011). The first is **emotional autonomy**—that aspect of independence related to changes in the individual's close relationships, especially with parents. The second is **behavioral autonomy**—the capacity to make independent decisions and follow through on them. And the third is **cognitive autonomy** (sometimes called "value autonomy"), which involves having independent values, opinions, and beliefs.

The Development of Emotional Autonomy

The relationship between children and their parents changes repeatedly over the life cycle. Changes in the expression of affection, the distribution of power, and patterns of interaction are likely to occur whenever important transformations take place in the child's or parents' competencies, concerns, and social roles.

By the end of adolescence, people are far less emotionally dependent on their parents than they were as children. We can see this in several ways. First, older adolescents do not generally rush to their parents when they are upset, worried, or in need of assistance. Second, they do not see their parents as all-knowing or all-powerful. Third, they often have a great deal of emotional energy wrapped up in relationships outside the family; they may feel more attached to a boyfriend or girlfriend than to their parents. And finally, older adolescents are able to see and interact with their parents as people—not just as their parents. Many parents find that they can confide in their adolescent children, which was not possible when their children were younger, or that their adolescent children can sympathize with them when they have had a hard day at work. These sorts of changes in the adolescent-parent relationship all reflect the development of emotional autonomy (McElhaney et al., 2009; Zimmer-Gembeck, Ducat, & Collins, 2011).

Emotional Autonomy: Detachment or Individuation?

Early writings about emotional autonomy were influenced by psychoanalytic thinkers such as Anna Freud (1958), who argued that the physical changes of puberty cause disruption and conflict inside the family, conflicts that are often expressed as increased tension, arguments, and discomfort in the family. As a consequence, early adolescents are driven to separate themselves from their parents emotionally, and they turn their emotional energies to relationships with peers—in particular, peers of the opposite sex. Psychoanalytic theorists call this process of separation **detachment** because to them it appears as though the adolescent is attempting to sever the attachments that were formed during infancy and strengthened throughout childhood.

Detachment Freud and her followers viewed detachment and the accompanying storm and stress inside the family as normal, healthy, and inevitable aspects of emotional development during adolescence. In fact, Freud believed that the absence of conflict between an adolescent and his or her parents signified that the young person was having problems growing up.

Studies of adolescents' family relationships have not supported Freud's view, however. In contrast to predictions that high levels of adolescent-parent tension are the norm, that adolescents detach themselves from relationships with their parents, and that adolescents are driven out of the household by unbearable levels of family conflict, every major study

emotional autonomy
The establishment of more adultlike and less childish close relationships with family members and peers.

behavioral autonomy
The capacity to make independent decisions and to follow through with them.

cognitive autonomy
The establishment of an independent set of values, opinions, and beliefs.

detachment
In psychoanalytic theory, the process through which adolescents sever emotional attachments to their parents or other authority figures.

In contrast to the view that tension between adolescents and their parents is the norm, every major study done to date of family relations in adolescence has shown that most teenagers and their parents get along quite well. Hero/age fotostock

done to date of teenagers' relations with their parents has shown that most families get along well during the adolescent years (McElhaney et al., 2009; Zimmer-Gembeck, Ducat, & Collins, 2011). Although parents and adolescents may bicker more often than they did during earlier periods of development, there is no evidence that this bickering diminishes closeness between them in any lasting way (Collins & Steinberg, 2006; Laursen & Collins, 2009). In fact, most individuals report becoming closer to their parents in late adolescence, especially after they have made the transition into college (Lefkowitz, 2005; McElhaney et al., 2009).

In other words, although teenagers and their parents modify their relationships during adolescence, their emotional bonds aren't severed. Emotional autonomy during adolescence involves a *transformation,* not a breaking off, of family relationships. Adolescents can become emotionally autonomous from their parents without becoming detached from them (Laursen & Collins, 2009; Van Petegem, Vansteenkiste, et al., 2015).

Individuation As an alternative to the classic psychoanalytic perspective on adolescent detachment, some theorists have suggested that we view the development of emotional autonomy in terms of the adolescent's developing sense of **individuation** (Blos, 1979). Individuation, which begins during infancy and continues into late adolescence, involves a gradual, progressive sharpening of one's sense of self as autonomous, competent, and separate from one's parents.

Individuation entails relinquishing childish dependencies

individuation
The progressive sharpening of an individual's sense of being an autonomous, independent person.

on parents in favor of a more mature, more responsible, and less dependent relationship (McElhaney et al., 2009). Adolescents who establish a healthy sense of autonomy accept responsibility for their choices and actions (Van Petegem et al., 2012). Rather than rebelling against her parents' midnight curfew by deliberately staying out later, a girl who has a healthy sense of individuation might take her parents aside before going out and say, "This party tonight is going to go later than midnight. If it does, I'd like to stay a bit longer. Why don't I call you at 11 and let you know when I'll be home?"

Research on Emotional Autonomy

The development of emotional autonomy is a long process, beginning early in adolescence and continuing into young adulthood (McElhaney et al., 2009). There are many indicators of this. Adolescents start to see their parents' flaws. They depend less on them to fix things that have gone wrong. As they individuate, teenagers realize that there are things about themselves that their parents aren't aware of (Steinberg & Silverberg, 1986). There often is a drop in the number of their friends whom their parents know, reflecting an increase in the size of teenagers' social networks and in their need for privacy (Feiring & Lewis, 1993). Adolescents' willingness to express negative emotions in front of their parents, such as anger or sadness, is lower during early adolescence than before or after because keeping some emotional distance from one's parents is a part of the individuation process (Zeman & Shipman, 1997).

Adolescents also become less likely to say that they have the same opinions as their parents or that they always agree with them (McElhaney et al., 2009; Zhang & Fuligni, 2006). This, in turn, is associated with changes in adolescents' beliefs about their parents' authority over them. Adolescents become increasingly likely to draw distinctions between aspects of their life that their parents have the right to regulate and those that they think are not really their parents' business (Chan, Brown, & Von Bank, 2015; Laird & Marrero, 2011; Perkins & Turiel, 2007).

De-Idealization Children place their parents on a pedestal; adolescents knock them off it. Psychologists believe that this "de-idealization" of parents may be one of the first aspects of emotional autonomy to develop because adolescents shed their childish images of their parents before replacing them with more mature ones. Even during the high school years, adolescents have some difficulty in seeing their parents as individuals beyond their roles as parents. This aspect of emotional autonomy may not develop until much later—perhaps not until young adulthood. Seeing one's parents as people, and not just as parents, typically develops later in adolescents' relations with their fathers than with their mothers because fathers interact less often with their adolescents in

As adolescents develop emotional autonomy, they often begin to question and challenge their parents more frequently.
Anna Bizoń/gpointstudio/123RF

ways that permit them to be seen as individuals (Smollar & Youniss, 1985).

The Importance of Maintaining the Connection

The development of emotional autonomy, and individuation in particular, may have different psychological effects on adolescents, depending on whether the parent-child relationship is a close one. Adolescents who become emotionally autonomous but who also feel distant from their parents score poorly on measures of psychological adjustment, whereas adolescents who demonstrate the same degree of emotional autonomy but who still feel close and attached to their parents are psychologically healthier than their peers (Allen et al., 2007; Vrolijk et al., 2020).

In other words, it is important to distinguish between separating from one's parents in a way that maintains emotional closeness in the relationship (which is healthy) and breaking away from one's parents in a fashion that involves alienation, conflict, and hostility (which is not) (Jager et al., 2015; Parra, Oliva, & Sánchez-Queija, 2015). For example, lying to one's parents and concealing undesirable things from them, which may be more an indicator of detachment than healthy individuation, is associated with psychological problems (Ahmad, Smetana, & Klimstra, 2015; Laird et al., 2013; Rote & Smetana, 2015; Tilton-Weaver, 2014). As individuals make the transition from adolescence into adulthood and work through much of the individuation process, they increasingly see lying to their parents as unacceptable (Jensen et al., 2004).

The Process of Individuation

What triggers individuation? Two different models have been suggested (Laursen & Collins, 2009). According to some researchers, puberty is the main catalyst (e.g., Holmbeck, 1996; Steinberg,

2000). Changes in the adolescent's physical appearance provoke changes in the way that adolescents are viewed—by themselves and by their parents—which, in turn, provoke changes in the ways in which parents and children interact. Shortly after puberty, most families experience an increase in bickering and squabbling. Adolescents' feelings of connectedness to their parents often decline in early adolescence, when bickering is more frequent, but increase in late adolescence after this temporary period of heightened squabbling is over (Pinquart & Silbereisen, 2002).

Other authors believe that adolescents' movement toward higher levels of individuation is stimulated by their cognitive development (Smetana, 1995a). The development of emotional autonomy in adolescence may be provoked by young people's development of more sophisticated understandings of themselves and their parents. Prior to adolescence, individuals accept their parents' views of themselves as accurate ("My parents think I am a good girl, so I must be"). But as individuals develop more differentiated self-conceptions in early and middle adolescence, they come to see that their parents' view is but one of many—and one that may not be entirely correct ("My parents think I am a good girl, but they don't know what I am really like"). By late adolescence, individuals are able to see that these discrepancies between their self-conceptions and their parents' views are perfectly understandable ("There are sides of me that my parents know and sides of me that they don't") (Harter, 2011).

Separating from one's parents is not always turbulent, but it often has its difficult moments. Even though the images children have of their parents as all-knowing and all-powerful may be naïve, these idealized pictures still provide emotional comfort. Leaving such images behind can be both liberating and frightening, for parents as well as teenagers. The development of emotional autonomy is associated not only with insecurity among adolescents but also with increased feelings of anxiety and rejection in their parents (Hock et al., 2001). Difficulties in the process of individuation also arise when adolescents push for independence at an earlier age than parents are willing to grant it. Adolescents usually believe that teenagers should be granted autonomy earlier than parents do (Ruck, Peterson-Badali, & Day, 2002).

Parenting and Emotional Autonomy

In Asian and Western countries alike, adolescents whose parents impede the individuation process are more likely to show signs of psychological distress (Campione-Barr, Bassett Greer, & Kruse, 2013; Kouros & Garber, 2014; Weltkamp & Seiffge-Krenke, 2019). Adolescents who do not feel good about themselves and who have very intrusive parents are especially vulnerable to depression (Pomerantz, 2001).

In contrast, around the world and across ethnic groups, adolescents whose parents provide support for

psychological control
Parenting that attempts to control the adolescent's emotions and opinions.

their growing interest in autonomy report better mental health than those whose parents do not (Kiang & Bhattacharjee, 2019; Nalipay, King, & Cai, 2020; Tran & Raffaeli, 2020). Teenagers who are provided sufficient support for their autonomy are more likely to disclose information about their social lives to their parents, which allows parents to be better at monitoring their children's behavior. This, in turn, may positively affect parents' own mental health (Wuyts et al., 2018). It's especially important that parents use positive reinforcement and praise, rather than punishment, to shape their teenagers' behavior (Fosco & LoBraico, 2019).

In contrast, adolescents whose parents use a lot of **psychological control**—parents who are emotionally close to the point of being intrusive or overprotective, who try to control their child by withdrawing love or making their child feel guilty or ashamed—may have difficulty individuating from them, which may lead to depression, anxiety, aggression, and feelings of incompetence and dependence (Brauer, 2017; A. Rogers et al., 2020; Van Petegem et al., 2020; Yu et al., 2019) (see Figure 9.1). This may be especially true when teenagers see these attempts at control as not in their best interests (Cheah et al., 2019). The effects of psychological control during early adolescence even persist into adulthood. People whose parents were very controlling were less psychologically mature and well-liked during mid-adolescence, which led to their being were less successful in school and less likely to be in romantic relationships in their 30s (Loeb et al., 2020).

Adolescents whose parents use a lot of psychological control also show patterns of behavior and brain activity that suggest potential problems in self-regulation (Marusak et al., 2017; Rogers et al., 2019). In some families, adolescents respond to excessive parental control by actively rebelling (Van Petegem et al., 2019) or lying (Gingo, Roded,

& Turiel, 2017), which may lead to problems in the parent-adolescent relationship (Flamant et al., 2020; Weymouth & Buehler, 2016). Helping parents to become more mindful about the way they parent may help them become less controlling, which may improve the quality of their relationship with their child as well as their child's mental health and feelings of competence (Bullock et al., 2018; Lippold et al., 2015).

Keep in mind, of course, that parents are also influenced by their teenagers: Adolescents who are anxious, timid, and withdrawn are more likely to elicit psychological control from their parents (Lin et al., 2020; Nelemans et al., 2020). Although parents' failure to support their teenager's developing sense of autonomy can lead to adolescent depression, the reverse is true as well (Duineveld et al., 2017; Werner et al., 2016) (see Figure 9.2). Similarly, adolescents with psychological problems are more likely to provoke conflict with their parents, which makes some parents more controlling (Steeger & Gondoli, 2013).

Emotional Autonomy and Parenting Style Responsibility, self-esteem, and positive mental health are all fostered by parents who are authoritative (friendly, fair, and firm) rather than authoritarian (excessively harsh), indulgent (excessively lenient), or indifferent (aloof to the point of being neglectful). As a result, the development of emotional autonomy follows different patterns in different types of households.

In authoritative families, guidelines are established for the adolescent's behavior, and standards are upheld, but they are flexible and open to discussion; parents are actively involved in monitoring their teenagers' behavior but in a way that supports the development of autonomy (Rodríguez-Meirinhos et al., 2020) Although parents may have the final say when it comes to their child's behavior, the decision that is reached usually comes after consultation and discussion—with the child included

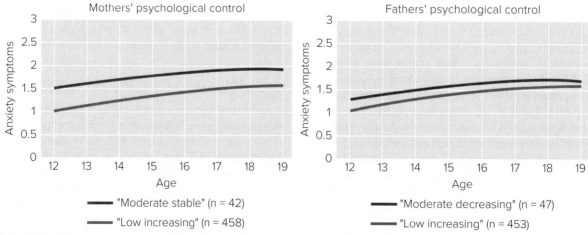

Figure 9.1 **Adolescents are more likely to develop anxiety when their parents use a lot of psychological control.**
(A. Rogers et al., 2020)

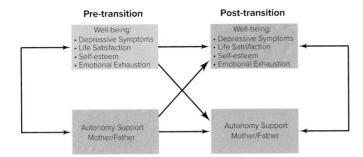

Figure 9.2 During the transition into high school, parents' autonomy support increases adolescent well-being, but the reverse is true as well: The better an adolescent's mental health, the more likely parents are to support his or her autonomy. (Adapted from Duineveld et al., 2017)

(Benish-Weisman, Levy, & Knafo, 2013; Mauras, Grolnick, & Friendly, 2013). In discussing an adolescent's curfew, for example, authoritative parents will sit down with their child and explain how they arrived at their decision and why they picked the hour they did. They will also ask the adolescent for his or her suggestions and consider them carefully in making a final decision.

It is not difficult to see why the sort of give-and-take found in authoritative families is well suited to the healthy development of emotional autonomy. Because standards and guidelines are flexible and adequately explained, it is not hard for the family to adjust and modify them as the child matures (Smetana & Asquith, 1994). Gradual changes in family relations that permit the young person more independence and encourage more responsibility but that do not threaten the emotional bond between parent and child—in other words, changes that promote increasing emotional autonomy—are relatively easy to make in a family that has been flexible all along (Vuchinich, Angeletti, & Gatherum, 1996). Plus, having a close relationship with one parent protects against the adverse effects of the other parent's psychological control (Murray et al., 2014).

In authoritarian households, where rules are rigidly enforced but rarely explained, adjusting to adolescence is more difficult. Authoritarian parents see the child's emotional independence as rebellious or disrespectful, and they resist their adolescent's growing need for independence, rather than accepting it. Seeing that their daughter is becoming interested in boys, an authoritarian parent may implement a rigid curfew in order to restrict the teenager's social life. Authoritarian parents may inadvertently maintain the dependencies of childhood by failing to give their children sufficient practice in making decisions and being responsible for their actions. In essence, authoritarian parenting may interfere with adolescent individuation.

When closeness, as well as support for autonomy, is absent, the problems are compounded. In families in which excessive parental control is accompanied by extreme coldness and punitiveness, adolescents may rebel against their parents' standards explicitly, in an attempt to assert their independence in a visible and demonstrable fashion (Kakihara et al., 2010). Today's technologies make

it easier for parents to stay in touch with their teenagers. But a little monitoring goes a long way. Adolescents are more likely to "act out"—to misbehave—when their parents are intrusive (van den Akker, Deković, & Prinzie, 2010); one study found that the more frequently parents called their adolescent's cell phone, the more dishonest the adolescent was (Weisskirch, 2009). Such rebellion is not indicative of genuine emotional autonomy; it's a demonstration of the adolescent's frustration with his or her parents' rigidity and lack of understanding.

In both indulgent and indifferent families, a different sort of problem arises. These parents do not provide sufficient guidance for their children, and as a result, the youngsters do not acquire adequate standards for behavior. In the absence of parental guidance and rules, permissively reared teenagers often turn to their peers for advice and emotional support—a practice that can be problematic when the peers are themselves still young and inexperienced. Adolescents whose parents have failed to provide sufficient guidance are likely to become psychologically dependent on their friends—emotionally detached from their parents, perhaps, but not genuinely autonomous.

Some parents who have raised their children permissively until adolescence are caught off guard by the consequences of not having been stricter earlier on. The greater orientation toward the peer group of permissively raised adolescents may involve the young person in behavior that his or her parents disapprove of. As a consequence, some parents who have been permissive throughout a youngster's childhood shift gears when he or she enters adolescence, becoming autocratic in an attempt to control a youngster over whom they feel they have lost their authority. Parents who have never placed any restrictions on their child's out-of-school activities during elementary school may suddenly begin monitoring her social life once she enters junior high school.

Shifts like these can be extremely hard on adolescents. Just at the time when they are seeking greater autonomy, their parents become more restrictive. Having become accustomed to relative leniency, adolescents whose parents change the rules in the middle of the game may find it difficult to accept standards that are being strictly enforced for the first time.

The Development of Behavioral Autonomy

Whereas the development of emotional autonomy is played out mainly in adolescents' relationships with their parents, the development of behavioral autonomy—the ability to act independently—is seen both inside and outside the family, in relationships with peers as well as parents. Broadly speaking, behavioral autonomy refers to the capacity for independent decision making. Researchers who have studied behavioral autonomy have looked at changes in *decision-making abilities* and in *susceptibility to the influence of others*.

Changes in Decision-Making Abilities

The more sophisticated reasoning processes used by adolescents permit them to hold multiple viewpoints in mind simultaneously, allowing them to compare people's different perspectives, which is crucial for weighing the opinions and advice of others. Because adolescents are better able than children to think in hypothetical terms, they also are more likely to contemplate the long-term consequences of their choices. With age, adolescents become more likely to consider both the risks and benefits associated with the decisions they make and more likely to weigh the long-term consequences of their choices, not just the immediate ones (Crone & van der Molen, 2007; Steinberg, Graham, et al., 2009). Moreover, the enhanced role-taking capabilities of adolescence permit teenagers to consider another person's opinion while taking into account that person's point of view. This is important in determining whether someone who has given advice has special areas of expertise, particular biases, or vested interests that the teenager should keep in mind. Taken together, these cognitive changes result in improved decision-making skills and, consequently, in the individual's enhanced ability to behave independently.

Improvements in Self-Regulation Many studies have documented important improvements in decision-making abilities during middle and late adolescence that are linked to gains in self-regulation (Allemand, Job, & Mroczek, 2019; Christakou, 2014). Across many different cultural contexts, strong self-regulation is one of the most robust predictors of success in life, whereas weak self-regulation is linked to all sorts of emotional and behavioral problems (Allemand, Job, & Mroczek, 2019; Galla & Duckworth, 2015; Memmott-Elison, Moilanen, & Padilla-Walker, 2020; Moffitt et al., 2011). For instance, adolescents with strong self-regulation are more likely to be engaged in school, which contributes not only to academic achievement but also to further improvements in self-regulation (Stefansson et al., 2018) On the other hand, adolescents with problems in self-regulation are more prone to extremes in negative emotions, such as

anger or sadness, as well as a wide range of behavioral and emotional problems (Laceulle et al., 2017; Rothenberg et al., 2019). Not surprisingly, teenagers who have poor self-regulation are more likely to become juvenile delinquents (Fosco et al., 2019), and those who are delinquent and have poor self-control are more likely to reoffend (Rocque, Beckley, & Piquero, 2019).

Improvements in self-regulation appear to be due to two separate but related developments (Duckworth & Steinberg, 2015; Shulman, Harden, et al., 2016). First, there is a decline over the course of adolescence in the extent to which decisions are influenced by their potential immediate rewards (de Water, Cillessen, & Scheres, 2014). Most situations in which we have to decide among alternative choices (Should I wear a protective face mask to my friend's party? Should I sleep with my girlfriend right now or wait until tomorrow night, when I'll make sure to have a condom?) present a combination of potential rewards and potential costs. What we decide to do is often the result of how strong those rewards and costs are. Someone who is just thinking about having fun with his friends or how good unprotected sex is going to feel will act differently than someone who is thinking about possible exposure to the coronavirus or the possibility of getting his girlfriend pregnant.

During early adolescence, individuals are much more drawn to the potential benefits of a decision than the potential costs. As they mature, the relative balance of reward and cost changes so that by late adolescence, these factors are weighed about evenly (Cauffman et al., 2010). Psychologists have now mapped this development onto changes in patterns of brain activation, showing that the regions of the brain that are especially sensitive to reward are more intensely activated during early and middle adolescence than in childhood or adulthood, especially when rewards are being anticipated, as they might be when adolescents are thinking about how much fun they are going to have before they head out for an evening (Galván, 2013; Van Leijenhorst, Zanolie, et al., 2010). Some of the heightened "reward sensitivity" seen among adolescents is not even conscious (Cauffman et al., 2010). In fact, adolescents are just as consciously aware as adults of the potential rewards and costs of a decision; they are just influenced more by the anticipated rewards (Van Leijenhorst, Westenberg, & Crone, 2008). Not only are younger adolescents more drawn to rewards than are adults, but they also seem especially drawn to *immediate* rewards (Steinberg, Graham, et al., 2009).

A second influence on changes in decision making concerns individuals' ability to control their impulses (Steinberg, Albert, et al., 2008; van Duijvenvoorde et al., 2012; Weiser & Reynolds, 2011). Regions of the brain that govern self-regulation are still developing during adolescence and early adulthood, as are connections between brain regions that control impulses and those that respond to rewards (Luna et al., 2013; Peper et al., 2013;

van den Bos et al., 2015). There is strong evidence, from studies all over the world, that adolescents are more likely to develop strong self-control if their parents engage in authoritative parenting—parenting that is both warm and firm (Li et al., 2019; Li et al., 2020).

This improvement in self-control has important implications for decision making. With age, individuals are better at thinking ahead, imagining and analyzing the consequences of their decisions, seeking and evaluating the advice of others, and making decisions that aren't hasty or excessively influenced by their emotions (Munakata, Snyder, & Chatham, 2012). The combination of heightened reward sensitivity and immature impulse control may lead adolescents to make a lot of risky—even dangerous—decisions. Some writers have suggested that one way to diminish adolescent risk taking is to encourage them to do things such as mindfulness meditation, which has been shown to increase self-regulation (Steinberg, 2014).

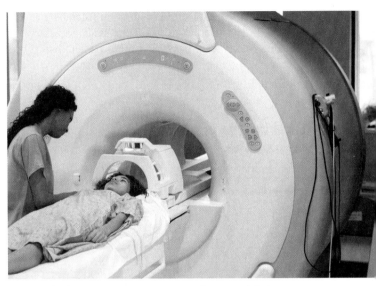

The brain's pleasure centers are more easily aroused during early adolescence than in childhood or adulthood, which makes adolescent decision making more influenced by the prospect of immediate rewards. ERproductions Ltd/Blend Images

When Do Adolescents Make Decisions as Well as Adults?

The recognition that individuals' decision-making skills improve over the course of adolescence has prompted numerous debates about young people's abilities to make decisions in the real world; for example, with regard to having access to medical care without their parents' approval or functioning as competent defendants in court. Many such debates revolve around where we should draw the legal boundary between adolescence and adulthood for such things as driving, purchasing alcohol or cigarettes, or being tried in adult court (Steinberg & Icenogle, 2019).

One relevant line of research has examined adolescents' legal decision making (Grisso et al., 2003; Kambam & Thompson, 2009). In the typical study, adolescents and adults are presented with vignettes involving an individual who had gotten into trouble with the law and then are asked how the individual should handle different situations: being interrogated by the police, consulting with an attorney, deciding whether to plead guilty in return for a lesser sentence versus going to trial, or taking her or his chances on the outcome. In these studies, adolescents are less likely than adults to think about the long-term implications of their decisions, more likely to focus on the immediate consequences of their decisions, and less able to understand the ways in which other people's positions might bias their interests. For example, when asked what a guilty individual should do when being interrogated by the police, younger adolescents are more likely than adults to say that they should confess (which is not what most attorneys would recommend) rather than remain silent (the most advisable thing to do). Younger adolescents are more inclined to think about the immediate consequences of their actions ("If I tell the police the truth, they'll let me go home"), not the longer-term implications ("If I confess, this information can be used against me in court").

One difficulty in making decisions about where to draw legal lines between adolescents and adults is that mature decision making is the product of both cognitive abilities (such as being able to reason logically) and emotional factors (such as being able to control one's impulses), aspects of development that proceed along somewhat different timetables (Icenogle et al., 2019; Steinberg, Cauffman, et al., 2009). The maturation of basic cognitive abilities is complete at around age 16. Many writers have argued that adolescents who have reached this age reason well enough to have the right to vote or to seek health care services (including abortions, contraception, substance abuse counseling, and vaccinations) without parental knowledge or consent. But because there are improvements in such things as impulse control, planning ahead, and risk assessment well into early adulthood, there is a period during which adolescents may *think* like adults but *behave* in a much more immature way. One study found that young adults were just as able as people in their mid-20s to exercise self-control under calm conditions but not when they were emotionally aroused (Cohen et al., 2016). Individuals who are opposed to trying juvenile offenders as adults use this evidence to argue in favor of treating juveniles who have committed crimes less harshly than adults because of their emotional immaturity (Scott & Steinberg, 2008).

One way of resolving this problem is to make sure our treatment of adolescents is consistent with what we know about psychological development in ways that are specific to the legal matters in question (Steinberg & Icenogle, 2019). In other words, if the skills necessary for making one type of decision mature earlier than those necessary for another, it would make sense to have a different age boundary for each.

making the practical connection

Based on what you have read about changes in decision-making abilities in adolescence, should adolescents be treated like adults under the law? If you were a lawmaker, where would you draw the line for issues concerning access to health care? For violations of the law?

Changes in Susceptibility to Influence

As adolescents come to spend more time outside the family, the opinions and advice of others—not only peers but adults as well—become more important. A variety of situations arise in which adolescents may feel that their parents' advice may be less valid than the opinions of others. Adolescents might seek the advice of friends, rather than their parents, about how to dress. They may turn to a teacher or guidance counselor for advice about what courses to take in school. Or they might talk something over with more than one person. A teenage girl who is trying to decide whether to take a part-time job after school might discuss the pros and cons with her parents but also ask friends for their advice. When different "advisors" disagree, adolescents must reconcile the differences of opinion and reach their own independent conclusions.

In situations in which parents and peers give conflicting advice, do teenagers tend to follow one group more often than the other? Adolescents are often portrayed as being extremely susceptible to the influence of peer pressure—more so than children or young adults—and as being stubbornly resistant to the influence of their parents. But is peer pressure really more potent during adolescence than at other times?

The Influence of Parents and Peers   Some researchers have studied conformity and peer pressure during adolescence by putting adolescents in situations in which they must choose between the wishes of their parents and those of their peers. An adolescent might be told to imagine that he and his friends discover the answer sheet to an upcoming test on the floor outside the teachers' lounge. His friends tell him that they should keep it a secret. But the adolescent tells his mother about it, and she advises him to tell the teacher. He then would be asked by the researcher to say what he would do.

Adolescents turn for advice to different people in different situations (Halpern-Felsher, 2011). In some situations, peers' opinions are more influential, but in others,

parents' views are more powerful. Adolescents are more likely to conform to peers' opinions when it comes to short-term, day-to-day, and social matters—styles of dress, tastes in music, choices among leisure activities, and so on. This is particularly true during the junior high school and early high school years.

When it comes to long-term questions concerning educational or occupational plans, however, or to issues concerning values, religious beliefs, or ethics, teenagers are primarily influenced by their parents (Collins & Steinberg, 2006). When adolescents' problems center on a relationship with a friend, they usually turn to a peer, a preference that becomes stronger with age. But adolescents' willingness to turn to an adult, such as a teacher or mentor, for advice with problems—especially those that involve getting along with their parents—remains very strong and increases as individuals move toward late adolescence. In one study in which the researchers compared the effect of advice given by a peer or an adult during a challenging gambling task, both teenagers and adults were more likely to follow the adult's recommendations (Lourenco et al., 2015).

Responding to Peer Pressure   Studies that contrast the influence of peers and adults do not really reveal all there is to know about peer pressure. Most peer pressure operates when adults are absent—when adolescents are at a party, driving home from school, or hanging out with their friends. To get closer to this issue, researchers have studied how adolescents respond when they must choose between pressure from their friends and their own opinions of what to do. For example, an adolescent might be asked whether he would go along with his friends' plans to vandalize some property even though he did not want to do so (e.g., Bámaca & Umaña-Taylor, 2006).

Most studies using this approach show that conformity to peers is higher during the first half of adolescence than later (Steinberg & Monahan, 2007). Susceptibility to peer pressure around age 14 is most often seen when the behavior in question is antisocial—such as cheating, stealing, or trespassing—especially in studies of boys (Erickson, Crosnoe, & Dornbusch, 2000). These findings are in line with studies of delinquent behavior, which is often committed by boys in groups, often during middle adolescence (Farrington, 2009), as well as experimental studies of peer influence, which have found that the impact of peers on adolescents' risky decision making is stronger among boys than girls (Defoe et al., 2020). Adolescents who are more susceptible to peer pressure to engage in delinquent activity actually are more likely to misbehave (Monahan et al., 2009; Walters, 2018).

The consequences of being especially susceptible to one's peers depend on who those peers are, though, as well as the context in which the peers are encountered (Ahmed et al., 2020; Ragan, 2020). For instance, whereas high susceptibility to peer influence predicts adolescents' antisocial behavior if their friends are antisocial, the same level of susceptibility is not predictive of problem behavior if their friends are not (Hofmann & Müller & 2018; Monahan, Steinberg, & Cauffman, 2009; Paternoster et al., 2013). And, of course, many adolescents have friends who pressure them *not* to get involved in questionable, illegal, or risky activities (Kam & Wang, 2015).

Although we know that conformity to peer pressure is high during early and middle adolescence, it isn't clear why. One possibility is that individuals' susceptibility to peer pressure doesn't change but that peer pressure may be especially strong around the time individuals are 14. In other words, adolescent peer groups may exert more pressure on their members to conform than do groups of younger or older individuals, and the pressure may be strong enough to make even the most autonomous teenagers comply.

Another possibility is that young adolescents are more susceptible to peer influence because of their heightened orientation toward other people in general (Nelson, Lau, & Jarcho, 2014; Somerville, 2013; Wolf et al., 2015) and toward peers in particular (Conson et al., 2017). In one experiment, people of different ages were asked to rate how risky various activities were, were then told how either a teenager or an adult had rated the same activities, and then were asked to re-rate them. All groups except the young adolescents were likely to change their ratings to be more consistent with what they were told the adult had said; the young adolescents were more likely to change their ratings to match what they thought other teenagers had said (Knoll et al., 2017; Knoll et al., 2015).

Keep in mind that not all peer influence is bad, however: When adolescents are actively discouraged from taking risks by their peers, they are likely to listen to them (de Boer & Harakeh, 2017), and in the presence of peers, adolescents engage in more prosocial behavior (Van Hoorn, Van Dijk, Güroglu, & Crone, 2016) and learn faster (Silva et al., 2016). During the COVID-19 pandemic, while many (including myself) worried that peer influences would lead adolescents to ignore guidelines for social distancing (Steinberg, 2020), others have suggested that we try to harness adolescents' susceptibility to peer influence to encourage safe behavior (Andrews, Foulkes, & Blakemore, 2020). The data are quite clear: In counties with universities where instruction continued in person after the pandemic had been identified, COVID cases rose immediately, but in counties in which universities switched to remote instruction, COVID cases were about as frequent as they were in counties without universities at all (Leidner et al., 2021) (see Figure 9.3).

Yet a third account is that being around other teenagers changes the way the adolescent brain functions. During adolescence, the mere presence of friends activates brain regions associated with the experience of reward, but no such effect is found when adolescents are with their parents, when adolescents are with a mix of peers and adults, or when adults are with *their* friends, as shown in Figure 9.4 (Chein et al., 2011; Silva, Chein, & Steinberg, 2016; Smith et al., 2015; Telzer, Ichien, & Qu, 2015). Even adolescent mice show an increase in sensitivity to rewards when with their "peers," something that isn't seen in adult mice (Logue et al., 2014).

Peer influence does not have to take the form of active peer pressure, however (Harakeh & de Boer, 2019). When adolescents are with their friends, they may be especially likely to pay attention to the potential rewards of a risky choice and less likely to notice the potential costs (Haddad et al., 2014; Smith, Chein, & Steinberg, 2014; Weigard et al., 2014). One study of adolescents' responses to Instagram posts found that when high school students were presented with photographs depicting risky activities, they showed decreased activation in brain regions known to govern self-control; this effect was not seen in college students, though (Sherman et al., 2018).

Because adolescents usually experience pleasure when they are with their peers, they are more likely to go along with the crowd to avoid being rejected (Blakemore, 2018). In experiments, adolescents who are led to believe they are interacting in a chat room with either high-status or low-status peers (which is manipulated by the researchers

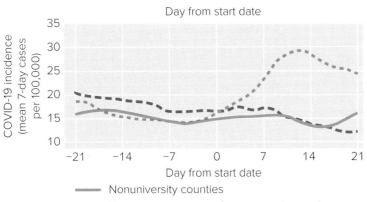

Figure 9.3 COVID-19 cases rose in counties with universities that continued in-person instruction but not in counties that switched to remote instruction, where cases were about the same as in counties without universities at all. (Leidner et al., 2021)

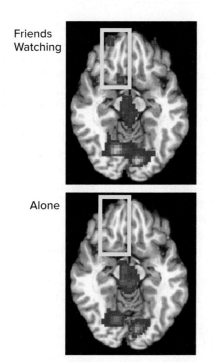

Friends
Watching

Alone

Figure 9.4 **Adolescents are more susceptible to peer influence than adults are. This figure shows two brain scans, one taken while adolescents were playing a driving game when their friends were watching, and the other taken when the adolescents were playing alone. The area surrounded by the yellow rectangle is a part of the brain that is activated when we experience reward. One reason adolescents may behave more recklessly when they are with their friends is that the presence of peers may make them pay more attention to the potential rewards of a risky choice.** (Chein et al., 2011)

in the way the peers are described) about the acceptability of various illegal or risky behaviors are more influenced by the opinions of high-status peers, an effect that is especially strong among adolescents who are particularly susceptible to peer influence (Choukas-Bradley et al., 2014). This creates a dilemma: Teenagers must strike a balance between asserting their independence and fitting in (Allen, Chango, & Szwedo, 2014). One of the difficult challenges of adolescence is that being popular with peers often requires a willingness to engage in behaviors that adults disapprove of, such as drinking. When adolescents view Instagram photos of other teenagers engaging in risky behavior, looking at photos with a large number of "likes" activates their brain's reward regions (Sherman et al., 2016).

Individual Differences in Susceptibility to Peer Influence Within a group of teenagers who are the same age, some are highly autonomous, others are easily influenced by their peers, others are oriented toward their parents, and still others are swayed by both peers and

parents, depending on the situation and the behavior in question (Prinstein, Brechwald, & Cohen, 2011; Sijtsema & Lindenberg, 2018). Girls are less susceptible to peer pressure than boys, as are Black adolescents in comparison to adolescents from other ethnic groups. Asian American adolescents, in contrast, seem especially susceptible to peer pressure, perhaps consistent with the greater emphasis placed on the importance of the group over the individual in Asian cultures (Steinberg & Monahan, 2007). Susceptibility to peer pressure is also higher among relatively more acculturated Latinx adolescents than their less acculturated peers and higher among Latinx adolescents who were born in the United States than those who were born abroad (Bámaca & Umaña-Taylor, 2006; Umaña-Taylor & Bámaca-Gómez, 2003). Adolescents from single-parent families, as well as those with less supportive or more controlling parents, appear especially susceptible to peer pressure (Chan & Chan, 2013). There also is evidence that adolescents with a particular genetic profile are relatively more susceptible than others to peer influence (Schlomer et al., 2021).

Studies of adolescent brain development have added to our growing understanding of differences among adolescents in their susceptibility to peer influence (Brechwald & Prinstein, 2011). Individuals who show a pattern of brain activity indicating heightened sensitivity to social evaluation are less able to resist peer influence (Falk et al., 2014; Guyer et al., 2014; Telzer et al., 2020), as are adolescents who are in the midst of puberty, perhaps because pubertal hormones make adolescents more sensitive to social influence (Kretsch & Harden, 2014), and those who are high in sensation seeking (Segalowitz et al., 2012) or fun seeking (Blankenstein et al., 2020). Being able to resist peer pressure is associated with stronger connections between areas of the brain active during decision making and other brain regions, perhaps because individuals who are more likely to stand up to their friends are better able to better control the impulsive, emotional decision making that often occurs in the peer group (Grosbras et al., 2007). Similarly, adolescents whose neural activity is indicative of better emotion regulation also report more resistance to peer influence (Pfeifer et al., 2011). This brain research is consistent with the idea that a key aspect of psychological maturation in adolescence, including resistance to peer influence, involves the development of self-regulation (Hinnant & Forman-Alberti, 2019; Monahan et al., 2009).

Parenting and Behavioral Autonomy Like emotional autonomy, behavioral autonomy appears to be associated with authoritative rather than permissive, authoritarian, or neglectful parenting (Collins & Steinberg, 2006). The impact of having authoritative parents on adolescents' susceptibility to peer pressure depends on the nature of the peer pressure, however. Adolescents from authoritative homes are less susceptible to

Peers have a powerful influence over adolescents' tastes in clothes, hairstyles, and other day-to-day decisions.
PhotoAlto/Laurence Mouton/Getty Images

antisocial peer pressure, but they may be *more* susceptible to the influence of positive peers. Adolescents from authoritative homes are less likely to be influenced by having drug-using friends, but they are more likely to be influenced by having friends who perform well in school (Mounts & Steinberg, 1995).

It is also important to distinguish between adolescents who are excessively dependent on their peers (and who forgo their parents' rules and pay less attention to their schoolwork for the sake of being popular with peers) and those who turn to peers for counsel but do not ignore their parents' guidance (Fuligni et al., 2001). Substituting peers for parents leads to problem behavior; adding peers to the list of persons one turns to for advice, so long as that list also includes parents, does not. In other words, the problem is being distant from one's parents, rather than being close to one's peers, something that parents who worry about the power of the peer group would do well to remember.

The ways in which parents and adolescents negotiate changes in behavioral autonomy have implications for adolescents' adjustment (Chen-Gaddini, 2012; Roche et al., 2014). Adolescents who have less positive relationships with their parents are more likely to be especially peer oriented, to affiliate with antisocial peers, and to spend time with friends in unsupervised settings, all of which heighten the risk for problem behavior.

But parents need to maintain a healthy balance between asserting control and granting autonomy. Granting too much autonomy before adolescents are ready for it or granting too little autonomy once adolescents are mature enough to handle it creates adolescents who are the most strongly peer oriented. Adolescents whose parents become more authoritarian over time (stricter and less likely to

permit the adolescent to make decisions) are the most peer oriented of all. Although many parents clamp down on their teenagers' independence out of fear that not doing so will allow the youngsters to fall under the "evil" influence of the peer group, this strategy often backfires. Having parents limit their autonomy at just the time when more independence is desired and expected makes adolescents turn away from the family and toward their friends.

Ethnic and Cultural Differences in Expectations for Autonomy

The development of behavioral autonomy varies across cultures because of differences in the age expectations that adolescents and parents have for independent behavior. Adolescents' mental health is best when their desire for autonomy matches their expectations for what their parents are willing to grant (Pérez, Cumsille, & Martínez, 2016). For example, within the same countries, white adolescents and their parents have earlier expectations for adolescent autonomy than do Asian adolescents and their parents. Because of this, Asian adolescents may be less likely to seek autonomy from their parents than white adolescents, white adolescents are less likely than Asian adolescents to define themselves in terms of their relationship with their parents (Pomerantz et al., 2009), and discrepancies between adolescents' and parents' expectations for autonomy don't cause the same degree of conflict in Asian homes as they do in Western ones (Jensen & Dost-Gözkan, 2015). Not surprisingly, increased autonomy is strongly associated with better emotional functioning among American youth (where being an independent person is highly valued) but less so among Asian adolescents (Qin, Pomerantz, & Wang, 2009).

Parents from different ethnic groups have different ideas about the appropriate age at which to grant adolescents autonomy.
Donald Iain Smith/Getty Images

In families that have immigrated to a new culture, parents and adolescents often have different expectations about granting autonomy (Romo, Mireles-Rios, & Lopez-Tello, 2014). As a rule, because adolescents generally acculturate more quickly to a new culture than do parents, a family that has moved from a culture in which it is normal to grant autonomy relatively later in adolescence (as in most Asian countries) to one in which it is normal to grant autonomy relatively earlier (as in the United States) may experience conflict as a result of differences in the expectations of adolescents and parents (Bámaca-Colbert et al., 2012). This is because adolescents' expectations for autonomy are shaped to a great extent by their perceptions of how much independence their friends have (Daddis, 2011).

The Development of Cognitive Autonomy

The development of cognitive autonomy entails changes in the adolescent's beliefs, opinions, and values. It has been studied mainly by looking at how adolescents think about moral, political, and religious issues.

Three trends in the development of cognitive autonomy are especially noteworthy. First, adolescents become increasingly abstract in the way they think about moral, political, and religious issues. This leads to more complicated decisions about how to act when one's beliefs about one issue conflict with one's beliefs about another. Consider an 18-year-old who is deciding whether to participate in a deliberately disruptive demonstration against policies he believes support the interests of environmental polluters. Instead of looking at the situation only in terms of the environmental issues, he might also think about the implications of knowingly violating the law by being disruptive.

Second, during adolescence, beliefs become increasingly rooted in general principles. An 18-year-old might say that demonstrating against pollution is acceptable because protecting the environment is more important than living in accord with the law, and so breaking a law is legitimate when the status quo leads to environmental degradation.

Finally, beliefs become increasingly founded in the young person's own values, not merely in a system of values passed on by parents or other authority figures. Thus, an 18-year-old may look at the issue of environmental protection in terms of what he himself believes, rather than in terms of what his parents think.

Much of the growth in cognitive autonomy can be traced to the cognitive changes characteristic of the period. With adolescents' enhanced reasoning capabilities and the further development of hypothetical thinking come a heightened interest in ideological and philosophical matters and a more sophisticated way of looking at them. The ability to consider alternate possibilities and to engage in thinking about thinking allows for the exploration of differing value systems, political ideologies, personal ethics, and religious beliefs. It also may permit the development of curiosity and open-mindedness (Baeher, 2017). The growth of cognitive autonomy is a relatively late development; it follows and is encouraged by the development of emotional and behavioral autonomy, which typically mature earlier in adolescence (Collins & Steinberg, 2006).

Why is cognitive autonomy stimulated by the development of emotional and behavioral autonomy? The establishment of emotional autonomy provides adolescents with the ability to look at their parents more objectively. When adolescents no longer see their parents as omnipotent and infallible, they may reevaluate the ideas and values that they accepted without question as children. And as adolescents begin to test the waters of independence behaviorally, they may experience a variety of cognitive conflicts caused by having to deal with competing pressures to behave in different ways.

These conflicts may prompt young people to consider in more serious and thoughtful terms what they really believe. For example, during adolescence, individuals become increasingly likely to say that it is permissible to lie to one's parents about disobeying them when they think their parents' advice is immoral (for instance, if the parents had forbidden their teenager to date someone from another race) (Perkins & Turiel, 2007). This struggle to clarify values, provoked in part by the exercise of behavioral autonomy, is a key component of the process of developing a sense of cognitive autonomy.

Moral Development During Adolescence

Moral development has been the most widely studied aspect of cognitive autonomy during adolescence. The study of moral development involves both reasoning (how individuals think about moral dilemmas) and behavior (how they behave in situations that call for moral judgments). Related to this is the study of **prosocial behavior,** acts people engage in to help others (Morris, Eisenberg, & Houltberg, 2011).

Assessing Moral Reasoning The dominant theoretical viewpoint in the study of moral reasoning is grounded in Piaget's theory of cognitive development. Cognitive-developmental theories of morality that stem from this viewpoint emphasize shifts in the type of reasoning that individuals use in making moral decisions, rather than changes in the content of the decisions they reach or the actions they take as a result (Eisenberg et al., 2009; Smetana & Villalobos, 2009).

prosocial behavior
Behaviors intended to help others.

Researchers assess individuals' moral reasoning by examining their responses to hypothetical dilemmas about difficult, real-world situations, such as the following (Gibbs et al., 2007):

The best-known dilemma used by researchers who study moral reasoning involves a man who had to choose between stealing a drug to save his wife or letting his wife remain mortally ill:

> In Europe, a woman was near death from a very bad disease, a special kind of cancer. There was one drug that the doctors thought might save her. It was a form of radium that a druggist in the same town had recently discovered. The drug was expensive to make, but the druggist was charging 10 times what the drug cost him to make. He paid $200 for the radium and charged $2,000 for a small dose of the drug. The sick woman's husband, Heinz, went to everyone he knew to borrow the money, but he could only get together about $1,000, which was half of what it cost. He told the druggist that his wife was dying and asked him to sell it cheaper or let him pay later. But the druggist said, "No, I discovered the drug and I'm going to make money from it." Heinz got desperate and broke into the man's store to steal the drug for his wife. *Should the husband have done that? Was it right or wrong?*

Stages of Moral Reasoning Whether or not you think that Heinz should have stolen the drug is less important than the reasoning behind your answers. According to the cognitive-developmental perspective, there are three levels of moral reasoning: **preconventional moral reasoning**, which is dominant during most of childhood; **conventional moral reasoning**, which is usually dominant during late childhood and early adolescence; and **postconventional moral reasoning** (sometimes called principled moral reasoning), which emerges sometime during the adolescent or young adult years.

Preconventional thinking is characterized by reference to external and physical events. Preconventional moral decisions are not based on society's standards, rules, or conventions (hence the label *pre*conventional). Children at this stage approach moral dilemmas in ways that focus on the rewards and punishments associated with different courses of action. One preconventional child might say that Heinz should not have stolen the drug because he could have been caught and sent to jail. Another might say that Heinz was right to steal the drug because people would have been angry with him if he had let his wife die. In either case, the chief concern to the preconventional thinker is what would happen to Heinz as a result of his choice.

Conventional thinking about moral issues focuses not so much on tangible rewards and punishments as on how an individual's behavior will be judged by others. In conventional moral reasoning, special importance is given to the roles people are expected to play and to society's rules, institutions, and conventions. Individuals behave properly because in so doing, they receive the approval of others and help to maintain the social order. The correctness of society's rules is not questioned, however; individuals do their duty by upholding and respecting the rules that people are supposed to follow. A conventional thinker might say that Heinz should not have stolen the drug because stealing is against the law. But another might counter that Heinz was right to steal the drug because it is what a good husband is expected to do. According to most studies of moral reasoning, the majority of adolescents and adults think primarily in conventional terms: They evaluate moral decisions in terms of a set of socially accepted rules that people are supposed to abide by.

Postconventional reasoning is relatively rare. At this level of reasoning, society's rules and conventions are seen as relative and subjective rather than as absolute and definitive. Individuals may have a moral duty to abide by society's standards for behavior—but only insofar as those standards support and serve moral ends. Occasions arise in which conventions ought to be questioned and when more important principles—such as justice, fairness, or the sanctity of human life—take precedence over established social norms. For instance, a postconventional response might be that Heinz should not have stolen the drug because in doing so he violated an implicit agreement among members of society—an agreement that gives each person the freedom to pursue his or her livelihood. However, another principled thinker might respond that Heinz was right to steal the drug because someone's life was at stake and because preserving human life is more important than respecting individual freedoms. Whereas conventional thinking is oriented toward society's rules, postconventional thinking is founded on more broadly based, abstract moral principles. For this reason, the development of postconventional reasoning is especially relevant to the discussion of cognitive autonomy.

Moral reasoning becomes more principled over the course of childhood and adolescence (Eisenberg et al., 2009). Preconventional reasoning dominates the responses of children; conventional responses begin to appear during preadolescence and continue into middle adolescence; and postconventional reasoning does not appear until late adolescence, if at all. Movement into higher stages of moral reasoning occurs when children

preconventional moral reasoning
The first level of moral reasoning, which is typical of children and is characterized by reasoning that is based on rewards and punishments associated with different courses of action.

conventional moral reasoning
The second level of moral development, which occurs during late childhood and early adolescence and is characterized by reasoning that is based on the rules and conventions of society.

postconventional moral reasoning
The level of moral reasoning during which society's rules and conventions are seen as relative and subjective rather than as authoritative; also called principled moral reasoning.

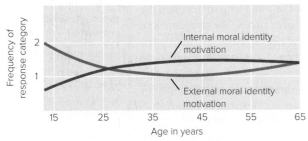

Figure 9.5 During adolescence, individuals increasingly define their moral identity in terms of how they see themselves (an internal motivation), rather than on how they want others to see them (an external motivation). (Krettenauer & Victor, 2017)

are developmentally "ready"—when their reasoning is predominantly at one stage but partially at the next higher one—and when they are exposed to the more advanced type of reasoning by other people, such as parents or peers (Eisenberg et al., 2009). The development of moral reasoning tends to follow a pattern in which individuals move from periods of consolidation (in which their reasoning is consistently at a particular stage of development), into periods of transition (in which there is more variability in their stages of reasoning), into new periods of consolidation (in which their reasoning is consistent but at a higher stage than during the previous period of consolidation) (Walker, Gustafson, & Hennig, 2001). These gains in moral reasoning are accompanied by changes in brain systems that permit us to behave less selfishly (Crone, 2013).

Although not all individuals enter a stage of consistent postconventional thinking during adolescence, many begin to place greater emphasis on abstract values and moral principles and to look inward (being moral is important because it reflects the sort of person you want to be), rather than outward (being moral is important because of what others will think of you), to define their moral identity (Krettenauer & Victor, 2017) (see Figure 9.5). Moreover, if individuals of different ages are presented with other peoples' moral arguments, older individuals are more often persuaded by justifications that are more advanced.

Thus, the appeal of postconventional moral reasoning increases over the course of adolescence, whereas the appeals of preconventional and of conventional reasoning both decline. The attractiveness of postconventional thinking appears to increase both with age and with schooling; most adults reach a plateau in moral reasoning after completing their formal education. Although for many years psychologists debated whether there were sex differences in the way that individuals approach moral problems and many popular books were based on the idea that men and women think differently about ethical issues, studies have not found this to be true (Smetana & Villalobos, 2009).

Moral Reasoning and Moral Behavior   It is one thing to reason about hypothetical moral problems in an advanced way; it is quite another to behave consistently with one's reasoning. After all, it is common for people to say one thing (cheating on a test is immoral) but do another (sneak a peek at a classmate's test when running out of time during an exam).

Although individuals do not always behave in ways that are absolutely consistent with their moral reasoning, on average, people who reason at higher stages are more ethical in their day-to-day behavior (Eisenberg et al., 2009). Adolescents who are capable of reasoning at higher stages are less likely to commit antisocial acts, less likely to cheat, and less likely to bow to the pressures of others, as well as be more tolerant of diversity, more likely to engage in political protests, more likely to volunteer their time, and more likely to assist others in need of help. They are also more likely to be influential over their friends in group decisions about moral problems (Gummerum et al., 2008). Conversely, those who reason at lower stages of moral thought are more aggressive, delinquent, accepting of violence, and accepting of others' misbehavior (Eisenberg et al., 2009).

Most of us have found ourselves in situations in which we behaved less morally than we would have liked to, often because of circumstances. For example, you probably realize in the abstract that complying with highway speed limits is important because such limits prevent accidents, and you likely obey these limits most of the time. But you may have found yourself in a situation in which you weighed your need to get somewhere in a hurry (maybe you were late for a job interview) against your belief in the importance of obeying speeding laws, and you decided that in this instance, you would knowingly behave in a way inconsistent with your belief.

The ways in which individuals think about moral dilemmas change during adolescence. Fertnig/Getty Images

The correlation between adolescents' moral reasoning and their moral behavior is especially likely to break down when they define issues as personal choices rather than ethical dilemmas (e.g., when using drugs is seen as a personal matter rather than a moral issue). This helps explain why adolescents' moral reasoning and risk taking are unrelated; people can be very advanced in their reasoning but still engage in risky behavior (Eisenberg et al., 2009). If people consider various risky behaviors (e.g., experimenting with drugs or having unprotected sex) to be personal decisions rather than ethical ones, their moral reasoning will be relatively unimportant in predicting how they will act.

It is not clear, however, whether viewing risk taking as a personal choice is likely to lead to more risk taking or whether individuals who've engaged in a risky activity are likely to redefine the issue as a personal rather than moral one as a way of justifying their behavior after the fact. In either case, this suggests that interventions designed to stimulate moral reasoning will have little impact on adolescents' risk taking if they fail to convince adolescents that the behavior in question involves a moral choice and not just a personal one. This is also why delinquency and aggression are more common among adolescents who score higher on measures of **moral disengagement** (the tendency to rationalize immoral behavior as legitimate, as when one justifies stealing from someone as a way of retaliating) (Bao et al., 2015).

Prosocial Reasoning, Prosocial Behavior, and Volunteerism

Although most research on the development of morality has focused on what adolescents do under circumstances in which a law might be broken or a rule violated, researchers have also studied reasoning and behavior in prosocial situations. In general, the ways in which individuals think about prosocial phenomena, such as honesty or kindness, become more sophisticated during late adolescence, just like their moral reasoning (Morris, Eisenberg, & Houltberg, 2011). Over the course of adolescence, individuals come to devalue prosocial acts that are done for self-serving reasons (to receive a reward, return a favor, or improve their image) and value those that are done out of genuine empathy, a pattern that has been observed across a variety of cultures (Eisenberg et al., 2009). During late adolescence, prosocial reasoning continues to become more advanced, leveling off sometime in the early 20s (Eisenberg et al., 2005). Some research connects these changes in reasoning to developments in regions of the brain that govern our ability to look at things from other people's perspectives (Crone, 2013). During adolescence, individuals become more likely to incorporate insights about their helpful behavior into their views of themselves, as this passage from an interview with a 16-year-old girl, about her helping a classmate, illustrates:

> *She has depression problems and she didn't have any friends in seventh grade—well she had friends but then they all like abandoned her or whatever. And I befriended her and . . . um she, she said, she had thoughts of suicide and she was cutting herself and all this crazy stuff and she was like "And now I don't think I would be here if it wasn't for you befriending me back then." . . . And . . . she told me that I was like a really good example to her and stuff.* (Recchia et al., 2015, p. 874)

making the personal connection

Did you grow up in a family that engaged in the sorts of discussions thought to promote more advanced levels of moral reasoning? What are some examples of the ways in which your family did (or did not) do this?

Generally, the same type of parenting that facilitates the growth of healthy emotional autonomy also contributes to the development of moral and prosocial reasoning. Adolescents whose parents engage them in discussion, elicit their point of view, and practice authoritative parenting display more advanced moral reasoning and prosocial behavior than their peers (Carlo et al., 2018; Recchia et al., 2015). It appears that authoritative parenting makes adolescents more likely to feel sympathy toward others, which in turn prompts prosocial behavior (Eisenberg, VanSchyndel, & Hofer, 2015; Shen, Carlo, & Knight, 2013). Growing up in a home that stresses familism (the importance of fulfilling one's obligations to the family) also leads adolescents to become more prosocial toward others (Knight, 2015). In addition, positive parenting helps facilitate the development of empathy and emotion regulation, both of which contribute to prosocial development (Padilla-Walker & Christensen, 2011; Wray-Lake & Flanagan, 2012).

Prosocial Reasoning and Prosocial Behavior

Adolescents who show more advanced prosocial reasoning and who place a high value on prosocial behavior behave in ways that are consistent with this (Hardy, Carlo, & Roesch, 2010). Adolescents who have volunteered considerable amounts of time in service activities score higher on measures of moral reasoning than their peers, are more committed to the betterment of society, and, as children, were made aware of the suffering of those who are less fortunate (Matsuba & Walker, 2005). Individuals who score high on measures of prosocial moral reasoning are more sympathetic and empathic (Carlo, Padilla-Walker, & Nielson, 2015; Van der Graaff et al., 2018), engage in more prosocial behavior (Eisenberg, Zhou, & Koller, 2001), and are less

moral disengagement
Rationalizing immoral behavior as legitimate, as a way of justifying one's own bad acts.

Figure 9.6 During middle adolescence, there is a marked decline in the extent to which people value being socially responsible, such as caring about one's school or community. (Wray-Lake, Syvertsen, & Flanagan, 2016)

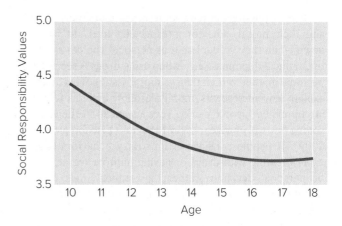

likely to behave violently after having witnessed violence themselves (Brookmeyer, Henrich, & Schwab-Stone, 2005). In general, adolescent girls score higher on measures of prosocial moral reasoning than do boys, as do both males and females who are relatively more feminine, consistent with the notion that helpfulness is a trait associated more with femininity than masculinity (Morris, Eisenberg, & Houltberg, 2011).

Although prosocial *reasoning* becomes more advanced over the course of adolescence, changes in prosocial *behavior* during adolescence are not as consistent. Some researchers have suggested that how adolescents *think* about behaving prosocially is less important than how they *feel* when they see others in need of help, and they have argued that fostering prosocial behavior may be more effectively done by encouraging the development of empathy rather than more advanced moral reasoning (Van der Graff et al., 2018). Encouraging the development of **emotional intelligence** may also be helpful. Given recent increases in immigration, for example, it is important to know that adolescents who are more empathic and skilled at perspective-taking are less likely to develop anti-immigrant attitudes (Miklikowska, 2018).

As a result, while some studies find that individuals become more empathic, sympathetic, and helpful as they move into and through adolescence (Padilla-Walker, Carlo, & Memmott-Elison, 2017), but many do not (Eisenberg et al., 2009). One reason for this inconsistency is that researchers have defined and measured prosocial behavior in many different ways, including helping, sharing, comforting, volunteering, and even etiquette (El Mallah, 2020). Being willing to comfort someone who needs it, volunteering for a community organization, and displaying good manners are entirely different things, but all have been used as measures of "prosocial" activities.

emotional intelligence The ability of individuals to accurately recognize and label their own emotions and those of others.

civic engagement Involvement in political and community affairs, as reflected in knowledge about politics and current affairs, participation in conventional and alternative political activities, and engaging in community service.

In fact, some studies even have found that teenagers become *less* helpful toward others as they get older and, especially during middle school, are markedly less likely to say that it is important to them to "help those who are less fortunate," "help my society," "help people in my community," "serve my country," "help other students in school," or "make new students feel welcome" (Wray-Lake, Syvertsen, & Flanagan, 2016) (see Figure 9.6). (This is consistent with other observations that early adolescence appears to be the height of meanness, laziness, and close-mindedness, at least in studies of American teens; Soto & Tackett, 2015). In experiments in which individuals are given money and must choose between keeping it all for themselves or giving half to an anonymous peer, older teenagers are *less* likely to share things equitably (Meuwese et al., 2015; van de Groep et al., 2020).

More consistent are research findings indicating that prosocial behavior is fairly stable with age (prosocial children grow up to be prosocial teenagers) and across different contexts (adolescents who are helpful to classmates in school are more likely to be helpful to strangers in the mall) (Padilla-Walker, Carlo, & Memmott-Elison, 2017). Also, girls are generally more caring and prosocial than boys, perhaps because parents emphasize prosocial development more in raising daughters than sons (Eisenberg et al., 2009). Encouraging adolescents to spend time thinking about what's important to them seems to increase their tendency to act prosocially (Thomaes et al., 2012). And having prosocial friends and classmates, as well as higher-quality friendships, leads to more prosocial behavior (Busching & Krahé, 2020; Stotsky, Bowker, & Etkin, 2020; Van Hoorn, Van Dijk, Meuwese, et al., 2016). Whereas children's prosocial behavior is influenced by the adult role models they have, by early adolescence, seeing peers behave prosocially is a more important influence (Ruggeri, et al., 2018).

Civic Engagement One of the most obvious ways in which adolescents can demonstrate prosocial behavior is through various types of civic engagement (Metzger, Ferris, & Oosterhoff, 2019). **Civic engagement** is a broad term for a category of activities that reflect involvement in political and community affairs, including staying knowledgeable about politics and current affairs, participating in conventional political activities (e.g., contacting a political representative about an issue, campaigning for a candidate, or voting in an election), participating in alternative political activities (e.g., being part of a demonstration or a boycott), and engaging in community service.

Because the minimum age for voting in most countries is 18 or older, little research has been conducted on adolescents' involvement in political activities, although a number of surveys have been conducted to measure students' knowledge and attitudes on a range of political issues. Most of these studies have found that only a small proportion of young people are politically engaged, not just in the United States but around the world. Nor does this change once people become old enough to vote. In the United States, election turnouts continue to be lower among young people than among adults, and, with the exception of a temporary spark in interest following major political and world events (such as the horrific 2018 school shooting in Parkland, Florida), adolescents' interest in and knowledge of political issues are meager (Sherrod & Lauckhardt, 2009).

Experts attribute this apathy in part to the widespread absence of civics education in American high schools, the absence of opportunities to become politically active in their communities, and the tendency of adolescents to focus their civic energies on organizations that they are more directly involved with, such as their schools, religious institutions, and extracurricular clubs, rather than local politics (Wray-Lake, 2019). Some writers, like me, believe that adolescents' participation in elections might be increased by lowering the voting age to 16 so that it becomes a habit at a time when it is easy to do (Steinberg, 2018). Voting at 18 may be more difficult because people this age often live out of the state in which they are registered.

Most research on civic engagement in adolescence has focused on community service. Volunteering in community service activities, sometimes referred to as **service learning,** is more common in the United States than in most other countries. Researchers have been interested in both the antecedents of volunteering (what leads adolescents to become involved in volunteer activities) and its consequences (how adolescents are affected by volunteering). Apart from attending a school in which some sort of community service is required, the best predictors of volunteerism in adolescence are being actively involved in religion (most probably because many volunteer activities are organized through religious institutions) and having parents who are active as volunteers in the community (Oosterhoff & Metzger, 2016; Rossi et al., 2016). Volunteers also tend to be female, more socially mature, more extraverted, and more altruistic (Eisenberg et al., 2009).

Engaging in community service leads to short-term gains in social responsibility, increases in the importance individuals place on helping others, and increased commitment to tolerance, equal opportunity, and cultural diversity.
Dmytro Zinkevych/Shutterstock

Many experts have noted that adolescents have a strong need to contribute to their communities and that doing so helps young people find purpose in their lives; simply put, adolescents need to feel that they matter to other people and to the community (Schmidt et al., 2020). Numerous writers have argued that involvement in local organizations, especially when the tasks assigned to adolescents are meaningful, can have a positive impact on the development of autonomy, identity, prosocial attitudes, and social competence. Unfortunately, society does not provide enough opportunities for teenagers to contribute to the well-being others, and even when such opportunities exist, they vary considerably in their quality (Fuligni, 2019).

Studies of volunteering indicate that engaging in community service leads to short-term gains in mental health and social responsibility; increases in the importance individuals place on helping others; and increased commitment to tolerance, equal opportunity, and cultural diversity (Ballard, Hoyt, & Pachuki, 2019; Eisenberg et al., 2009; Flanagan et al., 2015). There also is some evidence that volunteering in adolescence predicts volunteering in adulthood (Chan, Ou, & Reynolds, 2014). The extent to which these effects persist over time depends, in part, on how long the volunteer activity lasts; the shorter the activity, the more short-lived the effects (Horn, 2012).

Many school districts require community service of all students, a graduation requirement that has prompted both praise and criticism. Proponents argue that service activities help develop concern for the community and facilitate adolescents' prosocial

service learning
The process of learning through involvement in community service.

development. Opponents counter that forcing adolescents to do something they don't want to do will make them even *more* negative about community service and less likely to volunteer at later ages. Some worry that turning an activity that adolescents may want to do into a school requirement makes the activity less intrinsically rewarding.

Several studies have compared students who have volunteered for community service with those who have had it forced on them. It does not seem that requiring community service makes students develop negative attitudes about volunteering, regardless of whether they had been volunteers previously. But the evidence is mixed with regard to whether the effects of volunteering are different between adolescents who willingly participate and those who do it only because it is a requirement. Some studies find that participating in community service activities has positive effects regardless of whether the participation is voluntary or required (Hart et al., 2007; J. Schmidt, Shumow, & Kackar, 2007), but others do not (Horn, 2012), and still others find that participation has little effect regardless of whether it is mandatory or optional (Henderson et al., 2007).

One reason for these discrepancies is that students' volunteer experiences vary considerably in quality, ranging from ones that engage adolescents in helping others directly to those that occupy them in tedious clerical work (Ferreira, Azevedo, & Menezes, 2012; Henderson, Pancer, & Brown, 2014). Another is that community service only may be beneficial if adolescents are required to reflect on their experience, perhaps in classes that encourage this (van Goethem, van Hoof, Orobio de Castro, et al., 2014). One important difference between students who are forced into community service and those who volunteer is that volunteers are more likely to continue their service work after graduation. In other words, whatever the positive effects of participation, they are not enough to turn adolescents who aren't especially interested in community work into adults who are (Planty, Bozick, & Regnier, 2006). The potential benefits to the *recipients* of the adolescents' service (the children they tutor, the elderly they visit, or residents of the neighborhoods whose parks they clean up) may be greater than those to the volunteers.

Political Thinking During Adolescence

Less is known about the development of political thinking during adolescence than about moral development, but the way adolescents think about politics becomes more principled, more abstract, and more independent during the adolescent years, just as moral reasoning does. This pattern is linked both to the general cognitive developments of adolescence and to the growth of specific expertise, as the adolescent is exposed to more political information and ideas (Flanagan, 2004).

Changes in Political Thinking Political thinking changes during adolescence in several important ways (Flanagan, 2004). First, it becomes more abstract. In response to the question "What is the purpose of laws?" for example, 12- and 13-year-olds are likely to reply with concrete answers: "So people don't kill or steal," "So people don't get hurt," and so on. Older adolescents are likely to respond with more abstract and more general statements: "To ensure safety and enforce the government" or "They are basically guidelines for people. I mean, like this is wrong and this is right and to help them understand" (Adelson, 1972, p. 108).

Individuals' understanding of various rights—for example, their beliefs about whether children and adolescents have the right to have some control over their lives—also becomes more abstract with age (Ruck, Abramovitch, & Keating, 1998). With age, individuals are more likely to judge the appropriateness of having certain rights (e.g., freedom of speech) in light of characteristics of the individual (e.g., whether the individual is mature enough to act responsibly) and the context within which the right is expressed (e.g., whether the authority who is regulating speech is a parent or a government official) (Tenenbaum & Ruck, 2012). There is strong support among adolescents for fundamental democratic principles such as representation and majority rule, even in countries whose governments do not operate on these principles (Helwig et al., 2007; Smetana & Villalobos, 2009).

Second, political thinking during adolescence becomes less authoritarian and less rigid (Flanagan & Galay, 1995). Young adolescents are inclined toward obedience, authority, and an uncritical, trusting, and acquiescent stance toward government. For example, when asked what might be done in response to a law that is not working out as planned, an older teenager may suggest that the law needs to be reexamined and perhaps amended. A young adolescent, in contrast, will "propose that it be enforced more rigorously." Unlike older adolescents, younger adolescents are "more likely to favor one-man rule as [opposed to] representative democracy"; show "little sensitivity to individual or minority rights"; and be "indifferent to the claims of personal freedom" (Adelson, 1972, p. 108).

Living under the rule of a young adolescent would likely be unpleasant. A few years ago, I was a guest lecturer in a local 7th-grade social studies class, where we were discussing juvenile justice. When I presented the students with hypothetical situations about a crime committed by a young teenager, their suggestions for how the adolescent should be punished were far more harsh than those allowed under the law.

Finally, during late adolescence, people often develop a roughly coherent and consistent set of attitudes—a sort of ideology—that does not appear before this age and that is based on a set of overarching principles. These principles may concern a wide range of issues, including civil liberties, freedom of speech, and social equality (Flanagan & Galay, 1995; Helwig, 1995).

As is the case among adults, adolescents' views about political matters—the causes of unemployment, poverty, or homelessness, for example—are strongly linked to their social upbringing (Barreiro, Arsenio, & Wainryb, 2019). Adolescents from higher social classes tend to attribute unemployment, poverty, and homelessness to societal factors ("People are poor because not everyone receives the same skills or training and encouragement when they are young"), whereas adolescents from lower-class backgrounds are more likely to attribute these problems to individual factors ("People are poor because they are lazy and don't want to work hard"). As a consequence, adolescents from higher-socioeconomic-status (SES) backgrounds tend to want society to distribute resources on the basis of need, whereas those from lower-SES backgrounds favor distributing resources on the basis of merit (Kornbluh, Pykett, & Flanagan, 2019).

Socioeconomic differences in explanations of why some people are wealthy are not as striking, but they follow a similar pattern, with adolescents from lower-class backgrounds more likely to favor individual explanations ("People are rich because they stayed in school") than societal ones ("Some people are rich because they inherited money or a big business") (Flanagan et al., 2014). There also predictable socioeconomic differences in the extent to which U.S. adolescents perceive American society to be inequitable or egalitarian, with those from poorer backgrounds more likely to endorse the former and those from wealthier ones more likely to endorse the latter (Flanagan & Kornbluh, 2019) (see Figure 9.7).

Shifts in all three of these directions—increasing abstraction, decreasing authoritarianism, and increasing use of principles—are similar to the shifts observed in studies of moral development and consistent with the idea that cognitive autonomy emerges during late adolescence. The movement away from authoritarianism, obedience, and unquestioning acceptance of the rulings of authority indicates that an important psychological concern for older adolescents involves questioning the values and beliefs emanating from parents and other authority figures as they begin to establish their own priorities.

Political Thinking and Political Behavior   As is the case with moral development, there often are gaps between adolescents' political thinking in hypothetical situations and their actual attitudes and behavior. The most important influence on the political behavior of young people tends to be the experiences they've had growing up, such as having political discussions with parents and friends, discussing politics in classes, and being exposed to the news (Kim & Stattin, 2019; Quintelier, 2015). There is also evidence that adolescents who are victimized frequently expressed more discontent with government and are more likely to become politically

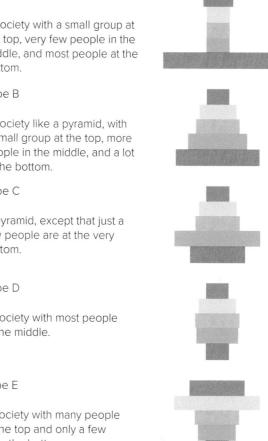

Type A

A society with a small group at the top, very few people in the middle, and most people at the bottom.

Type B

A society like a pyramid, with a small group at the top, more people in the middle, and a lot at the bottom.

Type C

A pyramid, except that just a few people are at the very bottom.

Type D

A society with most people in the middle.

Type E

A society with many people at the top and only a few near the bottom.

Figure 9.7   These images were used to assess how adolescents view American society. Those from poorer families were more likely to see society's stratification as closer to Type A, whereas those from wealthier backgrounds were more likely to see America as closer to Type E. (Flanagan & Kornbluh, 2019)

engaged (Oosterhoff et al., 2018). Minority adolescents, especially those living in environments in which there are limited economic opportunities, tend to be more cynical about politics than their white counterparts. Here are two comments from a recent study of ethnic minority youth living in Chicago:

> *The problems in the world that upset me are all the police brutality and the innocent killing [sic] of teen black males. These problems bother me because I feel it's unfair that we constantly fight for justice but we get nowhere.* (Roy et al., 2019, p. 554)
>
> *The problem . . . that I am most upset about is how people in urban and poverty filled neighborhoods don't have the same opportunities as someone in a "wealthy" neighborhood. This upsets me because people in poverty are judged based on the way that they have to survive based on limited opportunities.* (Roy et al., 2019, p. 554)

Although today's adolescents in the United States on average tend to lean Democratic, young people's

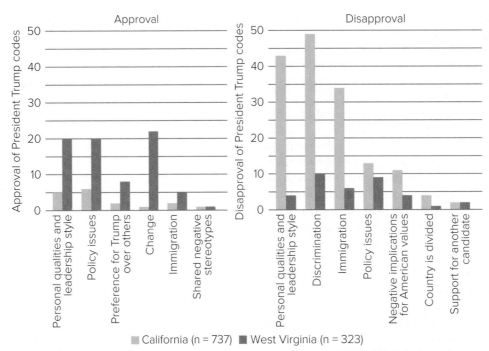

Figure 9.8   High school students' views of President Trump in California and West Virginia, based on a survey shortly after he was inaugurated. (Metzger et al., 2020)

political views usually mirror those of the adults in their lives. For example, in a survey of high school students conducted just after President Donald Trump's inauguration in 2017, there were significant differences between the views held by students in California (a famously liberal state, where Trump received 33% of the vote) and West Virginia (a famously conservative state, where Trump received 69% of the vote) (Metzger et al., 2020) (see Figure 9.8).

Adolescents' political concerns also change with the times. It is too soon to know how the Black Lives Matter movement and the economic havoc wrought by the COVID-19 pandemic have affected teenagers' attitudes about race relations and the economy, but it is likely that concerns about social justice and financial insecurity increased during recent years, as did concerns about climate change, as exemplified by the work of Greta Thunberg, who garnered international attention at the age of 15 for speaking out about adults' reluctance to address the problem (Sanson, Van Hoorn, & Burke, 2019). During the early 1990s, when racial tensions and crime were both on the rise, adolescents' concerns about race relations and violence increased; similarly, following the Great Recession of 2008, teenagers understandably were more worried about economic problems (Oosterhoff et al., 2019). In general, adolescent girls tend to be more concerned than boys about most social issues, such as hunger and poverty, perhaps because girls generally are more empathic and sensitive to the needs of others. Surprisingly, teenagers from different socioeconomic groups did not differ much in their priorities.

Environmental activist Greta Thunberg, then 17 years old, meets with the president of the European Commission in Belgium at the commission's weekly meeting. Thierry Monasse/Getty Images

Religious Beliefs During Adolescence

Despite the fact that religion plays an important role in the lives of many adolescents, the development of religious beliefs has been very much neglected by social scientists (Burg, Mayers, & Miller, 2011; Clardy & King, 2011).

Religious beliefs, like moral and political beliefs, become more abstract, more principled, and more independent during adolescence. Beliefs become more

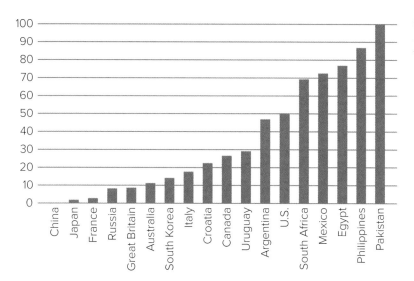

Figure 9.9 The proportion of adolescents from different countries who report that God is very important in their life. (Based on Clardy & King, 2011)

oriented toward spiritual and ideological matters and less oriented toward rituals, practices, and the strict observance of religious customs. Although more than 90% of all American adolescents pray and 95% believe in God, a substantial proportion of young people say that organized religion does not play a very important role in their lives (Wallace et al., 2003). Compared with children, adolescents place more emphasis on the internal aspects of religious commitment (such as what an individual believes) and less on the external manifestations (such as whether an individual goes to church) (Lopez, Huynh, & Fuligni, 2011). Adolescence is an important time for "spiritual questioning, doubting, and creating" (King & Roeser, 2009, p. 447). There are enormous differences around the world in the extent to which adolescents say that God is important in their life (see Figure 9.9).

the underlying growth of cognitive abilities and the shift from concrete to abstract reasoning that characterizes the adolescent transition. This fundamental shift in cognitive ability affects adolescents' thinking across a wide variety of topics.

During adolescence, religious beliefs become more oriented toward spiritual and ideological matters and less oriented toward rituals, practices, and the strict observance of religious customs. Mansoreh/Shutterstock

making the cultural connection

As shown in Figure 9.9, there is wide cultural variability around the world in the significance of religion in adolescents' lives. To what extent do you think this affects the nature of adolescence more generally? Is the experience of adolescence as a developmental period likely to be different for young people who grow up in a context where religion is important compared to those who grow up in one where it plays less of a role?

During late adolescence, individuals enter into a stage in which they begin to form a system of personal religious beliefs, rather than relying solely on the teachings of their parents (King & Roeser, 2009), which is similar to the transition to principled moral reasoning or the development of a coherent political ideology. Developments in all three domains—moral, political, and religious—reflect

religiosity
The degree to which one engages in religious practices, such as attending services.

spirituality
The degree to which one places importance on the quest for answers to questions about God and the meaning of life.

Patterns of Religious Involvement Religious development has two main components: **religiosity** (the religious practices one engages in) and **spirituality** (one's personal quest for answers to questions about God and the meaning of life) (King, Ramos, & Clardy, 2013). Although both can be part of the process of psychosocial development, religiosity may be more important for identity development, since it involves identification with a particular religious group and its practices and beliefs (not unlike identifying oneself with a particular ethnic group), whereas spirituality may be more closely linked to the development of cognitive autonomy, since it involves the development of self-awareness and of a particular personal meaning system and set of values. For most religious adolescents, religiosity and spirituality are deeply interconnected (French et al., 2008). But there are substantial numbers of adolescents who practice religion without giving much thought to its spiritual aspects (e.g., adolescents who attend religious services each week or celebrate religious holidays either because their parents expect them to or because they enjoy the familiarity and routine of regular observance), as well as many who devote a great deal of time and energy to thinking about spiritual matters but don't identify with an organized religion or practice customary religious rituals (Vasilenko & Espinosa-Hernández, 2019).

The stated importance of religion—and especially religiosity—declines during adolescence (Hardy et al., 2020) (see Figure 9.10), especially during the transition from adolescence to adulthood (Chan, Tsai, & Fuligini, 2015). Compared with older adolescents, younger ones are more likely to attend church regularly and to state that religion is important to them (Hardie, Pearce, & Denton, 2016). The early years of college are a time when many individuals reexamine and reevaluate the beliefs and values they grew up with. For some, this involves a decline in regular participation in organized religious activities (perhaps because the college environment doesn't encourage this)

but an increase in spirituality and religious faith (Lefkowitz, 2005). The religious context of the college environment plays an important role, though. Not surprisingly, religious commitment often becomes stronger among students who attend a college with a religious orientation (Barry & Nelson, 2005).

Although some parents interpret the adolescent decline in religiosity as indicating rebellion against the family's values, the development of religious thinking during late adolescence is better understood as part of the overall development of cognitive autonomy. As adolescents develop a stronger sense of independence, they may leave behind the unquestioning conventionality of their younger years as a first step toward finding a truly personal faith. Adolescents who continue to comply with their parents' religious beliefs without ever questioning them may actually be showing signs of immature conformity or identity foreclosure, not spiritual maturity.

Individual Differences in Religiosity Although individuals usually become less involved in formal religion during adolescence, adolescents differ in their degree of religiosity (Good, Willoughby, & Busseri, 2011). According to U.S. surveys, about 85% of American adolescents report an affiliation with a religious group; of the remaining 15%, about 10% report not being religious, 3% say they are uncertain, and another 3% describe themselves as atheist or agnostic (King, Ramos, & Clardy, 2013).

About half of all American adolescents say that formal religious participation is important in their life (King & Roeser, 2009). Approximately one-third report weekly attendance at religious services, one-sixth attend once or twice per month, and about 45% rarely or never attend services; regular attendance at religious services drops over the course of high school. Adolescent religious attendance declined gradually during the 1980s and 1990s but has changed very little since then.

About half of U.S. adolescents identify themselves as Protestant (and close to half of Protestants identify themselves as conservative Christians) and about one-fifth as Catholic. Adolescent girls are slightly more likely to be religious than adolescent boys (this sex difference is found among adults, too). In general, Black and Latinx adolescents are more religious than youth from other ethnic backgrounds, as are adolescents who live in the South or Midwest (King & Roeser, 2009). Rates of adolescents' religious participation are considerably higher in the United States than other parts of the world. In contrast to the 41.9% of American youth who participate in an organization sponsored by a religious group, the figures are 27.6% in Southern Europe, 19.9% in Asia/Pacific regions, 14.4% in Western Europe, 13.1% in Northern Europe, and 10.3% in Eastern Europe (King, Ramos, & Clardy, 2013).

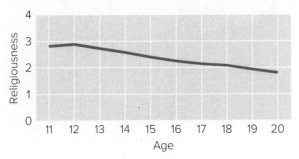

Figure 9.10   Individuals become less religious over the course of adolescence. (Hardy et al., 2020)

The Impact of Religious Involvement on Development
Religious adolescents are better adjusted and less

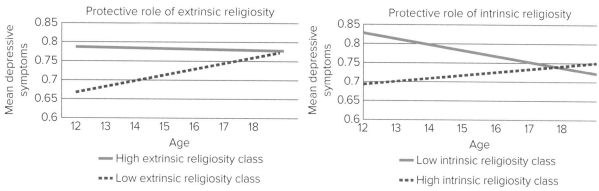

Figure 9.11 A study of urban Black youth found that the protective roles of both extrinsic (e.g., attending church services) and intrinsic (e.g., praying) religious involvement against the negative effects of stress weaken as adolescents get older. (Lee & Neblett, 2019)

depressed than other adolescents, less likely to have premarital sex, less likely to use drugs, and less likely to engage in delinquency (Davis & Kiang, 2016; Hardy et al., 2019; Taggart et al., 2019; Valisenko & Espinosa-Hernández, 2019). Some of the apparent beneficial effects of religious involvement are because adolescents who are involved in religion often have other positive influences in their life that promote positive development and prevent problem behavior, such as supportive parents, prosocial peers, or adults outside the immediate family who care about them (Hardy et al., 2019).

But being religious in and of itself improves self-regulation, deters problem behavior, and delays the onset of sexual activity (Good & Willoughby, 2014; Hardy et al., 2020; Holmes et al., 2019). Religious involvement may play an especially important role in buffering inner-city Black adolescents against the harmful effects of neighborhood disorganization and exposure to violence (Gooden & McMahon, 2016; Hope et al., 2019), and there is evidence that religious involvement may help protect against the adverse effects of family conflict, parental substance abuse, and other sources of stress (Debnam et al., 2018; Peviani et al., 2020), although the protective roles of different types of religious involvement, such as attending church services or praying, decline as adolescents grow older (Lee & Neblett, 2019) (see Figure 9.11). Nevertheless, religious involvement

appears to have an especially positive influence on the educational aspirations and future plans of low-SES inner-city youth (Lee & Pearce, 2019; Wright, Yendork, & Kliewer, 2018).

Some clues to the reasons that religious involvement may protect against involvement in problem behavior come from the finding that religiosity, rather than spirituality, is the stronger predictor of staying out of trouble (Good & Willoughby, 2014; Jang & Franzen, 2013; Kim-Spoon, Longo, & Holmes, 2015). Moreover, it does not appear to be attending religious services that matters; it is being a part of a community of individuals who share similar values and engage in similar activities (Hardy et al., 2019). As one adolescent put it:

I notice that my religious friends, they're more positive people. You know, they doing school and they not involved in a lot of other stuff. They keep theirselves (sic) *busy. They usually never have to worry about, I mean, they never think about using drugs or getting pregnant and all that—as opposed to my friends who are not so religious.* (Lee & Pearce, 2019, p. 375).

Seen in this light, the connection between religious participation and lower problem behavior is not surprising since some of the strongest predictors of adolescents' involvement in sex, drugs, and delinquency are the behavior and attitudes of their peers and the development of strong self-regulation.

10 Intimacy

Intimacy as an Adolescent Issue
    Puberty and the Development of Intimacy
    Cognitive Change and the Development
        of Intimacy
    Changes in Social Roles and the Development
        of Intimacy

Theoretical Perspectives on Adolescent Intimacy
    Sullivan's Theory of Interpersonal Development
    Interpersonal Development During Adolescence
    Attachment Theory

The Development of Intimacy in Adolescence
    Changes in the Nature of Friendship

Changes in the Display of Intimacy
Does Using Social Media Hurt the
    Development of Intimacy?
Sex Differences in Intimacy
Changes in the Targets of Intimacy
Friendships with the Other Sex

Dating and Romantic Relationships
    Dating and the Development of Intimacy
    The Development of Dating Relationships
    The Impact of Dating on Adolescent
        Development

Intimacy and Psychosocial Development

Westend61/Getty Images

One of the most remarkable things about adolescence is the way close relationships change during these years. Think about the friendships you had as a child and compare them with those you had as a teenager. Think about the boyfriends or girlfriends that children have and the boyfriends or girlfriends adolescents have. And think about relationships between parents and their children and about how these relationships change during adolescence. In all three cases, adolescents' relationships are closer, more personal, more involved, and more emotionally charged than children's. During adolescence, in short, relationships become more intimate.

To begin with, let's draw a distinction between intimacy and sexuality. The concept of intimacy—at least as it is used in the study of adolescence—does not have a sexual or physical connotation. Rather, an intimate relationship is an emotional attachment between two people that is characterized by concern for each other's well-being; a willingness to disclose private, and occasionally sensitive, topics; and a sharing of common interests and activities. (An easy way to remember this is "caring," "daring," and "sharing.") Two individuals can have an intimate relationship without having a sexual one. And, by the same token, two people can have a sexual relationship without being especially intimate.

Although the development of intimacy during adolescence is almost always studied in relation to friendships and romantic relationships with peers, adolescents' intimate relationships aren't limited to other teenagers. Parents often have intimate relationships with their adolescent children, especially once the children have reached a sufficient level of maturity. Siblings, even with many years between them, are often close confidants. Sometimes, young people form intimate relationships with adults who are not in their immediate family, such as teachers or mentors.

Obviously, one of the central issues in the study of intimacy during adolescence is the onset of dating. Although the young person's initiation into romantic relationships is undoubtedly important, it is not the only noteworthy change that occurs in close relationships during adolescence. Adolescence is also an important time for changes in what individuals look for in friends, in their capacity to be intimate with friends of both sexes, and in the way they express closeness to others.

Intimacy as an Adolescent Issue

Intimacy is an important concern throughout most of the life span. During childhood, not having friends is associated with a wide range of psychological and social problems (Rubin, Bukowski, & Parker, 2006). And during adulthood, having at least one intimate friendship is beneficial to an individual's health: People who have others to turn to for emotional support are less likely to suffer from psychological and physical disorders (Myers, Lindenthal, & Pepper, 1975). Without question, close relationships are extremely important to people of all ages. Why, then, is the development of intimacy especially important during adolescence?

One reason is that it is not until adolescence that truly intimate relationships—relationships characterized by openness, honesty, self-disclosure, and trust—emerge. Children certainly have important friendships, but their relationships are different from those formed during adolescence. Children's friendships are very concrete, built around games and shared activities. To children, friends are people who like to do the same things that they themselves like. But teenagers' close friendships are more likely to have a strong emotional foundation. They are built on the sorts of bonds that form between people who care about and know and understand each other in a special way (Kobak & Madsen, 2011).

Another reason for the importance of intimacy during adolescence concerns the changing nature of the adolescent's social world: during early adolescence, the increasing importance of peers in general, and during middle and late adolescence, the increasing importance of other-sex peers in particular (Furman, Brown, & Feiring, 1999). Although experiences in the family are important for the initial development of social skills, experiences in friendships, especially during adolescence, contribute above and beyond the benefits of good parenting to the development of social competence (Glick & Rose, 2011). In this chapter, we'll pay special attention to changes in adolescent peer relations in light of the development of intimacy.

Why do such important changes take place in close relationships during adolescence? Theorists point to significant links between the development of intimacy during adolescence and the biological, cognitive, and social changes of the period.

Puberty and the Development of Intimacy

The link between puberty and intimacy is obvious: Changes in sexual impulses at puberty provoke interest in sex, which leads to the development of romantic relationships. With romance and sexuality come new issues and concerns requiring serious, intimate discussions. Some young people feel hesitant to discuss sex and dating with their parents and turn instead to relationships outside the family. And some of the most intimate conversations adolescents have with their friends involve their relationships with actual or potential romantic partners. These concerns may also prompt the development of intimate friendships with other-sex peers, perhaps for the first time.

Cognitive Change and the Development of Intimacy

Advances in thinking—especially in the realm of social cognition—are also related to the development of intimacy (Rote & Smetana, 2011). Compared to children, adolescents have more sophisticated conceptions of social relationships, better communication skills, and more self-awareness. They know more about how to "repair" their emotions—how to get themselves out a negative mood and into a positive one (Hessel et al., 2016). These developments permit adolescents to establish and maintain relationships with greater empathy, self-disclosure, and sensitivity; they also contribute to adolescents' feelings of loneliness if they perceive themselves as socially isolated (Laursen & Hartl, 2013). Limitations in preadolescents' ability to look at things from another person's point of view may make intimate interpersonal relationships a cognitive impossibility because it is hard to be an intimate friend to someone with whom you are unable to empathize. Neuroimaging studies show that the maturation during adolescence of connections among brain regions involved in decision making, emotional experience, and processing social information goes hand in hand with improvements in interpersonal competence (Nelson, Jarcho, & Guyer, 2016).

Changes in Social Roles and the Development of Intimacy

We can also point to changes in the adolescent's social roles as potentially affecting the development of intimacy. The behavioral independence that often accompanies the transition into adolescence provides greater opportunities for adolescents to be alone with their friends, engaged in intimate discussion, either in person or online. Adolescents spend more time in conversation with their friends than in any other activity (Dijkstra & Veenstra, 2011). Moreover, the recognition of adolescents as "near adults" may prompt their parents and other adults to confide in them and turn to them for support. Shared experiences such as working, as well as the development of emotional autonomy, may help give young people and their parents more of a basis for friendship and communication (Youniss & Smollar, 1985). Finally, changes in the structure of schools during early adolescence—often giving younger teenagers more contact with older ones—may promote new types of peer relationships (Eccles & Roeser, 2009).

During the course of preadolescence and adolescence, relationships are gradually transformed from the friendly but activity-oriented friendships of childhood to the more self-conscious, analytical, and intimate relationships of adulthood. In the next section, we examine why and how this transformation occurs.

Theoretical Perspectives on Adolescent Intimacy

The most important theoretical perspectives on the development of intimacy during adolescence are those of Harry Stack Sullivan (1953a) and various writers who have studied attachment relationships in adolescence (Kobak & Madsen, 2011; McElhaney et al., 2009). Let's look at each of these views in turn.

Sullivan's Theory of Interpersonal Development

Sullivan took a far less biological view of development than other thinkers who have written about adolescence. Instead, he emphasized the social aspects of development, suggesting that psychological maturation can be best understood by looking at our relationships with others. In his view, the challenges of adolescence (actually, of the entire life cycle) revolve around trying to satisfy changing interpersonal needs (Buhrmester, 1996).

Stages of Interpersonal Needs   Sullivan's perspective starts from the premise that, as children develop, different interpersonal needs surface that lead either to feelings of security (when the needs are satisfied) or feelings of anxiety (when the needs are frustrated). Sullivan charted a developmental progression of needs, beginning in infancy and continuing through adolescence (Sullivan, 1953b). These changing interpersonal needs define the course of interpersonal development through different phases of the life span. During middle childhood, for example, youngsters need to be accepted into peer groups, or else they feel rejected and ostracized.

In Sullivan's view, the security that is derived from having satisfying relationships with others is the glue that holds one's sense of self together. Identity and self-esteem are gradually built up through interpersonal relationships. Sullivan viewed psychosocial development as cumulative: The frustrations and satisfactions individuals experience during earlier periods affect their later relationships and developing sense of identity. The child who as an infant has her need for contact or tenderness frustrated will approach interpersonal relationships at subsequent ages with greater anxiety, a more intense need for security, and a shakier sense of self. In contrast, the infant who has his interpersonal needs met will approach later relationships with confidence and optimism.

When important interpersonal transitions arise (for example, during childhood, when the social world is broadened to include significant relationships with peers), having a solid foundation of security in past relationships aids in the successful negotiation of the transition. An individual who is nervous about forming relationships with others is likely to have trouble forming new types of relationships because they threaten an already tentative sense of security. A child who does not have a strong sense of security may have many friends in elementary school but be too afraid to form intimate friendships upon reaching preadolescence. She may try to maintain friendships like those more typical of childhood—friendships that focus on activities, for example, rather than talking—long after friends have outgrown getting together to "play." As a result, that young person may be rejected by peers and come to feel lonely and isolated.

Interpersonal Development During Adolescence

Sullivan distinguished between intimacy and sexuality; perhaps more important, he suggested that the need for intimacy—which surfaces during preadolescence— precedes the development of romantic or sexual relationships, which do not emerge until adolescence. In other words, Sullivan believed that the capacity for intimacy first develops prior to adolescence and in the context of same-sex, not other-sex, relationships. This turns out to be one of the most important observations in Sullivan's theory because, as you will read, the quality of individuals' same-sex friendships is predictive of the quality of their later romantic relationships.

Not all youngsters feel secure enough as preadolescents to forge these more mature, intimate friendships. Their feelings of insecurity are so strong that anxiety holds them back. Some youngsters never fully develop the capacity to be intimate with others, a limitation that takes its toll on relationships throughout adolescence and adulthood. Sullivan felt that forming intimate friendships during preadolescence is a necessary precondition to forming close relationships—both sexual and nonsexual— as an adolescent or young adult.

According to Sullivan, preadolescence comes to an end with the onset of puberty. Early adolescence is marked by the emergence of sexuality, in the form of a powerful, biological sex drive. As a consequence of this development, the preferred "target" of the adolescent's need for intimacy changes. He or she must begin to make the shift from intimate relationships with members of the same sex to intimate relationships with members of the other sex. During the historical epoch when Sullivan was writing, homosexuality was considered abnormal, and like other writers of his era, Sullivan equated normal sexual development with the development of heterosexual relationships. Social scientists no longer hold this view,

As adolescents' needs for intimacy increase, so does the emphasis they place on intimacy as an important component of friendship. Dragosh Co/Shutterstock

however, and most would say that the crucial interpersonal challenge for the young adolescent is not the movement from same-sex to other-sex friendships, but the transition from nonromantic to romantic relationships.

Like all interpersonal transitions, the movement from nonromantic to romantic relationships can be fraught with anxiety. For adolescents who do not have a healthy sense of security, it can be scary to leave the safety of nonsexual friendships and venture into the world of dating and sexuality. Socially anxious adolescents are less likely to have satisfying friendships, which makes them less able to develop satisfying cross-sex friendships and romantic relationships (Hebert et al., 2013).

The overarching challenge of adolescence, according to Sullivan, is to integrate an established need for intimacy with an emerging need for sexual contact in a way that does not lead to excessive anxiety. Sullivan saw adolescence as a time of experimentation with different types of relationships. Some adolescents choose to date many different people to try to find out what they are looking for in a relationship. Others get involved very deeply with a boyfriend or girlfriend in a relationship that lasts throughout their entire adolescence. Others may have a series of serious relationships. Still others keep intimacy and sexuality separate. They may develop close **platonic relationships** (nonsexual relationships) with other-sex peers, for example, or they may have sexual relationships without getting very intimate with their sex partners.

Sullivan viewed the adolescent's experimentation with different types of relationships as a normal way of handling new feelings, new fears, and new interpersonal needs. For many

platonic relationships Nonsexual relationships with individuals who might otherwise be romantic partners.

young people, experimentation with sex and intimacy continues well into late adolescence. If the interpersonal tasks of adolescence have been negotiated successfully, we enter late adolescence able to be intimate, able to enjoy sex, and, most critically, able to experience intimacy and sexuality in the same relationship.

Attachment Theory

Today, a different theoretical perspective guides the study of intimate relationships in adolescence, one that draws on theories of the development of the attachment relationship during infancy (Kobak & Madsen, 2011). In many ways, the basic ideas developed by Sullivan (namely, that early relationships set the stage for later ones) were maintained, but a different perspective and vocabulary have come to dominate contemporary theory and research on adolescents' intimate relationships. In order to understand how attachment theory is applied to the study of adolescence, though, we need to look first at how the concept of "attachment" has been used to understand development in infancy.

attachment
The strong affectional bond that develops between an infant and a caregiver.

secure attachment
A healthy attachment between infant and caregiver, characterized by trust.

anxious-avoidant attachment
An insecure attachment between infant and caregiver, characterized by indifference on the part of the infant toward the caregiver.

anxious-resistant attachment
An insecure attachment between infant and caregiver, characterized by distress at separation and anger at reunion.

disorganized attachment
A relationship between infant and caregiver characterized by the absence of normal attachment behavior.

internal working model
The implicit model of interpersonal relationships that an individual employs throughout life, believed to be shaped by early attachment experiences.

rejection sensitivity
Heightened vulnerability to being rejected by others.

Attachment in Infancy In writings on infant development, an **attachment** is defined as a strong and enduring emotional bond. Virtually all infants form attachment relationships with their mother (and most do so with their father and other caregivers as well), but not all infants have attachment relationships of the same quality. Psychologists differentiate among four types of infant attachment: secure, anxious-avoidant, anxious-resistant, and disorganized. A **secure attachment** between infant and caregiver is characterized by trust; an **anxious-avoidant attachment** is characterized by indifference on the part of the infant toward the caregiver; an **anxious-resistant attachment** is characterized by ambivalence. Children who develop a **disorganized attachment**, which is characterized by the absence of normal attachment behavior, are most at risk for psychological problems (Kerns & Brumariu, 2014). The security of the early attachment

relationship is important because studies show that infants who have had a secure attachment are more likely to grow into psychologically healthy and socially skilled children (Matas, Arend, & Sroufe, 1978).

Does Infant Attachment Predict Adolescent Intimacy? Many theorists who study adolescent development believe that the nature of individuals' attachment to caregivers during infancy continues to have an influence on their capacity to form satisfying intimate relationships during adolescence and adulthood, two ways (McElhaney et al., 2009). First, some theorists have argued that the initial attachment relationship forms the basis for the model of interpersonal relationships we employ throughout life (Bowlby, 1969). This **internal working model** determines to a large measure whether people feel trusting or apprehensive in relationships with others and whether they see themselves as worthy of others' affection. An internal working model is a set of beliefs and expectations people draw on in forming close relationships with others—whether they go into relationships expecting acceptance or anticipating rejection. According to the theory, individuals who enjoyed a secure attachment relationship during infancy will have a more positive and healthy internal working model of relationships during adolescence, whereas individuals who were insecurely attached as infants will have a less positive one (Dykas et al., 2014; Kobak & Madsen, 2011; McElhaney et al., 2009).

Several studies have found that adolescents' working models for their relationships with parents are similar to their working models of relationships with friends and that adolescents' working models of relationships with friends are similar to their working models of relationships with romantic partners (e.g., Furman et al., 2002). In addition, a number of writers have suggested that individuals who emerge from infancy with an insecure attachment are more sensitive to being rejected by others in later romantic encounters, a trait that psychologists call **rejection sensitivity** (Norona et al., 2014; Rowe et al., 2015). Individuals who are high in rejection sensitivity and emotional insecurity are more likely to develop symptoms of depression and anxiety, which in turn, lead to further increases in rejection sensitivity (Chango et al., 2012; Davies et al., 2014; Hafen et al., 2014). Adolescents who are frequently teased about their physical appearance by parents or peers may become especially sensitive about being rejected by others because of how they look (Webb et al., 2015).

In recent years, several teams of neuroscientists have studied adolescents' neural responses to rejection by imaging their brain activity while the adolescents play an online game called "Cyberball" (White et al., 2013). Participants are told that they will be playing a ball-tossing game via the Internet with two other adolescents in other scanners (in actuality, there are no other players). On a screen inside the scanner, adolescents see cartoon images representing the other players, as well as a cartoon image of their own "hand" (see Figure 10.1). The ball is thrown back and forth among the three players, with the participant choosing which person to throw to and the throws of the other two "players" determined by the computer.

At the beginning of the game, the computerized players are equally likely to throw the ball to the participant or the other player. However, as the task progresses, the other players stop throwing to the participant. The researchers then compare participants' brain activity when they are excluded to that when they are included. Adolescents high in rejection sensitivity actually show a different pattern of brain activity in response to exclusion, and those who do so are more likely to develop symptoms of depression (Masten et al., 2011). As young adults, adolescents who spent a lot of time with their friends in adolescence show patterns of brain activity that indicate less sensitivity to rejection (Masten et al., 2012).

A second reason for the continued importance of early attachment relationships during adolescence is that interpersonal development is cumulative: What happens during infancy affects what happens in early childhood, which affects what happens in middle childhood, and so on (Boyer & Nelson, 2015). In other words, individuals who leave infancy with a secure attachment may be on a different interpersonal trajectory than those who leave infancy insecure. (Here's where you can see similarities between this perspective and Sullivan's.)

The only way to examine this proposition is to follow individuals over time and trace their interpersonal development. Numerous studies that have done this show that insecure children are more likely to develop psychological and social problems during childhood and adolescence, including poor peer relationships (e.g., Weinfield, Ogawa, & Sroufe, 1997) and poor self-regulation (M. J. Martin et al., 2017; Farley & Kim-Spoon, 2014), which may lead to risk taking (Delker, Bernstein, & Laurent, 2018). It is thought that these problems in peer relations during childhood affect the development of social competence

Attachment theory, which has been used mainly in the study of infancy, has influenced the study of close relationships in adolescence.
JGI/Blend Images LLC

during adolescence—in essence, forming a link between early experience and later relationships (Fraley et al., 2013). In contrast, secure infants are more likely to grow into socially competent teenagers and young adults (Raby et al., 2015). The benefits of positive relations with peers also extend beyond adolescence: People who establish healthy intimate relationships with age-mates during adolescence are psychologically healthier and more satisfied with their lives as adults (Raudino, Fergussson, & Horwood, 2013).

making the personal connection

Think about your own internal working model of relationships. Are there consistencies in the ways in which you approach close relationships with different people? Would you say that you are high or low in "rejection sensitivity"?

Of course, it is possible for interpersonal development to be cumulative without the root cause of this continuity being the individual's internal working model. Individuals who have positive peer relationships in childhood may simply learn how to get along better with others, and this may lead to more positive peer relationships in adolescence, which, in turn, may lead to better relationships in adulthood (Lansford, Yu et al., 2014). One study that followed individuals from birth through midlife found a cascade of interpersonal connections over time: low-quality parent-child relationships were linked to low-quality parent-adolescent relationships, which predicted low-quality romantic relationships in young adulthood and

You can throw the ball by clicking on the name or picture of another player

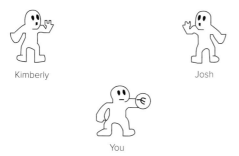

Kimberly   Josh

You

Figure 10.1 Using a computer game called "Cyberball," researchers scan adolescents' brains in order to better understand their responses to social exclusion.
(K. Williams et al., 2012)

adult attachment interview
A structured interview used to assess an individual's past attachment history and internal working model of relationships.

dissatisfaction with life in middle age (Overbeek et al., 2007). Individuals with more negative views of themselves disengage from peers, which may lead to poorer-quality peer relationships and peer rejection, thereby intensifying their negative self-image (M. S. Caldwell et al., 2004). Adolescents who have high-quality relationships with their parents are more likely to develop high self-esteem, which in turn facilitates the development of better romantic relationships in young adulthood (Johnson & Galambos, 2014).

How strong is the *direct* link between infant attachment and the quality of interpersonal relationships in adolescence and young adulthood? Do individuals who were securely attached as infants have more positive working models of relationships as adolescents or young adults?

Studies that have followed individuals from infancy all the way through adolescence and beyond have yielded conflicting results. Some have shown considerable continuity from infancy through adolescence (e.g., Hamilton, 2000; Waters et al., 2000), but others have shown no continuity whatsoever (Lewis, Feiring, & Rosenthal, 2000; Weinfield, Sroufe, & Egeland, 2000). Some researchers have suggested that individuals' security of attachment remains stable only in the absence of major life events that could upset the course of interpersonal development (such as the loss of a parent or parental divorce) and that the lack of continuity observed in some studies is due to the importance of intervening events (Waters et al., 2000; Weinfield, Sroufe, & Egeland, 2000). Others, however, argue that the significance of early attachment for later relationships is far outweighed by the importance of the experiences the individual has in childhood and the context in which he or she lives as an adolescent (Lewis, Feiring, & Rosenthal, 2000).

Attachment in Adolescence   In addition to employing the four-way attachment classification scheme to study the links among infancy, childhood, and adolescence, attachment theorists have applied similar classifications to the study of adolescents' attachments to others (e.g., McElhaney et al., 2009; Obsuth et al., 2014), as well as to adolescents' internal working models (e.g., Kobak et al., 1993). In some of these studies, adolescents' current relationships with parents and peers are assessed; in others, adolescents are asked to recount their childhood experiences through the use of a procedure called the **adult attachment interview** (Main, Kaplan, & Cassidy, 1985). The interview focuses on individuals' recollections of their early attachment experiences and obtains information on the ways in which the individual recounts his or her childhood history. A variety of schemes for coding responses to the interview have been devised, but most categorize individuals as "secure," "dismissing," or "preoccupied."

Many researchers have found that adolescents in different attachment categories differ in predictable ways (McElhaney et al., 2009). Compared with dismissing or preoccupied adolescents, secure adolescents interact with their mothers with less unhealthy anger and more appropriate assertiveness, suggesting fewer difficulties in establishing emotional autonomy (Kobak et al., 1993). Individuals with dismissive or preoccupied attachment profiles are more likely to show a range of emotional and behavior problems in adolescence, including depression, maladaptive coping, anxiety, eating disorders, conduct problems, and delinquency (J. Allen et al., 2007; Kobak, Zajac, & Smith, 2009). They are more likely to recall negative aspects of their interactions with others (Dykas et al., 2012). Not surprisingly, adolescents who are judged to have had a secure infant attachment have more stable romantic relationships than their insecure counterparts (Davis & Kirkpatrick, 1994). People's security of attachment in infancy predicts social competence in childhood, security of attachment to close friends in adolescence, and positive romantic relationships in adulthood (Nosko et al., 2011; Simpson et al., 2007) (Figure 10.2). Of course, it is hard to say whether social competence leads to healthier attachments or vice versa (most probably, both are true).

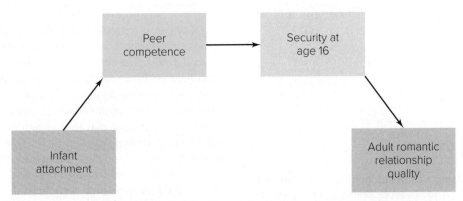

Figure 10.2   **The quality of infant attachment is linked to adult romantic relationships through effects on social development in childhood and adolescence.** (Simpson et al., 2007)

Numerous studies also have looked at the quality of adolescents' current attachments to parents and peers (Chango et al., 2015; McElhaney et al., 2009; Vandevivere, Braet, & Bosmans, 2015). Individuals who have secure attachments during adolescence are more socially competent, more successful in school, less likely to engage in substance use, and better adjusted than their insecure peers (Keiser, Helmerhorst, & van Rijn-van Gelderen, 2019; Kochendorfer & Kerns, 2017; Tan et al., 2016). Adolescents with secure attachments to their parents are more sensitive to their social environment and better able to use relationships with others to buffer the effects of stress on well-being (Gunnar, 2017). Security of attachment also predicts whether and at what age adolescents "leave the nest": Insecurely attached adolescents are more likely to delay moving out or to return to their parents' home than their more securely attached peers (Seiffge-Krenke, 2006).

Although attachment security is generally very stable over adolescence, it can change if adolescents are living in dysfunctional family situations or under a lot of stress (Jones et al., 2018; Kahn et al., 2020). By the same token, having supportive parents and positive peer relationships is associated with increases in attachment security between adolescence and adulthood, whereas having psychologically controlling parents or parents who fight with each other frequently are associated with decreases in security over time (Allen et al., 2018). In other words, early attachment security is not an "inoculation" that protects individuals from psychological problems forever, but rather a psychological advantage that increases the probability of developing in healthy ways. In general, attachments to parents become more secure over the course of adolescence (Ruhl, Dolan, & Buhrmester, 2015).

By the same token, the degree of security in an adolescent's attachment style interacts with other experiences to shape mental health and behavior: Positive experiences (such as having an authoritative parent) have even more positive effects among adolescents with a secure style, whereas negative experiences are not as harmful (Allen et al., 2002). And, among adolescents with an insecure attachment style, negative experiences (such as having excessively intrusive parents) have an even worse effect than they would otherwise (Marsh, McFarland, & Allen, 2003).

The Development of Intimacy in Adolescence

Psychologists interested in the development of intimacy during adolescence have focused mainly, but not exclusively, on relationships between adolescents and their peers. Among the most researched topics are how friendships change, how the display of intimacy changes (and whether and to what extent there are sex differences in the

During middle adolescence, concerns about jealousy often surface in adolescent girls' friendships. PeopleImages/Getty Images

ways intimacy is expressed), and, most recently, whether the increased use of social media has changed the way adolescents form and maintain close relationships.

Changes in the Nature of Friendship

When asked what makes someone a friend, both children and adolescents mention such things as sharing, helping, and common activities, but not until early adolescence do people mention such things as self-disclosure, common interests, similar attitudes and values, or loyalty. In childhood, friendship is defined by companionship; it is not until adolescence that intimacy is a part of the definition (Buhrmester & Furman, 1987). Adolescents report that the most important qualities in a friend are honesty, humor, kindness, and fairness (Wagner, 2018). And, whereas children's self-disclosure to friends tends to be superficial (e.g., "Sometimes I carry ChapStick"), adolescents' self-disclosure grows more intimate over time (e.g., "Sometimes I worry about kissing"). Some researchers have suggested that the superficial self-disclosure of childhood and early adolescence may set the stage for more intimate self-disclosure later in development (Vijayakumar et al., 2020).

making the cultural connection

Images of jealous adolescent girls pervade American movies and television shows that feature teenagers. Do you think this is a common phenomenon around the world? Or is it less likely to be found in cultures where dating is delayed until early adulthood?

The fact that conceptions of friendship come to place greater weight on such things as intimacy, loyalty, and shared values and attitudes during early adolescence is consistent with Sullivan's theory. As adolescents' needs for intimacy increase, so does the emphasis they place on intimacy as an important component of friendship. The findings are also consistent with what we know about other cognitive changes during early adolescence. Compared to children, adolescents are better at thinking about abstract concepts such as intimacy and loyalty, and their judgments of others are more sophisticated, more psychological, and less tied to concrete attributes such as how they look or the things they own.

Jealousy The importance of intimacy as a defining feature of close friendship continues to increase throughout early and middle adolescence (McNelles & Connolly, 1999; Phillipsen, 1999). But an interesting pattern of change occurs around age 14. During middle adolescence (between ages 13 and 15), particularly among girls, concerns about loyalty and anxieties over rejection become more pronounced and may temporarily overshadow concerns about intimate self-disclosure (Berndt & Perry, 1990). Adolescents who keep a lot of secrets from their friends report higher levels of depression (Laird, Bridges, & Marsee, 2013).

The sorts of conflicts adolescents have with their friends change during this time. Whereas older adolescents' conflicts are typically over private matters, younger adolescents' conflicts are often over perceived public disrespect (Shulman & Laursen, 2002). Adolescents who report high levels of peer conflict and low levels of peer support are more likely to engage in risky behavior, perhaps as a response to the stress caused by problems with their friends (Telzer, Fuligni, et al., 2015).

Girls in particular show a pronounced increase in jealousy over their friends' friends during early adolescence (Parker et al., 2005). Girls who have low self-esteem and are especially sensitive to rejection are especially likely to become envious of their friends' relationships with other girls. In some senses, then, intimate friendship is a mixed blessing for young adolescent girls: They get the benefits of having confidantes with whom they can easily talk about their problems, but their friendships are more fragile and more easily disrupted by feelings of betrayal. As a consequence, girls' friendships on average do not last as long as boys' do (Benenson & Christakos, 2003).

Conflict Adolescents' close friendships also are distinguished from their casual friendships in the types of conflicts they have and the ways in which disagreements are resolved (Laursen, 1996; Raffaelli, 1997). Although conflicts between adolescents and their close friends are less frequent than they are between adolescents and less intimate peers, arguments with close friends are more emotional, with lots of anger and hurt feelings. Conflicts

with friends both influence and are influenced by adolescent depression (Yang et al., 2020). Conflict between close friends is more likely to provoke efforts to restore the relationship than is conflict between casual friends. Nonetheless, some best friendships don't survive, and others are "downgraded" from best friend to "good friend" (Bowker, 2011).

Changes in the Display of Intimacy

In addition to placing greater emphasis on intimacy and loyalty in defining friendship than children do, teenagers are also more likely to *display* intimacy in their relationships, in what they know about their friends, how responsive they are, how empathic they are, and how they resolve disagreements.

Knowing Who Their Friends Are As individuals move into and through adolescence, they gain knowledge about more intimate aspects of their friends' lives. Although preadolescents and adolescents have comparable degrees of knowledge about characteristics of their best friends that are not especially personal (such as the friend's telephone number or birthday), adolescents know significantly more things about their friends that are intimate (such as what their friends worry about or what they are proud of) (Savin-Williams & Berndt, 1990).

Over the course of adolescence, adolescents' reports of friendship quality increase steadily. These improvements in friendship quality lead to gains in social competence and increases in positive affect, which in turn lead to further improvements in the quality of adolescents' friendships (Glick & Rose, 2011), creating what has been called an "upward spiral" (Ramsey & Gentzler, 2015). Although there are ethnic differences in average levels of friendship quality—Asian American adolescents report more dissatisfaction with their friendships than do other adolescents—the rate of improvement in friendship quality over time is the same in different ethnic groups (Way & Greene, 2006). And, despite fears that spending time socializing over the Internet will undermine adolescents' social competence, the people adolescents interact with online are mainly the same people they interact with offline (Reich, Subrahmanyam, & Espinosa, 2012) (see Figure 10.3). Actually, adolescents who use the Internet a lot for social networking are *less* socially isolated than their peers (Smahel, Brown, & Blinka, 2012).

Caring and Concern People also become more responsive to close friends, less controlling, and more tolerant of their friends' individuality during adolescence (Keller et al., 1998; Shulman et al., 1997). Before preadolescence, children are actually less likely to help and share with their friends than with other classmates (perhaps because children are more competitive with their friends than with other youngsters and do not want to feel inferior). By about

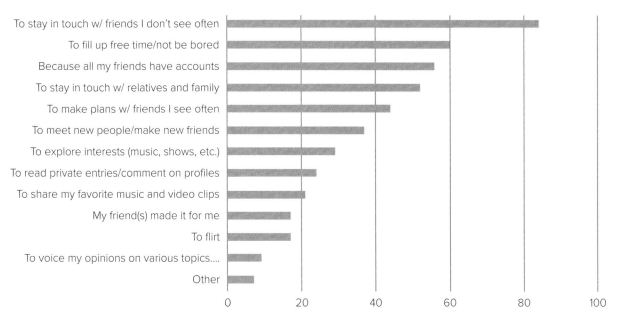

Figure 10.3   **Adolescents use social networking sites primarily to communicate with people they have offline relationships with.** (Reich, Subrahmanyam, & Espinosa, 2012)

age 9, children treat their friends and other classmates similarly when it comes to sharing and cooperation. But by the time they have reached early adolescence, friends are more helpful and generous toward each other than toward other classmates (Burnett Heyes et al., 2015). Experiments in which individuals play computer games with an anonymous partner find increases with age in both trust and reciprocity (van den Bos et al., 2010).

Adolescents also show greater levels of empathy and social understanding in situations in which they are helping or comforting others. Compared with children, adolescents are more likely to understand and acknowledge how their friends feel when those friends are having problems. Over the course of adolescence, attempts to help friends with personal problems become more centered on providing support and less aimed at distracting them from their troubles (Denton & Zarbatany, 1996).

Conflict Resolution   The ways in which close friends resolve conflict also change. As individuals move from childhood into adolescence and from adolescence into young adulthood, they become more likely to end their disagreements by negotiation (trying to compromise or find a solution that is acceptable to both friends) or disengagement (walking away from the situation) and less likely to end them with one person coercing or overpowering the other and getting his or her way; across cultures, negotiation is the main way that adolescents cope with conflicts they have with friends (Seiffge-Krenke et al., 2013). Generally speaking, the ways in which adolescents resolve conflicts with their friends are similar to the ways in which they resolved conflicts with their parents when they were younger and predictive of how they resolve conflicts with romantic partners when they are older (Staats et al., 2018).

Does Using Social Media Hurt the Development of Intimacy?

One of the most controversial topics in contemporary discussions of adolescent intimacy concerns the impact of social media on teenagers' social competence and friendships. Many social commentators have stoked fears that the increase in adolescents' use of digital devices to communicate with others is destroying young people's abilities to engage in meaningful face-to-face relationships (Turkle, 2015; Twenge et al., 2018).

Thankfully, there is very little evidence of this. Headlines about smartphones destroying adolescents' brains may sell a lot of books, but they have created unnecessary anxiety and panic among parents and educators. In fact, some scientists believe that using social media may actually *help* teenagers develop social competence (Reich, 2017).

There is no question that teenagers are using digital devices to stay in touch with their friends. But research clearly shows that digital communication among friends enhances, rather than detracts from, the quality of adolescents' friendships. One comprehensive review of three dozen studies published in peer-reviewed scientific journals (rather than in the popular press) looked at the impact of digital communication on a variety of relationship components, including self-disclosure, support, companionship, and conflict (Yau & Reich, 2017). The main conclusion of this review is that social media provide opportunities to engage in many of the same activities that adolescents do in person, without compromising these relationships.

For example, the authors found that digital communication helped adolescents seek social support and get

Although many people are sure that teenagers' use of social media has impaired their interpersonal development, there is very little evidence that this is the case.
wavebreakmediamicro/123RF

advice on a wide range of problems and that digital disclosure was effective in relieving emotional distress and increasing closeness between friends. Despite fears that adolescents don't appreciate the risks of disclosing sensitive information online, studies have found that adolescents, especially by the time they are in high school, are surprisingly thoughtful about what they share online and with whom they share it and that they clearly understand the difference between sharing personal information with close friends and sharing it with mere acquaintances (Blachnio et al., 2016; Xie & Kang, 2015).

A second conclusion about social media and adolescents' social development is that digital communication serves an important purpose in helping teenagers validate the importance of their friendships. For all the talk about cyberbullying, the fact is that far more online communication among adolescents involves positive communication about their relationships, the significance of their friendships, and their feelings of love, affection, and connectedness. Much of what is posted on popular social networking sites is reminiscent of what teenagers write in each other's yearbooks—"to my best buddy," "I love you soooo much," "you're so gorgeous," and so forth—except that these affirmations are viewed by many more people than would typically see yearbook inscriptions. And the nature of social media platforms permits friends to elaborate on their feelings or memories with pictures, emoticons, and, of course, "likes."

Third, digital communication has provided new ways for adolescents to enjoy their friends' companionship. Teenagers share jokes, things they find interesting, music, and YouTube videos. They play video games with their friends, either in person or jointly online. And while studies have found that joint activities done in person lead to stronger feelings of bonding than do shared online activities, the magnitude of the difference between reports of closeness during digital exchanges versus in-person contact is surprisingly small. An added benefit of digital communication is that it can take place in locations and at times of day when talking on the phone is inconvenient or difficult. Teenagers also report that social media are an important source of information about their romantic partners (Van Ouytsel et al., 2016).

Finally, many of the negative interactions that occur between teenagers online are the same as those that occur in person. Gossip, jealousy, criticism, and conflict are features of adolescents' relationships that are expressed online, but they are also things that are expressed in person. Whether these negative aspects of adolescents' interpersonal interactions are amplified or diminished when they occur online compared to when they take place in person isn't known; most likely, some adolescents are bothered more by slights that occur in person, while others are more bothered by ones that are posted online. There is some evidence, however, that online communications are especially likely to provoke jealousy between friends (Lennarz et al., 2017).

In sum, the impact of social media on adolescents' relationships appears to be far more positive than negative. As the authors of an extensive review concluded, "digital communication can provide greater opportunities for friends to disclose, spend time together, and display affection than in offline spaces alone. Rather than reducing intimacy in friendships, technology-mediated communication may provide the same benefits to teens as interactions that occur face-to-face" (Yau & Reich, 2017).

Sex Differences in Intimacy

There are striking sex differences in intimacy during adolescence.

How Females Are More Intimate When asked to name the people who are most important to them, adolescent girls—particularly in the middle adolescent years—list more friends than boys do, and girls are more likely to mention intimacy as a defining aspect of close friendship. In interviews, adolescent girls express greater interest in their close friendships, talk more frequently about their intimate conversations with friends, express greater concern about their friends' faithfulness and greater anxiety over rejection, and place greater emphasis on emotional closeness in their evaluation of romantic partners (Feiring, 1999; Parker et al., 2005).

Girls also are more likely than boys to make distinctions in the way they treat intimate and nonintimate friends and to fight about relationships; girls prefer to keep their friendships more exclusive and are less willing to include other classmates in their cliques' activities (Bukowski et al., 1993; Raffaelli, 1997). In conversations, girls are more collaborative, whereas boys are more controlling (Strough & Berg, 2000). In situations in which people need help, girls are more likely to provide it than boys (Van Rijsewijk et al., 2016). And girls are better than boys at seeing things from the perspective of others, especially, others who are less fortunate (Tucker Smith et al., 2016).

When self-disclosure is used as the measure of intimacy, boys' friendships with other boys aren't comparable to girls' friendships with other girls until late in adolescence, if at all (McNelles & Connolly, 1999; Radmacher & Azmitia, 2006). And girls are more sensitive and empathic than boys, especially in knowing when their friends are depressed or comforting them when they are distressed (Swenson & Rose, 2003; Van der Graaff et al., 2014). One reason girls are more likely than boys to confide in friends is that girls expect that self-disclosure will make them feel better, whereas boys expect it to be a waste of time that will make them feel "weird" (Rose et al., 2012). Girls value friendships characterized by emotional support and concern; boys place a premium on having fun (Rose & Asher, 2017). In these very numerous—and very important—respects, the expression of intimacy is more advanced among adolescent girls than among boys.

Although this carries many advantages for girls, it also carries some liabilities. Girls' mental health is more positively affected than boys' when things are going well with their friends, but girls suffer more when things are going poorly (Benner, Hou, & Jackson, 2019; Flook, 2011). Girls also are more likely than boys to spend excessive time discussing each other's problems—something called **co-rumination** (Rose, 2002; Rose et al., 2014). Co-rumination, often done in the context of discussing problems with romantic relationships, turns out to be a double-edged sword, especially for girls: It brings friends closer, but it also contributes to depression and anxiety (Bastin et al., 2018; Dirghangi et al., 2015).

Co-rumination among depressed adolescent girls is especially toxic (Bastin et al., 2015; Rose et al., 2017). In fact, co-rumination makes anxiety and depression "contagious," transmitting symptoms between the pair of individuals, either because listening to someone's problems is itself distressing (Smith & Rose, 2011) or through "emotional mimicry," where one person unconsciously takes on the feelings of another (Schwartz-Mette & Rose, 2012).

Among boys, co-rumination also improves friendships but does not increase depression or anxiety as much or as consistently as it does among girls (Rose, Carlson, & Waller, 2007), both because girls are more likely to get upset when they hear that their friends are having

problems (Smith & Rose, 2011) and because boys are more likely to also use humor when they are discussing problems with each other, which draws them closer (Rose et al., 2016). This doesn't mean that adolescents should avoid talking to friends about their feelings and problems; they just need to keep it in check and focus on gaining insight into the source of the problem, rather than just sitting around and brooding about it (Bastin et al., 2018). Adolescents also have to be careful not to engage in too much "negative feedback seeking" (asking other people to verify their flaws, as in, "My voice is so annoying, right?"). Too much of this leads to rejection by others, which then only makes people feel even worse (Borelli & Prinstein, 2006).

> **co-rumination**
> Excessive talking with another about problems.

There also are interesting sex differences in the nature of conflicts between close friends during adolescence. Boys' conflicts are briefer, typically over issues of power and control (such as whose turn it is in a game), more likely to escalate into physical aggression, and usually resolved without any explicit effort to do so, often by just "letting things slide." Boys are far less likely than girls to become jealous of their friends developing friendships with others (Rose & Asher, 2017). Although girls are better than boys at negotiating conflict (Baker & Exner-Cortens, 2020), girls' conflicts are longer (perhaps because it takes longer to negotiate a conflict than to simply let things slide), typically about some form of betrayal in the relationship (such as breaking a confidence or ignoring the other person), and only resolved when one of the friends apologizes (Noakes & Rinaldi, 2006). When friendships end, girls are more adversely affected than boys by the loss of the relationships (Bakker et al., 2010).

And How They Aren't On some measures of friendship, though, adolescent boys and girls show similar degrees of intimacy. Although girls are more likely to mention self-disclosure when asked to define close friendship and report more self-disclosure in their friendships, boys and girls have equivalent degrees of intimate knowledge about their best friends (McNelles & Connolly, 1999). When boys are with their friends, they are just as likely as girls to share each other's emotional state (McNelles & Connolly, 1999). Although girls are generally more considerate, sex differences in helpfulness are very small (Eisenberg et al., 2009).

There's no question that intimacy is a more conscious concern for adolescent girls than it is for adolescent boys. But this doesn't mean that intimacy is *absent* from boys' relationships or unimportant for their mental health (Way, 2013). Rather, they express intimacy in different ways. Boys' friendships are more oriented toward shared activities than toward the explicit satisfaction of emotional needs, as is often the case in girls' friendships. The

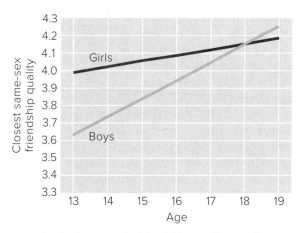

Figure 10.4 **Changes in friendship quality over time.**
(Way & Greene, 2006)

development of intimacy between adolescent males may be more subtle, reflected more in shared activities than in self-disclosure, even in young adulthood (Radmacher & Azmitia, 2006) and even in online communication (Valkenburg & Peter, 2007).

Another possibility is that the development of close friendships among males starts at a later age than it does among females. There are substantial sex differences in friendship quality at age 13, but by age 18, these are gone (see Figure 10.4) (Way & Greene, 2006). It's a familiar pattern: During early and middle adolescence, girls are more emotionally and socially mature than boys, but by late adolescence, boys have caught up. (I know that many female readers are shaking their heads at this, but that's what the research says.)

The Origins of Sex Differences   Many theorists have suggested that sex differences in intimacy are the result of different patterns of socialization. From an early age, females are more strongly encouraged to develop and express intimacy—especially verbal intimacy—than males. Other factors could be at work, however. Social pressures on males and females during adolescence are quite different and may lead to differences in expressions of intimacy. Boys are punished much more for acting in feminine ways (such as sharing feelings with others) than girls are for acting in masculine ways (such as holding strong emotions in). This is especially so within ethnic groups that stress the importance of "machismo" (a strong and sometimes exaggerated sense of masculinity), as is often the case among Mexican Americans (Stanton-Salazar & Spina, 2005). One reason that adolescent males may not be as intimate in their friendships as adolescent females may be that boys are nervous that expressions of intimacy will be taken as a sign of their lack of masculinity. Consistent with this, boys who are members of peer groups in which individuals express a lot of prejudice toward gay teenagers have less positive interactions with their friends (Poteat, Mereish, & Birkett, 2015).

making the scientific connection

Some sex differences in friendship quality predate adolescence—girls are more verbal than boys at an early age, for example—but others, such as differences in conflict resolution or in feelings of jealousy, do not seem to emerge until this developmental period. What aspects of the transition into adolescence differ for girls and boys that might account for sex differences in intimacy?

Changes in the Targets of Intimacy

Adolescence is a time of noteworthy changes in the "targets" of intimate behavior. During preadolescence and early adolescence, intimacy with peers is hypothesized to replace intimacy with parents, and during late adolescence, intimacy with peers of the other sex is thought to take the place of intimacy with same-sex friends. Actually, this view appears to be only somewhat accurate. As we'll see, new targets of intimacy do not *replace* old ones. Rather, new targets are *added to* old ones.

Parents and Peers as Targets of Intimacy   From early adolescence on, teenagers describe their relationships with their best friends and romantic partners as more intimate and less stressful than those with their mother or father (Persike & Seiffge-Krenke, 2014). Although there may be a slight drop in intimacy between adolescents and parents sometime during adolescence, the decline reverses as young people move toward young adulthood (Ebbert, Infurna, & Luthar, 2019; Keijsers & Poulin, 2013).

By virtually any measure, girls display more intimacy in their friendships than do boys. Blend Images/Shutterstock

Intimacy between individuals and their parents declines between the 5th and 10th grades but increases between 10th grade and young adulthood. Time spent in family activities declines throughout preadolescence and adolescence, but the amount of time adolescents spend alone with their mother or father follows a curvilinear pattern, increasing between preadolescence and middle adolescence and then declining (Lam, McHale, & Crouter, 2014). Intimacy with friends increases steadily throughout adolescence, although most dramatically during the early adolescent years. Intimacy with romantic partners also increases steadily throughout adolescence, but in this case, the most dramatic increase takes place during the late high school years (Szwedo et al., 2017).

In other words, while peers become relatively more important during adolescence as confidants and sources of emotional support, by no means do parents become unimportant (De Goede et al., 2009). When adolescents are asked to list the important people in their lives—people they care about, go to for advice, or do things with—the number of peers listed increases over the course of adolescence. At the same time, however, there are no changes over adolescence in the percentage of individuals listing their mother or father. More importantly, studies indicate that adolescents who spend a good deal of time with their parents also spend a good deal of time with their friends.

Thus, rather than drawing distinctions between parent-oriented and peer-oriented adolescents, it makes more sense to distinguish between adolescents who have a lot of social contact and enjoy a great deal of support from others (both family and friends) and those who are socially isolated or lonely (Scholte, van Lieshout, & van Aken, 2001). Chronically lonely teenagers are more sensitive to being rejected, less likely to expect social situations to be fun, and, as a consequence, less likely to accept invitations from others to get together, which only strengthens their sense of isolation (Vanhalst et al., 2015; Vanhalst et al., 2018). They do not experience the normal and adaptive **reaffiliation motive** that most of us have, which prompts us to reconnect with others when we feel lonely (Qualter et al., 2015). Similarly, brain scans of socially anxious teenagers show that they experience less activation in reward regions when anticipating feedback from peers (Spielberg, Jarcho, et al., 2015). Unfortunately, adolescents who have negative expectations of their peers are more likely to form hostile relationships with friends and romantic partners (Loeb et al., 2016).

Unfortunately, loneliness in adolescence is associated with all sorts of psychological and physical problems, including frequent illness, disturbed sleep, hyperawareness of social threats, and lower responsiveness to social rewards. As a consequence, lonely adolescents are more likely to hold negative views of themselves and others and to be especially sensitive to rejection. These reactions entrap lonely adolescents in a vicious cycle: The lonelier they feel, the more likely they are to notice things that

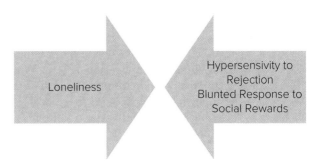

Figure 10.5 Lonely adolescents are more sensitive to social rejection and less sensitive to social rewards, increasing their feelings of isolation and making them feel even more lonely. (Goossens, 2018)

confirm their negative preconceptions about social relationships, which increases their feelings of social isolation (Goossens, 2018) (see Figure 10.5).

The quality of adolescents' peer and family relationships are closely linked (Flynn et al., 2018; Kretschmer et al., 2016). In other words, we can see features of adolescents' relationships with their parents and their parents' marital relationship—how close they are, how emotionally reactive they are, how they deal with conflict, and so forth—in their relationships with their friends and romantic partners (Ackerman et al., 2013; Cook, Blair, & Buehler, 2018; Fosco et al., 2016; Trifan & Stattin, 2015).

On a theoretical level, this provides support for both social learning and attachment-based views of adolescent intimacy, in that it suggests that the lessons young people learn in close relationships at home provide a template for the close relationships they form with others. Teenagers whose relationships with parents are emotionally close but not very individuated tend to stay longer in romantic relationships, even when the relationships are not very good, suggesting that difficulties in establishing healthy autonomy at home may carry over to romantic relationships (Smetana & Gettmen, 2006). One approach to improving the peer relationships of adolescents who are having difficulties might be to focus on improving the quality of their relationships at home (Updegraff et al., 2002).

Studies of adolescents' preferences for social support similarly show that the likelihood of turning to a peer during a time of trouble increases during adolescence but that the likelihood of turning to a parent does not change. Between ages 7 and 14, the amount of support children receive from their immediate family remains fairly constant, while the amount of support received from friends increases (Levitt, Guacci-Franci, & Levitt, 1993). In other words, even though adolescents begin to see their friends as increasingly important sources of emotional support, they do not cease needing

reaffiliation motive
The normal and adaptive motivation that most of us have, which prompts us to reconnect with others when we feel lonely.

or using their parents for the same purpose. What seems to occur, instead, is that adolescents develop preferences for social support that vary as a function of the specific issue. Nevertheless, among children, support from parents is more effective than support from friends in diminishing the adverse physiological effects of stress; during adolescence, the reverse is true (Hostinar, Johnson, & Gunnar, 2015; Miller et al., 2017).

Adolescents typically feel freer to express anger during arguments with family members than during arguments with friends, presumably because anger may lead to the end of a friendship but rarely would it cause the end of a family relationship (Laursen, 1993). Perhaps because of this, adolescents report more angry feelings after conflicts with their parents than after conflicts with their friends (Adams & Laursen, 2001). And when asked to recall key events in their past that contributed to their sense of identity, college students' reminiscences of their relationships with their parents more often emphasize conflict and separation, whereas their recollections of their relationships with their friends more often emphasize closeness (McLean & Thorne, 2003).

There are important differences between adolescents' relationships with mothers versus fathers. In general, adolescents interact much more often with, are closer to, and argue more with their mother than with their father, a pattern seen among males as well as females and across a variety of cultures (Fuligni, 1998). Of their two parents, adolescents see their mother as being more understanding, more accepting, and more willing to negotiate and as less judgmental, less guarded, and less defensive. The difference between perceptions of mothers and fathers is especially large among girls: As a rule, the mother-daughter relationship tends to be the closest, and the father-daughter relationship the least intimate, with mother-son and father-son relationships falling in between (Noller & Callan, 1990; Rice & Mulkeen, 1995).

In summary, an important transition in intimate relationships takes place during early adolescence. Peers become the most important source of companionship and intimate self-disclosure, surpassing parents and siblings (Larson & Richards, 1991; Villalobos Solís, Smetana, & Comer, 2015). Peers become increasingly important targets of intimacy not simply because they are similar in age but because they grow up in a different family. As adolescents begin the process of individuation, they often need to seek intimacy outside the family as a means of establishing an identity beyond their family role. Although this shift in intimacy is normative, a shift in primary attachment figures at this age is not: Adolescents who report that their strongest attachment is to a friend or romantic partner are more likely to have insecure attachments with their parents (Freeman & Brown, 2001).

social support
The extent to which an individual receives emotional or instrumental assistance from his or her social network.

The Different Roles of Parents and Peers Adolescents have very different sorts of intimate relationships with parents and peers, and these differences point to different ways in which mothers, fathers, and friends contribute to social development. Even in close families, parent-adolescent relations are characterized by an imbalance of power. Parents are nurturers, advice givers, and teachers whom adolescents turn to for their experience and expertise. Adolescents' interactions with their friends are more mutual, more balanced, and more likely to provide them with opportunities to express alternative views and engage in an equal exchange of feelings and beliefs. Conflicts between adolescents and their parents are relatively more likely to end with a "winner" and a "loser," whereas conflicts between adolescents and their friends are relatively more likely to end in compromise or, at least, equal outcomes (Adams & Laursen, 2001).

Rather than viewing one type of relationship as more or less intimate than the other, it is more accurate to say that intimacy with parents and with peers are both important. Intimacy with parents provides opportunities to learn from those older and wiser; intimacy with friends provides opportunities to share experiences with individuals who have a similar perspective and degree of expertise. Adolescents who have strong attachments to both parents and peers are better adjusted than those who have strong attachments in one type of relationship but not the other (Laible, Carlo, & Raffaelli, 2000). In addition, the positive impact of having supportive friends in adolescence is greater when an adolescent also has supportive parents (Helsen, Vollebergh, & Meeus, 2000). Shy adolescents seem especially likely to benefit from having supportive parents (Barstead et al., 2018).

The different functions of intimacy with parents and peers are nicely illustrated in studies of school transitions. Changing schools during adolescence can sometimes be stressful, and **social support**—emotional or instrumental assistance from others—can help buffer adolescents against the potential negative effects of stress (Hauser & Bowlds, 1990). Support from family members is more predictive of adaptation to the demands of the new school, as indexed by grades and attendance, but support from peers is more predictive of psychological well-being. The absence of peer support appears to be especially critical for boys, perhaps because girls are more likely than boys to seek out other sources of support when their peers do not provide it.

A lack of support from parents or from friends in school is associated with low self-worth and poorer social adjustment. Social support from one source (such as the family) can be especially important when other sources of support (such as friends) are lacking. Accordingly, having a supportive family is more important for the healthy adjustment of adolescents who do not have a close friend, whereas support from friends or romantic partners is more crucial among adolescents whose family relationships are strained (Szwedo, Hessel, & Allen, 2017). An absence of social support may be especially problematic for ethnic minority youth, who often rely on peers to provide emotional support in the face of stress and other difficulties associated with living in high-risk environments (Benner, 2011; Stanton-Salazar & Spina, 2005).

Having support from parents, siblings, or nonschool friends does not fully compensate for a lack of support from classmates, though, and having support from siblings, classmates, or others does not fully compensate for a lack of support from parents (East & Rook, 1992; Gore & Aseltine, 1995). Optimal social development during adolescence may require healthy relationships with *both* parents and peers (Ciarrochi et al., 2017; Jose, Ryan, & Pryor, 2012; Waters, Lester, & Cross, 2014). In other words, family relationships and peer relationships influence, rather than compete with, each other.

Although the importance of peer relationships undoubtedly increases during adolescence, the significance of family relationships does not decline so much as it narrows in focus. Parents do not cease to be important sources of influence or targets of intimacy. Throughout adolescence, parents and teenagers remain close, parents (especially mothers) remain important confidants, and both mothers and fathers continue to be significant influences on the adolescent's behavior and decisions. Having a supportive relationship with one parent can compensate somewhat from a less close relationship with the other (Rueger et al., 2014). That said, peers take on an increasingly important role in the individual's social life over the course of adolescence (Brown & Larson, 2009). Although peers do not replace parents, they make unique and influential contributions to the adolescent's social development.

Other Individuals as Targets of Intimacy Intimacy in sibling relationships is complicated and often includes a mix of affection and rivalry (East, 2009). Generally, adolescents say they are less intimate with siblings than with their parents or friends (Buhrmester & Furman, 1987). Adolescents fight more with brothers and sisters than they do with close friends, and their arguments with siblings tend to be resolved less often by giving in or by letting things slide than through the intervention of parents (Raffaelli, 1997). Over the course of adolescence, conflict between siblings decreases, but this may be due to the fact that siblings spend less time together in adolescence than they did in childhood as they become involved in close friendships, romantic relationships, and extracurricular activities. Although overt conflict between siblings declines during adolescence, so do warmth and closeness. Early adolescence is the low point in sibling relationships, but even college students report ambivalent feelings about their brothers and sisters (Stocker, Lanthier, & Furman, 1997).

Comparatively little is known about intimacy with members of adolescents' extended family or with nonfamilial adults such as teachers or coaches. Contact with extended family is infrequent for many adolescents because those family members often live outside the adolescent's immediate area. There is a slight increase in intimacy with extended family members during childhood but an especially steep drop-off in intimacy with grandparents and other extended family members between childhood and adolescence (Creasey & Kaliher, 1994; Levitt, Guacci-Franci, & Levitt, 1993). Nevertheless, adolescents benefit from having grandparents involved in their life (Yorgason, Padilla-Walker, & Jackson, 2011), and having frequent high-quality interactions with their grandparents is associated with more favorable feelings toward the elderly (Flamion et al., 2019).

Although a decline in intimacy with grandparents is often observed during adolescence, this is not as common among adolescents who are living with a single, divorced mother (Dunifon, 2013). Divorce is associated with increased contact between adolescents and their grandparents, especially between adolescents and their maternal grandfathers. Ties to grandmothers are especially strong among Black adolescents, particularly among girls from divorced households (Hirsch, Mickus, & Boerger, 2002).

Researchers also have asked whether relationships between adolescents and nonfamilial adults in schools, workplaces, or neighborhoods can play a significant role in teenagers' lives. Indeed, studies suggest that the development of relationships with nonfamilial adults is a normative part of adolescence, not a sign of difficulties at home (Beam, Chen, & Greenberger, 2002; Rhodes & Lowe, 2009), and that relationships with positive role models outside the family, such as mentors, contribute to healthy development above and beyond the contribution of family relationships and well into late adolescence and even adulthood (Chang et al., 2010; Haddad, Chen, & Greenberger, 2011; Miranda-Chan et al., 2016). Close friendships may develop naturally between adolescents and their teachers or work supervisors or can be cultivated through community organizations, such as Big Brothers/Big Sisters or similar programs designed to pair young people—especially those under stress—with supportive and caring adults. Unfortunately, low-income youth are less likely than their peers to develop relationships with naturally occurring mentors (as opposed to mentors whom they meet through organized programs) (Raposa et al., 2018).

Linking an adolescent with a mentor is one of the most important components of successful youth programs (Theokas & Lerner, 2006). The benefits of having a Big Brother or Big Sister are especially great among adolescents with more difficulties at home, such as those living in foster care (Rhodes, Haight, & Briggs, 1999).

Not all close relationships with nonparental adults benefit adolescents' development, however: Adolescent boys who have close friendships with young adult men are more likely to engage in antisocial behavior when they perceive their older friends as likely to condone or commit antisocial acts themselves (Greenberger, Chen, & Beam, 1998).

Friendships with the Other Sex

Not until late adolescence do close friendships with other-sex peers begin to be important. Studies of preadolescents and young teenagers point to very strong sex segregation in adolescents' friendships, with boys rarely reporting friendships with girls and girls rarely reporting friendships with boys, at least until middle adolescence (Galambos, Berenbaum, & McHale, 2009).

Origins of the "Sex Cleavage."　The schism between boys and girls during early adolescence results from various factors. First, despite whatever changes may have taken place in American society in sex-role socialization during the past 60 years, it is still the case that preadolescent and early adolescent boys and girls have different interests, engage in different sorts of peer activities, and perceive themselves to be different from each other (Galambos, Berenbaum, & McHale, 2009). The "sex cleavage" in adolescent friendships results more from adolescents' preferring members of the same sex—and the activities they engage in—than from their actually disliking members of the other sex. Boys express more positive feelings about their female classmates than vice versa (Bukowski, Sippola, & Hoza, 1999).

The transitional period—between same-sex nonsexual relationships and other-sex sexual ones—can be a trying time for adolescents. This period usually coincides with the peer group's shift from same-sex cliques to mixed-sex crowds. The interpersonal strains and anxieties inherent in the transition show up in the teasing, joking around, and overt discomfort that young adolescents so often display in situations that are a little too close to being romantic or sexual. One reason for the mutual physical playfulness that boys and girls engage in is that it satisfies normal curiosity about sexual feelings while being ambiguous enough to be denied as motivated by romantic interest. Whereas rough play—play fighting—between boys is typically done to show who is dominant, the same behavior between boys and girls is often semisexual in nature—what some have labeled "poke and push courtship" (Pellegrini, 2003).

These observations support the claim that intimacy between adolescent boys and girls is relatively slow to develop and generally is tinged with an air of sexuality. Contrary to the idea that cross-sex intimacy comes to replace intimacy with peers of the same sex, however, intimate friendships between adolescents of the same sex are not displaced by the emergence of intimacy between adolescent males and females. Although the likelihood of other-sex peers appearing on adolescents' lists of people who are important to them increases during early and middle adolescence and although the amount of time adolescents spend with other-sex peers increases as well, the number of same-sex peers listed also increases or remains constant, and time spent with same-sex peers does not decline. However, there are substantial individual differences in patterns of time allocation to same- and other-sex relationships. Some adolescents shift their energy from same-sex friends to other-sex relationships early and abruptly, others do so gradually over the course of high school, and still others do not shift their focus at all (Zimmer-Gembeck, 1999).

When females do include other-sex peers on their list of important people, the boys they mention are often older and often from another school; when boys list girls as important friends, they generally are of the same age or younger (Poulin & Pedersen, 2007). Consequently, the increase in time spent with other-sex peers that occurs in adolescence takes place much earlier among girls than boys; by 11th grade, the average girl spends 10 hours each week alone with a boy, compared to only 5 hours per week spent by the average boy alone with a girl. Young adolescents of both sexes spend a lot of time thinking about the other sex but relatively little time with them. As adolescents get older, the time they spend thinking about the other sex tends to be increasingly associated with negative moods, perhaps because the fantasies about the other sex experienced in early adolescence come to be replaced by unrequited longings for romantic companionship (Richards et al., 1998).

As cross-sex relationships begin to develop, adolescents may mask their anxieties by teasing and joking around with members of the other sex. Hammond HSN/Design Pics

Some Functions of Other-Sex Friendships

Although the emergence of close other-sex friendships in early adolescence is not explicitly in the context of romance, it sets the stage for later romantic experiences (Connolly & McIsaac, 2009; Savickaitė et al., 2019). In early and middle adolescence, age differences in other-sex friendships are similar to those seen between dating partners, with boys generally older than their female friends, rather than the reverse (Montgomery & Sorell, 1998). In addition, adolescents who have more other-sex friends than their peers early in adolescence tend to enter into romantic relationships at an earlier age and tend to have longer romantic relationships (Feiring, 1999). This could be due to many factors, including the adolescent's use of the pool of other-sex friends to "rehearse" for later romantic relationships (Kreager et al., 2016) or to develop a social network that is used to meet potential romantic partners later on (Connolly, Furman, & Konarski, 2000). In any case, even preadolescents as young as 9 differentiate between cross-sex relationships that are platonic and those that are romantic (Connolly et al., 1999).

Not all relationships between males and females in adolescence are romantic, of course, and having close, other-sex friendships is a common experience (Connolly & McIsaac, 2009; Kuttler, La Greca, & Prinstein, 1999). Interestingly, two very different types of adolescents appear to have close other-sex friends: adolescents who are socially competent and highly popular with same-sex peers, and adolescents who are socially incompetent and highly unpopular with same-sex peers (Bukowski, Sippola, & Hoza, 1999).

Among boys, having an other-sex friend compensates for not having same-sex friends, leading to more positive mental health than is seen among boys without any friends at all. Among girls, however, the results are mixed. Although some studies have found that for girls "there is no advantage, or perhaps there is even a disadvantage, to having a friendship with a boy" (Bukowski, Sippola, & Hoza, 1999, p. 457), others have found that, among less sexually advanced girls, having platonic friendships with boys is associated with a more positive body image—perhaps because these friendships permit girls to feel that boys like them for themselves, without the added cost of feeling pressured to have sex (Compian, Gowen, & Hayward, 2004). The downside is that having male friends increases girls' likelihood of being involved in antisocial behavior (Arndorfer & Stormshak, 2008; Mrug, Borch, & Cillessen, 2011; Poulin, Denalt, & Pedersen, 2011), especially if their male friends are antisocial (Cauffman, Farruggia, & Goldweber, 2008). (One of the ways through which parental monitoring deters adolescent girls' substance use is by limiting their friendships with boys [Poulin & Denault, 2012].) Another potential cost is that many cross-sex friendships draw females into caregiving roles, reinforcing traditional sex-role stereotypes.

Platonic friendships between adolescent males and females often prepare the adolescent for the transition into romantic relationships. Shutterstock

All things considered, boys have more to gain from friendships with girls than vice versa. Having an intimate relationship with an other-sex peer is more strongly related to boys' general level of interpersonal intimacy than it is to girls' (Buhrmester & Furman, 1987). Whereas boys report that their friendships with girls are more rewarding than their friendships with other boys, girls do not describe their friendships with boys as more rewarding than their friendships with other girls (Thomas & Daubman, 2001). These findings are not surprising, given that adolescents' friendships with girls (regardless of whether they themselves are male or female) tend to be more intimate and supportive than their friendships with boys (Kuttler, La Greca, & Prinstein, 1999).

Dating and Romantic Relationships

Dating plays a very different role in adolescents' lives today than it did in previous times (Connolly & McIsaac, 2009). In earlier eras, dating was not so much a recreational activity (as it is today) as a part of the process of courtship and mate selection. Individuals would date in order to ready themselves for marriage, and unmarried individuals would play the field—under the watchful eyes of chaperones—for a relatively long period before settling down (Montgomery, 1996). At the turn of the twentieth century, most individuals did not marry until their mid-20s. The first half of the twentieth century saw a gradual decline in the average age of marriage, however, and as a result, individuals began dating more seriously at an earlier age. By the mid-1950s, the average age at first marriage in the United States had fallen to 20 among women and 22 among men—which means that substantial numbers of individuals were in premarital relationships during high school and marrying during their late adolescent years.

The function of adolescent dating changed as individuals began to marry later and later—a trend that began in the mid-1950s and continues today (see Figure 10.6). Now, the average age at which people marry is considerably later than it was 50 years ago—about age 27 for women and 30 for men, although the age at which couples begin living together has not changed (Manning, Brown, & Payne, 2014; U.S. Census Bureau, 2020). This, of course, gives high school dating a whole new meaning because today it is clearly divorced from its function in mate selection. Adults continue to regulate and monitor adolescent dating in order to prevent rash or impulsive commitments to early marriage (Laursen & Jensen-Campbell, 1999), but in the minds of most young people, high school dating has little to do with finding a potential spouse. Nor do today's adolescents see cohabitation (living together) as a substitute for marriage (Manning, Longmore, & Giordano, 2007).

Romantic relationships during adolescence are very common: One-fourth of American 12-year-olds, one-half of 15-year-olds, and more than two-thirds of 18-year-olds report having had a romantic relationship in the past 18 months. Despite this, adolescent romance has not received a great deal of research attention. One reason researchers know so little about romantic relationships in adolescence is that few of them last more than a couple of months. In one study (Furman et al., 2019), the average respondent reported having had more than 10 romantic relationships before the age of 25!

There has been a substantial decline in the past three decades in the proportion of adolescents who have gone out on a date, however (see Figure 10.7). Whether this reflects a drop in adolescents' interest in romance and sex (which is probably unlikely) or a decrease in the popularity of going out isn't known for sure, although some have speculated that teenagers' interest in online socializing has led more of them to spend time at home (Twenge & Park, 2019). That is, fewer adolescents are "going out" on dates but are "dating" electronically instead through texts or social media. How this affects the development of interpersonal skills within romantic relationships is not known, although one study found that frequent use of technology-based communication with romantic partners was associated with lower social competence, especially among boys (Nesi et al., 2017).

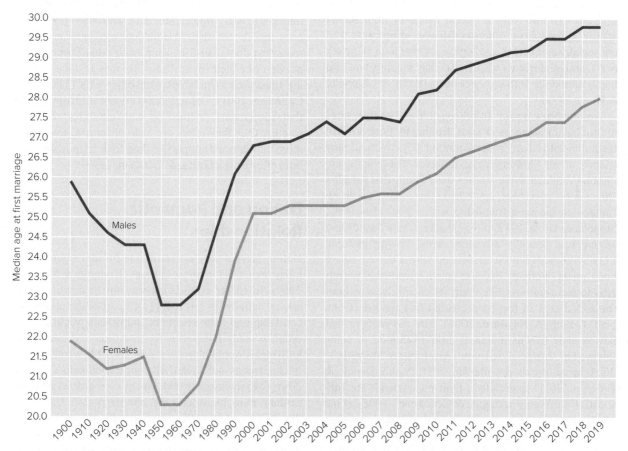

Figure 10.6 **The median age at marriage in the United States declined from 1900 through the mid-1950s but rose markedly during the second half of the twentieth century.**

Source: U.S. Census Bureau. (2020). Marriage rates in the US over the last century. *Current population survey.* Washington, DC: Author. https://www.census.gov/data/tables/time-series/demo/families/marital.html.

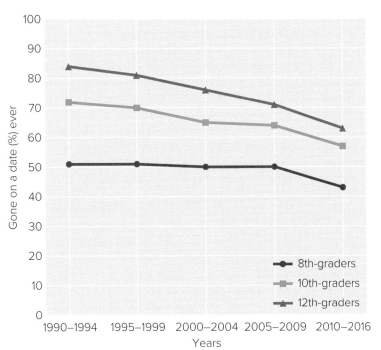

Figure 10.7 There has been a substantial decline in the past three decades in the proportions of 8th-, 10th-, and 12th-graders who have gone out on a date. (Twenge & Park, 2019)

As is the case with platonic cross-sex friendships, girls tend to become romantically involved with boys who are slightly older, whereas boys tend to become involved with girls who are the same age or younger. Because the average duration of romantic relationships during the middle high school years is about 6 months, most adolescents report having experienced a breakup during the last year. Perhaps as a way of protecting themselves from more pain than is necessary, most teenagers say that they were in control of the breakup (either alone or by mutual agreement) (Connolly & McIsaac, 2009). Nevertheless, as you will read later in this chapter, the breakup of a romantic relationship is a significant source of distress for many adolescents, and, as you read earlier, the ups and downs of romantic life often dominate conversations between friends.

Dating and the Development of Intimacy

Contemporary discussions of adolescent romance draw on Sullivan's theory of interpersonal development, attachment theory, and ecological perspectives on development (Connolly & McIsaac, 2009). From Sullivan comes the idea that there is a developmental progression in individuals' capacity for intimacy, with the emergence of romantic relationships occurring after individuals have experienced emotional closeness within same-sex friendships. From attachment theory comes the idea that individuals differ in the quality of their romantic relationships and that these differences are paralleled by differences in the relationships individuals have with parents and peers.

And from the ecological perspective comes the idea that romantic relationships, like all relationships, need to be viewed within the social context in which they occur.

The Nature and Significance of Romance The capacity for intimacy, which initially develops out of same-sex friendships, eventually is brought into romantic relationships, which for the vast majority of adolescents are with members of the other sex. In this sense, relationships between romantic partners are better thought of as a context in which intimacy is expressed rather than where it is learned. Consistent with this, the quality of adolescents' friendships is predictive of the quality of their subsequent romantic relationships, whereas the reverse is not true (Connolly, Furman, & Konarski, 2000).

Romantic relationships play a different role in the development of intimacy for females than for males. In many cultures, boys are not encouraged to develop the capacity to be emotionally expressive, particularly in their relationships with other males. During middle adolescence, girls are better than boys at self-disclosure and interpersonal understanding, so when adolescents first start having serious romantic relationships, girls generally are better at being intimate. Early sexual relationships are far more likely to revolve around love, emotional involvement, and intimacy for girls than for boys (Montgomery, 2005; Shulman & Scharf, 2000).

In other words, for girls romantic relationships provide a context for the further *expression* of intimacy, whereas for boys they provide a context for the further *development* of intimacy. Relationships with the other sex, therefore, play a more important role in the development of intimacy among boys than among girls, who, on average, develop and experience intimacy earlier with same-sex friends than boys do (Buhrmester & Furman, 1987). The way a girl interacts with her boyfriend is more strongly related to the girl's internal working model of relationships than the boy's, perhaps because girls' greater prior experience with intimacy has led them to better align how they behave with how they really feel (Furman & Simon, 2006).

Although boys' capacity for intimacy may lag behind girls', it is important not to confuse ability with aspiration. In the past, much was made of the different meanings of romantic relationships to adolescent males and females, but today it appears that the sexes are more similar than different in how their romantic relationships develop (Connolly & McIsaac, 2009). The stereotype of the emotionally stunted but swaggering boy who enters into a romantic relationship purely for sex and uses his power and influence to get it no longer appears accurate, although adolescent couples are more likely to have intercourse when the girl reports that her boyfriend holds the power in the relationship (Giordano, Manning, & Longmore, 2010). Boys are often more awkward and less confident than the girls they are dating and just as eager to be emotionally close. Here's a 17-year-old talking about his girlfriend:

> She kept insisting I wasn't going to work out and I kept insisting I wanted to try it and one night, and like I said I couldn't sleep, and I wrote her a letter, front and back, crying the whole time and then I handed the letter to her the next morning. . . . It was really emotional, like how she hurt me and how it wasn't right. (Giordano, Longmore, & Manning, 2006, p. 277)

Or how about this 18-year-old young man:

> I guess she was more mature than I was and I guess I wasn't on her level you know because she wanted to do it [have sex] more than I did. . . . she said that I wasn't mature enough and you know all that stuff. . . . I was too young, I was scared, I didn't know what I was doing I wasn't ready for it. I think I felt like I was too young. . . . she was my girlfriend and that's what she wanted. (Giordano, Longmore, & Manning, 2006, p. 281)

There are also important cultural differences in how adolescents approach dating: In one study, Latinx adolescents were more likely to emphasize romantic aspects of the relationship and were more willing to accept traditional views of the roles of males and females in relationships, whereas Black adolescents were more pragmatic and egalitarian in their attitudes (Milbrath, Ohlson, & Eyre, 2009).

The Role of Context The age at which dating begins is influenced by the norms and expectations in the adolescent's community. Romantic relationships are more common at a younger age in other industrialized countries than in North America, but by late adolescence, rates of dating are similar. Within the United States and Canada, Asian adolescents are less likely than other adolescents to date, whereas the prevalence of dating is very similar among Black, Latinx, Native American, and white adolescents, although some studies find that Latinx girls start dating at a later age than either Black or white girls (Connolly & McIsaac, 2009). Westernization is leading many adolescents from Asian cultures to develop interests in dating at an earlier age than is typical within their culture (Dhariwal & Connolly, 2013).

Although early maturers begin dating somewhat earlier than late maturers (Lam et al., 2002; Neemann, Hubbard, & Masten, 1995), age norms within the adolescent's school and peer group are more important in determining the age at which dating begins than is the adolescent's physical maturity. In other words, a physically immature 14-year-old who goes to school where it is expected that 14-year-olds will date is more likely to date than is a physically mature 14-year-old who lives in a community where dating is typically delayed until age 16. Consistent with this, adolescents who begin a romantic relationship at an earlier age than was normative in their school reported more problems than those whose dating began at an age that was more customary among their classmates (van Zantvliet, Ivanova, & Verbakel, 2020). (As you will read, early dating in general is associated with more psychological problems, but it isn't clear whether early dating is a cause or consequence of them.)

Early maturers whose peers are dating are especially likely to date early (Friedlander et al., 2007). Dating also begins earlier among adolescents who have older siblings, who are less close to their parents, and who live with single mothers, especially if the mother is sexually active (de Graaf et al., 2012; Tyrell et al., 2016). Family instability (changes in parents' marital status through divorce or remarriage) is associated with dating, especially among boys, with adolescents from more unstable families more likely to date and more likely to have multiple romantic partners (Valle & Tillman, 2014). Whether this is due to less vigilant parental monitoring, a desire on the part of the adolescent to escape a difficult home environment, or both is not known (Cavanagh, Crissey, & Raley, 2008).

Patterns of Dating "Dating" can mean a variety of different things, from group activities that bring males and females together (without much actual contact between the sexes), to group dates in which a group of boys and girls go out jointly (and spend part of the time in couples and part of the time in the larger group), to casual dating in couples, to serious involvement with a boyfriend or girlfriend (Carlson & Rose, 2012). Generally, casual socializing with other-sex peers and experiences in a mixed-sex social network occur before the development of romantic relationships (Connolly & McIsaac, 2009).

As a consequence, more adolescents have experience in mixed-sex group activities such as parties or dances than in dating, and more have dated than have had a serious boyfriend or girlfriend, or a sexual relationship (Connolly et al., 2004; O'Sullivan et al., 2007). However, involvement in one-on-one romantic relationships does not replace same-sex or mixed-sex group activities; like other aspects of intimacy in adolescence, new forms of relationships are added to the adolescent's repertoire while old ones are retained. The sequence of transitioning into romantic relationships follows similar patterns across ethnic groups, although Asian American youth appear to make this transition at a somewhat later stage than their peers from other backgrounds, consistent with other findings on ethnic differences in beliefs about the appropriate age at which adolescents should begin dating and engaging in other adultlike activities (Connolly et al., 2004).

Even for adolescents with a history of intimate friendships with same- and other-sex peers, the transition into romantic relationships can be difficult. In one study in which adolescents were asked to discuss social situations they thought were difficult, themes having to do with communicating with the other sex were mentioned frequently. Many adolescents discussed difficulty in initiating or maintaining conversations in person ("He will think I am an idiot," "Sometimes you don't know, if you're like sitting with a guy and you're watching a basketball game or something, you don't know if you should start talking or if you should just sit there") and on the phone ("I think it is hard to call. After it's done with, you don't know how to get off the phone"). Others mentioned problems in asking people out ("Asking a girl out on a first date—complete panic!") or in turning people down ("How about if you go on a date and you're really not interested, but he keeps calling?"). Still others noted problems in making or ending romantic commitments ("You don't know if you are going out with someone or if you are just seeing them," "It is hard to say, 'so, are we gonna make a commitment?'" "I avoided [breaking up] for two weeks because I was trying to think of what to say") (Grover & Nangle, 2003, pp. 133–134).

The Development of Dating Relationships

It is not until late adolescence that dating relationships begin to be characterized by a level of emotional depth and maturity that can be described as intimate, and it is not until late adolescence that individuals develop genuinely deep attachments to individuals other than their parents (Furman & Simon, 1999; Montgomery, 2005). One study comparing the way adolescents interacted with their mother, a close friend, and a romantic partner when discussing something like planning a celebration found that interactions with romantic partners were characterized by more conflict and fewer positive interactions than with friends and by more off-task behavior than with

mothers (Furman & Shomaker, 2008). Over the course of adolescence, the importance of a romantic partner—relative to other relationships—increases, and by college, individuals typically name their romantic partner first on a list of significant others (up from fourth in grade 7 and third in grade 10) (Buhrmester, 1996; Furman & Wehner, 1994).

The ways in which adolescents interact with romantic partners also changes with development, with increasing willingness to acknowledge, analyze, and work through disagreements. The major sources of conflict between boyfriends and girlfriends are issues related to how the relationship is going, such as jealousy, neglect, betrayal, dishonesty, and trust (McIsaac et al., 2008; Norona et al., 2017). Compared to young adults, adolescents' behavior toward their partners is more negative, more controlling, and more characterized by jealousy; younger couples who have been dating for a long time are especially likely to report these problems (Lantagne & Furman, 2017) (see Figure 10.8). One study of age differences in couples' conflict resolution found that whereas 70% of the adolescent couples either denied having conflicts or dismissed them as insignificant, only 20% of the young adults did. Adolescents whose conversations look more like those of the young adults are less likely to break up (Appel & Shulman, 2015; Shulman et al., 2006).

Reasons for Dating   Prior to middle or late adolescence, dating may be less important for the development of intimacy than it is for other purposes, including establishing emotional and behavioral autonomy from parents (Gray & Steinberg, 1999), furthering the development of gender identity (Feiring, 1999), learning about oneself as a romantic partner (Furman & Simon, 1999), and establishing and maintaining status and popularity in the peer

One of the fundamental developmental tasks of adolescence is to begin to develop the capacity for intimate, romantic relationships. Andrey_Popov/Shutterstock

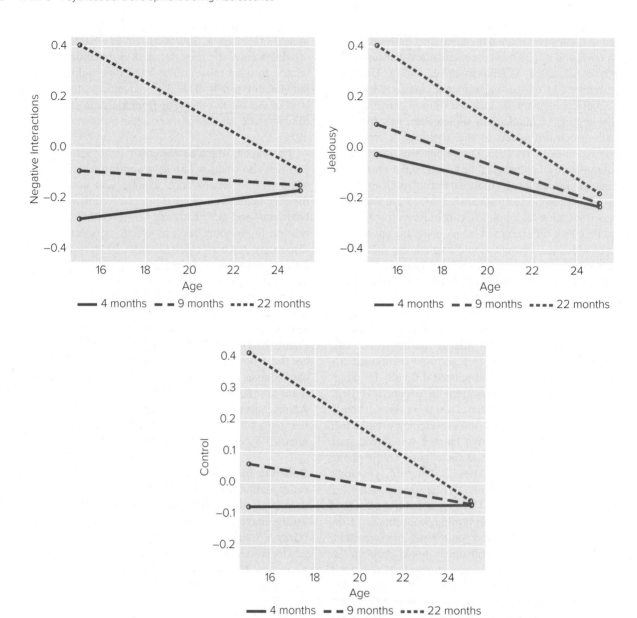

Figure 10.8 Compared to young adults, adolescents' behavior toward their partners is more negative, more controlling, and more characterized by jealousy; younger couples who have been dating for a long time (i.e., 22 months, in this study) are especially likely to report these problems. (Lantagne & Furman, 2017)

group (Brown, 2004). Younger adolescents' choice of dating partners may have more to do with how they will be seen by others (for example, as "grown up," "macho," or "popular") than with the actual quality of the relationship itself. This explains why, between elementary school and middle school, there is an increase in girls' attraction to "bad boys"–aggressive boys who enjoy high status in the peer group (Bukowski, Sippola, & Newcomb, 2000).

Phases of Romance The development of intimacy and more sophisticated social cognitive abilities is paralleled by changes in the ways adolescents think about and behave within romantic relationships (Connolly & McIsaac, 2009). The evolution of romance in the adolescent's life proceeds through three distinct phases. During the first phase (roughly between 11 and 13), adolescents first discover an interest in socializing with potential romantic and sexual partners. The focus of activity during this phase is primarily on learning about themselves, as adolescents broaden their self-conceptions to include seeing themselves as a potential romantic partner. Actual romantic relationships tend to be short-lived (the average romantic relationship at this age lasts only a few weeks), though, and are frequently based on superficial infatuations. Success in socializing with the other sex becomes an important determinant of status in the peer group, and high-status adolescents generally start dating before their lower-status peers. The main purpose of romantic activity at this age involves establishing, improving, or maintaining one's social status.

During the second phase (from about 14 to 16), adolescents slowly move toward more meaningful dyadic relationships. Dating is very casual and often occurs in a group context in which peer networks start to include couples who have a special relationship. Although adolescents are still learning about themselves as romantic and sexual partners and are still aware of the way their peers view their romantic relationships, they are now sufficiently involved in the emotional side of romance for this to completely overshadow the personal and status concerns that dominated the earlier phases of romantic involvement. Relationships become a source of passion and preoccupation—recalling the themes expressed in popular love songs that appeal to teenagers. Although relationships are more enduring at this age than they were during early adolescence, the average romance still lasts only about 6 months (Connolly & McIsaac, 2009). One reason for this is that "dating the 'wrong' person or conducting romantic relationships in the 'wrong' way can seriously damage one's standing in the group. . . .This makes it difficult to sustain relationships that are too heavily focused inward, on the quality of the interaction or needs of the couple" (Brown, 1999, p. 297).

Finally, toward the later years of high school (around 17 or 18), concerns about commitment begin to move to the forefront as adolescents begin to think about the long-term survival and growth of their romantic attachments. Often during this stage, there are tensions between partners' needs for intimacy (which draw them together) and their needs for autonomy (which distance them). As conceptions of romance develop, adolescents come to value commitment and caring as features of relationships that are as important as passion and pleasure, if not more so (Seiffge-Krenke, 2003). Relationships begin to look more like those seen among young adults, and couples increasingly spend time by themselves, rather than in the larger peer group. The average romantic relationship at age 18 lasts more than a year (Connolly & McIsaac, 2009). The quality of someone's romantic relationships has a much more significant impact on his or her mental health than it did at younger ages (Collibee & Furman, 2015).

Although the progression through the different phases of dating and romance may characterize the development of most adolescents, a number of writers interested in the experiences of lesbian, gay, bisexual, transgender, and questioning (LGBTQ) adolescents have pointed out that this picture may be less applicable to **LGBTQ youth**—adolescents who are not exclusively or conventionally heterosexual (Diamond, Savin-Williams, & Dubé, 1999). Although great strides have been made in increasing the public's tolerance and understanding of **sexual-minority youth,** stigmas and stereotypes still make the development of intimate relationships—whether nonsexual friendships, dating relationships, or sexual relationships—more complicated among LGBTQ youth than among their straight peers.

For example, because LGBTQ youth don't always have the freedom to publicly express their romantic and sexual interests, they often find it difficult, if not impossible, to engage in many of the social and interpersonal activities that their heterosexual friends are permitted to enjoy. Thus, many LGBTQ youth end up pursuing sexual activity *outside* the context of a dating relationship because the prejudices and harassment of others may preclude any public display of romantic intimacy with a same-sex partner. At the same time, for LGBTQ youth who are even somewhat open about their sexual identity, the development of close, nonsexual friendships with same-sex peers may be hampered by the suspicions and homophobia of others. As one group of writers explains the special predicament faced by LGBTQ adolescents, "A sexual-minority adolescent may already be privately plagued by the sense that he or she is profoundly different from other youths. To have this differentness acknowledged and perhaps ridiculed by peers may prove intolerable" (Diamond, Savin-Williams, & Dubé, 1999). Interestingly, a study of 15-year-olds from six different European countries found very similar percentages of boys and girls who said they had dated opposite-gender peers, same-gender peers, peers of both genders, or no one (Költő et al., 2018) (see Figure 10.9).

LGBTQ youth Lesbian, gay, bisexual, transgender, and questioning youth, sometimes referred to as sexual-minority youth.

sexual-minority youth Lesbian, gay, bisexual, transgender, and questioning (LGBTQ) youth.

Sex Differences in Partner Preferences   There are both age and sex differences in what adolescents look for in romantic partners, and these differences parallel what is known about age and sex differences in romantic

The interpersonal challenges of adolescence can be more complicated for LGBTQ youth. mangpor2004/Shutterstock

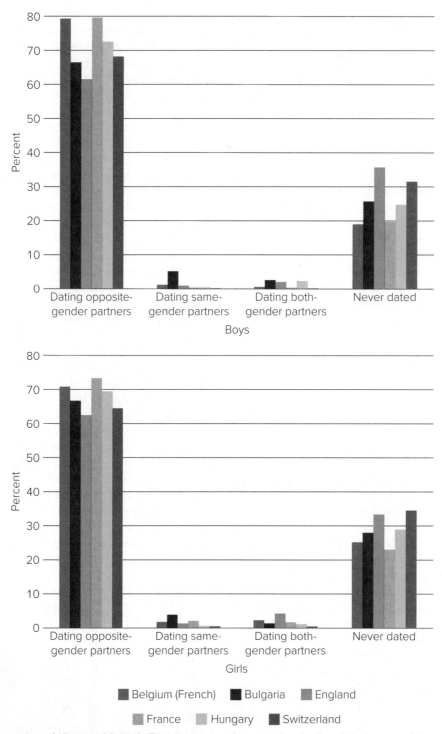

Figure 10.9   Proportion of 15-year-olds in six European countries reporting having dated peers of the opposite gender, same gender, or both, or who had never dated. (Költő et al., 2018)

relationships. During middle adolescence, boys are more likely than girls to emphasize physical attractiveness and girls are more likely than boys to place more weight on interpersonal qualities, such as support or intimacy, although controlled studies, in which characteristics of potential dates are experimentally manipulated, find that girls are influenced more by attractiveness than they think they are (Ha, Overbeek, & Engels, 2010). By late adolescence, both sexes emphasize interpersonal qualities, and the ingredients of a satisfying relationship are very similar for males and females (and quite similar to those mentioned by adults): passion, communication, commitment, emotional support, and togetherness (Collins, 2003).

The Impact of Dating on Adolescent Development

When considering the impact of dating on adolescents' development and mental health, it is important to differentiate between group and couple activities. Participating in mixed-sex activity in group situations—going to parties or dances, for example—has a positive impact on the psychological well-being of adolescents because at this stage of development, participating in these activities is status enhancing.

The impact of more serious dating is complicated and depends on the adolescent's age. Early starters (those who enter into dating relationships well before their peers) and late bloomers (those who do not have a romantic relationship until young adulthood) may both be at risk, although for different reasons and with different consequences. This is not to say that dating is not a valuable interpersonal experience for the adolescent, just that its benefits may only accrue among teenagers who begin dating at a certain age.

Early Starters Entering into a serious romantic relationship before it is normative (say, before age 15) is associated with a wide range of negative correlates (Connolly et al., 2013; Furman & Collibee, 2014; Orpinas et al., 2013). This is probably true for both sexes, but researchers have focused primarily on girls because boys are less likely to begin serious dating quite so early. Even so, the few studies that have looked at early dating among boys do not show consistent effects.

The links between early dating and poorer mental health have been reported consistently for more than 50 years. Girls who begin serious dating early are worse off psychologically than their peers: less mature socially, less imaginative, less oriented toward achievement, less happy with who they are and how they look, more depressed, more likely to engage in disordered eating, less likely to do well in school, and more likely to be involved in delinquency, substance use, and risky behavior (Beckmeyer, 2015; Connolly & McIsaac, 2009).

Early dating seems to have particularly negative implications for white girls (Compian, Gowen, & Hayward, 2004), girls whose family relationships are more strained (Doyle et al., 2003), girls who date older boys (Haydon & Halpern, 2010; Loftus, Kelly, & Mustillo, 2011), and girls who are early physical maturers (Natsuaki, Biehl, & Ge, 2009). Adolescents who are unpopular with same-sex peers are especially harmed by early serious dating, perhaps because having few same-sex friends makes the dating relationships all the more important (Brendgen et al., 2002). Research also shows that adolescents who begin dating early and who have multiple dating partners experience a drop in the quality of their relationships over time (Collins, 2003) and poorer quality relationships in young adulthood (Madsen & Collins, 2011). Adolescents

who begin dating early are also more likely to be victims of dating violence (Halpern et al., 2009).

A variety of explanations for the link between early dating and psychological problems have been offered, but before we get ahead of ourselves, let's keep in mind the difficulty in distinguishing between cause and effect. There are all sorts of reasons that girls with psychological problems are more likely to get involved in dating relationships at a younger age, and because we cannot randomly assign some teenagers to date and others to remain single, we cannot be sure that early dating actually *causes* problems.

Early dating may be part of a larger profile that includes precocious involvement in many adultlike activities (often because girls' dating partners are older), and there is a good deal of evidence that this sort of "pseudomaturity" is associated with a range of psychological problems (Simons et al., 2018). Because this profile is itself associated with many factors known to place adolescents at risk (poor parenting, early puberty, or family instability, for example), it is hard to pinpoint early dating as the culprit. One study found, for example, that individuals who had poorer-quality relationships *prior* to adolescence were more likely to be dating at age 15 (Roisman et al., 2009). Another found that early dating was associated not only with puberty but also with having a sibling who was involved in risky behavior, having excessively lax parents, and having delinquent friends (Low & Shortt, 2017). In sum, there is evidence that girls who get involved in serious romances at a young age are different from their peers even before they begin dating.

That said, it has been suggested that early dating actually has adverse effects on adolescents' psychological adjustment. The link between early dating and poor mental health

The impact of dating on adolescent development depends on the age of the adolescent and the intensity of the relationship. Early, serious dating may have a negative impact on psychological development. Luxy Images/Getty Images

may have something to do with pressures on girls to engage in sexual activity before they are willing or psychologically ready (Marin et al., 2006). Sexual coercion and date rape are common during the high school years (Brown, 2004), although as it has become all too clear in recent years, sexual harassment and sexual assault are by no means limited to teenagers. Although boys may feel peer pressure to become sexually active, this may be a very different sort of pressure—with very different consequences—from what girls feel. Because boys generally begin dating at a later age than girls and date people who are younger, dating may be less anxiety-provoking for boys, who have the advantage of a few additional years of "maturity."

To Date or Not to Date?   About 10% of late adolescents report having had no serious romantic relationships, and another 15% have not been in a relationship that lasted more than a few months (Connolly & McIsaac, 2009). In looking at the effects of being a "late bloomer," it is important to distinguish between adolescents who delay dating because it is culturally normative to do so (as is the case in many Asian American communities) and those who delay because they are shy, unattractive, or unpopular (Connolly & McIsaac, 2009). Although one would think that it is the latter group whose development is most at risk, not enough research has been done on late bloomers to draw definitive conclusions.

In general, adolescents who do not date at all show signs of retarded social development and feelings of insecurity (Connolly & McIsaac, 2009), whereas adolescents who date and go to parties regularly are more popular, have a stronger self-image, and report greater acceptance by their friends; they also are more skilled at relational aggression, which is often associated with social competence (Houser, Mayeux, & Cross, 2015). Conversely, stopping or cutting back on dating after having dated heavily is associated with a drop in self-image and an increase in symptoms of depression (Davies & Windle, 2000).

In contrast to the impact of early serious dating or not dating at all, romantic socializing that is developmentally appropriate is associated with psychosocial maturity, social competence, and school bonding, perhaps because school is a setting in which romantic partners have plenty of opportunities to see each other (Beckmeyer & Weybright, 2020). It is not clear, of course, whether age-appropriate dating leads to better social development or whether more socially advanced adolescents are simply more likely to date; both are probably true. But it does seem safe to conclude that a moderate degree of dating—and a delay in serious involvement until age 15 or so—appears to be the most potentially valuable pattern.

This conclusion must be tempered by the fact that characteristics of the romantic partner play a role in shaping the impact of dating on psychological development. Adolescents who are not all that popular to begin with but who date popular peers gain in popularity over time,

and adolescents with problems who date peers whose mental health is good show improvements in their psychological functioning over time (Simon, Aikins, & Prinstein, 2008). It is also the case, just as in the selection of friends, that adolescents tend to select romantic partners with whom they share certain attributes. (Generally speaking, the idea that "birds of a feather flock together" is more often true than "opposites attract.") And, as is the case with friendships, dating a romantic partner with a history of delinquent behavior leads to more antisocial behavior, especially among females (Herrera, Wiersma, & Cleveland, 2011; Monahan, Dmitrieva, & Cauffman, 2014). Indeed, once they are romantically involved, adolescents' pattern of drinking starts to resemble that of their romantic partner more than that of their friends (DeLay et al., 2016).

Regardless of the impact that dating does or doesn't have on adolescents' psychosocial development, studies show that romance has a powerful impact on their emotional state. Entering into a new relationship leads to increases in self-esteem—but only if the relationship is of high quality; if it is a low-quality relationship, self-esteem suffers (Luciano & Orth, 2017) (see Figure 10.10).

According to several studies, adolescents' real and fantasized relationships trigger more strong emotional feelings (one-third of girls' strong feelings and one-quarter of boys') than do family, school, or friends. Not surprisingly, the proportion of strong emotions attributed to romantic relationships increases dramatically between preadolescence and early adolescence and between early and middle adolescence as well. And although the majority of

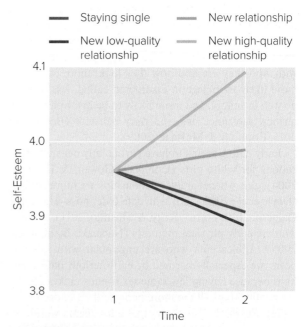

Figure 10.10   **Entering into a new relationship leads to increases in self-esteem—but only if the relationship is of high quality; if it is a low-quality relationship, self-esteem suffers.** (Luciano & Orth, 2017)

adolescents' feelings about their romantic relationships are positive, a substantial minority of their feelings—more than 40%, in fact—are negative, involving anxiety, anger, jealousy, and depression (Larson, Clore, & Wood, 1999).

Adolescents who have entered into a romantic relationship in the past year report more symptoms of depression than do those who have not (Joyner & Udry, 2000). One reason for this is that many adolescents who are involved romantically also experience breakups during the same time period (Chen et al., 2009; Collins, 2003), and the breakup of a romantic relationship is the single most common trigger of the first episode of major depression (Monroe et al., 1999). Breaking up is also associated with increases in substance use and delinquency (Hou et al., 2013; Larson & Sweeten, 2012).

Not surprisingly, having negative experiences in romantic relationships increases the risk of developing psychological problems, such as depression or anxiety (Reid et al., 2018). And, as you would expect, negative emotions associated with being in a relationship are more common among adolescents who are high in rejection sensitivity (Downey, Bonica, & Rincón, 1999) or who have an insecure working model, especially those who form preoccupied attachments to romantic partners (because they are unable to fully trust their partner or see themselves as worthy of their partner's affection) (Davila, 2008). Not surprisingly, adolescents whose parents are psychologically controlling, which can lead to anxiety, depression, and low self-esteem, are more likely to be high in rejection sensitivity (Rowe et al., 2015) and more prone to feelings of jealousy in their friendships (Kim, Parker, & Walker Marciano, 2017).

Breaking up does not have severe effects on all adolescents. Those who are most vulnerable to the potential negative consequences of ending a relationship are adolescents high in rejection sensitivity, those who have experienced a series of breakups, those who have other sorts of problems (such as binge drinking or involvement in delinquency), and, not surprisingly, those who identify themselves as the one who was broken up with (rather than the breaker-upper) (Connolly & McIsaac, 2009). Although breaking up often leads to a temporary drop in self-esteem, adolescents and young adults who are low in self-esteem are more likely to experience break-ups, in part because people with low self-esteem are less likely to have high-quality relationships (Luciano & Orth, 2017).

Violence in Dating Relationships Unfortunately, many romantic relationships in adolescence are characterized by hostility, aggression, and abuse (Exner-Cortens, 2014). More distressingly, a high proportion of young adolescents believe that physical violence in a relationship is acceptable. In a study of more than 5,000 American 6th-graders, over half said that it was acceptable for a girl to hit her boyfriend if he had made her mad or jealous, and a quarter of the students thought it was fine for

Unfortunately, a substantial number of teenagers end up in violent or abusive romantic relationships. Pixland/Getty Images

a boy to hit his girlfriend. Nearly a third of the girls in the sample and more than 25% of the boys who either were in or had been in a romantic relationship had been physically aggressive toward their partner (Simon et al., 2010). Although more than half of all parents talk to their adolescent about dating violence, parents are less likely to talk about this topic than about drugs, alcohol, family finances, money management, or even the economy (Rothman et al., 2011).

Estimates vary from study to study, but national surveys find that between 40% and 50% of American adolescents have been victims of stalking, harassment, or violence within the context of a romantic relationship at some time (Halpern et al., 2009; Rothman et al., 2020); 13% of high school girls and 4% of high school boys have been the victim of dating violence within the previous 12 months (Centers for Disease Control and Prevention, 2020). About 25% of dating teenagers report having been the victim of "cyber dating abuse" (abuse via technology and social media) during the past year (Zweig et al., 2013). As with other forms of cyberbullying, individuals who perpetrate cyber dating abuse are more likely to be abusive toward their partners in other ways, such as sexual coercion and violence (Cava et al., 2020; Temple et al., 2016; Zweig et al., 2014).

Dating abuse increases between early adolescence and mid-adolescence and then becomes somewhat less common (Foshee et al., 2009), and violence is often associated with drinking and drug use (East & Hokoda, 2015; H. Reyes et al., 2012; Temple et al., 2013) and exposure to stressful life events (Chen & Foshee, 2015). One recent study of young adults found, however, that drinking only elevates the likelihood of dating violence in relationships that are characterized by jealousy and negative interactions, which are risks for dating violence regardless of

Table 10.1   Percentages of students who witnessed situations and intervened when they had the opportunity.

Situation	Sample who witnessed the situation (%)	Who intervened among those who had the opportunity (%)
Expressed concern to a friend when I saw their boyfriend or girlfriend exhibiting very jealous behavior and trying to control my friend	36.7	61.5
Heard a friend insulting their partner, and said something to them	27.5	51.3
Indicated my displeasure when I heard sexist jokes	26.1	35.2
Indicated my displeasure when I heard catcalls (e.g., whistling at a girl)	20.2	31.2
Approached a friend I thought was in an abusive relationship and let them know that I'm here to help	17.9	54.2
Talked with friends about what makes a relationship abusive and what warning signs might be	17.9	28.3
Saw a man talking to a female friend. He was sitting very close to her, and by the look on her face, I could see she was uncomfortable. I asked her if she was okay or tried to start a conversation with her	14.2	47.7
Talked with my friends about sexual assault and relationship abuse as an issue for our community	11.9	18.4
Spoke up when I heard someone say, "She deserved to be raped"	11.5	56.8
Expressed disagreement with a friend who says having sex with someone who is passed out or very intoxicated is okay	10.6	44.2
Thought through the pros and cons of different ways I could help when I saw an instance of sexual assault	7.8	24.6
Stopped and checked in with my friend who looked very intoxicated when they were being taken upstairs at party	6.4	29.2
Went with my friend to talk with someone (e.g., police, counselor, crisis center) about an unwanted sexual experience or physical violence in their relationship	3.7	14.0

Percentage of sample who witnessed the situation consists of participants who had the opportunity to intervene, regardless of whether or not they actually intervened. The percentage of those who intervened among those who had the opportunity includes only the participants who intervened when given the opportunity.

(Edwards, Rodenhizer-Stampfli, & Eckstein, 2015)

whether the couple drinks (Collibee & Furman, 2018; Novak & Furman, 2016).

Because beliefs about the acceptability of violence in romantic relationships influence adolescents' behavior toward their partners (Fernández-González, Calvete, & Orue, 2019; McNaughton Reyes et al., 2016; Taylor, Sullivan, & Farrell, 2015), adolescents whose friends perpetrate dating violence are themselves more likely to do so (Aizpitarte, Alonso-Arbiol, & Van de Vaijver, 2017; Foshee et al., 2013), as are those who have been exposed to violent pornography (Rostad et al., 2019). One survey of high school students found that more than 90% of the sample had seen dating violence or sexual aggression or a situation likely to escalate into one or the other during the last year (Edwards, Rodenhizer-Stampfli, & Eckstein, 2015) (see Table 10.1). Some schools have adopted programs designed to promote bystander intervention in such circumstances.

Dating violence is more common in rural areas than in suburban or urban communities (Spencer & Bryant, 2000), and among ethnic minority adolescents, adolescents from single-parent households, adolescents from lower-socioeconomic homes, and LGBTQ youth (Dank et al., 2014; Foshee et al., 2009; Halpern et al., 2009; Luo, Stone, & Tharp, 2014; Martin-Storey, 2015). Individuals who are aggressive in romantic relationships are more likely to have had problems with aggression earlier in life (Humphrey & Vaillancourt, 2020; Vagi et al., 2013).

Being in a violent relationship also increases the chances of an adolescent girl behaving violently as a young adult (Herrera, Wiersma, & Cleveland, 2011). Adolescents who have been the victims of violence within the context of a romantic relationship are more likely to be depressed, contemplate suicide, use illegal drugs, become pregnant during adolescence, and drop out of school (Kim & Capaldi, 2004; Silverman et al., 2001), with many of these problems persisting into young adulthood (Adam et al., 2011). They are also more likely to be victimized again in the future (Cui et al., 2013; Exner-Cortens et al., 2017).

making the practical connection

What can be done to reduce the prevalence of violence in adolescents' dating relationships? Is this something that schools should become involved in?

We also know that adolescents behave in a variety of ways within dating relationships that are shaped by "scripts" for how males and females are expected to behave—scripts that are learned at home and from the mass media (Gray & Steinberg, 1999; Larson, Clore, & Wood, 1999). In general, adolescents' ways of dealing with conflict in their romantic relationships are linked to the models they've had at home (Fosco et al., 2016; Staats et al., 2018). Adolescents who have witnessed a great deal of conflict between their parents (either physical or verbal) report higher levels of verbal aggression, physical aggression, and relationship difficulties with their romantic partners, as both perpetrators and victims (Goldberg et al., 2019; Liu, Mumford, & Taylor, 2018; Low et al., 2017). Although exposure to violence in school is associated with dating violence (Jain et al., 2018; Sullivan et al., 2020), exposure to violence at home is a much stronger predictor of dating aggression, suggesting that there is something distinctive about the impact of being exposed to domestic violence, rather than violence in general (Cadely, Mrug, & Windle, 2019).

A number of different explanations for the **intergenerational transmission of violence** have been hypothesized, including the development of beliefs about the appropriateness of violence in close relationships and the adverse impact of exposure to violence on adolescents' mental health, which then leads to mental health problems and difficulties in regulating anger (Cascardi, 2016; Foshee et al., 2016; Madan Morris, Mrug, & Windle, 2015; McNaughton Reyes et al., 2015; Mumford, Liu, & Taylor, 2016). Other studies have found that adolescents who are either perpetrators or victims of violence in dating

relationships are more likely to have had parents who were abusive, harsh, or behaved inappropriately toward them, and many of these parents were themselves victims of abuse when they were children (Adams et al., 2019; Kaufman-Parks et al., Liu, Mumford, & Taylor, 2018) (see Figure 10.11). These studies, along with those discussed earlier about adolescent attachments, suggest that variations in adolescents' romantic relationships may have their origins—at least in part—in adolescents' family experiences.

> **intergenerational transmission of violence** The frequently observed connection between exposure to domestic violence while growing up and later violence in adolescents' own romantic relationships.

The main point to keep in mind is that the qualities of adolescents' relationships with others—whether with parents, siblings, friends, or romantic partners—are correlated across different types of relationships (Boele et al., 2019; Shulman et al., 2012). Adolescents who have supportive and satisfying relationships at home are more likely to have high-quality friendships, and adolescents who have high-quality friendships are more likely to have high-quality romantic relationships (Kochendorfer & Kerns, 2020). Individuals' early experiences in the family in interaction with their cumulative experiences with peers during childhood and preadolescence affect the nature and quality of their romantic relationships in adolescence (Dhariwal et al., 2009; Rauer et al., 2013), and the quality of adolescents' family relationships affects the quality of the romantic relationships they have in young adulthood (Sun, McHale, & Updegraff, 2019).

Intimacy and Psychosocial Development

Intimate relationships during adolescence—whether with peers or adults, inside or outside the family, sexual or nonsexual—play an important role in young people's overall psychological development. Close friends serve as a sounding board for adolescents' fantasies and questions about the future. Adolescents often talk to their friends about the careers they hope to have, the people they hope to get involved with, and the life they expect to lead after they leave home. Friends provide advice on a range of

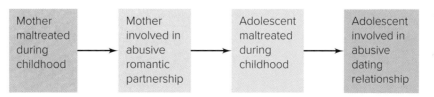

Figure 10.11 The intergenerational transmission of violence: Adolescents who are involved in abusive dating relationships were often abused by their parents, who themselves had histories of violence in their romantic relationships and maltreatment during childhood. (Based on Adams et al., 2019)

identity-related matters, from how to act in different situations to what sorts of occupational and educational paths to pursue. Having an intimate friendship is more central to adolescents' mental health than it is to children's (Buhrmester, 1990).

Keep in mind, however, that the effects of having an intimate friendship depend on who that friend is and what takes place in the relationship. Being popular is less important than genuinely having friends, and having friends is less important than having *good* friendships (Fontaine et al., 2009; Hussong, 2000). Not all friendships are consistently good, though. Some provide for positive things such as self-disclosure, intimacy, and companionship, but others give rise to insecurity, conflict, jealousy, and mistrust (Parker et al., 2005). Adolescents who are close to peers or romantic partners who have antisocial values or habits are themselves more likely to develop similar patterns of behavior (Cauffman et al., 2008; Hussong & Hicks, 2003). It is easy to forget but important to remember that not all close relationships foster positive developmental outcomes.

Nevertheless, studies consistently show that individuals with satisfying close friendships fare better than those without them, not only in adolescence but also in adulthood. And there appears to be an added benefit of being immersed in a larger peer group. One study found that "running with the pack" during adolescence—being embedded in the peer network—was predictive not only of mental health in adulthood but physical health as well (Allen, Uchino, & Hafen, 2015). Adolescence is an especially important time in the development of close relationships because many of the capacities and capabilities that permit intimacy in adult relationships make their debut in adolescence.

Sexuality

11

Sexuality as an Adolescent Issue
Puberty and Adolescent Sexuality
Cognitive Change and Adolescent Sexuality
Social Roles and Adolescent Sexuality

Sexual Activity During Adolescence
Stages of Sexual Activity
Sexual Intercourse During Adolescence

The Sexually Active Adolescent
Sexual Activity and Psychological Development
Causation or Correlation?
Hormonal and Contextual Influences on Sexual Activity

Parental and Peer Influences on Sexual Activity
Sex Differences in the Meaning of Sex
Sexual Orientation
Sexual Harassment, Rape, and Sexual Abuse During Adolescence

Risky Sex and Its Prevention
Adolescents' Reasons for Not Using Contraception
Improving Contraceptive Behavior
AIDS and Other Sexually Transmitted Diseases
Teen Pregnancy
Sex Education

Jupiterimages/Getty Images

293

American adults are ambivalent about adolescent sexuality. On the one hand, they are fascinated by it; it is nearly impossible to turn on the television and avoid seeing sexual imagery that either depicts or is directed at adolescents (Ward, 2016). On the other hand, adults deplore it; most adults (80%, in fact) say that teenage sex is always or almost always wrong (Diamond & Savin-Williams, 2009). Adults look, and then they look the other way, and then they look again. Talk about a love-hate relationship!

This same ambivalence is reflected in the way that social scientists have studied adolescent sexuality. Sex has always been a popular subject among adolescence researchers. But rather than try to understand it, most research focuses simply on enumerating it—counting how many people have done which things how often, at what age, and with whom. Until fairly recently, the problematic aspects of adolescent sexuality—precocious sex, promiscuous sex, unsafe sex, unwanted sex, and so forth—have received far more attention than its normative aspects (Tolman & McClelland, 2011).

This is not to make light of these problems, which for many adolescents are very real. But it is worth pointing out that the study of other aspects of adolescent psychosocial development is not similarly dominated by research on what can go wrong. Imagine if researchers interested in identity, autonomy, intimacy, or achievement studied only negative self-conceptions, angry rebellion, failed friendships, or flunking out. As you will read, and in contrast to adults' concerns, most of the time, sex during adolescence is not associated with problems.

Fortunately, in recent decades, there has been increased interest in positive sexual development (Diamond & Savin-Williams, 2009). There are four distinct aspects to positive sexuality in adolescence that can serve as the basis for how parents and educators discuss sex with teenagers. First, the adolescent needs to come to feel comfortable with his or her maturing body—its shape, size, and attractiveness. Second, the adolescent should accept having feelings of sexual arousal as normal and appropriate. Third, the adolescent needs to feel comfortable about choosing to engage in—or not to engage in—various sexual activities; that is, healthy sexual development involves understanding that sex is a *voluntary* activity for oneself and for one's partner. Finally, the adolescent (at least, one who is sexually active) must understand and practice safe sex—sex that avoids pregnancy and sexually transmitted diseases. One recent study of British 15-year-olds found that the majority of those who were sexually active were psychologically "ready" to have sex but that nearly 40% reported that the last time they had sex, they felt forced or regretful, had sex for the wrong reasons (e.g., to avoid being broken up with), or had unsafe sex (Heron et al., 2015).

Sexuality as an Adolescent Issue

Sexuality is not an entirely new issue that surfaces for the first time during adolescence, of course. Young children are curious about their sex organs and at a very early age derive pleasure from them. And although sexual development may be more dramatic and more obvious prior to adulthood, it by no means ceases at the end of adolescence. Nonetheless, most of us would agree that adolescence is a fundamentally important time—if not the most important time in life—for the development of sexuality. There are several reasons for this.

Puberty and Adolescent Sexuality

Perhaps most obvious is the link between adolescent sexuality and puberty (Bogin, 2011; Diamond & Savin-Williams, 2011). The substantial increase in the sex drive that takes place in early adolescence is the result of hormonal changes. Moreover, not until puberty do individuals become capable of sexual reproduction. Before puberty, children are capable of kissing, fondling, masturbating, and even having sexual intercourse, and erotic feelings are reported by individuals prior to adolescence. Sexual feelings do not suddenly switch on at puberty (Herdt & McClintock, 2000). But not until puberty can males ejaculate semen or do females ovulate, and the fact that pregnancy is a possible outcome of sexual activity changes the nature and meaning of sexual behavior markedly—for the adolescent and for others. Not until puberty do individuals develop the secondary sex characteristics that serve as a basis for sexual attraction and as dramatic indicators that the young person is no longer physically a child. And, in recent years, scientists have discovered that the hormonal changes of puberty affect the brain as well as the body, changing the ways in which we experience emotions, think about others, and process social information (Suleiman et al., 2017).

Cognitive Change and Adolescent Sexuality

The increased importance of sexuality at adolescence is not solely a result of puberty. The cognitive changes of adolescence play a part in the changed nature of sexuality as well. One obvious difference between the sex play

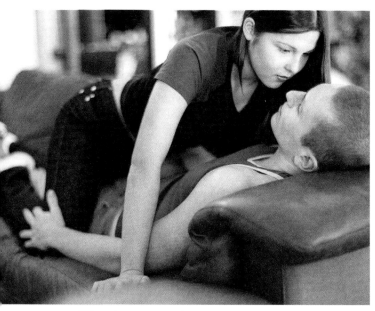

Although most research on adolescent sexuality has focused on sexual intercourse, adolescents' initial forays into the world of sex typically begin with less intimate sexual activity and gradually build toward intercourse. Jonathan Cavendish/Getty Images

of children and the sexual activity of adolescents is that children are not introspective or reflective about sexual behavior. In contrast, sex during adolescence is the subject of sometimes painful conjecture ("Will she or won't she?"), decision making ("Should I or shouldn't I?"), hypothetical thinking ("What if he wants to do it tonight?"), and self-conscious concern ("Am I good-looking enough?"). One of the chief tasks of adolescence is to figure out how to deal with sexual desires and how to incorporate sex successfully and appropriately into intimate relationships. Much of this task is cognitive in nature, and much of it is made possible by the expansion of intellectual abilities that takes place during the period.

Social Roles and Adolescent Sexuality

Adolescence also is a turning point in the development of sexuality because it marks the onset of deliberate sexually motivated behavior that is recognized, both by an adolescent and by others, as primarily and explicitly sexual in nature. Sexual activity in adolescence is motivated by more than hormones. For many adolescents, sex is motivated by love and the desire for the sort of serious emotional relationship that begins to take on features of adult romance. For many adolescents (especially boys, but girls as well), sex is motivated by a desire to enhance their status with peers (Diamond & Savin-Williams, 2009).

Sexual Activity During Adolescence

Given the field's historical focus on problematic aspects of adolescent sexuality, such as precocious sex (having sex at too young an age), promiscuous sex (having sex with too many partners), unwanted sex (having sex that isn't voluntary), or unsafe sex (having sex that can result in pregnancy or a sexually transmitted disease), most of the research conducted into the sexual behavior of adolescents has focused on sexual intercourse (Tolman & McClelland, 2011). With the possible exception of oral sex, adults have tended not to worry about sexual behavior other than intercourse, and worries about oral sex have surfaced only in recent years, in response to exaggerated media reports about teenagers reporting giving or receiving oral sex promiscuously. Although national surveys show that slightly more teenagers have had oral sex than intercourse, they also indicate that the vast majority of teenagers who have oral sex also engage in sexual intercourse and that promiscuity is not the norm for either activity (Hensel, Fortenberry, & Orr, 2008; Lindberg, Jones, & Santelli, 2008).

Although adolescents' involvement in sexual intercourse is an important topic, it is wise to remember that a good deal of the sexual activity of adolescents—even sexually experienced adolescents—involves activities other than sexual intercourse, such as kissing and touching parts of each other's body (technically referred to as "noncoital activity," or, to use a more familiar term, "fooling around") (Tolman & McClelland, 2011). Moreover, because most individuals do not begin their sexual experiences with intercourse but progress toward it through stages of gradually increasing intimacy, it is important to view intercourse as one activity in a long progression, rather than as an isolated behavior (Diamond & Savin-Williams, 2009).

Stages of Sexual Activity

Before we turn to statistics on adolescent sexual activity, a word of caution is in order. Reports of sexual behavior vary markedly as a function of the ways in which questions are worded and data are collected. When President Bill Clinton, referring to his affair with Monica Lewinsky, infamously said, "I did not have sexual relations with that woman," what he meant (we assume) is that he did not have vaginal intercourse with her. Whether the possibility that they engaged in oral sex makes his statement false depends on what one takes the expression "sexual relations" to mean.

If you were asked, "How old were you when you first had sex?", what would you answer? When adolescents respond to questions asking whether they have "had sex," have been "sexually active," or are "still a virgin," it is not clear how they interpret the question. Is genital touching "sex"? Are you a "virgin" if you have had anal sex but not vaginal intercourse?

autoerotic behavior
Sexual behavior that is experienced alone, such as masturbation or sexual fantasizing.

Adolescents, like adults, don't always agree. And to make things even more complicated, adolescents distinguish between acts that culminate in orgasm (which are more likely to be viewed as leading to a loss of virginity) and those that don't (Bersamin et al., 2007). Moreover, adolescents who have engaged in a specific behavior are more likely to say that the behavior doesn't "count" in their definition of losing one's virginity, which means that adolescents' responses to surveys about sex are biased by their actual experience. So bear in mind that all figures to follow are necessarily approximate.

Most adolescents' first experience with sex is what researchers call **autoerotic behavior**—sexual behavior that is experienced alone. The most common autoerotic activities reported by adolescents are having erotic fantasies (about three-quarters of all teenagers report having sexual fantasies) and masturbation (different surveys yield different estimates, depending on the age of the respondents and the wording of the questions, but about 80% all adolescent boys and about 60% of all adolescent girls masturbate prior to age 18) (Robbins et al., 2011).

By the time most adolescents reach high school, they have made the transition from autoerotic behavior to sexual activity that involves another person. By the time individuals have turned 16, about 80% have engaged in some type of noncoital activity with another person. ("Noncoital" refers to sexual activity other than intercourse.) By about 18, 80% have had either vaginal or oral sex; nearly all of those who hadn't by 18 have done so before the end of their 20s (Halpern & Haydon, 2012; Haydon et al., 2014). There have been large increases over the past half-century in the proportion of adolescents who engage in oral or anal sex (Lewis et al., 2017).

The developmental progression of sexual behaviors, from less intimate to more intimate, has not changed very much over the past 70 years, and the sequence in which males and females engage in various sexual activities is remarkably similar. According to recent, large-scale studies of American adolescents, holding hands comes first, followed (in this order) by kissing, making out (kissing for a long time), feeling breasts through clothes, feeling breasts under clothes, feeling a penis through clothes, feeling a penis under clothes or while naked, feeling a vagina through clothes, feeling a vagina under clothes or while naked, and intercourse or oral sex. For about half of all adolescents, intercourse precedes oral sex by about a year, and for another third, both types of sex are initiated around the same time; the rest report a range of different patterns (Halpern & Haydon, 2012; Haydon et al., 2012). One worrisome finding is that most adolescents report talking about contraception *after* they first have intercourse, rather than before (O'Sullivan et al., 2007).

For most adolescents, this sequence of increasingly advanced behaviors unfolds gradually over time, but for a significant minority, it is compressed into a shorter interval (de Graaf et al., 2009). One large study in Great Britain found that the length of time between adolescents' first sexual activity and the initiation of intercourse has narrowed considerably over the past 50 years (Lewis et al., 2017). The expected timetable for progressive sexual activities is faster among adolescents who expect a relatively faster timetable for achieving autonomy from parents and experimenting with drugs and alcohol, suggesting that earlier involvement in more intimate forms of sex may be part of a larger pattern of earlier involvement in "adult" activities (Rosenthal & Smith, 1997).

Sexual Intercourse During Adolescence

Prevalence of Sexual Intercourse Estimates of the prevalence of sexual intercourse among contemporary adolescents vary from study to study, depending on the nature of the sample surveyed, the year and region in which the study was undertaken, the reliability of the data gathered, and the wording of the questions (Santelli et al., 2000). Adolescents do not always report their sexual activity honestly or accurately. Males tend to overstate their level of activity, and females tend to understate it (Kaestle et al., 2005).

Although regional and ethnic variations make it difficult—if not misleading—to generalize about the average age at which American adolescents initiate sexual intercourse, national surveys indicate that fewer adolescents are sexually active today than several decades ago (Centers for Disease Control and Prevention, 2020). The best estimates we have are that about 34% of American high school sophomores have had heterosexual vaginal intercourse (these estimates, which are based on large national surveys, do not include same-sex intercourse or other types of sex, such as oral or anal sex). By senior year, this number has risen to about 57% (see Figure 11.1).

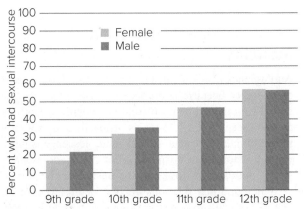

Figure 11.1　More than one-third of American 10th-graders have had sexual intercourse. By senior year, about 60% have.
(Centers for Disease Control and Prevention, 2020)

These numbers refer to the proportion of people who have *ever* had intercourse; fewer than one-third of high school students are "sexually active" (i.e., had intercourse at least once in the past 3 months). Nevertheless, one conclusion is inescapable: Sexual intercourse during high school continues to be a part of the normative experience of the majority American students.

American teenagers are neither promiscuous nor sexually precocious, however. Only about 10% of high school students have had sex with four or more different people, and only 3% of high school students report having had intercourse before age 13; sexual promiscuity and precocity are both much lower now than 30 years ago (see Figure 11.2) (Centers for Disease Control and Prevention, 2020). And contrary to media reports of large numbers of young people "hooking up," today's young adults are more likely to be sexually *inactive* than their counterparts from previous generations (Twenge, Sherman, & Wells, 2017).

Ethnic Differences in Age of Sexual Initiation The average age at which American teenagers have intercourse for the first time is around 17 (Guttmacher Institute, 2014). There are substantial ethnic differences in age of sexual initiation, especially among males (Centers for Disease Control and Prevention, 2020). About 11% of Black boys report having had sex for the first time by age 13, compared to 4% of Latinx boys, 2% of white boys, and 1% of Asian American boys. In all ethnic groups, the average reported age of first sex is slightly older among females than males (3%, 4%, 2%, and 1% of Black, Latinx, white, and Asian American girls, respectively). As you can see, ethnic differences in the age of sexual initiation are far smaller among females than males.

One reason for the relatively high rate of early sexual activity among Black males is the higher proportion of Black youth who grow up in single-parent homes and in poor neighborhoods, both of which, as you will read later in this chapter, are **risk factors** for early sexual activity. Although first-generation Mexican American girls are more likely to become sexually active than either immigrant youth or those who are second-generation Americans (Bamaca-Colbert et al., 2014; Killoren & Deutsch, 2014), girls who are more Americanized and who have expectations for earlier autonomy are more likely than their less acculturated peers to have sex at a younger age, to have multiple sex partners, to contract STDs, and to become pregnant (Lee & Hahm, 2010; Ma et al., 2014; McDonald, Manlove, & Ikramullah, 2009), and more acculturated Asian American girls are more likely to be sexually active than their less Americanized peers (Hahm, Lahiff, & Barreto, 2006).

Studies also indicate that, among all ethnic groups, rates of sexual activity are higher among economically disadvantaged youth, although the gap in rates of sexual activity between rich and poor is substantially narrower now than it was a decade ago, again pointing to the increasingly normative nature of sexual intercourse among American teenagers (Singh & Darroch, 1999). The average age at first intercourse varies considerably across nations; one survey of European adolescents found that the proportion of 15-year-olds who ever had intercourse ranged from 15% in Poland to 75% in Greenland (Madkour et al., 2010).

> **risk factors**
> Factors that increase the likelihood of some behavior or condition.

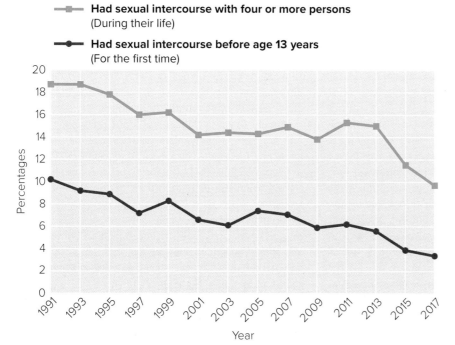

- ▬■▬ **Had sexual intercourse with four or more persons**
  (During their life)
- ▬●▬ **Had sexual intercourse before age 13 years**
  (For the first time)

Figure 11.2 Today's teenagers are less sexually precocious and less promiscuous than previous generations.
(Centers for Disease Control and Prevention, 2020)

For many teenagers, especially girls, their early sexual experiences are involuntary; 11% of female high school students and 3% of male high school students report having been physically forced to have sex (Centers for Disease Control and Prevention, 2020). Involuntary sex is especially frequent among girls who have sex for the first time when they are younger than 13 (Finer & Philbin, 2013); one-fourth of younger adolescents report that their first intercourse was against their will. Moreover, many other young women who report that they had sex voluntarily the first time nevertheless report that they did not really *want* to have sex; girls in relationships where the balance of power favors the boy are more likely to have sex than those whose relationship is more equal (Giordano, Manning, & Longmore, 2010). Young girls whose first partner was at least 7 years older are twice as likely as others to report having had voluntary but unwanted intercourse (Abma, Driscoll, & Moore, 1998). Young adolescents, both male and female, with a significantly older romantic partner are far more likely to have sexual intercourse than those whose partner is the same age (Kaestle, Morisky, & Wiley, 2002; Leitenberg & Saltzman, 2000; Loftus & Kelly, 2012).

About one-third of sexually active adolescents have had sex with someone they are not in a romantic relationship with. More often than not, though, "hooking up" involves teenagers who are friends, not strangers who have just met. Blend Images/Shutterstock

Changes in Sexual Activity over Time   Attitudes toward premarital intercourse during adolescence became more liberal beginning in the mid-1960s and, especially, during the early 1970s. Accompanying this shift in attitudes was an equally noteworthy shift in sexual behavior.

Three trends are of special interest. First, the overall percentage of American high school students who had engaged in sexual intercourse accelerated markedly during the early 1970s and again during the late 1980s, and then declined between 1995 and 2001. The percentage remained flat, at a little less than 50%, for about 10 years and then declined again, to around 38% as of 2019 (Centers for Disease Control and Prevention, 2020). The recent decline in the proportion of adolescents who have had sexual intercourse has not been paralleled by a decline in the proportion of adolescents who are having other types of sex; in fact, today's teenagers are far more "active" sexually than were previous generations (Diamond & Savin-Williams, 2009; Lewis et al., 2017). It is likely that the threat of AIDS and other sexually transmitted diseases has led many adolescents to substitute a safer type of sex—such as oral sex, which, although safer than vaginal or anal intercourse, still carries some risk—for intercourse, with what appear to be the desired results: Adolescents who engage in oral sex but not sexual intercourse are less likely to feel guilty or used and less likely to contract a sexually transmitted infection (Brady & Halpern-Felsher, 2007).

Second, the proportion of individuals who have sexual intercourse *early* in adolescence has declined in recent years, but it still is substantial. Although the median age at which adolescents first engage in intercourse has remained somewhere around 17 for some time, today, nearly one-fifth of all contemporary American adolescents have had intercourse by the time they are 9th-graders, and 3% have had intercourse by age 13 (Centers for Disease Control and Prevention, 2020). The figures on sexual activity among younger adolescents are noteworthy because the younger individuals are when they have sex, the more likely they are to have unprotected sex, exposing themselves to the risks of pregnancy and STDs (Diamond & Savin-Williams, 2009; Kaestle et al., 2005). (Because Black males initiate sex at an earlier age, they are also more likely than other adolescents to engage in unprotected sex; Centers for Disease Control and Prevention, 2020). The fact that a large number of adolescents are sexually active before high school is also an important factor in discussions of sex education because programs that do not begin until students' later years of high school are probably too late for a substantial number of young people.

Finally, the greatest increase in the prevalence of intercourse among adolescents and the greatest decline in the age at first intercourse have been among females (Diamond & Savin-Williams, 2009). Before 1965, there were substantial gaps between the proportions of sexually active boys and girls. Since about 1965, the proportion of sexually experienced high school males has nearly tripled, but the proportion of sexually experienced high school females is about *five* times higher today. Sex differences in rates of sexual intercourse today are negligible, especially by age 15 (when about half of both males and females have had intercourse). By the time they are high school seniors, nearly 60% of males and females have had sexual intercourse (Centers for Disease Control and Prevention, 2017b).

About one-third of sexually active adolescents have had intercourse outside of a romantic relationship (Manning, Longmore, & Giordano, 2005), and people who report having had a lot of casual sex as high school students are more likely to have casual sex and shorter romantic relationships as young adults (Shulman, Seiffge-Krenkle, & Walsh, 2017). Although many adults have expressed concern about adolescents having sex with someone outside the context of a dating relationship, or "hooking up," these encounters are usually with someone the adolescent knows well, such as a friend or ex-partner. And in one-third of these "nonromantic" encounters, one of the persons was hoping that the friendship would turn into (or return to) a romantic relationship (Manning, Giordano, & Longmore, 2005). In other words, the broad category of "casual sex" includes a wide range of behavior, from one-night stands to emotionally close sex with a desired (but not yet committed) romantic partner (Williams & Russell, 2013). "Hooking up" doesn't appear to have negative psychological consequences as long as the hookup was voluntary and desired (Vrangalova, 2015).

Sex and Drugs One particular cause for concern is that the percentage of adolescents who use alcohol or other drugs prior to having sex has increased in recent years; in one national survey, about one-fifth of American adolescents said they drank or used drugs before the last time they had sex (Centers for Disease Control and Prevention, 2020). Not surprisingly, sexual risk taking, casual sex, and nonconsensual sex are all more likely when alcohol, marijuana, or other drugs are involved, mainly because of impaired judgment and loss of control (Clayton et al., 2016; Felson, Savolainen, & Schwartz, 2020; Vasilenko et al., 2017). There also is evidence that becoming sexually active at a relatively early age (prior to 15) may lead to increased substance use, suggesting that the link between the two is probably bidirectional or due to a common underlying factor (Clark et al., 2020; El-Menshawi et al., 2019).

The Sexually Active Adolescent

For many years, researchers studied the psychological and social characteristics of sexually active adolescents with the assumption that these teenagers were more troubled than their peers (either before or as a consequence of becoming sexually active). This view has been replaced as sexual activity has become more prevalent among "normal" adolescents.

Sexual Activity and Psychological Development

Numerous studies show that sexual activity during adolescence is decidedly *not* associated with psychological disturbance (Diamond & Savin-Williams, 2011; Tolman & McClelland, 2011). Adolescents who are sexually active earlier than their peers have levels of self-esteem and life satisfaction similar to those of other adolescents (Vrangalova & Savin-Williams, 2011). Losing one's virginity does not have negative psychological repercussions, either in the short or long term (Bingham & Crockett, 1996; Langer, Zimmerman, & Katz, 1995), even when one's sexual debut is outside of a romantic relationship (Monahan & Lee, 2008). In short, the notion that only "troubled" adolescents have sex and the belief that sexual activity during adolescence leads to later psychological disturbance are both incorrect (Goodson, Buhi, & Dunsmore, 2006; Meier, 2007; Spriggs & Halpern, 2008).

It is important, however, to distinguish between predictors of being sexually active and predictors of engaging in *risky sex* (unprotected sex, sex with multiple partners, etc.). Risky sex is associated with the same sorts of psychological and behavioral factors correlated with other forms of risk taking, such as sensation seeking, impulsivity, and poor self-regulation (Crandall et al., 2017; Dogan et al., 2010; Khurana et al., 2015; Price & Hyde, 2011). One factor that *isn't* correlated with risky sexual behavior, however, is exposure to pornography (Luder et al., 2011; Martyniuk & Štulhofer, 2018).

Although sexually active adolescents do not differ psychologically from those who are not, *early* sexual activity (having intercourse before age 15) is associated with a more general attitudinal and behavioral profile that includes more permissive attitudes toward sex, experimentation with drugs and alcohol, minor delinquency, lower levels of religious involvement, lower interest in

Many adolescents have sex after drinking or using drugs, which increases the likelihood of sexual risk taking.
staticnak1983/Getty Images

academic achievement, and a stronger orientation toward independence (Cavazos-Rehg et al., 2010; Harden & Mendle, 2011; Kågesten & Blum, 2015; Lohman & Billings, 2008). One study that measured adolescents' likelihood of losing their virginity found that individuals who fit the profile in seventh or eighth grade were *25* times more likely to lose their virginity within the next 2 years than those who did not (L'Engle & Jackson, 2008). In contrast, studies of adolescents who become sexually active at *age 16 or later* do not find major differences between these youth and their virginal counterparts. One study found that having sex for the first time during high school or later (but not before high school) actually was associated with positive development (Golden, Furman, & Collibee, 2016).

The impact of early sexual activity on adolescents' mental health may depend on the extent to which the behavior is seen as culturally normative. In the United States and Mexico, early sexual intercourse is associated with higher rates of depression (Espinosa-Hernández & Vasilenko, 2015; Madkour et al., 2010; Vasilenko, Kugler, & Rice, 2016; Vasilenko, 2017) (see Figure 11.3), especially among girls and especially when it takes place outside the context of a romantic relationship (Mendle et al., 2013). In the Netherlands, however, where adults are more accepting of adolescent sexual activity, there is no link between depression and early sex (Nogueira Avelar e Silva et al., 2018). Furthermore, the relation between girls' early initiation into sex and depression may be fleeting. In one recent study, girls who started having sex at age 15 initially had higher rates of depression than those who didn't start until later in high school or who hadn't become sexually active by the end of high school, but one year later, the early starters weren't any more depressed than the other girls (Wesche et al., 2017).

Less is known about characteristics of individuals who do not have sex at all during adolescence, but the most consistent correlate of abstaining from sex until after age 18 is strong religious commitment (Zimmer-Gembeck & Helfand, 2008). Individuals who don't have sex for the first time until they are in their 20s are less likely to marry or cohabit, but those who do report better mental health and greater satisfaction with their relationship than people who started having sex during their teen years (Harden, 2012).

making the practical connection

Why do you think the psychological correlates of early sexual intercourse are different from the correlates of sexual intercourse when it is delayed until the last years of high school? Would you be in favor of sex education courses whose focus was on persuading adolescents to wait until they were 16 before having intercourse?

Causation or Correlation?

Although many studies have found a link between early sexual activity and small-scale deviance, why they are correlated is not entirely clear (Diamond & Savin-Williams, 2009; Zimmer-Gembeck, Siebenbruner, & Collins, 2004). There is little support for the idea that early sex leads to other types of risky or antisocial activity. Just the opposite: Several studies show that involvement in problem behavior (especially alcohol and drug use, but aggression and bullying as well) precedes early involvement with sex (Boislard et al., 2013; Doran & Waldron, 2017; Parkes et al., 2014; Skinner et al., 2015). Experimentation with

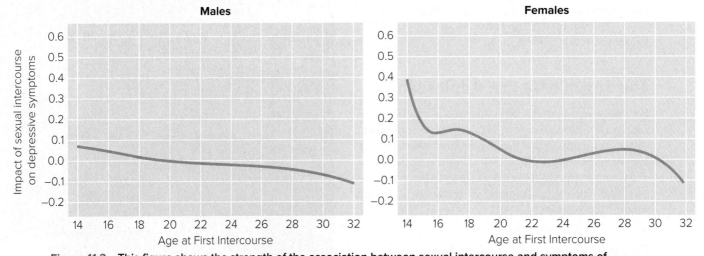

Figure 11.3 This figure shows the strength of the association between sexual intercourse and symptoms of depression: the greater the number on the vertical axis, the stronger the association. Among females, having sexual intercourse in adolescence, especially before age 16, is associated with reports of depression; this is not the case once women reach their early 20s. The connection between age at first intercourse and depression is virtually nonexistent among males. (Vasilenko, 2017)

deviant activity and early sex may be connected because they share some common underlying factor, such as impulsivity or the propensity to take risks (Derefinko et al., 2014; Harden et al., 2008).

Many experts believe that a general inclination toward problem behavior and lack of impulse control is behind an overarching pattern that includes minor delinquency, precocious or promiscuous sex, disengagement from school, and drug and alcohol use (Clark et al., 2020; Goldenberg et al., 2013; Khurana et al., 2012; Parkes et al., 2014). Engaging in delinquency and in casual sex are influenced by some of the same genes, but delinquency and sex within a romantic relationship are not, consistent with other research on the genetic bases of traits such as sensation-seeking and impulsivity (Harden & Mendle, 2011a). Risky sex is more likely among teenagers who are especially sensitive to immediate rewards and low in self-control (Kahn et al., 2015), a combination that is linked to virtually all forms of risky behavior (Duell et al., 2018). It probably makes sense to view sexual risk taking as a specific instance of risky behavior more generally (Madkour et al., 2010; Secor-Turner et al., 2013).

Another factor that affects adolescents' sexual activity is the extent to which they are supervised by their parents or other adults (Pain, 2020). Most sexual activity between teenagers takes place in one of the two individuals' homes—most often, the boy's. (The third most popular setting is at the home of another friend.) And the most common time for adolescents to have sex is not on the weekend but on weekdays, after school. Adolescents who are unsupervised after school and who do not participate in after-school programs are more likely to be sexually active, more likely to have multiple sexual partners, and more likely to contract an STD (Buhi & Goodson, 2007; Cohen et al., 2002).

Hormonal and Contextual Influences on Sexual Activity

One factor that is consistently related to the age at which adolescents initiate sex is physical maturation. Adolescents who mature earlier are also likely to have sex earlier, including both risky and safe sex (Baams et al., 2015; Diamond & Savin-Williams, 2009). Increased interest in sex at adolescence is likely to have social as well as biological causes, however. Adolescents become interested in sex in part because of increases in sex hormones at puberty and in part because sexual activity becomes accepted—even encouraged—in their peer group. A fuller understanding of adolescent sexual behavior necessitates looking at biological and social influences in interaction with each other, rather than at either set of influences alone (Halpern, 2003). And the story line is different for males than females.

Hormonal Influences Boys' and girls' initial interest in sex is influenced primarily by the surge in certain

Adolescents who go through puberty earlier than their peers are more likely to start having sex earlier, too. Susan Vogel/ UpperCut Images/Alamy Stock Photo

hormones at puberty—**testosterone,** to be specific. Adolescents with higher levels of androgens (testosterone is an androgen) are more likely than their peers to report masturbating, thinking about sex, and planning to have sexual intercourse within the next year. This hormonal change appears to increase adolescents' interest in sex as well as their arousal when exposed to sexual stimuli. This is true for both males and females, although females' interest in sex is also influenced by estrogen.

Motivation to have sex is one thing; becoming sexually active is another. How important is the rise in testosterone at puberty in triggering the onset of sexual intercourse? The answer differs between boys and girls.

Among boys, the increased level of androgens is directly related to the likelihood of being sexually active (Campbell, Prossinger, & Mbzivo, 2005). Younger boys who are more mature biologically are more likely to be sexually active than older boys whose hormone levels are lower. Early-maturing boys also are more likely than their peers to download pornography off the Internet (Skoog, Stattin, & Kerr, 2009).

Whether boys actually have sex is not entirely dependent on their hormone levels, however, because actually having sex depends on how receptive potential partners are to them. Sex hormones do not just contribute to increases in boys' sex drive; they also affect height, strength, and the development of secondary sex characteristics, such as facial hair. In other words, increases in androgens lead to boys' increased sexual activity

testosterone
One of the sex hormones secreted by the gonads, found in both sexes but in higher levels among males than females.

both because they increase their sex drive (which may make boys with higher testosterone levels want to have sex more) and because they change their physical appearance (which may make them more attractive to others).

Hormonal influences on sexual desire and physical appearance are easier to separate in girls. Although androgens also are responsible for increases in girls' sex drive, a different set of hormones—estrogens—is primarily responsible for changes in their appearance, including breast development. Because of this, it is possible to study whether increased sexual activity among girls after puberty is more influenced by increases in their sex drive or by changes in their physical appearance (both of which, presumably, influence their sexual attractiveness to boys). It turns out that differences in adolescent girls' sexual activity have little to do with differences in their androgen levels but are correlated with differences in their estrogen levels. In other words, estrogen influences girls' sexual activity mainly through its impact on their physical attractiveness to others.

Of course, girls' involvement in sex is not solely determined by whether others want them as sexual partners. Girls' own interest in sex and their receptivity to others' interest in them are also crucial. But in girls, it turns out, these factors are much more determined by context than by biology.

The Role of Context Social factors are far more important in influencing girls' involvement in sexual intercourse than boys' (Henry et al., 2007). Although increases in androgens lead to increased interest in sex among girls and increases in estrogens lead to increased attractiveness to others, whether this interest and attractiveness are translated into behavior depends largely on the social environment (Diamond & Savin-Williams, 2009). Among girls with high levels of androgens, for example, those who have sexually permissive attitudes and whose friends are sexually active are more likely to engage in intercourse. But girls whose social environment is less encouraging of sex—even those with high levels of androgens—are unlikely to be sexually active. In other words, whereas hormones seem to have a direct and powerful effect on the sexual behavior of boys, the impact of hormones on the sexual behavior of girls depends on the social context.

Why might this be? One explanation is that boys develop in an environment that usually is more tolerant and encouraging of sexual behavior than do girls. All that boys need to become sexually active is the biological jolt from the increase in androgens at puberty; usually, there is nothing in the environment to hold them back.

For girls, however, the environment is more varied. Some girls develop within a context that permits and even encourages sexual activity; others do not. Although the increase in androgens also provides a jolt to the sex drive of the adolescent girl and the increase in estrogens makes her more appealing to others, if she develops within a context that places strong social controls on girls' sexual activity, this hormonal awakening or change in attractiveness will not be translated into behavior.

Parental and Peer Influences on Sexual Activity

Many researchers have asked whether adolescents who become sexually active earlier than their peers have different sorts of relationships with their parents. The answer is clear: Not surprisingly, given the correlation between early sexual activity and other forms of problem behavior, adolescents from authoritative homes—that is, homes where parents are warm, are involved in their adolescent's life, and monitor their adolescent's behavior—are less likely to become sexually active at an early age and less likely to engage in risky sexual activity (Ethier et al., 2016; Simons et al., 2016). Parent-adolescent conflict is also associated with early sexual activity, especially among adolescents who are relatively more mature physically (McBride, Paikoff, & Holmbeck, 2003). These strong and consistent links between effective parenting and safer sexual behavior have been found across ethnic groups (Kerpelman et al., 2016; Nogueira Avelar e Silva et al., 2016). Effective parenting by fathers in particular diminishes adolescents' involvement with sexually promiscuous peers, which in turn lessens the likelihood of risky sex (DelPriore, Schlomer, & Ellis, 2017). Adolescents are especially likely to have sex early when their parents had little knowledge of their whereabouts and friends (Madkour et al., 2012).

Parent-Adolescent Communication A great deal of attention has been devoted to the study of parent-adolescent communication about sex, although it is quite clear from this research that any conclusions you might draw about the nature and impact of these conversations depends on whom you ask. Many more parents report communicating with their adolescent about sex than vice versa, and parents often say that they have communicated about a particular topic (such as AIDS) when their teenager says they haven't.

Other discrepancies abound as well. Parents underestimate their adolescents' sexual activity and unrealistically assume that if they simply disapprove of it, their adolescents are not likely to be sexually active. On the other hand, sexually active adolescents underestimate their parents' disapproval of sexual activity (Jaccard, Dittus, & Gordon, 1998). Generally, teenagers are more likely to talk about sex with mothers than fathers, and they rate their mothers as better sex educators (Raffaelli & Green, 2003). Adolescents also are likely to be more receptive to having multiple conversations over a period of time about sex than to having one "big talk" (Martino et al., 2008).

Talking to teenagers about sex does not increase their likelihood of becoming sexually active but may encourage adolescents to practice safe sex. SW Productions/Photodisc/Getty Images

Most discussions parents and teenagers have about sex focus on issues of safety (AIDS, condom use) rather than issues of sexual behavior or relationships (DiIorio, Kelley, & Hockenberry-Eaton, 1999). Adolescents are more likely to be well educated about sex when their conversations with their parents are genuinely interactive, rather than dominated by the parents (Lefkowitz et al., 2000).

It is often assumed that it is beneficial for adolescents to discuss sex with their parents, but the effect of parent-child communication on adolescents' sexual behavior depends on who is doing the communicating and what is being communicated. Overall, the impact of parent-adolescent communication on the likelihood of an adolescent being sexually active is very small (Miller, Benson, & Galbraith, 2001). However, parent-child communication specifically about contraception lowers the rate of *risky* sex (Aspy et al., 2007; Hutchinson et al., 2003), especially if the discussions take place before the adolescent becomes sexually active (Miller et al., 1998). Communication with older siblings about safe sex is also effective (Kolburn Kowal & Blinn-Pike, 2004).

Many studies find that what is most important are the attitudes and values communicated by parents during discussions of sex and the ways in which these attitudes and values are interpreted by the adolescent (Deutsch & Crockett, 2016; Longmore et al., 2009). For example, parents who emphasize the importance of love and respect

have sons who have less permissive attitudes and who are less likely to engage in sexual risk-taking (Overbeek, van de Bongardt, & Baams, 2018), whereas parents who actively communicate about sex, provide emotional support, and encourage autonomy have daughters with stronger feelings of agency about their own sexual behavior (Klein, Becker, & Štulhofer, 2018). It's important for parents to maintain a close relationship with their teenager after the adolescent has become sexually active and to resist the temptation to pull away in anger over the teenager's behavior (Ream & Savin-Williams, 2005). Adolescent girls who are open with their mothers about their sexual behavior are also more likely to report emotional intimacy with their partners and less likely to have permissive attitudes than girls whose primary disclosure targets are peers (Killoren et al., 2019).

In summary, parent-adolescent communication about sex is more effective in deterring *risky* sexual activity than in promoting abstinence, and even here, the effect that parents have is small. Thus, despite some parents' beliefs that they can prevent their adolescent's sexual activity by talking about it and despite other parents' fears that talking about sex will have the unintended effect of encouraging their teenager's sexual behavior, parent-adolescent communication about sex has surprisingly little impact on whether adolescents are sexually active, one way or the other. Adolescents' opportunity to have sex (for example, whether they are in a steady relationship or date frequently), their having sexually active friends, and their use of alcohol and drugs are far better predictors of early sexual initiation than is parent-adolescent communication.

Sexual Activity and Household Composition One family factor that does predict adolescent sexual involvement, however—especially among girls—is household composition. Adolescents whose parents are in the process of divorcing as well as those who live in single-parent households—regardless of when (or if) a divorce took place—are more likely to be sexually active earlier than their peers (Ellis et al., 2003; Ryan, 2015). Why might this be?

One hypothesis is that parental divorce temporarily disrupts the parent-child relationship, leading the adolescent into early involvement with drugs, alcohol, and minor delinquency, which, according to some studies, increases the likelihood of sex. In other words, it is not family structure per se but the quality of family relationships in divorced homes that helps explain why girls from single-parent homes are more sexually active at an earlier age (Davis & Friel, 2001). Another possibility is that some of the same personality characteristics that are associated with adults' marital instability, such as impulsivity and substance abuse, are transmitted genetically from parents to children, making adolescents with divorced parents more likely to engage in early sex; in other words, it may not only be what divorced parents do but who they are genetically (Mendle et al., 2009). Adolescents whose mothers had been sexually active at an early age are themselves more likely to begin having sex early (Mott et al., 1996).

Why does growing up in a single-parent home affect girls' sexual behavior more than boys'? At least three possibilities exist. One, as noted earlier, is that social influences on girls' sexual behavior are stronger and more varied than are the influences on boys' behavior. Parents simply may not attempt to exert much control over sons' sexual activity, regardless of whether the household has one parent or two, and as a result, boys from single- and two-parent homes may be equally likely to be sexually active. Girls' sexual behavior, in contrast, may be more subject to parental controls (Simons et al., 2016). Single-parent homes are typically more permissive than two-parent homes (Laursen & Collins, 2009), and this difference in control may be enough to make a difference in girls' sexual activity.

A second possibility is that many single-parent mothers are likely to be dating and, in so doing, may unknowingly be role models of sexual activity to their adolescents (Ivanova, Mills, & Veenstra, 2014). To the extent that this modeling effect is stronger between parents and children of the same sex, we would expect to find a more powerful effect of growing up in a single-parent home on the sexual behavior of daughters than sons. (There hasn't been enough research on boys' sexual behavior in families headed by single fathers who date to look at this possibility.) There is also evidence that dating may lead mothers to behave more permissively, which as you just read, increases the likelihood of adolescent girls' sexual activity (Zito & De Coster, 2016).

Finally, some researchers suggest that the link between growing up in a single-parent household and earlier involvement in sex is genetic in a way that is specific to girls. They have shown that the same gene that makes men more likely to leave their family may, when passed on to daughters, makes adolescent girls more likely to go through puberty early and become sexually active at an earlier age (Comings et al., 2002).

The Influence of Peers Generally, adolescents are more likely to be sexually active when their peers are (and more likely to engage in risky sex when their peers do) (Henry et al., 2007); when they *believe* that their friends are sexually active, whether or not their friends actually are (Babalola, 2004; Prinstein, Meade, & Cohen, 2003); and when they have older siblings who model more sexually advanced behavior (East, 2009). Popular adolescents are more likely to be sexually active by age 16, but they aren't any more likely than their peers to engage in risky sex (Wesche et al., 2019). Importantly, adolescents whose parents discuss sex with them in an open and understanding way are less influenced by having sexually active peers (Fasula & Miller, 2006; Whitaker & Miller, 2000).

Peer influences on adolescents' sexual activity appear to operate in two different, but compatible, ways. First, when an adolescent's peers are sexually active, they establish a normative standard that having sex is acceptable (Van de Bongardt et al., 2017; White & Warner, 2015). Boys and girls are susceptible to this sort of peer influence (Widman et al., 2016), but girls tend to "curate" their peer networks so that their friends have their sexual debuts at a similar age to their own, perhaps to avoid feeling ostracized by friends whose attitudes toward sex are different from theirs (Trinh et al., 2019).

Brain imaging studies find that adolescents who engage in risky sex are more sensitive to social rewards, which may make them more easily influenced by what they believe their friends will approve of (Eckstrand et al., 2017). One of the reasons that minor drug use is associated with earlier involvement in sexual activity is that drug use may lead an adolescent to form friendships with a different group of friends, a group that is sexually more permissive (French & Dishion, 2003). Adolescents' initiation of sexual activity varies from neighborhood to neighborhood, with earlier and riskier sexual activity more likely in poorer and relatively more disorganized neighborhoods, where adults have little control over teenagers and where peer groups are relatively more powerful (Carlson et al., 2014; Warner, 2018).

Several studies show that sexual activity spreads within a community of adolescents much like an epidemic, with sexually experienced adolescents initiating their less experienced partners into increasingly more advanced sex (Rodgers & Rowe, 1993). Once they become sexually experienced, previously inexperienced adolescents then "infect" other adolescents. Over time, the percentage of sexually experienced adolescents within a community grows and grows. Peers also influence each other's sexual behavior directly, either through communication among friends ("You haven't done it yet! What's the matter with you?" "You're thinking of doing what?"), or, more commonly, between sex partners. As one teenager noted, however, succumbing to peer pressure often led to regret:

I felt really uncomfortable . . . it [her relationship with a boy] didn't really start because I wanted it to be . . . It was kind of like peer pressure and that kind of thing. . . . It's my friends and I don't want to disappoint them, and it's kind of like, I just went with it. And then—just awful. Yeah, it was awful. (Suleiman & Deardorff, 2015, p. 770)

So did giving in to one's partner, as this girl explains:

. . . like he was my first sexual relationship. And I was like—I told him no but he kept telling me, "Come on, come on, let's do it." And like I guess—I guess I felt that pressure and I was like: oh, my God. And I can't even say no. Like it was hard for me to say no. And like to this day I feel—I feel sad about it you know. I wish he wasn't the first guy . . . I still feel like he shouldn't have been my first. (Suleiman & Deardorff, 2015, p. 770)

Ambivalence about introducing sex into a relationship is by no means limited to girls. Here's one boy's account:

Like when we're about to do certain things you know, it's just in the back of my mind like … but I'm just like damn, does she even really like want this or is she just doing this just because like I'm doing this, you know? (Suleiman & Deardorff, 2015, p. 772)

Researchers also have examined the role of the broader environment in influencing adolescent sexual behavior. Adolescents growing up in poor neighborhoods, for example, are more likely to engage in early sexual activity than adolescents from more affluent communities (Dupéré et al., 2008; Leventhal, Dupéré, & Brooks-Gunn, 2009). When adolescents grow up in poverty, they may see little hope for the future, and they therefore may be more likely to risk their occupational and economic future by becoming sexually active (Raiford et al., 2014). To a young person who believes that the chances of getting a good job are slim, an early pregnancy does not seem as costly as it might to someone who hopes to complete high school, attend college, and secure a good job.

Virginity Pledges   Over the past 40 years, several million American adolescents have taken a "virginity pledge," promising to abstain from sex until they are married. How effective are these vows? Not very. Virginity pledges work only for younger adolescents; they have no effect on high school students. Among high school students, "pledgers" are just as likely to have sex as "nonpledgers" (including intercourse, oral sex, and anal sex). And longitudinal studies show that after having sex, adolescents who had taken a virginity pledge frequently deny having made one (Hollander, 2006; Rosenbaum, 2006). One study found that 82% of the adolescents who took a virginity pledge denied having done so 5 years later (Rosenbaum, 2009)!

Ironically, one way in which those who take a virginity pledge differ from their nonpledging peers is that those who take the pledge are less likely to use contraception, suggesting that encouraging abstinence may actually promote unsafe sex, which increases the likelihood of getting

Over the past 4 decades, several million American adolescents have taken a virginity pledge, promising to abstain from sex until they are married. Research has found, however, that high school students who have pledged to remain virgins are just as likely to have sex as those who haven't made such pledges.
Andreas Keuchel/Alamy Stock Photo

pregnant (Paik, Sanchagrin, & Heimer, 2016) (see Figure 11.4). The impact of pledging also varies as a function of how many other adolescents in the same school have taken the pledge. Pledging has little effect in schools in which few students take virginity pledges (presumably because there is little encouragement of abstinence) or in schools in which nearly everyone pledges (because one of the ways in which pledging works is by allowing those who pledge to make a statement about their values). Making a promise to *oneself* to delay becoming sexually active is more effective than making a formal, public pledge (Bersamin et al., 2005).

Sex Differences in the Meaning of Sex

Any discussion of the psychosocial significance of sexual experience during adolescence must be sensitive to the

Figure 11.4   **Adolescents who take a virginity pledge but later break it are far more likely to become pregnant than adolescents who don't take such pledges.** (Paik, Sanchagrin, & Heimer, 2016)

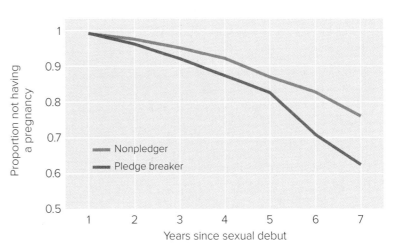

sexual socialization
The process through which adolescents are exposed to and educated about sexuality.

very substantial sex differences in how early sexual activity is experienced. Despite the convergence of males' and females' rates of sexual activity in recent decades, the early sexual experiences of adolescent boys and girls are still very different and, as a consequence, are imbued with very different meanings (Diamond & Savin-Williams, 2009). In other words, the sexual behavior of males and females may be similar, but the **sexual socialization** of males and females is quite different.

The Way Boys Feel   The typical boy's first sexual experience is masturbation in early adolescence (Diamond & Savin-Williams, 2009). At the outset, then, the sexual socialization of males typically places sex outside of an interpersonal context, a situation that has no doubt been furthered by boys' widespread use of and easy access to online pornography (Jones, 2018). Before adolescent boys begin dating, they have generally already experienced orgasm and know how to arouse themselves. For males, the development of sexuality during adolescence revolves around efforts to integrate the capacity to form close relationships into an already existing sense of sexual capability.

Perhaps because of this, at the time of first intercourse, boys are likely to keep matters of sex and intimacy separate. Boys often have as their first partner someone they just met or describe as a casual date, and it is generally the male partner of a couple who is likely to initiate sex (Diamond & Savin-Williams, 2009). Boys are more likely than girls to mention sexual arousal (rather than emotional factors) as a reason for having sex (Eyre & Millstein, 1999). And males typically report that the people to whom they describe their first sexual liaison—most probably, male peers—are overwhelmingly approving. The most common immediate reactions among adolescent males to having intercourse for the first time are excitement, satisfaction, exhilaration, and happiness (Diamond & Savin-Williams, 2009; Higgins et al., 2010). Here's how one 14-year-old boy described his first time, which was outside of a romantic relationship:

> It was really terrific . . . the sex itself felt good, yeah, but when you come, that's really the nicest feeling that I've ever had. . . . The sex itself, I thought that it would have been better, the whole time, but coming, I hadn't expected that it would be that good. (Symons, Vermeersch, & Van Houtte, 2014, pp. 547–548)

Or, consider this unemotional response from a 13-year-old:

> It wasn't the fairy tale story that I had imagined about losing virginity. I can't even say what it was. Yeah, sex, nothing more than that. (Symons, Vermeersch, & Van Houtte, 2014, p. 548)

The Way Girls Feel   The typical girl's first experience and feelings afterward are likely to be very different. Masturbation is far less prevalent among girls than boys, and it is far less regularly practiced (Diamond & Savin-Williams, 2009). As a consequence, the typical adolescent girl is more likely than the typical boy to experience sex for the first time with another person. For girls, unlike boys, the development of sexuality involves the integration of sexual activity into an already existing capacity for intimacy and emotional involvement. As a consequence, the girl's sexual script is one that, from the outset, tinges sex with romance, love, friendship, and intimacy.

Girls are more likely than boys to engage in sex in order to enhance an emotional connection (Diamond & Savin-Williams, 2009). Compare these 14-year-old girls' reactions to those of the two boys who were quoted earlier:

> It's a whole new experience and you love that person and you long for him, and yeah, it's a step further in your relationship . . . I think that you trust each other more, you give yourself more to that person and the bond grows. You get closer to each other. (Symons, Vermeersch, & Van Houtte, 2014, p. 547)
>
> It was fun, and intimate, mainly intimate actually. I mean, he was really sweet. But apart from that, I can't say that I really enjoyed it. I mean, it mainly just hurt. I thought "I just have to go through this." I think that, even if I had waited another year, it would have hurt just as much. (Symons, Vermeersch, & Van Houtte, 2014, pp. 548–549)

The adolescent girl's first sexual partner is likely to be someone she says she was in love with at the time. After losing her virginity, she is more likely to encounter disapproval or mixed feelings on the part of others in whom she confides (generally, peers) than is the typical boy. And although the majority of girls report more positive than negative feelings about their first sexual experience, girls are more likely than boys to report feeling afraid, guilty, or worried as well as happy or excited about the experience (Diamond & Savin-Williams, 2009; Higgins et al., 2010).

It's important to note that differences between males and females in the meaning of sex are neither inevitable nor consistent across cultures or historical time. Nor is it the case that all adolescent boys follow the male script and all adolescent girls follow the female one. In fact, "girls are more sexually oriented and boys more romantically oriented than previous research might suggest" (Diamond & Savin-Williams, 2009, p. 514). Moreover, as they mature, adolescent boys and girls become more similar in their motives to have sex (males increasingly emphasize the place of sex in an emotional relationship and place less importance on the role of sex in elevating their social status,

Sexual orientation is influenced by a complex interplay of biological and contextual factors. Rawpixel.com/Shutterstock

who later identify themselves as exclusively heterosexual. By the same token, studies show that the majority of gay, lesbian, and bisexual adults engaged in heterosexual activity during adolescence. As two experts noted, "contrary to the widespread notion that desire, behavior, and identity coalesce neatly in adolescence and young adulthood to signal an unambiguously heterosexual or homosexual orientation, the reality is much more complicated" (Diamond & Savin-Williams, 2009, p. 505).

The development of sexual orientation follows different patterns among sexual-minority males and females (Saewyc, 2011). Males are more likely to have had same-sex relations before identifying themselves as gay or bisexual, whereas the reverse sequence is more characteristic among females. And whereas more lesbian and bisexual females had heterosexual experiences before their first same-sex sexual activity, the opposite is true for males. In addition, females who have had same-sex contact during adolescence almost always pursue same-sex contact in adulthood (whereas the same is not true for males; only about 60% do) (Diamond & Savin-Williams, 2009).

The Antecedents of Homosexuality   Studies of the antecedents of homosexuality generally have focused on two sets of factors: biological influences, such as hormones, and social influences, such as the parent-child relationship. More is known about the development of homosexuality among men than among women, but the weight of the evidence suggests that an adolescent's sexual orientation is likely to be shaped by a complex interaction of social and biological influences (Saewyc, 2011; Savin-Williams, 2006).

Support for the contention that homosexuality is determined at least partly by biological factors comes from two sources. First, there is some evidence that gay and lesbian adults may have been exposed prenatally to certain hormones that, in theory, could affect sexual orientation and gender-atypical behavioral preferences through their effects on early brain organization (Saewyc, 2011). Second, some evidence indicates that homosexuality has a strong genetic component, since sexual orientation is more likely to be similar among close relatives than distant relatives and between identical twins than fraternal twins (Savin-Williams, 2006). Although environmental explanations for this similarity cannot be ruled out, chances are that at least some of the predisposition to develop a homosexual orientation is inherited (Saewyc, 2011). Same-sex attraction does not spread through adolescent social networks, which would be the case if its determinants were largely environmental (Brakefield et al., 2014).

Several studies suggest as well that a higher proportion of homosexuals than heterosexuals report having had problems in their early family relationships—specifically, in their relationship with their father. Although some studies point to certain factors that appear more often than not in the early histories of gay, lesbian, or bisexual individuals, all homosexual individuals do not have identical developmental histories, of course. Nonetheless, because of the bullying, rejection, and victimization, sexual-minority adolescents often experience at school and in the community, the support and acceptance of parents when their child comes out are critical, especially for younger teenagers, who are more likely to encounter harassment and discrimination than their peers who come out at a somewhat older age (Mills-Koonce, Rehder, & McCurdy, 2018).

making the scientific connection

Should social scientists be interested in the antecedents of homosexuality? Is it important to know whether homosexuality is biologically or contextually determined? Why or why not?

Sexual Harassment, Rape, and Sexual Abuse During Adolescence

Although most research on adolescent sexual activity has focused on voluntary sexual behavior between consenting individuals, there is growing public awareness that a large proportion of teenagers are sexually harassed and that a significant minority are forced to have sex against their will (Chiodo et al., 2009; Katz et al., 2019). This latter group includes adolescents who have been the victims of forcible rape by a stranger, sexual abuse within the family, or **date rape**— when someone, typically a woman, is forced by a date to

date rape
Being forced by a date to have sex against one's will.

have sex when she doesn't want to. Adolescents who are sexually coerced are more likely to report depression, behavior problems, and alcohol and drug use (Bucchianeri et al., 2014; Duncan, Zimmer-Gembeck, & Furman, 2019; Young, Furman, & Jones, 2012). Sexual coercion and sex under the influence of alcohol or drugs are more likely to occur when there is a large age difference (3 years or more) between a girl and her partner (Gowen et al., 2004).

Sexual Harassment and Date Rape For all the concern that is expressed about the sexual harassment of teenagers over the Internet, adolescents are far more at risk for harassment at school than online. Numerous studies indicate that sexual harassment—both cross-sex and between members of the same sex—is widespread within American public schools (Leaper & Brown, 2008; Young, Grey, & Boyd, 2009).

Sexual harassment is especially distressing to early-maturing girls, whose physical maturity, which makes them the targets of harassment, already makes them stand apart from their peers (Lindberg, Grabe, & Hyde, 2007; Skoog & Özdemir, 2016). Girls who are sexually harassed are more likely to focus on their appearance and develop eating disorders as a consequence (Petersen & Hyde, 2013).

Because the majority of those who had been sexually harassed had themselves harassed others and because many incidents occurred within full view of teachers and other school personnel—indeed, a significant percentage of students report having been sexually harassed by their *teachers*—numerous experts have suggested the need for significant changes in the moral and ethical climate of secondary schools (Timmerman, 2002; Young, Grey, & Boyd, 2009). This is easier said than done, however; one evaluation of a school-based program called Safe Dates found significant reductions in psychological abuse and sexual violence 1 month after the program was implemented, but these effects had disappeared within 1 year (Foshee et al., 2000). Other research, on the histories of individuals who commit dating violence, indicates that perpetrators themselves were likely to have been exposed to physical punishment and abuse at home (Basile et al., 2006; Ha et al., 2016). Given that sexual harassment is a form of bullying, it is not surprising that studies find considerable overlap between adolescents who bully others and those who harass others sexually (Espelage, Basile, & Hamburger, 2012; Reyes & Foshee, 2012).

Harassment of Sexual-Minority Youth A substantial number of LGBTQ youth are harassed, physically abused, or verbally abused by peers or adults while growing up (Hequembourg, Livingston, & Wang, 2020; Kaufman, Baams, & Veenstra, 2020; Sterzing et al., 2018; Toomey & Russell, 2016). Abuse of this sort, as well as having more distant family relationships, contributes to the relatively higher rates of truancy, depression, suicide, substance abuse, running away from home, and school

difficulties reported by sexual-minority adolescents (Birkett, Russell, & Corliss, 2014; Caputi et al., 2018; Mueller et al., 2015; Poteat et al., 2014), as well as mental health problems that persist into adulthood (Dermody et al., 2014; Marshal et al., 2013).

As with other types of discrimination, hostility toward sexual-minority youth is greater in small schools, rural schools, schools in lower-SES communities, less racially diverse schools, schools with fewer explicit rules for student behavior, and schools that tend to have climates that are more hostile toward sexual-minority youth (Hatzenbuehler et al., 2014; Martin-Storey et al., 2015). Perhaps because victims of harassment often channel their anger into the harassment of others, sexual-minority adolescents are significantly more likely than straight adolescents to bully students from other vulnerable groups, such as those who are overweight or have some sort of disability (Eisenberg et al., 2015).

Homophobic teasing and name-calling is most common in early adolescence, so much so that friends who tease peers about being gay or are homophobic actually are more likely to affiliate with peers with similar points of view (la Roi et al., 2020; Merrin et al., 2018). Victims of this sort of harassment, who are an age at which they may be unsure about their sexual orientation, may internalize some of these negative messages and become depressed (DeLay et al., 2017; DeLay et al., 2018; Tucker et al., 2016). Fortunately, over the course of adolescence, prejudice against both gay and lesbian individuals declines (see Figure 11.7) (Poteat & Anderson, 2012), and parental acceptance of their adolescents' sexual orientation increases (Samarova, Shilo, & Diamond, 2014). Given the extent to which lesbian, gay, bisexual, and transgender adolescents are victimized, many sexual-minority youth are understandably hesitant about coming out (disclosing their sexual orientation to others). However, hiding one's sexual orientation from others has its own set of problems, including diminished self-esteem and increased risk for depression (Kosciw, Palmer, & Kull, 2015).

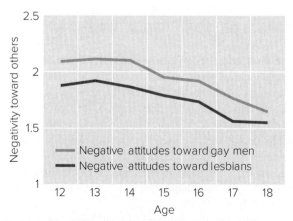

Figure 11.7 With age, adolescents become less prejudiced against gay and lesbian people. (Poteat & Anderson, 2012)

This has prompted many experts to call for more concerted efforts to implement school-based educational programs designed to promote tolerance. The attitudes of teachers and other school personnel also are important: Sexual-minority adolescents who feel they have the support of at least one adult at school are less likely to suffer from the adverse consequences of having been verbally abused (e.g., teased, sworn at, shamed) for their sexual orientation. Studies also find that the establishment of gay–straight alliances within schools have had positive effects on school climate for all students, regardless of their sexual orientation (Ioverno & Russell, 2020; Lessard, Watson, & Puhl, 2020; Marx & Kettrey, 2016). Expanding school and community resources and services for sexual-minority youth also has beneficial effects (Eisenberg et al., 2020; Zhang et al., 2020). Perhaps as a result of these efforts, there has been a significant drop in the victimization of LGBTQ youth in the past 2 decades, as well as in suicidal thoughts and behavior in this population, although there are still significant disparities between sexual-minority and other teenagers in these indicators (Liu et al., 2017; O'Malley Olsen et al., 2017; Raifman et al., 2020).

Sexual Abuse Because both perpetrators and victims of sexual assaults are often reluctant to admit their experiences, it is difficult to obtain accurate estimates of the numbers of adolescents who have been sexually victimized, although given new disclosures of widespread sexual harassment and sexual assault that began to come to the public's attention in 2017, these incidents are probably a lot more common than had been thought.

According to several studies, between 7% and 18% of American adolescents report having had nonvoluntary sexual intercourse before age 18; reports by females are substantially higher than those by males, but it is not known how much of this is due to different prevalence rates and how much to different willingness on the part of females and males to report having been raped (Diamond & Savin-Williams, 2009). (These figures on sexual abuse do not include adolescents who have been physically forced to engage in sexual activity other than intercourse and, as such, clearly underestimate the proportion of teenagers who have been sexually abused.) Women who were most likely to have been raped during adolescence were those who lived apart from their parents before age 16; who were physically, emotionally, or mentally impaired; who were raised at or below the poverty level; or whose parents abused alcohol or used other drugs. Indeed, two-thirds of all women who had three or more of these risk factors were raped as adolescents. In contrast to popular perception, adolescents are abused (sexually, physically, and emotionally) and neglected at a higher rate than are younger children (Cappelleri, Eckenrode, & Powers, 1993).

Several studies have examined the psychological consequences of having been the victim of sexual abuse during adolescence. Adolescents who have been sexually abused have relatively lower self-esteem, weaker self-efficacy, more academic difficulties, and higher rates of anxiety, fear, eating disorders, and depression (Perkins, Luster, & Jank, 2002; Miller et al., 2016); are more likely to engage in risky behavior (Tubman et al., 2004); and are more likely to be sexually active, have risky sex, have multiple sexual partners, be sexually victimized, become pregnant as teenagers, and engage in prostitution (Black et al., 2009; Homma et al., 2012; Noll et al., 2019; Wilson & Widom, 2010). Girls who have been chronically sexually abused by their biological father are at greatest risk for problems (Trickett et al., 2001). There is also some evidence that sexual abuse prior to adolescence may lead to precocious (that is, very early) puberty (Brown et al., 2004).

At the same time, it is worth noting that there are substantial differences among individuals in the extent to which they show problems as a result of having been sexually abused and in the form those problems take (Bauserman & Rind, 1997). Generally, individuals who have been both sexually and physically abused fare worse than those who experience sexual abuse alone. But adolescents who have been sexually abused fare better psychologically when they have parents (presumably not the perpetrators of the abuse) who are authoritative (firm and supportive) and when they are successful in school (Luster & Small, 1997).

Risky Sex and Its Prevention

One reason for the great concern among adults over the sexual activity of adolescents is the failure of many sexually active young people to use contraception regularly. Among sexually active high school students in the United States, nearly 45% report not having used a condom the last time they had sex. Adolescents' condom use increased significantly during the 1990s (from less than half of sexually active teens to close to 60%) but dropped between 2003 and 2019 (see Figure 11.8). Condom use is higher among younger high school students than older ones, most likely because nearly twice as many 12th-grade girls (27%) than 9th-grade girls (12%) are on the birth control pill. Of course, using the pill prevents pregnancy but provides no protection against sexually transmitted diseases (Centers for Disease Control and Prevention, 2020).

Among adolescents who do use contraception, the most popular method by far is using a condom, followed by the birth control pill; this is a significant change from previous generations of adolescents, who were far more likely to depend on the pill than on condoms (Everett et al., 2000). Withdrawal (pulling out before ejaculation), a highly ineffective method of preventing pregnancy and a practice that provides no protection against sexually transmitted diseases, unfortunately is still used by 10% teenagers (Centers for Disease Control and Prevention, 2020).

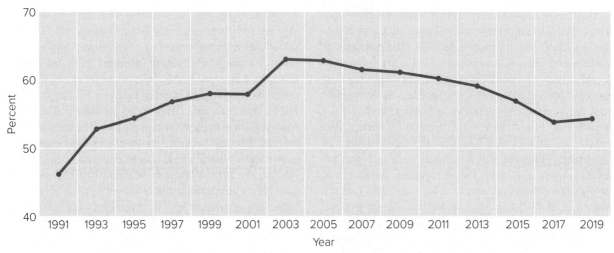

Figure 11.8 **Proportion of sexually active teens who used a condom the last time they had intercourse.** (Centers for Disease Control and Prevention, 2020)

One important recent trend has been an increase in the number of sexually active adolescent girls who use **long-acting reversible contraception** (LARC), such as intrauterine devices (IUDs) or contraceptive implants, although these methods are used by only 30% of high school students (Centers for Disease Control and Prevention, 2020). These methods work well in this age group because, once installed, they don't require any thinking on the part of teenagers, many of whom find themselves in situations in which they want to have sex but didn't plan for it in advance. Many experts believe that the increased use of LARC has contributed to the substantial drop in teen pregnancies seen in many years (Lindberg, Santelli, & Desai, 2018).

It is important to note, however, that LARC, like the birth control pill, does not provide protection against STDs. Unfortunately, fewer than 10% of girls who are on the pill or a longer-acting form of birth control report that they and their partner also used a condom the last time they had sex (Centers for Disease Control and Prevention, 2020).

Researchers estimate that the risk of teen pregnancy is about half due to the absence of contraceptive use and about half due to failed contraceptive use, which is more frequent among adolescents than adults (Blanc et al., 2010; Santelli et al., 2006). A large proportion of condom users do not use condoms correctly, for example (e.g., not putting the condom on before first entry or not holding onto the condom while withdrawing) (Oakley & Bogue, 1995), and many adolescents who might benefit from using emergency contraception (the "morning after pill," or "Plan B") do not know how to use it properly (Mollen et al., 2008). The rate of adolescent pregnancy is substantially higher in

long-acting reversible contraception (LARC) Methods of birth control that provide effective contraception for several years without requiring users to maintain them once they have been put in place, such as intrauterine devices (IUDs) and subdermal contraceptive implants.

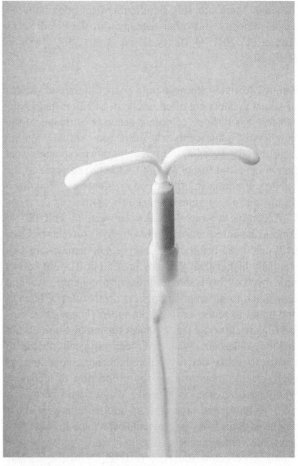

One of the reasons for adults' concern about adolescent sexual activity is the failure of many sexually active teenagers to use contraception regularly. The increasing popularity of long-acting, reversible contraceptives, such as the IUD, is a welcome sign. B. BOISSONNET/BSIP SA/Alamy Stock Photo

the United States than in other industrialized countries—despite the fact that the rate of teenage sexual activity in the United States is comparable to that in many other countries. For example, the average age at which young women become sexually active is 17 in both the United States and the Netherlands, but the U.S. teen pregnancy rate is *four times higher* (Sedgh et al., 2015).

Adolescents' Reasons for Not Using Contraception

Why do so few American adolescents use contraception regularly and effectively? Social scientists point to three broad factors: lack of planning, lack of access, and lack of knowledge.

By far the most important reason many adolescents fail to use birth control is that their sexual activity is unplanned (Kirby, 2007). This absence of planning may reflect adolescents' resistance to admitting that they are choosing to be sexually active, which may explain why adolescents who have taken virginity pledges often do not use contraception when they break their pledge and have sex (Brückner & Bearman, 2005; Rosenbaum, 2009) and why conservatively religious adolescents are less likely to be sexually active but also are less likely to consistently use birth control if they do have sex (Burdette et al., 2014). Adolescents' failure to use contraceptives also may reflect the fact that adolescents are just generally less likely to plan ahead, exercise self-control, and think about the future consequences of their behavior than adults (Hansen et al., 2018; Steinberg, 2014). Going on the pill or purchasing a condom requires an adolescent to acknowledge that he or she is having or is going to have sexual relations and engage in some advance planning. One reason long-acting reversible contraception is effective is that once the device is in place, no further planning is required.

One of the best predictors of condom use is the individual's intent to use a condom and willingness to communicate about it with his or her partner (Widman et al., 2006). When it comes to using a condom, males tend to have more influence than females (Vasilenko, Kreager, & Lefkowitz, 2015). Interventions designed to strengthen adolescents' intentions and their ability to communicate with their partner about contraception, and not just increase their knowledge, have been shown to be effective in promoting condom use, even within high-risk populations (DiClemente et al., 2004).

A second reason for adolescents' failure to use contraception, although a far less important one, is that some adolescents can't afford birth control or don't know where to obtain it (Kirby, 2007). Lack of access (whether real or perceived) is an especially important barrier among younger adolescents, who may feel uncomfortable discussing their sexual activity with parents or other adults whose help or consent may be necessary in order to obtain birth control. Having ready access to a free, confidential family planning service that does not require parents' consent is a strong predictor of whether adolescents will use contraceptives consistently or at all (Ryan, Franzetta, & Manlove, 2007). Teen pregnancies and

childbearing increase after states implement requirements that adolescents get their parents' consent in order to obtain contraception (Zavodny, 2004), and surveys of sexually active teenagers who use contraceptives indicate that one-fifth of them would stop using them if they had to notify their parents in order to get them (Jones et al., 2005). Some experts have called for changes in regulations that would permit adolescents to purchase oral contraceptives without a prescription, noting that today's birth control pills are safe and effective, even more so for adolescents than adults (Upadhaya et al., 2017).

Finally, many young people are insufficiently educated about sex, contraception, and pregnancy, which may leave them misinformed about when and how to use contraception (Kirby, 2007; Ryan, Franzetta, & Manlove, 2007). For example, although it is important for adolescents to understand the need to use contraception every time they have sex, a very large proportion of teenagers who have had sex with contraception have also had sex without contraception (Vasilenko, Kreager, & Lefkowitz, 2015). That said, knowledge alone does not seem to be sufficient to promote contraceptive use; individuals must be motivated to use contraception as well as know why they need to (Sheeran, Abraham, & Orbell, 1999).

Given all these reasons—lack of planning, lack of access, and lack of knowledge—it is not surprising that one of the best predictors of contraceptive use is the adolescent's age: Older teenagers are better at thinking ahead, less guilty about having sex, more likely to be able to discuss contraception with their partner, and better able to grasp the potential negative consequences of an unwanted pregnancy. Relatively younger women are even less likely to use contraception if their partner is older and more likely, as a result, to contract an STD (Pettifor et al., 2010; Ryan et al., 2008).

Improving Contraceptive Behavior

There is a great deal that adults can do to improve the contraceptive behavior of adolescents (Jones et al., 2011). First, adults can see that contraceptives are made accessible to young people who want them; many experts have called for increasing school-based condom distribution programs (Society for Adolescent Health and Medicine, 2017). Second, parents and schools can provide sex education at an early enough age to instruct young people in the fundamentals of contraceptive use before, rather than after, they've become sexually active; such education should try to strengthen adolescents' intentions to use contraception and not just increase their contraceptive knowledge. Third, parents can be more open and responsive in the ways in which they communicate with their teenagers about sex, and about safe sex in particular, so that when adolescents become sexually active, they find it easier to plan ahead without feeling guilty. Finally, adolescents can be encouraged to consider the potential future consequences of an unplanned pregnancy or a sexually transmitted disease. One way to do this is to engage adolescents in school, which may improve their aspirations for the future (Knowles et al., 2020; Manlove et al., 2013). Adolescents who do not believe that a pregnancy will be an impediment to their future goals are less likely to take steps to avoid getting pregnant (Mireles-Rios & Romo, 2014).

AIDS and Other Sexually Transmitted Diseases

Helping youngsters understand sex, pregnancy, and contraception is an important goal of sex education programs for adolescents. Helping them avoid the risks of **sexually transmitted diseases (STDs)** (also referred to as sexually transmitted infections, or STIs) is another. STDs are caused by viruses, bacteria, or parasites that are transmitted through sexual contact. About 10 million people between the ages of 15 and 24 are diagnosed with a sexually transmitted infection each year (Shannon & Klausner, 2018). Some of the most common STDs among adolescents are **gonorrhea** and **chlamydia** (both caused by a bacterium), **herpes** and **human papillomavirus (HPV)** (both caused by a virus), and **trichomoniasis** (caused by a parasite) (Forhan et al., 2009). One-fourth of all sexually active American young women between the ages of 14 and 19 have at least one of these five infections (Centers for Disease Control and Prevention, 2020). These infections pose a significant health risk because they are associated with increased rates of cancer and infertility. Countries vary considerably in rates of STD infection, with the United States having the highest rate in the developed world (World Population Review, 2020).

HIV/AIDS Since the 1980s, a new and far more serious STD has commanded the world's attention: **AIDS, or acquired immune deficiency syndrome**. The virus that causes AIDS, **human immunodeficiency virus (HIV),** is transmitted through bodily fluids, especially semen, during sex, or blood when drug users share needles. AIDS itself has no symptoms, but HIV attacks the body's immune system, interfering with the body's ability to defend itself

against life-threatening diseases such as pneumonia or cancer. Because there is a long period of time between HIV infection and the actual manifestation of illness—sometimes as long as 10 years—infected adolescents are likely to be asymptomatic carriers of the HIV virus who may develop AIDS in young adulthood. Although adolescents and young adults account for about one-fifth of new HIV infections each year, the rate of infection in this age group has dropped over the past 2 decades. Most new cases in this age group are among Black and Latinx gay young men (Centers for Disease Control and Prevention, 2019). The chances of contracting HIV are greatest among individuals who use drugs, have unprotected sex, have many sexual partners, and already have another STD (such as gonorrhea) (Elkington, Bauermeister, & Zimmerman, 2010). Because these risk factors are more common among young people than adults, the risk of HIV infection among adolescents is substantial.

Protecting Against STDs Adults often forget that adolescents' sexual behavior is as much, if not more, influenced by their perceptions of benefits (for example, the fun of having different partners or the physical sensation of unprotected intercourse) as it is by their perceptions of costs (for example, the risks of pregnancy or contracting an STD). Adolescents have sex because they want intimacy with their partner, status with their peers, and, of course, physical pleasure (Ott et al., 2006). In one large-scale study, among both males and females, the belief that condoms reduced pleasure was the main reason for nonuse (Higgins & Wang, 2015); along these lines, when condoms are not immediately available, young men are more likely to go ahead and have unprotected sex when they are relatively more attracted to their partner (Collado et al., 2017).

Short of abstinence, the best way for teenagers to protect themselves against contracting HIV and other STDs is by using condoms; adolescents who consistently use condoms are half as likely as those who do not to contract an STD (Crosby et al., 2003). One large-scale evaluation of a media campaign targeted at Black youth (who are five times more likely than other youth to have an STD; Centers for Disease Control and Prevention, 2019a) and designed to promote the messages that using condoms would make sex more worry-free and therefore more enjoyable, that waiting to have sex was a way of showing respect for one's partner, and that a "steady partner is a safe partner" was shown to be effective in changing adolescents' attitudes and condom use (Romer et al., 2009).

Teen Pregnancy

Given the high rate of sexual activity and relatively poor record of contraceptive use among contemporary adolescents, it comes as little surprise to learn that many young

---

sexually transmitted disease (STD)
Any of a group of infections—including HPV, gonorrhea, trichomoniasis, herpes, chlamydia, and AIDS—passed on through sexual contact.

gonorrhea
A sexually transmitted infection caused by a bacterium.

chlamydia
A sexually transmitted infection caused by a bacterium.

herpes
A sexually transmitted infection caused by a virus.

human papillomavirus (HPV)
One of several viruses that causes a sexually transmitted disease.

trichomoniasis
A sexually transmitted infection caused by a parasite.

AIDS (acquired immune deficiency syndrome)
A disease, caused by a virus transmitted by means of bodily fluids, that devastates the immune system.

HIV (human immunodeficiency virus)
The virus associated with AIDS.

women become pregnant before the end of adolescence. Each year, more than 200,000 American adolescents between 15 and 19 become pregnant—giving the United States the highest rate of teen pregnancy in the industrialized world (see Table 11.1) (Sedgh et al., 2015). The rate of unintended pregnancy is far greater among adolescents than adults once age differences in sexual activity are taken into account (Finer, 2010). Close to 90% of teen pregnancies are unintended (Committee on Adolescence, 2014). This is important because having an unintended pregnancy increases the odds that an adolescent mother will experience difficulties in parenting (East, Chien, & Barber, 2012).

making the cultural connection

Although rates of sexual activity are no higher in the United States than in many other industrialized countries, rates of STDs, teen pregnancy, and teen childbearing are. What factors do you think contribute to this?

Prevalence of Teen Pregnancy   About one-quarter of American young women become pregnant at least once by age 20 (Power to Decide, 2016). This rate is dramatically lower than it had been a few decades ago (it peaked in the early 1990s, when it was twice as high as it is today). Teen pregnancy has become less common mainly because of increased and improved contraceptive use (including the use of long-acting reversible contraception) (Lindberg, Santelli, & Desai, 2016). Rates of teen pregnancy vary considerably by ethnicity: The rate is nearly three times higher among Black youth and more than twice as high among Latinx youth than among white youth; the rate among Asian American adolescents is lowest of all (National Campaign to Prevent Teen and Unplanned Pregnancy, 2015).

Keep in mind that not all adolescent pregnancies result in childbirth, however. But as rates of teen pregnancy have fallen, so have rates of teen births (Martin et al., 2019) (see Figure 11.9). In the United States, about 25% of all teenage pregnancies are aborted, and slightly more than 15% end in miscarriage (Kost & Henshaw, 2014). Among American adolescents who carry their

Table 11.1   Rates of adolescent pregnancies, abortions, and births in Europe and the United States.

Country	Year	Rate per 1,000 females 15–19 years old			Pregnancies that end in abortion (%)
		Pregnancies	Abortions	Births	
Belgium	2009	21	8	10	38
Denmark	2011	21	14	5	67
England and Wales	2011	47	20	21	42
Estonia	2011	43	19	19	43
Finland	2011	23	13	8	55
France	2011	25	15	7	61
Hungary	2011	38	16	18	41
Iceland	2011	30	15	11	51
Israel	2011	23	8	13	32
Netherlands	2008	14	7	5	50
New Zealand	2011	51	18	26	36
Norway	2011	23	13	7	56
Portugal	2011	25	8	13	33
Scotland	2011	46	17	23	37
Singapore	2011	14	8	5	54
Slovakia	2011	33	6	22	17
Slovenia	2009	14	7	5	48
Spain	2011	26	13	10	50
Sweden	2010	29	20	6	69
Switzerland	2011	8	5	2	59
United States	2010	57	15	34	26

(Sedgh et al., 2015)

Figure 11.9 **Trends in teen births.**
*Data on teen births were not reported separately for Native Hawaiian and Other Pacific Islanders (NHOPI) until 2016.
(Martin et al., 2019)

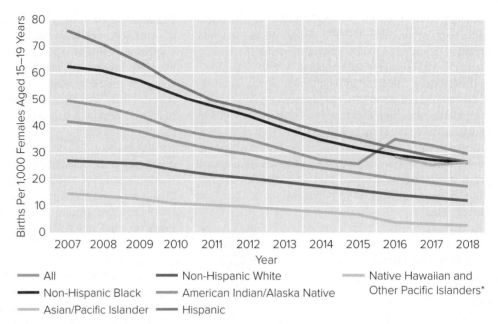

pregnancy full term, very few put the baby up for adoption. Thus, around 60% of teenage pregnancies in the United States result in the birth of an infant who will be raised by his or her mother (with or without the help of a partner or other family members). The proportion of teen pregnancies that are aborted differs from country to country, from a low of about 3% in Azerbaijan to a high of close to 70% in Sweden (Sedgh et al., 2015).

Abortion Researchers have asked whether teenagers who choose to abort an unwanted pregnancy are harmed psychologically by the experience. The consensus among experts is that they are not (Adler, Ozer, & Tschann, 2003). Several studies indicate that pregnant teenage women who abort their pregnancy are significantly better off, psychologically, socially, and economically, than women who give birth to their child, both in the United States (Zabin, Hirsch, & Emerson, 1989) and abroad (Jalanko et al., 2020) (see Figure 11.10). Among the most important differences between pregnant adolescents who abort their pregnancy and those who do not is that young women who terminate their pregnancy by abortion are less likely over the next 2 years to experience a subsequent pregnancy and are more likely to practice contraception.

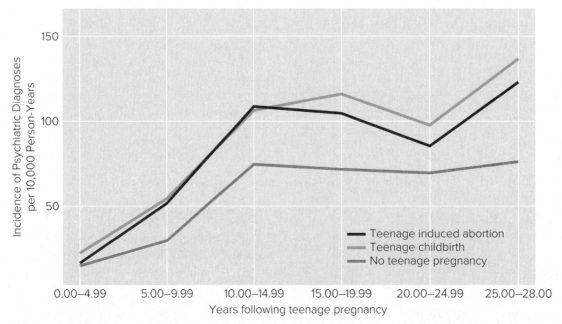

Figure 11.10 **Adolescents who abort their pregnancies are significantly less likely to develop a psychiatric disorder than those who give birth to the child, but more likely than those who were never pregnant.** (Jalanko et al., 2020)

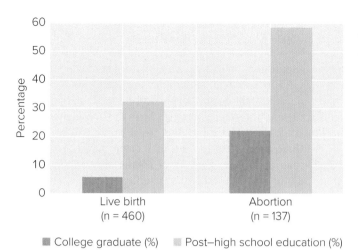

The benefits of terminating an unwanted pregnancy also extend to young men; men whose partners abort their pregnancy are more likely than those whose partners give birth to the child to complete high school and go to college (Everett et al., 2019) (see Figure 11.11).

Given the psychological and economic benefits of terminating an unwanted adolescent pregnancy, it is easy to understand why many social scientists have questioned the wisdom of court decisions designed to restrict adolescents' access to abortion services (ACLU, 2021). While some studies show that laws requiring parental notification or limiting access to legal abortion do, in fact, result in fewer terminated pregnancies among adolescents (e.g., Ralph et al., 2018), not all studies reach the same conclusion (e.g., Ramesh, Zimmerman, & Patel, 2016). Policies limiting access to abortion lead to higher rates of unintended childbearing, especially among Black, Latinx, and poor youth (Coles et al., 2010).

One reason to worry about parental notification laws is that there are many adolescents who don't want to tell their parents about their decision to abort a pregnancy because they fear their parents' reaction, either to the plans to abort the pregnancy or to simply the fact that they are sexually active. In response to this, several states have implemented laws that allow adolescents who are unwilling to involve their parents in their decision making to obtain permission from a judge to seek an abortion without notifying their parents, a procedure known as a **judicial bypass**. Although this sounds reasonable in principle, some studies find that adolescents who pursue this option describe the process as intimidating and humiliating and are emotionally distressed by judges who lecture or shame them and question whether they are sufficiently mature to make the decision without involving their parents (Coleman-Minahan et al., 2019).

Causes of Teen Pregnancy   Many myths permeate discussions of the causes of adolescent pregnancy and complicate what is actually a fairly simple matter. The most important differences between young women who do and do not become pregnant during adolescence are in their sexual activity and contraceptive use. As you have read, sexual intercourse among American young people is common (although not as common as it had been), while contraceptive use is sporadic and inadequate (although better than it had been). More than 80% of adolescent pregnancies are unintended (Finer & Zolna, 2016).

"Unintended" has different meanings, though, and the line between intended and unintended is often blurry. Here's an example: Imagine that you are going to a party and you've told yourself that you were only going to drink in moderation. You arrive at the party and see that things are pretty wild. After one drink, a friend offers you another, and as the evening went on and you found yourself having fun, this happened a few times, and you felt a little drunk. Would we say that you had "intended" to drink too much? Probably not. But surely you could have stopped this from happening if you had taken certain steps (e.g., left the party once you discovered what it was like, asked a friend to stop you from drinking, and so on). Although becoming intoxicated wasn't something you intended to do, you didn't do anything to stop this from happening. Under these circumstances, "unintended" may not be the right way to describe what happened.

Deep down inside, do adolescents who become pregnant actually intend to have a baby? This, too, is a difficult question to answer. According to national surveys, 75% of births to women ages 15 to 19 are not planned, so we know that the vast majority of adolescent mothers did not become pregnant intentionally (Finer & Zolna, 2016). Yet, studies that plumb the issue a bit deeper find that many young women who say they do not want to become pregnant are actually ambivalent and not unequivocally negative about the prospect of having a child

judicial bypass
A regulation in many states that allows adolescents who want to abort a pregnancy but who are unwilling or unable to involve their parents in the decision to obtain permission from a judge to seek an abortion.

(Jaccard, Dodge, & Dittus, 2003). For example, consider the following response from a 17-year-old Australian girl when asked about her pregnancy: "I knew it was going to happen, like I didn't stop it from happening so if it was going to happen it was going to happen and if it didn't, it didn't" (Smith, Skinner, & Fenwick, 2011, p. 628). She doesn't explicitly say that she wanted to get pregnant, but she doesn't say that she didn't want to either. Was her pregnancy intended or unintended?

Adolescents who are ambivalent about childbearing or who believe that having a child will be a positive experience are less likely to use contraception effectively (Unger, Molina, & Teran, 2002; Zabin, Astone, & Emerson, 1993). Thus, while the vast majority of sexually active teenagers do not actively wish to become pregnant, a significant minority feel less troubled by the prospect of early parenthood than do their peers, and these youngsters are more likely to risk pregnancy by having unprotected sex. As one team of authors wrote, "Adolescent childbearing is more an unintended result of risky behaviors than a result of rational choice" (Trent & Crowder, 1997, p. 532). Consistent with this, rates of unintended pregnancy are four times higher among adolescents with ADHD and other problems that are associated with risk taking (Owens & Hinshaw, 2020).

Adolescent Parenthood   It is important to distinguish between pregnancies and actual births—a distinction that often is lost in debates over the consequences of teenage pregnancy. Because 40% of teen pregnancies in the United States do not result in the birth of a child, the birth rate among adolescents is far lower than it would otherwise be, and it may surprise you to learn that the birth rate among adolescent women today is considerably lower than it was in previous eras. Contrary to the popular idea that teenage childbearing has reached epidemic proportions in this country, relatively more women gave birth to an infant before reaching adulthood in previous decades than do so today—and by a large margin. Nevertheless, the rate of teenage births in the United States continues to be more than twice as high as in Canada, three times greater than in Iceland, five times greater than in France, nine times greater than in Japan, and 17 times greater than in Switzerland (Sedgh et al., 2015).

All sorts of explanations for the astoundingly high rate of teenage childbearing in the United States have been offered (often, the finger is pointed at the mass media, which are blamed for pretty much everything adolescents do that adults disapprove of). More likely candidates are income inequality and school attendance: The greater the gap between rich and poor and the lower the rate of school attendance among young people, the higher the rate of teen childbearing. According to international data from the World Bank and the Organisation for Economic Co-operation and Development, among developed countries, the United States pretty much leads the list in income inequality and is below average in the proportion of adolescents who attend school regularly.

Rates of teenage childbearing also vary markedly across ethnic and socioeconomic groups. Middle-class women are far more likely to abort their pregnancies than are poor women, and as a consequence, the problem of teenage childbearing is densely concentrated among economically disadvantaged youth. Because minority adolescents are more likely to grow up poor, teenage childbearing is especially prevalent in nonwhite communities.

Children of Teen Mothers   Studies of the children of teen parents consistently find that they are more likely to have behavioral, psychological, and scholastic problems than their peers born to adult parents (Hoffman & Maynard, 2008). But because teenage childbearing tends to go hand in hand with a variety of other problems—the most critical of which is poverty—it is extremely difficult to know whether any problems of teenage mothers or their children result from the mother's young age or from other, correlated factors.

Separating the effects of early childbearing from poverty is a matter of more than theoretical importance: If early childbearing is, in fact, a problem in and of itself, it becomes important to direct preventive programs at deterring adolescent pregnancy (either by discouraging sexual activity or by encouraging effective contraceptive use) and childbearing (by encouraging adoption and abortion). But if poverty, not the mother's age, is the key, an entirely different set of strategies is called for, aimed not at youngsters' sexual behavior but at all individuals' economic circumstances. It is extremely important, therefore, to ask whether and in what ways a mother's age at

Each year, more than 600,000 American adolescents become pregnant—giving the United States the highest rate of teen pregnancy in the industrialized world. Katarzyna Białasiewicz/123RF

the time she gives birth affects her and her child's well-being.

In fact, many of the problems that afflict children born to adolescent mothers result primarily from poverty and single parenthood and from other qualities that often characterize young women who become teen parents (such as poor school achievement), rather than from the mother's youth (Levine, Emery, & Pollack, 2007; Pittard, Laditka, & Laditka, 2008). Babies born to middle-class adolescents differ little from their counterparts born to middle-class adults, and infants born to poor adolescents are similar to children born to equally poor adults.

One important exception to this general similarity between the children of adolescent and adult mothers is that adolescent mothers—even of similar socioeconomic status—may perceive their babies as being especially difficult and may interact with their infants less often in ways that are known to be beneficial to the child's cognitive and social development (Reid & Meadows-Oliver, 2007). Children born to adolescent mothers are more likely to have school problems, to be involved in misbehavior and delinquent activity, to be sexually active at an early age, and to become an adolescent parent (Campa & Eckenrode, 2006; Tang et al., 2016). In general, and for reasons that are not known, the cognitive and psychosocial problems of children born to adolescent mothers grow increasingly more apparent with age (that is, the differences between children born to teen versus adult mothers are more evident in adolescence than infancy).

Again, though, studies show that the adverse outcomes of being born to an adolescent mother—even outcomes not visible until the children have reached young adulthood—are attributable both to characteristics of young women who are likely to become teen parents (for example, the adverse effects of being raised by someone who is poorly educated) and to the circumstances that characterize the family environments of young mothers (for example, the adverse effects of growing up in poverty) (Jaffee et al., 2001; Pogarsky, Lizotte, & Thornberry, 2003). Because adolescent mothers are more likely than adult mothers to be both unmarried and poor, their children are at greater risk of developing a variety of psychological and social problems. Many of the problem behaviors seen among children of adolescent mothers are prevalent among poor children growing up in single-parent homes generally.

In other words, the greater incidence of problems among offspring of adolescent mothers may reflect the overall environment in which the children grow up, rather than the ways in which they are raised. Although in theory we can separate the effects of poverty on children from the effects of adolescent childbearing, in reality, the two usually go together, and the end result is that children born to adolescent mothers are more likely than other children to suffer the effects both of malnutrition—in the womb as well as in the world—and of environmental deprivation.

Consequences for Teen Mothers   Actually, the problems associated with teen parenthood may actually be greater for the mothers than for their children. In general, women who bear children early suffer disruptions in their educational and occupational careers (Gibb et al., 2014; Hoffman & Maynard, 2008). Not only are adolescent mothers more likely to come from a poor background and to have a history of academic difficulties, but they are also more likely to remain poor than their equally disadvantaged peers who delay childbearing until after their schooling is completed (Mollborn, 2007). However, many adolescent mothers were low-achieving students *before* becoming pregnant, and the limited educational attainment of teenage mothers is at least partly due to factors that were in play long before the pregnancy, perhaps even during early childhood (Fergusson & Woodward, 2000; Russell, 2002). In short, poverty and low achievement are both causes *and* consequences of early childbearing.

Having a child early in life does not inevitably cast in concrete a life of poverty and misery for the mother and her youngster, however. There is considerable diversity among teenage mothers in the routes that their adult lives take (Oxford et al., 2006). One study identified three distinct groups: a problem-prone group (15% of the sample), who had chronic problems in many areas of life, including antisocial behavior; a psychologically vulnerable group (42%), who had relatively high rates of mental health problems but who were able to transition into adult roles with some degree of success; and a normative group (43%), who defied common stereotypes of adolescent mothers as doomed to failure and poverty and who were able to make a successful transition to adulthood (Oxford et al., 2005).

In general, young mothers who remain in or return to high school and delay subsequent childbearing fare a great deal better over the long run—as do their children—than those who drop out of school or have more children relatively early (Dahl, 2010). Remaining in school and living at home with one's parents significantly diminishes the chances of a second unwanted pregnancy (Manlove, Mariner, & Papillo, 2000). Marriage, in contrast, is a high-risk strategy. When a stable relationship is formed and economic resources are available, marriage improves the mother's and the child's chances for life success; this seems to be especially true for women who marry somewhat later. However, a hasty decision to marry in the absence of a stable relationship and economic security exacerbates many other problems (Dahl, 2010).

After the Baby Is Born   Many of the negative effects of having children as a teenager can be prevented or at least minimized by lessening the disruptive economic impact of teenage parenthood on young women's lives (Development Services Group & Child Welfare Information Gateway, 2005). What do we know about the factors that work?

First, marrying the father of the child may place the adolescent mother at greater risk if the father is not capable of economically supporting himself, much less his family. If the father is able to find a good job and remain employed, he can be an important source of psychological and economic support and a healthy influence on the mother and child. However, it is all too likely that marriage may diminish, rather than enhance, an adolescent mother's economic circumstances. In addition, marriage places the adolescent mother at greater risk of having another child relatively soon, which further jeopardizes her already precarious economic situation. Moreover, teenage marriage is very likely to end in divorce, which itself is an additional stressor on the mother and child.

Adolescent mothers therefore cannot always look to the father of the child to help break the cycle of poverty. However, in many cases, they can look to their own parents for support, and this may be an effective strategy. Teenage mothers who move in with their own family for a short time—a practice far more common among Black than Latinx or white adolescents—are more likely to enjoy educational and occupational success than their counterparts who live on their own because the family's help allows the young mother to return to school or find employment. Without this help, many young mothers drop out of school and have to find and pay for child care, which often is more costly than the income their low-paying jobs generate. Without a high school diploma, these women have little chance of improving their economic situation or their child's opportunities.

One fact is certain: Adolescent mothers who receive social support fare better, are better parents, and have healthier children than do adolescent mothers who lack support (Riggs et al., 2004; Turner, Sorenson, & Turner, 2000). The best arrangement for a teenage mother is usually to live independently from her own parents but to rely on them for emotional support and child care (Coley & Chase-Lansdale, 1998).

Because it is so important for young mothers to have an adequate income and a chance for adequate employment, many policy makers have called for changes in the ways that schools and other social institutions treat pregnant students and changes in the provision of day care. Among the most important are adaptations in school schedules and the development of school-based child care centers so that pregnant students can remain in school after the birth of their child; the expansion of subsidized child care for young mothers who are out of school so that the economic benefits of having a job are not outweighed by the costs of child care; and the expansion of family planning services to adolescent mothers so that they can prevent another pregnancy.

Although there are stories of young women whose lives are not devastated by early childbearing, the successes are young women who have avoided poverty, rather

Because adolescent mothers are more likely than adult mothers to be both unmarried and poor, their children are at greater risk of developing a variety of psychological and social problems.
Ian Hooton/SPL/Alamy Stock Photo

than achieving great economic success. Although the picture of adolescent parenthood is less uniformly dire than typically painted in the media, there is still consensus among experts that it is important to try to prevent teenage pregnancy and childbearing.

Sex Education

Each year, millions of dollars are spent attempting to prevent teen pregnancy and the spread of sexually transmitted diseases. Many adolescents receive some sort of classroom instruction about sex—whether through high school health classes, biology classes, classes designated exclusively for the purpose of sex education, or educational programs administered through youth or religious organizations. Do these programs do any good?

The answer to this question is complicated and depends on the nature of the program and the outcome it is trying to achieve. A comprehensive review of more than 50 curriculum-based programs concluded that carefully constructed educational interventions can delay the initiation of sex and reduce rates of risky sexual activity among adolescents (Kirby & Laris, 2009), although the long-term effectiveness of these programs has not been adequately studied (Kågesten et al., 2014). One problem is that many schools do not use sex education curricula that have proven effectiveness (Bryan, Gillman, & Hansen, 2016); moreover, what is effective in one population (suburban middle-class teenagers) isn't necessarily effective in a different one (poor, inner-city teenagers) (Bull et al., 2016; Jenner et al., 2016). Generally speaking, programs are more effective in reducing risky sex than in reducing sexual activity more generally. But experts agree that successful interventions must do more than provide information about contraception, STDs, and pregnancy. They must also teach adolescents how to refuse unwanted sex and avoid unintended sex, increase adolescents' motivation to engage in safe sex, and change perceptions about peer norms and attitudes (Jaramillo et al., 2017). These approaches, collectively, are referred to as **comprehensive sex education.** Surveys of adolescents find that they overwhelming prefer this type of sex education (Corcoran et al., 2020).

Although many adults are concerned that teaching adolescents how to engage in safe sex sends a message encouraging more teenagers to become sexually active, evaluations of effective comprehensive sex education programs (even those that distribute condoms to teenagers) show that this is not the case (Kirby & Laris, 2009; Minguez et al., 2015). In fact, expanding access to family planning services and contraceptives is more effective than sex education in deterring teen childbearing without increasing adolescents' sexual activity or encouraging an early sexual debut (Algur et al., 2019; Beltz et al., 2015). This is consistent with evaluations of other health education interventions, which find that many are good at changing what teenagers know but not at changing how they behave (Abe et al., 2016; Kelsey et al., 2016; Gelfond et al., 2016; Steinberg, 2015).

We also know a fair amount about what *doesn't* work. Careful evaluations of **abstinence-only sex education** programs have shown unequivocally that they are not successful, either in changing adolescents' sexual behavior or in reducing rates of pregnancy or STDs (Santelli et al., 2017). In fact, abstinence-only education programs cause an *increase* in teen pregnancy and childbearing (Stanger-Hall & Hall, 2011; Yang & Gaydos, 2010). Programs that attempt to reduce sexual risk taking by reducing other forms of risky behavior (such as delinquency or substance use) also are not effective, consistent with the notion that sexual risk taking, while correlated with other types of risk taking, may have some unique causes (Santelli et al., 2009). The evidence on other types of programs designed to reduce unsafe sex, such as those designed to encourage safe sex indirectly by facilitating positive youth development, is inconclusive (Kirby, 2007).

Changing the context in which adolescents live may be a necessary addition to classroom-based education in order to change actual behavior (Shackleton et al., 2016). For example, providing adult-supervised, structured after-school activities for young adolescents would limit their opportunities to have sex during late afternoon hours, which is the most common time of day for young teenagers' sexual activity.

comprehensive sex education

Programs that not only provide information about contraception, STDs, and pregnancy but also teach adolescents how to refuse unwanted sex and avoid unintended sex, increase their motivation to engage in safe sex, and change perceptions about peer norms and attitudes.

abstinence-only sex education

Programs that encourage adolescents to avoid sexual activity but that do not provide information about safe sex.

Design Elements: (Brain): McGraw Hill Education; (Globe): Jupiterimages/Stockbyte/Getty Images; (Compass): Jacques Cornell/McGraw Hill Education; (Lightbulb): ansonsaw/Getty Images; (Girl with laptop): Africa Studio/Shutterstock.

12 Achievement

Achievement as an Adolescent Issue
Puberty and Achievement
Cognitive Change and Achievement
Social Roles and Achievement

The Importance of Noncognitive Factors
Achievement Motivation
Beliefs About Success and Failure

Environmental Influences on Achievement
The Influence of the Home Environment
The Influence of Friends

Educational Achievement
The Importance of Socioeconomic Status
Ethnic Differences in Educational Achievement
Changes in Educational Achievement over Time
Dropping Out of High School

Occupational Achievement
The Development of Occupational Plans
Influences on Occupational Choices

Relaximages/Cultura/Getty Images

Because adolescence is typically a time of preparation for the roles of adulthood, considerable attention has been paid to the development and expression of achievement during these years. Broadly defined, achievement concerns the development of motives, capabilities, interests, and behavior that have to do with performance in evaluative situations. The study of achievement during adolescence has focused on young people's performance in educational settings and on their hopes and plans for future scholastic and occupational careers.

Achievement is a particularly important consideration in the study of adolescence in contemporary society. Industrialized societies place an extraordinary emphasis on performance, competition, and success. During childhood and adolescence, youngsters are continually tested to determine how they stand in relation to their peers. In most industrialized societies, the amount of education a person has completed and the job he or she holds—two of the most important indicators of achievement—provide a basis for the individual's self-conceptions and image in the eyes of others.

A second reason for the importance of achievement in the study of adolescence concerns the range and rapidly changing nature of the choices faced by today's young people. Adolescents in modern societies are confronted with an array of difficult educational and occupational decisions before they turn 25. Beyond such fundamental questions as whether to continue with schooling after high school and what type of career to follow, adolescents must think about what specific sorts of jobs should be pursued within a particular career path, what kind of educational preparation would be most appropriate, and how to get a decent job.

Maybe you're considering a career as a therapist who works with teenagers. Is it better to major in some sort of counseling or to follow a more general, liberal arts course of study? How early do you have to decide which specific profession to specialize in (e.g., counseling, social work, psychology, psychiatry)? Is it necessary to go to graduate school right away, or is it better to get some work experience before applying? These are all difficult questions to answer. And they are made more difficult because the nature of work and the preparation one needs for specific careers change so rapidly. What might have been good advice 10 years ago might be terrible advice today.

Finally, achievement is a particularly important issue in the study of adolescence in contemporary society because individuals vary so widely in levels of educational and occupational success. By the end of high school, many adolescents demonstrate a high enough level of academic achievement to enter selective colleges and universities; at the other extreme are their peers who enter adulthood unable even to read a newspaper or understand a bus schedule. Although 70% of adolescents in the United States today go on to college immediately after high school, nearly 10% drop out of high school before graduating (the figure is even higher in many inner-city school districts). In this chapter, we'll look at the many factors that distinguish between young people who are successful and those who are not.

Achievement as an Adolescent Issue

Development in the realm of achievement neither begins nor ends during adolescence. Educational institutions—even for young children—stress performance, competition, and success on tests of knowledge and ability, even more so today than in the past. Concerns over achievement continue throughout adulthood as well. Like their younger counterparts, adults often place a premium on success, and in American society, someone's occupation is an important part of his or her identity.

Achievement during the adolescent years, though, merits special attention for several reasons. First, the fact that adolescence is a time of preparation for adult work roles raises questions about the nature of the preparation young people receive and the processes through which they sort themselves (or are sorted) into the jobs that may influence the remainder of their lives. Individuals' options for later school and work are often influenced by decisions they make during high school and college. It's important to ask how such options are perceived and defined, and how decisions are made.

Second, although differences in school performance and achievement are apparent as early as the first grade, not until adolescence do individuals begin to fully appreciate the implications of these differences for immediate and future accomplishment. Children's occupational plans are often the product of fantasy and passing interests, without any realistic assessment of their practicality or feasibility. During adolescence, individuals begin to evaluate their occupational choices in light of their actual talents, abilities, and opportunities and by comparing their own performance to that of those around them.

Third, the scholastic and occupational decisions made during adolescence are more numerous, and the consequences of such choices more serious, than those made during childhood. In most elementary schools, children generally are all exposed to fairly similar curricula and have few opportunities to veer from the academic program established by their school. In high school, however, students can decide how much science and math they want to take, whether they wish to study a foreign language, and whether they want to pursue a college-prep or vocational track—even whether they want to remain in school once they have reached the legal age for leaving school. Moreover, it is during adolescence that most individuals decide whether they want to go to college or enter a full-time job directly from high school. All these decisions have important implications for the sort of choices and plans the adolescent will make in the future, which, in turn, will influence earnings, lifestyle, identity, and subsequent psychosocial development.

How might the biological, cognitive, and social changes of adolescence affect the ways in which individuals respond in achievement-related situations?

Puberty and Achievement

Although the biological changes of puberty are less obvious influences on achievement than are the cognitive and social transitions of the period, they may nevertheless affect the development of achievement in important ways. As you will read, the transition into secondary school is usually marked by a temporary drop in individuals' motivation to achieve, and some of this may be related to puberty because it introduces new issues (such as dating and sex) into the adolescent's mix of concerns. To the extent that puberty changes what's important for maintaining status in the peer group, it may lead some adolescents to worry about whether trying too hard to do well will make them less attractive to their classmates. Puberty also increases adolescents' interest in risky behavior (such as experimenting with drugs), which may conflict or interfere with what's expected of them in school.

Cognitive Change and Achievement

The intellectual changes of the period obviously are important influences on achievement. Certain subjects, such as algebra, demand the use of the sorts of higher-order cognitive skills that don't fully mature until adolescence. Perhaps more important, not until adolescence are individuals cognitively capable of seeing the long-term consequences of their educational and occupational choices or of realistically considering the range of scholastic and work possibilities open to them (Sharp et al., 2020). Thus, a second reason for the prominence of achievement-related issues during adolescence is the advent of more sophisticated forms of thinking. The ability to think in hypothetical terms, for example, raises new achievement concerns for the individual ("Should I go to college after I graduate, or should I work for

noncognitive factors
Influences on achievement that do not have to do with intellectual ability, such as determination, perseverance, and grit.

a while?"); it also permits the young person to think through such questions in a logical and systematic fashion ("If I decide to go to college, then . . .").

Social Roles and Achievement

The main reason that many achievement-related issues take on new significance during adolescence, though, involves the social transition of the period. In virtually all societies, adolescence is the age when important educational and occupational decisions are made, and educational and work institutions are structured around this. In most societies, it is not until adolescence that individuals attain the status necessary to decide whether they will stop at high school or continue on to college. Similarly, it is not until adolescence that individuals are allowed to enter the labor force in an official capacity because child labor regulations typically prohibit the formal employment of youngsters under the age of 14 or so. In other words, the transition from school to work—one of the central issues in the study of achievement during adolescence—is a socially defined passage that society has determined will begin during adolescence, even if it is not complete until early adulthood.

In this chapter, we look at the nature of achievement during the adolescent years. As you'll see, the extent to which an adolescent is successful in school and in preparing for work is influenced by a complex array of personal and environmental factors. We begin with a look at one set of factors that reliably differentiates adolescents who are successful from their peers who are not. It turns out that **noncognitive factors,** such as how motivated someone is to achieve or what the person believes about the causes of successes and failure, are far more important than had been thought.

The Importance of Noncognitive Factors

In recent years, there has been growing interest in understanding the social and personality factors that predict success in school and work, especially things such as self-control and persistence (Padilla-Walker et al., 2013; Muenks et al., 2017). There is no question that success is partly determined by sheer ability (Bornstein, Hahn, & Wolke, 2013). But as many writers have pointed out, it takes more than talent to succeed; it also takes desire and determination—what some experts have called "grit" (Duckworth, 2016). Individuals differ in the extent to which they strive for success, and this differential striving—which can be measured independently of ability—helps to account for different degrees of actual achievement (Casillas et al., 2012; Mega, Ronconi, & De Beni, 2014). Let's look at some of the most important factors. As you read, stop and think about your own profile.

Achievement Motivation

How much do you care about succeeding in school? Two students may both score equally on an intelligence or aptitude test, but if one student simply tries much harder than the other, their actual grades will probably differ. I've been advising undergraduate and graduate students for more than 45 years, and I can assure you that the difference between those who are successful and those who are not usually has much more to do with their drive and capacity for self-direction than with their intelligence—an observation that is borne out by scientific study (Andersson & Bergman, 2011; Duckworth & Seligman, 2005; Pekrun, 2017). As far as success in school or work is concerned, a certain amount of intelligence is necessary, but it's more important to be determined than to be brilliant. Perseverance is especially important when schoolwork is uninteresting (Trautwein et al., 2015).

In a classic study conducted more than 50 years ago, preschoolers were asked to choose between receiving a single marshmallow immediately or waiting 15 minutes to get two of them. This test measured what psychologists call **delay of gratification,** the ability to wait longer to get a larger, better, or more valuable reward instead of a less attractive one available immediately. In the marshmallow study, children who had a stronger ability to delay gratification *when they were just preschoolers* were far more likely than the others to be successful in school throughout childhood and adolescence, and, as adults, at work (Mischel, 2014). Motivation becomes a more and more important determinant of success during adolescence, as individuals increasingly are expected to take charge of their own educational careers. By the time one enters college, doing well is influenced as much by conscientiousness as it is by intelligence (Poropat, 2009).

Fear of Failure

Being motivated to achieve is only part of the story, however. Even students who are determined to succeed are sometimes so afraid of failing that their strong achievement motivation is undermined. Fear of failure, which often creates feelings of anxiety during tests or in other evaluative situations, can interfere with successful performance.

Some anxiety before taking a test or beginning a project can be helpful, but a little goes a long way. Being a little anxious helps to focus attention (if, for example, the task is boring), and a small amount of anxiety may improve performance by increasing one's concentration, a phenomenon known as the **Yerkes-Dodson law** (Yerkes & Dodson, 1908) (see Figure 12.1). But the anxiety generated by a strong fear of failure interferes with successful performance. This often happens when the task involves learning something new or solving a complex problem. Studies of adolescents from affluent backgrounds who are under strong pressure to do well in school find that it isn't so much parents' pressure to do well that creates mental health problems but rather parents' criticism when their expectations aren't achieved (Luthar, Shoum, & Brown, 2006).

An adolescent's motivation to succeed and her or his fear of failure work together to pull the individual toward (or repel the individual from) achievement situations. Individuals with a relatively strong motivation to succeed and a relatively weak fear of failure are more likely to actively approach challenging achievement situations—by taking more difficult classes, for example—and to look forward to them. In contrast, adolescents whose fear of failure is intense and whose motivation to succeed is weak will dread challenging situations and do what they can to avoid them. Many students who have trouble persisting at tasks and who fear failure become **underachievers**—students whose grades are far lower than one would expect based on their intellectual ability.

Self-Handicapping

Distinguishing between students whose underachievement is due mainly to anxiety and those who underperform for other reasons is important (Klassen et al., 2009; Midgley, Arunkumar, & Urdan, 1996). Some students try appear uninterested in academics because in some schools, this presentation may garner more respect and admiration from peers than academic success. Others want to make sure that they have an excuse for poor performance other than a lack of ability (Nurmi, Onatsu, & Haavisto, 1995). Still others may downplay the importance of academics as a response to their poor performance (Loose et al., 2012). These students may

delay of gratification
The capacity to wait longer to get a larger, better, or more valuable reward instead of a smaller, less attractive, or less valuable one that is available immediately.

Yerkes-Dodson law
A basic psychological principle that states that performance is impaired by too little or too much arousal or anxiety.

underachievers
Individuals whose actual school performance is lower than what would be expected on the basis of objective measures of their aptitude or intelligence.

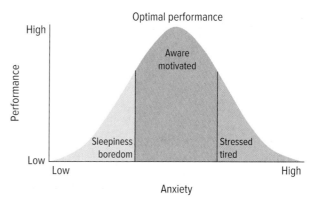

Figure 12.1   Insufficient anxiety can impair performance as a result of boredom, but excessive anxiety can impair performance because of stress, a phenomenon known as the Yerkes-Dodson law. (Yerkes & Dodson, 1908)

self-handicapping
Deliberately behaving in ways that will likely interfere with doing well in order to have an excuse for failing.

mastery motivation
Motivation to succeed based on the pleasure one will experience from mastering a task.

performance motivation
Motivation to succeed based on the rewards one will receive for successful performance.

use various **self-handicapping** strategies—such as joking around in class, procrastinating, turning in incomplete homework, or partying excessively the night before a big exam—as a way of self-protection ("I failed the test because I didn't try hard, not because I'm stupid") or as a means of enhancing their self-presentation ("I'm too cool to care about doing well in school").

Although self-handicapping is common among both males and females, there are sex differences in the ways in which adolescent girls and boys undermine their own success in school: Boys who self-handicap tend to attribute their poor performance to a lack of effort, whereas girls are more likely to mention emotional problems, such as being upset about a friendship that is going through a hard time (Warner & Moore, 2004). A number of writers have drawn special attention to the use of self-handicapping strategies among ethnic minority youth, who may disengage from school because they perceive their long-term prospects as being limited by discrimination and prejudice (Taylor et al., 1994).

Achievement Goal Orientation Two individuals can be equally motivated to achieve but for very different reasons. Psychologists draw a distinction between **mastery motivation** (similar to *intrinsic motivation*) and **performance motivation** (similar to *extrinsic motivation*). Individuals who have a strong mastery orientation strive to achieve because of the pleasure they get out of learning and mastering the material. Individuals who are mainly performance oriented strive to achieve to get the rewards for performing well (typically, good grades) and to avoid the punishments they receive for performing poorly (such as

Individuals who are intrinsically motivated strive to achieve because of the pleasure they get out of learning and mastering the material. Generally speaking, they perform better in school than students who are extrinsically motivated. svetikd/Getty Images

parental disapproval). Students with a strong commitment to achieve their educational goals are "grittier," which increases their school engagement and achievement (Tang et al., 2019). Achieving these goals, in turn, leads to increases in grit (Oi, 2019).

Individuals with a strong mastery orientation perform better in school than those whose motivation is mainly driven by performance goals because intrinsically motivated individuals are more confident about their ability and more likely to persist in the face of failure (Yeager et al., 2014). There is a drop in students' mastery motivation as they transition from elementary into secondary school (Bong, 2009; Wang & Pomerantz, 2009), in part because teachers themselves become more performance-oriented and less mastery-oriented during this time (Eccles & Roeser, 2011). Students who believe that their teachers value and encourage autonomy are less likely to show this decline in motivation (Hafen et al., 2012).

Important adults in the adolescent's life affect the extent to which an adolescent's achievement orientation is aimed more at mastery or at performance (Kim, Schallert, & Kim, 2010; Murayama & Elliot, 2009). It's valuable for students to have perfectionistic tendencies, but it's essential that this drive to do well comes from inside and not from the demands of others (Bong et al., 2014).

What happens at home is especially important. When parents attempt to control an adolescent's achievement behavior by rewarding good grades (e.g., giving prizes or money), punishing bad grades (e.g., restricting privileges), or excessively supervising their performance (e.g., constantly checking up on their homework), adolescents are more likely to develop a performance orientation and, as a result, are less likely to do well in school—just the opposite of their parents' intention. In contrast, adolescents whose parents and teachers encourage their autonomy, provide a cognitively stimulating home environment, and are supportive of school success (without rewarding it concretely) are more likely to develop a strong mastery orientation and perform better in school as a consequence (Dumont et al., 2014; Kim, Schallert, & Kim, 2010; Mouratidis et al., 2013).

Beliefs About Success and Failure

How we behave in achievement situations is also influenced by our beliefs about our abilities and our chances for success and failure. You may have a very strong motivation to achieve, but if you are put into a situation in which you see little likelihood of succeeding, you'll behave very differently than if you're in a situation in which you think your odds of doing well are good. For this reason, researchers have studied adolescents' beliefs about achievement and not simply their motives.

Adolescents make judgments about their likelihood of succeeding or failing and exert different degrees of effort accordingly (Dweck, 2002). Students who believe that they are good at math, for example, will take more, and more difficult, courses than their peers (Wang, 2012). This potentially has ramifications for the future: Course selection influences achievement (students who take more challenging math classes perform better on math tests), and achievement, in turn, influences students' beliefs about their abilities (students who do well on math tests come to see themselves as better math students). A cycle is set in motion in which students' beliefs, abilities, classroom engagement, and actual achievement have a reciprocal influence on each other (Poorthuis et al., 2014). One of the most interesting applications of this idea involves what psychologists call "stereotype threat."

Stereotype Threat Students' beliefs about their abilities and, as a consequence, their performance can also be affected by situational factors operating when they are being evaluated. In controlled experiments, psychologists have found that when students are led to believe that members of their ethnic group usually perform poorly on a particular test (for example, before the test is administered, students are told that previous studies have shown that members of their ethnic group do not score as well as other students), their performance actually suffers, whereas the reverse is true when students are told that members of their ethnic group usually perform better than others (Steele, 1997). This phenomenon is referred to as **stereotype threat.**

To the extent that adolescents believe widely held stereotypes about ethnic or sex differences in ability (for example, that boys are just better at math than girls or that Asians are more intelligent than individuals from other ethnic groups), their achievement may be enhanced or depressed, depending on how they think they are expected to perform (McKellar et al., 2019; Woodcock et al., 2012). For instance, biracial students who identify themselves as Black or Latinx (groups often stereotyped as poor achievers) achieve lower grades in school than those with identical backgrounds who identify themselves as white or Asian (groups often stereotyped as high achievers) (Herman, 2009). Certain stereotypes about ethnic differences in intelligence (e.g., that Asians are better at math) are present even before adolescence (Cvencek et al., 2015). Importantly, interventions designed to counter students' beliefs about their group's intellectual deficiencies have been successful (Hanselman et al., 2014). In fact, the "model minority" stereotype that many Asian teenagers encounter may actually have psychological benefits: It appears to protect against some of the negative consequences of discrimination (Kiang, Witkow, & Thompson, 2016).

Changing views of male and female intellectual ability have affected adolescent girls' test performance. For many years, experts were concerned about the achievement motives and beliefs of adolescent girls, particularly with regard to performance in math and science, but several studies have shown that many previously observed

Students who are good at math take more, and more difficult, math courses, which enhances their academic self-conceptions. This leads them to take more challenging math courses in the future. Pixtal/age fotostock

sex differences have gotten much smaller, at least in the United States (Reilly, Neumann, & Andrews, 2014; Watt et al., 2012). One possible reason for this is that stereotypes about sex differences in cognitive ability have weakened considerably. Many decades ago, raters in experiments judged successful females as less likable, less attractive, and less likely to be happy. Nowadays, similar experiments show the opposite effect, perhaps because we have become that much more accustomed to seeing successful girls and women in a variety of settings and endeavors (Quatman, Sokolik, & Smith, 2000). These days, people tend to be worried about the poor achievement of boys, not girls. On average, boys do not do as well in school, are less invested in doing well, are disciplined more often by their teachers, and are more likely to perceive their schools and teachers as unfair (Kiang et al., 2012; Pomerantz, Altermatt, & Saxon, 2002).

The Nature of Intelligence The way adolescents think about intelligence in general (in addition to how they view their own capability) also enters into the equation. What's especially crucial is whether you think of intelligence as something that is fixed or as something that is malleable—something that has been called a **growth mindset** (Rattan et al., 2015). Studies show that three factors interact to predict students' behavior in school: their mindset, whether they are oriented more toward performance or mastery, and whether they are confident

stereotype threat
The harmful effect that exposure to stereotypes about ethnic or sex differences in ability has on student performance.

growth mindset
Believing that intelligence is malleable and can be "grown" over time.

self-efficacy
The sense that an individual has some control over his or her life.

about their abilities, or, as some theorists have put it, have a strong sense of **self-efficacy** (Bandura et al., 1996). It's how these qualities are combined that really matters, though (De Castella, Byrne, & Covington, 2013; Martin et al., 2013).

Students who believe that intelligence is fixed tend to be oriented toward their performance and to be greatly affected by their degree of self-efficacy. If they are confident about their abilities, this is fine; they tend to work hard and to seek out challenges. If they are insecure, though, they tend to give up easily and feel helpless. In other words, if you believe that intelligence is fixed, you'd better have confidence in your own abilities. Not surprisingly, lower-achieving students who believe that intelligence is fixed are especially vulnerable to this effect (Hwang, Reyes, & Eccles, 2019).

Students who believe that intelligence is malleable approach achievement situations from a different perspective. They are more likely to be intrinsically than extrinsically motivated; for them, satisfaction comes from mastering the material, not simply from getting a good grade. They are also far less affected by their level of confidence because they are less concerned about their performance. Whether assured or insecure, these students exert extra effort and seek out challenges because they are motivated by learning rather than by performing (Purdie, Hattie, & Douglas, 1996). Beliefs in the capacity of people to change are especially helpful during times of stress (Yeager, Lee, & Jamieson, 2016). In contrast, compared to students who believe the intelligence is malleable, those who believe that intelligence is fixed are more likely to suffer the adverse health consequences of stress, such as elevated cortisol levels, after they have experienced a decline in their grades (Lee et al., 2019).

These newer models of the noncognitive aspects of achievement during adolescence illustrate how students' beliefs (about the nature of ability in general and the nature of their own ability in particular) influence their motivation, which, in turn, influences their performance and course selection (Bassi et al., 2007; Guo et al., 2015). Their performance, in turn, influences their beliefs about their competence (Williams & Williams, 2010) (Figure 12.2). Understanding how these forces work together has important implications for teachers because, as you will read, there are specific steps teachers can take that will help bring out the best in their students. Having a growth mindset about math seems to have particular benefits for young women (Degol et al., 2018).

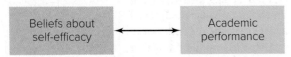

Figure 12.2 Individuals' sense of self-efficacy influences their academic performance, which further shapes their sense of self-efficacy. (Williams & Williams, 2010)

The Importance of Context Although students' orientation toward mastery versus performance is determined in part by psychological factors, the educational context matters as well. When classroom conditions change so that performance becomes more important than learning, students' motives and beliefs change as a result.

You've probably experienced this when you enrolled in a course in which the instructor stressed grades rather than mastery of the material. This sort of emphasis brings out the worst in students—literally. Under some circumstances, performance goals make students more extrinsically motivated, more insecure about their abilities, more hesitant to challenge themselves, and less likely to ask for help. This is especially likely when students are motivated mainly by trying to avoid looking stupid (which diminishes their performance) rather than by trying to compete with and outperform their classmates (which enhances their performance) (Pintrich, 2000). In classrooms in which teachers are very performance-oriented, students feel more alienated from school, have lower feelings of self-efficacy, and are more likely to engage in self-handicapping behavior (Kalil & Ziol-Guest, 2008; Patall, Cooper, & Wynn, 2010).

Students' feelings of self-efficacy influence, and are influenced by, their experiences, the messages they receive from teachers and parents, and the ways in which they compare themselves to their classmates (Gniewosz, Eccles, & Noack, 2015; Simpkins, 2015). Studies from around the world have found that adolescents also use peers as a basis of social comparison and develop beliefs about their academic competence by comparing their grades to the grades their friends get (Bissell-Havran, 2014; Marsh et al., 2014). Here is how Jamaal, an 8th-grade student who is high in self-efficacy, described his reaction to the performance of a high-achieving classmate:

I was real mad when Stacey had got a 100. I wasn't really mad, but I was kind of jealous. Like I envied it. Like I wished I was that one that got 100. I mean sometimes, now that, that's one of the things that give me the extra drive. That gives me the extra determination to work harder in math to get good grades like everyone else. (Usher, 2009, p. 295)

When he felt challenged by a math problem, Jamaal would give himself pep talks:

I'll be like, "Come on." I'll be thinking about different ways to solve problems and stuff like that. I'll be saying, "Come on, Jamaal, you can do this," and stuff like that. . . . I don't know what it does, but it's just like extra comfort to me. (Usher, 2009, p. 295)

Compare this sentiment to that expressed by Tanisha, a classmate of Jamaal's who is low in self-efficacy:

Some of my friends tell me about [algebra], and, you know, some of their tests that they told me about, they said it was hard. But, you know, that's kind of what makes me feel like I'm not going to do good in it. Because, like, if they can't do it, then I probably can't do it. (Usher, 2009, p. 297)

Attributions for Success and Failure How students interpret their successes and failures is also important. Researchers who are interested in **achievement attributions** have studied how the explanations that people give for their success or failure influence their performance (Dweck, 2002). According to these theorists, individuals attribute their performance to a combination of four factors: ability, effort, task difficulty, and luck. When people succeed and mainly attribute their success to internal causes, such as their ability or effort, they are more likely to approach future tasks confidently and with self-assurance. If, however, they attribute their success to external factors outside their control, such as luck or an easy task, they are more likely to remain unsure of their abilities. Successful students, who tend to be high in achievement motivation, are likely to attribute their successes to internal causes (Denner et al., 2019; Swinton et al., 2011). However, some experts have noted that too much praise for effort may inadvertently communicate the message that the adolescent has low ability, which can undermine achievement (Amemiya & Wang, 2018). Praising an adolescent's ability *and* his or her work ethic is probably the best way to encourage scholastic success.

making the personal connection

When you succeed in school, how do you explain your success? When you fail, how do you account for your failure? Have you had teachers who influenced your beliefs about your own abilities?

How adolescents interpret their failures is also key. Some students try harder in the face of failure, whereas others withdraw and exert less effort. When students attribute their failures to a lack of effort, they are more likely to try harder on future tasks (Dweck, 2002). In contrast, adolescents who attribute their failure to factors that they feel cannot be changed (such as bad luck, lack of intelligence, or task difficulty) are more likely to feel helpless and to exert less effort in subsequent situations.

Suppose a student takes the Scholastic Assessment Test (SAT) and receives a mediocre score. He then is told by his guidance counselor that the SAT is a measure of intelligence, that intelligence is fixed, and that his score reflects how smart he is. The counselor tells the student that he can retake the test if he wants to but that he should not expect to score much higher the next time. Now imagine a different student who has the same score on the test but a different counselor. She is told that effort has a great deal to do with scores on the SAT and that she can raise her score by trying harder. In all likelihood, the next time these students take the test, the first student will not try as hard as the second student because he is more likely to feel helpless.

Students who are led to believe that their efforts do not make a difference—by being told, for example, that

When teachers emphasize performance, rather than mastery, students are more likely to disengage from class.
adamkaz/Getty Images

they are not very smart or that the work is too difficult for them—develop what psychologists call **learned helplessness:** the belief that failure is inevitable (Dweck, 2002). As a result of learned helplessness, some students try less hard than their peers, and they don't do as well as they might. Students who suffer from learned helplessness and who use a lot of self-handicapping strategies tend not only to perform worse in school but also to have more overall adjustment problems than their peers (Määtä, Nurmi, & Stattin, 2007). Instead of dismissing low-achieving students as having "low needs for achievement" or "low intelligence," teachers and other school personnel can help students achieve more by helping them learn to attribute their performance to factors that are under their control (Blackwell, Trzesniewski, & Dweck, 2007).

The Drop in Motivation During the Transition into Secondary School Many studies find that students' motivation and school performance decline when they move into secondary school (Wang & Eccles, 2012). Why might this be?

One possibility is that this transition takes place at the time adolescents are becoming more emotionally autonomous from their parents and that this is associated with a drop in the extent to which adolescents feel a sense of obligation to do well in school (Qu & Pomerantz, 2015). The drop in engagement seen among students in the United States is not seen in China, where teenagers are more likely to believe that they have to do well in school out of a sense of responsibility to their family. In a comparison of early adolescents from the United States and China, for example,

achievement attributions
The beliefs an individual holds about the causes of her or his successes and failures.

learned helplessness
The acquired belief that an individual is not able to influence events through his or her own efforts or actions.

students were asked to name characteristics that were more typical of adolescents than children. Chinese students were more likely to mention that adolescents work hard to meet their parents' expectations, that they comply with their parents' requests, and that they are concerned about their parents' approval. In both countries, students who held this conception of adolescence were less likely to become disengaged during the transition into secondary school (Qu et al., 2016).

Another is that the drop in engagement is due to a shift on the part of teachers toward a more performance-oriented style of instruction and evaluation (Fine, 2014). Elementary school teachers tend to stress the importance of mastering the material. During secondary school, however, more of an emphasis is placed on grades. This shift undermines many students' intrinsic motivation and their self-confidence, which, in turn, diminishes their performance.

Indeed, during the early years of high school, there is a decline in adolescents' feelings of self-efficacy and their mastery motivation, and an increase in their use of self-handicapping strategies (Pintrich, 2000). This is unfortunate because being engaged in school is a significant predictor not only of future achievement but also of future mental health (Watson & Russell, 2016). In addition, beliefs about intelligence change as students move into and through adolescence, with older students more likely to view intelligence as stable (Ablard & Mills, 1996) and to endorse dysfunctional attributions (e.g., attributing failure to a lack of ability, rather than a lack of effort) (Swinton et al., 2011).

Several experiments have demonstrated that this decline does not have to be inevitable. In one, researchers randomly assigned students enrolled in 7th-grade math classes to one of two groups: an experimental group, which received two class sessions on how it is possible to "grow your intelligence" and on how experience can actually affect brain development, and a control group, which was taught strategies to improve memory (Blackwell, Trzesniewski, & Dweck, 2007). Although both groups showed a comparable drop in math grades initially, the group that was taught that intelligence is malleable improved after the intervention, whereas the control group continued to decline.

Other studies have found that interventions designed to promote the development of a growth mindset and strong perseverance also help foster student achievement, engagement, and feelings of self-efficacy (Paunesku et al., 2015; Schmidt, Shumow, & Kackar-Cam, 2017; Tang et al., 2019) (see Figure 12.3). Interventions designed to teach students the importance of deliberate practice also have been shown to improve achievement

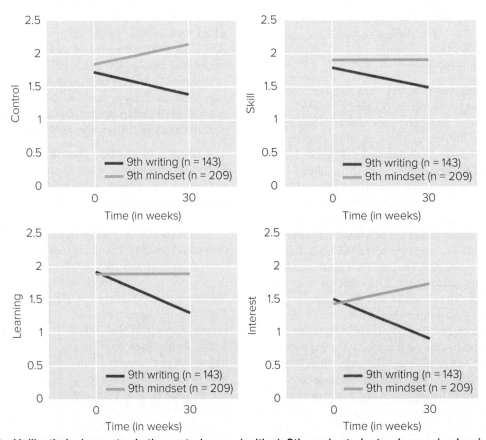

Figure 12.3 Unlike their classmates in the control group (writing), 9th-grade students who received an intervention to increase their growth mindset did not report declines over the school year in their sense of control, learning, interest, or skill. (Schmidt, Shumow, & Kackar-Cam, 2017)

(Eskreis-Winkler et al., 2016). Another study found that having students write essays about the potential benefits of the transition into high school helped maintain positive academic self-conceptions during this time (Facchin et al., 2014). Some commentators, however, have argued that the magnitude of the impact of these sorts of interventions is very small, that other beneficial practices need to be in place for them to succeed, and that educators should be careful not to embrace mindset interventions as some sort of silver bullet (Miller, 2019).

Environmental Influences on Achievement

Ability, beliefs, and motivation play a large role in influencing academic performance, but opportunity and situational factors also have a great deal to do with achievement. Many differences in achievement observed among adolescents aren't due to differences in their abilities, motives, or beliefs. They're a result of differences in the schools and classrooms where their abilities and motives are expressed.

School environments differ markedly—in physical facilities, in opportunities for pursuing academically enriched programs, and in classroom atmospheres. Unfortunately, many school districts that are plagued with shrinking tax bases have decaying school buildings, outdated equipment, and shortages of textbooks and teachers. In some schools, disciplinary problems and crime have become so overwhelming that dealing with them has taken precedence over learning and instruction.

As a result, many young people who genuinely want to succeed are impeded by a school environment that makes their academic success virtually impossible. Students who attend schools with a high concentration of poor, minority students are especially disadvantaged (Bankston & Caldas, 1998). The decline in school engagement seen during the transition from elementary to secondary school is especially pronounced among students in low-income neighborhoods (Benner & Wang, 2014a) and among disadvantaged students in schools in which they are a small minority (Benner & Wang, 2014b).

The Influence of the Home Environment

The school, of course, is not the only environment that makes a difference in adolescents' achievement, and few would argue that schools should accept full responsibility for adolescents who do not succeed at a level consonant with their abilities. If anything, important aspects of the home environment are better predictors of adolescents' academic achievement than are features of the school environment (Steinberg, 1996). Researchers have studied three ways in which the adolescent's home may influence his or her level of achievement (see Figure 12.4).

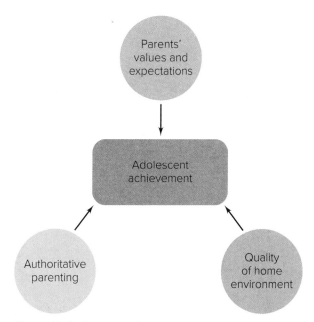

Figure 12.4 Parents influence adolescent achievement through three processes: their values and expectations, the way they parent, and the quality of the home environment.

Parental Values and Expectations Adolescents' achievement is directly related to their parents' values and expectations. Parental encouragement of academic success is manifested in a number of ways, all of which benefit adolescents' school performance. Three of the most effective forms of parental involvement are setting high standards for schoolwork, structuring the home environment to support academic pursuits, and maintaining an active role in their child's education. Let's take a look at how and why each type of involvement works.

First, parents who encourage school success set higher standards for their child's school performance and homework; they have higher aspirations for their child, which, in turn, contribute to school success. Parents' and adolescents' expectations influence each other over time, so that adolescents who grow up with parents who expect a lot come to expect a lot of themselves (Aceves, Bámaca-Colbert, & Robins, 2020; Day & Dotterer, 2018), whereas low parental expectations can contribute to a self-fulfilling prophecy, leading to poor achievement (Wood et al., 2010). The relation between parents' and adolescents' expectations is complicated, though: In the long run, adolescents achieve more when their parents' expectations for them actually exceed their own (perhaps because parents then provide encouragement that bolsters adolescents' school performance), but in the short term, they achieve less when they believe that their parents expect more of them than they are capable of (perhaps because this creates stress) (Ma, Shu, & Tse, 2018; Randall, Bohnert, & Travers, 2015; Murayama et al., 2016; Wang & Benner, 2014).

Second, parents who encourage school success also have values that are consistent with doing well in school.

Schools in the United States vary considerably in the resources their students have access to. SDI Productions/Getty Images

They structure the home environment to support academic pursuits so that the messages children receive from their teachers are echoed at home (Day & Dotterer, 2018; Grolnick et al., 2015). Even high school students profit from having parents who help them learn more effective time management strategies and healthier work habits (Xu, 2004). The evidence on the importance of parental involvement in adolescents' schoolwork at home, such as monitoring and checking homework, is mixed; one study found that it benefits Black and Latinx students but hurts white ones (Day & Dotterer, 2018).

Finally, parents who encourage success are likely to be more involved in their child's education—more likely to attend school programs, help in course selection, maintain interest in school activities and assignments, and the like, all of which contribute to students' success (Benner, Boyle, & Sadler, 2016; Day & Dotterer, 2018; Im, Hughes, & West, 2016; Kim & Hill, 2015). Parental involvement in schooling may make academic success seem both more important and more attainable to the adolescent, which may enhance the young person's academic self-conceptions (Ibañez et al., 2004); it also sends an important message to teachers (Kuperminc, Darnell, & Alvarez-Jiminez, 2008).

In contrast, parental disengagement from school makes students themselves more likely to disengage and do poorly. Parental involvement seems to be an especially strong influence on the achievement of Mexican American youth, perhaps because of the importance of the family in Mexican culture (Woolley, Kol, & Bowen, 2009). The way in which parents are involved matters, however: Encouraging and expecting achievement in school and being involved in school-based activities are both effective forms of parental involvement, whereas helping with homework is not (Hill & Tyson, 2009). Parental involvement in schooling has a more substantial effect when the adolescent attends a school in which a large proportion of other students' parents are involved as well (Darling & Steinberg, 1997) and in higher-income communities (Gordon & Cui, 2014).

Authoritative Parenting   A second way in which parents influence student achievement is through their general approach to parenting. Authoritative parenting is linked to school success during adolescence, as indexed by better grades, better attendance, higher expectations, more positive academic self-conceptions, and stronger engagement in the classroom (Hill & Wang, 2015; Lowe & Dotterer, 2013; Wang, Hill, & Hofkens, 2014). In contrast, parenting that is especially punitive, harsh, overcontrolling, or inept is associated with lower school engagement and diminished achievement (Blondal & Adalbjarnardottir, 2014; Wang, Pomerantz, & Chen, 2007). Adolescents fare best psychologically—and perform better in school—when their parents encourage achievement in a supportive way, have

Adolescents whose parents are involved in their schooling perform better than adolescents whose parents are not. One reason that students from higher social classes do better in school is that their parents tend to be more involved. Ariel Skelley/Blend Images/Getty Images

realistic expectations, and avoid criticism (Ciciolla et al., 2017; Wentzel, Russell, & Baker, 2016). Contrary to notions about the benefits of having a "Tiger Mother," this sort of aloof, demanding, and hypercritical parenting is associated with higher rates of adjustment problems, even among Chinese American students, especially when they are having difficulties in school (Kim et al., 2015; Qu, Yang, & Telzer, 2020).

Why do adolescents achieve more in school when they come from authoritative homes? Authoritative parenting promotes the development of a healthy achievement orientation—including an emphasis on mastery and a healthier attributional style—which, in turn, enhances adolescent school performance (Duchesne & Ratelle, 2010; Suizzo et al., 2012). This is in part because authoritative parents are more likely themselves to hold healthier beliefs about their child's achievement and less likely to be overly controlling—two factors that strengthen adolescents' work ethic and intrinsic motivation. Having a strong work orientation enhances achievement both directly, as we saw earlier, and indirectly, through the positive impression it makes on teachers.

In general, these findings are in line with a good deal of research suggesting that consistent, authoritative parenting is associated with a wide array of benefits to the adolescent, including higher achievement motivation, greater self-esteem, and enhanced competence (Steinberg, 2001). Authoritative parents also tend to be more involved in school activities, which is associated with scholastic success, although parents' involvement both affects and is affected by adolescents' achievement (Cheung & Pomerantz, 2012; Wang & Sheikh-Khalil, 2014).

The Quality of the Home Environment A third mechanism of familial influence is through the quality of the home environment, as measured by the presence of such items as a television, dictionary, encyclopedia, newspaper, and other indicators of family income. The quality of the home environment is more strongly correlated with academic achievement than is the quality of the physical facility of the school students attend, the background and training of their teachers, or their teachers' salaries (Armor, 1972). The extent to which parents provide **cultural capital**—by exposing the adolescent to art, music, literature, and so forth—exerts a positive impact on achievement above and beyond the effects of the parents' own level of education (Hardaway et al., 2020; Waithaka, 2014). Access to the Internet at home is important, too (Hofferth & Moon, 2012).

Several researchers have asked whether adolescents' school achievement is affected by genetic factors. Whereas intelligence and cognitive achievement both have strong genetic components (and influence grades through this mechanism), school performance is highly influenced by environmental factors, both inside and outside the family (Johnson, McGue, & Iacono, 2006).

With this in mind, it is important to point out that a disheartening number of young people in the United States live in overcrowded, inadequate housing and come from families that are under severe economic and social stress—so much so that parental encouragement and involvement are often undermined by neighborhood conditions. It is extremely difficult for a parent under severe economic stress to provide a supportive home environment. Stress at home, in turn, spills over into the adolescent's school life, leading to academic problems and lower achievement (Flook & Fuligni, 2008). The stress of living in poverty also interferes with the development of grit because poverty is often accompanied by chaos in the home environment, which interferes with the development of persistence (Fuller-Rowell et al., 2015). Interestingly, adolescents from homes in which there had been a lot of family instability do not do as well as other students when they attend schools that have a large proportion of high-achieving students; in schools with fewer high achievers, coming from an unstable family environment matters much less (Cavanagh & Fomby, 2012).

Many communities lack **social capital**—the support, encouragement, and involvement of adults necessary to facilitate youngsters' success (Coleman & Hoffer, 1987). (Whereas cultural capital refers to the quality of the home environment, social capital refers to the quality of the family's social network.) Social capital, which

cultural capital
The resources provided within a family through the exposure of the adolescent to art, music, literature, and other elements of "high culture."

social capital
The interpersonal resources available to an adolescent or family.

is strengthened when families have strong ties to other families in the community, is an important contributor to success in school, above and beyond the contribution of adolescents' family income, their parents' education, or their household composition (Waithaka, 2014). In contrast, students who can draw on resources provided not only by the family but also by friends, mentors, and teachers stand a far better chance of succeeding in school (Fruiht & Wray-Lake, 2013; Maulana, 2013; Rice et al., 2013).

The Influence of Friends

Friends also influence adolescents' achievement. In fact, friends, not parents, are the most salient influences on adolescents' day-to-day school behaviors, such as doing homework and exerting effort in class (Steinberg, 1996). One of the main reasons that adolescents growing up in poor neighborhoods achieve less is that they are often surrounded by peers who are disengaged from school (South, Baumer, & Lutz, 2003).

When most of us think about the influence of adolescents' peers on achievement, we tend to think of the ways in which peers undermine academic success. But the impact of friends on adolescents' school performance depends on the academic orientation of the peer group and the extent to which academically engaged students are also popular in school (Laninga-Wijnen et al., 2018; Shin, 2020; Zhang et al., 2019). Having friends who earn high grades and aspire to further education enhances adolescents' achievement, whereas having friends who earn low grades or disparage school success interferes with it (Steinberg, 1996). Feeling connected to one's classmates

Peers influence how much effort adolescents devote to school, for better and for worse. Eric Audras/PhotoAlto/Getty Images

increases students' engagement in the classroom, which, in turn, leads to higher achievement. Moreover, students whose friends are more engaged in school are themselves more engaged and less likely to drop out (Ream & Rumberger, 2008). Friends also influence course selection and play an important role in decisions to take math and science classes, which may be an especially powerful influence on girls' choice of classes (Leaper, Farkas, & Brown, 2012; Robnett & Leaper, 2013).

Students' grades change in parallel to the grades their friends get (Rambaran et al., 2017; Shin & Ryan, 2014). Students with best friends who achieve high grades in school are more likely to show improvements in their own grades than are students who begin at similar levels of achievement but whose friends are not high achievers. Perhaps because Asian American and white students tend to do better in school than students from other ethnic groups, having relatively more friends from these ethnic groups is associated with higher achievement (Chen, Saafir, & Graham, 2020).

Peers also exert a small but significant influence on each other's future plans (Kiuru et al., 2012). Among low-achieving adolescents, those with high-achieving friends are more likely to plan to continue their education than are those with low-achieving friends. The causal direction works the other way, too: When adolescents' grades go up, they tend to befriend more high-achieving classmates, but when their grades drop, they tend to become friends with lower-achieving peers (Flashman, 2012; Véronneau et al., 2010).

Although peers can influence achievement for better or for worse, many observers have noted that in the contemporary United States, the influence of the peer culture on academic achievement is far more negative than positive (Bishop et al., 2003). Perhaps because of this, adolescents with an extremely high orientation toward peers tend to perform worse in school (Fuligni & Eccles, 1993). Conversely, adolescents who are neglected by their peers often have a stronger academic orientation than relatively more popular students (Luthar & McMahon, 1996; Wentzel & Asher, 1995).

As they move into middle school, adolescents become increasingly worried about their friends' reactions to success in school. By eighth grade, students do not want their classmates to know that they work hard in school, even though they know that it would be helpful to convey this impression to their teachers (Juvonen & Murdock, 1995). High-achieving, popular students believe that it is important to hide their grades from their friends (Zook & Russotti, 2013), which may make sense in schools where high-achieving students are ostracized (Schwartz, Kelly, & Duong, 2013). One experiment found that students' decisions about whether to sign up for an SAT prep course were far more positive if they were told the decision would be kept private than if they were told it would be revealed to their classmates (Bursztyn & Jensen, 2015).

Doing well in school does not have to come at the cost of having a decent social life, however. A study in which adolescents maintained daily diaries of their time use sheds interesting light on the differences between high- and low-achieving students in how they spend their time (Witkow, 2009). Not surprisingly, students who earn higher grades than their peers spend more time studying, both on weekdays and on weekends. But as Figure 12.5 shows, a key difference between the groups is in how much—and when—they spend time with their friends. As you can see, high-achieving students spend less time with their friends than do low-achieving students on weekdays but not on weekends. In other words, high-achieving students are able to maintain an active social life by allocating their time more judiciously during the week. In all likelihood, one reason that high-achieving students spend less time with friends on weekdays is that their friends are also busy studying.

A number of researchers have studied how the influences of parents and peers operate together to affect adolescents' achievement. These studies show that the family environment has an effect on adolescents' choice of friends, which in turn influences school achievement (Brown et al., 1993). Having academically oriented peers is especially beneficial to adolescents from single-parent homes, where parental involvement in schooling is typically lower (Garg, Melanson, & Levin, 2007). By the same token, having friends who disparage school success may offset the benefits of authoritative parenting (Steinberg, 1996); as a consequence, having friends who are disengaged from school is especially detrimental to the achievement of students with more distant relationships at home (Espinoza et al., 2014; Marion et al., 2014).

Rather than asking whether family members or friends are the stronger influence on adolescents' school performance, it may make more sense to ask how these two forces—along with the influence of the school itself—work together. The same is true for understanding the joint impact of peers and teachers; having friends who are disengaged from school has a more negative impact on student engagement when they perceive their teachers as uninvolved (Vollet, Kindermann, & Skinner, 2017).

The broader context in which schooling takes place affects the degree to which peers and parents influence adolescents' achievement. Peers and parents more strongly influence student achievement in countries where schools serve more heterogeneous groups of students, as in the United States. In countries where students with different long-term educational aspirations attend different schools (for instance, in countries such as Germany, where there are separate schools for adolescents who are planning to go to college and those who are not), peers and parents are less influential (Buchmann & Dalton, 2002).

In summary, although psychological factors play a key role in determining scholastic success, it is important to take into account the broader environment in which individuals pursue their education (Li, Lerner, & Lerner, 2010; Steinberg, 1996). Distinguishing between psychological and environmental factors is hard, though, because they typically go hand in hand. Living in an environment that offers few opportunities for success induces feelings of learned helplessness, which, in turn, leads individuals to feel that exerting any effort to succeed is futile. Attending school in an environment in which achievement is not encouraged engenders attitudes and beliefs inconsistent with striving to do well. Rather than being determined by one single factor, such as ability or motivation, patterns of achievement are the result of a cumulative process that includes a long history of experience and socialization in school, at home, in the peer group, and in the community.

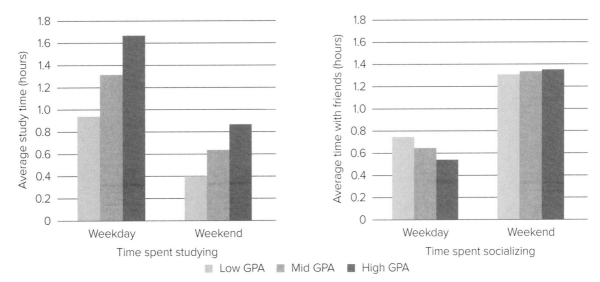

Figure 12.5 High- and low-achieving students allocate their time spent studying and socializing differently. (Witkow, 2009)

Educational Achievement

Educational achievement is usually defined in one of three ways: **school performance** (the grades students earn in school), **academic achievement** (their performance on standardized tests), or **educational attainment** (the number of years of schooling they complete). These different measures of educational achievement are interrelated, but they are less tied to each other than you might expect.

No single factor adequately accounts for differences in educational achievement. Intellectual ability as assessed by IQ tests is highly correlated with performance on achievement tests (hardly a surprise, since IQ tests and achievement tests are designed to tap similar abilities). But grades in school—and to an even greater extent, educational attainment—are influenced by a wider range of factors than intellectual abilities. Grades are influenced by teachers' judgments of students' mastery of the material, and these judgments are influenced by teachers' evaluations of students' efforts and behaviors in the classroom (Farkas, Grobe, & Shuan, 1990).

How many years of school an adolescent completes is likely to be influenced by his or her family background and living circumstances, as well as by school performance. Two adolescents may have similar grade point averages, but if one comes from a poor family and cannot afford to go to college, the two will have different levels of educational attainment. Even as early as elementary school, many inner-city youth have very limited occupational expectations, and these low expectations affect their educational achievement and attainment (Cook et al., 1996).

Regardless of what influences it, educational attainment has important implications for subsequent earnings and health (Ceci & Williams, 1999; Duke & MacMillan, 2016). The gap in earnings between high school graduates and college graduates is considerable, and this is true across all ethnic groups. When they enter the labor force, individuals with a college degree earn nearly twice as much per year as do individuals with only a high school diploma (Bureau of Labor Statistics, 2019). This state of affairs has led many to call for educational policies that encourage all students to "shoot for the stars." Although some experts had speculated that encouraging all students to strive to go to college would ultimately have negative effects on the mental health of students whose expectations are unrealistic, this has not proven to be true (Domina, Conley, & Farkas, 2011; Reynolds & Baird, 2010). It is important, however, that adolescents who are encouraged to go to college

school performance
A measure of achievement based on an individual's grades in school.

academic achievement
Achievement that is measured by standardized tests of scholastic ability or knowledge.

educational attainment
The number of years of schooling completed by an individual.

be given the information and skills they need in order to fulfill their plans and succeed (Roderick, Coca, & Nagaoka, 2011; Rosenbaum, 2011).

The Importance of Socioeconomic Status

One of the most powerful influences on educational achievement is the socioeconomic status of the adolescent's family. Although some of the socioeconomic gaps in school achievement have narrowed, disparities in achievement between the social classes remain strong, and the importance of socioeconomic status in determining educational achievement remains substantial across all ethnic groups and in different countries (Alessandri et al., 2017; Parker et al., 2012).

A Head Start for the More Affluent Five decades of studies have shown over and over that middle-class adolescents score higher on basic tests of academic skills and achievement, earn higher grades, and complete more years of schooling than their less affluent peers (Sackett et al., 2009; Sackett et al., 2012). Socioeconomic status also influences adolescent achievement through neighborhood processes. Poor Black students who live in neighborhoods with a relatively higher proportion of middle-class neighbors place more value on education and try harder in school than comparably poor students who live in disadvantaged neighborhoods (Ceballo, McLoyd, & Toyokawa, 2004; Stewart, Stewart, & Simons, 2007).

One big reason that family background is related to educational achievement is that children from lower socioeconomic levels are more likely to enter elementary school

Intervening in early childhood can help close the achievement gap between disadvantaged and affluent children. Jupiterimages/ Getty Images

scoring low on tests of basic academic competence (Rouse, Brooks-Gunn, & McLanahan, 2005). These initial differences reflect both genetic and environmental factors. Middle-class adults generally have higher IQs than lower-class adults, and this advantage is passed on to their children—both through genetics and through the benefit that middle-class youngsters receive from growing up under more favorable environmental conditions.

Growing up in a more affluent family also has been shown to affect brain development; adolescents from higher income groups have more gray matter in brain regions important to performance on achievement tests as well as measures of working memory, perhaps the most important executive function for scholastic success (Finn et al., 2017; Mackey et al., 2015). The disadvantages of poorer youngsters in achievement test scores persist—and may even increase—throughout elementary and secondary school (Rouse, Brooks-Gunn, & McLanahan, 2005). Because progress in high school depends so heavily on having a solid foundation of basic academic competence, adolescents who enter secondary school without having mastered basic academic skills quickly fall behind, and some leave high school before graduating.

One reason for the relatively poorer school performance of disadvantaged youth, therefore, is that these youngsters begin school at a distinct academic disadvantage. A second reason for the disparity is stress, both before and during adolescence. Stress adversely affects adolescents' mental health, well-being, and school performance (DuBois et al., 1992; Felner et al., 1995). In addition to their less frequent exposure to stress, teenagers from higher income families tend to have better coping abilities, which enables them to deal with stress more effectively (Alessandri et al., 2017).

making the scientific connection

In light of the profound impact that socioeconomic status has on student achievement, what would you suggest as policies or practices to raise the achievement of poor youth? Think about people you know who overcame economic disadvantage and were highly successful in school (maybe *you* are one of these persons). To what would you attribute this success?

Socioeconomic Status and Parental Involvement

Parents from higher social classes are more likely to be involved in their adolescent's education, especially through formal parent-teacher organizations such as the PTA or PTO (Shumow & Miller, 2001). Middle- and upper-middle-class parents are also more likely to have information about their child's school, to be responsive to their child's school problems, and to help select more rigorous courses for their child to take (Crosnoe &

Huston, 2007). Because adolescents whose parents are involved in their schooling perform better than those whose parents are not involved, youngsters from higher social classes achieve more in school than their less advantaged peers in part because of their parents' more active involvement (Henry, Cavanagh, & Oetting, 2011; Lee & Croninger, 1994).

Parents with greater economic resources also are able to provide their children with more cultural capital, which is an important contributor to school success (Waithaka, 2014). Teachers may involve students in classroom activities that allow students from middle-class families to display this home advantage (for example, asking students to read out loud, which is likely easier for those whose parents have read to them frequently), which may undermine the achievement of students from poorer families (Goudeau & Croizet, 2017). Adolescents from higher socioeconomic groups are also more likely to attribute their success to internal causes such as talent and effort, which, as you read earlier, is associated with higher achievement (Kay, Shane, & Heckhausen, 2017).

Socioeconomic differences in school achievement obviously reflect the cumulative and combined effects of a variety of influences, and it is simplistic to explain social class differences in achievement without considering these factors simultaneously. What is perhaps more interesting—and more worthy of scientific study than has been the case—is the question of what it is about the many youngsters from economically disadvantaged backgrounds who are successful that accounts for their overcoming the tremendous odds against them. The successful college student who comes from an environment of severe economic disadvantage has had to overcome incredible barriers. Researchers have been studying various types of interventions designed to encourage such students, many of whom are the first in their family to aspire to college, to make a successful transition into postsecondary education (Stephens, Hamedani, & Destin, 2014).

Although more research on successful students from poor backgrounds is sorely needed, it is impossible to overstate the importance of having warm and encouraging parents who raise their children authoritatively, take an interest in their children's academic progress, and hold high aspirations for their children's educational attainment, as well as the availability of peers who support and encourage academic success (Goza & Ryabov, 2009; Melby et al., 2008). In other words, positive relations at home and the encouragement of significant others can in some circumstances overcome the negative influence of socioeconomic disadvantage.

Ethnic Differences in Educational Achievement

Among the most controversial findings in research on American adolescents' achievement are those concerning ethnic differences in school success. On average, the educational achievement of Black and Latinx students—virtually however indexed—lags behind that of white students, and all three groups achieve less in school than Asian students. Although some of these differences can be attributed to socioeconomic differences among these ethnic groups, the group disparities persist even after socioeconomic factors are taken into account (Fuligni, Hughes, & Way, 2009).

The Success of Immigrants Of course, there are large and important variations in achievement *within* as well as between ethnic groups. First, there are differences in educational achievement among youngsters from different countries of origin who may be classified together by researchers into the same larger ethnic group for purposes of statistical comparison. For example, although both groups are classified as Asian, Chinese American adolescents have much higher academic achievement than Filipino Americans; similarly, there are large differences in academic achievement among Puerto Rican, Cuban American, and Mexican American adolescents, all of whom are classified as Latinx (Fuligni et al., 2009).

Second, studies of ethnic minority youngsters show that foreign-born adolescents, as well as those who are children of immigrants, tend to be more cognitively engaged (although less socially engaged) and achieve more in school than do minority youngsters who are second- or third-generation Americans, a finding that has now emerged in many studies of Asian, Latinx, and Caribbean youth (Chiu et al., 2012; Fuligni et al., 2009). One explanation for the so-called "immigrant paradox" has been that part of becoming acculturated to American society—at least among teenagers—may be learning to devalue academic success, which may lead to disengagement from school (Peguero, Bondy, & Hong, 2017; Santiago et al., 2014).

The exceptional achievement of immigrant youth is all the more remarkable in light of the fact that these adolescents typically have much greater family obligations—providing financial support to their parents, for instance—than their American-born peers (Fuligni & Witkow, 2004). However, a stronger sense of family obligation contributes to, rather than interferes with, school success, as long as this obligation doesn't burden students with the time demands of excessive household chores (Chang, 2013; Roche, Ghazarian, & Fernandez-Esquer, 2012; van Geel & Vedder, 2011).

The academic superiority of Asian students, whether American or foreign-born, tends to emerge during the transition into junior high school—when most other students' grades typically decline—and it persists through high school and into college (Fuligni & Witkow, 2004). What has been most intriguing to social scientists is that Black and Latinx students have educational aspirations

and attitudes that are similar to those of Asian and white students but significantly poorer academic skills, habits, and behavior (Ainsworth-Darnell & Downey, 1998). If Black and Latinx students have the same long-term goals as other students, why don't they behave in similar ways? Several theories have been advanced to explain this.

False Optimism Rather Than Realistic Pessimism
One set of theories involves the perceptions that adolescents have about the likely payoff of hard work in school. Some writers have argued that even though they have high aspirations in the abstract, many Black and Latinx students do not believe that educational success will have a substantial occupational payoff for them because discrimination and prejudice will limit their actual opportunities. Although intuitively appealing, this theory has not received convincing empirical support (Fuligni et al., 2009; Herman, 2009). It is true that adolescents who believe they have been victims of discrimination or who believe that their opportunities for occupational success are unfairly constrained achieve less in school and report more emotional distress than their peers who do not hold these beliefs (Fisher, Wallace, & Fenton, 2000). It is also true that students who are more confident about and oriented to the future do better in school (Beal & Crockett, 2010; Oyserman, Bybee, & Terry, 2006).

But it is not true that Black or Latinx youngsters are more likely than other adolescents to believe that their opportunities for success are blocked (Downey & Ainsworth-Darnell, 2002; Kao & Tienda, 1998). Indeed, several studies indicate that Black and Latinx youth have *more* optimistic beliefs and positive feelings about school than other students (e.g., Downey, Ainsworth, & Qian, 2009; Shernoff & Schmidt, 2008). Plus, some research suggests that beliefs about the likelihood of future discrimination may motivate adolescents to perform better in school (perhaps because they feel that they will need to be even better prepared than others to overcome prejudicial treatment), although feeling discriminated against in the present, by classmates or teachers, hinders academic achievement (perhaps by causing psychological distress, a loss of confidence, or hopelessness) (Benner, Crosnoe, & Eccles, 2015; Diemer et al., 2016).

All in all, however, adolescents' hopes and aspirations for the future are very similar across ethnic groups (Chang et al., 2006). Pessimism about the likely payoff of education is greater among teenagers who feel that they've been discriminated against, though (Cooper & Sánchez, 2016; Mroczkowski, Sánchez, & Carter, 2017). Feeling discriminated against by teachers is especially likely to lead to a sense of futility (D'hondt et al., 2016).

If anything, it may be adolescents' fear of failure, rather than their desire (or lack of desire) to succeed, that matters most. Asian youngsters not only believe in the value of school success but also are very anxious about the possible negative repercussions of not doing well in school, in terms of both occupational success and their parents' disappointment (Eaton & Dembo, 1997; Steinberg, 1996). Moreover, many Asian youth believe that the only way they can succeed in mainstream American society is through educational achievement (Sue & Okazaki, 1990). Asian students' sense of obligation to their parents—a factor frequently suggested as a reason for their high rates of school success—does not seem to play a very important role in predicting school achievement. If anything, being expected to assist the family by performing household chores and other family work—something that is especially salient in Asian and Latinx households—has a negative impact on school performance (Telzer & Fuligni, 2009).

Ethnic Differences in Beliefs A third account of ethnic differences in achievement stresses differences in beliefs about ability. We noted earlier that adolescents who believe that intelligence is malleable are more likely to be intrinsically motivated and, as a consequence, academically successful. It is therefore interesting that Asian cultures tend to place more emphasis on effort than on ability in explaining school success and are more likely to believe that all students have the capacity to succeed (Stevenson & Stigler, 1992). By and large, students from Asian backgrounds tend to be more invested in mastering the material than in simply performing well—an orientation that, as we saw earlier, contributes to school success (Li, 2006). It is also important to note that Asian students—both in the United States and in Asia—spend significantly more time each week than their peers on homework and other school-related activities and significantly less time socializing and watching television (Asakawa & Csikszentmihalyi, 2000; Steinberg, 1996).

It is sometimes claimed that pressure to do well takes a toll on the mental health of Asian teenagers. There is no evidence, however, that Asian students pay a price for their superior achievement in terms of increased anxiety, depression, stress, or social awkwardness; the suicide rate among American teenagers is higher than it is among Asian youth, for example (Wasserman, Cheng, & Jiang, 2005). One study of adolescents in China found that feeling academically competent fosters positive mental health and protects against depression and anxiety (Cohen et al., 2015). During regular periods of school in the United States, Asian students' moods while studying are significantly more positive than those of other students (Asakawa & Csikszentmihalyi, 1998), and the links between academic motivation and various indices of happiness and adjustment are stronger among Asian adolescents than other youth (Asakawa & Csikszentmihalyi, 2000). Among Asian students more than their peers from other ethnic groups, then, engagement in academics is linked to positive emotion and well-being.

One reason Asian students outperform adolescents from other ethnic groups is the widely held belief in Asian culture that success in school is a function of how hard one works. DragonImages/iStock/Getty Images

making the cultural connection

Many immigrant adolescents in the United States achieve more in school than their counterparts from the same ethnic group who were born in America—despite the fact that adolescents who are immigrants often arrive without proficiency in English or familiarity with American culture. How do you explain this?

It is important to keep in mind that, within all ethnic groups, students achieve more when they feel a sense of belonging to their school, when they see the connection between academic accomplishment and future success, when their friends and parents value and support educational achievement, and when their parents are effective monitors of their children's behavior and schooling (Hernández et al., 2016; Spees, Perreira, & Fuligni, 2017). The especially close and supportive relationships characteristic of immigrant families likely contribute to school success (Suárez-Orozco, Rhodes, & Milburn, 2009).

Changes in Educational Achievement over Time

Today, nearly 80% of high school graduates enroll in college by the time they are 20, nearly 70% of them immediately after graduation (National Center for Education Statistics, 2020). Although ethnic differences in educational

National Assessment of Educational Progress (NAEP)
A periodic testing of American 4th-, 8th-, and 12th-graders by the federal government, used to track achievement.

attainment have narrowed over the past 40 years, there remain substantial gaps in attainment between white and nonwhite individuals, and especially between white and Latinx individuals. Thus, whereas 40% of non-Latinx white adults ages 25 and over and 58% of Asian adults of this age are college graduates, about 26% of Black adults and only 19% of Latinx adults are (U.S. Census Bureau, 2020). Discrepancies in rates of high school graduation between Latinx and other Americans are also substantial: 96% of non-Latinx white adults have completed high school, compared with 88% of Blacks and 91% of Asian Americans, but only 72% of Latinx adults have (U.S. Census Bureau, 2020). In light of the rapidly increasing size of the Latinx population in the United States, the gap in educational attainment between Latinx and non-Latinx individuals is one of the most important challenges facing American educational institutions.

More Schooling But Less Learning Trends in academic achievement (what students know) have not paralleled trends in educational attainment (how many years of schooling they have completed). In other words, although more students are staying in school longer, they are not necessarily learning more.

For example, as Figure 12.6 indicates, between 1970 and 1980, average scores on the SAT declined by about 35 points on the verbal portion and 20 points on the math. Scores remained more or less flat between 1980 and 1990, when math (but not verbal) scores began to rise. Verbal, math, and writing scores all dropped slightly from 2005 on. (The one exception to this general trend is among Asian students, whose scores on both subscales have risen substantially in the last 10 years.) Moreover, the gap in SAT scores between Black and Latinx students on the one hand and Asian and white students on the other remains substantial and virtually unchanged over the past two decades (PrepScholar, 2020).

The relatively poor showing of American adolescents on standardized tests of achievement has been carefully documented in a series of reports based on the **National Assessment of Educational Progress (NAEP).** This national assessment of student achievement is conducted by the federal government in order to track trends in educational achievement over time. Because the NAEP tests have been administered regularly for more than 50 years, it is possible to compare the achievement levels of today's adolescents with their counterparts four decades ago.

According to recent NAEP reports, over the past 50 years, adolescent achievement in reading, writing, math, and science improved only slightly among 13-year-olds (although scores have dropped a bit in recent years) and not at all among 17-year-olds, despite massive national efforts at education reform. This is consistent with other trends in achievement data, which show that American elementary and middle school students have been making gains but that high school student achievement has not improved (Steinberg, 2014). Contemporary 17-year-olds, for example, score no better than their counterparts did in the early 1970s in reading or math and *worse* than their counterparts did in science.

Perhaps more important, most analyses of the NAEP data indicate that the modest gains in achievement that have occurred during recent years have been in relatively simple skills. Only a handful of students, at any age or in any subject area, score at a level that is designated "advanced" or "superior," whereas large proportions of

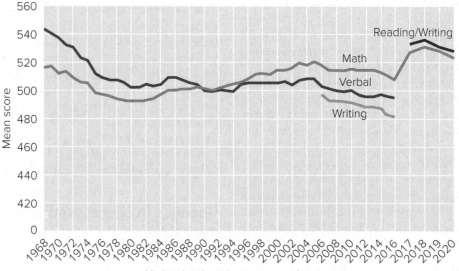

Figure 12.6 Changes in SAT scores over time.
Source: College Board, SAT data tables, 2020, https://collegereadiness.collegeboard.org/pdf/understanding-sat-scores.pdf.

students score in the lowest category, "below basic." When gains have been made (and they are generally very small), they tend to be in the proportion of students who have moved from the basic into the "proficient" range, rather than from "proficient" to "advanced."

As is the case in rates of high school graduation and SAT scores, the gap in achievement test performance among ethnic groups narrowed during the 1970s, but a wide disparity still exists. The achievement gap did not shrink at all during the 1980s, widened a bit during the 1990s, and has not changed since then. About three times as many white and Asian middle school students score in the proficient range in reading, for example, as do Black students, and about twice as many white and Asian students score in the proficient range as do Latinx students (National Center for Education Statistics, 2020a). The gaps are even larger in math. Obviously, the achievement gap has important implications for the labor market success of adolescents from different ethnic groups.

International Competitions Although the poor achievement test performance of Black and Latinx students is certainly cause for concern, there is no reason to be sanguine about the performance of high school students from other ethnic groups. Since the 1970s, their achievement test scores have remained more or less stagnant, and U.S. scores on standardized tests of math and science are mediocre in comparison with scores of other industrialized countries.

The gap between American students' performance and that of students from other countries widens as they move from elementary to middle to high school. That is, when elementary school students from around the world are compared, American students fare just about as well as students from other countries. When middle school students are compared, Americans perform more poorly than their counterparts from most industrialized Asian countries but at a level comparable to young adolescents from most western European countries and considerably better than adolescents from less developed nations (National Center for Education Statistics, 2009). But when the comparison focuses on high school students, the gap between the United States and other countries is substantial (Schmidt, 2003). According to recent international comparisons, 15-year-olds in the United States ranked slightly above average in reading and science but well below average in math (OECD, 2020) (see Table 12.1).

The relatively poor performance of American high school students in international competitions persists despite the fact that spending, per student, on education in the United States is the second highest in the world (OECD, 2020). Despite how much is spent, more than two-thirds of community college students and nearly one-third of students at 4-year public colleges and universities require some sort of remedial education (usually, two or more courses) in order to do college-level work (Ganga,

On tests of achievement, American high school students lag behind those from many European countries. Angelafoto/Getty Images

Mazzareillo, & Edgecombe, 2018). As a result, employers and postsecondary educational institutions alike today devote vast amounts of money to remedial education; colleges and universities spend an estimated $7 billion annually covering subject matter that students should have mastered before graduating from high school. And it's not just colleges that foot the bill: According to one estimate, college students and their families spend $1.3 billion each year on remedial courses.

If more American students are remaining in high school and so many are going on to college, why are their achievement test scores so low according to absolute, historical, and international standards? Experts suggest several reasons: that teachers are not challenging students to work hard; that very little time is spent on writing; that there has been a pervasive decline in the difficulty of textbooks; that parents are not encouraging academic pursuits at home; that students are not spending sufficient time on their studies outside of school; that students are permitted to choose what courses they take; and that students know that, thanks to "grade inflation," they can earn good grades without working very hard (Steinberg, 2014).

Dropping Out of High School

There was a time when leaving high school before graduating did not have the dire consequences that it does today. With changes in the labor force, however, have come changes in the educational requirements for entry into the world of work.

Today, educational attainment is a powerful predictor of adult occupational success and earnings. High school dropouts are far more likely than graduates to live at or near the poverty level, experience unemployment, have poor health, depend on government-subsidized income maintenance programs, become pregnant while still a teenager, use illicit drugs, and be involved in delinquent and criminal activity. This has led some experts to

Table 12.1 Average Scores in Mathematics, Reading, and Science Among 15-Year-Olds from Developed Nations

PISA Math		PISA Reading		Science	
Country (Ranked in Descending Order)	Score	Country (Ranked in Descending Order)	Score	Country (Ranked in Descending Order)	Score
OECD average	489	OECD average	487	OECD average	489
Japan	527	Estonia	523	Estonia	530
Korea, Republic of	526	Canada	520	Japan	529
Estonia	523	Finland	520	Finland	522
Netherlands	519	Ireland	518	Korea, Republic of	519
Poland	516	Korea, Republic of	514	Canada	518
Switzerland	515	Poland	512	Poland	511
Canada	512	Sweden	506	New Zealand	508
Denmark	509	New Zealand	506	Slovenia	507
Slovenia	509	United States	505	United Kingdom	505
Belgium	508	United Kingdom	504	Netherlands	503
Finland	507	Japan	504	Germany	503
Sweden	502	Australia	503	Australia	503
United Kingdom	502	Denmark	501	United States	502
Norway	501	Norway	499	Sweden	499
Germany	500	Germany	498	Belgium	499
Ireland	500	Slovenia	495	Czech Republic	497
Czech Republic	499	Belgium	493	Ireland	496
Austria	499	France	493	Switzerland	495
Latvia	496	Portugal	492	France	493
France	495	Czech Republic	490	Denmark	493
Iceland	495	Netherlands	485	Portugal	492
New Zealand	494	Austria	484	Norway	490
Portugal	492	Switzerland	484	Austria	490
Australia	491	Latvia	479	Latvia	487
Italy	487	Italy	476	Spain	483
Slovak Republic	486	Hungary	476	Lithuania	482
Luxembourg	483	Lithuania	476	Hungary	481
Spain	481	Iceland	474	Luxembourg	477
Lithuania	481	Israel	470	Iceland	475
Hungary	481	Luxembourg	470	Turkey	468
United States	478	Turkey	466	Italy	468
Israel	463	Slovak Republic	458	Slovak Republic	464
Turkey	454	Greece	457	Israel	462
Greece	451	Chile	452	Greece	452
Chile	417	Mexico	420	Chile	444
Mexico	409	Colombia	412	Mexico	419
Colombia	391	Spain	Unavailable	Colombia	413

(OECD, 2020)

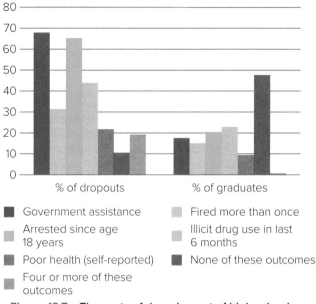

Figure 12.7 The costs of dropping out of high school are enormous. (Lansford et al., 2016)

characterize dropping out as a public health problem (Lansford et al., 2016) (see Figure 12.7).

Because there are different ways of counting dropouts, different studies often report very different figures. For example, many students drop out of school temporarily but return in their early 20s and obtain a diploma or GED; so while these students would be classified as dropouts at the age of 17, they would be classified as graduates if they were surveyed just a few years later. As you can see from Figure 12.8, although 85% of American adolescents graduate from high school on time, there are variations in graduation rates as a function of ethnicity (National Center for Education Statistics, 2020).

Correlates of Dropping Out Given the findings on educational achievement discussed earlier, the other correlates of dropping out come as no surprise. Adolescents

who leave high school before graduating are more likely to come from lower socioeconomic levels, poor communities, large families, single-parent families, permissive or disengaged families, and households where little reading material is available (Afia et al., 2019). Students from poor families are also relatively more likely to drop out because of poor health (Sznitman, Reisel, & Khurana, 2017). In short, adolescents who drop out of school are more likely to come from backgrounds with limited **family capital,** which has three components: economic capital, social capital, and cultural capital (Waithaka, 2014) (see Figure 12.9).

Coupled with this disadvantage in background, adolescents who drop out of high school also are more likely to have a history of poor school performance, low school involvement, multiple changes of schools, poor performance on standardized tests of achievement and intelligence, negative school experiences, adverse childhood experiences, and a variety of emotional and behavioral problems, some of which contribute to academic failure and some of which result from it. Many high school dropouts had to repeat one or more grades in elementary school; indeed, having been held back is one of the strongest predictors of dropping out (Gubbels, van der Put, & Assink, 2019; Morrow & Villodas, 2018; Rumberger, 2012; Wang & Fredricks, 2014).

In other words, dropping out of high school is not so much a discrete decision made during the adolescent years as

family capital
The economic, social, and cultural resources provided by the family.

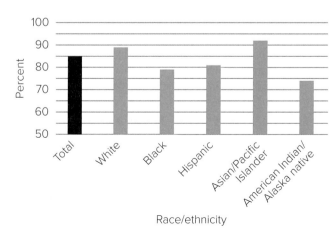

Figure 12.8 High school graduation rates of American adolescents. (National Center for Education Statistics, 2020)

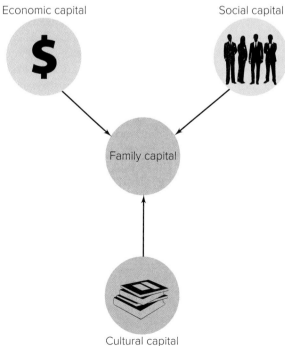

Figure 12.9 Families provide three kinds of capital: economic, social, and cultural. (Adapted from Waithaka, 2014)

social promotion
The practice of promoting students from one grade to the next automatically, regardless of their school performance.

it is the culmination of a long process (Rumberger, 2012; Sweeten, Bushway, & Paternoster, 2009). Specific factors may instigate a student's final decision to leave school—a suspension for misbehavior, a failed course, an unintended pregnancy, the lure of a job—but by and large, dropping out is a process characterized by a history of repeated academic failure and increasing alienation from school (Henry, Knight, & Thornberry, 2012; Samuel & Burger, 2020).

Although adolescents who drop out of school often share certain characteristics in common (for example, a history of poor school performance), there is nevertheless diversity within this population. According to one extensive study of Canadian students (Janosz et al., 2000), there are at least four distinct groups of dropouts: (1) quiet dropouts (whose histories and personal characteristics actually look very similar to those of students who do not drop out of school but who appear somewhat withdrawn; they almost seem to "fade out" rather than drop out, perhaps as a result of depression), (2) disengaged dropouts (whose dropping out appears mainly to be the result of low commitment to school and poor academic motivation), (3) low-achiever dropouts (whose dropping out is primarily the result of very poor school performance), and (4) maladjusted dropouts (whose dropping out is part of a larger constellation of behavioral and psychological problems).

The idea that different developmental histories lead to dropping out is important to the design of preventive interventions because it suggests that different sorts of programs may work for different sorts of students. For instance, dropping out early in high school is more likely to be the result of disciplinary problems at school, whereas dropping out later in high school is more likely to be driven by the desire to work and earn money (Stearns & Glennie, 2006). Other studies indicate that it is important to distinguish between students who temporarily drop out of school but return at some later point and obtain their GED—as do between one-third and one-half of all dropouts—and those who leave and never return (Entwisle, Alexander, & Olson, 2004).

making the practical connection

Based on what we know about the causes and consequences of dropping out, what steps should be taken to reduce the dropout rate?

School Factors   Although most research on the causes of dropping out has focused on characteristics of adolescents who leave school prematurely, some studies have focused on the schools that dropouts leave (Rumberger, 2012). In general, dropping out is less likely from schools where the environment is orderly, where academic pursuits are emphasized, where students are treated fairly, and where the faculty is supportive and committed (Peguero & Bracy, 2015). Students who are at particularly high risk of dropping out (low-achieving, economically disadvantaged, and foreign-born Latinx youth) are helped especially by having teachers who are sources of social support and guidance (Enriquez, 2011). Although some educators have expressed concern about the recent trend toward toughening graduation requirements and ending **social promotion**—the practice of promoting students from one grade to the next on the basis of age rather than actual achievement—evaluations of policies such as the use of high school exit examinations to determine whether students can graduate show that they do not increase the rate of dropping out or differentially affect minority and white students (Warren, Grodsky, & Lee, 2008).

Occupational Achievement

School, rather than work, is the setting in which achievement is most often studied by contemporary scholars interested in adolescence. Although many individuals in previous generations began their occupational careers during adolescence, this is very rare today in most industrialized societies, where the majority of individuals pursue some form of postsecondary education before entering into full-time work. With the exception of apprenticeships, which are popular in only a handful of European countries, the work individuals perform during adolescence is rarely relevant to their future careers; it is mainly a means of earning spending money. Work experiences in adolescence, in general, have little or no impact on adolescents' plans or aspirations for adult work, especially among students from nonpoor families (Entwisle, Alexander, & Olson, 2005; Johnson, 2002), although it is possible that the small minority of adolescents who hold "good" jobs may learn something about their career interests from them. Fast food, restaurant, and retail jobs provide the fewest opportunities to build career-related skills, whereas office and clerical jobs are among the best (Staff, Messersmith, & Schulenberg, 2009).

Researchers who are interested in occupational achievement during adolescence have examined several issues, including the ways in which young people make decisions about their careers and the influences on their occupational aspirations and expectations. We begin with a look at the development of adolescents' occupational plans.

The Development of Occupational Plans

The development of occupational plans during adolescence is one aspect of the process of developing a sense of identity

(Skorikov & Vondracek, 2007). Occupational development follows a sequence that involves an examination of one's traits, abilities, and interests; a period of experimentation with different work roles; and an integration of influences from one's past (primarily, identification with familial role models) with one's hopes for the future. And as is also the case with identity development, the development of an occupational identity is profoundly influenced by the social environment in which it takes place.

Changes in the broader environment in which adolescents develop—in this case, changes in the need for and accessibility of higher education—have exerted a powerful influence on the developmental course of occupational planning. For many individuals, the development of occupational plans may not take place until the final years of college, and deciding on a specific career may not even begin until well after college graduation.

Influences on Occupational Choices

What makes one individual choose to become an attorney and another decide to be a teacher? Why do some students pursue careers in psychology, while others major in engineering? Researchers have long been interested in the reasons that individuals end up in certain careers (Neuenschwander & Kracke, 2011).

Work Values When you think about your future work, what will you look for in a job? **Work values** refer to the sorts of rewards individuals seek from their jobs (e.g., Johnson, 2002). For example, are you most interested in making a lot of money, in having a secure job, or in having a job that permits you to have a lot of vacation time?

According to most theories of work values, seven basic types of work rewards define individuals' work values: extrinsic rewards (earning a high income), security (enjoying job stability), intrinsic rewards (being able to be creative or to learn things from work), influence (having authority over others or power over decision making), altruistic rewards (helping others), social rewards (working with people you like), and leisure (having an opportunity for free time or vacation). Individuals choose jobs based on the relative importance of these various work rewards to them (see Table 12.2).

Many contemporary adolescents have unrealistic and overly ambitious ideas about the rewards they will derive from their future work. A very large proportion of adolescents aspire to levels of work rewards that they are highly unlikely to attain (Schneider & Stevenson, 1999). One problem is that adolescents tend to rate almost all work rewards very highly, optimistically believing that they can find jobs that satisfy multiple rewards simultaneously. When they actually enter their first full-time adult jobs, though, they soon discover that it is difficult, if not impossible, to have a career in which one makes a lot of money, is creative, helps other people, enjoys job security, and

Table 12.2 People look for different things in a job. Which types of work values are most important to you?

Work Value	Example
Extrinsic	Earning a good income
Security	Enjoying job stability
Intrinsic	Having opportunities for creativity
Influence	Wielding power over others
Altruistic	Helping others
Social	Enjoying one's co-workers
Leisure	Having opportunities for vacation or time off

has a lot of free time. Over the course of young adulthood, one of the most important changes that occurs in the domain of occupational development is that individuals become both somewhat disillusioned and more focused on what they want from a job, abandoning the unrealistic notion that one can "have it all" (Roberts, O'Donnell, & Robins, 2004).

There are important limitations to theories of career choice that are based solely on reward preferences assessed in adolescence. First, interests and abilities are not fixed during adolescence but continue to develop and change during the adult years, and one of the most important influences on personality development during adulthood is work itself (Johnson, 2002). Through working in a job that emphasizes certain personality characteristics, requires certain abilities, or provides certain types of rewards, individuals begin to change their personality, skills, and values. As a result, a job that seems like a bad match during early adulthood may over time become a good match.

A second problem with theories of career choice that emphasize adolescents' work values is that they may underestimate the importance of other factors that influence and shape vocational decisions, most importantly, the social context in which adolescents make career decisions. Many career decisions are influenced more by individuals' beliefs about what sorts of jobs are accessible or "appropriate" for them than by their interests and preferences (Johnson, 2002). It is all well and good for an adolescent to discover that he is well suited for a career in medicine, but the realization is of little value if his family cannot afford the cost of college or medical school. An adolescent girl may discover through taking a vocational preference test that she is well suited for work in the area of construction or building but find that her parents, peers, teachers, and potential employers all discourage her from following this

work values
The particular sorts of rewards an individual looks for in a job (extrinsic, intrinsic, social, altruistic, security, influence, leisure).

avenue of employment because they think it is not appropriate for women.

The Influence of Parents and Peers No influence on occupational choice is stronger than socioeconomic status, and as a result, adolescents' occupational ambitions and achievements are highly correlated with the ambitions and achievements of those around them (Ashby & Schoon, 2012). Youngsters from middle-class families are more likely than their less advantaged peers to aspire to and enter middle-class occupations. Socioeconomic status also influences work values, with individuals from higher classes more likely to value intrinsic rewards and influence and less likely to value extrinsic rewards and security. The importance of social class as a determinant of what people look for in their jobs is strong and constant throughout adolescence and young adulthood (Johnson, 2002).

A variety of explanations have been offered for the fit between adolescents' ambitions and the socioeconomic status of those around them. First, and perhaps most important, **occupational attainment**—the prestige or status an individual achieves in the world of work—depends strongly on educational attainment (Elmore, 2009). As we saw earlier, educational attainment is greatly influenced by socioeconomic status. Because middle-class adolescents are likely to complete more years of schooling than their lower-class peers, economically advantaged adolescents are more likely to seek and enter higher-status occupations.

Second, middle-class parents, as noted earlier, are more likely to raise their children in ways that foster the development of strong achievement orientation and career exploration. The development of achievement motivation, which has an impact on school performance, also has an impact on youngsters' occupational ambitions—both directly (in that individuals with strong needs for achievement will express these needs by aspiring to occupations that provide opportunities to achieve status or wealth) and indirectly, through the effects of achievement motivation on academic achievement (in that youngsters who are successful in school are likely to be encouraged to seek higher-status occupations and engage in identity exploration). Parents influence their adolescents' career aspirations mainly by influencing their educational achievement (Jodl et al., 2001).

Finally, the same opportunities that favor economically advantaged youngsters in the world of education—better facilities, more opportunities for enrichment, greater accessibility of higher education—also favor middle-class youngsters in the world of work. Because their parents are more likely to work in positions of power and leadership, middle-class youngsters often have important family connections and sources of

occupational attainment
A measure of achievement based on the status or prestige of the job an individual holds.

An individual's choice of occupation is influenced by many factors, including the work values he or she has. Contextual factors, such as job opportunities, are important as well. nd3000/Shutterstock

information about the world of work that are less available to youngsters from poorer families. In addition, coming from a family that is economically well off may provide an adolescent with more time to explore career options and to wait for an especially desirable position, rather than having to take the first job that becomes available out of economic necessity. This advantage is particularly important during economic downturns, such as the one that took place during the COVID-19 pandemic, when it is often difficult to find employment.

The Broader Context of Occupational Choice Adolescents' occupational choices are made, of course, within a broader social context that profoundly influences the nature of their plans. Today's young people see work as a less central part of life than their counterparts did in the past. Contemporary young people, for example, are more likely than past generations to say that if they had enough money, they would not work; that they are less willing to work overtime to make sure their job was done well; and that it is important to have a job that allows sufficient time for leisure (Wray-Lake et al., 2009).

At different times, different employment opportunities arise, and young people—particularly by the time they reach the end of their formal schooling—are often very aware of the prospects for employment in different fields. Young people often tailor their plans in response to what they perceive as the future needs and demands of the labor market and the acceptability of given occupational choices within their community. In addition, whether an adolescent's occupational expectations are actually realized depends on many factors that are not in his or her control (as anyone graduating during the economic downturn of the previous decade could certainly attest).

Adolescents also tailor their plans based on their beliefs regarding which jobs society says are "acceptable" for individuals of a particular social class, ethnicity, or sex (Johnson, 2002; Master, Cheryan, & Meltzoff, 2016). One manifestation of this is seen in the disproportionate numbers of males who major in the sciences; much progress has been made in encouraging more young women to major in STEM fields (science, technology, engineering, and math), especially in biological and biomedical sciences, but there are still large gender gaps in physical sciences, engineering, and computer sciences.

One problem faced by all young people in making career plans is obtaining accurate information about the labor market needs of the future and the appropriate means of pursuing positions in various fields. The majority of young people do not have educational plans that are consistent with the educational requirements of the jobs they hope to enter, and many adolescents are overly optimistic about their chances for success (Chang et al., 2006). One goal of career educators is to help adolescents make more informed and more realistic choices about their careers and to free them from stereotypes that constrain their choices. Career counselors, especially on college campuses, have come to play an increasingly important role in individuals' career decision making because the rapid pace at which the labor market changes has made it less likely that adolescents will be able to obtain accurate information from their family.

13 Psychosocial Problems in Adolescence

Some General Principles About Problems in Adolescence

Most Problems Reflect Transitory Experimentation

Not All Problems Begin in Adolescence

Most Problems Do Not Persist into Adulthood

Problems During Adolescence Are Not Caused by Adolescence

Psychosocial Problems: Their Nature and Covariation

Comorbidity of Externalizing Problems

Comorbidity of Internalizing Problems

Substance Use and Abuse

Prevalence of Substance Use and Abuse

Causes and Consequences of Substance Use and Abuse

Drugs and the Adolescent Brain

Prevention and Treatment of Substance Use and Abuse

Externalizing Problems

Categories of Externalizing Problems

Developmental Progression of Antisocial Behavior

Changes in Juvenile Offending over Time

Causes of Antisocial Behavior

Prevention and Treatment of Externalizing Problems

Internalizing Problems

The Nature and Prevalence of Depression

Sex Differences in Depression

Suicide and Non-Suicidal Self-Injury

Causes of Depression and Internalizing Disorders

Treatment and Prevention of Internalizing Problems

Stress and Coping

Peter Dazeley/Getty Images

The majority of young people move through the adolescent years without major difficulty, but some experience serious psychological and behavioral problems, such as substance abuse, delinquency, and depression, that disrupt not only their lives but also the lives of those around them. These problems indirectly touch the lives of all of us, either directly, through the personal contact we may have with a troubled young person, or indirectly, through increased taxes for community services or heightened anxiety about the safety of our neighborhoods. In this chapter, we look at some of the more serious psychological problems we typically associate with adolescence.

Some General Principles About Problems in Adolescence

The mass media love to paint extreme pictures of the world in which we live, an exaggerated view that is obvious in the presentation of teenage problem behavior. Rarely are popular portrayals of adolescents' behavioral disorders, psychological distress, or drug use accurate: A breakup with a boyfriend is followed that evening by a suicide attempt. An after-school prank develops into a life of crime. A weekend of heavy drinking fades into a commercial, and when the program returns, the adolescent is on his way to a life of addiction, delinquency, and school failure. Those of you for whom adolescence was not that long ago know that these "facts" about adolescent problem behavior are rarely true. But we are so often bombarded with images of young people in trouble that it is easy to be fooled into believing that "adolescence" equals "problems."

We should not gloss over the fact that many healthy adolescents at one time or another experience self-doubt, family squabbles, academic setbacks, or broken hearts. But it is important to keep in mind as we look at psychosocial problems during adolescence that there is an important distinction between the normative, and usually temporary, difficulties encountered by many young people and the serious psychosocial problems experienced by a minority of youth. One of the purposes of this chapter is to put these problems in perspective. Before we look at several specific categories of problems in detail, it's helpful to lay out some general principles about adolescent psychosocial problems that apply to all of them.

Most Problems Reflect Transitory Experimentation

First, let's distinguish between occasional experimentation and enduring patterns of dangerous or troublesome behavior. In a period of development during which it is normal—maybe even expected—that individuals will seek independence and explore themselves and their relationships with others, it is hardly surprising that some of the experimentation in which individuals engage is risky (Haydon, McRee, & Halpern, 2011; Steinberg, 2008). For example, the majority of adolescents experiment with alcohol sometime before high school graduation, and

It is important to differentiate between occasional experimentation with risky or unhealthful activities and enduring patterns of troublesome behavior. Joshua Resnick/123RF

about 40% will have been drunk at least once (Miech et al., 2020). But relatively few teenagers develop drinking problems or permit alcohol to adversely affect their schooling or personal relationships, and as they move into adulthood, get married, and change their patterns of socializing, their drinking declines (Allen et al., 2020; Staff et al., 2010). Similarly, although the vast majority of teenagers do something during adolescence that is against the law, such as smoking marijuana or shoplifting, very few of these young people go on to have criminal careers.

Not All Problems Begin in Adolescence

Second, let's distinguish between problems that have their origins and onset during adolescence and those that have their roots during earlier periods of development (Drabick & Steinberg, 2011). Some teenagers fall into patterns of criminal or delinquent behavior during adolescence, and we tend to associate delinquency with the adolescent years. But most teenagers who have recurrent problems with the law had problems at home and at

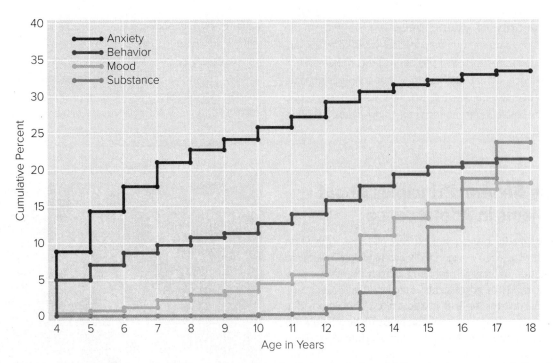

Figure 13.1 Anxiety disorders and behavioral disorders typically begin during childhood, whereas mood disorders and substance abuse usually first appear during adolescence. (Merikangas et al., 2010)

school from an early age; in some samples of delinquents, the problems were evident as early as preschool (Farrington, 2009; Hartung, Lefner, & Fedele, 2011). Many individuals who develop depression during adolescence suffered from other types of psychological distress, such as excessive anxiety, as children (Graber & Sontag, 2009). According to a study of more than 10,000 American adolescents, although one-third of all teenagers report having had an anxiety disorder by age 18, almost all of these individuals had developed an anxiety disorder before turning 12. Similarly, of the 20% of adolescents who reported having had a behavioral disorder at some point in time, two-thirds had the first occurrence before entering adolescence (Merikangas et al., 2010) (see Figure 13.1). A recent study of 1.3 million Danish youth found that about two-thirds of all boys and half of all girls who were diagnosed with a mental disorder by age 18 had the first occurrence before age 12 (Dalsgaard et al., 2020). In other words, simply because a problem may be displayed *during* adolescence does not mean that it is a problem *of* adolescence.

Most Problems Do Not Persist into Adulthood

Third, many of the behavioral problems experienced by adolescents are resolved by the beginning of adulthood, with few long-term repercussions. Substance abuse, delinquency, and eating disorders are three good examples: Rates of drug and alcohol use, delinquency, and disordered eating are all higher within the adolescent population than

in the adult population, but most individuals who abused drugs and alcohol, committed delinquent acts, or were bulimic as teenagers grow up to be sober, law-abiding adults without eating disorders. Nevertheless, we should not lose sight of the fact that adolescence is the most common age for the onset of a serious mental illness or that 20% of adolescents have a mental illness that will persist into adulthood (Lee et al., 2014). But individuals for whom problem behavior persists into adulthood are likely to have had a problematic childhood as well as a problematic adolescence.

Problems During Adolescence Are Not Caused by Adolescence

Finally, problem behavior during adolescence is virtually never a direct consequence of the normative changes of adolescence itself. Popular theories about "raging hormones" causing oppositional or deviant behavior have no scientific support whatsoever, nor do the widely held beliefs that problem behaviors are manifestations of an inherent need to rebel against authority or that bizarre behavior results from an identity crisis. The hormonal changes of puberty have only a modest direct effect on adolescent behavior; rebellion during adolescence is atypical, not normal; and few adolescents experience a tumultuous identity crisis. When a young person exhibits a serious psychosocial problem, such as depression, the worst possible interpretation is that it is a normal part of growing up. It is more likely a sign that something is wrong.

Psychosocial Problems: Their Nature and Covariation

Clinical practitioners (psychologists, psychiatrists, social workers, and counselors) and other experts on the development and treatment of psychosocial problems during adolescence distinguish among three broad categories of problems: substance abuse, externalizing disorders, and internalizing disorders. **Substance abuse** refers to the maladaptive use of drugs, including legal drugs such as alcohol or nicotine; illegal drugs such as marijuana (even in states that have legalized marijuana, it is still illegal for adolescents to use it without a prescription), cocaine, or LSD; and prescription drugs such as stimulants or sedatives. **Externalizing disorders** are those in which the young person's problems are turned outward and are manifested in behavioral problems (some writers use the expression "acting out" to refer to this set of problems). Common externalizing problems during adolescence are delinquency, antisocial aggression, and truancy. **Internalizing disorders** are those in which the young person's problems are turned inward and are manifested in emotional and cognitive distress, such as depression, anxiety, or disordered eating.

Although many people think of substance abuse as an externalizing disorder, research indicates that it is just as likely to accompany depression and other internalizing disorders as it is to be a part of "acting out" behavior (Baker et al., 2017; Conway et al., 2016; Siennick et al., 2016). We are simply more likely to be aware of substance abuse problems when they are seen among adolescents who are antisocial (such as a rowdy group of drunk delinquent youth) than when they occur along with internalizing problems (such as a depressed teenager who drinks herself to sleep each night). Because substance abuse problems co-occur, or are **comorbid,** with both externalizing and internalizing problems and because many adolescents who experiment with drugs have neither internalizing nor externalizing problems, we look at substance abuse as a separate category of problem behavior. One reason it is helpful to use the labels of "internalizing" and "externalizing" is that the specific problems within each broad category are often comorbid.

While the distinction between internalizing disorders and externalizing disorders is useful for organizing information about psychosocial problems during adolescence, it is important to bear in mind that some adolescents experience problems in both domains simultaneously (Yu et al., 2017). Some adolescents who engage in delinquency or show other behavior problems also suffer from depression (Jaggers et al., 2020; Martinez-Ferrer & Stattin, 2017; McDonough-Caplan, Klein, & Beauchaine, 2018). Many depressed or anxious adolescents, as well as many antisocial adolescents, also abuse drugs and alcohol (Scalco et al., 2020; Maslowsky, Schulenberg, & Zucker, 2014; Monahan et al., 2014).

It is important to distinguish among adolescents who exhibit one specific problem without any others (for example, depressed adolescents who do not have other internalizing or externalizing problems), adolescents who exhibit more than one problem within the same general category (for example, violent delinquent youth or anxious-depressed youth), and adolescents who exhibit both internalizing and externalizing problems (for example, depressed delinquents). Multiproblem adolescents tend not only to have more problems but more *serious* problems (Kessler et al., 2012). These adolescents may have followed very different developmental pathways and may require very different types of treatment. Multiproblem teenagers typically have had far worse family experiences than those with one problem (Chen & Simons-Morton, 2009; Yong et al., 2014).

The links between co-occurring internalizing and externalizing problems are different among females than among males (Klostermann, Connell, & Stormshak, 2016). In girls, internalizing problems, such as depression, usually precede conduct problems. Girls who are depressed often experience problems with their peers, which may lead them into antisocial peer groups, where their chances of developing conduct problems increase. Boys, on the other hand, are more likely to have conduct problems that lead to depression, often because their conduct problems lead to academic difficulties, which cause emotional distress. One important implication of research on comorbidity is that successfully treating one sort of problem (e.g., antisocial behavior) may also help reduce other sorts of problems as well (e.g., depression) (Monahan et al., 2014).

Comorbidity of Externalizing Problems

Adolescents who demonstrate one type of behavioral problem, such as aggression, often demonstrate another, such as criminal behavior. It is well-documented that delinquency is often associated with problems such as truancy, defiance, sexual promiscuity, academic difficulties, substance abuse, and violence (Farrington, 2009; Savolainen et al., 2012).

substance abuse
The misuse of alcohol or other drugs to a degree that causes problems in the individual's life.

externalizing disorders
Psychosocial problems that are manifested in a turning of the symptoms outward, as in aggression or delinquency.

internalizing disorders
Psychosocial problems that are manifested in a turning of the symptoms inward, as in depression or anxiety.

comorbid
Co-occurring, as when an individual has more than one problem at the same time.

Problem Behavior Syndrome   One highly influential approach to understanding comorbidity among externalizing problems has described a **problem behavior syndrome** (Jessor & Jessor, 1977). According to many proponents of this view, the underlying cause of problem behavior syndrome is unconventionality in both the adolescent's personality and environment. Unconventional individuals are tolerant of deviance, not highly connected to educational or religious institutions, and very liberal in their views. Unconventional environments are those in which a large number of individuals share these same attitudes. Unconventional individuals in unconventional environments are more likely to engage in a wide variety of risk-taking behavior, including experimentation with illegal drugs, risky sex, delinquent activity, and risky driving (Cooper et al., 2003; Monshouwer et al., 2012). A comparison of adolescents in the United States and China found that the same factors heighten or diminish adolescents' risk for problem behavior in both countries (Jessor et al., 2003).

A number of possibilities have been proposed about the origins of unconventionality. One set of theories emphasizes the biological underpinnings of the trait and argues that a predisposition toward deviance may actually be inherited (McAdams et al., 2012). A second view stresses biologically based differences (either inherited or acquired through experience) among individuals in arousal, sensation seeking, and fearlessness (e.g., Dunlop & Romer, 2010; Ortiz & Raine, 2004). Yet a third view emphasizes the early family context in which deviance-prone children are reared and frames problem behavior as a sort of adaptive response to a hostile environment (Belsky, Steinberg, & Draper, 1991). Indeed, many writers have argued that some types of antisocial behavior in adolescence, especially those that involve risk taking, actually make a lot of evolutionary sense because in most species, adolescence is a time when individuals must establish independence and venture out into the world without the protection of their parents (Ellis et al., 2012).

Problems Lead to Other Problems   An alternative to the view that an underlying trait drives all problem behavior is that different types of deviance have different origins but involvement in a given problem behavior may lead to involvement in a second one. Thus, problem behaviors cluster together not because of a common underlying trait such as unconventionality, but because engaging in some problematic activities (such as drug and alcohol use) leads to others (such as delinquency) (Bingham & Shope, 2004; Hussong, Curran, & Moffitt, 2004). Some writers have talked about "cascading" effects, where one sort of problem causes another, which triggers a third (Burt & Roisman, 2010; Lynne-Landsman, Bradshaw, & Ialongo, 2010a; Negriff, 2018). One study of individuals followed from preadolescence into adulthood found that externalizing problems in childhood led to academic difficulties in adolescence, which, in turn, led to internalizing problems in adulthood (see Figure 13.2) (Masten et al., 2005). Studies of the relationship between drug use and depression, and between drug use and conduct problems have found similar sorts of cascades (Felton et al., 2015; Jones et al., 2016; Sitnick, Shaw, & Hyde, 2014).

Social Control Theory   According to a third view, **social control theory** (Gottfredson & Hirschi, 1990), individuals who do not have strong bonds to society's institutions—such as the family, school, or workplace—will be likely to behave unconventionally in a variety of ways. Thus, the clustering of different problem behaviors may stem not from a problem "in" the person (such as a biological predisposition toward risky behavior) but from an underlying weakness in the individual's attachment to society. This underlying problem leads to the development of an unconventional attitude, to membership in an unconventional peer group, or to involvement in one or several problem behaviors that may set a chain of problem activities in motion. Social control theory helps to explain why behavior problems are not just clustered together but are far more prevalent among poor, inner-city, minority youngsters.

Overstating the Case?   Finally, a number of researchers stress that we should be careful about overstating the case for a single problem behavior "syndrome" (Simons et al., 2016; Willoughby, Chalmers, & Busseri, 2004). They note that although engaging in one type of problem behavior increases the likelihood of engaging in another, the overlap among behavior problems is far from perfect. Other studies suggest that it is

---

problem behavior syndrome
The covariation among various types of externalizing disorders believed to result from an underlying trait of unconventionality.

social control theory
A theory of delinquency that links deviance with the absence of bonds to society's main institutions.

Figure 13.2   **One explanation for comorbidity is that problems in one domain can create problems in another.** (Masten et al., 2005)

important to differentiate between problem behavior that adults disapprove of but that many adolescents consider normative (such as smoking, drinking, or having sex) versus problem behavior that both adults and adolescents view as serious (such as violent crime) (Sullivan, Childs, & O'Connell, 2010; Warren et al., 2016). Context matters, too: One international comparison found that adolescent alcohol use was predictive of violence in Scandinavia and Eastern Europe but not in Mediterranean countries, in part because adolescents in Mediterranean countries are less likely to drink to intoxication and more likely to drink in settings where adults are present (Felson et al., 2011).

Comorbidity of Internalizing Problems

There is also a good deal of comorbidity in internalizing disorders, which tend to have in common the subjective state of distress. For example, depressed adolescents are more likely than their peers to experience anxiety, panic, phobia, obsessional thinking, suicidal ideation, eating disorders, and various psychosomatic disturbances (physical problems that have psychological causes) (Ask et al., 2016; Danneel et al., 2020; Hankin et al., 2016). Some experts question whether it even makes sense to consider some of these problems as separate entities when speaking about children or adolescents (for example, to draw a distinction between anxiety and depression) because rates of comorbidity are so high (Graber & Sontag, 2009).

Just as different externalizing problems are hypothesized to reflect an underlying antisocial syndrome, various indicators of internalizing problems may be thought of as different manifestations of a common underlying factor, **negative emotionality** (Class et al., 2019; Hankin et al., 2016; Rudolph, Davis, & Monti, 2017). Individuals who are high in negative emotionality—who become distressed easily—are at greater risk for depression, anxiety disorders, and a range of internalizing problems, as are individuals who are **anhedonic**—who have difficulty experiencing positive emotions like joy—are especially prone to depression (Luking et al., 2016). An alternative view is that the core underlying trait that links different types of internalizing problems is cognitive in nature; depressed and anxious individuals, for example, are especially prone to self-criticism, rumination, and hopelessness (Hankin, Snyder, & Gulley, 2016). As with externalizing problems, the underpinnings of internalizing problems are believed to have both biological and environmental origins, including high levels of biological reactivity to stress (Susman et al., 1997).

In this chapter, we examine the nature, prevalence, consequences, and amelioration of the three sets of problems often seen during adolescence: substance abuse, antisocial behavior and other externalizing problems, and depression and other internalizing problems. In each case, we ask four central questions: (1) What is the nature

of this sort of problem in adolescence? (2) How many, and which, young people have these problems? (3) What do we know about factors that contribute to these problems? and (4) What approaches to prevention and intervention appear to have the most promise?

negative emotionality
The presumed underlying cause of internalizing disorders, characterized by high levels of subjective distress.

anhedonic
Having difficulty experiencing positive emotions, a risk factor for depression.

Substance Use and Abuse

Society sends young people contradictory messages about drugs and alcohol. Television programs aimed at preadolescents urge viewers to "just say no!" but the football games and sitcoms that many of these same viewers watch tell them, no less subtly, that having a good time with friends is impossible without something alcoholic to drink. Many celebrities who are idolized by teenagers speak out against cocaine and marijuana, but many equally famous stars admit to using these same drugs. Tobacco and alcohol companies label their products as causing health problems, but they spend enormous amounts of money marketing their cigarettes and beverages to teenagers.

The mixed signals sent to young people about drugs reflect the inconsistent way that we view these substances as a society: Some drugs (such as alcohol or Adderall) are fine, as long as they are not abused, but others (such as cocaine or meth) are not; some drinking (enough to relax at a party) is socially appropriate, but too much (enough to impair driving or lead to nonconsensual sex) is not; some people (those over 21) are old enough to handle drugs, but others (those under 21) are not. It is easy to see why teenagers do not follow the dictates of their elders when it comes to alcohol and other drugs. How, then, should we view substance use and abuse among teenagers when our backdrop is a society that much of the time tolerates, if not actively encourages, adults who use these same substances?

As with most of the problem behaviors that are common during adolescence, discussions of teenage substance use are often filled more with rhetoric than reality. The popular stereotype of contemporary young people is that they use and abuse a wide range of drugs more than their counterparts did previously, that the main reason adolescents use drugs is peer pressure, and that the "epidemic" level of substance use among American teenagers is behind many of the other problems associated with this age group—including academic underachievement, early pregnancy, suicide, and crime. The simplicity of these assertions is undeniably tempting; after all, what could be more reassuring than to identify the "real" culprit (drugs) and the "real" causes (peers and mass media) of all the maladies of young people? And what could be even more

Monitoring the Future
An annual survey of a nationwide sample of American 8th-, 10th-, and 12th-graders, mainly known for its data on adolescent substance use.

binge drinking
Consuming five or more drinks in a row on one occasion, an indicator of alcohol abuse.

comforting than the belief that if we simply teach young people to "just say no," these problems will disappear?

Unfortunately, what we might like to believe about adolescent substance use is not necessarily correct. As we shall see, there are grains of truth to many of the popular claims about the causes, nature, and consequences of teenage substance use and abuse, but there are many widely held misconceptions about the subject, too.

Prevalence of Substance Use and Abuse

Each year since 1975, a group of researchers from the University of Michigan has surveyed a nationally representative sample of about 15,000 American high school seniors on several aspects of their lifestyle and values, including their use and abuse of a variety of drugs. Beginning in 1991, comparable samples of 8th- and 10th-graders were added to the annual survey. Because of the size and representativeness of the sample of respondents, this survey, called **Monitoring the Future** (Miech et al., 2020), is an excellent source of information about patterns of adolescent drug and alcohol use, at least among young people who have not dropped out of school. (The latest survey results can be accessed at www.monitoringthefuture.org.)

Drugs of Choice   The surveys consistently indicate that alcohol is by far the most commonly used and abused substance in terms of both prevalence (the percentage of teenagers who have ever used the drug) and recency of use (the percentage of teenagers who have used the drug within the last month), followed by vaping nicotine and marijuana (about the same percentages for each) and cigarettes. By the time they are seniors in high school, 59% of teenagers have tried alcohol, 44% have tried marijuana, 41% have vaped nicotine, and 22% have smoked cigarettes. After cigarettes, however, the percentage of young people who have tried various other drugs drops precipitously, and only about 5% of high school seniors have used an illicit drug other than marijuana within the last month (Miech et al., 2020) (see Figure 13.3).

Although there was once a time when drug use was more common among adolescent males than females, today sex differences in the prevalence of drug use are virtually nonexistent with respect to drinking, smoking marijuana, vaping nicotine, and smoking cigarettes. Girls are more likely than boys to try these drugs before high school, but by the time they are seniors, male and female adolescents report comparable patterns of use (Johnston et al., 2020). Although alcohol and tobacco use among adolescents in most European countries is substantially

higher than it is in the United States, twice as many American than European adolescents regularly use illicit drugs (mainly marijuana) (ESPAD, 2019).

Prevalence statistics, especially those that tap whether an individual has ever tried the substance in question, tell us little about the nature and extent of drug use from the standpoint of adolescents' health and well-being. It is one thing to have *tried* alcohol or marijuana; it is something else to use either of these substances so often that one's life and behavior are markedly affected.

One of the best ways to examine this issue is to look at the percentage of young people who report using various substances daily or nearly daily. Daily use is infrequent, even among older teens. Marijuana is used daily by 6% of seniors, only 2% of high school seniors smoke cigarettes daily, and daily use of alcohol is extremely rare (fewer than 2% of seniors drink daily). However, about 14% of all 12th-graders, 8% of all 10th-graders, and 4% of all 8th-graders report having abused alcohol (had more than five drinks in a row, sometimes called **binge drinking**) at least once during the last month, and 10% of 8th-graders, 20% of 10th-graders, and 25% of 12-graders had vaped nicotine (Miech et al., 2020). Also worrisome is that 6% of high school seniors report having driven a car after drinking at least once in the past month, and 16% reported having ridden in a car with a driver who had been drinking (Centers for Disease Control and Prevention, 2020).

making the cultural connection

The use of illicit drugs is more common among American teenagers than their European counterparts, but adolescent smoking and drinking are more common in Europe. Why do you think this is?

Alcohol and marijuana remain the main drugs of choice among American adolescents. Lucky winner/Alamy Stock Photo

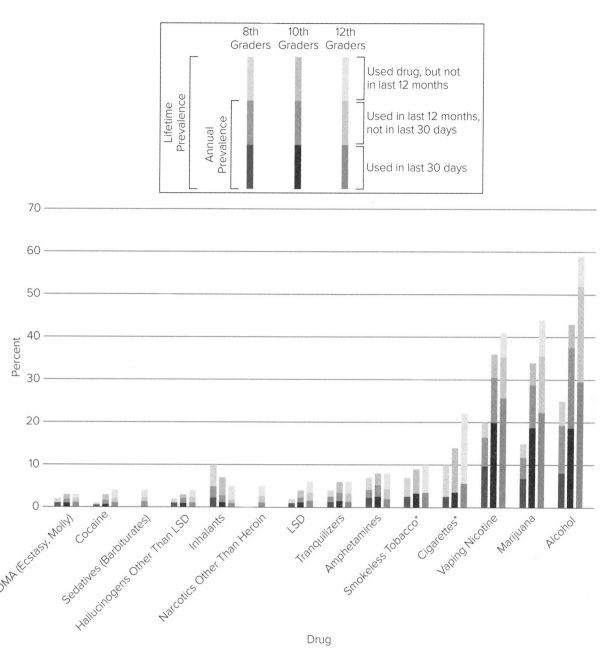

Figure 13.3 **Prevalence of substance use among American 8th-, 10th-, and 12th-graders.** (Miech et al., 2020)

Taken together, the findings from these surveys cast doubt on some of the most fervently held stereotypes about adolescent drug use in the United States. Many adolescents who drink do so to excess: About one-fifth of all seniors and nearly 10% of all sophomores have been drunk at least once in the last month (Miech et al., 2020). But only a very small proportion of young people have serious drug dependency problems (which would lead to daily use) or use hard drugs at all. Moreover, it is very unlikely that drug and alcohol use lurks behind the wide assortment of adolescent problems for which it is so frequently blamed.

Rather, the pattern suggests that most adolescents have experimented with alcohol; that nearly half have tried marijuana or vaping nicotine; that many have used

one or more of these drugs regularly; that alcohol is clearly the drug of choice among teenagers (a substantial proportion of whom drink to excess); and that most teenagers have not experimented with other drugs. One point worth noting is that many high school students have used opioids (such as Vicodin), amphetamines (such as Adderall), tranquilizers (such as Xanax), and sedatives (such as Seconal) that they have obtained without a prescription, a pattern that also is seen on college campuses (McCabe & West, 2013; Young, Glover, & Havens, 2012).

Changes in Substance Use over Time The Monitoring the Future study has also been used to chart changes over time in adolescent substance use. Recent

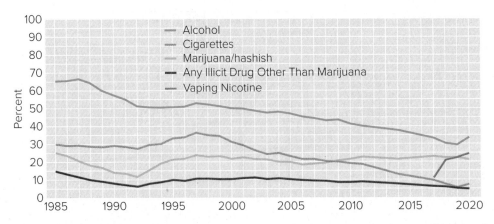

Figure 13.4 Over-time trends in the proportion of high school seniors who report having used various drugs in the 30 days preceding the survey. Questions about vaping nicotine were not included in the survey until 2017. (Johnston et al., 2015, and Meich et al., 2020)

administrations of the survey have given experts both cause for relief and cause for concern (Miech et al., 2020) (see Figure 13.4). Things haven't gotten worse, but for the most part, they haven't gotten better, either. Marijuana use, which had been on a steady decline since the late 1970s, rose quite sharply during the mid-1990s, has not declined to its former levels, and has not changed appreciably in recent years. Alcohol use, which declined steadily during the 1980s (from more than 70% of seniors drinking monthly to about 50%), has declined steadily but more slowly since then and actually has increased a bit in recent years.

One bit of very good news is that teen smoking, which increased during the 1990s, has declined dramatically and continues to fall—probably because there has been a gargantuan increase in the price of cigarettes during the past 25 years, which has hit teenagers, who do not have a lot of discretionary income, especially hard (Hawkins, Bach, & Baum, 2016). Several states have raised the legal minimum purchase age for tobacco to 21, which will undoubtedly lead to further declines in teen smoking. The high price of cigarettes is a far more powerful deterrent to teen smoking than antitobacco education, as is setting the minimum legal purchase age higher (Institute of Medicine, 2015).

A new concern, however, is the large number of teenagers who report vaping nicotine: According to recent surveys, 10% of 8th-graders, 20% of sophomores, and 25% of high school seniors vape on a monthly basis (Miech et al., 2020). Most adolescents view electronic cigarettes as less harmful and addictive than cigarettes (Amrock, Lee, & Weitzman, 2016; Owotomo, Maslowsky, & Loukas, 2018). Although regular cigarettes have more harmful health consequences than e-cigarettes, nicotine, whether introduced into the bloodstream through smoking or vaping, is highly addictive, and e-cigarettes also contain chemicals that are potentially harmful to adolescents' health and brain development (Hildick-Smith et al., 2015;

Holliday & Gould, 2016; Tobore, 2019). Adolescents who use e-cigarettes frequently are more likely than those who don't vape or smoke to binge drink, smoke marijuana, and use other illicit drugs (McCabe et al., 2017), although it isn't clear whether vaping leads to the use of these substances or is simply correlated with them.

Although pundits and political commentators frequently claim to have discovered the "real" reason for changes in rates of adolescent substance use, no one really knows why rates of adolescent substance use fluctuate over time, except, perhaps, because of fluctuations in price and availability. We know that adolescents' drug use fluctuates with changes in their perceptions of how normative, harmful, and disapproved of drug use is (Keyes et al., 2012), but scientists have not been able to determine what influences these perceptions, although it is likely that the messages teenagers receive about drugs—from parents, teachers, and mass media—are important. Still, many historical patterns are puzzling and hard to make sense of. For instance, during the same time period that heavy drinking among high school seniors declined dramatically (between 1976 and 2004), it increased just as significantly among college students who were just a few years older (Jager, Keyes, & Schulenberg, 2015). And during this very same era, rates of marijuana use were far more stable at both ages (Jager et al., 2013).

Perhaps the most encouraging finding to emerge in recent surveys is that experimentation with alcohol, marijuana, and tobacco is less common among younger teens than 20 years ago (Miech et al., 2020). In the mid-1990s, about 25% of all 8th-graders reported drinking at least once a month; by 2019, fewer than 7% of young adolescents did. In the mid-1990s, 10% of 8th-graders were regular smokers; today, it is 1%. Nevertheless, one-fourth of all 8th-graders have tried alcohol and 1 in 6 has tried marijuana. Curiously, while young adolescents' attitudes toward heavy drinking and regular smoking have gotten progressively more negative over the years, their views of marijuana have not changed much, perhaps because many states have legalized the sale of marijuana to adults. Rates of marijuana use among adolescents have also held steady over the past two decades.

Rates of substance use among 8th-graders are important to watch because the chances of becoming addicted to alcohol or nicotine are dramatically increased when substance use begins prior to age 15 (Patton, Coffey, Carlin, Sawyer, & Wakefield, 2006). Because the typical adolescent who smokes cigarettes begins around the seventh or eighth grade, looking at changes in the number of 8th-graders who smoke is a good way of forecasting rates of smoking among adults in the future. Fortunately, smoking among 8th-graders has declined markedly since the 1990s, when close to half of all 8th-graders had tried cigarettes; today, fewer than 10% have (Miech et al., 2020).

Ethnic Differences in Substance Use Several national surveys have examined ethnic differences in rates of adolescent substance use and abuse. In general, white, Latinx, and Native American adolescents are more likely to drink than Black youth (illicit drug use among Black youth is comparable to that among white and Latinx youth), and Asian youth are less likely to drink or use drugs than any other ethnic group (Johnston et al., 2020; Kane et al., 2017; Substance Abuse and Mental Health Services Administration, 2016). Foreign-born and less Americanized minority youngsters—whether Asian or Latinx in background—use alcohol, drugs, and tobacco at a lower rate than do American-born and more acculturated immigrant youth (Alamilla et al., 2018; Barsties et al., 2017).

Does Substance Use Follow a Particular Progression?
Young people experiment with beer and wine before trying cigarettes or hard liquor, which precedes marijuana use, which, in turn, precedes the use of other illicit drugs (Atherton et al., 2016). However, although experimentation may follow this sequence, this does not mean that alcohol use or smoking invariably lead to marijuana use or that marijuana use necessarily leads to experimentation with harder drugs (van Leeuwen et al., 2011).

The fact that there is a fairly standard sequence of drug use suggests that virtually all users of hard drugs have also tried alcohol, tobacco, and marijuana and, moreover, that one way to prevent adolescents from experimenting with more serious drugs might be to stop them from drinking, smoking cigarettes or vaping nicotine, and using marijuana. Adolescents who have not experimented with alcohol or marijuana by the time they are in their 20s are unlikely ever to use these or any other drugs (Chen & Kandel, 1996). For this reason, tobacco, alcohol, and marijuana are considered **gateway drugs,** in the sense that they represent a gate through which individuals pass on the way to using harder drugs.

Alcohol and nicotine exposure sensitize the adolescent brain to other drugs, such as cocaine, and make future abuse and addiction more likely (Griffin et al., 2017; Keyes, Hamilton, & Kandel, 2016; Yuan et al., 2015). Whether an individual passes through the gate is influenced by many factors beyond his or her previous patterns of drug use, though, including the era in which he or she grows up.

> **gateway drugs**
> Drugs that, when used over time, lead to the use of other, more dangerous substances.
>
> **developmental trajectories**
> Patterns of change over time.

On average, drinking and illicit drug use (and problematic drinking in particular) increase during adolescence, peak in the early 20s, and then decline (Reich et al., 2015), but not all individuals follow this pattern. Researchers have identified several distinct **developmental trajectories** of alcohol, tobacco, and drug use. In one study, six distinct groups were identified (Table 13.1). Nonusers (one-third of the sample) rarely experimented with substances at any point in adolescence. Alcohol experimenters (25% of the sample) first tried alcohol early in adolescence and continued to drink occasionally but did not try other drugs and did not increase their

Exposure to nicotine, whether through tobacco or e-cigarettes, may sensitize the adolescent brain to other substances, increasing the likelihood of future substance abuse. librakv/123RF

Table 13.1 Developmental trajectories of substance use

Adolescent Group	Percentage of Sample	Characteristic Behavior
Nonusers	33%	Rarely experiment with any substances in adolescence
Alcohol experimenters	25%	First try alcohol early in adolescence, continue to drink occasionally, but do not try other drugs and do not increase their drinking over time
Low escalators	5%	Begin using substances early in adolescence and increase use slowly and steadily over time
Early starters	6%	Show very high substance use in early adolescence that gradually escalates over time. By the end of high school, they smoke and drink frequently and experiment with drugs.
Late starters	20%	Use substances infrequently during early adolescence but rapidly increase use so by the end of adolescence, they nearly match early starters
High escalators	8%	Show moderate substance use in early adolescence that escalates rapidly and continues to increase throughout high school

(Adapted from Zapert, Snow, & Tebes, 2002)

drinking over time. Low escalators (5%) began using substances early in adolescence and increased their use slowly but steadily over time. Early starters (6%) showed very high substance use in early adolescence and escalated gradually over time, so that by the end of high school, they were smoking and drinking frequently and experimenting with drugs. Late starters (20%) used substances infrequently during early adolescence but increased their use rapidly during high school—so much so that by the end of high school, their substance use was similar to that of the early starters. Finally, high escalators (8%) showed moderate use in early adolescence, escalated rapidly between early and middle adolescence, and continued to increase their use throughout high school (Zapert, Snow, & Tebes, 2002). Adolescents whose substance use begins early or escalates rapidly, as well as those with a history of solitary use, are most at risk for substance use problems as adults (Nelson, Van Ryzin, & Dishion, 2015; Tucker et al., 2014).

Causes and Consequences of Substance Use and Abuse

In looking at the causes and consequences of substance use and abuse in adolescence, it is especially important to keep in mind the distinction between occasional experimentation and problematic use.

Users, Abusers, and Abstainers   Because the majority of adolescents have experimented with alcohol and close to half have tried marijuana, it stands to reason that there are plenty of normal, healthy young people who have used these drugs at least once. And, indeed, adolescents who experiment with alcohol and marijuana are no worse adjusted than their peers who abstain from them (Alex Mason & Spoth, 2011; Tucker et al., 2006).

In order to understand the relation between substance use and psychological adjustment, it is important to differentiate among four groups of adolescents: frequent drug users (for example, at least once a week); hard-drug users (that is, drugs other than alcohol, tobacco, or marijuana); those who experiment with marijuana and alcohol but who do not use them frequently (that is, no more than once a month); and those who abstain (Connell et al., 2010; Ehrenreich et al., 2015). Experimenters and abstainers score higher on measures of psychological adjustment than frequent users. The age at which adolescents experiment with substances is also important. One study of people in their mid-20s found that those who had experimented with substance use at age 17 (when experimentation is normative, at least in the United States) generally were better adjusted than those who had been abstainers, abusers, or problematic users (Englund et al., 2013) (see Figure 13.5).

Longer-term follow-up studies also show that moderate alcohol use during adolescence does not have negative long-term effects (Haller et al., 2010; Warren et al., 2016). In contrast, cigarette use during adolescence has more harmful long-term health consequences because nicotine is a more addictive drug and its use is more likely to persist into middle adulthood (Chen & Kandel, 1996; Elders et al., 1994; Pierce & Gilpin, 1996).

This does not mean that occasional experimentation with drugs during adolescence *leads* to better adjustment, of course. In fact, the psychological advantages observed among adolescents who experiment with alcohol and marijuana were evident well before they began experimenting, even when they were young children (Shedler & Block, 1990). Well-adjusted adolescents are more socially competent and are more likely to be in social situations in which other teenagers are drinking and smoking marijuana (Ludden & Eccles, 2007). In this sense,

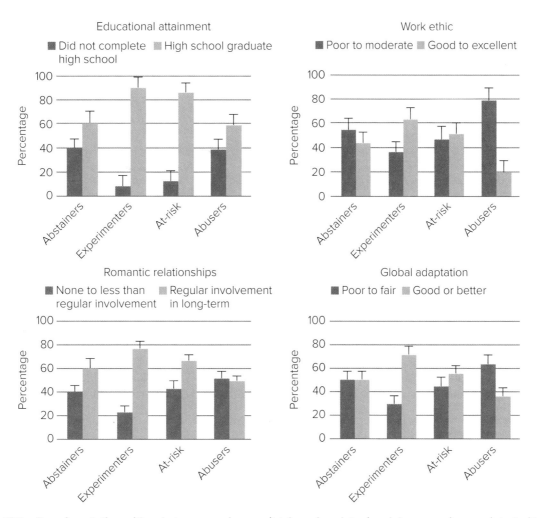

Figure 13.5   Experimentation with substances, as long as it takes place later in adolescence, is associated with better adjustment in young adulthood than is abstaining, abusing, or using drugs problematically (which places the teenager at risk for abuse). (Englund et al., 2013)

psychological adjustment increases the likelihood of alcohol and marijuana use, rather than the reverse.

Taken together, research indicates that moderate alcohol and marijuana use has become normative among adolescents in contemporary society (however troublesome some adults may find this), that these substances are typically used in social situations, and that better-adjusted and more interpersonally competent young people are likely to participate in social activities in which alcohol and other drugs are present.

Predictors and Consequences of Substance Abuse

Substance abuse (using drugs in a way that causes significant problems at home, school, work, or with the law) is a different matter (see Table 13.2). Adolescents who are frequent users of alcohol, tobacco, and other drugs score lower on measures of psychological adjustment as teenagers and were more likely to have been maladjusted as children (Hicks et al., 2014). Drug and alcohol abuse during adolescence is often a symptom of prior psychological disturbance.

Substance abuse during adolescence, whatever its antecedents, is associated with a host of other problems. Young people who abuse alcohol, tobacco, and other drugs are more likely to experience problems at school; suffer from psychological distress and depression; become involved in dangerous or deviant activities, including crime, delinquency, and truancy; and engage in unprotected sexual activity. Alcohol and other drugs are often implicated in adolescent automobile crashes, the leading cause of death and disability among American teenagers (Centers for Disease Control and Prevention, 2019b), and in other fatal and nonfatal accidents, such as drownings, falls, and burns (Hingson & Zha, 2009).

The effects of adolescent substance abuse also last long into adulthood. As adults, adolescent substance abusers are more likely to have physical health problems, experience unemployment and out-of-wedlock childbearing, and continue to have substance abuse problems (Chassin, Hussong, & Beltran, 2009; Green & Ensminger, 2006; Stuart & Green, 2008). Adolescent substance abusers also expose themselves to the long-term physical

Table 13.2 DSM—5 diagnostic criteria for substance use disorder

The DSM-5 defines a substance use disorder as the presence of at least 2 of 11 criteria, which are clustered in four groups:

1. *Impaired control:* (1) taking more or for longer than intended, (2) unsuccessful efforts to stop or cut down use, (3) spending a great deal of time obtaining, using, or recovering from use, (4) craving for substance.

2. *Social impairment:* (5) failure to fulfill major obligations due to use, (6) continued use despite problems caused or exacerbated by use, (7) important activities given up or reduced because of substance use.

3. *Risky use:* (8) recurrent use in hazardous situations, (9) continued use despite physical or psychological problems that are caused or exacerbated by substance use.

4. *Pharmacologic dependence:* (10) tolerance to effects of the substance, (11) withdrawal symptoms when not using or using less.*

*Persons who are prescribed medications such as opioids may exhibit these two criteria but would not necessarily be considered to have a substance use disorder.

(American Psychiatric Association, 2013)

health risks of excessive drug use. In the case of cigarettes, alcohol, and marijuana, these risks are substantial and well documented—among them, cancer, heart disease, and kidney and liver damage. It is also now well established that heavy cigarette smoking during adolescence can exacerbate feelings of emotional distress and lead to depression and anxiety disorders (Chassin, Hussong, & Beltran, 2009).

Risk Factors for Substance Abuse Because alcohol and marijuana use are both so common among American teenagers, it does not make sense to talk about risk factors (that is, things that make some teenagers more likely to try alcohol or marijuana) for using these substances. Researchers have asked, however, which adolescents are most likely to become substance *abusers*? Generally, four sets of risk factors—psychological, familial, social, and contextual—have been identified, and the more risk factors that are present for an individual, the more likely she or he is to use and abuse drugs (Bountress, Chassin, & Lemery-Chalfant, 2017; Carliner et al., 2016; Defoe et al., 2016).

These same risk factors have been found across a variety of studies and in samples of adolescents from a wide range of ethnic and socioeconomic backgrounds, although there is evidence that family factors may be more influential in early adolescence and peer factors more so in middle adolescence (Cleveland et al., 2008). In other words, the factors that place an adolescent at risk for substance abuse are more or less the same regardless of the adolescent's sex, social class, or ethnicity (Aspy et al., 2014; Choi et al., 2005). This is good news, because it suggests that preventive interventions do not need to be specifically tailored to different subgroups of adolescents (Hu, Davies, & Kandel, 2006).

The first set of risk factors is psychological. Individuals with certain personality characteristics—which typically are present prior to adolescence—are more likely to develop drug and alcohol problems than their peers.

These characteristics include anger, impulsivity, inattentiveness, and sensation seeking (Lydon-Staley & Geier, 2018; Oshri et al., 2018; Quach et al., 2020; Scalco & Colder, 2017). The combination of poor impulse control and heightened sensation seeking is especially problematic (Khurana et al., 2015; Willoughby & Fortner, 2015); moreover, the same traits that lead to drinking are themselves amplified by using alcohol—creating a vicious cycle (Peterson, Davis, & Smith, 2018).

Many of these traits have a strong genetic component (Su et al., 2019; Trucco et al., 2018; Wang et al., 2018), although the effects of having a genetic propensity toward substance use are amplified in contexts in which other teenagers are using drugs and alcohol (Russell, Wang, & Odgers, 2016) but diminished by contexts that discourage smoking or drinking (Li et al., 2011; Park et al., 2011). In addition, individuals who have more tolerant attitudes about drug use (and about deviance in general) are at greater risk for drug abuse (Petraitis, Flay, & Miller, 1995), as are those who expect alcohol or other drugs to improve their social relationships (Griffin et al., 2001).

Second, individuals with distant, hostile, or conflicted family relationships are more likely to develop substance abuse problems than their peers who grow up in close, nurturing families (Neppl, Dhalewadikar, & Lohman, 2016; Wen, 2017). Drug-abusing youngsters are also more likely than their peers to have parents who are excessively permissive, uninvolved, neglectful, or rejecting (Elam et al., 2020; Mun et al., 2018; Savage et al., 2018). In addition, they are more likely to come from homes where one or more other family members (parents or siblings) smoke, drink, or use drugs (as a result of both genetics and the environment) (Gottfredson et al., 2017; Griesler et al., 2019; Mays et al., 2014; Parra et al., 2020). One explanation for especially high rates of substance use among affluent suburban teenagers is that their parents often are tolerant of this behavior (Luthar & Goldstein, 2008).

Third, individuals with substance abuse problems are more likely to have friends who use and tolerate the use of drugs (Armenta, Sittner, & Whitbeck, 2016; Meisel & Colder, 2020; Wesche, Kreager, & Lefkowitz, 2019). Whether and how often adolescents use drugs is an important defining characteristic of peer groups; abstainers tend to have other abstainers as friends, and users tend to be friends with other users. Drug-using adolescents seek drug-using peers, and drug-using peers encourage even more drug use among their friends (Leung et al., 2016). Substance-using adolescents who have many substance-using friends may also overestimate how common substance use is because they are so much more likely to see other people engaged in it (Park et al., 2017).

Finally, adolescents who become substance abusers are more likely to live in a social context that makes drug use easier (Chassin, Hussong, & Beltran, 2009; Stanley, Henry, & Swaim, 2011). Important factors are the availability of drugs, the community's norms regarding drug use, the degree to which drug laws are enforced, and the ways in which drug use is presented via the mass media (Bendtsen et al., 2013; Su & Supple, 2016; Thrul et al., 2014). Lowering the minimum purchase age for alcohol (as was done in New Zealand) significantly increases the rate of alcohol-related car crashes among younger drivers, whereas raising it (as was done in the United States) decreases crashes (Kypri et al., 2006). Rates of binge drinking and drinking while driving are higher among adolescents who live in neighborhoods with relatively more retail outlets for alcohol (Milam et al., 2016; Resko et al., 2010), and smoking is more common among adolescents who live in neighborhoods with relatively more stores that sell cigarettes or electronic cigarettes (Giovenco et al., 2016; McCarthy et al., 2009) or who attend schools where a high proportion of other students smoke (Sabiston et al., 2009). Adolescent marijuana use is not higher in states that have legalized the drug for medical use, however (Choo et al., 2014; Lynne-Landsman, Livingston, & Wagenaar, 2013).

Researchers have also identified important **protective factors** that decrease the likelihood of adolescents' engaging in substance abuse (Jessor & Turbin, 2014). Among the most important are positive mental health (including high self-esteem and the absence of depression), high academic achievement, engagement in school, close family relationships, and involvement in religious activities (Eiden et al., 2016; Martin et al., 2015; Sanchez et al., 2011). These protective factors appear to operate over and above the effects of the risk factors discussed previously. As with the factors that place adolescents at risk for substance abuse, the protective factors identified operate similarly among adolescents from different ethnic groups and explain why some groups of adolescents use drugs more than others do (Ennett et al., 2008; Flannery, Vazsonyi, & Rowe, 1996). And, as with risk factors, the more protective factors an adolescent has in his or her life, the lower the risk for drug use (Lenzi et al., 2015).

Drugs and the Adolescent Brain

> **protective factors**
> Factors that limit individual vulnerability to harm.
>
> **dopamine**
> A neurotransmitter especially important in the brain circuits that regulate the experience of reward.

Scientists have long speculated that because the brain is still very malleable early in adolescence, experimentation with drugs is more harmful then than later in development. Experimental research in which scientists have compared the brains of animals exposed to drugs, either close to the time of puberty or after reaching full maturity, has illuminated some of the specific neurobiological pathways that explain why the potential for addiction is much greater in adolescence than adulthood (Jobson et al., 2019; Reynolds et al., 2019; Walker et al., 2017). In order to understand what these studies say, we need to digress slightly and look at certain aspects of adolescent brain development.

Changes in the limbic system during adolescence, a region of the brain that is important for the experience of reward and punishment, affect receptors for **dopamine,** one of the neurotransmitters that influence our experience of pleasure. We experience things such as great sex or fabulous food as enjoyable because they result in higher levels of dopamine in the brain; these higher levels permit more neural activity through the synapses that connect the circuits in the brain that regulate feelings of pleasure.

Recreational drugs make users feel good primarily because they affect the same receptors that are sensitive to the dopamine that is in the brain naturally. The molecules of addictive drugs are so similar to dopamine

Studies of juvenile mice have furthered our understanding of the impact of drinking on adolescent brain development.
Adam Gault/OJO Images/Getty Images

molecules that dopamine receptors act in the same way in their presence as they do in the presence of natural dopamine. As a result, when drugs enter the brain (which is where they go whether they enter the body through the mouth, nose, or blood vessels), they are "read" by dopamine receptors as the real thing. On the positive side, this makes the user feel good (the same way that natural dopamine does)—which, of course, is why people use drugs.

The problem, though, is that frequent drug use during adolescence interferes with the normal maturation of the brain's reward processing regions (Cservenka, Jones, & Nagel, 2015; Weissman et al., 2015). The animal studies referred to earlier have shown that experiences in early adolescence, when the limbic system is especially malleable, or "plastic," can *permanently* affect the way the brain functions (Spear & Swartzwelder, 2014). Repeated exposure to drugs during this period of heightened plasticity in the limbic system can affect the brain in ways that make it *necessary* to use drugs in order to experience normal amounts of pleasure.

How many exposures to a drug does it take to permanently alter the adolescent brain's dopamine system? No one knows for sure, and the answer varies from person to person, largely because of genetic factors (this is why some people are more likely to develop addictions than others) (Jordan & Andersen, 2017; Schlomer et al., 2017). People with more responsive reward centers, for example, are more likely to drink (Braams et al., 2016). We do know, though, that a permanent alteration in the dopamine system as a result of drug exposure is more likely to happen in adolescence, when the limbic system is still malleable, than in adulthood, when it is less plastic.

This is why exposure to drugs during adolescence is more likely to lead to abuse, addiction, and other psychological problems than is the same amount of exposure during adulthood (Bolland et al., 2016; Epstein et al., 2015; Scalco & Colder, 2017; Sittner, 2016; Swendsen et al., 2012). Compared with people who delay drinking until they are 21, people who begin in early adolescence (before age 14) are *seven times* more likely to binge drink as teenagers and *five times* more likely to develop a substance abuse or dependence disorder at some point in life (Hingson, Heeren, & Winter, 2006). Similarly, people who begin smoking regularly before age 14 are at much greater risk for nicotine dependence as adults than are those who start in late adolescence (Orlando et al., 2004). It's not simply that people who start using drugs early are different from those who wait in ways that make them more prone to addiction. Experimental studies with animals, in which some are randomly assigned to drug exposure shortly after puberty and others to exposure in adulthood, have proven that it is easier to become addicted during adolescence than during adulthood (Spear, 2016).

The increased vulnerability of the adolescent brain to the addicting effects of alcohol is compounded by the fact that adolescents don't feel the negative consequences of drinking as profoundly as adults do (this can only be studied experimentally in animals because researchers are not allowed to give teenagers alcohol). Studies comparing juvenile rodents with adult rodents find that juveniles can drink more than adults before they become tired or have their reflexes slow, and the unpleasant physical consequences of drinking too much (otherwise known as a hangover) are less intense among juveniles than adults. To make matters worse, juveniles feel the positive effects of alcohol more intensely than adults; alcohol makes juvenile rodents want to socialize, but it makes adults want to be left alone (Spear, 2013). And whereas the presence of "peers" increases alcohol consumption among juvenile rodents, it has no such effect among adult animals (Logue et al., 2014). Similarly, juvenile rodents are more likely to experience the rewarding aspects of nicotine exposure, including enhanced learning, than are older animals (Holliday & Gould, 2016).

Although the short-term effects of alcohol are less severe in adolescents than adults, the lasting effects of alcohol on brain functioning are worse in adolescence than in adulthood—again, because the brain is more vulnerable to influences during periods of plasticity. One area of the adolescent brain that is especially vulnerable to the harmful effects of alcohol and other drugs is the hippocampus, which is important for memory and, with the prefrontal cortex, for "putting the brakes" on impulsive behavior (Boulos et al., 2016; Silveri et al., 2016). Alcohol also has harmful effects on the development of regions of the brain involved in higher-order cognitive abilities, such as planning and decision making, and in self-regulation (Müller-Oehring et al., 2018; Nasrallah et al., 2011), although some of the association between heavy drinking and poor self-regulation is due to the fact that adolescents with weak self-control are more likely to drink (Peeters et al., 2015). Nonetheless, the fact that early exposure is more likely to lead to addiction and long-term use indicates that interventions designed to prevent substance abuse should begin prior to adolescence.

In recent years, scientists have conducted many studies of the impact of marijuana use on adolescent brain development (Hurd et al., 2019). It is now well-established that chronic use may be associated with brain abnormalities in many of the same areas that are also affected by drinking, including the hippocampus and prefrontal cortex, regions that play an important role in memory, advanced thinking abilities, and emotion regulation (Batalla et al., 2013; Camchong, Lim, & Kumura, 2017; Heitzeg et al., 2015; Lopez-Larson, Rogowska, & Yurgelun-Todd, 2015). Both early and heavy marijuana use are associated with worse outcomes than later or less frequent use, including cognitive deficits and diminished educational attainment (Castellanos-Ryan et al., 2017; Jacobus et al., 2015; Maggs et al., 2015; Sagar et al., 2015). There also is evidence that early marijuana use may lead to brain changes that increase the risk for depression, suicidal ideation, schizophrenia, and other psychotic disorders (Bourque, Afzali, & Conrod, 2018; Gobbi et al., 2019; Jones et al., 2018; Renard et al., 2017). Fortunately, there is some evidence that the adverse effects of marijuana use can be reversed by sustained abstinence (Scott et al., 2018).

Prevention and Treatment of Substance Use and Abuse

Efforts to prevent substance use and abuse among teenagers focus on one of three factors: the supply of drugs, the environment in which teenagers may be exposed to drugs, and characteristics of the potential drug user. One huge problem is that two of the three most commonly used and abused drugs—cigarettes and alcohol—are both legal and widely available, and laws prohibiting the sale of these substances to minors are not well enforced (Centers for Disease Control and Prevention, 2006). Research does show, however, that raising the price of alcohol and cigarettes reduces adolescents' use of them (Bishai, Mercer, & Tapales, 2005; Lovato et al., 2013), that raising the minimum legal drinking age leads to a decline in binge drinking among teenagers (but not young adults) (Andersen et al., 2014; Grucza, Norberg, & Bierut, 2009), and that raising the minimum purchase age for tobacco products lowers rates of teen smoking (Institute of Medicine, 2015). Attempts to enforce laws governing the purchase of cigarettes are less effective than those governing alcohol, in part because many adolescents obtain cigarettes through means other than purchasing them from stores (for example, bumming them from older friends or stealing them from parents) (Porkorny, Jason, & Schoeny, 2006).

Many different types of drug abuse prevention interventions have been tried, either alone or in combination. In programs designed to change some characteristic of the adolescent, drug use is targeted indirectly either by attempting to enhance adolescents' psychological development in general or by helping adolescents develop other interests and participate in other activities that will make drug use less likely. One reason that substance use is more common among teenagers from lower socioeconomic backgrounds is that they have fewer opportunities to engage in pleasurable activities that don't involve drugs (Lee et al., 2018). The idea behind these sorts of efforts is that adolescents who have high self-esteem, for example, or who are gainfully employed will be less likely to use drugs. In other programs, the intervention is directly focused on preventing drug use. These programs include information-based efforts (in which adolescents are educated about the dangers of drugs), social skills training (in which adolescents are taught how to turn down drugs), and some combination of informational and general psychological intervention (in which adolescents are educated about drug abuse and exposed to a program designed to enhance their self-esteem or social skills).

The results of research designed to evaluate these sorts of individual-focused approaches have not been encouraging. Careful evaluations of Project DARE—the most widely implemented drug education program in the United States—show that the program is largely ineffective (Ennett et al., 1994). Experts are now fairly confident that drug education alone, whether based on rational information or scare tactics, does not prevent drug use (Steinberg, 2015). This is reminiscent of research on sex education, which has shown that informational programs are simply not effective on their own. As a rule, educational programs may change individuals' knowledge, but they rarely affect their behavior. Research on the effectiveness of drug testing in schools has yielded inconsistent findings (James-Burdumy et al., 2012; Yamaguchi, Johnston, & O'Malley, 2003).

Successful Approaches The most encouraging results have been found in programs that do not focus only on the individual adolescent but rather combine some sort of social competence training with a communitywide intervention aimed not only at adolescents but also at their peers, parents, and teachers (Anderson-Carpenter et al., 2016; Liddle et al., 2009; Oesterle et al., 2018). These multifaceted efforts have been shown to be effective in reducing adolescents' use of alcohol, cigarettes, and other drugs, especially if the programs begin when youngsters are preadolescents and continue well into high school (Bruvold, 1993; Ellickson, Bell, & McGuigan, 1993; Flynn et al., 1994; Perry et al., 1996). Overall, most experts agree that efforts designed simply to change the potential adolescent drug user without transforming the environment in which the adolescent lives are not likely to succeed. Despite their intuitive appeal, efforts to help adolescents "just say no" have been remarkably unsuccessful.

One of the problems with all prevention programs is that they often do not distinguish between drug *use* and drug *abuse*. Trying to stop teenagers from *ever* using alcohol, for instance, is both unlikely to succeed and probably not a very wise allocation of resources, whereas preventing binge drinking and drunk driving are far more important—and attainable—goals.

Distinguishing between use and abuse is also important in treatment. Some experts worry that adolescents who are mistakenly enrolled in treatment programs (because their parents have overreacted to the adolescent's normative and probably harmless experimentation with drugs) may end up more alienated and more distressed—and more likely to become drug abusers—as a result of the "treatment." Evaluations of treatment programs for adolescents who are genuine drug abusers suggest that efforts that involve the adolescent's family, and not just the teenager, are more likely to be successful (Liddle et al., 2009). Unfortunately, many adolescents who would benefit from substance abuse treatment, especially those from ethnic minority groups, do not receive it, often because they can't afford it or have inadequate health insurance (Cummings, Wen, & Druss, 2011).

conduct disorder

A repetitive and persistent pattern of antisocial behavior that results in problems at school or work, or in relationships with others.

oppositional-defiant disorder

A disorder of childhood and adolescence characterized by excessive anger, spite, and stubbornness.

antisocial personality disorder

A disorder of adulthood characterized by antisocial behavior and persistent disregard for the rules of society and the rights of others.

psychopaths

Individuals who are not only antisocial but also manipulative, superficially charming, impulsive, and indifferent to the feelings of others.

Externalizing Problems

Experts distinguish among three main categories of externalizing problems in adolescence: conduct disorder, aggression, and delinquency. Although these three classes of problems are highly interrelated, their definitions differ.

Categories of Externalizing Problems

Conduct Disorder The first category of externalizing problems is **conduct disorder,** which is a clinical diagnosis that refers to a repetitive and persistent pattern of antisocial behavior in which the rights of others or age-appropriate societal norms are violated and, as a result of this behavior, the individual has problems in social relationships, school, or the workplace (see Table 13.3) (Farrington, 2009). (A related, but less serious, diagnosis is **oppositional-defiant disorder,** which refers to behavior that is spiteful, angry, and argumentative but not necessarily aggressive.) An estimated 6% to 16% of adolescent males and 2% to 9% of adolescent females have conduct disorder (Farrington, 2009). Conduct disorder is very stable between childhood and adolescence; about half of all individuals who are diagnosed with it as children are also diagnosed with it as teenagers, and many had oppositional-defiant disorder when they were younger. One reason for this is that the risk factors for these two disorders are pretty much the same (Boden, Fergusson, & Horwood, 2011).

Individuals who have been diagnosed with conduct disorder and who persist in their antisocial behavior after age 18 may subsequently be diagnosed with **antisocial personality disorder,** which is characterized by a lack of regard for the moral or legal standards of the community and a marked inability to get along with others or abide by societal rules. Some individuals with antisocial personality disorder are **psychopaths**—individuals who are not only antisocial in their behavior but manipulative, superficially charming, impulsive, and indifferent to the

Table 13.3 DSM-5 diagnostic criteria for conduct disorder

In conduct disorder, a repetitive and persistent pattern of behavior occurs in which the basic rights of others or major age-appropriate societal norms or rules are violated. This manifests as the presence of at least 3 of the following 15 criteria in the past 12 months from any of the categories below, with at least 1 criterion present in the past 6 months:

Aggression to people and animals:	• Often bullies, threatens, or intimidates others
	• Often initiates physical fights
	• Has used a weapon that can cause serious physical harm to others (e.g., a bat, brick, broken bottle, knife, gun)
	• Has been physically cruel to people
	• Has been physically cruel to animals
	• Has stolen while confronting a victim (e.g., mugging, purse snatching, extortion, armed robbery)
	• Has forced someone into sexual activity
Destruction of property:	• Has deliberately engaged in fire setting with the intention of causing serious damage
	• Has deliberately destroyed others' property (other than by fire setting)
Deceitfulness or theft:	• Has broken into someone else's house, building, or car
	• Often lies to obtain goods or favors or to avoid obligations (i.e., "cons" others)
	• Has stolen items of nontrivial value without confronting a victim (e.g., shoplifting, but without breaking and entering; forgery)
Serious violations of rules:	• Often stays out at night despite parental prohibitions, beginning before age 13 years
	• Has run away from home overnight at least twice while living in the parental or parental surrogate home or once without returning for a lengthy period
	• Is often truant from school, beginning before age 13 years

The disturbance in behavior causes clinically significant impairment in social, academic, or occupational functioning.

(American Psychiatric Association, 2013)

feelings of others, a cluster of characteristics referred to as **callous-unemotional (CU) traits** (Frick & White, 2008; Shirtcliff et al., 2009). Because the terms *antisocial personality disorder* and *psychopath* imply a deep-seated personality problem that is unlikely to change, experts advise against applying them to people younger than 18 because, as you will read, most individuals who engage in antisocial behavior as teenagers do not continue to do so after their mid-20s.

Social scientists disagree about whether it is possible to identify "juvenile psychopaths" or "fledgling psychopaths"—individuals who, despite their youth, exhibit many of the same characteristics as adult psychopaths and are likely to grow into them. Some contend that it is possible to do so (Frick et al., 2005; Lynam et al., 2009), while others note that some of the distinguishing features of adult psychopaths that are considered pathological (impulsivity, irresponsibility, instability in romantic relationships) may be transient characteristics that reflect immaturity, not pathology (Hawes et al., 2014; Vincent et al., 2003). Nevertheless, some adolescents have stronger psychopathic tendencies than others (Edens, Marcus, & Vaughn, 2011; Thornton et al., 2015), and while not all teenagers who score high on measures of CU traits grow up to be adult psychopaths, they are more likely to commit crimes as adolescents and as adults (McMahon et al., 2010; Moran et al., 2009). For this reason, when making a diagnosis of conduct disorder, practitioners distinguish between conduct-disordered adolescents with CU traits and those without them (Kimonis, Graham, & Cauffman, 2018).

Aggression   A second category of externalizing problems is **aggression,** which is behavior that is done to intentionally hurt someone. *Aggression* is a very broad term that includes physical fighting, relational aggression, and intimidation, and it can be either instrumental (planned) or reactive (unplanned).

It is very difficult to estimate the prevalence of aggression during adolescence because the category is so far-reaching. Virtually everyone has done *something* aggressive at one time or another, and about one-fourth of high school students report having been in a fight during the past year (Centers for Disease Control and Prevention, 2020). Most psychologists are concerned with adolescents whose aggression is persistent and causes serious injury to others. Aggressive behavior actually declines over the course of childhood and adolescence; in sheer quantity, the most aggressive period of development is the preschool years, when children frequently hit, kick, or bite each other, although aggression committed by adolescents is usually more serious than that committed by children (Bongers et al., 2004). Like conduct disorder, aggression is also very stable, although much more so in boys than girls (Broidy et al., 2003). One likely reason for this sex difference is that aggressive

little girls are more often forced to curtail their bad behavior than aggressive little boys are.

Juvenile Offending   The third main category of externalizing problems is **juvenile offending,** which includes **delinquency** (crimes committed by minors that are dealt with in the juvenile justice system), **criminal behavior** (crimes that are dealt with in the criminal justice system, regardless of the age of the offender), and **status offenses,** a special category of delinquent acts that are not against the law for adults but that nevertheless violate established codes of conduct for juveniles, such as truancy or running away from home (Woolard & Scott, 2009). Unlike conduct disorder or aggression, which are defined in terms of behavior, juvenile offending is defined legally. A large proportion of juvenile offenders have conduct disorder, and most are aggressive, but not all adolescents who have conduct disorder or who are aggressive are juvenile offenders because that depends entirely on whether they have broken the law.

Both violent crimes (such as assault, rape, robbery, and murder) and property crimes (such as burglary, theft, and arson) increase in frequency between the preadolescent and adolescent years, peak during the late high school

callous-unemotional traits (CU)
A cluster of traits characteristic of psychopathic individuals, which includes a lack of empathy and indifference toward the feelings of others.

aggression
Acts done to be intentionally harmful.

juvenile offending
An externalizing problem that includes delinquency and criminal behavior.

delinquency
Juvenile offending that is processed within the juvenile justice system.

criminal behavior
Crimes that are dealt with in the criminal justice system, regardless of the age of the offender.

status offenses
Violations of the law that pertain to minors but not adults.

Arrests for both violent and nonviolent crime peak in late adolescence. Carline Jean/AP Images

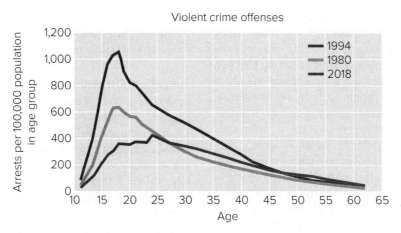

Figure 13.6 **Although the overall violent crime rate has fallen since it peaked in the early 1990s, the age-crime curve has barely changed.** (Federal Bureau of Investigation, 2020)

age–crime curve
The relationship between chronological age and offending, showing that the prevalence of offending peaks in late adolescence.

authority conflicts
A type of antisocial behavior characterized by stubbornness and rebelliousness.

covert antisocial behavior
A type of antisocial behavior characterized by misdeeds that are not always detected by others, such as lying or stealing.

overt antisocial behavior
A type of antisocial behavior characterized by aggression toward others.

years, and decline during young adulthood (Sweeten, Piquero, & Steinberg, 2013), a pattern seen for externalizing problems more generally (Petersen et al., 2015). The so-called **age-crime curve** has been remarkably stable over time and is generally seen around the world (Piquero, Farrington, & Blumstein 2003) (see Figure 13.6). In the United States, individuals under 18 account for 10% of all violent crimes, 11% of all property crimes, and 5% of all drug crimes (Federal Bureau of Investigation, 2020). The onset of serious delinquency generally begins between the ages of 13 and 16 (Farrington, 2009).

making the scientific connection

The age-crime curve is found all over the world. How do you account for this in light of the fact that the contexts in which adolescents develop vary so much?

Developmental Progression of Antisocial Behavior

Antisocial behavior can take different forms: **authority conflicts** (such as truancy or running away from home), **covert antisocial behavior** (such as stealing), and **overt antisocial behavior** (such as attacking someone with a

weapon). Within these broad categories, there are some fairly predictable progressions (Loeber & Burke, 2011). Authority conflicts usually first appear as stubborn behavior, which escalates into defiance and disobedience, and then progresses to more serious signs of problems with authority, such as truancy and running away from home. Covert antisocial behavior typically begins with such acts as lying and shoplifting; progresses to property damage, such as vandalism; and then to more serious property crimes, such as burglary. Overt antisocial behavior generally first presents itself as fighting or bullying, which escalates to such things as gang fighting and, ultimately, to violent criminal activity.

This is not to say that all bullies grow up to be violent criminals or that all stubborn preschoolers run away from home as teenagers. But the reverse is almost always true. Virtually all violent juveniles have a history of escalating aggressive behavior, most adolescents who commit serious property crimes started with less serious forms of overt behavior, and most chronically rebellious teenagers were oppositional children.

Some juveniles commit all three types of acts. Generally, the more serious an adolescent's behavior is in one category, the more likely he or she is to have displayed the others. That is, most adolescents who commit violent crimes have also engaged in covert and authority-related antisocial behavior, but not all adolescents who have conflicts with authority or who engage in covert antisocial behavior are necessarily aggressive (Van Lier et al., 2009). The authority conflict pathway almost always starts in childhood (contrary to the stereotype, few people suddenly develop serious authority problems for the first time as teenagers). The covert and overt pathways, in contrast, can begin either in childhood or in adolescence. As you will read, individuals whose antisocial behavior begins in childhood are very different from those whose antisocial behavior doesn't start until adolescence.

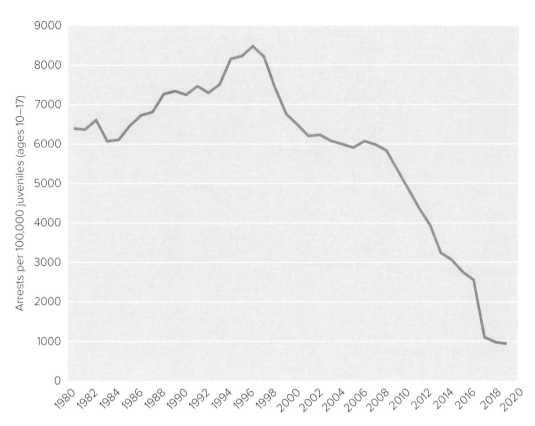

Figure 13.7 Rates of juvenile crime in the United States are lower than they have been at any time in the past **30 years.** (Office of Juvenile Justice and Delinquency Prevention, 2020)

Changes in Juvenile Offending over Time

When social scientists track changes in adolescents' antisocial behavior over time, they generally look at juvenile offending because statistics are kept on the numbers of juveniles arrested each year and the crimes with which they have been charged. Between 1965 and 1988, and especially after 1984, arrests increased substantially among young people. After 1996, crime among young people declined dramatically. As of 2016, crime among adolescents was at its lowest level since the 1970s (Office of Juvenile Justice and Delinquency Prevention, 2020) (see Figure 13.7). This is true for both violent and nonviolent crime; rates of fighting and violence that are not recorded as crimes have fallen as well (Salas-Wright et al., 2017).

Bad Girls Much attention has been devoted to what appears to be a substantial reduction in the gender gap in serious offenses over the past several decades (Sela-Shayovitz, 2016). Although antisocial behavior is still far more common among males than females, the male-to-female ratio in juvenile arrests for violent crime today is about 3.5 to 1—less than half of what it was in 1980 (National Center for Juvenile Justice, 2020).

It is not clear whether this change is mainly due to changes in actual offending or to changes in arrest practices. Changes in arrest rates can occur without there being any changes in actual offending (if, for example, the police crack down on crime, more people will be arrested, even if more people are not offending), and studies that rely on official statistics often reach conclusions different from those that rely on police or court records (Farrington, Loeber, & Stouthamer-Loeber, 2003). In fact, an analysis of data on actual offending found that there has *not* been an increase in violent acts committed by adolescent girls; rather, girls are simply being arrested more frequently for the same things they did in the past but were not arrested for (Steffensmeier et al., 2005). Analyses of underage drinking among girls have reached a similar conclusion: Although the proportion of girls who drink illegally has not increased in recent years, there has been a disproportionate increase in girls who are arrested for underage drinking (Zhong & Schwartz, 2010).

The ratio of males to females who have been arrested has changed not so much because of an increase in female offending but because the drop in juvenile offending since 1993 was much steeper for males than females (see Figure 13.8). If female offending remained relatively flat but male offending dropped by more than 50%, the ratio of male-to-female offending would be cut in half. Regardless of the size or causes of the gender gap in arrests, violent females have significantly more mental health problems than do violent males, consistent with

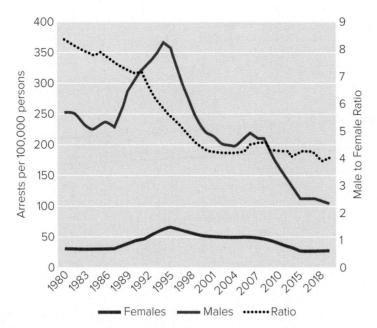

Figure 13.8 The gender gap in arrests for violent offending has closed over time, mainly because male arrests have dropped considerably while female arrests have not changed much. (National Center for Juvenile Justice, 2020)

the notion that gender-inappropriate displays of aggression may be indicative of greater maladjustment (Beaudry et al., 2021). Girls' antisocial behavior may be especially influenced by the boys who are their friends and boyfriends (Cauffman, Farruggia, & Goldweber, 2008; Lonardo et al., 2009).

Adolescents as Crime Victims Violent crime among young people is a significant and understandable source of worry to adults. But crime is also a major source of worry to adolescents themselves, who are the age group most likely to be *victims* of crimes such as theft, robbery, rape, and assault. Adolescents are twice as likely as adults to be the victim of a violent crime (Hullenaar & Ruback, 2020). In addition, worldwide nearly one-third of 11- to 16-year-olds say that they have been bullied or maltreated; few of these incidents are reported to legal authorities and are therefore not captured in crime statistics (Elgar et al., 2015; Fisher et al., 2015). Adolescent victims of violent crimes are more likely to report a wide range of problems than are other adolescents, including posttraumatic stress disorder, depressed mood, sleep deprivation, and academic difficulties, and they are more likely themselves to engage in aggression and antisocial behavior (Wylie & Rufino, 2018; Yu et al., 2018).

Adolescents living in single-parent homes in the inner city are disproportionately likely to be the victims of violent crime; although Black and Latinx adolescents are more likely to be victimized than white adolescents, this is due to the higher proportion of nonwhite adolescents living in single-parent homes in poor neighborhoods (Wright & Younts, 2009). For many adolescents growing

up in the inner city, gang violence and victimization are chronic problems. Among American 15- to 19-year-olds, homicide accounts for 43% of all deaths among Blacks and 17% of all deaths among Latinx youth but about 8% of deaths among Native Americans, 5% among Asian Americans, and 4% among whites (National Center for Health Statistics, 2015).

Violence and aggression among youth are strongly linked to poverty for a number of reasons (Stoddard et al., 2013; Stoddard, Zimmerman, & Bauermeister, 2012). First, as you've read, when families live in impoverished neighborhoods, parents are less effective in nurturing and monitoring their children, and this diminished effectiveness leads to increased aggression and crime. Second, concentrated poverty upsets the social fabric of a neighborhood, making it more difficult for adults and social institutions to provide the guidance and supervision that adolescents need. Third, in many inner-city communities devastated by unemployment, aggression is used by males to demonstrate their standing and power—characteristics that are typically demonstrated in middle-class communities through occupational success (Wilson & Daly, 1985).

Finally, the widespread prevalence of guns in inner-city neighborhoods changes the sorts of interactions that take place when adolescents fight, transforming what might have been aggressive disputes into lethal exchanges (Cook & Ludwig, 2004). The significance of neighborhood influences on violence has been confirmed in experiments in which poor families with adolescents were randomly selected to be relocated into better neighborhoods: After their relocation, rates of violent behavior among the

Table 13.4 Some major descriptive differences between street shootings and school shootings

Street Shootings	School Shootings
Less rare	Extremely rare
Concentrated in inner cities	Concentrated in rural towns and suburbs
Nonwhite offenders overrepresented	Mostly white offenders
Guns usually obtained from illegal gun market	Guns often obtained from family members who purchased them legally
Preferred weapon is a handgun.	Often multiple guns used, including semiautomatic rifles with high-capacity magazines
Many committed by recidivist violent offenders	Uncommonly committed by recidivist violent offenders
Offender commonly has a history of discipline problems.	Offender does not commonly have a history of discipline problems.
Co-offending typical	Solo offending typical
Prior criminal victimization common	Prior criminal victimization uncommon
Suicide combined with homicide uncommon	Suicide and homicide very common
Victims are mostly of same sex and race (often Black males)	Victims are usually mixed-sex (male and female) but of the same race
Victimization of family members highly unusual	Victimization of family members can occur prior to the school shooting.
Mostly from low-income families	Mostly from middle-class families
Offender substance use common	Offender substance use uncommon
Uncommon for offender to receive treatment for mental illness	Uncommon for offender to receive treatment for mental illness, but some symptoms of mental illness may be present
Generally, offender is below average in academic achievement.	Generally, offender is average or above in intellectual functioning and academic achievement.
Generally, offender personally knows someone who has killed or been killed.	Generally, offender does not personally know anyone who has killed.
Offenders avoid media attention for shootings because they don't want to be caught and prosecuted.	Offenders seek media attention for shootings.

(Bushman et al., 2016)

juveniles dropped significantly (Kling, Ludwig, & Katz, 2005), although some studies have found that these interventions are not universally successful (Nguyen et al., 2016).

School Shootings Several horrific school shootings, in which a young person murdered multiple students, have prompted recent debates about the nature, prevention, and causes of these events. Several conclusions have emerged from analyses of these incidents (Bushman et al., 2016) (see Table 13.4). First, school shootings are far more rare than shootings that take place on the street; the former are more likely to occur in rural or suburban communities, whereas the latter are more likely to take place in the inner city. Second, whereas perpetrators of street shootings typically use an illegally obtained handgun, school shooters typically use legally purchased, multiple weapons (often, semiautomatic assault rifles) that they obtained from family members.

Third, substance use is often associated with street shootings but rarely with school shootings; the reverse is true with respect to mental health problems, however. Fourth, whereas street shooters usually have extensive histories of violent offending, discipline problems, and exposure to violence (either as victims or witnesses), school shooters do not.

With regard to the prevention of these occurrences, most experts agree that it is far easier to prevent street violence than school shootings, oddly enough, because street shootings are so much more common. Massive amounts of information make the prediction of frequent events much easier than extremely rare ones, especially since the advent of data mining. As a result, many cities have implemented data-based statistical models that can map "hot spots" and identify individuals who are more likely than others to commit these sorts of crimes (because, as noted earlier, many are repeat offenders).

In contrast, because school shootings are so rare (despite the tremendous publicity they receive), it is impossible to predict which individuals will commit them or where they will occur. In the United States, around 1,500 school-aged individuals are murdered each year—but only 1% of these homicides take place in or around schools, and only a small portion of these are multiple-victim shootings (National Center for Education Statistics, 2020). While it is often pointed out that school shooters are more likely to suffer from mental health problems, the proportion of individuals with mental illness who commit violent crimes is very small. Any attempt to identify which teenagers with a mental illness will commit a school shooting will result in a massive number of "false positives" (things that are identified as having happened when they actually did not). Instead, limiting young people's access to firearms (and to assault weapons in particular) and encouraging students and others in the community to alert school personnel or law authorities when they have heard rumblings that "something bad is going to happen" would likely be far more effective.

Official Statistics Versus Adolescents' Reports

Official figures about adolescent crime both underreport and selectively report rates of juvenile offending (Farrington, Loeber, & Stouthamer-Loeber, 2003). Underreporting results from the fact that many adolescents commit offenses that are undetected by authorities or that are handled outside official reporting procedures, as when an adolescent who is caught shoplifting is reprimanded by the storekeeper instead of being referred to the police. Selective reporting results from the fact that poor and minority youngsters are more likely to be arrested and, if convicted, to be treated more harshly than other youngsters who commit similar offenses, so that official statistics may artificially inflate the proportion of crimes committed by poor, minority youth (Chauhan et al., 2010; Kakade et al., 2012; Rodriguez, 2010).

People hold such strong negative stereotypes about Black males that when provided with information about a crime committed by a male teenager and asked to evaluate the perpetrator, individuals who were unconsciously led to believe that the offender was Black were significantly more likely than those who were not to rate him as likely to reoffend in the future and as deserving of harsh punishment, an effect that was consistent regardless of the race of the rater (Graham & Lowery, 2004). Racial bias is especially strong in the processing of relatively more *minor* crimes, such as drug possession. When a very serious crime such as armed robbery is committed, juveniles of different ethnic backgrounds are likely to receive similar treatment because in many states, sentences for serious violent crimes are mandated by state law, and not up to the discretion of the judge (Cauffman et al., 2007).

An alternative to relying on official records is to go to adolescents directly and ask them about their involvement in various criminal or status offenses. Several researchers have done this, promising the respondents anonymity and confidentiality. The results of these surveys do not necessarily provide a more accurate picture of juvenile crime, but they certainly paint a different one. Two conclusions are especially interesting.

First, a very large proportion of adolescents—between 60% and 80%, depending on the survey sample—report having engaged in delinquent behavior at one time or another; nearly one-third of American 17-year-old boys have committed a violent crime in the past year, and nearly half of all males report being responsible for an assault sometime during adolescence (Farrington, 2009). Second, ethnic differences in the prevalence of self-reported offending are smaller than those derived from official records (Farrington, Loeber, & Stouthamer-Loeber, 2003). More minority than white youth admit to having committed a serious crime, but ethnic differences in self-reported offending are far smaller than ethnic differences arrest rates. There also are social class and neighborhood differences in rates of serious criminal activity, and because minority youth are overrepresented among the poor, they are also overrepresented among those who commit crimes (McNulty & Bellair, 2003). Delinquency is by no means limited to poor adolescents, however. Many adolescents in affluent neighborhoods report involvement in violent and serious delinquency (Singer, 2017).

Although studies indicate that most adolescents—regardless of their social backgrounds—do something that violates the law at one time or another, the vast majority of teenagers who violate the law do so only once and not violently. In fact, a relatively small number of adolescents—between 5% and 10%, depending on the study—account for most serious criminal activity (Piquero et al., 2003). It is important, therefore, in thinking about the causes of delinquent behavior, to distinguish between delinquent behavior that is serious and chronic and delinquent behavior that is less worrisome. As you will see, these two sets of delinquent behavior have very different antecedents (Moffitt, 2006).

Causes of Antisocial Behavior

The earlier an adolescent's "criminal career" begins—in particular, if it begins before adolescence—the more likely he or she is to become a chronic offender, to commit serious and violent crimes, and to continue committing crimes as an adult (Farrington, 2009). Conversely, the older an adolescent is when the delinquent activity first appears, the less worrisome his or her behavior is likely to become. For purposes of discussion, therefore, it is helpful to distinguish between youngsters who begin misbehaving before adolescence and those whose delinquent activity first appears during adolescence.

Two Types of Offenders   One of the most influential ways of characterizing these two groups of delinquents distinguishes between **life-course-persistent offenders** and **adolescence-limited offenders** (Moffitt, 2006). The first group demonstrates antisocial behavior before adolescence, is involved in delinquency during adolescence, and is at great risk for continuing criminal activity in adulthood. The second group engages in antisocial behavior *only* during adolescence; some adolescence-limited offenders become involved in crime relatively early in adolescence, whereas others begin during mid-adolescence (Fergusson & Horwood, 2002).

Some researchers have suggested that there are other groups of offenders as well (for example, individuals who do not start offending until adolescence but who continue on into adulthood and those who display antisocial behavior as children but desist before adulthood) (Evans, Simons, & Simons, 2016; Piquero, Farrington, & Blumstein, 2003; Veenstra et al., 2009), and others have pointed out that virtually everybody desists from crime by midlife, so that there really is no such thing as "life-course-persistent" offending (Sampson & Laub, 2003). Nevertheless, experts agree that the causes and consequences of delinquent behavior that begins during childhood or preadolescence are quite different from those of delinquency that begins—and typically ends— during adolescence or young adulthood (e.g., Dandreaux & Frick, 2009; Moffitt, 2006). Although many more males than females are life-course-persistent offenders, the risk factors for early-onset antisocial behavior are similar for the sexes (Fergusson & Horwood, 2002; Storvoll & Wichstrøm, 2002).

In other words, it's necessary to have information on the juvenile's behavior and history *before* adolescence in order to predict whether her or his offending is likely to be adolescence-limited or life-course-persistent because the best predictor of continued offending in adulthood isn't whether someone is antisocial in adolescence. It's the presence of serious antisocial behavior in childhood. Social scientists who have attempted to assess juvenile offenders' risk for future reoffending based solely on their adolescent characteristics have a remarkably poor track record (Mulvey et al., 2004).

Life-Course-Persistent Offenders   Youngsters whose problems with the law begin before adolescence are

It is important to distinguish between adolescents whose "criminal careers" begin early and those who do not engage in delinquency until they are teenagers. Early-onset offending is a risk factor for chronic criminality. Robert Nickelsberg/Getty Images

often psychologically troubled. Most of these delinquents are male, many are poor, and a disproportionate number come from homes in which divorce has occurred (Farrington, 2009). More important, chronic delinquents typically come from disorganized families with hostile, inept, or neglectful parents who have mistreated their children and failed to instill in them proper standards of behavior or the psychological foundations of self-control (Milojevich, Norwalk, & Sheridan, 2019; Thomas et al., 2018).

As Figure 13.9 illustrates, serious adolescent violence is typically the result of a cascade that begins early in life (Dodge et al., 2008). Early economic disadvantage in the home leads to harsh and inconsistent parenting, which leads to cognitive and social deficits. These deficits, in turn, lead to conduct problems, which contribute to peer rejection and academic failure in elementary school

life-course-persistent offenders

Individuals who begin demonstrating antisocial or aggressive behavior during childhood and continue their antisocial behavior throughout adolescence and into adulthood.

adolescence-limited offenders

Antisocial adolescents whose delinquent or violent behavior begins and ends during adolescence.

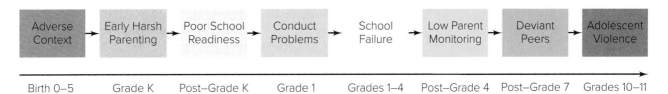

| Adverse Context | Early Harsh Parenting | Poor School Readiness | Conduct Problems | School Failure | Low Parent Monitoring | Deviant Peers | Adolescent Violence |

| Birth 0–5 | Grade K | Post–Grade K | Grade 1 | Grades 1–4 | Post–Grade 4 | Post–Grade 7 | Grades 10–11 |

Figure 13.9   Adolescent violence is often the long-term consequence of a process that begins early in life. (Dodge et al., 2008)

and, over time, a reduction in parental supervision and monitoring (Ettekal & Ladd, 2015). Once poorly monitored, adolescents tend to drift into antisocial peer groups, which heightens their involvement in violence.

The idea that family factors may underlie chronic delinquency—because of genetic factors, environmental influences, or both—is supported by observations that preadolescent delinquency tends to run in families. Many adolescents who have been in trouble with the law from an early age have siblings and parents who have had similar problems (Farrington, 2009; Tzoumakis, Lussier, & Corrado, 2012). Although studies have identified genetic influences on all types of antisocial behavior (Newsome & Sullivan, 2014), aggression is especially heritable (Deater-Deckard & Plomin, 1999; Eley, Lichtenstein, & Stevenson, 1999).

In addition to family factors, certain characteristics distinguish persistently delinquent youngsters from their peers at a relatively early age. First and most important, children who become delinquent—especially those who engage in violence—have histories of aggressive and antisocial behavior that are identifiable early in childhood (Okado & Bierman, 2015; Staff et al., 2015). Although this has been confirmed in hundreds of studies, it is important to keep in mind that the majority of children who have histories of aggressive behavior problems do *not* grow up to be delinquent. (If this seems confusing, think about it this way: The majority of delinquents probably have eaten in fast-food restaurants at some point in their childhood, but the majority of children who eat in fast-food restaurants don't grow up to be delinquent.)

Second, studies show that many children who become persistent offenders have problems in self-regulation (Fine et al., 2017; Mann et al., 2018; Modecki, Zimmer-Gembeck, & Guerra, 2017). They are more impulsive, less able to control their anger, and more likely than their peers to suffer from attention deficit/hyperactivity disorder (ADHD) (Ahmad & Hinshaw, 2017; Mohr-Jensen et al., 2019). ADHD is primarily biological in origin, strongly influenced by genes, and characterized by impulsivity, inattentiveness, restlessness, and inappropriately high levels of activity, especially in learning situations (Greven, Rijsdijk, & Plomin, 2011). Although ADHD does not directly cause antisocial behavior, it does elevate the risk for other family and academic problems, which, in turn, increase the likelihood of an adolescent developing externalizing problems (Sibley et al., 2014; von Polier, Vloet, & Herpetz-Dahlmann, 2012).

Current thinking is that chronically conduct-disordered adolescents are born with strong biological predispositions toward antisocial behavior, some of which are genetic in origin, including low levels of serotonin (which diminish their ability to delay gratification), an emotional system that is easily aroused and difficult to regulate, and a temperament that makes them hard to control and increases their

likelihood of rejection by peers (Buil et al., 2017; Piehler et al., 2020; Wang et al., 2017). One brain imaging study found that the connections between brain regions that are important for impulse control are less well developed among juvenile offenders (Shannon et al., 2011). Poor self-regulation is an especially potent risk factor for continued problem behavior (Chen & Vazsonyi, 2011; Gardner, Dishion, & Connell, 2008; Monahan et al., 2009).

Many researchers have examined the biological underpinnings of chronic antisocial behavior. There is considerable evidence that antisocial adolescents, especially those who are callous and unemotional (CU), have a significantly lower resting heart rate than other youth, which may indicate a biologically inherited tendency toward this trait (Latvala et al., 2015; Saunders et al., 2019). In addition, CU adolescents show a blunted biological response to emotional and painful stimuli, as evidenced both in neuroimaging studies (Blair, Leibenluft, & Pine, 2014) and in studies of reactivity to aversive stimuli (Haltigan et al., 2011; Rydell & Brocki, 2019). Because individuals high in CU traits don't experience distress as easily or often as others, they are less likely to empathize with others or behave prosocially (Shirtcliff et al., 2009). Some antisocial adolescents, especially those who have CU traits, show abnormal brain development in regions that govern how we process emotionally arousing stimuli (Herpers et al., 2014; Hyde, Shaw, & Hariri, 2013; Pincham, Bryce, & Pasco Fearon, 2015; Weissman et al., 2018).

All CU adolescents do not become delinquents, however; it also takes a willingness to engage in antisocial activity, sometimes referred to as "moral disengagement" (Cardinale et al., 2018; Hyde, Shaw, & Moilanen, 2010; Shulman et al., 2011). The identification of the biological underpinnings of problematic functioning does not necessarily mean that they are inborn or hard-wired. Child maltreatment, for example, has been shown to affect children's stress reactivity, which may be one reason that abused and neglected children are at greater risk for developing subsequent behavior problems (Trickett et al., 2011). There is also research showing that engaging in antisocial behavior can lead adolescents to become more morally disengaged (Sijtsema et al., 2019).

Third, and probably as a result of these biological inclinations, children who become chronically delinquent are more likely than their peers to score low on standardized tests of intelligence and neuropsychological functioning and to perform poorly in school (Cauffman, Steinberg, & Piquero, 2005; Raine et al., 2005). Some of this is due to genetic factors, but some is also due to conditions surrounding their birth and prenatal care. A disproportionate number of persistently violent adolescents were born to mothers who abused drugs during pregnancy and had medical complications during delivery that likely affected their baby's neuropsychological and intellectual development (Liu et al., 2009).

Especially aggressive youngsters also are likely to suffer from a tendency toward what has been called a **hostile attributional bias** (Dodge & Pettit, 2003; Fontaine et al., 2008). Individuals with this predisposition are likely to interpret ambiguous interactions with other children as deliberately hostile and to react aggressively. What might be viewed by the average adolescent as an innocent and accidental bump on the cafeteria line may be interpreted as an intentional shove by someone with a biased viewpoint, and it may lead to a fight.

Adolescents with a hostile attributional bias are more likely to believe that people's personalities are unlikely to change (Yeager et al., 2013). In addition, some adolescents have more positive views about using aggression to solve problems, and this inclination, in combination with a hostile attributional bias, leads to aggressive behavior that is almost automatic (Griffith Fontaine, Salzer Burks, & Dodge, 2002). This research has led to the development of interventions designed to change the way aggressive adolescents think about their interactions with others. Evaluations of Fast Track, a program designed to prevent disruptive behavior by improving individuals' social skills, found that reducing individuals' hostile attributional biases, as well as the extent to which they value aggression as a response to problems, led to a modest reduction in antisocial behavior (Dodge, Godwin, & Conduct Problems Prevention Research Group, 2013).

Because aggressiveness, impulsivity, hyperactivity, and intelligence are relatively stable, there is a great deal of continuity in problem behaviors over time (Wang et al., 2016). Studies that have followed individuals from childhood through adolescence and into adulthood find very high correlations between behavior problems at one point in time and antisocial behavior later in life (Farrington, 2009; Lussier, Farrington, & Moffitt, 2009). This does not mean that all individuals who show antisocial behavior early invariably show it later; in fact, the majority do not. Nevertheless, many chronically antisocial adolescents grow up to be adults who persist in their antisocial behavior and who are at increased risk for other problems as well, such as substance abuse and depression (Wiesner & Windle, 2006).

Adolescence-Limited Offenders In contrast to youngsters who begin their delinquent activity prior to adolescence (and who often continue their antisocial behavior into adulthood), those who begin during adolescence do not ordinarily show signs of serious psychological abnormality or severe family pathology (Moffitt, 2006; Van Lier, Wanner, & Vitaro, 2007). However, some individuals are genetically inclined to experience a greater-than-average increase in sensation-seeking during early adolescence, which contributes to increased delinquency as well (Harden, Quinn, & Tucker-Drob, 2012). Typically, the offenses committed by these youngsters do not develop into serious criminality, and these individuals

Some aggressive adolescents are prone to having a "hostile attributional bias"—they are more likely to interpret ambiguous interactions with others as intentionally hostile. Ken Karp/ McGraw Hill

do not commit serious violations of the law after adolescence, although they may be more likely to have subsequent problems with drugs and alcohol (Nagin, Farrington, & Moffitt, 1995).

In general, individuals who are involved in adolescence-limited antisocial activities have learned the norms and standards of society and are far better socialized than life-course-persistent antisocial individuals. Nor do adolescence-limited offenders show the sorts of temperamental difficulties and neuropsychological problems seen among life-course-persistent offenders (Moffitt et al., 2002). In contrast to the greatly disproportionate number of males who make up the life-course-persistent population (10 times more of these offenders are males than females), the ratio of males to females whose delinquency begins in adolescence is much smaller (about 1.5 to 1) (Moffitt & Caspi, 2001).

Although adolescence-limited offenders do not show the same degree of pathology as life-course-persistent offenders, they nevertheless have more problems during adolescence and early adulthood than youth who are not at all delinquent (Roisman et al., 2010; Sentse et al., 2017); although studies have found that many antisocial adolescents are nevertheless popular with their peers, there is no evidence that abstaining from antisocial behavior leads to peer rejection (Rulison, Kreager, & Osgood, 2014). One long-term follow-up of individuals who had earlier been classified as life-course-persistent offenders, adolescence-limited offenders, or neither found that the adolescence-limited offenders had more mental health, substance abuse, and financial problems as young adults than individuals who had not been

hostile attributional bias The tendency to interpret ambiguous interactions with others as deliberately hostile.

evidence-based practices
Programs and practices that have a proven scientific basis.

multisystemic family therapy
An intervention designed to reduce antisocial behavior that has been proven to be effective.

delinquent as teenagers (Moffitt et al., 2002). It is incorrect, therefore, to assume that just because an adolescent's antisocial behavior is limited to adolescence that he or she is not troubled. Their serious offending may be limited to adolescence, but other problems may persist into early adulthood.

The main risk factors for adolescence-limited offending are well established: poor parenting (especially poor monitoring) and affiliation with antisocial peers (Mercer et al., 2016; Ray et al., 2017; Wiesner, Capaldi, & Kim, 2012). The first of these (poor parenting) usually leads to the second (hanging around with antisocial peers) (Allen et al., 2019), often through the impact of poor parenting on school problems. Adolescents who have problems in school start spending time with antisocial peers, which leads to violence and other types of antisocial behavior (Dishion, Véronneau, & Myers, 2010). Influences on adolescence-limited offending are virtually identical for males and females and among adolescents from different ethnic groups and parts of the world (Fite, Wynn, & Pardini, 2009; Maldonado-Molina et al., 2009; Miller, Malone, & Dodge, 2010; Parks et al., 2020).

One of the strongest predictors of delinquency and other forms of problem behavior is the extent to which the adolescent spends unsupervised time in unstructured activities with peers—activities such as hanging out, driving around, and going to parties (Osgood et al., 1996). Most delinquent activity occurs in situations in which adolescents are pressured by their friends to go along with the group (Zimring, 1998). It is not coincidental that the peak years of susceptibility to peer pressure overlap with the peak years for this sort of delinquency. Indeed, adolescence-limited offending is largely done in an effort to impress other teenagers with one's bravado and independence from adult authority; nondelinquent youth often mimic antisocial peers to increase their status and popularity (Moffitt, 2006; Rebellon, 2006).

Prevention and Treatment of Externalizing Problems

Given the important differences between the causes of life-course-persistent and adolescence-limited antisocial behavior, it makes sense that these two groups of adolescents would be best served by different sorts of preventive and after-the-fact interventions. In order to lower the rate of chronic antisocial behavior, experts argue that we need mainly to prevent disruption in early family relationships and head off early academic problems through a combination of family support and preschool intervention (Loeber & Farrington, 2000; Tolan & Gorman-Smith, 2002).

There is also some evidence that interventions designed to improve the transition into school and work roles in young adulthood may prove helpful (Roisman, Aguilar, & Egeland, 2004; Stouthamer-Loeber, Wei, & Loeber, 2004). These sorts of preventive strategies are easier proposed than done, however. Society is hesitant to intervene to prevent family problems, and we typically wait until we see a sign of trouble in a family before acting.

Unfortunately, research shows that the outlook for delinquents who have begun criminal careers early is not very good, although evaluations of a variety of interventions that follow **evidence-based practices** (programs that have a proven track record) have been encouraging (Lipsey, 2009). This is the case for approaches that employ individual psychotherapy, family-based interventions, and diversion programs designed to remove delinquents from the juvenile justice system and provide them with alternative opportunities for productive behavior. One analysis found that every dollar spent on **multisystemic family therapy,** a proven intervention for antisocial youth (Weiss et al., 2013), saved taxpayers five times that amount (Dopp et al., 2014). In contrast, interventions that group antisocial youth together tend to be less effective because they may inadvertently foster friendships among delinquent peers, and more antisocial adolescents may teach less antisocial ones some of the "tricks of the trade" (Mager et al., 2005).

The prognosis for delinquents whose antisocial behavior is adolescence-limited is considerably better. Many juvenile offenders "age out" of crime; as they settle into adult roles, a criminal lifestyle becomes more difficult and less attractive (Massoglia & Uggen, 2010). Others go through a period of self-discovery, during which they decide that they want to change their lifestyle and become successful members of the community (Amemiya, Kieta, & Monahan, 2017). Because they have internalized a basic foundation of norms and moral standards, it is easier to help these youngsters control their own behavior and stop misbehaving.

Four types of strategies have been proposed. First, we can teach delinquent adolescents how to learn to resist peer pressure and to settle conflicts without resorting to aggression (Conduct Problems Prevention Research Group, 1999). Second, we can train parents to monitor their children more effectively, thereby minimizing opportunities adolescents have to engage in peer-oriented misbehavior (Forgatch et al., 2009). Third, by intervening within classrooms, schools, and neighborhoods, we may be able to alter the broader climate to discourage antisocial behavior and encourage prosocial behavior (Beets et al., 2009). Finally, by treating delinquency seriously when it occurs—by making sure that an adolescent knows that misbehavior has definite consequences—we can deter the teenager from doing the same thing again in the future (Scott & Steinberg, 2008). Treating juvenile offending seriously does not require that we incarcerate juveniles for long periods, however; this has been shown to be ineffective in deterring future crime (Loughran et al., 2009). In fact, policies that lead juvenile offenders to become more seriously involved in the justice system are more likely to increase reoffending over time than to reduce it (Beardslee et al., 2019).

Internalizing Problems

Most individuals emerge from adolescence confident with a healthy sense of who they are and where they are headed. But for some, the changes and demands of adolescence create feelings of helplessness, confusion, and pessimism. Although minor fluctuations in self-esteem during early adolescence are commonplace, it is not normal for adolescents (or adults, for that matter) to feel a prolonged or intense sense of hopelessness or frustration. Such young people are likely to be psychologically depressed and in need of professional help. Depression is by far the most significant internalizing problem that has its onset in adolescence.

Many adolescents have experienced bouts of severe anxiety as well, but these generally make their first appearance in childhood (Dalsgaard et al., 2020; Merikangas et al., 2010) (see Figure 13.10). Moreover, there is considerable comorbidity (the simultaneous occurrence of multiple health problems) between anxiety and depression in adolescence, with about 75% of adolescents with depression reporting symptoms of anxiety as well (Cohen et al., 2014). Although they are not the same, anxiety and depression share many of the same risk factors and respond to similar treatments (Silk et al., 2019).

The Nature and Prevalence of Depression

In its mild form, **depression** is the most common psychological disturbance among adolescents (Graber & Sontag, 2009). Although we associate depression with feelings of sadness, there are other symptoms that are important signs of the disorder, and sadness alone without any other symptoms may not indicate depression, at least in the clinical sense of the term. Depression has emotional symptoms, including dejection, decreased enjoyment of pleasurable activities, and low self-esteem. It has cognitive symptoms, such as pessimism and hopelessness. It has motivational symptoms, including apathy and boredom. Finally, it often has physical symptoms, such as a loss of appetite, difficulty sleeping, and loss of energy. The symptoms of major depression are the same in adolescence as in adulthood and among males and females, although, as you'll read, there are large sex differences in the prevalence of the illness (Lewinsohn et al., 2003).

Mood, Syndromes, and Disorder It is important to distinguish among depressed mood (feeling sad), depressive syndromes (having multiple symptoms of depression), and depressive disorder (having enough symptoms to be diagnosed with the illness) (Graber & Sontag, 2009). According to a large-scale survey of a representative sample of American teenagers, 37% of all high school students (and nearly half of all

depression
A psychological disturbance characterized by low self-esteem, decreased motivation, sadness, and difficulty in finding pleasure in formerly pleasurable activities.

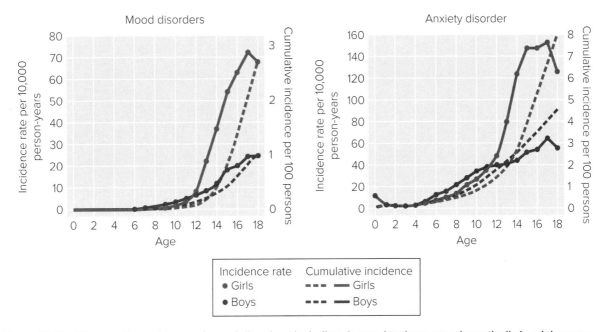

Figure 13.10 Whereas the incidence of mood disorders, including depression, increases dramatically in adolescence, the incidence of anxiety disorders increases most in childhood. (Dalsgaard et al., 2020)

Table 13.5 DSM-5 diagnostic criteria for persistent depressive disorder

The essential feature of persistent depressive disorder is a depressed mood that occurs for most of the day, for more days than not, for at least 2 years (at least 1 year for children and adolescents). Individuals with persistent depressive disorder describe their mood as sad or "down in the dumps." During periods of depressed mood (in children and adolescents, the mood can be irritable), at least two of the following six symptoms are present:

- Poor appetite or overeating
- Insomnia or hypersomnia
- Low energy or fatigue
- Low self-esteem
- Poor concentration or difficulty making decisions
- Feelings of hopelessness

Because these symptoms have become a part of the individual's day-to-day experience, particularly in the case of early onset (e.g., "I've always been this way"), they may not be reported unless the individual is directly prompted. During the 2-year period (1 year for children or adolescents), any symptom-free intervals last no longer than 2 months. The symptoms may not be due to the direct physiological effects of the use or abuse of a substance (for instance, alcohol, drugs, or medications) or a general medical condition (e.g., cancer or a stroke). The symptoms must also cause significant distress or impairment in social, occupational, educational, or other important areas of functioning.

(American Psychiatric Association, 2013)

high school girls) feel so sad and hopeless so often that they stop engaging in their usual activities, and each year, 19% of this age group seriously contemplate committing suicide (Centers for Disease Control and Prevention, 2020).

Fewer individuals report a pattern of depressive symptoms that includes a wider range of symptoms than sadness alone. About 13% of American teenagers between the ages of 12 and 17 (and 20% of girls this age) meet the DSM diagnostic criteria for a depressive disorder during the past year (Substance Abuse and Mental Health Services Administration, 2018) (see Table 13.5). As many as 15% of individuals will experience at least one bout of depression by the age of 18 (Merikangas et al., 2010). Visits to psychiatrists have increased at a much faster rate in recent decades among adolescents than adults (Olfson et al., 2014).

Depressed mood, depressive syndrome, and depressive disorder all become more common over adolescence, in part because of the increasing prevalence of stressful events during the adolescent years (Graber & Sontag, 2009) and in part because the cognitive changes of adolescence permit the introspection, self-criticism, and rumination that often accompany depression (Avenevoli & Steinberg, 2001). There is also a significant decline in positive mood over the adolescent years (Weinstein et al., 2007).

There is an especially dramatic increase in the prevalence of depressive feelings around the time of puberty; depression is one-third as common during childhood as it is during adolescence (Graber & Sontag, 2009). Symptoms of depression increase steadily throughout adolescence and then start to decline—making middle adolescence the period of the life span with the highest risk for the disorder. And because depression becomes increasingly more common with age among adolescent girls than boys, by age 17, 36% of girls and 14% of boys will have had at least one depressive episode (Breslau

et al., 2017). The increase in depression in early adolescence is so striking that some experts have called for universal screening in order to identify teenagers who may be especially vulnerable to the disorder (Hankin, 2020).

One intriguing idea links the increase in depression to the same changes in the brain's dopamine system that increase the vulnerability to alcohol and other drugs (Davey, Yücel, & Allen, 2008). According to this theory, the coincidence of increased reward seeking caused by this brain change with changes in the adolescent's social world leads to an intensification in adolescents' desire for the rewards of intimate friendships and romantic relationships. If these rewards don't materialize, adolescents may become frustrated and depressed. One reason that depression declines after late adolescence is that individuals report a significant decline in stress during this period (Seiffge-Krenke, Aunola, & Nurmi, 2009).

For reasons that are not entirely clear, there have been increases over time in the prevalence of depression, anxiety, and other signs of internalized distress, especially among adolescent girls (Substance Abuse and Mental Health Services Administration, 2018) (see Figure 13.11). Some writers have suggested that this trend is attributable to the increased reliance of adolescents, and adolescent girls in particular, on smartphones and social media for social comparison and self-affirmation and, as a consequence, their vulnerability to distress when they receive feedback indicating that they are unpopular or unattractive (Twenge et al., 2018). While this is an intriguing possibility, to date there is insufficient evidence to confirm or refute it. Other hypothesized contributors are increased academic pressure and uncertainty about the future (Denizet-Lewis, 2017). And, like their adult counterparts, adolescents' already high levels of anxiety have been exacerbated by the COVID-19 pandemic (Courtney et al., 2020).

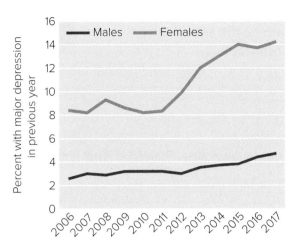

Figure 13.11 Rates of depression among American adolescents have increased substantially in recent years, especially among girls. (Mojtabai, Olfson, & Han, 2016)

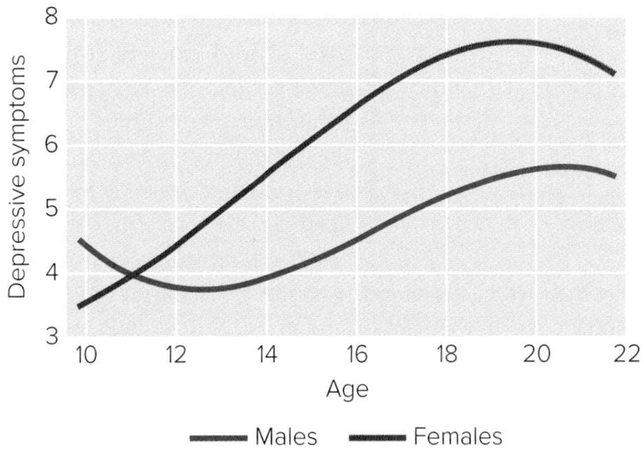

Figure 13.12 The sex difference in rates of depression emerges in adolescence but declines in early adulthood. (Kwong et al., 2019)

Sex Differences in Depression

One of the most consistent findings in the study of adolescent depression involves the emergence of a very large sex difference in rates of depression in early adolescence (Avenevoli et al., 2015). Before adolescence, boys are somewhat more likely to exhibit depressive symptoms than girls, but after puberty, the sex difference in prevalence of depression reverses. From early adolescence until very late in adulthood, twice as many females as males suffer from depressive disorder, and females are somewhat more likely than males to report depressed mood (Avenevoli et al., 2015). The increased risk for depression among girls emerges during puberty, rather than at a particular age or grade in school (Patton et al., 2008). It is well-known that rates of depression are about twice as high among adult women than men; it is less well-known that this sex difference is *entirely* due to the higher prevalence of depression among girls than boys, which persists into adulthood. Sex differences in the appearance of depression for the first time after adolescence (which is rare in either gender) are very small (Kwong et al., 2019) (see Figure 13.12).

Do Gender Roles Put Girls at Risk for Depression?

Social scientists speculate that the emergence of sex differences in depression has something to do with the social role that the adolescent girl may find herself in as she enters the world of boy-girl relationships, which may bring heightened self-consciousness over her physical appearance and increased concern over popularity with peers (Wichstrøm, 1999). Because many of these feelings may provoke helplessness, hopelessness, and anxiety, adolescent girls may be more susceptible to depressive feelings. To make matters worse, pressures on young women to behave in sex-stereotyped ways may lead girls to adopt some behaviors and dispositions—passivity, dependency, and fragility, for example—that they have been socialized to believe are part of the feminine role and that may contribute to their depressed mood. Depression in girls is significantly correlated with having a poor body image and being low in masculinity (Bearman & Stice, 2008; Eberhart et al., 2006). The gender-role hypothesis is only one explanation for sex differences in the prevalence of depression during adolescence. Three other accounts focus on sex differences in the degree to which adolescence is stressful, in how people cope with stress, and in vulnerability to different types of stressors.

Stress, Rumination, and Sensitivity to Others

The link between stress and depression during adolescence is well documented among both males and females; individuals who experience more stress are more vulnerable to depression and other internalizing problems, such as anxiety (Ge et al., 2009). But early adolescence is generally a more stressful time for girls than boys (Charbonneau, Mezulis, & Hyde, 2009). This is because the bodily changes of puberty, especially when they occur early in adolescence, are more likely to be stressful for girls than boys; because girls are more likely than boys to experience multiple stressors at the same time (for example, going through puberty while making the transition into junior high school); and because girls are likely to experience more stressful life events than boys, including sexual abuse and harassment (Graber & Sontag, 2009; Vaughan & Halpern, 2010). Although sex differences in major depression persist beyond adolescence, reports of depressive symptoms tend to diminish in early adulthood, but the decline is steeper among females, perhaps because they experience a greater drop in stress as they leave adolescence behind (Ge, Natsuaki, & Conger, 2006; Meadows, Brown, & Elder, Jr., 2006).

oxytocin
A hormone known to influence emotional bonding to others.

suicidal ideation
Thinking about ending one's life.

Second, girls are more likely than boys to react to stress by turning their feelings inward—for instance, by brooding about the problem and feeling helpless—whereas boys are more likely to respond either by distracting themselves or by turning their feelings outward, in aggressive behavior or in drug and alcohol abuse (LeMoult et al., 2019; Padilla Paredes & Calvete Zumalde, 2015). Girls' greater tendency to coruminate with their friends likely contributes to their greater risk for depression, too (Bastin et al., 2015; Stone et al., 2011). As a result, even when exposed to the same degree of stress, girls are more likely than boys to respond to the stressors by becoming depressed (Kiang & Buchanan, 2014; Rood et al., 2012). This difference in the ways that boys and girls react to stress helps explain why the prevalence of externalizing disorders is higher in boys, while the prevalence of internalizing disorders is higher in girls. Girls are also more likely than boys to tamp down positive feelings about themselves (Gomez-Baya et al., 2017).

A third explanation emphasizes girls' generally greater orientation toward and sensitivity to interpersonal relations (Guyer et al., 2009; Hankin, Stone, & Wright, 2010). Sex differences in levels of the hormone **oxytocin** may both encourage females to invest more in their close relationships and make them more vulnerable to the adverse consequences of relational disruptions and interpersonal difficulties (Bakker et al., 2010). Girls are much more likely than boys to develop emotional problems as a result of family discord or problems with peers (Owens et al., 2019; St. Clair et al., 2015; Telzer & Fuligni, 2013). Because adolescence is a time of many changes in relationships—in the family, with friends, and with romantic partners—the capacity of females to invest heavily in their relationships with others may be both a strength and a source of vulnerability.

making the practical connection

In light of what we know about the likely causes of sex differences in depression, what preventive interventions should be targeted at young adolescent girls?

Suicide and Non-Suicidal Self-Injury

According to recent national surveys, in any given year, nearly 11% of American female high school students and about 7% of males attempt suicide; nearly one-third of these attempts are serious enough to require treatment by a physician or nurse. More than twice as many adolescents think about killing themselves—referred to as **suicidal ideation**—than actually attempt suicide, but more than 80% of teenagers who have thought about committing suicide have gone so far as to make a plan (Centers for Disease Control and Prevention, 2020). Adolescents who attempt to kill themselves usually have made appeals for help and have tried but failed to get emotional support from family or friends. They report feeling trapped, lonely, worthless, and hopeless (Kidd, 2004).

The adolescent suicide rate among 15- to 19-year-olds increased alarmingly between 1950 and 1990, fueled by the increased use of drugs and alcohol and the increased availability of firearms (Judge & Billick, 2004). The rate peaked and declined somewhat during the 1990s. But the adolescent suicide rate began increasing again in 2007 and is higher now than it was 10 years ago (Centers for Disease Control and Prevention, 2020) (see Figure 13.13).

You may have read that suicide is a leading cause of death among young people (along with automobile crashes and homicide), but this is primarily because in the developed world, very few young people die from disease or illness. Although the rate of suicide rises rapidly during the middle adolescent years, it continues to rise

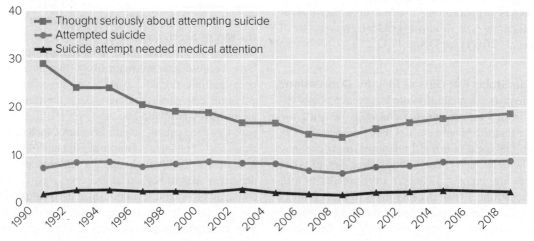

Figure 13.13 Suicidal thoughts and suicide attempts among U.S. adolescents, which had been declining, are on the rise. (Centers for Disease Control and Prevention, 2020)

throughout adulthood, and suicide is a much more common cause of death among adults than it is among young people, largely because very few suicide attempts by adolescents are successful. The most common method of suicide among adolescent and young adult males is using a firearm, followed by hanging or suffocation, and poisoning; among females, hanging or suffocation is most common, followed by using a firearm, and poisoning (Suicide Prevention Resource Center, 2020). Attempted suicide is most common among Native American and Alaskan Native adolescents and least common among Black, Asian, and Latinx adolescents; the rate among white adolescents falls between these extremes (Centers for Disease Control and Prevention, 2020).

Non-Suicidal Self-Injury Many adolescents do not contemplate suicide but commit acts of **non-suicidal self-injury (NSSI),** such as deliberately burning or cutting themselves (Nock, Prinstein, & Sterba, 2009). Nearly one-fifth of adolescents have engaged in NSSI (Valencia-Agudo et al., 2018). Many of the same risk factors associated with suicide, such as depression, hopelessness, or problematic family relationships, are also associated with NSSI (Gong et al., 2019; Zhu, Chen, & Su, 2020). There is also evidence that adolescents who commit NSSI score high on measures of impulsivity (Aldrich, Wielgus, & Mezulis, 2018; Hamza & Willoughby, 2019).

The most common reasons given for NSSI are to reduce feelings of tension, anger, anxiety, or depression, or to prompt feelings when none exists (Valencia-Agudo et al., 2018). Less is known about this group of adolescents than about those who attempt suicide, but levels of depressive symptomatology among adolescents who attempt to harm themselves, as well as risk factors for depression, fall somewhere between non-suicidal and suicidal adolescents (Brausch & Gutierrez, 2010; Guan, Fox, & Prinstein, 2012). Adolescents who engage in NSSI often have the same cognitive vulnerabilities associated with depression, which may actually lead to more rumination (Buelens et al., 2019; Tatnell et al., 2014; Voon, Hasking, & Martin, 2014). They are also more likely than other adolescents to have a friend who has attempted NSSI (Hasking, Andrews, & Martin, 2013; Schwartz-Mette & Lawrence, 2019).

Risk Factors for Suicide There are four established sets of risk factors for thinking about or attempting suicide during adolescence, and they are similar for males and females and among adolescents from different ethnic groups and different parts of the world: having a psychiatric problem, especially depression or substance abuse; having a history of suicide in the family; being under stress, especially in the areas of achievement; being victimized or bullied; and, especially, experiencing parental rejection, maltreatment, family disruption,

Some studies estimate that about one-fifth of American adolescents have engaged in non-suicidal self-injury (NSSI).
Sasa Prudkov/Shutterstock

or extensive family conflict (Forster et al., 2020; Holland et al., 2017; Koyanagi et al., 2019; Miller, Esposito-Smythers, & Leichtweis, 2015). Adolescents who have one of these risk factors are significantly more likely to attempt suicide than their peers, and adolescents who have more than one risk factor are dramatically more likely to try to kill themselves. Adolescents who have attempted suicide once are at risk for attempting it again (Lewinsohn, Rohde, & Seely, 1994).

One fascinating observation about suicide among adolescent girls is that the risk for suicide attempts may be greater during certain phases of the menstrual cycle (Owens, Eisenlohr-Moul, & Prinstein, 2020). Specifically, during the perimenstrual phase, which occurs about 2 weeks before menstruation, there is higher than usual variability in hormones that in some young women is associated with physical symptoms (e.g., headache, muscle pain), negative affect (e.g., depression, irritability), relationship problems (e.g., interpersonal conflict, rejection sensitivity), and diminished self-control

non-suicidal self-injury (NSSI) Deliberate attempts to hurt oneself in nonlethal ways, including cutting or burning one's skin.

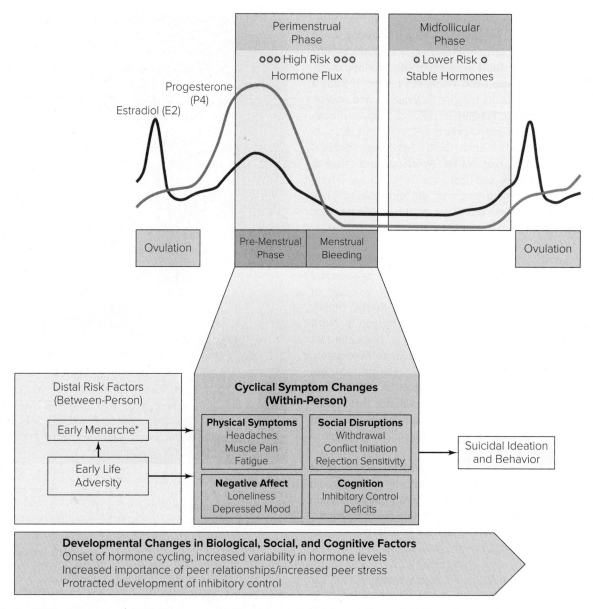

Figure 13.14 Women are more likely to attempt suicide during the perimenstrual phase of their menstrual cycle.
(Owens, Eisenlohr-Moul, & Prinstein, 2020)

suicide contagion
The process through which learning about another's suicide can lead people to try to take their own lives.

(e.g., impulsivity, emotionality) (see Figure 13.14). Although only a small number of girls are diagnosed with premenstrual dysphoric disorder (PMDD), many more have subclinical symptoms. These problems may be more pronounced during adolescence, when levels of various sex hormones are still fluctuating, and in combination with other risk factors, such as stress due to family problems or achievement pressures, they may prompt some girls to attempt suicide.

Suicide Contagion Adolescents are also more likely to attempt suicide if one of their friends or someone else in their community has committed suicide, which is

referred to as **suicide contagion** (Abrutyn & Mueller, 2014; Institute of Medicine, 2013). Teenagers are more susceptible to suicide contagion than adults. Studies of media reports show that adolescents are susceptible to both fictionalized (e.g., television dramas) and news reports of suicide, especially those involving celebrities.

The way in which a suicide victim is portrayed in the media has a significant impact on the likelihood that adolescents will copy the behavior. When the victim is portrayed as someone who is suffering from some sort of abnormality or psychopathology, there is far less chance that the suicide will be "contagious." When the victim is portrayed in a positive light, though, it increases the odds that adolescents who learn about it will attempt to take their own lives. Following the 2017 release of the Netflix

Following the 2017 release of the Netflix show 13 Reasons Why, *a series in which a young woman commits suicide, the suicide rate among American teenagers at the height of public interest in the program increased.* PictureLux/The Hollywood Archive/Alamy Stock Photo

show *13 Reasons Why,* a series in which a young woman commits suicide, the suicide rate among American teenagers at the height of public interest in the program increased 12% among males and 22% among females; no such increase was seen in any other age group (Bridge et al., 2020; Niederkrotenthaler et al., 2019). This is especially the case when coverage of the death presents a celebrity suicide as having been a means of liberating himself or herself from a painful situation. Suicide experts prefer that media coverage of celebrity suicides (which is inevitable) emphasize the fact that individuals who are under duress or hopeless seek treatment for their mental health.

Causes of Depression and Internalizing Disorders

A variety of theories have been proposed to account for the onset of depression and other types of internalizing problems during adolescence. The current consensus is that internalizing problems are likely to result from interacting environmental conditions and individual predispositions rather than either set of factors alone. Today, most experts endorse a **diathesis–stress model of depression,** which suggests that depression may occur when individuals who are predisposed toward internalizing problems (a diathesis is a predisposition to develop a particular illness or medical condition) are exposed to chronic or acute stressors that precipitate a depressive reaction (Auerbach, Eberhart, & Abela, 2010; Lewinsohn, Joiner, & Rohde, 2001). Individuals without the diathesis—who are not predisposed toward depression—are able to withstand a great deal of stress, for instance, without developing any psychological problems. In contrast, individuals who have strong predispositions toward the disorder may become depressed in the face of mildly stressful circumstances that most of us would consider to be normal.

Research has focused on both the diathesis and the stress—on identifying individual predispositions toward depression and on identifying the environmental circumstances likely to precipitate the disorder.

The Diathesis Two categories of predispositions have received the most attention. First, because depression has been found to have a strong genetic component, it is believed that at least some of the diathesis is biological in origin and may be related to problematic patterns of neuroendocrine functioning (**neuroendocrine** refers to hormonal activity in the brain and nervous system) with respect to how we react to stress and negative events (Kuhlman et al., 2018; LeMoult et al., 2015; Rakesh, Allen, & Whittle, 2020; Schuler et al., 2017). In particular, researchers have focused on the predisposition toward intense problems in the regulation of neural activity in brain regions that play a crucial role in stress reactivity (Paten, 2013). This biological predisposition may make it difficult for individuals to regulate their emotions, which, in turn, may make them susceptible to depression and other psychological problems (Miller et al., 2015; Silk et al., 2007).

Abnormalities in one of several genes, in particular, may make some individuals more likely to develop depression in the face of stress (Caspi et al., 2003; Hankin et al., 2015; Little et al., 2015). Not surprisingly, given the role that genes play in the development of depression, vulnerability to depression tends to run in families (Monti & Rudolph, 2017): Adolescents with a depressed parent are 3 times as likely to develop depression as are other youth (Graber & Sontag, 2009). There is also evidence that depression is more common among individuals whose reward centers show a blunted response to positive stimuli (Toenders et al., 2019).

Other researchers have focused more on the cognitive style of depressed individuals, suggesting that people with tendencies toward hopelessness, pessimism, and self-blame are more likely to interpret events in their lives in ways that lead to the development of depression (Burke et al., 2016; Koch, Mendle, & Beam, 2020; Mac Giollabhui et al., 2018; Shapero et al., 2017). These sorts of cognitive sets, which may be linked to the ways in which children think they are viewed, first by their parents and later by peers, develop during childhood and are thought to play a role in the onset of depression during adolescence (Abela & Hankin, 2011). Individuals who tend to ruminate in the face of stress are especially at risk for the development of depression and anxiety (Michl et al., 2013). And, as is true for reactivity to stress, there is some evidence that individuals' cognitive style is stable and

diathesis–stress model of depression
A perspective on depression that posits that problems are the result of an interaction between a preexisting condition (the diathesis) and exposure to a stressful event or condition.

neuroendocrine
Referring to activity in the brain and nervous system.

moderately heritable (Rudolph & Klein, 2009). There is also evidence that depressed adolescents show a blunted response to reward, praise, and other positive experiences but an exaggerated response to criticism and negative experiences (Fussner, Luebbe, & Bell, 2015; Silk et al., 2017; Stephanou et al., 2017).

The Stress Researchers who have been more concerned with the stress component of the diathesis–stress model—that is, with environmental influences on depression—have focused on three broad sets of stressors. First, depression is more common among adolescents from families characterized by high conflict and low cohesion, and rates are higher among adolescents from divorced homes (Griffiths et al., 2019; Hamza & Willoughby, 2011; Wang et al., 2020). Second, depression is more prevalent among adolescents who are unpopular, have poor peer relations, are bullied, or have friends who are depressed (Agoston & Rudolph, 2011; Mendle et al., 2010; Oppenheimer, Hankin, & Young, 2018; Swearer & Hymel, 2015; Van Zalk et al., 2010). Third, depressed adolescents report more chronic and acute adversity than nondepressed adolescents do, such as the loss of a parent, maltreatment, and poverty (Askeland et al., 2020; Lim, Rice, & Rhoades, 2016; McLaughlin et al., 2012). There is also evidence that academic difficulties are correlated with depression, especially among affluent suburban youth in the United States (Luthar & Becker, 2002). Although all sorts of stressors have been linked to the onset of psychological problems, the single most common trigger of the first episode of major depression in adolescence is the breakup of a romantic relationship (Monroe et al., 1999).

You read earlier that the prevalence of depression rises during adolescence. Can diathesis–stress models of depression account for this increase? For the most part, they can. Biological theorists can point to the hormonal changes of puberty because one of the effects of pubertal hormones is to make individuals more reactive to stress (Edwards et al., 2011; Heller & Casey, 2016; Walker, Sabuwalla, & Huot, 2004). Consistent with this, many studies show that the increase in depression in adolescence is more closely linked to puberty than age (Conley & Rudolph, 2009), although it is difficult to pinpoint puberty as the *cause* of the problem, since many other changes typically occur around the same time (such as the transition out of elementary school or changes in peer relationships).

cognitive behavioral therapy (CBT)
A type of psychotherapy, commonly used to treat depression and anxiety, in which the focus is on changing maladaptive and habitual patterns of thinking and acting.

interpersonal therapy (IPT)
A type of psychotherapy, commonly used to treat depression and anxiety, in which the focus is on changing dysfunctional patterns of interacting with others.

selective serotonin reuptake inhibitors (SSRIs)
A class of antidepressant medications that has proven to be effective with adolescents suffering from internalizing problems, such as depression.

Cognitive theorists can point to the onset of hypothetical thinking at adolescence, which may result in new (and perhaps potentially more depressing) ways of viewing the world (Kuhn, 2009). And theorists who emphasize environmental factors draw attention to the new environmental demands of adolescence, such as changing schools, beginning to date, or coping with transformations in family relationships—all of which may be stressful (Morris, Ciesla, & Garber, 2010). Thus, there are many good reasons to expect that the prevalence of depression would increase as individuals pass from childhood into adolescence. Individuals who develop internalizing disorders such as depression and anxiety in adolescence are at elevated risk to suffer from these problems as adults (Lewinsohn et al., 2003).

Treatment and Prevention of Internalizing Problems

The treatment of depression during adolescence is very similar to its treatment at other points in the life span. Clinicians use a wide range of approaches, including biological therapies employing antidepressant medication (these address the neuroendocrine problem, if one exists); psychotherapies designed to help depressed adolescents understand the roots of their depression, to increase the degree to which they experience pleasure in their daily activities, or to change the nature of their cognitive style; and family therapy, which focuses on changing patterns of family relationships that may be contributing to the adolescent's symptoms.

A recent comprehensive review found that psychotherapy with depressed and anxious adolescents has a very modest impact, leading some experts to call for more intense scrutiny of the factors that distinguish successful from unsuccessful approaches (Weisz et al., 2019). Although most of the treatment studies employed **cognitive behavioral therapy,** the review found that other evidence-based practices, such as **interpersonal therapy**, were equally, if not more, effective (Eckshtain et al., 2020). Importantly, evidence-based approaches are superior to approaches that do not have a scientific basis, which, unfortunately, are widely used (Beardslee et al., 2013; Weisz et al., 2009). With regard to antidepressants, research has confirmed the effectiveness of a class of drugs called **selective serotonin reuptake inhibitors (SSRIs)** in the treatment of depression in adolescence (Graber & Sontag, 2009). These medications are also effective in treating other types of internalizing problems, such as anxiety disorders and social phobias, especially when used in conjunction with cognitive-behavioral therapy (Brent et al., 2008; Kennard et al., 2009; Walkup et al., 2008). The use of antidepressant medications among adolescents has nearly doubled since the 1990s (Olfson, Druss, & Marcus, 2015).

Stress and Coping

Many adolescents report difficulty in coping with stressful situations at home or at school. These stressors include major life changes (such as a parental divorce, changing schools, or having someone in the family suddenly become seriously ill), chronically stressful conditions (such as poverty, a disabling illness, or constant family conflict), and day-to-day hassles (such as school exams, fights with friends, and arguments with siblings and parents) (Compas & Reeslund, 2009).

Stress can affect individuals in different ways (Steinberg & Avenevoli, 2000). For some teenagers, it can lead to internalized disorders, such as anxiety, depression, headaches, and indigestion—even compromised immune system functioning (Birmaher et al., 1994). For others, the consequences of stress are externalized, in behavior and conduct problems. For still others, the impact of stress is manifested in drug and alcohol abuse. These links between stress and psychosocial problems have been documented in studies of youngsters from all ethnic groups and family backgrounds and among youth exposed to both relatively common stressors (such as breaking up with a romantic partner) and relatively severe ones (such as exposure to war, terrorism, or natural disasters) (Gershoff et al., 2010; La Greca & Silverman, 2009).

Yet, for some adolescents, the very same sources and levels of stress do not seem to be associated with psychological or physical upset at all. Thus, although we tend to think of stress as having negative effects on our well-being, the connection between stress and dysfunction is not clear-cut. Some adolescents show enormous **resilience** in the face of enormous adversity (Compas & Reeslund, 2009). What makes some adolescents more vulnerable to the effects of stress than others? Psychologists point to three sets of factors.

First, the effect of any one stressor is exacerbated if it is accompanied by other stressors. Stress tends to have a multiplicative effect: An adolescent who faces two stressors at the same time (parental divorce and a change of schools, for example) is more than twice as likely to experience psychological problems as someone who has experienced only one of the two stressors (Compas & Reeslund, 2009; Sharma et al., 2019).

Second, adolescents who have other resources—either internal resources, such as high self-esteem, mindfulness, high intelligence, strong feelings of competence, or belief in the capacity for people to change, or external resources, such as social support from others—are better able than their peers to cope with stress (Galla, 2016; Monahan et al., 2016; Skinner & Saxton, 2019; Yeager, Lee, & Jamieson, 2016). Adolescents with close friends and good social skills seem to be better able to handle stressors such as parental divorce or starting junior high school than are teenagers who lack close friendships or have fewer interpersonal resources. Studies consistently show that the presence of a close parent-adolescent relationship is probably the single most important factor in protecting adolescents from psychological harm (Askeland et al., 2020; Raffaelli et al., 2013). The importance of social support as a buffer against the adverse effects of stress has been documented in studies of adolescents around the world.

Finally, some adolescents use more effective coping strategies than do others. Specialists who study coping strategies distinguish between strategies that involve taking steps to change the source of the stress, called **primary control strategies,** and those that involve efforts to adapt to the problem, called **secondary control strategies** (Compas & Reeslund, 2009). For instance, if you are very worried about an upcoming exam, a primary control strategy might be to form a study group with other students in order to review the material, whereas a secondary control strategy might be to go out to a movie or for a run in order to relax yourself. Individuals who use primary or secondary control strategies are better adjusted, less depressed, and less likely to have behavioral problems than those who react to stress through disengagement or avoidance (Carothers et al., 2016; Compas & Reeslund, 2009; Weisz, Francis, & Bearman, 2010; Sladek, Doane, & Stroud, 2017).

> **resilience**
> The ability of an individual to continue to function competently in the face of adversity or stress.
>
> **primary control strategies**
> Coping strategies in which an individual attempts to change the stressor.
>
> **secondary control strategies**
> Coping strategies that involve attempts by the individual to adapt to the stressor.

making the personal connection

How do you cope with stress? Are you more likely to use primary or secondary control strategies?

We tend to think of primary control strategies as particularly desirable, but in some situations, secondary control strategies are very effective. These tend to be stressful situations that are clearly uncontrollable, such as being diagnosed with a serious illness or learning that one's parents are getting a divorce (Hall et al., 2006). In these instances, trying to distract and calm oneself may help alleviate some of the stress, whereas trying to exert control over an uncontrollable situation may only make matters worse (Jaser et al., 2007). That said, adolescents who employ primary control strategies when the source of the stress is controllable are less vulnerable to its detrimental health consequences, which is a good reason to help teenagers develop these kinds of coping skills (Clarke, 2006).

Glossary

A

abstinence-only sex education   Programs that encourage adolescents to avoid sexual activity but that do not provide information about safe sex.

academic achievement   Achievement that is measured by standardized tests of scholastic ability or knowledge.

achievement   The psychosocial domain concerning behaviors and feelings in evaluative situations.

achievement attributions   The beliefs an individual holds about the causes of her or his successes and failures.

adolescence   The stage of development that begins with puberty and ends when individuals make the transition into adult roles, roughly speaking, from about age 10 until the early 20s.

adolescence-limited offenders   Antisocial adolescents whose delinquent or violent behavior begins and ends during adolescence.

adolescent egocentrism   Extreme self-absorption, often a consequence of too much "thinking about thinking."

adolescent growth spurt   The dramatic increase in height and weight that occurs during puberty.

adrenarche   The maturation of the adrenal glands that takes place during adolescence.

adult attachment interview   A structured interview used to assess an individual's past attachment history and internal working model of relationships.

adult plasticity   Relatively minor changes in brain circuits as a result of experiences during adulthood, after the brain has matured.

age–crime curve   The relationship between chronological age and offending, showing that the prevalence of offending peaks in late adolescence.

age grading   The process of grouping individuals within social institutions on the basis of age.

age of majority   The designated age at which an individual is recognized as an adult.

agency   The sense that one has an impact on one's world.

aggression   Acts done to be intentionally harmful.

AIDS (acquired immune deficiency syndrome)   A disease, caused by a virus transmitted by means of bodily fluids, that devastates the immune system.

alleles   Different versions of the same gene.

androgens   A class of sex hormones secreted by the gonads, found in both sexes but in higher levels among males than females following puberty.

anhedonic   Having difficulty experiencing positive emotions, a risk factor for depression.

anorexia nervosa   An eating disorder found chiefly among young women, characterized by dramatic and severe self-induced weight loss.

antisocial personality disorder   A disorder of adulthood characterized by antisocial behavior and persistent disregard for the rules of society and the rights of others.

anxious-avoidant attachment   An insecure attachment between infant and caregiver, characterized by indifference on the part of the infant toward the caregiver.

anxious-resistant attachment   An insecure attachment between infant and caregiver, characterized by distress at separation and anger at reunion.

attachment   The strong affectional bond that develops between an infant and a caregiver.

attention deficit/hyperactivity disorder (ADHD)   A biologically based psychological disorder characterized by impulsivity, inattentiveness, and restlessness, often in school situations.

authoritarian parents   Parents who use punitive, absolute, and forceful discipline, and who place a premium on obedience and conformity.

authoritative parents   Parents who use warmth, firm control, and rational, issue-oriented discipline, in which emphasis is placed on the development of self-direction.

authority conflicts   A type of antisocial behavior characterized by stubbornness and rebelliousness.

autobiographical memory   The recall of personally meaningful past events.

autoerotic behavior   Sexual behavior that is experienced alone, such as masturbation or sexual fantasizing.

autonomy   The psychosocial domain concerning the development and expression of independence.

B

baby boom   The period following World War II, during which the number of infants born was extremely large.

Bar (Bas) Mitzvah   In Judaism, the religious ceremony marking the young person's transition to adulthood.

basal metabolism rate   The minimal amount of energy used by the body during a resting state.

behavioral autonomy   The capacity to make independent decisions and to follow through with them.

behavioral decision theory   An approach to understanding adolescent risk taking, in which behaviors are seen as the outcome of systematic decision-making processes.

behavioral genetics   The scientific study of genetic influences on behavior.

big fish–little pond effect   The reason that individuals who attend high school with high-achieving peers feel worse about themselves than comparably successful individuals with lower-achieving peers.

binge drinking   Consuming five or more drinks in a row on one occasion, an indicator of alcohol abuse.

binge eating disorder   An eating disorder characterized by a pattern of binge eating that is not accompanied by drastic attempts to lose weight.

biosocial theories   Theories of adolescence that emphasize the biological changes of the period.

body mass index (BMI) A measure of an individual's body fat, the ratio of weight to height; used to gauge overweight and obesity.

brain function Patterns of brain activity.

brain structure The physical form and organization of the brain.

bulimia An eating disorder found primarily among young women, characterized by a pattern of binge eating and extreme weight-loss measures, including self-induced vomiting.

C

callous-unemotional traits (CU) A cluster of traits characteristic of psychopathic individuals, which includes a lack of empathy and indifference toward the feelings of others.

causation The correlation between two things attributable to the effect one thing has on the other.

charter schools Public schools that have been given the autonomy to establish their own curricula and teaching practices.

child protectionists Individuals who argued, early in the twentieth century, that adolescents needed to be kept out of the labor force in order to protect them from the hazards of the workplace.

chlamydia A sexually transmitted infection caused by a bacterium.

civic engagement Involvement in political and community affairs, as reflected in knowledge about politics and current affairs, participation in conventional and alternative political activities, and engaging in community service.

cliques Small, tightly knit groups of between 2 and 12 friends, generally of the same sex and age.

cofigurative cultures Cultures in which young people are socialized both by adults and by each other.

cognitive autonomy The establishment of an independent set of values, opinions, and beliefs.

cognitive behavioral therapy (CBT) A type of psychotherapy, commonly used to treat depression and anxiety, in which the focus is on changing maladaptive and habitual patterns of thinking and acting.

cognitive-developmental view A perspective on development, based on the work of Piaget, that takes a qualitative, stage-theory approach.

cohort A group of individuals born during the same general historical era.

collective efficacy A community's social capital, derived from its members' common values and goals.

Common Core A proposed set of standards in language arts and mathematics that all American schools would be expected to use.

comorbid Co-occurring, as when an individual has more than one problem at the same time.

comprehensive high school An educational institution that evolved during the first half of the twentieth century, offering a varied curriculum and designed to meet the needs of a diverse population of adolescents.

comprehensive sex education Programs that not only provide information about contraception, STDs, and pregnancy but also teach adolescents how to refuse unwanted sex and avoid unintended sex, increase their motivation to engage in safe sex, and change perceptions about peer norms and attitudes.

compulsive Internet use (CIU) Internet addiction.

concrete operations The third stage of cognitive development, according to Piaget, spanning the period roughly between age 6 and early adolescence.

conduct disorder A repetitive and persistent pattern of antisocial behavior that results in problems at school or work, or in relationships with others.

continuous transitions Passages into adulthood in which adult roles and statuses are entered into gradually.

conventional moral reasoning The second level of moral development, which occurs during late childhood and early adolescence and is characterized by reasoning that is based on the rules and conventions of society.

correlation The extent to which two things vary systematically with each other.

cortisol A hormone produced when a person is exposed to stress.

co-rumination Excessive talking with another about problems.

covert antisocial behavior A type of antisocial behavior characterized by misdeeds that are not always detected by others, such as lying or stealing.

criminal behavior Crimes that are dealt with in the criminal justice system, regardless of the age of the offender.

criminal justice system The system of courts and related institutions developed to handle adult crime.

critical thinking Thinking that involves analyzing, evaluating, and interpreting information, rather than simply memorizing it.

cross-sectional study A study that compares two or more groups of individuals at one point in time.

crowds Large, loosely organized groups of young people, composed of several cliques and typically organized around a common shared activity.

cultivation theory A perspective on media use that emphasizes the impact media exposure has on individuals.

cultural capital The resources provided within a family through the exposure of the adolescent to art, music, literature, and other elements of "high culture."

cyberbullying Bullying that occurs over the Internet or via cell phones.

D

date rape Being forced by a date to have sex against one's will.

delay of gratification The capacity to wait longer to get a larger, better, or more valuable reward instead of a smaller, less attractive, or less valuable one that is available immediately.

delayed phase preference A pattern of sleep characterized by later sleep and wake times, which usually emerges during puberty.

delinquency Juvenile offending that is processed within the juvenile justice system.

depression A psychological disturbance characterized by low self-esteem, decreased motivation, sadness, and difficulty in finding pleasure in formerly pleasurable activities.

detachment In psychoanalytic theory, the process through which adolescents sever emotional attachments to their parents or other authority figures.

developmental plasticity Extensive remodeling of the brain's circuitry in response to experiences during childhood and adolescence, while the brain is still maturing.

developmental trajectories Patterns of change over time.

diathesis-stress model A perspective on psychological disorder that posits that problems are the result of an interaction between a preexisting condition (the diathesis) and exposure to stress in the environment.

diathesis–stress model of depression A perspective on depression that posits that problems are the result of an interaction between a preexisting condition (the diathesis) and exposure to a stressful event or condition.

differential susceptibility theory The idea that the same genetic tendencies that make an individual especially susceptible to develop problems when exposed to adverse environmental influences also make him or her especially likely to thrive when exposed to positive environmental influences.

diffusion tensor imaging (DTI) A technique used to produce images of the brain that shows connections among different regions.

discontinuous transitions Passages into adulthood in which adult roles and statuses are entered into abruptly.

disordered eating Mild, moderate, or severe disturbance in eating habits and attitudes.

disorganized attachment A relationship between infant and caregiver characterized by the absence of normal attachment behavior.

divided attention The process of paying attention to two or more stimuli at the same time.

dopamine A neurotransmitter especially important in the brain circuits that regulate the experience of reward.

dyscalculia Impaired ability in arithmetic.

dysgraphia Impaired ability in handwriting.

dyslexia Impaired ability in reading or spelling.

E

early adolescence The period spanning roughly ages 10 to 13, corresponding roughly to the junior high or middle school years.

ecological perspective on human development A perspective on development that emphasizes the broader context in which development occurs.

educational attainment The number of years of schooling completed by an individual.

emerging adulthood The period spanning roughly ages 18 to 25, during which individuals make the transition from adolescence to adulthood.

emotional autonomy The establishment of more adultlike and less childish close relationships with family members and peers.

emotional intelligence The ability of individuals to accurately recognize and label their own emotions and those of others.

endocrine system The system of the body that produces, circulates, and regulates hormones.

epiphysis The closing of the ends of the bones, which terminates growth after the adolescent growth spurt has been completed.

estrogens A class of sex hormones secreted by the gonads, found in both sexes but in higher levels among females than males following puberty.

ethnic identity The aspect of individuals' sense of identity concerning ancestry or racial group membership.

ethnic socialization The process through which individuals develop an understanding of their ethnic or racial background, also referred to as racial socialization.

evidence-based practices Programs and practices that have a proven scientific basis.

executive function More advanced thinking abilities, enabled chiefly by the maturation of the prefrontal cortex, especially in early adolescence.

experience sampling method (ESM) A method of collecting data about adolescents' emotional states, in which individuals are signaled and asked to report on their mood and activity.

externalizing disorders Psychosocial problems that are manifested in a turning of the symptoms outward, as in aggression or delinquency.

F

false-self behavior Behavior that intentionally presents a false impression to others.

familism An orientation toward life in which the needs of one's family take precedence over the needs of the individual.

family capital The economic, social, and cultural resources provided by the family.

family systems theory A perspective on family functioning that emphasizes interconnections among different family relationships (such as marital, parent–child, sibling).

fear of missing out (FOMO) Excessive worry that others are having rewarding experiences that don't include you.

feedback loop A cycle through which two or more bodily functions respond to and regulate each other, such as that formed by the hypothalamus, the pituitary gland, and the gonads.

five-factor model The theory that there are five basic dimensions to personality: extraversion, agreeableness, conscientiousness, neuroticism, and openness to experience.

formal operations The fourth stage of cognitive development, according to Piaget, spanning the period from early adolescence through adulthood.

foster care A placement in a temporary living arrangement when a child's parents are not able to provide care, nurturance, or safety.

functional connectivity The extent to which multiple brain regions function at the same time, which improves during adolescence.

functional magnetic resonance imaging (fMRI) A technique used to produce images of the brain, often while the subject is performing some sort of mental task.

future orientation The extent to which an individual is able and inclined to think about the potential consequences of decisions and choices.

G

gangs Organized peer groups of antisocial individuals.

gateway drugs Drugs that, when used over time, lead to the use of other, more dangerous substances.

gender identity One's sense of oneself as male, female, or transgender.

gender intensification hypothesis The idea that pressures to behave in sex-appropriate ways intensify during adolescence.

gender-role behavior The extent to which an individual behaves in traditionally "masculine" or "feminine" ways.

generational dissonance Divergence of views between adolescents and parents that is common in families of immigrant parents and American-born adolescents.

gifted students Students who are unusually talented in some aspect of intellectual performance.

glands Organs that stimulate particular parts of the body to respond in specific ways to particular hormones.

gonadotropin-releasing hormone (GnRH) neurons Specialized neurons that are activated by certain pubertal hormones.

gonads The glands that secrete sex hormones: in males, the testes; in females, the ovaries.

gonorrhea A sexually transmitted infection caused by a bacterium.

growth mindset Believing that intelligence is malleable and can be "grown" over time.

H

herpes A sexually transmitted infection caused by a virus.

HIV (human immunodeficiency virus) The virus associated with AIDS.

hormones Highly specialized substances secreted by one or more endocrine glands.

hostile attributional bias The tendency to interpret ambiguous interactions with others as deliberately hostile.

human papillomavirus (HPV) One of several viruses that cause a sexually transmitted disease.

hypothalamus A part of the brain that controls the functioning of the pituitary gland.

I

iatrogenic effects Unintended adverse consequences of a treatment or intervention.

identity The domain of psychosocial development involving self-conceptions, self-esteem, and the sense of who one is.

identity diffusion The incoherent, disjointed, incomplete sense of self characteristic of not having resolved the crisis of identity.

identity foreclosure The premature establishment of a sense of identity, before sufficient role experimentation has occurred.

identity status The point in the identity development process that characterizes an adolescent at a given time.

identity versus identity diffusion According to Erikson, the normative crisis characteristic of the fifth stage of psychosocial development, predominant during adolescence.

imaginary audience The belief, often brought on by the heightened self-consciousness of early adolescence, that everyone is watching and evaluating one's behavior.

immigrant paradox The fact that on many measures of psychological functioning and mental health, adolescents who have immigrated more recently to the United States score higher on measures of adjustment than adolescents from the same ethnic group whose family has lived in the United States for several generations.

indifferent parents Parents who are characterized by low levels of both responsiveness and demandingness.

individuation The progressive sharpening of an individual's sense of being an autonomous, independent person.

indulgent parents Parents who are characterized by responsiveness but low demandingness and who are mainly concerned with the child's happiness.

information-processing perspective A perspective on cognition that derives from the study of artificial intelligence and attempts to explain cognitive development in terms of the growth of specific components of the thinking process (such as memory).

initiation ceremony The formal induction of a young person into adulthood.

intergenerational transmission of violence The frequently observed connection between exposure to domestic violence while growing up and later violence in adolescents' own romantic relationships.

internal working model The implicit model of interpersonal relationships that an individual employs throughout life, believed to be shaped by early attachment experiences.

internalizing disorders Psychosocial problems that are manifested in a turning of the symptoms inward, as in depression or anxiety.

Internet addiction A disorder in which an individual's use of the Internet is pathological, defined by six symptoms: salience, mood change, tolerance, withdrawal, conflict, and relapse and reinstatement.

interpersonal therapy (IPT) A type of psychotherapy, commonly used to treat depression and anxiety, in which the focus is on changing dysfunctional patterns of interacting with others.

intimacy The psychosocial domain concerning the formation, maintenance, and termination of close relationships.

inventionists Theorists who argue that the period of adolescence is mainly a social invention.

J

judicial bypass A regulation in many states that allows adolescents who want to abort a pregnancy but who are unwilling or unable to involve their parents in the decision to obtain permission from a judge to seek an abortion.

junior high school An educational institution designed during the early era of public secondary education in which young adolescents are schooled separately from older adolescents.

juvenile justice system A separate system of courts and related institutions developed to handle juvenile crime and delinquency.

juvenile offending An externalizing problem that includes delinquency and criminal behavior.

K

kisspeptin A brain chemical believed to trigger the onset of puberty.

L

late adolescence The period spanning roughly ages 18 to 21, corresponding approximately to the college years.

learned helplessness The acquired belief that an individual is not able to influence events through his or her own efforts or actions.

learning disability A difficulty with academic tasks that cannot be traced to an emotional problem or sensory dysfunction.

learning theories Theories of adolescence that emphasize the ways in which patterns of behavior are acquired through reinforcement and punishment or through observation and imitation.

leptin A protein produced by the fat cells that may play a role in the onset of puberty through its impact on kisspeptin.

LGBTQ youth Lesbian, gay, bisexual, transgender, and questioning youth, sometimes referred to as sexual-minority youth.

life-course-persistent offenders Individuals who begin demonstrating antisocial or aggressive behavior during childhood and continue their antisocial behavior throughout adolescence and into adulthood.

limbic system An area of the brain that plays an important role in the processing of emotional experience, social information, and reward and punishment.

long-acting reversible contraception (LARC) Methods of birth control that provide effective contraception for several years without requiring users to maintain them once they have been put in place, such as intrauterine devices (IUDs) and subdermal contraceptive implants.

longitudinal study A study that follows the same group of individuals over time.

long-term memory The ability to recall something from a long time ago.

M

mainstreaming The integration of adolescents who have educational handicaps into regular classrooms.

mastery motivation Motivation to succeed based on the pleasure one will experience from mastering a task.

media practice model A perspective on media use that emphasizes the fact that adolescents not only choose what media they are exposed to but also interpret the media in ways that shape their impact.

melatonin A hormone secreted by the brain that contributes to sleepiness and that triggers the onset of puberty through its impact on kisspeptin.

menarche The time of first menstruation, one of the most important changes to occur among females during puberty.

mentalizing The ability to understand someone else's mental state.

metacognition The process of thinking about thinking itself.

middle adolescence The period spanning roughly ages 14 to 17, corresponding to the high school years.

middle school An educational institution housing 7th- and 8th-grade students along with adolescents who are 1 or 2 years younger.

midlife crisis A psychological crisis over identity believed to occur between the ages of 35 and 45, the age range of most adolescents' parents.

molecular genetics The scientific study of the structure and function of genes.

Monitoring the Future An annual survey of a nationwide sample of American 8th-, 10th-, and 12th-graders, mainly known for its data on adolescent substance use.

moral disengagement Rationalizing immoral behavior as legitimate, as a way of justifying one's own bad acts.

multidimensional model of racial identity A perspective on ethnic identity that emphasizes three different phenomena: racial centrality (how important race is in defining individuals' identity), private regard (how individuals feel about being a member of their race), and public regard (how individuals think others feel about their race).

multiethnic Having two parents of different ethnic or racial backgrounds.

multisystemic family therapy An intervention designed to reduce antisocial behavior that has been proven to be effective.

myelination The process through which brain circuits are insulated with myelin, which improves the efficiency of information processing.

N

National Assessment of Educational Progress (NAEP) A periodic testing of American 4th-, 8th-, and 12th-graders by the federal government, used to track achievement.

negative emotionality The presumed underlying cause of internalizing disorders, characterized by high levels of subjective distress.

negative identity The selection of an identity that is obviously undesirable in the eyes of significant others and the broader community.

neuroendocrine Referring to activity in the brain and nervous system.

neurons Nerve cells.

neurotransmitters Specialized chemicals that carry electrical impulses between neurons.

new media Digital media typically accessed via computers, smartphones, or other Internet-based devices.

noncognitive factors Influences on achievement that do not have to do with intellectual ability, such as determination, perseverance, and grit.

nonshared environmental influences The nongenetic influences in individuals' lives that make them different from people they live with.

non-suicidal self-injury (NSSI) Deliberate attempts to hurt oneself in nonlethal ways, including cutting or burning one's skin.

O

occupational attainment A measure of achievement based on the status or prestige of the job an individual holds.

oppositional-defiant disorder A disorder of childhood and adolescence characterized by excessive anger, spite, and stubbornness.

organismic theories Theories of adolescence that emphasize the interaction between the biological changes of the period and the contexts in which they take place.

ovaries The female gonads.

overt antisocial behavior A type of antisocial behavior characterized by aggression toward others.

oxytocin A hormone known to influence emotional bonding to others.

P

parental demandingness One of two important dimensions of parenting; demandingness refers to the degree to which the parent expects and insists on mature, responsible behavior from the child.

parental responsiveness One of the two important dimensions of parenting; responsiveness refers to the degree to which the parent responds to the child's needs in an accepting, supportive manner.

peer groups Groups of individuals of approximately the same age.

perceived popularity How much status or prestige an individual has.

performance motivation Motivation to succeed based on the rewards one will receive for successful performance.

personal fable An adolescent's belief that he or she is unique and therefore not subject to the rules that govern other people's behavior.

pheromones A class of chemicals secreted by animals that stimulate certain behaviors in other members of the species.

pituitary gland One of the chief glands responsible for regulating levels of hormones in the body.

plasticity The capacity of the brain to change in response to experience.

platonic relationships Nonsexual relationships with individuals who might otherwise be romantic partners.

positive risk taking Risk taking that promotes healthy psychological development

positive youth development The goal of programs designed to facilitate healthy psychosocial development and not simply to deter problematic development.

possible selves The various identities an adolescent might imagine for him- or herself.

postconventional moral reasoning The level of moral reasoning during which society's rules and conventions are seen as relative and subjective rather than as authoritative; also called principled moral reasoning.

postfigurative cultures Cultures in which the socialization of young people is done primarily by adults.

preconventional moral reasoning The first level of moral reasoning, which is typical of children and is characterized by reasoning that is based on rewards and punishments associated with different courses of action.

prefigurative cultures Cultures in which society is changing so quickly that adults are frequently socialized by young people, rather than the reverse.

prefrontal cortex The region of the brain most important for sophisticated thinking abilities, such as planning, thinking ahead, weighing risks and rewards, and controlling impulses.

preoperational period The second stage of cognitive development, according to Piaget, spanning roughly ages 2 to 5.

primary control strategies Coping strategies in which an individual attempts to change the stressor.

proactive aggression Aggressive behavior that is deliberate and planned.

problem behavior syndrome The covariation among various types of externalizing disorders believed to result from an underlying trait of unconventionality.

prosocial behavior Behaviors intended to help others.

protective factors Factors that limit individual vulnerability to harm.

psychological control Parenting that attempts to control the adolescent's emotions and opinions.

psychopaths Individuals who are not only antisocial but also manipulative, superficially charming, impulsive, and indifferent to the feelings of others.

psychosocial Referring to aspects of development that are both psychological and social in nature, such as developing a sense of identity or sexuality.

psychosocial moratorium A period during which individuals are free from excessive obligations and responsibilities and can therefore experiment with different roles and personalities.

puberty The biological changes of adolescence.

Q

quinceañera An elaborate sort of "coming-out" celebration for adolescent girls that is practiced in many Latinx communities.

R

reactive aggression Aggressive behavior that is unplanned and impulsive.

reaffiliation motive The normal and adaptive motivation that most of us have, which prompts us to reconnect with others when we feel lonely.

reference group A group against which an individual compares him or herself.

rejection sensitivity Heightened vulnerability to being rejected by others.

relational aggression Acts intended to harm another through the manipulation of his or her relationships with others, as in malicious gossip.

religiosity The degree to which one engages in religious practices, such as attending services.

reminiscence bump The fact that experiences from adolescence are generally recalled more than experiences from other stages of life.

resilience The ability of an individual to continue to function competently in the face of adversity or stress.

response inhibition The suppression of a behavior that is inappropriate or no longer required.

reverse causation Relationship in which the correlation between two things is due not to the first thing causing the second but to the second causing the first.

risk factors Factors that increase the likelihood of some behavior or condition.

rite of passage A ceremony or ritual marking an individual's transition from one social status to another, especially marking the young person's transition to adulthood.

routine activity theory A perspective on adolescence that views unstructured, unsupervised time with peers as a main cause of misbehavior.

S

scaffolding Structuring a learning situation so that it is just within the reach of the student.

scarification The intentional creation of scars on some part or parts of the body, often done as part of an initiation ceremony.

school performance A measure of achievement based on an individual's grades in school.

schools within schools Subdivisions of the student body within large schools created to foster feelings of belongingness.

secondary control strategies Coping strategies that involve attempts by the individual to adapt to the stressor.

secondary education Middle schools, junior high schools, and high schools.

secondary sex characteristics The manifestations of sexual maturity at puberty, including the development of breasts, the growth of facial and body hair, and changes in the voice.

secular trend The tendency, over the past two centuries, for individuals to be larger in stature and to reach puberty earlier, primarily because of improvements in health and nutrition.

secure attachment A healthy attachment between infant and caregiver, characterized by trust.

selective attention The process by which we focus on one stimulus while tuning out another.

selective serotonin reuptake inhibitors (SSRIs) A class of antidepressant medications that has proven to be effective with adolescents suffering from internalizing problems, such as depression.

self-conceptions The collection of traits and attributes that individuals use to describe or characterize themselves.

self-consciousness The degree to which an individual is preoccupied with his or her self-image.

self-efficacy The sense that an individual has some control over his or her life.

self-esteem The degree to which individuals feel positively or negatively about themselves.

self-fulfilling prophecy The idea that individuals' behavior is influenced by others' expectations for them.

self-handicapping Deliberately behaving in ways that will likely interfere with doing well in order to have an excuse for failing.

self-image stability The degree to which an individual's self-image changes from day to day.

sensation seeking The pursuit of experiences that are novel or exciting.

sense of identity The extent to which individuals feel secure about who they are and who they are becoming.

sensorimotor period The first stage of cognitive development, according to Piaget, spanning the period roughly between birth and age 2.

serotonin A neurotransmitter that is especially important for the experience of different moods.

service learning The process of learning through involvement in community service.

set point A physiological level or setting (e.g., of a specific hormone) that the body attempts to maintain through a self-regulating system.

sexting Sending sexually explicit content, usually pictures, over the Internet.

sexual orientation Whether one is sexually attracted to individuals of the same sex, other sex, or both.

sexual socialization The process through which adolescents are exposed to and educated about sexuality.

sexuality The psychosocial domain concerning the development and expression of sexual feelings.

sexually transmitted disease (STD) Any of a group of infections—including HPV, gonorrhea, trichomoniasis, herpes, chlamydia, and AIDS—passed on through sexual contact.

sexual-minority youth Lesbian, gay, bisexual, transgender, and questioning (LGBTQ) youth.

shared environmental influences Nongenetic influences that make individuals living in the same family similar to each other.

sibling rivalry Competition between siblings, often for parental attention.

social capital The interpersonal resources available to an adolescent or family.

social cognition The aspect of cognition that concerns thinking about other people, about interpersonal relations, and about social institutions.

social control theory A theory of delinquency that links deviance with the absence of bonds to society's main institutions.

social conventions The norms that govern everyday behavior in social situations.

social promotion The practice of promoting students from one grade to the next automatically, regardless of their school performance.

social redefinition The process through which an individual's position or status is redefined by society.

social support The extent to which an individual receives emotional or instrumental assistance from his or her social network.

sociological theories Theories of adolescence that emphasize the ways in which adolescents, as a group, are treated by society.

sociometric popularity How well-liked an individual is.

spirituality The degree to which one places importance on the quest for answers to questions about God and the meaning of life.

spurious causation Relationship in which the correlation between two things is due to the fact that each of them is correlated with some third factor.

standards-based reform Policies designed to improve achievement by holding schools and students to a predetermined set of standards measured by achievement tests.

status offense A violation of the law that pertains to minors but not adults.

statutory rape Sex between two individuals, even when it is consensual, when at least one of the persons is below the legal age of consent; in the United States, the specific age of consent varies from state to state.

stereotype threat The harmful effect that exposure to stereotypes about ethnic or sex differences in ability has on student performance.

student engagement The extent to which students are psychologically committed to learning and mastering the material rather than simply completing the assigned work.

subjective social status Where one believes he or she ranks socio-economically (regardless of his or her actual socioeconomic class).

substance abuse The misuse of alcohol or other drugs to a degree that causes problems in the individual's life.

suicidal ideation Thinking about ending one's life.

suicide contagion The process through which learning about another's suicide can lead people to try to take their own lives.

synapse The gap in space between neurons, across which neurotransmitters carry electrical impulses.

synaptic pruning The process through which unnecessary connections between neurons are eliminated, improving the efficiency of information processing.

T

Tanner stages A widely used system that describes the five stages of pubertal development.

teenager A term popularized about 50 years ago to refer to young people; it connoted a more frivolous and lighthearted image than did *adolescent*.

testes The male gonads.

testosterone One of the sex hormones secreted by the gonads, found in both sexes but in higher levels among males than females.

theory of mind The ability to understand that others have beliefs, intentions, and knowledge that may be different from one's own.

tracking The practice of separating students into ability groups, so that they take classes with peers at the same skill level.

transgender Having a gender identity that differs from the sex one was assigned at birth.

trichomoniasis A sexually transmitted infection caused by a parasite.

U

underachievers Individuals whose actual school performance is lower than what would be expected on the basis of objective measures of their aptitude or intelligence.

uses and gratification approach A perspective on media use that emphasizes the active role users play in selecting the media to which they are exposed.

V

vouchers Government-subsidized vouchers that can be used for private school tuition.

W

work values The particular sorts of rewards an individual looks for in a job (extrinsic, intrinsic, social, altruistic, security, influence, leisure).

working memory That aspect of memory in which information is held for a short time while a problem is being solved.

Y

Yerkes-Dodson law A basic psychological principle that states that performance is impaired by too little or too much arousal or anxiety.

youth Today, a term used to refer to individuals ages 18 to 22; it once referred to individuals ages 12 to 24.

Z

zero tolerance A get-tough approach to adolescent misbehavior that responds seriously or excessively to the first infraction.

zone of proximal development In Vygotsky's theory, the level of challenge that is still within the individual's reach but that forces an individual to develop more advanced skills.

References

Abar, C. C., Jackson, K. M., Colby, S. M., & Barnett, N. P. (2015). Parent-child discrepancies in reports of parental monitoring and their relationship to adolescent alcohol-related behaviors. *Journal of Youth and Adolescence, 44,* 1688-1701.

Abe, Y., Barker, L. T., Chan, V., & Eucogo, J. (2016). Culturally responsive adolescent pregnancy and sexually transmitted infection prevention program for middle school students in Hawai'i. *American Journal of Public Health, 106,* S110-S116.

Abela, J., & Hankin, B. (2011). Rumination as a vulnerability factor to depression during the transition from early to middle adolescence: A multiwave longitudinal study. *Journal of Abnormal Psychology, 120,* 259-271.

Ablard, K., & Mills, C. (1996). Implicit theories of intelligence and self-perceptions of academically talented adolescents and children. *Journal of Youth and Adolescence, 25,* 137-148.

Abma, J., Driscoll, A., & Moore, K. (1998). Young women's degree of control over first intercourse: An exploratory analysis. *Family Planning Perspectives, 30,* 12-18.

Abo-Zena, M. (2019). Being young, Muslim, and female: Youth perspectives on the intersection of religious and gender identities. *Journal of Research on Adolescence, 29,* 308-320.

Abrutyn, S., & Mueller, A. (2014). Are suicidal behaviors contagious in adolescence? Using longitudinal data to examine suicide suggestion. *American Sociological Review, 79,* 211-227.

Aceves, L., Bámaca-Colbert, M., & Robins, R. (2020). Longitudinal linkages among parents' educational expectations, youth's educational expectations, and competence in Mexican-origin families. *Journal of Youth and Adolescence, 49,* 32-48.

Ackerman, R., Kashy, D., Donnellan, M., Neppl, T., Lorenz, F., & Conger, R. D. (2013). The interpersonal legacy of a positive family climate in adolescence. *Psychological Science, 24,* 243-250.

ACLU. (2021). Laws restricting teenagers' access to abortion. https://www.aclu.org/other/laws-restricting-teenagers-access-abortion. Accessed on January 14, 2021.

Adachi, P., & Willoughby, T. (2013a). More than just fun and games: The longitudinal relationships between strategic video games, self-reported problem solving skills, and academic grades. *Journal of Youth & Adolescence, 42,* 1041-1052.

Adachi, P., & Willoughby, T. (2013b). Demolishing the competition: The longitudinal link between competitive video games, competitive gambling, and aggression. *Journal of Youth & Adolescence, 42,* 1090-1104.

Adachi, P., & Willoughby, T. (2015). From the couch to the sports field: The longitudinal associations between sports video game play, self-esteem, and involvement in sports. *Psychology of Popular Media Culture, 4,* 329-341.

Adachi, P., & Willoughby, T. (2016). The longitudinal association between competitive video game play and aggression among adolescents and young adults. *Child Development, 87,* 1877-1892.

Adachi, P. J. C., & Willoughby, T. (2017). The link between playing video games and positive youth outcomes. *Child Development Perspectives, 11,* 202-206.

Adam, E., Chyu, L., Hoyt, L., Doane, L., Boisjoly, J., Duncan, G., & McDade, T. (2011). Adverse adolescent relationship histories and young adult health: Cumulative effects of loneliness, low parental support, relationship instability, intimate partner violence, and loss. *Journal of Adolescent Health, 49,* 278-286.

Adams, R., & Laursen, B. (2001). The organization and dynamics of adolescent conflict with parents and friends. *Journal of Marriage and the Family, 63,* 97-110.

Adams, R., Bukowski, W., & Bagwell, C. (2005). Stability of aggression during early adolescence as moderated by reciprocated friendship status and friend's aggression. *International Journal of Behavioral Development, 29,* 139.

Adams, T., Handley, E., Manly, J., Cicchetti, D., & Toth, S. (2019). Intimate partner violence as a mechanism underlying the intergenerational transmission of maltreatment among economically disadvantaged mothers and their adolescent daughters. *Development and Psychopathology, 31,* 83-93.

Adelson, J. (1972). The political imagination of the young adolescent. In J. Kagan & R. Coles (Eds.), *Twelve to sixteen: Early adolescence.* New York: Norton.

Adhia, A., Drolette, L., Vander Stoep, A., Valencia, E., & Kernic, M. (2019). The impact of exposure to parental intimate partner violence on adolescent precocious transitions to adulthood. *Journal of Adolescence, 77,* 179-187.

Adiele, I., & Olatokun, W. (2014). Prevalence and determinants of Internet addiction among adolescents. *Computers in Human Behavior, 32,* 100-110.

Adler, N., Ozer, E. J., & Tschann, J. (2003). Abortion among adolescents. *American Psychologist, 58,* 211-217.

Adolescent Sleep Working Group, Committee on Adolescence, Council on School Health. (2014). School start times for adolescents. *Pediatrics, 134,* 642-649.

Adrian, M., Jenness, J., Kuehn, K., Smith, M., & McLaughlin, K. (2019). Emotion regulation processes linking peer victimization to anxiety and depression symptoms in adolescence. *Development and Psychopathology, 31,* 999-1009.

Affrunti, N., Suárez, L., & Simpson, D. (2018). Community violence and posttraumatic stress disorder symptoms in urban youth: The moderating influence of friend and parent support. *Journal of Community Psychology, 46,* 636-650.

Afia, K., Dion, E., Dupéré, V., Archambault, I., & Toste, J. (2019). Parenting practices during middle adolescence and high school dropout. *Journal of Adolescence, 76,* 55-64.

Agans, J., Johnson, S., & Lerner, R. (2017). Adolescent athletic participation patterns and self-perceived competence: Associations with later participation, depressive symptoms, and health. *Journal of Research on Adolescence, 27,* 594-610.

Agoston, A., & Rudolph, K. (2011). Transactional associations between youths' responses to peer stress and depression: The moderating roles of sex and stress exposure. *Journal of Abnormal Child Psychology, 39,* 159-171.

Ahmad, I., Smetana, J., & Klimstra, T. (2015). Maternal monitoring, adolescent disclosure, and adolescent adjustment among Palestinian refugee youth in Jordan. *Journal of Research on Adolescence, 25,* 403-411.

Ahmad, S., & Hinshaw, S. (2017). Attention-deficit/hyperactivity disorder, trait impulsivity, and externalizing behavior in a longitudinal sample. *Journal of Abnormal Child Psychology, 45,* 1077-1089.

Ahmed, S., Foulkes, L., Leung, J. T., Griffin, C., Sakhardande, A., Bennett, M., . . . Blakemore, S.-J. (2020). Susceptibility to prosocial and antisocial influence in adolescence. *Journal of Adolescence, 84,* 56-68.

Ahmed, S. F., Tang, S., Waters, N. E., & Davis-Kean, P. (2019). Executive function and academic achievement: Longitudinal relations from early childhood to adolescence. *Journal of Educational Psychology, 111,* 446.

Ainsworth-Darnell, J., & Downey, D. (1998). Assessing the oppositional culture explanation for racial/ethnic differences in school performance. *American Sociological Review, 63,* 536-553.

Aite, A., Cassotti, M., Linzarini, A., Osmont, A., Houde, O., & Borst, G. (2017). Adolescents' inhibitory control: Keep it cool or lose control. *Developmental Science,* e12491.

Aizpitarte, A., Alonso-Arbiol, I., & Van de Vaijver, F. (2017). An explanatory model of dating violence and risk factors in Spanish adolescents. *Journal of Research on Adolescence, 27,* 797-809.

Aizpitarte, A., Atherton, O., Zheng, L., Alonso-Arbiol, I., & Robins, R. (2019). Developmental precursors of relational aggression from late childhood through adolescence. *Child Development, 90,* 117-126.

Akın, R. I., Breeman, L. D., Meeus, W., & Branje, S. (2020). Parent-adolescent relationship quality as a predictor of leaving home. *Journal of Adolescence, 79,* 81-90.

Alamilla, S., Barney, B., Small, R., Wang, S., Schwartz, S., Donovan, R., & Lewis, C. (2020) Explaining the immigrant paradox: The influence of acculturation, enculturation, and acculturative stress on problematic alcohol consumption. *Behavioral Medicine, 46,* 21-33.

Albert, D., & Steinberg, L. (2011a). Age differences in strategic planning as indexed by the Tower of London. *Child Development, 82,* 1501-1517.

Albert, D., & Steinberg, L. (2011b). Judgment and decision making in adolescence. *Journal of Research on Adolescence, 21,* 211-224.

Albert, D., Chein, J., & Steinberg, L. (2013). The teenage brain: Peer influences on adolescent decision making. *Current Directions in Psychological Science, 22,* 114-120.

Aldrich, J., Wielgus, M., & Mezulis, A. (2018). Low physiological arousal and high impulsivity as predictors of self-injurious thoughts and behaviors among adolescents. *Journal of Adolescence, 62*, 55-60.

Alessandri, G., Zuffiano, A., Eisenberg, N., & Pastorelli, C. (2017). The role of ego-resiliency as mediator of the longitudinal relationship between family socio-economic status and school grades. *Journal of Youth and Adolescence, 46*, 2157-2168.

Alex Mason, W., & Spoth, R. (2011). Longitudinal associations of alcohol involvement with subjective well-being in adolescence and prediction to alcohol problems in early adulthood. *Journal of Youth and Adolescence, 40*, 1215-1224.

Algur, E., Wang, E., Friedman, H., & Deperthes, B. (2019). A systematic global review of condom availability programs in high schools. *Journal of Adolescent Health, 64*, 292-304.

Ali, M. M., Rizzo, J. A., & Heiland, F. W. (2013). Big and beautiful? Evidence of racial differences in perceived attractiveness of obese females. *Journal of Adolescence, 36*, 539-549.

Allemand, M., Job, V., & Mroczek, D. (2019). Self-control development in adolescence predicts love and work in adulthood. *Journal of Personality and Social Psychology, 117*, 621-634.

Allen, J., Grande, L., Tan, J., & Loeb, E. (2018). Parent and peer predictors of change in attachment security from adolescence to adulthood. *Child Development, 89*, 1120-1132.

Allen, J., Hauser, S., O'Connor, T., & Bell, K. (2002). Prediction of peer-rated adult hostility from autonomy struggles in adolescent-family interactions. *Development and Psychopathology, 14*, 123-137.

Allen, J., Narr, R., Loeb, E., & Davis, A. (2019). Beyond deviancy-training: Deviant adolescent friendships and long-term social development. *Development and Psychopathology, 31*, 1609-1618.

Allen, J., Porter, M., McFarland, C., McElhaney, K., & Marsh, P. (2007). The relation of attachment security to adolescents' paternal and peer relationships, depression, and externalizing behavior. *Child Development, 78*, 1222-1239.

Allen, J., Porter, M., McFarland, F., Marsh, P., & McElhaney, K. (2005). The two faces of adolescents' success with peers: Adolescent popularity, social adaptation, and deviant behavior. *Child Development, 76*, 747-760.

Allen, J., Schad, M., Oudekerk, B., & Chango, J. (2014). What ever happened to the "cool" kids? Long-term sequelae of early adolescent pseudomature behavior. *Child Development, 85*, 1866-1880.

Allen, J., Uchino, B., & Hafen, C. (2015). Running with the pack. *Psychological Science, 26*, 1574-1583.

Allen, J. P., Loeb, E. L., Narr, R. K., & Costello, M. A. (2020). Different factors predict adolescent substance use versus adult substance abuse: Lessons from a social-developmental approach. *Development and Psychopathology,* early view.

Allen, J. P., Chango, J., & Szwedo, D. (2014). The adolescent relational dialectic and the peer roots of adult social functioning. *Child Development, 85*, 192-204.

Allen, M. L., Elliott, M. N., Morales, L. S., Diamant, A. L., Hambarsoomian, K., & Schuster, M. A. (2007). Adolescent participation in preventive health behaviors, physical activity, and nutrition: Differences across immigrant generations for Asians and Latinos compared with Whites. *American Journal of Public Health, 97*, 337-343.

Alm, S., Låftman, S. B., Sandahl, J., & Modin, B. (2019). School effectiveness and students' future orientation: A multilevel analysis of upper secondary schools in Stockholm, Sweden. *Journal of Adolescence, 70*, 62-73.

Alt, D., & Boniel-Nissim, M. (2018). Parent-adolescent communication and problematic internet use: the mediating role of Fear of Missing Out (FoMO). *Journal of Family Issues, 39*, 3391-3409.

Amato, P., & Booth, A. (1996). A prospective study of divorce and parent–child relationships. *Journal of Marriage and the Family, 58*, 356-365.

Amato, P., & Cheadle, J. (2008). Parental divorce, marital conflict, and children's behavior problems: A comparison of adopted and biological children. *Social Forces, 86*, 1139-1161.

Amato, P., & Sobolewski, J. M. (2001). The effects of divorce and marital discord on adult children's psychological well being. *American Sociological Review, 66*, 900-921.

Amato, P. R., & Anthony, C. J. (2014). Estimating the effects of parental divorce and death with fixed effects models. *Journal of Marriage and Family, 76*, 370-386.

Amato, P. R., King, V., & Thorsen, M. L. (2016). Parent-child relationships in stepfather families and adolescent adjustment: A latent class analysis. *Journal of Marriage and Family, 78*, 482-497.

Ambrosia, M., Eckstrand, K., Morgan, J., Allen, N., Jones, N., Sheeber, L., . . . Forbes, E. (2018). Temptations of friends: adolescents' neural and behavioral responses to best friends predict risky behavior. *Social Cognitive and Affective Neuroscience, 13*, 483-491.

Amemiya, J., & Wang, M.-T. (2018). Why effort praise can backfire in adolescence. *Child Development Perspectives, 12*(3), 199-203.

Amemiya, J., Fine, A., & Wang, M.-T. (2020). Trust and discipline: Adolescents' institutional and teacher trust predict classroom behavioral engagement following teacher discipline. *Child Development, 91*, 661-678.

Amemiya, J., Kieta, J., & Monahan, K. (2017). Adolescent offenders' qualitative reflections on desistance from crime. *Journal of Research on Adolescence, 27*, 765-781.

Amemiya, J., Mortenson, E., & Wang, M. T. (2020). Minor infractions are not minor: School infractions for minor misconduct may increase adolescents' defiant behavior and contribute to racial disparities in school discipline. *American Psychologist, 75*(1), 23-36.

American Psychiatric Association. (2013). *Diagnostic and statistical manual of the American Psychiatric Association (DSM-V).* Washington: Author.

Amrock, S., Lee, L., & Weitzman, M. (2016). Perceptions of e-cigarettes and noncigarette tobacco products among US youth. *Pediatrics, 138*, e20154306.

Amso, D., Haas, S., McShane, L., & Badre, D. (2014). Working memory updating and the development of rule-guided behavior. *Cognition, 133*, 201-210.

Analitis, F., Velderman, M., Ravens-Sieberer, U., Detmar, S., Erhart, M., Herdman, M., & European Kidscreen Group. (2009). Being bullied: Associated factors in children and adolescents 8 to 18 years old in 11 European countries. *Pediatrics, 123*, 569-577.

Ananat, E. O., Gassman-Pines, A., Francis, D. V., & Gibson-Davis, C. M. (2017). Linking job loss, inequality, mental health, and education. *Science, 356*, 1127-1128.

Anandakumar, J., Mills, K. L., Earl, E. A., Irwin, L., Miranda-Dominguez, O., Demeter, D. V., . . . Fair, D. A. (2018). Individual differences in functional brain connectivity predict temporal discounting preference in the transition to adolescence. *Developmental Cognitive Neuroscience, 34*, 101-113.

Anderman, E. (2002). School effects on psychological outcomes during adolescence. *Journal of Educational Psychology, 94*, 795-809.

Andersen, A., Rasmussen, M., Bendtsen, P., Due, P., & Holstein, B. (2014). Secular trends in alcohol drinking among Danish 15-year-olds: Comparable representative samples from 1988 to 2010. *Journal of Research on Adolescence, 24*, 748-756.

Andersen, S. H. (2021). Association of youth age at exposure to household dysfunction with outcomes in early adulthood. *JAMA Network Open, 4*, e2032769.

Anderson, C. A., Carnagey, N., & Eubanks, J. (2003). Exposure to violent media: The effects of songs with violent lyrics on aggressive thoughts and feelings. *Journal of Personality and Social Psychology, 84*, 960-971.

Anderson, M., Kaufman, J., Simon, T. R., Barrios, L., Paulozzi, L., Ryan, G., School Associated Violent Deaths Study Group. (2001). School-associated violent deaths in the United States, 1994-1999. *Journal of the American Medical Association, 286*, 2695-2702.

Anderson, R., Jones, S., Anyiwo, N., McKenny, M., & Gaylord-Harden, N. (2019). What's race got to do with it? Racial socialization's contribution to Black adolescent coping. *Journal of Research on Adolescence, 29*, 822-831.

Anderson, S., & Leventhal, T. (2017). Residential mobility and adolescent achievement and behavior: Understanding timing and extent of mobility. *Journal of Research on Adolescence, 27*, 328-343.

Anderson, S. E., Dallal, G. E., & Must, A. (2003). Relative weight and race influence average age at menarche: Results from two nationally representative surveys of U.S. girls studied 25 years apart. *Pediatrics, 111*, 844-891.

Anderson-Carpenter, K., Watson-Thompson, J., Chaney, L., & Jones, M. (2016). Reducing binge drinking in adolescents through implementation of the Strategic Prevention Framework. *American Journal of Community Psychology, 57*, 36-46.

Andersson, H., & Bergman, L. (2011). The role of task persistence in young adolescence for successful educational and occupational attainment in middle adulthood. *Developmental Psychology, 47*, 950-960.

Andrew, T., Tiggemann, M., & Clark, L. (2016). Predictors and health-related outcomes of positive body image in adolescent girls: A prospective study. *Developmental Psychology, 52*, 463-474.

Andrews, J., Foulkes, L., & Blakemore, S-J. (2020). Peer influence in adolescence: Public-health implications for COVID-19. *Trends in Cognitive Sciences, 24,* 585-587.

Andrews, J., Mills, K., Flournoy, J., Flannery, J., Mobasser, A., Ross, G., . . . Pfeifer, J. (2020). Expectations of social consequences impact anticipated involvement in health-risk behavior during adolescence. *Journal of Research on Adolescence, 30,* 1008-1024.

Andrews, N., Hanish, L., & Santos, C. (2017). Reciprocal associations between delinquent behavior and social network position during middle school. *Journal of Youth and Adolescence, 46,* 1918-1932.

Andrews, N., Hanish, L., Updegraff, K., Martin, C., & Santos, C. (2016). Targeted victimization: Exploring linear and curvilinear associations between social network prestige and victimization. *Journal of Youth and Adolescence, 45,* 1772-1785.

Anguiano, R. (2018). Language brokering among Latino immigrant families: Moderating variables and youth outcomes. *Journal of Youth and Adolescence, 47,* 222-242.

Antshel, K., & Barkley, R. (2011). Attention deficit/hyperactivity disorder. (2011). In B. Brown & M. Prinstein (Eds.), *Encyclopedia of adolescence* (Vol. 3, pp. 56-61). New York: Academic Press.

Anyon, Y., Zhang, D., & Hazel, C. (2016). Race, exclusionary discipline, and connectedness to adults in secondary schools. *American Journal of Community Psychology, 57,* 342-352.

Appel, I., & Shulman, S. (2015). The role of romantic attraction and conflict resolution in predicting shorter and longer relationship maintenance among adolescents. *Archives of Sexual Behavior, 44,* 777-782.

Archibald, A., Graber, J., & Brooks-Gunn, J. (1999). Associations among parent–adolescent relationships, pubertal growth, dieting, and body image in young adolescent girls: A short-term longitudinal study. *Journal of Research on Adolescence, 9,* 395-415.

Arens, A., Yeung, A., Craven, R., & Hasselhorn, M. (2011). The twofold multidimensionality of academic self-concept: Domain specificity and separation between competence and affect components. *Journal of Educational Psychology, 103,* 970-981.

Armenta, B., Sittner, K., & Whitbeck, B. (2016). Predicting the onset of alcohol use and the development of alcohol use disorder among indigenous adolescents. *Child Development, 87,* 870-882.

Armor, D. (1972). School and family effects on Black and White achievement: A reexamination of the USOE data. In F. Mosteller & D. Moynihan (Eds.), *On equality of educational opportunity.* New York: Random House.

Arndorfer, C., & Stormshak, E. (2008). Same-sex versus other-sex best friendship in early adolescence: Longitudinal predictors of antisocial behavior throughout adolescence. *Journal of Youth and Adolescence, 37,* 1059-1070.

Arnett, J. (2004). *Emerging adulthood: The winding road from the late teens through the twenties.* New York: Oxford University Press.

Arnett, J. (2009). Emerging adulthood: What is it, and what is it good for? *Child Development Perspectives, 1,* 68-73.

Arnett, J. J., & Padilla-Walker, L. M. (2015). Brief report: Danish emerging adults' conceptions of adulthood. *Journal of Adolescence, 38,* 39-44.

Arnold, A. L., Lucier-Greer, M., Mancini, J. A., Ford, J. L., & Wickrama, K. A. S. (2017). How family structures and processes interrelate: The case of adolescent mental health and academic success in military families. *Journal of Family Issues, 38,* 858-879.

Asakawa, K., & Csikszentmihalyi, M. (1998). The quality of experience of Asian American adolescents in academic activities: An exploration of educational achievement. *Journal of Research on Adolescence, 8,* 241-262.

Asakawa, K., & Csikszentmihalyi, M. (2000). Feelings of connectedness and internalization of values in Asian American adolescents. *Journal of Youth and Adolescence, 29,* 121-145.

Aseltine, R., & Gore, S. (2005). Work, postsecondary education, and psychosocial functioning following the transition from high school. *Journal of Adolescent Research, 20,* 615-639.

Ashby, J., & Schoon, I. (2012). Living the dream? A qualitative retrospective study exploring the role of adolescent aspirations across the life span. *Developmental Psychology, 48,* 1694-1706.

Asher, S., Parker, J., & Walker, D. (1996). Distinguishing friendship from acceptance: Implications for intervention and assessment. In W. Bukowski, A. Newcomb, & W. Hartup (Eds.), *The company they keep: Friendship in childhood and adolescence* (pp. 366-405). New York: Cambridge University Press.

Ask, H., Waaktaar, T., Brobakke Seglem, K., & Torgersen, S. (2016). Common etiological sources of anxiety, depression, and somatic complaints in adolescents: A multiple rater twin study. *Journal of Abnormal Child Psychology, 44,* 101-114.

Askeland, K. G., Bøe, T., Breivik, K., La Greca, A. M., Sivertsen, B., & Hysing, M. (2020). Life events and adolescent depressive symptoms: Protective factors associated with resilience. *PLOS ONE, 15,* e0234109.

Askeland, K. G., Hysing, M., La Greca, A. M., Aaro, L. E., Tell, G. S., & Sivertsen, B. (2017). Mental health in internationally adopted adolescents: A meta-analysis. *Journal of the American Academy of Child & Adolescent Psychiatry, 56,* 202-213.

Aspy, C., Tolma, E., Oman, R., & Vesely, S. (2014). The influence of assets and environmental factors on gender differences in adolescent drug use. *Journal of Adolescence, 37,* 827-837.

Aspy, C., Vesely, S., Oman, R., Rodine, S., Marshall, L., & McLeroy, K. (2007). Parental communication and youth sexual behaviour. *Journal of Adolescence, 30,* 449-466.

Atherton, O., Conger, R., Ferrer, E., & Robins, R. (2016). Risk and protective factors for early substance use initiation: A longitudinal study of Mexican-origin youth. *Journal of Research on Adolescence, 26,* 864-879.

Atherton, O., Schofield, T., Sitka, A., Conger, R., & Robins, R. (2016). Unsupervised self-care predicts conduct problems: The moderating roles of hostile aggression and gender. *Journal of Adolescence, 48,* 1-10.

Auerbach, R., Eberhart, N., & Abela, J. (2010). Cognitive vulnerability to depression in Canadian and Chinese adolescents. *Journal of Abnormal Child Psychology, 38,* 57-68.

Augustyn, M., Thornberry, T., & Krohn, M. (2014). Gang membership and pathways to maladaptive parenting. *Journal of Research on Adolescence, 24,* 252-267.

Austin, L., Parnes, M., Jarjoura, G., Keller, T., Herrera, C., Tanyu, M., & Schwartz, S. (2020). Connecting youth: The role of mentoring approach. *Journal of Youth and Adolescence, 49*(12), 2409-2428.

Auxier, B. (2020). *8 facts about Americans and Instagram.* Washington: Pew Research Center.

Avenevoli, S., & Steinberg, L. (2001). The continuity of depression across the adolescent transition. In H. Reese & R. Kail (Eds.), *Advances in child development and behavior* (Vol. 28, pp. 139-173). New York: Academic Press.

Avenevoli, S., Swendsen, J., He, J., Burstein, M., & Merikangas, K. (2015). Major depression in the National Comorbidity Survey-Adolescent Supplement: Prevalence, correlates, and treatment. *Journal of the American Academy of Child & Adolescent Psychiatry, 54,* 37-44.

Aylwin, C. F., Toro, C. A., Shirtcliff, E., & Lomniczi, A. (2019). Emerging genetic and epigenetic mechanisms underlying pubertal maturation in adolescence. *Journal of Research on Adolescence, 29,* 54-79.

Baams, L., Dubas, J., Overbeek, G., & van Aken, M. (2015). Transitions in body and behavior: A meta-analytic study on the relationship between pubertal development and adolescent sexual behavior. *Journal of Adolescent Health, 56,* 586-598.

Baams, L., Grossman, A. H., & Russell, S. T. (2015). Minority stress and mechanisms of risk for depression and suicidal ideation among lesbian, gay, and bisexual youth. *Developmental Psychology, 51,* 688-696.

Baams, L., Overbeek, G., Dubas, J., Doornwaard, S., Rommes, E., & van Aken, M. (2015). Perceived realism moderates the relation between sexualized media consumption and permissive sexual attitudes in Dutch adolescents. *Archives of Sexual Behavior, 44,* 743-754.

Babalola, S. (2004). Perceived peer behavior and the timing of sexual debut in Rwanda: A survival analysis of youth data. *Journal of Youth and Adolescence, 33,* 353-363.

Bachman, J., Staff, J., O'Malley, P., & Freedman-Doan, P. (2013). Adolescent work intensity, school performance, and substance use: Links vary by race/ethnicity and socioeconomic status. *Developmental Psychology, 49,* 2125-2134.

Bachman, J., Staff, J., O'Malley, P., Schulenberg, J., & Freedman-Doan, P. (2011). Twelfth-grade student work intensity linked to later educational attainment and substance use: New longitudinal evidence. *Developmental Psychology, 47,* 344-363.

Bae, D., Wickrama, K. A. S., & O'Neal, C. W. (2014). Social consequences of early socioeconomic adversity and youth BMI trajectories: Gender and race/ethnicity differences. *Journal of Adolescence, 37,* 883-892.

Baeher, J. (2017). The varieties of character and some implications for character education. *Journal of Youth and Adolescence, 46,* 1153-1161.

Bai, Y., Chen, S., Laurson, K., Kim, Y., Saint-Maurice, P., & Welk, G. (2016). The associations of youth physical activity and screen time with fatness and fitness: The 2012 NHANES National Youth Fitness Survey. *PLOS ONE, 11,* e0148038.

Baird, A., Fugelsang, J., & Bennett, C. (2005, April). "What were you thinking?": An fMRI study of adolescent decision making. Poster presented at the 12th Annual Cognitive Neuroscience Society (CNS) Meeting, New York.

Bakan, D. (1972). Adolescence in America: From idea to social fact. In J. Kagan & R. Coles (Eds.), *Twelve to sixteen: Early adolescence.* New York: Norton.

Baker, E., & Exner-Cortens, D. (2020). Adolescents' interpersonal negotiation strategies: Does competence vary by context? *Journal of Research on Adolescence, 30,* 1059-1050.

Baker, J., Munn-Chernoff, M., Lichtenstein, P., Larsson, H., Maes, H., & Kendler, K. (2017). Shared familial risk between bulimic symptoms and alcohol involvement during adolescence. *Journal of Abnormal Psychology, 126,* 506-518.

Baker, S. T. E., Lubman, D. I., Yucel, M., Allen, N. B., Whittle, S., Fulcher, B. D., . . . Fornito, A. (2015). Developmental changes in brain network hub connectivity in late adolescence. *The Journal of Neuroscience, 35,* 9078-9087.

Baker, T., & Velez, W. (1996). Access to and opportunity in postsecondary education in the United States: A review. *Sociology of Education, Extra Issue, 69,* 82-101.

Bakker, M., Ormel, J., Verhulst, F., & Oldehinkel, A. (2010). Peer stressors and gender differences in adolescents' mental health: The TRAILS study. *Journal of Adolescent Health, 46,* 444-450.

Ballard, P., Hoyt, L., & Pachucki, M. (2019). Impacts of adolescent and young adult civic engagement on health and socioeconomic status in adulthood. *Child Development, 90,* 1138-1154.

Balsa, A., Homer, J., French, M., & Norton, E. (2011). Alcohol use and popularity: Social payoffs from conforming to peers' behavior. *Journal of Research on Adolescence, 21,* 559-568.

Balsano, A., Theokas, C., & Bobek, D. (2009). A shared commitment to youth: The integration of theory, research, practice, and policy. In R. Lerner & L. Steinberg (Eds.), *Handbook of adolescent psychology* (3rd ed., Vol. 2, pp. 623-650). New York: Wiley.

Bámaca, M., & Umaña-Taylor, A. (2006). Testing a model of resistance to peer pressure among Mexican-origin adolescents. *Journal of Youth and Adolescence, 35,* 631-645.

Bamaca-Colbert, M., Greene, K., Killoren, S., & Noah, A. (2014). Contextual and developmental predictors of sexual initiation timing among Mexican-origin girls. *Developmental Psychology, 50,* 2353-2359.

Bámaca-Colbert, M., Umaña-Taylor, A., Espinosa-Hernández, G., & Brown, A. (2012). Behavioral autonomy age expectations among Mexican-origin mother-daughter dyads: An examination of within-group variability. *Journal of Adolescence, 35,* 691-700.

Bañales, J., Marchand, A., Skinner, O., Anyiwo, N., Rowley, S., & Kurtz-Costes, B. (2020). Black adolescents' critical reflection development: Parents' racial socialization and attributions about race achievement gaps. *Journal of Research on Adolescence, 30*(S2), 403-417.

Bandura, A., & Walters, R. (1959). *Adolescent aggression.* New York: Ronald Press.

Bandura, A., Barbaranelli, C., Caprara, G., & Pastorelli, C. (1996). Multifaceted impact of self-efficacy beliefs on academic functioning. *Child Development, 67,* 1206-1222.

Banerjee, M., Byrd, C., & Rowley, S. (2018). The relationships of school-based discrimination and ethnic-racial socialization to African American adolescents' achievement outcomes. *Social Sciences, 7,* 208.

Banister, E. (1999). Women's midlife experience of their changing bodies. *Qualitative Health Research, 9,* 520-537.

Bank, L., Burraston, B., & Snyder, J. (2004). Sibling conflict and ineffective parenting as predictors of adolescent boys' antisocial behavior and peer difficulties: Additive and interactional effects. *Journal of Research on Adolescence, 14,* 99-125.

Bankston, C. L., III, & Caldas, S. (1998). Family structure, schoolmates, and racial inequalities in school achievement. *Journal of Marriage & the Family, 60,* 715-723.

Banny, A., Heilbron, N., Ames, A., & Prinstein, M. (2011). Relational benefits of relational aggression: Adaptive and maladaptive associations with adolescent friendship quality. *Developmental Psychology, 47,* 1153-1166.

Banyard, V., Edwards, K., Jones, L., & Mitchell, K. (2020). Poly-strengths and peer violence perpetration: What strengths can add to risk factor analyses. *Journal of Youth and Adolescence, 49,* 735-746.

Banzon-Librojo, L., Garabiles, M., & Peña Alampay, L. (2017). Relations between harsh discipline from teachers, perceived teacher support, and bullying victimization among high school students. *Journal of Adolescence, 57,* 18-22.

Bao, Z., Zhang, W., Lai, X., Sun, W., & Wang, Y. (2015). Parental attachment and Chinese adolescents' delinquency: The mediating role of moral disengagement. *Journal of Adolescence, 44,* 37-47.

Barkley-Levenson, E., & Galván, A. (2017). Eye blink rate predicts reward decisions in adolescents. *Developmental Science, 20,* e123412.

Barlett, C. P., & Fennel, M. (2018). Examining the relation between parental ignorance and youths' cyberbullying perpetration. *Psychology of Popular Media Culture, 7,* 547-560.

Barnes, J., & Motz, R. (2018). Reducing racial inequalities in adulthood arrest by reducing inequalities in school discipline: Evidence from the school-to-prison pipeline. *Developmental Psychology, 54,* 2328-2340.

Barnes, R. (2007, June 29). Divided court limits use of race by school districts. *Washington Post,* p. A01.

Barreiro, A., Arsenio, W., & Wainryb, C. (2019). Adolescents' conceptions of wealth and societal fairness amid extreme inequality: An Argentine sample. *Developmental Psychology, 55,* 498-508.

Barry, C. M., & Nelson, L. J. (2005). The role of religion in the transition to adulthood for young emerging adults. *Journal of Youth and Adolescence 34,* 245-255.

Barstead, M., Smith, K., Laursen, B., Booth-LaForce, C., King, S., & Rubin, K. (2018). Shyness, preference for solitude, and adolescent internalizing: The roles of maternal, paternal, and best-friend support. *Journal of Research on Adolescence, 28,* 488-504.

Barsties, L, Walsh, S, Huijts, T., Bendtsen, P., Molcho, M., Buijs, T., . . . Stevens, G. (2017). Alcohol consumption among first- and second-generation immigrant and native adolescents in 23 countries: Testing the importance of origin and receiving country alcohol prevalence rates. *Drug and Alcohol Review, 36,* 769-778.

Basile, K., Black, M., Simon, T., Arias, I., Brener, N., & Saltzman, L. (2006). The association between self-reported lifetime history of forced sexual intercourse and recent health-risk behaviors: Findings from the 2003 national youth risk behavior survey. *Journal of Adolescent Health, 39,* e1-e7.

Bassi, M., Steca, P., Delle Fave, A., & Caprara, G. (2007). Academic self-efficacy beliefs and quality of experience in learning. *Journal of Youth and Adolescence, 36,* 301-312.

Bastin, M., Mezulis, A., Ahles, J., Raes, F., & Bijttebier, P. (2015). Moderating effects of brooding and co-rumination on the relationship between stress and depressive symptoms in early adolescence: A multi-wave study. *Journal of Abnormal Child Psychology, 43,* 607-618.

Bastin, M., Vanhalst, J., Raes, F., & Bijttebier, P. (2018). Co-brooding and co-reflection as differential predictors of depressive symptoms and friendship quality in adolescents: Investigating the moderating role of gender. *Journal of Youth and Adolescence, 47,* 1037-1051.

Batalla, A., Bhattacharyya, S., Yücel, M., Fusar-Poli, P., Crippa, J., Nogué, S., . . . Martin-Santos, R. (2013). Structural and functional imaging studies in chronic cannabis users: A systematic review of adolescent and adult findings. *PLOS ONE, 8,* 55821.

Baumer, E. P., & South, S. J. (2001). Community effects on youth sexual activity. *Journal of Marriage and the Family, 63,* 540-554.

Baumrind, D. (1978). Parental disciplinary patterns and social competence in children. *Youth and Society, 9,* 239-276.

Bauserman, R., & Rind, B. (1997). Psychological correlates of male child and adolescent sexual experiences with adults: A review of the nonclinical literature. *Archives of Sexual Behavior, 26,* 105-141.

Bayram Özdemir, S., & Stattin, H. (2014). Why and when is ethnic harassment a risk for immigrant adolescents' school adjustment? Understanding the processes and conditions. *Journal of Youth & Adolescence, 43,* 1252-1265.

Bayram Özdemir, S., Sun, S., Korol, L., Özdemir, M., & Stattin, H. (2018). Adolescents' engagement in ethnic harassment: Prejudiced beliefs in social networks and classroom ethnic diversity. *Journal of Youth and Adolescence, 47*(6), 1151-1163.

Baysu, G., Celeste, L., Brown, R., Verschueren, K., & Phalet, K. (2016). Minority adolescents in ethnically diverse schools: Perception of equal treatment buffer threat effects. *Child Development, 87,* 1352-1366.

Beal, S., & Crockett, L. (2010). Adolescents' occupational and educational aspirations and expectations: Links to high school activities and adult educational attainment. *Developmental Psychology, 46,* 258-265.

Beal, S. J., Crockett, L. J., & Peugh, J. (2016). Adolescents' changing future expectations predict the timing of adult role transitions. *Developmental Psychology, 52,* 1606-1618.

Beal, S. J., Grimm, K. J., Dron, L. D., & Susman, E. J. (2016). Morningness-eveningness and physical activity in adolescent girls: Menarche as a transition point. *Child Development, 87,* 1106-1114.

Beam, M., Chen, C., & Greenberger, E. (2002). The nature of adolescents' relationship with their "very important" nonparental adults. *American Journal of Community Psychology, 30,* 305-325.

Beardslee, J., Miltimore, S., Fine, A., Frick, P., Steinberg, L., & Cauffman, E. (2019). Under the radar or under arrest: How is adolescent boys' first contact with the juvenile justice system related to future offending and arrests? *Law and Human Behavior, 43,* 342-357.

Beardslee, W., Brent, D., Weersing, V., Clarke, G., Porta, G., Hollon, S., . . . Garber, J. (2013). Prevention of depression in at-risk adolescents: Longer-term effects. *JAMA Psychiatry, 70,* 1161-1170.

Bearman, S., & Stice, E. (2008). Testing a gender additive model: The role of body image in adolescent depression. *Journal of Abnormal Child Psychology, 36,* 1251-1263.

Beaudry, G., Yu, R., Långström, N., & Seena Fazel, F. (2021). An updated systematic review and meta-regression analysis: Mental disorders among adolescents in juvenile detention and correctional facilities. *Journal of the American Academy of Child & Adolescent Psychiatry, 60,* 46-60.

Beaver, K., Barnes, J., & Boutwell, B. (2016). Exploring the relationship between violent behavior and participation in football during adolescence. *Youth & Society, 48,* 786-809.

Beaver, K. M., Schwartz, J. A., Connolly, E. J., Al-Ghamdi, M. S., & Kobeisy, A. N. (2015). The role of parenting in the prediction of criminal involvement: Findings from a nationally representative sample of youth and a sample of adopted youth. *Developmental Psychology, 51,* 301-308.

Becht, A., Bos, M., Nelemans, S., Peters, S., Vollebergh, W., Branje, S., . . . Crone, E. (2018). Goal-directed correlates and neurobiological underpinnings of adolescent identity: A multimethod multisample longitudinal approach. *Child Development, 89,* 823-836.

Becht, A., Nelemans, S., Branje, S., Vollebergh, W., Koot, H., Denissen, J., & Meeus, W. (2016). The quest for identity in adolescence: Heterogeneity in daily identity formation and psychosocial adjustment across 5 years. *Developmental Psychology, 52,* 2010-2021.

Becht, A., Nelemans, S., Dijk, M., Branje, S., Van Lier, P., Denissen, J., . . . van Dijk, M. (2017). Clear self, better relationships: Adolescents' self-concept clarity and relationship quality with parents and peers across 5 years. *Child Development, 88,* 1823-1833.

Beck, S. R., & Riggs, K. J. (2014). Developing thoughts about what might have been. *Child Development Perspectives, 8,* 175-179.

Becker, B. E., & Luthar, S. S. (2007). Peer-perceived admiration and social preference: Contextual correlates of positive peer regard among suburban and urban adolescents. *Journal of Research on Adolescence, 17,* 117-144.

Becker, M., Neumann, M., Tetzner, J., Böse, S., Knoppick, H., Maaz, K., Baumert, J., & Lehmann, R. (2014). Is early ability grouping good for high-achieving students' psychosocial development? Effects of the transition into academically

selective schools. *Journal of Educational Psychology, 106,* 555-568.

Beckmeyer, J. (2015). Comparing the associations between three types of adolescents' romantic involvement and their engagement in substance use. *Journal of Adolescence, 42,* 140-147.

Beckmeyer, J., & Weybright, E. (2020). Exploring the associations between middle adolescent romantic activity and positive youth development. *Journal of Adolescence, 80,* 214-219.

Beets, M., Flay, B., Vuchinich, S., Snyder, F., Acock, A., Li, K., . . . Durlack, J. (2009). Use of a social and character development program to prevent substance use, violent behaviors, and sexual activity among elementary-school students in Hawaii. *American Journal of Public Health, 99,* 1438-1445.

Bellmore, A. (2011). Peer rejection and unpopularity: Associations with GPAs across the transition to middle school. *Journal of Educational Psychology, 103,* 282-295.

Bellmore, A., Villarreal, V., & Ho, A. (2011). Staying cool across the first year of middle school. *Journal of Youth and Adolescence, 40,* 776-785.

Belsky, J. (2019). Early-life adversity accelerates child and adolescent development. *Current Directions in Psychological Science, 28,* 241-246.

Belsky, J., & Pluess, M. (2009). Beyond diathesis-stress: Differential susceptibility to environmental influences. *Psychological Bulletin, 135,* 885-908.

Belsky, J., & Pluess, M. (2013). Beyond risk, resilience and dysregulation: Phenotypic plasticity and human development. *Development and Psychopathology, 25,* 1243-1261.

Belsky, J., & Shalev, I. (2016). Contextual adversity, telomere erosion, pubertal development, and health: Two models of accelerated aging, or one? *Development and Psychopathology, 28,* 1367-1383.

Belsky, J., Ruttle, P. L., Boyce, W. T., Armstrong, J. M., & Essex, M. J. (2015). Early adversity, elevated stress physiology, accelerated sexual maturation, and poor health in females. *Developmental Psychology, 51,* 816-822.

Belsky, J., Steinberg, L., & Draper, P. (1991). Childhood experience, interpersonal development, and reproductive strategy: An evolutionary theory of socialization. *Child Development, 62,* 647-670.

Beltz, A., Corley, R., Wadsworth, S., DiLalla, L., & Berenbaum, S. (2020). Does puberty affect the development of behavior problems as a mediator, moderator, or unique predictor? *Development and Psychopathology, 32,* 1473-1485

Beltz, A. M. (2018). Gendered mechanisms underlie the relation between pubertal timing and adult depressive symptoms. *Journal of Adolescent Health, 62,* 722-728.

Beltz, A. M., Corley, R. P., Wadsworth, S. J., DiLalla, L. F., & Berenbaum, S. A. (2019). Does puberty affect the development of behavior problems as a mediator, moderator, or unique predictor? *Development and Psychopathology, 32,* 1-13.

Beltz, M., Sacks, V., Moore, K., & Terzian, M. (2015). State policy and teen childbearing: A review of research studies. *Journal of Adolescent Health, 56,* 130-138.

BeLue, R., Francis, L. A., & Colaco, B. (2009). Mental health problems and overweight in a nationally representative sample of adolescents:

Effects of race and ethnicity. *Pediatrics, 123,* 697-702.

Bendtsen, P., Damsgaard, M., Tolstrup, J., Ersbøll, A., & Holstein, B. (2013). Adolescent alcohol use reflects community-level alcohol consumption irrespective of parental drinking. *Journal of Adolescent Health, 53,* 368-373.

Benedict, R. (1934). *Patterns of culture.* New York: Houghton Mifflin.

Benenson, J., & Christakos, A. (2003). The greater fragility of females' versus males' closest same-sex friendships. *Child Development, 74,* 1123-1129.

Benish-Weisman, M., Levy, S., & Knafo, A. (2013). Parents differentiate between their personal values and their socialization values: The role of adolescents' values. *Journal of Research on Adolescence, 23,* 614-620.

Benjet, C., & Hernández-Guzmán, L. (2002). A short-term longitudinal study of pubertal change, gender, and psychological well-being of Mexican early adolescents. *Journal of Youth and Adolescence, 31,* 429-442.

Benner, A. (2011). Latino adolescents' loneliness, academic performance, and the buffering nature of friendships. *Journal of Youth and Adolescence, 40,* 556-567.

Benner, A., & Wang, Y. (2014a). Demographic marginalization, social integration, and adolescents' educational success. *Journal of Youth and Adolescence, 43,* 1611-1627.

Benner, A., & Wang, Y. (2014b). Shifting attendance trajectories from middle to high school: Influences of school transitions and changing school contexts. *Developmental Psychology, 50,* 1288-1301.

Benner, A., & Wang, Y. (2017). Racial/ethnic discrimination and adolescents' well-being: The role of cross-ethnic friendships and friends' experiences of discrimination. *Child Development, 88,* 493-504.

Benner, A., Boyle, A. & Sadler, S. (2016). Parental involvement and adolescents' educational success: The roles of prior achievement and socioeconomic status. *Journal of Youth and Adolescence, 45,* 1053-1064.

Benner, A., Crosnoe, R., & Eccles, J. (2015). Schools, peers, and prejudice in adolescence. *Journal of Research on Adolescence, 25,* 173-188.

Benner, A., Hou, Y., & Jackson, K. (2019). The consequences of friend-related stress across early adolescence. *The Journal of Early Adolescence, 40,* 249-272.

Benner, A., Wang, Y., Shen, Y., Boyle, A., Polk, R., & Cheng, Y. (2018). Racial/ethnic discrimination and well-being during adolescence: A meta-analytic review. *American Psychologist, 73,* 855-883.

Benner, A. D., & Graham, S. (2009). The transition to high school as a developmental process among multiethnic urban youth. *Child Development, 80,* 356-376.

Benner, A. D., & Mistry, R. S. (2007). Congruence of mother and teacher educational expectations and low-income youth's academic competence. *Journal of Educational Psychology, 99,* 140-153.

Benner, A. D., & Wang, Y. (2015). Adolescent substance use: The role of demographic marginalization and socioemotional distress. *Developmental Psychology, 51,* 1086-1097.

Benner, A. D., Boyle, A., & Bakhtiari, F. (2017). Understanding students' transition to high school: Demographic variation and the role of supportive relationships. *Journal of Youth and Adolescence, 46,* 2129-2142.

Bennett, M., Roche, K., Huebner, D., & Lambert, S. (2020). School discrimination and changes in Latinx adolescents' internalizing and externalizing symptoms. *Journal of Youth and Adolescence, 49,* 2020-2033.

Bennett, P., Lutz, A., & Jayaram, L. (2012). Beyond the schoolyard: The role of parenting logics, financial resources, and social institutions in the social class gap in a structured activity participation. *Sociology of Education, 85,* 131-157.

Benoit, A., Lacourse, E., & Claes, M. (2013). Pubertal timing and depressive symptoms in late adolescence: The moderating role of individual, peer, and parental factors. *Development and Psychopathology, 25,* 455-471.

Benson, M. J., & Buehler, C. (2012). Family process and peer deviance influences on adolescent aggression: Longitudinal effects across early and middle adolescence. *Child Development, 83,* 1213-1228.

Berg, N., Kiviruusu, O., Karvonen, S., Rahkonen, O., & Huurre, T. (2017). Pathways from problems in adolescent family relationships to midlife mental health via early adulthood disadvantages—a 26-year longitudinal study. *PLOS ONE, 12,* e0178136.

Berge, J., Wall, M., Loth, K., & Neumark-Sztainer, D. (2010). Parenting style as a predictor of adolescent weight and weight-related behaviors. *Journal of Adolescent Health, 46,* 331-338.

Berger, C., & Dijkstra, J. (2013). Competition, envy, or snobbism? How popularity and friendships shape antipathy networks of adolescents. *Journal of Research on Adolescence, 23,* 586-595.

Berkel, C., Murry, V., Hurt, T., Chen, Y., Brody, G., Simons, R. L., . . . Gibbons, F. (2009). It takes a village: Protecting rural African American youth in the context of racism. *Journal of Youth and Adolescence, 38,* 175-188.

Berndt, T., & Perry, T. (1990). Distinctive features and effects of early adolescent friendships. In R. Montemayor, G. Adams, & T. Gullota (Eds.), *Advances in adolescence research* (Vol. 2, pp. 269-287). Beverly Hills, CA: Sage.

Berninger, V., & Miller, B. (2011). Adolescent specific learning disabilities. In B. Brown & M. Prinstein (Eds.), *Encyclopedia of adolescence* (Vol. 3, pp. 21-29). New York: Academic Press.

Bersamin, M., Fisher, D., Walker, S., Hill, D., & Grube, J. (2007). Defining virginity and abstinence: Adolescents' interpretations of sexual behaviors. *Journal of Adolescent Health, 41,* 182-188.

Beyers, W., & Goossens, L. (2008). Dynamics of perceived parenting and identity formation in late adolescence. *Journal of Adolescence, 31,* 165-184.

Beyers, W., & Luyckx, K. (2016). Ruminative exploration and reconsideration of commitment as risk factors for suboptimal identity development in adolescence and emerging adulthood. *Journal of Adolescence, 47,* 169-178.

Beyth-Marom, R., Austin, L., Fischoff, B., Palmgren, C., & Jacobs-Quadrel, M. (1993). Perceived consequences of risky behaviors: Adults and adolescents. *Developmental Psychology, 29,* 549-563.

Bezold, C. P., Konty, K. J., Day, S. E., Berger, M., Harr, L., Larkin, M., . . . Stark, J. H. (2014). The effects of changes in physical fitness on academic performance among New York City youth. *Journal of Adolescent Health, 55,* 774-781.

Biehl, M. C., Natsuaki, M. N., & Ge, X. (2007). The influence of pubertal timing on alcohol use and heavy drinking trajectories. *Journal of Youth and Adolescence, 36,* 153-167.

Bierman, K., & Wargo, J. (1995). Predicting the longitudinal course associated with aggressive-rejected, aggressive-nonrejected, and rejected non-aggressive status. *Development and Psychopathology, 7,* 669-682.

Bills, D., Helms, L., & Ozcan, M. (1995). The impact of student employment on teachers' attitudes and behaviors toward working students. *Youth and Society, 27,* 169-193.

Bingham, C., & Crockett, L. (1996). Longitudinal adjustment patterns of boys and girls experiencing early, middle, and late sexual intercourse. *Developmental Psychology, 32,* 647-658.

Bingham, C., & Shope, J. (2004). Adolescent problem behavior and problem driving in young adulthood. *Journal of Adolescent Research, 19,* 205-223.

Birkeland, M., Melkevik, O., Holsen, I., & Wold, B. (2012). Trajectories of global self-esteem development during adolescence. *Journal of Adolescence, 35,* 43-54.

Birkeland, M. S., Breivik, K., & Wold, B. (2014). Peer acceptance protects global self-esteem from negative effect of low closeness to parents during adolescence and early adulthood. *Journal of Youth & Adolescence, 43,* 70-80.

Birkett, M., Russell, S., & Corliss, H. (2014). Sexual-orientation disparities in school: The mediational role of indicators of victimization in achievement and truancy because of feeling unsafe. *American Journal of Public Health, 104,* 1124-1128.

Birmaher, B., Rabin, B., Garcia, M., Jain, U., Whiteside, T., Williamson, D., . . . Ryan, N. (1994). Cellular immunity in depressed, conduct disorder, and normal adolescents: Role of adverse life events. *Journal of the American Academy of Child and Adolescent Psychiatry, 33,* 671-678.

Biro, F., Striegel-Moore, R., Franko, D. L., Padgett, J., & Bean, J. A. (2006). Self-esteem in adolescent females. *Journal of Adolescent Health, 39,* 501-507.

Bishai, D., Mercer, D., & Tapales, A. (2005). Can government policies help adolescents avoid risky behavior? *Preventive Medicine, 40,* 197-202.

Bishop, J., Bishop, M., Gelbwasser, L., Green, S., & Zuckerman, A. (2003). Why do we harass nerds and freaks? Towards a theory of student culture and norms. In D. Ravitch (Ed.), *Brookings papers on education policy.* Washington, DC: Brookings Institution.

Bissell-Havran, J. (2014). Dispositional hope as a moderator of the link between social comparison with friends and eighth-grade students' perceptions of academic competence. *The Journal of Adolescence, 35*(8).

Blachnio, A., Przepiorka, A., Balakier, E., & Boruch, W. (2016). Who discloses the most on Facebook? *Computers in Human Behavior, 55,* 664-667.

Black, M., Oberlander, S., Lewis, T., Knight, E., Zolotor, A., & Litrownik, A., & English, D. (2009). Sexual intercourse among adolescents maltreated before age 12: A prospective investigation. *Pediatrics, 124,* 941-949.

Blackwell, L., Trzesniewski, K., & Dweck, C. (2007). Implicit theories of intelligence predict achievement across an adolescent transition: A longitudinal study and an intervention. *Child Development, 78,* 246-263.

Blair, R., Leibenluft, E., & Pine, D. (2014). Conduct disorder and callous-unemotional traits in youth. *The New England Journal of Medicine, 371,* 2207-2216.

Blakemore, S-J. (2018). Avoiding social risk in adolescence. *Current Directions in Psychological Science, 27,* 116-122.

Blakemore, S-J. (2012). Imaging brain development: The adolescent brain. *Neuroimage, 61,* 397-406.

Blakemore, S-J. (2018). *Inventing ourselves: The secret life of the teenage brain.* New York: Public Affairs.

Blanc, A., Tsui, A., Croft, T., & Trevitt, J. (2010). Patterns and trends in adolescents' contraceptive use and discontinuation in developing countries and comparisons with adult women. *International Perspectives on Sexual and Reproductive Health, 35,* 63-71.

Blankenstein, N., Telzer, E., Do, K., van Duijvenvoorde, A., & Crone, E. (2020). Behavioral and neural pathways supporting the development of prosocial and risk-taking behavior across adolescence. *Child Development, 91,* e665-e681.

Bleakley, A., Hennessy, M., Fishbein, M., & Jordan, A. (2008). It works both ways: The relationship between sexual content in the media and adolescent sexual behavior. *Media Psychology, 11,* 443-461.

Bleakley, A., Jamieson, P., & Romer, D. (2012). Trends of sexual and violent content by gender in top-grossing U.S. films, 1950-2006. *Journal of Adolescent Health, 51,* 73-79.

Bleidorn, W. (2015). What accounts for personality maturation in early adulthood? *Current Directions in Psychological Science, 24,* 245-252.

Bleidorn, W., Arsland, R. C., Denissen, J. J. A., Rentfrow, P. J., Gebauer, J. E., Potter, J., & Gosling, S. D. (2016). Age and gender differences in self-esteem—A cross-cultural window. *Journal of Personality and Social Psychology, 111,* 396-410.

Blondal, K., & Adalbjarnardottir, S. (2014). Parenting in relation to school dropout through student engagement: A longitudinal study. *Journal of Marriage and Family, 76,* 778-795.

Blos, P. (1979). *The adolescent passage.* New York: International Universities Press.

Blum, R., & Rinehart, P. (2000). *Reducing the risk: Connections that make a difference in the lives of youth.* Minneapolis: Division of General Pediatrics and Adolescent Health, University of Minnesota.

Blumenthal, H., Leen-Feldner, E. W., Babson, K. A., Gahr, J. L., Trainor, C. D., & Frala, J. L. (2011). Elevated social anxiety among early maturing girls. *Developmental Psychology, 47,* 1133-1140.

Blyth, D., Simmons, R., & Zakin, D. (1985). Satisfaction with body image for early adolescent females: The impact of pubertal timing within different school environments. *Journal of Youth and Adolescence, 14,* 227-236.

Bodell, L., Wildes, J., Goldschmidt, A., Lepage, R., Keenan, K., Guyer, A., . . . Forbes, E. (2018). Associations between neural reward processing and binge eating among adolescent girls. *Journal of Adolescent Health, 62,* 107–113.

Bodell, L. P., Wildes, J. E., Cheng, Y., Goldschmidt, A. B., Keenan, K., Hipwell, A. E., & Stepp, S. D. (2018). Associations between race and eating disorder symptom trajectories in black and white girls. *Journal of Abnormal Child Psychology, 46,* 625–638.

Boden, J., Fergusson, D., & Horwood, J. (2011). Age of menarche and psychosocial outcomes in a New Zealand birth cohort. *Journal of the American Academy of Child & Adolescent Psychiatry, 50,* 132–140.

Bodner, N., Kuppens, P., Allen, N., Sheeber, L., & Ceulemans, E. (2018). Affective family interactions and their associations with adolescent depression: A dynamic network approach. *Development and Psychopathology, 30,* 1459–1473.

Boele, S., Van der Graaff, J., de Wied, M., Van der Valk, I., Crocetti, E., & Branje, S. (2019). Linking parent–child and peer relationship quality to empathy in adolescence: A multilevel meta-analysis. *Journal of Youth and Adolescence, 48,* 1033–1055.

Boer, M., Stevens, G., Finkenauer, C., & van den Eijnden, R. (2020). Attention Deficit Hyperactivity Disorder—symptoms, social media use intensity, and social media use problems in adolescents: Investigating directionality. *Child Development, 91,* e853–e865.

Bogaerts, A., Claes, L., Schwartz, S., Becht, A., Verschueren, M., Gandhi, A., & Luyckx, K. (2019). Identity structure and processes in adolescence: Examining the directionality of between- and within-person associations. *Journal of Youth and Adolescence, 48,* 891–907.

Bogin, B. (2011). Puberty and adolescence: An evolutionary perspective. In B. Brown & M. Prinstein (Eds.), *Encyclopedia of adolescence* (Vol. 1, pp. 275–286). New York: Academic Press.

Boislard, M., Dussault, F., Brendgen, M., & Vitaro, F. (2013). Internalizing and externalizing behaviors as predictors of sexual onset in early adolescence. *Journal of Early Adolescence, 33,* 920–945.

Boivin, J., Piekarski, D., Thomas, A., & Wilbrecht, L. (2018). Adolescent pruning and stabilization of dendritic spines on cortical layer 5 pyramidal neurons do not depend on gonadal hormones. *Developmental Cognitive Neuroscience, 30,* 100–107.

Boivin, J. R., Piekarski, D. J., Thomas, A. W., & Wilbrecht, L. (2018). Adolescent pruning and stabilization of dendritic spines on cortical layer 5 pyramidal neurons do not depend on gonadal hormones. *Developmental Cognitive Neuroscience, 30,* 100–107.

Bolland, K. A., Bolland, J. M., Tomek, S., Devereaux, R. S., Mrug, S., & Wimberly, J. C. (2016). Trajectories of adolescent alcohol use by gender and early initiation status. *Youth & Society, 48,* 3–32.

Bolling, D., Pitskel, N., Deen, B., Crowley, M., Mayes, L., & Pelphrey, K. (2011). Development of neural systems for processing social exclusion from childhood to adolescence. *Developmental Psychology, 14,* 1431–1444.

Bonanno, R. A., & Hymel, S. (2013). Cyber bullying and internalizing difficulties: Above and beyond the impact of traditional forms of bullying. *Journal of Youth & Adolescence, 42,* 685–697.

Bond, R. M., & Bushman, B. J. (2016). The contagious spread of violence among US adolescents through social networks. *American Journal of Public Health, 106,* 288–294.

Bong, M. (2009). Age-related differences in achievement goal differentiation. *Journal of Educational Psychology, 101,* 879–896.

Bong, M., Hwang, A., Noh, A., & Kim, S-i. (2014). Perfectionism and motivation of adolescents in academic contexts. *Journal of Educational Psychology, 106,* 711–729.

Bongers, I., Koot, H., van der Ende, J., & Verhulst, F. (2004). Developmental trajectories of externalizing behaviors in childhood and adolescence. *Child Development, 75,* 1523–1537.

Boniel-Nissim, M., & Sasson, H. (2018). Bullying victimization and poor relationships with parents as risk factors of problematic internet use in adolescence. *Computers in Human Behavior, 88,* 176–183.

Booth, A., Scott, M., & King, V. (2010). Father residence and adolescent problem behavior: Are youth always better off in two-parent families? *Journal of Family Issues, 31,* 585–605.

Booth, J. M., & Shaw, D. S. (2020). Relations among perceptions of neighborhood cohesion and control and parental monitoring across adolescence. *Journal of Youth and Adolescence, 49,* 74–86.

Booth, M. Z., & Gerard, J. M. (2014). Adolescents' stage-environment fit in middle and high school: The relationship between students' perceptions of their schools and themselves. *Youth & Society, 46,* 735–755.

Booth, M. Z., & Sheehan, H. C. (2008). Perceptions of people and place: Young adolescents' interpretation of their schools in the United States and the United Kingdom. *Journal of Adolescent Research, 23,* 722–744.

Borelli, J. L., & Prinstein, M. J. (2006). Reciprocal, longitudinal associations among adolescents' negative feedback-seeking, depressive symptoms, and peer relations. *Journal of Abnormal Child Psychology, 34,* 159–169.

Borghuis, J., Denissen, J., Oberski, D., Sijtsma, K., Meeus, W., Branje, S., . . . Bleidorn, W. (2017). Big five personality stability, change, and codevelopment across adolescence and early adulthood. *Journal of Personality and Social Psychology, 113,* 641–657.

Bornstein, M., Hahn, C., & Wolke, D. (2013). Systems and cascades in cognitive development and academic achievement. *Child Development, 84,* 154–162.

Borzekowski, D., Fobil, J., & Asante, K. (2006). Online access by adolescents in Accra: Ghanaian teens' use of the Internet for health information. *Developmental Psychology, 42,* 450–458.

Bos, H., & Sandfort, T. (2015). Gender nonconformity, sexual orientation, and Dutch adolescents' relationship with peers. *Archives of Sexual Behavior, 44,* 1269–1279.

Bottiani, J., Bradshaw, C., & Mendelson, T. (2016). Inequality in Black and White high school students' perceptions of school support: An examination of race in context. *Journal of Youth and Adolescence, 45,* 1176–1191.

Bouchard, K., Smith, J., & Woods, H. (2021). Individual and social-contextual factors underlying adolescents' commitment to victimizing friendships: A qualitative analysis. *The Journal of Early Adolescence, 41,* 70–96.

Bouchey, H. A., Shoulberg, E. K., Jodl, K. M., & Eccles, J. S. (2010). Longitudinal links between older sibling features and younger siblings' academic adjustment during early adolescence. *Journal of Educational Psychology, 102,* 197–211.

Boulos, P., Dalwani, M., Tanabe, J., Mikulich-Gilbertson, S., Banich, M., Crowley, T., . . . Sakai, J. (2016). Brain cortical thickness differences in adolescent females with substance use disorders. *PLOS ONE, 11,* e0152983.

Bountress, K., Chassin, L., & Lemery-Chalfant, K. (2017). Parent and peer influence on emerging adult substance use disorder: A genetically informed study. *Development and Psychopathology, 29,* 121–142.

Bourque, J., Afzali, M., & Conrod, P. (2018). Association of cannabis use with adolescent psychotic symptoms. *JAMA Psychiatry, 75,* 864–866.

Bower, A., Nishina, A., Witkow, M., & Bellmore, A. (2015). Nice guys and gals finish last? Not in early adolescence when empathic, accepted, and popular peers are desirable. *Journal of Youth and Adolescence, 44,* 2275–2288.

Bowers, E., Geldhof, G., Johnson, S., Lerner, J., & Lerner, R. (2014). Special issue introduction: Thriving across the adolescent years: A view of the issues. *Journal of Youth & Adolescence, 43,* 859–868.

Bowker, A. (2004). Predicting friendship stability during early adolescence. *Journal of Early Adolescence, 24,* 85–112.

Bowker, J. (2011). Examining two types of best friendship dissolution during early adolescence. *Journal of Early Adolescence, 31,* 656–670.

Bowker, J., & Etkin, R. (2014). Does humor explain why relationally aggressive adolescents are popular? *Journal of Youth and Adolescence, 43,* 1322–1332.

Bowker, J., & Spencer, S. (2010). Friendship and adjustment: A focus on mixed-grade friendships. *Journal of Youth and Adolescence, 39,* 1318–1329.

Bowlby, J. (1969). *Attachment and loss:* Vol. 1. *Attachment.* New York: Basic Books.

Boyce, T. (2019). *The orchid and the dandelion.* New York: Vintage.

Boyd, D. (2014). *It's complicated: The social life of networked teens.* New Haven: Yale University Press.

Boyer, B., & Nelson, J. (2015). Longitudinal associations of childhood parenting and adolescent health: The mediating influence of social competence. *Child Development, 86,* 828–843.

Boyer, T. W. (2006). The development of risk-taking: A multi-perspective review. *Developmental Review, 26,* 291–345.

Boyle, M. H., Georgiades, K., Racine, Y., & Mustard, C. (2007). Neighborhood and family influences on educational attainment: Results from the Ontario Child Health Study follow-up 2001. *Child Development, 78,* 168–189.

Braams, B., Davidow, J., & Somerville, L. (2020). Developmental patterns of change in the influence of safe and risky peer choices on risky decision-making. *Developmental Science, 22,* e12717.

Braams, B., Peper, J., van der Heide, D., Peters, S., & Crone, E. (2016). Nucleus accumbens response to rewards and testosterone levels are related to alcohol use in adolescents and young adults. *Developmental Cognitive Neuroscience, 17,* 83–93.

Braams, B. R., & Crone, E. A. (2017). Longitudinal changes in social brain development: Processing outcomes for friend and self. *Child Development, 88,* 1952–1965.

Bradbury, S., Dubow, E., & Domoff, S. (2018). How do adolescents learn cyber-victimization coping skills? An examination of parent and peer coping socialization. *Journal of Youth and Adolescence, 47,* 1866–1879.

Brady, S., & Halpern-Felsher, B. (2007). Adolescents' reported consequences of having oral sex versus vaginal sex. *Pediatrics, 119,* 229–236.

Brain Development Cooperative Group. (2012). Total and regional brain volumes in a population-based normative sample from 4 to 18 years: The NIH MRI Study of Normal Brain Development. *Cerebral Cortex, 22,* 1–12.

Braithwaite, I., Stewart, A., Hancox, R., Beasley, R., Murphy, R., Mitchell, E., & ISAAC Phase Three Study Group. (2013). The worldwide association between television viewing and obesity in children and adolescents: Cross sectional study. *PLOS ONE, 8,* 74263.

Brakefield, T., Mednick, S., Wilson, H., De Neve, J., Christakis, N., & Fowler, J. (2014). Same-sex sexual attraction does not spread in adolescent social networks. *Archives of Sexual Behavior, 43,* 335–344.

Bramen, J. E., Hranilovich, J. A., Dahl, R. E., Chen, J., Rosso, C., Forbes, E. E., Dinov, I. D., Worthman, C. M., & Sowell, E. R. (2012). Sex matters during adolescence: Testosterone-related cortical thickness maturation differs between boys and girls. *PLOS One, 7,* 33850.

Branje, S. (2018). Development of parent–adolescent relationships: Conflict interactions as a mechanism of change. *Child Development Perspectives, 12,* 171–176.

Brauer, J. (2017). Cultivating conformists or raising rebels? Connecting parental control and autonomy support to adolescent delinquency. *Journal of Research on Adolescence, 27,* 452–470.

Brauner, E., Busch, A., Lind, C, Koch, T., Hickey, M., & Juul, A. (2020). Trends in the incidence of central precocious puberty and normal variant puberty among children in Denmark, 1998 to 2010. *JAMA Open, 3,* e2015665.

Brausch, A., & Gutierrez, P. (2010). Differences in non-suicidal self-injury and suicide attempts in adolescents. *Journal of Youth and Adolescence, 39,* 233–242.

Brechwald, W., & Prinstein, M. (2011). Beyond homophily: A decade of advances in understanding peer influence processes. *Journal of Research on Adolescence, 21,* 166–179.

Brendgen, M., & Poulin, F. (2018). Continued bullying victimization from childhood to young adulthood: A longitudinal study of mediating and protective factors. *Journal of Abnormal Child Psychology, 46,* 27–39.

Brendgen, M., Vitaro, F., & Bukowski, W. (2000). Deviant friends and early adolescents' emotional and behavioral adjustment. *Journal of Research on Adolescence, 10,* 173–189.

Brendgen, M., Vitaro, F., Doyle, A., Markiewicz, D., & Bukowski, W. (2002). Same-sex peer relations and romantic relationships during early adolescence: Interactive links to emotional, behavioral, and academic adjustment. *Merrill-Palmer Quarterly, 48,* 77–103.

Brenick, A., & Killen, M. (2014). Moral judgements about Jewish-Arab intergroup exclusion: The role of cultural identity and contact. *Developmental Psychology, 50,* 86–99.

Brent, D., Emslie, G., Clarke, G., Wagner, K., Asarnow, J., Keller, M., . . . Zelazny, J. (2008). Switching to another SSRI or to venlafaxine with or without cognitive behavioral therapy for adolescents with SSRI-resistant depression: The TORDIA randomized controlled trial. *JAMA, 299,* 901–913.

Breslau, J., Gilman, S. E., Stein, B. D., Ruder, T., Gmelin, T., & Miller, E. (2017). Sex differences in recent first-onset depression in an epidemiological sample of adolescents. *Translational Psychiatry, 7*(5), e1139.

Breslend, N., Shoulberg, E., McQuade, J., & Murray-Close, D. (2018). Social costs for wannabes: moderating effects of popularity and gender on the links between popularity goals and negative peer experiences. *Journal of Youth and Adolescence, 47,* 1894–1906.

Breuer, J., Vogelgesang, J., Quandt, T., & Festl, R. (2015). Violent video games and physical aggression: Evidence for a selection effect among adolescents. *Psychology of Popular Media Culture, 4,* 305–328.

Brewer, G., & Kerslake, J. (2015). Cyberbullying, self-esteem, empathy and loneliness. *Computers in Human Behavior, 48,* 255–260.

Bridge, J., Greenhouse, J., Ruch, D., Stevens, J., Ackerman, J., Sheftall, A., . . . Campo, J. (2020). Association between the release of Netflix's *13 Reasons Why* and suicide rates in the United States: An interrupted time series analysis. *Journal of the American Academy of Child & Adolescent Psychiatry, 59,* 236–243.

Brieant, A., Peviani, K., Lee, J., King-Casas, B., & Kim-Spoon, J. (2020). Socioeconomic risk for adolescent cognitive control and emerging risk-taking Behaviors. *Journal of Research on Adolescence,* in press.

Briley, D. A., & Tucker-Drob, E. M. (2013). Explaining the increasing heritability of cognitive ability across development: A meta-analysis of longitudinal twin and adoption studies. *Psychological Science, 24,* 1704–1713.

Brinch, C., & Galloway, T. (2012). Schooling in adolescence raises IQ scores. *Proceedings of the National Academy of Sciences, 109,* 425–430.

Brody, G., Chen, Y., Murry, V., Ge, X., Simons, R., Gibbons, F., . . . Cutrona, C. (2006). Perceived discrimination and the adjustment of African American youths: A five-year longitudinal analysis with contextual moderation effects. *Child Development, 77,* 1170–1189.

Brody, G., Miller, G., Tianyi, Y., Beach, S., & Chen, E. (2016). Supportive family environments ameliorate the link between racial discrimination and epigenetic aging: A replication across two longitudinal cohorts. *Psychological Science, 27,* 530–541.

Brody, G., Stoneman, Z., & Flor, D. (1996). Parental religiosity, family processes, and youth competence in rural, two-parent African-American families. *Developmental Psychology, 32,* 696–706.

Brody, G., Yu, T., & Beach, S. (2015). A differential susceptibility analysis reveals the "who and how" about adolescents' responses to preventive interventions: Tests of first- and second-generation gene × intervention hypotheses. *Development and Psychopathology, 27,* 37–49.

Brody, G., Yu, T., Miller, G., & Chen, E. (2015). Discrimination, racial identity, and cytokine levels among African-American adolescents. *Adolescent Health, 56,* 496–501.

Brody, G. H., Yu, T., Nusslock, R., Barton, A. W., Miller, G. E., Chen, E., Holmes, C., McCormick, M., & Sweet, L. H. (2019). The protective effects of supportive parenting on the relationship between adolescent poverty and resting-state functional brain connectivity during adulthood. *Psychological Science, 30,* 1040–1049.

Broidy, L., Nagin, D., Tremblay, R., Bates, J., Brame, B., Dodge, K., . . . Vitaro, F. (2003). Developmental trajectories of childhood disruptive behaviors and adolescent delinquency: A six-site, cross-national study. *Developmental Psychology, 39,* 222–245.

Bromberg, U., Wiehler, A., & Peters, J. (2015). Episodic future thinking is related to impulsive decision making in healthy adolescents. *Child Development, 86,* 1458–1468.

Bronfenbrenner, U. (1979). *The ecology of human development.* Cambridge, MA: Harvard University Press.

Brookmeyer, K., Henrich, C., & Schwab-Stone, M. (2005). Adolescents who witness community violence: Can parent support and prosocial cognitions protect them from committing violence? *Child Development, 76,* 917–929.

Brooks-Gunn, J., & Warren, M. (1985). The effects of delayed menarche in different contexts: Dance and nondance students. *Journal of Youth and Adolescence, 14,* 285–300.

Brooks-Gunn, J., Graber, J., & Paikoff, R. (1994). Studying links between hormones and negative affect: Models and measures. *Journal of Research on Adolescence, 4,* 469–486.

Brown, B. (1990). Peer groups. In S. Feldman & G. Elliott (Eds.), *At the threshold: The developing adolescent* (pp. 171–196). Cambridge, MA: Harvard University Press.

Brown, B. (2004). Adolescents' relationships with peers. In R. Lerner & L. Steinberg (Eds.), *Handbook of adolescent psychology* (pp. 363–394). New York: Wiley.

Brown, B., & Larson, J. (2009). Peer relationships in adolescence. In R. Lerner & L. Steinberg (Eds.), *Handbook of adolescent psychology* (3rd ed., Vol. 2, pp. 74–103). New York: Wiley.

Brown, B., Herman, M., Hamm, J., & Heck, D. (2008). Ethnicity and image: Correlates of minority adolescents' affiliation with individual-based versus ethnically defined peer crowds. *Child Development, 79,* 529–546.

Brown, B., Mory, M., & Kinney, D. (1994). Casting crowds in a relational perspective: Caricature, channel, and context. In R. Montemayor, G. Adams, & T. Gullotta (Eds.), *Advances in adolescent development:* Vol. 5. *Personal relationships during adolescence.* Newbury Park, CA: Sage.

Brown, B., Mounts, N., Lamborn, S., & Steinberg, L. (1993). Parenting practices and peer group affiliation in adolescence. *Child Development, 64,* 467-482.

Brown, B., Von Bank, H., & Steinberg, L. (2008). Smoke in the looking glass: Effects of discordance between self- and peer-rated crowd affiliation on adolescent anxiety, depression, and self-feelings. *Journal of Youth and Adolescence, 37,* 1163-1177.

Brown, B. B. (1999). "You're going out with who?": Peer group influences on adolescent romantic relationships. In W. Furman, B. B. Brown, & C. Feiring (Eds.), *Cambridge studies in social and emotional development. The development of romantic relationships in adolescence* (p. 291-329). New York: Cambridge University Press.

Brown, C., Alabi, B., Huynh, V., & Masten, C. (2011). Ethnicity and gender in late childhood and early adolescence: Group identity and awareness of bias. *Developmental Psychology, 47,* 463-471.

Brown, J., & Bobkowski, P. (2011a). Media, influence of. In B. Brown & M. Prinstein (Eds.), *Encyclopedia of adolescence* (Vol. 2, pp. 189-195). New York: Academic Press.

Brown, J., & Bobkowski, P. (2011b). Older and newer media: Patterns of use and effects on adolescents' health and well-being. *Journal of Research on Adolescence, 21,* 95-113.

Brown, J., Cohen, P., Chen, H., Smailes, E., & Johnson, J. (2004). Sexual trajectories of abused and neglected youths. *Journal of Developmental & Behavioral Pediatrics, 25,* 77-82.

Browning, C. R., Gardner, M., Maimon, D., & Brooks-Gunn, J. (2014). Collective efficacy and the contingent consequences of exposure to life-threatening violence. *Developmental Psychology, 50,* 1878-1890.

Brubacher, J., & Rudy, W. (1976). *Higher education in transition* (3rd ed.). New York: Harper & Row.

Brückner, H., & Bearman, P. (2005). After the promise: The STD consequences of adolescent virginity pledges. *Journal of Adolescent Health, 36,* 271-278.

Brunborg, G., & Burdzovic Andreas, J. (2019). Increase in time spent on social media is associated with modest increase in depression, conduct problems, and episodic heavy drinking. *Journal of Adolescence, 74,* 201-209.

Bruvold, W. (1993). A meta-analysis of adolescent smoking prevention programs. *American Journal of Public Health, 83,* 872-880.

Bryan, A., Gillman, A., & Hansen, N. (2016). Changing the context is important and necessary, but not sufficient, for reducing adolescent risky sexual behavior: A reply to Steinberg (2015). *Perspectives on Psychological Science, 11,* 535-538.

Bryan, M. A., Rowhani-Rahbar, A., Comstock, R., & Rivara, F. (2016). Sports- and recreation-related concussions in US youth. *Pediatrics, 138,* e20154635.

Bryant, A., & Zimmerman, M. (2003). Role models and psychosocial outcomes among African American adolescents. *Journal of Adolescent Research, 18,* 36-67.

Bucchianeri, M., Eisenberg, M., Wall, M., Piran, N., & Neumark-Sztainer, D. (2014). Multiple types of harassment: Associations with emotional well-being and unhealthy behaviors in adolescents. *Journal of Adolescent Health, 54,* 724-729.

Bucci, R., & Staff, J. (2020). Pubertal timing and adolescent delinquency. *Criminology, 58,* 537-567.

Buchanan, C., Eccles, J., & Becker, J. (1992). Are adolescents the victims of raging hormones? Evidence for activational effects of hormones on moods and behavior at adolescence. *Psychological Bulletin, 111,* 62-107.

Buchanan, C., Maccoby, E., & Dornbusch, S. (1996). *Adolescents after divorce.* Cambridge, MA: Harvard University Press.

Buchmann, C., & Dalton, B. (2002). Interpersonal influences and educational aspirations in 12 countries: The importance of institutional context. *Sociology of Education, 75,* 99-122.

Buehler, C. (2020). Family processes and children's and adolescents' well-being. *Journal of Marriage and Family, 82,* 145-174.

Buelens, T., Luyckx, K., Gandhi, A., Kiekens, G., & Claes, L. (2019). Non-suicidal self-injury in adolescence: Longitudinal associations with psychological distress and rumination. *Journal of Abnormal Child Psychology, 47,* 1569-1581.

Buelga, S., Martinez-Ferrer, B., & Cava, M. (2017). Differences in family climate and family communication among cyberbullies, cybervictims, and cyber bully-victims in adolescents. *Computers in Human Behavior, 76,* 164-173.

Buelow, M., Okdie, B., & Cooper, A. (2015). The influence of video games on executive functions in college students. *Computers in Human Behavior, 45,* 228-234.

Buhi, E., & Goodson, P. (2007). Predictors of adolescent sexual behavior and intention: A theory-guided systematic review. *Journal of Adolescent Health, 40,* 4-21.

Buhrmester, D. (1990). Intimacy of friendship, interpersonal competence, and adjustment during preadolescence and adolescence. *Child Development, 61,* 1101-1111.

Buhrmester, D. (1996). Need fulfillment, interpersonal competence, and the developmental contexts of early adolescent friendship. In W. Bukowski, A. Newcomb, & W. Hartup, (Eds.), *The company they keep: Friendship in childhood and adolescence* (pp. 158-185). New York: Cambridge University Press.

Buhrmester, D., & Furman, W. (1987). The development of companionship and intimacy. *Child Development, 58,* 1101-1113.

Buil, J., van Lier, P., Brendgen, M., Koot, H., & Vitaro, F. (2017). Developmental pathways linking childhood temperament with antisocial behavior and substance use in adolescence: Explanatory mechanisms in the peer environment. *Journal of Personality and Social Psychology, 112,* 948-966.

Bukowski, W., Gauze, C., Hoza, B., & Newcomb, A. (1993). Differences and consistency between same-sex and other-sex peer relationships during early adolescence. *Developmental Psychology, 29,* 255-263.

Bukowski, W., Sippola, L., & Hoza, B. (1999). Same and other: Interdependency between participation in same- and other-sex friendships. *Journal of Youth and Adolescence, 28,* 439-459.

Bukowski, W., Sippola, L., & Newcomb, A. (2000). Variations in patterns of attraction of same- and other-sex peers during early adolescence. *Developmental Psychology, 36,* 147-154.

Bull, S., Devine, S., Schmiege, S., Pickard, L., Campbell, J., & Shlay, J. (2016). Text messaging, teen outreach program, and sexual health behavior: A cluster randomized trial. *American Journal of Public Health, 106,* S117-S125.

Bullock, A., Liu, J., Cheah, C., Coplan, R., Chen, X., & Li, D. (2018). The role of adolescents' perceived parental psychological control in the links between shyness and socio-emotional adjustment among youth. *Journal of Adolescence, 68,* 117-126.

Burdette, A., & Needham, B. (2012). Neighborhood environment and body mass index trajectories from adolescence to adulthood. *Journal of Adolescent Health, 50,* 30-37.

Burdette, A., Haynes, S., Hill, T., & Bartkowski, J. (2014). Religious variations in perceived infertility and inconsistent contraceptive use among unmarried young adults in the United States. *Journal of Adolescent Health, 54,* 704-709.

Bureau of Labor Statistics. (2019). *Current population survey.* Washington: Author.

Bureau of Labor Statistics. (2020). *Employment characteristics of families.* Washington: Author.

Burg, S., Mayers, R., & Miller, L. (2011). Spirituality, religion, and healthy development in adolescents. In B. Brown & M. Prinstein (Eds.), *Encyclopedia of adolescence* (Vol. 1, pp. 353-359). New York: Academic Press.

Burke, A. R., McCormick, C. M., Pellis, S. M., & Lukkes, J. L. (2017). Impact of adolescent social experiences on behavior and neural circuits implicated in mental illnesses. *Neuroscience & Biobehavioral Reviews, 76,* 280-300.

Burke, T., Connolly, S., Hamilton, J., Stange, J., Abramson, L., & Alloy, L. (2016). Cognitive risk and protective factors for suicidal ideation: A two year longitudinal study in adolescence. *Journal of Abnormal Child Psychology, 44,* 1145-1160.

Burke, T., Sticca, F., & Perren, S. (2017). Everything's gonna be alright! The longitudinal interplay among social support, peer victimization, and depressive symptoms. *Journal of Youth and Adolescence, 46,* 1999-2014.

Burnett Heyes, S., Jih, Y-R., Bock, P., Hiu, C-F., Holmes, E., & Lau, J. (2015). Relationship reciprocation modulates resource allocation in adolescent social networks: Developmental effects. *Child Development, 86,* 1489-1506.

Burnett, S., Sebastian, C., Kadosh, K., & Blakemore, S-J. (2011). The social brain in adolescence: Evidence from functional magnetic resonance imaging and behavioural studies. *Neuroscience and Biobehavioral Reviews, 35,* 1654-1664.

Burns, E. C. (2020). Factors that support high school completion: A longitudinal examination of quality teacher-student relationships and intentions to graduate. *Journal of Adolescence, 84,* 180-189.

Burnside, A. N., & Gaylord-Harden, N. K. (2019). Hopelessness and delinquent behavior as predictors of community violence exposure in ethnic minority male adolescent offenders. *Journal of Abnormal Child Psychology, 47,* 801-810.

Bursztyn, L., & Jensen, R. (2015). How does peer pressure affect educational investments? *Quarterly Journal of Economics,* 1329-1367.

Burt, K. B., & Paysnick, A. A. (2012). Resilience in the transition to adulthood. *Development and Psychopathology, 24,* 493-505.

Burt, K., & Roisman, G. (2010). Competence and psychopathology: Cascade effects in the NICHD Study of Early Child Care and Youth Development. *Development and Psychopathology, 22,* 557-567.

Burt, K., Obradović, J., Long, J., & Masten, A. (2008). The interplay of social competence and psychopathology over 20 years: Testing transactional and cascade models. *Child Development, 79,* 359-374.

Burt, S. A., Barnes, A. R., McGue, M., & Iacono, W. G. (2008). Parental divorce and adolescent delinquency: Ruling out the impact of common genes. *Developmental Psychology, 44,* 1668-1677.

Burt, S. A., McGue, M., Krueger, R. F., & Iacono, W. G. (2007). Environmental contributions to adolescent delinquency: A fresh look at the shared environment. *Journal of Abnormal Child Psychology, 35,* 787-800.

Burton, L. (2007). Childhood adultification in economically disadvantaged families: A conceptual model. *Family Relations, 56,* 329-345.

Busching, R., & Krahé, B. (2020). With a little help from their peers: The impact of classmates on adolescents' development of prosocial behavior. *Journal of Youth and Adolescence, 49*(9), 1849-1863.

Bushman, B., Newman, K., Calvert, S., Downey, G., Dredze, M., Gottfredson, M., . . . Webster, D. (2016). Youth violence: What we know and what we need to know. *American Psychologist, 71,* 17-39.

Butler-Barnes, S., Richardson, B., Chavous, T., & Zhu, J. (2019). The importance of racial socialization: School-based racial discrimination and racial identity among African American adolescent boys and girls. *Journal of Research on Adolescence, 29,* 432-448.

Butterfield, R., Silk, J., Lee, K., Siegle, G., Dahl, R., Forbes, E., . . . & Ladouceur, C. (2020). Parents still matter! Parental warmth predicts adolescent brain function and anxiety and depressive symptoms two years later. *Development and Psychopathology, 32,* 1-14.

Bygren, M. (2016). Ability grouping's effects on grades and the attainment of higher education. *Sociology of Education, 89,* 118-136.

Byrd, C., & Chavous, T. (2011). Racial identity, school racial climate, and school intrinsic motivation among African American youth: The importance of person-context congruence. *Journal of Research on Adolescence, 21,* 849-860.

Cadely, H., Mrug, S., & Windle, M. (2019). Comparisons of types of exposure to violence within and across contexts in predicting the perpetration of dating aggression. *Journal of Youth and Adolescence, 48,* 2377-2390.

Calabro, F. J., Murty, V. P., Jalbrzikowski, M., Tervo-Clemmens, B., & Luna, B. (2020). Development of hippocampal–prefrontal cortex interactions through adolescence. *Cerebral Cortex, 30,* 1548-1558.

Caldwell, L., & Darling, N. (1999). Leisure context, parental control, and resistance to peer pressure as predictors of adolescent partying and substance use: An ecological perspective. *Journal of Leisure Research, 31,* 57-77.

Caldwell, M. S., Rudolph, K., Troop-Gordon, W., & Kim, D. (2004). Reciprocal influence among relational self-views, social disengagement, and peer stress during early adolescence. *Child Development, 75,* 1140-1154.

Callahan, R. (2005). Tracking and English learners: Limiting opportunity to learn. *American Educational Research Journal, 42,* 305-328.

Calzo, J. P., Sonneville, K. R., Haines, J., Blood, E. A., Field, A. E., & Austin, S. B. (2012). The development of associations among body mass index, body dissatisfaction, and weight and shape concern in adolescent boys and girls. *Journal of Adolescent Health, 51,* 517-523.

Camacho, D., & Fuligni, A. (2015). Extracurricular participation among adolescents from immigrant families. *Journal of Youth and Adolescence, 44,* 1251-1262.

Camacho-Thompson, D., and Vargas, R. (2018). Organized community activity participation and the dynamic roles of neighborhood violence and gender among Latino adolescents. *American Journal of Community Psychology, 62,* 87-100.

Camacho-Thompson, D. E., Gillen-O'Neel, C., Gonzales, N. A., & Fuligni, A. J. (2016). Financial strain, major family life events, and parental academic involvement during adolescence. *Journal of Youth and Adolescence, 45,* 1065-1074.

Cambron, C., Kosterman, R., Catalano, R. F., Guttmannova, K., & Hawkins, J. D. (2018). Neighborhood, family, and peer factors associated with early adolescent smoking and alcohol use. *Journal of Youth and Adolescence, 47,* 369-382.

Camchong, J., Lim, K., & Kumra, S. (2017). Adverse effects of cannabis on adolescent brain development: A longitudinal study. *Cerebral Cortex, 27,* 1922-1930.

Campa, M., & Eckenrode, J. (2006). Pathways to intergenerational adolescent childbearing in a high-risk sample. *Journal of Marriage and Family, 68,* 558-572.

Campbell, B. (2011). Adrenarche and middle childhood. *Human Nature, 22,* 327-349.

Campbell, B., Prossinger, H., & Mbzivo, M. (2005). Timing of pubertal maturation and the onset of sexual behavior among Zimbabwe school boys. *Archives of Sexual Behavior, 34,* 505-516.

Campbell, F., Pungello, E., Miller-Johnson, S., Burchinal, M., & Ramey, C. (2001). The development of cognitive and academic abilities: Growth curves from an early childhood educational experiment. *Developmental Psychology, 37,* 231-242.

Campione-Barr, N., & Killoren, S. E. (2019). Love them and hate them: The developmental appropriateness of ambivalence in the adolescent sibling relationship. *Child Development Perspectives, 13,* 221-226.

Campione-Barr, N., Bassett Greer, K., & Kruse, A. (2013). Differential associations between domains of sibling conflict and adolescent emotional adjustment. *Child Development, 84,* 938-954.

Cappelleri, J., Eckenrode, J., & Powers, J. (1993). The epidemiology of child abuse: Findings from the Second National Incidence and Prevalence Study of Child Abuse and Neglect. *American Journal of Public Health, 83,* 1622-1624.

Caputi, T., Smith, L., Strathdee, S., & Ayers, J. (2018). Substance use among lesbian, gay, bisexual, and questioning adolescents in the United States, 2015. *American Journal of Public Health, 108,* 1031-1034.

Carbonaro, W. (2005). Tracking, students' effort, and academic achievement. *Sociology of Education, 78,* 27-49.

Carbonaro, W., & Covay, E. (2010). School sector and student achievement in the era of standards-based reforms. *Sociology of Education, 83,* 160-182.

Card, N., Stucky, B., Sawalani, G., & Little, T. (2008). Direct and indirect aggression during childhood and adolescence: A meta-analytic review of gender differences, intercorrelations, and relations to maladjustment. *Child Development, 79,* 1185-1229.

Cardinale, E., Breeden, A., Robertson, E., Lozier, L., Vanmeter, J., & Marsh, A. (2018). Externalizing behavior severity in youths with callous-unemotional traits corresponds to patterns of amygdala activity and connectivity during judgments of causing fear. *Development and Psychopathology, 30,* 191-201.

Carliner, H., Keyes, K., McLaughlin, K., Meyers, J., Dunn, E., & Martins, S. (2016). Childhood trauma and illicit drug use in adolescence: A population-based national comorbidity survey replication-adolescent supplement study. *Journal of the American Academy of Child & Adolescent Psychiatry, 55,* 701-708.

Carlo, G., Padilla-Walker, L. P., & Day, R. (2011). A test of the economic strain model on adolescents' prosocial behaviors. *Journal of Research on Adolescence, 21,* 842-848.

Carlo, G., Padilla-Walker, L., & Nielson, M. (2015). Longitudinal bidirectional relations between adolescents' sympathy and prosocial behavior. *Developmental Psychology, 51,* 1771-1777.

Carlo, G., White, R., Streit, C., Knight, G., & Zeiders, K. (2018). Longitudinal relations among parenting styles, prosocial behaviors, and academic outcomes in U.S. Mexican adolescents. *Child Development, 89,* 577-592.

Carlson, D., McNulty, T., Bellair, P., & Watts, S. (2014). Neighborhoods and racial/ethnic disparities in adolescent sexual risk behavior. *Journal of Youth and Adolescence, 43,* 1536-1549.

Carlson, W., & Rose, A. (2012). Activities in heterosexual romantic relationships: Grade differences and associations with relationship satisfaction. *Journal of Adolescence, 35,* 219-224.

Carothers, K., Arizaga, J., Smith Carter, J., Taylor, J., & Grant, K. (2016). The costs and benefits of active coping for adolescents residing in urban poverty. *Journal of Youth and Adolescence, 45,* 1323-1337.

Carriedo, N., Corral, A., Montor, P. R., Herrero, L., & Rucian, M. (2016). Development of the updating executive function: From 7-year-olds to young adults. *Developmental Psychology, 52,* 666-678.

Carrion, V. G., & Wong, S. S. (2012). Can traumatic stress alter the brain? Understanding the implications of early trauma on brain development and learning. *Journal of Adolescent Health, 51,* S23-S28.

Carroll, J. S., Willoughby, B., Badger, S., Nelson, L. J., Barry, C. M., & Madsen, S. D. (2007). So close, yet so far away: The impact of varying marital horizons on emerging adulthood. *Journal of Adolescent Research, 22,* 219-247.

Carskadon, M., & Acebo, C. (2002). Regulation of sleepiness in adolescence: Update, insights, and speculation. *Sleep, 25,* 606-616.

Carter, R., Caldwell, C. H., Matusko, N., Antonucci, T., & Jackson, J. S. (2011). Ethnicity, perceived pubertal timing, externalizing behaviors, and depressive symptoms among Black adolescent girls. *Journal of Youth and Adolescence, 40,* 1394-1406.

Carter, R., Halawah, A., & Trinh, S. L. (2018). Peer exclusion during the pubertal transition: The role of social competence. *Journal of Youth and Adolescence, 47,* 121-134.

Carter, R., Seaton, E., & Blazek, J. (2020). Comparing associations between puberty, ethnic-racial identity, self-concept, and depressive symptoms among African American and Caribbean Black boys. *Child Development, 91*(6), 2019-2041.

Casas, J., Ojeda, M., Elipe, P., & Del Rey, R. (2019). Exploring which factors contribute to teens' participation in sexting. *Computers in Human Behavior, 100,* 60-69.

Cascardi, M. (2016). From violence in the home to physical dating violence victimization: The mediating role of psychological distress in a prospective study of female adolescents. *Journal of Youth and Adolescence, 45,* 777-792.

Casella, R. (2003). Zero tolerance policy in schools: Rationale, consequences, and alternatives. *Teachers College Review, 105,* 872-892.

Casement, M. D., Shaw, D. S., Sitnick, S. L., Musselman, S. C., & Forbes, E. E. (2015). Life stress in adolescence predicts early adult reward-related brain function and alcohol dependence. *Social Cognitive and Affective Neuroscience, 10,* 416-423.

Casey, B. J., & Caudle, K. (2013). The teenage brain: Self control. *Current Directions in Psychological Science, 22,* 82-87.

Casey, B. J., Duhoux, S., & Cohen, M. (2010). Adolescence: What do transmission, transition, and translation have to do with it? *Neuron, 67,* 749-760.

Casey, B. J., Galván, A., & Somerville, L. H. (2016). Beyond simple models of adolescence to an integrated circuit-based account: A commentary. *Developmental Cognitive Neuroscience, 17,* 128-130.

Casey, B. J., Heller, A., Gee, D., & Cohen, A. (2019). Development of the emotional brain. *Neuroscience Letters, 693,* 29-34.

Casey, B. J., Jones, R., & Somerville, L. (2011). Braking and accelerating of the adolescent brain. *Journal of Research on Adolescence, 21,* 21-33.

Casey, B. J., Tottenham, N., Liston, C., & Durston, S. (2005). Imaging the developing brain: What have we learned about cognitive development? *Trends in Cognitive Science, 9,* 104-110.

Cash, T. F., Morrow, J., Hrabosky, J. I., & Perry, A. A. (2004). How has body image changed? A cross-sectional investigation of college women and men from 1983 to 2001. *Journal of Consulting and Clinical Psychology, 72,* 1081-1089.

Casillas, A., Robbins, S., Allen, J., Kuo, Y.-L., Hanson, M., & Schmeiser, C. (2012). Predicting early academic failure in high school from prior academic achievement, psychosocial characteristics, and behavior. *Journal of Educational Psychology, 104,* 407-420.

Casper, D., & Card, N. (2010). "We were best friends, but . . .": Two studies of antipathetic relationships emerging from broken friendships. *Journal of Adolescent Research, 25,* 499-526.

Casper, D., & Card, N. (2017). Overt and relational victimization: A meta-analytic review of their overlap and associations with social-psychological adjustment. *Child Development, 88,* 466-483.

Casper, D., Card, N., & Barlow, C. (2020). Relational aggression and victimization during adolescence: A meta-analytic review of unique associations with popularity, peer acceptance, rejection, and friendship characteristics. *Journal of Adolescence, 80,* 41-52.

Caspi, A., Begg, D., Dickson, N., Harrington, H., Langley, J., Moffitt, T., & Silva, P. (1997). Personality traits predict health-risk behaviors in young adulthood: Evidence from a longitudinal study. *Journal of Personality and Social Psychology, 73,* 1052-1063.

Caspi, A., Henry, B., McGee, R., Moffitt, T., & Silva, P. (1995). Temperamental origins of child and adolescent behavior problems: From age 3 to age 15. *Child Development, 66,* 55-68.

Caspi, A., Lynam, D., Moffitt, T., & Silva, P. (1993). Unraveling girls' delinquency: Biological, dispositional, and contextual contributions to adolescent misbehavior. *Developmental Psychology, 29,* 19-30.

Caspi, A., Sugden, K., Moffitt, T., Taylor, A., Craig, I., Harrington, H., . . . Poulton, R. (2003). Influence of life stress on depression: Moderation by a polymorphism in the 5-HTT gene. *Science, 301,* 386-389.

Castellanos-Ryan, N., Pingault, J.-B., Parent, S., Vitaro, F., Tremblay, R., & Séguin, J. (2017). Adolescent cannabis use, change in neurocognitive function, and high-school graduation: A longitudinal study from early adolescence to young adulthood. *Development and Psychopathology, 29,* 1253-1266.

Castro-Schilo, L., Ferrer, E., Hernández, M. M., & Conger, R. D. (2016). Developmental outcomes of school attachment among students of Mexican origin. *Journal of Research on Adolescence, 26,* 753-768.

Cauffman, E., Farruggia, S., & Goldweber, A. (2008). Bad boys or poor parents: Relations to female juvenile delinquency. *Journal of Research on Adolescence, 18,* 699-712.

Cauffman, E., Piquero, A., Kimonis, E., Steinberg, L., & Chassin, L. (2007). Legal, individual, and contextual predictors of court disposition. *Law and Human Behavior, 31,* 519-535.

Cauffman, E., Shulman, E., Bechtold, J., & Steinberg, L. (2015). Children and the law. In R. M. Lerner (Series Ed.) & M. Bornstein & T. Leventhal (Vol. Eds.), *Handbook of child psychology and developmental science* (7th ed.). *Volume 4: Ecological settings and processes in developmental systems* (pp. 616-653). New York: Wiley.

Cauffman, E., Shulman, E., Steinberg, L., Claus, E., Banich, M., Graham, S., & Woolard, J. (2010). Age differences in affective decision making as indexed by performance on the Iowa Gambling Task. *Developmental Psychology, 46,* 193-207.

Cauffman, E., Steinberg, L., & Piquero, A. (2005). Psychological, neuropsychological and physiological correlates of serious antisocial behavior in adolescence: The role of self-control. *Criminology, 43,* 133-175.

Cava, M., Martínez-Ferrer, B., Buelga, S., & Carrascosa, L. (2020). Sexist attitudes, romantic myths, and offline dating violence as predictors of cyber dating violence perpetration in adolescents. *Computers in Human Behavior, 106449.*

Cavanagh, S., & Fomby, P. (2012). School context, family instability, and the academic careers of adolescents. *Sociology of Education, 85,* 81-97.

Cavanagh, S., Crissey, S., & Raley, R. (2008). Family structure history and adolescent romance. *Journal of Marriage and Family, 70,* 698-714.

Cavanagh, S. E., Stritzel, H., Smith, C., & Crosnoe, R. (2018). Family instability and exposure to violence in the early life course. *Journal of Research on Adolescence, 28,* 456-472.

Cavanaugh, A., Stein, G., Supple, A., Gonzalez., L., & Kiang, L. (2018). Protective and promotive effects of Latino early adolescents' cultural assets against multiple types of discrimination. *Journal of Research on Adolescence, 28,* 310-326.

Cavazos-Rehg, P., Spitznagel, E., Bucholz, K., Nurnberger, J., Edenberg, H., Kramer, J., . . . Beirut, L. (2010). Predictors of sexual debut at age 16 or younger. *Archives of Sexual Behavior, 39,* 664-673.

Ceballo, R., McLoyd, V., & Toyokawa, T. (2004). The influence of neighborhood quality on adolescents' educational values and school effort. *Journal of Adolescent Research, 19,* 716-739.

Ceci, S., & Williams, W. (1999). Schooling, intelligence, and income. *American Psychologist, 52,* 1051-1058.

Cédric, P., Koolschijn, P. C., Peper, J. S., & Crone, E. A. (2014). The influence of sex steroids on structural brain maturation in adolescence. *PLOS ONE, 9,* 83929.

Ceglarek, P. J. D., & Ward, L. M. (2016). A tool for help or harm? How associations between social networking use, social support, and mental health differ for sexual minority and heterosexual youth. *Computers in Human Behavior, 65,* 201-209.

Centers for Disease Control and Prevention. (2006). Youth behavior surveillance—United States, 2005. *Morbidity and Mortality Weekly Report, 55,* SS-5.

Centers for Disease Control and Prevention. (2019). *HIV surveillance report, 2018 (preliminary), 30.* http://www.cdc.gov/hiv/library/reports/hiv-surveillance.html. Accessed on January 15, 2021.

Centers for Disease Control and Prevention. (2019a). *Sexually transmitted disease and prevention, 2018.* Washington: Author.

Centers for Disease Control and Prevention. (2019b). *Teen drivers: Get the facts.* Washington: Author.

Centers for Disease Control and Prevention. (2019c). *Youth risk behavior survey, 2019.* Author: Washington.

Centers for Disease Control and Prevention. (2020). *Youth risk behavior surveillance, 2019.* Washington, DC: Author.

Cepa, K., & Furstenberg, F. F. (2020). Reaching adulthood: Persistent beliefs about the importance and timing of adult milestones. *Journal of Family Issues,* in press.

Cerniglia, L., Zoratto, F., Cimino, S., Laviola, G., Ammaniti, M., & Adriana, W. (2017). Internet addiction in adolescence: Neurobiological, psychosocial and clinical issues. *Neuroscience & BioBehavioral Review, 76,* 174–184.

Cervantes, R., & Cordova, D. (2011). Life experiences of Hispanic adolescents: Developmental and language considerations in acculturation stress. *Journal of Community Psychology, 39,* 336–352.

Chaloupka, F. (2004). The effects of price on alcohol use, abuse, and their consequences. In R. Bonnie & M. O'Connell (Eds.), *Reducing underage drinking: A collective responsibility.* Washington: The National Academies Press.

Chan, H.-Y., Brown, B., & Von Bank, H. (2015). Adolescent disclosure of information about peers: The mediating role of perceptions of parents' right to know. *Journal of Youth and Adolescence, 44,* 1048–1065.

Chan, M., Kiang, L., & Witkow, M. (2020). Correlates of ethnicity-related dating preferences among Asian American adolescents across the high school years. *Journal of Research on Adolescence, 30,* 669–686.

Chan, M., Tsai, K. M., & Fuligni, A. J. (2015). Changes in religiosity across the transition to young adulthood. *Journal of Youth and Adolescence, 44,* 1555–1566.

Chan, S., & Chan, K. (2013). Adolescents' susceptibility to peer pressure: Relations to parent–adolescent relationship and adolescents' emotional autonomy from parents. *Youth & Society, 45,* 286–302.

Chan, W., Ou, S. & Reynolds, A. (2014). Adolescent civic engagement and adult outcomes: An examination among urban racial minorities. *Journal of Youth & Adolescence, 43,* 1829–1843.

Chang, E. (2013). Negotiating family obligations and educational goals among college-enrolled youth on Jeju Island, Korea. *Journal of Research on Adolescence, 23,* 25–34.

Chang, E., Chen, C., Greenberger, E., Dooley, D., & Heckhausen, J. (2006). What do they want in life? The life goals of a multi-ethnic, multigenerational sample of high school seniors. *Journal of Youth and Adolescence, 35,* 321–332.

Chang, E., Greenberger, E., Chen, C., Heckhausen, J., & Farruggia, S. (2010). Nonparental adults as social resources in the transition to adulthood. *Journal of Research on Adolescence, 20,* 1065–1082.

Chang, Z., Lichtenstein, P., Asherson, P., & Larsson, H. (2013). Developmental twin study of attention problems high heritabilities throughout development. *JAMA Psychiatry, 70,* 311–318.

Chango, J., Allen, J. P., Szwedo, D., & Schad, M. (2015). Early adolescent peer foundations of late adolescent and young adult psychological adjustment. *Journal of Research on Adolescence, 25,* 685–699.

Chango, J., McElhaney, K., Allen, J., Schad, M., & Marston, E. (2012). Relational stressors and depressive symptoms in late adolescence:

Rejection sensitivity as a vulnerability. *Journal of Abnormal Child Psychology, 40,* 369–379.

Chao, R., & Otsuki-Clutter, M. (2011). Racial and ethnic differences: Sociocultural and contextual explanations. *Journal of Research on Adolescence, 21,* 47–60.

Charbonneau, A., Mezulis, A., & Hyde, J. (2009). Stress and emotional reactivity as explanations for gender differences in adolescents' depressive symptoms. *Journal of Youth and Adolescence, 38,* 1050–1058.

Chassin, L., Hussong, A., & Beltran, I. (2009). Adolescent substance use. In R. Lerner & L. Steinberg (Eds.), *Handbook of adolescent psychology* (3rd ed., Vol. 1, pp. 723–764). New York: Wiley.

Chauhan, P., Reppucci, N., & Turkheimer, E. (2009). Racial differences in the associations of neighborhood disadvantage, exposure to violence, and criminal recidivism among female juvenile offenders. *Behavioral Sciences & the Law, 27,* 531–552.

Chauhan, P., Reppucci, N., Burnette, M., & Reiner, S. (2010). Race, neighborhood disadvantage, and antisocial behavior among female juvenile offenders. *Journal of Community Psychology, 38,* 532–540.

Chavez, R., & Heatherton, T. (2015). Multimodal frontostriatal connectivity underlies individual differences in self-esteem. *Social Cognitive Affective Neuroscience, 10,* 364–370.

Cheah, C., Leung, C., & Bayram Özdemir, S. (2018). Chinese Malaysian adolescents' social-cognitive reasoning regarding filial piety dilemmas. *Child Development, 89,* 383–396.

Cheah, C. S. L., Leung, C. Y. Y., & Bayram Özdemir, S. (2018). Chinese Malaysian adolescents' social-cognitive reasoning regarding filial piety dilemmas. *Child Development, 89,* 383–396.

Cheah, C. S. L., Yu, J., Liu, J., & Coplan, R. J. (2019). Children's cognitive appraisal moderates associations between psychologically controlling parenting and children's depressive symptoms. *Journal of Adolescence, 76,* 109–119.

Chein, J., Albert, D., O'Brien, L., Uckert, K., & Steinberg, L. (2011). Peers increase adolescent risk taking by enhancing activity in the brain's reward circuitry. *Developmental Psychology, 14,* F1–F10.

Chen, F. R., Raine, A., & Granger, D. A. (2018). Testosterone and proactive-reactive aggression in youth: The moderating role of harsh discipline. *Journal of Abnormal Child Psychology, 46,* 1599–1612.

Chen, F. R., Rothman, E. F., & Jaffee, S. R. (2017). Early puberty, friendship group characteristics, and dating abuse in US girls. *Pediatrics, 139,* e20162847.

Chen, K., & Kandel, D. (1996). The natural history of drug use from adolescence to the mid-thirties in a general population sample. *American Journal of Public Health, 85,* 41–47.

Chen, L., & Chen, X. (2019). Affiliation with depressive peer groups and social and school adjustment in Chinese adolescents. *Development and Psychopathology, 32,* 1087–1095.

Chen, L., Zhang, W., Ji, L., & Deater-Deckard, K. (2019). Developmental trajectories of Chinese adolescents' relational aggression: Associations

with changes in social-psychological adjustment. *Child Development, 90,* 2153–2170.

Chen, M., & Foshee, V. (2015). Stressful life events and the perpetration of adolescent dating abuse. *Journal of Youth and Adolescence, 44,* 696–707.

Chen, P., & Vazsonyi, A. (2011). Future orientation, impulsivity, and problem behaviors: A longitudinal moderation model. *Developmental Psychology, 47,* 1633–1645.

Chen, R., & Simons-Morton, B. (2009). Concurrent changes in conduct problems and depressive symptoms in early adolescents: A developmental person-centered approach. *Development and Psychopathology, 21,* 285–307.

Chen, X. (2012). Culture, peer interaction, and socioemotional development. *Child Development Perspectives, 6,* 27–34.

Chen, X., & Graham, S. (2017). Same-ethnic, interethnic, and interracial friendships among Asian early adolescents. *Journal of Research on Adolescence, 27,* 705–713.

Chen, X., Saafir, A., & Graham, S. (2020). Ethnicity, peers, and academic achievement: Who wants to be friends with the smart kids? *Journal of Youth and Adolescence, 49,* 1030–1042.

Chen, Z., Guo, F., Yang, X., Li, X., Duan, Q., Zhang, J., & Ge, X. (2009). Emotional and behavioral effects of romantic relationships in Chinese adolescents. *Journal of Youth and Adolescence, 38,* 1282–1293.

Chen-Gaddini, M. (2012). Chinese mothers and adolescents' views of authority and autonomy: A study of parent–adolescent conflict in urban and rural china. *Child Development, 83,* 1846–1852.

Chen-Gaddini, M., Liu, J., & Nucci, L. (2020). "It's my own business!": Parental control over personal issues in the context of everyday adolescent–parent conflicts and internalizing disorders among urban Chinese adolescents. *Developmental Psychology, 56,* 1775–1786.

Cherlin, A., Chase-Lansdale, P., & McRae, C. (1998). Effects of parental divorce on mental health throughout the life course. *American Sociological Review, 63,* 239–249.

Cherlin, A., Ribar, D., & Yasutake, S. (2016). Nonmarital first births, marriage, and income inequality. *American Sociological Review, 81,* 749–770.

Cheung, C., & Pomerantz, E. (2012). Why does parents' involvement enhance children's achievement? The role of parent-oriented motivation. *Journal of Educational Psychology, 104,* 820–832.

Cheung, R. Y. M., Cummings, E. M., Zhang, Z., & Davies, P. T. (2016). Trivariate modeling of interparental conflict and adolescent emotional security: An examination of mother-father-child dynamics. *Journal of Youth and Adolescence, 45,* 2336–2352.

Chhangur, R. R., Overbeek, G., Verhagen, M., Weeland, J., Matthys, W., & Engels, R. C. M. E. (2015). *DRD4* and *DRD2* genes, parenting, and adolescent delinquency: Longitudinal evidence for a gene by environment interaction. *Journal of Abnormal Psychology, 124,* 791–802.

Chiodo, D., Wolfe, D., Crooks, C., Hughes, R., & Jaffe, P. (2009). Impact of sexual harassment victimization by peers on subsequent adolescent victimization and adjustment: A longitudinal study. *Journal of Adolescent Health, 45,* 246–252.

Chisholm, L., & Hurrelmann, K. (1995). Adolescence in modern Europe: Pluralized transition patterns and their implications for personal and social risks. *Journal of Adolescence, 18,* 129–158.

Chiu, M., Pong, S., Mori, I., & Chow, B. (2012). Immigrant students' emotional and cognitive engagement at school: A multilevel analysis of students in 41 countries. *Journal of Youth & Adolescence, 41,* 1409–1425.

Choi, B., & Park, S. (2018). Who becomes a bullying perpetrator after the experience of bullying victimization? The moderating role of self-esteem. *Journal of Youth and Adolescence, 47,* 2414–2423.

Choi, H., Mori, C., Van Ouytsel, J., Madigan, S., & Temple, J. (2019). Adolescent sexting involvement over 4 years and associations with sexual activity. *Journal of Adolescent Health, 65,* 738–744.

Choi, Y., Harachi, T., Gillmore, M., & Catalano, R. (2005). Applicability of the social development model to urban ethnic minority youth: Examining the relationship between external constraints, family socialization, and problem behaviors. *Journal of Research on Adolescence, 15,* 505–534.

Choi, Y., Park, M., Lee, J. P., Yasui, M., & Kim, T. (2018). Explicating acculturation strategies among Asian American Youth: Subtypes and Correlates across Filipino and Korean Americans. *Journal of Youth and Adolescence, 47*(10), 2181–2205.

Choo, E., Benz, M., Zaller, N., Warren, O., Rising, K., & McConnell, K. (2014). The impact of state medical marijuana legislation on adolescent marijuana use. *Journal of Adolescent Health, 55,* 160–166.

Choudhury, S., Blakemore, S-J., & Charman, T. (2006). Social cognitive development during adolescence. *Social Cognitive and Affective Neuroscience, 3,* 165–174.

Choukas-Bradley, S., Giletta, M., Cohen, G., & Prinstein, & M. (2015). Peer influence, peer status, and prosocial behavior: An experimental investigation of peer socialization of adolescents' intentions to volunteer. *Journal of Youth and Adolescence, 44,* 2197–2210.

Choukas-Bradley, S., Giletta, M., Neblett, E., & Prinstein, M. (2015a). Ethnic differences in associations among popularity, likability, and trajectories of adolescents' alcohol use and frequency. *Child Development, 86,* 519–535.

Choukas-Bradley, S., Giletta, M., Widman, L., Cohen, G., & Prinstein, M. J. (2014). Experimentally measured susceptibility to peer influence and adolescent sexual behavior trajectories: A preliminary study. *Developmental Psychology, 50,* 2221–2227.

Chow, A., Kiuru, N., Parker, P., Eccles, J., & Salmela-Aro, K. (2018). Development of friendship and task values in a new school: friend selection for the arts and physical education but socialization for academic subjects. *Journal of Youth and Adolescence, 47,* 1966–1977.

Christakou, A. (2014). Present simple and continuous: Emergence of self-regulation and contextual sophistication in adolescent decision-making. *Neuropsychologia, 65,* 302–312.

Christensen, K., Hagler, M., Stams, G.-J., Raposa, E., Burton, S., & Rhodes, J. E. (2020). Non-specific versus targeted approaches to youth mentoring: A follow-up meta-analysis. *Journal of Youth and Adolescence, 49,* 959–972.

Chua, A. (2011). *Battle hymn of the Tiger Mother.* New York: Penguin.

Chua, L. W., Milfont, T. L., & Jose, P. E. (2015). Coping skills help explain how future-oriented adolescents accrue greater well-being over time. *Journal of Youth and Adolescence, 44,* 2028–2041.

Chua, T., & Chang, L. (2016). Follow me and like my beautiful selfies: Singapore teenage girls' engagement in self-presentation and peer comparison on social media. *Computers in Human Behavior, 55,* 190–197.

Chue, A. E., Gunthert, K. C., Kim, R. W., Alfano, C. A., & Ruggiero, A. R. (2018). The role of sleep in adolescents' daily stress recovery: Negative affect spillover and positive affect bounce-back effects. *Journal of Adolescence, 66,* 101–111.

Chumlea, W., Schubert, C., Roche, A., Kulin, H., Lee, P., . . . Himes, J. (2003). Age at menarche and racial comparisons in U.S. girls. *Pediatrics, 111,* 110–113.

Chung, G., Flook, L., & Fuligni, A. (2009). Daily family conflict and emotional distress among adolescents from Latin American, Asian, and European backgrounds. *Developmental Psychology, 45,* 1406–1415.

Chung, G. H., Flook, L., & Fuligni, A. (2011). Reciprocal associations between family and peer conflict in adolescents' daily lives. *Child Development, 82,* 1390–1396.

Chung, J., Robins, R., Trzesniewski, K., Noftle, E., Roberts, B., & Widaman, K. (2014). Continuity and change in self-esteem during emerging adulthood. *Journal of Personality and Social Psychology, 106,* 469–483.

Church, J. A., Bunge, S. A., Petersen, S. E., & Schlaggar, B. L. (2017). Preparatory engagement of cognitive control networks increases late in childhood. *Cerebral Cortex, 27,* 2139–2153.

Church, R. (1976). *Education in the United States.* New York: Free Press.

Ciarrochi, J., Morin, A., Sahdra, B., Litalien, D., & Parker, P. (2017). A longitudinal person-centered perspective on youth social support: Relations with psychological wellbeing. *Developmental Psychology, 53,* 1154–1169.

Ciarrochi, J., Parker, P., Sahdra, B., Marshall, S., Jackson, C., Gloster, A. T., & Heaven, P. (2016). The development of compulsive internet use and mental health: A four-year study of adolescence. *Developmental Psychology, 52,* 272–283.

Ciciolla, L., Curlee, A., Karageorge, J., & Luthar, S. (2017). When mothers and fathers are seen as disproportionately valuing achievements: Implications for adjustment among upper middle class youth. *Journal of Youth and Adolescence, 46,* 1057–1075.

Ciocanel, O., Power, K., Eriksen, A., & Gillings, K. (2017). Effectiveness of positive youth development interventions: A meta-analysis of randomized controlled trials. *Journal of Youth and Adolescence, 46,* 483–504.

Clardy, C., & King, P. (2011). Religious involvement. In B. Brown & M. Prinstein (Eds.), *Encyclopedia of adolescence* (Vol. 2, pp. 279–288). New York: Academic Press.

Clark, D., Donnellan, M., Durbin, C., Nuttall, A., Hicks, B., & Robins, R. (2020) Sex, drugs and early emerging risk: Examining the association between sexual debut and substance use across adolescence. *PLOS ONE, 15,* e0228432

Clark, D., Durbin, C., Heitzeg, M., Iacono, W., McGue, M., & Hicks, B. (2020). Adolescent sexual development and peer groups: reciprocal associations and shared genetic and environmental influences. *Archives of Sexual Behavior, Early View.*

Clarke, A. (2006). Coping with interpersonal stress and psychosocial health among children and adolescents: A meta-analysis. *Journal of Youth and Adolescence, 35,* 11–24.

Clarke, A., Kuosmanen, T., & Barry, M. (2015). A systematic review of online youth mental health promotion and prevention interventions. *Journal of Youth and Adolescence, 44,* 90–113.

Clasen, D., & Brown, B. (1985). The multidimensionality of peer pressure in adolescence. *Journal of Youth and Adolescence, 14,* 451–468.

Class, Q., Van Hulle, C., Rathouz, P., Applegate, B., Zald, D., & Lahey, B. (2019). Socioemotional dispositions of children and adolescents predict general and specific second-order factors of psychopathology in early adulthood: A 12-year prospective study. *Journal of Abnormal Psychology, 128,* 574.

Clayton, H., Lowry, R., August, E., & Jones, S. (2016). Nonmedical use of prescription drugs and sexual risk behaviors. *Pediatrics, 137,* 1–10.

Clentifanti, L. C. M., Modecki, K. L., MacLellan, S., & Gowling, H. (2014). Driving under the influence of risky peers: An experimental study of adolescent risk taking. *Journal of Research on Adolescence, Early view.* DOI: 10.1111/jora.12187

Cleveland, M., Feinberg, M., Bontempo, D., & Greenberg, M. (2008). The role of risk and protective factors in substance use across adolescence. *Journal of Adolescent Health, 43,* 157–164.

Cleveland, M. J., Feinberg, M. E., & Greenberg, M. T. (2010). Protective families in high- and low-risk environments: Implications for adolescent substance use. *Journal of Youth and Adolescence, 39,* 114–126.

Coatsworth, J., & Conroy, D. (2009). The effects of autonomy-supportive coaching, need satisfaction, and self-perceptions on initiative and identity in youth swimmers. *Developmental Psychology, 45,* 320–328.

Coelho, V., & Marchante, M. (2018). Trajectories of social and emotional competencies according to cyberbullying roles: a longitudinal multilevel analysis. *Journal of Youth and Adolescence, 47,* 1952–1965.

Cohen, A., Breiner, K., Steinberg, L., Bonnie, R., Scott, E., Taylor-Thompson, K., . . . Casey, B. J. (2016). When is an adolescent an adult: Assessing cognitive control in emotional and nonemotional contexts. *Psychological Science, 27,* 549–562.

Cohen, D., Farley, T., Taylor, S., Martin, D., & Schuster, M. (2002). When and where do youths have sex? The potential role of adult supervision. *Pediatrics, 110,* E66.

Cohen, G., & Prinstein, M. (2006). Peer contagion of aggression and health risk behavior among adolescent males: An experimental investigation of effects on public conduct and private attitudes. *Child Development, 77,* 967–983.

Cohen, J., Sheshko, D., Ames, A., Young, J., Hansford, A., Zhu, X., . . . Abela, J. R. Z. (2015). Self-perceived competence in mainland China: A multiwave longitudinal examination of internalizing symptoms in Chinese adolescents. *Journal of Research on Adolescence, 25,* 564-579.

Cohen, J., Young, J., Gibb, B., Hankin, B., & Abela, J. (2014). Why are anxiety and depressive symptoms comorbid in youth? A multi-wave, longitudinal examination of competing etiological models. *Journal of Affective Disorders, 161,* 21-29.

Cohen, P. K., Chen, H., Hartmark, C., & Gordon, K. (2003). Variations in patterns of developmental transmissions in the emerging adulthood period. *Developmental Psychology, 39,* 657-669.

Cohen-Gilbert, J. E., & Thomas, K. M. (2013). Inhibitory control during emotional distraction across adolescence and early adulthood. *Child Development, 84,* 1954-1966.

Cole, D. A., Zelkowitz, R. L., Nick, E., Martin, N. C., Roeder, K. M., Sinclair-McBride, K., & Spinelli, T. (2016). Longitudinal and incremental relation of cybervictimization to negative self-cognitions and depressive symptoms in young adolescents. *Journal of Abnormal Child Psychology, 44,* 1321-1332.

Cole, M. W., Yarkoni, T., Repovš, G., Anticevic, A., & Braver, T. S. (2012). Global connectivity of prefrontal cortex predicts cognitive control and intelligence. *Journal of Neuroscience, 32,* 8988-8999.

Coleman, J. (1961). *The adolescent society.* Glencoe, IL: Free Press.

Coleman, J., & Hoffer, T. (1987). *Public and private high schools: The impact of communities.* New York: Basic Books.

Coleman, J., Hoffer, T., & Kilgore, S. (1982). *High school achievement: Public, Catholic and other private schools compared.* New York: Basic Books.

Coleman-Minahan, K., Stevenson, A., Obront, E., & Hays, S. (2019). Young women's experiences obtaining judicial bypass for abortion in Texas. *Journal of Adolescent Health, 64,* 20-25.

Coles, M., Makino, K., Stanwood, N., Dozier, A., & Klein, J. (2010). How are restrictive abortion statutes associated with unintended teen birth? *Journal of Adolescent Health, 47,* 160-167.

Coley, R., & Chase-Lansdale, P. L. (1998). Adolescent pregnancy and parenthood: Recent evidence and future directions. *American Psychologist, 53,* 152-166.

Coley, R., O'Brien, M., & Spielvogel, B. (2019). Secular trends in adolescent depressive symptoms: Growing disparities between advantaged and disadvantaged schools. *Journal of Youth and Adolescence, 48,* 2087-2098.

Coley, R., Sims, J., Dearing, E., & Spielvogel, B. (2018). Locating economic risks for adolescent mental and behavioral health: poverty and affluence in families, neighborhoods, and schools. *Child Development, 89,* 360-369.

Coley, R. L., Morris, J., & Hernandez, D. (2004). Out-of-school care and problem behavior trajectories among low-income adolescents: Individual, family, and neighborhood characteristics as added risks. *Child Development, 75,* 948-965.

Collado, A., Johnson, P., Loya, J., Johnson, M., & Yi, R. (2017). Discounting of condom-protected sex as a measure of high risk for sexually transmitted infection among college students. *Archives of Sexual Behavior, 46,* 2187-2195.

Collibee, C., & Furman, W. (2015). Quality counts: Developmental shifts in associations between romantic relationship qualities and psychosocial adjustment. *Child Development, 86,* 1639-1652.

Collibee, C., & Furman, W. (2018). A moderator model of alcohol use and dating aggression among young adults. *Journal of Youth and Adolescence, 47,* 534-546.

Collier, K., Coyne, S., Rasumussen, E., Hawkins, A., Padilla-Walker, L., Erickson, S., & Memmott-Elison, M. (2016). Does parental mediation of media influence child outcomes? A meta-analysis on media time, aggression, substance use, and sexual behavior. *Developmental Psychology, 52,* 798-812.

Collins, R., Martino, S., Elliott, M., & Miu, A. (2011). Relationships between adolescent sexual outcomes and exposure to sex in media: Robustness to propensity-based analysis. *Developmental Psychology, 47,* 585-591.

Collins, W. A. (2003). More than a myth: The developmental significance of romantic relationships during adolescence. *Journal of Research on Adolescents, 13,* 1-24.

Collins, W. A., Maccoby, E., Steinberg, L., Hetherington, E. M., & Bornstein, M. (2000). Contemporary research on parenting: The case for nature and nurture. *American Psychologist, 55,* 218-232.

Collins, W. A., & Steinberg, L. (2006). Adolescent development in interpersonal context. In W. Damon & R. Lerner (Ser. Eds.) & N. Eisenberg (Vol. Ed.), *Handbook of child psychology: Vol. 3. Social, emotional, and personality development* (6th ed., pp. 1003-1067). New York: Wiley.

Comings, D., Muhleman, D., Johnson, J., & Mac-Murray, J. (2002). Parent–daughter transmission of the androgen receptor gene as an explanation of the effect of father absence on age of menarche. *Child Development, 73,* 1046-1051.

Committee on Adolescence. (2014). Addendum—Adolescent pregnancy: Current trends and issues. *Pediatrics, 133,* 954-957.

Compas, B., & Reeslund, K. (2009). Processes of risk and resilience during adolescence. In R. Lerner & L. Steinberg (Eds.), *Handbook of adolescent psychology* (3rd ed., Vol. 1, pp. 561-588). New York: Wiley.

Compian, L., Gowen, L., & Hayward, C. (2004). Peripubertal girls' romantic and platonic involvement with boys: Associations with body image and depression symptoms. *Journal of Research on Adolescence, 14,* 23-47.

Conduct Problems Prevention Research Group. (1999). Initial impact of the Fast Track Prevention Trial for Conduct Problems, II: Classroom effects. *Journal of Consulting and Clinical Psychology, 67,* 648-657.

Conger, R., Ge, X., Elder, G., Jr., Lorenz, F. and Simons, R. (1994). Economic stress, coercive family process, and developmental problems of adolescents. *Child Development, 65,* 541-561.

Conley, C., & Rudolph, K. (2009). The emerging sex difference in adolescent depression: Interacting contributions of puberty and peer stress. *Development and Psychopathology, 21,* 593-620.

Connell, A. M., & Dishion, T. J. (2008). Reducing depression among at-risk early adolescents: Three-year effects of a family-centered intervention embedded within schools. *Journal of Family Psychology, 22,* 574-585.

Connell, C., Gilreath, T., Aklin, W., & Brex, R. (2010). Social-ecological influences on patterns of substance use among non-metropolitan high school students. *American Journal of Community Psychology, 45,* 36-48.

Conner, J., & Pope, D. (2013). Not just robo-students: Why full engagement matters and how school can promote it. *Journal of Youth & Adolescence, 42,* 1426-1442.

Connolly, J., & McIsaac, C. (2009). Romantic relationships in adolescence. In R. Lerner & L. Steinberg (Eds.), *Handbook of adolescent psychology* (3rd ed., Vol. 2, pp. 104-151). New York: Wiley.

Connolly, J., Craig, W., Goldberg, A., & Pepler, D. (1999). Conceptions of cross-sex friendships and romantic relationships in early adolescence. *Journal of Youth and Adolescence, 28,* 481-494.

Connolly, J., Craig, W., Goldberg, A., & Pepler, D. (2004). Mixed-gender groups, dating, and romantic relationships in early adolescence. *Journal of Research on Adolescence, 14,* 185-207.

Connolly, J., Furman, W., & Konarski, R. (2000). The role of peers in the emergence of heterosexual romantic relationships in adolescence. *Child Development, 71,* 1395-1408.

Connolly, J., Nguyen, H., Pepler, D., Craig, W., & Jiang, D. (2013). Developmental trajectories of romantic stages and associations with problem behaviours during adolescence. *Journal of Adolescence, 36,* 1013-1024.

Connolly, M., Zervos, M., Barone, C., Johnson, C., & Joseph, C. (2016). The mental health of transgender youth: Advances in understanding. *Journal of Adolescent Health, 59,* 489-495.

Conson, M., Salzano, S., Frolli, A., & Mazzarella, E. (2017). The peer's point of view: Observing a peer performing an action enhances third-person perspective in adolescents. *Journal of Adolescence, 56,* 84-90.

Conway, K., Swendsen, J., Husky, M., He, J., & Merikangas, K. (2016). Association of lifetime mental disorders and subsequent alcohol and illicit drug use: Results from the national comorbidity survey—adolescent supplement. *Journal of the American Academy of Child & Adolescent Psychiatry, 55,* 280-288.

Cooc, N., & Gee, K. (2014). National trends in school victimization among Asian American adolescents. *Journal of Adolescence, 37,* 839-849.

Cook, E., Blair, B., & Buehler, C. (2018). Individual differences in adolescents' emotional reactivity across relationship contexts. *Journal of Youth and Adolescence, 47,* 290-305.

Cook, P., & Ludwig, J. (2004). Does gun prevalence affect teen gun carrying after all? *Criminology, 42,* 27-54.

Cook, T., Church, M., Ajanaku, S., Shadish, W., Jr., Kim, J., & Cohen, R. (1996). The development of occupational aspirations and expectations among inner-city boys. *Child Development, 67,* 3368-3385.

Cook, T., Deng, Y., & Morgano, E. (2007). Friendship influences during early adolescence: The special role of friends' grade point average. *Journal of Research on Adolescence, 17,* 325-356.

Cooksey, E. C., Mott, F. L., & Neubauer, S. A. (2002). Friendships and early relationships: Links to sexual initiation among American adolescents born to young mothers. *Perspectives on Sexual and Reproductive Health, 34,* 118-126.

Cooper, A., & Sánchez, B. (2016). The roles of racial discrimination, cultural mistrust, and gender in Latina/o youth's school attitudes and academic achievement. *Journal of Research on Adolescence, 26,* 1036-1047.

Cooper, K., Quayle, E., Jonsson, L., & Svedin, C. (2016). Adolescents and self-taken sexual images: A review of the literature. *Computers in Human Behavior, 55,* 706-716.

Cooper, M., Wood, P., Orcutt, H., & Albino, A. (2003). Personality and the predisposition to engage in risky or problem behaviors during adolescence. *Journal of Personality and Social Psychology, 84,* 390-410.

Copeland, W. E., Worthman, C., Shanahan, L., Costello, E. J., & Angold, A. (2019). Early pubertal timing and testosterone associated with higher levels of adolescent depression in girls. *Journal of the American Academy of Child & Adolescent Psychiatry, 58,* 1197-1206.

Coplan, R. J., Rose-Krasnor, L., Weeks, M., Kingsbury, A., Kingsbury, M., & Bullock, A. (2013). Alone in a crowd: Social motivations, social withdrawal, and socioemotional functioning in later childhood. *Developmental Psychology, 49,* 861-875.

Corcoran, J., Davies, S., Knight, C., Lanzi, R., Li, P., & Ladores, S. (2020). Adolescents' perceptions of sexual health education programs: An integrative review. *Journal of Adolescence, 84,* 96-112.

Corenblum, B. (2014). Relationships between racial-ethnic identity, self-esteem and in-group attitudes among first nation children. *Journal of Youth & Adolescence, 43,* 387-404.

Cornell, D., & Huang, F. (2016). Authoritative school climate and high school student risk behavior: A cross-sectional multi-level analysis of student self-reports. *Journal of Youth and Adolescence, 45,* 2246-2259.

Cornell, D., & Limber, S. (2015). Law and policy on the concept of bullying at school. *American Psychologist, 70,* 333-343.

Cornell, D., Gregory, A., Huang, F., & Fan, X. (2013). Perceived prevalence of teasing and bullying predicts high school dropout rates. *Journal of Educational Psychology, 105,* 138-149.

Cornell, D., Shukla, K., & Konold, T. (2015). Peer victimization and authoritative school climate: A multilevel approach. *Journal of Educational Psychology, 107,* 1186-1201.

Cortina, K., & Arel, S. (2011). Schools and schooling. In B. Brown & M. Prinstein (Eds.), *Encyclopedia of adolescence* (Vol. 2, pp. 299-305). New York: Academic Press.

Côté, J. (2000). *Arrested adulthood: The changing nature of maturity and identity.* New York: New York University Press.

Côté, J. (2009). Identity formation and self development in adolescence. In R. Lerner & L. Steinberg (Eds.), *Handbook of adolescent psychology* (3rd ed., Vol. 1, pp. 266-304). New York: Wiley.

Côté, J. (2014). The dangerous myth of emerging adulthood: An evidence-based critique of a flawed developmental theory. *Applied Developmental Science, 18,* 177-188.

Côté, J., & Bynner, J. (2008). Changes in the transition to adulthood in the UK and Canada: The role of structure and agency in emerging adulthood. *Journal of Youth Studies, 11,* 251-268.

Couperus, J. W., & Nelson, C. A. (2006). Early brain development and plasticity. In K. McCartney & D. Phillips (Eds.), *Blackwell handbook of early childhood development* (pp. 85-105). Malden, MA: Blackwell Publishing.

Courtney, D., Watson, P., Battaglia, M., Mulsant, B., & Szatmari, P. (2020). COVID-19 impacts on child and youth anxiety and depression: Challenges and opportunities. *The Canadian Journal of Psychiatry, 65,* 688-691.

Cox, M., Wang, F., & Gustafsson, H. (2011). Family organization and adolescent development. In B. Brown & M. Prinstein (Eds.), *Encyclopedia of adolescence* (Vol. 2, pp. 75-83). New York: Academic Press.

Coyne, S., Padilla-Walker, L., & Holmgren, H. (2018). A six-year longitudinal study of texting trajectories during adolescence. *Child Development, 89,* 58-65.

Coyne, S., Padilla-Walker, L., Holmgren, H., & Stockdale, L. (2019). Instagrowth: A longitudinal growth mixture model of social media time use across adolescence. *Journal of Research on Adolescence, 29,* 897-907.

Coyne, S., Rogers, A., Zurcher, J., Stockdale, L., & Booth, M. (2020). Does time spent using social media impact mental health? An eight year longitudinal study. *Computers in Human Behavior, 104,* 106160.

Coyne, S., Stockdale, L., Warburton, W., Gentile, D., Yang, C., & Merrill, B. (2020). Pathological video game symptoms from adolescence to emerging adulthood: A 6-year longitudinal study of trajectories, predictors, and outcomes. *Developmental Psychology, 56,* 1385-1396.

Coyne, S., Warburton, W., Essig, L., & Stockdale, L. (2018). Violent video games, externalizing behavior, and prosocial behavior: A five-year longitudinal study during adolescence. *Developmental Psychology, 54,* 1868-1880.

Coyne, S. M. (2016). Effects of viewing relational aggression on television on aggressive behavior in adolescents: A three-year longitudinal study. *Developmental Psychology, 52,* 284-295.

Coyne, S. M., & Padilla-Walker, L. (2015). Sex, violence, & rock n' roll: Longitudinal effects of music on aggression, sex, and prosocial behavior during adolescence. *Journal of Adolescence, 41,* 96-104.

Coyne, S. M., Ward, L. M., Kroff, S. L., Davis, E. J., Holmgren, H. G., Jensen, A. C., . . . Essig, L. W. (2019). Contributions of mainstream sexual media exposure to sexual attitudes, perceived peer norms, and sexual behavior: A meta-analysis. *Journal of Adolescent Health, 64*(4), 430-436.

Crandall, A., Magnusson, B., Novilla, M., Novilla, L., & Dyer, W. (2017). Family financial stress and adolescent sexual risk-taking: The role of self-regulation. *Journal of Youth and Adolescence, 46,* 45-62.

Crean, H. F. (2012). Youth activity involvement, neighborhood adult support, individual decision making skills, and early adolescent delinquent behaviors: Testing a conceptual model. *Journal of Applied Developmental Psychology, 33,* 175-188.

Creasey, G., & Kaliher, G. (1994). Age differences in grandchildren's perceptions of relations with grandparents. *Journal of Adolescence, 17,* 411-426.

Cribb, V., & Haase, A. (2016). Girls feeling good at school: School gender environment, internalization and awareness of socio-cultural attitudes associations with self-esteem in adolescent girls. *Journal of Adolescence, 46,* 107-114.

Crick, N. (1996). The role of overt aggression, relational aggression, and prosocial behavior in the prediction of children's future social adjustment. *Child Development, 67,* 2317-2327.

Crick, N., & Dodge, K. (1994). A review and reformulation of social information-processing mechanisms in children's social adjustment. *Psychological Bulletin, 115,* 74-101.

Criss, M. M., & Shaw, D. (2005). Sibling relationships as contexts for delinquency training in low-income families. *Journal of Family Psychology, 19,* 592-600.

Criss, M. M., Sheffield Morris, A., Ponce-Garcia, E., Cui, L., & Silk, J. S. (2016). Pathways to adaptive emotion regulation among adolescents from low-income families. *Family Relations, 65,* 517-529.

Crocetti, E. (2017). Identity formation in adolescence: The dynamic of forming and consolidating identity commitments. *Child Development Perspectives, 11,* 145-150.

Crocetti, E., Klimstra, T., Keijsers, L., Hale, W., & Meeus, W. (2009). Anxiety trajectories and identity development in adolescence: A five-wave longitudinal study. *Journal of Youth and Adolescence, 38,* 839-849.

Crockett, L., Brown, J., Russell, S. T., & Shen, Y. (2007). The meaning of good parent–child relationships for Mexican American adolescents. *Journal of Research on Adolescence, 17,* 639-668.

Croll, J., Neumark-Sztainer, D., Story, M., & Ireland, M. (2002). Prevalence and risk and protective factors related to disordered eating behaviors among adolescents: Relationship to gender and ethnicity. *Journal of Adolescent Health, 31,* 166-175.

Crone, E. (2013). Considerations of fairness in the adolescent brain. *Child Development Perspectives, 7,* 97-103.

Crone, E. A., & Steinbeis, N. (2017). Neural perspectives on cognitive control development during childhood and adolescence. *Trends in Cognitive Sciences, 21,* 205-215.

Crone, E., & van der Molen, M. (2007). Development of decision making in school-aged children and adolescents: Evidence from heart rate and skin conductance analysis. *Child Development, 78,* 1288-1301.

Crone, E., Somsen, R., Zanolie, K., & Van der Molen, M. (2006). A heart rate analysis of developmental change in feedback processing and rule shifting from childhood to early adulthood. *Journal of Experimental Child Psychology, 95,* 99-116.

Crosby, R., DiClemente, R., Wingood, G., Lang, D., & Harrington, K. (2003). Value of consistent condom use: A study of sexually transmitted disease prevention among African American adolescent females. *American Journal of Public Health, 93,* 901-902.

Crosnoe, R. (2002). High school curriculum track and adolescent association with delinquent friends. *Journal of Adolescent Research, 17,* 143-167.

Crosnoe, R. (2009). Low-income students and the socioeconomic composition of public high schools. *American Sociological Review, 74,* 709-730.

Crosnoe, R., & Cavanagh, S. (2010). Families with children and adolescents: A review, critique, and future agenda. *Journal of Marriage and Family, 72,* 594-611.

Crosnoe, R., & Huston, A. (2007). Socioeconomic status, schooling, and the developmental trajectories of adolescents. *Developmental Psychology, 43,* 1097-1110.

Crosnoe, R., & Needham, B. (2004). Holism, contextual variability, and the study of friendships in adolescent development. *Child Development, 75,* 264-279.

Crosnoe, R., Mistry, R. S., & Elder, G. H., Jr. (2002). Economic disadvantage, family dynamics, and adolescent enrollment in higher education. *Journal of Marriage and the Family, 64,* 690-702.

Cross, F., Agi, A., Montoro, J. Medina, M., Miller-Tejada, S., Pinetta, B., Tran-Dubongco, M., & Rivas-Drake, D. (2020). Illuminating ethnic-racial socialization among undocumented Latinx parents and its implications for adolescent psychosocial functioning. *Developmental Psychology, 56,* 1458-1474.

Cross, F., Hoffman, A., Constante, K., & Rivas-Drake, D. (2018). Ethnic-racial identity content and the development of depressive symptoms among Latino adolescents. *Development and Psychopathology, 30,* 1557-1569.

Crouter, A., Bumpus, M., Davis, K., & McHale, S. (2005). How do parents learn about adolescents' experiences? Implications for parental knowledge and adolescent risky behavior. *Child Development, 76,* 869-882.

Crowley, S. J., Wolfson, A. R., Tarokh, L., & Carskadon, M. A. (2018). An update on adolescent sleep: New evidence informing the perfect storm model. *Journal of Adolescence, 67,* 55-65.

Cruz, R., King, K., Cauce, A., Conger, R., & Robins, R. (2017). Cultural orientation trajectories and substance use: Findings from a longitudinal study of Mexican-origin youth. *Child Development, 88,* 555-572.

Cruz, R. A., King, K. M., Mechammic, M., Bamaca-Colbert, M., & Robins, R. W. (2018). Mexican-origin youth substance use trajectories: Associations with cultural and family factors. *Developmental Psychology, 54,* 111-126.

Cservenka, A., Jones, S., & Nagel, B. (2015). Reduced cerebellar brain activity during reward processing in adolescent binge drinkers. *Developmental Cognitive Neuroscience, 16,* 110-120.

Cuadros, O., & Berger, C. (2016). The protective role of friendship quality on the wellbeing of adolescents victimized by peers. *Journal of Youth and Adolescence, 45,* 1877-1888.

Cui, M., & Conger, R. (2008). Parenting behavior as mediator and moderator of the association between marital problems and adolescent maladjustment. *Journal of Research on Adolescence, 18,* 261-284.

Cui, M., Donnellan, M. B., & Conger, R. (2007). Reciprocal influences between parents' marital problems and adolescent internalizing and externalizing behavior. *Developmental Psychology, 43,* 1544-1552.

Cui, M., Ueno, K., Gordon, M., & Fincham, F. D. (2013). The continuation of intimate partner violence from adolescence to young adulthood. *Journal of Marriage and Family, 75,* 300-313.

Cummings, E. M., Koss, K. J., & Davies, P. T. (2015). Prospective relations between family conflict and adolescent maladjustment: Security in the family system as a mediating process. *Journal of Abnormal Child Psychology, 43,* 503-515.

Cummings, J., Wen, H., & Druss, B. (2011). Racial/ethnic differences in treatment for substance use disorders among U.S. adolescents. *Journal of the American Academy of Child & Adolescent Psychiatry, 50,* 1265-1274.

Cunningham, M. (1999). African-American adolescent males' perceptions of their community resources and constraints: A longitudinal analysis. *Journal of Community Psychology, 27,* 569-588.

Currie, C., Ahluwalia, N., Godeau, E., Nic Gabhainn, S., Due, P., & Currie, D. B. (2012). Is obesity at individual and national level associated with lower age at menarche? Evidence from 34 countries in the health behaviour in school-aged children study. *Journal of Adolescent Health, 50,* 621-626.

Cvencek, D., Nasir, N., O'Connor, K., Wischnia, S., & Meltzoff, A. (2015). The development of math-race stereotypes: "They say Chinese people are the best at math." *Journal of Research on Adolescence, 25,* 603-637.

D'hondt, F., Eccles, J., Van Houte, M., & Stevens, P. (2016). Perceived ethnic discrimination by teachers and ethnic minority students' academic futility: Can parents prepare their youth for better or for worse? *Journal of Youth and Adolescence, 45,* 1075-1089.

D'Onofrio, B. M., Turkheimer, E., Emery, R. E., Slurske, W. S., Heath, A. C., . . . Madden, P. A. (2006). A genetically informed study of the processes underlying the association between parental marital instaility and offspring adjustment. *Developmental Psychology, 42,* 486-499.

Daddis, C. (2011). Desire for increased autonomy and adolescents' perceptions of peer autonomy: "Everyone else can; Why can't I?" *Child Development, 82,* 1310-1326.

Daha, M. (2011). Contextual factors contributing to ethnic identity development of second-generation Iranian American adolescents. *Journal of Adolescent Research, 26,* 543-569.

Dahl, G. (2010). Early teen marriage and poverty. *Demography, 47,* 689-718.

Dahl, R. (2008). Biological, developmental, and neurobehavioral factors relevant to adolescent driving risks. *American Journal of Preventive Medicine, 35,* S278-S284.

Dahl, R., & Hariri, A. (2005). Lessons from G. Stanley Hall: Connecting new research in biological science to the study of adolescent development. *Journal of Research on Adolescence, 15,* 367-382.

Dahl, R. E. (2016). The developmental neuroscience of adolescence: Revisiting, refining, and extending seminal models. *Developmental Cognitive Neuroscience, 17,* 101-102.

Dallago, L., Perkins, D., Santinello, M., Boyce, W., Molcho, M., & Morgan, A. (2009). Adolescent place attachment, social capital, and perceived safety: A comparison of 13 countries. *American Journal of Community Psychology, 44,* 148-160.

Dalsgaard, S., Thorsteinsson, E., Trabjerg, B., Schullehner, J., Plana-Ripoll, O., Brikell, I., . . . Schendel, D. (2020). Incidence rates and cumulative incidences of the full spectrum of diagnosed mental disorders in childhood and adolescence. *JAMA Psychiatry, 77,* 155-164.

Damian, R., Spengler, M., Sutu, A., & Roberts, B. (2019). Sixteen going on sixty-six: A longitudinal study of personality stability and change across 50 years. *Journal of Personality and Social Psychology, 117,* 674.

Dandreaux, D., & Frick, P. (2009). Developmental pathways to conduct problems: A further test of the childhood and adolescent-onset distinction. *Journal of Abnormal Child Psychology, 37,* 375-385.

Daniels, E., & Leaper, C. (2011). Gender issues. In B. Brown & M. Prinstein (Eds.), *Encyclopedia of adolescence* (Vol. 1, pp. 151-159). New York: Academic Press.

Daniels, E., & Zurbriggen, E. (2016). The price of sexy: Viewers' perceptions of a sexualized versus nonsexualized Facebook profile photograph. *Psychology of Popular Media Culture, 5,* 2-14.

Dank, M., Lachman, P., Zweig, J. M., & Yahner, J. (2014). Dating violence experiences of lesbian, gay, bisexual, and transgender youth. *Journal of Youth and Adolescence, 43,* 846-857.

Danneel, S., Geukens, F., Maes, M., Bastin, M., Bijttebier, P., Colpin, H., . . . Goossens, L. (2020). Loneliness, social anxiety symptoms, and depressive symptoms in adolescence: Longitudinal distinctiveness and correlated change. *Journal of Youth and Adolescence, 49,* 2246-2264.

Darki, F., & Klingberg, T. (2015). The role of fronto-parietal and fronto-striatal networks in the development of working memory: A longitudinal study. *Cerebral Cortex, 25,* 1587-1595.

Darling, N., & Steinberg, L. (1993). Parenting style as context: An integrative model. *Psychological Bulletin, 113,* 487-496.

Darling, N., & Steinberg, L. (1997). Community influences on adolescent achievement and deviance. In J. Brooks-Gunn, G. Duncan, & L. Aber (Eds.), *Neighborhood poverty: Context and consequences for children: Vol. 2. Conceptual, methodological, and policy approaches to studying neighborhoods* (pp. 120-131). New York: Russell Sage Foundation.

Darling, N., & Tilton-Weaver, L. (2019). All in the family: Within-family differences in parental monitoring and adolescent information management. *Developmental Psychology, 55,* 390-402.

Darling, N., Cumsille, P., & Martínez, M. L. (2007). Adolescents as active agents in the socialization process: Legitimacy of parental authority and obligation to obey as predictors of obedience. *Journal of Adolescence, 30,* 297-311.

Darling-Hammond, L. (1997). *The right to learn.* San Francisco: Jossey-Bass.

Darling-Hammond, L. (2006). No child left behind and high school reform. *Harvard Educational Review, 76,* 642-667.

Daryanani, I., Hamilton, J. L., Abramson, L. Y., & Alloy, L. B. (2016). Single mother parenting and adolescent psychopathology. *Journal of Abnormal Child Psychology, 44,* 1411-1423.

Daryanani, I., Hamilton, J. L., McArthur, B. A., Steinberg, L., Abramson, L. Y., & Alloy, L. B. (2017). Cognitive vulnerabilities to depression for adolescents in single-mother and two-parent families. *Journal of Youth and Adolescence, 46*, 213–227.

Dauber, S., Alexander, K., & Entwisle, D. (1996). Tracking and transitions through the middle grades: Channeling educational trajectories. *Sociology of Education, 69*, 290–307.

Daukantaitė, D., Lundh, L., & Wångby-Lundh, M. (2019). Association of direct and indirect aggression and victimization with self-harm in young adolescents: A person-oriented approach. *Development and Psychopathology, 31*, 727–739.

Davey, C. G., Yücel, M., & Allen, N. B. (2008). The emergence of depression in adolescence: Development of the prefrontal cortex and the representation of reward. *Neuroscience & Biobehavioral Reviews, 32*, 1–19.

DaViera, A. L., Roy, A. L., Uriostegui, M., and Fiesta, D. (2020), Safe spaces embedded in dangerous contexts: How Chicago youth navigate daily life and demonstrate resilience in high-crime neighborhoods. *American Journal of Community Psychology, 66*, 65–80.

Davies, P. T., Martin, M. J., Coe, J. L., & Cummings, E. M. (2016). Transactional cascades of destructive interparental conflict, children's emotional insecurity, and psychological problems across childhood and adolescence. *Development and Psychopathology, 28*, 653–671.

Davies, P., & Windle, M. (2000). Middle adolescents' dating pathways and psychosocial adjustment. *Merrill-Palmer Quarterly, 46*, 90–118.

Davies, P., Parry, L., Bascoe, S., Cicchetti, D., & Cummings, E. (2020a). Interparental conflict as a curvilinear risk factor of youth emotional and cortisol reactivity. *Developmental Psychology, 56*, 1787–1802.

Davies, P., Sturge-Apple, M., Bascoe, S., & Cummings, E. M. (2014). The legacy of early insecurity histories in shaping adolescent adaptation to interparental conflict. *Child Development, 85*, 338–354.

Davies, P., Thompson, M., Martin, M., & Cummings, E. (2020b). The vestiges of childhood interparental conflict: Adolescent sensitization to recent interparental conflict. *Child Development,* online ahead of print.

Davila, J. (2008). Depressive symptoms and adolescent romance: Theory, research, and implications. *Child Development Perspectives, 2,* 26–31.

Davis, E., & Friel, L. (2001). Adolescent sexuality: Disentangling the effects of family structure and family context. *Journal of Marriage and the Family, 63,* 669–681.

Davis, H. A., Guller, L., & Smith, G. T. (2016). Developmental trajectories of boys' driven exercise and fasting during the middle school years. *Journal of Abnormal Child Psychology, 44,* 1309–1319.

Davis, J. P., Pedersen, E. R., Tucker, J. S., Dunbar, M. S., Seelam, R., Shih, R., & D'Amico, E. J. (2019). Long-term associations between substance use-related media exposure, descriptive norms, and alcohol use from adolescence to young adulthood. *Journal of Youth and Adolescence, 48*(7), 1311–1326.

Davis, K. (2013). Young people's digital lives: The impact of interpersonal relationships and digital media use on adolescents' sense of identity. *Computers in Human Behavior, 29,* 2281–2293.

Davis, K., & Kirkpatrick, L. (1994). Attachment style, gender, and relationship stability: A longitudinal analysis. *Journal of Personality and Social Psychology, 66,* 502–512.

Davis, R., & Kiang, L. (2016). Religious identity, religious participation, and psychological well-being in Asian American adolescents. *Journal of Youth and Adolescence, 45,* 532–546.

Davis, S., Scott, E., Wadlington, W., & Weithorn, C. (2013). *Children in the legal system* (5th ed.). St. Paul, MN: Foundation Press.

Davis-Kean, P., Huesmann, L. R., Jager, J., Collins, W. A., Bates, J. E., & Lansford, J. E. (2008). Changes in the relation of self-efficacy beliefs and behaviors across development. *Child Development, 79,* 1257–1269.

Davison, T., & McCabe, M. (2011). Physical attractiveness. In B. Brown & M. Prinstein (Eds.), *Encyclopedia of adolescence* (Vol. 1, pp. 269–274). New York: Academic Press.

Dawes, N., & Larson, R. (2011). How youth get engaged: Grounded-theory research on motivational development in organized youth programs. *Developmental Psychology, 47,* 259–269.

Day, E., & Dotterer, A. M. (2018). Parental involvement and adolescent academic outcomes: Exploring differences in beneficial strategies across racial/ethnic groups. *Journal of Youth and Adolescence, 47,* 1332–1349.

Day, J., Fish, J., Grossman, A., & Russell, S. (2020). Gay-straight alliances, inclusive policy, and school climate: LGBTQ youths' experiences of social support and bullying. *Journal of Research on Adolescence, 30*(S2), 418–430.

Day, J., Perez-Brumer, A., & Russell, S. (2018). Safe schools? Transgender youth's school experiences and perceptions of school climate. *Journal of Youth and Adolescence, 47,* 1731–1742.

de Boer, A., & Harakeh, Z. (2017). The effect of active and passive peer discouragement on adolescent risk taking: An experimental study. *Journal of Research on Adolescence, 27,* 878–889.

de Boer, H., Bosker, R., & van der Werf, M. (2010). Sustainability of teacher expectation bias effects on long-term student performance. *Journal of Educational Psychology, 102,* 168–179.

De Bolle, M., De Fruyt, F., McCrae, R., Löckenhoff, C., Costa Jr., P., Aguilar-Vafaie, M., . . . Terracciano, A. (2015). The emergence of sex differences in personality traits in early adolescence: A cross-sectional, cross-cultural study. *Journal of Personality and Social Psychology, 108,* 171–185.

de Bruyn, E., & Cillessen, A. (2006). Heterogeneity of girls' consensual popularity: Academic and interpersonal behavioral profiles. *Journal of Youth and Adolescence, 35,* 435–445.

De Castella, K., Byrne, D., & Covington, M. (2013). Unmotivated or motivated to fail? A cross-cultural study of achievement motivation, fear of failure, and student disengagement. *Journal of Educational Psychology, 105,* 861–880.

De Goede, I., Branje, S. Delsing, M., & Meeus, W. (2009). Linkages over time between adolescents' relationships with parents and friends. *Journal of Youth and Adolescence, 38,* 1304–1315.

De Goede, I., Branje, S., & Meeus, W. (2009). Developmental changes in adolescents' perceptions of relationships with their parents. *Journal of Youth and Adolescence, 38,* 75–88.

de Graaf, H., van de Schoot, R., Woertman, L., Hawk, S., & Meeus, W. (2012). Family cohesion and romantic and sexual initiation: A three wave longitudinal study. *Journal of Youth & Adolescence, 41,* 583–592.

de Graaf, H., Vanwesenbeeck, I., Meijer, S., Woertman, L., & Meeus, W. (2009). Sexual trajectories during adolescence: Relation to demographic characteristics and sexual risk. *Archives of Sexual Behavior, 38,* 276–282.

de la Haye, K., Green, H. D. Jr., Kennedy, D. P., Pollard, M. S., & Tucker, J. S. (2013). Selection and influence mechanisms associated with marijuana initiation and use in adolescent friendship networks. *Journal of Research on Adolescence, 23,* 474–486.

de la Haye, K., Green, H., Pollard, M., Kennedy, D., & Tucker, J. (2015). Befriending risky peers: Factors driving adolescents' selection of friends with similar marijuana use. *Journal of Youth and Adolescence, 44,* 1914–1928.

de la Haye, K., Robins, G., Mohr, P., & Wilson, C. (2013). Adolescents' intake of junk food: Processes and mechanisms driving consumption similarities among friends. *Journal of Research on Adolescence, 23,* 524–536.

De Los Reyes, A., Ohannessian, C., & Racz, S. (2019). Discrepancies between adolescent and parent reports about family relationships. *Child Development Perspectives, 13,* 53–58.

De vries, D., Peter, J., de Graaf, H., & Nikken, P. (2016). Adolescents' social network site use, peer appearance-related feedback, and body dissatisfaction: Testing a mediation model. *Journal of Youth and Adolescence, 45,* 211–224.

de Water, E., Cillessen, A. H. N., & Scheres, A. (2014). Distinct age-related differences in temporal discounting and risk taking in adolescents and young adults. *Child Development, 85,* 1881–1897.

Deane, C., Vijayakumar, N., Allen, N. B., Schwartz, O., Simmons, J. G., Bousman, C. A., . . . Whittle, S. (2020). Parenting × Brain Development interactions as predictors of adolescent depressive symptoms and well-being: Differential susceptibility or diathesis-stress? *Development and Psychopathology, 32,* 139–150.

Deane, K., Richards, M., & Santiago, C. (2020). Violence exposure, posttraumatic stress, and affect variability among African American youth: A time sampling approach. *Development and Psychopathology,* online ahead of print.

Deardorff, J., Cham, H., Gonzales, N. A., White, R. M. B., Tein, J. Y., Wong, J. J., & Roosa, M. W. (2013). Pubertal timing and Mexican-origin girls' internalizing and externalizing symptoms: The influence of harsh parenting. *Developmental Psychology, 49,* 1790–1804.

Deardorff, J., Gonzales, N. A., Christopher, F. S., Roosa, M. W., & Millsap, R. E. (2005). Early puberty and adolescent pregnancy: The influence of alcohol use. *Pediatrics 116,* 1451–1456.

Deater-Deckard, K. (2014). Family matters: Intergenerational and interpersonal processes of executive function and attentive behavior. *Current Directions in Psychological Science, 23,* 230–236.

Deater-Deckard, K., & Plomin, R. (1999). An adoption study of etiology of teacher and parent reports of externalizing behavior problems in middle childhood. *Child Development, 70,* 144–154.

Deater-Deckard, K., Godwin, J., Lansford, J. E., Tirado, L. M. U., Yotanyamaneewong, S., Alampay, L. P., . . . & Di Giunta, L. (2019). Chaos, danger, and maternal parenting in families: Links with adolescent adjustment in low- and middle-income countries. *Developmental science, 22,* e12855.

Deater-Deckard, K., Godwin, J., Lansford, J., Bacchini, D., Bombi, A., Bornstein, M., . . . Al-Hassan, S. (2018). Within- and between-person and group variance in behavior and beliefs in cross-cultural longitudinal data. *Journal of Adolescence, 62,* 207–217.

Debnam, K., Johnson, S., Waasdorp, T., & Bradshaw, C. (2014). Equity, connection, and engagement in the school context to promote positive youth development. *Journal of Research on Adolescence, 24,* 447–459.

Debnam, K., Milam, A., Mullen, M., Lacey, K., & Bradshaw, C. (2018). The moderating role of spirituality in the association between stress and substance use among adolescents: Differences by gender. *Journal of Youth and Adolescence, 47,* 818–828.

DeCamp, W., & Ferguson, C. (2017). The impact of degree of exposure to violent video games, family background, and other factors on youth violence. *Journal of Youth and Adolescence, 46,* 388–400.

Defoe, I., Dubas, J., Dalmaijer, E., & van Aken, M. (2020). Is the peer presence effect on heightened adolescent risky decision-making only present in males? *Journal of Youth and Adolescence, 49,* 693–705.

Defoe, I., Dubas, J., Somerville, L., Lugtig, P., & van Aken, M. (2016). The unique roles of intrapersonal and social factors in adolescent smoking development. *Developmental Psychology, 52,* 2044–2056.

Defoe, I. N., Dubas, J. S., Figner, B., & van Aken, M. A. (2015). A meta-analysis on age differences in risky decision making: Adolescents versus children and adults. *Psychological Bulletin, 141,* 48–84.

Değirmencioğilu, S., Urberg, K., Tolson, J., & Richard, P. (1998). Adolescent friendship networks: Continuity and change over the school year. *Merrill-Palmer Quarterly, 44,* 313–337.

Degol, J., Wang, M.-T., Zhang, Y., & Allerton, J. (2018). Do growth mindsets in math benefit females? Identifying pathways between gender, mindset, and motivation. *Journal of Youth and Adolescence, 47,* 976–990.

Del Toro, J., Hughes, D., & Way, N. (2020). Interrelations between ethnic-racial discrimination and ethnic-racial identity among early adolescents. *Child Development,* DOI:10.1111/cdev.13424.

DeLay, D., Hanish, L., Zhang, L., & Martin, C. (2017). Assessing the impact of homophobic name calling on early adolescent mental health: A longitudinal social network analysis of competing peer influence effects. *Journal of Youth and Adolescence, 46,* 955–969.

DeLay, D., Laursen, B., Bukowski, W., Kerr, M., & Stattin, H. (2016). Adolescent friend similarity

on alcohol abuse as a function of participation in romantic relationships: Sometimes a new love comes between old friends. *Developmental Psychology, 52,* 117–129.

DeLay, D., Laursen, B., Kiuru, N., Salmela-Aro, K., & Nurmi, J. E. (2013). Selecting and retaining friends on the basis of cigarette smoking similarity. *Journal of Research on Adolescence, 23,* 464–473.

DeLay, D., Martin, C., Cook, R., & Hanish, L. (2018). The influence of peers during adolescence: Does homophobic name calling by peers change gender identity? *Journal of Youth and Adolescence, 47,* 636–649.

Delevi, R., & Weisskirch, R. (2013). Personality factors as predictors of sexting. *Computers in Human Behavior, 29,* 2589–2594.

Delgado, M., Updegraff, K., Roosa, M., & Umaña-Taylor, A. (2011). Discrimination and Mexican-origin adolescents' adjustment: The moderating roles of adolescents', mothers', and fathers' cultural orientations and values. *Journal of Youth and Adolescence, 40,* 125–139.

Delker, B., Bernstein, R., & Laurent, H. (2018). Out of harm's way: Secure versus insecure-disorganized attachment predicts less adolescent risk taking related to childhood poverty. *Development and Psychopathology, 30,* 283–296.

DelPriore, D., Schlomer, G., & Ellis, B. (2017). Impact of fathers on parental monitoring of daughters and their affiliation with sexually promiscuous peers: A genetically and environmentally controlled sibling study. *Developmental Psychology, 53,* 1330–1343.

Delsing, M. J. M. H., ter Bogt, T. F. M., Engels, R. C. M. E., & Meeus, W. H. J. (2007). Adolescents' peer crowd identification in the Netherlands: Structure and associations with problem behaviors. *Journal of Research on Adolescence, 17,* 467–480.

DeLuca, H., Claxton, S., & van Dulmen, M. (2019). The peer relationships of those who have experienced adoption or foster care: A meta-analysis. *Journal of Research on Adolescence, 29,* 796–813.

Demo, D., & Acock, A. (1996). Family structure, family process, and adolescent well-being. *Journal of Research on Adolescence, 6,* 457–488.

Demurie, E., Roeyers, H., Baeyens, D., & Sonuga-Barke, E. (2012). Temporal discounting of monetary rewards in children and adolescents with ADHD and autism spectrum disorders. *Developmental Science, 15,* 791–800.

Denault, A., & Guay, F. (2017). Motivation towards extracurricular activities and motivation at school: A test of the generalization effect hypothesis. *Journal of Adolescence, 54,* 94–103,

Denault, A.-S., & Poulin, F. (2009). Predictors of adolescent participation to organized activities: A five-year longitudinal study. *Journal of Research on Adolescence, 19,* 347–371.

Denizet-Lewis, A. (2017, October 15). Why are more American teenagers than ever suffering from severe anxiety? *The New York Times Magazine,* p. 39 and ff.

Denner, J., Valdes, O., Dickson, D. J., & Laursen, B. (2019). Math interest and self-concept among latino/a students: Reciprocal influences across the transition to middle school. *Journal of Adolescence, 75,* 22–36.

Denton, K., & Zarbatany, L. (1996). Age differences in support processes in conversations between friends. *Child Development, 67,* 1360–1373.

Derefinko, K., Peters, J. Eisenlohr-Moul, T., Walsh, E., Adams, Z., & Lynam, D. (2014). Relations between trait impulsivity, behavioral impulsivity, physiological arousal, and risky sexual behavior among young men. *Archives of Sexual Behavior, 43,* 1149–1158.

Derlan, C., Umaña-Taylor, A., Toomey, R., Updegraff, K., Jahromi, L., & Flores, L. (2014). Perceived discrimination and ethnic affirmation: Anglo culture orientation as a moderator among Mexican-origin adolescent mothers. *Child Development, 85,* 1357–1365.

Dermody, S. S., Marshal, M. P., Cheong, J., Burton, C., Hughes, T., Aranda, F., & Friedman, M. S. (2014). Longitudinal disparities of hazardous drinking between sexual minority and heterosexual individuals from adolescence to young adulthood. *Journal of Youth & Adolescence, 43,* 30–39.

DeRose, L. M., Shiyko, M. P., Foster, H., & Brooks-Gunn, J. (2011). Associations between menarcheal timing and behavioral developmental trajectories for girls from age 6 to age 15. *Journal of Youth and Adolescence, 40,* 1329–1342.

Desjardins, T., & Leadbeater, B. (2011). Relational victimization and depressive symptoms in adolescence: Moderating effects of mother, father, and peer emotional support. *Journal of Youth and Adolescence, 40,* 531–544.

DesRoches, A., & Willoughby, T. (2014). Bidirectional associations between valued activities and adolescent positive adjustment in a longitudinal study: Positive mood as a mediator. *Journal of Youth & Adolescence, 43,* 208–220.

Deutsch, A., & Crockett, L. (2016). Gender, generational status, and parent-adolescent sexual communication: Implications for Latino/a adolescent sexual behavior. *Journal of Research on Adolescence, 26,* 300–315.

Development Services Group, Inc., & Child Welfare Information Gateway. (2015). *Promoting protective factors for pregnant and parenting teens: A guide for practitioners.* Washington, DC: U.S. Department of Health and Human Services, Administration on Children, Youth and Families, Children's Bureau.

Dhariwal, A., & Connolly, J. (2013). Romantic experiences of homeland and diaspora South Asian youth: Westernizing processes of media and friends. *Journal of Research on Adolescence, 23,* 45–56.

Dhariwal, A., Connolly, J., Paciello, M., & Caprara, G. (2009). Adolescent peer relationships and emerging adult romantic styles: A longitudinal study of youth in an Italian community. *Journal of Adolescent Research, 24,* 579–600.

Di Giunta, L., Rothenberg, W. A., Lunetti, C., Lansford, J. E., Pastorelli, C., Eisenberg, N., . . . Uribe Tirado, L. M. (2020). Longitudinal associations between mothers' and fathers' anger/irritability expressiveness, harsh parenting, and adolescents' socioemotional functioning in nine countries. *Developmental Psychology, 56,* 458–474.

Diamond, L. (1998). Development of sexual orientation among adolescent and young adult women. *Developmental Psychology, 34,* 1085–1095.

Diamond, L. (2008). Female bisexuality from adolescence to adulthood: Results from a 10-year longitudinal study. *Developmental Psychology, 44,* 5–14.

Diamond, L., & Dubé, E. M. (2002). Friendship and attachment among heterosexual and sexual-minority youths: Does the gender of your friend matter? *Journal of Youth and Adolescence, 31,* 155–166.

Diamond, L., & Savin-Williams, R. (2009). Adolescent sexuality. In R. Lerner & L. Steinberg (Eds.), *Handbook of adolescent psychology* (3rd ed., Vol. 1, pp. 479–523). New York: Wiley.

Diamond, L., & Savin-Williams, R. (2011). Sexuality. In B. Brown & M. Prinstein (Eds.), *Encyclopedia of adolescence* (Vol. 2, pp. 314–321). New York: Academic Press.

Diamond, L., Savin-Williams, R., & Dubé, E. (1999). Sex, dating, passionate friendships, and romance: Intimate peer relations among lesbian, gay, and bisexual adolescents. In W. Furman, B. Brown, & C. Feiring (Eds.), *Contemporary perspectives on adolescent romantic relationships* (pp. 175–210). New York: Cambridge University Press.

Diamond, L. M. (2020). Gender fluidity and nonbinary gender identities among children and adolescents. *Child Development Perspectives, 14,* 110–115.

Diazgranados, S., & Selman, R. (2014). How students' perceptions of the school climate influence their choice to upstand, bystand, or join perpetrators of bullying. *Harvard Educational Review, 84,* 162–187.

Dick, D. (2011). Developmental changes in genetic influences on alcohol use and dependence. *Child Development Perspectives, 5,* 223–230.

Dick, D. M., Adkins, A. E., & Kuo, S. I-C. (2016). Genetic influences on adolescent behavior. *Neuroscience & Biobehavioral Reviews, 70,* 198–205.

Dickerson, K. L., Milojevich, H. M., & Quas, J. A. (2019). Early environmental unpredictability: Implications for youth's perceptions and social functioning. *Journal of Youth and Adolescence, 48,* 1754–1764.

DiClemente, R., Wingood, G., Harrington, K., Lang, D., Davies, S., . . . Hook, E. (2004). Efficacy of an HIV prevention intervention for African American adolescent girls: A randomized controlled trial. *Journal of the American Medical Association, 292,* 171–179.

Diehl, L., Vicary, J., & Deike, R. (1997). Longitudinal trajectories of self-esteem from early to middle adolescence and related psychosocial variables among rural adolescents. *Journal of Research on Adolescence, 7,* 393–411.

Diemer, M., Marchand, A., McKellar, S., & Malachuk, O. (2016). Promotive and corrosive factors in African American students' math beliefs and achievement. *Journal of Youth and Adolescence, 45,* 1208–1225.

DiIorio, C., Kelley, M., & Hockenberry-Eaton, M. (1999). Communication about sexual issues: Mothers, fathers, and friends. *Journal of Adolescent Health, 24,* 181–189.

Dijkstra, J., & Veenstra, R. (2011). Peer relations. In B. Brown & M. Prinstein (Eds.), *Encyclopedia of adolescence* (Vol. 2, pp. 255–259). New York: Academic Press.

Dijkstra, J., Cillessen, A. H., & Borch, C. (2013). Popularity and adolescent friendship networks: Selection and influence dynamics. *Developmental Psychology, 49,* 1242–1252.

Dijkstra, J., Cillessen, A., Lindenberg, S., & Veenstra, R. (2010). Basking in reflected glory and its

limits: Why adolescents hang out with popular peers. *Journal of Research on Adolescence, 20,* 942–958.

Dirghangi, S., Kahn, G., Laursen, B., Brendgen, M., Vitaro, F., Dionne, G., & Boivin, M. (2015). Co-rumination cultivates anxiety: A genetically informed study of friend influence during early adolescence. *Developmental Psychology, 51,* 564–571.

Dirks, M. A., Cuttini, L. A., Mott, A., & Henry, D. B. (2017). Associations between victimization and adolescents' self-reported responses to peer provocation are moderated by peer-reported aggressiveness. *Journal of Research on Adolescence, 27,* 436–451.

Dishion, T., McCord, J., & Poulin, F. (1999). When interventions harm: Peer groups and problem behavior. *American Psychologist, 54,* 755–764.

Dishion, T., Véronneau, M.-H., & Myers, M. (2010). Cascading peer dynamics underlying the progression from problem behavior to violence in early to late adolescence. *Development and Psychopathology, 22,* 603–619.

Dmitrieva, J., Gibson, L., Steinberg, L., Piquero, A., & Fagan, J. (2014). Predictors and consequences of gang membership: Comparing gang members, gang leaders, and non-gang-affiliated adjudicated youth. *Journal of Research on Adolescence, 24,* 220–234.

Do, K., Guassi Moreira, J., & Telzer, E. (2017). But is helping you worth the risk? Defining prosocial risk taking in adolescence. *Developmental Cognitive Neuroscience, 25,* 260–271.

Do, K., Sharp, P., & Telzer, E. (2020). Modernizing conceptions of valuation and cognitive-control deployment in adolescent risk taking, *Current Directions in Psychological Science, 29,* 102–109.

Doane, L., Breitenstein, R., Beekman, C., Clifford, S., Smith, T., & Lemery-Chalfant, K. (2019). Early life socioeconomic disparities in children's sleep: The mediating role of the current home environment. *Journal of Youth and Adolescence, 48,* 56–70.

Dodge, K., & Pettit, G. (2003). A biopsychosocial model of the development of chronic conduct problems in adolescence. *Developmental Psychology, 39,* 349–371.

Dodge, K., Coie, J., & Lynam, D. (2006). Aggression and antisocial behavior in youth. In W. Damon & R. Lerner (Ser. Eds.) & N. Eisenberg (Vol. Ed.), *Handbook of child psychology: Vol. 3. Social, emotional, and personality development* (6th ed., pp. 719–788). New York: Wiley.

Dodge, K., Greenberg, M., Malone, P., & Conduct Problems Prevention Research Group. (2008). Testing an idealized dynamic cascade model of the development of serious violence in adolescence. *Child Development, 79,* 1907–1927.

Dodge, K. A., Godwin, J., & Conduct Problems Prevention Research Group. (2013). Social-information-processing patterns mediate the impact of preventive intervention on adolescent antisocial behavior. *Psychological Science, 24,* 456–465.

Dogan, S., Stockdale, G., Widaman, K., & Conger, R. (2010). Developmental relations and patterns of change between alcohol use and number of sexual partners from adolescence through adulthood. *Developmental Psychology, 46,* 1747–1759.

Doi, H., & Shinohara, K. (2018). Attention allocation towards own face is pronounced during

middle adolescence: An eye-tracking study. *Developmental Science, 21,* e12490.

Dolev-Cohen, M., & Barak, A. (2013). Adolescents' use of Instant Messaging as a means of emotional relief. *Computers in Human Behavior, 29,* 58–63.

Domina, T., Conley, A., & Farkas, G. (2011). The link between educational expectations and effort in the college-for-all era. *Sociology of Education, 84,* 93–112.

Donahue, K. L., D'Onofrio, B. M., Bates, J. E., Lansford, J. E., Dodge, K. A., & Pettit, G. S. (2010). Early exposure to parents' relationship instability: Implications for sexual behavior and depression in adolescence. *Journal of Adolescent Health, 47,* 547–554.

Donoghue, C., & Meltzer, L. J. (2018). Sleep it off: Bullying and sleep disturbances in adolescents. *Journal of Adolescence, 68,* 87–93.

Doornwaard, S., Bickham, D., Rich, M., ter Bogt, T., & van den Eijnden, R. (2015). Adolescents' use of sexually explicit Internet material and their sexual attitudes and behavior: Parallel development and directional effects. *Developmental Psychology, 51,* 1476–1488.

Doornwaard, S. M., Branje, S., Meeus, W. H., & ter Bogt, T. F. (2012). Development of adolescents' peer crowd identification in relation to changes in problem behaviors. *Developmental Psychology, 48,* 1366–1380.

Dopp, A., Borduin, C., Wagner, D., & Sawyer, A. (2014). The economic impact of multisystemic therapy through midlife: A cost-benefit analysis with serious juvenile offenders and their siblings. *Journal of Consulting and Clinical Psychology, 82,* 694–705.

Doran, K., & Waldron, M. (2017). Timing of first alcohol use and first sex in male and female adolescents. *Journal of Adolescent Health, 61,* 606–611.

Doremus-Fitzwater, T. L., & Spear, L. P. (2016). Reward-centricity and attenuated aversions: An adolescent phenotype emerging from studies in laboratory animals. *Neuroscience & Biobehavioral Reviews, 70,* 121–134.

Dorn, L. D., Hostinar, C. E., Susman, E. J., & Pervanidou, P. (2019). Conceptualizing puberty as a window of opportunity for Impacting health and well-being across the life span. *Journal of Research on Adolescence, 29,* 155–176.

Dosenbach, N., Nardos, B., Cohen, A., Fair, D., Power, J., Church, J. A., . . . Schlaggar, B. (2010). Prediction of individual brain maturity using fMRI. *Science, 329,* 1358–1361.

Dosenbach, N. U. F., Petersen, S. E., & Schlaggar, B. (2013). The teenage brain: Functional connectivity. *Current Directions in Psychological Science, 22,* 101–107.

Dotterer, A., McHale, S., & Crouter, A. (2007). Implications of out-of-school activities for school engagement in African American adolescents. *Journal of Youth and Adolescence, 36,* 391–401.

Dotterer, A., McHale, S., & Crouter, A. C. (2009). The development and correlates of academic interests from childhood through adolescence. *Journal of Educational Psychology, 101,* 509–519.

Dotterer, A. M., & Day, E. (2019). Parental knowledge discrepancies: Examining the roles of warmth and self-disclosure. *Journal of Youth and Adolescence, 48,* 459–468.

Doughty, S. E., Lam, C. B., Stanik, C. E., & McHale, S. M. (2015). Links between sibling experiences and romantic competence from adolescence through young adulthood. *Journal of Youth and Adolescence, 44,* 2054-2066.

Doughty, S. E., McHale, S. M., & Feinberg, M. E. (2015). Sibling experiences as predictors of romantic relationship qualities in adolescence. *Journal of Family Issues, 36,* 589-608.

Douglass, S., & Umaña-Taylor, A. (2017). Examining discrimination, ethnic-racial identity status, and youth public regard among Black, Latino, and White adolescents. *Journal of Research on Adolescence, 27,* 155-172.

Douglass, S., & Umaña-Taylor, A. J. (2015). Development of ethnic-racial identity among Latino adolescents and the role of family. *Journal of Applied Developmental Psychology, 41,* 90-98.

Douglass, S., & Umaña-Taylor, A. J. (2016). Time-varying effects of family ethnic socialization on ethnic-racial identity development among Latino adolescents. *Developmental Psychology, 52,* 1904-1912.

Douglass, S., Mirpuri, S., & Yip, T. (2017). Considering friends within the context of peers in school for the development of ethnic/racial identity. *Journal of Youth and Adolescence, 46,* 300-316.

Douglass, S., Yip, T., & Shelton, J. N. (2014). Intragroup contact and anxiety among ethnic minority adolescents: Considering ethnic identity and school diversity transitions. *Journal of Youth & Adolescence, 43,* 1628-1641.

Downey, D., & Ainsworth-Darnell, J. (2002). The search for oppositional culture among Black students. *American Sociological Review, 67,* 156-164.

Downey, D., Ainsworth, J., & Qian, Z. (2009). Rethinking the attitude-achievement paradox among Blacks. *Sociology of Education, 82,* 1-19.

Downey, G., Bonica, C., & Rincón, C. (1999). Rejection sensitivity and adolescent romantic relationships. In W. Furman, B. Brown, & C. Feiring (Eds.), *Contemporary perspectives on adolescent romantic relationships* (pp. 148-174). New York: Cambridge University Press.

Doyle, A., Brendgen, R., Markiewicz, D., & Kamkar-Parsi, K. (2003). Family relationships as moderators of the significance of romantic relationships for adjustment in early adolescence. *Journal of Early Adolescence, 23,* 316-340.

Drabick, D., & Steinberg, L. (2011). Developmental psychopathology. In B. Brown & M. Prinstein (Eds.), *Encyclopedia of adolescence* (Vol. 3, pp. 135-142). New York: Academic Press.

Dreyfuss, M., Caudle, K., Drysdale, A. T., Johnston, N. E., Cohen, A. O., Somerville, L. H., Galván, A., Tottenham, N., Hare, T. A., & Casey, B. J. (2014). Teens impulsively react rather than retreat from threat. *Developmental Neuroscience, 36,* 220-227.

Drumm, P., & Jackson, D. (1996). Developmental changes in questioning strategies during adolescence. *Journal of Adolescent Research, 11,* 285-305.

Drummond, A., & Sauer, J. (2014). Video-games do not negatively impact adolescent academic performance in science, mathematics or reading. *PLOS ONE, 9,* 87943.

Du, H., Chi, P., & King, R. B. (2019). Economic inequality is associated with long-term harm on adolescent well-being in China. *Child Development, 90*(4), 1016-1026.

Dubé, E., & Savin-Williams, R. (1999). Sexual identity development among ethnic sexual-minority male youths. *Developmental Psychology, 35,* 1389-1398.

DuBois, D., & Silverthorn, N. (2005). Natural mentoring relationships and adolescent health: Evidence from a national study. *American Journal of Public Health, 95,* 518-524.

DuBois, D., Burk-Braxton, C., Swenson, L., Tevendale, H., & Hardesty, J. (2002). Race and gender influences on adjustment in early adolescence: Investigation of an integrative model. *Child Development, 73,* 1573-1592.

DuBois, D., Felner, R., Brand, S., & George, G. (1999). Profiles of self-esteem in early adolescence: Identification and investigation of adaptive correlates. *American Journal of Community Psychology, 27,* 899-932.

DuBois, D., Felner, R., Brand, S., Adan, A., & Evans, E. (1992). A prospective study of life stress, social support, and adaptation in early adolescence. *Child Development, 63,* 542-557.

DuBois, D., Tevendale, H., Burk-Braxton, C., Swenson, L., & Hardesty, J. (2000). Self-system influences during early adolescence: Investigation of an integrative model. *Journal of Early Adolescence, 20,* 12-43.

Duchesne, S., & Ratelle, C. (2010). Parental behaviors and adolescents' achievement goals at the beginning of middle school: Emotional problems as potential mediators. *Journal of Educational Psychology, 102,* 497-507.

Duckworth, A. (2016). *Grit: The power of passion and perseverance.* New York: Scribner.

Duckworth, A., & Seligman, M. (2005). Self-discipline outdoes IQ in predicting academic performance of adolescents. *Psychological Science, 16,* 939-944.

Duckworth, A., & Steinberg, L. (2015). Unpacking self-control. *Child Development Perspectives, 9,* 32-37.

Duckworth, A. L., Quinn, P. D., & Tsukayama, E. (2012). What No Child Left Behind leaves behind: The roles of IQ and self-control in predicting standardized achievement test scores and report card grades. *Journal of Educational Psychology, 104,* 439-451.

Due, P., Merlo, J., Harel-Fisch, Y., Damsgaard, M., Holstein, B., Hetland, J., . . . Lynch, J. (2009). Socioeconomic inequality in exposure to bullying during adolescence: a comparative, cross-sectional, multilevel study in 35 countries. *American Journal of Public Health, 99,* 907-915.

Duell, N., & Steinberg, L. (2019). Positive risk taking in adolescence. *Child Development Perspectives, 13,* 48-52.

Duell, N., & Steinberg, L. (2020). Differential correlates of positive and negative risk taking in adolescence. *Journal of Youth and Adolescence, 49,* 1162-1178.

Duell, N., Steinberg, L., Chein, J., Al-Hassan, S. M., Bacchini, D., Chang, L., . . . Alampay, L. P. (2016). Interaction of reward seeking and self-regulation in the prediction of risk taking: A cross-national test of the dual systems model. *Developmental Psychology, 52,* 1593-1605.

Duell, N., Steinberg, L., Icenogle, G., Chein, J., Chaudhary, N., Di Giunta, L., . . . Chang, L. (2018). Age patterns in risk taking across the world. *Journal of Youth and Adolescence, 47,* 1052-1072.

Duineveld, J., Parker, P., Ryan, R., Ciarrochi, J., & Salmela-Aro, K. (2017). The link between perceived maternal and paternal autonomy support and adolescent well-being across three major educational transitions. *Developmental Psychology, 53,* 1978-1994.

Duke, N., & Macmillan, R. (2016). Schooling, skills, and self-rated health: A test of conventional wisdom on the relationship between educational attainment and health. *Sociology of Education, 89,* 171-206.

Duke, S. A., Balzer, B. W. R., & Steinbeck, K. S. (2014). Testosterone and its effects on human male adolescent mood and behavior: A systematic review. *Journal of Adolescent Health, 55,* 315-322.

Dumas, T., Davis, J., & Ellis, W. (2019). Is it good to be bad? A longitudinal analysis of adolescent popularity motivations as a predictor of engagement in relational aggression and risk behaviors. *Youth & Society, 51,* 659-679.

Dumas, T. M., Lawford, H., Tieu, T.-T., & Pratt, M. W. (2009). Positive parenting in adolescence and its relation to low-point narration and identity status in emerging adulthood: A longitudinal analysis. *Developmental Psychology, 45,* 1531-1544.

Dumont, H., Trautwein, U., Nagy, G., & Nagengast, B. (2014). Quality of parental homework involvement: Predictors and reciprocal relations with academic functioning in the reading domain. *Journal of Educational Psychology, 106,* 144-161.

Dumontheil, I., Apperly, I., & Blakemore, S.-J. (2010). Online usage of theory of mind continues to develop in late adolescence. *Developmental Science, 13,* 331-338.

Dunbar, A., Leerkes, E., Coard, S., Supple, A., & Calkins, S. (2017). An integrative conceptual model of parental racial/ethnic and emotion socialization and links to children's social-emotional development among African American families. *Child Development Perspectives, 11,* 16-22.

Duncan, N., Zimmer-Gembeck, M., & Furman, W. (2019). Sexual harassment and appearance-based peer victimization: Unique associations with emotional adjustment by gender and age. *Journal of Adolescence, 75,* 12-21.

Dunifon, R. (2013). The influence of grandparents on the lives of children and dolescents. *Child Development Perspectives, 7,* 55-60.

Dunlop, S., & Romer, D. (2010). Adolescent and young adult crash risk: Sensation seeking, substance use propensity, and substance use behaviors. *Journal of Adolescent Health, 46,* 90-92.

Dunn, E. C., Milliren, C. E., Evans, C. R., Subramanian, S. V., & Richmond, T. K. (2015). Disentangling the relative influence of schools and neighborhoods of adolescents' risk for depressive symptoms. *American Journal of Public Health, 105,* 732-740.

Dupéré, V., Lacourse, E., Willms, D., Leventhal, T., & Tremblay, R. (2008). Neighborhood poverty and early transition to sexual activity in young adolescents: A developmental ecological approach. *Child Development, 79,* 1463-1476.

DuPont-Reyes, M. J., & Villatoro, A. P. (2019). The role of school race/ethnic composition in mental health outcomes: A systematic literature review. *Journal of Adolescence, 74,* 71-82.

Durwood, L., McLaughlin, K. A., & Olson, K. R. (2017). Mental health and self-worth in socially transitioned transgender youth. *Journal of the American Academy of Child & Adolescent Psychiatry, 56,* 116-123.

Dweck, C. (2002). The development of ability conceptions. In A. Wigfield & J. Eccles (Eds.), *The development of achievement motivation* (pp. 57-88). New York: Academic Press.

Dykas, M., Woodhouse, S., Ehrlich, K., & Cassidy, J. (2012). Attachment-related differences in perceptions of an initial peer interaction emerge over time: Evidence of reconstructive memory processes in adolescents. *Developmental Psychology, 48,* 1381-1389.

Dykas, M., Woodhouse, S., Jones, J., & Cassidy, J. (2014). Attachment-related biases in adolescents' memory. *Child Development, 85,* 2185-2201.

East, P. (2009). Adolescents' relationships with siblings. In R. Lerner & L. Steinberg (Eds.), *Handbook of adolescent psychology* (3rd ed., Vol. 2, pp. 43-73). New York: Wiley.

East, P., & Hokoda, A. (2015). Risk and protective factors for sexual and dating violence victimization: A longitudinal, prospective study of Latino and African American adolescents. *Journal of Youth and Adolescence, 44,* 1288-1300.

East, P., & Rook, K. (1992). Compensatory patterns of support among children's peer relationships: A test using school friends, nonschool friends, and siblings. *Developmental Psychology, 28,* 163-172.

East, P., Chien, N., & Barber, J. (2012). Adolescents' pregnancy intention, wantedness, and regret: Cross-lagged relations with mental health and harsh parenting. *Journal of Marriage and Family, 74,* 167-185.

East, P., Reyes, B. T., & Horn, E. J. (2007). Association between adolescent pregnancy and a family history of teenage births. *Perspectives on Sexual and Reproductive Health, 39,* 108-115.

Eastman, M., Foshee, V., Ennett, S., Sotres-Alvarez, D., Reyes, H. L. M., Faris, R., & North, K. (2018). Profiles of internalizing and externalizing symptoms associated with bullying victimization. *Journal of Adolescence, 65,* 101-110.

Eaton, M., & Dembo, M. (1997). Differences in the motivational beliefs of Asian American and non-Asian students. *Journal of Educational Psychology, 89,* 433-440.

Ebbert, A. M., Infurna, F. J., & Luthar, S. S. (2019). Mapping developmental changes in perceived parent-adolescent relationship quality throughout middle school and high school. *Development and Psychopathology, 31,* 1541-1556.

Eberhart, N., Shih, J., Hammen, C., & Brennan, P. (2006). Understanding the sex difference in vulnerability to adolescent depression: An examination of child and parent characteristics. *Journal of Abnormal Child Psychology, 34,* 495-508.

Eccles, J. (2004). Schools, academic motivation, and stage-environment fit. In R. Lerner & L. Steinberg (Eds.), *Handbook of adolescent psychology.* New York: Wiley.

Eccles, J., & Roeser, R. (2009). Schools, academic motivation, and stage-environment fit. In R. Lerner & L. Steinberg (Eds.), *Handbook of adolescent psychology* (3rd ed., Vol. 1, pp. 404-434). New York: Wiley.

Eccles, J., & Roeser, R. (2011). Schools as developmental contexts during adolescence. *Journal of Research on Adolescence, 21,* 225-241.

Eccles, J., Lord, S. E., & Roeser, R. (1996). Round holes, square pegs, rocky roads, and sore feet: The impact of stage/environment fit on young adolescents' experiences in schools and families. In S. L. Toth & D. Cicchetti (Eds.), *Adolescence: Opportunities and challenges* (Vol. 7, pp. 49-93). Rochester, NY: University of Rochester Press.

Echols, L., & Graham, S. (2016). For better or worse: Friendship choices and peer victimization among ethnically diverse youth in the first year of middle school. *Journal of Youth and Adolescence, 45,* 1862-1876.

Eckshtain, D., Kuppens, S., Ugueto, A., Ng, M., Vaughn-Coaxum, R., Corteselli, K., & Weisz, J. (2020). Meta-analysis: 13-year follow-up of psychotherapy effects on youth depression. *Journal of the American Academy of Child & Adolescent Psychiatry, 59,* 45-63.

Eckstrand, K., Choukas-Bradley, S., Mohanty, A., Cross, M., Allen, N., Silk, J., Jones, N., & Forbes, E. (2017). Heightened activity in social reward networks is associated with adolescents' risky sexual behaviors. *Developmental Cognitive Neuroscience, 27,* 1-9.

Edens, J., Marcus, D., & Vaughn, M. (2011). Exploring the taxometric status of psychopathy among youthful offenders: Is there a juvenile psychopath taxon? *Law and Human Behavior, 35,* 13-24.

Eder, D. (1985). The cycle of popularity: Interpersonal relations among female adolescence. *Sociology of Education, 58,* 154-165.

Edwards, A., Rose, R., Kaprio, J., & Dick, D. (2011). Pubertal development moderates the importance of environmental influences on depressive symptoms in adolescent girls and boys. *Journal of Youth and Adolescence, 40,* 1383-1393.

Edwards, K., Rodenhizer-Stampfli, K., & Eckstein, R. (2015). Bystander action in situations of dating and sexual aggression: A mixed methodological study of high school youth. *Journal of Youth and Adolescence, 44,* 2321-2336.

Ehrenreich, H., Nahapetyan, L., Orpinas, P., & Song, X. (2015). Marijuana use from middle to high school: Co-occurring problem behaviors, teacher-rated academic skills and sixth-grade predictors. *Journal of Youth and Adolescence, 44,* 1929-1940.

Ehrenreich, S., Beron, K., Burnell, K., Meter, D., & Underwood, M. (2020). How adolescents use text messaging through their high school years. *Journal of Research on Adolescence, 30,* 521-540.

Ehrenreich, S., Meter, D. Jouriles, E., & Underwood, M. (2019). Adolescents' externalizing behaviors and antisocial text messaging across the broader peer network: Implications for socialization and selection effects. *Development and Psychopathology, 31,* 1619-1631.

Ehrlich, K. B., Richards, J. M., Lejuez, C. W., & Cassidy, J. (2016). When parents and adolescents disagree about disagreeing: Observed parent-adolescent communication predicts informant discrepancies about conflict. *Journal of Research on Adolescence, 265,* 380-389.

Eichen, D. M., Conner, B. T., Daly, B. P., & Fauber, R. L. (2012). Weight perception, substance use, and disordered eating behaviors: Comparing normal weight and overweight high-school students. *Journal of Youth and Adolescence, 41,* 1-13.

Eiden, R., Lessard, J., Colder, C., Livingston, J., Casey, M., & Leonard, K. (2016). Developmental cascade model for adolescent substance use from infancy to late adolescence. *Developmental Psychology, 52,* 1619-1633.

Eisenberg, M., Erickson, D., Gower, A., Kne, L., Watson, R., Corliss, H., & Saewyc, E. (2020). Supportive community resources are associated with lower risk of substance use among lesbian, gay, bisexual, and questioning adolescents in Minnesota. *Journal of Youth and Adolescence, 49,* 836-848.

Eisenberg, M., Gower, A., McMorris, B., & Bucchianeri, M. (2015). Vulnerable bullies: Perpetration of peer harassment among youths across sexual orientation, weight and disability status. *American Journal of Public Health, 105,* 1784-1791.

Eisenberg, N., Cumberland, A., Guthrie, I., Murphy, B., & Shepard, S. (2005). Age changes in prosocial responding and moral reasoning in adolescence and early adulthood. *Journal of Research on Adolescence, 15,* 235-260.

Eisenberg, N., Morris, A., McDaniel, B., & Spinrad, T. (2009). Moral cognitions and prosocial responding in adolescence. In R. Lerner & L. Steinberg (Eds.), *Handbook of adolescent psychology* (3rd ed., Vol. 1, pp. 229-265). New York: Wiley.

Eisenberg, N., VanSchyndel, S., & Hofer, C. (2015). The association of maternal socialization in childhood and adolescence with adult offsprings' sympathy/caring. *Developmental Psychology, 51,* 7-16.

Eisenberg, N., Zhou, Q., & Koller, S. (2001). Brazilian adolescents' prosocial moral judgment and behavior: Relations to sympathy, perspective taking, gender-role orientation, and demographic characteristics. *Child Development, 72,* 518-534.

Eisman, A., Lee, D., Hsieh, H.-F., Stoddard, S., & Zimmerman, M. (2018). More than just keeping busy: The protective effects of organized activity participation on violence and substance use among urban youth. *Journal of Youth and Adolescence, 47,* 2231-2242.

El Mallah, S. (2020). Conceptualization and measurement of adolescent prosocial behavior: looking back and moving forward. *Journal of Research on Adolescence, 30*(S1), 15-38.

Elam, K., Sandler, I., Wolchik, S., & Tein, J.-Y. (2016). Non-residential father-child involvement, interparental conflict and mental health of children following divorce: A person-focused approach. *Journal of Youth and Adolescence, 45,* 581-593.

Elam, K., Sternberg, A., Waddell, J., Blake, A., & Chassin, L. (2020). Mother and father prescription opioid misuse, alcohol use disorder, and parent knowledge in pathways to adolescent alcohol use. *Journal of Youth and Adolescence, 49,* 1663-1673.

Elder, G. H., Jr. (1980). Adolescence in historical perspective. In J. Adelson (Ed.). *Handbook of adolescent psychology.* New York: Wiley.

Elders, M., Perry, C., Eriksen, M., & Giovino, G. (1994). The report of the Surgeon General: Preventing tobacco use among young people. *American Journal of Public Health, 84,* 543–547.

Eley, T., Lichenstein, P., & Stevenson, J. (1999). Sex differences in the etiology of aggressive and non-aggressive antisocial behavior: Results from two twin studies. *Child Development, 70,* 155–168.

Elfassi, Y., Braun-Lewensohn, O., Krumer-Nevo, M., & Sagy, S. (2016). Community sense of coherence among adolescents as related to their involvement in risk behaviors. *Journal of Community Psychology, 44,* 22–37.

Elgar, F., McKinnon, B., Walsh, S., Freeman, J., Donnelly, P., Gaspar de Matos, M., . . . Currie, C. (2015). Structural determinants of youth bullying and fighting in 79 countries. *Journal of Adolescent Health, 57,* 643–650.

Elkind, D. (1967). Egocentrism in adolescence. *Child Development, 38,* 1025–1034.

Elkington, K., Bauermeister, J., & Zimmerman, M. (2010). Psychological distress, substance use, and HIV/STI risk behaviors among youth. *Journal of Youth and Adolescence, 39,* 514–527.

Ellickson, P., Bell, R., & McGuigan, K. (1993). Preventing adolescent drug use: Long-term results of a junior high program. *American Journal of Public Health, 83,* 856–861.

Elliott, M. C., Leventhal, T., Shuey, E. A., Lynch, A. D., & Coley, R. L. (2016). The home and the 'hood: Associations between housing and neighborhood contexts and adolescent functioning. *Journal of Research on Adolescence, 26,* 194–206.

Ellis, B., Bates, J., Dodge, K., Fergusson, D., Horwood, L., . . . Pettit, G. (2003). Does father absence place daughters at special risk for early sexual activity and teenage pregnancy? *Child Development, 74,* 801–821.

Ellis, B., Del Guidice, M., Dishion, T., Figueredo, A., Gray, G., Griskevicius, G., . . . Wilson, D. (2012). The evolutionary basis of risky adolescent behavior: Implications for science, policy, and practice. *Developmental Psychology, 48,* 598–623.

Ellis, B., Shirtcliff, E., Boyce, W., Deardorff, J., & Essex, M. (2011). Quality of early family relationships and the timing and tempo of puberty: Effects depend on biological sensitivity to context. *Development and Psychopathology, 23,* 85–99.

Ellis, B. J., Schlomer, G. L., Tilley, E. H., & Butler, E. A. (2012). Impact of fathers on risky sexual behavior in daughters: A genetically and environmentally controlled sibling study. *Development and Psychopathology, 24,* 317–332.

Ellis, W., & Zarbatany, L. (2017). Understanding processes of peer clique influence in late childhood and early adolescence. *Child Development Perspectives, 11,* 227–232.

Ellwood-Lowe, M., Humphreys, K., Ordaz, S., Camacho, M., Sacchet, M., & Gotlib, I. (2018). Time-varying effects of income on hippocampal volume trajectories in adolescent girls. *Developmental Cognitive Neuroscience, 30,* 41–50.

El-Menshawi, M., Castro, G., Rodriguez de la Vega, P., Ruiz Peláez, J. G., & Barengo, N. C. (2019). First time cannabis use and sexual debut in U.S. high school adolescents. *Journal of Adolescent Health, 64,* 194–200.

Elmore, R. (2009). Schooling adolescents. In R. Lerner & L. Steinberg (Eds.), *Handbook of adolescent psychology* (3rd ed., Vol. 2, pp. 193–227). New York: Wiley.

Elsharnouby, E., & Dost-Gözkan, A. (2020). Adolescents' well-being with respect to the patterns of disclosure to and secrecy from parents and the best friend: A person-centered examination. *Journal of Youth and Adolescence, 49,* 1687–1701.

El-Sheikh, M., Shimizu, M., Philbrook, L. E., Erath, S. A., & Buckhalt, J. A. (2020). Sleep and development in adolescence in the context of socioeconomic disadvantage. *Journal of Adolescence, 83,* 1–11

Engels, M. C., Phalet, K., Gremmen, M. C., Dijkstra, J. K., & Verschueren, K. (2020). Adolescents' engagement trajectories in multicultural classrooms: The role of the classroom context. *Journal of Applied Developmental Psychology, 69,* 101156.

Englund, M., Siebenbruner, J., Oliva, E., Egeland, B., Chung, C., & Long, J. (2013). The developmental significance of late adolescent substance use for early adult functioning. *Developmental Psychology, 49,* 1554–1564.

Ennett, S., & Bauman, K. (1996). Adolescent social networks: School, demographic, and longitudinal considerations. *Journal of Adolescent Research, 11,* 194–215.

Ennett, S., Foshee, V., Bauman, K., Hussong, A., Faris, R., . . . Durant, R. (2008). The social ecology of adolescent alcohol misuse. *Child Development, 79,* 1777–1791.

Ennett, S., Tobler, N., Ringwalt, C., & Flewelling, R. (1994). How effective is drug abuse resistance education? A meta-analysis of Project DARE outcome evaluations. *American Journal of Public Health, 84,* 1394–1401.

Enriquez, L. (2011). "Because we feel the pressure and we also feel the support": Examining the educational success of undocumented immigrant Latina/o students. *Harvard Educational Review, 81,* 476–499.

Entwisle, D. (1990). Schools and the adolescent. In S. Feldman & G. Elliott (Eds.), *At the threshold: The developing adolescent* (pp. 197–224). Cambridge, MA: Harvard University Press.

Entwisle, D., Alexander, K., & Olson, L. (2004). Temporary as compared to permanent high school dropout. *Social Forces, 82,* 1181–1205.

Entwisle, D., Alexander, K., & Olson, L. (2005). Urban teenagers work and dropout. *Youth and Society, 37,* 3–32.

Epstein, M., Hill, K. G., Nevell, A. M., Guttmannova, K., Bailey, J. A., Abbott, R. D., . . . Hawkins, J. D. (2015). Trajectories of marijuana use from adolescence into adulthood: Environmental and individual correlates. *Developmental Psychology, 51,* 1650–1663.

Epstein, R. (2007). *The case against adolescence: Rediscovering the adult in every teen.* Sanger, CA: Quill Driver Books.

Erath, S., Flanagan, K., & Bierman, K. (2007). Social anxiety and peer relations in early adolescence: Behavioral and cognitive factors. *Journal of Abnormal Child Psychology, 35,* 405–416.

Erickson, K., Crosnoe, R., & Dornbusch, S. (2000). A social process model of adolescent deviance: Combining social control and differential association perspectives. *Journal of Youth and Adolescence, 29,* 395–425.

Erikson, E. (1959). Identity and the life cycle. *Psychological Issues, 1,* 1–171.

Erikson, E. (1968). *Identity: Youth and crisis.* New York: Norton.

Erkut, S., Szalacha, L. A., Garcia Coll, C., & Alarcon, O. (2000). Puerto Rican early adolescents' self-esteem patterns. *Journal of Research on Adolescence, 10,* 339–364.

Erol, R., & Orth, U. (2011). Self-esteem development from age 14 to 30 years: A longitudinal study. *Journal of Personality and Social Psychology, 101,* 607–619.

Erus, G., Battapady, H., Satterthwaite, T. D., Hakonarson, H., Gur, R. E., Davatzikos, C., & Gur, R. C. (2015). Imaging patterns of brain development and their relationship to cognition. *Cerebral Cortex, 25,* 1676–1684.

Eskreis-Winkler, L., Shulman, E., Young, V., Tsukayama, E., Brunwasser, S., & Duckworth, A. (2016). Using wise interventions to motivate deliberate practice. *Journal of Personality and Social Psychology, 111,* 728–744.

Esnaola, I., Sesé, A., Antonio-Agirre, I., & Azpiazu, L. (2020). The development of multiple self-concept dimensions during adolescence. *Journal of Research on Adolescence, 30*(S1), 100–114.

ESPAD Group (2020), ESPAD Report 2019: Results from the European School Survey Project on Alcohol and Other Drugs, EMCDDA Joint Publications, Publications Office of the European Union, Luxembourg

Espelage, D., Anderman, E. M., Brown, V. E., Jones, A., Lane, K. L., McMahon, S. D., et al. (2013). Understanding and preventing violence directed against teachers: Recommendations for a national research, practice, and policy agenda. *American Psychologist, 68,* 75–87.

Espelage, D., Basile, K., & Hamburger, M. (2012). Bullying perpetration and subsequent sexual violence perpetration among middle school students. *Journal of Adolescent Health, 50,* 60–65.

Espelage, D., Merrin, G., Hong, J., & Resko, S. (2018). Applying social cognitive theory to explore relational aggression across early adolescence: A within- and between-person analysis. *Journal of Youth and Adolescence, 47,* 2401–2413.

Espenshade, T., Hale, L., & Chung, C. (2005). The frog pond revisited: High school academic context, class rank, and elite college admission. *Sociology of Education, 78,* 269–293.

Espinosa-Hernández, G., & Vasilenko, S. (2015). Patterns of relationship and sexual behaviors in Mexican adolescents and associations with well-being: A latent class approach. *Journal of Adolescence, 44,* 280–290.

Espinoza, G. (2015). Daily cyberbullying among Latino adolescents: Links with emotional, physical and school adjustment. *Journal of Applied Developmental Psychology, 38,* 39–48.

Espinoza, G., Gillen-O'Neel, C., Gonzales, N., & Fuligni, A. (2014). Friend affiliations and school adjustment among Mexican-American adolescents: The moderating role of peer and parent support. *Journal of Youth and Adolescence, 43,* 1969–1981.

Espinoza, G., Gonzales, N., & Fuligni, A. (2016). Parent discrimination predicts Mexican-American adolescent psychological adjustment 1 year later. *Child Development, 87,* 1079-1089.

Espinoza, G., Schacter, H., & Juvonen, J. (2020). School and cybervictimization across high school: Normative developmental trajectories and bidirectional links with loneliness. *Journal of Research on Adolescence, 30,* 787-799.

Espinoza, P., Penelo, E., Mora, M., Francisco, R., González, M. L., & Raich, R. M. (2018). Bidirectional relations between disordered eating, internalization of beauty ideals, and self-esteem: A longitudinal study with adolescents. *The Journal of Early Adolescence, 39*(9), 1244-1260.

Estévez, E., Jiménez, T., & Segura, L. (2019). Emotional intelligence and empathy in aggressors and victims of school violence. *Journal of educational psychology, 111,* 488.

Ethier, K., Harper, C., Hoo, E., & Dittus, P. (2016). The longitudinal impact of perceptions of parental monitoring on adolescent initiation of sexual activity. *Journal of Adolescent Health, 59,* 570-576.

Ettekal, I., & Ladd, G. (2015). Costs and benefits of children's physical and relational aggression trajectories on peer rejection, acceptance, and friendships: Variations by aggression subtypes, gender, and age. *Developmental Psychology, 51,* 1756-1770.

Evans, A. D., & Lee, K. (2011). Verbal deception from late childhood to middle adolescence and its relation to executive functioning skills. *Developmental Psychology, 47,* 1108-1116.

Evans, A., Banerjee, M., Meyer, R., Aldana, A., Foust, M., & Rowley, S. (2012). Racial socialization as a mechanism for positive development among African American youth. *Child Development Perspectives, 6,* 251-257.

Evans, B., Huizink, A., Greaves-Lord, K., Tulen, J., Roelofs, K., & van der Ende, J. (2020) Urbanicity, biological stress system functioning and mental health in adolescents. *PLOS ONE, 15,* e0228659.

Evans, C., & Smokowski, P. (2015). Prosocial bystander behavior in bullying dynamics: Assessing the impact of social capital. *Journal of Youth and Adolescence, 44,* 2289-2307.

Evans, S., Simons, L., & Simons, R. (2016). Factors that influence trajectories of delinquency throughout adolescence. *Journal of Youth and Adolescence, 45,* 156-171.

Eveleth, P., & Tanner, J. (1990). *Worldwide variation in human growth* (2nd ed.). New York: Cambridge University Press.

Everett, B., Myers, K., Sanders, J., & Turok, D. (2019). Male abortion beneficiaries: Exploring the long-term educational and economic associations of abortion among men who report teen pregnancy. *Journal of Adolescent Health, 65,* 520-526.

Everett, S., Warren, C., Santelli, J., Kann, L., Collins, J., & Kolbe, L. (2000). Use of birth control pills, condoms, and withdrawal among U.S. high school students. *Journal of Adolescent Health, 27,* 112-118.

Evers, K., Chen, S., Rothmann, S., Dhir, A., & Pallesen, S. (2020). Investigating the relation among disturbed sleep due to social media use, school burnout, and academic performance. *Journal of Adolescence, 84,* 156-164.

Exner-Cortens, D. (2014). Theory and teen dating violence victimization: Considering adolescent development. *Developmental Review, 34,* 168-188.

Exner-Cortens, D., Eckenrode, J., Bunge, J., & Rothman, E. (2017). Revictimization after adolescent dating violence in a matched, national sample of youth. *Journal of Adolescent Health, 60,* 176-183.

Eyre, S., & Millstein, S. (1999). What leads to sex? Adolescent preferred partners and reasons for sex. *Journal of Research on Adolescence, 9,* 277-307.

Facchin, F., Margola, D., Molgora, S., & Revenson, T. (2014). Effects of benefit-focused versus standard expressive writing on adolescents' self-concept during the high school transition. *Journal of Research on Adolescence, 24,* 131-144.

Fairweather-Schmidt, A. K., & Wade, T. D. (2016). Characterizing and predicting trajectories of disordered eating over adolescence. *Journal of Abnormal Psychology, 125,* 369-380.

Falk, E., Cascio, C., O'Donnell, M., Carp, J., Tinney, F. Jr., Bingham, C., . . . Simons-Morton, B. (2014). Neural responses to exclusion predict susceptibility to social influence. *Journal of Adolescent Health, 54,* S22-S31.

Farb, A., & Matjasko, J. (2012). Recent advances in research on school-based extracurricular activities and adolescent development. *Developmental Review, 32,* 1-48.

Fardouly, J., Magson, N., Johnco, C., Oar, E., & Rapee, R. (2018). Parental control of the time preadolescents spend on social media: Links with preadolescents' social media appearance comparisons and mental health. *Journal of Youth and Adolescence, 47,* 1456-1468.

Farkas, G., Grobe, R., & Shuan, Y. (1990). Cultural resources and school success: Gender, ethnicity, and poverty groups within an urban school district. *American Sociological Review, 55,* 127-142.

Farley, J., & Kim-Spoon, J. (2014). The development of adolescent self-regulation: Reviewing the role of parent, peer, friend, and romantic relationships. *Journal of Adolescence, 37,* 433-440.

Farr, R. H. (2017). Does parental sexual orientation matter? A longitudinal follow-up of adoptive families with school-age children. *Developmental Psychology, 53,* 252-264.

Farrell, A. D., Erwin, E. H., Allison, K. W., Meyer, A., Sullivan, T., Camou, S., . . . Esposito, L. (2007). Problematic situations in the lives of urban African American middle school students: A qualitative study. *Journal of Research on Adolescence, 17,* 413-454.

Farrell, A. D., Mehari, K. R., Kramer-Kuhn., A., & Goncy, E. A. (2014). The impact of victimization and witnessing violence on physical aggression among high-risk adolescents. *Child Development, 85,* 1694-1710.

Farrell, A., Goncy, E., Sullivan, T., & Thompson, E. (2018). Victimization, aggression, and other problem behaviors: Trajectories of change within and across middle school grades. *Journal of Research on Adolescence, 28,* 438-455.

Farrell, A., Thompson, E., Curran, P., & Sullivan, T. (2020). Bidirectional relations between witnessing violence, victimization, life events, and physical aggression among adolescents in urban schools. *Journal of Youth and Adolescence, 49,* 1309-1327.

Farrington, D. (2009). Conduct disorder, aggression, and delinquency. In R. Lerner & L. Steinberg (Eds.), *Handbook of adolescent psychology* (3rd ed., Vol. 1, pp. 683-722). New York: Wiley.

Farrington, D., Loeber, R., & Stouthamer-Loeber, M. (2003). How can the relationship between race and violence be explained? In D. Hawkins (Ed.), *Violent crimes: Assessing race and ethnic differences* (pp. 213-237). New York: Cambridge University Press.

Farruggia S. P., Bullen, P., & Davidson, J. (2013). Important nonparental adults as an academic resource for youth. *The Journal of Early Adolescence, 33,* 498-522.

Fasick, F. (1994). On the "invention" of adolescence. *Journal of Early Adolescence, 14,* 6-23.

Fasula, A., & Miller, K. (2006). African-American and Hispanic adolescents' intentions to delay first intercourse: Parental communication as a buffer for sexually active peers. *Journal of Adolescent Health, 38,* 193-200.

Fauth, R. C., Leventhal, T., & Brooks-Gunn, J. (2007). Welcome to the neighborhood? Long-term impacts of moving to low-poverty neighborhoods on poor children's and adolescents' outcomes. *Journal of Research on Adolescence, 17,* 249-284.

Federal Bureau of Investigation. (2020). *Crime in the United States, 2019.* Washington: Author.

Federal Interagency Forum on Child and Family Statistics. (2005). *America's children.* Washington: Author.

Feinberg, M., McHale, S., Crouter, A., & Cumsille, P. (2003). Sibling differentiation: Sibling and parent relationship trajectories in adolescence. *Child Development, 74,* 1261-1274.

Feinberg, M., Neiderhiser, J., Simmens, S., Reiss, D., & Hetherington, E. (2000). Sibling comparison of differential parental treatment in adolescence: Gender, self-esteem, and emotionality as mediators of the parenting-adjustment association. *Child Development, 71,* 1611-1628.

Feiring, C. (1999). Gender identity and the development of romantic relationships in adolescence. In W. Furman, B. Brown, & C. Feiring (Eds.), *Contemporary perspectives on adolescent romantic relationships* (pp. 211-232). New York: Cambridge University Press.

Feiring, C., & Lewis, M. (1993). Do mothers know their teenagers' friends? Implications for individuation in early adolescence. *Journal of Youth and Adolescence, 22,* 337-354.

Felner, R., Brand, S., DuBois, D., Adan, A., Mulhall, P., & Evans, E. (1995). Socioeconomic disadvantage, proximal environmental experiences, and socioemotional and academic adjustment in early adolescence: Investigation of a mediated effects model. *Child Development, 66,* 774-792.

Felson, R., Savolainen, J., & Schwartz, J. (2020). The influence of alcohol intoxication on adolescent sexual intercourse and contraception use. *Youth & Society, 52,* 1395-1413.

Felson, R., Savolainen, J., Bjarnason, T., Anderson, A., & Zohra, I. (2011). The cultural context of adolescent drinking and violence in 30 European countries. *Criminology, 49,* 699-728.

Felton, J., Kofler, M., Lopez, C., Saunders, B., & Kilpatrick, D. (2015). The emergence of co-occurring adolescent polysubstance use and depressive symptoms: A latent growth modeling approach. *Development and Psychopathology, 27,* 1367-1383.

Fenzel, L. (2001). Prospective study of changes in global self-worth and strain during the transition to middle school. *Journal of Early Adolescence, 20,* 93-116.

Ferdinand, A. O., Menachemi, N., Blackburn, J. L., Sen, B., Nelson, L., & Morrisey, M. (2015). The impact of texting bans on motor vehicle crash-related hospitalizations. *American Journal of Public Health, 105,* 859-865.

Ferguson, C. (2020). Links between screen use and depressive symptoms in adolescents over 16 years: Is there evidence for increased harm? *Developmental Science,* e13008.

Ferguson, C., & Beresin, E. (2017). Social science's curious war with pop culture and how it was lost: The media violence debate and the risks it holds for social science. *Preventive Medicine, 99,* 69-76.

Ferguson, C., & Colwell, J. (2018). A meaner, more callous digital world for youth? The relationship between violent digital games, motivation, bullying, and civic behavior among children. *Psychology of Popular Media Culture, 7,* 202-215.

Ferguson, C., & Olson, C. (2014). Video game violence use among "vulnerable" populations: The impact of violent games on delinquency and bullying among children with clinically elevated depression or attention deficit symptoms. *Journal of Youth & Adolescence, 43,* 127-136.

Ferguson, C., & Wang, J. (2019). Aggressive video games are not a risk factor for future aggression in youth: A longitudinal study. *Journal of Youth and Adolescence, 48,* 1439-1451.

Ferguson, C., Barr, H., Figueroa, G., Foley, K., Gallimore, A., LaQuea, R., . . . Garza, A. (2015). Digital poison? Three studies examining the influence of violent video games on youth. *Computers in Human Behavior, 50,* 399-410.

Ferguson, C. J., Muñoz, M., Garza, A., and Galindo, M. (2014). Concurrent and prospective analyses of peer, television and social media influences on body dissatisfaction, eating disorder symptoms and life satisfaction in adolescent girls. *Journal of Youth and Adolescence, 43,* 1-14.

Ferguson, G., Nelson, M., Fiese, B., Meeks Gardner, J., Koester, B., & JUS Media Programme Study Team. (2020). U.S. media enjoyment without strong media literacy undermines adolescents' and mothers' reported efforts to reduce unhealthy eating in Jamaica. *Journal of Research on Adolescence, 30,* 928-942.

Ferguson, S., & Ryan, A. (2019). It's lonely at the top: Adolescent students' peer-perceived popularity and self-perceived social contentment. *Journal of Youth and Adolescence, 48,* 341-358.

Fergusson, D., & Horwood, L. (2002). Male and female offending trajectories. *Development and Psychopathology, 14,* 159-177.

Fergusson, D., & Woodward, L. (2000). Teenage pregnancy and female educational underachievement: A prospective study of a New Zealand birth cohort. *Journal of Marriage and the Family, 62,* 147-161.

Fernández-González, L., Calvete, E., & Orue, I. (2019). The role of acceptance of violence beliefs and social information processing on dating violence perpetration. *Journal of Research on Adolescence, 29,* 763-776.

Ferrar, S., Stack, D., Dickson, D., & Serbin, L. (2020). Conflict resolution and emotional expression in mother-preadolescent dyads: longitudinal associations with children's socioemotional development. *Journal of Youth and Adolescence, 49,* 2388-2406.

Ferreira, P., Azevedo, C., & Menezes, I. (2012). The developmental quality of participation experiences: Beyond the rhetoric that "participation is always good!" *Journal of Adolescence, 35,* 599-610.

Ferreiro, F., Wichstrøm, L., Seoane, G., & Senra, C. (2014). Reciprocal associations between depressive symptoms and disordered eating among adolescent girls and boys: A multiwave, prospective study. *Journal of Abnormal Child Psychology, 42,* 803-812.

Ferrer, E., Whitaker, K. J., Steele, J. S., Green, C. T., Wendelken, C., & Bunge, S. A. (2013). White matter maturation supports the development of reasoning ability through its influence on processing speed. *Developmental Science, 16,* 941-951.

Ferschmann, L., Fjell, A. M., Vollrath, M. E., Grydeland, H., Walhovd, K. B., & Tamnes, C. K. (2018). Personality traits are associated with cortical development across adolescence: A longitudinal structural MRI Study. *Child Development, 89*(3), 811-822.

Ferschmann, L., Vijayakumar, N., Grydeland, H., Overbye, K., Sederevicius, D., Due-Tønnessen, P., . . . Tamnes, C. K. (2019). Prosocial behavior relates to the rate and timing of cortical thinning from adolescence to young adulthood. *Developmental Cognitive Neuroscience, 40,* 100734.

Festl, R., Vogelgesang, J., Scharkow, M., & Quandt, T. (2017). Longitudinal patterns of involvement in cyberbullying: Results from a latent transition analysis. *Computers in Human Behavior, 66,* 7-15.

Fields, J. (2003). *Children's living arrangements and characteristics: March 2002.* Current Population Reports P20-547. Washington, DC: U.S. Census Bureau.

Figner, B., & Weber, E. (2011). Who takes risks when and why? Determinants of risk taking. *Current Directions in Psychological Science, 20,* 211-216.

Filardo, E. (1996). Gender patterns in African American and White adolescents' social interactions in same-race, mixed-gender groups. *Journal of Personality and Social Psychology, 71,* 71-82.

Filion, N., Fenelon, A., & Boudreaux, M. (2018). Immigration, citizenship, and the mental health of adolescents. *PLOS ONE, 13,* e0196859.

Fine, A., Mahler, A., Steinberg, L., Frick, P., & Cauffman, E. (2017). Individual in context: The role of impulse control on the association between the home, school, and neighborhood developmental contexts and adolescent delinquency. *Journal of Youth and Adolescence, 46,* 1488-1502.

Fine, S. (2014). "A slow revolution": Toward a theory of intellectual playfulness in high school classrooms. *Harvard Educational Review, 84,* 1-23, 134-135.

Finer, L., & Philbin, J. (2013). Sexual initiation, contraceptive use, and pregnancy among young adolescents. *Pediatrics, 131,* 886-891.

Finer, L., & Zolna, M. (2016). Declines in unintended pregnancy in the United States, 2008-2011. *New England Journal of Medicine, 374,* 843-852.

Finer, L. B. (2010). Unintended pregnancy among U.S. adolescents: Accounting for sexual activity. *Journal of Adolescent Health, 47,* 312-314.

Finn, A., Kraft, M., West, M., Leonard, J., Bish, C., Martin, R., . . . Gabrieli, J. (2014). Cognitive skills, student achievement test, and schools. *Psychological Science, 25,* 736-744.

Finn, A., Minas, J., Leonard, J., Mackey, A., Salvatore, J., Goetz, C., . . . Gabrieli, J. (2017). Functional brain organization of working memory in adolescents varies in relation to family income and academic achievement. *Developmental Science, 20,* e12450.

Finn, J., Gerber, S. B., & Boyd-Zaharias, J. (2005). Small classes in the early grades, academic achievement, and graduating from high school. *Journal of Educational Psychology, 97,* 214-223.

Fischer, D., Lombardi, D. A., Marucci-Wellman, H., & Ronneberg, T. (2017). Chronotypes in the US—Influence of age and sex. *PLOS ONE, 12,* e0178782.

Fisher, B., Gardella, J., & Teurbe-Tolon, A. (2016). Peer cybervictimization among adolescents and the associated internalizing and externalizing problems: A meta-analysis. *Journal of Youth and Adolescence, 45,* 1727-1743.

Fisher, C., Wallace, S., & Fenton, R. (2000). Discrimination distress during adolescence. *Journal of Youth and Adolescence, 29,* 679-695.

Fisher, H. L., Caspi, A., Moffitt, T., Wertz, J., Gray, R., Newbury, J., . . . Arseneault, L. (2015). Measuring adolescents' exposure to victimization: The Environmental Risk (E-Risk) Longitudinal Twin Study. *Development and Psychopathology, 27,* 1399-1416.

Fisher, M., Golden, N., Katzman, D., Kriepe, R., Rees, J., Schebendach, J., . . . Hoberman, H. (1995). Eating disorders in adolescents: A background paper. *Journal of Adolescent Health, 16,* 420-437.

Fisher, P., Stoolmiller, M., Mannering, A., Takahashi, A., & Chamberlain, P. (2011). Foster placement disruptions associated with problem behavior: Mitigating a threshold effect. *Journal of Consulting and Clinical Psychology, 79,* 481-487.

Fite, P., Wynn, P., & Pardini, D. (2009). Explaining discrepancies in arrest rates between Black and White male juveniles. *Journal of Consulting and Clinical Psychology, 77,* 916-927.

Flamant, N., Haerens, L., Mabbe, E., Vansteenkiste, M., & Soenens, B. (2020). How do adolescents deal with intrusive parenting? The role of coping with psychologically controlling parenting in internalizing and externalizing problems. *Journal of Adolescence, 84,* 200-212.

Flament, M. F., Henderson, K., Buchholz, A., Obeid, N., Nguyen, H. N. T., Birmingham, M., & Goldfield, G. (2015). Weight status and DSM-5 diagnoses of eating disorders in adolescents from the community. *Journal of the American Academy of Child & Adolescent Psychiatry, 54,* 403-411.

Flamion, A., Missotten, P., Marquet, M., & Adam, S. (2019). Impact of contact with grandparents on children's and adolescents' views on the elderly. *Child Development, 90,* 1155-1169.

Flamm, E. S., & Grolnick, W. S. (2013). Adolescent adjustment in the context of life change: The supportive role of parental structure provision. *Journal of Adolescence, 36,* 899-912.

Flanagan, C. (2004). Volunteerism, leadership, political socialization, and civic engagement. In R. Lerner & L. Steinberg (Eds.), *Handbook of adolescent psychology.* New York: Wiley.

Flanagan, C., & Galay, L. (1995). Reframing the meaning of "political" in research with adolescents. *Perspectives on Political Science, 24,* 34-41.

Flanagan, C., & Stout, M. (2010). Developmental patterns of social trust between early and late adolescence: Age and school climate effects. *Journal of Research on Adolescence, 20,* 748-773.

Flanagan, C., Kim, T., Collura, J., & Kopish, M. (2015). Community service and adolescents' social capital. *Journal of Research on Adolescence, 25,* 295-309.

Flanagan, C., Kim, T., Pykett, A., Finlay, A., Gallay, E., & Pancer, M. (2014). Adolescents' theories about economic inequality: Why are some people poor while others are rich? *Developmental Psychology, 50,* 2512-2525.

Flanagan, C. A., & Kornbluh, M. (2019). How unequal is the United States? Adolescents' images of social stratification. *Child Development, 90*(3), 957-969.

Flannery, D., Torquati, J., & Lindemeier, L. (1994). The method and meaning of emotional expression and experience during adolescence. *Journal of Adolescent Research, 9,* 8-27.

Flannery, D., Vazsonyi, A., & Rowe, D. (1996). Caucasian and Hispanic early adolescent substance use: Parenting, personality, and school adjustment. *Journal of Early Adolescence, 16,* 71-89.

Flannery, D., Weseter, K., & Singer, M. (2004). Impact of exposure to violence in school on child and adolescent mental health and behavior. *Journal of Community Psychology, 32,* 559-573.

Flashman, J. (2012). Academic achievement and its impact on friend dynamics. *Sociology of Education, 85,* 61-80.

Flook, L. (2011). Gender differences in adolescents' daily interpersonal events and well-being. *Child Development, 82,* 454-461.

Flook, L., & Fuligni, A. (2008). Family and school spillover in adolescents' daily lives. *Child Development, 79,* 776-787.

Flora, C. (2018). Are smartphones really destroying the adolescent brain? *Scientific American, 318,* 30-37.

Flynn, B., Worden, J., Secker-Walker, R., Pirie, P., Badger, G., Carpenter, J., & Geller, B. (1994). Mass media and school interventions for cigarette smoking prevention: Effects 2 years after completion. *American Journal of Public Health, 84,* 1148-1150.

Flynn, H., Felmlee, D., Shu, X., & Conger, R. (2018). Mothers and fathers matter: The influence of parental support, hostility, and problem solving on adolescent friendships. *Journal of Family Issues, 39,* 2389-2412.

Fomby, P., & Bosick, S. J. (2013). Family instability and the transition to adulthood. *Journal of Marriage and Family, 75,* 1266-1287.

Fomby, P., Goode, J. A., Truong-Vu, K.-P., & Mollborn, S. (2019, August). Adolescent technology, sleep, and physical activity time in two U.S. cohorts. *Youth & Society.*

Fontaine, R. G., Yang, C., Burks, V., Dodge, K., Price, J., Pettit, G., & Bates, J. (2009).

Loneliness as a partial mediator of the relation between low social preference in childhood and anxious/depressed symptoms in adolescence. *Development and Psychopathology, 21,* 479.

Fontaine, R., Yang, C., Dodge, K., Bates, J., & Pettit, G. (2008). Testing an individual systems model of response evaluation and decision (RED) and antisocial behavior across adolescence. *Child Development, 79,* 462-475.

Forbes, E. E., Phillips, M. L., Silk, J. S., Ryan, N. D., & Dahl, R. E. (2011). Neural systems of threat processing in adolescents: Role of pubertal maturation and relation to measures of negative affect. *Developmental Neuropsychology, 36,* 429-452.

Ford, K., Hurd, N., Jagers, R., & Sellers, R. (2013). Caregiver experiences of discrimination and African American adolescents' psychological health over time. *Child Development, 84,* 485-499.

Fordham, C., & Ogbu, J. (1986). Black students' school success: Coping with the burden of "acting White." *Urban Review, 18,* 176-206.

Forest, A. & Wood, J. (2012). When social networking is not working: Individuals with low self-esteem recognize but do not reap the benefits of self-disclosure on Facebook. *Psychological Science, 23,* 295-302.

Forgatch, M., Patterson, G., Degarmo, D., & Beldavs, Z. (2009). Testing the Oregon delinquency model with 9-year follow-up of the Oregon Divorce Study. *Development and Psychopathology, 21,* 637-660.

Forgatch, M., Snyder, J., Patterson, G., Pauldine, M., Chaw, Y., Elish, K., . . . Richardson, E. (2016). Resurrecting the chimera: Progressions in parenting and peer processes. *Development and Psychopathology, 28,* 689-706.

Forhan, S., Gottlieb, S., Sternberg, M., Xu, F., Datta, S., McQuillan, G., . . . Markowitz, L. (2009). Prevalence of sexually transmitted infections among female adolescents aged 14 to 19 in the United States. *Pediatrics, 124,* 1505-1512.

Forrest, W., Hay, C., Widdowson, A., & Rocque, M. (2019). Development of impulsivity and risk-seeking: Implications for the dimensionality and stability of self control. *Criminology, 57,* 512-543.

Forster, M., Grigsby, T., Gower, A., Mehus, C., & McMorris, B. (2020). The role of social support in the association between childhood adversity and adolescent self-injury and suicide: Findings from a statewide sample of high school students. *Journal of Youth and Adolescence, 49,* 1195-1208.

Fortner, M., Crouter, A., & McHale, S. (2004). Is parents' work involvement responsive to the quality of relationships with adolescent offspring? *Journal of Family Psychology, 19,* 530-538.

Fortuin, J., van Geel, M., & Vedder, P. (2015). Peer influences on internalizing and externalizing problems among adolescents: A longitudinal social network analysis. *Journal of Youth and Adolescence, 44,* 887-897.

Fosco, G., & LoBraico, E. (2019). Elaborating on premature adolescent autonomy: Linking variation in daily family processes to developmental risk. *Development and Psychopathology, 31,* 1741-1755.

Fosco, G., Xia, M., Lynn, M., & Grych, J. (2016). Triangulation and parent-adolescent relationships: Implications for adolescent dating

competence and abuse. *Journal of Research on Adolescence, 26,* 524-537.

Fosco, W. D., Hawk, L. W., Colder, C. R., Meisel, S. N., & Lengua, L. J. (2019). The development of inhibitory control in adolescence and prospective relations with delinquency. *Journal of Adolescence, 76,* 37-47.

Foshee, V., Bauman, K., Greene, W., Koch, G., Linder, G., & MacDougall, J. (2000). The safe dates program: 1-year follow-up results. *American Journal of Public Health, 90,* 1619-1622.

Foshee, V., Benefield, T., Reyes, H., Ennett, S., Faris, R., Chang, L., . . . Suchindran, C. (2013). The peer context and the development of the perpetration of adolescent dating violence. *Journal of Youth and Adolescence, 42,* 471-486.

Foshee, V., Benefield, T., Suchindran, C., Ennett, S., Bauman, K., Karriker-Jaffe, K., . . . Mathias, J. (2009). The development of four types of adolescent dating abuse and selected demographic correlates. *Journal of Research on Adolescence, 19,* 380-400.

Foshee, V. A., McNaughton Reyes, H. L., Chen, M. S., Ennett, S. T., Basile, K. C., DeGue, S., . . . Bowling, J. M. (2016). Shared risk factors for the perpetration of physical dating violence, bullying, and sexual harassment among adolescents exposed to domestic violence. *Journal of Youth and Adolescence, 45,* 672-686.

Foss, R. D., & Goodwin, A. H. (2014). Distracted driver behaviors and distracting conditions among adolescent drivers: Findings from a naturalistic driving study. *Journal of Adolescent Health, 54,* S50-S60.

Foster, H., & Brooks-Gunn, J. (2012). Neighborhood, family and individual influences on school physical victimization. *Journal of Youth and Adolescence, 42,* 1596-1610.

Foulkes, L., & Blakemore, S-J. (2018). Studying individual differences in human adolescent brain development. *Nature Neuroscience, 21,* 315-323.

Fowler, P., Tompsett, C., Braciszewski, J., Jacques-Tiura, A., & Baltes, B. (2010). Community violence: A meta-analysis on the effect of exposure and mental health outcomes of children and adolescents. *Development and Psychopathology, 21,* 227-259.

Fowler, P., Toro, P., & Miles, B. (2009). Pathways to and from homelessness and associated psychosocial outcomes among adolescents leaving the foster care system. *American Journal of Public Health, 99,* 1453-1458.

Fox, J. A., & Fridel, E. E. (2018). The three R's of school shootings: Risk, readiness, and response. In H. Shapiro, ed., *The Wiley Handbook on Violence in Education: Forms, Factors, and Preventions.* New York: Wiley/Blackwell.

Fraley, R., Roisman, G., Booth-LaForce, C., Owen, M., & Holland, A. (2013). Interpersonal and genetic origins of adult attachment styles: A longitudinal study from infancy to early adulthood. *Journal of Personality and Social Psychology, 104,* 817-838.

Francisco, R., Espinoza, P., González, M. L., Penelo, E., Mora, M., Rosés, R., & Raich, R. M. (2015). Body dissatisfaction and disordered eating among Portuguese and Spanish adolescents: The role of individual characteristics and internalization of sociocultural ideals. *Journal of Adolescence, 41,* 7-16.

Frank, K., Muller, C., Schiller, K., Riegle-Crumb, C., Mueller, A., Crosnoe, R., & Pearson, J. (2008). The social dynamics of mathematics coursetaking in high school. *American Journal of Sociology, 113,* 1645-1696.

Franken, A., Keijsers, L., Dijkstra, J., & ter Bogt, T. (2017). Music preferences, friendship, and externalizing behavior in early adolescence: A SIENA examination of the music marker theory using the SNARE study. *Journal of Youth and Adolescence, 46,* 1839-1850.

Franken, A., Prinstein, M. J., Dijkstra, J. K., Steglich, C. E. G., Harakeh, Z., & Vollebergh, W. A. M. (2016). Early adolescent friendship selection based on externalizing behavior: The moderating role of pubertal development. The SNARE study. *Journal of Abnormal Child Psychology, 44,* 1647-1657.

Frankenhuis, W., & Walasek, N. (2020). Modeling the evolution of sensitive periods. *Developmental Cognitive Neuroscience, 41,* 100715.

Franzoi, S., Davis, M., & Vasquez-Suson, K. (1994). Two social worlds: Social correlates and stability of adolescent status groups. *Journal of Personality and Social Psychology, 67,* 462-473.

Freeman, H., & Brown, B. (2001). Primary attachment to parents and peers during adolescence: Differences by attachment style. *Journal of Youth and Adolescence, 30,* 653-674.

French, D., & Dishion, T. (2003). Predictors of early initiation of sexual intercourse among high-risk adolescents. *Journal of Early Adolescence, 23,* 295-315.

French, D., Eisenberg, N., Vaughan, J., Purwono, U., & Suryanti, T. (2008). Religious involvement and the social competence and adjustment of Indonesian Muslim adolescents. *Developmental Psychology, 44,* 597-611.

French, S. E., Seidman, E., Allen, L., & Aber, J. L. (2006). The development of ethnic identity during adolescence. *Developmental Psychology, 42,* 1-10.

Freud, A. (1958). Adolescence. *Psychoanalytic Study of the Child, 13,* 255-278.

Freud, S. (1938). *An outline of psychoanalysis.* London: Hogarth Press.

Frick, P., & White, S. (2008). The importance of callous-unemotional traits for the development of aggressive and antisocial behavior. *Journal of Child Psychology and Psychiatry, 49,* 359-375.

Frick, P., Kotov, R., Loney, B., & Vasey, M. (2005). The latent structure of psychopathy in youth: A taxometric investigation. *Journal of Abnormal Child Psychology, 33.*

Fried, M., & Fried, M. (1980). *Transitions: Four rituals in eight cultures.* New York: Norton.

Friedenberg, E. (1959). *The vanishing adolescent.* Boston: Beacon Press.

Friedenberg, E. (1967). *Coming of age in America.* New York: Vintage Books.

Friedlander, L., Connolly, J., Pepler, D., & Craig, W. (2007). Biological, familial, and peer influences on dating in early adolescence. *Archives of Sexual Behavior, 36,* 821-830.

Frison, E., Subrahmanyam, K., & Eggermont, S. (2016). The short-term longitudinal and reciprocal relations between peer victimization on Facebook and adolescents' well-being. *Journal of Youth and Adolescence, 45,* 1755-1771.

Fromme, K., Corbin, W. R., & Kruse, M. I. (2008). Behavioral risks during the transition from high school to college. *Developmental Psychology, 44,* 1497-1504.

Frøyland, L., Bakken, A., & von Soest, T. (2020). Physical fighting and leisure activities among norwegian adolescents--investigating co-occurring changes from 2015 to 2018. *Journal of Youth and Adolescence, 49,* 2298-2310.

Fruiht, V., & Wray-Lake, L. (2013). The role of mentor type and timing in predicting educational attainment. *Journal of Youth and Adolescence, 42,* 1459-1472.

Fry, R. (2016). *For the first time in modern era, living with parents edges out other living arrangements for 18- to 34-year-olds.* Washington: Pew Research Center.

Fry, R., Passel, J., & Cohn, D. (2020). *A majority of young adults in the U.S. live with their parents for the first time since the Great Depression.* Washington: Pew Research Center.

Fuhrmann, D., Knoll, L. J., & Blakemore, S-J. (2015). Adolescence as a sensitive period of brain development. *Trends in Cognitive Sciences, 19,* 558-566.

Fujimoto, K., Unger, J., & Valente, T. (2012). A network method of measuring affiliation-based peer influence: Assessing the influences of teammates' smoking on adolescent smoking. *Child Development, 83,* 442-451.

Fuligni, A. (1998). Authority, autonomy, and parent-adolescent conflict and cohesion: A study of adolescents from Mexican, Chinese, Filipino, and European backgrounds. *Developmental Psychology, 34,* 782-792.

Fuligni, A. (2019). The need to contribute during adolescence. *Perspectives on Psychological Science, 14,* 331-343.

Fuligni, A., & Eccles, J. (1993). Perceived parent-child relationships and early adolescents' orientation toward peers. *Developmental Psychology, 29,* 622-632.

Fuligni, A., & Witkow, M. (2004). The postsecondary educational progress of youth from immigrant families. *Journal of Research on Adolescence, 14,* 159-183.

Fuligni, A., Eccles, J., Barber, B., & Clements, P. (2001). Early adolescent peer orientation and adjustment during high school. *Developmental Psychology, 37,* 28-36.

Fuligni, A., Hughes, D., & Way, N. (2009). Ethnicity and immigration. In R. Lerner & L. Steinberg (Eds.), *Handbook of adolescent psychology* (3rd ed., Vol. 2, pp. 527-569). New York: Wiley.

Fuligni, A., Kiang, L., Witkow, M., & Baldelomar, O. (2008). Stability and change in ethnic labeling among adolescents from Asian and Latin American immigrant families. *Child Development, 79,* 944-956.

Fuligni, A., Witkow, M., & Garcia, C. (2005). Ethnic identity and the academic adjustment of adolescents from Mexican, Chinese, and European backgrounds. *Developmental Psychology, 41,* 799-811.

Fuligni, A. J., Arruda, E. H., Krull, J. L., & Gonzales, N. A. (2018). Adolescent sleep duration, variability, and peak levels of achievement and mental health. *Child Development, 89,* e18-e28.

Fuller-Rowell, T., Evans, G., Paul, E., & Curtis, D. (2015). The role of poverty and chaos in the development of task persistence among adolescents. *Journal of Research on Adolescence, 25,* 606-613.

Furman, W., & Collibee, C. (2014). A matter of timing: Developmental theories of romantic involvement and psychosocial adjustment. *Development and Psychopathology, 26,* 1149-1160.

Furman, W., & Shomaker, L. (2008). Patterns of interaction in adolescent romantic relationships: Distinct features and links to other close relationships. *Journal of Adolescence, 31,* 771-788.

Furman, W., & Simon, V. (1999). Cognitive representations of adolescent romantic relationships. In W. Furman, B. Brown, & C. Feiring (Eds.), *Contemporary perspectives on adolescent romantic relationships* (pp. 75-98). New York: Cambridge University Press.

Furman, W., & Simon, V. (2006). Actor and partner effects of adolescents' romantic working models and styles on interactions with romantic partners. *Child Development, 77,* 588-604.

Furman, W., & Wehner, E. (1994). Romantic views: Toward a theory of adolescent romantic relationships. In R. Montemayor (Ed.), *Advances in adolescent development:* Vol. 3. *Relationships in adolescence* (pp. 168-195). Newbury Park, CA: Sage.

Furman, W., Brown, B., & Feiring, C. (Eds.). (1999). *Contemporary perspectives on adolescent romantic relationships.* New York: Cambridge University Press.

Furman, W., Collibee, C., Lantagne, A., & Golden, R. (2019). Making movies instead of taking snapshots: Studying change in youth's romantic relationships. *Child Development Perspectives, 13,* 135-140.

Furman, W., Simon, V., Shaffer, L., & Bouchey, H. (2002). Adolescents' working models and styles for relationships with parents, friends, and romantic partners. *Child Development, 73,* 241-255.

Furstenberg, F., Jr. (2006, March). *Diverging development: The not-so-invisible hand of social class in the United States.* Invited address, Society for Research on Adolescence, San Francisco.

Fussner, L., Luebbe, A., & Bell, D. (2015). Dynamics of positive emotion regulation: Associations with youth depressive symptoms. *Journal of Abnormal Child Psychology, 43,* 475-488.

Gaarde, J., Hoyt, L. T., Ozer, E. J., Maslowsky, J., Deardorff, J., & Kyauk, C. K. (2020). So much to do before I sleep: Investigating adolescent-perceived barriers and facilitators to sleep. *Youth & Society, 52,* 592-617.

Gage, J., Overpeck, M., Nansel, T., & Kogan, M. (2005). Peer activity in the evenings and participation in aggressive and problem behaviors. *Journal of Adolescent Health, 37,* 517.e7-517.e14.

Gaias, L., Lindstrom Johnson, S., White, R., Pettigrew, J. and Dumka, L. (2019). Positive school climate as a moderator of violence exposure for Colombian adolescents. *American Journal of Community Psychology, 63,* 17-31.

Galambos, N., Barker, E., & Krahn, H. (2006). Depression, self-esteem, and anger in emerging adulthood: Seven-year trajectories. *Developmental Psychology, 42,* 350-365.

Galambos, N., Barker, E., & Tilton-Weaver, L. (2003). Who gets caught at maturity gap? A study of pseudomature, immature, and mature adolescents. *International Journal of Behavioral Development, 27,* 253–263.

Galambos, N., Berenbaum, S., & McHale, S. (2009). Gender development in adolescence. In R. Lerner & L. Steinberg (Eds.), *Handbook of adolescent psychology* (3rd ed., Vol. 1, pp. 305–357). New York: Wiley.

Galambos, N., Kolaric, G., Sears, H., & Maggs, J. (1999). Adolescents' subjective age: An indicator of perceived maturity. *Journal of Research on Adolescence, 9,* 309–337.

Galambos, N., Turner, P., & Tilton-Weaver, L. (2005). Chronological and subjective age in emerging adulthood: The crossover effect. *Journal of Adolescent Research, 20,* 538–556.

Galla, B. (2016). Within-person changes in mindfulness and self-compassion predict enhanced emotional well-being in healthy, but stressed adolescents. *Journal of Adolescence, 49,* 204–217.

Galla, B., & Duckworth, A. (2015). More than resisting temptation: Beneficial habits mediate the relationship between self-control and positive life outcomes. *Journal of Personality and Social Psychology, 109,* 508–525.

Gallagher, A., Updegraff, K., Padilla, J., & McHale, S. (2018). Longitudinal associations between sibling relational aggression and adolescent adjustment. *Journal of Youth and Adolescence, 47,* 2100–2113.

Galván, A. (2010). Adolescent development of the reward system. *Frontiers in Neuroscience, 4,* 1–9.

Galván, A. (2013). The teenage brain: Sensitivity to rewards. *Current Directions in Psychological Science, 22,* 88–93.

Galván, A. (2020). The need for sleep in the adolescent brain. *Trends in Cognitive Sciences, 24,* 79–89.

Gámez-Guadix, M., & Gini, G. (2016). Individual and class justification of cyberbullying and cyberbullying perpetration: A longitudinal analysis among adolescents. *Journal of Applied Developmental Psychology, 44,* 81–89.

Gámez-Guadix, M., & Mateos-Pérez, E. (2019). Longitudinal and reciprocal relationships between sexting, online sexual solicitations, and cyberbullying among minors. *Computers in Human Behavior, 94,* 70–76.

Gamoran, A. (1996). Curriculum standardization and equality of opportunity in Scottish secondary education: 1984–90. *Sociology of Education, 69,* 1–21.

Ganga, E., Mazzareillo, A., & Edgecombe, N. (2018). *Developmental education.* Denver: Education Commission of the States.

Garceau, C., & Ronis, S. (2019). A qualitative investigation of expected versus actual initial sexual experiences before age 16. *Journal of Adolescence, 71,* 38–49.

Garcia, N. V., & Scherf, K. S. (2015). Emerging sensitivity to socially complex expressions: A unique role for adolescence? *Child Development Perspectives, 9,* 84–90.

Gardner, M., & Brooks-Gunn, J. (2009). Adolescents' exposure to community violence: Are neighborhood youth organizations protective? *Journal of Community Psychology, 37,* 505–525.

Gardner, M., & Steinberg, L. (2005). Peer influence on risk taking, risk preference, and risky decision making in adolescence and adulthood: An experimental study. *Developmental Psychology, 41,* 625–635.

Gardner, M., Browning, C., & Brooks-Gunn, J. (2012). Can organized youth activities protect against internalizing problems among adolescents living in violent homes? *Journal of Research on Adolescence, 22,* 662–667.

Gardner, M., Hutt, S., Kamentz, D., Duckworth, A., & D'Mello, S. (2020). How does high school extracurricular participation predict bachelor's degree attainment? It is Complicated. *Journal of Research on Adolescence, 30,* 753–768.

Gardner, T., Dishion, T., & Connell, A. (2008). Adolescent self-regulation as resilience: Resistance to antisocial behavior within the deviant peer context. *Journal of Abnormal Child Psychology, 36,* 273–284.

Garduno, L. S., & Brancale, J. M. (2017). Examining the risk and protective factors of gang involvement among Hispanic youth in Maryland. *Journal of Community Psychology, 45,* 765–782.

Garg, R., Melanson, S., & Levin, E. (2007). Educational aspirations of male and female adolescents from single-parent and two biological parent families: A comparison of influential factors. *Journal of Youth and Adolescence, 36,* 1010–1023.

Gartner, M., Kiang, L., & Supple, A. (2014). Prospective links between ethnic socialization, ethnic and American identity, and well-being among Asian-American adolescents. *Journal of Youth & Adolescence, 43,* 1715–1727.

Gartrell, N., Bos, H., Peyser, H., Deck, A., & Rodas, C. (2011). Family characteristics, custody arrangements, and adolescent psychological well-being after lesbian mothers break up. *Family Relations, 60,* 572–585.

Gartstein, M., Seamon, E., & Dishion, T. J. (2014). Geospatial ecology of adolescent problem behavior: Contributions of community factors and parental monitoring. *Journal of Community Psychology, 42,* 299–315.

Gathercole, S. E., Pickering, S. J., Ambridge, B., & Wearing, H. (2004). The structure of working memory from 4 to 15 years of age. *Developmental Psychology, 40,* 177–190.

Gaudreau, P., Amiot, C., & Vallerand, R. (2009). Trajectories of affective states in adolescent hockey players: Turning point and motivational antecedents. *Developmental Psychology, 45,* 307–319.

Gaylord-Harden, N., Ragsdale, B. L., Mandara, J., Richards, M. H., & Petersen, A. C. (2007). Perceived support and internalizing symptoms in African American adolescents: Self-esteem and ethnic identity as mediators. *Journal of Youth and Adolescence, 36,* 77–88.

Ge, X., Best, K., Conger, R., & Simons, R. (1996). Parenting behaviors and the occurrence and co-occurrence of adolescent depressive symptoms and conduct problems. *Developmental Psychology, 32,* 717–731.

Ge, X., Kim, I. J., Brody, G., Conger, R., Simons, R., Gibbons, F., & Cutrona, C. (2003). It's about timing and change: Pubertal transition effects on symptoms of major depression among African American youths. *Developmental Psychology, 39,* 430–439.

Ge, X., Natsuaki, M., & Conger, R. (2006). Trajectories of depressive symptoms and stressful life events among male and female adolescents in divorced and nondivorced families. *Development and Psychopathology, 18,* 253–273.

Ge, X., Natsuaki, M., Neiderhiser, J., & Reiss, D. (2007). Genetic and environmental influences on pubertal timing: Results from two national sibling studies. *Journal of Research on Adolescence, 17,* 767–788.

Ge, X., Natsuaki, M., Neiderhiser, J., & Reiss, D. (2009). The longitudinal effects of stressful life events on adolescent depression are buffered by parent–child closeness. *Development and Psychopathology, 21,* 621–635.

Gecas, V., & Seff, M. (1990). Families and adolescents: A review of the 1980s. *Journal of Marriage and the Family, 52,* 941–958.

Gee, D., Bath, K., Johnson, C., Meyer, H., Murty, V., van den Bos, W., & Hartley, C. (2018). Neurocognitive development of motivated behavior: Dynamic changes across childhood and adolescence. *Journal of Neuroscience, 38,* 9433–9445.

Gelfond, J., Dierschke, N., Lowe, D., & Plastin, K. (2016). Preventing pregnancy in high school students: Observations from a 3-year longitudinal quasi-experimental study. *American Journal of Public Health, 106,* S97–S102.

Gentile, D., Swing, E., Lim, C., & Khoo, A. (2012). Video game playing, attention problems, and impulsiveness: Evidence of bidirectional causality. *Psychology of Popular Media Culture, 1,* 62–70.

George, M., & Odgers, C. L. (2015). Seven fears and the science of how mobile technologies may be influencing adolescents in the digital age. *Perspectives on Psychological Science, 10,* 832–851.

Gerard, J., & Buehler, C. (2004). Cumulative environmental risk and youth maladjustment: The role of youth attributes. *Child Development, 75,* 1832–1849.

Gerbner, G., Gross, L., Morgan, M., & Signorelli, N. (1994). Growing up with television: The cultivation perspective. In J. Bryant & D. Zillman (Eds.), *Media effects: Advances in theory and research* (pp. 17–41). Hillsdale, NJ: Erlbaum.

Gershoff, E., Aber, J., Ware, A., & Kotler, J. (2010). Exposure to 9/11 among youth and their mothers in New York City: Enduring associations with mental health and sociopolitical attitudes. *Child Development, 81,* 1142–1160.

Gest, S. (1997). Behavioral inhibition: Stability and associations with adaptation from childhood to early adulthood. *Journal of Personality and Social Psychology, 72,* 467–475.

Gewirtz O'Brien, J., Edinburgh, L., Barnes, A., & McRee, A-L. (2020). Mental health outcomes among homeless, runaway, and stably housed youth. *Pediatrics, 145,* e20192674.

Gibb, S., Fergusson, D., Horwood, L., & Boden, J. (2014). Early motherhood and long-term economic outcomes: Findings from a 30-year longitudinal study. *Journal of Research on Adolescence, 25,* 163–172.

Gibbs, J., Basinger, K., Grime, R., & Snarney, J. (2007). Moral judgment development across cultures: Revisiting Kohlberg's universality claims. *Developmental Review, 27,* 443–500.

Giedd, J. N. (2015). Adolescent neuroscience of addiction: A new era. *Developmental Cognitive Neuroscience, 16,* 192-193.

Gillespie, B. (2020). Adolescent intergenerational relationship dynamics and leaving and returning to the parental home. *Journal of Marriage and Family, 82,* 997-1014.

Gilman, A. B., Hill, K. G., & Hawkins, J. D. (2014). Long-term consequences of adolescent gang membership for adult functioning. *American Journal of Public Health, 104,* 938-994.

Gilman, A. B., Hill, K. G., Hawkins, J. D., Howell, J. C., & Kosterman, R. (2014). The development dynamics of joining a gang in adolescence: Patterns and predictors of gang membership. *Journal of Research on Adolescence, 24,* 204-219.

Gingo, M., Roded, A., & Turiel, E. (2017). Authority, autonomy, and deception: Evaluating the legitimacy of parental authority and adolescent deceit. *Journal of Research on Adolescence, 27,* 862-877.

Gingo, M., Roded, A., & Turiel, E. (2020). What they don't know won't hurt them: Parents' judgments about lying to their adolescents. *Journal of Research on Adolescence, 30,* 95-108.

Giordano, P., Longmore, M., & Manning, W. (2006). Gender and the meanings of adolescent romantic relationships: A focus on boys. *American Sociological Review, 71,* 260-287.

Giordano, P., Manning, W., & Longmore, M. (2010). Affairs of the heart: Qualities of adolescent romantic relationships and sexual behavior. *Journal of Research on Adolescence, 20,* 983-1013.

Giovenco, D., Casseus, M., Duncan, D., Coups, E., Lewis, M., & Delnevo, C. (2016). Association between electronic cigarette marketing near schools and e-cigarette use among youth. *Journal of Adolescent Health, 59,* 627-634.

Glenwright, M., & Pexman, P. (2010). Development of children's ability to distinguish sarcasm and verbal irony. *Journal of Child Language, 37,* 429-451.

Glick, G., & Rose, A. (2011). Prospective associations between friendship adjustment and social strategies: Friendship as a context for building social skills. *Developmental Psychology, 47,* 1117-1132.

Gniewosz, B., Eccles, J., & Noack, P. (2015). Early adolescents' development of academic self-concept and intrinsic task value: The role of contextual feedback. *Journal of Research on Adolescence, 25,* 459-473.

Gobbi, G., Atkin, T., Zytynski, T., Wang, S., Askari, S., Boruff, J., . . . Mayo, N. (2019). Association of cannabis use in adolescence and risk of depression, anxiety, and suicidality in young adulthood: a systematic review and meta-analysis. *JAMA Psychiatry, 76,* 426-434.

Goddings, A.-L., Beltz, A., Peper, J. S., Crone, E. A., & Braams, B. R. (2019). Understanding the role of puberty in structural and functional development of the adolescent brain. *Journal of Research on Adolescence, 29,* 32-53.

Gold, S., Edin, K., & Nelson, T. (2020). Does time with Dad in childhood pay off in adolescence? *Journal of Marriage and Family, 82*(5), 1587-1605.

Goldbach, J., Sterzing, P., & Stuart, M. (2018). Challenging conventions of bullying thresholds: exploring differences between low and high levels of bully-only, victim-only, and bully-victim roles. *Journal of Youth and Adolescence, 47,* 586-600.

Goldberg, R., Tienda, M., Eilers, M., & McLanahan, S. (2019). Adolescent relationship quality: Is there an intergenerational link? *Journal of Marriage and Family, 81,* 812-829.

Golden, R., Furman, W., & Collibee, C. (2016). The risks and rewards of sexual debut. *Developmental Psychology, 52,* 1913-1925.

Goldenberg, D., Telzer, E. H., Lieberman, M. D., Fuligni, A., & Galván, A. (2013). Neural mechanisms of impulse control in sexually risky adolescents. *Developmental Cognitive Neuroscience, 6,* 23-29.

Goldschmidt, A. B., Wall, M. W., Zhang, J., Loth, K. A., & Neumark-Sztainer, D. (2016). Overeating and binge eating in emerging adulthood: 10-year stability and risk factors. *Developmental Psychology, 52,* 475-483.

Goldstein, B. (1976). *Introduction to human sexuality.* Belmont, CA: Star.

Goldstick, J., Heinze, J., Stoddard, S., Cunningham, R., & Zimmerman, M. (2019). Age-specific associations between violence exposure and past 30-day marijuana and alcohol use. *Journal of Research on Adolescence, 29,* 480-492.

Golombok, S., Rust, J., Zervoulis, K., Golding, J., & Hines, M. (2012). Continuity in sex-typed behavior from preschool to adolescence: A longitudinal population study of boys and girls aged 3-13 years. *Archives of Sexual Behavior, 41,* 591-597.

Gomez-Baya, D., Mendoza, R., Paino, S., & Gillham, J. (2017). A two-year longitudinal study of gender differences in responses to positive affect and depressive symptoms during middle adolescence. *Journal of Adolescence, 56,* 11-23.

Gommans, R., Muller, C., Stevens, G., Cillessen, A., & Ter Bogt, T. (2017). Individual popularity, peer group popularity composition and adolescents' alcohol consumption. *Journal of Youth and Adolescence, 46,* 1716-1726.

Gong, T., Ren, Y., Wu, J., Jiang, Y., Hu, W., & You, J. (2019). The associations among self-criticism, hopelessness, rumination, and NSSI in adolescents: A moderated mediation model. *Journal of Adolescence, 72,* 1-9.

Gonzales, R. (2011). Learning to be illegal: Undocumented youth and shifting legal contexts in the transition to adulthood. *American Sociological Review, 76,* 602-619.

Gonzales-Backen, M., Bamaca-Colbert, M., & Allen, K. (2016). Ethnic identity trajectories among Mexican-origin girls during early and middle adolescence: Predicting future psychosocial adjustment. *Developmental Psychology, 52,* 790-797.

Gonzales-Backen, M., Meca, A., Lorenzo-Blanco, E., Des Rosiers, S., Córdova, D., Soto, D., . . . Unger, J. (2018). Examining the temporal order of ethnic identity and perceived discrimination among Hispanic immigrant adolescents. *Developmental Psychology, 54,* 929-937.

Gonzalez, M. Z., Allen, J. P., & Coan, J. A. (2016). Lower neighborhood quality in adolescence predicts higher mesolimbic sensitivity to reward anticipation in adulthood. *Developmental Cognitive Neuroscience, 22,* 48-57.

Good, M., & Willoughby, T. (2014). Institutional and personal spirituality/religiosity and psychosocial adjustment in adolescence: Concurrent and longitudinal associations. *Journal of Youth & Adolescence, 43,* 757-774.

Good, M., Willoughby, T., & Busseri, M. (2011). Stability and change in adolescent spirituality/religiosity: A person-centered approach. *Developmental Psychology, 47,* 538-550.

Gooden, A., & McMahon, S. (2016). Thriving among African-American adolescents: Religiosity, religious support, and communalism. *American Journal of Community Psychology, 57,* 118-128.

Goodson, P., Buhi, E., & Dunsmore, S. (2006). Self-esteem and adolescent sexual behaviors, attitudes, and intentions: A systematic review. *Journal of Adolescent Health, 38,* 310-319.

Goossens, L. (2018). Loneliness in adolescence: Insights from Cacioppo's evolutionary model. *Child Development Perspectives, 12,* 230-234.

Goossens, L., Seiffge-Krenke, I., & Marcoen, A. (1992). The many faces of adolescent egocentrism: Two European replications. *Journal of Adolescent Research, 7,* 43-58.

Gordon, M., & Cui, M. (2014). School-related parental involvement and adolescent academic achievement: The role of community poverty. *Family Relations, 63,* 616-626.

Gordon, R. A., Rowe, H. L., Pardini, D., Loeber, R., White, H. R., & Farrington, D. P. (2014). Serious delinquency and gang participation: Combining and specializing in drug selling, theft, and violence. *Journal of Research on Adolescence, 24,* 235-251.

Gore, S., & Aseltine, R., Jr. (1995). Protective processes in adolescence: Matching stressors with social resources. *American Journal of Community Psychology, 23,* 301-327.

Görzig, A. (2016). Adolescents' experience of offline and online risks: Separate and joint propensities. *Computers in Human Behavior, 56,* 9-13.

Gottfredson, D., & DiPietro, S. (2011). School size, social capital, and student victimization. *Sociology of Education, 84,* 69-89.

Gottfredson, M., & Hirschi, T. (1990). *A general theory of crime.* Stanford, CA: Stanford University Press.

Gottfredson, N., Hussong, A., Ennett, S., & Rothenberg, A. (2017). The role of parental engagement in the intergenerational transmission of smoking behavior and identity. *Journal of Adolescent Health, 60,* 599-605.

Goudeau, S., & Croizet, J-C. (2017). Hidden advantages and disadvantages of social class: How classroom settings reproduce social inequality by staging unfair comparison. *Psychological Science, 28,* 162-170.

Gowen, L., Feldman, S., Diaz, R., & Yisrael, D. (2004). A comparison of the sexual behaviors and attitudes of adolescent girls with older vs. similar-aged boyfriends. *Journal of Youth and Adolescence, 33,* 167-175.

Gowen, L., Hayward, C., Killen, J., Robinson, T., & Taylor, C. (1999). Acculturation and eating disorder symptoms in adolescent girls. *Journal of Research on Adolescence, 9,* 67-83.

Goza, F., & Ryabov, I. (2009). Adolescents' educational outcomes: Racial and ethnic variations in peer network importance. *Journal of Youth and Adolescence, 38,* 1264-1279.

Graber, J., & Sontag, L. (2009). Internalizing problems during adolescence. In R. Lerner & L. Steinberg (Eds.), *Handbook of adolescent psychology* (3rd ed., Vol. 1, pp. 642–682). New York: Wiley.

Graber, J., Brooks-Gunn, J., & Warren, M. P. (2006). Pubertal effects on adjustment in girls: Moving from demonstrating effects to identifying pathways. *Journal of Youth and Adolescence, 35,* 391–401.

Graber, J., Seeley, J., Brooks-Gunn, J., & Lewinsohn, P. (2004). Is pubertal timing associated with psychopathology in young adulthood? *Journal of the American Academy of Child and Adolescent Psychiatry, 43,* 718–726.

Graf, G., Biroli, P., & Belsky, D. (2021). Critical periods in child development and the transition to adulthood. *JAMA Network Open, 4,* e2033359

Graham, S., & Lowery, B. (2004). Priming unconscious racial stereotypes about adolescent offenders. *Law and Human Behavior, 28,* 483–504.

Graham, S., Bellmore, A., Nishina, A., & Juvonen, J. (2009). "It must be 'me'": Ethnic diversity and attributions for peer victimization in middle school. *Journal of Youth and Adolescence, 38,* 487–499.

Graham, S., Munniksma, A., & Juvonen, J. (2014). Psychosocial benefits of cross-ethnic friendships in urban middle schools. *Child Development, 85,* 469–483.

Graif, C. (2015). Delinquency and gender moderation in the Moving to Opportunity intervention: The role of extended neighborhoods. *Criminology, 53,* 366–398.

Granberg, E., Simons, L., & Simons, R. (2009). Body size and social self-image among adolescent African American girls: The moderating influence of family racial socialization. *Youth & Society, 41,* 256–277.

Granic, I., Hollenstein, T., Dishion, T. K., & Patterson, G. R. (2003). Longitudinal analysis of flexibility and reorganization in early adolescence: A dynamic systems study of family interactions. *Developmental Psychology, 39,* 606–617.

Gray, M., & Steinberg, L. (1999). Adolescent romance and the parent–child relationship: A contextual perspective. In W. Furman, B. Brown, & C. Feiring (Eds.), *Contemporary perspectives on adolescent romantic relationships* (pp. 235–265). New York: Cambridge University Press.

Gray-Little, B., & Hafdahl, A. (2000). Factors influencing racial comparisons of self-esteem: A quantitative review. *Psychological Bulletin, 126,* 26–54.

Green, K., & Ensminger, M. (2006). Adult social behavioral effects of heavy adolescent marijuana use among African Americans. *Developmental Psychology, 42,* 1168–1178.

Greenberger, E., Chen, C., & Beam, M. (1998). The role of "very important" nonparental adults in adolescent development. *Journal of Youth and Adolescence, 27,* 321–343.

Greene, M., Way, N., & Pahl, K. (2006). Trajectories of perceived adult and peer discrimination among Black, Latino, and Asian American adolescents: Patterns and psychological correlates. *Developmental Psychology, 42,* 218–236.

Greene, M. L., & Way, N. (2005). Self-esteem trajectories among ethnic minority adolescents: A growth curve analysis of the patterns and predictors of change. *Journal of Research on Adolescence, 15,* 151–177.

Green-Hennessy, S. (2014). Homeschooled adolescents in the United States: Developmental outcomes. *Journal of Adolescence, 37,* 441–449.

Greenspan, L., & Deardorff, J. (2014). *The new puberty.* New York: Rodale.

Gregory, A., Cornell, D., & Fan, X. (2011). The relationship of school structure and support to suspension rates for Black and White high school students. *American Educational Research Journal, 48,* 904–934.

Gregory, E. (2007). *Ready: Why women are embracing the new later motherhood.* New York: Basic Books.

Gremmen, M., Berger, C., Ryan, A., Steglich, C., Veenstra, R., & Dijkstra, J. (2019). Adolescents' friendships, academic achievement, and risk behaviors: Same-behavior and cross-behavior selection and influence processes. *Child Development, 90,* e192–e211.

Gremmen, M., Dijkstra, J., Steglich, C., & Veenstra, R. (2017). First selection, then influence: Developmental differences in friendship dynamics regarding academic achievement. *Developmental Psychology, 53,* 1356–1370.

Greven, C., Rijsdijk, F., & Plomin, R. (2011). A twin study of ADHD symptoms in early adolescence: Hyperactivity-impulsivity and inattentiveness show substantial genetic overlap but also genetic specificity. *Journal of Abnormal Child Psychology, 39,* 265–275.

Griesler, P., Hu, M.-C., Wall, M., & Kandel, D. (2019). Nonmedical prescription opioid use by parents and adolescents in the US. *Pediatrics, 143,* e20182354.

Griffin, Jr., E., Melas, P., Zhou, R., Li, Y., Mercado, P., Kempadoo, K., . . . Kandel, D. (2017). Prior alcohol use enhances vulnerability to compulsive cocaine self-administration by promoting degradation of HDAC4 and HDAC5. *Science Advances, 3,* e1701682.

Griffin, K., Epstein, J., Botvin, G., & Spoth, R. (2001). Social competence and substance use among rural youth: Mediating role of social benefit expectancies of use. *Journal of Youth and Adolescence, 30,* 485–498.

Griffith, J., Crawford, C., Oppenheimer, C., Young, J., & Hankin, B. (2019). Parenting and youth onset of depression across three years: Examining the influence of observed parenting on child and adolescent depressive outcomes. *Journal of Abnormal Child Psychology, 47,* 1969–1980.

Griffith, J. M., Silk, J. S., Oppenheimer, C. W., Morgan, J. K., Ladouceur, C. D., Forbes, E. E., & Dahl, R. E. (2018). Maternal affective expression and adolescents' subjective experience of positive affect in natural settings. *Journal of Research on Adolescence, 18,* 28, 537–550.

Griffith Fontaine, R., Salzer Burks, V., & Dodge, K. (2002). Response decision processes and externalizing behavior problems in adolescents. *Development and Psychopathology, 14,* 107–122.

Grisso, T., Steinberg, L., Woolard, J., Cauffman, E., Scott, E., Graham, S., . . . Schwartz, R. (2003). Juveniles' competence to stand trial: A comparison of adolescents' and adults' capacities as trial defendants. *Law and Human Behavior, 27,* 333–363.

Grolnick, W., Raftery-Helmer, J., Flamm, E., Marbell, K., & Cardemil, E. (2015). Parental provision of academic structure and the transition to middle school. *Journal of Research on Adolescence, 25,* 668–684.

Grosbras, M., Jansen, M., Leonard, G., McIntosh, A., Osswald, K., Poulsen, C., . . . Paus, T. (2007). Neural mechanisms of resistance to peer influence in early adolescence. *Journal of Neuroscience, 27,* 8040–8045.

Grossman, J. M., & Charmaraman, L. (2009). Race, context, and privilege: White adolescents' explanations of racial-ethnic centrality. *Journal of Youth and Adolescence, 38,* 139–152.

Grotevant, H. D., Lo, A. Y. H., Fiorenzo, L., & Dunbar, N. D. (2017). Adoptive identity and adjustment from adolescence to emerging adulthood: A person-centered approach. *Developmental Psychology, 53,* 2195–2204.

Grover, R., & Nangle, D. (2003). Adolescent perceptions of problematic heterosocial situations: A focus group study. *Journal of Youth and Adolescence, 32,* 129–139.

Grucza, R., Norberg, K., & Bierut, L. (2009). Binge drinking among youths and young adults in the United States: 1979–2006. *Journal of the American Academy of Child and Adolescent Psychiatry, 48,* 692–702.

Gruenenfelder-Steiger, A., Harris, M., & Fend, H. (2016). Subjective and objective peer approval evaluations and self-esteem development: A test of reciprocal, prospective, and long-term effects. *Developmental Psychology, 52,* 1563–1577.

Grumbach, M., Roth, J., Kaplan, S., & Kelch, R. (1974). Hypothalamic-pituitary regulation of puberty in man: Evidence and concepts derived from clinical research. In M. Grumbach, G. Grave, & F. Mayer (Eds.), *Control of the onset of puberty.* Philadelphia: Lippincott Williams & Wilkins.

Guan, K., Fox, K., & Prinstein, M. (2012). Nonsuicidal self-injury as a time-invariant predictor of adolescent suicide ideation and attempts in a diverse community sample. *Journal of Consulting and Clinical Psychology, 80,* 842–849.

Guarini, T. Marks, A., Patton, F., & Garcia Coll, C. (2015). The immigrant paradox in pregnancy: Explaining the first-generation advantage for Latina adolescent. *Journal of Research on Adolescence, 25,* 14–19.

Guassi Moreira, J. F., & Telzer, E. H. (2016). Mother still knows best: Maternal influence uniquely modulates adolescent reward sensitivity during risk taking. *Developmental Science,* e12484.

Gubbels, J., van der Put, C., & Assink, M. (2019). Risk factors for school absenteeism and dropout: A meta-analytic review. *Journal of Youth and Adolescence, 48,* 1637–1667.

Gummerum, M., Keller, M., Takezawa, M., & Mata, J. (2008). To give or not to give: Children's and adolescents' sharing and moral negotiations in economic decision situations. *Child Development, 79,* 562–576.

Gunnar, M. (2017). Social buffering of stress in development: A career perspective. *Perspectives on Psychological Science, 12,* 355–373.

Guo, J., Parker, P., Marsh, H., & Morin, A. (2015). Achievement, motivation, and educational choices: A longitudinal study of expectancy and value using a multiplicative perspective. *Developmental Psychology, 51,* 1163–1176.

Gupta, T., Way, N., McGill, R. K., Hughes, D., Santos, C., Jia, Y., Yoshikawa, H., Chen, X., & Deng, H. (2013). Gender-typed behaviors in friendships and well-being: A cross-cultural study of Chinese and American boys. *Journal of Research on Adolescence, 23,* 57-68.

Gur, R. E., & Gur, R. C. (2016). Sex differences in brain and behavior in adolescence: Findings from the Philadelphia Neurodevelopmental Cohort. *Neuroscience & Biobehavioral Reviews, 70,* 159-170.

Güroğlu, B., Haselager, G., van Lieshout, C., & Scholte, R. (2009). Antagonists in mutual antipathies: A person-oriented approach. *Journal of Research on Adolescence, 19,* 35-46.

Gutman, L., & Midgley, C. (2000). The role of protective factors in supporting the academic achievement of poor African American students during the middle school transition. *Journal of Youth and Adolescence, 29,* 223-248.

Guttmacher Institute. (2014). American teens' sexual and reproductive health. www.guttmacher.org/pubs/FB-ATSRH.html. Accessed on July 13, 2015.

Guyer, A., McClure-Tone, E., Shiffrin, N., Pine, D., & Nelson, E. (2009). Probing the neural correlates of anticipated peer evaluation in adolescence. *Child Development, 80,* 1000-1015.

Guyer, A. E. (2020). Adolescent psychopathology: The role of brain-based diatheses, sensitivities, and susceptibilities. *Child Development Perspectives, 14,* 104-109.

Guyer, A. E., Benson, B., Choate, V., Bar-Haim, Y., Perez-Edgar, K., Jarcho, J., . . . Nelson, E. (2014). Lasting associations between early-childhood temperament and late-adolescent reward circuitry response to peer feedback. *Development and Psychopathology, 26,* 229-243.

Guyer, A. E., Choate, V. R., Pine, D. S., & Nelson, E. E. (2012). Neural circuitry underlying affective response to peer feedback in adolescence. *Social Cognitive Affective Neuroscience, 7,* 81-92.

Guyer, A. E., Jarcho, J. M., Perez-Edgar, K., Degnan, K. A., Pine, D. S., Fox, N. A., & Nelson, E. E. (2015). Temperament and parenting styles in early childhood differentially influence neural response to peer evaluation in adolescence. *Journal of Abnormal Child Psychology, 43,* 863-874.

Guyer, A. E., Silk, J. S., & Nelson, E. E. (2016). The neurobiology of the emotional adolescent: From the inside out. *Neuroscience & Biobehavioral Reviews, 70,* 74-85.

Guzmán-Rocha, M., McLeod, D., & Bohnert, A. (2017). Dimensions of organized activity involvement among Latino youth: Impact on well-being. *Journal of Adolescence, 60,* 130-139.

Ha, T., Kim, H., Christopher, C., Caruthers, A., & Dishion, T. (2016). Predicting sexual coercion in early adulthood: The transaction among maltreatment, gang affiliation, and adolescent socialization of coercive relationship norms. *Development and Psychopathology, 28,* 707-720.

Ha, T., Overbeek, G., & Engels, R. (2010). Effects of attractiveness and social status on dating desire in heterosexual adolescents: An experimental study. *Archives of Sexual Behavior, 39,* 1063-1071.

Habermas, T., & de Silveira, C. (2008). The development of global coherence in life narratives across adolescence: Temporal, causal, and thematic aspects. *Developmental Psychology, 44,* 707-721.

Haddad, A., Harrison, F., Norman, T., & Lau, J. (2014). Adolescent and adult risk-taking in virtual social contexts. *Developmental Psychology, 5,* 1-7.

Haddad, E., Chen, C., & Greenberger, E. (2011). The pole of important nonparental adults (VIPs) in the lives of older adolescents: A comparison of three ethnic groups. *Journal of Youth and Adolescence, 40,* 310-319.

Hadiwijaya, H., Klimstra, T. A., Vermunt, J. K., Branje, S. J. T., & Meeus, W. H. J. (2017). On the development of harmony, turbulence, and independence in parent–adolescent relationships: A five-wave longitudinal study. *Journal of Youth and Adolescence, 46,* 1771-1788.

Hafen, C., Allen, J., Mikami, A., Gregory, A., Hamre, B., & Pianta, R. (2012). The pivotal role of adolescent autonomy in secondary school classrooms. *Journal of Youth & Adolescence, 41,* 245-255.

Hafen, C., Spilker, A., Chango, J., Marston, E., & Allen, J. (2014). To accept or reject? The impact of adolescent rejection sensitivity on early adult romantic relationships. *Journal of Research on Adolescence, 24,* 55-64.

Haghighat, M., & Knifsend, C. (2019). The longitudinal influence of 10th grade extracurricular activity involvement: Implications for 12th grade academic practices and future educational attainment. *Journal of Youth and Adolescence, 48,* 609-619.

Hahm, H., Lahiff, M., & Barreto, R. (2006). Asian American adolescents' first sexual intercourse: Gender and acculturation differences. *Perspectives on Sexual and Reproductive Health, 38,* 28-36.

Hall, G. S. (1904). *Adolescence.* New York: Appleton.

Hall, N., Chipperfield, J., Perry, R., Ruthig, J., & Goetz, T. (2006). Primary and secondary control in academic development: Gender-specific implications for stress and health in college students. *Anxiety, Stress & Coping: An International Journal, 19,* 189-210.

Haller, M., Handley, E., Chassin, L., & Bountress, K. (2010). Developmental cascades: Linking adolescent substance use, affiliation with substance use promoting peers, and academic achievement to adult substance use disorders. *Development and Psychopathology, 22,* 899-916.

Halligan, S., & Philips, K. (2010). Are you thinking what I'm thinking? Peer group similarities in adolescent hostile attribution tendencies. *Developmental Psychology, 46,* 1385-1388.

Hallinan, M. (1996). Track mobility in secondary school. *Social Forces, 74,* 983-1002.

Hallinan, M., & Kubitschek, W. (2012). A comparison of academic achievement and adherence to the common school ideal in public and Catholic schools. *Sociology of Education, 85,* 1-22.

Hallinan, M., & Williams, R. (1989). Interracial friendship choices in secondary schools. *American Sociological Review, 54,* 67-78.

Halpern, C. (2003). Biological influences on adolescent romantic and sexual behavior. In P. Florsheim (Ed.), *Adolescent romantic relations and sexual behavior: Theory, research, and practical implications* (pp. 57-84). Mahwah, NJ: Lawrence Erlbaum.

Halpern, C., & Haydon, A. (2012). Sexual timetables for oral-genital, vaginal, and anal intercourse: Sociodemographic comparisons in a nationally representative sample of adolescents. *American Journal of Public Health, 102,* 1221-1228.

Halpern, C., King, R., Oslak, S., & Udry, J. (2005). Body mass index, dieting, romance, and sexual activity in adolescent girls: Relationships over time. *Journal of Research on Adolescence, 15,* 535-559.

Halpern, C., Spriggs, A., Martin, S., & Kupper, L. (2009). Patterns of intimate partner violence victimization from adolescence to young adulthood in a nationally representative sample. *Journal of Adolescent Health, 45,* 508-516.

Halpern, C., Udry, J., Campbell, B., & Suchindran, C. (1999). Effects of body fat on weight concerns, dating, and sexual activity: A longitudinal analysis of Black and White adolescent girls. *Developmental Psychology, 35,* 721-736.

Halpern-Felsher, B. (2011). Adolescent decision-making. In B. Brown & M. Prinstein (Eds.), *Encyclopedia of adolescence* (Vol. 1, pp. 30-37). New York: Academic Press.

Halpern-Meekin, S., & Tach, L. (2008). Heterogeneity in two-parent families and adolescent well-being. *Journal of Marriage and Family, 70,* 435-451.

Haltigan, J., Roisman, G., Susman, E., Barnett-Walker, K., & Monahan, K. (2011). Elevated trajectories of externalizing problems are associated with lower awakening cortisol levels in midadolescence. *Developmental Psychology, 47,* 472-478.

Haltigan, J. D., & Vaillancourt, T. (2014). Joint trajectories of bullying and peer victimization across elementary and middle school and associations with symptoms of psychopathology. *Developmental Psychology, 50,* 2426-2436.

Hamilton, C. (2000). Continuity and discontinuity of attachment from infancy through adolescence. *Child Development, 71,* 690-694.

Hamilton, J. L., Chand, S., Reinhardt, L., Ladouceur, C., Silk, J., Moreno, M., . . . Bylsma, L. (2020). Social media use predicts later sleep timing and greater sleep variability: An ecological momentary assessment study of youth at high and low familial risk for depression. *Journal of Adolescence, 83,* 122-130.

Hamilton, J. L., Hamlat, E. J., Strange, J. P., Abramson, L. Y., & Alloy, L. B. (2014). Pubertal timing and vulnerabilities to depression in early adolescence: Differential pathways to depressive symptoms by sex. *Journal of Adolescence, 37,* 165-174.

Hamm, J., Brown, B., & Heck, D. (2005). Bridging the ethnic divide: Student and school characteristics in African American, Asian-descent, Latino, and White adolescents' cross-ethnic friend nominations. *Journal of Research on Adolescence, 15,* 21-46.

Hammons, A., & Fiese, B. (2011). Is frequency of shared family meals related to the nutritional health of children and adolescents? *Pediatrics, 127,* 1565-1574.

Hamza, C., & Willoughby, T. (2011). Perceived parental monitoring, adolescent disclosure, and adolescent depressive symptoms: A longitudinal examination. *Journal of Youth and Adolescence, 40,* 902-915.

Hamza, C. A., & Willoughby, T. (2019). Impulsivity and nonsuicidal self-injury: A longitudinal examination among emerging adults. *Journal of Adolescence, 75*, 37–46.

Hankin, B. (2020). Screening for and personalization prevention of adolescent depression. *Current Directions in Psychological Science, 29*, 327–332.

Hankin, B., Snyder, H., & Gulley, L. (2016). Cognitive risks in developmental psychopathology. In D. Cicchetti (Ed.), *Developmental psychopathology: Vol. 3. Maladaptation and psychopathology* (2nd ed., pp. 312–385). Hoboken, NJ: Wiley.

Hankin, B., Snyder, H., Gulley, L., Schweizer, T., Bijttebier, P., Nelis, S., . . . Vasey, M. (2016). Understanding comorbidity among internalizing problems: Integrating hierarchical structural models of psychopathology and risk mechanisms. *Development and Psychopathology, 28*, 987–1012.

Hankin, B., Stone, L., & Wright, P. (2010). Corumination, interpersonal stress generation, and internalizing symptoms: Accumulating effects and transactional influences in a multiwave study of adolescents. *Development and Psychopathology, 22*, 217–235.

Hankin, B. L., Young, J. F., Abela, J. R. Z., Smolen, A., Jenness, J. L., Gulley, L. D., . . . Oppenheimer, C. W. (2015). Depression from childhood into late adolescence: Influence of gender, development, genetic susceptibility, and peer stress. *Journal of Abnormal Psychology, 124*, 803–816.

Hannigan, L. J., McAdams, T. A., Plomin, R., & Eley, T. C. (2017). Parent- and child-driven effects during the transition to adolescence: A longitudinal, genetic analysis of the home environment. *Developmental Science, 20*, e12432.

Hanselman, P., Bruch, S., Gamoran, A., & Borman, G. (2014). Threat in context: School moderation of the impact of social identity threat on racial/ethnic achievement gaps. *Sociology of Education, 87*, 106–124.

Hansen, D. M., Janssen, I., Schiff, A., Zee, P. C., & Dubocovich, M. L. (2005). The impact of school daily schedule on adolescent sleep. *Pediatrics, 115*, 1555–1561.

Hansen, D. M., Moore, E., & Jessop, N. (2018). Youth program adult leader's directive assistance and autonomy support and development of adolescents' agency capacity. *Journal of Research on Adolescence, 28*, 505–519.

Hansen, D., Moore, E., & Jessop, N. (2018). Youth program adult leader's directive assistance and autonomy support and development of adolescents' agency capacity. *Journal of Research on Adolescence, 28*, 505–519.

Hansen, N., Thayer, R., Feldstein Ewing, S., Sabbineni, A., & Bryan, A. (2018). Neural correlates of risky sex and response inhibition in high-risk adolescents. *Journal of Research on Adolescence, 28*, 56–69.

Hanson, J. L., Adluru, N., Chung, M. K., Alexander, A. L., Davidson, R. J., & Pollak, S. D. (2013). Early neglect is associated with alterations in white matter integrity and cognitive functioning. *Child Development, 84*, 1566–1578.

Hanson, J. L., Chung, M. K., Avants, B. B., Rudolph, K. D., Shirtcliff, E. A., Gee, J. C., et al. (2012). Structural variations in prefrontal cortex mediate the relationship between early childhood

stress and spatial working memory. *Journal of Neuroscience, 32*, 7917–7925.

Hanson, T., McLanahan, S., & Thomson, E. (1996). Double jeopardy: Parental conflict and stepfamily outcomes for children. *Journal of Marriage and the Family, 58*, 141–154.

Hanusshek, E. (2016). What matters for student achievement. *Education Next, Spring*, 19–26.

Hao, L., & Woo, H. S. (2012). Distinct trajectories in the transition to adulthood: Are children of immigrants advantaged? *Child Development, 83*, 1623–1639.

Harakeh, Z., & de Boer, A. (2019). The effect of active and passive peer encouragement on adolescent risk-taking. *Journal of Adolescence, 71*, 10–17.

Harber, K. D., Gorman, J. L., Gengaro, F. P., Butisingh, S., Tsang W., & Ouellette, R. (2012). Students' race and teachers' social support affect the positive feedback bias in public schools. *Journal of Educational Psychology, 104*, 1149–1161.

Harcourt, T. H., Adler-Baeder, F., Erath, S., & Pettit, G. S. (2015). Examining family structure and half-sibling influence on adolescent well-being. *Journal of Family Issues, 36*, 250–272.

Hardaway, C., Sterrett-Hong, E., De Genna, N., & Cornelius, M. (2020). The role of cognitive stimulation in the home and maternal responses to low grades in low-income African American adolescents' academic achievement. *Journal of Youth and Adolescence, 49*, 1043–1056.

Hardaway, C. R., Sterrett-Hong, E., Larkby, C. A., & Cornelius, M. D. (2016). Family resources as protective factors for low-income youth exposed to community violence. *Journal of Youth and Adolescence, 45*, 1309–1322.

Harden, K. P. (2012). True love waits? A sibling-comparison study of age at first sexual intercourse and romantic relationships in young adulthood. *Psychological Science, 23*, 1324–1336.

Harden, K. P. & Mann, F. D. (2015). Biological risk for the development of problem behavior in adolescence: Integrating insights from behavioral genetics and neuroscience. *Child Development Perspectives, 9*, 211–216.

Harden, K. P., & Mendle, J. (2011). Adolescent sexual activity and the development of delinquent behavior: The role of relationship context. *Journal of Youth and Adolescence, 40*, 825–838.

Harden, K. P., & Mendle, J. (2012). Gene-environment interplay in the association between pubertal timing and delinquency in adolescent girls. *Journal of Abnormal Psychology, 121*, 73–87.

Harden, K. P., & Tucker-Drob, E. M. (2011). Individual differences in the development of sensation seeking and impulsivity during adolescence: Further evidence for a dual systems model. *Developmental Psychology, 47*, 739–746.

Harden, K. P., Mann, F., Grozinger, A., Patterson, M., Steinberg, L., Tackett, J., & Tucker-Drob, E. (2018). Developmental differences in reward sensitivity and sensation seeking in adolescence: Testing sex-specific associations with gonadal hormones and pubertal development. *Journal of Personality and Social Psychology: Personality Processes and Individual Differences, 115*, 161–178.

Harden, K. P., Mendle, J., Hill, J., Turkheimer, E., & Emery, R. (2008). Rethinking timing of first sex

and delinquency. *Journal of Youth and Adolescence, 37*, 373–385.

Harden, K. P., Quinn, T., & Tucker-Drob, E. (2012). Genetically influenced change in sensation seeking drives the rise of delinquent behavior during adolescence. *Developmental Science, 15*, 150–163.

Hardie, J. H., & Tyson, K. (2013). Other people's racism: Race, rednecks, and riots in a southern high school. *Sociology of Education, 86*, 83–102.

Hardie, J. H., Pearce, L. D., & Denton, M. L. (2016). The dynamics and correlates of religious service attendance in adolescence. *Youth & Society, 48*, 151–175.

Hardway, C., & Fuligni, A. (2006). Dimensions of family connectedness among adolescents with Mexican, Chinese, and European backgrounds. *Developmental Psychology, 42*, 1246–1258.

Hardy, S. A., Nelson, J. M., Moore, J. P., & King, P. E. (2019). Processes of religious and spiritual influence in adolescence: a systematic review of 30 years of research. *Journal of Research on Adolescence, 29*(2), 254–275.

Hardy, S., Baldwin, C., Herd, T., & Kim-Spoon, J. (2020). Dynamic associations between religiousness and self-regulation across adolescence into young adulthood. *Developmental Psychology, 56*, 180–197.

Hardy, S., Carlo, G., & Roesch, S. (2010). Links between adolescents' expected parental reactions and prosocial behavioral tendencies: The mediating role of prosocial values. *Journal of Youth and Adolescence, 39*, 84–95.

Hardy, S., Nelson, J., Moore, J., & King, P. (2019). Processes of religious and spiritual influence in adolescence: A systematic review of 30 years of research. *Journal of Research on Adolescence, 29*, 254–275.

Harenski, C. L., Harenski, K. A., Shane, M. S., & Kiehl, K. A. (2012). Neural development of mentalizing in moral judgment from adolescence to adulthood. *Development Cognitive Neuroscience, 2*, 162–173.

Harper, J. M., Padilla-Walker, L. M., & Jensen, A. C. (2016). Do siblings matter independent of both parents and friends? Sympathy as a mediator between sibling relationship quality and adolescent outcomes. *Journal of Research on Adolescence, 26*, 101–114.

Harris, C., Vazsonyi, A. T., & Bolland, J. M. (2017). Bidirectional relationships between parenting processes and deviance in a sample of inner-city African American youth. *Journal of Research on Adolescence, 27*, 201–213.

Harris, C., Vazsonyi, A., Özdemir, Y., & Sağkal, A. (2020). Family environment and school engagement: An investigation of cross-lagged effects. *Journal of Adolescence, 84*, 171–179.

Harris, J. (1998). *The nurture assumption: Why children turn out the way they do.* New York: Free Press.

Harris, M., Gruenenfelder-Steiger, A., Ferrer, E., Donnellan, M., Allemand, M., Fend, H., . . . Trzesniewski, K. (2015). Do parents foster self-esteem? Testing the prospective impact of parent closeness on adolescent self-esteem. *Child Development, 86*, 995–1015.

Harrison, K., & Heffner, V. (2008). Media, body image, and eating disorders. In S. L. Calvert & B. J. Wilson (Eds.), *The handbook of children, media, and development* (pp. 381–406). Oxford: Wiley-Blackwell.

Hart, D., Donnelly, T. M., Youniss, J., & Atkins, R. (2007). High school community service as a predictor of adult voting and volunteering. *American Educational Research Journal, 44,* 197–219.

Hart, D., Hofmann, V., Edelstein, W., & Keller, M. (1997). The relation of childhood personality types to adolescent behavior and development: A longitudinal study of Icelandic children. *Developmental Psychology, 33,* 195–205.

Harter, S. (2011). Self-development during adolescence. In B. Brown & M. Prinstein (Eds.), *Encyclopedia of adolescence* (Vol. 1, pp. 307–315). New York: Academic Press.

Harter, S., & Monsour, A. (1992). Developmental analysis of conflict caused by opposing attributes in the adolescent self-portrait. *Developmental Psychology, 28,* 251–260.

Harter, S., Marold, D., Whitesell, N., & Cobbs, G. (1996). A model of the effects of parent and peer support on adolescent false-self behavior. *Child Development, 67,* 360–374.

Harter, S., Stocker, C., & Robinson, N. (1996). The perceived directionality of the link between approval and self-worth: The liabilities of a looking glass self orientation among young adolescents. *Journal of Research on Adolescence, 6,* 285–308.

Harter, S., Waters, P., & Whitesell, N. (1998). Relational self-worth: Differences in perceived worth as a person across interpersonal contexts among adolescents. *Child Development, 69,* 756–766.

Hartl, A., Laursen, B., & Cillessen, A. (2015). A survival analysis of adolescent friendships. *Psychological Science, 26,* 1304–1315.

Hartman, S., Widaman, K. F., & Belsky, J. (2015). Genetic moderation of effects of maternal sensitivity on girl's age of menarche: Replication of the Manuck et al. Study. *Development and Psychopathology, 27,* 747–756.

Hartney, C. (2006). *Youth under 18 in the criminal justice system.* Oakland: National Council on Crime and Delinquency.

Hartung, C., Lefner, E., & Fedele, D. (2011). Disruptive behaviors and aggression. In B. Brown & M. Prinstein (Eds.), *Encyclopedia of adolescence* (Vol. 3, pp. 143–150). New York: Academic Press.

Hasking, P., Andrews, T., & Martin, G. (2013). The role of exposure to self-injury among peers in predicting later self-injury. *Journal of Youth & Adolescence, 42,* 1543–1556.

Hastings, J., & Weinstein, J. (2008). Information, school choices, and academic achievement: Evidence from two experiments. *Quarterly Journal of Economics, 123,* 1373–1414.

Hatano, K., & Sugimura, K. (2017). Is adolescence a period of identity formation for all youth? Insights from a four-wave longitudinal study of identity dynamics in Japan. *Developmental Psychology, 53,* 2113–2126.

Hatano, K., Sugimura, K., & Crocetti, E. (2016). Looking at the dark and bright sides of identity formation: New insights from adolescents and emerging adults in Japan. *Journal of Adolescence, 47,* 156–168.

Hatzenbuehler, M., Birkett, M., Van Wagenen, A., & Meyer, I. (2014). Protective school climates and reduced risk for suicide ideation in sexual minority youths. *American Journal of Public Health, 104,* 279–286.

Hauser, S., & Bowlds, M. (1990). Stress, coping, and adaptation. In S. Feldman & G. Elliott (Eds.), *At the threshold: The developing adolescent* (pp. 388–413). Cambridge, MA: Harvard University Press.

Hawes, S., Mulvey, E., Schubert, C., & Pardini, D. (2014). Structural coherence and temporal stability of psychopathic personality features during emerging adulthood. *Journal of Abnormal Psychology, 123,* 623–633.

Hawk, S., Keijsers, L., Frijns, T., Hale, W., Branje, S., & Meeus, W. (2013). "I still haven't found what I'm looking for": Parental privacy invasion predicts reduced parental knowledge. *Developmental Psychology, 49,* 1286–1298.

Hawk, S. T., Becht, A., & Branje, S. (2016). "Snooping" as a distinct parental monitoring strategy: Comparisons with overt solicitation and control. *Journal of Research on Adolescence, 26,* 443–458.

Hawkins, D. N., Amato, P. R., & King, V. (2006). Parent-adolescent involvement: The relative influence of parent gender and residence. *Journal of Marriage and Family, 68,* 125–136.

Hawkins, S., Bach, N., & Baum, C. (2016). Impact of tobacco control policies on adolescent smoking. *Journal of Adolescent Health, 58,* 679–685.

Hay, C., Fortson, E. N., Hollist, D. R., Altheimer, I., & Schaible, L. M. (2007). Compounded risk: The implications for delinquency of coming from a poor family that lives in a poor community. *Journal of Youth and Adolescence, 36,* 593–605.

Haydon, A., & Halpern, C. (2010). Older romantic partners and depressive symptoms during adolescence. *Journal of Youth and Adolescence, 39,* 1240–1251.

Haydon, A., Cheng, M., Herring, A., McRee, A., & Halpern, C. (2014). Prevalence and predictors of sexual inexperience in adulthood. *Archives of Sexual Behavior, 43,* 221–230.

Haydon, A., Herring, A., Prinstein, M., & Halpern, C. (2012). Beyond age at first sex: Patterns of emerging sexual behavior in adolescence and young adulthood. *Journal of Adolescent Health, 50,* 456–463.

Haydon, A., McRee, A-L., & Halpern, C. (2011). Risk-taking behavior. In B. Brown & M. Prinstein (Eds.), *Encyclopedia of adolescence* (Vol. 3, pp. 255–263). New York: Academic Press.

Haynie, D., Doogan, N., & Soller, B. (2014). Gender, friendship networks, and delinquency: A dynamic network approach. *Criminology, 52,* 688–722.

Hazel, N. A., Oppenheimer, C. W., Technow, J. R., Young, J. F., & Hankin, B. L. (2014). Parent relationship quality buffers against the effect of peer stressors on depressive symptoms from middle childhood to adolescence. *Developmental Psychology, 50,* 2115–2123.

Heard, H. E. (2007). The family structure trajectory and adolescent school performance: Differential effects by race and ethnicity. *Journal of Family Issues, 28,* 319–354.

Hebert, K., Fales, J., Nangle, D., Papadakis, A., & Grover, R. (2013). Linking social anxiety and adolescent romantic relationship functioning: Indirect effects and the importance of peers. *Journal of Youth & Adolescence, 42,* 1708–1720.

Hechinger, F. (1993). Schools for teenagers: A historic dilemma. *Teachers College Record, 94,* 522–539.

Heck, R. H., Price, C. L., & Thomas, S. L. (2004). Tracks as emergent structures: A network analysis of student differentiation in a high school. *American Journal of Education, 110,* 321–353.

Heinze, J. E., Stoddard, S. A., Aiyer, S. M., Eisman, A. B., & Zimmerman, M. A. (2017). Exposure to violence during adolescence as a predictor of perceived stress trajectories in emerging adulthood. *Journal of Applied Developmental Psychology, 49,* 31–38.

Heitzeg, M., Cope, L., Martz, M., Hardee, J., & Zucker, R. (2015). Brain activation to negative stimuli mediates a relationship between adolescent marijuana use and later emotional functioning. *Developmental Cognitive Neuroscience, 16,* 71–83.

Heleniak, C., King, K. M., Monahan, K. C., & McLaughlin, K. A. (2018). Disruptions in emotion regulation as a mechanism linking community violence exposure to adolescent internalizing problems. *Journal of Research on Adolescence, 28,* 229–244.

Heller, A., & Casey, B. J. (2016). The neurodynamics of emotion: Delineating typical and atypical emotional processes during adolescence. *Developmental Science, 19,* 3–18.

Hellström, C., Nilsson, K. W., Leppert, J., & Öslund, C. (2012). Influences of motives to play and time spent gaming on the negative consequences of adolescent online computer gaming. *Computers in Human Behavior, 28,* 1379–1387.

Helms, S., Choukas-Bradley, S., Widman, L., Giletta, M., Cohen, G., & Prinstein, M. (2014). Adolescents misperceive and are influenced by high-status peers' health risk, deviant, and adaptive behavior. *Developmental Psychology, 50,* 2697–2714.

Helsen, M., Vollebergh, W., & Meeus, W. (2000). Social support from parents and friends and emotional problems in adolescence. *Journal of Youth and Adolescence, 29,* 319–335.

Helwig, C. (1995). Adolescents' and young adults' conceptions of civil liberties: Freedom of speech and religion. *Child Development, 66,* 152–166.

Helwig, C., Arnold, M., Tan, D., & Boyd, D. (2007). Mainland Chinese and Canadian adolescents' judgments and reasoning about the fairness of democratic and other forms of government. *Cognitive Development, 22,* 96–109.

Helwig, C., Yang, S., Tan, D., Liu, C., & Shao, T. (2011). Urban and rural Chinese adolescents' judgments and reasoning about personal and group jurisdiction. *Child Development, 82,* 701–716.

Henderson, A., Brown, S., Pancer, S., & Ellis-Hale, K. (2007). Mandated community service in high school and subsequent civic engagement: The case of the "double cohort" in Ontario, Canada. *Journal of Youth and Adolescence, 36,* 849–860.

Henderson, A., Pancer, S. M., & Brown, S. D. (2014). Creating effective civic engagement policy for adolescents: Quantitative and qualitative evaluations of compulsory community service. *Journal of Adolescent Research, 29,* 120–154.

Henderson, C., Hayslip, B., Sanders, L., & Louden, L. (2009). Grandmother-grandchild relationship quality predicts psychological adjustment among youth from divorced families. *Journal of Family Issues, 30,* 1245-1264.

Henry, D., Schoeny, M., Deptula, D., & Slavick, J. (2007). Peer selection and socialization effects on adolescent intercourse without a condom and attitudes about the costs of sex. *Child Development, 78,* 825-838.

Henry, K., Cavanagh, T., & Oetting, E. (2011). Perceived parental investment in school as a mediator of the relationship between socio-economic indicators and educational outcomes in rural America. *Journal of Youth and Adolescence, 40,* 1164-1177.

Henry, K., Knight, K., & Thornberry, T. (2012). School disengagement as a predictor of dropout, delinquency, and problem substance use during adolescence and early adulthood. *Journal of Youth and Adolescence, 41,* 156-166.

Hensel, D., Fortenberry, J., & Orr, D. (2008). Variations in coital and noncoital sexual repertoire among adolescent women. *Journal of Adolescent Health, 42,* 170-176.

Hentges, R., Shaw, D., & Wang, M. (2018). Early childhood parenting and child impulsivity as precursors to aggression, substance use, and risky sexual behavior in adolescence and early adulthood. *Development and Psychopathology, 30,* 1305-1319.

Hequembourg, A., Livingston, J., & Wang, W. (2020). Prospective associations among relationship abuse, sexual harassment and bullying in a community sample of sexual minority and exclusively heterosexual youth. *Journal of Adolescence, 83,* 52-61.

Herbers, J. E., Reynolds, A. J., & Chen, C. C. (2013). School mobility and developmental outcomes in young adulthood. *Development and Psychopathology, 25,* 501-515.

Herd, T., King-Casas, B., & Kim-Spoon, J. (2020). Developmental changes in emotion regulation during adolescence: associations with socioeconomic risk and family emotional context. *Journal of Youth and Adolescence, 49,* 1545-1557.

Herdt, G., & McClintock, M. (2000). The magical age of 10. *Archives of Sexual Behavior, 29,* 587-606.

Herman, M. (2004). Forced to choose: Some determinants of racial identification in multiracial adolescents. *Child Development, 75,* 730-748.

Herman, M. (2009). The Black-White-other achievement gap: Testing theories of academic performance among multiracial and monoracial adolescents. *Sociology of Education, 82,* 20-46.

Herman-Giddens, M., Slora, E., Wasserman, R., Bourdony, C., Bhapkar, M., Koch, G., . . . Hasemeier, C. (1997). Secondary sexual characteristics and menses in young girls seen in office practice: A study from the Pediatric Research in Office Settings Network. *Pediatrics, 88,* 505-512.

Herman-Giddens, M., Steffes, J., Harris, D., Slora, E., Hussey, M., Dowshen, S., . . . Reiter, E. (2012, October 20). Secondary sexual characteristics in boys: Data from the Pediatric Research in Office Settings Network. *Pediatrics,* published online doi: 10.1542/peds.2011-3291.

Hernandez, M., Conger, R., Robins, R., Bacher, K., & Widaman, K. (2014). Cultural socialization and ethnic pride among Mexican-origin adolescents during the transition to middle school. *Child Development, 85,* 695-708

Hernández, M., Robins, R., Widaman, K., & Conger, R. (2016). School belonging, generational status, and socioeconomic effects on Mexican-origin children's later academic competence and expectations. *Journal of Research on Adolescence, 26,* 241-256.

Heron, J., Low, N., Lewis, G., Macleod, J., Ness, A., & Waylen, A. (2015). Social factors associated with readiness for sexual activity in adolescents: A population-based cohort study. *Archives of Sexual Behavior, 44,* 669-678.

Herpers, P., Scheepers, F., Bons, D., Buitelaar, J., & Rommelse, N. (2014). The cognitive and neural correlates of psychopathy and especially callous–unemotional traits in youths: A systematic review of the evidence. *Development and Psychopathology, 26,* 245-273.

Herrera, V., Wiersma, J., & Cleveland, H. (2011). Romantic partners' contribution to the continuity of male and female delinquent and violent behavior. *Journal of Research on Adolescence, 21,* 608-618.

Herting, M. M., Colby, J. B., Sowell, E. R., & Nagel, B. J. (2014). White matter connectivity and aerobic fitness in male adolescents. *Developmental Cognitive Neuroscience, 7,* 65-75.

Herting, M. M., Maxwell, E. C., Irvine, C., & Nagel, B. J. (2012). The impact of sex, puberty, and hormones on white matter microstructure in adolescents. *Cerebral Cortex, 22,* 1979-1992.

Hessel, E. T., Loeb, E. L., Szwedo, d. E., & Allen, J. P. (2016). Predictions from early adolescent emotional repair abilities to functioning in future relationships. *Journal of Research on Adolescence, 26,* 776-789.

Hetherington, E. M., Bridges, M., & Insabella, G. (1998). What matters? What does not? Five perspectives on the association between marital transitions and children's adjustment. *American Psychologist, 53,* 167-184.

Hetherington, E. M., Henderson, S., & Reiss, D. (1999). Adolescent siblings in stepfamilies: Family functioning and adolescent adjustment. *Monographs of the Society for Research in Child Development, 64,* Serial No. 259.

Hicks, B., Johnson, W., Durbin, C., Blonigen, D., Iacono, W., & McGue, M. (2014). Delineating selection and mediation effects among childhood personality and environmental risk factors in the development of adolescent substance abuse. *Journal of Abnormal Child Psychology, 42,* 845-859.

Higgins, J., & Wang, Y. (2015). The role of young adults' pleasure attitudes in shaping condom use. *American Journal of Public Health, 105,* 1329-1332.

Higgins, J., Trussell, J., Moore, N., & Davidson, J. (2010). Virginity lost, satisfaction gained? Physiological and psychological sexual satisfaction at heterosexual debut. *Journal of Sex Research, 47,* 384-394.

Hildick-Smith, G., Pesko, M., Shearer, L., Hughes, J., Chang, J., Loughlin, G., & Ipp, L. (2015). A practitioner's guide to electronic cigarettes in the adolescent population. *Journal of Adolescent Health, 57,* 574-579.

Hill, J. P. (1983). Early adolescence: A framework. *Journal of Early Adolescence, 3,* 1-21.

Hill, N., & Wang, M. (2015). From middle school to college: Developing aspirations, promoting engagement, and indirect pathways from parenting to post high school enrollment. *Developmental Psychology, 51,* 224-235.

Hill, N. E., & Tyson, D. (2009). Parental involvement in middle school: A meta-analytic assessment of the strategies that promote achievement. *Developmental Psychology, 45,* 740-763.

Hill, N. E., Liang, B., Bravo, D. Y., Price, M., Polk, W., Perella, J., & Savitz-Romer, M. (2018). Adolescents' perceptions of the economy: Its association with academic engagement and the role of school-based and parental relationships. *Journal of Youth and Adolescence, 47*(5), 895-915.

Hill, P. L., Burrow, A. L., & Sumner, R. (2013). Addressing important questions in the field of adolescent purpose. *Child Development Perspectives, 7,* 232-236.

Hine, T. (1999). *The rise and fall of the American teenager.* New York: Bard Books.

Hingson, R., & Zha, W. (2009). Age of drinking onset, alcohol use disorders, frequent heavy drinking, and unintentionally injuring oneself and others after drinking. *Pediatrics, 123,* 1477-1484.

Hingson, R., Heeren, T., & Winter, M. (2006). Age at drinking onset and alcohol dependence: Age at onset, duration, and severity. *Archives of Pediatric and Adolescent Medicine, 160,* 739-746.

Hinnant, J., & Forman-Alberti, A. (2019). Deviant peer behavior and adolescent delinquency: protective effects of inhibitory control, planning, or decision making? *Journal of Research on Adolescence, 29,* 682-695.

Hirsch, B., Mickus, M., & Boerger, R. (2002). Ties to influential adults among Black and White adolescents: Culture, social class, and family networks. *American Journal of Community Psychology, 30,* 289-303.

Hobbes, M. (2017). Millennials are screwed. *HuffPost Highline.* (Accessed at https://highline.huffingtonpost.com/articles/en/poor-millennials/ on February 11, 2021).

Hock, E., Eberly, M., Bartle-Haring, S., Ellwanger, P., & Widaman, K. (2001). Separation anxiety in parents of adolescents: Theoretical significance and scale development. *Child Development, 72,* 284-298.

Hofer, M., Womack, S., & Wilson, M. (2020). An examination of the influence of procedurally just strategies on legal cynicism among urban youth experiencing police contact. *Journal of Community Psychology, 48,* 104-123.

Hoff, K. A., Song, Q., Einarsdóttir, S., Briley, D. A., & Rounds, J. (2020). Developmental structure of personality and interests: A four-wave, 8-year longitudinal study. *Journal of Personality and Social Psychology, 118*(5), 1044.

Hofferth, S., & Moon, U. (2012). Electronic play, study, communication, and adolescent achievement, 2003-2008. *Journal of Research on Adolescence, 22,* 215-224.

Hoffman, A., Dumas, F., Loose, F., Smeding, A., Kurtz-Costes, B., & Régner, I. (2019). Development of gender typicality and felt pressure in

European French and North African French adolescents. *Child Development, 90*, e306–e321.

Hoffman, S., & Maynard, R. (2008). *Kids having kids: Economic costs and social consequences of teen pregnancy.* Washington: Urban Institute Press.

Hofmann, V., & Müller, C. M. (2018). Avoiding anti-social behavior among adolescents: The positive influence of classmates' prosocial behavior. *Journal of Adolescence, 68*, 136–145.

Hogue, A., & Steinberg, L. (1995). Homophily of internalized distress in adolescent peer groups. *Developmental Psychology, 31*, 897–906.

Holas, I., & Huston, A. C. (2012). Are middle schools harmful? The role of transition timing, classroom quality and school characteristics. *Journal of Youth & Adolescence, 41*, 333–345.

Holfeld, B., & Leadbeater, B. (2017). Concurrent and longitudinal associations between early adolescents' experiences of school climate and cyber victimization. *Computers in Human Behavior, 76*, 321–328.

Holfeld, B., & Mishna, F. (2019). Internalizing symptoms and externalizing problems: Risk factors for or consequences of cyber victimization? *Journal of Youth and Adolescence, 48*, 567–580.

Holland, K., Vivolo-Kantor, A., Logan, J., & Leemis, R. (2017). Antecedents of suicide among youth aged 11–15: A multistate mixed methods analysis. *Journal of Youth and Adolescence, 46*, 1598–1610.

Holland, M. (2012). Only here for the day: The social integration of minority students at a majority white high school. *Sociology of Education, 85*, 101–120.

Hollander, D. (2006). Many teenagers who say they have taken a virginity pledge retract that statement after having intercourse. *Perspectives on Sexual and Reproductive Health, 38*, 168.

Hollenstein, T., & Lougheed, J. P. (2013). Beyond storm and stress: Typicality, transactions, timing, and temperament to account for adolescent change. *American Psychologist, 68*, 444–454.

Holliday, E., & Gould, T. (2016). Nicotine, adolescence, and stress: A review of how stress can modulate the negative consequences of adolescent nicotine abuse. *Neuroscience & Biobehavioral Reviews, 65*, 173–184.

Holmbeck, G. (1996). A model of family relational transformations during the transition to adolescence: Parent-adolescent conflict and adaptation. In J. Graber, J. Brooks-Gunn, & A. Petersen (Eds.), *Transitions through adolescence: Interpersonal domains and context* (pp. 167–199). Mahwah, NJ: Erlbaum.

Holmes, C., Brieant, A., King-Casas, B., & Kim-Spoon, J. (2019). How Is religiousness associated with adolescent risk-taking? The roles of emotion regulation and executive function. *Journal of Research on Adolescence, 29*, 334–344.

Holmes, C., Kim-Spoon, J., & Deater-Deckard, K. (2016). Linking executive function and peer problems from early childhood through middle adolescence. *Journal of Abnormal Child Psychology, 44*, 31–42.

Holoyda, B., Landess, J., Sorrentino, R., & Friedman, S. (2018). Trouble at teens' fingertips: Youth sexting and the law. *Behavioral Sciences & the Law, 36*, 170–181.

Homma, Y., Wang, N., Saewyc, E., & Kishor, N. (2012). The relationship between sexual abuse and risky sexual behavior among adolescent boys: A meta-analysis. *Journal of Adolescent Health, 51*, 18–24.

Hope, M., Lee, D., Hsieh, H.-F., Hurd, N., Sparks, H., and Zimmerman, M. (2019). Violence exposure and sexual risk behaviors for African American adolescent girls: The protective role of natural mentorship and organizational religious involvement. *American Journal of Community Psychology, 64*, 242–255.

Horan, P., & Hargis, P. (1991). Children's work and schooling in the late nineteenth-century family economy. *American Sociological Review, 56*, 583–596.

Horn, A. (2012). The cultivation of a prosocial value orientation through community service: An examination of organizational context, social facilitation, and duration. *Journal of Youth & Adolescence, 41*, 948–968.

Horn, S. S. (2003). Adolescents' reasoning about exclusion from social groups. *Developmental Psychology, 39*, 71–84.

Horvat, E. M., & Lewis, K. S. (2003). Reassessing the "burden of 'acting White'": The importance of peer group in managing academic success. *Sociology of Education, 76*, 265–280.

Horvath, G., Knopik, V. S., & Marceau, K. (2020). Polygenic influences on pubertal timing and tempo and depressive symptoms in boys and girls. *Journal of Research on Adolescence, 30*, 78–94.

Hostinar, C., Johnson, A., & Gunnar, M. (2015). Parent support is less effective in buffering cortisol stress reactivity for adolescents compared to children. *Developmental Science, 18*, 281–297.

Hou, J., Natsuaki, M., Zhang, J., Guo, F., Huang, Z., Wang, M., & Chen, Z. (2013). Romantic relationships and adjustment problems in China: The moderating effect of classroom romantic context. *Journal of Adolescence, 36*, 171–180.

Hou, Y., Benner, A., Kim, S., Chen, S., Spitz, S., Shi, Y., & Beretvas, T. (2020). Discordance in parents' and adolescents' reports of parenting: A meta-analysis and qualitative review. *American Psychologist, 75*, 329–348.

Hou, Y., Kim, S. Y., & Wang, Y. (2016). Parental acculturative stressors and adolescent adjustment through interparental and parent–child relationships in Chinese American families. *Journal of Youth and Adolescence, 45*, 1466–1481.

Houghton, S., Lawrence, D., Hunter, S., Rosenberg, M., Zadow, C., Wood, L., & Shilton, T. (2018). Reciprocal relationships between trajectories of depressive symptoms and screen media use during adolescence. *Journal of Youth and Adolescence, 47*, 2453–2467.

Houser, J., Mayeux, L., & Cross, C. (2015). Peer status and aggression as predictors of dating popularity in adolescence. *Journal of Youth and Adolescence, 44*, 683–695.

Houston, S.L., II, Pearman, F.A., II and McGee, E.O. (2020). Risk, protection, and identity development in high-achieving Black males in high school. *Journal of Research on Adolescence, 30*, 875–895.

Howard, A., & Galambos, N. (2011). Transitions to adulthood. In B. Brown & M. Prinstein (Eds.), *Encyclopedia of adolescence* (Vol. 1, pp. 376–383). New York: Academic Press.

Howard, D., Debnam, K., & Strausser, A. (2017). "I'm a stalker and proud of it": Adolescent girls' perceptions of the mixed utilities associated with Internet and social networking use in their dating relationships. *Youth & Society, 51*, 773–792.

Hoyt, L. T., Kushi, L. H., Leung, C. W., Nickleach, D. C., Adler, N., Laraia, B. A., Hiatt, R. A., & Yen, I. H. (2014). Neighborhood influences on girls' obesity risk across the transition to adolescence. *Pediatrics, 134*, 942–949.

Hu, M., Davies, M., & Kandel, D. (2006). Epidemiology and correlates of daily smoking and nicotine dependence among young adults in the United States. *American Journal of Public Health, 96*, 299–308.

Hudson, J., Hiripi, E., Pope, H., Jr., & Kessler, R. (2007). The prevalence and correlates of eating disorders in the National Comorbidity Survey Replication. *Biological Psychiatry, 61*, 348–358.

Huey, M., Laursen, B., Kaniušonytė, G., Malinauskienė, O., & Žukauskienė, R. (2020). Self-esteem mediates longitudinal associations from adolescent perceptions of parenting to adjustment. *Journal of Abnormal Child Psychology, 48*(3), 331–341.

Hughes, D., Del Toro, J., Harding, J., Way, N., & Rarick, J. (2016). Trajectories of discrimination across adolescence: Associations with academic, psychological, and behavioral outcomes. *Child Development, 87*, 1337–1351.

Hughes, D., Way, N., & Rivas-Drake, D. (2011). Stability and change in private and public ethnic regard among African American, Puerto Rican, Dominican, and Chinese American early adolescents. *Journal of Research on Adolescence, 21*, 861–870.

Hughes, D. L., Del Toro, J., & Way, N. (2017). Interrelations among dimensions of ethnic-racial identity during adolescence. *Developmental Psychology, 53*, 2139–2153.

Hughes, J. N., Im, M., Kwok, O., Cham, H., & West, S. G. (2015). Latino students' transition to middle school: Role of bilingual education and school ethnic context. *Journal of Research on Adolescence, 25*, 443–458.

Huh, D., Stice, E., Shaw, H., & Boutelle, K. (2012). Female overweight and obesity in adolescence: Developmental trends and ethnic differences in prevalence, incidence, and remission. *Journal of Youth and Adolescence, 41*, 76–85.

Hulleman, C. S., & Harackiewicz, J. M. (2009). Promoting interest and performance in high school science classes. *Science, 326*(5958), 1410–1412.

Hullenaar, K., & Ruback, R. (2020). *Juvenile violent victimization, 1995–2018.* Washington, DC: Office of Juvenile Justice and Delinquency Prevention.

Hummer, D. L., & Lee, T. M. (2016). Daily timing of the adolescent sleep phase: Insights from a cross-species comparison. *Neuroscience & Biobehavioral Reviews, 70*, 171–181.

Humphrey, T., & Vaillancourt, T. (2020). Longitudinal relations between bullying perpetration, sexual harassment, homophobic taunting, and dating violence: Evidence of heterotypic continuity. *Journal of Youth and Adolescence, 49*, 1976–1986.

Humphreys, K., Watts, E., Dennis, E., King, L., Thompson, P., & Gotlib, I. (2019). Stressful life events, ADHD symptoms, and brain structure in early adolescence. *Journal of Abnormal Child Psychology, 47,* 421-432.

Hurd, N. M., Sánchez, B., Zimmerman, M. A., & Caldwell, C. H. (2012). Natural mentors, racial identity, and educational attainment among African American adolescents: Exploring pathways to success. *Child Development, 83,* 1196-1212.

Hurd, N. M., Varner, F. A., & Rowley, S. J. (2013). Involved-vigilant parenting and socio-emotional well-being among black youth: The moderating influence of natural mentoring relationships. *Journal of Youth & Adolescence, 42,* 1583-1595.

Hurd, Y., Manzoni, O., Pletnikov, M., Lee, F., Bhattacharyya, S., & Melis, M. (2019). Cannabis and the developing brain: Insights into its long-lasting effects. *Journal of Neuroscience, 39,* 8250-8258.

Hurley, D. (2005, April 19). Divorce rate: It's not as high as you think. *The New York Times.*

Hussong, A. (2000). Perceived peer context and adolescent adjustment. *Journal of Research on Adolescence, 10,* 391-415.

Hussong, A., & Hicks, R. (2003). Affect and peer context interactively impact adolescent substance use. *Journal of Abnormal Child Psychology, 31,* 413-426.

Hussong, A., Curran, P., & Moffitt, T. (2004). Substance abuse hinders desistance in young adults' antisocial behavior. *Development and Psychopathology, 16,* 1029-1046.

Hutchinson, M., Jemmott, J., III, Jemmott, L., Braverman, P., & Fong, G. (2003). The role of mother-daughter sexual risk communication in reducing sexual risk-behaviors among urban adolescent females: A prospective study. *Journal of Adolescent Health, 33,* 98-107.

Hwang, N., & Domina, T. (2017). The links between youth employment and educational attainment across racial groups. *Journal of Research on Adolescence, 27,* 312-327.

Hwang, N., Reyes, M., & Eccles, J. S. (2019). Who holds a fixed mindset and whom does it harm in mathematics? *Youth & Society, 51,* 247-267.

Hyde, L., Shaw, D., & Hariri, A. (2013). Understanding youth antisocial behavior using neuroscience through a developmental psychopathology lens: Review, integration, and directions for research. *Developmental Review, 33,* 168-223.

Hyde, L., Shaw, D., & Moilanen, K. (2010). Developmental precursors of moral disengagement and the role of moral disengagement in the development of antisocial behavior. *Journal of Abnormal Child Psychology, 38,* 197-209.

Hymel, S., & Swearer, S. (2015). Four decades of research on school bullying: An introduction. *American Psychologist, 70,* 293-299.

Iannotti, R. J., & Wang, J. (2013). Patterns of physical activity, sedentary behavior, and diet in U.S. adolescents. *Journal of Adolescent Health, 53,* 280-286.

Ibañez, G., Kuperminc, G., Jurkovic, G., & Perilla, J. (2004). Cultural attributes and adaptations linked to achievement motivation among Latino adolescents. *Journal of Youth and Adolescence, 33,* 559-568.

Icenogle, G., Steinberg, L., Duell, N., Chein, J., Chang, L., Chaudary, N., . . . Bacchini, D.

(2019). Adolescents' cognitive capacity reaches adult levels prior to their psychosocial maturity: Evidence for a "maturity gap" in a multinational sample. *Law and Human Behavior, 43,* 69-85.

Icenogle, G., Steinberg, L., Olino, T. M., Shulman, E. P., Chein, J., Alampay, L. P., . . . Sorbring, E. (2017). Puberty predicts approach but not avoidance on the Iowa gambling task in a multinational sample. *Child Development, 88,* 1598-1614.

Im, M., Hughes, J., & West, S. (2016). Effect of trajectories of friends' and parents' school involvement on adolescents' engagement and achievement. *Journal of Research on Adolescence, 26,* 963-978.

Inhelder, B., & Piaget, J. (1958). *The growth of logical thinking from childhood to adolescence.* New York: Basic Books.

Insel, C., & Somerville, L. H. (2018). Asymmetric neural tracking of gain and loss magnitude during adolescence. *Social Cognitive and Affective Neuroscience, 13,* 785-796.

Institute of Medicine. (2013). *Contagion of violence: Workshop summary.* Washington, DC: National Academies Press.

Institute of Medicine of the National Academies (2015). *Public health implications of raising the minimum age of legal access to tobacco products.* Washington: Author.

IOM (Institute of Medicine) and NRC (National Research Council). (2006). *Food marketing to children and youth: Threat or opportunity?* Washington, DC: National Academies Press.

IOM (Institute of Medicine) and NRC (National Research Council). (2011b). *The health of lesbian, gay, bisexual, and transgender people: Building a foundation for better understanding.* Washington, DC: The National Academies Press.

IOM (Institute of Medicine) and NRC (National Research Council). (2011). *The science of adolescent risk-taking: Workshop report.* Committee on the Science of Adolescence. Washington, DC: The National Academies Press.

Ioverno, S., & Russell, S. (2020). Homophobic bullying in positive and negative school climates: The moderating role of gender sexuality alliances. *Journal of Youth and Adolescence*, early view.

Irwin, K. (2004). The violence of adolescent life experiencing and managing everyday threats. *Youth and Society, 35,* 452-479.

Isakson, K., & Jarvis, P. (1999). The adjustment of adolescents during the transition into high school: A short-term longitudinal study. *Journal of Youth and Adolescence, 28,* 1-26.

Iselin, A. M., Mulvey, E. P., Loughran, T. A., Chung, H. L., & Schubert, C. A. (2012). A longitudinal examination of serious adolescent offenders' perceptions of chances for success and engagement in behaviors accomplishing goals. *Journal of Abnormal Child Psychology, 40,* 237-249.

Ispa-Landa, S. (2013). Gender, race, and justifications for group exclusion: Urban black students bussed to affluent suburban schools. *Sociology of Education, 86,* 218-233.

Ivanova, K., Mills, M., & Veenstra, R. (2011). The initiation of dating in adolescence: The effect of parental divorce. The TRAILS study. *Journal of Research on Adolescence, 21,* 769-775.

Ivanova, K., Mills, M., & Veenstra, R. (2014). Parental residential and partnering transitions and the initiation of adolescent romantic relationships. *Journal of Marriage and Family, 76,* 465-475.

Ivers, R., Senserrick, T., Boufous, S., Stevenson, M., Chen, H., Woodward, M., & Norton, R. (2009). Novice drivers' risky driving behavior, risk perception, and crash risk: Findings from the DRIVE study. *American Journal of Public Health, 99,* 1638-1644.

Jaccard, J., Dittus, P., & Gordon, V. (1998). Parent-adolescent congruency in reports of adolescent sexual behavior and in communications about sexual behavior. *Child Development, 69,* 247-261.

Jaccard, J., Dodge, T., & Dittus, P. (2003). Do adolescents want to avoid pregnancy? Atttitudes toward pregnancy as predictors of pregnancy. *Journal of Adolescent Health, 33,* 79-83.

Jackson, K. M., & Schulenberg, J. E. (2013). Alcohol use during the transition from middle school to high school: National panel data on prevalence and moderators. *Developmental Psychology, 49,* 2147-2158.

Jackson, L. (2008). Adolescents and the Internet. In P. Jamieson & D. Romer (Eds.), *The changing portrayal of adolescents in the media since 1950* (pp. 377-411). New York: Oxford University Press.

Jackson, T., & Chen, H. (2014). Risk factors for disordered eating during early and middle adolescence: A two year longitudinal study of mainland Chinese boys and girls. *Journal of Abnormal Child Psychology, 42,* 791-802.

Jacobs, J. E., Chin, C. S., & Shaver, K. (2005). Longitudinal links between perceptions of adolescence and the social beliefs of adolescents: Are parents' stereotypes related to beliefs held about and by their children? *Journal of Youth and Adolescence, 34,* 61-72.

Jacobs, J. E., Lanza, S., Osgood, D. W., Eccles, J., & Wigfield, A. (2002). Changes in children's self-competence and values: Gender and domain differences across grades one through twelve. *Child Development, 73,* 509-527.

Jacobsen, W. (2020). School punishment and interpersonal exclusion: Rejection, withdrawal, and separation from friends. *Criminology, 58,* 35-69.

Jacobson, K., & Rowe, D. (1999). Genetic and environmental influences on the relationships between family connectedness, school connectedness, and adolescent depressed mood: Sex differences. *Developmental Psychology, 35,* 926-939.

Jacobus, J., Squeglia, L., Meruelo, A., Castro, N., Brumback, T., Giedd, J., & Tapert, S. (2015). Cortical thickness in adolescent marijuana and alcohol users: A three-year prospective study from adolescence to young adulthood. *Developmental Cognitive Neuroscience, 16,* 101-109.

Jaffee, S., Caspi, A., Moffitt, T., Belsky, J., & Silva, P. (2001). Why are children born to teen mothers at risk for adverse outcomes in young adulthood? Results from a 20-year longitudinal study. *Development and Psychopathology, 13,* 377-397.

Jager, J., Keyes, K., & Schulenberg, J. (2015). Historical variation in young adult binge drinking trajectories and its link to historical variation in social roles and minimum legal drinking age. *Developmental Psychology, 51,* 962-974.

Jager, J., Schulenberg, J., O'Malley, P., & Bachman, J. (2013). Historical variation in drug use trajectories across the transition to adulthood: The trend toward lower intercepts and steeper, ascending slopes. *Development and Psychopathology, 25,* 527-543.

Jager, J., Yuen, C., Putnick, D., Hendricks, C., & Bornstein, M. (2015). Adolescent-peer relationships, separation and detachment from parents, and internalizing and externalizing behaviors: Linkages and interactions. *The Journal of Early Adolescence, 35,* 511-537.

Jaggers, J., Sonsteng-Person, M., Griffiths, A., Gabbard, W., & Turner, M. (2020). Behavioral problems and psychological distress among seriously delinquent youth: Assessing a mediational pathway of parental monitoring, peer delinquency, and violence exposure. *Youth & Society,* early view.

Jaggers, J. W., Prattini, R. J., & Church, W. T. (2016). Traumatic stress among seriously delinquent youth: Considering the consequences of neighborhood circumstance. *American Journal of Community Psychology, 58,* 69-79.

Jain, S., Cohen, A., Paglisotti, T., Subramanyam, M., Chopel, A., & Miller, E. (2018). School climate and physical adolescent relationship abuse: Differences by sex, socioeconomic status, and bullying. *Journal of Adolescence, 66,* 71-82.

Jalanko, E., Leppälahti, S., Heikinheimo, O., & Gissler, M. (2020). The risk of psychiatric morbidity following teenage induced abortion and childbirth: A longitudinal study from Finland. *Journal of Adolescent Health, 66,* 345-351.

James-Burdumy, S., Goesling, B., Deke, J., & Einspruch, E. (2012). The effectiveness of mandatory-random student drug testing: A cluster randomized trial. *Journal of Adolescent Health, 50,* 172-178.

Jang, S., & Franzen, A. (2013). Is being "spiritual" enough without being religious? A study of violent and property crimes among emerging adults. *Criminology, 51,* 595-627.

Janosz, M., Archambault, I., Pagani, L., Pascal, S., Morin, A., & Bowen, F. (2008). Are there detrimental effects of witnessing school violence in early adolescence? *Journal of Adolescent Health, 43,* 600-608.

Janosz, M., LeBlanc, M., Boulerice, B., & Tremblay, R. (2000). Predicting different types of school dropouts: A typological approach with two longitudinal samples. *Journal of Educational Psychology, 92,* 171-190.

Janssen, S., Chessa, A., & Murre, J. (2007). Temporal distribution of favourite books, movies, and records: Differential encoding and re-sampling. *Memory, 15,* 755-67.

Janssen, T., Cox, M., Stoolmiller, M., Barnett, N., & Jackson, K. (2018). The role of sensation seeking and R-rated movie watching in early substance use initiation. *Journal of Youth and Adolescence, 47,* 991-1006.

Janssens, A., Van Den Noortgate, W., Goossens, L., Colpin, H., Verschueren, K., Claes, S., & Van Leeuwen, K. (2017). Externalizing problem behavior in adolescence: Parenting interacting with DAT1 and DRD4 genes. *Journal of Research on Adolescence, 27,* 278-297.

Janssens, A., Van Den Noortgate, W., Goossens, L., Verschueren, K., Colpin, H., De Laet, S., . . . Van Leeuwen, K. (2015). Externalizing problem behavior in adolescence: Dopaminergic genes in interaction with peer acceptance and rejection. *Journal of Youth and Adolescence, 44,* 1441-1456.

Jaramillo, J., Mello, Z., & Worrell, F. (2016). Ethnic identity, stereotype threat, and perceived discrimination among Native American adolescents. *Journal of Research on Adolescence, 26,* 769-775.

Jaramillo, N., Buhi, E., Elder, J., & Corliss, H. (2017). Associations between sex education and contraceptive use among heterosexually active, adolescent males in the United States. *Journal of Adolescent Health, 60,* 534-540.

Jaser, S., Champion, J., Reeslund, K., Keller, G., Merchant, M., Benson, M., & Compas, B. (2007). Cross-situational coping with peer and family stressors in adolescent offspring of depressed parents. *Journal of Adolescence, 30,* 917-932.

Jenner, E., Jenner, L., Walsh, S., Demby, H., Gregory, A., & Davis, E. (2016). Impact of an intervention designed to reduce sexual health risk behaviors of African American adolescents: Results of a randomized controlled trial. *American Journal of Public Health, 106,* S78-S84.

Jensen, A., & McHale, S. (2017). Mothers', fathers', and siblings' perceptions of parents' differential treatment of siblings: Links with family relationship qualities. *Journal of Adolescence, 60,* 119-129.

Jensen, A. C., Pond, A. M., & Padilla-Walker, L. M. (2015). Why can't I be more like my brother? The role and correlates of sibling social comparison orientation. *Journal of Youth and Adolescence, 44,* 2067-2078.

Jensen, L., & Dost-Gözkan, A. (2015). Adolescent-parent relations in Asian Indian and Salvadoran immigrant families: A cultural-developmental analysis of autonomy, authority, conflict, and cohesion. *Journal of Research on Adolescence, 25,* 340-351.

Jensen, L. A., Arnett, J. J., Feldman, S. S., & Cauffman, E. (2004). The right to do wrong: Lying to parents among adolescents and emerging adults. *Journal of Youth and Adolescence, 33,* 101-112.

Jensen, M., Chassin, L., & Gonzales, N. A. (2017). Neighborhood moderation of sensation seeking effects on adolescent substance use initiation. *Journal of Youth and Adolescence, 46,* 1953-1967.

Jensen, T. (2020). Stepfamily processes and youth adjustment: the role of perceived neighborhood collective efficacy. *Journal of Research on Adolescence, 30*(S2), 545-561.

Jessor, R., & Jessor, S. (1977). *Problem behavior and psychosocial development: A longitudinal study of youth.* New York: Academic Press.

Jessor, R., & Turbin, M. (2014). Parsing protection and risk for problem behavior versus pro-social behavior among U.S. and Chinese adolescents. *Journal of Youth & Adolescence, 43,* 1037-1051.

Jessor, R., Turbin, M. S., Costa, F. M., Dong, Q., Zhang, H., & Wang, C. (2003). Adolescent problem behavior in China and the United States: A cross-national study of psychosocial protective factors. *Journal of Research on Adolescence, 13,* 329-360.

Jewell, J., Brown, C., & Perry, B. (2015). All my friends are doing it: Potentially offensive sexual behavior perpetration within adolescent social networks. *Journal of Research on Adolescence, 25, 592-604.*

Jewett, R., Sabiston, C. M., Brunet, J., O'Loughlin, E. K., Scarapicchia, T., & O'Loughlin, J. (2014). School sport participation during adolescence and mental health in early adulthood. *Journal of Adolescent Health, 55,* 640-644.

Jeynes, W. (2001). The effects of recent parental divorce on their children's consumption of alcohol. *Journal of Youth and Adolescence, 30,* 305-319.

Jeynes, W. (2002). A meta-analysis of the effects of attending religious schools and religiosity on Black and Hispanic academic achievement. *Education and Urban Society, 35,* 27-49.

Jia, Y., Way, N., Ling, G., Yoskikawa, H., Chen, X., Hughes, D., . . . Lu, Z. (2009). The influence of student perceptions of school climate on socioemotional and academic adjustment: A comparison of Chinese and American adolescents. *Child Development, 80,* 1514-1530.

Jiang, J. (2018). *Teens who are constantly online are just as likely to socialize with their friends offline.* Washington: Pew Research Center.

Jiang, Y., Granja, M. R., & Koball, H. (2017, January). Basic facts about low-income children: Children 12 through 17 years, 2015. National Center for Children in Poverty.

Jobson, C., Renard, J., Szkudlarek, H., Rosen, L., Pereira, B., Wright, D., . . . Laviolette, S. R. (2019). Adolescent nicotine exposure induces dysregulation of mesocorticolimbic activity states and depressive and anxiety-like prefrontal cortical molecular phenotypes persisting into adulthood. *Cerebral Cortex, 29,* 3140-3153.

Jodl, K. M., Michael, A., Malanchuk, O., Eccles, J., & Sameroff, A. (2001). Parents' roles in shaping early adolescents' occupational aspirations. *Child Development, 72,* 1247-1265.

John, O., Caspi, A., Robins, R., Moffitt, T., & Stouthamer-Loeber, M. (1994). The "Little Five": Exploring the nomological network of the five-factor model of personality in adolescent boys. *Child Development, 65,* 160-178.

Johnson, M. (2002). Social origins, adolescent experiences, and work value trajectories during the transition to adulthood. *Social Forces, 80,* 1307-1341.

Johnson, M. D., & Galambos, N. L. (2014). Paths to intimate relationship quality from parent-adolescent relations and mental health. *Journal of Marriage and Family, 76,* 145-160.

Johnson, W., McGue, M., & Iacono, W. (2006). Genetic and environmental influences on academic achievement trajectories during adolescence. *Developmental Psychology, 42,* 514-532.

Johnson, W., McGue, M., & Iacono, W. G. (2009). School performance and genetic and environmental variance in antisocial behavior at the transition from adolescence to adulthood. *Developmental Psychology, 45,* 973-987.

Johnston, L., Miech, R., O'Malley, P., Bachman, J., Schulenberg, J., & Patrick, M. (2020). *Demographic subgroup trends among adolescents in the use of various licit and illicit drugs, 1975-2019* (Monitoring the Future Occasional Paper No. 94). Ann Arbor, MI: Institute for Social Research, University of Michigan

Johnston, L., O'Malley, P., Miech, R., Bachman, J., & Schulenberg, J. (2015). *Monitoring the Future national survey results on drug use: 1975-2014: Overview, key findings on adolescent drug use.* Ann Arbor: Institute for Social Research, The University of Michigan.

Jolles, D., Kleibeuker, S., Rombouts, S. A. R. B., & Crone, E. A. (2011). Developmental differences in prefrontal activation during working memory maintenance and manipulation for different memory loads. *Developmental Science, 14,* 713-724.

Jones, D., & Smolak, L. (2011). Body image during adolescence: A developmental perspective. In B. Brown & M. Prinstein (Eds.), *Encyclopedia of adolescence* (Vol. 1, pp. 77-86). New York: Academic Press.

Jones, D. C., Vigfusdottir, T. H., & Lee, Y. (2004). Body image and the appearance culture among adolescent girls and boys: An examination of friend conversations, peer criticism, appearance magazines, and the internalization of appearance ideals. *Journal of Adolescent Research, 19,* 323-339.

Jones, D. J., Loiselle, R., & Highlander, A. (2018). Parent-adolescent socialization of social class in low-income white families: Theory, research, and future directions. *Journal of Research on Adolescence, 28,* 622-636.

Jones, H., Gage, S., Heron, J., Hickman, M., Lewis, G., Munafò, M., & Zammit, S. (2018). Association of combined patterns of tobacco and cannabis use in adolescence with psychotic experiences. *JAMA Psychiatry, 75,* 240-246.

Jones, J. D., Fraley, R. C., Ehrlich, K. B., Stern, J. A., Lejuez, C. W., Shaver, P. R., & Cassidy, J. (2018). Stability of attachment style in adolescence: an empirical test of alternative developmental processes. *Child Development, 89*(3), 871-880.

Jones, M. (February 7, 2018). What teenagers are learning from online porn. *The New York Times Magazine,* pp. 30-35 and ff.

Jones, M., Luce, K., Osborne, M., Taylor, K., Cunning, D., Doyle, A., & Taylor, C. (2008). Randomized, controlled trial of an Internet-facilitated intervention for reducing binge eating and overweight in adolescents. *Pediatrics, 121,* 453-462.

Jones, R., Biddlecom, A., Hebert, L., & Mellor, R. (2011). Teens reflect on their sources of contraceptive information. *Journal of Adolescent Research, 26,* 423-446.

Jones, R., Purcell, A., Singh, S., & Finer, L. (2005). Adolescents' reports of parental knowledge of adolescents' use of sexual health services and their reactions to mandated parental notification for prescription contraception. *Journal of the American Medical Association, 293,* 340-348.

Jones, T., Hill, K., Epstein, M., Lee, J., Hawkins, J., & Catalano, R. (2016). Understanding the interplay of individual and social-developmental factors in the progression of substance use and mental health from childhood to adulthood. *Development and Psychopathology, 28,* 721-741.

Jonkmann, K., Trautwein, U., & Lüdtke, O. (2009). Social dominance in adolescence: The moderating role of the classroom context and behavioral heterogeneity. *Child Development, 80,* 338-355.

Joos, C., Wodzinski, A., Wadsworth, M., & Dorn, L. (2018). Neither antecedent nor consequence: Developmental integration of chronic stress, pubertal timing, and conditionally adapted stress response. *Developmental Review, 48,* 1-23.

Jordan, C., & Andersen, S. (2017). Sensitive periods of substance abuse: Early risk for the transition to dependence. *Developmental Cognitive Neuroscience, 25,* 29-44.

Jordán-Conde, Z., Mennecke, B., & Townsend, A. (2014). Late adolescent identity definition and intimate disclosure on Facebook. *Computers in Human Behavior, 33,* 356-366.

Jose, P., & Vierling, A. (2018). Cybervictimisation of adolescents predicts higher rumination, which in turn, predicts worse sleep over time. *Journal of Adolescence, 68,* 127-135.

Jose, P., Ryan, N., & Pryor, J. (2012). Does social connectedness promote a greater sense of well-being in adolescence over time? *Journal of Research on Adolescence, 22,* 235-251.

Joshi, S., Peter, J., & Valkenburg, P. (2014). Virginity loss and pregnancy in U.S. and Dutch teen girl magazines: A content-analytic comparison. *Youth & Society, 46,* 70-88.

Joyner, K., & Udry, J. (2000). You don't bring me anything but down: Adolescent romance and depression. *Journal of Health and Social Behavior, 41,* 369-391.

Juang, L., & Alvarez, A. (2010). Discrimination and adjustment among Chinese American adolescents: Family conflict and family cohesion as vulnerability and protective factors. *American Journal of Public Health, 100,* 2403-2409.

Juang, L., Simpson, J., Lee, R., Rothman, A., Titzmann, P., Schachner, M., . . . Betsch, C. (2018). Using attachment and relational perspectives to understand adaptation and resilience among immigrant and refugee youth. *American Psychologist, 73,* 797-811.

Juarascio, A., Felton, J., Borges, A., Manasse, S., Murray, H., & Lejuez, C. (2016). An investigation of negative affect, reactivity, and distress tolerance as predictors of disordered eating attitudes across adolescence. *Journal of Adolescence, 49,* 91-98.

Judge, B., & Billick, S. B. (2004). Suicidality in adolescence: Review and legal considerations. *Behavioral Sciences and the Law, 22,* 681-695.

Jung, J., & Forbes, G. B. (2013). Body dissatisfaction and characteristics of disordered eating among black and white early adolescent girls and boys. *The Journal of Early Adolescence, 33,* 737-764.

Jungert, T., Piroddi, B., & Thornberg, R. (2016). Early adolescents' motivations to defend victims in school bullying and their perceptions of student-teacher relationships: A self-determination theory approach. *Journal of Adolescence, 53,* 75-90.

Juonala, M., Magnussen, C., & Berenson, G. (2011). Childhood adiposity, adult adiposity, and cardiovascular risk factors. *New England Journal of Medicine, 365,* 1876-1885.

Jussim, L., Eccles, J., & Madon, S. (1996). Social perception, social stereotypes, and teacher expectations: Accuracy and the quest for the powerful self-fulfilling prophecy. *Advances in Experimental Social Psychology, 28,* 281-388.

Juvonen, J., & Gross, E. (2008). Extending the school grounds? Bullying experiences in cyberspace. *Journal of School Health, 78,* 496-505.

Juvonen, J., & Murdock, T. (1995). Grade-level differences in the social value of effort: Implications for self-presentation tactics of early adolescents. *Child Development, 66,* 1694-1705.

Juvonen, J., Lessard, L. M., Schacter, H. L., & Enders, C. (2019). The effects of middle school weight climate on youth with higher body weight. *Journal of Research on Adolescence, 29,* 466-479.

Juvonen, J., Nishina, A., & Graham, S. (2006). Ethnic diversity and perceptions of safety in urban middle schools. *Psychological Science, 17,* 393-400.

Juvonen, J., Wang, Y., & Espinoza, G. (2013). Physical aggression, spreading of rumors, and social prominence in early adolescence: Reciprocal effects supporting gender similarities. *Journal of Youth and Adolescence, 42,* 1801-1810.

Kaestle, C., Halpern, C., Miller, W., & Ford, C. (2005). Young age at first sexual intercourse and sexually transmitted infections in adolescents and young adults. *American Journal of Epidemiology, 161,* 774-780.

Kaestle, C., Morisky, D., & Wiley, D. (2002). Sexual intercourse and the age difference between adolescent females and their romantic partners. *Perspectives on Sexual and Reproductive Health, 34,* 304-305.

Kågesten, A., & Blum, R. (2015). Characteristics of youth who report early sexual experiences in Sweden. *Archives of Sexual Behavior, 44,* 679-694.

Kågesten, A., Parekh, J., Tunçalp, Ö., Turke, S., & Blum, R. (2014). Comprehensive adolescent health programs that include sexual and reproductive health services: A systematic review. *American Journal of Public Health, 104,* 23-36.

Kahn, R., Holmes, C., Farley, J., & Kim-Spoon, J. (2015). Delay discounting mediates parent-adolescent relationship quality and risky sexual behavior for low self-control adolescents. *Journal of Youth and Adolescence, 44,* 1674-1687.

Kahneman, D. (2011). *Thinking, fast and slow.* New York: Farrar, Straus, and Giroux.

Kail, R. V., & Ferrer, E. (2007). Processing speed in childhood and adolescence: Longitudinal models for examining developmental change. *Child Development, 78,* 1760-1770.

Kakade, M., Duarte, C., Liu, X., Fuller, C., Drucker, E., Hoven, C., . . . Wu, P. (2012). Adolescent substance use and other illegal behaviors and racial disparities in criminal justice system involvement: Findings from a US national survey. *American Journal of Public Health, 102,* 1307-1310.

Kakihara, F., Tilton-Weaver, L., Kerr, M., & Stattin, H. (2010). The relationship of parental control to youth adjustment: Do youths' feelings about their parents play a role? *Journal of Youth and Adolescence, 39,* 1442-1456.

Kalakoski, V., & Nurmi, J.-E. (1998). Identity and educational transitions: Age differences in adolescent exploration and commitment related to education, occupation, and family. *Journal of Research on Adolescence, 8,* 29-47.

Kalil, A., & Ziol-Guest, K. (2008). Teacher support, school goal structures, and teenage mothers' school engagement. *Youth and Society, 39,* 524-548.

Kam, J., & Wang, N. (2015). Longitudinal effects of best-friend communication against substance use for Latino and non-Latino white early adolescents. *Journal of Research on Adolescence, 25,* 534-550.

Kambam, P., & Thompson, C. (2009). The development of decision-making capacities in children and adolescents: Psychological and neurological perspectives and their implications for juvenile defendants. *Behavioral Sciences & the Law, 27,* 173-190.

Kamenetz, A. (2006, May 30). Take this internship and shove it. *The New York Times,* p. A19.

Kan, E., Knowles, A., Peniche, M., Frick, P., Steinberg, L., & Cauffman, E. (2020). Neighborhood disorder and risk-taking among justice-involved youth: The mediating role of life expectancy. *Journal of Research on Adolescence,* in press.

Kandler, C. (2012). Nature and nurture in personality development: The case of neuroticism and extraversion. *Current Directions in Psychological Science, 21,* 290-296.

Kane, J., Damian, A., Fairman, B., Bass, J., Iwamoto, D., & Johnson, R. (2017). Differences in alcohol use patterns between adolescent Asian American ethnic groups: Representative estimates from the National Survey on Drug Use and Health 2002-2013. *Addictive Behavior, 64,* 154-158.

Kao, G., & Tienda, M. (1998). Educational aspirations of minority youth. *American Journal of Education, 106,* 349-384.

Kapetanovic, S., Rothenberg, W., Lansford, J., Bornstein, M., Chang, L., Deater-Deckard, K., . . . Bacchini, D. (2020). Cross-cultural examination of links between parent-adolescent communication and adolescent psychological problems in 12 cultural groups. *Journal of Youth and Adolescence, 49,* 1225-1244.

Karre, J. K., & Mounts, N. S. (2012). Nonresident fathers' parenting style and the adjustment of late-adolescent boys. *Journal of Family Issues, 33,* 1642-1657.

Karriker-Jaffe, K., Foshee, V., Ennett, S., & Suchindran, C. (2009). Sex differences in the effects of neighborhood socioeconomic disadvantage and social organization on rural adolescents' aggression trajectories. *American Journal of Community Psychology, 43,* 189-203.

Katz, A., Hensel, D., Hunt, A., Zaban, L., Hensley, M., & Ott, M. (2019). Only yes means yes: Sexual coercion in rural adolescent relationships. *Journal of Adolescent Health, 65,* 423-425.

Katz, E., Blumler, J., & Gurevitch, M. (1974). Uses and gratifications research. *Public Opinion Quarterly, 37,* 509-523.

Katz, M. (1975). *The people of Hamilton, Canada West: Family and class in a mid-nineteenth-century city.* Cambridge, MA: Harvard University Press.

Kaufman, T., Baams, L., & Veenstra, R. (2020). Disparities in persistent victimization and associated internalizing symptoms for heterosexual versus sexual minority youth. *Journal of Research on Adolescence, 30*(S2), 516-531.

Kaufman, T., Lee, H., Benner, A., & Yeager, D. (2020). How school contexts shape the relations among adolescents' beliefs, peer victimization, and depressive symptoms. *Journal of Research on Adolescence, 30,* 769-786.

Kaufman-Parks, A., DeMaris, A., Giordano, P., Manning, W., & Longmore, M. (2018). Familial effects on intimate partner violence perpetration across adolescence and young adulthood. *Journal of Family Issues, 39,* 1933-1961.

Kawabata, Y., Alink, L., Tseng, W., van IJzendoorn, M., & Crick, N. (2011). Maternal and paternal parenting styles associated with relational aggression in children and adolescents: A conceptual analysis and meta-analytic review. *Developmental Review, 31,* 240-278.

Kay, J., Shane, J., & Heckhausen, J. (2017). Youth's causal beliefs about success: Socioeconomic differences and prediction of early career development. *Journal of Youth and Adolescence, 46,* 2169-2180.

Keating, D. (2004). Cognitive and brain development. In R. Lerner & L. Steinberg (Eds.), *Handbook of adolescent psychology* (2nd ed.). New York: Wiley.

Keating, D. (2011). Cognitive development. In B. Brown & M. Prinstein (Eds.), *Encyclopedia of adolescence* (Vol. 1, pp. 106-114). New York: Academic Press.

Keel, P. K., & Klump, K. L. (2003). Are eating disorders culture-bound syndromes? Implications for conceptualizing their etiology. *Psychological Bulletin, 129,* 747-769.

Keijsers, L., & Laird, R. D. (2014). Mother-adolescent monitoring dynamics and the legitimacy of parental authority. *Journal of Adolescence, 37,* 515-524.

Keijsers, L., & Poulin, F. (2013). Developmental changes in parent-child communication throughout adolescence. *Developmental Psychology, 49,* 2301-2308.

Keijsers, L., Branje, S., Frijns, T., Finkenauer, C., & Meeus, W. (2010). Gender differences in keeping secrets from parents in adolescence. *Developmental Psychology, 46,* 293-298.

Keijsers, L., Branje, S., Hawk, S., Schwartz, S., Frijns, T., Koot, H., . . . Meuss, W. (2012). Forbidden friends as forbidden fruit: Parental supervision of friendships, contact with deviant peers, and adolescent delinquency. *Child Development, 83,* 651-656.

Keizer, R., Helmerhorst, K., & van Rijn-van Gelderen, L. (2019). Perceived quality of the mother-adolescent and father-adolescent attachment relationship and adolescents' self-esteem. *Journal of Youth and Adolescence, 48,* 1203-1217.

Kelleghan, A., Mali, L., Malamut, S., Badaly, D., Duong, M., & Schwartz, D. (2019). Cross-ethnic friendships, intergroup attitudes, intragroup social costs, and depressive symptoms among Asian-American and Latino-American youth. *Journal of Youth and Adolescence, 48,* 2165-2178.

Keller, M., Edelstein, W., Schmid, C., Fang, F., & Fang, G. (1998). Reasoning about responsibilities and obligations in close relationships: A comparison across two cultures. *Developmental Psychology, 34,* 731-741.

Kelly, A., Wall, M., Eisenberg, M., Story, M., & Neumark-Sztainer, D. (2005). Adolescent girls with high body satisfaction: Who are they and what can they teach us? *Journal of Adolescent Health, 37,* 391-396.

Kelly, S. (2009). The Black-White gap in mathematics course taking. *Sociology of Education, 82,* 47-69.

Kelsey, M., Layzer, C., Layzer, J., Price, C., Juras, R., Blocklin, M., & Mendez, J. (2016). Replicating ¡Cuidate!: 6-month impact findings of a randomized controlled trial. *American Journal of Public Health, 106,* S70-S77.

Kendig, S. M., Mattingly, M. J., & Bianchi, S. M. (2014). Childhood poverty and the transition to adulthood. *Family Relations, 63,* 271-286.

Keniston, K. (1970). Youth: A "new" stage of life. *American Scholar, 39,* 631-641.

Kennard, B., Silva, S., Tonev, S., Rohde, P., Hughes, J., Vitiello, B., . . . March, J. (2009). Remission and recovery in the treatment for adolescents with depression study (TADS): Acute and long-term outcomes. *Journal of the American Academy of Child and Adolescent Psychiatry, 48,* 186-195.

Kennedy, T. M., & Ceballo, R. (2016). Emotionally numb: Desensitization to community violence exposure among urban youth. *Developmental Psychology, 52,* 778-789.

Kenyon, D. B., Rankin, L. A., Koerner, S. S., & Dennison, R. P. (2007). What makes an adult? Examining descriptions from adolescents of divorce. *Journal of Youth and Adolescence, 36,* 813-823.

Kern, M., Benson, L., Steinberg, E., & Steinberg, L. (2016). The EPOCH measure of adolescent well-being. *Psychological Assessment, 5,* 586-597.

Kerns, K., & Brumariu, L. (2014). Is insecure parent-child attachment a risk factor for the development of anxiety in childhood or adolescence? *Child Development Perspectives, 8,* 12-17.

Kerpelman, J., McElwain, A., Pittman, J., & Adler-Baeder, F. (2016). Engagement in risky sexual behavior: Adolescents' perceptions of self and the parent-child relationship matter. *Youth & Society, 48,* 101-125.

Kerr, M., Stattin, H., & Özdemir, M. (2012). Perceived parenting style and adolescent adjustment: Revisiting directions of effects and the role of parental knowledge. *Developmental Psychology, 48,* 1540-1553.

Kessler, R., Avenevoli, S., Costello, J., Green, J., Gruber, M., McLaughlin, K., . . . Merikangas, K. R. (2012). Severity of 12-month DSM-IV disorders in the national comorbidity survey replication adolescent supplement. *Archives of General Psychiatry, 69,* 381-389.

Kessler, R., Berglun, P., Demler, O., Jin, R., Merikangas, K., & Walters, E. (2005). Lifetime prevalence and age-of-onset distributions of DSM-IV disorders in the National Comorbidity Survey Replication. *Archives of General Psychiatry, 62*(6), 593-602.

Kett, J. (1977). *Rites of passage: Adolescence in America, 1790 to the present.* New York: Basic Books.

Keyes, K., Gary, D., Beardslee, J., Prins, S., O'Malley, P., Rutherford, C., & Schulenberg, J. (2018). Joint effects of age, period, and cohort effects on conduct problems among American adolescents from 1991 through 2015. *American Journal of Epidemiology, 187,* 548-557.

Keyes, K., Hamilton, A., & Kandel, D. (2016). Birth cohorts analysis of adolescent cigarette smoking and subsequent marijuana and cocaine use. *American Journal of Public Health, 106,* 1143-1149.

Keyes, K., Schulenberg, J., O'Malley, P., Johnston, L., Bachman, J., Li, G., & Hasin, D. (2012). Birth cohort effects on adolescent alcohol use: The influence of social norms from 1976 to 2007. *Archives of General Psychiatry, 69,* 1304-1313.

Keyes, K. M., Maslowsky, J., Hamilton, A., & Schulenberg, J. (2015). The great sleep recession: Changes in sleep duration among US adolescents, 1991-2012. *Pediatrics, 135,* 460-468.

Khalife, N., Kantomaa, M., Glover, V., Tammelin, T., Laitinen, J., Ebeling, H., . . . Rodriguez, A. (2014). Childhood attention-deficit/hyperactivity disorder symptoms are risk factors for obesity and physical inactivity in adolescence. *Journal of the American Academy of Child & Adolescent Psychiatry, 53,* 425-436.

Khan, F., Chong, J., Theisen, J., Fraley, R., Young, J., & Hankin, B. (2020). Development and change in attachment: A multiwave assessment of attachment and its correlates across childhood and adolescence. *Journal of Personality and Social Psychology, 118,* 1188-1206.

Khan, S., Gagné, M., Yang, L., & Shapka, J. (2016). Exploring the relationship between adolescents' self-concept and their offline and online social worlds. *Computers in Human Behavior, 55,* 940-945.

Khundrakpam, B., Lewis, J., Zhao, L., Chouinard-Decorte, F., & Evans, A. (2016). Brain connectivity in normally developing children and adolescents. *Neuroimage, 134,* 192-203.

Khurana, A., Bleakley, A., Jordan, A., & Romer, D. (2015). The protective effects of parental monitoring and internet restriction on adolescents' risk of online harassment. *Journal of Youth and Adolescence, 44,* 1039-1047.

Khurana, A., Romer, D., Betancourt, L. M., & Hurt, H. (2018). Modeling trajectories of sensation seeking and impulsivity dimensions from early to late adolescence: Universal trends or distinct sub-groups? *Journal of Youth and Adolescence, 47,* 1992-2005.

Khurana, A., Romer, D., Betancourt, L., Brodsky, N., Giannetta, J., & Hurt, H. (2012). Early adolescent sexual debut: The mediating role of working memory ability, sensation seeking, and impulsivity. *Developmental Psychology, 48,* 1416-1428.

Kiang, L., & Bhattacharjee, K. (2019). Developmental change and correlates of autonomy in Asian American adolescents. *Journal of Youth and Adolescence, 48,* 410-421.

Kiang, L., & Buchanan, C. (2014). Daily stress and emotional well-being among Asian American adolescents: Same-day, lagged, and chronic associations. *Developmental Psychology, 50,* 611-621.

Kiang, L., & Fuligni, A. (2009). Ethnic identity and family processes among adolescents from Latin American, Asian, and European backgrounds. *Journal of Youth and Adolescence, 38,* 228-241.

Kiang, L., & Fuligni, A. (2010). Meaning in life as a mediator of ethnic identity and adjustment among adolescents from Latin, Asian, and European American backgrounds. *Journal of Youth and Adolescence, 39,* 1253-1264.

Kiang, L., & Witkow, M. (2018). Identifying as American among adolescents from Asian backgrounds. *Journal of Youth and Adolescence, 47,* 64-76.

Kiang, L., Andrews, K., Stein, G. L., Supple, A. J., & Gonzales, L. M. (2013). Socioeconomic stress and academic adjustment among Asian American adolescents: The protective role of family

obligation. *Journal of Youth & Adolescence, 42,* 837-847.

Kiang, L., Peterson, J. L., & Thompson, T. L. (2011). Ethnic peer preferences among Asian American adolescents in emerging immigrant communities. *Journal of Research on Adolescence, 21,* 754-761.

Kiang, L., Supple, A., & Stein, G. (2019). Latent profiles of discrimination and socialization predicting ethnic identity and well-being among Asian American Adolescents. *Journal of Research on Adolescence, 29,* 523-538.

Kiang, L., Supple, A., Stein, G., & Gonzales, L. (2012). Gendered academic adjustment among Asian American adolescents in an emerging immigrant community. *Journal of Youth & Adolescence, 41,* 283-294.

Kiang, L., Witkow, M., & Thompson, T. (2016). Model minority stereotyping, perceived discrimination, and adjustment among adolescents from Asian American backgrounds. *Journal of Youth and Adolescence, 45,* 1366-1379.

Kiang, L., Witkow, M., Baldelomar, O., & Fuligni, A.(2010). Change in ethnic identity across the high school years among adolescents with Latin American, Asian, and European backgrounds. *Journal of Youth and Adolescence, 39,* 683-693.

Kidd, S. A. (2004). "The walls were closing in, and we were trapped": A qualitative analysis of street youth suicide. *Youth and Society, 36,* 30-55.

Kiefer, S., & Wang, J. (2016). Associations of coolness and social goals with aggression and engagement during adolescence. *Journal of Applied Developmental Psychology, 44,* 52-62.

Kiesner, J., Poulin, F., & Nicotra, E. (2003). Peer relations across contexts: Individual-network homophily and network inclusion in and after school. *Child Development, 74,* 1328-1343.

Kilford, E. J., Garrett, E., & Blakemore, S-J. (2016). The development of social cognition in adolescence: An integrated perspective. *Neuroscience and Biobehavioral Reviews, 70,* 106-120.

Killen, M., Rutland, A., Abrams, D., Mulvey, K. L., & Hitti, A. (2013). Development of intra- and intergroup judgments in the context of moral and social-conventional norms. *Child Development, 84,* 1063-1080.

Killoren, S., & Deutsch, A. (2014). A longitudinal examination of parenting processes and Latino youth's risky sexual behaviors. *Journal of Youth & Adolescence, 43,* 1982-1993.

Killoren, S., Campione-Barr, N., Jones, S., & Giron, S. (2019). Adolescent girls' disclosure about dating and sexuality. *Journal of Family Issues, 40,* 887-910.

Kim, H., & Capaldi, D. (2004). The association of antisocial behavior and depressive symptoms between partners and risk for aggression in romantic relationships. *Journal of Family Psychology, 18,* 82-96.

Kim, H., Parker, J., & Walker Marciano, A. (2017). Interplay of self-esteem, emotion regulation, and parenting in young adolescents' friendship jealousy. *Journal of Applied Developmental Psychology, 52,* 170-180.

Kim, J.-I., Schallert, D., & Kim, M. (2010). An integrative cultural view of achievement motivation: Parental and classroom predictors of children's goal orientations when learning mathematics in

Korea. *Journal of Educational Psychology, 102,* 418-437.

Kim, S., & Hill, N. (2015). Including fathers in the picture: A meta-analysis of parental involvement and students' academic achievement. *Journal of Educational Psychology, 107,* 919-934.

Kim, S., Colwell, S., Kata, A., Boyle, M., & Georgiades, K. (2018). Cyberbullying victimization and adolescent mental health: Evidence of differential effects by sex and mental health problem type. *Journal of Youth and Adolescence, 47,* 661-672.

Kim, S., Wang, Y., Deng, S., Alvarez, R., & Li, J. (2011). Accent, perpetual foreigner stereotype, and perceived discrimination as indirect links between English proficiency and depressive symptoms in Chinese American adolescents. *Developmental Psychology, 47,* 289-301.

Kim, S., Wang, Y., Shen, Y., & Hou, Y. (2015). Stability and change in adjustment profiles among Chinese American adolescents: The role of parenting. *Journal of Youth and Adolescence, 44,* 1735-1751.

Kim, Y., & Stattin, H. (2019). Parent-youth discussions about politics from age 13 to 28. *Journal of Applied Developmental Psychology, 62,* 249-259.

Kimonis, E., Graham, N., & Cauffman, E. (2018). Aggressive male juvenile offenders with callous-unemotional traits show aberrant attentional orienting to distress cues. *Journal of Abnormal Child Psychology, 46,* 519-527.

Kim-Spoon, J., Deater-Deckard, K., Lauharatanahirun, N., Farley, J. P., Chiu, P. H., Bickel, W. K., & King-Casas, B. (2017). Neural interaction between risk sensitivity and cognitive control predicting health risk behaviors among late adolescents. *Journal of Research on Adolescence, 27,* 674-682.

Kim-Spoon, J., Longo, G., & Holmes, C. (2015). Bifactor modeling of general vs. specific factors of religiousness differentially predicting substance use risk in adolescence. *Journal of Adolescence, 43,* 15-19.

King, M. D., Jennings, J., & Fletcher, J. M. (2014). Medical adaptation to academic pressure schooling, stimulant use, and socioeconomic status. *American Sociological Review, 79,* 1039-1066.

King, P., & Roeser, R. (2009). Religion and spirituality in adolescent development. In R. Lerner & L. Steinberg (Eds.), *Handbook of adolescent psychology* (3rd ed., Vol. 1, pp. 435-478). New York: Wiley.

King, P., Ramos, J., & Clardy, C. (2013). Searching for the sacred: Religious and spiritual development among adolescents. In K. I. Pargament, J. Exline, & J. Jones (Eds.), *APA handbook of psychology, religion and spirituality.* Washington D.C.: American Psychological Association.

King, V., & Mrug, S. (2016). The relationship between violence exposure and academic achievement in African American adolescents is moderated by emotion regulation. *The Journal of Early Adolescence, 38,* 497-512.

King, V., Boyd, L., & Pragg, B. (2018). Parent-adolescent closeness, family belonging, and adolescent well-being across family structures. *Journal of Family Issues, 39,* 2007-2036.

Kirby, D. (2007). *Emerging answers 2007: Research findings on programs to reduce teen pregnancy and sexually transmitted diseases.* Washington,

DC: National Campaign to Prevent Teen and Unplanned Pregnancy.

Kirby, D., & Laris, B. (2009). Effective curriculum-based sex and STD/HIV education programs for adolescents. *Child Development Perspectives, 3,* 21-29.

Kircanski, K., Sisk, L. M., Ho, T. C., Humphreys, K. L., King, L. S., Colich, N. L., . . . & Gotlib, I. H. (2019). Early life stress, cortisol, frontolimbic connectivity, and depressive symptoms during puberty. *Development and Psychopathology, 31,* 1011-1022.

Kirk, D. (2009). Unraveling the contextual effects on student suspension and juvenile arrest: The independent and interdependent influences of school, neighborhood, and family social controls. *Criminology, 47,* 479-520.

Kirschenbaum, D. S., & Gierut, K. (2013). Treatment of childhood and adolescent obesity: An integrative review of recent recommendations from five expert groups. *Journal of Consulting and Clinical Psychology, 81,* 347-360.

Kistler, M., Rodgers, K., Power, T., Austin, E., & Hill, L. (2010). Adolescents and music media: Toward an involvement-mediational model of consumption and self-concept. *Journal of Research on Adolescence, 20,* 616-630.

Kiuru, N., Burk, W., Laursen, B., Nurmi, J., & Salmela-Aro, K. (2012). Is depression contagious? A test of alternative peer socialization mechanisms of depressive symptoms in adolescent peer networks. *Journal of Adolescent Health, 50,* 250-255.

Kiuru, N., Salmela-Aro, K., Nurmi, J. E., Zettergren, P., Andersson, H., & Bergman, L. (2012). Best friends in adolescence show similar educational careers in early adulthood. *Journal of Applied Developmental Psychology, 33,* 102-111.

Kiuru, N., Wang, M.-T., Salmela-Aro, K., Kannas, L., Ahonen, T., & Hirvonen, R. (2020). Associations between adolescents' interpersonal relationships, school well-being, and academic achievement during educational transitions. *Journal of Youth and Adolescence, 49,* 1057-1072.

Klahr, A., McGue, M., Iacono, W., & Burt, S. (2011). The association between parent-child conflict and adolescent conduct problems over time: Results from a longitudinal adoption study. *Journal of Abnormal Psychology, 120,* 46-56.

Klahr, A., Rueter, M., McGue, M., Iacono, W., & Burt, S. (2011). The relationship between parent-child conflict and adolescent antisocial behavior: Confirming shared environmental mediation. *Journal of Abnormal Child Psychology, 39,* 683-694.

Klassen, R., Ang, R., Chong, W., Krawchuk, L., Huan, V., Wong, I., & Yeo, L. (2009). A cross-cultural study of adolescent procrastination. *Journal of Research on Adolescence, 19,* 799-811.

Kleibeuker, S. W., Koolschijn, P. C., Jolles, D. D., De Dreu, C. K., & Crone, E. A. (2013). The neural coding of creative idea generation across adolescence and early adulthood. *Frontiers in Human Neuroscience, 7,* 905.

Kleibeuker, S. W., Stevenson, C. E., van der Aar, L., Overgaauw, S., van Duijvenvoorde, A. C., & Crone, E. A. (2017). Training in the adolescent brain: An fMRI training study on divergent thinking. *Developmental Psychology, 53,* 353-365.

Klein, J., & Cornell, D. (2010). Is the link between large high schools and student victimization an illusion? *Journal of Educational Psychology, 102,* 933-946.

Klein, V., Becker, I., & Štulhofer, A. (2018). Parenting, communication about sexuality, and the development of adolescent womens' sexual agency: A longitudinal assessment. *Journal of Youth and Adolescence, 47,* 1486-1498.

Kleinepier, T., & van Ham, M. (2018). The temporal dynamics of neighborhood disadvantage in childhood and subsequent problem behavior in adolescence. *Journal of Youth and Adolescence, 47,* 1611-1628.

Klimstra, T., Hale, W., Raaijmakers, Q., Branje, S., & Meeus, W. (2009). Maturation of personality in adolescence. *Journal of Personality and Social Psychology, 96,* 898-912.

Klimstra, T., Hale, W., Raaijmakers, Q., Branje, S., & Meeus, W. (2010). Identity formation in adolescence: Change or stability? *Journal of Youth and Adolescence, 39,* 150-162.

Kling, J., Ludwig, J., & Katz, L. F. (2005). Neighborhood effects on crime for female and male youth: Evidence from a randomized housing voucher experiment. *Quarterly Journal of Economics, 120,* 87-130.

Klingberg, T. (2006). Development of a superior frontal-intraparietal network for visuo-spatial working memory. *Neuropsychologia, 44,* 2171-2177.

Klodnick, V. V., Guterman, N., Haj-Yahia, M. M., & Leshem, B. (2014). Exploring adolescent community violence exposure and posttraumatic stress cross-culturally in Israel. *Journal of Community Psychology, 42,* 47-60.

Kloep, M., & Hendry, L. B. (2014). Some ideas on the emerging future of developmental research. *Journal of Adolescence, 37,* 1541-1545.

Klopack, E., Sutton, T., Simons, R., & Simons, L. (2020). Disentangling the effects of boys' pubertal timing: The importance of social context. *Journal of Youth and Adolescence, 49,* 1393-1405.

Klostermann, S., Connell, A., & Stormshak, E. (2016). Gender differences in the developmental links between conduct problems and depression across early adolescence. *Journal of Research on Adolescence, 26,* 76-89.

Knecht, A., Burk, W., Weesie, J., & Steglich, C. (2011). Friendship and alcohol use in early adolescence: A multilevel social network approach. *Journal of Research on Adolescence, 21,* 475-487.

Knifsend, C., & Graham, S. (2012). Too much of a good thing? How breadth of extracurricular participation relates to school-related affect and academic outcomes during adolescence. *Journal of Youth & Adolescence, 41,* 379-389.

Knifsend, C., & Juvonen, J. (2014). Social identity complexity, cross-ethnic friendships, and intergroup attitudes in urban middle schools. *Child Development, 85,* 709-721.

Knifsend, C., & Juvonen, J. (2017). Extracurricular activities in multiethnic middle schools: Ideal context for positive intergroup attitudes? *Journal of Research on Adolescence, 27,* 407-422.

Knifsend, C., Camacho-Thompson, D., Juvonen, J., & Graham, S. (2018). Friends in activities, school-related affect, and academic outcomes in diverse middle schools. *Journal of Youth and Adolescence, 47,* 1208-1220.

Knight, G., Carlo, G., Basilio, C., & Jacobson, R. (2015). Familism values, perspective taking, and prosocial moral reasoning: Predicting prosocial tendencies among Mexican American adolescents. *Journal of Research on Adolescence, 25,* 717-727.

Knight, G. P., Mazza, G. L., & Carlo, G. (2018). Trajectories of familism values and the prosocial tendencies of Mexican American adolescents. *Developmental Psychology, 54,* 378-384.

Knite, G., Carlo, G., Streit, C., & White, R. (2017). A model of maternal and paternal ethnic socialization of Mexican-American adolescents' self-views. *Child Development, 88,* 1885-1896.

Knoester, C., Haynie, D. L., & Stephens, C. M. (2006). Parenting practices and adolescents' friendship networks. *Journal of Marriage and Family, 68,* 1247-1260.

Knoll, L., Leung, J., Foulkes, L., & Blakemore, S-J. (2017). Age-related differences in social influence on risk perception depend on the direction of influence. *Journal of Adolescence, 60,* 53-63.

Knoll, L., Magis-Weinberg, L., Speekenbrink, M., & Blakemore, S-J. (2015). Social influence on risk perception during adolescence. *Psychological Science, 26,* 583-592.

Knoll, L. J., Fuhrmann, D., Sakhardande, A. L., Stamp, F., Speekenbrink, M., & Blakemore, S-J. (2016). A window of opportunity for cognitive training in adolescence. *Psychological Science, 27,* 1620-1631.

Knowles, A., Rinehart, J., Steinberg, L., Frick, P., & Cauffman, E. (2020). Risky sexual behavior among arrested adolescent males: The role of future expectations and impulse control. *Journal of Research on Adolescence, 30*(S2), 562-579.

Knutson, B., & Adcock, R. (2005). Remembrance of rewards past. *Neuron, 45,* 331-332.

Ko, L., & Perreira, K. (2010). "It turned my world upside down": Latino youths' perspectives on immigration. *Journal of Adolescent Research, 25,* 465-493.

Kobak, R., & Madsen, S. (2011). Attachment. In B. Brown & M. Prinstein (Eds.), *Encyclopedia of adolescence* (Vol. 2, pp. 18-24). New York: Academic Press.

Kobak, R., Cole, H., Ferenz-Gillies, R., Fleming, W., & Gamble, W. (1993). Attachment and emotion regulation during mother-teen problem-solving: A control theory analysis. *Child Development, 64,* 231-245.

Kobak, R., Zajac, K., & Smith, C. (2009). Adolescent attachment and trajectories of hostile-impulsive behavior: Implications for the development of personality disorders. *Development and Psychopathology, 21,* 839.

Koch, M., Mendle, J., & Beam, C. (2020). Psychological distress amid change: Role disruption in girls during the adolescent transition. *Journal of Abnormal Child Psychology, 48,* 1211-1222.

Kochel, K., Miller, C., Updegraff, K., Ladd, G., & Kochenderfer-Ladd, B. (2012). Associations between fifth graders' gender atypical problem behavior and peer relationships: a short-term longitudinal study. *Journal of Youth & Adolescence, 41,* 1022-1034.

Kochel, K. P., Ladd, G. W., Bagwell, C. L., & Yabko, B. A. (2015). Bully/victim profiles' differential risk for worsening peer acceptance: The role of friendship. *Journal of Applied Developmental Psychology, 41,* 38-45.

Kochendorfer, L., & Kerns, K. (2017). Perceptions of parent-child attachment relationships and friendship qualities: Predictors of romantic relationship involvement and quality in adolescence. *Journal of Youth and Adolescence, 46,* 1009-1021.

Kochendorfer, L., & Kerns, K. (2020). A meta-analysis of friendship qualities and romantic relationship outcomes in adolescence. *Journal of Research on Adolescence, 30,* 4-25.

Koff, E., & Rierdan, J. (1996). Premenarcheal expectations and postmenarcheal experiences of positive and negative menstrual related changes. *Journal of Adolescent Health, 18,* 286-291.

Kogan, S., Yu, T., Allen, K., & Brody, G. (2015). Racial microstressors, racial self-concept, and depressive symptoms among male African Americans during the transition to adulthood. *Journal of Youth and Adolescence, 44,* 898-909.

Kogan, S. M., Cho, J., Simons, L. G., Allen, K. A., Beach, S. R. H., Simons, R. L., & Gibbons, F. X. (2015). Pubertal timing and sexual risk behaviors among rural African American male youth: Testing a model based on life history theory. *Archives of Sexual Behavior, 44,* 609-618.

Kohler, J. K., Grotevant, H. D., & McRoy, R. G. (2002). Adopted adolescents' preoccupation with adoption: The impact on adoptive family relationships. *Journal of Marriage and Family, 64,* 93-104.

Kolburn Kowal, A., & Blinn-Pike, L. (2004). Sibling influences on adolescents' attitudes toward safe sex practices. *Family Relations, 53,* 377-384.

Kolla, B., He, J-P., Mansukhani, M., Kotagal, S., Frye, M., & Merikangas, K. (2020). Prevalence and correlates of hypersomnolence symptoms in US teens. *Journal of the American Academy of Child and Adolescent Psychiatry, 58,* 712-720.

Kollerová, L., Yanagida, T., Mazzone, A., Soukup, P., & Strohmeier, D. (2018). "They think that I should defend": Effects of peer and teacher injunctive norms on defending victimized classmates in early adolescents. *Journal of Youth and Adolescence, 47,* 2424-2439.

Költó, A., Young, H., Burke, L., Moreau, N., Cosma, A., Magnusson, J., . . . Gabhainn, S. N. (2018). Love and dating patterns for same- and both-gender attracted adolescents across Europe. *Journal of Research on Adolescence, 28,* 772-778.

Kornbluh, M., Pykett, A., & Flanagan, C. (2019). Exploring the associations between youths' explanations of poverty at the societal level and judgements of distributive justice. *Developmental Psychology, 55,* 488-497.

Kornienko, O., Ha, T., & Dishion, T. (2020). Dynamic pathways between rejection and antisocial behavior in peer networks: Update and test of confluence model. *Development and Psychopathology, 32,* 175-188.

Kornienko, O., Santos, C. E., Martin, C. L., & Granger, K. L. (2016). Peer influence on gender identity development in adolescence. *Developmental Psychology, 52,* 1578-1592.

Kosciw, J., Palmer, N., & Kull, R. (2015). Reflecting resiliency: Openness about sexual orientation and/or gender identity and its relationship to well-being and educational outcomes for LGBT students. *American Journal of Community Psychology, 55,* 167-178.

Kosir, K., Horvat, M., Aram, U., Jurinec, N., & Tement, S. (2016). Does being on Facebook make me (feel) accepted in the classroom? The relationships between early adolescents' Facebook usage, classroom peer acceptance and self-concept. *Computers in Human Behavior, 62,* 375-384.

Kost, K., & Henshaw, S. (2014). US teen pregnancies, births, and abortions. New York: Guttmacher Institute. Available online at http://www.childtrends.org/wp-content/uploads/2012/07/27_fig1.jpg. Accessed on July 14, 2015.

Kotchick, B., Whitsett, D. & Sherman, M. (2020). Food insecurity and adolescent psychosocial adjustment: Indirect pathways through caregiver adjustment and caregiver-adolescent relationship quality. *Journal of Youth and Adolescence,* online ahead of print.

Kouros, C. D., & Garber, J. (2014). Trajectories of individual depressive symptoms in adolescents: Gender and family relationships as predictors. *Developmental Psychology, 50,* 2633-2643.

Kowal, A., & Kramer, L. (1997). Children's understanding of parental differential treatment. *Child Development, 68,* 113-126.

Kowaleski-Jones, L., & Dunifon, R. (2006). Family structure and community context: Evaluating influences on adolescent outcomes. *Youth and Society, 38,* 110-130.

Koyanagi, A., Oh, H., Carvalho, A., Smith, L., Haro, J., Vancampfort, D., . . . DeVylder, J. (2019). Bullying victimization and suicide attempt among adolescents aged 12-15 years from 48 countries. *Journal of the American Academy of Child & Adolescent Psychiatry, 58,* 907-918.

Krahé, B., Busching, R., & Möller, I. (2012). Media violence use and aggression among German adolescents: Associations and trajectories of change in a three-wave longitudinal study. *Psychology of Popular Media Culture, 1,* 152-166.

Kramer, L., & Kowal, A. K. (2005). Sibling relationship quality from birth to adolescence: The enduring contributions of friends. *Journal of Family Psychology, 19,* 503-511.

Krauss, S., Orth, U., & Robins, R. W. (2020). Family environment and self-esteem development: A longitudinal study from age 10 to 16. *Journal of Personality and Social Psychology, 119*(2), 457.

Kreager, D., & Haynie, D. (2011). Dangerous liaisons? Dating and drinking diffusion in adolescent peer networks. *American Sociological Review, 76,* 737-763.

Kreager, D., Molloy, L., Moody, J., & Feinberg, M. (2016). Friends first? The peer network origins of adolescent dating. *Journal of Research on Adolescence, 26,* 257-269.

Kreager, D. A. (2007a). When it's good to be "bad": Violence and adolescent peer acceptance. *Criminology: An Interdisciplinary Journal, 45,* 893-923.

Kreager, D. A. (2007b). Unnecessary roughness? School sports, peer networks, and male adolescent violence. *American Sociological Review, 72,* 705-724.

Kretsch, N., & Harden, K. P. (2014). Pubertal development and peer influence on risky decision making. *The Journal of Early Adolescence, 34,* 339-359.

Kretsch, N., Mendle, J., & Harden, P. (2016). A twin study of objective and subjective pubertal timing and peer influence on risk-taking. *Journal of Research on Adolescence, 26,* 45-59.

Kretschmer, T., Oliver, B. R., & Maughan, B. (2014). Pubertal development, spare time activities, and adolescent delinquency: Testing the contextual amplification hypothesis. *Journal of Youth and Adolescence, 43,* 1346-1360.

Kretschmer, T., Sentse, M., Meeus, W., Verhulst, F., Veenstra, R., & Oldehinkel, A. (2016). Configurations of adolescents' peer experiences: Associations with parent-child relationship quality and parental problem behavior. *Journal of Research on Adolescence, 26,* 474-491.

Krettenauer, T., & Victor, R. (2017). Why be moral? Moral identity motivation and age. *Developmental Psychology, 53,* 1589-1596.

Kroger, J. (1993). The role of historical context in the identity formation process of late adolescence. *Youth and Society, 24,* 363-376.

Kroger, J. (2003). Identity development during adolescence. In G. R. Adams, & M. D. Berzonsky (Eds.), *Blackwell handbook of adolescence* (pp. 205-226). Malden, MA: Blackwell.

Kroger, J., & Green, K. (1996). Events associated with identity status change. *Journal of Adolescence, 19,* 477-490.

Krygsman, A., & Vaillancourt, T. (2017). Longitudinal associations between depression symptoms and peer experiences: Evidence of symptoms-driven pathways. *Journal of Applied Developmental Psychology, 51,* 20-34.

Kubiszewski, V., Fontaine, R., Potard, C., & Auzoult, L. (2015). Does cyberbullying overlap with school bullying when taking modality of involvement into account? *Computers in Human Behavior, 43,* 49-57.

Kuhlman, K., Geiss, E., Vargas, I., & Lopez-Duran, N. (2018). HPA-axis activation as a key moderator of childhood trauma exposure and adolescent mental health. *Journal of Abnormal Child Psychology, 46,* 149-157.

Kuhlman, K., Chiang, J., Bower, J., Irwin, M., Seeman, T., McCreath, H. E., . . . Fuligni, A. J. (2020). Sleep problems in adolescence are prospectively linked to later depressive symptoms via the cortisol awakening response. *Development and Psychopathology, 32,* 997-1006.

Kuhn, D. (2009). Adolescent thinking. In R. Lerner & L. Steinberg (Eds.), *Handbook of adolescent psychology* (3rd ed., Vol. 1, pp. 152-186). New York: Wiley.

Kuhn, E. S., Phan, J. M., & Laird, R. D. (2014). Compliance with parents' rules: Between-person and within-person predictions. *Journal of Youth & Adolescence, 43,* 245-256.

Kulis, S., Marsiglia, F., & Hurdle, D. (2003). Gender identity, ethnicity, acculturation, and drug use: Exploring differences among adolescents in the Southwest. *Journal of Community Psychology, 31,* 167-188.

Kumpfer, K. L., & Alvarado, R. (2003). Family-strengthening approaches for the prevention of youth problem behaviors. *American Psychologist, 58,* 457-465.

Kunkel, D., Eyal, E., Finnerty, K., Biely, E., & Donnerstein, E. (2005). *Sex on TV.* Menlo Park, CA: Kaiser Family Foundation.

Kuperminc, G., Darnell, A., & Alvarez-Jimenez, A. (2008). Parent involvement in the academic adjustment of Latino middle and high school youth: Teacher expectations and school belonging as mediators. *Journal of Adolescence, 31,* 469–483.

Kurdek, L., & Fine, M. (1993). The relation between family structure and young adolescents' appraisals of family climate and parenting behavior. *Journal of Family Issues, 14,* 279–290.

Kurlychek, M., & Johnson, B. (2010). Juvenility and punishment: Sentencing juveniles in adult criminal court. *Criminology, 48,* 725–758.

Kuttler, A., & La Greca, A. (2004). Linkages among adolescent girls' romantic relationships, best friendships, and peer networks. *Journal of Adolescence, 27,* 395–414.

Kuttler, A., La Greca, A., & Prinstein, M. (1999). Friendship qualities and social–emotional functioning of adolescents with close, cross-sex friendships. *Journal of Research on Adolescence, 9,* 339–366.

Kwon, J.-S., & Park, S. (2018). Adaptation to transition: Meaning of menarche for female adolescents in South Korea. *The Journal of Early Adolescence, 39,* 520–538.

Kwong, A., Manley, D., Timpson, N., Pearson, R., Heron, J., Sallis, H., . . . Leckie, G. (2019). Identifying critical points of trajectories of depressive symptoms from childhood to young adulthood. *Journal of Youth and Adolescence, 48,* 815–827.

Kypri, K., Voas, R., Langley, J., Stephenson, S., Begg, D., Tippetts, A., & Davie, G. (2006). Minimum purchasing age for alcohol and traffic crash injuries among 15- to 19-year-olds in New Zealand. *American Journal of Public Health, 96,* 126–131.

L'Engle, K., & Jackson, C. (2008). Socialization influences on early adolescents' cognitive susceptibility and transition to sexual intercourse. *Journal of Research on Adolescence, 18,* 353–378.

L'Engle, K., Brown, J., & Kenneavy, K. (2006). The mass media are an important context for adolescents' sexual behavior. *Journal of Adolescent Health, 38,* 186–192.

La Greca, A., & Silverman, W. (2009). Treatment and prevention of posttraumatic stress reactions in children and adolescents exposed to disasters and terrorism: What is the evidence? *Child Development Perspectives, 3,* 4–10.

la Roi, C., Dijkstra, J., Kretschmer, T., Savickaitė, R., & Veenstra, R. (2020). Peers and homophobic attitudes in adolescence: Examining selection and influence processes in friendships and antipathies. *Journal of Youth and Adolescence, 49,* 2229–2245.

Laceulle, O., Veenstra, R., Vollebergh, W., & Ormel, J. (2017). Sequences of maladaptation: Preadolescent self-regulation, adolescent negative social interactions, and young adult psychopathology. *Development and Psychopathology, 12,* 1–14.

Lachman, M. (2004). Development in midlife. *Annual Review of Psychology, 55,* 305–331.

Ladd, G., Ettekal, I., & Kochenderfer-Ladd, B. (2017). Peer victimization trajectories from kindergarten through high school: Differential pathways for children's school engagement and achievement? *Journal of Educational Psychology, 109,* 826–841.

Ladd, G., Ettekal, I., Kochenderfer-Ladd, B., Rudolph, K., & Andrews, R. (2014). Relations among chronic peer group rejection, maladaptive behavioral dispositions, and early adolescents' peer perceptions. *Child Development, 85,* 971–988.

Ladouceur, C. D., Dahl, R. E., & Carter, C. S. (2007). Development of action monitoring through adolescence into adulthood: ERP and source localization. *Developmental Science, 10,* 874–891.

LaFleur, L., Zhao, Y., Zeringue, M., & Laird, R. (2016). Warmth and legitimacy beliefs contextualize adolescents' negative reactions to parental monitoring. *Journal of Adolescence, 51,* 58–67.

Lahat, A., Helwig, C. C., & Zelazo, P. D. (2013). An event-related potential study of adolescents' and young adults' judgments of moral and social conventional violations. *Child Development, 84,* 938–954.

Lai, T., & Kao, G. (2018). Hit, robbed, and put down (but not bullied): Underreporting of bullying by minority and male students. *Journal of Youth and Adolescence, 47,* 619–635.

Laible, D., Carlo, G., & Raffaelli, M. (2000). The differential relations of parent and peer attachment to adolescent adjustment. *Journal of Youth and Adolescence, 29,* 45–59.

Laird, R., & Marrero, M. (2011). Mothers' knowledge of early adolescents' activities following the middle school transition and pubertal maturation. *Journal of Early Adolescence, 31,* 209–233.

Laird, R., Marrero, M., & Sentse, M. (2010). Revisiting parental monitoring: Evidence that parental solicitation can be effective when needed most. *Journal of Youth and Adolescence, 39,* 1431–1441.

Laird, R., Marrero, M., Melching, J., & Kuhn, E. (2013). Information management strategies in early adolescence: Developmental change in use and transactional associations with psychological adjustment. *Developmental Psychology, 49,* 928–937.

Laird, R., Pettit, G., Dodge, K., & Bates, J. (2005). Peer relationship antecedents of delinquent behavior in late adolescence: Is there evidence of demographic group differences in developmental processes? *Development and Psychopathology, 17,* 127–144.

Laird, R. D., Bridges, B. J., & Marsee, M. A. (2013). Secrets from friends and parents: Longitudinal links with depression and antisocial behavior. *Journal of Adolescence, 36,* 685–693.

Lakon, C., Hipp, J., Wang, C., Butts, C., & Jose, R. (2015). Simulating dynamic network models and adolescent smoking: The impact of varying peer influence and peer selection. *American Journal of Public Health, 105,* 2438–2448.

Lam, C. B., McHale, S. M., & Crouter, A. C. (2014). Time with peers from middle childhood to late adolescence: Developmental course and adjustment correlates. *Child Development, 85,* 1677–1693.

Lam, C., & McHale, S. (2015). Time use as cause and consequence of youth development. *Child Development Perspectives, 9,* 20–25.

Lam, C., McHale, S., & Crouter, A. (2014). Time with peers from middle childhood to late adolescence: Developmental course and adjustment correlates. *Child Development, 85,* 1677–1693.

Lam, T., Shi, H., Ho, L., Stewart, S. M., & Fan, S. (2002). Timing of pubertal maturation and heterosexual behavior among Hong Kong Chinese adolescents. *Archives of Sexual Behavior, 31,* 359–366.

Lambert, H. K., King, K. M., Monahan, K. C., & McLaughlin, K. A. (2017). Differential associations of threat and deprivation with emotion regulation and cognitive control in adolescence. *Development and Psychopathology, 29,* 929–940.

Lampard, A. M., MacLehose, R. F., Eisenberg, M. E., Neumark-Sztainer, D., & Davison, K. K. (2014). Weight-related teasing in the school environment: Associations with psychosocial health and weight control practices among adolescent boys and girls. *Journal of Youth and Adolescence, 43,* 1770–1780.

Landoll, R., La Greca, A., Lai, B., Chan, S., & Herge, W. (2015). Cyber victimization by peers: Prospective associations with adolescent social anxiety and depressive symptoms. *Journal of Adolescence, 42,* 77–86.

Lang, F., & Carstensen, L. (2002). Time counts: Future time perspective, goals, and social relationships. *Psychology and Aging, 17,* 125–139.

Langer, L., Zimmerman, R., & Katz, J. (1995). Virgins' expectations and nonvirgins' reports: How adolescents feel about themselves. *Journal of Adolescent Research, 10,* 291–306.

Laninga-Wijnen, L., Harakeh, Z., Garandeau, C., Dijkstra, J., Veenstra, R., & Vollebergh, W. (2019). Classroom popularity hierarchy predicts prosocial and aggressive popularity norms across the school year. *Child Development, 90,* e637–e653.

Laninga-Wijnen, L., Harakeh, Z., Steglich, C., Dijkstra, J., Veenstra, R., & Vollebergh, W. (2017). The norms of popular peers moderate friendship dynamics of adolescent aggression. *Child Development, 88,* 1265–1283.

Laninga-Wijnen, L., Ryan, A., Harakeh, Z., Shin, H., & Vollebergh, W. (2018). The moderating role of popular peers' achievement goals in 5th-and 6th-graders' achievement-related friendships: A social network analysis. *Journal of Educational Psychology, 110,* 289.

Laninga-Wijnen, L., Steglich, C., Harakeh, Z., Vollebergh, W., Veenstra, R., & Dijkstra, J. (2020). The role of prosocial and aggressive popularity norm combinations in prosocial and aggressive friendship processes. *Journal of Youth and Adolescence, 49,* 645–663.

Lansford, J., Dodge, K., Pettit, G., & Bates, J. (2016). A public health perspective on school dropout and adult outcomes: A prospective study of risk and protective factors from age 5 to 27 years. *Journal of Adolescent Health, 58,* 652–658.

Lansford, J., Yu, T., Pettit, G., Bates, J., & Dodge, K. (2014). Pathways of peer relationships from childhood to young adulthood. *Journal of Applied Developmental Psychology, 35,* 111–117.

Lansford, J. E., Rothenberg, W. A., Riley, J., Uribe Tirado, L. M., Yotanyamaneewong, S., Alampay, L. P., . . . Steinberg, L. (2021). Longitudinal trajectories of four domains of parenting in relation to adolescent age and puberty in nine countries. *Child Development,* in press.

Lansford, J. E., Rothenberg, W., Jensen, T., Lippold, M., Bacchini, D., Bornstein, M., . . . Al-Hassan, S. (2018). Bidirectional relations between parenting and behavior problems from age 8 to 13 in nine countries. *Journal of Research on Adolescence, 28,* 571–590.

Lansu, T., & Cillessen, A. (2011). Peer status in emerging adulthood: Associations of popularity and preference with social roles and behavior. *Journal of Adolescent Research, 27,* 132–150.

Lansu, T., Cillessen, A., & Karremans, J. (2012). Implicit associations with popularity in early adolescence: An approach-avoidance analysis. *Developmental Psychology, 48,* 65–75.

Lansu, T. A. M., Cillessen, A. H. N., & Karremans, J. C. (2014). Adolescents' selective visual attention for high-status peers: The role of perceiver status and gender. *Child Development, 85,* 421–428.

Lantagne, A., & Furman, W. (2017). Romantic relationship development: The interplay between age and relationship length. *Developmental Psychology, 53,* 1738–1749.

Lardier, D., Barrios, V., Forenza, B., Herr, K., Bergeson, C., Suazo, C., . . . Reid, R. (2020). Contextualizing negative sense of community and disconnection among urban youth of color: "Community. . . We ain't got that." *Journal of Community Psychology, 48,* 834–848.

Lardier, D., Opara, I., Bergeson, C., Herrera, A., Garcia-Reid, P., & Reid, R. (2019). A study of psychological sense of community as a mediator between supportive social systems, school belongingness, and outcome behaviors among urban high school students of color. *Journal of Community Psychology, 47,* 1131–1150.

Larsen, B., Verstynen, T., Yeh, F., & Luna, B. (2018). Developmental changes in the integration of affective and cognitive corticostriatal pathways are associated with reward-driven behavior. *Cerebral Cortex, 28,* 2834–2845.

Larson, M., & Sweeten, G. (2012). Breaking up is hard to do: Romantic dissolution, offending, and substance use during the transition to adulthood. *Criminology, 50,* 605–636.

Larson, R. (1983). Adolescents' daily experience with family and friends: Contrasting opportunity systems. *Journal of Marriage and the Family, 11,* 739–750.

Larson, R. (2000). Toward a psychology of positive youth development. *American Psychologist, 55,* 170–183.

Larson, R., & Angus, R. (2011). Adolescents' development of skills for agency in youth programs: Learning to think strategically. *Child Development, 82,* 277–294.

Larson, R., & Brown, J. (2007). Emotional development in adolescence: What can be learned from a high school theater program? *Child Development, 78,* 1083–1099.

Larson, R., & Richards, M. (1991). Daily companionship in late childhood and early adolescence: Changing developmental contexts. *Child Development, 62,* 284–300.

Larson, R., & Richards, M. (1998). Waiting for the weekend: Friday and Saturday night as the emotional climax of the week. *New Directions for Child and Adolescent Development, Winter,* 37–51.

Larson, R., Clore, G., & Wood, G. (1999). The emotions of romantic relationships: Do they wreak havoc on adolescents? In W. Furman, B. Brown, & C. Feiring (Eds.), *Contemporary perspectives on adolescent romantic relationships* (pp. 19–49). New York: Cambridge University Press.

Larson, R., Hansen, D., & Moneta, G. (2006). Differing profiles of developmental experiences across types of organized youth activities. *Developmental Psychology, 42,* 849–863.

Larson, R., Moneta, G., Richards, M., & Wilson, S. (2002). Continuity, stability, and change in daily emotional experience across adolescence. *Child Development, 73,* 1151–1165.

Larson, R., Pearce, N., Sullivan, P., & Jarrett, R. (2007). Participation in youth programs as a catalyst for negotiation of family autonomy with connection. *Journal of Youth and Adolescence, 36,* 31–45.

Larson, R., Wilson, S., & Rickman, A. (2009). Globalization, societal change, and adolescence across the world. In R. Lerner & L. Steinberg (Eds.), *Handbook of adolescent psychology* (3rd ed., Vol. 2, pp. 590–622). New York: Wiley.

Larson, R. W., Izenstark, D., Rodriguez, G., & Perry, S. (2016). The art of restraint: How experienced program leaders use their authority to support youth agency. *Journal of Research on Adolescence, 26,* 845–863.

Latvala, A., Kuja-Halkola, R., Almqvist, C., Larsson, H., & Lichtenstein, P. (2015). A longitudinal study of resting heart rate and violent criminality in more than 700,000 men. *JAMA Psychiatry, 72,* 971–978.

Laube, C., Lorenz, R., & van den Bos, W. (2020). Pubertal testosterone correlates with adolescent impatience and dorsal striatal activity. *Developmental Cognitive Neuroscience, 42,* 100749.

Laube, C., van den Bos, W., & Fandakova, Y. (2020). The relationship between pubertal hormones and brain plasticity: Implications for cognitive training in adolescence. *Developmental Cognitive Neuroscience, 42,* 100753.

Laursen, B. (1993). The perceived impact of conflict on adolescent relationships. *Merrill-Palmer Quarterly, 39,* 535–550.

Laursen, B. (1996). Closeness and conflict in adolescent peer relationships: Interdependence with friends and romantic partners. In W. Bukowski, A. Newcomb, & W. Hartup (Eds.), *The company they keep: Friendship in childhood and adolescence* (pp. 186–210). New York: Cambridge University Press.

Laursen, B. (2017). Making and keeping friends: The importance of being similar. *Child Development Perspectives, 11,* 282–289.

Laursen, B., & Collins, W. A. (2009). Parent–child relationships during adolescence. In R. Lerner & L. Steinberg (Eds.), *Handbook of adolescent psychology* (3rd ed., Vol. 2, pp. 3–42). New York: Wiley.

Laursen, B., & DeLay, D. (2011). Parent-child relationship. In B. Brown & M. Prinstein (Eds.), *Encyclopedia of adolescence* (Vol. 2, pp. 233–240). New York: Academic Press.

Laursen, B., & Hartl, A. C. (2013). Understanding loneliness during adolescence: Developmental changes that increase the risk of perceived social isolation. *Journal of Adolescence, 36,* 1261–1268.

Laursen, B., & Jensen-Campbell, L. (1999). The nature and functions of social exchange in adolescent romantic relationships. In W. Furman, B. Brown, & C. Feiring (Eds.), *Contemporary perspectives on adolescent romantic relationships* (pp. 50–74). New York: Cambridge University Press.

Laursen, B., Coy, K., & Collins, W. A. (1998). Reconsidering changes in parent–child conflict across adolescence: A meta-analysis. *Child Development, 69,* 817–832.

Laursen, B., DeLay, D., & Adams, R. E. (2010). Trajectories of perceived support in mother–adolescent relationships: The poor (quality) get poorer. *Developmental Psychology, 46,* 1792–1798.

Laursen, B., Hartl, A. C., Vitaro, F., Brendgen, M., Dionne, G., & Biovin, M. (2017). The spread of substance use and delinquency between adolescent twins. *Developmental Psychology, 53,* 329–339.

Lavagnino, L., Arnone, D., Cao, B., Soares, J. C., & Selvaraj, S. (2016). Inhibitory control in obesity and binge eating disorder: A systematic review and meta-analysis of neurocognitive and neuroimaging studies. *Neuroscience and Biobehavioral Reviews, 68,* 714–726.

Lawford, H. L., & Ramey, H. L. (2015). "Now I know I can make a difference": Generativity and activity engagement as predictors or meaning making in adolescents and emerging adults. *Developmental Psychology, 561,* 1395–1406.

Lawler, M., & Nixon, E. (2011). Body dissatisfaction among adolescent boys and girls: The effects of body mass, peer appearance culture and internalization of appearance ideals. *Journal of Youth and Adolescence, 40,* 59–71.

Leaper, C., & Brown, C. (2008). Perceived experiences with sexism among adolescent girls. *Child Development, 79,* 685–704.

Leaper, C., & Brown, C. S. (2018). Sexism in childhood and adolescence: Recent trends and advances in research. *Child Development Perspectives, 12,* 10–15.

Leaper, C., Farkas, T., & Brown, C. (2012). Adolescent girls' experiences and gender-related beliefs in relation to their motivation in math/science and English. *Journal of Youth and Adolescence, 41,* 268–282.

Leatherdale, S. T., & Papadakis, S. (2011). A multilevel examination of the association between older social models in the school environment and overweight and obesity among younger students. *Journal of Youth and Adolescence, 40,* 361–372.

Lee, B., & Pearce, L. (2019). Understanding why religious involvement's relationship with education varies by social class. *Journal of Research on Adolescence, 29,* 369–389.

Lee, D., & Neblett, E. (2019). Religious development in African American adolescents: Growth patterns that offer protection. *Child Development, 90,* 245–259.

Lee, H., Jamieson, J., Miu, A., Josephs, R., & Yeager, D. (2019). An entity theory of intelligence predicts higher cortisol levels when high school grades are declining. *Child Development, 90,* e849–e867.

Lee, H., Jamieson, J., Reis, H., Beevers, C., Josephs, R., Mullarkey, M., . . . Yeager, D. (2020). Getting fewer "likes" than others on social media elicits emotional distress among victimized adolescents. *Child Development, 91,* 2141–2159.

Lee, H. J., Park, S., Kim, C. I., Choi, D. W., Lee, J. S., Oh, S. M. . . . & Oh, S. W. (2013). The association between disturbed eating behavior and socioeconomic status: The online Korean adolescent panel survey (OnKAPS). *PLOS ONE, 8,* 57880.

Lee, J. (2008). "A Kotex and a Smile": Mothers and daughters at menarche. *Journal of Family Issues, 29,* 1325–1347.

Lee, J., & Hahm, H. (2010). Acculturation and sexual risk behaviors among Latina adolescents transitioning to young adulthood. *Journal of Youth and Adolescence, 39,* 414–427.

Lee, J., Cho, J., Yoon, Y., Bello, M., Khoddam, R., & Leventhal, A. (2018). Developmental pathways from parental socioeconomic status to adolescent substance use: Alternative and complementary reinforcement. *Journal of Youth and Adolescence, 47,* 334–348.

Lee, J. M., Wasserman, R., Kaciroti, N., Gebremariam, A., Steffes, J., Dowshen, S., . . . Herman-Giddens, M. E. (2016). Timing of puberty in overweight versus obese boys. *Pediatrics, 137,* e20150164.

Lee, K., Siegle, G., Dahl, R., Hooley, J., & Silk, J. (2014). Neural responses to maternal criticism in healthy youth. *Social Cognitive Affective Neuroscience, 10,* 902–912.

Lee, K. S., & Vaillancourt, T. (2018). Longitudinal associations among bullying by peers, disordered eating behavior, and symptoms of depression during adolescence. *JAMA Psychiatry, 75,* 605–612.

Lee, K. T. H., Lewis, R. W., Kataoka, S., Schenke, K., & Vandell, D. L. (2018). Out-of-school time and behaviors during adolescence. *Journal of Research on Adolescence, 28*(2), 284–293.

Lee, M., Oi-yeung Lam, B., Ju, E., & Dean, J. (2017). Part-time employment and problem behaviors: Evidence from adolescents in South Korea. *Journal of Research on Adolescence, 27,* 88–104.

Lee, T. K., Wickrama, K. A. S., & Simons, L. G. (2013). Chronic family economic hardship, family processes and progression of mental and physical health symptoms in adolescence. *Journal of Youth & Adolescence, 42,* 821–836.

Lee, V., & Croninger, R. (1994). The relative importance of home and school in the development of literacy skills for middle-grade students. *American Journal of Education, 102,* 286–329.

Lee, V., & Smith, J. (1997). High school size: Which works best, and for whom? *Educational Evaluation and Policy Analysis, 19,* 205–227.

Lee, V., Burkam, D., Zimiles, H., & Ladewski, B. (1994). Family structure and its effect on behavioral and emotional problems in young adolescents. *Journal of Research on Adolescence, 4,* 405–437.

Lee, V., Smith, J., & Croninger, R. (1997). How high school organization influences the equitable distribution of learning in mathematics and science. *Sociology of Education, 70,* 128–150.

Leets, L., & Sunwolf. (2005). Adolescent rules for social exclusion: When is it fair to exclude someone else? *Journal of Moral Education, 34,* 343–362.

Lefkowitz, E. (2005). "Things have gotten better": Developmental changes among emerging adults after the transition to university. *Journal of Adolescent Research, 20,* 40–63.

Lefkowitz, E., Romo, L., Corona, R., Au, T., & Sigman, M. (2000). How Latino American and European American adolescents discuss conflicts, sexuality, and AIDS with their mothers. *Developmental Psychology, 36,* 315–325.

Lehman, B. (2020). Good grades and a bad reputation: Gender, academics, and relational aggression. *Youth & Society, 52,* 490–509.

Lei, H., Li, S., Chiu, M., & Lu, M. (2018). Social support and Internet addiction among mainland Chinese teenagers and young adults: A meta-analysis. *Computers in Human Behavior, 85,* 200–209.

Leichtman Research Group. (2020). Pay-TV in the U.S., 2020. Accessed at https://www.leichtman-research.com.

Leidner A., Barry V., Bowen V., Silver, R., Musial, T., Kang, G., . . . Pevzner, E. (2021). Opening of large institutions of higher education and county-level COVID-19 Incidence — United States, July 6–September 17, 2020. *Morbidity and Mortality Weekly Report, 70,* 14–19.

Leitenberg, H., & Saltzman, H. (2000). A statewide survey of age at first intercourse for adolescent females and age of their male partners: Relation to other risk behaviors and statutory rape implications. *Archives of Sexual Behavior, 29,* 203–215.

LeMoult, J., Humphreys, K., King, L., Colich, N., Price, A., Ordaz, S., & Gotlib, I. (2019). Associations among early life stress, rumination, symptoms of psychopathology, and sex in youth in the early stages of puberty: A moderated mediation analysis. *Journal of Abnormal Child Psychology, 47,* 199–207.

LeMoult, J., Ordaz, S., Kircanski, K., Singh, M., & Gotlib, I. (2015). Predicting first onset of depression in young girls: Interaction of diurnal cortisol and negative life events. *Journal of Abnormal Psychology, 124,* 850–859.

Lenhart, A. (2012). *Teens, smartphones, and texting.* Washington: Pew Research Center.

Lenhart, A. (2015). *Teens, social media, and technology.* Washington: Pew Research Center.

Lenhart, A., Madden, M., Smith, A., Purcell, K., Zickuhr, K., & Rainie, L. (2011). *Teens, kindness and cruelty on social network sites.* Washington: Pew Research Center.

Lenhart, A., Purcell, K., Smith, A., & Zickuhr, K. (2020). *Social media and Internet use among teens and young adults.* Washington: Pew Research Center.

Lennarz, H., Lichtwarck-Aschoff, A., Finkenauer, C., & Granic, I. (2017). Jealousy in adolescents' daily lives: How does it relate to interpersonal context and well-being? *Journal of Adolescence, 54,* 18–31.

Lenroot, R. K., & Giedd, J. N. (2008). The changing impact of genes and environment on brain development during childhood and adolescence: Initial findings from a neuroimaging study of pediatric twins. *Development and Psychopathology, 20,* 1161–1175.

Lenzi, M., Dougherty, D., Furlong, M., Sharkey, J., & Dowdy, E. (2015). The configuration protective model: Factors associated with adolescent behavioral and emotional problems. *Journal of Applied Developmental Psychology, 38,* 49–59.

Lenzi, M., Vieno, A., Perkins, D. D., Pastore, M., Santinello, M., & Mazzardis, S. (2012). Perceived neighborhood social resources as determinants of prosocial behavior in early adolescence. *American Journal of Community Psychology, 50,* 37–49.

Leon, G., Fulkerson, J. A., Perry, C. L., Keel, P. K., & Klump, K. L. (1999). Three to four year prospective evaluation of personality and behavioral risk factors for later disordered eating in adolescent girls and boys. *Journal of Youth and Adolescence, 28,* 181–196.

Lerner, J., Phelps, E., Forman, Y., & Bowers, E. (2009). Positive youth development. In R. Lerner & L. Steinberg (Eds.), *Handbook of adolescent psychology* (3rd ed., Vol. 1, pp. 524–558). New York: Wiley.

Lerner, R., & Steinberg, L. (Eds.) (2009). *Handbook of adolescent psychology* (3rd ed.). New York: Wiley.

Lerner, R., Lerner, J. V., Almerigi, J. B., Theokas, C., Phelps, E., Gestsdottir, S., . . . von Eye, A. (2005). Positive youth development, participation in community youth development programs, and community contributions of fifth-grade adolescents findings from the first wave of the 4-H study of positive youth development. *Journal of Early Adolescence, 25,* 17–71.

Lerner, R., von Eye, A., Lerner, J., Lewin-Bizan, S., & Bowers, E. (2010). Special issue introduction: The meaning and measurement of thriving: A view of the issues. *Journal of Youth and Adolescence, 39,* 707–719.

Lessard, L., & Juvonen, J. (2018). Friendless adolescents: do perceptions of social threat account for their internalizing difficulties and continued friendlessness? *Journal of Research on Adolescence, 28,* 277–283.

Lessard, L., Kogachi, K., & Juvonen, J. (2019). Quality and stability of cross-ethnic friendships: Effects of classroom diversity and out-of-school contact. *Journal of Youth and Adolescence, 48,* 554–566.

Lessard, L., Watson, R., & Puhl, R. (2020). Bias-based bullying and school adjustment among sexual and gender minority adolescents: The role of Gay-Straight Alliances. *Journal of Youth and Adolescence, 49,* 1094–1109.

Leung, R., Toumbourou, J., Hemphill, S., & Catalano, R. (2016). Peer group patterns of alcohol-using behaviors among early adolescents in Victoria, Australia, and Washington State, United States. *Journal of Research on Adolescence, 26,* 902–917.

Leventhal, T., & Brooks-Gunn, J. (2004). Diversity in developmental trajectories across adolescence: Neighborhood influences. In R. Lerner & L. Steinberg (Eds.), *Handbook of adolescent psychology.* New York: Wiley.

Leventhal, T., & Brooks-Gunn, J. (2011). Changes in neighborhood poverty from 1990 to 2000 and youth's problem behaviors. *Developmental Psychology, 47,* 1680–1698.

Leventhal, T., Dupéré, V., & Brooks-Gunn, J. (2009). Neighborhood influences on adolescent development. In R. Lerner & L. Steinberg (Eds.), *Handbook of adolescent psychology* (3rd ed., Vol. 2, pp. 411–443). New York: Wiley.

Leventhal, T., Fauth, R. C., & Brooks-Gunn, J. (2005). Neighborhood poverty and public policy: A 5-year follow-up of children's educational outcomes in the New York City Moving to Opportunity demonstration. *Developmental Psychology, 41,* 933–952.

Leversen, I., Danielsen, A., Birkeland, M., & Samdal, O. (2012). Basic psychological need satisfaction in leisure activities and adolescents' life satisfaction. *Journal of Youth & Adolescence, 41,* 1588–1599.

Levine, J., Emery, C., & Pollack, H. (2007). The well-being of children born to teen mothers. *Journal of Marriage and Family, 69,* 105–122.

Levine, P. (2001). The sexual activity and birth control use of American teenagers. In J. Gruber (Ed.), *Risky behavior among youths: An economic analysis* (pp. 167–218). Chicago: University of Chicago Press.

Levitt, M., Guacci-Franci, N., & Levitt, J. (1993). Convoys of social support in childhood and early adolescence: Structure and function. *Developmental Psychology, 29,* 811–818.

Levitt, S., & Dubner, S. (2005). *Freakonomics.* New York: William Morrow.

Lewin, K. (1951). *Field theory and social science.* New York: Harper & Row.

Lewinsohn, P., Joiner, T. E., Jr., & Rohde, P. (2001). Evaluation of cognitive diathesis–stress models in predicting major depressive disorder in adolescents. *Journal of Abnormal Psychology, 110,* 203–215.

Lewinsohn, P., Pettit, J., Joiner, T., Jr., & Seeley, J. (2003). The symptomatic expression of major depressive disorder in adolescents and young adults. *Journal of Abnormal Psychology, 112,* 244–252.

Lewinsohn, P., Rohde, P., & Seeley, J. (1994). Psychosocial risk factors for future adolescent suicide attempts. *Journal of Consulting and Clinical Psychology, 62,* 297–305.

Lewinsohn, P., Rohde, P., Seeley, J., Klein, D., & Gotlib, I. (2003). Psychosocial functioning of young adults who have experienced and recovered from major depressive disorder during adolescence. *Journal of Abnormal Psychology, 112,* 353–363.

Lewis, G., Ioannidis, K., van Harmelen, A-L., Neufeld, S., Stochl, J., Lewis, G., . . . Goodyer, I. (2018) The association between pubertal status and depressive symptoms and diagnoses in adolescent females: A population-based cohort study. *PLOS ONE, 13,* e0198804.

Lewis, J., Nishina, A., Hall, A., Cain, S., Bellmore, A., & Witkow, M. (2018). Early adolescents' peer experiences with ethnic diversity in middle school: Implications for academic outcomes. *Journal of Youth and Adolescence, 47,* 194–206.

Lewis, M., Feiring, C., & Rosenthal, S. (2000). Attachment over time. *Child Development, 71,* 707–720.

Lewis, R., Tanton, C., Mercer, C., Mitchell, K., Palmer, M., Macdowall, W., & Wellings, K. (2017). Heterosexual practices among young people in Britain: Evidence from three national surveys of sexual attitudes and lifestyles. *Journal of Adolescent Health, 61,* 694–702.

Lewis-Smith, H., Bray, I., Salmon, D., & Slater, A. (2020). Prospective pathways to depressive symptoms and disordered eating in adolescence: A 7-year longitudinal cohort study. *Journal of Youth and Adolescence, 49,* 2060–2074.

Li, D., London, S. J., Liu, J., Lee, W., Jiang, X., Van Den Berg, D., . . . Conti, D. (2011). Association of the calcyon neuron-specific vesicular protein gene (CALY) with adolescent smoking initiation in China and California. *American Journal of Epidemiology, 173,* 1039–1048.

Li, G., & Davis, J. (2020). Sexual experimentation in heterosexual, bisexual, lesbian/gay, and questioning adolescents from ages 11 to 15. *Journal of Research on Adolescence, 30,* 423–439.

Li, J. (2006). Self in learning: Chinese adolescents' goals and sense of agency. *Child Development, 77,* 482–501.

Li, J. (2009). Forging the future between two different worlds: Recent Chinese immigrant adolescents tell their cross-cultural experiences. *Journal of Adolescent Research, 24,* 477–504.

Li, J., Willems, Y., Stok, F., Deković, M., Bartels, M., & Finkenauer, C. (2019). Parenting and self-control across early to late adolescence: A three-level meta-analysis. *Perspectives on Psychological Science, 14,* 967–1005.

Li, J. L., Berk, M. S., & Lee, S. S. (2013). Differential susceptibility in longitudinal models of gene–environment interaction for adolescent depression. *Development and Psychopathology, 25,* 991–1003.

Li, M., Chen, J., Li, X., & Deater-Deckard, K. (2015). Moderation of harsh parenting on genetic and environmental contributions to child and adolescent deviant peer affiliation: A longitudinal twin study. *Journal of Youth and Adolescence, 44,* 1396–1412.

Li, X., Newman, J., Li, D., & Zhang, H. (2016). Temperament and adolescent problematic Internet use: The mediating role of deviant peer affiliation. *Computers in Human Behavior, 60,* 342–350.

Li, Y., & Lerner, R. M. (2011). Trajectories of school engagement during adolescence: Implications for grades, depression, delinquency, and substance use. *Developmental Psychology, 47,* 233–247.

Li, Y., Lerner, J., & Lerner, R. (2010). Personal and ecological assets and academic competence in early adolescence: The mediating role of school engagement. *Journal of Youth and Adolescence, 39,* 801–815.

Li, Z., Sturge-Apple, M., Russell, J., Martin, M., & Davies, P. (2020). The role of emotion processing in the association between parental discipline and adolescent socio-emotional development. *Journal of Research on Adolescence,* DOI: 10.1111/jora.12584.

Liddle, H., Rowe, C., Dakof, G., Henderson, C., & Greenbaum, P. (2009). Multidimensional family therapy for young adolescent substance abuse: Twelve-month outcomes of a randomized controlled trial. *Journal of Consulting and Clinical Psychology, 77,* 12–25.

Lillard, A., & Erisir, A. (2011). Old dogs learning new tricks: Neuroplasticity beyond the juvenile period. *Developmental Review, 31,* 207–239.

Lim, C., Rice, E., & Rhoades, H. (2016). Depressive symptoms and their association with adverse environmental factors and substance use in runaway and homeless youths. *Journal of Research on Adolescence, 26,* 403–417.

Lin, H., Harrist, A., Lansford, J., Pettit, G., Bates, J., & Dodge, K. (2020). Adolescent social withdrawal, parental psychological control, and parental knowledge across seven years: A developmental cascade model. *Journal of Adolescence, 81,* 124–134.

Lin, W., Cheong, P., Kim, Y., & Jung, J. (2010). Becoming citizens: Youths' civic uses of new media in five digital cities in East Asia. *Journal of Adolescent Research, 25,* 839–857.

Lindberg, L., Jones, R., & Santelli, J. (2008). Noncoital sexual activities among adolescents. *Journal of Adolescent Health, 43,* 231–238.

Lindberg, L., Santelli, J., & Desai, S. (2016). Understanding the decline in adolescent fertility in the United States, 2007–2012. *Journal of Adolescent Health, 59,* 577–583.

Lindberg, L., Santelli, J., & Desai, S. (2018). Changing patterns of contraceptive use and the decline in rates of pregnancy and birth among U.S. adolescents, 2007. *Journal of Adolescent Health, 63,* 253–256.

Lindberg, S., Grabe, S., & Hyde, J. (2007). Gender, pubertal development, and peer sexual harassment predict objectified body consciousness in early adolescence. *Journal of Research on Adolescence, 17,* 723–742.

Lindstrom, J. S., Jones, V., & Cheng, T. L. (2015). Promoting "Healthy Futures" to reduce risk behaviors in urban youth: A randomized controlled trial. *American Journal of Community Psychology, 56,* 36–45.

Lindstrom Johnson, S., Pas, E., & Bradshaw, C. (2016). Understanding the association between school climate and future orientation. *Journal of Youth and Adolescence, 45,* 1575–1586.

Linver, M., Roth, J., & Brooks-Gunn, J. (2009). Patterns of adolescents' participation in organized activities: Are sports best when combined with other activities? *Developmental Psychology, 45,* 354–367.

Linver, M. R., Brooks-Gunn, J., & Kohen, D. E. (2002). Family processes as pathways from income to young children's development. *Developmental Psychology, 38,* 719–734.

Lippold, M., Duncan, L., Coatsworth, J., Nix, R., & Greenberg, M. (2015). Understanding how mindful parenting may be linked to mother-adolescent communication. *Journal of Youth and Adolescence, 44,* 1663–1673.

Lippold, M. A., Greenberg, M. T., Graham, J. W., & Feinberg, M. E. (2014). Unpacking the effect of parental monitoring on early adolescent problem behavior: Mediation by parental knowledge and moderation by parent–youth warmth. *Journal of Family Issues, 35,* 1800–1823.

Lippold, M. A., McHale, S. M., Davis, K. D., Almeida, D. M., & King, R. B. (2016). Experiences with parents and youth physical health symptoms and cortisol: A daily diary investigation. *Journal of Research on Adolescence, 26,* 226–240.

Lipsey, M. (2009). The primary factors that characterize effective interventions with juvenile offenders: A meta-analytic overview. *Victims and Offenders, 4,* 124–147.

Liptak, A. (June 24, 2021). Justices rein in schools' power to limit speech. *The New York Times,* pp. A1 and ff.

Lister-Landman, K., Domoff, S., & Dubow, E. (2017). The role of compulsive texting in adolescents' academic functioning. *Psychology of Popular Media Culture, 6,* 311–325.

Little, K., Olsson, C., Whittle, S., Macdonald, J., Sheeber, L., Youssef, G., . . . Allen, N. (2019). Sometimes it's good to be short: The serotonin transporter gene, positive parenting, and adolescent depression. *Child Development, 90,* 1061–1079.

Little, K., Olsson, C., Youssef, G., Whittle, S., Simmons, J., Yücel, M., . . . Allen, N. (2015). Linking the serotonin transporter gene, family environments, hippocampal volume and depression onset: A prospective imaging gene x environment analysis. *Journal of Abnormal Psychology, 124,* 834–849.

Little, S. A., & Garber, J. (2004). Interpersonal and achievement orientations and specific stressors predict depressive and aggressive symptoms. *Journal of Adolescent Research, 19,* 63–84.

Litwack, S., Aikins, J., & Cillessen, A. (2012). The distinct roles of sociometric and perceived popularity in friendship: Implications for adolescent depressive affect and self-esteem. *The Journal of Early Adolescence, 32,* 226–251.

Liu, D., & Xin, Z. (2014). Birth cohort and age changes in the self-esteem of Chinese adolescents: A cross-temporal meta-analysis, 1996–2009. *Journal of Research on Adolescence, 25,* 366–376.

Liu, D., Chen, D., & Brown, B. B. (2020). Do parenting practices and child disclosure predict parental knowledge? A meta-analysis. *Journal of Youth and Adolescence, 49,* 1–16.

Liu, J., Bowker, J., Coplan, R., Yang, P., Li, D., & Chen, X. (2019). Evaluating links among shyness, peer relations, and internalizing problems in Chinese young adolescents. *Journal of Research on Adolescence, 29,* 696–709.

Liu, J., Mustanski, B., Dick, D., Bolland, J., & Kertes, D. A. (2017). Risk and protective factors for comorbid internalizing and externalizing problems among economically disadvantaged African American youth. *Development and Psychopathology, 29,* 1043–1056.

Liu, J., Raine, A., Wuerker, A., Venables, P., & Mednick, S. (2009). The association of birth complications and externalizing behavior in early adolescents: Direct and mediating effects. *Journal of Research on Adolescence, 19,* 93–111.

Liu, R., Walsh, R., Sheehan, A., Cheek, S., & Carter, S. (2020). Suicidal ideation and behavior among sexual minority and heterosexual youth: 1995–2017. *Pediatrics, 145,* e20192221.

Liu, W., Mumford, E., & Taylor, B. (2018). The relationship between parents' intimate partner victimization and youths' adolescent relationship abuse. *Journal of Youth and Adolescence, 47,* 321–333.

Livingston, G. (2014). *Four in 10 couples are saying "I do" again.* Washington: Pew Research Center.

Livingston, G. (2017). *The rise of multiracial and multiethnic babies in the U.S.* Washington: Pew Research Center.

Livingston, G. (2019). *The way U.S. teens spend their time is changing, but differences between boys and girls persist.* Washington, DC: Pew Research Center.

Lobel, A., Engels, R., Stone, L., Burk, W., & Granic, I. (2017). Video gaming and children's psychosocial wellbeing: A longitudinal study. *Journal of Youth and Adolescence, 46,* 884–897.

Loeb, E. L., Kansky, J., Tan, J. S., Costello, M. A., & Allen, J. P. (2021). Perceived psychological control in early adolescence predicts lower levels of adaptation into mid-adulthood. *Child Development,* DOI: 10.1111/cdev.13377.

Loeb, E., Tan, J., Hessel, E., & Allen, J. (2018). Getting what you expect: Negative social expectations in early adolescence predict hostile romantic partnerships and friendships Into adulthood. *Journal of Early Adolescence, 38,* 475–496.

Loeber, R., & Burke, J. (2011). Developmental pathways in juvenile externalizing and internalizing problems. *Journal of Research on Adolescence, 21,* 34–46.

Loeber, R., & Farrington, D. (2000). Young children who commit crime: Epidemiology, developmental origins, risk factors, early interventions, and policy implications. *Development and Psychopathology, 12,* 737–762.

Loehlin, J. C., Neiderhiser, J. M., & Reiss, D. (2005). Genetic and environmental components of adolescent adjustment and parental behavior: A multivariate analysis. *Child Development, 76,* 1104–1115.

Loftus, J., & Kelly, B. (2012). Short-term sexual health effects of relationships with significantly older females on adolescent boys. *Journal of Adolescent Health, 50,* 195–197.

Loftus, J., Kelly, B., & Mustillo, S. (2011). Depressive symptoms among adolescent girls in relationships with older partners: Causes and lasting effects? *Journal of Youth and Adolescence, 40,* 800–813.

Logis, H., Rodkin, P., Gest, S., & Ahn, H. (2013). Popularity as an organizing factor of preadolescent friendship networks: Beyond prosocial and aggressive behavior. *Journal of Research on Adolescence, 23,* 413–423.

Logue, S., Chein, J., Gould, T., Holliday, E., & Steinberg, L. (2014). Adolescent mice, unlike adults, consume more alcohol in the presence of peers than alone. *Developmental Science, 17,* 79–85.

Lohman, B., & Billings, A. (2008). Protective and risk factors associated with adolescent boys' early sexual debut and risky sexual behaviors. *Journal of Youth and Adolescence, 37,* 723–735.

Lonardo, R., Giordano, P., Longmore, M., & Manning, W. (2009). Parents, friends, and romantic partners: Enmeshment in deviant networks and adolescent delinquency involvement. *Journal of Youth and Adolescence, 38,* 367–383.

Longest, K., & Shanahan, M. (2007). Adolescent work intensity and substance use: The mediational and moderational roles of parenting. *Journal of Marriage and Family, 69,* 703–720.

Longmore, M., Eng, A., Giordano, P., & Manning, W. (2009). Parenting and adolescents' sexual initiation. *Journal of Marriage and Family, 71,* 969–982.

Loose, F., Régner, I., Morin, A., & Florence, D. (2012). Are academic discounting and devaluing double-edged swords? Their relations to global self-esteem, achievement goals, and performance among stigmatized students. *Journal of Educational Psychology, 104,* 713–725.

Looze, M. E., Huijts, T., Stevens, G. W. J. M., Torsheim, T., & Vollebergh, W. A. M. (2018). The happiest kids on earth. gender equality and adolescent life satisfaction in Europe and North America. *Journal of Youth and Adolescence, 47*(5), 1073–1085.

Lopez, A., Huynh, V., & Fuligni, A. (2011). A longitudinal study of religious identity and participation during adolescence. *Child Development, 82,* 1297–1309.

Lopez, E., Wishard, A., Gallimore, R., & Rivera, W. (2006). Latino high school students' perceptions of gangs and crews. *Journal of Adolescent Research, 21,* 299–318.

Lopez-Larson, M., Anderson, J., Ferguson, M., & Yurgelun-Todd, D. A. (2011). Local brain connectivity and associations with gender and age. *Developmental Cognitive Neuroscience, 1,* 187–197.

Lopez-Larson, M., Rogowska, J., & Yurgelun-Todd, D. (2015). Aberrant orbitofrontal connectivity in marijuana smoking adolescents. *Developmental Cognitive Neuroscience, 16,* 54–62.

Lougheed, J. P., Hollenstein, T., & Lewis, M. D. (2016). Maternal regulation of daughters' emotion during conflicts from early to mid-adolescence. *Journal of Research on Adolescence, 26,* 610–616.

Loughran, T., Mulvey, E., Schubert, C., Fagan, J., Piquero, A., & Losoya, S.(2009). Estimating a dose-response relationship between length of stay and future recidivism in serious juvenile offenders. *Criminology, 47,* 699–740.

Loughran, T. A., Reid, J. A., Collins, M. E., & Mulvey, E. P. (2016). Effect of gun carrying on perceptions of risk among adolescent offenders. *American Journal of Public Health, 106,* 350–352.

Louis, K., & Smith, B. (1992). Breaking the iron law of social class: The renewal of teachers' professional status and engagement. In F. Newmann (Ed.), *Student engagement and achievement in American high schools.* New York: Teachers College Press.

Loukas, A. (2009). Examining temporal associations between perceived maternal psychological control and early adolescent internalizing problems. *Journal of Abnormal Child Psychology, 37,* 1113–1122.

Loukas, A., Roalson, L., & Herrera, D. (2010). School connectedness buffers the effects of negative family relations and poor effortful control on early adolescent conduct problems. *Journal of Research on Adolescence, 20,* 13–22.

Lourenco, F., Decker, J., Pedersen, G., Dellarco, D., Casey, B. J., & Hartley, C. (2015). Consider the source: Adolescents and adults similarly follow older adult advice more than peer advice. *PLOS ONE,* e0128047.

Lovato, C., Watts, A., Brown, K., Lee, D., Sabiston, C., Nykiforuk, C. . . . Thompson, M. (2013). School and community predictors of smoking: A longitudinal study of Canadian high schools. *American Journal of Public Health, 103,* 362–368.

Loveless, T. (2002). *How well are American students learning? The 2002 Brown Center Report on American Education.* Washington, DC: Brookings Institution.

Low, S., & Shortt, J. (2017). Family, peer, and pubertal determinants of dating involvement among adolescents. *Journal of Research on Adolescence, 27,* 78–87.

Low, S., Polanin, J., & Espelage, D. (2013). The role of social networks in physical and relational aggression among young adolescents. *Journal of Youth & Adolescence, 42,* 1078–1089.

Low, S., Tiberio, S., Shortt, J., Mulford, C., Eddy, J., & Capaldi, D. (2019). Intergenerational transmission of violence: The mediating role of adolescent psychopathology symptoms. *Development and Psychopathology, 31,* 233–245.

Lowe, K., & Dotterer, A. (2013). Parental monitoring, parental warmth, and minority youths' academic outcomes: Exploring the integrative model of parenting. *Journal of Youth & Adolescence, 42,* 1413-1425.

Lozada, F., & Tynes, B. (2017). Longitudinal effects of online experiences on empathy among African American adolescents. *Journal of Applied Developmental Psychology, 52,* 181-190.

Lozano-Blasco, R., Cortés-Pascual, A., & Latorre-Martínez, P. (2020). Being a cybervictim and a cyberbully-The duality of cyberbullying: A meta-analysis. *Computers in Human Behavior,* 106444.

Lu, T., Jin, S., Li, L., Niu, L., Chen, X., & French, D. (2018). Longitudinal associations between popularity and aggression in Chinese middle and high school adolescents. *Developmental Psychology, 54,* 2291-2301.

Lubienski, S. T., & Lubienski, C. (2006). School sector and academic achievement: A multilevel analysis of NAEP mathematics data. *American Education Research Journal, 43,* 651-698.

Lucas, S., & Berends, M. (2002). Sociodemographic diversity, correlated achievement, and de facto tracking. *Sociology of Education, 75,* 328-348.

Lucas-Thompson, R. G., Lunkenheimer, E. S., & Granger, D. A. (2017). Adolescent conflict appraisals moderate the link between marital conflict and physiological stress reactivity. *Journal of Research on Adolescence, 27,* 173-188.

Lucas-Thompson, R. G., McKernan, C. J., & Henry, K. L. (2018). Unraveling current and future adolescent depressive symptoms: The role of stress reactivity across physiological systems. *Developmental Psychology, 54,* 1650-1660.

Luciana, M. (2013). Adolescent brain development in normality and psychopathology. *Development and Psychopathology, 25,* 1325-1345.

Luciana, M., Conklin, H. M., Hooper, C. J., & Yarger, R. S. (2005). The development of nonverbal working memory and executive control processes in adolescents. *Child Development, 76,* 697.

Luciano, E., & Orth, U. (2017). Transitions in romantic relationships and development of self-esteem. *Journal of Personality and Social Psychology, 112,* 307-328.

Ludden, A., & Eccles, J. (2007). Psychosocial, motivational, and contextual profiles of youth reporting different patterns of substance use during adolescence. *Journal of Research on Adolescence, 17,* 51-88.

Luder, M., Pittet, I., Berchtold, A., Akré, C., Michaud, P., & Suris, J. (2011). Associations between online pornography and sexual behavior among adolescents: Myth or reality? *Archives of Sexual Behavior, 40,* 1027-1035.

Luebbe, A., Tu, C., & Fredrick, J. (2018). Socialization goals, parental psychological control, and youth anxiety in Chinese students: Moderated indirect effects based on school type. *Journal of Youth and Adolescence, 47,* 413-429.

Luengo Kanacri, B. P., Eisenberg, N., Thartori, E., Pastorelli, C., Uribe Tirado, L. M., Gerbino, M., & Capara, G. V. (2017). Longitudinal relations among positivity, perceived positive school climate, and prosocial behavior in Colombian adolescents. *Child Development, 88,* 1100-1114.

Luking, K., Pagliaccio, D., Luby, J., & Barch, D. (2016). Reward processing and risk for depression across development. *Trends in Cognitive Sciences, 20,* 456-468.

Luna, B., Paulsen, D., Padmanabhan, A., & Geier, C. (2013). The teenage brain: Cognitive control and motivation. *Current Directions in Psychological Science, 22,* 94-100.

Lund, T. J., Dearing, E., & Zachrisson, H. D. (2017). Is affluence a risk for adolescents in Norway? *Journal of Research on Adolescence, 27,* 628-643.

Luo, F., Stone, D., & Tharp, A. (2014). Physical dating violence victimization among sexual minority youth. *American Journal of Public Health, 104,* 66-73.

Lussier, P., Farrington, D., & Moffitt, T. (2009). Is the antisocial child father of the abusive man? A 40-year prospective longitudinal study on the developmental antecedents of intimate partner violence. *Criminology, 47,* 741-779.

Luster, T., & Small, S. (1997). Sexual abuse history and problems in adolescence: Exploring the effects of moderating variables. *Journal of Marriage and the Family, 59,* 131-142.

Luthar, S., & Becker, B. (2002). Privileged but pressured? A study of affluent youth. *Child Development, 73,* 1593-1610.

Luthar, S., & Goldstein, A. (2008). Substance use and related behaviors among suburban late adolescents: The importance of perceived parent containment. *Development and Psychopathology, 20,* 591-614.

Luthar, S., & McMahon, T. (1996). Peer reputation among inner-city adolescents: Structure and correlates. *Journal of Research on Adolescence, 6,* 581-603.

Luthar, S., Shoum, K., & Brown, P. (2006). Extracurricular involvement among affluent youth: A scapegoat for "ubiquitous achievement pressures"? *Developmental Psychology, 42,* 583-597.

Luthar, S., Small, P., & Ciciolla, L. (2018). Adolescents from upper middle class communities: Substance misuse and addiction across early adulthood. *Development and Psychopathology, 30,* 315-335.

Luthar, S. S., Barkin, S., & Crossman, E. (2013). "I can, therefore I must": Fragility in the upper-middle classes. *Development and Psychopathology, 25,* 1529-1549.

Lydon-Staley, D. M., & Geier, C. F. (2018). Age-varying associations between cigarette smoking, sensation seeking, and impulse control through adolescence and young adulthood. *Journal of Research on Adolescence, 18,* 354-367.

Lynam, D., Charnigo, R., Moffitt, T., Raine, A., Loeber, R., & Stouthamer-Loeber, M. (2009). The stability of psychopathy across adolescence. *Development and Psychopathology, 21,* 1133-1153.

Lynne-Landsman, S., Bradshaw, C., & Ialongo, N. (2010a). Testing a developmental cascade model of adolescent substance use trajectories and young adult adjustment. *Development and Psychopathology, 22,* 933-948.

Lynne-Landsman, S., Livingston, M., & Wagenaar, A. (2013). Effects of state medical marijuana laws on adolescent marijuana use. *American Journal of Public Health, 103,* 1500-1506.

Lynne-Landsman, S. D., Graber, J. A., & Andrews, J. A. (2010b). Do trajectories of household risk in childhood moderate pubertal-timing effects on substance initiation in middle school? *Developmental Psychology, 46,* 853-868.

Ma, J., Flanders, W., Ward, E., & Jemal, A. (2011). Body mass index in young adulthood and premature death: Analyses of the US National Health Interview Survey linked mortality files. *American Journal of Epidemiology, 174,* 934-944.

Ma, M., Malcolm, L. R., Diaz-Albertini, K., Klinoff, V. A., Leeder, E., Barrientos, S., & Kibler, J. (2014). Latino cultural values as protective factors against sexual risks among adolescents. *Journal of Adolescence, 37,* 1215-1225.

Ma, Y., Siu, A., & Tse, W. (2018). The role of high parental expectations in adolescents' academic performance and depression in Hong Kong. *Journal of Family Issues, 39,* 2505-2522.

Maas, M. K., Bray, B. C., & Noll, J. G. (2018). A latent class analysis of online sexual experiences and offline sexual behaviors among female adolescents. *Journal of Research on Adolescence, 28*(3), 731-747.

Määttä, S., Nurmi, J., & Stattin, H. (2007). Achievement orientations, school adjustment, and well-being: A longitudinal study. *Journal of Research on Adolescence, 17,* 789-812.

Mac Cárthaigh, S., Griffin, C., & Perry, J. (2020). The relationship between sleep and problematic smartphone use among adolescents: A systematic review. *Developmental Review, 55,* 100897.

Mac Giollabhui, N., Hamilton, J., Nielsen, J., Connolly, S., Stange, J., Varga, S., . . . Alloy, L. (2018). Negative cognitive style interacts with negative life events to predict first onset of a major depressive episode in adolescence via hopelessness. *Journal of Abnormal Psychology, 127,* 1-11.

Maccoby, E. (1990). Gender and relationships: A developmental account. *American Psychologist, 45,* 513-520

Maccoby, E., & Martin, J. (1983). Socialization in the context of the family: Parent-child interaction. In E. M. Hetherington (Ed.), *Handbook of child psychology:* Vol. 4. *Socialization, personality, and social development* (pp. 1-101). New York: Wiley.

Maciejewski, D., Keijsers, L., van Lier, P., Branje, S., Meeus, W., & Koot, H. (2019). Most fare well—But some do not: Distinct profiles of mood variability development and their association with adjustment during adolescence. *Developmental Psychology, 55,* 434-448.

Maciejewski, D., van Lier, P., Neumann, A., Van der Giessen, D., Branje, S., Meeus, W. & Koot, H. (2014). The development of adolescent generalized anxiety and depressive symptoms in the context of adolescent mood variability and parent-adolescent negative interactions. *Journal of Abnormal Child Psychology, 42,* 515-526.

Maciejewski, D. F., van Lier, P. A. C., Branje, S. J. T., Meeus, W. H. J., & Koot, H. M. (2015). A 5-year longitudinal study on mood variability across adolescence using daily diaries. *Child Development, 86,* 1908-1921.

Mackey, A., Finn, A., Leonard, J., Jacoby-Senghor, D., West, M., Gabrieli, C., & Gabrieli, J. (2015). Neuroanatomical correlates of the income-achievement gap. *Psychological Science, 26,* 925-933

Madan Morris, A., Mrug, S., & Windle, M. (2015). From family violence to dating violence: Testing a dual pathway model. *Journal of Youth and Adolescence, 44,* 1819–1835.

Madigan, S., Villani, V., Azzopardi, C., Laut, D., Smith, T., Temple, J., . . . Dimitropoulos, G. (2018). The prevalence of unwanted online sexual exposure and solicitation among youth: A meta-analysis. *Journal of Adolescent Health, 63,* 133–141.

Madkour, A., Farhat, T., Halpern, C., Gabhainn, N., & Godeau, E. (2012). Parents' support and knowledge of their daughters' lives, and females' early sexual initiation in nine European countries. *Perspectives on Sexual & Reproductive Health, 44,* 167–175.

Madkour, A., Farhat, T., Halpern, C., Godeau, E., & Gabhainn, S. (2010). Early adolescent sexual initiation as a problem behavior: A comparative study of five nations. *Journal of Adolescent Health, 47,* 389–398.

Madkour, A. S., Farhat, T., Halpern, C. T., Godeau, E., & Gabhainn, S. (2010). Early adolescent sexual initiation and physical/psychological symptoms: A comparative analysis of five nations. *Journal of Youth and Adolescence, 39,* 1211–1225.

Madon, S., Willard, J., Guyll, M., Trudeau, L., & Spoth, R. (2006). Self-fulfilling prophecy effects of mothers' beliefs on children's alcohol use: Accumulation, dissipation, and stability over time. *Journal of Personality and Social Psychology, 90,* 911–926.

Madsen, S., & Collins, W. A. (2011). The salience of adolescent romantic experiences for romantic relationship qualities in young adulthood. *Journal of Research on Adolescence, 21,* 789–801.

Mager, W., Milich, R., Harris, M., & Howard, A. (2005). Intervention groups for adolescents with conduct problems: Is aggregation harmful or helpful? *Journal of Abnormal Child Psychology, 33,* 349–362.

Maggs, J., Staff, J., Kloska, D., Patrick, M., O'Malley, P., & Schulenberg, J. (2015). Predicting young adult degree attainment by late adolescent marijuana use. *Journal of Adolescent Health, 57,* 205–211.

Magis-Weinberg, L., Custers, R., & Dumontheil, I. (2019). Rewards enhance proactive and reactive control in adolescence and adulthood. *Social Cognitive and Affective Neuroscience, 14,* 1219–1232.

Magnusson, D., Stattin, H., & Allen, V. (1986). Differential maturation among girls and its relation to social adjustment in a longitudinal perspective. In P. Baltes, D. Featherman, & R. Lerner (Eds.), *Life span development and behavior* (Vol. 7, pp. 135–172). Hillsdale, NJ: Erlbaum.

Maheux, A., Evans, R., Widman, L., Nesi, J., Prinstein, M., & Choukas-Bradley, S. (2020). Popular peer norms and adolescent sexting behavior. *Journal of Adolescence, 78,* 62–66.

Mahler, A., Fine, A., Frick, P. J., Steinberg, L., & Cauffman, E. (2018). Expecting the unexpected? Expectations for future success among adolescent first-time offenders. *Child Development, 89,* e535–e551.

Mahoney, J., & Parente, M. (2009). Should we care about adolescents who care for themselves? What we have learned and what we need to know about youth in self-care. *Child Development Perspectives, 3,* 189–195.

Mahoney, J., Larson, R., Eccles, J., & Lord, H. (2005). Organized activities as developmental contexts for children and adolescents. In J. Mahoney, R. Larson, & J. Eccles (Eds.), *Organized activities as contexts of development* (pp. 3–22). Hillsdale, NJ: Erlbaum.

Mahoney, J., Stattin, H., & Lord, H. (2004). Unstructured youth recreation centre participation and antisocial behaviour development: Selective influences and the moderating role of antisocial peers. *International Journal of Behavioral Development, 28,* 553–560.

Mahoney, J., Vandell, D., Simpkins, S., & Zarrett, N. (2009). Adolescent out-of-school activities. In R. Lerner & L. Steinberg (Eds.), *Handbook of adolescent psychology* (3rd ed., Vol. 2, pp. 228–269). New York: Wiley.

Mahoney, J. L., & Vest, A. E. (2012). The over-scheduling hypothesis revisited: Intensity of organized activity participation during adolescence and young adult outcomes. *Journal of Research on Adolescence, 22,* 409–418.

Main, M., Kaplan, N., & Cassidy, J. (1985). Security in infancy, childhood, and adulthood: A move to the level of representation. In I. Bretherton and E. Waters (Eds.), *Growing points of attachment theory and research, Monographs of the Society for Research on Child Development, 50*(1–2), Serial No. 209, pp. 66–106.

Majeno, A., Tsai, K., Huynh, V., McCreath, H., & Fuligni, A. (2018). Discrimination and sleep difficulties during adolescence: The mediating roles of loneliness and perceived stress. *Journal of Youth and Adolescence, 47,* 135–147.

Mak, H. W., Fosco, G. M., & Feinberg, M. E. (2018). The role of family for youth friendships: Examining a social anxiety mechanism. *Journal of Youth and Adolescence, 47,* 306–320.

Makara, K. A., & Madjar, N. (2015). The role of goal structures and peer climate in trajectories of social achievement goals during high school. *Developmental Psychology, 51,* 473–488.

Makel, M. C., Lee, S.-Y., Olszewki-Kubilius, P., & Putallaz, M. (2012). Changing the pond, not the fish: Following high-ability students across different educational environments. *Journal of Educational Psychology, 104,* 778–792.

Malamut, S., Luo, T., & Schwartz, D. (2020). Prospective associations between popularity, victimization, and aggression in early adolescence. *Journal of Youth and Adolescence, 49,* 2347–2357.

Malamut, S., van den Berg, Y., Lansu, T., & Cillessen, A. (2021). Bidirectional associations between popularity, popularity goal, and aggression, alcohol use and prosocial behaviors in adolescence: A 3-year prospective longitudinal study. *Journal of Youth and Adolescence, 50,* 298–313.

Maldonado-Molina, M., Piquero, A., Jennings, W., Bird, H., & Canino, G. (2009). Trajectories of delinquency among Puerto Rican children and adolescents at two sites. *Journal of Research in Crime and Delinquency, 46,* 144–181.

Mali, L., Schwartz, D., Badaly, D., Luo, T., Malamut, S., Ross, A., & Duong, M. (2019). Unpopularity with same-and cross-ethnicity peers as predictors of depressive symptoms during adolescence. *Journal of Applied Developmental Psychology, 62,* 93–101.

Malin, H., Liauw, I., & Damon, W. (2017). Purpose and character development in early adolescence. *Journal of Youth and Adolescence, 46,* 1200–1215.

Manago, A., Brown, G., Lawley, K., & Anderson, G. (2020). Adolescents' daily face-to-face and computer-mediated communication: Associations with autonomy and closeness to parents and friends. *Developmental Psychology, 56,* 153–164.

Manlove, J., Mariner, C., & Papillo, A. (2000). Subsequent fertility among teen mothers: Longitudinal analyses of recent national data. *Journal of Marriage and the Family, 62,* 430–448.

Manlove, J., Steward-Streng, N., Peterson, K., Scott, M., & Wildsmith, E. (2013). Racial and ethnic differences in the transition to a teenage birth in the United States. *Perspectives on Sexual & Reproductive Health, 45,* 89–100.

Mann, F., Paul, S., Tackett, J., Tucker-Drob, E., & Harden, K. (2018). Personality risk for antisocial behavior: Testing the intersections between callous-unemotional traits, sensation seeking, and impulse control in adolescence. *Development and Psychopathology, 30,* 267–282.

Mann, F. D., Patterson, M. W., Grotzinger, A. D., Kretsch, N., Tackett, J. L., Tucker-Drob, E. M., & Harden, K. P. (2016). Sensation seeking, peer deviance, and genetic influences on adolescent delinquency: Evidence for person-environment correlation and interaction. *Journal of Abnormal Psychology, 125,* 679–691.

Mannheim, K. (1952). The problem of generations. In K. Mannheim (Ed.), *Essays on the sociology of knowledge.* London: Routledge & Kegan Paul.

Manning, W., Brown, S., & Payne, K. (2014). Two decades of stability and change in age at first union formation. *Journal of Marriage and Family, 76,* 247–260.

Manning, W., Longmore, M., & Giordano, P. (2005). Adolescents' involvement in nonromantic sexual activity. *Social Science Research, 34,* 384–407.

Manning, W. D., Longmore, M. A., & Giordano, P. (2007). The changing institution of marriage: Adolescents' expectations to cohabit and to marry. *Journal of Marriage and Family, 69,* 559–575.

Marceau, K., Abar, C. C., & Jackson, K. M. (2015). Parental knowledge is a contextual amplifier of associations of pubertal maturation and substance use. *Journal of Youth and Adolescence, 44,* 1720–1734.

Marceau, K., Ram, N., & Susman, E. J. (2015). Development and lability in the parent-child relationship during adolescence: Associations with pubertal timing and tempo. *Journal of Research on Adolescence, 25,* 474–489.

Marcia, J. (1966). Development and validation of ego identity status. *Journal of Personality and Social Psychology, 3,* 551–558.

Marin, B., Kirby, D., Hudes, E., Coyle, K., & Gomez, C. (2006). Boyfriends, girlfriends, and teenagers' risk of sexual involvement. *Perspectives on Sexual and Reproductive Health, 38,* 76–83.

Marion, D., Laursen, B., Kiuru, N., Nurmi, J. E., & Salmela-Aro, K. (2014). Maternal affection moderates friend influence on schoolwork engagement. *Developmental Psychology, 50,* 766–771.

Marion, D., Laursen, B., Zettergren, P., & Bergman, L. (2013). Predicting life satisfaction during middle adulthood from peer relationships during mid-adolescence. *Journal of Youth and Adolescence, 42,* 1299–1307.

Markey, P., Markey, C., & French, J. (2015). Violent video games and real-world violence: Rhetoric versus data. *Psychology of Popular Media Culture, 4, 277–295.*

Markovic, A., Kaess, M., & Tarokh, L. (2020). Environmental factors shape sleep EEG connectivity during early adolescence. *Cerebral Cortex, 30,* 5780–5791.

Markowitz, A. J., & Ryan, R. M. (2016). Father absence and adolescent depression and delinquency: A comparison of siblings approach. *Journal of Marriage and Family, 78,* 1300–1314.

Marks, A., Ejesi, K., & Garcia Coll, C. (2014). Understanding the U.S. immigrant paradox in childhood and adolescence. *Child Development Perspectives, 8,* 59–64.

Marks, H. M. (2000). Student engagement in instructional activity: Patterns in the elementary, middle, and high school years. *American Educational Research Journal, 37,* 153–184.

Marks, J., de la Haye, K., Barnett, L., & Allender, S. (2015). Friendship network characteristics are associated with physical activity and sedentary behavior in early adolescence. *PLOS ONE, 10,* e0145344.

Markstrom, C. (2011). Initiation ceremonies and rites of passage. In B. Brown & M. Prinstein (Eds.), *Encyclopedia of adolescence* (Vol. 2, pp. 152–159). New York: Academic Press.

Markstrom, C. (2011a). Identity formation of American Indian adolescents: Local, national, and global considerations. *Journal of Research on Adolescence, 21,* 519–535.

Markstrom, C. (2011b). Initiation ceremonies and rites of passage. In B. Brown & M. Prinstein (Eds.), *Encyclopedia of adolescence* (Vol. 2, pp. 152–159). New York: Academic Press.

Markus, H., & Nurius, P. (1986). Possible selves. *American Psychologist, 41,* 954–969.

Marsh, H. W., Abduljabbar, A. S., Morin, A. J. S., Parker, P., Abdelfattah, F., Bagengast, B., & Abu-Hilal, M. M. (2015). The big-fish-little-pond effect: Generalizability of social comparison processes over two age cohorts from Western Asian, and Middle Eastern Islamic countries. *Journal of Educational Psychology, 107,* 258–271.

Marsh, H., & Hau, K. (2003). Big-fish–little-pond effect on academic self-concept: A cross-cultural (26-country) test of the negative effects of academically selective schools. *American Psychologist, 58,* 364–376.

Marsh, H., & Hau, K. (2004). Explaining paradoxical relationship between academic self-concepts and achievements: Cross-cultural generalizability of the internal/external frame of reference predictions across 26 countries. *Journal of Educational Psychology, 96,* 56–67.

Marsh, H., & Kleitman, S. (2005). Consequences of employment during high school: Character building, subversion of academic goals, or a threshold? *American Educational Research Journal, 42,* 331–369.

Marsh, H., Chessor, D., Craven, R., & Roche, L. (1995). The effects of gifted and talented programs on academic self-concept: The big fish strikes again. *American Educational Research Journal, 32,* 285–319.

Marsh, H., Craven, R., Parker, P., Parada, R., Guo, J., Dicke, T., & Abduljabbar, A. (2016). Temporal ordering effects of adolescent depression, relational aggression, and victimization over six waves: Fully latent reciprocal effects models. *Developmental Psychology, 52,* 1994–2009.

Marsh, H., Trautwein, U., Ludtke, O., Baumert, J., & Koller, O. (2007). The big-fish–little-pond effect: Persistent negative effects of selective high schools on self-concept after graduation. *American Education Research Journal, 44,* 631–669.

Marsh, P., McFarland, F., & Allen, J. (2003). Attachment, autonomy, and multifinality in adolescent internalizing and risky behavioral symptoms. *Development and Psychopathology, 15,* 451–467.

Marshal, M., Dermody, S., Cheong, J., Burton, C., Friedman, M., Aranda, F., & Hughes, T. (2013). Trajectories of depressive symptoms and suicidality among heterosexual and sexual minority youth. *Journal of Youth and Adolescence, 42,* 1243–1256.

Marshall, S., Parker, P., Ciarrochi, J., & Heaven, P. (2014). Is self-esteem a cause or consequence of social support? A 4-year longitudinal study. *Child Development, 85,* 1275–1291.

Marshall, W. (1978). Puberty. In F. Faulkner & J. Tanner (Eds.), *Human growth* (Vol. 2, pp. 141–181). New York: Plenum.

Marshall, W., & Tanner, J. (1969). Variations in the pattern of pubertal change in girls. *Archive of Diseases of Childhood, 44,* 130.

Marsiglia, F., Nagoshi, J., Parsai, M., Booth, J., & Castro, G. (2014). The parent-child acculturation gap, parental monitoring, and substance use in Mexican heritage adolescents in Mexican neighborhoods of the Southwest U.S. *Journal of Community Psychology, 42,* 530–543.

Martin, A., & Collie, R. (2019). Teacher–student relationships and students' engagement in high school: Does the number of negative and positive relationships with teachers matter? *Journal of Educational Psychology, 111,* 861.

Martin, A., Nejad, H., Colmar, S., & Liem, G. (2013). Adaptability: How students' responses to uncertainty and novelty predict their academic and non-academic outcomes. *Journal of Educational Psychology, 105,* 728–746.

Martin, J., Hamilton, B., Osterman, M., & Driscoll, A. (2019). Births: Final data for 2018. *National Vital Statistics Reports, 68.* Hyattsville, MD: National Center for Health Statistics.

Martin, M., Bacher, K., Conger, R., & Robins, R. (2019). Prospective relationships between ethnic discrimination and substance use by Mexican-American adolescents. *Child Development, 90,* 2019–2034.

Martin, M., Bascoe, S., & Davies, P. (2011). Family relationships. In B. Brown & M. Prinstein (Eds.), *Encyclopedia of adolescence* (Vol. 2, pp. 84–94). New York: Academic Press.

Martin, M., Conger, R., Sitnick, S., Masarik, A., Forbes, E., & Shaw, D. (2015). Reducing risk for substance use by economically disadvantaged young men: Positive family environments and pathways to educational attainment. *Child Development, 86,* 1719–1737.

Martin, M., Davies, P., Cummings, E., & Cicchetti, D. (2017). The mediating roles of cortisol reactivity and executive functioning difficulties in the pathways between childhood histories of emotional insecurity and adolescent school problems. *Development and Psychopathology, 29,* 1483–1498.

Martin, M. J., Sturge-Apple, M. L., Davies, P. T., & Romero, C. V. (2017). Mothers' implicit appraisals of their adolescents as unlovable: Explanatory factor linking family conflict and harsh parenting. *Developmental Psychology, 53,* 1344–1355.

Martinez-Ferrer, B., & Stattin, H. (2017). A mutual hostility explanation for the co-occurrence of delinquency and depressive mood in adolescence. *Journal of Abnormal Child Psychology, 45,* 1399–1412.

Martino, S., Elliott, M., Corona, R., Kanouse, E., & Schuster, M. (2008). Beyond the "big talk": The roles of breadth and repetition in parent–adolescent communication about sexual topics. *Pediatrics, 121,* 612–618.

Martin-Storey, A. (2015). Prevalence of dating violence among sexual minority youth: Variation across gender, sexual minority identity and gender of sexual partners. *Journal of Youth & Adolescence, 44,* 211–224.

Martin-Storey, A. (2016). Gender, sexuality, and gender nonconformity: Understanding variation in functioning. *Child Development Perspectives, 10,* 257–262.

Martin-Storey, A., & Benner, A. (2019). Externalizing behaviors exacerbate the link between discrimination and adolescent health risk behaviors. *Journal of Youth and Adolescence, 48,* 1724–1735.

Martin-Storey, A., Cheadle, J., Skalamera, J., & Crosnoe, R. (2015). Exploring the social integration of sexual minority youth across high school contexts. *Child Development, 86,* 965–975.

Martyniuk, U., & Štulhofer, A. (2018). A longitudinal exploration of the relationship between pornography use and sexual permissiveness in female and male adolescents. *Journal of Adolescence, 69,* 80–87.

Martz, M. E., Schulenberg, J. E., Patrick, M. E., & Kloska, D. D. (2018). "I am so bored!": Prevalence rates and sociodemographic and contextual correlates of high boredom among American adolescents. *Youth & Society, 50*(5), 688–710.

Marusak, H., Thomason, M., Sala-Hamrick, K., Crespo, L., & Rabinak, C. (2017). What's parenting got to do with it: Emotional autonomy and brain and behavioral responses to emotional conflict in children and adolescents. *Developmental Science,* e12605.

Marx, R., & Kettrey, H. (2016). Gay-straight alliances are associated with lower levels of school-based victimization of LGBTQ+ youth: A systematic review and meta-analysis. *Journal of Youth and Adolescence, 45,* 1269–1282.

Maslowsky, J., & Ozer, E. J. (2014). Developmental trends in sleep duration in adolescence and young adulthood: Evidence from a national

United States sample. *Journal of Adolescent Health, 54,* 691-697.

Maslowsky, J., Owotomo, O., Huntley, E., & Keating, D. (2019). Adolescent risk behavior: Differentiating reasoned and reactive risk-taking. *Journal of Youth and Adolescence, 48,* 243-255.

Maslowsky, J., Schulenberg, J., & Zucker, R. (2014). Influence of conduct problems and depressive symptomatology on adolescent substance use: Developmentally proximal versus distal effects. *Developmental Psychology, 50,* 1179-1189.

Mason, W. (2001). Self-esteem and delinquency revisited (again): A test of Kaplan's self-derogation theory of delinquency using latent growth curve modeling. *Journal of Youth and Adolescence, 30,* 83-102.

Masselink, M., Van Roekel, E., & Oldehinkel, A. J. (2018). Self-esteem in early adolescence as predictor of depressive symptoms in late adolescence and early adulthood: The mediating role of motivational and social factors. *Journal of Youth and Adolescence, 47,* 932-946.

Massoglia, M., & Uggen, C. (2010). Settling down and aging out: Toward an interactionist theory of desistance and the transition to adulthood. *American Journal of Sociology, 116,* 543-582.

Masten, A., Roisman, G., Long, J., Burt, K., Obradovic, J., Riley, J., . . . Tellegen, A. (2005). Developmental cascades: Linking academic achievement and externalizing and internalizing symptoms over 20 years. *Developmental Psychology, 41,* 733-746.

Masten, C. L., Eisenberger, N. I., Pfeifer, J. H., & Dapretto, M. (2013). Neural responses to witnessing peer rejection after being socially excluded: fMRI as a window into adolescents' emotional processing. *Developmental Science, 16,* 743-759.

Masten, C., Eisenberger, N., Borofsky, L., McNealy, K., Pfeifer, J., & Dapretto, M. (2011). Subgenual anterior cingulate responses to peer rejection: A marker of adolescents' risk for depression. *Development and Psychopathology, 23,* 283-292.

Masten, C., Telzer, E., Fuligni, A., Lieberman, M., & Eisenberger, N. (2012). Time spent with friends in adolescence relates to less neural sensitivity to later peer rejection. *Social Cognitive Affective Neuroscience, 7,* 106-114.

Masten, S. V., Foss, R. D., & Marshall, S. W. (2011). Graduated driver licensing and fatal crashes involving 16- to 19-year-old drivers. *JAMA, 306,* 1098-1103.

Master, A., Cheryan, S., & Meltzoff, A. (2016). Computing whether she belongs: Stereotypes undermine girls' interest and sense of belonging in computer science. *Journal of Educational Psychology, 108,* 424-437.

Masters, S., Hixson, K., & Hayes, A. (2020). Perceptions of gender norm violations among middle school students: An experimental study of the effects of violation type on exclusion expectations. *The Journal of Early Adolescence,* DOI: 10.1177/0272431620931193.

Mastrotheodoros, S., Canário, C., Cristina Gugliandolo, M., Merkas, M., & Keijsers, L. (2020). Family functioning and adolescent internalizing and externalizing problems: disentangling between-, and within-family associations. *Journal of Youth and Adolescence, 49,* 804-817.

Matas, L., Arend, R., & Sroufe, L. (1978). Continuity in adaptation in the second year: The relationship between quality of attachment and later competence. *Child Development, 49,* 547-556.

Mathieson, L. C., Klimes-Dougan, B., & Crick, N. C. (2014). Dwelling on it may make it worse: The links between relational victimization, relational aggression, rumination, and depressive symptoms in adolescents. *Development and Psychopathology, 26,* 735-747.

Matsuba, M., & Walker, L. (2005). Young adult moral exemplars: The making of self through stories. *Journal of Research on Adolescence, 15,* 275-297.

Matthews, T., Odgers, C., Danese, A., Fisher, H., Newbury, J., Caspi, A., Moffitt, T. & Arseneault, L. (2019). Loneliness and neighborhood characteristics: a multi-informant, nationally representative study of young adults. *Psychological Science, 30,* 765-775.

Maulana, R., Opdenakker, M., Stroet, K., & Bosker, R. (2013). Changes in teachers' involvement versus rejection and links with academic motivation during the first year of secondary education: A multilevel growth curve analysis. *Journal of Youth and Adolescence, 42,* 1348-1371.

Mauras, C., Grolnick, W., & Friendly, R. (2013). Time for "the talk" . . . Now what? Autonomy support and structure in mother-daughter conversations about sex. *The Journal of Early Adolescence, 33,* 458-481.

Mayberry, M., Espelage, D., & Koenig, B. (2009). Multilevel modeling of direct effects and interactions of peers, parents, school, and community influences on adolescent substance use. *Journal of Youth and Adolescence, 38,* 1038-1049.

Mayeux, L., Sandstrom, M., & Cillessen, A. (2008). Is being popular a risky proposition? *Journal of Research on Adolescence, 18,* 49-74.

Mays, D., & Thompson, N. (2009). Alcohol-related risk behaviors and sports participation among adolescents: An analysis of 2005 youth risk behavior survey data. *Journal of Adolescent Health, 44,* 87-89.

Mays, D., Gilman, S., Rende, R., Luta, G., Tercyak, K., & Niaura, R. (2014). Parental smoking exposure and adolescent smoking trajectories. *Pediatrics, 133,* 983-991.

Mazzer, K., Bauducco, S., Linton, S. J., & Boersma, K. (2018). Longitudinal associations between time spent using technology and sleep duration among adolescents. *Journal of Adolescence, 66,* 112-119.

McAdams, T., Rowe, R., Rijsdijk, F., Maughan, B., & Eley, T. (2012). The covariation of antisocial behavior and substance use in adolescence: A behavioral genetic perspective. *Journal of Research on Adolescence, 22,* 100-112.

McBride, C., Paikoff, R., & Holmbeck, G. (2003). Individual and familial influences on the onset of sexual intercourse among urban African American adolescents. *Journal of Consulting and Clinical Psychology, 71,* 159-167.

McCabe, K., Modecki, K., & Barber, B. (2016). Participation in organized activities protects against adolescents' risky substance use, even beyond development in conscientiousness. *Journal of Youth and Adolescence, 45,* 2292-2306.

McCabe, S., & West, B. (2013). Medical and non-medical use of prescription stimulants: Results from a national multicohort study. *Journal of the American Academy of Child & Adolescent Psychiatry, 52,* 1272-1280.

McCabe, S., West, B., Veliz, P., & Boyd, C. (2017). E-cigarette use, cigarette smoking, dual use, and problem behaviors among U.S. adolescents: Results from a national survey. *Journal of Adolescent Health, 61,* 155-162.

McCarthy, W. J., Mistry, R., Lu, Y., Patel, M., Zheng, H., & Dietsch, B. (2009). Density of tobacco retailers near schools: Effects of tobacco use among students. *American Journal of Public Health, 99,* 2006-2013.

McCauley Ohannessian, C., Laird, R., & De Los Reyes, A. (2016). Discrepancies in adolescents' and mothers' perceptions of the family and mothers' psychological symptomatology. *Journal of Youth and Adolescence, 45,* 2011-2021.

McClean, S. A., Paxton, S. J., & Wertheim, E. H. (2016). Does media literacy mitigate risk for reduced body satisfaction following exposure to thin-ideal media? *Journal of Youth and Adolescence, 45,* 1678-1695.

McConnachie, A., Ayed, N., Foley, S., Lamb, M., Jadva, V., Tasker, F., & Golombok, S. (2021). Adoptive gay father families: A longitudinal study of children's adjustment at early adolescence. *Child Development, 92*(1), 425-443.

McCormick, E., Perino, M., & Telzer, E. (2018). Not just social sensitivity: Adolescent neural suppression of social feedback during risk taking. *Developmental Cognitive Neuroscience, 30,* 134-141.

McCormick, E., van Hoorn, J., Cohen, J., & Telzer, E. (2018). Functional connectivity in the social brain across childhood and adolescence. *Social Cognitive and Affective Neuroscience, 13,* 819-830.

McCrae, R., & John, O. (1992). An introduction to the five-factor model and its applications. *Journal of Personality, 60,* 175-215.

McCrae, R., Costa, P. T., Jr., Terracciano, A., Parker, W., Mills, C., De Fruyt, F., & Mervielde, I. (2002). Personality trait development from age 12 to age 18: Longitudinal, cross-sectional, and cross-cultural analyses. *Journal of Personality and Social Psychology, 83,* 1456-1468.

McDermott, E. Umaña-Taylor, A., & Martinez-Fuentes, S. (2018). Family ethnic socialization predicts better academic outcomes via proactive coping with discrimination and increased self-efficacy. *Journal of Adolescence, 65,* 189-195.

McDermott, E., Umaña-Taylor, A., & Zeiders, K. (2019). Profiles of coping with ethnic-racial discrimination and Latina/o adolescents' adjustment. *Journal of Youth and Adolescence, 48,* 908-923.

McDonald, J., Manlove, J., & Ikramullah, E. (2009). Immigration measures and reproductive health among Hispanic youth: Findings from the National Longitudinal Survey of Youth, 1997-2003. *Journal of Adolescent Health, 44,* 14-24.

McDonald, K., & Asher, S. (2018). Pacifists and revenge-seekers in response to unambiguous peer provocation. *Journal of Youth and Adolescence, 47,* 1907-1925.

McDonough-Caplan, H., Klein, D., & Beauchaine, T. (2018). Comorbidity and continuity of depression and conduct problems from elementary school to adolescence. *Journal of Abnormal Psychology, 127,* 326-337.

McElhaney, K., Allen, J., Stephenson, J., & Hare, A. (2009). Attachment and autonomy during adolescence. In R. Lerner & L. Steinberg (Eds.), *Handbook of adolescent psychology* (3rd ed., Vol. 1, pp. 358-403). New York: Wiley.

McElhaney, K., Antonishak, J., & Allen, J. (2008). "They like me, they like me not": Popularity and adolescents' perceptions of acceptance predicting social functioning over time. *Child Development, 79,* 720-731.

McGill, R., Hughes, D., Alicea, S., & Way, N. (2012). Academic adjustment across middle school: The role of public regard and parenting. *Development Psychology, 48,* 1003-1018.

McGloin, J., Sullivan, C., & Thomas, K. (2014). Peer influence and context: the interdependence of friendship groups, schoolmates and network density in predicting substance use. *Journal of Youth and Adolescence, 43,* 1436-1452.

McGrady, P. B., & Reynolds, J. R. (2013). Racial mismatch in the classroom: Beyond black-white difference. *Sociology of Education, 86,* 3-17.

McGue, M., Sharma, A., & Benson, P. (1996). The effects of common rearing on adolescent adjustment: Evidence from a U.S. adoption cohort. *Developmental Psychology, 32,* 604-613.

McGuire, S., Manke, B., Saudino, K., Reiss, D., Hetherington, E. M., & Plomin R. (1999). Perceived competence and self-worth during adolescence: A longitudinal behavioral genetic study. *Child Development, 70,* 1283-1296.

McHale, S., Crouter, A., & Tucker, C. (2001). Free time activities in middle childhood: Links with adjustment in early adolescence. *Child Development, 72,* 1764-1778.

McHale, S., Crouter, A., Kim, J., Burton, L., Davis, K., . . . Dotterer, A. (2006). Mothers' and fathers' racial socialization in African American families: Implications for youth. *Child Development, 77,* 1387-1402.

McHale, S. M., Corneal, D., Crouter, A., & Birch, L. (2001). Gender and weight concerns in early and middle adolescence: Links with well-being and family characteristics. *Journal of Clinical Child Psychology, 30,* 338-348.

McHale, S. M., Kim, J., Dotterer, A., Crouter, A., & Booth, A. (2009). The development of gendered interests and personality qualities from middle childhood through adolescence: A biosocial analysis. *Child Development, 80,* 482-495.

McHale, S. M., Kim, J., Whiteman, S., & Crouter, A. C. (2004). Links between sex-typed time use in middle childhood and gender development in early adolescence. *Developmental Psychology, 40,* 868-881.

McIsaac, C., Connolly, J., McKenney, K., Pepler, D., & Craig, W. (2008). Conflict negotiation and autonomy processes in adolescent romantic relationships: An observational study of interdependency in boyfriend and girlfriend effects. *Journal of Adolescence, 31,* 691-707.

McKellar, S., Marchand, A., Diemer, M., Malanchuk, O., & Eccles, J. (2019). Threats and supports to female students' math beliefs and achievement. *Journal of Research on Adolescence, 29,* 449-465.

McKenney, S., & Bigler, R. (2014). High heels, low grades: Internalized sexualization and academic orientation among adolescent girls. *Journal of Research on Adolescence, Early view.* DOI: 10.1111/jora.12179

McLaughlin, K., Green, J., Gruber, M., Sampson, N., Zaslavsky, A., & Kessler, R. (2012). Childhood adversities and first onset of psychiatric disorders in a national sample of US adolescents. *Archives of General Psychiatry, 69,* 1151-1160.

McLean, K., & Thorne, A. (2003). Late adolescents' self-defining memories about relationships. *Developmental Psychology, 39,* 635-645.

McLean, K., Breen, A., & Fournier, M. (2010). Constructing the self in early, middle, and late adolescent boys: Narrative identity, individuation, and well-being. *Journal of Research on Adolescence, 20,* 166-187.

McLoyd, V., Kaplan, R., Purtell, K., Bagley, E., Hardaway, C., & Smalls, C. (2009). Poverty and socioeconomic disadvantage in adolescence. In R. Lerner & L. Steinberg (Eds.), *Handbook of adolescent psychology* (3rd ed., Vol. 2, pp. 444-491). New York: Wiley.

McMahon, R., Witkiewitz, K., Kotler, J., & Conduct Problems Prevention Research Group. (2010). Predictive validity of callous-unemotional traits measured in early adolescence with respect to multiple antisocial outcomes. *Journal of Abnormal Psychology, 119,* 752-763.

McNaughton Reyes, H., Foshee, V., Fortson, B., Valle, L., Breiding, M., & Merrick, M. (2015). Longitudinal mediators of relations between family violence and adolescent dating aggression perpetration. *Journal of Marriage and Family, 77,* 1016-1030.

McNaughton Reyes, H., Foshee, V., Holditch Niolon, P., Reidy, D., & Hall, J. (2016). Gender role attitudes and male adolescent dating violence perpetration: Normative beliefs as moderators. *Journal of Youth and Adolescence, 45,* 350-360.

McNelles, L., & Connolly, J. (1999). Intimacy between adolescent friends: Age and gender differences in intimate affect and intimate behaviors. *Journal of Research on Adolescence, 9,* 143-159.

McNulty, T., & Bellair, P. (2003). Explaining racial and ethnic differences in serious adolescent violent behavior. *Criminology, 41,* 709-748.

McPhie, M. L., & Rawana, J. S. (2015). The effect of physical activity on depression in adolescence and emerging adulthood: A growth-curve analysis. *Journal of Adolescence, 40,* 83-92.

Mead, M. (1978). *Coming of age in Samoa.* New York: Morrow. (Original work published 1928).

Meadows, S., Brown, J., & Elder, G. H. Jr. (2006). Depressive symptoms, stress, and support: Gendered trajectories from adolescence to young adulthood. *Journal of Youth and Adolescence, 35,* 93-103.

Meca, A., Gonzales-Backen, M., Davis, R., Rodil, J., Soto, D., & Unger, J. (2020). Discrimination and ethnic identity: Establishing directionality among Latino/a youth. *Developmental Psychology, 56,* 982-992.

Meca, A., Rodil, J. C., Paulson, J. F., Kelley, M., Schwartz, S. J., Unger, J. B., . . . Zamboanga, B. L. (2019). Examining the directionality between identity development and depressive symptoms among recently immigrated Hispanic Adolescents. *Journal of Youth and Adolescence, 48*(11), 2114-2124.

Meeus, W. (2011). The study of adolescent identity formation 2000-2010: A review of longitudinal research. *Journal of Research on Adolescence, 21,* 75-94.

Meeus, W., Iedema, J., & Vollebergh, W. (1999). Rejoinder: Identity formation re-revisited: A rejoinder to Waterman in developmental and cross-cultural issues. *Developmental Review, 19,* 480-496.

Meeus, W., van de Schoot, R., Keijsers, L., & Branje, S. (2012). Identity statuses as developmental trajectories: A five-wave longitudinal study in early-to-middle and middle-to-late adolescents. *Journal of Youth & Adolescence, 41,* 1008-1021.

Meeus, W., van de Schoot, R., Keijsers, L., Schwartz, S., & Branje, S. (2010). On the progression and stability of adolescent identity formation: A five-wave longitudinal study in early-to-middle and middle-to-late adolescence. *Child Development, 81,* 1565-1581.

Mega, C., Ronconi, L., & De Beni, R. (2014). What makes a good student? How emotions, self-regulated learning, and motivation contribute to academic achievement. *Journal of Educational Psychology, 106,* 121-131.

Mehari, K., & Farrell, A. (2015). The relation between peer victimization and adolescents' well-being: The moderating role of ethnicity within context. *Journal of Research on Adolescence, 25,* 118-134.

Mehta, C., & Strough, J. (2009). Sex segregation in friendships and normative contexts across the life span. *Developmental Review, 29,* 201-220.

Meier, A. (2007). Adolescent first sex and subsequent mental health. *American Journal of Sociology, 112,* 1811-1847.

Meier, A., Hartmann, B., & Larson, R. (2018). A quarter century of participation in school-based extracurricular activities: Inequalities by race, class, gender and age? *Journal of Youth and Adolescence, 47,* 1299-1316.

Meisel, S., & Colder, C. (2020). Adolescent social norms and alcohol use: Separating between- and within-person associations to test reciprocal determinism. *Journal of Research on Adolescence, 30*(S2), 499-515.

Meisel, S., Colder, C., Bowker, J., & Hussong, A. (2018). A longitudinal examination of mediational pathways linking chronic victimization and exclusion to adolescent alcohol use. *Developmental Psychology, 54,* 1795-1807.

Melby, J., Conger, R., Fang, S., Wickrama, K., & Conger, K. (2008). Adolescent family experiences and educational attainment during early adulthood. *Developmental Psychology, 44,* 1519-1536.

Melde, C., & Esbensen, F. (2011). Gang membership as the turning point in the life course. *Criminology, 49,* 513-552.

Meldrum, R., & Barnes, J. (2017). Unstructured socializing with peers and delinquent behavior: A genetically informed analysis. *Journal of Youth and Adolescence, 46,* 1968-1981.

Memmert, D. (2014). Inattentional blindness to unexpected events in 8-15-year-olds. *Cognitive Development, 32,* 103-109

Memmott-Elison, M., Moilanen, K., & Padilla-Walker, L. (2020). Latent growth in self-regulatory subdimensions in relation to adjustment outcomes in youth aged 12-19. *Journal of Research on Adolescence, 30,* 651-668.

Mendle, J. (2014). Beyond pubertal timing: New directions for studying individual differences in development. *Current Directions in Psychological Science, 23,* 215-219.

Mendle, J., & Ferrero, J. (2012). Detrimental psychological outcomes associated with pubertal timing in adolescent boys. *Developmental Review, 32,* 49-66.

Mendle, J., Ferrero, J., Moore, S., & Harden, K. P. (2013). Depression and adolescent sexual activity in romantic and nonromantic relational contexts: A genetically informative sibling comparison. *Journal of Abnormal Psychology, 122,* 51-63.

Mendle, J., Harden, K. P., Brooks-Gunn, J., & Graber, J. (2010). Development's tortoise and hare: Pubertal timing, pubertal tempo, and depressive symptoms in boys and girls. *Developmental Psychology, 46,* 1341-1353.

Mendle, J., Harden, K. P., Turkheimer, E., Van Hulle, C., D'Onofrio, B., Brooks-Gunn, J., . . . Lahey, B. (2009). Associations between father absence and age of first sexual intercourse. *Child Development, 80,* 1463-1480.

Mendle, J., Ryan, R. M., & McKone, K. M. (2016). Early childhood maltreatment and pubertal development: Replication in a population-based sample. *Journal of Research on Adolescence, 26,* 595-602.

Mendle, J., Ryan, R., & McKone, K. (2018). Age at menarche, depression, and antisocial behavior in adulthood. *Pediatrics, 141,* e20171703.

Mendle, J., Turkheimer, E., & Emery, R. E. (2007). Detrimental psychological outcomes associated with early pubertal timing in adolescent girls. *Developmental Review, 27,* 151-171.

Meng, X., Li, S., Duan, W., Sun, Y., & Jia, C. (2017). Secular trend of age of menarche in Chinese adolescents born from 1973-2004. *Pediatrics, 140,* e20170085.

Menning, C. L. (2002). Absent parents are more than money: The joint effect of activities and financial support on youths' educational attainment. *Journal of Family Issues, 23,* 648-671.

Menon, M. (2011). Does felt gender compatibility mediate influences of self-perceived gender nonconformity on early adolescents' psychosocial adjustment? *Child Development, 82,* 1152-1162.

Menzer, M., & Torney-Purta, J. (2012). Individualism and socioeconomic diversity at school as related to perceptions of the frequency of peer aggression in fifteen countries. *Journal of Adolescence, 35,* 1285-1294.

Menzies, L., Goddings, A. L., Whitaker, K. J., Blakemore, S-J., & Viner, R. M. (2015). The effects of puberty on white matter development in boys. *Developmental Cognitive Neuroscience, 11,* 116-128.

Mercer, N., Crocetti, E., Branje, S., van Lier, P., & Meeus, W. (2017). Linking delinquency and personal identity formation across adolescence: Examining between- and within-person associations. *Developmental Psychology, 53,* 2182-2194.

Mercer, N., Keijsers, L., Crocetti, E., Branje, S., & Meeus, W. (2016). Adolescent abstention from delinquency: Examining the mediating role of time spent with (delinquent) peers. *Journal of Research on Adolescence, 26,* 947-962.

Merikangas, K., He, J., Burstein, M., Swanson, S., Avenevoli, S., Cui, L., . . . Swendsen, J. (2010). Lifetime prevalence of mental disorders in U.S. adolescents: Results from the National Comorbidity Survey Replication–Adolescent Supplement (NCS-A). *Journal of the American Academy of Child & Adolescent Psychiatry, 49,* 980-989.

Merrin, G., de la Haye, K., Espelage, D., Ewing, B., Tucker, J., Hoover, M., & Green, H. (2018). The co-evolution of bullying perpetration, homophobic teasing, and a school friendship network. *Journal of Youth and Adolescence, 47,* 601-618.

Merskin, D. (1999). Adolescence, advertising, and the ideology of menstruation. *Sex Roles, 40,* 941-957.

Merten, D. (1997). The meaning of meanness: Popularity, competition and conflict among junior high school girls. *Sociology of Education, 70,* 175-191.

Mesch, G., & Talmud, I. (2007). Similarity and the quality of online and offline social relationships among adolescents in Israel. *Journal of Research on Adolescence, 17,* 455-466.

Meter, D., & Card, N. (2015). Defenders of victims of peer aggression: Interdependence theory and an exploration of individual, interpersonal, and contextual effects on the defender participant role. *Developmental Review, 38,* 222-240.

Metzger, A., Alvis, L., Romm, K., Wray-Lake, L., & Syvertsen, A. (2020). Adolescents' evaluations of political leaders: The case of President Donald Trump. *Journal of Research on Adolescence, 30,* 314-330.

Metzger, A., Ferris, K., & Oosterhoff, B. (2019). Adolescents' civic engagement: Concordant and longitudinal associations among civic beliefs and civic involvement. *Journal of Research on Adolescence, 29,* 879-896.

Meuwese, R., Crone, E., de Rooij, M., & Güroğlu, B. (2015). Development of equity preferences in boys and girls across adolescence. *Child Development, 86,* 145-158.

Michl, L., McLaughlin, K., Shepherd, K., & Nolen-Hoeksema, S. (2013). Rumination as a mechanism linking stressful life events to symptoms of depression and anxiety: Longitudinal evidence in early adolescents and adults. *Journal of Abnormal Psychology, 122,* 339-352.

Midgley, C., Arunkumar, R., & Urdan T. (1996). If I don't do well tomorrow, there's a reason: Predictors of adolescents' use of academic self-handicapping strategies. *Journal of Educational Psychology, 88,* 423-434.

Midgley, C., Berman, E., & Hicks, L. (1995). Differences between elementary and middle school teachers and students: A goal theory approach. *Journal of Early Adolescence, 15,* 90-113.

Miech, R., Johnston, L., O'Malley, P., Bachman, J., Schulenberg, J., & Patrick, M. (2020). *National Survey on Drug Use, 1975-2019. Volume 1, Secondary School Students.* Ann Arbor, MI: Institute for Social Research, University of Michigan.

Mikami, A., Szwedo, D., Khalis, A., Jia, M., & Na, J. (2019). Online social interactions predict academic and emotional adjustment in the transition to university. *Journal of Research on Adolescence, 29,* 210-224.

Miklikowska, M. (2018). Empathy trumps prejudice: The longitudinal relation between empathy and anti-immigrant attitudes in adolescence. *Developmental Psychology, 54,* 703-717.

Miklikowska, M., Bohman, A., & Titzmann, P. F. (2019). Driven by context? The interrelated effects of parents, peers, classrooms on development of prejudice among Swedish majority adolescents. *Developmental Psychology, 55*(11), 2451-2463.

Miklikowska, M., Thijs, J., & Hjerm, M. (2019). The impact of perceived teacher support on anti-immigrant attitudes from early to late adolescence. *Journal of Youth and Adolescence, 48,* 1175-1189.

Mikuška, J., & Vazsonyi, A. (2018). Developmental links between gaming and depressive symptoms. *Journal of Research on Adolescence, 28,* 680-697.

Milam, A., Lindstrom Johnson, S., Furr-Holden, C., & Bradshaw, C. (2016). Alcohol outlets and substance use among high schoolers. *Journal of Community Psychology, 44,* 819-832.

Milbrath, C., Ohlson, B., & Eyre, S. (2009). Analyzing cultural models in adolescent accounts of romantic relationships. *Journal of Research on Adolescence, 19,* 313-351.

Milkie, M. A., Nomaguchi, K. M., & Denny, K. E. (2015). Does the amount of time mothers spend with children or adolescents matter? *Journal of Marriage and Family, 77,* 355-372.

Miller, A., Esposito-Smythers, C., & Leichtweis, R. (2015). Role of social support in adolescent suicidal ideation and suicide attempts. *Journal of Adolescent Health, 56,* 286-292.

Miller, B., Benson, B., & Galbraith, K. (2001). Family relationships and adolescent pregnancy risk: A research synthesis. *Developmental Review, 21,* 1-38.

Miller, C. (2014, December 2). The divorce surge is over, but the myth lives on. *The New York Times.* Accessed on January 22, 2018 at https://www.nytimes.com/2014/12/02/upshot/the-divorce-surge-is-over-but-the-myth-lives-on.html

Miller, C., Hamilton, J., Sacchet, M., & Gotlib, I. (2015). Meta-analysis of functional neuroimaging of major depressive disorder in youth. *JAMA Psychiatry, 72,* 1045-1053.

Miller, D. (2019). When do growth mindset interventions work? *Trends in Cognitive Sciences, 23,* 910-912.

Miller, D. I., & Halpern, D. F. (2014). The new science of cognitive sex differences. *Trends in Cognitive Sciences, 18,* 37-45.

Miller, J., Smith, E., Coffman, D., Mathews, C., & Wegner, L. (2016). Forced sexual experiences and sexual situation self-efficacy among South African youth. *Journal of Research on Adolescence, 26,* 673-686.

Miller, K., Levin, M., Whitaker, D., & Xu, X. (1998). Patterns of condom use among adolescents: The impact of mother-adolescent communication. *American Journal of Public Health, 88,* 1542-1544.

Miller, K., Margolin, G., Shapiro, L., & Timmons, A. (2017). Adolescent life stress and the cortisol awakening response: The moderating roles of attachment and sex. *Journal of Research on Adolescence, 27,* 34-48.

Miller, N. (1928). *The child in primitive society.* New York: Brentano's.

Miller, S., Malone, P., & Dodge, K. (2010). Developmental trajectories of boys' and girls' delinquency: Sex differences and links to later adolescent outcomes. *Journal of Abnormal Child Psychology, 38,* 1021-1032.

Miller-Cotto, D., & Byrnes, J. P. (2016). Ethnic/racial identity and academic achievement: A meta-analytic review. *Developmental Review, 41,* 51-70.

Mills, B., Reyna, V., & Estrada, S. (2008). Explaining contradictory relations between risk perception and risk taking. *Psychological Science, 19,* 429-433.

Mills, K. (2014). Effects of internet use on the adolescent brain: Despite popular claims, experimental evidence remains scarce. *Trends in Cognitive Sciences, 18,* 385-387.

Mills, K. L., Goddings, A. L., Clasen, L. S., Giedd, J. N., & Blakemore, S-J. (2014). The developmental mismatch in structural brain maturation during adolescence. *Developmental Neuroscience, 36,* 147-160.

Mills, K. L., Lalonde, F., Clasen, L. S., Giedd, J. N., & Blakemore, S. J. (2014b). Developmental changes in the structure of the social brain in late childhood and adolescence. *Social Cognitive Affective Neuroscience, 9,* 123-131.

Mills-Koonce, W., Rehder, P., & McCurdy, A. (2018). The significance of parenting and parent–child relationships for sexual and gender minority adolescents. *Journal of Research on Adolescence, 28,* 637-649.

Milnitsky-Sapiro, C., Turiel, E., & Nucci, L. (2006). Brazilian adolescents' conceptions of autonomy and parental authority. *Cognitive Development, 21,* 317-331.

Milojevich, H., Norwalk, K., & Sheridan, M. (2019). Deprivation and threat, emotion dysregulation, and psychopathology: Concurrent and longitudinal associations. *Development and Psychopathology, 31,* 847-857.

Minguez, M., Santelli, J., Gibson, E., Orr, M., & Samant, S. (2015). Reproductive health impact of a school health center. *Journal of Adolescent Health, 56,* 338-344.

Minor, K., & Benner, A. (2018). School climate and college attendance for Black adolescents: Moving beyond college-going culture. *Journal of Research on Adolescence, 28,* 160-168.

Miranda-Chan, T., Fruiht, V., Dubon, C., & Wray-Lake, L. (2016). The functions and longitudinal outcomes of adolescents' naturally occurring mentorships. *American Journal of Community Psychology, 57,* 47-59.

Mireles-Rios, R., & Romo, L. (2014). Latina daughters' childbearing attitudes: The role of maternal expectations and education communication. *Developmental Psychology, 50,* 1553-1563.

Mischel, W. (2014). *The marshmallow effect.* New York: Little, Brown.

Mitchell, J., Pate, R., Beets, M., & Nader, P. (2013). Time spent in sedentary behavior and changes in childhood BMI: A longitudinal study from ages 9 to 15 years. *International Journal of Obesity, 37,* 54-60.

Mitchell, K. J., Wells, M., Priebe, G., & Ybarra, M. L. (2014). Exposure to websites that encourage self-harm and suicide: Prevalence rates and association with actual thoughts of self-harm and thoughts of suicide in the United States. *Journal of Adolescence, 37,* 1335-1344.

Mizuno, K., Tanaka, M., Fukuda, S., Sasabe, T., Imai-Matsumura, K., & Watanabe, Y. (2011). Changes in cognitive functions of students in the transitional period from elementary school to junior high school. *Brain Development, 33,* 412-420.

Modecki, K., Minchin, J., Harbaugh, A., Guerra, N., & Runions, K. (2014). Bullying prevalence across contexts: A meta-analysis measuring cyber and traditional bullying. *Journal of Adolescent Health, 55,* 602-611.

Modecki, K., Zimmer-Gembeck, M., & Guerra, N. (2017). Emotion regulation, coping, and decision making: Three linked skills for preventing externalizing problems in adolescence. *Child Development, 88,* 417-426.

Modecki, K. L. (2016). Do risks matter? Variable and person-centered approaches to adolescents' problem behavior. *Journal of Applied Developmental Psychology, 42,* 8-20.

Modell, J., & Goodman, M. (1990). Historical perspectives. In S. Feldman & G. Elliott (Eds.), *At the threshold: The developing adolescent* (pp. 93-122). Cambridge, MA: Harvard University Press.

Modell, J., Furstenberg, F., Jr., & Hershberg, T. (1976). Social change and transitions to adulthood in historical perspective. *Journal of Family History, 1,* 7-32.

Moed, A., Gershoff, E. T., Eisenberg, N., Hofer, C., Losoya, S., Spinrad, T. L., & Liew, J. (2015). Parent–adolescent conflict as sequences of reciprocal negative emotion: Links with conflict resolution and adolescents' behavior problems. *Journal of Youth and Adolescence, 44,* 1607-1622.

Moffitt, T. (2006). Life-course persistent versus adolescence-limited antisocial behavior. In D. Cicchetti & D. Cohen (Eds.), *Developmental psychopathology* (2nd ed.). New York: Wiley.

Moffitt, T., & Caspi, A. (2001). Childhood predictors differentiate life-course-persistent and adolescence-limited antisocial pathways among males and females. *Development and Psychopathology, 13,* 355-375.

Moffitt, T., Arseneault, L., Belsky, D., Dickson, N., Hancox, R., Harrington H., . . . Caspi, A. (2011). A gradient of childhood self control predicts health, wealth, and public safety. *PNAS, 108,* 2693-2698.

Moffitt, T., Caspi, A., Harrington, H., & Milne, B. (2002). Males on the life-course-persistent and adolescence-limited antisocial pathways: Follow-up at age 26 years. *Development and Psychopathology, 14,* 179-207.

Mohr-Jensen, C., Bisgaard, C., Boldsen, S., & Steinhausen, H. (2019). Attention-deficit/hyperactivity disorder in childhood and adolescence and the risk of crime in young adulthood in a Danish nationwide study. *Journal of the American Academy of Child & Adolescent Psychiatry, 58,* 443-452.

Moilanen, K., Shaw, D., & Maxwell K. (2010). Developmental cascades: Externalizing, internalizing, and academic competence from middle childhood to early adolescence. *Development and Psychopathology, 22,* 635-653.

Mollborn, S. (2007). Making the best of a bad situation: Material resources and teenage parenthood. *Journal of Marriage and Family, 69,* 92-104.

Mollen, C., Barg, F., Hayes, K., Gotcsik, M., Blades, N., & Schwarz, D. (2008). Assessing attitudes about emergency contraception among urban, minority adolescent girls: An in-depth interview study. *Pediatrics, 122,* 395-401.

Molloy, L. E., Gest, S. D., Feinberg, M. E., & Osgood, D. W. (2014). Emergence of mixed-sex friendship groups during adolescence: Developmental associations with substance use and delinquency. *Developmental Psychology, 50,* 2449-2461.

Molloy, L. E., Ram, N., & Gest, S. D. (2011). The storm and stress (or calm) of early adolescent self-concepts: Within- and between-subjects variability. *Developmental Psychology, 47,* 1589-1607.

Molnar, B. E., Cerda, M., Roberts, A. L., & Buka, S. L. (2008). Effects of neighborhood resources on aggressive and delinquent behaviors among urban youths. *American Journal of Public Health, 98,* 1086-1093.

Monahan, K., & Booth-LaForce, C. (2016). Deflected pathways: Becoming aggressive, socially withdrawn, or prosocial with peers during the transition to adolescence. *Journal of Research on Adolescence, 26,* 270-285.

Monahan, K., & Lee, J. (2008). Adolescent sexual activity: Links between relational context and depressive symptoms. *Journal of Youth and Adolescence, 37,* 917-927.

Monahan, K., & Steinberg, L. (2011). Accentuation of individual differences in social competence during the transition to adolescence. *Journal of Research on Adolescence, 21,* 576-585.

Monahan, K., Dmitrieva, J., & Cauffman, E. (2014). Bad romance: Sex differences in the longitudinal association between romantic relationships and deviant behavior. *Journal of Research on Adolescence, 24,* 12-26.

Monahan, K., Guyer, A., Silk, J., Fitzwater, T., & Steinberg, L. (2016). Integration of developmental neuroscience and contextual approaches to the study of adolescent psychopathology. In D. Cicchetti (Ed.), *Developmental psychopathology* (3rd ed., pp. 720-765). New York: Wiley.

Monahan, K., Lee, J., & Steinberg, L. (2011). Revisiting the negative impact of part-time work on adolescent adjustment: Distinguishing between selection and socialization using propensity score matching. *Child Development, 82,* 96-112.

Monahan, K., Oesterle, S., Rhew, I., & Hawkins, J. (2014). The relation between risk and protective factors for problem behaviors and depressive symptoms, antisocial behavior, and alcohol use in use in adolescence. *Journal of Community Psychology, 42,* 621-638.

Monahan, K., Rhew, I., Hawkins, J., & Brown, E. (2014). Adolescent pathway to co-occurring problem behavior: The effects of peer delinquency and peer substance use. *Journal of Research on Adolescence, 24,* 630-645.

Monahan, K., Steinberg, L., & Cauffman, E. (2009). Affiliation with antisocial peers, susceptibility to peer influence, and desistance from antisocial behavior during the transition to adulthood. *Developmental Psychology, 45,* 1520-1530.

Monahan, K., Steinberg, L., & Cauffman, E. (2013). Age differences in the impact of employment on antisocial behavior. *Child Development, 84,* 791-801.

Monahan, K., Steinberg, L., Cauffman, E., & Mulvey, E. (2009). Trajectories of antisocial behavior and psychosocial maturity from adolescence to young adulthood. *Developmental Psychology, 45,* 1654-1668.

Monroe, S., Rohde, P., Seeley, J., & Lewinsohn, P. (1999). Life events and depression in adolescence: Relationship loss as a prospective risk factor for first onset of major depressive disorder. *Journal of Abnormal Psychology, 108,* 606-614.

Monshouwer, K., Harakeh, Z., Lugtig, P., Huizink, A., Creemers, H., Reijneveld, S., . . . Vollebergh, W. (2012). Predicting transitions in low and high levels of risk behavior from early to middle adolescence: The TRAILS study. *Journal of Abnormal Child Psychology, 40,* 923-931.

Montgomery, M. (1996). "The fruit that hangs highest": Courtship and chaperonage in New York high society, 1880-1920. *Journal of Family History, 21,* 172-191.

Montgomery, M. (2005). Psychosocial intimacy and identity: From early adolescence to emerging adulthood. *Journal of Adolescent Research, 20,* 346-374.

Montgomery, M., & Sorell, G. (1998). Love and dating experience in early and middle adolescence: Grade and gender comparisons. *Journal of Adolescence, 21,* 677-689.

Monti, J., & Rudolph, K. (2017). Maternal depression and trajectories of adolescent depression: The role of stress responses in youth risk and resilience. *Development and Psychopathology, 29,* 1413-1429.

Moore, C., Hubbard, J., Bookhout, M., & Mlawer, F. (2019). Relations between reactive and proactive aggression and daily emotions in adolescents. *Journal of Abnormal Child Psychology, 47,* 1495-1507.

Moore, M., Petrie, C., Braga, A., & McLaughlin, B. (2003). *Deadly lessons: Understanding lethal school violence.* Washington, DC: National Academies Press.

Moore, M. R., & Chase-Lansdale, P. L. (2001). Sexual intercourse and pregnancy among African American girls in high-poverty neighborhoods: The role of family and perceived community environment. *Journal of Marriage and the Family, 63,* 1146-1157.

Moore, S. (1995). Girls' understanding and social construction of menarche. *Journal of Adolescence, 18,* 87-104.

Moore, S., McKone, K., & Mendle, J. (2016). Recollections of puberty and disordered eating in young women. *Journal of Adolescence, 53,* 180-188.

Moore, S., Scott, J., Thomas, H., Sly, P., Whitehouse, A., Zubrick, S., & Norman, R. (2016). Impact of adolescent peer aggression on later educational and employment outcomes in an Australian cohort. *Journal of Adolescence, 43,* 39-49.

Moore, S. R., Harden, K. P., & Mendle, J. (2014). Pubertal timing and adolescent sexual behavior in girls. *Developmental Psychology, 50,* 1734-1745.

Morales-Chicas, J., & Graham, S. (2015). Pubertal timing of Latinas and school connectedness during the transition to middle school. *Journal of Youth and Adolescence, 44,* 1275-1287.

Morales-Chicas, J., & Graham, S. (2017). Latinos' changing ethnic group representation from elementary to middle school: Perceived belonging and academic achievement. *Journal of Research on Adolescence, 27,* 537-549.

Moran, P., Rowe, R., Flach, C., Briskman, J., Ford, T., Maughan, B., . . . Goodman, R. (2009). Predictive value of callous-unemotional traits in a large community sample. *Journal of the American Academy of Child and Adolescent Psychiatry, 48,* 1079-1084.

Morin, A., Maïano, C., Marsh, H., Nagengast, B., & Janosz, M. (2013). School life and adolescents' self-esteem trajectories. *Child Development, 84,* 1967-1988.

Morisi, T. (2008). Youth enrollment and employment during the school year. *Monthly Labor Review, 131,* 51-63.

Morris, A., Eisenberg, N., & Houltberg, B. (2011). Adolescent moral development. In B. Brown & M. Prinstein (Eds.), *Encyclopedia of adolescence* (Vol. 1, pp. 48-55). New York: Academic Press.

Morris, M., Ciesla, J., & Garber, J. (2010). A prospective study of stress autonomy versus stress sensitization in adolescents at varied risk for depression. *Journal of Abnormal Psychology, 119,* 341-354.

Morris, N., & Udry, J. (1980). Validation of a self-administered instrument to assess stage of adolescent development. *Journal of Youth and Adolescence, 9,* 271-280.

Morrow, A., & Villodas, M. (2018). Direct and indirect pathways from adverse childhood experiences to high school dropout among high-risk adolescents. *Journal of Research on Adolescence, 28,* 327-341.

Mortimer, J. (2003). *Working and growing up in America.* Cambridge, MA: Harvard University Press.

Mortimer, J., & Larson, R. (2002). Adolescence in the 21st century: A worldwide perspective. Introduction: Macro societal trends and the changing experiences of adolescence. In J. Mortimer & R. Larson (Eds.), *The future of adolescent experience: Societal trends and the transition to adulthood.* New York: Cambridge University Press.

Mortimer, J., Pimentel, E., Ryu, S., Nash, K., & Lee, C. (1996). Part-time work and occupational value formation in adolescence. *Social Forces, 74,* 1405-1418.

Mosteller, F., Light, R., & Sachs, J. (1996). Sustained inquiry in education: Lessons from skill grouping and class size. *Harvard Educational Review, 66,* 797-842.

Motl, R., McAuley, E., Birnbaum, A. & Lytle, L. (2006). Naturally occurring changes in time spent watching television are inversely related to frequency of physical activity during early adolescence. *Journal of Adolescence, 29,* 19-32.

Mott, F., Fondell, M., Hu, P., Kowaleski-Jones, P., & Menaghan, E. (1996). The determinants of first sex by age 14 in a high-risk adolescent population. *Family Planning Perspectives, 28,* 13-18.

Motta-Mena, N. V., & Scherf, S. (2017). Pubertal development shapes perception of complex facial expressions. *Developmental Science, 20,* e12451.

Motti-Stefanidi, F. (2018). Resilience among immigrant youth: The role of culture, development and acculturation. *Developmental Review, 50,* 99-109.

Motti-Stefanidi, F. (2019). Resilience among immigrant youths: Who adapts well, and why? *Current Directions in Psychological Science, 28,* 510-517.

Motti-Stefanidi, F., Pavlopoulos, V., & Asendorpf, J. B. (2018). Immigrant youth acculturation and perceived discrimination: Longitudinal mediation by immigrant peers' acceptance/rejection. *Journal of Applied Developmental Psychology, 59,* 36-45.

Mõttus, R., Briley, D., Zheng, A., Mann, F., Engelhardt, L., Tackett, J., & Tucker-Drob, E. (2019). Kids becoming less alike: A behavioral genetic analysis of developmental increases in personality variance from childhood to adolescence. *Journal of Personality and Social Psychology, 117,* 635.

Moua, M., & Lamborn, S. (2010). Hmong American adolescents' perceptions of ethnic socialization practices. *Journal of Adolescent Research, 25,* 416-440.

Mounts, N. (2004). Adolescents' perceptions of parental management of peer relationships in an ethnically diverse sample. *Journal of Adolescent Research, 19,* 446-467.

Mounts, N. (2011). Parental management of peer relationships and early adolescents' social skills. *Journal of Youth and Adolescence, 40,* 416-427.

Mounts, N., & Steinberg, L. (1995). An ecological analysis of peer influence on adolescent grade point average and drug use. *Developmental Psychology, 31,* 915-922.

Mouratidis, A., Vansteenkiste, M., Lens, W., Michou, A., & Soenens, B. (2013). Within-person configurations and temporal relations of personal and perceived parent-promoted aspirations to school correlates among adolescents. *Journal of Educational Psychology, 105,* 895-910.

Mouw, T., & Entwisle, B. (2006). Residential segregation and interracial friendship in schools. *American Journal of Sociology, 112,* 394-441.

Mroczkowski, A., Sánchez, B., & Carter, J. (2017). The perceived payoff of education: Do generational status and racial discrimination matter? *Journal of Research on Adolescence, 27,* 690-696.

Mrug, S., Borch, C., & Cillessen, A. (2011). Other-sex friendships in late adolescence: Risky associations for substance use and sexual debut? *Journal of Youth and Adolescence, 40,* 875-888.

Mrug, S., Madan, A., & Windle, M. (2016). Emotional desensitization to violence contributes to adolescents' violent behavior. *Journal of Abnormal Child Psychology, 44,* 75-86.

Mueller, A., James, W., Abrutyn, S., & Levin, M. (2015). Suicide ideation and bullying among US adolescents: Examining the intersections of sexual orientation, gender, and race/ethnicity. *American Journal of Public Health, 105,* 980-985.

Muenks, K., Wigfield, A., Yang, J., & O'Neal, C. (2017). How true is grit? Assessing its relations to high school and college students' personality characteristics, self-regulation, engagement, and achievement. *Journal of Educational Psychology, 109,* 599-620.

Mulgrew, K., Volcevski-Kostas, D., & Rendell, P. (2014). The effect of music video clips on adolescent boys' body image, mood, and schema activation. *Journal of Youth & Adolescence, 43,* 92-103.

Müller, C., Hofmann, V., Fleischli, J., & Studer, F. (2016). Effects of classroom composition on the development of antisocial behavior in lower secondary school. *Journal of Research on Adolescence, 26,* 345-369.

Müller-Oehring, E., Kwon, D., Nagel, B., Sullivan, E., Chu, W., Rohlfing, T., . . . Brown, S. (2018). Influences of age, sex, and moderate alcohol drinking on the intrinsic functional architecture of adolescent brains. *Cerebral Cortex, 28,* 1049-1063.

Mulvey, E., & Cauffman, E. (2001). The inherent limits of predicting school violence. *American Psychologist, 56,* 797-802.

Mulvey, E., Steinberg, L., Fagan, J., Cauffman, E., Piquero, A., Chassin, L., . . . Losoya, S. (2004). Theory and research on desistance from antisocial activity among serious adolescent offenders. *Youth Violence and Juvenile Justice, 2,* 213-236.

Mulvey, K., Gönültaş, S., Goff, E., Irdam, G., Carlson, R., DiStefano, C., & Irvin, M. (2019). School and family factors predicting adolescent cognition regarding bystander intervention in response to bullying and victim retaliation. *Journal of Youth and Adolescence, 48,* 581-596.

Mulvey, K. L., & Killen, M. (2015). Challenging gender stereotypes: Resistance and exclusion. *Child Development, 86,* 681-694.

Mumford, E., Liu, W., & Taylor, B. (2016). Parenting profiles and adolescent dating relationship abuse: Attitudes and experiences. *Journal of Youth and Adolescence, 45,* 959-972.

Mun, C., Dishion, T., Tein, J., & Otten, R. (2018). Adolescence effortful control as a mediator between family ecology and problematic substance use in early adulthood: A 16-year prospective study. *Development and Psychopathology, 30,* 1355-1369.

Munakata, Y., Snyder, H., & Chatham, C. (2012). Developing cognitive control: Three key transitions. *Current Directions in Psychological Science, 21,* 71-77.

Munniksma, A., Scheepers, P., Stark, T. H., & Tolsma, J. (2017). The impact of adolescents' classroom and neighborhood ethnic diversity on same- and cross-ethnic friendships within classrooms. *Journal of Research on Adolescence, 27,* 20-33.

Murayama, K., & Elliot, A. J. (2009). The joint influence of personal achievement goals and classroom goal structures on achievement-relevant outcomes. *Journal of Educational Psychology, 101,* 432-447.

Murayama, K., Pekrun, R., Suzuki, M., Marsh, H., & Lichtenfeld, S. (2016). Don't aim too high for your kids: Parental overaspiration undermines students' learning in mathematics. *Journal of Personality and Social Psychology, 111,* 766-779.

Murchison, G., Agénor, M., Reisner, S., & Watson, R. (2019). School restroom and locker room restrictions and sexual assault risk among transgender youth. *Pediatrics, 143*(6), e20182902.

Murdock, K., Gorman, S., & Robbins, M. (2015). Co-rumination via cellphone moderates the association of perceived interpersonal stress and psychosocial well-being in emerging adults. *Journal of Adolescence, 38,* 27-37.

Murdock, T., Anderman, L. H., & Hodge, S. A. (2000). Middle-grade predictors of students' motivation and behavior in high school. *Journal of Adolescent Research, 15,* 327-351.

Murray, A. L., Booth, T., Eisner, M., Auyeung, B., Murray, G., & Ribeaud, D. (2019). Sex differences in ADHD trajectories across childhood and adolescence. *Developmental Science, 22,* e12721.

Murray, K., Dwyer, K., Rubin, K., Knighton-Wisor, S., & Booth-LaForce, C. (2014). Parent-child relationships, parental psychological control, and aggression: Maternal and paternal relationships. *Journal of Youth & Adolescence, 43,* 1362-1373.

Murry, V., & Lippold, M. (2018). Parenting practices in diverse family structures: Examination of adolescents' development and adjustment. *Journal of Research on Adolescence, 28,* 650-664.

Mustanski, B. S., Viken, R. J., Kaprio, J., Pulkkinen, L., & Rose, R. J. (2004). Genetic and environmental influences on pubertal development: Longitudinal data from Finnish twins at ages 11 and 14. *Developmental Psychology, 40,* 1188-1198.

Musu-Gillette, L., Zhang, A., Wang, K., Zhang, J., & Oudekerk, B. A. (2017*). Indicators of school crime and safety: 2016.* Washington, DC: National Center for Education Statistics, U.S. Department of Education, and Bureau of Justice Statistics, Office of Justice Programs, U.S. Department of Justice.

Mychasiuk, R., & Metz, G. A. S. (2016). Epigenetic and gene expression changes in the adolescent brain: What have we learned from animal models? *Neuroscience & Biobehavioral Reviews, 70,* 189-197.

Myers, J., Lindentthal, J., & Pepper, M. (1975). Life events, social integration, and psychiatric symptomatology. *Journal of Health and Social Behavior, 16,* 421-429.

Myers, T., Salcedo, A., Frick, P., Ray, J., Thornton, L., Steinberg, L., & Cauffman, E. (2018). Understanding the link between exposure to violence and aggression in justice-involved adolescents. *Development and Psychopathology, 30,* 593-603.

Nadeem, E., & Graham, S. (2005). Early puberty, peer victimization, and internalizing symptoms in ethnic minority adolescents. *Journal of Early Adolescence, 25,* 197-222.

Nader, P., Bradley, R., Houts, R., McRitchie, S., & O'Brien, M. (2008). Moderate-to-vigorous physical activity from ages 9 to 15 years. *Journal of the American Medical Association, 300,* 295-305.

Nagata, J. M., Bibbins-Domingo, K., Garber, A. K., Griffiths, S., Vittinghoff, E., & Murray, S. B. (2019). Boys, bulk, and body ideals: Sex differences in weight-gain attempts among adolescents in the United States. *Journal of Adolescent Health, 64,* 450-453.

Nagata, J. M., Garber, A. K., Tabler, J. L., Murray, S. B., & Bibbins-Domingo, K. (2018). Differential risk factors for unhealthy weight control behaviors by sex and weight status among U.S. adolescents. *Journal of Adolescent Health, 63,* 335-341.

Nagengast, B., & Marsh, H. W. (2012). Big fish in little ponds aspire more: Mediation and cross-cultural generalizability of school-average ability effects on self-concept and career aspirations in science. *Journal of Educational Psychology, 104,* 1033-1053.

Nagengast, B., Marsh, H., Chiorri, C., & Hau, K.-T. (2014). Character building or subversive consequences of employment during high school: Causal effects based on propensity score models for categorical treatments. *Journal of Educational Psychology, 106,* 584-603.

Nagin, D., Farrington, D., & Moffitt, T. (1995). Life-course trajectories of different types of offenders. *Criminology, 33,* 111-139.

Nair, R. L., Roche, K. M., & White, R. M. B. (2018). Acculturation gap distress among Latino youth: Prospective links to family processes and youth depressive symptoms, alcohol use, and academic performance. *Journal of Youth and Adolescence, 47,* 105-120.

Nalipay, M., King, R., & Cai, Y. (2020). Autonomy is equally important across East and West: Testing the cross-cultural universality of self-determination theory. *Journal of Adolescence, 78,* 67-72.

Nasrallah, N., Clark, J., Collins, A., Akers, C., Phillips, P., & Bernstein, I. (2011). Risk preference following adolescent alcohol use is associated with corrupted encoding of costs but not rewards by mesolimbic dopamine. *Proceedings from the National Academy of Sciences, 108,* 5466-5471.

National Campaign to Prevent Teen and Unplanned Pregnancy. (2015). Fact sheet. Available at www.thenationalcampaign.org. Accessed on July 14, 2015.

National Center for Education Statistics. (2005). *Youth indicators, 2005.* Washington, DC: Author.

National Center for Education Statistics. (2009). *The condition of education 2009.* Washington: Author.

National Center for Education Statistics. (2012). *The condition of education 2012.* Washington: Author.

National Center for Education Statistics. (2019). *Digest of education statistics.* Washington: Author.

National Center for Education Statistics. (2019a). *The nation's report card.* Washington: Author.

National Center for Education Statistics. (2020). *The condition of education.* Washington: Author.

National Center for Education Statistics. (2020). *Violent deaths at school and away from school and school shootings.* Washington, DC: Author.

National Center for Education Statistics. (2020a). *The nation's report card.* Washington: Author.

National Center for Health Statistics. (2015). *National vital statistics system.* Washington: Author.

National Center for Juvenile Justice. (2020). Arrest rates of offense and age group. Accessed on March 20, 2018, at www.ojjdp.gov/ojstatbb/crime

National Commission on Social, Emotional, and Academic Development. (2018). *How learning happens.* Washington, DC: The Aspen Institute.

National Conference of State Legislatures. (2016). *Homeless and runaway youth.* Accessed on January 22, 2018 at http://www.ncsl.org/research/human-services/homeless-and-runaway-youth.aspx.

National Research Council. (1998). *Protecting youth at work.* Washington, DC: National Academy Press.

National Research Council. (2005). *Growing up global.* Washington, DC: National Academies Press.

National Runaway Safeline. (2018). *Runaway youth statistics and facts.* Accessed on February 26, 2018, at https://www.1800runaway.org/runaway-statistics/

Natsuaki, M., Biehl, M., & Ge, X. (2009). Trajectories of depressed mood from early adolescence to young adulthood: The effects of pubertal timing and adolescent dating. *Journal of Research on Adolescence, 19,* 47-74.

Neal, J. (2010). Social aggression and social position in middle childhood and early adolescence: Burning bridges or building them? *Journal of Early Adolescence, 30,* 122-137.

Neblett, E., Jr., Gaskin, A., Lee, D., & Carter, S. (2011). Discrimination, racial and ethnic. In B. Brown & M. Prinstein (Eds.), *Encyclopedia of adolescence* (Vol. 2, pp. 53-58). New York: Academic Press.

Neemann, J., Hubbard, J., & Masten, A. (1995). The changing importance of romantic relationship involvement to competence from late childhood to late adolescence. *Development and Psychopathology, 7,* 727-750.

Negriff, S. (2018). Developmental pathways from maltreatment to risk behavior: Sexual behavior as a catalyst. *Development and Psychopathology, 30,* 683-693.

Negriff, S., & Susman, E. J. (2011). Pubertal timing, depression, and externalizing problems: A framework, review, and examination of gender differences. *Journal of Research on Adolescence, 21,* 717-746.

Negriff, S., Blankson, A. N., & Trickett, P. K. (2015). Pubertal timing and tempo: Associations with childhood maltreatment. *Journal of Research on Adolescence, 25,* 201-213.

Negriff, S., Ji, J., & Trickett, P. (2011a). Exposure to peer delinquency as a mediator between self-report pubertal timing and delinquency: A longitudinal study of mediation. *Development and Psychopathology, 23,* 293-304.

Negriff, S., Susman, E. J., & Trickett, P. K. (2011b). The developmental pathway from pubertal timing to delinquency and sexual activity from early to late adolescence. *Journal of Youth and Adolescence, 40,* 1343-1356.

Negru-Subtirica, O., Pop, E., Luyckx, K., Dezutter, J., & Steger, M. (2016). The meaningful identity: A longitudinal look at the interplay between identity and meaning in life in adolescence. *Developmental Psychology, 52,* 1926-1936.

Neiderhiser, J. M., Reiss, D., Pedersen, N. L., Lictenstein, P., Spotts, E. L., Hansson, K., . . . Ellhammer, O. (2004). Genetic and environmental influences on mothering of adolescents: A comparison of two samples. *Developmental Psychology, 40,* 335-351.

Nelemans, S., Hale, W. W., Branje, S. J., Meeus, W. H., & Rudolph, K. D. (2018). Individual differences in anxiety trajectories from grades 2 to 8: Impact of the middle school transition. *Development and Psychopathology, 30*(4), 1487-1501.

Nelemans, S., Keijsers, L., Colpin, H., van Leeuwen, K., Bijttebier, P., Verschueren, K., & Goossens, L. (2020). Transactional links between social anxiety symptoms and parenting across adolescence: Between- and within-person associations. *Child Development, 91,* 814-828.

Nelson, E., Lau, J., & Jarcho, J. (2014). Growing pains and pleasures: How emotional learning guides development. *Trends in Cognitive Sciences, 18,* 99-108.

Nelson, E., Leibenluft, E., McClure, E., & Pine, D. (2005). The social re-orientation of adolescence: A neuroscience perspective on the process and its relation to psychopathology. *Psychological Medicine, 35,* 163-174.

Nelson, E. E., Jarcho, J. M., & Guyer, A. E. (2016). Social re-orientation and brain development: An expanded and updated view. *Developmental Cognitive Neuroscience, 17,* 118-127.

Nelson, I. A., & Gastic, B. (2009). Street ball, swim team and the sour cream machine: A cluster analysis of out of school time participation portfolios. *Journal of Youth and Adolescence, 38,* 1172-1186.

Nelson, L. J., & Barry, C. M. (2005). Distinguishing features of emerging adulthood. *Journal of Adolescent Research, 20,* 242-262.

Nelson, M., O'Neil, S., Wisnowski, J., Hart, D., Sawardekar, S., Rauh, V., . . . Algermissen, M. (2019). Maturation of brain microstructure and metabolism associates with increased capacity for self-regulation during the transition from childhood to adolescence. *Journal of Neuroscience, 39*(42), 8362-8375.

Nelson, S., Syed, M., Tran, A., Hu, A. W., & Lee, R. (2018). Pathways to ethnic-racial identity development and psychological adjustment: The differential associations of cultural socialization by parents and peers. *Developmental Psychology, 54,* 2166-2180.

Nelson, S., Van Ryzin, M., & Dishion, T. (2015). Alcohol, marijuana, and tobacco use trajectories from age 12 to 24 years: Demographic correlates and young adult substance use problems. *Development and Psychopathology, 27,* 253-277.

Neppl, T., Dhalewadikar, J., & Lohman, B. (2016). Harsh parenting, deviant peers, adolescent risk behavior: Understanding the mediational effect of attitudes and intentions. *Journal of Research on Adolescence, 26,* 538-551.

Neppl, T. K., Jeon, S., Schofield, T. J., & Donnellan, M. B. (2015). The impact of economic pressure on parent positivity, parenting, and adolescent positivity into emerging adulthood. *Family Relations, 64,* 80-92.

Nesbit, K. C., Kolobe, T. H., Sisson, S. B., & Ghement, I. R. (2014). A model of environmental correlates of adolescent obesity in the United States. *Journal of Adolescent Health, 55,* 394-401.

Nesi, J., Miller, A., & Prinstein, M. J. (2017). Adolescents' depressive symptoms and subsequent technology-based interpersonal behaviors: A multi-wave study. *Journal of Applied Developmental Psychology, 51,* 12-19.

Nesi, J., Widman, L., Choukas-Bradley, S., & Prinstein, M. J. (2017). Technology-based communication and the development of interpersonal competencies within adolescent romantic relationships: A preliminary investigation. *Journal of Research on Adolescence, 27,* 471-477.

Neuenschwander, M., & Kracke, B. (2011). Career development. In B. Brown & M. Prinstein (Eds.), *Encyclopedia of adolescence* (Vol. 1, pp. 97-105). New York: Academic Press.

Neumark-Sztainer, D., Paxton, S. J., Hannan, P. J., Haines, J., & Story, M. (2006). Does body satisfaction matter? Five-year longitudinal associations between body satisfaction and health behaviors in adolescent females and males. *Journal of Adolescent Health, 39,* 244-251.

Neumark-Sztainer, D., Story, M., Dixon, L., & Murray, D. (1998). Adolescents engaging in unhealthy weight control behaviors: Are they at risk for other health-compromising behaviors? *American Journal of Public Health, 88,* 952-955.

Neumark-Sztainer, D., Wall, M., Story, M., & Standish, A. R. (2012). Dieting and unhealthy weight control behaviors during adolescence: Associations with 10-year changes in body mass index. *Journal of Adolescent Health, 50,* 80-86.

New York Times. (2020). Tracking the coronavirus at U.S. colleges and universities. Retrieved from https://www.nytimes.com/interactive/2020/us/covid-college-cases-tracker.html on October 23, 2020.

Newman, B., & Newman, P. (2001). Group identity and alienation: Giving the we its due. *Journal of Youth and Adolescence, 30,* 515-538.

Newman, B., & Newman, P. (2011). Adolescence, theories of. In B. Brown & M. Prinstein (Eds.), *Encyclopedia of adolescence* (Vol. 1, pp. 20-29). New York: Academic Press.

Newsome, J., & Sullivan, C. (2014). Resilience and vulnerability in adolescents: Genetic influences on differential response to risk for delinquency. *Journal of Youth & Adolescence, 43,* 1080-1095.

Neyt, B., Omey, E., Verhaest, D., & Baert, S. (2017). *Does student work really affect educational outcomes? A review of the literature.* Bonn, Germany: IZA Institute of Labor Economics.

Nguyen, J., & Brown, B. (2010). Making meanings, meaning identity: Hmong adolescent perceptions and use of language and style as identity symbols. *Journal of Research on Adolescence, 20,* 849-868.

Nguyen, Q., Rehkopf, D., Schmidt, N., & Osypuk, T. (2016). Heterogeneous effects of housing vouchers on the mental health of US adolescents. *American Journal of Public Health, 106,* 755-762.

Niederkrotenthaler, T., Stack, S., Till, B., Sinyor, M., Pirkis, J., Garcia, D., . . . & Tran, U. S. (2019). Association of increased youth suicides in the United States with the release of *13 Reasons Why. JAMA Psychiatry, 76*(9), 933-940.

Nieuwenhuis, J., van Ham, M., Yu, R., Branje, S., Meeus, W., & Hooimeijer, P. (2017). Being poorer than the rest of the neighborhood: Relative deprivation and problem behavior of youth. *Journal of Youth and Adolescence, 46,* 1891-1904.

Nishina, A. (2012). Microcontextual characteristics of peer victimization experiences and adolescents' daily well-being. *Journal of Youth and Adolescence, 41,* 191-201.

Nishina, A., & Juvonen, J. (2005). Daily reports of witnessing and experiencing peer harassment in middle school. *Child Development, 76,* 435-450.

Nishina, A., & Witkow, M. (2020). Why developmental researchers should care about biracial, multiracial, and multiethnic youth. *Child Development Perspectives, 14,* 21-27.

Nishina, A., Bellmore, A., Witkow, M., & Nylund-Gibson, K. (2010). Longitudinal consistency of adolescent ethnic identification across varying school ethnic contexts. *Developmental Psychology, 46,* 1389-1401.

Nishina, A., Bellmore, A., Witkow, M. R., Nylund-Gibson, K., & Graham, S. (2018). Mismatches in self-reported and meta-perceived ethnic identification across the high school years. *Journal of Youth and Adolescence, 47,* 51-63.

Niwa, E. Y., Way, N., & Hughes, D. L. (2014). Trajectories of ethnic-racial discrimination among ethnically diverse early adolescents: Associations with psychological and social adjustment. *Child Development, 85,* 2339-2354.

Noakes, M., & Rinaldi, C. (2006). Age and gender differences in peer conflict. *Journal of Youth and Adolescence, 35,* 881-891.

Noble, K. G., Korgaonkar, M. S., Grieve, S. M., & Brickman, A. M. (2013). Higher education is an age-independent predictor of white matter integrity and cognitive control in late adolescence. *Developmental Science, 16,* 653-664.

Nock, M., Prinstein, M., & Sterba, S. (2009). Revealing the form and function of self-injurious thoughts and behaviors: A real-time ecological assessment study among adolescents and young adults. *Journal of Abnormal Psychology, 118,* 816-827.

Nogueira Avelar e Silva, R., van de Bongardt, D., Baams, L., & Raat, H. (2018). Bidirectional associations between adolescents' sexual behaviors and psychological well-being. *Journal of Adolescent Health, 62,* 63-71.

Nogueira Avelar e Silva, R., van de Bongardt, D., van de Looij-Jansen, P., Wijtzes, A., & Raat, H. (2016). Mother- and father-adolescent relationships and early sexual intercourse. *Pediatrics, 138,* e20160782.

Noll, J., Guastaferro, K., Beal, S., Schreier, H., Barnes, J., Reader, J., & Font, S. (2019). Is sexual abuse a unique predictor of sexual risk behaviors, pregnancy, and motherhood in adolescence? *Journal of Research on Adolescence, 29,* 967-983.

Nolle, K., Guerino, P., & Dinkes, R. (2007). *Crime, violence, discipline, and safety in U.S. public schools: Findings from the School Survey on Crime and Safety: 2005-06.* Washington, DC: National Center for Education Statistics, Institute of Education Sciences, U.S. Department of Education.

Noller, P., & Callan, V. (1990). Adolescents' perceptions of the nature of their communication with parents. *Journal of Youth and Adolescence, 19,* 349-362.

Norona, J., Salvatore, J., Welsh, D., & Darling, N. (2014). Rejection sensitivity and adolescents' perceptions of romantic interactions. *Journal of Adolescence, 37,* 1257-1267.

Norona, J., Welsh, D., Olmstead, S., & Bliton, C. (2017). The symbolic nature of trust in heterosexual adolescent romantic relationships. *Archives of Sexual Behavior, 46,* 1673-1684.

North, E., Ryan, A., Cortina, K., & Brass, N. (2019). Social status and classroom behavior in math and science during early adolescence. *Journal of Youth and Adolescence, 48,* 597-608.

Nosko, A., Tieu, T.-T., Lawford, H., & Pratt, M. (2011). How do I love thee? Let me count the ways: Parenting during adolescence, attachment styles, and romantic narratives in emerging adulthood. *Developmental Psychology, 47,* 645-657.

Novak, J., & Furman, W. (2016). Partner violence during adolescence and young adulthood: Individual and relationship level risk factors. *Journal of Youth and Adolescence, 45,* 1849-1861.

Nuñez, A. (2009). Latino students' transitions to college: A social and intercultural capital perspective. *Harvard Educational Review, 79,* 22-49.

Nurmi, J. (2004). Socialization and self-development: Channeling, selection, adjustment, and reflection. In R. Lerner & L. Steinberg (Eds.), *Handbook of adolescent psychology* (pp. 85-124). New York: Wiley.

Nurmi, J., Onatsu, T., & Haavisto, T. (1995). Underachievers' cognitive and behavioral strategies: Self-handicapping at school. *Contemporary Educational Psychology, 20,* 188-200.

O'Brien, L., Albert, D., Chein, J., & Steinberg, L. (2011). Adolescents prefer more immediate rewards when in the presence of their peers. *Journal of Research on Adolescence, 21,* 747-753.

O'Connor, S. M., Burt, A., VanHuysse, J. L., & Klump, K. L. (2016). What drives the association between weight-conscious peer groups and disordered eating? Disentangling genetic and environmental selection from pure socialization effects. *Journal of Abnormal Psychology, 125,* 356-368.

O'Connor, T., Caspi, A., DeFries, J., & Plomin, R. (2000). Are associations between parental divorce and children's adjustment genetically mediated? An adoption study. *Developmental Psychology, 36,* 429-437.

O'Connor, T., Deater-Deckard, K., Fulker, D., Rutter, M., & Plomin, R. (1998). Genotype-environment correlations in late childhood and early adolescence: Antisocial behavioral problems and coercive parenting. *Developmental Psychology, 34,* 970-981.

O'Hara, R., Gibbons, F., Gerrard, M., Li, Z., & Sargent, J. (2012). Greater exposure to sexual content in popular movies predicts earlier sexual debut and increased sexual risk taking. *Psychological Science, 23,* 984-993.

O'Hare, E. D., Lu, L. H., Houston, S. M., Bookheimer, S. Y., & Sowell, E. R. (2008). Neurodevelopmental changes in verbal working memory load-dependency: An fMRI investigation. *Neuroimage, 42,* 1678-1685.

O'Keefe, G., Clarke-Pearson, K., & Council on Communications and Media. (2011). The impact of social media on children, adolescents, and families. *Pediatrics, 127,* 800-804.

O'Malley Olsen, E., Vivolo-Kantor, A., Kann, L., & Milligan, C. (2017). Trends in school-related victimization of lesbian, gay, and bisexual youths—Massachusetts, 1995-2015. *American Journal of Public Health, 107,* 1116-1118.

O'Sullivan, L., Cheng, M., Harris, K., & Brooks-Gunn, J. (2007). I wanna hold your hand: The progression of social, romantic, and sexual events in adolescent relationships. *Perspectives on Sexual and Reproductive Health, 39,* 100-107.

Oakes, J. (1995). Two cities' tracking and within-school segregation. *Teachers College Record, 96,* 681-690.

Oakes, J. (2005) *Keeping track: How schools structure inequality.* New Haven: Yale University Press.

Oakley, D., & Bogue, E. (1995). Quality of condom use as reported by female clients of a family planning clinic. *American Journal of Public Health, 85,* 1526-1530.

Obeidallah, D., Brennan, R. T., Brooks-Gunn, J., & Earls, F. (2004). Links between pubertal timing and neighborhood contexts: Implications for girls' violent behavior. *Journal of the American Academy of Child and Adolescent Psychiatry, 43,* 1460-1468.

Obergefell v. Hodges. 576 U.S.__2015.

Oberle, E., Ji, X., Guhn, M., Schonert-Reichl, K., & Gadermann, A. (2019). Benefits of extracurricular participation in early adolescence: Associations with peer belonging and mental health. *Journal of Youth and Adolescence, 48,* 2255-2270.

Obsuth, I., Hennighausen, K., Brumariu, L., & Lyons-Ruth, K. (2014). Disorganized behavior in adolescent-parent interaction: Relations to attachment state of mind, partner abuse, and psychopathology. *Child Development, 85,* 370-387.

Odgers, C. L., Caspi, A., Russell, M. A., Sampson, R. J., Arseneault, L., & Moffitt, T. E. (2012). Supportive parenting mediates neighborhood socioeconomic disparities in children's antisocial behavior from ages 5 to 12. *Development and Psychopathology, 24,* 705-721.

Odudu, C., Williams, M., & Campione-Barr,, N. (2020). Associations between domain differentiated sibling conflict and adolescent problem behavior. *Journal of Marriage and Family, 82,* 1015-1025.

OECD (2020). *PISA 2018 Results.* Paris: Author.

OECD. (2020). *Education at a glance.* Paris: Author.

Oelsner, J., Lippold, M., & Greenberg, M. (2011). Factors influencing the development of school bonding among middle school students. *Journal of Early Adolescence, 31,* 463-487.

Oesterle, S., Kuklinski, M., Hawkins, J., Skinner, M., Guttmannova, K., & Rhew, I. (2018). Long-term effects of the Communities That Care trial on substance use, antisocial behavior, and violence through age 21 years. *American Journal of Public Health, 108,* 659-665.

Oettinger, G. (1999). Does high school employment affect high school academic performance? *Industrial and Labor Relations Review, 53,* 136-151.

Offer, S. (2013). Family time activities and adolescents' emotional well-being. *Journal of Marriage and Family, 75,* 26-41.

Office of Juvenile Justice and Delinquency Prevention. (2020). *Arrest rates by offense and age.* Washington: Author.

Ogle, J. P., & Damhorst, M. L. (2003). Mothers' and daughters' interpersonal approaches to body and dieting. *Journal of Family Influence, 24,* 448-487.

Ohannessian, C. M., & Vannucci, A. (2020). Adolescent psychological functioning and membership in latent adolescent-parent communication dual trajectory classes. *Journal of Research on Adolescence, 30*(S1), 66-86.

Oi, K. (2019). Does degree completion improve non-cognitive skills during early adulthood and adulthood? *Journal of Adolescence, 71,* 50-62.

Ojeda, M., Del Rey, R., & Hunter, S. (2019). Longitudinal relationships between sexting and involvement in both bullying and cyberbullying. *Journal of Adolescence, 77,* 81-89.

Okado, Y., & Bierman, K. (2015). Differential risk for late adolescent conduct problems and mood dysregulation among children with early externalizing behavior problems. *Journal of Abnormal Child Psychology, 43,* 735-747.

Okonofua, J., & Eberhardt, J. (2015). Two strikes: Race and the disciplining of young students. *Psychological Science, 26,* 617-624.

Olfson, M., Blanco, C., Wang, S., Laje, G., & Correll, C. U. (2014). National trends in the mental health care of children, adolescents, and adults by office-based physicians. *JAMA Psychiatry, 71,* 81-90.

Olfson, M., Druss, B., & Marcus, S. (2015). Trends in mental health care among children and adolescents. *New England Journal of Medicine, 372,* 2029-2038.

Olvera, N., McCarley, K., Rodriguez, A. X., Noor, N., & Hernández-Valero, M. (2015). Body image disturbances and predictors of body dissatisfaction among Hispanic and white preadolescents. *Journal of Research of Adolescence, 25,* 728-738.

Oosterhoff, B., & Metzger, A. (2016). Mother-adolescent civic messages: Associations with adolescent civic behavior and civic judgments. *Journal of Applied Developmental Psychology, 43,* 62-70.

Oosterhoff, B., & Metzger, A. (2017). Domain specificity in adolescents' concepts of laws: Associations among beliefs and behavior. *Journal of Research on Adolescence, 27,* 139-154.

Oosterhoff, B., Kaplow, J., Layne, C., & Pynoos, R. (2018). Civilization and its discontented: Links between youth victimization, beliefs about government, and political participation across seven American presidencies. *American Psychologist, 73,* 230-242.

Oosterhoff, B., Kaplow, J., Wray-Lake, L., & Gallagher, K. (2017). Activity-specific pathways among duration of organized activity involvement, social support, and adolescent well-being: Findings from a nationally representative sample. *Journal of Adolescence, 60,* 83-93.

Oosterhoff, B., Wray-Lake, L., Palmer, C. A., & Kaplow, J. B. (2019). Historical trends in concerns about social issues across four decades among U.S. adolescents. *Journal of Research on Adolescence, 30*(S2), 485-498.

Op de Macks, Z. A., Bunge, S. A., Bell, R. N., Kriegsfeld, L. J., Kayser, A. S., & Dahl, R. E. (2017). The effect of social rank feedback on risk taking and associated reward processes in adolescent girls. *Social Cognitive and Affective Neuroscience, 12,* 240-250.

Oppenheimer, C., Hankin, B., & Young, J. (2018). Effect of parenting and peer stressors on cognitive vulnerability and risk for depression among youth. *Journal of Abnormal Child Psychology, 46,* 597-612.

Oransky, M., & Marecek, J. (2009). "I'm not going to be a girl": Masculinity and emotions in boys' friendships and peer groups. *Journal of Adolescent Research, 24,* 218-241.

Orben, A., & Przybylski, A. K. (2019). The association between adolescent well-being and digital technology use. *Nature Human Behaviour, 3,* 173-182.

Ordaz, S. J., Fritz, B. L., Forbes, E. E., & Luna, B. (2017). The influence of pubertal maturation on antisaccade performance. *Developmental Science, e12568.*

Orihuela, C. A., Mrug, S., Davies, S., Elliott, M. N., Tortolero Emery, S., Peskin, M. F., . . . Schuster, M. A. (2020). Neighborhood disorder, family functioning, and risky sexual behaviors in adolescence. *Journal of Youth and Adolescence, 49,* 991-1004.

Orlando, M., Tucker, J., Ellickson, P., & Klein, D. (2004). Developmental trajectories of cigarette smoking and their correlates from early

adolescence to young adulthood. *Journal of Consulting and Clinical Psychology, 72,* 400-410.

Orpinas, P., Horne, A., Song, X., Reeves, P., & Hsieh, H. (2013). Dating trajectories from middle to high school: Association with academic performance and drug use. *Journal of Research on Adolescence, 23,* 772-784.

Ortega, F. B., Konstabel, K., Pasquali, E., Ruiz, J. R., Hurtig-Wennlöf, A., Mäestu, J., . . . Sjöström, M. (2013). Objectively measured physical activity and sedentary time during childhood, adolescence and young adulthood: A cohort study. *PLOS ONE, 8,* 60871.

Orth, U., & Robins, R. W. (2013). Understanding the link between low self-esteem and depression. *Current Directions in Psychological Science, 22,* 455-460.

Orth, U., & Robins, R. W. (2014). The development of self-esteem. *Current Directions in Psychological Science, 23,* 381-387.

Orth, U., Maes, J., & Schmitt, M. (2015). Self-esteem development across the life span: A longitudinal study with a large sample from Germany. *Developmental Psychology, 51,* 248-259.

Orth, U., Robins, R., Widaman, K., & Conger, R. (2014). Is low self-esteem a risk factor for depression? Findings from a longitudinal study of Mexican-origin youth. *Developmental Psychology, 50,* 622-633.

Ortiz, J., & Raine, A. (2004). Heart rate level and antisocial behavior in children and adolescents. *Journal of the American Academy of Child and Adolescent Psychiatry, 43,* 154-162.

Osgerby, B. (2008). Understanding the "Jackpot Market": Media, marketing, and the rise of the American teenager. In P. Jamieson & D. Romer (Eds.), *The changing portrayal of adolescents in the media since 1950* (pp. 27-58). New York: Oxford University Press.

Osgood, D. W., Ruth, G., Eccles, J., Jacobs, J., & Barber, B. (2005). Six paths to adulthood. In R. Settersten, F. Furstenberg, Jr., & R. Rumbaut (Eds.), *On the frontier of adulthood* (pp. 340-355). Chicago: University of Chicago Press.

Osgood, D. W., Wilson, J., O'Malley, P., Bachman, J., & Johnston, L. (1996). Routine activities and individual deviant behavior. *American Sociological Review, 61,* 635-655.

Oshri, A., Kogan, S., Kwon, J., Wickrama, K., Vanderbroek, L., Palmer, A., & Mackillop, J. (2018). Impulsivity as a mechanism linking child abuse and neglect with substance use in adolescence and adulthood. *Development and Psychopathology, 30,* 417-435.

Osypuk, T. L., Tchetgen, E. J., Acevedo-Garcia, D., Earls, F. J., Lincoln, A., Schmidt, N. M., & Glymour, M. (2012). Differential mental health effects of neighborhood relocation among youth in vulnerable families: Results from a randomized trial. *Archives of General Psychiatry, 69,* 1284-1294.

Ott, M. A., Millstein, S. G., Ofner, S., & Halpern-Felsher, B. L. (2006). Greater expectations: Adolescents' positive motivations for sex. *Perspectives on Sexual and Reproductive Health, 38,* 84-89.

Overbeek, G., Stattin, H., Vermulst, A., Ha, T., & Engels, R. (2007). Parent-child relationships, partner relationships, and emotional adjustment: A birth-to-maturity prospective study. *Developmental Psychology, 43,* 429-437.

Overbeek, G., van de Bongardt, D., & Baams, L. (2018). Buffer or brake? The role of sexuality-specific parenting in adolescents' sexualized media consumption and sexual development. *Journal of Youth and Adolescence, 47,* 1427-1439.

Owens, A. (2010). Neighborhoods and schools as competing and reinforcing contexts for educational attainment. *Sociology of Education, 83,* 287-311.

Owens, E., & Hinshaw, S. (2020). Adolescent mediators of unplanned pregnancy among women with and without childhood ADHD, *Journal of Clinical Child and Adolescent Psychology, 49,* 229-238.

Owens, S., Helms, S., Rudolph, K., Hastings, P., Nock, M., & Prinstein, M. (2019). Interpersonal stress severity longitudinally predicts adolescent girls' depressive symptoms: The moderating role of subjective and HPA axis stress responses. *Journal of Abnormal Child Psychology, 47,* 895-905.

Owens, S. A., Eisenlohr-Moul, T. A., and Prinstein, M. J. (2020), Understanding when and why some adolescent girls attempt suicide: An emerging framework integrating menstrual cycle fluctuations in risk. *Child Development Perspectives, 14,* 116-123.

Owotomo, O., Maslowsky, J., & Loukas, A. (2018). Perceptions of the harm and addictiveness of conventional cigarette smoking among adolescent e-cigarette users. *Journal of Adolescent Health, 62,* 87-93.

Oxford, M., Gilchrist, L., Gillmore, M., & Lohr, M. (2006). Predicting variation in the life course of adolescent mothers as they enter adulthood. *Journal of Adolescent Health, 39,* 20-26.

Oxford, M., Gilchrist, L., Lohr, M., Gillmore, M., Morrison, D., & Spieker, S. (2005). Life course heterogeneity in the transition from adolescence to adulthood among adolescent mothers. *Journal of Research on Adolescence, 15,* 479-504.

Oyserman, D., Bybee, D., & Terry, K. (2006). Possible selves and academic outcomes: How and when possible selves impel action. *Journal of Personality and Social Psychology, 91,* 188-204.

Pabian, S., Vandebosch, H., Poels, K., Van Cleemput, K., & Bastiaensens, S. (2016). Exposure to cyberbullying as a bystander: An investigation of desensitization effects among early adolescents. *Computers in Human Behavior, 62,* 480-487.

Paceley, M., Sattler, P., Goffnett, J., Jen, S. (2020). "It feels like home": Transgender youth in the Midwest and conceptualizations of community climate. *Journal of Community Psychology, 48,* 1863-1881.

Padilla Paredes, P., & Calvete Zumalde, E. (2015). A test of the vulnerability-stress model with brooding and reflection to explain depressive symptoms in adolescence. *Journal of Youth and Adolescence, 44,* 860-869.

Padilla-Walker, L. (2008). Domain-appropriateness of maternal discipline as a predictor of adolescents' positive and negative outcomes. *Journal of Family Psychology, 22,* 456-464.

Padilla-Walker, L., Carlo, G., & Memmott-Elison, M. (2017). Longitudinal change in adolescents' prosocial behavior toward strangers, friends, and family. *Journal of Research on Adolescence, 28*(3), 698-710.

Padilla-Walker, L., Coyne, S., & Collier, K. (2016). Longitudinal relations between parental media monitoring and adolescent aggression, prosocial behavior, and externalizing problems. *Journal of Adolescence, 46,* 86-97.

Padilla-Walker, L., Day, R., Dyer, W., & Black, B. (2013). "Keep on keeping on, even when it's hard!": Predictors and outcomes of adolescent persistence. *The Journal of Early Adolescence, 33,* 433-457.

Padilla-Walker, L. M., & Christensen, K. J. (2011). Empathy and self-regulation as mediators between parenting and adolescents' prosocial behaviors toward strangers, friends, and family. *Journal of Research on Adolescence, 21,* 545-551.

Padmanabhan, A., Geier, C., Ordaz, S., Teslovich, T., & Luna, B. (2011). Developmental changes in brain function underlying the influence of reward processing on inhibitory control. *Developmental Cognitive Neuroscience, 1,* 517-529.

Pahl, K., & Way, N. (2006). Longitudinal trajectories of ethnic identity among urban Black and Latino adolescents. *Child Development, 77,* 1403-1415.

Paik, A., Sanchagrin, K., & Heimer, K. (2016). Broken promises: Abstinence pledging and sexual and reproductive health. *Journal of Marriage and Family, 78,* 546-561.

Pain, E. (2020). Is teen risk of having sex with strangers associated with family environment? Family processes, household structure, and adolescent sex with strangers. *Youth & Society, 52,* 894-911.

Pál, J., Stadtfeld, C., Grow, A., & Takács, K. (2016). Status perceptions matter: Understanding disliking among adolescents. *Journal of Research on Adolescence, 26,* 805-818.

Palladino, G. (1996). *Teenagers: An American history.* New York: Basic Books.

Pallock, L., & Lamborn, S. (2006). Beyond parenting practices: Extended kinship support and the academic adjustment of African-American and European-American teens. *Journal of Adolescence, 29,* 813-828.

Pan, Y., Yang, C., Liu, G., Chan, M., Liu, C., & Zhang, D. (2020). Peer victimization and problem behaviors: the roles of self-esteem and parental attachment among Chinese adolescents. *Child Development, 91,* e968-e983.

Pardini, D., Loeber, R., & Stouthamer-Loeber, M. (2005). Developmental shifts in parent and peer influences on boys' beliefs about delinquent behavior. *Journal of Research on Adolescence 15,* 299-323.

Park, A., Kim, J., Zaso, M., Glatt, S., Sher, K., Scott-Sheldon, L., . . . Carey, M. (2017). The interaction between the dopamine receptor D4 (DRD4) variable number tandem repeat polymorphism and perceived peer drinking norms in adolescent alcohol use and misuse. *Development and Psychopathology, 29,* 173-183.

Park, A., Sher, K., Todorov, A., & Heath, A. (2011). Interaction between the DRD4 VNTR polymorphism and proximal and distal environments in alcohol dependence during emerging and young adulthood. *Journal of Abnormal Psychology, 120,* 585-595.

Park, I., Wang, L., Williams, D., & Alegria, M. (2017). Does anger regulation mediate the discrimination-mental health link among Mexican-origin adolescents? A longitudinal mediation analysis using multilevel modeling. *Developmental Psychology, 53,* 340-352.

Park, M. J., Scott, J. T., Adams, S. H., Brindis, C. D., & Irwin, C. E., Jr. (2014). Adolescent and young adult health in the United States in the past decade: Little improvement and young adults remain worse off than adolescents. *Journal of Adolescent Health, 55,* 3-16.

Parker, J., Low, C., Walker, A. & Gamm, B. (2005). Friendship jealousy in young adolescents: Individual differences and links to sex, self-esteem, aggression, and social adjustment. *Developmental Psychology, 41,* 235-250.

Parker, K. (2012). *The boomerang generation.* Washington: Pew Research Center.

Parker, K. F., & Reckdenwald, A. (2008). Concentrated disadvantage, traditional male role models, and African-American juvenile violence. *Criminology, 46,* 711-735.

Parker, P., Schoon, I., Tsai, Y., Nagy, G., Trautwein, U., & Eccles, J. (2012). Achievement, agency, gender, and socioeconomic background as predictors of postschool choices: A multicontext study. *Developmental Psychology, 48,* 1629-1642.

Parkes, A., Waylen, A., Saval, K., Heron, J., Henderson, M., Wight, D., & Mcleoud, J. (2014). Which behavioral, emotional and school problems in middle-childhood predict early sexual behavior? *Journal of Youth & Adolescence, 43,* 507-527.

Parkin, C. M., & Kuczynski, L. (2012). Adolescent perspectives on rules and resistance within the parent-child relationship. *Journal of Adolescent Research, 27,* 632-658.

Parks, M., Solomon, R., Solomon, S., Rowland, B., Hemphill, S., Patton, G., & Toumbourou, J. (2020). Delinquency, school context, and risk factors in India, Australia, and the United States: Implications for prevention. *Journal of Research on Adolescence, 30*(S1), 143-157.

Parra, A., Oliva, A., & Sánchez-Queija, I. (2015). Development of emotional autonomy from adolescence to young adulthood in Spain. *Journal of Adolescence, 38,* 57-67.

Parra, G., Patwardhan, I., Mason, W., Chmelka, M., Savolainen, J., Miettunen, J., & Järvelin, M.-R. (2020). Parental alcohol use and the alcohol misuse of their offspring in a Finnish birth cohort: Investigation of developmental timing. *Journal of Youth and Adolescence, 49,* 1702-1715.

Pascarella, E., & Terenzini, P. (2005). *How college affects students: Vol. 2. A third decade of research.* San Francisco: Jossey-Bass.

Pasch, K. E., Latimer, L. A., Duncan Cance, J., Moe, S. G., & Lytle, L. A. (2012). Longitudinal bi-directional relationships between sleep and youth substance use. *Journal of Youth and Adolescence, 41,* 1184-1196.

Patall, E., Cooper, H., & Wynn, S. R. (2010). The effectiveness and relative importance of choice in the classroom. *Journal of Educational Psychology, 102,* 896-915.

Patchin, J., & Hinduja, S. (2019). The nature and extent of sexting among a national sample of middle and high school students in the US. *Archives of Sexual Behavior, 48,* 2333-2343.

Paten, S. (2013). Major depression epidemiology from a diathesis-stress conceptualization. *BMC Psychiatry, 13,* 19.

Paternoster, R., McGloin, J., Nguyen, H., & Thomas, K. (2013). The causal impact of exposure to deviant peers: An experimental investigation. *Journal of Research in Crime and Delinquency, 50,* 476-503.

Patterson, C. J. (2009). Children of lesbian and gay parents: Psychology, law, and policy. *American Psychologist, 64,* 727-736.

Patton, D., Hong, J., Ranney, M., Patel, S., Kelley, C., Eschmann, R., & Washington, T. (2014). Social media as a vector for youth violence: A review of the literature. *Computers in Human Behavior, 35,* 548-553.

Patton, D., Leonard, P., Elaesser, C., Eschmann, R., Patel, S., & Crosby, S. (2019). What's a threat on social media? How Black and Latino Chicago young men define and navigate threats online. *Youth & Society, 51,* 756-772.

Patton, G., Coffey, C., Carlin, J., Sawyer, S., & Wakefield, M. (2006). Teen smokers reach their mid twenties. *Journal of Adolescent Health, 39,* 214-220.

Patton, G., Olsson, C., Bond, L., Toumbourou, J., Carlin, J., . . . Hemphill, S.(2008). Predicting female depression across puberty: A two-nation longitudinal study. *Journal of the American Academy of Child & Adolescent Psychiatry, 47,* 1424-1432.

Paunesku, D., Walton, G., Romero, C., Smith, E., Yeager, D., & Dweck, C. (2015). Mind-set interventions are a scalable treatment for academic underachievement. *Psychological Science, 26,* 784-793.

Paus, T. (2009). Brain development. In R. Lerner & L. Steinberg (Eds.), *Handbook of adolescent psychology* (3rd ed., Vol. 1, pp. 95-115). New York: Wiley.

Paus, T., Keshavan, B., & Giedd, J. (2008). Why do so many psychiatric disorders emerge during adolescence? *Nature Reviews Neuroscience, 9,* 947-957.

Paxton, S., Wertheim, E., Gibbons, K., Szmukler, G., Hillier, L., & Petrovich, J. (1991). Body image satisfaction, dieting beliefs, and weight loss behaviors in adolescent girls and boys. *Journal of Youth and Adolescence, 20,* 361-380.

Payne, A., & Hutzell, K. (2017). Old wine, new bottle? Comparing interpersonal bullying and cyberbullying victimization. *Youth & Society, 49,* 1149-1178.

Pearce, L., Hayward, G., Chassin, L., & Curran, P. (2018). The increasing diversity and complexity of family structures for adolescents. *Journal of Research on Adolescence, 28,* 591-608.

Pearson, C. M., & Smith, G. T. (2015). Bulimic symptom onset in young girls: A longitudinal trajectory analysis. *Journal of Abnormal Psychology, 124,* 1003-1013.

Pedersen, S., Vitaro, F., Barker, E., & Borge, A. (2007). The timing of middle-childhood peer rejection and friendship: Linking early behavior to early-adolescent adjustment. *Child Development, 78,* 1037-1051.

Peeters, M., Janssen, T., Monshouwer, K., Boendermaker, W., Pronk, T., Wiers, R., & Vollebergh, W. (2015). Weaknesses in executive functioning predict the initiating of adolescents' alcohol use. *Developmental Cognitive Neuroscience, 16,* 139-146.

Peguero, A., & Bracy, N. (2015). School order, justice, and education: Climate, discipline practices, and dropping out. *Journal of Research on Adolescence, 25,* 412-426.

Peguero, A., Bondy, J., & Hong, J. (2017). Social bonds across immigrant generations: Bonding to school and examining the relevance of assimilation. *Youth & Society, 49,* 733-754.

Pekrun, R. (2017). Emotion and achievement during adolescence. *Child Development Perspectives, 11,* 215-221.

Pellegrini, A. (2003). Perceptions and functions of play and real fighting in early adolescence. *Child Development, 74,* 1522-1533.

Pellegrini, A. D., & Long, J. D. (2007). An observational study of early heterosexual interaction at middle-school dances. *Journal of Research on Adolescence, 17,* 613-638.

Pellerin, L. (2005). Student disengagement and the socialization styles of high schools. *Social Forces, 84,* 1159-1179.

Peng, C.-Z., Grant, J., Heath, A., Reiersen, A., Mulligan, R., & Anokhin, A. (2016). Familial influences on the full range of variability in attention and activity levels during adolescence: A longitudinal twin study. *Development and Psychopathology, 28,* 517-526.

Peper, J., Mandl, R., Braams, B., de Water, E., Heijboer, A., Koolschijn, P., & Crone, E. (2013). Delay discounting and frontostriatal fiber tracts: A combined DTI and MTR study on impulsive choices in healthy young adults. *Cerebral Cortex, 23,* 1695-1702.

Pepin, J., & Cotter, D. (2018). Separating spheres? Diverging trends in youth's gender attitudes about work and family. *Journal of Marriage and Family, 80,* 7-24.

Pérez, J., Cumsille, P., & Martínez, M. (2016). Brief report: Agreement between parent and adolescent autonomy expectations and its relationship to adolescent adjustment. *Journal of Adolescence, 53,* 10-15.

Perez-Brumer, A., Day, J., Russell, S., & Hatzenbuehler, M. (2017). Prevalence and correlates of suicidal ideation among transgender youth in California: Findings from a representative, population-based sample of high school students. *Journal of the American Academy of Child & Adolescent Psychiatry, 56,* 739-746.

Perino, M. T., Miernicki, M. E., & Telzer, E. H. (2016). Letting the good times roll: Adolescence as a period of reduced inhibition to appetitive social cues. *Social Cognitive and Affective Neuroscience, 11,* 1762-1771.

Perkins, D., Luster, T., & Jank, W. (2002). Protective factors, physical abuse, and purging from community-wide surveys of female adolescents. *Journal of Adolescent Research, 17,* 377-400.

Perkins, S. A., & Turiel, E. (2007). To lie or not to lie: To whom and under what circumstances. *Child Development, 78,* 609-621.

Perrino, T., Brincks, A., Lee, T., Quintana, K., & Prado, G. (2019). Screen-based sedentary behaviors and internalizing symptoms across time among U.S. Hispanic adolescents. *Journal of Adolescence, 72,* 91-100.

Perry, C., Williams, C., Veblen-Mortenson, S., Toomey, T., Komro, K., Anstine, P., McGovern, P., . . . Wolfson, M. (1996). Project Northland: Outcomes of a communitywide alcohol use prevention program during early adolescence. *American Journal of Public Health, 86,* 956-965.

Perry, D., & Pauletti, R. (2011). Gender and adolescent development. *Journal of Research on Adolescence, 21,* 61-74.

Persike, M., & Seiffge-Krenke, I. (2014). Is stress perceived differently in relationships with parents and peers? Inter- and intra-regional comparisons on adolescents from 21 nations. *Journal of Adolescence, 37,* 493-504.

Persson, A., Kerr, M., & Stattin, H. (2007). Staying in or moving away from structured activities: Explanations involving parents and peers. *Developmental Psychology, 43,* 197-207.

Peters, S., Peper, J. S., van Duijvenvoorde, A. C. K., Braams, B. R., & Crone, E. A. (2017). Amygdala-orbitofrontal connectivity predicts alcohol use two years later: A longitudinal neuroimaging study on alcohol use in adolescence. *Developmental Science, 20,* e12448.

Petersen, A. (1988). Adolescent development. *Annual Review of Psychology, 39,* 583-607.

Petersen, I., Bates, J., Dodge, K., Lansford, J., & Pettit, G. (2015). Describing and predicting developmental profiles of externalizing problems from childhood to adulthood. *Development and Psychopathology, 27,* 791-818.

Petersen, J., & Hyde, J. (2013). Peer sexual harassment and disordered eating in early adolescence. *Developmental Psychology, 49,* 184-195.

Peterson, S., Davis, H., & Smith, G. (2018). Personality and learning predictors of adolescent alcohol consumption trajectories. *Journal of Abnormal Psychology, 127,* 482-495.

Petraitis, J., Flay, B., & Miller, T. (1995). Reviewing theories of adolescent substance use: Organizing pieces in the puzzle. *Psychological Bulletin, 117,* 67-86.

Pettifor, A., O'Brien, K., MacPhail, C., Miller, W., & Rees, H. (2010). Early coital debut and associated HIV risk factors among young women and men in South Africa. *International Perspectives on Sexual and Reproductive Health, 35,* 74-82.

Pettit, G., Bates, J., Dodge, K., & Meece, D. (1999). The impact of after-school peer contact on early adolescent externalizing problems is moderated by parental monitoring, perceived neighborhood safety, and prior adjustment. *Child Development, 70,* 768-778.

Peviani, K., Brieant, A., Holmes, C., King-Casas, B., & Kim-Spoon, J. (2020). Religious social support protects against social risks for adolescent substance use. *Journal of Research on Adolescence, 30,* 361-371.

Pfeifer, J., & Blakemore, S-J. (2012). Adolescent social cognitive and affective neuroscience: past, present, and future. *Social Cognitive and Affective Neuroscience, 7,* 1-10.

Pfeifer, J., & Peake, S. (2012). Self-development: Integrating cognitive, socioemotional, and neuroimaging perspectives. *Developmental Cognitive Neuroscience, 2,* 55-69.

Pfeifer, J., Masten, C., Borofsky, L., Dapretto, M., Fuligni, A., & Lieberman, M. (2009). Neural correlates of direct and reflected self-appraisals in adolescents and adults: When social perspective-taking informs self-perception. *Child Development, 80,* 1016-1038.

Pfeifer, J., Masten, C., Moore, W., III, & Oswald, T. (2011). Entering adolescence: Resistance to peer influence, risky behavior, and neural changes in emotion reactivity. *Neuron, 69,* 1029-1036.

Pfeifer, J. H., Kahn, L. E., Merchant, J. S., Peake, S. A., Veroude, K., Masten, C. L., Lieberman, M. D., Mazziotta, J. C., & Dapretto, M. (2013). Longitudinal change in the neural bases of adolescent social self-evaluations: Effects of age and pubertal development. *Journal of Neuroscience, 24,* 7415-7419.

Phillipsen, L. C. (1999). Associations between age, gender, and group acceptance and three components of friendship quality. *Journal of Early Adolescence, 19,* 438-464.

Phinney, J., Ferguson, D., & Tate, J. (1997). Intergroup attitudes among ethnic minority adolescents: A causal model. *Child Development, 68,* 955-969.

Picci, G., & Scherf, K. S. (2016). From caregivers to peers: Puberty shapes human face perception. *Psychological Science, 27,* 1461-1473.

Piccoli, V., Carnaghi, A., Grassi, M., Stragà, M., & Bianchi, M. (2020). Cyberbullying through the lens of social influence: Predicting cyberbullying perpetration from perceived peer-norm, cyberspace regulations and ingroup processes. *Computers in Human Behavior, 102,* 260-273.

Piccolo, L. R., Merz, E. C., He, X., Sowell, E. R., Noble, K. G., & Pediatric Imaging, Neurocognition, and Genetics Study. (2016). Age-related differences in cortical thickness vary by socioeconomic status. *PLOS ONE, 11,* e0162511.

Piccolo, L. R., Merz, E. C., Noble, K. G., & Pediatric Imaging, Neurocognition, and Genetics Study. (2019). School climate is associated with cortical thickness and executive function in children and adolescents. *Developmental Science, 22*(1), e12719.

Piehler, T., & Dishion, T. (2014). Dyadic coregulation and deviant talk in adolescent friendships: Interaction patterns associated with problematic substance use in early adulthood. *Developmental Psychology, 50,* 1160-1169.

Piehler, T., Distefano, R., Ausherbauer, K., Bloomquist, M., Almy, B., & August, G. (2020). Self-regulatory profiles and conduct problems in youth referred to juvenile diversion. *Journal of Research on Adolescence, 30,* 372-388.

Pierce, J., & Gilpin, E. (1996). How long will today's new adolescent smoker be addicted to cigarettes? *American Journal of Public Health, 86,* 253-256.

Pietiläinen, K. H., Kaprio, J., Rasanen, M., Winter, T., Rissanen, A., & Rose, R. (2001). Tracking of body size from birth to late adolescence: Contributions of birth length, birth weight, duration of gestation, parents' body size, and twinship. *American Journal of Epidemiology, 154,* 21-29.

Pike, A., McGuire, S., Hetherington, E. M., Reiss, D., et al. (1996). Family environment and adolescent depressive symptoms and antisocial behavior: A multivariate genetic analysis. *Developmental Psychology, 32,* 590-604.

Pimentel, P. S., Arndorfer, A., & Malloy, L. C. (2015). Taking the blame for someone else's wrongdoing: The effects of age and reciprocity. *Law and Human Behavior, 39,* 219-231.

Pincham, H., Bryce, D., & Pasco Fearon, R. (2015). The neural correlates of emotion processing in juvenile offenders. *Developmental Science, 18,* 994-1005.

Pinderhughes, E., Jones Harden, B., & Guyer, A. (2007). Children in foster care. In D. Phillips, L. Aber, L. Allen, & S. Jones (Eds.), *Child development and social policy: Knowledge for action.* Washington: American Psychological Association.

Pingault, J-B., Viding, E., Galera, C., Greven, C. U., Zheng, Y., Plomin, R., & Rijsdijk, F. (2015). Genetic and environmental influences on the developmental course of attention-deficit/hyperactivity disorder symptoms from childhood to adolescence. *JAMA Psychiatry, 72,* 651-658.

Pinquart, M. (2017). Associations of parenting dimensions and styles with externalizing problems of children and adolescents: An updated meta-analysis. *Developmental Psychology, 53,* 873-932.

Pinquart, M., & Silbereisen, R. (2002). Changes in adolescents' and mothers' autonomy and connectedness in conflict discussions: An observation study. *Journal of Adolescence, 25,* 509-522.

Pintrich, P. (2000). Multiple goals, multiple pathways: The role of goal orientation in learning and achievement. *Journal of Educational Psychology, 92,* 544-555.

Piquero, A., Farrington, D., & Blumstein, A. (2003). The criminal career paradigm: Background and recent developments. *Crime and Justice: A Review of Research, 30,* 359-506.

Pittard, W., Laditka, J., & Laditka, S. (2008). Associations between maternal age and infant health outcomes among Medicaid-insured infants in South Carolina: Mediating effects of socioeconomic factors. *Pediatrics, 122,* e100-e106.

Planty, M., Bozick, R., & Regnier, M. (2006). Helping because you have to or helping because you want to? Sustaining participation in service work from adolescence through young adulthood. *Youth and Society, 38,* 177-202.

Pogarsky, G., Lizotte, A., & Thornberry, T. (2003). The delinquency of children born to young mothers: Results from the Rochester Youth Development Study. *Criminology, 41,* 1249-1286.

Pokorny, S., Jason, L., & Schoeny, M. (2006). Youth supplying tobacco to other minors: Evaluating individual and town-level correlates. *Journal of Youth and Adolescence, 35,* 705-715.

Pollak, Y., Oz, A., Neventsal, O., Rabi, O., Kitrossky, L., & Maeir, A. (2016). Do adolescents with attention-deficit/hyperactivity disorder show risk seeking? Disentangling probabilistic decision making by equalizing the favorability of alternatives. *Journal of Abnormal Psychology, 125,* 387-398.

Pomerantz, E. (2001). Parent-child socialization: Implications for the development of depressive symptoms. *Journal of Family Psychology, 15,* 510-525.

Pomerantz, E., Altermatt, E., & Saxon, J. (2002). Making the grade but feeling distressed: Gender differences in academic performance and internal distress. *Journal of Educational Psychology, 94,* 396-404.

Pomerantz, E., Qin, L., Wang, Q., & Chen, H. (2009). American and Chinese early adolescents' inclusion of their relationships with their parents in their self-construals. *Child Development, 80,* 792-807.

Pong, S., & Ju, D. (2000). The effects of change in family structure and income on dropping out in middle and high school. *Journal of Family Issues, 21,* 147-169.

Ponnet, K., Van Leeuwen, K., Wouters, E., & Mortelmans, D. (2015). A family system approach to investigate family-based pathways between financial stress and adolescent problem behavior. *Journal of Research on Adolescence, 25,* 675-780.

Ponnet, K., Wouters, E., Goedemé, T., & Mortelmans, D. (2016). Family financial stress, parenting and problem behavior in adolescents: An actor-partner interdependence approach. *Journal of Family Issues, 37,* 574-597.

Poorthuis, A., Juvonen, J., Thomaes, S., Denissen, J., Orobio de Castro, B., & van Aken, M. (2014). Do grades shape students' school engagement? The psychological consequences of report card grades at the beginning of secondary school. *Journal of Educational Psychology, 107,* 842-854.

Poropat, A. (2009). A meta-analysis of the five-factor model of personality and academic performance. *Psychological Bulletin, 135,* 322-338.

Poteat, V., & Anderson, C. (2012). Developmental changes in sexual prejudice from early to late adolescence: The effects of gender, race, and ideology on different patterns of change. *Developmental Psychology, 48,* 1403-1415.

Poteat, V., Mereish, E., & Birkett, M. (2015). The negative effects of prejudice on interpersonal relationships within adolescent peer groups. *Developmental Psychology, 51,* 544-553.

Poteat, V., Scheer, J., DiGiovanni, C., & Mereish, E. (2014). Short-term prospective effects of homophobic victimization on the mental health of heterosexual adolescents. *Journal of Youth and Adolescence, 43,* 1240-1251.

Poulin, F., & Chan, A. (2010). Friendship stability and change in childhood and adolescence. *Developmental Review, 30,* 257-272.

Poulin, F., & Denault, A. S. (2012). Other-sex friendships as a mediator between parental monitoring and substance use in girls and boys. *Journal of Youth & Adolescence, 41,* 1488-1501.

Poulin, F., & Pedersen, S. (2007). Developmental changes in gender composition of friendship networks in adolescent girls and boys. *Developmental Psychology, 43,* 1484-1496.

Poulin, F., Denault, A.-S., & Pedersen, S. (2011). Longitudinal associations between other-sex friendships and substance use in adolescence. *Journal of Research on Adolescence, 21,* 776-788.

Pouwels, J., Salmivalli, C., Saarento, S., van den Berg, Y., Lansu, T., & Cillessen, A. (2018). Predicting adolescents' bullying participation from developmental trajectories of social status and behavior. *Child Development, 89,* 1157-1176.

Power to Decide (formerly The National Campaign to Prevent Teen and Unplanned Pregnancy). (2016). *Teen Pregnancy in the United States.* Washington, DC: Author.

Pradhan, A. K., Li, K., Bingham, C. R., Simons-Morton, B. G., Ouimet, M. C., & Shope, J. T. (2014). Peer passenger influences on male adolescent drivers' visual scanning behavior during simulated driving. *Journal of Adolescent Health, 54,* S42-S49.

PrepScholar (2020). *SAT scores over time.* https://blog.prepscholar.com/average-sat-scores-over-time. Accessed on January 18, 2021.

Price, M. N., & Hyde, J. (2011). Perceived and observed maternal relationship quality predict sexual debut by age 15. *Journal of Youth and Adolescence, 40,* 1595-1606.

Priess, H., & Hyde, J. (2011). Gender roles. In B. Brown & M. Prinstein (Eds.), *Encyclopedia of adolescence* (Vol. 2, pp. 99-108). New York: Academic Press.

Priess, H., Lindberg, S., & Hyde, J. (2009). Adolescent gender-role identity and mental health: Gender intensification revisited. *Child Development, 80,* 1531-1544.

Prinstein, M. J., & La Greca, A. M. (2002). Peer crowd affiliation and internalizing distress in childhood and adolescence: A longitudinal follow-back study. *Journal of Research on Adolescence, 12,* 325-351.

Prinstein, M., & Aikins, J. (2004). Cognitive moderators of the longitudinal association between peer rejection and adolescent depressive symptoms. *Journal of Abnormal Child Psychology, 32,* 147-158.

Prinstein, M., Brechwald, W., & Cohen, G. (2011). Susceptibility to peer influence: Using a performance-based measure to identify adolescent males at heightened risk for deviant peer socialization. *Developmental Psychology, 47,* 1167-1172.

Prinstein, M., Meade, C., & Cohen, G. (2003). Adolescent oral sex, peer popularity, and perceptions of best friends' sexual behavior. *Journal of Pediatric Psychology, 28,* 243-249.

Pronk, R., & Zimmer-Gembeck, M. (2010). It's 'mean,' but what does it mean to adolescents? Relational aggression described by victims, aggressors, and their peers. *Journal of Adolescent Research, 25,* 175-204.

Prot, S., Gentile, D., Suzuki, K., Lim, K., Horiuchi, Y., Jelic, M. . . . Lam, B. (2013). Long-term relationships among prosocial-media use, empathy, and prosocial behavior. *Psychological Science, 25,* 358-368.

Przepiorka, A., & Blachnio, A. (2020). The role of Facebook intrusion, depression, and future time perspective in sleep problems among adolescents. *Journal of Research on Adolescence, 30,* 559-569.

Przybylski, A., & Mishkin, A. (2016). How the quantity and quality of electronic gaming relates to adolescents' academic engagement and psychosocial adjustment. *Psychology of Popular Media Culture, 5,* 145-156.

Przybylski, A., & Weinstein, N. (2017). A large-scale test of the Goldilocks hypothesis: Quantifying the relations between digital-screen use and the mental well-being of adolescents. *Psychological Science, 28,* 204-215.

Purdie, N., Hattie, J., & Douglas, G. (1996). Student conceptions of learning and their use of self-regulated learning strategies: A cross-cultural comparison. *Journal of Educational Psychology, 88,* 87-100.

Purtell, K. M., & McLoyd, V. C. (2013). A longitudinal investigation of employment among low-income youth: Patterns, predictors, and correlates. *Youth & Society, 45,* 243-264.

Pyrooz, D. C. (2014). From colors and guns to caps and gowns? The effects of gang membership on educational attainment. *Journal of Research in Crime and Delinquency, 51,* 56-87.

Qin, D. (2009). Being "good" or being "popular": Gender and ethnic identity negotiations of Chinese immigrant adolescents. *Journal of Adolescent Research, 24,* 37-66.

Qin, D., Way, N., & Mukherjee, P. (2008). The other side of the model minority story: The familial and peer challenges faced by Chinese American adolescents. *Youth and Society, 39,* 480-506.

Qin, L., Pomerantz, E., & Wang, Q. (2009). Are gains in decision-making autonomy during early adolescence beneficial for emotional functioning? The case of the United States and China. *Child Development, 80,* 1705-1721.

Qu, Y., & Pomerantz, E. (2015). Divergent school trajectories in early adolescence in the United States and China: An examination of underlying mechanisms. *Journal of Youth and Adolescence, 44,* 2095-2109.

Qu, Y., Fuligni, A. J., Galván, A., & Telzer, E. H. (2015). Buffering effect of positive parent-child relationships on adolescent risk taking: A longitudinal neuroimaging investigation. *Developmental Cognitive Neuroscience, 15,* 26-34.

Qu, Y., Pomerantz, E. M., & Deng, C. (2016). Mothers' goals for adolescents in the United States and China: Content and transmission. *Journal of Research on Adolescence, 26,* 126-141.

Qu, Y., Pomerantz, E., McCormick, E., & Telzer, E. (2018). Youths' perceptions of adolescence predict longitudinal changes in prefrontal cortex activation and risk taking during adolescence. *Child Development, 89,* 773-783.

Qu, Y., Pomerantz, E., Wang, M., Cheung, C., & Cimpian, A. (2016). Conceptions of adolescence: Implications for differences in engagement in school over early adolescence in the United States and China. *Journal of Youth and Adolescence, 45,* 1512-1526.

Qu, Y., Rompilla, D. B., Wang, Q., & Ng, F. F.-Y. (2020). Youth's negative stereotypes of teen emotionality: Reciprocal relations with emotional functioning in Hong Kong and mainland China. *Journal of Youth and Adolescence, 49,* 2003-2019.

Qu, Y., Yang, B., & Telzer, E. (2020). The cost of academic focus: Daily school problems and biopsychological adjustment in Chinese American families. *Journal of Youth and Adolescence, 49,* 1631-1644.

Quach, A., Tervo-Clemmens, B., Foran, W., Calabro, F., Chung, T., Clark, D., & Luna, B. (2020). Adolescent development of inhibitory control and substance use vulnerability: A longitudinal neuroimaging study. *Developmental Cognitive Neuroscience, 42,* 100771.

Qualter, P., Hurley, R., Eccles, A., Abbott, J., Boivin, M., & Tremblay, R. (2018). Reciprocal prospective relationships between loneliness and weight status in late childhood and early adolescence.

Journal of Youth and Adolescence, 47, 1385-1397.

Qualter, P., Vanhalst, J., Harris, R., Van Roekel, E., Lodder, G., Bangee, M., Maes, M., & Verhagen, M. (2015). Loneliness across the lifespan. *Perspectives on Psychological Science, 10,* 250-264.

Quatman, T., Sokolik, E., & Smith, K. (2000). Adolescent perception of peer success: A gendered perspective over time. *Sex Roles, 43,* 61-84.

Quillian, L., & Campbell, M. E. (2003). Beyond Black and White: The present and future of multiracial friendship segregation. *American Sociological Review, 68,* 540-566.

Quinn, K., Pacella, M., Dickson-Gomez, J., & Nydegger, L. (2017). Childhood adversity and the continued exposure to trauma and violence among adolescent gang members. *American Journal of Community Psychology, 59,* 36-49.

Quintelier, E. (2015). Engaging adolescents in politics: The longitudinal effect of political socialization agents. *Youth & Society, 47,* 51-69.

Raby, K., Roisman, G., Fraley, R., & Simpson, J. (2015). The enduring predictive significance of early maternal sensitivity: Social and academic competence through age 32 years. *Child Development, 86,* 695-708.

Radmacher, K., & Azmitia, M. (2006). Are there gendered pathways to intimacy in early adolescents' and emerging adults' friendships? *Journal of Adolescent Research, 21,* 415-448.

Raffaelli, M. (1997). Young adolescents' conflicts with siblings and friends. *Journal of Youth and Adolescence, 26,* 539-558.

Raffaelli, M., & Green, S. (2003). Parent-adolescent communication about sex: Retrospective reports by Latino college students. *Journal of Marriage and the Family, 65,* 474.

Raffaelli, M., Andrade, F., Wiley, A., Sanchez-Armass, O., Edwards, L., & Aradillas-Garcia, C. (2013). Stress, social support, and depression: A test of the stress-buffering hypothesis in a Mexican sample. *Journal of Research on Adolescence, 23,* 283-289.

Ragan, D. (2020). Similarity between deviant peers: Developmental trends in influence and selection. *Criminology, 58,* 336-369.

Rahal, D., Huynh, V., Cole, S., Seeman, T., & Fuligni, A. (2020). Subjective social status and health during high school and young adulthood. *Developmental Psychology, 56,* 1220-1232.

Raifman, J., Charlton, B., Arrington-Sanders, R., Chan, P., Rusley, J., Mayer, K., . . . McConnell, M. (2020). Sexual orientation and suicide attempt disparities among US adolescents: 2009-2017. *Pediatrics, 145,* 20191658.

Raiford, J., Herbst, J., Carry, M., Browne, F., Doherty, I., & Wechsberg, W. (2014). Low prospects and high risk: Structural determinants of health associated with sexual risk among young African American women residing in resource-poor communities in the South. *American Journal of Community Psychology, 54,* 243-250.

Raine, A., Loeber, R., Stouthamer-Loeber, M., Moffitt, T., Caspi, A., & Lynam, D. (2005). Neurocognitive impairments in boys on the life-course-persistent antisocial path. *Journal of Abnormal Psychology, 114,* 38-49.

Rakesh, D., Allen, N., & Whittle, S. (2020). Balancing act: Neural correlates of affect dysregulation

in youth depression and substance use – A systematic review of functional neuroimaging studies. *Developmental Cognitive Neuroscience, 42,* 100775.

Ralph, L., King, E., Belusa, E., Foster, D., Brindis, C., & Biggs, M. (2018). The impact of a parental notification requirement on Illinois minors' access to and decision-making around abortion. *Journal of Adolescent Health, 62,* 281-287.

Rambaran, J., Hopmeyer, A., Schwartz, D., Steglich, C., Badaly, D., & Veenstra, R. (2017). Academic functioning and peer influences: A short-term longitudinal study of network-behavior dynamics in middle adolescence. *Child Development, 88,* 523-543.

Ramesh, S., Zimmerman, L., & Patel, A. (2016). Impact of parental notification on Illinois minors seeking abortion. *Journal of Adolescent Health, 58,* 290-294.

Ramsden, S., Richardson, F., Josse, G., Thomas, M., & Ellis, C. (2011). Verbal and non-verbal intelligence changes in the teenage brain. *Nature, 479,* 113-116.

Ramsey, M., & Gentzler, A. (2015). An upward spiral: Bidirectional associations between positive affect and positive aspects of close relationships across the life span. *Developmental Review, 36,* 58-104.

Randall, E., Bohnert, A., & Travers, L. (2015). Understanding affluent adolescent adjustment: The interplay of parental perfectionism, perceived parental pressure, and organized activity involvement. *Journal of Adolescence, 41,* 56-66.

Ranney, J., & Troop-Gordon, W. (2020). The role of popularity and digital self-monitoring in adolescents' cyberbehaviors and cybervictimization. *Computers in Human Behavior, 102,* 293-302.

Raposa, E, Erickson, L, Hagler, M. and Rhodes, J. (2018). How economic disadvantage affects the availability and nature of mentoring relationships during the transition to adulthood. *American Journal of Community Psychology, 61,* 191-203.

Raposa, E. B., Rhodes, J., Stams, G. J. J. M., Card, N., Burton, S., Schwartz, S., . . . Hussain, S. (2019). The effects of youth mentoring programs: A meta-analysis of outcome studies. *Journal of Youth and Adolescence, 48,* 423-443.

Rapuano, K. M., Huckins, J. F., Sargent, J. D., Heatherton, T. F., & Kelley, W. M. (2016). Individual differences in reward and somatosensory-motor brain regions correlate with adiposity in adolescents. *Cerebral Cortex, 26,* 2602-2611.

Rastogi, R., & Juvonen, J. (2019). Interminority friendships and intergroup attitudes across middle school: Quantity and stability of Black-Latino ties. *Journal of Youth and Adolescence, 48,* 1619-1630.

Rattan, A., Savani, K., Chugh, D., & Dweck, C. (2015). Leveraging mindsets to promote academic achievement. *Perspectives on Psychological Science, 10,* 721-726.

Raudino, A., Fergusson, D., & Horwood, L. (2013). The quality of parent/child relationships in adolescence is associated with poor adult psychosocial adjustment. *Journal of Adolescence, 36,* 331-340.

Rauer, A., Pettit, G., Lansford, J., Bates, J., & Dodge, K. (2013). Romantic relationship patterns in young adulthood and their developmental antecedents. *Developmental Psychology, 49,* 2159-2171.

Rauscher, K., Wegman, D., Wooding, J., Davis, L., & Junkin, R. (2013). Adolescent work quality: A view from today's youth. *Journal of Adolescent Research, 28,* 557-590.

Ravitch, D. (2000). *Left back: A century of failed school reforms.* New York: Simon & Schuster.

Ravitch, D. (Ed.). (2001). *Brookings papers on education policy.* Washington, DC: Brookings Institution.

Ray, J., Frick, P., Thornton, L., Wall Myers, T., Steinberg, L., & Cauffman, E. (2017). Callous-unemotional traits predict self-reported offending in adolescent boys: The mediating role of delinquent peers and the moderating role of parenting practices. *Developmental Psychology, 53,* 319-328.

Ready, D. D., Lee, V., & Welner, K. G. (2004). Educational equity and school structure: School size, overcrowding, and schools-within-schools. *Teachers College Review, 106,* 1989-2014.

Ream, G., & Savin-Williams, R. (2005). Reciprocal associations between adolescent sexual activity and quality of youth-parent interactions. *Journal of Family Psychology, 19,* 171-179.

Ream, R., & Rumberger, R. (2008). Student engagement, peer social capital, and school dropout among Mexican American and non-Latino White students. *Sociology of Education, 81,* 109-139.

Rebellon, C. (2006). Do adolescents engage in delinquency to attract the social attention of peers?: An extension and longitudinal test of the social reinforcement hypothesis. *Journal of Research in Crime and Delinquency, 43,* 387-411.

Recchia, H., Wainryb, C., & Pasupathi, M. (2013). "Two for flinching": Children's and adolescents' narrative accounts of harming their friends and siblings. *Child Development, 84,* 1459-1474.

Recchia, H. E., Brehl, B. A., & Wainryb, C. (2012). Children's and adolescents' reasons for socially excluding others. *Cognitive Development, 27,* 195-203.

Recchia, H. E., Wainryb, C., Bourne, S., & Pasupathi, M. (2015). Children's and adolescents' accounts of helping and hurting others: Lessons about the development of moral agency. *Child Development, 86,* 864-876.

Redlich, A. D., & Shteynberg, R. V. (2016). To plead or not to plead: A comparison of juvenile and adult true and false plea decisions. *Law and Human Behavior, 40,* 611-625.

Reese, E., Jack, F., & White, N. (2010). Origins of adolescents' autobiographical memories. *Cognitive Development, 25,* 352-367.

Reich, R., Cummings, J., Greenbaum, P., Moltisanti, A., & Goldman, M. (2015). The temporal "pulse" of drinking: Tracking 5 years of binge drinking in emerging adults. *Journal of Abnormal Psychology, 124,* 635-647.

Reich, S. (2010). Adolescents' sense of community on Myspace and Facebook: A mixed-methods approach. *Journal of Community Psychology, 38,* 688-705.

Reich, S. (2017). Connecting offline social competence to online peer interactions. *Psychology of Popular Media Culture, 6,* 291-310.

Reich, S., Subrahmanyam, K., & Espinosa, G. (2012). Friending, IMing, and hanging out face-to-face: Overlap in adolescents' online and offline social networks. *Developmental Psychology, 48,* 356-368.

Reid, A., Halgunseth, L., Espinosa-Hernandez, G., & Vasilenko, S. (2018). Sociocultural influences on the association between negative romantic experiences and psychological maladjustment in Mexican adolescents. *Journal of Research on Adolescence, 28,* 888-901.

Reid, V., & Meadows-Oliver, M. (2007). Postpartum depression in adolescent mothers: An integrative review of the literature. *Journal of Pediatric Health Care, 21,* 289-298.

Reilly, D., Neumann, D., & Andrews, G. (2015). Sex differences in mathematics and science achievement: A meta-analysis of National Assessment of Educational Progress assessments. *Journal of Educational Psychology, 107,* 645-662.

Reisner, S., Katz-Wise, S., Gordon, A., Corliss, H., & Austin, S. (2016). Social epidemiology of depression and anxiety by gender identity. *Journal of Adolescent Health, 59,* 203-208.

Reisner, S., Vetters, R., Leclerc, M., Zaslow, S., Wolfrum, S., Shumer, D., & Mimiaga, M. (2015). Mental health of transgender youth in care at an adolescent urban community health center: A matched retrospective cohort study. *Journal of Adolescent Health, 56,* 274-279.

Rekker, R., Keijsers, L., Branje, S., Koot, H., & Meeus, W. (2017). The interplay of parental monitoring and socioeconomic status in predicting minor delinquency between and within adolescents. *Journal of Adolescence, 59,* 155-165.

Renard, J., Rosen, L., Loureiro, M., De Oliveira, C., Schmid, S., Rushlow, W., & Laviolette, S. (2017). Adolescent cannabinoid exposure induces a persistent sub-cortical hyper-dopaminergic state and associated molecular adaptations in the prefrontal cortex. *Cerebral Cortex, 26,* 1297-1310.

Reniers, R. L. E. P., Murphy, L., Lin, A., Bartolomé, S. P., & Wood, S. J. (2016). Risk perception and risk-taking behavior during adolescence: The influence of personality and gender. *PLOS ONE, 11,* e0153842.

Resett, S., & Gamez-Guadix, M. (2017). Traditional bullying and cyberbullying: Differences in emotional problems, and personality. Are cyberbullies more Machiavellians? *Journal of Adolescence, 61,* 113-116.

Resko, S., Walton, M., Bingham, C., Shope, J., Zimmerman, M., Chermack, S., . . . Cunningham, R. (2010). Alcohol availability and violence among inner-city adolescents: A multi-level analysis of the role of alcohol outlet density. *American Journal of Community Psychology, 46,* 253-262.

Resnik, F., & Bellmore, A. (2019). Connecting online and offline social skills to adolescents' peer victimization and psychological adjustment. *Journal of Youth and Adolescence, 48,* 386-398.

Reuman, D. (1989). How social comparison mediates the relation between ability-grouping practices and students' achievement expectancies in mathematics. *Journal of Educational Psychology, 81,* 178-189.

Reyes, H., & Foshee, V. (2013). Sexual dating aggression across grades 8 through 12: Timing and predictors of onset. *Journal of Youth & Adolescence, 42,* 581-595.

Reyes, H., Foshee, V., Bauer, D., & Ennett, S. (2012). Developmental associations between adolescent alcohol use and dating aggression. *Journal of Research on Adolescence, 22,* 526-541.

Reyna, V., & Farley, F. (2006). Risk and rationality in adolescent decision making: Implications for theory, practice, and public policy. *Psychological Science in the Public Interest, 7,* 1-44.

Reyna, V. F., Weldon, R. B., & McCormick, M. (2015). Educating intuition. *Current Directions in Psychological Science, 24,* 392-398.

Reyna, V. F., Wilhelms, E. A., McCormick, M. J., & Weldon, R. B. (2015). Development of risky decision making: Fuzzy-trace theory and neurobiological perspectives. *Child Development Perspectives, 9,* 122-127.

Reynolds, B. M., & Juvonen, J. (2011). The role of early maturation, perceived popularity, and rumors in the emergence of internalizing symptoms among adolescent girls. *Journal of Youth and Adolescence, 40,* 1407-1422.

Reynolds, J., & Baird, C. (2010). Is there a downside to shooting for the stars? Unrealized educational expectations and symptoms of depression. *American Sociological Review, 75,* 151-172.

Reynolds, L., Yetnikoff, L., Pokinko, M., Wodzinski, M., Epelbaum, J., Lambert, L., . . . Flores, C. (2019). Early adolescence is a critical period for the maturation of inhibitory behavior. *Cerebral Cortex, 29,* 3676-3686.

Rhodes, J. (2004). *Stand by me.* Cambridge, MA: Harvard University Press.

Rhodes, J., & Lowe, S. (2009). Mentoring in adolescence. In R. Lerner & L. Steinberg (Eds.), *Handbook of adolescent psychology* (3rd ed., Vol. 2, pp. 152-190). New York: Wiley.

Rhodes, J., Haight, W., & Briggs, E. (1999). The influence of mentoring on the peer relationships of foster youth in relative and nonrelative care. *Journal of Research on Adolescence, 9,* 185-201.

Ricciardelli, L. A., & McCabe, M. P. (2004). A biopsychosocial model of disorder eating and the pursuit of muscularity in adolescent boys. *Psychological Bulletin, 130,* 179-205.

Rice, E., Craddock, J., Hemler, M., Rusow, J., Plant, A., Montoya, J., & Kordic, T. (2018). Associations between sexting behaviors and sexual behaviors among mobile phone-owning teens in Los Angeles. *Child Development, 89,* 110-117.

Rice, K., & Mulkeen, P. (1995). Relationships with parents and peers: A longitudinal study of adolescent intimacy. *Journal of Adolescent Research, 10,* 338-357.

Rice, L., Barth, J., Guadagno, R., Smith, G., McCallum, D., & ASERT. (2013). The role of social support in students' perceived abilities and attitudes toward math and science. *Journal of Youth & Adolescence, 42,* 1028-1040.

Richards, M., Crowe, P., Larson, R., & Swarr, A. (1998). Developmental patterns and gender differences in the experience of peer companionship during adolescence. *Child Development, 69,* 154-163.

Richardson, J. (2009). Men do matter: Ethnographic insights on the socially supportive role of the African American uncle in the lives of inner-city African American youth. *Journal of Family Issues, 30,* 1041-1069.

Richman, S. B., & Mandara, J. (2013). Do socialization goals explain differences in parental control between black and white parents? *Family Relations, 62,* 625-636.

Rideout, V., and Robb, M. (2019). *The Common Sense census: Media use by tweens and teens, 2019.* San Francisco: Common Sense Media.

Rideout, V., Foeher, U., & Roberts, D. (2010). *Generation M²: Media in the lives of 8- to 18-year-olds.* Palo Alto: Kaiser Family Foundation.

Rieger, S., Gollner, R., Trautwein, U., & Roberts, B. W. (2016). Low self-esteems prospectively predicts depression in the transition to young adulthood: A replication of Orth, Robins, and Roberts (2008). *Journal of Personality and Social Psychology, 110,* e16-e22.

Riggs, L., Holmbeck, G., Paikoff, R., & Bryant, F. (2004). Teen mothers parenting their own teen offspring: The moderating role of parenting support. *Journal of Early Adolescence, 24,* 200-230.

Riina, E., Martin, A., Gardner, M., & Brooks-Gunn, J. (2013). Context matters: Links between location of discrimination, neighborhood cohesion and African American adolescents? *Journal of Youth and Adolescence, 42,* 136-146.

Rioux, C., Castellanos-Ryan, N., Parent, S., & Seguin, J. R. (2016). The interaction between temperament and the family environment in adolescent substance use and externalizing behaviors: Support for diathesis-stress or differential susceptibility? *Developmental Review, 40,* 117-150.

Risch, S., Jodl, K., & Eccles, J. (2004). Role of the father-adolescent relationship in shaping adolescents' attitudes toward divorce. *Journal of Marriage and the Family, 66,* 46.

Rivas-Drake, D., & Witherspoon, D. (2013). Racial identity from adolescence to young adulthood: Does prior neighborhood experience matter? *Child Development, 84,* 1918-1932.

Rivas-Drake, D., Hughes, D., & Way, N. (2009). A preliminary analysis of associations among ethnic racial socialization, ethnic discrimination, and ethnic identity among urban sixth graders. *Journal of Research on Adolescence, 19,* 558-584.

Rivenbark, J., Copeland, W., Davisson, E., Gassman-Pines, A., Hoyle, R., . . . Odgers, C. (2019). Perceived social status and mental health among young adolescents: Evidence from census data to cellphones. *Developmental Psychology, 55,* 574-585.

Rivers, S., Reyna, V., & Mills, B. (2008). Risk taking under the influence: A fuzzy-trace theory of emotion in adolescence. *Developmental Review, 28,* 107-144.

Robbins, C., Schick, V., Reece, M., Herbenick, D., Sanders, S., & Dodge, B. (2011). Prevalence, frequency, and associations of masturbation with partnered sexual behaviors among US adolescents. *Archives of Pediatric and Adolescent Medicine, 165,* 1087-1093.

Roberts, A., Rosario, M., Slopen, N., Calzo, J., & Austin, S. (2013). Childhood gender nonconformity, bullying victimization, and depressive symptoms across adolescence and early adulthood: An 11-year longitudinal study. *Journal of the American Academy of Child & Adolescent Psychiatry, 52,* 143-152.

Roberts, B., O'Donnell, M., & Robins, R. (2004). Goal and personality trait development in

emerging adulthood. *Journal of Personality and Social Psychology, 87,* 541-550.

Roberts, D., Foehr, U., & Rideout, V. (2005). *Generation M: Media in the lives of 8-18-year-olds.* Menlo Park, CA: Kaiser Family Foundation.

Roberts, D., Henriksen, L., & Foehr, U. (2009). Adolescence, adolescents, and media. In R. Lerner & L. Steinberg (Eds.), *Handbook of adolescent psychology* (3rd ed., Vol. 2, pp. 314-344). New York: Wiley.

Roberts, M., Gibbons, F., Gerard, M., Weng, C., Murry, V., Simons, L., . . . Lorenz, F. (2012). From racial discrimination to risky sex: Prospective relations involving peers and parents. *Developmental Psychology, 48,* 89-102.

Robertson, L., McAnally, H., & Hancox, R. (2013). Childhood and adolescent television viewing and antisocial behavior in early adulthood. *Pediatrics, 131,* 439-446.

Robinson, B. (2018). Conditional families and lesbian, gay, bisexual, transgender, and queer youth homelessness: Gender, sexuality, family instability, and rejection. *Journal of Marriage and Family, 80,* 383-396.

Robnett, R., & Leaper, C. (2013). Friendship groups, personal motivation, and gender in relation to high school students' STEM career interest. *Journal of Research on Adolescence, 23,* 652-664.

Roche, K., Caughy, M., Schuster, M., Bogart, L., Dittus, P., & Franzini, L. (2014). Cultural orientations, parental beliefs and practices, and Latino adolescents' autonomy and independence. *Journal of Youth & Adolescence, 43,* 1389-1403.

Roche, K., Ghazarian, S., & Fernandez-Esquer, M. (2012). Unpacking acculturation: Cultural orientation and educational attainment among Mexican-origin youth. *Journal of Youth & Adolescence, 41,* 920-931.

Roche, K. M., Ensminger, M. E., & Cherlin, A. J. (2007). Variations in parenting and adolescent outcomes among African American and Latino families living in low-income, urban areas. *Journal of Family Issues, 28,* 882-909.

Roche, K. M., Lambert, S. F., Ghazarian, S. R., & Little, T. D. (2015). Adolescent language brokering in diverse contexts: Associations with parenting and parent–youth relationships in a new immigrant destination area. *Journal of Youth and Adolescence, 44,* 77-89.

Rocque, M., Beckley, A. L., & Piquero, A. R. (2019). Psychosocial maturation, race, and desistance from crime. *Journal of Youth and Adolescence, 48*(7), 1403-1417.

Roderick, M., Coca, V., & Nagaoka, J. (2011). Potholes on the road to college: High school effects in shaping urban students' participation in college application, four-year college enrollment, and college match. *Sociology of Education, 84,* 178-211.

Rodgers, J., & Rowe, D. (1993). Social contagion and adolescent sexual behavior: A developmental EMOSA model. *Psychological Review, 100,* 479-510.

Rodgers, R. F., McLean, S. A., & Paxton, S. J. (2015). Longitudinal relationships among internalization of the media ideal, peer social comparison, and body dissatisfaction: Implications for the tripartite influence model. *Developmental Psychology, 51,* 706-713.

Rodgers, R. F., McLean, S. A., Marques, M., Dunstan, C. J., & Paxton, S. J. (2016). Trajectories of body dissatisfaction and dietary restriction in early adolescent girls: A latent class growth analysis. *Journal of Youth and Adolescence, 45,* 1664-1677.

Rodkin, P., Espelage, D., & Hanish, L. (2015). A relational framework for understanding bullying: Developmental antecedents and outcomes. *American Psychologist, 70,* 311-321.

Rodkin, P., Farmer, T., Pearl, R., & Van Acker, R. (2000). Heterogeneity of popular boys: Antisocial and prosocial configurations. *Developmental Psychology, 36,* 14-24.

Rodríguez De Jesús, S. A., Updegraff, K. A., Umaña-Taylor, A. J., McHale, S. M., & Zeiders, K. H. (2019). Mexican-origin youth's cultural orientations and values: Do older sisters and brothers matter? *Child Development, 90*(6), e675-e687.

Rodriguez, N. (2010). The cumulative effect of race and ethnicity in juvenile court outcomes and why preadjudication detention matters. *Journal of Research in Crime & Delinquency, 47,* 391-413.

Rodríguez-Meirinhos, A., Vansteenkiste, M., Soenens, B., Oliva, A., Brenning, K., & Antolín-Suárez, L. (2020). When is parental monitoring effective? a person-centered analysis of the role of autonomy-supportive and psychologically controlling parenting in referred and non-referred adolescents. *Journal of Youth and Adolescence, 49,* 352-368.

Rogers, A., Memmott-Elison, M., Padilla-Walker, L., & Byon, J. (2019). Perceived parental psychological control predicts intraindividual decrements in self-regulation throughout adolescence. *Developmental Psychology, 55,* 2352-2364.

Rogers, A., Padilla-Walker, L., McLean, R., & Hurst, J. (2020). Trajectories of perceived parental psychological control across adolescence and implications for the development of depressive and anxiety symptoms. *Journal of Youth and Adolescence, 49,* 136-149.

Rogers, C., Guyer, A., Nishina, A., & Conger, K. (2018). Developmental change in sibling support and school commitment across adolescence. *Journal of Research on Adolescence, 28,* 858-874.

Rogers, C. R., Lee, T.-H., Fry, C. M., & Telzer, E. H. (2020). Where you lead, I will follow: Exploring sibling similarity in brain and behavior during risky decision making. *Journal of Research on Adolescence,* online ahead of print.

Rogers, L., Scott, M., & Way, N. (2015). Racial and gender identity among black adolescent males: An intersectionality perspective. *Child Development, 86,* 407-424.

Rogers, L., Yang, R., Way, N., Weinberg, S., & Bennet, A. (2020). "We're supposed to look like girls, but act like boys": Adolescent girls' adherence to masculinity norms. *Journal of Research on Adolescence, 30*(S1), 270-285.

Rohrer, J., Egloff, B., Kosinski, M., Stillwell, D., & Schmukle, S. (2018). In your eyes only? Discrepancies and agreement between self-and other-reports of personality from age 14 to 29. *Journal of Personality and Social Psychology, 115,* 304-320.

Roisman, G., Aguilar, B., & Egeland, B. (2004). Antisocial behavior in the transition to adulthood: The independent and interactive roles of developmental history and emerging developmental tasks. *Development and Psychopathology, 16,* 857-871.

Roisman, G., Booth-LaForce, C., Cauffman, E., Spieker, S., & The NICHD Early Child Care Research Network. (2009). The developmental significance of adolescent romantic relationships: Parent and peer predictors of engagement and quality at age 15. *Journal of Youth and Adolescence, 38,* 1294-1303.

Roisman, G., Monahan, K., Campbell, S., Steinberg, L., Cauffman, E., & The National Institute of Child Health and Human Development Early Child Care Research Network. (2010). Is adolescence-onset antisocial behavior developmentally normative? *Development and Psychopathology, 22,* 295-311.

Romer, D., Betancourt, L., Brodsky, N., Giannetta, J., Yang, W., & Hurt, H. (2011). Does adolescent risk taking imply weak executive function? A prospective study of relations between working memory performance, impulsivity, and risk taking in early adolescence. *Developmental Science, 14,* 1119-1133.

Romer, D., Reyna, V. F., & Satterthwaite, T. D. (2017). Beyond stereotypes of adolescent risk taking: Placing the adolescent brain in developmental context. *Developmental Cognitive Neuroscience, 27,* 19-34.

Romer, D., Sznitman, S., DiClemente, R., Salazar, L. F., Vanable, P. A., Carey, M. P., . . . Juzang, I. (2009). Mass media as an HIV-prevention strategy: Using culturally sensitive messages to reduce HIV-associated sexual behavior of at-risk African American youth. *American Journal of Public Health, 99,* 2150-2159.

Romero, E., Richards, M. H., Harrison, P. R., Garbarino, J., & Mozley, M. (2015). The role of neighborhood in the development of aggression in urban African American youth: A multilevel analysis. *American Journal of Community Psychology, 56,* 156-169.

Romo, L., Mireles-Rios, R., & Lopez-Tello, G. (2014). Latina mothers' and daughters' expectations for autonomy at age 15 (La Quinceañera). *Journal of Adolescent Research, 29,* 271-294.

Rood, L., Roelofs, J., Bögels, S., & Meesters, C. (2012). Stress-reactive rumination, negative cognitive style, and stressors in relationship to depressive symptoms in non-clinical youth. *Journal of Youth & Adolescence, 41,* 414-425.

Rose, A. (2002). Co-rumination in the friendships of girls and boys. *Child Development, 73,* 1830-1843.

Rose, A., & Asher, S. (2017). The social tasks of friendship: Do boys and girls excel in different tasks? *Child Development Perspectives, 11,* 3-8.

Rose, A., & Swenson, L. (2009). Do perceived popular adolescents who aggress against others experience emotional adjustment problems themselves? *Developmental Psychology, 45,* 868-872.

Rose, A., Glick, G., Smith, R., Schwartz-Mette, R., & Borowski, S. (2017). Co-rumination exacerbates stress generation among adolescents with depressive symptoms. *Journal of Abnormal Child Psychology, 45,* 985-995.

Rose, A., Schwartz-Mette, R., Glick, G., Smith, R., & Luebbe, A. (2014). An observational study of co-rumination in adolescent friendships. *Developmental Psychology, 50,* 2199-2209.

Rose, A., Schwartz-Mette, R., Smith, R., Asher, S., Swenson, L., Carlson, W., & Waller, E. (2012). How girls and boys expect that talking about problems will make them feel: Associations with disclosure to friends in childhood and adolescence. *Child Development, 83,* 844-863.

Rose, A. J., Carlson, W., & Waller, E. M. (2007). Prospective associations of co-rumination with friendship and emotional adjustment: Considering the socioemotional trade-offs of co-rumination. *Developmental Psychology, 43,* 1019-1031.

Rose, A. J., Smith, R. L., Glick, G. C., & Schwartz-Mette, R. A. (2016). Girls' and boys' problem talk: Implications for emotional closeness in friendships. *Developmental Psychology, 52,* 629-639.

Rosen, L., Lim, A., Felt, J., Carrier, L., Cheever, N., Lara-Ruiz, J. . . . & Rokkum, J. (2014). Media and technology use predicts ill-being among children, preteens and teenagers independent of the negative health impacts of exercise and eating habits. *Computers in Human Behavior, 35,* 364-375.

Rosen, M. L., Sheridan, M. A., Sambrook, K. A., Dennison, M. J., Jenness, J. L., Askren, M. K., . . . McLaughlin, K. A. (2018). Salience network response to changes in emotional expressions of others in heightened during early adolescence: Relevance for social functioning. *Developmental Science, 21,* e12571.

Rosenbaum, G., Venkatraman, V., Steinberg, L., & Chein, J. (2018). The influences of described and experienced information on adolescent risky decision making. *Developmental Review, 47,* 23-43.

Rosenbaum, J. (2006). Reborn a virgin: Adolescents' retracting of virginity pledges and sexual histories. *American Journal of Public Health, 96,* 1098-1103.

Rosenbaum, J. (2009). Patient teenagers? A comparison of the sexual behavior of virginity pledgers and matched nonpledgers. *Pediatrics, 123,* e110-120.

Rosenbaum, J. (2020). Educational and criminal justice outcomes 12 years after school suspension. *Youth & Society, 52,* 515-547.

Rosenbaum, J. E. (2011). The complexities of college for all: Beyond fairy-tale dreams. *Sociology of Education, 84,* 113-117.

Rosenblum, G., & Lewis, M. (1999). The relations among body image, physical attractiveness, and body mass in adolescence. *Child Development, 70,* 50-64.

Rosenthal, D., & Smith, A. (1997). Adolescent sexual timetable. *Journal of Youth and Adolescence, 26,* 619-636.

Roseth, C. J., Johnson, D. W., & Johnson, R. T. (2008). Promoting early adolescents' achievement and peer relationships: The effects of cooperative, competitive, and individualistic goal structures. *Psychological Bulletin, 134,* 223-246.

Rossi, G., Lenzi, M., Sharkey, J., Vieno, A., & Santinello, M. (2016). Factors associated with civic engagement in adolescence: The effects of neighborhood, school, family, and peer contexts. *Journal of Community Psychology, 44,* 1040-1058.

Rostad, W., Gittins-Stone, D., Huntington, C., Rizzo, C., Pearlman, D., & Orchowski, L.

(2019). The association between exposure to violent pornography and teen dating violence in grade 10 high school students. *Archives of Sexual Behavior, 48,* 2137-2147.

Rote, W., & Smetana, J. (2011). Social cognition. In B. Brown & M. Prinstein (Eds.), *Encyclopedia of adolescence* (Vol. 1, pp. 333-341). New York: Academic Press.

Rote, W., & Smetana, J. (2018). Within-family dyadic patterns of parental monitoring and adolescent information management. *Developmental Psychology, 54,* 2302-2315

Rote, W., Smetana, J., & Feliscar, L. (2020). Longitudinal associations between adolescent information management and mother-teen relationship quality: Between- versus within-family differences. *Developmental Psychology, 56,* 1935-1947.

Rote, W. M., & Smetana, J. (2015). Acceptability of information management strategies: Adolescents' and parents' judgments and links with adjustment and relationships. *Journal of Research on Adolescence, 25,* 490-505.

Rothbart, M. K., & Posner, M. I. (2015). The developing brain in a multitasking world. *Developmental Review, 35,* 42-63.

Rothenberg, W., Di Giunta, L., Lansford, J., Lunetti, C., Fiasconaro, I., Basili, E., . . . Cirimele, F. (2019). Daily associations between emotions and aggressive and depressive symptoms in adolescence: The mediating and moderating role of emotion dysregulation. *Journal of Youth and Adolescence, 48,* 2207-2221.

Rothenberg, W. A., Hussong, A. M., & Chassin, L. (2017). Modeling trajectories of adolescent-perceived family conflict: Effects of marital dissatisfaction and parental alcoholism. *Journal of Research on Adolescence, 27,* 105-121.

Rothenberg, W. A., Lansford, J., Alampay, L., Al-Hassan, S., Bacchini, D., Bornstein, M., . . . Yotanyamaneewong, S. (2020). Examining effects of mother and father warmth and control on child externalizing and internalizing problems from age 8 to 13 in nine countries. *Development and Psychopathology, 32,* 1113-1137.

Rothman, E., Bahrami, E., Okeke, N., & Mumford, E. (2020). Prevalence of and risk markers for dating abuse-related stalking and harassment victimization and perpetration in a nationally representative sample of U.S. adolescents. *Youth & Society, early view.*

Rothman, E., Miller, E., Terpeluk, A., Glauber, A., & Randel, J. (2011). The proportion of U.S. parents who talk with their adolescent children about dating abuse. *Journal of Adolescent Health, 49,* 216-218.

Rouse, C., Brooks-Gunn, J., & McLanahan, S. (Eds.) (2005). *The Future of Children 2005: School Readiness: Closing Racial and Ethnic Gaps.* Washington, DC: Brookings Institution.

Rousseau, A., & Eggermont, S. (2017). Tween television and peers: Reinforcing social agents in early adolescents' body surveillance and self-objectification. *Journal of Research on Adolescence, 28,* 807-823.

Rousseau, A., Eggermont, S., & Frison, E. (2017). The reciprocal and indirect relationships between passive Facebook use, comparison on Facebook, and adolescents' body dissatisfaction. *Computers in Human Behavior, 73,* 336-344.

Rousseau, A., Frison, E., & Eggermont, S. (2019). The reciprocal relations between Facebook relationship maintenance behaviors and adolescents' closeness to friends. *Journal of Adolescence, 76,* 173-184.

Rowe, D., Vazsonyi, A., & Flannery, D. (1994). No more than skin deep: Ethnic and racial similarity in developmental processes. *Psychological Review, 101,* 396-413.

Rowe, S., Zimmer Gembeck, M., Rudolph, J., & Nesdale, D. (2015). A longitudinal study of rejecting and autonomy-restrictive parenting, rejection sensitivity, and socioemotional symptoms in early adolescents. *Journal of Abnormal Child Psychology, 43,* 1107-1118.

Rowland, B., Toumbourou, J. W., & Livingston, M. (2015). The association of alcohol outlet density with illegal underage adolescent purchasing of alcohol. *Journal of Adolescent Health, 56,* 146-152.

Roy, A., Raver, C., Masucci, M., & DeJoseph, M. (2019). "If they focus on giving us a chance in life we can actually do something in this world": Poverty, inequality, and youths' critical consciousness. *Developmental Psychology, 55,* 550-561.

Rozek, C., & Gaither, S. (2020). Not quite White or Black: Biracial students' perceptions of threat and belonging across school contexts. *The Journal of Early Adolescence,* DOI:10.1177/0272431620950476.

Rubin, D., et al. (1986). Autobiographical memory across the adult life span. In D. Rubin (Ed.), *Autobiographical Memory* (pp. 202-221). Cambridge, UK: Cambridge University Press.

Rubin, K., Bukowski, W., & Parker, J. (2006). Peer interactions, relationships, and groups. In W. Damon & R. Lerner (Series Eds.), & N. Eisenberg (Vol. Ed.), *Handbook of child-psychology: Vol 3. Social, emotional, and personality development* (6th ed., pp. 571-645). Hoboken, NJ: Wiley.

Rubin, K., LeMare, L., & Lollis, S. (1990). Social withdrawal in childhood: Developmental pathways to peer rejection. In S. Asher & J. Coie (Eds.), *Peer rejection in childhood* (pp. 217-249). New York: Cambridge University Press.

Ruck, M., Abramovitch, R., & Keating, D. (1998). Children and adolescents' understanding of rights: Balancing nurturance and self-determination. *Child Development, 64,* 404-417.

Ruck, M., Peterson-Badali, M., & Day, D. (2002). Adolescents' and mothers' understanding of children's rights in the home. *Journal of Research on Adolescence, 12,* 373-398.

Ruck, M. D., Park, H., Crystal, D. S., & Killen, M. (2015). Intergroup contact is related to evaluations of interracial peer exclusion in African American students. *Journal of Youth and Adolescence, 44,* 1226-1240.

Rudolph, K., & Klein, D. (2009). Exploring depressive personality traits in youth: Origins, correlates, and developmental consequences. *Development and Psychopathology, 21,* 1155-1180.

Rudolph, K., Davis, M., & Monti, J. (2017). Cognition–emotion interaction as a predictor of adolescent depressive symptoms. *Developmental Psychology, 53,* 2377-2383.

Rudolph, K., Miernicki, M., Troop-Gordon, W., Davis, M., & Telzer, E. (2016). Adding insult to injury: Neural sensitivity to social exclusion is associated with internalizing symptoms in chronically peer-victimized girls. *Social Cognitive and Affective Neuroscience, 11,* 829-842.

Rudolph, K., Monti, J., Modi, H., Sze, W., & Troop-Gordon, W. (2020). Protecting youth against the adverse effects of peer victimization: Why do parents matter? *Journal of Abnormal Child Psychology, 48,* 163-176.

Rueger, S., Chen, P., Jenkins, L., & Choe, H. (2014). Effects of perceived support from mothers, fathers, and teachers on depressive symptoms during the transition to middle school. *Journal of Youth & Adolescence, 43,* 655-670.

Ruggeri, A., Luan, S., Keller, M., & Gummerum, M. (2018). The influence of adult and peer role models on children' and adolescents' sharing decisions. *Child Development, 89,* 1589-1598.

Ruhl, H., Dolan, E., & Buhrmester, D. (2015). Adolescent attachment trajectories with mothers and fathers: The importance of parent-child relationship experiences and gender. *Journal of Research on Adolescence, 25,* 427-442.

Rulison, K., Kreager, D., & Osgood, D. W. (2014). Delinquency and peer acceptance in adolescence: A within-person test of Moffitt's hypotheses. *Developmental Psychology, 50,* 2437-2448.

Rumberger, R. (2012). *Dropping out.* Cambridge, MA: Harvard University Press.

Rumberger, R., & Palardy, G. (2005). Test scores, dropout rates, and transfer rates as alternative indicators of high school performance. *American Education Research Journal, 42,* 3-42.

Rusby, J., Forrester, K., Biglan, A., & Metzler, C. (2005). Relationships between peer harassment and adolescent problem behaviors. *Journal of Early Adolescence, 25,* 453-477.

Russell, M., & Odgers, C. (2020). Adolescents' subjective social status predicts day-to-day mental health and future substance use. *Journal of Research on Adolescence, 30*(S2), 532-544.

Russell, M. A., Wang, L., & Odgers, C. (2016). Witnessing substance use increases same-day antisocial behavior among at-risk adolescents: Gene-environment interaction in a 30-day ecological momentary assessment study. *Development and Psychopathology, 28,* 1441-1456.

Russell, S. (2002). Childhood development risk for teen childbearing in Britain. *Journal of Research on Adolescence, 12,* 305-324.

Ryan, J., Marshall, J., Herz, D., & Hernandez, P. (2008). Juvenile delinquency in child welfare: Investigating group home effects. *Children and Youth Services Review, 30,* 1088-1099.

Ryan, R. (2015). Nonresident fatherhood and adolescent sexual behavior: A comparison of siblings approach. *Developmental Psychology, 51,* 211-223.

Ryan, S., Franzetta, K., & Manlove, J. (2007). Knowledge, perceptions, and motivations for contraception: Influence on teens' contraceptive consistency. *Youth and Society, 39,* 182-208.

Ryan, S., Franzetta, K., Manlove, J., & Schelar, E. (2008). Older sexual partners during adolescence: Links to reproductive health outcomes in young adulthood. *Perspectives on Sexual and Reproductive Health, 40,* 17-26.

Rydell, A., & Brocki, K. (2019). Cognitive and emotional profiles of CU traits and disruptive behavior in adolescence: A prospective study. *Journal of Abnormal Child Psychology, 47,* 1039-1051.

Sabiston, C., Lovato, C., Ahmed, R., Pullman, A., Hadd, V., Campbell, H., . . . Brown, K. (2009). School smoking policy characteristics and individual perceptions of the school tobacco context: Are they linked to students' smoking status? *Journal of Youth and Adolescence, 38,* 1374-1387.

Sackett, P., Kuncel, N., Arneson, J., Cooper, S., & Waters, S. (2009). Does socioeconomic status explain the relationship between admissions tests and post-secondary academic performance? *Psychological Bulletin, 135,* 1-22.

Sackett, P. R., Kuncel, N. R., Beatty, A. S., Rigdon, J. L., Shen, W., & Kiger, T. B. (2012). The role of socioeconomic status in SAT-grade relationships and in college admissions decision. *Psychological Science, 23,* 1000-1007.

Saewyc, E. (2011). Research on adolescent sexual orientation: Development, health disparities, stigma, and resilience. *Journal of Research on Adolescence, 21,* 256-272.

Sagar, K., Dahlgren, M., Gonenc, A., Racine, M., Dreman, M., & Gruber, S. (2015). The impact of initiation: Early onset marijuana smokers demonstrate altered Stroop performance and brain activation. *Developmental Cognitive Neuroscience, 16,* 84-92.

Sagrestano, L., McCormick, S., Paikoff, R., & Holmbeck, G. (1999). Pubertal development and parent–child conflict in low-income, urban, African American adolescents. *Journal of Research on Adolescence, 9,* 85-107.

Saint-Georges, Z., & Vaillancourt, T. (2020). The temporal sequence of depressive symptoms, peer victimization, and self-esteem across adolescence: Evidence for an integrated self-perception driven model. *Development and Psychopathology, 32,* 975-984.

Salafia, E., & Gondoli, D. (2011). A 4-year longitudinal investigation of the processes by which parents and peers influence the development of early adolescent girls' bulimic symptoms. *Journal of Early Adolescence, 31,* 390-414.

Salas-Wright, C., Nelson, E., Vaughn, M., Reingle Gonzalez, J., & Córdova, D. (2017). Trends in fighting and violence among adolescents in the United States, 2002-2014. *American Journal of Public Health, 107,* 977-982.

Saleem, F., Busby, D., & Lambert, S. Neighborhood social processes as moderators between racial discrimination and depressive symptoms for African American adolescents. *Journal of Community Psychology, 46,* 747-761.

Salmela-Aro, K., Upadyaya, K., Hakkarainen, K., Lonka, K., & Alho, K. (2017). The dark side of internet use: Two longitudinal studies of excessive internet use, depressive symptoms, school burnout and engagement among Finnish early and late adolescents. *Journal of Youth and Adolescence, 46,* 343-357.

Salmivalli, C. (1998). Intelligent, attractive, well-behaving, unhappy: The structure of adolescents' self-concept and its relations to their social behavior. *Journal of Research on Adolescence, 8,* 333-354.

Salusky, I., Larson, R., Griffith, A., Wu, J., Raffaelli, M., Sugimura, N., & Guzman, M. (2014). How adolescents develop responsibility: What can be learned from youth programs. *Journal of Research on Adolescence, 24,* 417-430.

Salzinger, S., Feldman, R., Rosario, M., & Ng-Mak, D. (2011). Role of parent and peer relationships and individual characteristics in middle school children's behavioral outcomes in the face of community violence. *Journal of Research on Adolescence, 21,* 395–407.

Samarova, V., Shilo, G., & Diamond, G. (2014). Changes in youths' perceived parental acceptance of their sexual minority status over time. *Journal of Research on Adolescence, 24,* 681–688.

Samek, D. R., Goodman, R. J., Riley, L., McGue, M., & Iacono, W. G. (2018). The developmental unfolding of sibling influences on alcohol use over time. *Journal of Youth and Adolescence, 47,* 349–368.

Samek, D. R., Hicks, B. M., Keyes, M. A., Iacono, W. G., & McGue, M. (2017). Antisocial peer affiliation and externalizing disorders: Evidence for gene × environment × development interaction. *Development and Psychopathology, 29,* 155–172.

Samela-Aro, K. (2011). Stages of adolescence. In B. Brown & M. Prinstein (Eds.), *Encyclopedia of adolescence* (Vol. 1, pp. 360–368). New York: Academic Press.

Sampson, R., & Laub, J. (2003). Life-course desistors? Trajectories of crime among delinquent boys followed to age 70. *Criminology, 41,* 555–592.

Sampson, R., Raudenbusch, S., & Earls, F. (1997). Neighborhoods and violent crime: A multilevel study of collective efficacy for children. *Science, 277,* 918–924.

Samuel, R., & Burger, K. (2020). Negative life events, self-efficacy, and social support: Risk and protective factors for school dropout intentions and dropout. *Journal of Educational Psychology, 112,* 973–986.

Sanchez, Z., Opaleye, E., Chaves, T., Noto, A., & Nappo, S. (2011). God forbids or mom disapproves? Religious beliefs that prevent drug use among youth. *Journal of Adolescent Research, 26,* 591–616.

Sandberg-Thoma, S. E., Snyder, A. R., & Jang, B. J. (2015). Exiting and returning to the parental home for boomerang kids. *Journal of Marriage and Family, 77,* 806–818.

Sanson, A., Van Hoorn, J., & Burke, S. (2019). Responding to the impacts of the climate crisis on children and youth. *Child Development Perspectives, 13,* 201–207.

Santelli, J., Carter, M., Orr, M., & Dittus, P. (2009). Trends in sexual risk behaviors, by nonsexual risk behavior involvement, U.S. high school students, 1991–2007. *Journal of Adolescent Health, 44,* 372–379.

Santelli, J., Kantor, L., Grilo, S., Speizer, I., Lindberg, L., Heitel, J., . . . Ott, M. (2017). Abstinence-only-until-marriage: An updated review of U.S. policies and programs and their impact. *Journal of Adolescent Health, 61,* 273–280.

Santelli, J., Lindberg, L., Abma, J., McNeely, C., & Resnick, M. (2000). Adolescent sexual behavior: Estimates and trends from four nationally representative surveys. *Family Planning Perspectives, 32,* 156–165.

Santelli, J., Morrow, B., Anderson, J., & Lindberg, L. (2006). Contraceptive use and pregnancy risk among U.S. high school students, 1991–2003. *Perspectives on Sexual and Reproductive Health, 38,* 106–111.

Santiago, C. D., Brewer, S. K., Fuller, A. K., Torres, S. A., Papadakis, J. L., & Ros, A. M. (2017).

Stress, coping, and mood among Latino adolescents: A daily diary study. *Journal of Research on Adolescence, 27,* 566–580.

Santiago, D., Gudiño, O., Baweja, S., & Nadeem, E. (2014). Academic achievement among immigrant and U.S.-born Latino adolescents: Associations with cultural, family, and acculturation factors. *Journal of Community Psychology, 42,* 735–747.

Santo, J., Martin-Storey, A., Recchia, H., & Bukowski, W. (2018). Self-continuity moderates the association between peer victimization and depressed affect. *Journal of Research on Adolescence, 28,* 875–887.

Santos, C., Kornienko, O., & Rivas-Drake, D. (2017). Peer influence on ethnic-racial identity development: A multi-site investigation. *Child Development, 88,* 725–742.

Saporito, S., & Sohoni, D. (2006). Coloring outside the lines: Racial segregation in public schools and their attendance boundaries. *Sociology of Education, 79,* 81–105.

Sarwer, D. B., & Dilks, R. J. (2012). Invited commentary: Childhood and adolescent obesity: Psychological and behavioral issues in weight loss treatment. *Journal of Youth and Adolescence, 41,* 98–104.

Satterthwaite, T. D., Wolf, D. H., Roalf, D. R., Ruparel, K., Erus, G., Vandekar, S., . . . Gur, R. C. (2015). Linked sex differences in cognition and functional connectivity in youth. *Cerebral Cortex, 25,* 2383–2394.

Saunders, J. F., & Frazier, L. D. (2017). Body dissatisfaction in early adolescence: The coactive roles of cognitive and sociocultural factors. *Journal of Youth and Adolescence, 46,* 1246–1261.

Saunders, M., Anckarsäter, H., Lundström, S., Hellner, C., Lichtenstein, P., & Fontaine, N. (2019). The associations between callous-unemotional traits and symptoms of conduct problems, hyperactivity and emotional problems: A study of adolescent twins screened for neurodevelopmental problems. *Journal of Abnormal Child Psychology, 47,* 447–457.

Savage, J., Rose, R., Pulkkinen, L., Silventoinen, K., Korhonen, T., Kaprio, J., . . . Dick, D. (2018). Early maturation and substance use across adolescence and young adulthood: A longitudinal study of Finnish twins. *Development and Psychopathology, 30,* 79–82.

Savickaitė, R., Dijkstra, J. K., Kreager, D., Ivanova, K., & Veenstra, R. (2019). Friendships, perceived popularity, and adolescent romantic relationship debut. *Journal of Early Adolescence, 40,* 377–399.

Savin-Williams, R. (2006). Who's gay? Does it matter? *Current Directions in Psychological Science, 15,* 40–44.

Savin-Williams, R., & Berndt, T. (1990). Friendship and peer relations. In S. Feldman & G. Elliott (Eds.), *At the threshold: The developing adolescent* (pp. 277–307). Cambridge, MA: Harvard University Press.

Savin-Williams, R. C., & Vrangalova, Z. (2013). Mostly heterosexual as a distinct sexual orientation group: A systematic review of the empirical evidence. *Developmental Review, 33,* 58–88.

Savin-Williams, R. C., Joyner, K., & Rieger, G. (2012). Prevalence and stability of self-reported

sexual orientation identity during young adulthood. *Archives of Sexual Behavior, 41,* 103–110.

Savolainen, J., Hughes, L., Mason, W., Hurtig, T., Ebeling, H., Moilanen, I., . . . Taanila, A. (2012). Antisocial propensity, adolescent school outcomes, and the risk of criminal conviction. *Journal of Research on Adolescence, 22,* 54–64.

Savolainen, J., Mason, W. A., Hughes, L. A., Ebeling, H., Hurtig, T. M., & Taanila, A. M. (2015). Pubertal development and sexual intercourse among adolescent girls: An examination of direct, mediated, and spurious pathways. *Youth & Society, 47,* 520–538.

Saxbe, D., Khoddam, H., Piero, L., Stoycos, S., Gimbel, S., Margolin, G., & Kaplan, J. (2018). Community violence exposure in early adolescence: longitudinal associations with hippocampal and amygdala volume and resting state connectivity. *Developmental Science, 21,* e12686.

Saxbe, D. E., Margolin, G., Spies Shapiro, L. A., & Baucom, B. R. (2012). Does dampened physiological reactivity protect youth in aggressive family environments? *Child Development, 83,* 821–830.

Saxbe, D. E., Negriff, S., Susman, E. J., & Trickett, P. K. (2015). Attenuated hypothalamic-pituitary-adrenal axis functioning predicts accelerated pubertal development in girls 1 year later. *Development and Psychopathology, 27,* 819–828.

Sayal, K., Washbrook, E., & Propper, C. (2015). Childhood behavior problems and academic outcomes in adolescence: Longitudinal population-based study. *Journal of the American Academy of Child & Adolescent Psychiatry, 54,* 360–368.

Sayre Smith, D., & Juvonen, J. (2017). Do I fit in? Psychosocial ramifications of low gender typicality in early adolescence. *Journal of Adolescence, 60,* 161–170.

Scalco, M., & Colder, C. R. (2017). Trajectories of marijuana use from late childhood to late adolescence: Can temperament x experience interactions discriminate different trajectories of marijuana use? *Development and Psychopathology, 29,* 775–790.

Scalco, M., Colder, C., Read, J., Lengua, L., Wieczorek, W., & Hawk, L. (2020). Testing alternative cascades from internalizing and externalizing symptoms to adolescent alcohol use and alcohol use disorder through co-occurring symptoms and peer delinquency. *Development and Psychopathology,* early view.

Scalco, M., Trucco, E., Coffman, D., & Colder, C. (2015). Selection and socialization effects in early adolescent alcohol use: A propensity score analysis. *Journal of Abnormal Child Psychology, 43,* 1131–1143.

Scanlan, T., Babkes, M., & Scanlan, L. (2005). Participation in sport: A developmental glimpse at emotion. In J. Mahoney, R. Larson, & J. Eccles (Eds.), *Organized activities as contexts of development* (pp. 275–309). Hillsdale, NJ: Erlbaum.

Schacter, H., & Juvonen, J. (2017). Depressive symptoms, friend distress, and self-blame: Risk factors for adolescent peer victimization. *Journal of Applied Developmental Psychology, 51,* 35–43.

Schacter, H., Lessard, L., & Juvonen, J. (2019). Peer rejection as a precursor of romantic dysfunction in adolescence: Can friendships protect? *Journal of Adolescence, 77,* 70-80.

Schacter, H. L., & Juvonen, J. (2015). The effects of school-level victimization on self-blame: Evidence for contextualized social cognitions. *Developmental Psychology, 51,* 841-847.

Schaefer, D., & Simpkins, S. (2014). Using social network analysis to clarify the role of obesity in selection of adolescent friends. *American Journal of Public Health, 104,* 1223-1229.

Schaefer, D., Simpkins, S., Vest, A., & Price, C. (2011). The contribution of extracurricular activities to adolescent friendships: New insights through social network analysis. *Developmental Psychology, 47,* 1141-1152.

Scheier, L., Botvin, G., Griffin, K., & Diaz, T. (2000). Dynamic growth models of self-esteem and adolescent alcohol use. *Journal of Early Adolescence, 20,* 178-209.

Schiller, K. (1999). Effects of feeder patterns on students' transition to high school. *Sociology of Education, 72,* 216-233.

Schlegel, A. (2009). Cross-cultural issues in the study of adolescent development. In R. Lerner & L. Steinberg (Eds.), *Handbook of adolescent psychology* (3rd ed., Vol. 2, pp. 570-589). New York: Wiley.

Schlegel, A., & Barry, H. (1991). *Adolescence: An anthropological inquiry.* New York: Free Press.

Schlomer, G., Cleveland, H., Feinberg, M., Murray, J., & Vandenbergh, D. (2021), Longitudinal links between adolescent and peer conduct problems and moderation by a sensitivity genetic index. *Journal of Research on Adolescence,* DOI: 10.1111/jora.12592.

Schlomer, G., Cleveland, H., Feinberg, M., Wolf, P., Greenberg, M., Spoth, R., . . . Vandenbergh, D. J. (2017). Extending previous cGxI findings on 5-HTTLPR's moderation of intervention effects on adolescent substance misuse initiation. *Child Development, 88,* 2001-2012.

Schmidt, C., Stoddard, S., Heinze, J., Caldwell, C., & Zimmerman, M. (2020). Examining contextual and relational factors influencing perceptions of societal and interpersonal mattering among rural youth. *Journal of Community Psychology, 48,* 2013-2032.

Schmidt, C. J., Pierce, J., & Stoddard, S. A. (2016). The mediating effect of future expectations on the relationship between neighborhood context and adolescent bullying perpetration. *Journal of Community Psychology, 44,* 232-248.

Schmidt, J. (2003). Correlates of reduced misconduct among adolescents facing adversity. *Journal of Youth and Adolescence, 32,* 439-452.

Schmidt, J., & Padilla, B. (2003). Self-esteem and family challenge: An investigation of their effects on achievement. *Journal of Youth and Adolescence, 32,* 37-46.

Schmidt, J., Shumow, L., & Kackar, H. (2007). Adolescents' participation in service activities and its impact on academic, behavioral, and civic outcomes. *Journal of Youth and Adolescence, 36,* 127-140.

Schmidt, J., Shumow, L., & Kackar-Cam, H. (2017). Does mindset intervention predict students' daily experience in classrooms? A comparison of seventh and ninth graders' trajectories. *Journal of Youth and Adolescence, 46,* 582-602.

Schmidt, N., Krohn, M., & Osypuk, T. (2018). Modification of housing mobility experimental effects on delinquency and educational problems: Middle adolescence as a sensitive period. *Journal of Youth and Adolescence, 47,* 2009-2026.

Schmiedek, F., Lövdén, M., & Lindenberger, U. (2014). Younger adults show long-term effects of cognitive training on broad cognitive abilities over 2 years. *Developmental Psychology, 50,* 2304-2310.

Schneider, B., & Stevenson, D. (1999). *The ambitious generations: America's teenagers, motivated but directionless.* New Haven, CT: Yale University Press.

Schneiders, J., Nicolson, N. A., Berkhof, J., Feron, F. J., van Os, J., & deVries, M. W. (2006). Mood reactivity to daily negative events in early adolescence: Relationship to risk for psychopathology. *Developmental Psychology, 42,* 543-554.

Schofield, T. J., Toro, R. I., Parke, R. D., Cookston, J. T., Fabricius, W. V., & Coltrane, S. (2017). Parenting and later substance use among Mexican-origin youth: Moderation by preference for a common language. *Developmental Psychology, 53,* 778-786.

Scholte, R., van Lieshout, C., & van Aken, C. (2001). Perceived relational support in adolescence: Dimensions, configurations, and adolescent adjustment. *Journal of Research on Adolescence, 11,* 71-94.

Schooler, D., Sorsoli, C., Kim, J., & Tolman, D. (2009). Beyond exposure: A person-oriented approach to adolescent media diets. *Journal of Research on Adolescence, 19,* 484-508.

Schriber, R. A., & Guyer, A. E. (2016). Adolescent neurobiological susceptibility to social context. *Developmental Cognitive Neuroscience, 19,* 1-18.

Schulenberg, J., Bryant, A. L., & O'Malley, P. (2004). Taking hold of some kind of life: How developmental tasks relate to trajectories of well-being during the transition to adulthood. *Development and Psychopathology, 16,* 1119-1140.

Schuler, K., Ruggero, C., Goldstein, B., Perlman, G., Klein, D., & Kotov, R. (2017). Diurnal cortisol interacts with stressful events to prospectively predict depressive symptoms in adolescent girls. *Journal of Adolescent Health, 61,* 767-772.

Schulz, K. M., & Sisk, C. L. (2016). The organizing actions of adolescent gonadal steroid hormones on brain and behavioral development. *Neuroscience & Biobehavioral Reviews, 70,* 148-158.

Schwartz, D., Kelly, B. M., & Duong, M. T. (2013). Do academically-engaged adolescents experience social sanctions from the peer group? *Journal of Youth and Adolescence, 42,* 1319-1330.

Schwartz, D., Kelly, B. M., Mali, L. V., & Duong, M. T. (2016). Exposure to violence in the community predicts friendships with academically disengaged peers during middle adolescence. *Journal of Youth and Adolescence, 45,* 1786-1799.

Schwartz, S., Côté, J. E., & Arnett, J. (2005). Identity and agency in emerging adulthood: Two developmental routes in the individualization process. *Youth and Society, 37,* 201-229.

Schwartz, S., Des Rosiers, S., Huang, S., Zamboanga, B., Unger, J., Knight, G. P., & Szapocznik, P. (2013). Developmental trajectories of acculturation in Hispanic adolescents: Associations with family functioning and adolescent risk behavior. *Child Development, 84,* 1355-1372.

Schwartz, S., Hardy, S., Zamboanga, B., Meca, A., Waterman, A., Picariello, S., . . . Forthun, L. (2015). Identity in young adulthood: Links with mental health and risky behavior. *Journal of Applied Developmental Psychology, 36,* 39-52.

Schwartz, S., Unger, J., Meca, A., Lorenzo-Blanco, E., Baezconde-Garbanati, L., Cano, M., . . . Pattarroyo, M. (2017). Personal identity development in Hispanic immigrant adolescents: Links with positive psychosocial functioning, depressive symptoms, and externalizing problems. *Journal of Youth and Adolescence, 46,* 898-913.

Schwartz, S. E. O., Rhodes, J. E., Chan, C. S., & Herrera, C. (2011). The impact of school-based mentoring on youths with different relational profiles. *Developmental Psychology, 47,* 450-462.

Schwartz-Mette, R., & Lawrence, H. (2019). Peer socialization of non-suicidal self-injury in adolescents' close friendships. *Journal of Abnormal Child Psychology, 47,* 1851-1862.

Schwartz-Mette, R., & Rose, A. (2012). Co-rumination mediates contagion of internalizing symptoms within youths' friendships. *Developmental Psychology, 48,* 1355-1365.

Schweder, R. (Ed.). (1998). *Welcome to middle age! And other cultural fictions.* Chicago: University of Chicago Press.

Scott, E., & Steinberg, L. (2008). *Rethinking juvenile justice.* Cambridge, MA: Harvard University Press.

Scott, E., Bonnie, R., & Steinberg, L. (2016). Young adulthood as a transitional legal category: science, social change, and justice policy. *Fordham Law Review, 85,* 641-666.

Scott, H., & Woods, H. C. (2018). Fear of missing out and sleep: Cognitive behavioural factors in adolescents' nighttime social media use. *Journal of Adolescence, 68,* 61-65.

Scott, J., Slomiak, S., Jones, J., Rosen, A., Moore, T., & Gur, R. (2018). Association of cannabis with cognitive functioning in adolescents and young adults: A systematic review and meta-analysis. *JAMA Psychiatry, 75,* 585-595.

Scull, T., Kupersmidt, J., & Erausquin, J. (2014). The impact of media-related cognitions on children's substance use outcomes in the context of parental and peer substance use. *Journal of Youth & Adolescence, 43,* 717-728.

Seaton, E., & Gilbert, A. (2011). Ethnic/racial identity among minority youth. In B. Brown & M. Prinstein (Eds.), *Encyclopedia of adolescence* (Vol. 2, pp. 68-74). New York: Academic Press.

Seaton, E., & Iida, M. (2019). Racial discrimination and racial identity: Daily moderation among Black youth. *American Psychologist, 74,* 117-127.

Seaton, E., & Tyson, K. (2019). The intersection of race and gender among Black American adolescents. *Child Development, 90,* 62-70.

Seaton, E., & Yip, T. (2009). School and neighborhood contexts, perceptions of racial discrimination, and psychological well-being among African American adolescents. *Journal of Youth and Adolescence, 38,* 153-163.

Seaton, E., Caldwell, C., Sellers, R., & Jackson, J. (2010). An intersectional approach for understanding perceived discrimination and psychological well-being among African American and Caribbean Black youth. *Developmental Psychology, 46,* 1372–1379.

Seaton, E., Scottham, K., & Sellers, R. (2006). The status model of racial identity development in African American adolescents: Evidence of structure, trajectories, and well-being. *Child Development, 77,* 1416–1426.

Seaton, E., Upton, R., Gilbert, A., & Volpe, V. (2014). A moderated mediation model: Racial discrimination, coping strategies, and racial identity among Black adolescents. *Child Development, 85,* 882–890.

Seaton, E., Yip, T., & Sellers, R. (2009). A longitudinal examination of racial identity and racial discrimination among African American adolescents. *Child Development, 80,* 406–417.

Sebastian, C., Burnett, S., & Blakemore, S. (2008). Development of the self-concept during adolescence. *Trends in Cognitive Science, 12,* 441–446.

Secor-Turner, M., McMorris, B., Sieving, R., & Bearinger, L. (2013). Life experiences of instability and sexual risk behaviors among high-risk adolescent females. *Perspectives on Sexual & Reproductive Health, 45,* 101–107.

Sedgh, G., Finer, L., Bankole, A., Eilers, M., & Singh, S. (2015). Adolescent pregnancy, birth, and abortion rates across countries: Levels and recent trends. *Journal of Adolescent Health, 56,* 223–230.

Segalowitz, S., Santesso, D., Willoughby, T., Reker, D., Campbell, K., Chalmers, H., & Rose-Krasnor, L. (2012). Adolescent peer interaction and trait surgery weaken medial prefrontal cortex responses to failure. *Social Cognitive Affective Neuroscience, 7,* 115–124.

Seider, S., Jayawickreme, E., & Lerner, R. (2017). Theoretical and empirical bases of character development in adolescence: A view of the issues. *Journal of Youth and Adolescence, 46,* 1149–1152.

Seidman, E., Lambert, L. E., Allen, L., & Aber, J. L. (2003). Urban adolescents' transition to junior high school and protective family transactions. *Journal of Early Adolescence, 23,* 166–193.

Seiffge-Krenke, I. (2003). Testing theories of romantic development from adolescence to young adulthood: Evidence of a developmental sequence. *International Journal of Behavioral Development, 27,* 519–531.

Seiffge-Krenke, I. (2006). Leaving home or still in the nest? Parent–child relationships and psychological health as predictors of different leaving home patterns. *Developmental Psychology, 42,* 864–876.

Seiffge-Krenke, I., Aunola, K., & Nurmi, J.-E. (2009). Changes in stress perception and coping during adolescence: The role of situational and personal factors. *Child Development, 80,* 259–279.

Seiffge-Krenke, I., Persike, M., Karaman, N. G., Cok, F., Herrera, D., Rohail, I., . . . & Hyeyoun, H. (2013). Stress with parents and peers: How adolescents from six nations cope with relationship stress. *Journal of Research on Adolescence, 23,* 103–117.

Sela, Y., Zach, M., Amichay-Hamburger, Y., Mishali, M., & Omer, H. (2020). Family environment and problematic internet use among adolescents: the mediating roles of depression and fear of missing out. *Computers in Human Behavior, 106,* 106226.

Sela-Shayovitz, R. (2016). Where are the girls? Gender trends in juvenile crime. *Journal of Social Science Studies, 4,* 71–85.

Selemon, L. (2013). A role for synaptic plasticity in the adolescent development of executive function. *Translational Psychiatry, 3,* e238 and ff.

Sellers, R., Copeland-Linder, N., Martin, P., & Lewis, R. (2006). Racial identity matters: The relationship between racial discrimination and psychological functioning in African American adolescents. *Journal of Research on Adolescence, 16,* 187–216.

Sentse, M., Kretschmer, T., de Haan, A., & Prinzie, P. (2017). Conduct problem trajectories between age 4 and 17 and their association with behavioral adjustment in emerging adulthood. *Journal of Youth and Adolescence, 46,* 1633–1642.

Serra Poirier, C., Brendgen, M., Vitaro, F., Dionne, G., & Biovin, M. (2017). Contagion of anxiety symptoms among adolescent siblings: A twin study. *Journal of Research on Adolescence, 27,* 65–77.

Setoh, P., Qin, L., Zhang, X., & Pomerantz, E. (2015). The social self in early adolescence: Two longitudinal investigations in the United States and China. *Developmental Psychology, 51,* 949–962.

Seymour, K., Chronis-Tuscano, A., Iwamoto, D., Kurdziel, G., & MacPherson, L. (2014). Emotion regulation mediates the association between ADHD and depressive symptoms in a community sample of youth. *Journal of Abnormal Child Psychology, 42,* 611–621.

Shackleton, N., Jamal, F., Viner, R., Dickson, K., Patton, G., & Bonell, C. (2016). School-based interventions going beyond health education to promote adolescent health: Systematic review of reviews. *Journal of Adolescent Health, 58,* 382–396.

Shanahan, L., McHale, S., Crouter, A., & Osgood, D. W. (2008). Linkages between parents' differential treatment, youth depressive symptoms, and sibling relationships. *Journal of Marriage and Family, 70,* 480–494.

Shanahan, L., McHale, S., Osgood, D. W., & Crouter, A. (2007). Conflict frequency with mothers and fathers from middle childhood to late adolescence: Within- and between-families comparisons. *Developmental Psychology, 43,* 539–550.

Shanahan, M. J., & Bauer, D. J. (2004). Developmental properties of transactional models: The case of life events and mastery from adolescence to young adulthood. *Development and Psychopathology, 16,* 1095–1117.

Shannon, B., Raichle, M., Snyder, A., Fair, D., Mills, K., Zhang, D., . . . Kiehl, K. (2011). Premotor functional connectivity predicts impulsivity in juvenile offenders. *Proceedings of the National Academy of Sciences, 108(27),* 11241–11245.

Shannon, C., & Klausner, J. (2018). The growing epidemic of sexually transmitted infections in adolescents: A neglected population. *Current Opinion in Pediatrics, 30,* 137–143.

Shapero, B., McClung, G., Bangasser, D., Abramson, L., & Alloy, L. (2017). Interaction of biological stress recovery and cognitive vulnerability for depression in adolescence. *Journal of Youth and Adolescence, 46,* 91–103.

Sharma, S., Mustanski, B., Dick, D., Bolland, J., & Kertes, D. A. (2019). Protective factors buffer life stress and behavioral health outcomes among high-risk youth. *Journal of Abnormal Child Psychology, 47(8),* 1289–1301.

Sharp, E., Seaman, J., Tucker, C., Van Gundy, K., & Rebellon, C. (2020). Adolescents' future aspirations and expectations in the context of a shifting rural economy. *Journal of Youth and Adolescence, 49,* 534–548.

Sharpe, H., Patalay, P., Choo, T. H., Wall, M., Mason, S. M., Goldschmidt, A. B., & Neumark-Sztainer, D. (2018). Bidirectional associations between body dissatisfaction and depressive symptoms from adolescence through early adulthood. *Development and Psychopathology, 30,* 1447–1458.

Sharp, E. H., Tucker, C. J., Baril, M. E., Van Gundy, K. T., & Rebellon, C. J. (2015). Breadth of participation in organized and unstructured leisure activities over time and rural adolescents' functioning. *Journal of Youth and Adolescence, 44,* 62–76.

Shaw, D. J., Mareček, R., Grosbras, M.-H., Leonard, G., Pike, G. B., & Paus, T. (2016). Co-ordinated structural and functional covariance in the adolescent brain underlies face processing performance. *Social Cognitive and Affective Neuroscience, 11,* 556–568.

Shaw, P., Gilliam, M., Liverpool, M., Weddle, C., Malek, M., Sharp, W., . . . Giedd, J. (2011). Cortical development in typically developing children with symptoms of hyperactivity and impulsivity: Support for a dimensional view of Attention Deficit Hyperactivity Disorder. *American Journal of Psychiatry, 168,* 143–151.

Shaw, P., Greenstein, D., Lerch, J., Klasen, L., Lenroot, R., Gogtay, N., . . . Giedd, J. (2006). Intellectual ability and cortical development in children and adolescents. *Nature, 440,* 676–679.

Shedler, J., & Block, J. (1990). Adolescent drug use and psychological health: A longitudinal inquiry. *American Psychologist, 45,* 612–630.

Sheeran, P., Abraham, C., & Orbell, S. (1999). Psychosocial correlates of heterosexual condom use: A meta-analysis. *Psychological Bulletin, 125,* 90–132.

Shek, D. (2007). A longitudinal study of perceived differences in parental control and parent–child relational qualities in Chinese adolescents in Hong Kong. *Journal of Adolescent Research, 22,* 156–188.

Shen, Y., Carlo, G., & Knight, G. (2013). Relations between parental discipline, empathy-related traits, and prosocial moral reasoning: A multicultural examination. *The Journal of Early Adolescence, 33,* 994–1021.

Sherman, L. E., Rudie, J. D., Pfeifer, J. H., Masten, C. L., McNealy, K., & Dapretto, M. (2014). Development of the default mode and central executive networks across early adolescence: A longitudinal study. *Developmental Cognitive Neuroscience, 10,* 148–159.

Sherman, L., Greenfield, P., Hernandez, L., & Dapretto, M. (2018). Peer influence via Instagram: Effects on brain and behavior in adolescence and young adulthood. *Child Development, 89,* 37–47.

Sherman, L., Payton, A., Hernandez, L., Greenfield, P., & Dapretto, M. (2016). The power of the like in adolescence: Effects of peer influence on neural and behavioral responses to social media. *Psychological Science, 27,* 1027–1035.

Shernoff, D., & Schmidt, J. (2008). Further evidence of an engagement–achievement paradox among U.S. high school students. *Journal of Youth and Adolescence, 37,* 564–580.

Shernoff, D., & Vandell, D. (2007). Engagement in after-school program activities: Quality of experience from the perspective of participants. *Journal of Youth and Adolescence, 36,* 891–903.

Sherrod, L., & Lauckhardt, J. (2009). The development of citizenship. In R. Lerner & L. Steinberg (Eds.), *Handbook of adolescent psychology* (3rd ed., Vol. 2, pp. 372–408). New York: Wiley.

Shifrer, D., Pearson, J., Muller, C., & Wilkinson, L. (2015). College-going benefits of high school sports participation: Race and gender differences over three decades. *Youth & Society, 47,* 295–318.

Shin, H. (2017). Friendship dynamics of adolescent aggression, prosocial behavior, and social status: The moderating role of gender. *Journal of Youth and Adolescence, 46,* 2305–2320.

Shin, H. (2020). Who are popular, liked, and admired? Longitudinal associations between three social status and academic-social behavior. *Journal of Youth and Adolescence, 49,* 1783–1792.

Shin, H., & Ryan, A. (2014). Early adolescent friendships and academic adjustment: Examining selection and influence processes with longitudinal social network analysis. *Developmental Psychology, 50,* 2462–2472.

Shin, H., & Ryan, A. (2017). Friend influence on early adolescent disruptive behavior in the classroom: Teacher emotional support matters. *Developmental Psychology, 53,* 114–125.

Shin, W., & Kang, H. (2016). Adolescents' privacy concerns and information disclosure online: The role of parents and the Internet. *Computers in Human Behavior, 54,* 114–123.

Shiner, R. L., Masten, A. S., & Tellegen, A. (2002). A developmental perspective on personality in emerging adulthood: Childhood antecedents and concurrent adaptation. *Journal of Personality and Social Psychology, 83,* 1165–1177.

Shirtcliff, E., Vitacco, M., Graf, A., Gostisha, A., Merz, J., & Zahn-Waxler, C. (2009). Neurobiology of empathy and callousness: Implications for the development of antisocial behavior. *Behavioral Sciences & the Law, 27,* 137–171.

Shubert, J., Wray-Lake, L., & McKay, B. (2020). Looking ahead and working hard: how school experiences foster adolescents' future orientation and perseverance. *Journal of Research on Adolescence, 30*(4), 989–1007.

Shukla, K., Konold, T., & Cornell, D. (2016). Profiles of student perceptions of school climate: Relations with risk behaviors and academic outcomes. *American Journal of Community Psychology, 57,* 291–307.

Shulman, E., Cauffman, E., Piquero, A., & Fagan, J. (2011). Moral disengagement among serious juvenile offenders: A longitudinal study of the relations between morally disengaged attitudes and offending. *Developmental Psychology, 47,* 1619–1632.

Shulman, E., Harden, K., Chein, J., & Steinberg, L. (2016). The development of impulse control and sensation-seeking in adolescence: Independent or interdependent processes? *Journal of Research on Adolescence, 26,* 37–44.

Shulman, E., Smith, A., Silva, K., Icenogle, G., Duell, N., Chein, J., & Steinberg, L. (2016). The dual systems model: Review, reappraisal, and reaffirmation. *Developmental Cognitive Neuroscience, 17,* 103–117.

Shulman, E. P., & Cauffman, E. (2014). Deciding in the dark: Age differences in intuitive risk judgment. *Developmental Psychology, 50,* 167–177.

Shulman, E. P., Harden, K. P., Chein, J. M., & Steinberg, L. (2016). The development of impulse control and sensation-seeking in adolescence: Independent or interdependent processes? *Journal of Research on Adolescence, 26,* 37–44.

Shulman, E. P., Monahan, K. C., & Steinberg, L. (2017). Severe violence during adolescence and early adulthood and its relation to anticipated rewards and costs. *Child Development, 88,* 16–26.

Shulman, S., & Laursen, B. (2002). Adolescent perceptions of conflict in interdependent and disengaged friendships. *Journal of Research on Adolescence, 12,* 353–372.

Shulman, S., & Scharf, M. (2000). Adolescent romantic behaviors and perceptions: Age- and gender-related differences, and links with family and peer relationships. *Journal of Research on Adolescence, 10,* 99–118.

Shulman, S., Connolly, J., & McIssac, C. (2011). Romantic relationships. In B. Brown & M. Prinstein (Eds.), *Encyclopedia of adolescence* (Vol. 2, pp. 289–298). New York: Academic Press.

Shulman, S., Laursen, B., Kalman, Z., & Karpovsky, S. (1997). Adolescent intimacy revisited. *Journal of Youth and Adolescence, 26,* 597–617.

Shulman, S., Seiffge-Krenke, I., & Walsh, S. (2017). Is sexual activity during adolescence good for future romantic relationships? *Journal of Youth and Adolescence, 46,* 1867–1877.

Shulman, S., Tuval-Mashiach, R., Levran, E., & Anbar, S. (2006). Conflict resolution patterns and longevity of adolescent romantic couples: A 2-year follow-up study. *Journal of Adolescence, 29,* 575–588.

Shulman, S., Zlotnik, A., Shachar-Shapira, L., Connolly, J., & Bohr, Y. (2012). Adolescent daughters' romantic competence, quality of parenting, and maternal romantic history. *Journal of Youth and Adolescence, 41,* 593–606.

Shumow, L., & Miller, J. (2001). Parents' at-home and at-school academic involvement with youth adolescents. *Journal of Early Adolescence, 21,* 68–91.

Shumow, L., Smith, T., & Smith, M. (2009). Academic and behavioral characteristics of young adolescents in self-care. *Journal of Early Adolescence, 29,* 233–257.

Sibinga, E. M. S., Webb, L., Ghazarian, S. R., & Ellen, J. M. (2016). School-based mindfulness instruction: An RCT. *Pediatrics, 137,* 1–8.

Sibley, M., Pelham, W., Molina, B., Coxe, S., Kipp, H., Gnagy, E., . . . Lahey, B. (2014). The role of early childhood ADHD and subsequent CD in the initiation and escalation of adolescent cigarette, alcohol, and marijuana use. *Journal of Abnormal Psychology, 123,* 362–374.

Sibley, M. H., Pelham, W. E., Jr., Molina, B. S. G., Gnagy, E. M., Waschbusch, D. A., Garefino, A. C. . . . Karch, K. M. (2012). Diagnosing ADHD in adolescence. *Journal of Consulting and Clinical Psychology, 80,* 139–150.

Siegel, A., & Scovill, L. C. (2000). Problem behavior: The double symptom of adolescence. *Development and Psychopathology, 12,* 763–793.

Siegler, R. (2006). Microgenetic analyses of learning. In W. Damon & R. Lerner (Series Eds.) & D. Kuhn & R. Siegler (Eds.), *Handbook of child psychology: Vol. 2. Cognition, perception, and language* (6th ed., pp. 464–510). Hoboken, NJ: Wiley.

Siennick, S., & Osgood, D. W. (2012). Hanging out with which friends? Friendship-level predictors of unstructured and unsupervised socializing in adolescence. *Journal of Research on Adolescence, 22,* 646–661.

Siennick, S., Widdowson, A., Woessner, M., & Feinberg, M. (2016). Internalizing symptoms, peer substance use, and substance use initiation. *Journal of Research on Adolescence, 26,* 645–657.

Sijtsema, J., & Lindenberg, S. (2018). Peer influence in the development of adolescent antisocial behavior: Advances from dynamic social network studies. *Developmental Review, 50,* 140–154.

Sijtsema, J., Garofalo, C., Jansen, K., & Klimstra, T. (2019). Disengaging from evil: Longitudinal associations between the dark triad, moral disengagement, and antisocial behavior in adolescence. *Journal of Abnormal Child Psychology, 47,* 1351–1365.

Sijtsema, J., Rambaran, J., Caravita, S., & Gini, G. (2014). Friendship selection and influence in bullying and defending: Effects of moral disengagement. *Developmental Psychology, 50,* 2093–2104.

Silbereisen, R., Petersen, A., Albrecht, H., & Kracke, B. (1989). Maturational timing and the development of problem behavior: Longitudinal studies in adolescence. *Journal of Early Adolescence, 9,* 247–268.

Silk, J., Lee, K., Elliott, R., Hooley, J., Dahl, R., Barber, A., & Siegle, G. (2017). "Mom—I don't want to hear it": Brain response to maternal praise and criticism in adolescents with major depressive disorder. *Social Cognitive and Affective Neuroscience, 12,* 452–460.

Silk, J., Price, R., Rosen, D., Ryan, N., Forbes, E., Siegle, G., . . . Ladouceur, C. (2019). A longitudinal follow-up study examining adolescent depressive symptoms as a function of prior anxiety treatment. *Journal of the American Academy of Child & Adolescent Psychiatry, 58,* 359–367.

Silk, J., Vanderbilt-Adriance, E., Shaw, D. S., Forbes, E. E., Whalen, D. J., Ryan, N. D., . . . Dahl, R. (2007). Resilience among children and adolescents at risk for depression: Mediation and moderation across social and neurobiological context. *Development and Psychopathology, 19,* 841–865.

Silk, J. S., Stroud, L. R., Siegle, G. J., Dahl, R. E., Lee, K. H., & Nelson, E. E. (2012). Peer acceptance and rejection through the eyes of youth: Pupillary, eyetracking and ecological data from the Chatroom Interact task. *Social Cognitive Affective Neuroscience, 7,* 93–105.

Silva, K., Chein, J., & Steinberg, L. (2016). Adolescents in peer groups make more prudent decisions when a slightly older adult is present. *Psychological Science, 27,* 322–330.

Silva, K., Patrianakos, J., Chein, J., & Steinberg, L. (2017). Joint effects of peer presence and fatigue on risk and reward processing in late adolescence. *Journal of Youth and Adolescence, 46,* 1878–1890.

Silva, K., Shulman, E., Chein, J., & Steinberg, L. (2016). Peers increase late adolescents' exploratory behavior and sensitivity to positive and negative feedback. *Journal of Research on Adolescence, 26,* 696–705.

Silverberg, S., Marczak, M., & Gondoli, D. (1996). Maternal depressive symptoms and achievement-related outcomes among adolescent daughters: Variations by family structure. *Journal of Early Adolescence, 16,* 90–109.

Silveri, M., Dager, A., Cohen-Gilbert, J., & Sneider, J. (2016). Neurobiological signatures associated with alcohol and drug use in the human adolescent brain. *Neuroscience & Biobehavioral Reviews, 70,* 244–259.

Silverman, J., Raj, A., Mucci, L., & Hathaway, J. (2001). Dating violence against adolescent girls and associated substance abuse, unhealthy weight control, sexual risk behavior, pregnancy, and suicidality. *Journal of the American Medical Association, 286,* 572–579.

Silvers, J. A., Insel, C., Powers, A., Franz, P., Helion, C., Martin, R. E., . . . Ochsner, K. N. (2017b). vlPFC-vmPFC-amygdala interactions underlie age-related differences in cognitive regulation of emotion. *Cerebral Cortex, 27,* 3502–3514.

Silvers, J. A., Insel, C., Powers, A., Franz, P., Helion, C., Martin, R., . . . Ochsner, K. N. (2017a). The transition from childhood to adolescence is marked by a general decrease in amygdala reactivity and an affect-specific ventral-to-dorsal shift in medial prefrontal recruitment. *Developmental Cognitive Neuroscience, 25,* 128–137.

Silvers, J. A., Insel, C., Powers, A., Franz, P., Weber, J., Mischel, W., & Ochsner, K. N. (2014). Curbing craving: Behavioral and brain evidence that children regulate craving when instructed to do so but have higher baseline craving than adults. *Psychological Science, 25,* 1932–1942.

Silvers, J. A., Shu, J., Hubbard, A. D., Weber, J., & Ochsner, K. N. (2015). Concurrent and lasting effects of emotion regulation on amygdala response in adolescence and young adulthood. *Developmental Science, 18,* 771–784.

Sim, T. N., & Yeo, G. H. (2012). Peer crowds in Singapore. *Youth & Society, 44,* 201–216.

Simmons, C., Steinberg, L., Frick, P. J., & Cauffman, E. (2018). The differential influence of absent and harsh fathers on juvenile delinquency. *Journal of Adolescence, 62,* 9–17.

Simmons, R. (2003). *Odd girl out.* New York: Harvest Books.

Simmons, R., Blyth, D., & McKinney, K. (1983). The social and psychological effects of puberty on White females. In J. Brooks-Gunn & A. Petersen (Eds.), *Girls at puberty* (pp. 229–272). New York: Plenum.

Simmons, R., Rosenberg, F., & Rosenberg, M. (1973). Disturbance in the self-image at adolescence. *American Sociological Review, 38,* 553–568.

Simon, T., Miller, S., Gorman-Smith, D., Orpinas, P., & Sullivan, T. (2010). Physical dating violence norms and behavior among sixth-grade students from four U.S. sites. *Journal of Early Adolescence, 30,* 395–409.

Simon, V., Aikins, J., & Prinstein, M. (2008). Romantic partner selection and socialization during early adolescence. *Child Development, 79,* 1676–1692.

Simone, M., Long, E., & Lockhart, G. (2018). The dynamic relationship between unhealthy weight control and adolescent friendships: A social network approach. *Journal of Youth and Adolescence, 47,* 1373–1384.

Simons, L., & Conger, R. (2007). Linking mother–father differences in parenting to a typology of family parenting styles and adolescent outcomes. *Journal of Family Issues, 28,* 212–241.

Simons, L., & Steele, M. (2020). The negative impact of economic hardship on adolescent academic engagement: An examination parental investment and family stress processes. *Journal of Youth and Adolescence, 49,* 973–990.

Simons, L., Sutton, T., Shannon, S., Berg, M., & Gibbons, F. (2018). The cost of being cool: How adolescent pseudomature behavior maps onto adult adjustment. *Journal of Youth and Adolescence, 47,* 1007–1021.

Simons, L., Sutton, T., Simons, R., Gibbons, F., & McBride Murry, V. (2016). Mechanisms that link parenting practices to adolescents' risky sexual behavior: A test of six competing theories. *Journal of Youth and Adolescence, 45,* 255–270.

Simons, L., Wickrama, K., Lee, T., Landers-Potts, M., Cutrona, C., & Conger, R. D. (2016). Testing family stress and family investment explanations for conduct problems among African American adolescents. *Journal of Marriage and Family, 78,* 498–515.

Simons, L. G., Simons, R. L., & Su, X. (2013). Consequences of corporal punishment among African Americans: The importance of context and outcome. *Journal of Youth & Adolescence, 42,* 1273–1285.

Simons-Morton, B., & Chen, R. (2009). Peer and parent influences on school engagement among early adolescents. *Youth & Society, 41,* 3–25.

Simons-Morton, B., Ouimet, M., Zhang, Z., Klauer, S., Lee, S., Wang, J., . . . Dingus, T. (2011). The effect of passengers and risk-taking friends on risky driving and crashes/near crashes among novice teenagers. *Journal of Adolescent Health, 49,* 587–593.

Simpkins, S. D. (2015). The role of parents in the ontogeny of achievement-related motivation and behavioral choices. *Monographs of the Society for Research in Child Development, 80,* 1–169.

Simpkins, S. D., Schaefer, D. R., Price, C. D., & Vest, A. E. (2013). Adolescent friendships, BMI, and physical activity: Untangling selection and influence through longitudinal social network analysis. *Journal of Research on Adolescence, 23,* 537–549.

Simpson, J., Collins, W. A., Tran, S., & Haydon, K. (2007). Attachment and the experience and expression of emotions in romantic relationships: A developmental perspective. *Journal of Personality and Social Psychology, 92,* 355–367.

Singer, S. (2017). Middle class crime and criminality. *Oxford Bibliographies.* https://www.oxford-bibliographies.com/view/document/obo-9780195396607/obo-9780195396607-0212.

xml#obo-9780195396607-0212-bibItem-0008. Accessed on January 19, 2021.

Singh, P., & Bussey, K. (2011). Peer victimization and psychological maladjustment: The mediating role of coping self-efficacy. *Journal of Research on Adolescence, 21,* 420–433.

Singh, S., & Darroch, J. (1999). Trends in sexual activity among adolescent American women: 1982–1995. *Family Planning Perspectives, 31,* 212–219.

Sirin, S., Rogers-Sirin, L., Cressen, J., Gupta, T., Ahmed, S., & Novoa, A. (2015). Discrimination-related stress effects on the development of internalizing symptoms among Latino adolescents. *Child Development, 86,* 709–725.

Sisk, C., & Romeo, R. (2019). *Coming of age: The neurobiology and psychobiology of puberty and adolescence.* New York: Oxford University Press.

Sitnick, S., Shaw, D., & Hyde, L. (2014). Precursors of adolescent substance use from early childhood and early adolescence: Testing a developmental cascade model. *Development and Psychopathology, 26,* 125–140.

Sittner, K. J. (2016). Trajectories of substance use: Onset and adverse outcomes among North American indigenous adolescents. *Journal of Research on Adolescence, 26,* 830–844.

Skinner, A., Ravanbakht, S., Skelton, J., Perrin, E., & Armstrong, S. (2018). Prevalence of obesity and severe obesity in US children, 1999–2016. *Pediatrics, 141,* e20173459

Skinner, B. F. (1953). *Science and human behavior.* New York: Free Press.

Skinner, E., & Saxton, E. (2019). The development of academic coping in children and youth: A comprehensive review and critique. *Developmental Review, 53,* 100870.

Skinner, S. R., Robinson, M., Smith, M. A., Mattes, E., Cannon, J., Rosenthal, S., . . . Doherty, D. A. (2015). Childhood behavior problems and age at first sexual intercourse: A prospective birth cohort study. *Pediatrics, 135,* 255–263.

Skoog, T., & Özdemir, S. (2016). Explaining why early-maturing girls are more exposed to sexual harassment in early adolescence. *Journal of Early Adolescence, 36,* 490–509.

Skoog, T., Ozdemir, S. B., & Stattin, H. (2016). Understanding the link between pubertal timing in girls and the development of depressive symptoms: The role of sexual harassment. *Journal of Youth and Adolescence, 45,* 316–327.

Skoog, T., Stattin, H., & Kerr, M. (2009). The role of pubertal timing in what adolescent boys do online. *Journal of Research on Adolescence, 19,* 1–7.

Skorikov, V. B., & Vondracek, F. W. (2007). Vocational identity. In V. B. Skorikov & W. Patton (Eds.), *Career development in childhood and adolescence* (pp. 143–168). Rotterdam, The Netherlands: Sense.

Sladek, M., Doane, L., & Stroud, C. (2017). Individual and day-to-day differences in active coping predict diurnal cortisol patterns among early adolescent girls. *Journal of Youth and Adolescence, 46,* 121–135.

Slater, A., Tiggemann, M., Hawkins, K., & Werchon, D. (2012). Just one click: A content analysis of advertisements on teen web sites. *Journal of Adolescent Health, 50,* 339–345.

Slocum, L., & Wiley, S. (2018). "Experience of the expected?" Race and ethnicity differences in the effects of police contact on youth. *Criminology, 56,* 402–432.

Smahel, D., Brown, B., & Blinka, L. (2012). Associations between online friendship and internet addiction among adolescents and emerging adults. *Developmental Psychology, 48,* 381–388.

Smetana, J. (1989). Adolescents' and parents' reasoning about actual family conflict. *Child Development, 59,* 1052–1067.

Smetana, J. (1995). Parenting styles and conceptions of parental authority during adolescence. *Child Development, 66,* 299–316.

Smetana, J. (1995a). Conflict and coordination in adolescent–parent relationships. In S. Shulman (Ed.), *Close relationships and socioemotional development* (pp. 155–184). Norwood, NJ: Ablex.

Smetana, J. (2005). Adolescent–parent conflict: Resistance and subversion as developmental process. In L. Nucci (Ed.), *Conflict, contradiction, and contrarian elements in moral development and education* (pp. 69–91). Mahwah, NJ: Erlbaum.

Smetana, J., & Asquith, P. (1994). Adolescents' and parents' conceptions of parental authority and personal autonomy. *Child Development, 65,* 1147–1162.

Smetana, J., & Bitz, B. (1996). Adolescents' conceptions of teachers' authority and their relations to rule violations in school. *Child Development, 67,* 1153–1172.

Smetana, J., & Daddis, C. (2002). Domain-specific antecedents of parental psychological control and monitoring: The role of parenting beliefs and practices. *Child Development, 73,* 563–580.

Smetana, J., & Gettman, D. (2006). Autonomy and relatedness with parents and romantic development in African American adolescents. *Developmental Psychology, 42,* 1347–1351.

Smetana, J., & Rote, W. (2015). What do mothers want to know about teens' activities? Levels, trajectories, and correlates. *Journal of Adolescence, 38,* 5–15.

Smetana, J., & Villalobos, M. (2009). Social cognitive development in adolescence. In R. Lerner & L. Steinberg (Eds.), *Handbook of adolescent psychology* (3rd ed., Vol. 1, pp. 187–228). New York: Wiley.

Smetana, J., Crean, H. F., & Daddis, C. (2002). Family processes and problem behaviors in middle-class African American adolescents. *Journal of Research on Adolescence, 12,* 275–304.

Smetana, J., Daddis, C., & Chuang, S. (2003). "Clean your room!" *Journal of Adolescent Research, 18,* 631–650.

Smetana, J. G., & Ahmad, I. (2018). Heterogeneity in perceptions of parenting among Arab refugee adolescents in Jordan. *Child Development, 89,* 1786–1802.

Smirnov, I., & Thurner, S. (2017). Formation of homophily in academic performance: Students change their friends rather than performance. *PLOS ONE 12,* e0183473.

Smith, A., Chein, J., & Steinberg, L. (2014). Peers increase adolescent risk taking even when the probabilities of negative outcomes are known. *Developmental Psychology, 50,* 1564–1568.

Smith, A., Steinberg, L., Strang, N., & Chein, J. (2015). Age differences in the impact of peers on adolescents' and adults' neural response to reward. *Development Cognitive Neuroscience, 11,* 75–82.

Smith, D. G., Xiao, L., & Bechara, A. (2012). Decision making in children and adolescents: Impaired Iowa gambling task performance in early adolescence. *Developmental Psychology, 48,* 1180–1187.

Smith, D. S., Schacter, H. L., Enders, C., & Juvonen, J. (2018). Gender norm salience across middle schools: Contextual variations in associations between gender typicality and socioemotional distress. *Journal of Youth and Adolescence, 47,* 947–960.

Smith, E. P., Faulk, M., & Sizer, M. A. (2016). Exploring the meso-system: The roles of community, family, and peers in adolescent delinquency and positive youth development. *Youth & Society, 48,* 318–343.

Smith, J., Skinner, S., & Fenwick, J. (2011). How Australian female adolescents prioritize pregnancy protection: A grounded theory study of contraceptive histories. *Journal of Adolescent Research, 26,* 617–644.

Smith, R., & Rose, A. (2011). The "cost of caring" in youths' friendships: Considering associations among social perspective-taking, co-rumination, and empathetic distress. *Developmental Psychology, 47,* 1792–1803.

Smith, S., Maas, I., & van Tubergen, F. (2015). Parental influence on friendships between native and immigrant adolescents. *Journal of Research on Adolescence, 25,* 580–591.

Smith-Bynum, M., Lambert, S., English, D., & Ialongo, N. (2014). Associations between trajectories of perceived racial discrimination and psychological symptoms among African American adolescents. *Development and Psychopathology, 26,* 1049–1065.

Smolak, L., Levine, M., & Gralen, S. (1993). The impact of puberty and dating on eating problems among middle school girls. *Journal of Youth and Adolescence, 22,* 355–368.

Smoll, F., & Schutz, R. (1990). Quantifying gender differences in physical performance: A developmental perspective. *Developmental Psychology, 26,* 360–369.

Smollar, J., & Youniss, J. (1985). *Transformation in adolescents' perceptions of parents.* Paper presented at the biennial meetings of the Society for Research in Child Development, Baltimore.

Snedker, K. A., & Herting, J. R. (2016). Adolescent mental health: Neighborhood stress and emotional distress. *Youth & Society, 48,* 695–719.

Snell, E., Adam, E., & Duncan, G. (2007). Sleep and the body mass index and overweight status of children and adolescents. *Child Development, 78,* 309–323.

Snyder, J., Bank, L., & Burraston, B. (2005). The consequences of antisocial behavior in older male siblings for younger brothers and sisters. *Journal of Family Psychology, 19,* 643–653.

Society for Adolescent Health and Medicine. (2017). Condom availability in schools: A practical approach to the prevention of sexually transmitted infection/HIV and unintended pregnancy. *Journal of Adolescent Health, 60,* 754–757.

Sole-Padulles, C., Castro-Fornieles, J., de la Serna, E., Calvo, R., Baeza, I., Moya, J., . . . Sugranyes, G. (2016). Intrinsic connectivity networks from childhood to late adolescence: Effects of age and sex. *Developmental Cognitive Neuroscience, 17,* 35–44.

Somerville, L. H. (2013). The teenage brain: Sensitivity to social evaluation. *Current Directions in Psychological Science, 22,* 121–127.

Somerville, L. H., Ruberry, E. J., Dyke, J. P., Glover, G., & Casey, B. J. (2013). The medial prefrontal cortex and the emergence of self-conscious emotion in adolescence. *Psychological Science, 24,* 1554–1562.

Sontag, L., Clemans, K., Graber, J., & Lyndon, S. (2011). Traditional and cyber aggressors and victims: A comparison of psychosocial characteristics. *Journal of Youth and Adolescence, 40,* 392–404.

Sorhagen, N. S. (2013). Early teacher expectations disproportionately affect poor children's high school performance. *Journal of Educational Psychology, 105,* 465–477.

Sorkkila, M., Ryba, T., Selänne, H., & Aunola, K. (2020). Development of school and sport burnout in adolescent student-athletes: A longitudinal mixed-methods study. *Journal of Research on Adolescence, 30*(S1), 115–133.

Soto, C., & Tackett, J. (2015). Personality traits in childhood and adolescence. *Current Directions in Psychological Science, 24,* 358–362.

South, S., Baumer, E., & Lutz, A. (2003). Interpreting community effects on youth educational attainment. *Youth and Society, 35,* 3–36.

Spaans, J., Will, G.-J., van Hoorn, J., & Güroğlu, B. (2019). Turning a blind eye? Punishment of friends and unfamiliar peers after observed exclusion in adolescence. *Journal of Research on Adolescence, 29,* 508–522.

Sparks, S. (2015, May 24). Study points to fewer "dropout factory" schools. *Education Week.*

Spear, L. (2010). *The behavioral neuroscience of adolescence.* New York: Norton.

Spear, L. (2013). The teenage brain: Adolescents and alcohol. *Current Directions in Psychological Science, 22,* 152–157.

Spear, L. (2013a). Adolescent neurodevelopment. *Journal of Adolescent Health, 52,* S7–S13.

Spear, L. (2016). Consequences of adolescent use of alcohol and other drugs: Studies using rodent models. *Neuroscience & Biobehavioral Reviews, 70,* 228–243.

Spear, L., & Silveri, M. (2016). Special issue on the adolescent brain. *Neuroscience and Biobehavioral Reviews, 70,* 1–3.

Spear, L., & Swartzwelder, H. (2014). Adolescent alcohol exposure and persistence of adolescent-typical phenotypes into adulthood: A mini-review. *Neuroscience and Biobehavioral Reviews, 45,* 1–8.

Specht, J., Luhmann, M., & Geiser, C. (2014). On the consistency of personality types across adulthood: Latent profile analyses in two large-scale panel studies. *Journal of Personality and Social Psychology, 107,* 540–556.

Spees, L., Perreira, K., & Fuligni, A. (2017). Family matters: Promoting the academic adaptation of Latino youth in new and established destination. *Journal of Family Issues, 38,* 457–479.

Spencer, G., & Bryant, S. (2000). Dating violence: A comparison of rural, suburban, and urban teens. *Journal of Adolescent Health, 27,* 302–305.

Spencer, R., Tugenberg, T., Ocean, M., Schwartz, S. E. O., & Rhodes, J. E. (2016). "Somebody who was on my side": A qualitative examination of youth initiated mentoring. *Youth & Society, 48,* 402-424.

Spiegler, O., Wölfer, R., & Hewstone, M. (2019). Dual identity development and adjustment in Muslim minority adolescents. *Journal of Youth and Adolescence, 48,* 1924-1937.

Spielberg, J., Jarcho, J., Dahl, R., Pine, D., Ernst, M., & Nelson, E. (2015). Anticipation of peer evaluation in anxious adolescents: Divergence in neural activation and maturation. *Social Cognitive and Affective Neuroscience, 10,* 1084-1091.

Spielberg, J. M., Olino, T. M., Forbes, E. E., & Dahl, R. E. (2014). Exciting fear in adolescence: Does pubertal development alter threat processing? *Development Cognitive Neuroscience, 8,* 86-95.

Spriggs, A., & Halpern, C. (2008). Sexual debut timing and depressive symptoms in emerging adulthood. *Journal of Youth and Adolescence, 37,* 1085-1096.

Spruijt-Metz, D. S. (2011). Etiology, treatment, and prevention of obesity in childhood and adolescence: A decade in review. *Journal of Research on Adolescence, 129,* 129-152.

Srikanth, S., Petrie, T. A., Greenleaf, C., & Martin, S. B. (2015). The relationship of physical fitness, self-beliefs, and social support to the academic performance of middle school boys and girls. *The Journal of Early Adolescence, 35,* 353-377.

St Clair, M. C., Croudace, T., Dunn, V. J., Jones, P. B., Herbert, J., & Goodyer, L. M. (2015). Childhood adversity subtypes and depressive symptoms in early and late adolescence. *Development and Psychopathology, 27,* 885-899.

St. George, I., Williams, S., & Silva, P. (1994). Body size and menarche: The Dunedin study. *Journal of Adolescent Health, 15,* 573-576.

Staats, S., van der Valk, I., Meeus, W., & Branje, S. (2018). Longitudinal transmission of conflict management styles across inter-parental and adolescent relationships. *Journal of Research on Adolescence, 28,* 169-185.

Staff, J., Messersmith, E., & Schulenberg, J. (2009). Adolescents and the world of work. In R. Lerner & L. Steinberg (Eds.), *Handbook of adolescent psychology* (3rd ed., Vol. 2, pp. 270-313). New York: Wiley.

Staff, J., Osgood, D. W., Schulenberg, J., Bachman, J., & Messersmith, E. (2010). Explaining the relationship between employment and juvenile delinquency. *Criminology, 48,* 1101-1131.

Staff, J., Schulenberg, J., Maslowsky, J., Bachman, J., O'Malley, P., Maggs, J., & Johnston, L. (2010). Substance use changes and social role transitions: Proximal developmental effects on ongoing trajectories from late adolescence through early adulthood. *Development and Psychopathology, 22,* 917-932.

Staff, J., VanEseltine, M., Woolnough, A., Silver, E., & Burrington, L. (2012). Adolescent work experiences and family formation behaviors. *Journal of Research on Adolescence, 22,* 150-164.

Staff, J., Whichard, C., Siennick, S., & Maggs, J. (2015). Early life risks, antisocial tendencies, and preteen delinquency. *Criminology, 54,* 677-701.

Staff, J., Yetter, A., Cundiff, K., Ramirez, N., Vuolo, M., & Mortimer, J. (2020). Is adolescent employment still a risk factor for high school dropout? *Journal of Research on Adolescence, 30,* 406-422.

Stanger-Hall, K., & Hall, D. (2011). Abstinence-only education and teen pregnancy rates: Why we need comprehensive sex education in the U.S. *PLOS ONE, 6,* e24658.

Stanley, L., Henry, K., & Swaim, R.(2011). Physical, social, and perceived availabilities of alcohol and last month alcohol use in rural and small urban communities. *Journal of Youth and Adolescence, 40,* 1203-1214.

Stanton-Salazar, R., & Spina, S. (2005). Adolescent peer networks as a context for social and emotional support. *Youth and Society, 36,* 379-417.

Stattin, H., & Latina, D. (2018). The severity and spread of adjustment problems of adolescents involved in mutually hostile interactions with others. *Journal of Adolescence, 63,* 51-63.

Stattin, H., Kerr, M., & Skoog, T. (2011). Early pubertal timing and girls' problem behavior: Integrating two hypotheses. *Journal of Youth and Adolescence, 40,* 1271-1287.

Stearns, E. (2004). Interracial friendliness and the social organization of schools. *Youth and Society 35,* 395-419.

Stearns, E., & Glennie, E. J. (2006). When and why dropouts leave high school. *Youth and Society, 38,* 29-57.

Steeger, C. M., & Gondoli, D. M. (2013). Mother-adolescent conflict as a mediator between adolescent problem behaviors and maternal psychological control. *Developmental Psychology, 49,* 804-814.

Steele, C. (1997). A threat in the air: How stereotypes shape intellectual identity and performance. *American Psychologist, 52,* 613-619.

Steele, J., & Brown, J. (1995). Adolescent room culture: Studying media in the context of everyday life. *Journal of Youth and Adolescence, 24,* 551-576.

Steele, M., Simons, L., Sutton, T., & Gibbons, F. (2020). Family context and adolescent risky sexual behavior: An examination of the influence of family structure, family transitions and parenting. *Journal of Youth and Adolescence, 49,* 1179-1194.

Stefansson, K., Gestsdottir, S., Birgisdottir, F., & Lerner, R. (2018). School engagement and intentional self-regulation: A reciprocal relation in adolescence. *Journal of Adolescence, 64,* 23-33.

Stefansson, K. K., Gestsdottir, S., Birgisdottir, F., & Lerner, R. M. (2018). School engagement and intentional self-regulation: A reciprocal relation in adolescence. *Journal of Adolescence, 64,* 23-33.

Steffensmeier, D., Schwartz, J., Zhong, H., & Ackerman, J. (2005). An assessment of recent trends in girls' violence using diverse longitudinal sources: Is the gender gap closing? *Criminology, 43,* 355-406.

Stein, G., Coard, S., Kiang, L., Smith, R., & Mejia, Y. (2018). The intersection of racial-ethnic socialization and adolescence: A closer examination at stage-salient issues. *Journal of Research on Adolescence, 28,* 609-621.

Stein, G., Mejia, Y., Gonzalez, L., Kiang, L., & Supple, A. (2020). Familism in action in an emerging immigrant community: An examination of indirect effects in early adolescence. *Developmental Psychology, 56,* 1475-1483.

Stein, G., Supple, A., Huq, N., Dunbar, A., & Prinstein, M. (2016). A longitudinal examination of perceived discrimination and depressive symptoms in ethnic minority youth: The roles of attributional style, positive ethnic/racial affect, and emotional reactivity. *Developmental Psychology, 52,* 259-271.

Stein, G. L., Coard, S. I., Kiang, L., Smith, R. K., & Mejia, Y. C. (2018). the intersection of racial-ethnic socialization and adolescence: A closer examination at stage-salient issues. *Journal of Research on Adolescence, 28*(3), 609-621.

Stein, J., & Reiser, L. (1994). A study of White middle-class adolescent boys' responses to "semenarche" (the first ejaculation). *Journal of Youth and Adolescence, 23,* 373-384.

Steinbeis, N., Haushofer, J., Fehr, E., & Singer, T. (2016). Development of behavioral control and associated vmPFC-DLPFC connectivity explains children's increased resistance to temptation in intertemporal choice. *Cerebral Cortex, 26,* 32-42.

Steinberg, D., Simon, V., Victor, B., Kernsmith, P., & Smith-Darden, J. (2019). Onset trajectories of sexting and other sexual behaviors across high school: A longitudinal growth mixture modeling approach. *Archives of Sexual Behavior, 48,* 2321-2331.

Steinberg, L. (1996). *Beyond the classroom: Why school reform has failed and what parents need to do.* New York: Simon & Schuster.

Steinberg, L. (2000). Youth violence: Do parents and families make a difference? *National Institute of Justice Journal, April,* 30-38.

Steinberg, L. (2001). We know some things: Adolescent-parent relationships in retrospect and prospect. *Journal of Research on Adolescence, 11,* 1-19.

Steinberg, L. (2005). *The 10 basic principles of good parenting.* New York: Simon & Schuster.

Steinberg, L. (2008). A social neuroscience perspective on adolescent risk-taking. *Developmental Review, 28,* 78-106.

Steinberg, L. (2010). A dual systems model of adolescent risk-taking. *Developmental Psychobiology, 52,* 216-224.

Steinberg, L. (2011). *You and your adolescent: The essential guide for ages 10-25.* New York: Simon & Schuster.

Steinberg, L. (2014a). *Age of opportunity: Lessons from the new science of adolescence.* New York: Houghton Mffflin Harcourt.

Steinberg, L. (2014b, September 21). The case for delayed adulthood. *The New York Times, Sunday Review,* p. 12.

Steinberg, L. (2014c, October 31). Injuries. Stress. Divided attention. Are coaches damaging our kids? *TIME.*

Steinberg, L. (2015). How to improve the health of American adolescents. *Perspectives on Psychological Science, 10,* 711-715.

Steinberg, L. (2018, March 4). Why we should lower the voting age to 16. *The New York Times Sunday Review,* p. 6.

Steinberg, L. (2020, June 16). Expecting students to play it safe if colleges reopen is a fantasy. *The New York Times,* p. A31.

Steinberg, L., & Avenevoli, S. (2000). The role of context in the development of psychopathology: A conceptual framework and some speculative propositions. *Child Development, 71,* 66-74.

Steinberg, L., & Belsky, J. (1996). A sociobiological perspective on psychopathology in adolescence. In D. Cicchetti and S. Toth (Eds.), *Rochester Symposium on Developmental Psychopathology* (Vol. 7, pp. 93-124). Rochester, NY: University of Rochester Press.

Steinberg, L., & Dornbusch, S. (1991). Negative correlates of part-time work in adolescence: Replication and elaboration. *Developmental Psychology, 17,* 304-313.

Steinberg, L., & Icenogle, G. (2019). Using developmental science to distinguish adolescents and adults under the law. *Annual Review of Developmental Psychology, 1,* 21-40.

Steinberg, L., & Monahan, K. (2007). Age differences in resistance to peer influence. *Developmental Psychology, 43,* 1531-1543.

Steinberg, L., & Monahan, K. (2011). Adolescents' exposure to sexy media does not hasten the initiation of sexual intercourse. *Developmental Psychology, 47,* 562-576.

Steinberg, L., & Silk, J. (2002). Parenting adolescents. In M. Bornstein (Ed.), *Handbook of parenting: Vol. 1. Children and parenting* (2nd ed., pp. 103-133). Mahwah, NJ: Erlbaum.

Steinberg, L., & Silverberg, S. (1986). The vicissitudes of autonomy in early adolescence. *Child Development, 57,* 841-851.

Steinberg, L., & Steinberg, W. (1994). *Crossing paths: How your child's adolescence triggers your own crisis.* New York: Simon & Schuster.

Steinberg, L., Albert, D., Cauffman, E., Banich, M., Graham, S., & Woolard, J. (2008). Age differences in sensation seeking and impulsivity as indexed by behavior and self-report: Evidence for a dual systems model. *Developmental Psychology, 44,* 1764-1778.

Steinberg, L., Cauffman, E., Woolard, J., Graham, S., & Banich, M. (2009). Are adolescents less mature than adults? Minors' access to abortion, the juvenile death penalty, and the alleged APA "flip-flop." *American Psychologist, 64,* 583-594.

Steinberg, L., Graham, S., O'Brien, L., Woolard, J., Cauffman, E., & Banich, M. (2009). Age differences in future orientation and delay discounting. *Child Development, 80,* 28-44.

Steinberg, L., Icenogle, G., Shulman, E. P., Breiner, K., Chein, J., Bacchini, D., . . . Takash, H. M. S. (2018). Around the world, adolescence is a time of heightened sensation seeking and immature self-regulation. *Developmental Science, 21,* 1-13.

Steiner, R., & Rasberry, C. (2015). Brief report: Associations between in-person and electronic bullying victimization and missing school because of safety concerns among U.S. high school students. *Journal of Adolescence, 43,* 1-4.

Stepanyan, S. T., Natsuaki, M. N., Cheong, Y., Hastings, P. D., Zahn-Waxler, C., & Klimes-Dougan, B. (2020). Early pubertal maturation and externalizing behaviors: Examination of peer delinquency as mediator and cognitive flexibility as a moderator. *Journal of Adolescence, 84,* 45-55.

Stephanou, K., Davey, C. G., Kerestes, R., Whittle, S., & Harrison, B. J. (2017). Hard to look on the bright side: Neural correlates of impaired emotion regulation in depressed youth. *Social Cognitive and Affective Neuroscience, 12,* 1138-1148.

Stephens, L. (1996). Will Johnny see Daddy this week? An empirical test of three theoretical perspectives of postdivorce contact. *Journal of Family Issues, 17,* 466-494.

Stephens, N., Hamedani, M., & Destin, M. (2014). Closing the social-class achievement gap: A difference-education intervention improves first-generation students' academic performance and all students' college transition. *Psychological Science, 25,* 943-953.

Sterzing, P. R., Gibbs, J. J., Gartner, R. E., & Goldbach, J. T. (2018). Bullying victimization trajectories for sexual minority adolescents: stable victims, desisters, and late-onset victims. *Journal of Research on Adolescence, 28*(2), 368-378.

Stevens, G., Boer, M., Titzmann, P., Cosma, A., & Walsh, S. (2020). Immigration status and bullying victimization: Associations across national and school contexts. *Journal of Applied Developmental Psychology, 66,* 101075.

Stevens, M. C. (2016). The contributions of resting state and task-based functional connectivity studies to our understanding of adolescent brain network maturation. *Neuroscience & Biobehavioral Reviews, 70,* 13-32.

Stevenson, H., & Stigler, J. (1992). *The learning gap: Why our schools are failing and what we can learn from Japanese and Chinese education.* New York: Simon & Schuster.

Stewart, E. B., Stewart, E. A., & Simons, R. (2007). The effect of neighborhood context on the college aspirations of African American adolescents. *American Education Research Journal, 44,* 896-919.

Stewart, J., Spivey, L., Widman, L., Choukas-Bradley, S., & Prinstein, M. (2019). Developmental patterns of sexual identity, romantic attraction, and sexual behavior among adolescents over three years. *Journal of Adolescence, 77,* 90-97.

Stice, E., & Bearman, S. (2001). Body-image and eating disturbances prospectively predict increases in depressive symptoms in adolescent girls: A growth curve analysis. *Developmental Psychology, 37,* 597-607.

Stice, E., & Van Ryzin, M. J. (2019). A prospective test of the temporal sequencing of risk factor emergence in the dual pathway model of eating disorders. *Journal of Abnormal Psychology, 128,* 119.

Stice, E., Hayward, C., Cameron, R. P., Killen, J., & Taylor, C. (2000). Body-image and eating disturbances predict onset of depression among female adolescents: A longitudinal study. *Journal of Abnormal Psychology, 109,* 438-444.

Stice, E., Presnell, K., Shaw, H., & Rohde, P. (2005). Psychological and behavioral risk factors for obesity onset in adolescent girls: A prospective study. *Journal of Consulting and Clinical Psychology, 73,* 195-202.

Stice, E., Shaw, H., & Marti, C. N. (2006). A meta-analytic review of obesity prevention programs for children and adolescents: The skinny on interventions that work. *Psychological Bulletin, 132,* 667-691.

Stice, E., Shaw, H., & Ochner, C. (2011). Eating disorders. In B. Brown & M. Prinstein (Eds.), *Encyclopedia of adolescence* (Vol. 3, pp. 151-159). New York: Academic Press.

Stockdale, L., & Coyne, S. (2020). Bored and online: Reasons for using social media, problematic social networking site use, and behavioral outcomes across the transition from adolescence to emerging adulthood. *Journal of Adolescence, 79,* 173-183.

Stockdale, L., Coyne, S., & Padilla-Walker, L. (2018). Parent and child technoference and socioemotional behavioral outcomes: A nationally representative study of 10-to 20-year-old adolescents. *Computers in Human Behavior, 88,* 219-226.

Stocker, C., Lanthier, R., & Furman, W. (1997). Sibling relationships in early adulthood. *Journal of Family Psychology, 11,* 210-221.

Stocker, C. M., Masarik, A. S., Widaman, K. F., Reeb, B. T., Boardman, J. D., Smolen, A., . . . Conger, K. J. (2017). Parenting and adolescents' psychological adjustment: Longitudinal moderation by adolescents' genetic sensitivity. *Development and Psychopathology, 29,* 1289-1304.

Stoddard, S., Whiteside, L., Zimmerman, M., Cunningham, R., Chermack, S., & Walton, M. (2013). The relationship between cumulative risk and promotive factors and violent behavior among urban adolescents. *American Journal of Community Psychology, 51,* 57-65.

Stoddard, S., Zimmerman, M., & Bauermeister, J. (2012). A longitudinal analysis of cumulative risks, cumulative promotive factors, and adolescent violent behavior. *Journal of Research on Adolescence, 22,* 542-555.

Stone, J. (2011). Employment. In B. Brown & M. Prinstein (Eds.), *Encyclopedia of adolescence* (Vol. 2, pp. 59-67). New York: Academic Press.

Stone, L., Hankin, B., Gibb, B., & Abela, J. (2011). Co-rumination predicts the onset of depressive disorders during adolescence. *Journal of Abnormal Psychology, 120,* 752-757.

Storvoll, E., & Wichstrøm, L. (2002). Do the risk factors associated with conduct problems vary according to gender? *Journal of Adolescence, 25,* 183-202.

Stotsky, M., Bowker, J., & Etkin, R. (2020). Receiving prosocial behavior: Examining the reciprocal associations between positive peer treatment and psychosocial and behavioral outcomes. *Journal of Research on Adolescence, 30,* 458-470.

Stouthamer-Loeber, M., Wei, E., & Loeber, R. (2004). Desistance from persistent serious delinquency in the transition to adulthood. *Development and Psychopathology, 16,* 897-918.

Strang, N. M., & Pollak, S. D. (2014). Development continuity in reward-related enhancement of cognitive control. *Development Cognitive Neuroscience, 10,* 34-43.

Strasburger, V., Jordan, A., & Donnerstein, E. (2010). Health effects of media on children and adolescents. *Pediatrics, 125,* 756-767.

Strenziok, M., Krueger, F., Pulaski, S., Openshaw, A., Zamboni, G., van de Meer, E., & Grafman, J. (2010). Lower lateral orbitofrontal cortex density associated with more frequent exposure to television and movie violence in male adolescents. *Journal of Adolescent Health, 46,* 607-609.

Stroud, L., Foster, E., Papandonatos, G., Handwerger, K., Granger, D., Kivlighan, K., ... Niaura, R. (2009). Stress response and the adolescent transition: Performance versus peer rejection stressors. *Development and Psychopathology, 21,* 47–68.

Strough, J., & Berg, C. (2000). Goals as a mediator of gender differences in high-affiliation dyadic conversations. *Developmental Psychology, 36,* 117–125.

Stuart, E., & Green, K. (2008). Using full matching to estimate causal effects in nonexperimental studies: Examining the relationship between adolescent marijuana use and adult outcomes. *Developmental Psychology, 44,* 395–406.

Stumper, A., Olino, T. M., Abramson, L. Y., & Alloy, L. B. (2019). Pubertal timing and substance use in adolescence: An investigation of two cognitive moderators. *Journal of Abnormal Child Psychology, 47,* 1509–1520.

Su, J., & Supple, A. (2016). School substance use norms and racial composition moderate parental and peer influences on adolescent substance use. *American Journal of Community Psychology, 57,* 280–290.

Su, J., Supple, A., Leerkes, E., Sally, I., & Kuo, C. (2019). Latent trajectories of alcohol use from early adolescence to young adulthood: Interaction effects between 5-HTTLPR and parenting quality and gender differences. *Development and Psychopathology, 31,* 457–469.

Su, Q., Chen, Z., Li, R., Elgar, F. J., Liu, Z., & Lian, Q. (2018). Association between early menarche and school bullying. *Journal of Adolescent Health, 63,* 213–218.

Suárez-Orozco, C., Rhodes, J., & Milburn, M. (2009). Unraveling the immigrant paradox: Academic engagement and disengagement among recently arrived immigrant youth. *Youth & Society, 41,* 151–185.

Substance Abuse and Mental Health Services Administration. (2016). *Racial and ethnic minority populations.* Washington: Author.

Substance Abuse and Mental Health Services Administration. (2018). *Key substance use and mental health indicators in the United States: Results from the 2017 National Survey on Drug Use and Health.* Rockville, MD: Author

Suchert, V., Hanewinkel, H., & Isensee, B. (2016). Screen time, weight status and the self-concept of physical attractiveness in adolescents. *Journal of Adolescence, 48,* 11–17.

Sue, S., & Okazaki, S. (1990). Asian-American educational achievements: A phenomenon in search of an explanation. *American Psychologist, 45,* 913–920.

Sugimura, K. (2020). Adolescent identity development in Japan. *Child Development Perspectives, 14,* 71–77.

Suicide Prevention Resource Center. (2020). Means of suicide. Accessed at https://www.sprc.org/scope/means-suicide on January 19, 2021.

Suizzo, M., Jackson, K., Pahlke, E., Marroquin, Y., Blondeau, L., & Martinez, A. (2012). Pathways to achievement: How low-income Mexican-origin parents promote their adolescents through school. *Family Relations, 61,* 533–547.

Suleiman, A., & Deardorff, J. (2015). Multiple dimensions of peer influence in adolescent romantic and sexual relationships: A descriptive, qualitative perspective. *Archives of Sexual Behavior, 44,* 765–775.

Suleiman, A., Galvan, A., Harden, K. P., & Dahl, R. (2017). Becoming a sexual being: The "elephant in the room" of adolescent brain development. *Developmental Cognitive Neuroscience, 25,* 209–220.

Sullivan, C., Childs, K., & O'Connell, D. (2010). Adolescent risk behavior subgroups: An empirical assessment. *Journal of Youth and Adolescence, 39,* 541–562.

Sullivan, H. S. (1953a). *The interpersonal theory of psychiatry.* New York: Norton.

Sullivan, H. S. (1953b). *Conceptions of modern psychiatry.* New York: Norton.

Sullivan, T., Goncy, E., Garthe, R., Carlson, M., Behrhorst, K., & Farrell, A. (2020). Patterns of dating aggression and victimization in relation to school environment factors among middle school students. *Youth & Society, 52,* 1128–1152.

Sun, Q., Geeraert, N., & Simpson, A. (2020). Never mind the acculturation gap: Migrant youth's wellbeing benefit when they retain their heritage culture but their parents adopt the settlement culture. *Journal of Youth and Adolescence, 49,* 520–533.

Sun, X., McHale, S., & Updegraff, K. (2019). Sibling dynamics in adolescence predict young adult orientations to couple relationships: A dyadic approach. *Journal of Adolescence, 77,* 129–138.

Sun, Y. (2001). Family environment and adolescents' well-being before and after parents' marital disruption: A longitudinal analysis. *Journal of Marriage and the Family, 63,* 697–713.

Sun, Y., Mensah, F. K., Azzopardi, P., Patton, G. C., & Wake, M. (2017). Childhood social disadvantage and pubertal timing: A national birth cohort from Australia. *Pediatrics, 139,* e20164099.

Susman, E., & Dorn, L. (2009). Puberty: Its role in development. In R. Lerner & L. Steinberg (Eds.), *Handbook of adolescent psychology* (3rd ed., Vol. 1, pp. 116–151). New York: Wiley.

Susman, E., Dorn, L., Inoff-Germain, G., Nottelmann, E., & Chrousos, G. (1997). Cortisol reactivity, distress behavior, and behavioral and psychological problems in young adolescents: A longitudinal perspective. *Journal of Research on Adolescence, 7,* 81–105.

Sutin, A., & Terracciano, A. (2015). Body weight misperception in adolescence and incident obesity in young adulthood. *Psychological Science, 26,* 507–511.

Svensson, R., & Shannon, D. (2020). Immigrant background and crime among young people: An examination of the importance of delinquent friends based on national self-report data. *Youth & Society,* early view.

Swearer, S., & Hymel, S. (2015). Understanding the psychology of bullying: Moving toward a social-ecological diathesis-stress model. *American Psychologist, 70,* 344–353.

Sweeten, G., Bushway, S. D., & Paternoster, R. (2009). Does dropping out of school mean dropping into delinquency? *Criminology: An Interdisciplinary Journal, 47,* 47–91.

Sweeten, G., Piquero, A., & Steinberg, L. (2013). Age and the explanation of crime, revisited. *Journal of Youth & Adolescence, 42,* 921–938.

Swendsen, J., Burstein, M., Case, B., Conway, K., Dierker, L., He, J., & Merikangas, K. (2012). Use and abuse of alcohol and illicit drugs in US adolescents: Results of the national comorbidity survey-adolescent supplement. *Archives of General Psychiatry, 69,* 390–398.

Swenson, L., & Rose, A. (2003). Friends as reporters of children's and adolescents' depressive symptoms. *Journal of Abnormal Child Psychology, 31,* 619–631.

Swinton, A., Kurtz-Costes, B., Rowley, S., & Okeke-Adeyanju, N. (2011). A longitudinal examination of African American adolescents' attributions about achievement outcomes. *Child Development, 82,* 1486–1500.

Syed, M., & Azmitia, M. (2008). A narrative approach to ethnic identity in emerging adulthood: Bringing life to the identity status model. *Developmental Psychology, 44,* 1012–1027.

Syed, M., & Seiffge-Krenke, I. (2013). Personality development from adolescence to emerging adulthood: Linking trajectories of ego development to the family context and identity formation. *Journal of Personality and Social Psychology, 104,* 371–384.

Symons, K., Ponnet, K., Emmery, K., Walrave, M., & Heirman, W. (2017). Parental knowledge of adolescents' online content and contact risks. *Journal of Youth and Adolescence, 46,* 401–416.

Symons, K., Vermeersch, H., & Van Houtte, M. (2014). The emotional experiences of early first intercourse: A multi-method study. *Journal of Adolescent Research, 29,* 533–560.

Syvertsen, A., Flanagan, C., & Stout, M. (2009). Code of silence: Students' perceptions of school climate and willingness to intervene in a peer's dangerous plan. *Journal of Educational Psychology, 101,* 219–232.

Sznitman, G., Zimmermann, G., & Van Petegem, S. (2019). Further insight into adolescent personal identity statuses: Differences based on self-esteem, family climate, and family communication. *Journal of Adolescence, 71,* 99–109.

Sznitman, S., Reisel, L., & Khurana, A. (2017). Socioeconomic background and high school completion: Mediation by health and moderation by national context. *Journal of Adolescence, 56,* 118–126.

Szwedo, D., Hessel, E., & Allen, J. (2017). Supportive romantic relationships as predictors of resilience against early adolescent maternal negativity. *Journal of Youth and Adolescence, 46,* 454–465.

Szwedo, D., Mikami, A., & Allen, J. (2011). Qualities of peer relations on social networking websites: Predictions from negative mother–teen interactions. *Journal of Research on Adolescence, 21,* 595–607.

Szwedo, D., Mikami, A., & Allen, J. (2012). Social networking site use predicts changes in young adults' psychological adjustment. *Journal of Research on Adolescence, 22,* 453–466.

Szwedo, D. E., Hessel, E., Loeb, E., Hafen, C., & Allen, J. (2017). Adolescent support seeking as a path to adult functional independence. *Developmental Psychology, 53,* 949–961.

Taggart, T., Powell, W., Gottfredson, N., Ennett, S., Eng, E., & Chatters, L. M. (2019). A person-centered approach to the study of black adolescent religiosity, racial identity, and sexual initiation. *Journal of Research on Adolescence, 29*(2), 402–413.

Talwar, V., Gomez-Garibello, C., & Shariff, S. (2014). Adolescents' moral evaluations and ratings of cyberbullying: The effect of veracity and intentionality behind the event. *Computers in Human Behavior, 36,* 122–128.

Tamnes, C. K., Herting, M. M., Goddings, A-L., Meuwese, R., Blakemore, S-J., Dahl, R. E., . . . Mills, K. L. (2017). Development of the cerebral cortex across adolescence: A multisample study of inter-related longitudinal changes in cortical volume, surface area, and thickness. *Journal of Neuroscience, 37,* 3402–3412.

Tamnes, C., Overbye, K., Ferschmann, L., Fjell, A., Walhovd, K., Blakemore, S.-J., & Dumontheil, I. (2018). Social perspective taking is associated with self-reported prosocial behavior and regional cortical thickness across adolescence. *Developmental Psychology, 54,* 1745–1757.

Tan, J., Hessel, E., Loeb, E., Schad, M., Allen, J., & Chango, J. (2016). Long-term predictions from early adolescent attachment state of mind to romantic relationship behaviors. *Journal of Research on Adolescence, 26,* 1022–1035.

Tanaka, C., Matsui, M., Uematsu, A., Noguchi, K., & Miyawaki, T. (2012) Developmental trajectories of the fronto-temporal lobes from infancy to early adulthood in healthy individuals. *Developmental Neuroscience, 34,* 477–487.

Tang, C. S., Yeung, D. Y., & Lee, A. M. (2003). Psychosocial correlates of emotional responses to menarche among Chinese adolescent girls. *Journal of Adolescent Health, 33,* 193–201.

Tang, C. S., Yeung, D. Y., & Lee, A. M. (2004). A comparison of premenarcheal expectations and postmenarcheal experiences in Chinese early adolescents. *Journal of Early Adolescence, 24,* 180–195.

Tang, S., Davis-Kean, P., Chen, M., & Sexton, H. (2016). Adolescent pregnancy's intergenerational effects: Does an adolescent mother's education have consequences for her children's achievement? *Journal of Research on Adolescence, 26,* 180–193.

Tang, S., McLoyd, V., & Hallman, S. (2016). Racial socialization, racial identity, and academic attitudes among African American adolescents: Examining the moderating influence of parent–adolescent communication. *Journal of Youth and Adolescence, 45,* 1141–1155.

Tang, X., Wang, M.-T., Guo, J., & Salmela-Aro, K. (2019). Building grit: The longitudinal pathways between mindset, commitment, grit, and academic outcomes. *Journal of Youth and Adolescence, 48*(5), 850–863.

Tanner, D. (1972). *Secondary education.* New York: Macmillan.

Tanner, J. (1972). Sequence, tempo, and individual variation in growth and development of boys and girls aged twelve to sixteen. In J. Kagan & R. Coles (Eds.), *Twelve to sixteen: Early adolescence.* New York: Norton.

Tanner-Smith, E. E. (2010). Negotiating the early developing body: Pubertal timing, body weight, and adolescent girls' substance use. *Journal of Youth and Adolescence, 39,* 1402–1416.

Tanner-Smith, E. E., & Fisher, B. W. (2016). Visible school security measures and student academic performance, attendance, and postsecondary

aspirations. *Journal of Youth and Adolescence, 45,* 195–210.

Tanofsky-Kraff, M., Schvey, N., & Grilo, C. (2020). A developmental framework of binge-eating disorder based on pediatric loss of control eating. *American Psychologist, 75,* 189–203.

Tarokh, L., Saletin, J. M., & Carskadon, M. A. (2016). Sleep in adolescence: Physiology, cognition, and mental health. *Neuroscience & Biobehavioral Reviews, 70,* 182–188.

Tartakovsky, E. (2009). Cultural identities of adolescent immigrants: A three-year longitudinal study including the pre-migration period. *Journal of Youth and Adolescence, 38,* 654–671.

Tashjian, S. M., Goldenberg, D., Monti, M. M., & Galván, A. (2018). Sleep quality and adolescent default mode network connectivity. *Social Cognitive and Affective Neuroscience, 13*(3), 290–299.

Tatnell, R., Kelada, L., Hasking, P., & Martin, G. (2014). Longitudinal analysis of adolescent NSSI: The role of intrapersonal and interpersonal factors. *Journal of Abnormal Child Psychology, 42,* 885–896.

Tavernier, R., & Willoughby, T. (2012). Adolescent turning points: The association between meaning-making and psychological well-being. *Developmental Psychology, 48,* 1058–1068.

Tavernier, R., & Willoughby, T. (2015). A longitudinal examination of the bidirectional association between sleep problems and social ties at university: The mediating role of emotion regulation. *Journal of Youth and Adolescence, 44,* 317–330.

Taylor, K., Sullivan, T., & Farrell, A. (2015). Longitudinal relationships between individual and class norms supporting dating violence and perpetration of dating violence. *Journal of Youth and Adolescence, 44,* 745–760.

Taylor, R., & Roberts, D. (1995). Kinship support and maternal and adolescent well-being in economically disadvantaged African-American families. *Child Development, 66,* 1585–1597.

Taylor, R., Casten, R., Flickinger, S., Roberts, D., & Fulmore, C. (1994). Explaining the school performance of African-American adolescents. *Journal of Research on Adolescence, 4,* 21–44.

Taylor, R. D. (2016). Association of demanding kin relations with psychological distress and school achievement among low-income, African American mothers and adolescents: Moderating effects of family routine. *Journal of Research on Adolescence, 26,* 638–644.

Taylor, Z. E., Widaman, K. F., & Robins, R. W. (2018). Longitudinal relations of economic hardship and effortful control to active coping in Latino youth. *Journal of Research on Adolescence, 28,* 396–411.

Teachman, J., Paasch, K., & Carver, K. (1996). Social capital and dropping out of school early. *Journal of Marriage and the Family, 58,* 773–783.

Tejada-Gallardo, C., Blasco-Belled, A., Torrelles-Nadal, C., & Alsinet, C. (2020). Effects of school-based multicomponent positive psychology interventions on well-being and distress in adolescents: A systematic review and meta-analysis. *Journal of Youth and Adolescence, 49,* 1943–1960.

Telzer, E., & Fuligni, A. (2009). A longitudinal daily diary study of family assistance and academic

achievement among adolescents from Mexican, Chinese, and European backgrounds. *Journal of Youth and Adolescence, 38,* 560–571.

Telzer, E., & Fuligni, A. (2013). Positive daily family interactions eliminate gender differences in internalizing symptoms among adolescents. *Journal of Youth & Adolescence, 42,* 1498–1511.

Telzer, E., Fowler, C., Davis, M., & Rudolph, K. (2019). Hungry for inclusion: Exposure to peer victimization and heightened social monitoring in adolescent girls. *Development and Psychopathology, 32,* 1495–1508.

Telzer, E., Fuligni, A., Lieberman, M., Miernicki, M., & Galván, A. (2015). The quality of adolescents' peer relationships modulates neural sensitivity to risk taking. *Social Cognitive Affective Neuroscience, 10,* 389–398.

Telzer, E., Ichien, N., & Qu, Y. (2015). Mothers know best: Redirecting adolescent reward sensitivity towards safe behavior during risk taking. *Social Cognitive Affective Neuroscience, 10,* 1383–1391.

Telzer, E., Jorgensen, N., Prinstein, M., & Lindquist, K. (2020). Neurobiological sensitivity to social rewards and punishments moderates link between peer norms and adolescent risk taking. *Child Development,* DOI: 10.1111/cdev.13466.

Telzer, E., Rogers, C., & Van Hoorn, J. (2017). Neural correlates of social influence on risk taking and substance use in adolescents. *Current Addiction Reports, 4,* 333–341.

Telzer, E. H. (2016). Dopaminergic reward sensitivity can promote adolescent health: A new perspective on the mechanism of ventral striatum activation. *Developmental Cognitive Neuroscience, 17,* 57–67.

Telzer, E. H., Yuen, C., Gonzales, N., & Fuligni, A. J. (2016). Filling gaps in the acculturation gap-distress model: Heritage cultural maintenance and adjustment in Mexican–American families. *Journal of Youth and Adolescence, 45,* 1412–1425.

Temple, J., Choi, H., Brem, M., Woldford-Clevenger, C., Stuart, G., Fleschler Peskin, M., & Elmquist, J. (2016). The temporal association between traditional and cyber dating abuse among adolescents. *Journal of Youth and Adolescence, 45,* 340–349.

Temple, J., Shorey, R., Fite, P., Stuart, G., & Le, V. (2013). Substance use as a longitudinal predictor of the perpetration of teen dating violence. *Journal of Youth & Adolescence, 42,* 596–606.

Tenenbaum, H., & Ruck, M. (2012). British adolescents' and young adults' understanding and reasoning about the religious and nonreligious rights of asylum-seeker youth. *Child Development, 83,* 1102–1115.

Teng, Z., Nie, Q., Guo, C., Zhang, Q., Liu, Y., & Bushman, B. (2019). A longitudinal study of link between exposure to violent video games and aggression in Chinese adolescents: The mediating role of moral disengagement. *Developmental Psychology, 55,* 184–195.

Terry, M., Ferris, J., Tehranifar, P., Wei, Y., & Flom, J. (2009). Birth weight, postnatal growth, and age at menarche. *American Journal of Epidemiology, 170,* 72–79.

Terry, R., & Winston, C. (2010). Personality characteristic adaptations: Multiracial adolescents' patterns of racial self-identification change.

Journal of Research on Adolescence, 20, 432-455.

Teslovich, T., Mulder, M., Franklin, N. T., Ruberry, E. J., Millner, A., Somerville, L. J., . . . & Casey, B. J. (2014). Adolescents let sufficient evidence accumulate before making a decision when large incentives are at stake. *Developmental Science, 17,* 59-70.

Tevendale, H., DuBois, D., Lopez, C., & Prindiville, S. (1997). Self-esteem stability and early adolescent adjustment: An exploratory study. *Journal of Early Adolescence, 17,* 216-237.

Theokas, C., & Lerner, R. (2006). Promoting positive development in adolescence: The role of ecological assets in families, schools, and neighborhoods. *Applied Developmental Science, 10,* 61-74.

Thijs, J., Verkuyten, M., & Helmond, P. (2010). A further examination of the big-fish-little-pond effect: Perceived position in class, class size, and gender comparisons. *Sociology of Education, 83,* 333-345.

Thillay, A., Roux, S., Gissot, V., Carteau-Martin, I., Knight, R. T., Bonnet-Brilhault, F., & Bidet-Caulet, A. (2015). Sustained attention and prediction: Distinct brain maturation trajectories during adolescence. *Frontiers in Human Neuroscience, 9,* 519.

Thomaes, S., Bushman, B., de Castro, B., & Reijntjes, A. (2012). Arousing "gentle passions" in young adolescents: Sustained experimental effects of value affirmations on prosocial feelings and behaviors. *Developmental Psychology, 48,* 103-110.

Thomaes, S., Poorthuis, A., & Nelemans, S. (2011). Self-esteem. In B. Brown & M. Prinstein (Eds.), *Encyclopedia of adolescence* (Vol. 1, pp. 316-324). New York: Academic Press.

Thomaes, S., Sedikides, C., van den Bos, N., Hutteman, R., & Reijntjes, A. (2017). Happy to be "me"? Authenticity, psychological need satisfaction, and subjective well-being in adolescence. *Child Development, 88,* 1045-1056.

Thomann, C., & Suyemoto, K. (2017). Developing an antiracist stance: How white youth understand structural racism. *The Journal of Early Adolescence, 38,* 745-771.

Thomas, A., Ozbardakci, N., Fine, A., Steinberg, L., Frick, P., & Cauffman, E. (2018). Effects of physical and emotional maternal hostility on adolescents' depression and reoffending. *Journal of Research on Adolescence, 28,* 427-437.

Thomas, J., & Daubman, K. A. (2001). The relationship between friendship quality and self-esteem in adolescent girls and boys. *Sex Roles, 45,* 53-65.

Thomas, K., Rodrigues, H., de Oliveira, R., & Mangino, A. (2020). What predicts pre-adolescent compliance with family rules? A longitudinal analysis of parental discipline, procedural justice, and legitimacy evaluations. *Journal of Youth and Adolescence, 49,* 936-950.

Thomas, K. J. (2015). Delinquent peer influence on offending versatility: Can peers promote specialized delinquency? *Criminology, 53,* 280-308.

Thomas, R., Sanders, S., Doust, J., Beller, E., & Glasziou, P. (2015). Prevalence of attention-deficit/hyperactivity disorder: A systematic review and meta-analysis. *Pediatrics, 135,* e994-e1001.

Thomas, V., & Azmitia, M. (2019). Motivation matters: Development and validation of the Motivation for Solitude Scale–Short Form (MSS-SF). *Journal of Adolescence, 70,* 33-42.

Thorne, A. (2000). Personal memory telling and personality development. *Personality and Social Psychology Review, 4,* 45-56.

Thornton, L., Frick, P., Shulman, E., Ray, J., Steinberg, L., & Cauffman, E. (2015). Callous-unemotional traits and adolescents' role in group crime. *Law and Human Behavior, 39,* 368-377.

Threlfall, J. (2018). Parenting in the shadow of Ferguson: Racial socialization practices in context. *Youth & Society, 50,* 255-273.

Thrul, J., Lipperman-Kreda, S., Grube, J., & Friend, K. (2014). Community-level adult daily smoking prevalence moderates the association between adolescents' cigarette smoking and perceived smoking by friends. *Journal of Youth & Adolescence, 43,* 1527-1535.

Tiggemann, M., & Slater, A. (2014). NetTweens: The internet and body image concerns in preteenage girls. *Journal of Early Adolescence, 34,* 606-620.

Tilton-Weaver, L. (2014). Adolescents' information management: Comparing ideas about why adolescents disclose to or keep secrets from their parents. *Journal of Youth & Adolescence, 43,* 803-813.

Tilton-Weaver, L., Burk, W., Kerr, M., & Stattin, H. (2013). Can parental monitoring and peer management reduce the selection or influence of delinquent peers? Testing the question using a dynamic social network approach. *Developmental Psychology, 49,* 2057-2070.

Timeo, S., Riva, P., & Paladino, M. (2020). Being liked or not being liked: A study on social-media exclusion in a preadolescent population. *Journal of Adolescence, 80,* 173-181.

Timmerman, G. (2002). A comparison between unwanted sexual behavior by teachers and by peers in secondary schools. *Journal of Youth and Adolescence, 31,* 397-404.

Timmons, A. C., & Margolin, G. (2015). Family conflict, mood, and adolescents' daily school problems: Moderating roles of internalizing and externalizing symptoms. *Child Development, 86,* 241-258.

Timpe, Z. C., & Lunkenheimer, E. (2015). The long-term economic benefits of natural mentoring relationships for youth. *American Journal of Community Psychology, 56,* 12-24.

Titzmann, P. F. (2014). Immigrant adolescents' adaptation to a new context: Ethnic friendship homophily and its predictors. *Child Development Perspectives, 8,* 107-112.

Tobore, T. (2019). On the potential harmful effects of e-cigarettes (EC) on the developing brain: The relationship between vaping-induced oxidative stress and adolescent/young adults social maladjustment. *Journal of Adolescence, 76,* 202-209.

Toenders, Y., van Velzen, L., Heideman, I., Harrison, B., Davey, C., & Schmaal, L. (2019). Neuroimaging predictors of onset and course of depression in childhood and adolescence: A systematic review of longitudinal studies. *Developmental Cognitive Neuroscience, 39,* 100700.

Tolan, P., & Gorman-Smith, D. (2002). What violence prevention research can tell us about developmental psychopathology. *Development and Psychopathology, 14,* 713-729.

Tolan, P., & Larsen, R. (2014). Trajectories of life satisfaction during middle school: Relations to developmental-ecological microsystems and student functioning. *Journal of Research on Adolescence, 24,* 497-511.

Tolan, P., Gorman-Smith, D., & Henry, D. (2003). The developmental ecology of urban males' youth violence. *Developmental Psychology, 39,* 274-291.

Tolman, D., & McClelland, S. (2011). Normative sexuality development in adolescence: A decade in review, 2000-2009. *Journal of Research on Adolescence, 21,* 242-255.

Tomasi, D., & Volkow, N. D. (2012). Laterality patterns of brain functional connectivity: Gender effects. *Cerebral Cortex, 22,* 1455-1462.

Tomasik, M., & Silbereisen, R. (2011). Globalization and adolescence. In B. Brown & M. Prinstein (Eds.), *Encyclopedia of adolescence* (Vol. 2, pp. 109-117). New York: Academic Press.

Tomasik, M. J., & Silbereisen, R. K. (2012). Social change and adolescent developmental tasks: The case of postcommunist Europe. *Child Development Perspectives, 6,* 326-334.

Tomasik, M. J., Napolitano, C. M., & Moser, U. (2019). Trajectories of academic performance across compulsory schooling and thriving in young adulthood. *Child Development, 90*(6), e745-e762.

Tompsett, C. J., Veits, G. M., & Amrhein, K. E. (2016). Peer delinquency and where adolescents spend time with peers: Mediation and moderation of home neighborhood effects on self-reported delinquency. *Journal of Community Psychology, 44,* 263-270.

Toomey, R., & Russell, S. (2016). The role of sexual orientation in school-based victimization: A meta-analysis. *Youth & Society, 48,* 176-201.

Toomey, R., Ryan, C., Diaz, R., Card, N., & Russell, S. (2010). Gender-nonconforming lesbian, gay, bisexual, and transgender youth: School victimization and young adult psychosocial adjustment. *Developmental Psychology, 46,* 1580-1589.

Torres, S. A., Santiago, C. D., Walts, K. K., & Richards, M. H. (2018). Immigration policy, practices, and procedures: The impact on the mental health of Mexican and Central American youth and families. *American Psychologist, 73*(7), 843.

Torres-Gomez, B., Alonso-Arbiol, I., & Gallarin, M. (2020). Attachment to parents and aggressiveness in adopted adolescents: A multi-sample comparison study. *Journal of Research on Adolescence, 30,* 46-54.

Tottenham, N., & Galván, A. (2016). Stress and the adolescent brain: Amygdala-prefrontal cortex circuitry and ventral striatum as developmental targets. *Neuroscience & Biobehavioral Reviews, 70,* 217-227.

Totura, C., Karver, M., & Gesten, E. (2014). Psychological distress and student engagement as mediators of the relationship between peer victimization and achievement in middle school youth. *Journal of Youth and Adolescence, 43,* 40-52.

Tough, P. (2008). *Whatever it takes: Geoffrey Canada's quest to change Harlem and America.* New York: Houghton Mifflin Harcourt.

Toyokawa, N., & Toyokawa, T. (2019). Interaction effect of familism and socioeconomic status on academic outcomes of adolescent children of Latino immigrant families. *Journal of Adolescence, 71,* 138-149.

Tran, S., & Raffaelli, M. (2020). Configurations of autonomy and relatedness in a multiethnic U.S. sample of parent-adolescent dyads. *Journal of Research on Adolescence, 30,* 203-218.

Trautwein, U., Ludtke, O., Nagy, N., Lenski, A., Niggli, A., & Schnyder, I. (2015). Using individual interest and conscientiousness to predict academic effort: Additive, synergistic or compensatory effects? *Journal of Personality and Social Psychology, 109,* 142-162.

Trejos-Castillo, E., & Vazsonyi, A. (2011). Transitions into adolescence. In B. Brown & M. Prinstein (Eds.), *Encyclopedia of adolescence* (Vol. 1, pp. 369-375). New York: Academic Press.

Trekels, J., & Eggermont, S. (2017). Linking magazine exposure to social appearance anxiety: The role of appearance norms in early adolescence. *Journal of Research on Adolescence, 27,* 736-751.

Trekels, J., Karsay, K., Eggermont, S., & Vandenbosch, L. (2018). How social and mass media relate to youth's self-sexualization: Taking a cross-national perspective on rewarded appearance ideals. *Journal of Youth and Adolescence, 47,* 1440-1455.

Trent, K., & Crowder, K. (1997). Adolescent birth intentions, social disadvantage, and behavioral outcomes. *Journal of Marriage and the Family, 59,* 523-535.

Trickett, P., Negriff, S., Ji, J., & Peckins, M. (2011). Child maltreatment and adolescent development. *Journal of Research on Adolescence, 21,* 3-20.

Trickett, P., Noll, J., Reiffman, A., & Putnam, F. (2001). Variants of intrafamilial sexual abuse experience: Implications for short- and long-term development. *Development and Psychopathology, 13,* 1001-1019.

Trifan, T., & Stattin, H. (2015). Are adolescents' mutually hostile interactions at home reproduced in other everyday life contexts? *Journal of Youth & Adolescence, 44,* 598-615.

Trinh, S., Lee, J., Halpern, C., & Moody, J. (2019). Our buddies, ourselves: The role of sexual homophily in adolescent friendship networks. *Child Development, 90,* e132-e147.

Trompeter, N., Bussey, K., & Fitzpatrick, S. (2018). Cyber victimization and internalizing difficulties: The mediating roles of coping self-efficacy and emotion dysregulation. *Journal of Abnormal Child Psychology, 46,* 1129-1139.

Trucco, E., Villafuerte, S., Hussong, A., Burmeister, M., & Zucker, R. (2018). Biological underpinnings of an internalizing pathway to alcohol, cigarette, and marijuana use. *Journal of Abnormal Psychology, 127,* 79-91.

Trucco, E. M., Colder, C. R., Wieczorek, W. F., Lengua, L. J., & Hawk, L. W. (2014). Early adolescent alcohol use in context: How neighborhoods, parents, and peers impact youth. *Development and Psychopathology, 26,* 425-436.

Trucco, E. M., Hicks, B. M., Villafuerte, S., Nigg, J. T., Burmeister, M., & Zucker, R. A. (2016). Temperament and externalizing behavior as mediators of genetic risk on adolescent substance use. *Journal of Abnormal Psychology, 125,* 565-575.

Trudeau, L., Mason, W., Randall, G., Spoth, R., & Ralston, E. (2012). Effects of parenting and deviant peers on early to mid-adolescent conduct problems. *Journal of Abnormal Child Psychology, 40,* 1249-1264.

Truelove-Hill, M., Erus, G., Bashyam, V., Varol, E., Sako, C., Gur, R., . . . Wolf, D. H. (2020). A multidimensional Neural Maturation Index reveals reproducible developmental patterns in children and adolescents. *Journal of Neuroscience, 40,* 1265-1275.

Trzesniewski, K., & Donnellan, M. (2009). Reevaluating the evidence for increasingly positive self-views among high school students: More evidence for consistency across generations (1976-2006). *Psychological Science, 20,* 920-922.

Trzesniewski, K., Donnellan, M., & Robins, R. (2003). Stability of self-esteem across the life span. *Journal of Personality and Social Psychology, 84,* 205-220.

Trzesniewski, K., Donnellan, M., Moffitt, T., Robins, R., Poulton, R., & Caspi, A. (2006). Low self-esteem during adolescence predicts poor health, criminal behavior, and limited economic prospects during adulthood. *Developmental Psychology, 42,* 381-390.

Tsai, K., & Fuligni, A. (2012). Change in ethnic identity across the college transition. *Developmental Psychology, 48,* 56-64.

Tsai, K., Telzer, E., Gonzales, N., & Fuligni, A. (2015). Parental cultural socialization of Mexican-American adolescents' family obligation values and behaviors. *Child Development, 86,* 1241-1252.

Tsai, K. M., Gonzales, N. A., & Fuligni, A. J. (2016). Mexican American adolescents' emotional support to the family in response to parental stress. *Journal of Research on Adolescence, 26,* 658-672.

Tsai, K. M., Telzer, E. H., & Fuligni, A. J. (2013). Continuity and discontinuity in perceptions of family relationships from adolescence to young adulthood. *Child Development, 84,* 471-484.

Tseng, W., Kawabata, Y., Gau, S., & Crick, N. (2014). Symptoms of attention-deficit/hyperactivity disorder and peer functioning: A transactional model of development. *Journal of Abnormal Child Psychology, 42,* 1353-1365.

Tsitsika, A., Janikian, M., Wójcik, S., Makaruk, K., Tzavela, E., Tzavara, C., . . . Richardson, C. (2015). Cyberbullying victimization prevalence and associations with internalizing and externalizing problems among adolescents in six European countries. *Computers in Human Behavior, 51,* 1-7.

Tu, K., Erath, S., & Flanagan, K. (2012). Can socially adept friends protect peer victimized early adolescents against lower academic competence? *Journal of Applied Developmental Psychology, 33,* 24-30.

Tubman, J., Montgomery, M., Gil, A., & Wagner, E. (2004). Abuse experiences in a community sample of young adults: Relations with psychiatric disorders, sexual risk behaviors, and sexually transmitted diseases. *American Journal of Community Psychology, 34,* 147-162.

Tucker Smith, C., Shepperd, J., Miller W., & Graber, J. (2016). Perspective taking explains gender differences in late adolescents' attitudes toward disadvantaged groups. *Journal of Youth and Adolescence, 45,* 1283-1293.

Tucker, C. J., & Wiesen-Martin, D. (2015). Adolescent siblings' suicide ideation. *Journal of Family Issues, 36,* 609-625.

Tucker, C., Updegraff, K. A., & Baril, M. E. (2010). Who's the boss? Patterns of control in adolescents' sibling relationships. *Family Relations, 59,* 520-532.

Tucker, J., Ellickson, P., Collins, R., & Klein, D. (2006). Are drug experimenters better adjusted than abstainers and users? A longitudinal study of adolescent marijuana use. *Journal of Adolescent Health, 39,* 488-494.

Tucker, J., Ewing, B., Espelage, D., Green, H., de la Haye, K., & Pollard, M. (2016). Longitudinal associations of homophobic name-calling victimization with psychological distress and alcohol use during adolescence. *Journal of Adolescent Health, 59,* 110-115.

Tucker, J., Pedersen, E., Miles, J., Ewing, B., Shih, R., & D'Amico, E. (2014). Alcohol and marijuana use in middle school: Comparing solitary and social-only users. *Journal of Adolescent Health, 55,* 744-749.

Tucker-Drob, E., & Harden, K. (2012). Intellectual interest mediates gene-socioeconomic status interaction on adolescent academic achievement. *Child Development, 83,* 743-757.

Tucker-Drob, E. M., Briley, D. A., & Harden, K. P. (2013). Genetic and environmental influences on cognition across development and context. *Current Directions in Psychological Science, 22,* 349-355.

Tung, I., Noroña, A. N., Morgan, J. E., Caplan, B., Lee, S. S., & Baker, B. L. (2019). Patterns of sensitivity to parenting and peer environments: early temperament and adolescent externalizing behavior. *Journal of Research on Adolescence, 29,* 225-239.

Turanovic, J. & Young, J. (2016). Violent offending and victimization in adolescence: Social network mechanisms and homophily. *Criminology, 54,* 487-519.

Turel, O., Romashkin, A., & Morrison, K. M. (2016). Health outcomes of information system use lifestyles among adolescents: Videogame addiction, sleep curtailment, and cardio-metabolic deficiencies. *PLOS ONE, 11,* e0154764.

Turkheimer, E., & Waldron, M. (2000). Nonshared environment: A theoretical, methodological, and quantitative review. *Psychological Bulletin, 126,* 78-108.

Turkle, S. (2015). *Reclaiming conversation.* New York: Penguin.

Turner, H., Finkelhor, D., Hamby, S., Shattuck, A., & Ormrod, R. (2011). Specifying type and location of peer victimization in a national sample of children and youth. *Journal of Youth and Adolescence, 40,* 1052-1067.

Turner, R., Sorenson, A., & Turner, J. (2000). Social contingencies in mental health: A seven-year follow-up study of teenage mothers. *Journal of Marriage and the Family, 62,* 777-791.

Turney, K., & Halpern-Meekin, S. (2020). Parental relationship churning and adolescent well-being: Examining instability within families. *Journal of Marriage and Family, 82,* 965-980.

Twenge, J., & Crocker, J. (2002). Race and self-esteem: Meta-analyses comparing Whites, Blacks, Hispanics, Asians, and American Indians and comment on Gray-Little and Hafdahl. *Psychological Bulletin, 128,* 371-408.

Twenge, J., & Martin, G. (2020). Gender differences in associations between digital media use and psychological well-being: Evidence from three large datasets. *Journal of Adolescence, 79,* 91–102.

Twenge, J., & Park, H. (2019). The decline in adult activities among U.S. adolescents, 1976–2016. *Child Development, 90,* 638–654.

Twenge, J., Joiner, T., Rogers, M., & Martin, G. (2018). Increases in depressive symptoms, suicide-related outcomes, and suicide rates among U.S. adolescents after 2010 and links to increased new media screen time. *Clinical Psychological Science, 6,* 3–17.

Twenge, J., Sherman, R., & Wells, B. (2017). Sexual inactivity during young adulthood is more common among U.S. Millennials and iGen: Age, period, and cohort effects on having no sexual partners after age 18. *Archives of Sexual Behavior, 46,* 433–440.

Twigg, L., Duncan, C., & Weich, S. (2020). Is social media use associated with children's well-being? Results from the UK Household Longitudinal Study. *Journal of Adolescence, 80,* 73–83.

Tyler, K., Schmitz, R., & Ray, C. (2018). Role of social environmental protective factors on anxiety and depressive symptoms among Midwestern homeless youth. *Journal of Research on Adolescence, 28,* 199–210.

Tynes, B. (2007). Role taking in online "classrooms": What adolescents are learning about race and ethnicity. *Developmental Psychology, 43,* 1312–1320.

Tynes, B., Umaña-Taylor, A., Rose, C., Lin, J., & Anderson, C. (2012). Online racial discrimination and the protective function of ethnic identity and self-esteem for African American adolescents. *Developmental Psychology, 48,* 343–355.

Tyrell, F., Wheeler, L., Gonzales, N., Dumka, L., & Millsap, R. (2016). Family influences on Mexican American adolescents' romantic relationships: Moderation by gender and culture. *Journal of Research on Adolescence, 26,* 142–158.

Tyrka, A. R., Graber, J. A., & Brooks-Gunn, J. (2000). The development of disordered eating: Correlate and predictors of eating problems in the context of adolescence. In A. J. Sameroff, M. Lewis, & S. M. Miller (Eds.), *Handbook of developmental psychopathology* (2nd ed., pp. 607–624). New York: Kluwer Academic/ Plenum.

Tyson, K., Darity, W., & Castellino, D. R. (2005). It's not "a Black thing." Understanding the burden of acting White and other dilemmas of high achievement. *American Sociological Review, 70,* 582–605.

Tzoumakis, S., Lussier, P., & Corrado, R. (2012). Female juvenile delinquency, motherhood, and the intergenerational transmission of aggression and antisocial behavior. *Behavioral Sciences & the Law, 30,* 211–237.

U.S. Census Bureau. (2019). *Current population survey.* Washington: Author.

U.S. Census Bureau. (2020). *Current population survey.* Washington: Author.

U.S. Census Bureau. (2020a). Age and sex composition in the United States, 2019. Washington: Author.

U.S. Census Bureau. (2021, January 8). *Current population survey.* Washington: Author.

U.S. Department of Commerce, Bureau of the Census. (1940). *Characteristics of the population.* Washington, DC: U.S. Government Printing Office.

U.S. Department of Education. (2006). *No Child Left Behind.* Available at www.ed.gov.

U.S. Department of Education. (2009). Creating common standards, turning around schools. Retrieved from http://www.ed.gov/index.jhtml.

U.S. Senate Committee on the Judiciary. (1955, March). *Comic books and juvenile delinquency, Interim report.* Washington: Author.

Uhls, Y. (2015). *Media moms and digital dads.* Brookline, MA: Bibliomotion.

Umaña-Taylor, A. (2016). A post-racial society in which ethnic-racial discrimination still exists and has significant consequences for youth's adjustment. *Current Directions in Psychological Science, 25,* 111–118.

Umaña-Taylor, A., Gonzales-Backen, M., & Guimond, A. (2009). Latino adolescents' ethnic identity: Is there a developmental progression and does growth in ethnic identity predict growth in self-esteem? *Child Development, 80,* 391–405.

Umaña-Taylor, A., Kornienko, O., Bayless, S., & Updegraff, K. (2018). A universal intervention program increases ethnic-racial identity exploration and resolution to predict adolescent psychosocial functioning one year later. *Journal of Youth and Adolescence, 47,* 1–15.

Umaña-Taylor, A., Kornienko, O., McDermott, E., & Motti-Stefanidi, F. (2020). National identity development and friendship network dynamics among immigrant and non-immigrant youth. Journal of Youth and Adolescence, 49, 706–723.

Umaña-Taylor, A., Tynes, B., Toomey, R., Williams, D., & Mitchell, K. (2015). Latino adolescents' perceived discrimination in online and offline settings: An examination of cultural risk and protective factors. *Developmental Psychology, 51,* 87–100.

Umaña-Taylor, A. J., & Bámaca-Gómez, M. Y. (2003). Generational differences in resistance to peer pressure among Mexican-origin adolescents. *Youth and Society, 35,* 183–203.

Umaña-Taylor, A. J., Alfaro, E. C., Bámaca, M. Y., & Guimond, A. B. (2009). The central role of familial ethnic socialization in Latino adolescents' cultural orientation. *Journal of Marriage and the Family, 71,* 46–90.

Umaña-Taylor, A. J., Quintana, S. M., Lee, R. M., Cross Jr., W. E., Rivas-Drake, D., Schwartz, S. J. . . . & the Ethnic and Racial Identity in the 21st Century Study Group. (2014). Ethnic and racial identity during adolescence and into young adulthood: An integrated conceptualization. *Child Development, 85,* 21–39.

Uncapher, M. R., Thieu, M., & Wagner, A. (2016). Media multitasking and memory: Differences in working memory and long-term memory. *Psychonomic Bulletin and Review, 23,* 483–490.

Underwood, M., & Ehrenreich, S. (2017). The power and the pain of adolescents' digital communication: Cyber victimization and the perils of lurking. *American Psychologist, 72,* 144–158.

Underwood, M., Ehrenreich, S., More, D., Solis, J., & Brinkley, D. (2013). The BlackBerry project: The hidden world of adolescents' text messaging and relations with internalizing symptoms. *Journal of Research on Adolescence, 25,* 101–117.

Unger J., Molina G., & Teran, L. (2002). Perceived consequences of teenage childbearing among adolescent girls in an urban sample. *Journal of Adolescent Health, 26,* 205–212.

United Nations Department of Economic and Social Affairs, Population Division. (2019). *World population prospects.* New York: Author.

United Nations. (2014). *The state of world population.* New York: Author.

United Nations. (2015). *UNICEF global databases.* New York: Author.

United Nations. (2018). *Participation in education.* New York: UNESCO Institute of Statistics.

Upadhya, K., Santelli, J., Raine-Bennett, T., Kottke, M., & Grossman, D. (2017). Over-the-counter access to oral contraceptives for adolescents. *Journal of Adolescent Health, 60,* 634–640.

Updegraff, K., Kim, J., Killoren, S., & Thayer, S. (2010). Mexican American parents' involvement in adolescents' peer relationships: Exploring the role of culture and adolescents' peer experiences. *Journal of Research on Adolescence, 20,* 65–87.

Updegraff, K., Madden-Derdich, D., Estrada, A., Sales, L., & Leonard, S. (2002). Young adolescents' experiences with parents and friends: Exploring the connections. *Family Relations, 51,* 72–80.

Updegraff, K., McHale, S., Whiteman, S., Thayer, S., & Crouter, A. (2006). The nature and correlates of Mexican-American adolescents' time with parents and peers. *Child Development, 77,* 1470–1486.

Updegraff, K., Umaña-Taylor, A., McHale, S., Wheeler, L., & Perez-Brena, N. (2012). Mexican-origin youth's cultural orientations and adjustment: Changes from early to late adolescence. *Child Development, 83,* 1655–1671.

Urberg, K., Değirmencioğilu, S., Tolson, J., & Halliday-Scher, K. (1995). The structure of adolescent peer networks. *Developmental Psychology, 31,* 540–547.

Usher, E. L. (2009). Sources of middle school students' self-efficacy in mathematics: A qualitative investigation. *American Educational Research Journal, 46,* 275–314.

Uy, J., Goldenberg, D., Tashjian, S., Do, K., & Galván, A. (2019). Physical home environment is associated with prefrontal cortical thickness in adolescents. *Developmental Science, 22,* e12834.

Vagi, K., Rothman, E., Latzman, N., Tharp, A., Hall, D., & Breiding, M. (2013). Beyond correlates: A review of risk and protective factors for adolescent dating violence perpetration. *Journal of Youth and Adolescence, 42,* 633–649.

Valencia-Agudo, F., Burcher, G., Ezpeleta, L., & Kramer, T. (2018). Nonsuicidal self-injury in community adolescents: A systematic review of prospective predictors, mediators and moderators. *Journal of Adolescence, 65,* 25–38.

Valkenburg, P., & Peter, J. (2007). Preadolescents' and adolescents' online communication and their closeness to friends. *Developmental Psychology, 43,* 267–277.

Valkenburg, P., & Peter, J. (2011). Online communication among adolescents: An integrated model of its attraction, opportunities, and risks. *Journal of Adolescent Health, 48,* 121-127.

Valkenburg, P., Koutamanis, M., & Vossen, H. (2017). The concurrent and longitudinal relationships between adolescents' use of social network sites and their social self-esteem. *Computers in Human Behavior, 76,* 35-41.

Valle, G., & Tillman, K. H. (2014). Childhood family structure and romantic relationships during the transition to adulthood. *Journal of Family Issues, 35,* 97-124.

Van Boekel, M., Mulut, O., Stanke, L., Palma Zamora, J., Jang, Y., Kang, Y., & Nickodem, K. (2016). Effects of participation in school sports on academic and social functioning. *Journal of Applied Developmental Psychology, 46,* 31-40.

Van de Bongardt, D., Reitz, E., Overbeek, G., Boislard, M.-A., Burk, B., & Deković, M. (2017). Observed normativity and deviance in friendship dyads' conversations about sex and the relations with youths' perceived sexual peer norms. *Archives of Sexual Behavior, 46,* 1793-1806.

van de Groep, S., Meuwese, R., Zanolie, K., Güroğlu, B., & Crone, E. (2020). Developmental changes and individual differences in trust and reciprocity in adolescence. *Journal of Research on Adolescence, 30*(S1), 192-208.

van den Akker, A., Deković, M., & Prinzie, P. (2010). Transitioning to adolescence: How changes in child personality and overreactive parenting predict adolescent adjustment problems. *Development and Psychopathology, 22,* 151-163.

Van den Akker, A. L., Deković, M., Asscher, J., & Prinzie, P. (2014). Mean-level personality development across childhood and adolescence: A temporary defiance of the maturity principle and bidirectional associations with parenting. *Journal of Personality and Social Psychology, 107,* 736-750.

van den Berg, P., Mond, J., Eisenberg, M., Ackard, D., & Neumark-Sztainer, D. (2010). The link between body dissatisfaction and self-esteem in adolescents: Similarities across gender, age, weight status, race/ethnicity, and socioeconomic status. *Journal of Adolescent Health, 47,* 290-296.

van den Berg, P., Neumark-Sztainer, D., Hannan, P., & Haines, J. (2007). Is dieting advice from magazines helpful or harmful? Five-year associations with weight-control behaviors and psychological outcomes in adolescents. *Pediatrics, 119,* 30-37.

van den Berg, Y., Burk, W., & Cillessen, A. (2019). The functions of aggression in gaining, maintaining, and losing popularity during adolescence: A multiple-cohort design. *Developmental Psychology, 55,* 2159-2168.

van den Berg, Y., Lansu, T., & Cillessen, A. (2020). Preference and popularity as distinct forms of status: A meta-analytic review of 20 years of research. *Journal of Adolescence, 84,* 78-95.

van den Berg, Y. H. M., Burk, W. J., & Cillessen, A. H. N. (2015). Identifying subtypes of peer status by combining popularity and preference: A cohort-sequential approach. *The Journal of Early Adolescence, 35, 1108-1137.*

van den Bos, E., van Duijvenvoorde, A. C. K., & Westenberg, P. M. (2016). Effects of adolescent sociocognitive development on the cortisol response to social evaluation. *Developmental Psychology, 52,* 1151-1163.

van den Bos, W., Crone, E., Güroğlu, B. (2012). Brain Function during probabilistic learning in relation to IQ and level of education. *Developmental Cognitive Neuroscience, 15,* S78-89.

van den Bos, W., Rodriguez, C., Schweitzer, J., & McClure, S. (2015). Adolescent impatience decreases with frontostriatal connectivity. *PNAS, 112,* e3765-e3774.

van den Bos, W., Westenberg, M., van Dijk, E., & Crone, E. (2010). Development of trust and reciprocity in adolescence. *Cognitive Development, 25,* 90-102.

van den Broek, N., Deutz, M., Schoneveld, E., Burke, W., & Cillessen, A. (2016). Behavioral correlates of prioritizing popularity in adolescence. *Journal of Youth and Adolescence, 45,* 2444-2454.

van den Eijnden, R., Meerkerk, G., Vermulst, A., Spijkerman, R., & Engels, R. (2008). Online communication, compulsive Internet use, and psychosocial well-being among adolescents: A longitudinal study. *Developmental Psychology, 44,* 655-665.

van der Aa, N., Overbeek, G., Engels, R., Scholte, R., Meerkerk, G.-J., & Eijnden, R. (2009). Daily and compulsive internet use and well-being in adolescence: A diathesis-stress model based on big five personality traits. *Journal of Youth and Adolescence, 38,* 765-776.

Van der Cruijsen, R., Buisman, R., Green, K., Peters, S., & Crone, E. A. (2019). Neural responses for evaluating self and mother traits in adolescence depend on mother–adolescent relationships. *Social Cognitive and Affective Neuroscience, 14,* 481-492.

Van der Graaff, J., Branje, S., De Wied, M., Hawk, S., Van Lier, P., & Meeus, W. (2014). Perspective taking and empathic concern in adolescence: Gender differences in developmental changes. *Developmental Psychology, 50,* 881-888.

Van der Graaff, J., Carlo, G., Crocetti, E., Koot, H., & Branje, S. (2018). Prosocial behavior in adolescence: Gender differences in development and links with empathy. *Journal of Youth and Adolescence, 47,* 1086-1099.

van der Lely, S., Frey, S., Garbazza, C., Wirz-Justice, A., Jenni, O. G., Steiner, R., . . . & Schmidt, C. (2015). Blue blocker glasses as a countermeasure for alerting effects of evening light-emitting diode screen exposure in male teenagers. *Journal of Adolescent Health, 56,* 113-119.

Van Dijk, M., Branje, S., Keijsers, L., Hawk, S., Hale, W. W. 3rd., & Meeus, W. (2014). Self-concept clarity across adolescence: Longitudinal associations with open communication with parents and internalizing symptoms. *Journal of Youth & Adolescence, 43,* 1861-1876.

Van Doorn, M. D., Branje, S. J. T., & Meeus, W. H. J. (2011). Developmental changes in conflict resolution styles in parent–adolescent relationships: A four-wave longitudinal study. *Journal of Youth and Adolescence, 40,* 97-107.

van Duijvenvoorde, A., Jansen, B. R. J., Bredman, J. C., & Huizenga, H. M. (2012). Age-related changes in decision making: Comparing informed and noninformed situations. *Developmental Psychology, 48,* 192-203.

van Duijvenvoorde, A., Jansen, B., Visser, I., & Huizenga, H. M. (2010). Affective and cognitive decision-making in adolescents. *Developmental Neuropsychology, 35,* 539-554.

van Duijvenvoorde, A. C. K., Huizenga, H. M., Somerville, L. H., Delgado, M. R., Powers, A., Weeda, W. D., Casey, B. J., Weber, E. U., & Figner, B. (2015). Neural correlates of expected risks and returns in risky choice across development. *Journal of Neuroscience, 35,* 1549-1560.

van Duijvenvoorde, A. C. K., Peters, S., Braams, B. R., & Crone, E. A. (2016). What motivates adolescents? Neural responses to rewards and their influence on adolescents' risk taking, learning, and cognitive control. *Neuroscience & Biobehavioral Reviews, 70,* 135-147.

van Geel, M., & Vedder, P. (2011). The role of family obligations and school adjustment in explaining the immigrant paradox. *Journal of Youth and Adolescence, 40,* 187-196.

van Geel, M., Goemans, A., Zwaanswijk, W., Gini, G., & Vedder, P. (2018). Does peer victimization predict low self-esteem, or does low self-esteem predict peer victimization? Meta-analyses on longitudinal studies. *Developmental Review, 49,* 31-40.

Van Gelder, J.-L., Luciano, E. C., Weulen Kranenburg, M., & Hershfield, H. E. (2015). Friends with my future self: Longitudinal vividness intervention reduces delinquency. *Criminology, 53,* 158-179.

van Goethem, A., van Hoof A., Orobio de Castro, B., Van Aken, M., & Hart, D. (2014). The role of reflection in the effects of community service on adolescent development: A meta-Analysis. *Child Development, 85,* 2114-2130.

Van Hoorn, J., Crone, E. A., & Van Leijenhorst, L. (2017). Hanging out with the right crowd: Peer influence on risk-taking behavior in adolescence. *Journal of Research on Adolescence, 27,* 189-200.

van Hoorn, J., McCormick, E., & Telzer, E. (2018). Moderate social sensitivity in a risky context supports adaptive decision making in adolescence: Evidence from brain and behavior. *Social Cognitive and Affective Neuroscience, 13,* 546-556.

Van Hoorn, J., Van Dijk, E., Güroglu, B., & Crone, E. A. (2016). Neural correlates of prosocial peer influence on public goods game donations during adolescence. Social Cognitive and Affective Neuroscience, 11, 923-933.

Van Hoorn, J., Van Dijk, E., Meuwese, R., Rieffe, C., & Crone, E. (2016). Peer influence on prosocial behavior in adolescence. *Journal of Research on Adolescence, 26,* 90-100.

van Leeuwen, A., Verhulst, F., Reijneveld, S., Vollebergh, W., Ormel, J., & Huizink, A. (2011). Can the gateway hypothesis, the common liability model and/or, the route of administration model predict initiation of cannabis use during adolescence? A survival analysis—The TRAILS study. *Journal of Adolescent Health, 48,* 73-78.

Van Leijenhorst, L., Westenberg, P. M., & Crone, E. A. (2008). A developmental study of risky decisions on the cake gambling task: Age and gender analyses of probability estimation and reward evaluation. *Developmental Neuropsychology, 33,* 179-196.

Van Leijenhorst, L., Zanolie, K., Van Meel, C., Westenberg, P. M., Rombouts, S. A. R. B., & Crone, E. A. (2010). What motivates the adolescent? Brain regions mediating reward sensitivity across adolescence. *Cerebral Cortex, 20,* 61-69.

Van Lier, P., Vitaro, F., Barker, E., Koot, H., & Tremblay, R. (2009). Developmental links between trajectories of physical violence, vandalism, theft, and alcohol-drug use from childhood to adolescence. *Journal of Abnormal Child Psychology, 37,* 481-492.

Van Lier, P., Wanner, B., & Vitaro, F. (2007). Onset of antisocial behavior, affiliation with deviant friends, and childhood maladjustment: A test of the childhood- and adolescent-onset models. *Development and Psychopathology, 19,* 167-185.

Van Lissa, C. J., Hawk, S. T., Koot, H. M., Branje, S., & Meeus, W. H. J. (2017). The cost of empathy: Parent-adolescent conflict predicts emotion dysregulation for highly empathic youth. *Developmental Psychology, 53,* 1722-1737.

Van Noorden, T., Haselager, G., Cillessen, A., & Bukowski, W. (2015). Empathy and involvement in bullying in children and adolescents: A systematic review. *Journal of Youth and Adolescence, 44,* 637-657.

Van Oosten, J., Peter, J., & Boot, I. (2015). Exploring associations between exposure to sexy online self-presentations and adolescents' sexual attitudes and behavior. *Journal of Youth and Adolescence, 44,* 1078-1091.

Van Ouytsel, J., Van Gool, E., Walrave, M., Ponnet, K., & Peeters, E. (2016). Exploring the role of social networking sites within adolescent romantic relationships and dating experiences. *Computers in Human Behavior, 55,* 76-86.

Van Ouytsel, J., Walrave, M., Lu, Y., Temple, J., & Ponnet, K. (2018). The associations between substance use, sexual behavior, deviant behaviors and adolescents' engagement in sexting: Does relationship context matter? *Journal of Youth and Adolescence, 47,* 2353-2370.

Van Petegem, S., Antonietti, J.-P., Eira Nunes, C., Kins, E., & Soenens, B. (2020). The relationship between maternal overprotection, adolescent internalizing and externalizing problems, and psychological need frustration: A multi-informant study using response surface analysis. *Journal of Youth and Adolescence, 49,* 162-177.

Van Petegem, S., Beyers, W., Vansteenkiste, M., & Soenens, B. (2012). On the association between adolescent autonomy and psychosocial functioning: Examining decisional independence from a self-determination theory perspective. *Developmental Psychology, 48,* 76-88.

Van Petegem, S., Vansteenkiste, M., Soenens, B., Beyers, W., & Aelterman, N. (2015). Examining the longitudinal association between oppositional defiance and autonomy in adolescence. *Developmental Psychology, 51,* 67-74.

Van Petegem, S., Vansteenkiste, M., Soenens, B., Zimmermann, G., Antonietti, J.-P., Baudat, S., & Audenaert, E. (2017). When do adolescents accept or defy to maternal prohibitions? The role of social domain and communication style. *Journal of Youth and Adolescence, 46,* 1022-1037.

Van Petegem, S., Zimmer-Gembeck, M., Baudat, S., Soenens, B., Vansteenkiste, M., & Zimmermann, G. (2019). Adolescents' responses to parental regulation: The role of communication style and self-determination. *Journal of Applied Developmental Psychology, 65,* 101073.

van Reijmersdal, E., & van Dam, S. (2020). How age and disclosures of sponsored influencer videos affect adolescents' knowledge of persuasion and persuasion. *Journal of Youth and Adolescence, 49,* 1531-1544.

Van Rijsewijk, L., Dijkstra, J., Pattiselanno, K., Steglich, C., & Veenstra, R. (2016). Who helps whom? Investigating the development of adolescent prosocial relationships. *Developmental Psychology, 52,* 894-908.

Van Zalk, M., Kerr, M., Branje, S., Stattin, H., & Meeus, W. (2010). It takes three: Selection, influence, and de-selection processes of depression in adolescent friendship networks. *Developmental Psychology, 46,* 927-938.

van Zantvliet, P., Ivanova, K., & Verbakel, E. (2020). Adolescents' involvement in romantic relationships and problem behavior: The moderating effect of peer norms. *Youth & Society, 52,* 574-591.

Vandenbosch, L., & Eggermont, S. (2013). Sexually explicit websites and sexual initiation: Reciprocal relationships and the moderating role of pubertal status. *Journal of Research on Adolescence, 23,* 621-634.

Vandevivere, E., Braet, C., & Bosmans, G. (2015). Under which conditions do early adolescents need maternal support? *Journal of Early Adolescence, 35,* 162-169.

Vanhalst, J., Luyckx, K., Scholte, R. H., Engels, R. C., & Goossens, L. (2013). Low self-esteem as a risk factor for loneliness in adolescence: Perceived—but not actual—social acceptance as an underlying mechanism. *Journal of Abnormal Child Psychology, 41,* 1067-1081.

Vanhalst, J., Luyckx, K., Van Petegem, S., & Soenens, B. (2018). The detrimental effects of adolescents' chronic loneliness on motivation and emotion regulation in social situations. *Journal of Youth and Adolescence, 47,* 162-176.

Vanhalst, J., Soenens, B., Luyckx, K., Van Petegem, S., Weeks, M. S., & Asher, S. R. (2015). Why do the lonely stay lonely? Chronically lonely adolescents' attributions and emotions in situations of social inclusions and exclusion. *Journal of Personality and Social Psychology, 109,* 932-948.

Vannucci, A., & Ohannessian, C. (2018). Self-competence and depressive symptom trajectories during adolescence. *Journal of Abnormal Child Psychology, 46*(5), 1089-1109.

Vannucci, A., & Ohannessian, C. (2019). Social media use subgroups differentially predict psychosocial well-being during early adolescence. *Journal of Youth and Adolescence, 48,* 1469-1493.

Vannucci, A., Simpson, E., Gagnon, S., & Ohannessian, C. (2020). Social media use and risky behaviors in adolescents: A meta-analysis. *Journal of Adolescence, 79,* 258-274.

Vaquera, E., & Kao, G. (2012). Educational achievement of immigrant adolescents in Spain: Do gender and region of origin matter? *Child Development, 83,* 1560-1576.

Varner, F., & Mandara, J. (2013). Discrimination concerns and expectations as explanations for gendered socialization in African American families. *Child Development, 84,* 875-890.

Váša, F., Seidlitz, J., Romero-Garcia, R., Whitaker, K. J., Rosenthal, G., Vértes, P. E., . . . & Jones, P. B. (2018). Adolescent tuning of association cortex in human structural brain networks. *Cerebral Cortex, 28*(1), 281-294.

Vasilenko, S. (2017). Age-varying associations between nonmarital sexual behavior and depressive symptoms across adolescence and young adulthood. *Developmental Psychology, 53,* 366-378.

Vasilenko, S., Kreager, D., & Lefkowitz, E. (2015). Gender, contraceptive attitudes, and condom use in adolescent romantic relationships: A dyadic approach. *Journal of Research on Adolescence, 25,* 51-62.

Vasilenko, S., Kugler, K., & Rice, C. (2016). Timing of first sexual intercourse and young adult health outcomes. *Journal of Adolescent Health, 59,* 291-297.

Vasilenko, S., Linden-Carmichael, A., Lanza, S., & Patrick, M. (2018). Sexual behavior and heavy episodic drinking across the transition to adulthood: Differences by college attendance. *Journal of Research on Adolescence, 28,* 473-487.

Vasilenko, S. A., & Espinosa-Hernández, G. (2019). Multidimensional profiles of religiosity among adolescents: associations with sexual behaviors and romantic relationships. *Journal of Research on Adolescence, 29*(2), 414-428.

Vaughan, C., & Halpern, C. (2010). Gender differences in depressive symptoms during adolescence: The contributions of weight-related concerns and behaviors. *Journal of Research on Adolescence, 20,* 389-419.

Vaughan, E. B., Van Hulle, C. A., Beasley, W. H., Rodgers, J. L., & D'Onofrio, B. M. (2015). Clarifying the associations between age at menarche and adolescent emotional and behavioral problems. *Journal of Youth and Adolescence, 44,* 922-939.

Veed, G. J., McGinley, M., & Crockett, L. J. (2019). Friendship network influence on the development of internalizing symptoms during adolescence. *Journal of Applied Developmental Psychology, 60,* 157-165.

Veenstra, R., Lindenberg, S., Huitsing, G., Sainio, M., & Salmivalli, C. (2014). The role of teachers in bullying: The relation between antibullying attitudes, efficacy, and efforts to reduce bullying. *Journal of Educational Psychology, 106,* 1135-1143.

Veenstra, R., Lindenberg, S., Verhulst, F., & Ormel, J. (2009). Childhood-limited versus persistent antisocial behavior: Why do some recover and others do not? The TRAILS study. *Journal of Early Adolescence, 29,* 718-742.

Verheijen, G., Stoltz, S., van den Berg, Y., & Cillessen, A. (2019). The influence of competitive and cooperative video games on behavior during play and friendship quality in adolescence. *Computers in Human Behavior, 91,* 297-304.

Verhoef, M., van den Eijnden, R. J. J. M., Koning, I. M., & Vollebergh, W. A. M. (2014). Age of menarche and adolescent alcohol use. *Journal of Youth and Adolescence, 43,* 1333-1345.

Verma, S., Allen, N., Trinder, J., & Bei, B. (2017). Highs and lows: Naturalistic changes in mood and everyday hassles over school and vacation periods in adolescents. *Journal of Adolescence, 61,* 17-21.

Vernon, L., Modecki, K., & Barber, B. (2018). Mobile phones in the bedroom: Trajectories of sleep habits and subsequent adolescent psychosocial development. *Child Development, 89,* 66-77.

Véronneau, M., & Dishion, T. (2011). Middle school friendships and academic achievement in early adolescence: A longitudinal analysis. *Journal of Early Adolescence, 31,* 99-124.

Véronneau, M.-H., Vitaro, F., Brendgen, M., Dishion, T., & Tremblay, R. (2010). Transactional analysis of the reciprocal links between peer experiences and academic achievement from middle childhood to early adolescence. *Developmental Psychology, 46,* 773–790.

Verschueren, M., Claes, L., Palmeroni, N., Bogaerts, A., Gandhi, A., Moons, P., & Luyckx, K. (2020). Eating disorder symptomatology in adolescent boys and girls: Identifying distinct developmental trajectory classes. *Journal of Youth and Adolescence, 49,* 410–426.

Viau, A., & Poulin, F. (2015). Youths' organized activities and adjustment in emerging adulthood: A multidimensional conception of participation. *Journal of Research on Adolescence, 25,* 652–667.

Viau, A., Denault, A.-S., & Poulin, F. (2015). Organized activities during high school and adjustment one year post high school: Identifying social mediators. *Journal of Youth and Adolescence, 44,* 1638–1651.

Victor, E. C., & Hariri, A. R. (2016). A neuroscience perspective on sexual risk behavior in adolescence and emerging adulthood. *Development and Psychopathology, 28,* 471–487.

Vigen, T. (2015). *Spurious correlations.* New York: Hachette.

Vijayakumar, N., Flournoy, J., Mills, K., Cheng, T., Mobasser, A., Flannery, J., . . . Pfeifer, J. (2019). Getting to know me better: An fMRI study of intimate and superficial self-disclosure to friends during adolescence. *Journal of Personality and Social Psychology, 118,* 885–899

Vilhjalmsdottir, A., Gardarsdottir, R., Bernburg, J., & Sigfusdottir, I. (2016). Neighborhood income inequality, social capital and emotional distress among adolescents: A population-based study. *Journal of Adolescence, 51,* 92–102.

Viljoen, J., McLachlan, K., Wingrove, T., & Penner, E. (2010). Defense attorneys' concerns about the competence of adolescent defendants. *Behavioral Sciences & the Law, 28,* 630–646.

Villalobos Solis, M., Smetana, J., & Comer, J. (2015). Associations among solicitation, relationship quality, and adolescents' disclosure and secrecy with mothers and best friends. *Journal of Adolescence, 43,* 193–205.

Vincent, G., Vitacco, M., Grisso, T., & Corrado, R. (2003). Subtypes of adolescent offenders: Affective traits and antisocial behavior patterns. *Behavioral Sciences and the Law, 21,* 695–712.

Vitaro, F., Brendgen, M., Girard, A., Boivin, M., Dionne, G., & Tremblay, R. E. (2015). The expression of genetic risk for aggressive and non-aggressive antisocial behavior is moderated by peer group norms. *Journal of Youth and Adolescence, 44,* 1379–1395.

Vogel, M., & Barton, M. S. (2013). Impulsivity, school context, and school misconduct. *Youth & Society, 45,* 455–479.

Vogel, M., & Van Ham, M. (2018). Unpacking the relationships between impulsivity, neighborhood disadvantage, and adolescent violence: an application of a neighborhood-based group decomposition. *Journal of Youth and Adolescence, 47,* 859–871.

Vollet, J., George, M., Burnell, K., & Underwood, M. (2020). Exploring text messaging as a platform for peer socialization of social aggression. *Developmental Psychology, 56,* 138–152.

Vollet, J., Kindermann, T., & Skinner, E. (2017). In peer matters, teachers matter: Peer group influences on students' engagement depend on teacher involvement. *Journal of Educational Psychology, 109,* 635–652.

Von Polier, G., Vloet, T., & Herpertz-Dahlmann, B. (2012). ADHD and delinquency: A developmental perspective. *Behavioral Sciences & the Law, 30,* 121–139.

Von Rhein, D., Cools, R., Zwiers, M. P., van der Schaaf, M., Franke, B., Luman, M., . . . Buitelaar, J. (2015). Increased neural responses to reward in adolescents and young adults with attention-deficit/hyperactivity disorder and their unaffected siblings. *Journal of the American Academy of Child & Adolescent Psychiatry, 54,* 394–402.

Von Soest, T., Wichstrom, L., & Lundin Kvalem, I. (2016). The development of global and domain-specific self-esteem from age 13 to 31. *Journal of Personality and Social Psychology, 110,* 592–608.

Voon, D., Hasking, P., & Martin G. (2014). Change in emotion regulation strategy use and its impact on adolescent nonsuicidal self-injury: A three-year longitudinal analysis using latent growth modeling. *Journal of Abnormal Psychology, 123,* 487–498.

Vossen, H. G. M., & Valkenburg, P. M. (2016). Do social media foster or curtail adolescents' empathy? A longitudinal study. *Computers in Human Behavior, 63,* 118–124.

Vrangalova, Z. (2015). Does casual sex harm college students' well-being? A longitudinal investigation of the role of motivation. *Archives of Sexual Behavior, 44,* 945–959.

Vrangalova, Z., & Savin-Williams, R. (2011). Adolescent sexuality and positive well-being: A group-norms approach. *Journal of Youth and Adolescence, 40,* 931–944.

Vrolijk, P., Van Lissa, C., Branje, S., Meeus, W., & Keizer, R. (2020). Longitudinal linkages between father and mother autonomy support and adolescent problem behaviors: between-family differences and within-family effects. *Journal of Youth and Adolescence, 49,* 2372–2387.

Vuchinich, S., Angeletti, J., & Gatherum, A. (1996). Context and development in family problem solving with preadolescent children. *Child Development, 67,* 1276–1288.

Vygotsky, L. (1978). *Mind in society.* Cambridge, MA: Harvard University Press. (Original work published 1930)

Waasdorp, T., & Bradshaw, C. (2011). Examining student responses to frequent bullying: A latent class approach. *Journal of Educational Psychology, 103,* 336–352.

Waasdorp, T., & Bradshaw, C. (2015). The overlap between cyberbullying and traditional bullying. *Journal of Adolescent Health, 56,* 483–488.

Wadman, R., Hiller, R., & St Clair, M. (2020). The influence of early familial adversity on adolescent risk behaviors and mental health: Stability and transition in family adversity profiles in a cohort sample. *Development and Psychopathology, 32,* 437–454.

Wagner, L. (2018). Good character is what we look for in a friend: Character strengths are positively related to peer acceptance and friendship quality in early adolescents. *The Journal of Early Adolescence, 39,* 864–903.

Waite, E. B., Shanahan, L., Calkins, S. D., Keane, S. P., & O'Brien, M. (2011). Life events, sibling warmth, and youths' adjustment. *Journal of Marriage and Family, 73,* 902–912.

Waithaka, E. (2014). Family capital: Conceptual model to unpack the intergenerational transfer of advantage in transitions to adulthood. *Journal of Research on Adolescence, 24,* 471–484.

Waizenhofer, R., Buchanan, C. M., & Jackson-Newsom, J. (2004). Mothers' and fathers' knowledge of adolescents' daily activities: Its sources and its links with adolescent adjustment. *Journal of Family Psychology, 18,* 348–360.

Wald, M. (2005). Foreword. In D. W. Osgood, M. Foster, C. Flanagan, & G. Ruth (Eds.), *On your own without a net: The transition to adulthood for vulnerable populations* (pp. vii–xi). Chicago: University of Chicago Press.

Walker, D., Bell, M., Flores, C., Gulley, J., Willing, J., & Paul, M. (2017). Adolescence and reward: Making sense of the neural and behavioral changes amid the chaos. *The Journal of Neuroscience, 37,* 10855–10866.

Walker, E., Sabuwalla, Z., & Huot, R. (2004). Pubertal neuromaturation, stress sensitivity, and psychopathology. *Development and Psychopathology, 16,* 807–824.

Walker, L., Gustafson, P., & Hennig, K. (2001). The consolidation/transition model in moral reasoning development. *Developmental Psychology, 37,* 187–197.

Walkup, J., Albano, A., Piacentini, J., Birmaher, B., Compton, S., . . . Sherrill, J. (2008). Cognitive behavioral therapy, sertraline, or a combination in childhood anxiety. *New England Journal of Medicine, 359,* 2753–2766.

Wallace, J., Forman, T., Caldwell, C., & Willis, D. S. (2003). Religion and U.S. secondary school students: Current patterns, recent trends, and sociodemographic correlates. *Youth and Society, 35,* 98–125.

Walsh, B., Kaplan, A., Attia, E., Olmsted, M., Parides, M., . . . Carter, J. (2006). Fluoxetine after weight restoration in anorexia nervosa: A randomized controlled trial. *Journal of the American Medical Association, 295,* 2605–2612.

Walters, G. (2018). Resistance to peer influence and crime desistance in emerging adulthood: A moderated mediation analysis. *Law and Human Behavior, 42,* 520–530.

Walters, G. (2019). Tracing the delinquency acquisition sequence from older siblings, to friends, to self: A mediation analysis. *Journal of Adolescence, 75,* 113–122.

Wang, C., Ryoo, J., Swearer, S., Turner, R., & Goldberg, T. (2017). Longitudinal relationships between bullying and moral disengagement among adolescents. *Journal of Youth and Adolescence, 46,* 1304–1317.

Wang, D., Choi, J.-K., & Shin, J. (2020). Long-term neighborhood effects on adolescent outcomes: mediated through adverse childhood experiences and parenting stress. *Journal of Youth and Adolescence, 49,* 2160–2173.

Wang, F., Chassin, L., Lee, M., Haller, M., & King, K. (2017). Roles of response inhibition and gene-environment interplay in pathways to adolescents' externalizing problems. *Journal of Research on Adolescence, 27,* 258-277.

Wang, F., Eisenberg, N., Valiente, C., & Spinrad, T. (2016). Role of temperament in early adolescent pure and co-occurring internalizing and externalizing problems using a bifactor model: Moderation by parenting and gender. *Development and Psychopathology, 28,* 1487-1504.

Wang, F. L., Chassin, L., Bates, J., Dick, D., Lansford, J., Pettit, G., & Dodge, K. (2018). Serotonin functioning and adolescents' alcohol use: A genetically informed study examining mechanisms of risk. *Development and Psychopathology, 30,* 213-233.

Wang, K., Frison, E., Eggermont, S., & Vandenbosch, L. (2018). Active public Facebook use and adolescents' feelings of loneliness: Evidence for a curvilinear relationship. *Journal of Adolescence, 67,* 35-44.

Wang, L., Huettel, S., & De Bellis, M. D. (2008). Neural substrates for processing task-irrelevant sad images in adolescents. *Developmental Science, 11,* 23-32.

Wang, M. (2012). Educational and career interests in math: A longitudinal examination of the links between classroom environment, motivational beliefs, and interests. *Developmental Psychology, 48,* 1643-1657.

Wang, M, & Eccles, J. (2012b). Social support matters: Longitudinal effects of social support on three dimensions of school engagement from middle to high school. *Child Development, 83,* 877-895.

Wang, M., & Eccles, J. (2012). Adolescent behavioral, emotional, and cognitive engagement trajectories in school and their differential relations to educational success. *Journal of Research on Adolescence, 22,* 31-39.

Wang, M., & Holcombe, R. (2010). Adolescents' perceptions of school environment, engagement, and academic achievement in middle school. *American Educational Research Journal, 47,* 633-662.

Wang, M., & Sheikh-Khalil, S. (2014). Does parental involvement matter for student achievement and mental health in high school? *Child Development, 85,* 610-625.

Wang, M., Hill, N., & Hofkens, T. (2014). Parental involvement and African American and European American adolescents' academic, behavioral, and emotional development in secondary school. *Child Development, 85,* 2151-2168.

Wang, M. T., & Fredricks, J. A. (2014). The reciprocal links between school engagement, youth problem behaviors, and school dropout during adolescence. *Child Development, 85,* 722-737.

Wang, M. T., & Kenny, S. (2014). Longitudinal links between fathers' and mothers' harsh verbal discipline and adolescents' conduct problems and depressive symptoms. *Child Development, 85,* 908-923.

Wang, M. T., & Peck, S. C. (2013). Adolescent educational success and mental health vary across school engagement profiles. *Developmental Psychology, 49,* 1266-1276.

Wang, M. T., Brinkworth, M., & Eccles, J. (2013). Moderating effects of teacher-student relationship in adolescent trajectories of emotional and behavioral adjustment. *Developmental Psychology, 49,* 690-705.

Wang, M.-T., Degol, J., & Amemiya, J. (2019). Older siblings as academic socialization agents for younger siblings: Developmental pathways across adolescence. *Journal of Youth and Adolescence, 48,* 1218-1233

Wang, Q., & Pomerantz, E. (2009). The motivational landscape of early adolescence in the United States and China: A longitudinal investigation. *Child Development, 80,* 1272-1287.

Wang, Q., Pomerantz, E., & Chen, H. (2007). The role of parents' control in early adolescents' psychological functioning: A longitudinal investigation in the United States and China. *Child Development, 78,* 1592-1610.

Wang, S.-C., and Fowler, P. (2019). Social cohesion, neighborhood collective efficacy, and adolescent subjective well-being in urban and rural Taiwan. *AmericanJournal of Community Psychology, 63,* 499-510.

Wang, X., Gao, L., Yang, J., Zhao, F., & Wang, P. (2020). Parental phubbing and adolescents' depressive symptoms: self-esteem and perceived social support as moderators. *Journal of Youth and Adolescence, 49,* 427-437.

Wang, Y., & Benner, A. (2014). Parent-child discrepancies in educational expectations: Differential effects of actual versus perceived discrepancies. *Child Development, 85,* 891-900.

Wang, Y., & Benner, A. (2016). Cultural socialization across contexts: Family-peer congruence and adolescent well-being. *Journal of Youth and Adolescence, 45,* 594-611.

Wang, Y., & Yip, T. (2020). Parallel changes in ethnic/racial discrimination and identity in high school. *Journal of Youth and Adolescence, 49,* 1517-1530.

Wang, Y., Douglass, S., & Yip, T. (2017). Longitudinal relations between ethnic/racial identity process and content: Exploration, commitment, and salience among diverse adolescents. *Developmental Psychology, 53,* 2154-2169.

Wang, Y., Tian, L., Guo, L., & Huebner, E. (2020). Family dysfunction and adolescents' anxiety and depression: A multiple mediation model. *Journal of Applied Developmental Psychology, 66,* 101090.

Wangqvist, M., Lamb, M., Frisen, A., & Hwang, C. (2015). Child and adolescent predictors of personality in early adulthood. *Child Development, 86,* 1253-1261.

Wang-Schweig, M., Miller, B.A. (2019). Examining the interdependence of parent-adolescent acculturation gaps on acculturation-based conflict: using the actor-partner interdependence model. *J Youth Adolescence, 48,* 648-649.

Ward, L. (2016). Media and sexualization: State of empirical research, 1995-2015. *Journal of Sex Research, 53,* 560-577.

Ward, L., Vandenbosch, L., & Eggermont, S. (2015). The impact of men's magazines on adolescent boys' objectification and courtship beliefs. *Journal of Adolescence, 39,* 49-58.

Warner, S., & Moore, S. (2004). Excuses, excuses: Self-handicapping in an Australian adolescent sample. *Journal of Youth and Adolescence, 33,* 271-281.

Warner, T. D. (2018). Adolescent sexual risk taking: The distribution of youth behaviors and perceived peer attitudes across neighborhood contexts. *Journal of Adolescent Health, 62,* 226-233.

Warren, J., Grodsky, E., & Lee, J. (2008). State high school exit examinations and postsecondary labor market outcomes. *Sociology of Education, 81,* 77-107.

Warren, M., Wray-Lake, L., Rote, W., & Shubert, J. (2016). Thriving while engaging in risk? Examining trajectories of adaptive functioning, delinquency, and substance use in a nationally representative sample of U.S. adolescents. *Developmental Psychology, 52,* 296-310.

Warren, R., & Aloia, L. (2018). Parent-adolescent communication via mobile devices: Influences on relational closeness. *Journal of Family Issues, 39,* 3778-3803.

Wartberg, L., Kriston, L., & Thomasius, R. (2020). Internet gaming disorder and problematic social media use in a representative sample of German adolescents: Prevalence estimates, comorbid depressive symptoms and related psychosocial aspects. *Computers in Human Behavior, 103,* 31-36.

Wasserman, A. M., Crockett, L. J., & Hoffman, L. (2017). Reward seeking and cognitive control: Using the dual systems model to predict adolescent sexual behavior. *Journal of Research on Adolescence, 27,* 907-913.

Wasserman, D., Cheng, Q., & Jiang, G. (2005). Global suicide rates among young people aged 15-19. *World Psychiatry, 4,* 114-120.

Waters, E., Merrick, S., Treboux, D., Crowell, J., & Albersheim, L. (2000). Attachment security in infancy and early adulthood: A twenty-year longitudinal study. *Child Development, 71,* 684-689.

Waters, S., Lester, L., & Cross, D. (2014). How does support from peers compare with support from adults as students transition to secondary school? *Journal of Adolescent Health, 54,* 543-549.

Watson, R., Wheldon, C., & Puhl, R. (2020). Evidence of diverse identities in a large national sample of sexual and gender minority adolescents. *Journal of Research on Adolescence, 30,* 431-442.

Watson, R. J., & Russell, S. T. (2016). Disengaged or bookwork: Academics, mental health, and success for sexual minority youth. *Journal of Research on Adolescence, 26,* 159-165.

Watt, H., Shapka, J., Morris, Z., Durik, A., Keating, D., & Eccles, J. (2012). Gendered motivational processes affecting high school mathematics participation, educational aspirations, and career plans: A comparison of samples from Australia, Canada, and the United States. *Developmental Psychology, 48,* 1594-1611.

Watt, T. T. (2003). Are small schools and private schools better for adolescents' emotional adjustment? *Sociology of Education, 76,* 344-367.

Way, N. (2013). Boys' friendships during adolescence: Intimacy, desire, and loss. *Journal of Research on Adolescence, 23,* 201-213.

Way, N., & Greene, M. (2006). Trajectories of perceived friendship quality during adolescence: The patterns and contextual predictors. *Journal of Research on Adolescence, 16,* 293-320.

Way, N., & Robinson, M. (2003). A longitudinal study of the effects of family, friends, and school experiences on the psychological adjustment of ethnic minority, low-SES adolescents. *Journal of Adolescent Research, 18,* 324-346.

Way, N., Reddy, R., & Rhodes, J. (2007). Students' perceptions of school climate during the middle school years: Associations with trajectories of psychological and behavioral adjustment. *American Journal of Community Psychology, 40,* 194-213.

Webb, H., Zimmer-Gembeck, M., Mastro, S., Farrell, L., Waters, A., & Lavell, C. (2015). Young adolescents' body dysmorphic symptoms: Associations with same- and cross-sex peer teasing via appearance-based rejection sensitivity. *Journal of Abnormal Child Psychology, 43,* 1161-1173.

Webb, H. J., & Zimmer-Gembeck, M. J. (2014). The role of friends and peers in adolescent body dissatisfaction: A review and critique of 15 years of research. *Journal of Research on Adolescence, 24,* 564-590.

Weerman, F. (2011). Delinquent peers in context: A longitudinal network analysis of selection and influence effects. *Criminology, 49,* 253-286.

Wegge, D., Vandebosch, H., Eggermont, S., & Pabian, S. (2014). Popularity through online harm: The longitudinal associations between cyberbullying and sociometric status in early adolescence. *The Journal of Early Adolescence, 36,* 86-107.

Weigard, A., Chein, J., Albert, D., Smith, A., & Steinberg, L. (2014). Effects of anonymous peer observation on adolescents' preference for immediate rewards. *Developmental Science, 17,* 71-78.

Weinfield, N., Ogawa, J., & Sroufe, L. (1997). Early attachment as a pathway to adolescent peer competence. *Journal of Research on Adolescence, 7,* 241-265.

Weinfield, N., Sroufe, A., & Egeland, B. (2000). Attachment from infancy to early adulthood in a high-risk sample: Continuity, discontinuity, and their correlates. *Child Development, 71,* 695-702.

Weinstein, S. M., Mermelstein, R. J., Hankin, B. L., Hedeker, D., & Flay, B. R. (2007). Longitudinal patterns of daily affect and global mood during adolescence. *Journal of Research on Adolescence, 17,* 587-600.

Weiser, J., & Reynolds, B. (2011). Impulsivity and adolescence. In B. Brown & M. Prinstein (Eds.), *Encyclopedia of adolescence* (Vol. 1, pp. 187-192). New York: Academic Press.

Weiss, B., Han, S., Harris, V., Catron, T., Ngo, V., Caron, A. . . . & Guth, C. (2013). An independent randomized clinical trial of multisystemic therapy with non-court-referred adolescents with serious conduct problems. *Journal of Consulting and Clinical Psychology, 81,* 1027-1039.

Weiss, C., & Baker-Smith, E. (2010). Eighth-grade school form and resilience in the transition to high school: A comparison of middle schools and K-8 schools. *Journal of Research on Adolescence, 20,* 825-839.

Weiss, C., Carolan, B. V., & Baker-Smith, E. C. (2010). Big school, small school: (Re)Testing assumptions about high school size, school engagement and mathematics achievement. *Journal of Youth and Adolescence, 39,* 163-176.

Weisskirch, R. S. (2009). Parenting by cell phone: Parental monitoring of adolescents and family relations. *Journal of Youth and Adolescence, 38,* 1123-1139.

Weissman, D., Conger, R., Robins, R., Hastings, P., & Guyer, A. (2018). Income change alters default mode network connectivity for adolescents in poverty. *Developmental Cognitive Neuroscience, 30,* 93-99.

Weissman, D., Gelardi, K., Conger, R., Robins, R., Hastings, P., & Guyer, A. (2018). Adolescent externalizing problems: Contributions of community crime exposure and neural function during emotion introspection in Mexican-origin youth. *Journal of Research on Adolescence, 28,* 551-563.

Weissman, D., Schriber, R., Fassbender, C., Atherton, O., Krafft, C., Robins, R., . . . Guyer, A. (2015). Earlier adolescent substance use onset predicts stronger connectivity between reward and cognitive control brain networks. *Developmental Cognitive Neuroscience, 16,* 121-129.

Weisz, J., Francis, S., & Bearman, S. (2010). Assessing secondary control and its association with youth depression symptoms. *Journal of Abnormal Child Psychology, 38,* 883-893.

Weisz, J., Kuppens, S., Ng, M., Vaughn-Coaxum, R., Ugueto, A., Eckshtain, D., & Corteselli, K. (2019). Are psychotherapies for young people growing stronger? Tracking trends over time for youth anxiety, depression, attention-deficit/hyperactivity disorder, and conduct problems. *Perspectives on Psychological Science, 14,* 216-237.

Weisz, J. R., Southam-Gerow, M. A., Gordis, E. B., Connor-Smith, J. K., Chu, B. C., Langer, D. A., . . . Weiss, B. (2009). Cognitive-behavioral therapy versus usual clinical care for youth depression: An initial test of transportability to community clinics and clinicians. *Journal of Consulting and Clinical Psychology, 77,* 383-396.

Weitkamp, K., & Seiffge-Krenke, I. (2019). The association between parental rearing dimensions and adolescent psychopathology: A cross-cultural study. *Journal of Youth and Adolescence, 48,* 469-483.

Welborn, B. L., Lieberman, M. D., Goldenberg, D., Fuligni, A. J., Galván, A., & Telzer, E. H. (2016). Neural mechanisms of social influence in adolescence. *Social Cognitive and Affective Neuroscience, 11,* 100-109.

Wells, A., & Serna, I. (1996). The politics of culture: Understanding local political resistance to detracking in racially mixed schools. *Harvard Educational Review, 66,* 93-118.

Wen, M. (2017). Social capital and adolescent substance use: The role of family, school, and neighborhood contexts. *Journal of Research on Adolescence, 27,* 362-378.

Wendelken, C., Ferrer, E., Ghetti, S., Bailey, S. K., Cutting, L., & Bunge, S. A. (2017). Frontoparietal structural connectivity in childhood predicts development of functional connectivity and reasoning ability: A large-scale longitudinal investigation. *Journal of Neuroscience, 37,* 8549-8558.

Wendelken, C., Ferrer, E., Whitaker, K. J., & Bunge, S. A. (2016). Fronto-parietal network configuration supports the development of reasoning ability. *Cerebral Cortex, 26,* 2178-2190.

Wentzel, K., & Asher, S. (1995). The academic lives of neglected, rejected, popular, and controversial children. *Child Development, 66,* 754-763.

Wentzel, K., Barry, C., & Caldwell, K. (2004). Friendships in middle school: Influences on motivation and school adjustment. *Journal of Educational Psychology, 96,* 195-203.

Wentzel, K., Russell, S., & Baker, S. (2016). Emotional support and expectations from parents, teachers, and peers predict adolescent competence at school. *Journal of Educational Psychology, 108,* 242-255.

Werner, L., Van der Graaf, J., Meeus, W., & Branje, S. (2016). Depressive symptoms in adolescence: Longitudinal links with maternal empathy and psychological control. *Journal of Abnormal Child Psychology, 44,* 1121-1132.

Wertz, J., Nottingham, K., Agnew-Blais, J., Matthews, T., Pariante, C. M., Moffitt, T. E., & Arseneault, L. (2016). Parental monitoring and knowledge: Testing bidirectional associations with youths' antisocial behavior. *Development and Psychopathology, 28,* 623-638.

Wesche, R., Kreager, D., & Lefkowitz, E. (2019). Sources of social influence on adolescents' alcohol use. *Journal of Research on Adolescence, 29,* 984-1000.

Wesche, R., Kreager, D., Feinberg, M., & Lefkowitz, E. (2019). Peer acceptance and sexual behaviors from adolescence to young adulthood. *Journal of Youth and Adolescence, 48,* 996-1008.

Wesche, R., Kreager, D., Lefkowitz, E., & Siennick, S. (2017). Early sexual initiation and mental health: A fleeting association or enduring change? *Journal of Research on Adolescence, 27,* 611-627.

Weymouth, B., & Buehler, C. (2016). Adolescent and parental contributions to parent-adolescent hostility across early adolescence. *Journal of Youth and Adolescence, 45,* 713-729.

Weymouth, B., Fosco, G., & Feinberg, M. (2019). Nurturant-involved parenting and adolescent substance use: Examining an internalizing pathway through adolescent social anxiety symptoms and substance refusal efficacy. *Development and Psychopathology, 31,* 247-260.

Weyns, T., Colpin, H., De Laet, S., Engels, M., & Verschueren, K. (2018). Teacher support, peer acceptance, and engagement in the classroom: A three-wave longitudinal study in late childhood. *Journal of Youth and Adolescence, 47,* 1139-1150.

Wheeler, L., Arora, P., & Delgado, M. (2020). The distal role of adolescents' awareness of and perceived discrimination on young adults' socioeconomic attainment among Mexican-origin immigrant families. *Journal of Youth and Adolescence, 49,* 2441-2458.

Wheeler, L., Killoren, S., Whiteman, S. Updegraff, K., McHale, S., & Umana-Taylor, A. (2016). Romantic relationship experiences from late adolescence to young adulthood: The role of older siblings in Mexican-origin families. *Journal of Youth and Adolescence, 45,* 900-915.

Wheeler, L. A., Zeiders, K. H., Updegraff, K. A., Umana-Taylor, A. J., Rodriguez de Jesus, S. a., & Perez-Brena, N. J. (2017). Mexican-origin youth's risk behavior from adolescence to young adulthood: The role of familism values. *Developmental Psychology, 53,* 126-137.

Whitaker, D., & Miller, K. (2000). Parent-adolescent discussions about sex and condoms: Impact on peer influences of sexual risk behavior. *Journal of Adolescent Research, 15,* 251-273.

White, C., & Warner, L. (2015). Influence of family and school-level factors on age of sexual initiation. *Journal of Adolescent Health, 56,* 231-237.

White, G. (2014, December 18). Inequality between America's rich and poor is at a 30-year high. *The Atlantic.* Retrieved from http://www.theatlantic.com/business/archive/2014/12/inequality-between-americas-rich-and-americas-poor-at-30-year-high/383866/ on February 21, 2018.

White, H. R., Fleming, C. B., Kim, M. J., Catalano, R. F., & McMorris, B. J. (2008). Identifying two potential mechanisms for changes in alcohol use among college-attending and non-college-attending emerging adults. *Developmental Psychology, 44,* 1625-1639.

White, L., Wu, J., Borelli, J., Mayes, L., & Crowley, M. (2013). Play it again: Neural responses to reunion with excluders predicted by attachment patterns. *Developmental Science, 16,* 850-863.

White, R., Knight, G., Jensen, M., & Gonzales, N. (2018). Ethnic socialization in neighborhood contexts: Implications for ethnic attitude and identity development among Mexican-origin adolescents. *Child Development, 89,* 1004-1021.

White, R., Zeiders, K., & Safa, M. (2018). Neighborhood structural characteristics and Mexican-origin adolescents' development. *Development and psychopathology, 30,* 1679-1698.

White, R. M., Liu, Y., Nair, R. L., & Tein, J. Y. (2015). Longitudinal and integrative tests of family stress model effects on Mexican-origin adolescents. *Developmental Psychology, 51,* 649-662.

White, R. M. B., Liu, Y., Gonzales, N. A., Knight, G. P., & Tein, J.-Y. (2016). Neighborhood qualification of the association between parenting and problem behavior trajectories among Mexican-origin father-adolescent dyads. *Journal of Research on Adolescence, 26,* 927-946.

White, R. M. B., Updegraff, K., Umana-Taylor, A., Zeiders, K., Perez-Brena, N., & Burleson, E. (2017). Neighborhood and school ethnic structuring and cultural adaptations among Mexican-origin adolescents. *Developmental Psychology, 53,* 511-524.

White, S., Voss, J., Chiang, J., Wang, L., McLaughlin, K., & Miller, G. (2019). Exposure to violence and low family income are associated with heightened amygdala responsiveness to threat among adolescents. *Developmental Cognitive Neuroscience, 40,* 100709.

Whitehead, K. A., Ainsworth, A. T., Wittig, M. A., & Gadino, B. (2009). Implications of ethnic identity exploration and ethnic identity affirmation and belonging for intergroup attitudes among adolescents. *Journal of Research on Adolescence, 19,* 123-135.

Whiteman, S. D., Solmeyer, A. R., & McHale, S. M. (2015). Sibling relationships and adolescent adjustment: Longitudinal associations in two-parent African American families. *Journal of Youth and Adolescence, 44,* 2042-2053.

Whiteman, S., McHale, S. M., & Crouter, A. C. (2011). Family relationships from adolescence to early adulthood: Changes in the family system following firstborns' leaving home. *Journal of Research on Adolescence, 21,* 461-474.

Whitesell, N., Mitchell, C., Kaufman, C., & Spicer, P. (2006). Developmental trajectories of personal and collective self-concept among American Indian adolescents. *Child Development, 77,* 1487-1503.

Wichstrøm, L. (1999). The emergence of gender difference in depressed mood during adolescence: The role of intensified gender socialization. *Developmental Psychology, 35,* 232-245.

Widman, L., Choukas-Bradley, S., Helms, S., & Prinstein, M. (2016). Adolescent susceptibility to peer influence in sexual situations. *Journal of Adolescent Health, 58,* 323-329.

Widman, L., Welsh, D., McNulty, J., & Little, K. (2006). Sexual communication and contraceptive use in adolescent dating couples. *Journal of Adolescent Health, 39,* 893-899.

Wierenga, L. M., Sexton, J. A., Laake, P., Giedd, J. N., Tamnes, C. K., & Pediatric Imaging, Neurocognition, and Genetics Study. (2018). A key characteristic of sex differences in the developing brain: Greater variability in brain structure of boys than girls. *Cerebral Cortex, 28,* 2741-2751.

Wiesner, M., & Windle, M. (2006). Young adult substance use and depression as a consequence of delinquency trajectories during middle adolescence. *Journal of Research on Adolescence, 16,* 239-264.

Wiesner, M., Capaldi, D., & Kim, H. (2012). General versus specific predictors of male arrest trajectories: A test of the Moffitt and Patterson theories. *Journal of Youth and Adolescence, 41,* 217-228.

Wigfield, A., Ho, A., & Mason-Singh, A. (2011). Achievement motivation. In B. Brown & M. Prinstein (Eds.), *Encyclopedia of adolescence* (Vol. 1, pp. 10-19). New York: Academic Press.

Wiley, S., Slocum, L., O'Neill, J., & Esbensen, F.-A. (2020). Beyond the breakfast club: Variability in the effects of suspensions by school context. *Youth & Society, 52,* 1259-1284.

Will, G., van Lier, P., Crone, E., & Güroğlu, B. (2016). Chronic childhood peer rejection is associated with heightened neural responses to social exclusion during adolescence. *Journal of Abnormal Child Psychology, 44,* 43-55.

Williams, J., Aiyer, S., Durkee, M., & Tolan, P. (2014). The protective role of ethnic identity for urban adolescent males facing multiple stressors. *Journal of Youth & Adolescence, 43,* 1728-1741.

Williams, J., Tolan, P., Durkee, M., Francois, A., & Anderson, R. (2012). Integrating racial and ethnic identity research into developmental understanding of adolescents. *Child Development Perspectives, 6,* 304-311.

Williams, K., Yeager, D., Cheung, C., & Choi, W. (2012). Cyberball (version 4.0) [Software]. Available from https://cyberball.wikispaces.com.

Williams, L., & Russell, S. (2013). Shared social and emotional activities within adolescent romantic and non-romantic sexual relationships. *Archives of Sexual Behavior, 42,* 649-658.

Williams, T., & Williams, K. (2010). Self-efficacy and performance in mathematics: Reciprocal determinism in 33 nations. *Journal of Educational Psychology, 102,* 453-466.

Willoughby, B., James, S., Marsee, I., Memmott, M., & Dennison, R. (2020). "I'm scared because divorce sucks": Parental divorce and the marital paradigms of emerging adults. *Journal of Family Issues, 41,* 711-738.

Willoughby, T., & Fortner, A. (2015). At-risk depressive symptoms and alcohol use trajectories in adolescence: A person-centered analysis of co-occurrence. *Journal of Youth & Adolescence, 44,* 793-805.

Willoughby, T., Chalmers, H., & Busseri, M. (2004). Where is the syndrome? Examining co-occurrence among multiple problem behaviors in adolescence. *Journal of Consulting and Clinical Psychology, 72,* 1022-1037.

Willroth, E. C., Atherton, O. E., & Robins, R. W. (2020). Life satisfaction trajectories during adolescence and the transition to young adulthood: Findings from a longitudinal study of Mexican-origin youth. *Journal of Personality and Social Psychology,* in press.

Wilson, H., & Widom, C. (2010). The role of youth problem behaviors in the path from child abuse and neglect to prostitution: A prospective examination. *Journal of Research on Adolescence, 20,* 210-236.

Wilson, J. L., Peebles, R., Hardy, K., & Litt, I. (2006). Surfing for thinness: A pilot study of pro-eating disorder web site usage in adolescents with eating disorders. *Pediatrics, 118,* 1635-1643.

Wilson, M., & Daly, M. (1985). Competitiveness, risk taking, and violence: The young male syndrome. *Ethology and Sociobiology, 6,* 59-73.

Winsler, A., Deutsch, A., Vorona, R. D., Payne, P. A., & Szklo-Coxe, M. (2015). Sleepless in Fairfax: The difference one more hour of sleep can make for teen hopelessness, suicidal ideation, and substance use. *Journal of Youth and Adolescence, 44,* 362-378.

Wiseman, R. (2003). *Queen bees and wannabes.* New York: Three Rivers Press.

Witkow, M. (2009). Academic achievement and adolescents' daily time use in the social and academic domains. *Journal of Research on Adolescence, 19,* 151-172.

Witkow, M., & Fuligni, A. (2010). In-school versus out-of-school friendships and academic achievement among an ethnically diverse sample of adolescents. *Journal of Research on Adolescence, 20,* 631-650.

Witvliet, M., Brendgen, M., van Lier, P., Koot, H., & Vitaro, F. (2010). Early adolescent depressive symptoms: Prediction from clique isolation, loneliness, and perceived social acceptance. *Journal of Abnormal Child Psychology, 38,* 1045-1056.

Wolak, J., Finkelhor, D., & Mitchell, K. J. (2012). How often are teens arrested for sexting? Data from a national sample of police cases. *Pediatrics, 129,* 4-12.

Wolak, J., Finkelhor, D., Walsh, W., & Treitman, L. (2018). Sextortion of minors: Characteristics and dynamics. *Journal of Adolescent Health, 62,* 72-79.

Wolf, L., Bazargani, N., Kilford, E., Dumontheil, I., & Blakemore, S-J. (2015). The audience effect in adolescence depends on who's looking over your shoulder. *Journal of Adolescence, 43,* 5-14.

Wölfer, R., & Hewstone, M. (2018). What buffers ethnic homophily? Explaining the development of outgroup contact in adolescence. *Developmental Psychology, 54,* 1507-1518.

Wolfer, R., Schmid, K., Hewstone, M., Wolfer, R., & van Zalk, M. (2016). Developmental dynamics of intergroup contact and intergroup attitudes: Long-term effects in adolescence and early adulthood. *Child Development, 87,* 1466-1478.

Wolfers, J. (2014, December 3). How we know the divorce rate is falling. *The New York Times.* (Accessed on January 22, 2018, at https://www.nytimes.com/2014/12/04/upshot/how-we-know-the-divorce-rate-is-falling.html

Wolff, J. M., & Crockett, L. J. (2011). The role of deliberative decision making, parenting, and friends in adolescent risk behaviors. *Journal of Youth and Adolescence, 40,* 1607-1622.

Wolfson, A., & Carskadon, M. (1998). Sleep schedules and daytime functioning in adolescents. *Child Development, 69,* 875-887.

Wolke, D., Copeland, W., Angold, A., & Costello, E. (2013). Impact of bullying in childhood on adult health, wealth, crime, and social outcomes. *Psychological Science, 24,* 1958-1970.

Wood, D., Kurtz-Costes, B., Rowley, S., & Okeke-Adeyanju, N. (2010). Mothers' academic gender stereotypes and education-related beliefs about sons and daughters in African American families. *Journal of Educational Psychology, 102,* 521-530.

Wood, D., Larson, R., & Brown, J. (2009). How adolescents come to see themselves as more responsible through participation in youth programs. *Child Development, 80,* 295-309.

Woodcock, A., Hernandez, P., Estrada, M., & Schultz, P. (2012). The consequences of chronic stereotype threat: Domain disidentification and abandonment. *Journal of Personality and Social Psychology, 103,* 635-646.

Woolard, J., & Scott, E. (2009). The legal regulation of adolescence. In R. Lerner & L. Steinberg (Eds.), *Handbook of adolescent psychology* (3rd ed., Vol. 2, pp. 345-371). New York: Wiley.

Woolley, M., Kol, K., & Bowen, G. (2009). The social context of school success for Latino middle school students: Direct and indirect influences of teachers, family, and friends. *Journal of Early Adolescence, 29,* 43-70.

World Population Review. (2020). *STD rates by country.* https://worldpopulationreview.com/country-rankings/std-rates-by-country. Accessed on January 14, 2021.

Worthman, C., Dockray, S., & Marceau, K. (2019). Puberty and the evolution of developmental science. *Journal of Research on Adolescence, 29,* 9-31.

Wouters, S., De Fraine, B., Colpin, H., Van Damme, J., & Verschueren, K. (2012). The effect of track changes on the development of academic self concept in high school: A dynamic test of the big-fish-little-pond effect. *Journal of Educational Psychology, 104,* 793-805.

Wray-Lake, L. (2019). How do young people become politically engaged? *Child Development Perspectives, 13,* 127-132.

Wray-Lake, L., & Flanagan, C. (2012). Parenting practices and the development of adolescents' social trust. *Journal of Adolescence, 35,* 549-560.

Wray-Lake, L., Syvertsen, A., & Flanagan, C. (2016). Developmental change in social responsibility during adolescence: An ecological perspective. *Developmental Psychology, 52,* 130-142.

Wray-Lake, L., Syvertsen, A., Briddell, L., Osgood, D. W., & Flanagan, C. (2009). *Exploring the changing meaning of work for American high school seniors from 1976 to 2005.* Unpublished paper, Pennsylvania State University, University Park, PA.

Wray-Lake, L., Syvertsen, A., Briddell, L., Osgood, D. W., & Flanagan, C. (2011). Exploring the changing meaning of work for American high school seniors from 1976 to 2005. *Youth & Society, 43,* 1110-1135.

Wright, A., Yendork, J., & Kliewer, W. (2018). Patterns of spiritual connectedness during adolescence: Links to coping and adjustment in low-income urban youth. *Journal of Youth and Adolescence, 47,* 2608-2624.

Wright, B., & Younts, C. (2009). Reconsidering the relationship between race and crime: Positive and negative predictors of crime among African American youth. *Journal of Research in Crime and Delinquency, 46,* 327-352.

Wright, M. F. (2017). Adolescents' emotional distress and attributions for face-to-face and cyber victimization: Longitudinal linkages to later aggression. *Journal of Applied Developmental Psychology, 48,* 1-13.

Wright, M. F., & Wachs, S. (2019). Does social support moderate the relationship between racial discrimination and aggression among Latinx adolescents? A longitudinal study. *Journal of Adolescence, 73,* 85-94.

Wrzus, C., Wagner, G., & Riediger, M. (2016). Personality-situation transactions from adolescence to old age. *Journal of Personality and Social Psychology, 110,* 782-799.

Wu, C., & Chao, R. K. (2011). Intergenerational cultural dissonance in parent–adolescent relationships among Chinese and European Americans. *Developmental Psychology, 47,* 493-508.

Wuyts, D., Soenens, B., Vansteenkiste, M., & Van Petegem, S. (2018). The role of observed autonomy support, reciprocity, and need satisfaction in adolescent disclosure about friends. *Journal of Adolescence, 65,* 141-154.

Wylie, L., & Rufino, K. (2018). The impact of victimization and mental health symptoms on recidivism for early system-involved juvenile offenders. *Law and Human Behavior, 42,* 558-569.

Xiao, Y., Romanelli, M., Vélez-Grau, C., & Lindsay, M. (2020). Unpacking racial/ethnic differences in the associations between neighborhood disadvantage and academic achievement: Mediation of future orientation and moderation of parental support. *Journal of Youth and Adolescence, 50*(1), 103-125.

Xie, W., & Kang, C. (2015). See you, see me: Teenagers' self-disclosure and regret of posting on social network site. *Computers in Human Behavior, 52,* 398-407.

Xu, J. (2004). Family help and homework management in urban and rural secondary schools. *Teachers College Review, 106,* 1786-1803.

Yamaguchi, R., Johnston, L., & O'Malley, P. (2003). Relationship between student illicit drug use and school drug-testing policies. *Journal of School Health, 73,* 159-164.

Yang, Y., Chen, L., Zhang, L., Ji, L., & Zhang, W. (2020). Developmental changes in associations between depressive symptoms and peer relationships: A four-year follow-up of Chinese adolescents. *Journal of Youth and Adolescence, 49,* 1913-1927.

Yang, Z., & Gaydos, L. (2010). Reasons for and challenges of recent increases in teen birth rates: A study of family planning service policies and demographic changes at the state level. *Journal of Adolescent Health, 46,* 517-524.

Yap, M., Schwartz, O., Byrne, M., Simmons, J., & Allen, N. (2010). Maternal positive and negative interaction behaviors and early adolescents' depressive symptoms: Adolescent emotion regulation as a mediator. *Journal of Research on Adolescence, 20,* 1014-1043.

Yarnell, L., Pasch, K., Brown, H., Perry, C., & Jomro, K. (2014). Cross-gender social normative effects for violence in middle school: Do girls carry a social multiplier effect for at-risk boys? *Journal of Youth and Adolescence, 43,* 1465-1485.

Yau, J., & Reich, S. (2017). Are the qualities of adolescents' offline friendships present in digital interactions? *Adolescent Research Review.* DOI: 10.1007/s40894-017-0059-y.

Yau, J., & Reich, S. (2019). "It's just a lot of work": Adolescents' self-presentation norms and practices on Facebook and Instagram. *Journal of Research on Adolescence, 29,* 196-209.

Yau, J., & Smetana, J. (2003). Adolescent–parent conflict in Hong Kong and Shenzhen: A comparison of youth in two cultural contexts. *International Journal of Behavioral Development, 27,* 201-211.

Ybarra, M., & Mitchell, K. (2014). "Sexting" and its relation to sexual activity and sexual risk behavior in a national survey of adolescents. *Journal of Adolescent Health, 55,* 757-764.

Ybarra, M., Espelage, D., Valido, A., Hong, J., & Prescott, T. (2019). Perceptions of middle school youth about school bullying. *Journal of Adolescence, 75,* 175-187.

Yeager, D. (2018). *Unpublished data analysis based on the 4-H Study of Positive Youth Development.* Department of Psychology, University of Texas, Austin, TX.

Yeager, D., Fong, C., Lee, H., & Espelage, D. (2015). Declines in efficacy of anti-bullying programs among older adolescents: Theory and a three-level meta-analysis. *Journal of Applied Developmental Psychology, 37,* 36-51.

Yeager, D., Henderson, M., Paunesku, D., Walton, G., D'Mello, S., Spitzer, B., et al. (2014). Boring but important: A self-transcendent purpose for learning fosters academic self-regulation. *Journal of Personality and Social Psychology, 107,* 559-580.

Yeager, D., Lee, H., & Jamieson, J. (2016). How to improve adolescent stress responses: Insights from integrating implicit theories of personality and biopsychosocial models. *Psychological Science, 27,* 1078-1091.

Yeager, D. S. (2017). Dealing with social difficulty during adolescence: The role of implicit theories of personality. *Child Development Perspectives, 11,* 196-201.

Yeager, D. S., Miu, A., Powers, J., & Dweck, C. (2013). Implicit theories of personality and attributions of hostile intent: A meta-analysis, an experiment, and a longitudinal intervention. *Child Development, 84,* 1651-1667.

Yerkes R., & Dodson, J. (1908). The relation of strength of stimulus to rapidity of habit-formation. *Journal of Comparative Neurology and Psychology, 18*, 459–482.

Yeung Thompson, R., & Leadbeater, B. (2013). Peer victimization and internalizing symptoms from adolescence into young adulthood: Building strength through emotional support. *Journal of Research on Adolescence, 23*, 290–303.

Yildiz, M., Demirhan, E., & Gurbuz, S. (2019). Contextual socioeconomic disadvantage and adolescent suicide attempts: A multilevel investigation. *Journal of Youth and Adolescence, 48*, 802–814.

Yip, T. (2014). Ethnic identity in everyday life: The influence of identity development status. *Child Development, 85*, 205–219.

Yip, T., Cham, H., Wang, Y., & El-Sheikh, M. (2020). Discrimination and sleep mediate ethnic/racial identity and adolescent adjustment: Uncovering change processes with slope-as-mediator mediation. *Child Development, 91*, 1021–1043.

Yip, T., Douglass, S., & Shelton, J. (2013). Daily intragroup contact in diverse settings: Implications for Asian adolescents' ethnic identity. *Child Development, 84*, 1425–1441.

Yip, T., Seaton, E., & Sellers, R. (2010). Interracial and intraracial contact, school-level diversity, and change in racial identity status among African American adolescents. *Child Development, 81*, 1431–1444.

YMCA. (2006). Information on the history of the organization is available at www.ymca.net.

Yong, M., Fleming, C., McCarty, C., & Catalano, R. (2014). Mediators of the associations between externalizing behaviors and internalizing symptoms in late childhood and early adolescence. *The Journal of Early Adolescence, 34*, 967–1000.

Yoon, J., Barton, E., & Taiarol, J. (2004). Relational aggression in middle school: Educational implications of developmental research. *Journal of Early Adolescence, 24*, 303–318.

Yorgason, J., Padilla-Walker, L., & Jackson, J. (2011). Nonresidential grandparents' emotional and financial involvement in relation to early adolescent grandchild outcomes. *Journal of Research on Adolescence, 21*, 552–558.

Yoshikawa, H., Aber, J. L., & Beardslee, W. R. (2012). The effects of poverty on the mental, emotional, and behavioral health of children and youth: Implications for prevention. *American Psychologist, 67*, 272–284.

Young, A., Glover, N., & Havens, J. (2012). Nonmedical use of prescription medications among adolescents in the United States: A systematic review. *Journal of Adolescent Health, 51*, 6–17.

Young, A., Grey, M., & Boyd, C. (2009). Adolescents' experiences of sexual assault by peers: Prevalence and nature of victimization occurring within and outside of school. *Journal of Youth and Adolescence, 38*, 1072–1083.

Young, B., Furman, W., & Jones, M. (2012). Changes in adolescents' risk factors following peer sexual coercion: Evidence for a feedback loop. *Development and Psychopathology, 24*, 559–571.

Young, J. (2014). "Role magnets"? An empirical investigation of popularity trajectories for life-course persistent individuals during adolescence. *Journal of Youth and Adolescence, 43*, 104–115.

Youniss, J., & Smollar, J. (1985). *Adolescent relations with mothers, fathers, and friends.* Chicago: University of Chicago Press.

Yu, C., Li, X., Wang, S., & Zhang, W. (2016). Teacher autonomy support reduces adolescent anxiety and depression: An 18-month longitudinal study. *Journal of Adolescence, 49*, 115–123.

Yu, J., Putnick, D., Hendricks, C., & Bornstein, M. (2019). Long-term effects of parenting and adolescent self-competence for the development of optimism and neuroticism. *Journal of Youth and Adolescence, 48*, 1544–1554.

Yu, R., Aaltonen, M., Branje, S., Ristikari, T., Meeus, W., Salmela-Aro, K., . . . Fazel, S. (2017). Depression and violence in adolescence and young adults: Findings from three longitudinal cohorts. *Journal of the American Academy of Child & Adolescent Psychiatry, 56*, 652–658.

Yu, R., Branje, S., Meeus, W., Koot, H., Van Lier, P., & Fazel, S. (2018). Victimization mediates the longitudinal association between depressive symptoms and violent behaviors in adolescence. *Journal of Abnormal Child Psychology, 46*, 839–848.

Yuan, A. S. V., & Hamilton, H. A. (2006). Stepfather involvement and adolescent well-being: Do mothers and nonresidential fathers matter? *Journal of Family Issues, 27*, 1191–1213.

Yuan, M., Cross, S., Loughlin, S., & Leslie, F. (2015). Nicotine and the adolescent brain. *Journal of Physiology, 593*, 3397–3412.

Yuen, C. X., Fuligni, A. J., Gonzales, N., & Telzer, E. H. (2018). Family first? The costs and benefits of family centrality for adolescents with high-conflict families. *Journal of Youth and Adolescence, 47*, 245–259.

Yun, H., & Juvonen, J. (2020). Navigating the healthy context paradox: identifying classroom characteristics that improve the psychological adjustment of bullying victims. *Journal of Youth and Adolescence, 49*, 2203–2213.

Yun, H.-Y., & Graham, S. (2019). Too tough at the top: Using latent class growth analysis to assess cool status during middle school. *Journal of Adolescence, 75*, 47–52.

Zabin, L., Astone, N., & Emerson, M. (1993). Do adolescents want babies? The relationship between attitudes and behavior. *Journal of Research on Adolescence, 3*, 67–86.

Zabin, L., Hirsch, M., & Emerson, M. (1989). When urban adolescents choose abortion: Effects on education, psychological status, and subsequent pregnancy. *Family Planning Perspectives, 21*, 248–255.

Zametkin, A. J., Zoon, C. K., Klein, H. W., & Munson, S. (2004). Psychiatric aspects of child and adolescent obesity: A review of the past 10 years. *Journal of the American Academy of Child and Adolescent Psychiatry, 43*, 134–150.

Zapert, K., Snow, D., & Tebes, J. (2002). Patterns of substance use in early through late adolescence. *American Journal of Community Psychology, 30*, 835–852.

Zapolski, T., Yu, T., Brody, G., Banks, D., & Barton, A. (2020). Why now? Examining antecedents for substance use initiation among African American adolescents. *Development and Psychopathology, 32*, 719–734.

Zarrett, N., Fay, K., Li, Y., Carrano, J., Phelps, E., & Lerner, R. (2009). More than child's play: Variable- and pattern-centered approaches for examining effects of sports participation on youth development. *Developmental Psychology, 45*, 368–382.

Zavodny, M. (2004). Fertility and parental consent for minors to receive contraceptives. *American Journal of Public Health, 94*, 1347–1351.

Zelazo, P. D., & Carlson, S. M. (2012). Hot and cool executive function in childhood and adolescence: Development and plasticity. *Child Development Perspectives, 6*, 354–360.

Zeldin, S., & Topitzes, D. (2002). Neighborhood experiences, community connection, and positive beliefs about adolescents among urban adults and youth. *Journal of Community Psychology, 30*, 647–669.

Zeman, J., & Shipman, K. (1997). Social-contextual influences on expectancies for managing anger and sadness: The transition from middle childhood to adolescence. *Developmental Psychology, 33*, 917–924.

Zentner, M., & Renaud, O. (2007). Origins of adolescents' ideal self: An intergenerational perspective. *Journal of Personality and Social Psychology, 92*, 557–574.

Zhang, J., Seo, D., Kolbe, L., Lee, A., Middlestadt, S., Zhao, W., & Huang, S. (2011). Comparison of overweight, weight perception, and weight-related practices among high school students in three large Chinese cities and two large US cities. *Journal of Adolescent Health, 48*, 366–372.

Zhang, L., Finan, L., Bersamin, M., & Fisher, D. (2020). Sexual orientation–based depression and suicidality health disparities: The protective role of school-based health centers. *Journal of Research on Adolescence, 30*(S1), 134–142.

Zhang, W., & Fuligni, A. (2006). Authority, autonomy, and family relationships among adolescents in urban and rural China. *Journal of Research on Adolescence, 16*, 527–537.

Zhang, W., Wei, X., Ji, L., Chen, L., & Deater-Deckard, K. (2017). Reconsidering parenting in Chinese culture: Subtypes, stability, and change of maternal parenting style during early adolescence. *Journal of Youth and Adolescence, 46*, 1117–1136.

Zhang, X., Pomerantz, E., Qin, L., Logis, H., Ryan, A., & Wang, M. (2019). Early adolescent social status and academic engagement: Selection and influence processes in the United States and China. *Journal of Educational Psychology, 111*, 1300.

Zhang, X., Pomerantz, E. M., Qin, L., Logis, H., Ryan, A. M., & Wang, M. (2018). Characteristics of likability, perceived popularity, and admiration in the early adolescent peer system in the United States and China. *Developmental Psychology, 54*, 1568–1581.

Zhang, Z., Solazzo, A., & Gorman, B. (2020). Education and health: The joint role of gender and sexual identity. *SSM - Population Health, 12*, 100668.

Zhao, X., & Gao, M. (2014). "No time for friendship": Shanghai mothers' views of adult and adolescent friendships. *Journal of Adolescent Research, 29*, 587–615.

Zhong, H., & Schwartz, J. (2010). Exploring gender-specific trends in underage drinking across adolescent age groups and measures of drinking: Is girls' drinking catching up with boys'? *Journal of Youth and Adolescence, 39*, 911–926.

Zhu, J., Chen, Y., & Su, B. (2020). Non-suicidal self-injury in adolescence: Longitudinal evidence of recursive associations with adolescent depression and parental rejection. *Journal of Adolescence, 84*, 36-44.

Zick, C. (2010). The shifting balance of adolescent time use. *Youth & Society, 41*, 569-596.

Zimmer-Gembeck, M. (1999). Stability, change and individual differences in involvement with friends and romantic partners among adolescent females. *Journal of Youth and Adolescence, 28*, 419-438.

Zimmer-Gembeck, M. (2016). Peer rejection, victimization, and relational self-system processes in adolescence: Toward a transactional model of stress, coping, and developing sensitivities. *Child Development Perspectives, 10*, 122-127.

Zimmer-Gembeck, M., & Helfand, M. (2008). Ten years of longitudinal research on U.S. adolescent sexual behavior: Developmental correlates of sexual intercourse, and the importance of age, gender, and ethnic background. *Developmental Review, 28*, 153-224.

Zimmer-Gembeck, M., Ducat, W., & Collins, W. A. (2011). Autonomy, development of. In B. Brown & M. Prinstein (Eds.), *Encyclopedia of adolescence* (Vol. 1, pp. 66-76). New York: Academic Press.

Zimmer-Gembeck, M., Siebenbruner, J., & Collins, W. A. (2004). A prospective study of intraindividual and peer influences on adolescents' heterosexual romantic and sexual behavior. *Archives of Sexual Behavior, 33*, 381-394.

Zimmer-Gembeck, M. J., Trevaskis, S., Nesdale, D., & Downey, G. (2014). Relational victimization, loneliness and depressive symptoms: Indirect associations between self and peer reports of rejection sensitivity. *Journal of Youth and Adolescence, 43*, 568-582.

Zimmer-Gembeck, M. J., Webb, H. J., Farrell, L. J., & Waters, A. M. (2018). Girls' and boys' trajectories of appearance anxiety from age 10 to 15 years are associated with earlier maturation and appearance-related teasing. *Development and Psychopathology, 30*, 337-350.

Zimmerman, G. M., & Farrell, C. (2017). Parents, peers, perceived risk of harm, and the neighborhood: Contextualizing key influences on adolescent substance use. *Journal of Youth and Adolescence, 46*, 228-247.

Zimmermann, F., Schütte, K., Taskinen, P., & Köller, O. (2013). Reciprocal effects between adolescent externalizing problems and measures of achievement. *Journal of Educational Psychology, 105*, 747-761.

Zimring, F. (1998). *American youth violence.* New York: Oxford University Press.

Zito, R., & De Coster, S. (2016). Family structure, maternal dating, and sexual debut: Extending the conceptualization of instability. *Journal of Youth and Adolescence, 45*, 1003-1019.

Zito, R. C. (2015). Family structure history and teenage cohabitation: Instability, socioeconomic disadvantage, or transmission? *Journal of Family Issues, 36*, 299-325.

Zohar, A., Zwir, I., Wang, J., Cloninger, C., & Anokhin, A. (2019). The development of temperament and character during adolescence: The processes and phases of change. *Development and Psychopathology, 31*, 601-617.

Zook, J., & Russotti, J. (2013). Academic self-presentation strategies and popularity in middle school. *The Journal of Early Adolescence, 33*, 765-785.

Zottoli, T. M., & Daftary-Kapur, T. (2019). Guilty pleas of youths and adults: Differences in legal knowledge and decision making. *Law and Human Behavior, 43*, 166.

Zweig, J., Dank, M., Yahner, J., & Lachman, P. (2013). The rate of cyber dating abuse among teens and how it relates to other forms of teen dating violence. *Journal of Youth & Adolescence, 42*, 1063-1077.

Zweig, J., Lachman, P., Yahner, J., & Dank, M. (2014). Correlates of cyber dating abuse among teens. *Journal of Youth & Adolescence, 43*, 1306-1321.

Name Index

A

Aaltonen, M., 351
Aaro, L. E., 119
Abar, C. C., 33, 100
Abbott, J., 34
Abbott, R. D., 362
Abdelfattah, F., 163
Abduljabbar, A., 147, 328
Abduljabbar, A. S., 163
Abe, Y., 321
Abela, J., 375, 378, 381
Abela, J. R. Z., 339, 381
Aber, J., 383
Aber, J. L., 87, 117, 160, 224
Ablard, K., 330
Abma, J., 296, 298
Abo-Zena, M., 224
Abraham, C., 313
Abramovitch, R., 256
Abrams, D., 61
Abramson, L., 381
Abramson, L. Y., 32, 114
Abrutyn, S., 310, 380
Abu-Hilal, M., 328
Abu-Hilal, M. M., 163
Acebo, C., 27
Acevedo-Garcia, D., 89
Ackard, D., 215, 216
Ackerman, J., 367, 381
Ackerman, R., 275
ACLU, 317
Acock, A., 113, 374
Adachi, P., 192, 193, 199
Adachi, P. J. C., 199
Adalbjarnardottir, S., 332
Adam, E., 27, 291
Adam, S., 277
Adams, R., 101, 138, 276
Adams, R. E., 95
Adams, S. H., 37
Adams, T., 291
Adams, Z., 301
Adan, A., 337
Adcock, R., 46
Adelson, J., 256
Adhia, A., 115
Adiele, I., 204
Adkins, A. E., 108
Adler, N., 35, 316
Adler-Baeder, F., 116, 302
Adluru, N., 35
Adolescent Sleep Working Group, 28
Adrian, M., 147
Adriana, W., 204

Aelterman, N., 240
Affrunti, N., 92
Afia, K., 343
Afzali, M., 363
Agans, J., 187
Agénor, M., 231
Agi, A., 225
Agnew-Blais, J., 107
Agoston, A., 382
Aguilar, B., 374
Aguilar-Vafaie, M., 213
Ahles, J., 273, 378
Ahluwalia, N., 24
Ahmad, I., 105, 241
Ahmad, S., 372
Ahmed, R., 361
Ahmed, S., 227, 246
Ahmed, S. F., 46
Ahn, H., 140
Ahonen, T., 161
Aikins, J., 138, 139, 144, 288
Ainsworth, A. T., 224
Ainsworth, J., 338
Ainsworth-Darnell, J., 338
Aite, A., 52
Aiyer, S., 228
Aiyer, S. M., 92
Aizpitarte, A., 143, 290
Ajanaku, S., 336
Akers, C., 362
Akın, R. I., 120
Aklin, W., 358
Akré, C., 299
Alabi, B., 228
Alamilla, S., 357
Alampay, L., 107
Alampay, L. P., 17, 25, 54, 64, 92, 117
Alarcon, O., 216
Albano, A., 382
Albersheim, L., 268
Albert, D., 47, 65, 238, 245, 247, 248
Albino, A., 352
Albrecht, H., 33
Aldana, A., 225
Aldrich, J., 379
Alegria, M., 227
Alessandri, G., 336, 337
Alexander, A. L., 35
Alexander, K., 161, 162, 344
Alex Mason, W., 358
Alfano, C. A., 29
Alfaro, E. C., 225, 226
Algermissen, M., 51

Al-Ghamdi, M. S., 108
Algur, E., 321
Al-Hassan, S., 106, 107
Al-Hassan, S. M., 64
Alho, K., 193
Ali, M. M., 19
Alicea, S., 225
Alink, L., 143
Allemand, M., 217, 244
Allen, J., 7, 136, 137, 140, 142, 202, 204, 237, 239, 240, 241, 264, 266, 268, 269, 275, 277, 292, 324, 326, 374
Allen, J. P., 92, 242, 248, 264, 269, 349
Allen, K., 224, 228
Allen, K. A., 30
Allen, L., 160, 224
Allen, M. L., 34
Allen, N., 27, 56, 99, 109, 117, 304, 381
Allen, N. B., 53, 110, 376
Allen, V., 33
Allender, S., 35, 138
Allerton, J., 328
Allison, K. W., 157
Alloy, L., 381
Alloy, L. B., 32, 114
Alm, S., 167
Almeida, D. M., 101
Almerigi, J. B., 191
Almqvist, C., 372
Almy, B., 372
Aloia, L., 100
Alonso-Arbiol, I., 119, 143, 290
Alsinet, C., 190
Alt, D., 100
Altermatt, E., 327
Altheimer, I., 92
Alvarado, R., 120
Alvarez, A., 228
Alvarez, R., 227
Alvarez-Jimenez, A., 170, 332
Alvis, L., 258
Amato, P., 114, 115
Amato, P. R., 112, 113, 116, 117
Ambridge, B., 47
Ambrosia, M., 56
Amemiya, J., 108, 168, 169, 174, 329, 374
American Psychiatric Association, 360, 364, 376
Ames, A., 143, 339
Amichay-Hamburger, Y., 204
Amico, E., 358
Amico, E. J., 201

Amiot, C., 187
Ammaniti, M., 204
Amrhein, K. E., 92
Amrock, S., 356
Amso, D., 46
Analitis, F., 145
Ananat, E. O., 86
Anandakumar, J., 53
Anbar, S., 283
Anckarsäter, H., 372
Anderman, E., 158, 165
Anderman, E. M., 173
Anderman, L. H., 160
Andersen, A., 363
Andersen, S., 362
Andersen, S. H., 26
Anderson, A., 353
Anderson, C., 228, 310
Anderson, C. A., 200
Anderson, G., 202
Anderson, J., 48, 312
Anderson, M., 174
Anderson, R., 225, 226
Anderson, S., 112
Anderson, S. E., 22
Anderson-Carpenter, K., 363
Andersson, H., 135, 325, 334
Andrade, F., 383
Andrew, T., 37
Andrews, G., 327
Andrews, J., 63, 247
Andrews, J. A., 32
Andrews, K., 99
Andrews, N., 140, 141
Andrews, R., 142
Andrews, T., 379
Ang, R., 325
Angeletti, J., 243
Angold, A., 31, 147
Anguiano, R., 99
Angus, R., 191
Anokhin, A., 164, 212
Anstine, P., 363
Anthony, C. J., 113
Anticevic, A., 58
Antolin-Suárez, L., 107, 242
Antonietti, J.-P., 60, 242
Antonio-Agirre, I., 215
Antonishak, J., 142
Antonucci, T., 33
Antshel, K., 164, 165
Anyiwo, N., 226, 228
Anyon, Y., 174
Appel, I., 283
Apperly, I., 59

Applegate, B., 353
Aradillas-Garcia, C., 383
Aram, U., 202
Aranda, F., 310
Archambault, I., 145, 343
Archibald, A., 36
Arel, S., 6
Arend, R., 266
Arens, A., 215
Arias, I., 310
Arizaga, J., 383
Armenta, B., 361
Armor, D., 333
Armstrong, J. M., 23
Armstrong, S., 34
Arndorfer, A., 77
Arndorfer, C., 279
Arneson, J., 336
Arnett, J., 4, 73, 74, 222, 223
Arnett, J. J., 80, 241
Arnold, A. L., 113
Arnold, M., 256
Arnone, D., 34
Arora, P., 228
Arrington-Sanders, R., 311
Arruda, E. H., 29
Arseneault, L., 92, 105, 107, 173,
    244, 368
Arsenio, W., 257
Arsland, R. C., 216
Arunkumar, R., 325
Asakawa, K., 339
Asante, K., 195
Asarnow, J., 382
Aseltine, R., 177
Aseltine, R., Jr., 277
Asendorpf, J. B., 134
Ashby, J., 346
Asher, S., 142, 143, 273, 334
Asher, S. R., 275
Asherson, P., 164
Ask, H., 353
Askari, S., 363
Askeland, K. G., 119, 382, 383
Askren, M. K., 56
Aspy, C., 303, 360
Asquith, P., 243
Asscher, J., 212
Assink, M., 343
Astone, N., 318
Atherton, O., 143, 188, 357, 362
Atherton, O. E., 74
Atkin, T., 363
Atkins, R., 256
Attia, E., 38
Au, T., 303
Audenaert, E., 60
Auerbach, R., 381
August, E., 299
August, G., 372
Augustyn, M., 136

Aunola, K., 188, 376
Ausherbauer, K., 372
Austin, E., 215
Austin, L., 62
Austin, S., 231, 234
Austin, S. B., 19, 37
Auxier, B., 192
Auyeung, B., 164
Auzoult, L., 149
Avants, B. B., 46
Avenevoli, S., 350, 351, 375, 376,
    377, 383
Ayed, N., 119
Ayers, J., 310
Aylwin, C. F., 14, 16
Azevedo, C., 256
Azmitia, M., 206, 224, 273, 274
Azpiazu, L., 215
Azzopardi, C., 198
Azzopardi, P., 23

B

Baams, L., 30, 33, 145, 198, 230,
    300, 301, 303, 310
Babalola, S., 304
Babkes, M., 188
Babson, K. A., 32
Bacchini, D., 47, 57, 62, 64, 84, 97,
    106, 107, 245
Bach, N., 356
Bacher, K., 225, 227
Bachman, J., 184, 189, 349, 354,
    355, 356, 357, 374
Badaly, D., 134, 135, 334
Badger, G., 363
Badger, S., 74
Badre, D., 46
Bae, D., 35
Baeher, J., 250
Baert, S., 6
Baeyens, D., 164
Baeza, I., 46
Baezconde-Garbanati, L., 222
Bagengast, B., 163
Bagley, E., 86, 88
Bagwell, C., 138
Bagwell, C. L., 145
Bahrami, E., 289
Bai, Y., 35, 195
Bailey, J. A., 362
Bailey, S. K., 51
Baird, A., 66
Baird, C., 336
Bakan, D., 11, 154
Baker, B. L., 110
Baker, E., 273
Baker, J., 351
Baker, S., 333
Baker, S. T. E., 53
Baker, T., 175

Baker-Smith, E., 159
Baker-Smith, E. C., 158
Bakken, A., 188
Bakker, M., 273, 378
Balakier, E., 204, 272
Baldelomar, O., 224, 225
Baldwin, C., 260, 261
Ballard, P., 255
Balsa, A., 140
Balsano, A., 88
Baltes, B., 92
Balzer, B. W. R., 26
Bámaca, M., 246, 248
Bámaca, M. Y., 225, 226
Bamaca-Colbert, M., 99, 224,
    250, 297
Bámaca-Gómez, M. Y., 248
Bañales, J., 228
Bandura, A., 10, 328
Banerjee, M., 225, 227
Bangasser, D., 381
Bangee, M., 145, 275
Banich, M., 63, 210, 244, 245, 362
Banister, E., 98
Bank, L., 108
Bankole, A., 313, 315, 316, 318
Banks, D., 227
Bankston, C. L., III, 331
Banny, A., 143
Banyard, V., 149
Banzon-Librojo, L., 168
Bao, Z., 253
Barak, A., 202
Barbaranelli, C., 328
Barber, A., 382
Barber, B., 4, 187, 188, 189, 194, 249
Barber, J., 315
Barch, D., 353
Barengo, N. C., 299
Barg, F., 312
Bar-Haim, Y., 248
Baril, M. E., 107, 180
Barker, E., 30, 74, 76, 144, 366
Barker, L. T., 321
Barkin, S., 90, 187
Barkley, R., 164, 165
Barkley-Levenson, E., 53
Barlett, C. P., 150
Barlow, C., 143
Barnes, A., 118
Barnes, A. R., 114
Barnes, J., 174, 188, 311
Barnes, R., 165
Barnett, L., 35, 138
Barnett, N., 201
Barnett, N. P., 100
Barnett-Walker, K., 372
Barney, B., 357
Barone, C., 231
Barr, H., 200
Barreiro, A., 257

Barreto, R., 297
Barrientos, S., 297
Barrios, L., 174
Barrios, V., 93
Barry, C., 161
Barry, C. M., 74, 222, 260
Barry, H., 79
Barry, M., 195
Barstead, M., 276
Bartels, M., 103, 106, 107, 245
Barth, J., 334
Bartkowski, J., 313
Bartle-Haring, S., 241
Bartolomé, S. P., 66
Barton, A., 227
Barton, A. W., 92
Barton, E., 143
Barton, M. S., 174
Bascoe, S., 6, 96, 104, 115, 266
Bashyam, V., 52
Basile, K., 310
Basile, K. C., 291
Basili, E., 244
Basilio, C., 253
Basinger, K., 251
Bass, J., 357
Bassett Greer, K., 241
Bassi, M., 328
Bastiaensens, S., 150
Bastin, M., 273, 353, 378
Batalla, A., 362
Bates, J., 59, 144, 190, 242, 267,
    291, 292, 303, 343, 360,
    365, 366, 373
Bates, J. E., 115, 210
Bath, K., 51
Battaglia, M., 376
Battapady, H., 58
Baucom, B. R., 114
Baudat, S., 60, 242
Bauducco, S., 28, 195
Bauer, D., 289
Bauer, D. J., 75
Bauermeister, J., 314, 368
Baum, C., 356
Bauman, K., 133, 134, 289, 290,
    310, 361
Baumer, E., 334
Baumer, E. P., 92
Baumert, J., 163
Baumrind, D., 104
Bauserman, R., 311
Baweja, S., 338
Bayless, S., 225
Bayram Özdemir, S., 60, 87, 96,
    97, 227
Baysu, G., 170
Bazargani, N., 55, 247
Beach, S., 110, 227
Beach, S. R. H., 30
Beal, S., 311, 338

Beal, S. J., 4, 35, 74
Beam, C., 381
Beam, M., 277, 278
Bean, J. A., 216
Beardslee, J., 189, 375
Beardslee, W., 382
Beardslee, W. R., 87, 117
Bearinger, L., 301
Bearman, P., 313
Bearman, S., 37, 377, 383
Beasley, R., 34, 35, 195
Beasley, W. H., 33
Beatty, A. S., 336
Beauchaine, T., 351
Beaudry, G., 368
Beaver, K., 188
Beaver, K. M., 108
Bechara, A., 64
Becht, A., 96, 211, 219, 221, 222
Bechtold, J., 69, 70, 77, 78
Beck, S. R., 41
Becker, B., 382
Becker, B. E., 140
Becker, I., 303
Becker, J., 26
Becker, M., 163
Beckley, A. L., 244
Beckmeyer, J., 287, 288
Beekman, C., 29
Beets, M., 195, 374
Beevers, C., 202, 203
Begg, D., 212, 361
Behrhorst, K., 291
Bei, B., 27
Beirut, L., 300
Beldavs, Z., 374
Bell, D., 382
Bell, K., 269
Bell, M., 55, 361
Bell, R., 363
Bell, R. N., 27
Bellair, P., 91, 304, 370
Beller, E., 164
Bellmore, A., 140, 141, 144, 146,
    150, 169, 225, 229
Bello, M., 363
Belsky, D., 51, 244
Belsky, J., 23, 26, 29, 33, 110,
    319, 352
Beltran, I., 8, 359, 360, 361
Beltz, A., 17, 25, 26, 33, 48, 53, 55
Beltz, A. M., 30, 31
Beltz, M., 321
BeLue, R., 34
Belusa, E., 317
Bendtsen, P., 357, 361, 363
Benedict, R., 11, 76
Benefield, T., 289, 290
Benenson, J., 270
Benish-Weisman, M., 243
Benjet, C., 29

Benner, A., 100, 147, 161, 165, 167,
    226, 227, 273, 277, 331,
    332, 338
Benner, A. D., 161, 165, 170
Bennet, A., 235
Bennett, C., 66
Bennett, M., 227, 246
Bennett, P., 186
Benoit, A., 33
Benson, B., 248, 303
Benson, L., 190
Benson, M., 383
Benson, M. J., 137
Benson, P., 109
Benz, M., 361
Berchtold, A., 299
Berenbaum, S., 33, 134, 232, 233,
    234, 278
Berenbaum, S. A., 30
Berends, M., 162
Berenson, G., 35
Beresin, E., 200
Beretvas, T., 100
Berg, C., 273
Berg, M., 140, 287
Berg, N., 101
Berge, J., 35
Berger, C., 138, 140, 145
Berger, M., 35
Bergeson, C., 92, 93
Berglun, P., 8
Bergman, L., 135, 151, 325, 334
Berk, M. S., 109
Berkel, C., 228
Berkhof, J., 27
Berman, E., 160
Bernburg, J., 90
Berndt, T., 270
Berninger, V., 163, 164
Bernstein, I., 362
Bernstein, R., 267
Beron, K., 192, 193
Bersamin, M., 296, 305, 311
Best, K., 32
Betancourt, L., 25, 57, 301
Betancourt, L. M., 63
Betsch, C., 217
Beyers, W., 222, 223, 240
Beyth-Marom, R., 62
Bezold, C. P., 35
Bhapkar, M., 22
Bhattacharjee, K., 242
Bhattacharyya, S., 362
Bianchi, M., 150
Bianchi, S. M., 88
Bibbins-Domingo, K., 37, 38
Bickel, W. K., 63
Bickham, D., 204
Biddlecom, A., 313
Bidet-Caulet, A., 45
Biehl, M., 287

Biehl, M. C., 30
Biely, E., 197
Bierman, K., 142, 372
Bierut, L., 363
Biggs, M., 317
Biglan, A., 147
Bigler, R., 234
Bijttebier, P., 161, 242, 273, 353, 378
Billick, S. B., 378
Billings, A., 300
Bills, D., 184
Bingham, C., 144, 248, 299, 352, 361
Bingham, C. R., 65
Biovin, M., 108, 109
Birch, L., 234
Bird, H., 374
Birgisdottir, F., 171, 244
Birkeland, M., 206, 214
Birkeland, M. S., 217
Birkett, M., 274, 310
Birmaher, B., 382, 383
Birmingham, M., 36
Birnbaum, A., 195
Biro, F., 216
Biroli, P., 51
Bisgaard, C., 372
Bish, C., 178
Bishai, D., 363
Bishop, J., 334
Bishop, M., 334
Bissell-Havran, J., 328
Bitz, B., 60
Bjarnason, T., 353
Blachnio, A., 204, 272
Black, B., 324
Black, M., 310, 311
Blackburn, J. L., 66
Blackwell, L., 329, 330
Blades, N., 312
Blair, B., 275
Blair, R., 372
Blake, A., 360
Blakemore, S., 209
Blakemore, S-J., 43, 47, 49, 50, 51,
    52, 53, 54, 55, 56, 59, 63,
    100, 209, 210, 246, 247
Blanc, A., 312
Blanco, C., 376
Blankenstein, N., 248
Blankson, A. N., 23
Blasco-Belled, A., 190
Blazek, J., 30
Bleakley, A., 150, 198, 199, 299,
    360
Bleidorn, W., 212, 213, 216
Blinka, L., 204, 270
Blinn-Pike, L., 303
Bliton, C., 283
Block, J., 358
Blocklin, M., 321
Blondal, K., 332

Blondeau, L., 333
Blonigen, D., 359
Blood, E. A., 19, 37
Bloomquist, M., 372
Blos, P., 240
Blum, R., 120, 300, 321
Blumenthal, H., 32
Blumler, J., 196
Blumstein, A., 366, 370, 371
Blyth, D., 32
Boardman, J. D., 110
Bobek, D., 88
Bobkowski, P., 6, 195, 196, 199
Bock, P., 271
Bodell, L., 53
Bodell, L. P., 37
Boden, J., 319, 364
Bodner, N., 117
Bøe, T., 382, 383
Boele, S., 291
Boendermaker, W., 362
Boer, M., 87, 204
Boerger, R., 277
Boersma, K., 28, 195
Bogaerts, A., 37, 38, 222
Bogart, L., 249
Bögels, S., 378
Bogin, B., 18, 21, 22, 23, 294
Bogue, E., 312
Bohman, A., 87
Bohnert, A., 187, 332
Bohr, Y., 115, 291
Boisjoly, J., 291
Boislard, M., 300
Boislard, M.-A., 304
Boivin, J., 25, 48
Boivin, J. R., 25, 48
Boivin, M., 34, 109, 273
Boldsen, S., 372
Bolland, J., 91, 311, 383
Bolland, J. M., 107, 362
Bolland, K. A., 362
Bolling, D., 142
Bombi, A., 106
Bonanno, R. A., 149
Bond, L., 377
Bond, R. M., 92, 136
Bondy, J., 338
Bonell, C., 321
Bong, M., 326
Bongers, I., 365
Bonica, C., 289
Boniel-Nissim, M., 100, 150
Bonnet-Brilhault, F., 45
Bonnie, R., 57, 77, 245
Bons, D., 372
Bontempo, D., 92, 360
Bookheimer, S. Y., 47
Bookhout, M., 141
Boot, I., 204
Booth, A., 114, 115, 234

Booth, J., 226
Booth, J. M., 91
Booth, M., 193, 201
Booth, M. Z., 160, 178
Booth, T., 164
Booth-LaForce, C., 142, 243, 267, 276, 287
Borch, C., 140, 279
Borduin, C., 374
Borelli, J., 266
Borelli, J. L., 273
Borge, A., 144
Borges, A., 38
Borghuis, J., 213
Borman, G., 327
Bornstein, M., 97, 103, 106, 107, 108, 241, 242, 324
Borofsky, L., 211, 267
Borowski, S., 273
Borst, G., 52
Boruch, W., 204, 272
Boruff, J., 363
Borzekowski, D., 195
Bos, H., 115, 233
Bos, M., 221, 222
Böse, S., 163
Bosick, S. J., 116
Bosker, R., 169, 334
Bosmans, G., 269
Bottiani, J., 169
Botvin, G., 218, 360
Bouchard, K., 145
Bouchey, H., 266
Bouchey, H. A., 111
Boudreaux, M., 226
Boufous, S., 63
Boulerice, B., 344
Boulos, P., 362
Bountress, K., 358, 360
Bourdony, C., 22
Bourne, S., 253
Bourque, J., 363
Bousman, C. A., 110
Boutelle, K., 34
Boutwell, B., 188
Bowen, F., 145
Bowen, G., 332
Bower, A., 141
Bower, J., 29
Bowers, E., 190
Bowker, A., 138
Bowker, J., 133, 143, 144, 145, 254, 270
Bowlby, J., 266
Bowlds, M., 276
Bowling, J. M., 291
Boyce, T., 110
Boyce, W., 23, 92
Boyce, W. T., 23
Boyd, C., 310, 356
Boyd, D., 193, 256

Boyd, L., 113
Boyd-Zaharias, J., 159
Boyer, B., 267
Boyer, T. W., 64
Boyle, A., 161, 227, 332
Boyle, M., 150
Boyle, M. H., 89
Bozick, R., 256
Braams, B., 64, 65, 245, 362
Braams, B. R., 17, 25, 26, 48, 53, 54, 55
Braciszewski, J., 92
Bracy, N., 344
Bradbury, S., 150
Bradley, R., 195
Bradshaw, C., 149, 150, 168, 169, 170, 261, 352, 361
Brady, S., 298
Braet, C., 269
Braga, A., 174
Brain Development Cooperative Group, 50
Braithwaite, I., 34, 35, 195
Brakefield, T., 309
Brame, B., 365
Bramen, J. E., 48
Brancale, J. M., 136
Brand, S., 217, 337
Branje, S., 12, 26, 90, 95, 96, 100, 101, 118, 120, 132, 137, 211, 213, 214, 219, 220, 221, 222, 223, 241, 242, 253, 254, 271, 273, 275, 291, 351, 368, 374, 382
Branje, S. J. T., 26, 100, 101, 102
Brass, N., 140
Brauer, J., 242
Brauner, E., 24
Braun-Lewensohn, O., 91
Brausch, A., 379
Braver, T. S., 58
Braverman, P., 303
Bravo, D. Y., 173
Bray, B. C., 105
Bray, I., 39
Brechwald, W., 132, 248
Bredman, J. C., 245
Breeden, A., 372
Breeman, L. D., 120
Breen, A., 223
Brehl, B. A., 60
Breiding, M., 290, 291
Breiner, K., 57, 64, 77, 84, 245
Breitenstein, R., 29
Breivik, K., 217, 382, 383
Brem, M., 289
Brendgen, M., 108, 109, 136, 147, 151, 273, 287, 300, 334, 372
Brendgen, R., 287
Brener, N., 310
Brenick, A., 60
Brennan, P., 377

Brennan, R. T., 33
Brenning, K., 107, 242
Brent, D., 382
Breslau, J., 376
Breslend, N., 142
Breuer, J., 199
Brewer, G., 150
Brewer, S. K., 27
Brex, R., 358
Brickman, A. M., 51
Briddell, L., 181, 346
Bridge, J., 381
Bridges, B. J., 241, 270
Bridges, M., 114
Brieant, A., 87, 261
Brien, J., 118
Brien, K., 313
Brien, L., 65, 210, 244, 245, 247, 248
Brien, M., 88, 108, 195
Briggs, E., 277
Brikell, I., 350, 375
Briley, D., 212
Briley, D. A., 109, 212
Brinch, C., 178
Brincks, A., 202
Brindis, C., 317
Brindis, C. D., 37
Brinkley, D., 202
Brinkworth, M., 160
Briskman, J., 365
Brobakke Seglem, K., 353
Brocki, K., 372
Brodsky, N., 25, 57, 301
Brody, G., 30, 32, 106, 110, 118, 227, 228
Brody, G. H., 92
Broidy, L., 365
Bromberg, U., 210
Bronfenbrenner, U., 6
Brookmeyer, K., 254
Brooks-Gunn, J., 27, 30, 31, 32, 33, 36, 89, 90, 91, 92, 93, 114, 187, 188, 283, 296, 304, 305, 337, 382
Brown, A., 250
Brown, B., 7, 122, 126, 127, 128, 129, 130, 131, 132, 134, 137, 138, 204, 224, 225, 240, 263, 270, 276, 277, 284, 288, 335
Brown, B. B., 107, 285
Brown, C., 138, 228, 310, 334
Brown, C. S., 232
Brown, E., 351
Brown, G., 202
Brown, H., 136
Brown, J., 6, 103, 187, 195, 196, 198, 199, 238, 311, 377
Brown, K., 361, 363
Brown, P., 325
Brown, R., 170

Brown, S., 256, 280, 362
Brown, S. D., 256
Brown, V. E., 173
Browne, F., 305
Browning, C., 187
Browning, C. R., 92
Brubacher, J., 175
Bruch, S., 327
Brückner, H., 313
Brumariu, L., 266, 268
Brumback, T., 362
Brunborg, G., 204
Brunet, J., 187
Brunwasser, S., 331
Bruvold, W., 363
Bryan, A., 313, 321
Bryan, M. A., 188
Bryant, A., 89
Bryant, A. L., 74, 75
Bryant, F., 320
Bryant, S., 290
Bryce, D., 372
Bucchianeri, M., 310
Bucci, R., 30
Buchanan, C., 26, 115, 116, 117, 378
Buchanan, C. M., 103
Buchholz, A., 36
Buchmann, C., 335
Bucholz, K., 300
Buckhalt, J. A., 29
Buehler, C., 102, 113, 120, 137, 217, 242, 275
Buelens, T., 379
Buelga, S., 150, 289
Buelow, M., 193
Buhi, E., 299, 301, 321
Buhrmester, D., 264, 269, 277, 279, 282, 283, 292
Buijs, T., 357
Buil, J., 372
Buisman, R., 100
Buitelaar, J., 165, 372
Buka, S. L., 93
Bukowski, W., 136, 138, 145, 149, 263, 273, 278, 279, 284, 287, 288
Bull, S., 321
Bullen, P., 88
Bullock, A., 142, 242
Bumpus, M., 103
Bunge, J., 291
Bunge, S. A., 27, 46, 47, 51
Burcher, G., 379
Burchinal, M., 58
Burdette, A., 34, 313
Burdzovic Andreas, J., 204
Bureau of Labor Statistics, 176, 177, 189, 336
Burg, S., 258
Burger, K., 344
Burk, B., 304

Burk, W., 106, 137, 138, 140, 141, 199
Burk, W. J., 140
Burkam, D., 116
Burk-Braxton, C., 215, 216
Burke, A. R., 15
Burke, J., 366
Burke, L., 285, 286
Burke, S., 258
Burke, T., 147, 381
Burke, W., 141
Burks, V., 292
Burleson, E., 225
Burmeister, M., 110, 360
Burnell, K., 143, 192, 193
Burnett, S., 56, 59, 209
Burnette, M., 370
Burnett Heyes, S., 271
Burns, E. C., 167
Burnside, A. N., 90
Burraston, B., 108
Burrington, L., 184
Burrow, A. L., 218
Burstein, M., 350, 362, 375, 376, 377
Bursztyn, L., 334
Burt, A., 19
Burt, K., 76, 352
Burt, K. B., 88
Burt, S., 101
Burt, S. A., 109, 114
Burton, C., 310
Burton, L., 225, 237
Burton, S., 89
Busby, D., 92
Busch, A., 24
Busching, R., 199, 254
Bushman, B., 174, 199, 254, 369
Bushman, B. J., 92, 136
Bushway, S. D., 344
Busseri, M., 260, 352
Bussey, K., 149, 150
Butisingh, S., 170
Butler, E. A., 110
Butler-Barnes, S., 225
Butterfield, R., 56
Butts, C., 138
Bybee, D., 338
Bygren, M., 162
Bylsma, L., 28, 203
Bylsma, L. M., 28, 203
Bynner, J., 4
Byon, J., 242
Byrd, C., 227
Byrne, D., 328
Byrne, M., 99
Byrnes, J. P., 225

C

Cadely, H., 291
Cai, Y., 242

Cain, S., 169
Calabro, F., 360
Calabro, F. J., 53
Caldas, S., 331
Caldwell, C., 227, 255, 259
Caldwell, C. H., 33, 89
Caldwell, K., 161
Caldwell, L., 190
Caldwell, M. S., 268
Calkins, S., 226
Calkins, S. D., 108
Callahan, R., 162
Callan, V., 276
Calvert, S., 174, 369
Calvete, E., 290
Calvete Zumalde, E., 378
Calvo, R., 46
Calzo, J., 234
Calzo, J. P., 19, 37
Camacho, D., 187
Camacho, M., 87
Camacho-Thompson, D., 92, 187
Camacho-Thompson, D. E., 118
Cambron, C., 90
Camchong, J., 362
Cameron, R. P., 37
Camou, S., 157
Campa, M., 319
Campbell, B., 15, 37, 301
Campbell, F., 58
Campbell, H., 361
Campbell, J., 321
Campbell, K., 248
Campbell, M. E., 134
Campbell, S., 373
Campione-Barr, N., 107, 241, 303
Campo, J., 381
Canário, C., 103
Canino, G., 374
Cannon, J., 300
Cano, M., 222
Cao, B., 34
Capaldi, D., 290, 374
Capara, G. V., 167
Caplan, B., 110
Cappelleri, J., 311
Caprara, G., 291, 328
Caputi, T., 310
Caravita, S., 138
Carbonaro, W., 162, 166
Card, N., 89, 139, 143, 147, 149, 233
Cardemil, E., 332
Cardinale, E., 372
Carey, M., 361
Carey, M. P., 314
Carlin, J., 357, 377
Carliner, H., 360
Carlo, G., 99, 118, 225–226, 253, 254, 276
Carlson, D., 91, 304
Carlson, M., 291

Carlson, R., 149
Carlson, S. M., 50
Carlson, W., 273, 282
Carnagey, N., 200
Carnaghi, A., 150
Carolan, B. V., 158
Caron, A., 374
Carothers, K., 383
Carp, J., 144, 248
Carpenter, J., 363
Carrano, J., 188
Carrascosa, L., 289
Carriedo, N., 46, 52
Carrier, L., 195
Carrion, V. G., 15
Carroll, J. S., 74
Carry, M., 305
Carskadon, M., 27, 29
Carskadon, M. A., 27, 28, 29
Carstensen, L., 98
Carteau-Martin, I., 45
Carter, C. S., 42
Carter, J., 38, 226, 338
Carter, M., 321
Carter, R., 30, 32, 33
Carter, S., 86
Caruthers, A., 310
Carvalho, A., 147, 379
Carver, K., 167
Casas, J., 204
Cascardi, M., 291
Cascio, C., 144, 248
Case, B., 362
Casella, R., 174
Casement, M. D., 53
Casey, B. J., 9, 43, 46, 51, 52, 53, 54, 57, 62, 77, 237, 238, 245, 246, 382
Casey, M., 361
Cash, T. F., 37
Casillas, A., 324
Casper, D., 139, 143, 147
Caspi, A., 33, 92, 105, 108, 114, 173, 212, 213, 217, 244, 319, 368, 372, 373, 374, 381
Casseus, M., 361
Cassidy, J., 101, 266, 268, 269
Cassotti, M., 52
Castellanos-Ryan, N., 109, 110, 362
Castellino, D. R., 133
Casten, R., 326
Castro, G., 226, 299
Castro, N., 362
Castro-Fornieles, J., 46
Castro-Schilo, L., 159
Catalano, R., 138, 351, 352, 360, 361
Catalano, R. F., 85, 90
Catron, T., 374
Cauce, A., 226
Caudle, K., 46, 53

Carlson, R., 149
Cauffman, E., 61, 63, 64, 69, 70, 77, 78, 90, 91, 92, 105, 114, 138, 174, 184, 210, 241, 244, 245, 246, 247, 248, 279, 287, 288, 292, 314, 365, 368, 370, 371, 372, 373, 374, 375
Caughy, M., 249
Cava, M., 150, 289
Cavanagh, S., 114, 282, 333
Cavanagh, S. E., 116
Cavanagh, T., 337
Cavanaugh, A., 227
Cavazos-Rehg, P., 300
Ceballo, R., 92, 336
Ceci, S., 58, 336
Cédric, P., 48
Ceglarek, P. J. D., 230
Celeste, L., 170
Centers for Disease Control and Prevention, 62, 157, 192, 289, 296, 297, 298, 299, 308, 311, 312, 314, 354, 359, 363, 365, 376, 378, 379
Cepa, K., 73
Cerda, M., 93
Cerniglia, L., 204
Cervantes, R., 226
Ceulemans, E., 117
Chalmers, H., 248, 352
Chaloupka, F., 67
Cham, H., 33, 160, 227
Chamberlain, P., 120
Champion, J., 383
Chan, A., 138, 139
Chan, C. S., 89
Chan, H.-Y., 240
Chan, K., 248
Chan, M., 147, 224, 260
Chan, P., 311
Chan, S., 150, 248
Chan, V., 321
Chan, W., 255
Chand, S., 28, 203
Chaney, L., 363
Chang, E., 277, 338, 347
Chang, J., 356
Chang, L., 2, 47, 57, 62, 64, 97, 198, 216, 245, 290, 301
Chang, Z., 164
Chango, J., 140, 248, 266, 269
Chao, R., 106, 224, 226
Chao, R. K., 100
Charbonneau, A., 377
Charlton, B., 311
Charman, T., 59
Charmaraman, L., 224
Charnigo, R., 365
Chase-Lansdale, P., 115
Chase-Lansdale, P. L., 115, 320
Chassin, L., 8, 90, 111, 112, 115, 358, 359, 360, 361, 370, 371, 372

Chatham, C., 245
Chatters, L. M., 261
Chaudary, N., 47, 57, 62, 245
Chaudhary, N., 2, 62, 301
Chauhan, P., 89, 370
Chaves, T., 361
Chavez, R., 215
Chavous, T., 225, 227
Chaw, Y., 137
Cheadle, J., 114, 310
Cheah, C., 60, 96, 97, 242
Cheah, C. S. L., 96, 97, 242
Cheever, N., 195
Chein, J., 2, 9, 17, 47, 48, 54, 57, 62, 63, 64, 65, 66, 84, 123, 244, 245, 247, 248, 301, 362
Chein, J. M., 9, 244, 283
Chen, C., 277, 278, 338, 347
Chen, C. C., 160
Chen, D., 107
Chen, E., 92, 227
Chen, F. R., 27, 32
Chen, H., 39, 63, 82, 249, 311, 332
Chen, J., 48, 137
Chen, K., 357, 358
Chen, L., 106, 138, 143, 270
Chen, M., 289, 319
Chen, M. S., 291
Chen, P., 277, 372
Chen, R., 173, 351
Chen, S., 35, 100, 194, 195
Chen, X., 127, 138, 140, 145, 168, 225, 234, 242, 334
Chen, Y., 106, 228, 379
Chen, Z., 32, 289
Cheng, M., 283, 296
Cheng, Q., 339
Cheng, T., 269
Cheng, T. L., 210
Cheng, Y., 37, 227
Chen-Gaddini, M., 60, 96, 249
Cheong, J., 310
Cheong, P., 195
Cheong, Y., 30
Cherlin, A., 112, 115
Cherlin, A. J., 92
Chermack, S., 361, 368
Cheryan, S., 347
Chessa, A., 46
Chessor, D., 162
Cheung, C., 267, 330, 333
Cheung, R. Y. M., 115
Chhangur, R. R., 109
Chi, P., 88
Chiang, J., 29, 92
Chien, N., 315
Childs, K., 353
Child Welfare Information Gateway, 319
Chin, C. S., 95
Chiodo, D., 309

Chiorri, C., 183
Chipperfield, J., 383
Chisholm, L., 84
Chiu, M., 204, 338
Chiu, P. H., 63
Chmelka, M., 360
Cho, J., 30, 363
Choate, V., 248
Choate, V. R., 55
Choe, H., 277
Choi, B., 148
Choi, D. W., 37
Choi, H., 205, 289
Choi, J.-K., 91, 92
Choi, W., 267
Choi, Y., 225, 360
Chong, W., 325
Choo, E., 361
Choo, T. H., 37
Chopel, A., 291
Choudhury, S., 59
Chouinard-Decorte, F., 51
Choukas-Bradley, S., 56, 140, 204, 248, 280, 304, 308
Chow, A., 135
Chow, B., 338
Christakis, N., 309
Christakos, A., 270
Christakou, A., 244
Christensen, K., 89
Christensen, K. J., 253
Christopher, C., 310
Christopher, F. S., 33
Chronis-Tuscano, A., 164
Chrousos, G., 353
Chu, B. C., 382
Chu, W., 362
Chua, A., 106
Chua, L. W., 210
Chua, T., 198, 216
Chuang, S., 96
Chue, A. E., 29
Chugh, D., 327
Chumlea, W., 22
Chung, C., 163, 358, 359
Chung, G., 101
Chung, G. H., 101
Chung, H. L., 86
Chung, J., 214
Chung, M. K., 35, 46
Chung, T., 360
Church, J. A., 46, 47, 54
Church, M., 336
Church, R., 154, 175
Church, W. T., 92
Chyu, L., 291
Ciarrochi, J., 204, 217, 242, 243, 277
Cicchetti, D., 115, 291
Ciciolla, L., 90, 333
Ciesla, J., 382

Cillessen, A., 132, 139, 140, 141, 145, 199, 279
Cillessen, A. H., 140
Cillessen, A. H. N., 63, 132, 140, 244
Cimino, S., 204
Cimpian, A., 330
Ciocanel, O., 191
Cirimele, F., 244
Claes, L., 37, 38, 222, 379
Claes, M., 33
Claes, S., 110
Clardy, C., 258, 259, 260
Clark, D., 299, 301, 360
Clark, J., 362
Clark, L., 37
Clarke, A., 195, 383
Clarke, G., 382
Clarke-Pearson, K., 203
Clasen, D., 132
Clasen, L. S., 43, 54
Class, Q., 353
Claus, E., 63, 244
Claxton, S., 119
Clayton, H., 299
Clemans, K., 150
Clements, P., 249
Clentifanti, L. C. M., 65
Cleveland, H., 136, 248, 288, 290, 362
Cleveland, M., 92, 360
Cleveland, M. J., 92
Clifford, S., 29
Cloninger, C., 212
Clore, G., 289, 291
Coan, J. A., 92
Coard, S., 226
Coard, S. I., 226
Coatsworth, J., 191, 238, 242
Cobbs, G., 212
Coca, V., 336
Coe, J. L., 115
Coelho, V., 150
Coffey, C., 357
Coffman, D., 138, 311
Cohen, A., 47, 52, 54, 57, 77, 245, 291
Cohen, A. O., 53
Cohen, D., 301
Cohen, G., 140, 248, 304
Cohen, J., 54, 339, 375
Cohen, M., 237, 238
Cohen, P., 311
Cohen, P. K., 82
Cohen, R., 336
Cohen-Gilbert, J., 362
Cohen-Gilbert, J. E., 56
Cohn, D., 85
Coie, J., 59
Cok, F., 271
Colaco, B., 34

Colby, J. B., 51
Colby, S. M., 100
Colder, C., 138, 144, 351, 361
Colder, C. R., 91, 244, 360, 362
Cole, D. A., 150
Cole, H., 268
Cole, M. W., 58
Cole, S., 88
Coleman, J., 10, 167, 333
Coleman-Minahan, K., 317
Coles, M., 317
Coley, R., 88, 90, 320
Coley, R. L., 92, 190
Colich, N., 378
Colich, N. L., 15
Collado, A., 314
Collibee, C., 280, 285, 287, 290, 300
Collie, R., 168
Collier, K., 195, 206
Collins, A., 362
Collins, J., 311
Collins, M. E., 63
Collins, R., 197, 358
Collins, W. A., 7, 29, 95, 101, 103, 108, 185, 210, 237, 238, 239, 240, 241, 246, 248, 250, 268, 286, 287, 289, 300, 304
Collura, J., 255
Colmar, S., 328
Colpin, H., 110, 161, 163, 167, 242, 353
Coltrane, S., 99
Colwell, J., 199
Colwell, S., 150
Comer, J., 276
Comings, D., 304
Compas, B., 383
Compian, L., 279, 287
Compton, S., 382
Comstock, R., 188
Conduct Problems Prevention Research Group, 145, 374
Conger, K., 108, 337
Conger, K. J., 110
Conger, R., 30, 32, 87, 92, 105, 114, 115, 117, 188, 217, 225, 226, 227, 275, 299, 337, 339, 357, 361, 372, 377
Conger, R. D., 159, 275, 352
Conklin, H. M., 47
Conley, A., 336
Conley, C., 382
Connell, A., 351, 372
Connell, A. M., 106
Connell, C., 358
Connell, D., 353
Conner, B. T., 36
Conner, J., 172
Connolly, E. J., 108
Connolly, J., 7, 115, 129, 270, 273, 279, 281, 282, 283, 284, 285, 287, 288, 289, 291

Connolly, M., 231
Connolly, S., 381
Connor, K., 327
Connor, S. M., 19
Connor, T., 103, 114, 269
Connor-Smith, J. K., 382
Conrod, P., 363
Conroy, D., 191, 238
Conson, M., 59, 247
Constante, K., 225
Conti, D., 360
Conway, K., 351, 362
Cooc, N., 134
Cook, E., 275
Cook, P., 368
Cook, R., 310
Cook, T., 135, 336
Cooksey, E. C., 129
Cookston, J. T., 99
Cools, R., 165
Cooper, A., 193, 338
Cooper, H., 328
Cooper, K., 205
Cooper, M., 352
Cooper, S., 336
Cope, L., 362
Copeland, W., 88, 147
Copeland, W. E., 31
Copeland-Linder, N., 227–228
Coplan, R., 145, 242
Coplan, R. J., 142, 242
Corbin, W. R., 85
Corcoran, J., 321
Córdova, D., 226, 228, 367
Corenblum, B., 224
Corley, R., 33
Corley, R. P., 30
Corliss, H., 231, 310, 311, 321
Corneal, D., 234
Cornelius, M., 333
Cornelius, M. D., 92
Cornell, D., 147, 148, 158, 168
Corona, R., 302, 303
Corrado, R., 365, 372
Corral, A., 46, 52
Correll, C. U., 376
Corteselli, K., 382
Cortés-Pascual, A., 150
Cortina, K., 6, 140
Cosma, A., 87, 285, 286
Costa, F. M., 352
Costa, P., Jr., 213
Costa, P. T., Jr., 212
Costello, E., 147
Costello, E. J., 31
Costello, J., 351
Costello, M. A., 242, 349
Côté, J., 4, 74, 76, 210, 215, 220, 222, 223
Cotter, D., 233
Couperus, J. W., 49

Coups, E., 361
Courtney, D., 376
Covay, E., 166
Covington, M., 328
Cox, M., 6, 201
Coxe, S., 372
Coy, K., 29
Coyle, K., 288
Coyne, S., 150, 192, 193, 195, 199, 201, 203, 204, 206
Coyne, S. M., 198, 200
Craddock, J., 204
Craig, I., 108, 381
Craig, W., 279, 282, 283, 287
Crandall, A., 299
Craven, R., 147, 162, 215
Crawford, C., 382
Crean, H. F., 106, 188
Creasey, G., 277
Creemers, H., 352
Crespo, L., 242
Cressen, J., 227
Cribb, V., 216
Crick, N., 143, 144, 164
Crick, N. C., 144
Crippa, J., 362
Criss, M. M., 92, 108, 136
Crissey, S., 282
Cristina Gugliandolo, M., 103
Crocetti, E., 220, 221, 223, 253, 254, 291, 374
Crocker, J., 216
Crockett, L., 103, 299, 303, 338
Crockett, L. J., 4, 35, 64, 66, 74, 138
Croft, T., 312
Croizet, J-C., 337
Croll, J., 37
Crone, E., 42, 58, 142, 144, 221, 222, 244, 245, 247, 248, 252, 253, 254, 271, 362
Crone, E. A., 17, 25, 26, 46, 47, 48, 52, 53, 54, 55, 58, 63, 100, 132, 245
Croninger, R., 177, 178, 337
Crooks, C., 309
Crosby, R., 314
Crosby, S., 201
Crosnoe, R., 114, 116, 118, 135, 161, 165, 246, 310, 337, 338
Cross, C., 288
Cross, D., 277
Cross, F., 225
Cross, M., 56, 304
Cross, S., 357
Cross, W. E., Jr., 225
Crossman, E., 90, 187
Crouter, A., 99, 102, 103, 111, 122, 127, 134, 173, 186, 188, 225, 234, 275
Crouter, A. C., 103, 107, 122, 127, 159, 233, 275

Crowder, K., 318
Crowe, P., 278
Crowell, J., 268
Crowley, M., 142, 266
Crowley, S. J., 27, 28, 29
Crowley, T., 362
Cruz, R., 226
Cruz, R. A., 99
Crystal, D. S., 60
Cservenka, A., 362
Csikszentmihalyi, M., 339
Cuadros, O., 145
Cui, L., 92, 136, 350, 375, 376
Cui, M., 114, 115, 291, 332
Cumberland, A., 253
Cummings, E., 115
Cummings, E. M., 115, 266
Cummings, J., 357, 363
Cumsille, P., 96, 111, 249
Cundiff, K., 181, 184
Cunning, D., 195
Cunningham, M., 234
Cunningham, R., 92, 361, 368
Curlee, A., 333
Curran, P., 92, 111, 112, 352
Currie, C., 24, 368
Currie, D. B., 24
Curtis, D., 333
Custers, R., 53
Cutrona, C., 30, 32, 106, 352
Cutting, L., 51
Cuttini, L. A., 149
Cvencek, D., 327

D

Daddis, C., 96, 106, 250
Daftary-Kapur, T., 77
Dager, A., 362
Daha, M., 227
Dahl, G., 319
Dahl, R., 9, 56, 63, 275, 294, 350, 381, 382
Dahl, R. E., 27, 42, 47, 48, 49, 53, 55, 101
Dahlgren, M., 362
Dakof, G., 363
Dallago, L., 92
Dallal, G. E., 22
Dalmaijer, E., 246
Dalsgaard, S., 350, 375
Dalton, B., 335
Dalwani, M., 362
Daly, B. P., 36
Daly, M., 368
Damhorst, M. L., 36
Damian, A., 357
Damian, R., 213
Damon, W., 210
Damsgaard, M., 145, 146, 361
Dandreaux, D., 371

Danese, A., 92
Daniels, E., 233, 234
Danielsen, A., 206
Dank, M., 289, 290
Danneel, S., 353
Dapretto, M., 43, 53, 56, 142, 204, 211, 247, 248, 267
Darity, W., 133
Darki, F., 51
Darling, N., 96, 106, 110, 190, 266, 332
Darling-Hammond, L., 155, 161, 162
Darnell, A., 170, 332
Darroch, J., 297
Daryanani, I., 114
Datta, S., 314
Dauber, S., 161, 162
Daubman, K. A., 279
Daukantaitė, D., 148
Davatzikos, C., 58
Davey, C., 381
Davey, C. G., 376, 382
Davidow, J., 64, 65
Davidson, J., 88, 306
Davidson, R. J., 35
Davie, G., 361
DaViera, A. L., 92, 93
Davies, M., 360
Davies, P., 6, 96, 104, 115, 245, 266, 288
Davies, P. T., 95, 115, 267
Davies, S., 91, 313, 321
Davila, J., 289
Davis, A., 136, 137, 374
Davis, E., 303, 321
Davis, E. J., 198
Davis, H., 360
Davis, H. A., 38
Davis, J., 143, 308
Davis, J. P., 201
Davis, K., 103, 218, 224, 225, 268
Davis, K. D., 101
Davis, L., 183
Davis, M., 57, 142, 144, 147, 148, 353
Davis, R., 228, 261
Davis, S., 76
Davis-Kean, P., 46, 210, 319
Davison, K. K., 34
Davison, T., 36
Davisson, E., 88
Dawes, N., 191
Day, D., 241
Day, E., 107, 332
Day, J., 168, 231
Day, R., 118, 324
Day, S. E., 35
Dean, J., 184
Deane, C., 110
Deane, K., 92
Deardorff, J., 16, 22, 23, 25, 28, 31, 33, 38, 304, 305

Dearing, E., 90
Deater-Deckard, K., 63, 92, 97, 103, 106, 117, 137, 143, 147, 372
De Bellis, M. D., 47
De Beni, R., 324
Debnam, K., 170, 201, 261
de Boer, A., 247
de Boer, H., 169
De Bolle, M., 213
de Bruyn, E., 141
DeCamp, W., 199
De Castella, K., 328
de Castro, B., 254
Deck, A., 115
Decker, J., 246
De Coster, S., 304
De Dreu, C. K., 47
Deen, B., 142
Defoe, I., 246, 360
Defoe, I. N., 61
De Fraine, B., 163
DeFries, J., 114
De Fruyt, F., 212, 213
Degarmo, D., 374
De Genna, N., 333
Değirmencioğlu, S., 129, 138
Degnan, K. A., 103
De Goede, I., 100, 275
Degol, J., 108, 328
de Graaf, H., 38, 199, 282, 296
DeGue, S., 291
de Haan, A., 373
Deike, R., 215
DeJoseph, M., 257
Deke, J., 363
Deković, M., 103, 106, 107, 245, 304
De Laet, S., 110, 167
de la Haye, K., 35, 138, 310
de la Serna, E., 46
de la Vega, P., 299
DeLay, D., 95, 96, 99, 101, 138, 288, 310
Delevi, R., 205
Delgado, M., 228
Delgado, M. R., 62
Del Guidice, M., 352
Delker, B., 267
Dellarco, D., 246
Delle Fave, A., 328
Delnevo, C., 361
de Looij-Jansen, P., 302
De Los Reyes, A., 100, 101
DelPriore, D., 302
Del Rey, R., 204, 205
Delsing, M., 275
Delsing, M. J. M. H., 128
Del Toro, J., 224, 227
DeLuca, H., 119
DeMaris, A., 291
Dembo, M., 339
Demby, H., 321

Demeter, D. V., 53
Demirhan, E., 92
Demler, O., 8
Demo, D., 113
Demurie, E., 164
Denault, A., 187
Denault, A.-S., 129, 187, 188, 279
De Neve, J., 309
Deng, C., 106
Deng, H., 234
Deng, S., 227
Deng, Y., 135
Denissen, J., 211, 213, 219, 221, 327
Denissen, J. J. A., 216
Denizet-Lewis, A., 376
Denner, J., 329
Dennis, E., 164
Dennison, M. J., 56
Dennison, R., 115
Dennison, R. P., 81
Denny, K. E., 103
Denton, K., 271
Denton, M. L., 260
De Oliveira, C., 363
de Oliveira, R., 60
Deperthes, B., 321
Deptula, D., 302, 304
Derefinko, K., 301
Derlan, C., 227
Dermody, S., 310
Dermody, S. S., 310
de Rooij, M., 254
DeRose, L. M., 33
Desai, S., 312, 315
de Silveira, C., 223
Desjardins, T., 143
DesRoches, A., 206
Des Rosiers, S., 226, 228
Destin, M., 337
Detmar, S., 145
Deutsch, A., 29, 297, 303
Deutz, M., 141
Development Services Group, Inc., 319
Devereaux, R. S., 362
Devine, S., 321
De vries, D., 38, 199
deVries, M. W., 27
DeVylder, J., 147, 379
de Water, E., 63, 244, 245
de Wied, M., 273, 291
Dezutter, J., 221
Dhalewadikar, J., 360
Dhariwal, A., 282, 291
Dhir, A., 194
D'hondt, F., 338
Diamant, A. L., 34
Diamond, G., 310
Diamond, L., 7, 134, 230, 285, 294, 295, 298, 299, 300, 301, 302, 306, 308, 309, 311

Diamond, L. M., 231
Diaz, R., 233, 310
Diaz, T., 218
Diaz-Albertini, K., 297
Diazgranados, S., 148
Dick, D., 91, 109, 311, 360, 382, 383
Dick, D. M., 108
Dicke, T., 147
Dickerson, K. L., 105
Dickson, D., 102
Dickson, D. J., 329
Dickson, K., 321
Dickson, N., 212, 244
Dickson-Gomez, J., 136
DiClemente, R., 313, 314
Diehl, L., 215
Diemer, M., 327, 338
Dierker, L., 362
Dierschke, N., 321
Dietsch, B., 361
DiGiovanni, C., 310
Di Giunta, L., 2, 62, 92, 117, 244, 301
DiIorio, C., 303
Dijk, M., 211
Dijkstra, J., 6, 122, 127, 130, 135, 138, 140, 141, 264, 273, 310
Dijkstra, J. K., 33, 167, 279
DiLalla, L., 33
DiLalla, L. F., 30
Dilks, R. J., 35
Dimitropoulos, G., 198
Dingus, T., 65
Dinkes, R., 173
Dinov, I. D., 48
Dion, E., 343
Dionne, G., 108, 109, 273
DiPietro, S., 158
Dirghangi, S., 273
Dirks, M. A., 149
Dishion, T., 135, 137, 304, 310, 334, 352, 358, 360, 372, 374
Dishion, T. J., 92, 106
Dishion, T. K., 95
DiStefano, C., 149
Distefano, R., 372
Dittus, P., 249, 302, 318, 321
Dixon, L., 36
Dmitrieva, J., 136, 288
Do, K., 54, 63, 65, 67, 88, 248
Doane, L., 29, 291, 383
Dockray, S., 5, 14
Dodge, B., 296
Dodge, K., 59, 144, 190, 242, 267, 291, 292, 303, 343, 360, 365, 366, 371, 373, 374
Dodge, K. A., 115, 144, 373
Dodge, T., 318
Dodson, J., 325
Dogan, S., 299
Doherty, D. A., 300

Doherty, I., 305
Doi, H., 214
Dolan, E., 269
Dolev-Cohen, M., 202
Domina, T., 184, 336
Domoff, S., 150, 194
Donahue, K. L., 115
Dong, Q., 352
Donnell, M., 144, 248, 345
Donnellan, M., 213, 217, 275, 299
Donnellan, M. B., 114, 117
Donnelly, P., 368
Donnelly, T. M., 256
Donnerstein, E., 195, 196, 197, 199, 200
Donoghue, C., 146
Donovan, R., 357
Doogan, N., 138
Dooley, D., 338, 347
Doornwaard, S., 30, 198, 204
Doornwaard, S. M., 132
Dopp, A., 374
Doran, K., 300
Doremus-Fitzwater, T. L., 47
Dorn, L., 18, 23, 26, 353
Dorn, L. D., 14, 26
Dornbusch, S., 115, 116, 117, 184, 246
Dosenbach, N., 47, 54
Dosenbach, N. U. F., 53
Dost-Gözkan, A., 97, 249
Dotterer, A., 159, 173, 188, 225, 234, 332
Dotterer, A. M., 107, 332
Dougherty, D., 361
Doughty, S. E., 108
Douglas, G., 328
Douglass, S., 220, 225, 228
Doust, J., 164
Dowdy, E., 361
Downey, D., 338
Downey, G., 144, 174, 289, 369
Dowshen, S., 16, 24
Doyle, A., 195, 287
Dozier, A., 317
Drabick, D., 349
Draper, P., 352
Dredze, M., 174, 369
Dreman, M., 362
Dreyfuss, M., 53
Driscoll, A., 298, 315, 316
Drolette, L., 115
Dron, L. D., 35
Drucker, E., 370
Drumm, P., 47
Drummond, A., 193
Druss, B., 8, 363, 382
Drysdale, A. T., 53
Du, H., 88
Duan, Q., 289
Duan, W., 24

Duarte, C., 370
Dubas, J., 30, 198, 246, 301, 360
Dubas, J. S., 61
Dubé, E., 230, 285
Dubé, E. M., 134
Dubner, S., 155
Dubocovich, M. L., 28
DuBois, D., 89, 214, 215, 216, 217, 337
Dubon, C., 89, 277
Dubow, E., 150, 194
Ducat, W., 7, 237, 238, 239, 240
Duchesne, S., 333
Duckworth, A., 63, 155, 187, 244, 324, 325, 331
Due, P., 24, 145, 146, 363
Duell, N., 2, 9, 47, 54, 57, 62, 64, 245, 301
Due-Tønnessen, P., 52
Duhoux, S., 237, 238
Duineveld, J., 242, 243
Duke, N., 336
Duke, S. A., 26
Dumas, F., 235
Dumas, T., 143
Dumas, T. M., 222
Dumka, L., 92, 168, 282
Dumont, H., 326
Dumontheil, I., 53, 55, 56, 59, 247
Dunbar, A., 226, 227
Dunbar, M. S., 201
Dunbar, N. D., 119
Duncan, C., 204
Duncan, D., 361
Duncan, G., 27, 291
Duncan, L., 242
Duncan, N., 310
Duncan Cance, J., 29
Dunifon, R., 114, 277
Dunlop, S., 352
Dunn, E., 360
Dunn, E. C., 91
Dunn, V. J., 378
Dunsmore, S., 299
Dunstan, C. J., 37, 38
Duong, M., 134, 135
Duong, M. T., 92, 100, 133, 334
Dupéré, V., 89, 90, 91, 305, 343
DuPont-Reyes, M. J., 166
Durant, R., 361
Durbin, C., 299, 301, 359
Durik, A., 327
Durkee, M., 225, 228
Durlack, J., 374
Durston, S., 51
Durwood, L., 231
Dussault, F., 300
Dweck, C., 144, 326, 327, 329, 330, 373
Dwyer, K., 243
Dyer, W., 299, 324

Dykas, M., 266, 268
Dyke, J. P., 43

E

Earl, E. A., 53
Earls, F., 33, 91
Earls, F. J., 89
East, P., 107, 108, 277, 289, 304, 315
Eastman, M., 146
Eaton, M., 339
Ebbert, A., 102, 274
Ebbert, A. M., 274
Ebeling, H., 33, 164, 351
Eberhardt, J., 170
Eberhart, N., 377, 381
Eberly, M., 241
Eccles, A., 34
Eccles, J., 4, 26, 117, 135, 159, 160, 161, 168, 169, 173, 177, 178, 185, 188, 189, 214, 249, 264, 326, 327, 328, 329, 334, 336, 338, 346, 358
Eccles, J. S., 111, 328
Echols, L., 146
Eckenrode, J., 291, 311, 319
Eckshtain, D., 382
Eckstein, R., 290
Eckstrand, K., 56, 304
Edelstein, W., 213, 270
Edenberg, H., 300
Edens, J., 365
Eder, D., 141
Edgecombe, N., 341
Edin, K., 116
Edinburgh, L., 118
Edwards, A., 382
Edwards, K., 149, 290
Edwards, L., 383
Egeland, B., 268, 358, 359, 374
Eggermont, S., 19, 150, 197, 198, 199, 202, 204
Egloff, B., 213
Ehrenreich, H., 358
Ehrenreich, S., 136, 150, 192, 193, 202, 203
Ehrlich, K., 268
Ehrlich, K. B., 101, 269
Eichen, D. M., 36
Eiden, R., 361
Eijnden, R., 203
Eilers, M., 291, 313, 315, 316, 318
Einarsdóttir, S., 212
Einspruch, E., 363
Eira Nunes, C., 242
Eisenberg, M., 35, 215, 216, 310, 311
Eisenberg, M. E., 34
Eisenberg, N., 7, 61, 102, 106, 117, 167, 238, 250, 251, 252, 253, 254, 255, 260, 273, 336, 337, 373

Eisenberger, N., 267
Eisenberger, N. I., 56
Eisenlohr-Moul, T., 301
Eisenlohr-Moul, T. A., 379, 380
Eisman, A., 187
Eisman, A. B., 92
Eisner, M., 164
Ejesi, K., 226
Elaesser, C., 201
Elam, K., 116, 360
Elder, G., Jr., 117
Elder, G. H., Jr., 11, 80, 118, 377
Elder, J., 321
Elders, M., 358
Eley, T., 352, 372
Eley, T. C., 103
Elfassi, Y., 91
Elgar, F., 368
Elgar, F. J., 32
Elipe, P., 204
Elish, K., 137
Elkind, D., 43
Elkington, K., 314
Ellen, J. M., 92
Ellhammer, O., 108
Ellickson, P., 358, 362, 363
Elliot, A. J., 326
Elliott, M., 197, 302
Elliott, M. C., 92
Elliott, M. N., 34, 91
Elliott, R., 382
Ellis, B., 23, 302, 303, 352
Ellis, B. J., 110
Ellis, C., 58
Ellis, W., 138, 143
Ellis-Hale, K., 256
Ellwanger, P., 241
Ellwood-Lowe, M., 87
El Mallah, S., 254
El-Menshawi, M., 299
Elmore, R., 155, 159, 346
Elmquist, J., 289
Elsharnouby, E., 97
El-Sheikh, M., 29, 227
Emerson, M., 316, 318
Emery, C., 319
Emery, R., 301
Emery, R. E., 31, 114
Emmery, K., 107, 206
Emslie, G., 382
Enders, C., 34, 234
Eng, A., 303
Eng, E., 261
Engelhardt, L., 212
Engels, M., 167
Engels, M. C., 167
Engels, R., 199, 203, 268, 286
Engels, R. C., 217
Engels, R. C. M. E., 109, 128
Engle, K., 198, 300
English, D., 227, 311

Englund, M., 358, 359
Ennett, S., 133, 134, 143, 146, 261, 289, 290, 360, 361, 363
Ennett, S. T., 291
Enriquez, L., 344
Ensminger, M., 359
Ensminger, M. E., 92
Entwisle, B., 134
Entwisle, D., 161, 162, 165, 344
Epelbaum, J., 361
Epstein, J., 360
Epstein, M., 352, 362
Epstein, R., 10
Erath, S., 116, 142, 149
Erath, S. A., 29
Erausquin, J., 201
Erhart, M., 145
Erickson, D., 311
Erickson, K., 246
Erickson, S., 206
Eriksen, A., 191
Eriksen, M., 358
Erikson, E., 9, 218
Erisir, A., 50
Erkut, S., 216
Ernst, M., 275
Erol, R., 213, 216
Ersbøll, A., 361
Erus, G., 48, 52, 58
Erwin, E. H., 157
Esbensen, F., 136
Esbensen, F.-A., 174
Eschmann, R., 149, 201
Eskreis-Winkler, L., 331
Esnaola, I., 215
ESPAD Group, 354
Espelage, D., 138, 143, 145, 148, 149, 173, 178, 310
Espenshade, T., 163
Espinosa, G., 270, 271
Espinosa-Hernández, G., 250, 260, 261, 289, 300
Espinoza, G., 143, 149, 150, 226, 335
Espinoza, P., 37, 198
Esposito, L., 157
Esposito-Smythers, C., 379, 381
Essex, M., 23
Essex, M. J., 23
Essig, L., 199
Essig, L. W., 198
Estévez, E., 174
Estrada, A., 275
Estrada, M., 327
Estrada, S., 63
Ethier, K., 302
Ethnic and Racial Identity in the 21st Century Study Group, 225
Etkin, R., 143, 254
Ettekal, I., 141, 142, 143, 145, 372
Eubanks, J., 200

Eucogo, J., 321
European Kidscreen Group, 145
Evans, A., 51, 225
Evans, A. D., 59
Evans, B., 92
Evans, C., 149
Evans, C. R., 91
Evans, E., 337
Evans, G., 333
Evans, R., 204
Evans, S., 371
Eveleth, P., 24
Everett, B., 317
Everett, S., 311
Evers, K., 194
Ewing, B., 310, 358
Exner-Cortens, D., 273, 289, 291
Eyal, E., 197
Eyre, S., 282, 306
Ezpeleta, L., 379

F

Fabricius, W. V., 99
Facchin, F., 331
Fagan, J., 136, 371, 372, 375
Fair, D., 47, 54, 372
Fair, D. A., 53
Fairman, B., 357
Fairweather-Schmidt, A. K., 38
Fales, J., 265
Falk, E., 144, 248
Fan, S., 282
Fan, X., 147, 168
Fandakova, Y., 50, 51
Fang, F., 270
Fang, G., 270
Fang, S., 337
Farb, A., 6, 186, 187
Fardouly, J., 204
Farhat, T., 297, 300, 301, 302
Faris, R., 146, 290, 361
Farkas, G., 336
Farkas, T., 334
Farley, F., 63
Farley, J., 267, 269, 301
Farley, J. P., 63
Farley, T., 301
Farmer, T., 141
Farr, R. H., 119
Farrell, A., 92, 146, 290, 291
Farrell, A. D., 92, 157
Farrell, C., 92
Farrell, L., 19, 266
Farrington, D., 8, 246, 350, 351,
    364, 366, 367, 370, 371, 372,
    373, 374
Farrington, D. P., 136
Farruggia, S., 277, 279, 292, 368
Fasick, F., 71, 72
Fassbender, C., 362

Fasula, A., 304
Fauber, R. L., 36
Faulk, M., 93
Fauth, R. C., 89
Fay, K., 188
Fazel, S., 351, 368
Fedele, D., 350
Federal Bureau of Investigation, 366
Federal Interagency Forum
    on Child and Family
    Statistics, 87
Fehr, E., 54
Feinberg, M., 92, 105, 111, 136, 248,
    279, 304, 351, 360, 362
Feinberg, M. E., 92, 96, 105,
    108, 129
Feiring, C., 240, 263, 268, 272,
    279, 283
Feldman, R., 92
Feldman, S., 310
Feldman, S. S., 241
Feldstein Ewing, S., 313
Feliscar, L., 97
Felmlee, D., 275
Felner, R., 217, 337
Felson, R., 299, 353
Felt, J., 195
Felton, J., 38, 352
Fend, H., 142, 217
Fenelon, A., 226
Fennel, M., 150
Fenton, R., 338
Fenwick, J., 318
Fenzel, L., 160
Ferdinand, A. O., 66
Ferenz-Gillies, R., 268
Ferguson, C., 199, 200, 201
Ferguson, C. J., 19
Ferguson, D., 225
Ferguson, G., 199
Ferguson, M., 48
Ferguson, S., 142
Fergusson, D., 267, 303, 319,
    364, 371
Fernandez-Esquer, M., 338
Fernández-González, L., 290
Feron, F. J., 27
Ferrar, S., 102
Ferreira, P., 256
Ferreiro, F., 37
Ferrer, E., 46, 47, 51, 159, 217, 357
Ferrero, J., 24, 30, 300
Ferris, J., 23
Ferris, K., 254
Ferschmann, L., 52, 56, 212
Festl, R., 150, 199
Fiasconaro, I., 244
Field, A. E., 19, 37
Fields, J., 112
Fiese, B., 35, 199
Fiesta, D., 92, 93

Figner, B., 61, 62, 63
Figueredo, A., 352
Figueroa, G., 200
Filardo, E., 133
Filion, N., 226
Finan, L., 311
Fincham, F. D., 291
Fine, A., 91, 105, 371, 372, 375
Fine, M., 116
Fine, S., 172, 330
Finer, L., 298, 313, 315, 316,
    317, 318
Finer, L. B., 315
Finkelhor, D., 149, 205, 206
Finkenauer, C., 101, 103, 106, 107,
    204, 245, 272
Finlay, A., 257
Finn, A., 178, 337
Finn, J., 159
Finnerty, K., 197
Fiorenzo, L., 119
Fischer, D., 28
Fischoff, B., 62
Fish, J., 168
Fishbein, M., 198
Fisher, B., 150
Fisher, B. W., 174
Fisher, C., 338
Fisher, D., 296, 305, 311
Fisher, H., 92
Fisher, H. L., 105, 173, 368
Fisher, M., 35
Fisher, P., 120
Fite, P., 289, 374
Fitzpatrick, S., 150
Fitzwater, T., 15, 383
Fjell, A., 56
Fjell, A. M., 212
Flach, C., 365
Flamant, N., 96, 242
Flament, M. F., 36
Flamion, A., 277
Flamm, E., 332
Flamm, E. S., 106
Flanagan, C., 174, 181, 253, 254,
    255, 256, 257, 346
Flanagan, C. A., 257
Flanagan, K., 142, 149
Flanders, W., 34
Flannery, D., 29, 173, 212, 361
Flannery, J., 63, 269
Flashman, J., 135, 334
Flay, B., 360, 374
Flay, B. R., 376
Fleischli, J., 136
Fleming, C., 351
Fleming, C. B., 85
Fleming, W., 268
Fleschler Peskin, M., 289
Fletcher, J. M., 165
Flewelling, R., 363

Flickinger, S., 326
Flom, J., 23
Flook, L., 101, 202, 273, 333
Flor, D., 118
Flora, C., 201
Florence, D., 325
Flores, C., 55, 361
Flores, L., 227
Flournoy, J., 63, 269
Flynn, B., 363
Flynn, H., 275
Fobil, J., 195
Foeher, U., 195
Foehr, U., 180, 195, 198, 199,
    200, 201
Foley, K., 200
Foley, S., 119
Fomby, P., 116, 194, 333
Fondell, M., 304
Fong, C., 148, 149
Fong, G., 303
Font, S., 311
Fontaine, N., 372
Fontaine, R., 59, 149, 373
Fontaine, R. G., 292
Foran, W., 360
Forbes, E., 53, 56, 304, 361, 375
Forbes, E. E., 27, 48, 53, 54,
    101, 381
Forbes, G. B., 19
Ford, C., 296, 298
Ford, J. L., 113
Ford, K., 226
Ford, T., 365
Fordham, C., 133
Forenza, B., 93
Forest, A., 202
Forgatch, M., 137, 374
Forhan, S., 314
Forman, T., 259
Forman, Y., 190
Forman-Alberti, A., 248
Fornito, A., 53
Forrest, W., 63
Forrester, K., 147
Forster, M., 379
Fortenberry, J., 295
Forthun, L., 222
Fortner, A., 360
Fortner, M., 99
Fortson, B., 291
Fortson, E. N., 92
Fortuin, J., 138
Fosco, G., 105, 242, 275, 291
Fosco, G. M., 105
Fosco, W. D., 244
Foshee, V., 143, 146, 289, 290, 291,
    310, 361
Foshee, V. A., 291
Foss, R. D., 65, 67
Foster, D., 317

Foster, E., 142
Foster, H., 33, 90
Foulkes, L., 52, 53, 246, 247
Fournier, M., 223
Foust, M., 225
Fowler, C., 147, 148
Fowler, J., 309
Fowler, P., 92, 120
Fox, J. A., 174
Fox, K., 379
Fox, N. A., 103
Frala, J. L., 32
Fraley, R., 267
Fraley, R. C., 269
Francis, D. V., 86
Francis, L. A., 34
Francis, S., 383
Francisco, R., 37, 198
Francois, A., 225
Frank, K., 135
Franke, B., 165
Franken, A., 33, 138
Frankenhuis, W., 55
Franklin, N. T., 53
Franko, D. L., 216
Franz, P., 35, 51, 54
Franzen, A., 261
Franzetta, K., 119, 313
Franzini, L., 249
Franzoi, S., 142
Frazier, L. D., 38
Fredrick, J., 106
Fredricks, J. A., 172, 343
Freedman-Doan, P., 184
Freeman, H., 276
Freeman, J., 368
French, D., 140, 260, 304
French, J., 200
French, M., 140
French, S. E., 224
Freud, A., 9, 239
Freud, S., 9
Frey, S., 28
Frick, P., 90, 91, 92, 105, 314, 365,
    371, 372, 374, 375
Frick, P. J., 91, 114
Fridel, E. E., 174
Fried, M., 79
Friedenberg, E., 10, 178
Friedlander, L., 282
Friedman, H., 321
Friedman, M., 310
Friedman, M. S., 310
Friedman, S., 206
Friel, L., 303
Friend, K., 361
Friendly, R., 243
Frijns, T., 12, 101, 137
Frisen, A., 213
Frison, E., 199, 202, 204
Fritz, B. L., 54

Frolli, A., 59, 247
Fromme, K., 85
Frøyland, L., 188
Fruiht, V., 89, 277, 334
Fry, C. M., 108
Fry, R., 85
Frye, M., 29
Fugelsang, J., 66
Fuhrmann, D., 50, 59
Fujimoto, K., 138
Fukuda, S., 45
Fulcher, B. D., 53
Fuligini, A., 301
Fuligni, A., 87, 88, 99, 101, 135, 175,
    187, 211, 224, 225, 226, 227,
    240, 249, 255, 259, 267, 270,
    276, 333, 334, 335, 338,
    339, 378
Fuligni, A. J., 29, 54, 55, 65, 99,
    100, 101, 118, 260
Fulker, D., 103
Fulkerson, J. A., 36
Fuller, A. K., 27
Fuller, C., 370
Fuller-Rowell, T., 333
Fulmore, C., 326
Furlong, M., 361
Furman, W., 129, 263, 266, 269,
    277, 279, 280, 281, 282, 283,
    284, 285, 287, 290, 300, 310
Furr-Holden, C., 361
Furstenberg, F., Jr., 84, 86
Furstenberg, F. F., 73
Fusar-Poli, P., 362
Fussner, L., 382

G

Gaarde, J., 28
Gabbard, W., 351
Gabhainn, N., 302
Gabhainn, S., 297, 300, 301
Gabhainn, S. N., 285, 286
Gabrieli, C., 337
Gabrieli, J., 178, 337
Gadermann, A., 187
Gadino, B., 224
Gage, J., 189
Gage, S., 363
Gagné, M., 203
Gagnon, S., 202
Gahr, J. L., 32
Gaias, L., 92, 168
Gaias, L. M., 92, 168
Gaither, S., 229
Galambos, N., 3, 30, 74, 76, 81, 134,
    232, 233, 234, 278
Galambos, N. L., 268
Galay, L., 256, 257
Galbraith, K., 303
Galera, C., 164

Galindo, M., 19
Galla, B., 244, 383
Gallagher, A., 108
Gallagher, K., 187
Gallarin, M., 119
Gallay, E., 257
Gallimore, A., 200
Gallimore, R., 136
Galloway, T., 178
Galván, A., 27, 29, 51, 52, 53,
    54, 55, 65, 88, 245, 270,
    294, 301
Gamble, W., 268
Gámez-Guadix, M., 150, 205
Gamm, B., 270, 272, 292
Gamoran, A., 162, 327
Gandhi, A., 37, 38, 222, 379
Ganga, E., 341
Gao, L., 195
Gao, M., 135
Garabiles, M., 168
Garandeau, C., 141
Garbarino, J., 91
Garbazza, C., 28
Garber, A. K., 37, 38
Garber, J., 160, 241, 382
Garceau, C., 307
Garcia, C., 224
Garcia, D., 381
Garcia, M., 383
Garcia, N. V., 55
Garcia Coll, C., 216, 226
Garcia-Reid, P., 92
Gardarsdottir, R., 90
Gardella, J., 150
Gardner, M., 65, 91, 92, 93,
    187, 188
Gardner, T., 372
Garduno, L. S., 136
Garefino, A. C., 164
Garg, R., 335
Garofalo, C., 372
Garrett, E., 54
Garthe, R., 291
Gartner, M., 225
Gartner, R. E., 310
Gartrell, N., 115
Gartstein, M., 92
Gary, D., 189
Garza, A., 19, 200
Gaskin, A., 86
Gaspar de Matos, M., 368
Gassman-Pines, A., 86, 88
Gastic, B., 180
Gathercole, S. E., 47
Gatherum, A., 243
Gau, S., 164
Gaudreau, P., 187
Gauze, C., 273
Gaydos, L., 321
Gaylord-Harden, N., 216, 226

Gaylord-Harden, N. K., 90
Ge, X., 23, 30, 32, 106, 117, 287,
    289, 377
Gebauer, J. E., 216
Gebremariam, A., 16
Gecas, V., 99
Gee, D., 51, 52
Gee, J. C., 46
Gee, K., 134
Geeraert, N., 100
Geier, C., 54, 64, 245, 360
Geier, C. F., 64, 360
Geiser, C., 213
Geiss, E., 381
Gelardi, K., 92, 372
Gelbwasser, L., 334
Geldhof, G., 190
Gelfond, J., 321
Geller, B., 363
Gengaro, F. P., 170
Gentile, D., 193, 199
Gentzler, A., 270
George, G., 217
George, M., 143, 202
Georgiades, K., 89, 150
Gerard, J., 217
Gerard, J. M., 160
Gerard, M., 227
Gerber, S. B., 159
Gerbino, M., 167
Gerbner, G., 196
Gerrard, M., 197
Gershoff, E., 383
Gershoff, E. T., 102
Gest, S., 140, 213
Gest, S. D., 129, 214
Gesten, E., 147
Gestsdottir, S., 171, 191, 244
Gettman, D., 275
Geukens, F., 353
Ghazarian, S., 338
Ghazarian, S. R., 92, 99
Ghement, I. R., 35
Ghetti, S., 51
Giannetta, J., 25, 57, 301
Gibb, B., 375, 378
Gibb, S., 319
Gibbons, F., 30, 32, 106, 116, 140,
    197, 227, 228, 287, 302, 304
Gibbons, F. X., 30
Gibbons, K., 37
Gibbs, J., 251
Gibbs, J. J., 310
Gibson, E., 321
Gibson, L., 136
Gibson-Davis, C. M., 86
Giedd, J., 26, 58, 165, 362
Giedd, J. N., 43, 48, 51, 54, 109
Gierut, K., 35
Gil, A., 311
Gilbert, A., 224, 227

Gilchrist, L., 319
Giletta, M., 140, 248
Gillespie, B., 120
Gillham, J., 378
Gilliam, M., 165
Gillings, K., 191
Gillman, A., 321
Gillmore, M., 319, 360
Gilman, A. B., 136
Gilman, S., 360
Gilman, S. E., 376
Gilpin, E., 358
Gilreath, T., 358
Gimbel, S., 92
Gingo, M., 60, 97, 242
Gini, G., 138, 144, 150, 217
Giordano, P., 280, 282, 291, 298,
    299, 303, 368
Giovenco, D., 361
Giovino, G., 358
Girard, A., 109
Giron, S., 303
Gissler, M., 316
Gissot, V., 45
Gittins-Stone, D., 290
Glasziou, P., 164
Glatt, S., 361
Glauber, A., 289
Glennie, E. J., 344
Glenwright, M., 44
Glick, G., 263, 270, 273
Glick, G. C., 273
Gloster, A. T., 204
Glover, G., 43
Glover, N., 355
Glover, V., 164
Glymour, M., 89
Gmelin, T., 376
Gnagy, E., 372
Gnagy, E. M., 164
Gniewosz, B., 328
Gobbi, G., 363
Goddings, A.-L., 17, 25, 26, 48, 49,
    51, 53, 54, 55
Godeau, E., 24, 297, 300, 301, 302
Godwin, J., 92, 106, 117, 144, 373
Goedemé, T., 117
Goemans, A., 144, 217
Goesling, B., 363
Goetz, C., 337
Goetz, T., 383
Goff, E., 149
Goffnett, J., 231
Gogtay, N., 58
Gold, S., 116
Goldbach, J., 145
Goldbach, J. T., 310
Goldberg, A., 279, 283
Goldberg, R., 291
Goldberg, T., 145
Golden, N., 35

Golden, R., 280, 300
Goldenberg, D., 53, 55, 88, 301
Goldfield, G., 36
Golding, J., 234
Goldman, M., 357
Goldschmidt, A., 53
Goldschmidt, A. B., 37, 38
Goldstein, A., 360
Goldstein, B., 19, 381
Goldstick, J., 92
Goldweber, A., 279, 292, 368
Gollner, R., 217
Golombok, S., 119, 234
Gomez, C., 288
Gomez-Baya, D., 378
Gomez-Garibello, C., 150
Gommans, R., 140
Goncy, E., 146, 291
Goncy, E. A., 92
Gondoli, D., 38, 99
Gondoli, D. M., 242
Gonenc, A., 362
Gong, T., 379
Gönültaş, S., 149
Gonzales, L., 327
Gonzales, L. M., 99
Gonzales, N., 54, 100, 225, 226,
    282, 335
Gonzales, N. A., 29, 33, 90, 99,
    106, 118
Gonzales, R., 226
Gonzales-Backen, M., 224, 228
Gonzalez, L., 99
González, M. L., 37, 198
Gonzalez, M. Z., 92
Good, M., 260, 261
Goode, J. A., 194
Gooden, A., 261
Goodman, M., 71, 72, 73, 84
Goodman, R., 365
Goodman, R. J., 108
Goodson, P., 299, 301
Goodwin, A. H., 65
Goodyer, I., 31
Goodyer, L. M., 378
Goossens, L., 43, 110, 161, 217, 222,
    242, 275, 353
Gordis, E. B., 382
Gordon, A., 231
Gordon, K., 82
Gordon, M., 291, 332
Gordon, R. A., 136
Gordon, V., 302
Gore, S., 177, 277
Gorman, B., 308
Gorman, J. L., 170
Gorman, S., 202
Gorman-Smith, D., 136, 289, 374
Göröglu, B., 58
Görzig, A., 205
Gosling, S. D., 216

Gostisha, A., 365, 372
Gotcsik, M., 312
Gotlib, I., 87, 164, 375, 378,
    381, 382
Gotlib, I. H., 15
Gottfredson, D., 158
Gottfredson, M., 174, 352, 369
Gottfredson, N., 261, 360
Gottlieb, S., 314
Goudeau, S., 337
Gould, T., 247, 356, 362
Gowen, L., 36, 279, 287, 310
Gower, A., 310, 311, 379
Gowling, H., 65
Goza, F., 337
Grabe, S., 310
Graber, J., 8, 27, 30, 31, 33, 36, 150,
    273, 350, 353, 375, 376, 377,
    381, 382
Graber, J. A., 32, 36
Graf, A., 365, 372
Graf, G., 51
Grafman, J., 200
Graham, J. W., 96
Graham, N., 365
Graham, S., 30, 32, 63, 77, 134, 142,
    146, 161, 165, 187, 210, 225,
    229, 244, 245, 334, 370
Graif, C., 89
Gralen, S., 19
Granberg, E., 19
Grande, L., 269
Granger, D., 142
Granger, D. A., 27, 115
Granger, K. L., 232
Granic, I., 95, 199, 272
Granja, M. R., 112, 113
Grant, J., 164
Grant, K., 383
Grassi, M., 150
Gray, G., 352
Gray, M., 283, 291
Gray, R., 105, 173, 368
Gray-Little, B., 216
Greaves-Lord, K., 92
Green, C. T., 51
Green, H., 138, 310
Green, H. D., Jr., 138
Green, J., 351, 382
Green, K., 100, 223, 359
Green, S., 302, 334
Greenbaum, P., 357, 363
Greenberg, M., 92, 160, 242, 360,
    362, 371
Greenberg, M. T., 92, 96
Greenberger, E., 277, 278, 338, 347
Greene, K., 297
Greene, M., 134, 270, 274
Greene, M. L., 216
Greene, W., 310
Greenfield, P., 142, 204, 247, 248

Green-Hennessy, S., 166
Greenhouse, J., 381
Greenleaf, C., 35
Greenspan, L., 16, 22, 25, 31, 38
Greenstein, D., 58
Gregory, A., 147, 168, 321, 326
Gregory, E., 98
Gremmen, M., 135, 138
Gremmen, M. C., 167
Greven, C., 372
Greven, C. U., 164
Grey, M., 310
Griesler, P., 360
Grieve, S. M., 51
Griffin, C., 194, 246
Griffin, E., Jr., 357
Griffin, K., 218, 360
Griffith, A., 191
Griffith, J., 382
Griffith, J. M., 101
Griffith Fontaine, R., 373
Griffiths, A., 351
Griffiths, S., 37
Grigsby, T., 379
Grilo, C., 36
Grilo, S., 321
Grime, R., 251
Grimm, K. J., 35
Griskevicius, G., 352
Grisso, T., 77, 245, 365
Grobe, R., 336
Grodsky, E., 344
Grolnick, W., 243, 332
Grolnick, W. S., 106
Grosbras, M., 248
Grosbras, M.-H., 55
Gross, E., 150
Gross, L., 196
Grossman, A., 168
Grossman, A. H., 33, 230
Grossman, D., 313
Grossman, J. M., 224
Grotevant, H. D., 119
Grotzinger, A. D., 136
Grover, R., 265, 283
Grow, A., 132
Grozinger, A., 64
Grube, J., 296, 305, 361
Gruber, M., 351, 382
Gruber, S., 362
Grucza, R., 363
Gruenenfelder-Steiger, A., 142, 217
Grumbach, M., 15
Grych, J., 275, 291
Grydeland, H., 52, 212
Guacci-Franci, N., 275, 277
Guadagno, R., 334
Guan, K., 379
Guarini, T., 226
Guassi Moreira, J., 65, 67
Guassi Moreira, J. F., 65

Guastaferro, K., 311
Guay, F., 187
Gubbels, J., 343
Gudiño, O., 338
Guerino, P., 173
Guerra, N., 57, 149, 372
Guhn, M., 187
Guimond, A., 224
Guimond, A. B., 225, 226
Guller, L., 38
Gulley, J., 55, 361
Gulley, L., 353
Gulley, L. D., 381
Gummerum, M., 252, 254
Gunnar, M., 269, 276
Gunthert, K. C., 29
Guo, C., 199
Guo, F., 289
Guo, J., 147, 326, 328, 330
Guo, L., 382
Gupta, T., 227, 234
Gur, R., 52, 363
Gur, R. C., 48, 58
Gur, R. E., 48, 58
Gurbuz, S., 92
Gurevitch, M., 196
Güroğlu, B., 143, 144, 145, 254
Gustafson, P., 252
Gustafsson, H., 6
Guterman, N., 92
Guth, C., 374
Guthrie, I., 253
Gutierrez, P., 379
Gutman, L., 161
Guttmacher Institute, 297
Guttmannova, K., 90, 362, 363
Guyer, A., 15, 53, 87, 92, 108, 119, 362, 372, 378, 383
Guyer, A. E., 53, 55, 56, 103, 110, 248, 264
Guyll, M., 12
Guzman, M., 191
Guzmán-Rocha, M., 187

H

Ha, T., 137, 268, 286, 310
Haas, S., 46
Haase, A., 216
Haavisto, T., 325
Habermas, T., 223
Hadd, V., 361
Haddad, A., 247
Haddad, E., 277
Hadiwijaya, H., 100, 101
Haerens, L., 96, 242
Hafdahl, A., 216
Hafen, C., 266, 275, 292, 326
Haghighat, M., 187
Hagler, M., 89, 277
Hahm, H., 297

Hahn, C., 324
Haight, W., 277
Haines, J., 19, 37, 39, 198
Haj-Yahia, M. M., 92
Hakkarainen, K., 193
Hakonarson, H., 58
Halawah, A., 32
Hale, L., 163
Hale, W., 12, 213, 222, 223
Hale, W. W., 211
Halgunseth, L., 289
Hall, A., 169
Hall, D., 290, 321
Hall, G. S., 8–9, 11, 71
Hall, J., 290
Hall, N., 383
Haller, M., 358, 372
Halliday-Scher, K., 129
Halligan, S., 144
Hallinan, M., 134, 161, 162, 166
Hallman, S., 226
Halpern, C., 37, 287, 289, 290, 296, 297, 298, 299, 300, 301, 302, 304, 349, 377
Halpern, C. T., 297, 300, 301
Halpern, D. F., 48
Halpern-Felsher, B., 238, 246, 298
Halpern-Felsher, B. L., 314
Halpern-Meekin, S., 111, 113
Haltigan, J., 372
Haltigan, J. D., 148
Hambarsoomian, K., 34
Hamburger, M., 310
Hamby, S., 149
Hamedani, M., 337
Hamilton, A., 28, 29, 357
Hamilton, B., 315, 316
Hamilton, C., 268
Hamilton, H. A., 117
Hamilton, J., 381
Hamilton, J. L., 28, 32, 114, 203
Hamlat, E. J., 32
Hamm, J., 134, 225
Hammen, C., 377
Hammons, A., 35
Hamre, B., 326
Hamza, C., 379, 382
Hamza, C. A., 379
Han, S., 374
Hancox, R., 34, 35, 195, 200, 244
Handley, E., 291, 358
Handwerger, K., 142
Hanewinkel, H., 35, 195
Hanish, L., 140, 141, 145, 310
Hankin, B., 353, 375, 376, 378, 381, 382
Hankin, B. L., 106, 376, 381
Hannan, P., 198
Hannan, P. J., 39
Hannigan, L. J., 103
Hansen, D., 188, 191

Hansen, D. M., 28
Hansen, N., 313, 321
Hansford, A., 339
Hanson, J. L., 35, 46
Hanson, M., 324
Hanson, T., 116
Hansson, K., 108
Hanusshek, E., 157
Hao, L., 226
Hara, R., 197
Harachi, T., 360
Harackiewicz, J. M., 173
Harakeh, Z., 33, 140, 141, 247, 334, 352
Harbaugh, A., 149
Harber, K. D., 170
Harcourt, T. H., 116
Hardaway, C., 86, 88, 333
Hardaway, C. R., 92
Hardee, J., 362
Harden, K., 109, 244, 372
Harden, K. P., 9, 30, 33, 63, 64, 109, 136, 244, 248, 283, 294, 300, 301, 304, 373, 382
Harden, P., 30
Hardesty, J., 215, 216
Hardie, J. H., 133, 260
Harding, J., 227
Hardway, C., 99
Hardy, K., 195
Hardy, S., 222, 253, 260, 261
Hardy, S. A., 261
Hare, A., 7, 237, 239, 240, 264, 266, 268, 269
Hare, E. D., 47
Hare, T. A., 53
Harel-Fisch, Y., 145, 146
Harenski, C. L., 59
Harenski, K. A., 59
Hargis, P., 181
Hariri, A., 9, 372
Hariri, A. R., 63
Haro, J., 147, 379
Harper, C., 302
Harper, J. M., 108
Harr, L., 35
Harrington, H., 108, 212, 373, 374, 381
Harrington, K., 313, 314
Harris, C., 107, 173
Harris, D., 24
Harris, J., 137
Harris, K., 283, 296
Harris, M., 142, 217, 374
Harris, R., 145, 275
Harris, V., 374
Harrison, B., 381
Harrison, B. J., 382
Harrison, F., 247
Harrison, K., 198
Harrison, P. R., 91

Harrist, A., 242
Hart, D., 51, 213, 256
Harter, S., 7, 210, 211, 212, 215, 217, 241
Hartl, A., 139
Hartl, A. C., 109, 264
Hartley, C., 51, 246
Hartman, S., 23
Hartmann, B., 186
Hartmark, C., 82
Hartney, C., 81
Hartung, C., 350
Haselager, G., 145
Hasemeier, C., 22
Hasin, D., 356
Hasking, P., 379
Hasselhorn, M., 215
Hastings, J., 166
Hastings, P., 87, 92, 372, 378
Hastings, P. D., 30
Hatano, K., 222, 223
Hathaway, J., 290
Hattie, J., 328
Hatzenbuehler, M., 231, 310
Hau, K., 163, 215
Hau, K.-T., 183
Hauser, S., 269, 276
Haushofer, J., 54
Havens, J., 355
Hawes, S., 365
Hawk, L., 351
Hawk, L. W., 91, 244
Hawk, S., 12, 137, 211, 273, 282
Hawk, S. T., 96, 100
Hawkins, A., 206
Hawkins, D. N., 112, 116
Hawkins, J., 351, 352, 363
Hawkins, J. D., 90, 136, 362
Hawkins, K., 198
Hawkins, S., 356
Hay, C., 63, 92
Haydon, A., 287, 296, 349
Haydon, K., 268
Hayes, A., 234
Hayes, K., 312
Haynes, S., 313
Haynie, D., 138
Haynie, D. L., 106
Hays, S., 317
Hayslip, B., 114
Hayward, C., 36, 37, 279, 287
Hayward, G., 111, 112
Hazel, C., 174
Hazel, N. A., 106
He, J., 350, 351, 362, 375, 376, 377
He, J-P., 29
He, X., 87
Heard, H. E., 114
Heath, A., 164, 360
Heath, A. C., 114
Heatherton, T., 215

Heatherton, T. F., 34
Heaven, P., 204, 217
Hebert, K., 265
Hebert, L., 313
Hechinger, F., 159
Heck, D., 134, 225
Heck, R. H., 162
Heckhausen, J., 277, 337, 338, 347
Hedeker, D., 376
Heeren, T., 362
Heffner, V., 198
Heideman, I., 381
Heijboer, A., 245
Heikinheimo, O., 316
Heiland, F. W., 19
Heilbron, N., 143
Heimer, K., 305
Heinze, J., 92, 255
Heinze, J. E., 92
Heirman, W., 107, 206
Heitel, J., 321
Heitzeg, M., 301, 362
Heleniak, C., 92
Helfand, M., 300
Helion, C., 51, 54
Heller, A., 52, 382
Hellner, C., 372
Hellström, C., 199
Helmerhorst, K., 269
Helmond, P., 163
Helms, L., 184
Helms, S., 140, 304, 378
Helsen, M., 276
Helwig, C., 60, 256, 257
Helwig, C. C., 60
Hemler, M., 204
Hemphill, S., 138, 361, 374, 377
Henderson, A., 256
Henderson, C., 114, 363
Henderson, K., 36
Henderson, M., 300, 301, 326
Henderson, S., 116
Hendricks, C., 241, 242
Hendry, L. B., 4
Hennessy, M., 198
Hennig, K., 252
Hennighausen, K., 268
Henrich, C., 254
Henriksen, L., 180, 195, 198, 199, 200, 201
Henry, B., 213
Henry, D., 136, 302, 304
Henry, D. B., 149
Henry, K., 337, 344, 361
Henry, K. L., 15
Hensel, D., 295, 309
Henshaw, S., 315
Hensley, M., 309
Hentges, R., 103
Herbenick, D., 296

Herbers, J. E., 160
Herbert, J., 378
Herbst, J., 305
Herd, T., 117, 260, 261
Herdman, M., 145
Herdt, G., 15, 294
Herge, W., 150
Herman, M., 134, 216, 225, 327, 338
Herman-Giddens, M., 22, 24
Herman-Giddens, M. E., 16
Hernandez, D., 190
Hernandez, L., 142, 204, 247, 248
Hernández, M., 225, 339
Hernández, M. M., 159
Hernandez, P., 119, 327
Hernández-Guzmán, L., 29
Hernández-Valero, M., 37
Heron, J., 294, 300, 301, 363, 377
Herpers, P., 372
Herpertz-Dahlmann, B., 372
Herr, K., 93
Herrera, A., 92
Herrera, C., 89
Herrera, D., 160, 271
Herrera, V., 288, 290
Herrero, L., 46, 52
Herring, A., 296
Hershberg, T., 84
Hershfield, H. E., 210
Herting, J. R., 90
Herting, M. M., 48, 49, 51
Herz, D., 119
Hessel, E., 269, 275, 277
Hessel, E. T., 264
Hetherington, E., 111
Hetherington, E. M., 103, 108, 109, 114, 116
Hetland, J., 145, 146
Hewstone, M., 134, 135, 225
Hiatt, R. A., 35
Hickey, M., 24
Hickman, M., 363
Hicks, B., 299, 301, 359
Hicks, B. M., 136
Hicks, L., 160
Hicks, R., 292
Higgins, J., 306, 314
Highlander, A., 88, 90
Hildick-Smith, G., 356
Hill, D., 296, 305
Hill, J., 301
Hill, J. P., 4
Hill, K., 352
Hill, K. G., 136, 362
Hill, L., 215
Hill, N., 332
Hill, N. E., 173, 332
Hill, P. L., 218
Hill, T., 313
Hiller, R., 115

Hillier, L., 37
Himes, J., 22
Hinduja, S., 204
Hine, T., 11, 73, 180
Hines, M., 234
Hingson, R., 359, 362
Hinnant, J., 248
Hinshaw, S., 318, 372
Hipp, J., 138
Hipwell, A. E., 37
Hiripi, E., 36
Hirsch, B., 277
Hirsch, M., 316
Hirschi, T., 352
Hirvonen, R., 161
Hitti, A., 61
Hiu, C-F., 271
Hixson, K., 234
Hjerm, M., 167
Ho, A., 8, 140
Ho, L., 282
Ho, T. C., 15
Hobbes, M., 10
Hoberman, H., 35
Hock, E., 241
Hockenberry-Eaton, M., 303
Hodge, S. A., 160
Hofer, C., 102, 253
Hofer, M., 60
Hoff, K. A., 212
Hoffer, T., 167, 333
Hofferth, S., 193, 333
Hoffman, A., 225, 235
Hoffman, L., 64
Hoffman, S., 318, 319
Hofkens, T., 332
Hofmann, V., 136, 213, 247
Hogue, A., 138
Hokoda, A., 289
Holas, I., 158, 159
Holcombe, R., 160
Holditch Niolon, P., 290
Holfeld, B., 149, 151, 168
Holland, A., 267
Holland, K., 379
Holland, M., 166
Hollander, D., 305
Hollenstein, T., 9, 25, 95
Holliday, E., 247, 356, 362
Hollist, D. R., 92
Hollon, S., 382
Holmbeck, G., 29, 241, 302, 320
Holmes, C., 92, 147, 261, 269, 301
Holmes, E., 271
Holmgren, H., 192, 204
Holmgren, H. G., 198
Holoyda, B., 206
Holsen, I., 214
Holstein, B., 145, 146, 361, 363
Homer, J., 140
Homma, Y., 311

Hong, J., 143, 148, 149, 338
Hoo, E., 302
Hooimeijer, P., 90
Hook, E., 313
Hooley, J., 56, 350, 382
Hooper, C. J., 47
Hoover, M., 310
Hopmeyer, A., 334
Horan, P., 181
Horiuchi, Y., 199
Horn, A., 255, 256
Horn, E. J., 108
Horn, S. S., 130, 131
Horne, A., 287
Horvat, E. M., 133
Horvat, M., 202
Horvath, G., 16
Horwood, J., 364
Horwood, L., 267, 303, 319, 371
Hostinar, C., 276
Hostinar, C. E., 14, 26
Hou, J., 289
Hou, Y., 100, 106, 115, 273, 333
Houde, O., 52
Houghton, S., 195
Houltberg, B., 7, 238, 250, 253, 254
Houser, J., 288
Houston, S. L., II, 169
Houston, S. M., 47
Houts, R., 195
Hoven, C., 370
Howard, A., 3, 374
Howard, D., 201
Howell, J. C., 136
Hoyle, R., 88
Hoyt, L., 255, 291
Hoyt, L. T., 28, 35
Hoza, B., 273, 278, 279
Hrabosky, J. I., 37
Hranilovich, J. A., 48
Hsieh, H., 287
Hsieh, H.-F., 187
Hu, A. W., 226
Hu, M., 360
Hu, M.-C., 360
Hu, P., 304
Hu, W., 379
Huan, V., 325
Huang, F., 147, 168
Huang, S., 35, 226
Huang, Z., 289
Hubbard, A. D., 54
Hubbard, J., 141, 282
Huckins, J. F., 34
Hudes, E., 288
Hudson, J., 36
Huebner, D., 227
Huebner, E., 382
Huesmann, L. R., 210
Huettel, S., 47
Huey, M., 217

Hughes, D., 87, 168, 224, 225, 226, 227, 228, 234, 338
Hughes, D. L., 216, 224
Hughes, J., 332, 356, 382
Hughes, J. N., 160
Hughes, L., 351
Hughes, L. A., 33
Hughes, R., 309
Hughes, T., 310
Huh, D., 34
Huijts, T., 232, 233, 357
Huitsing, G., 148
Huizenga, H. M., 62, 63, 245
Huizink, A., 92, 352, 357
Hulleman, C. S., 173
Hullenaar, K., 368
Hummer, D. L., 27
Humphrey, T., 290
Humphreys, K., 87, 164, 378
Humphreys, K. L., 15
Hunt, A., 309
Hunter, S., 195, 205
Huntington, C., 290
Huntley, E., 54
Huot, R., 382
Huq, N., 227
Hurd, N., 226
Hurd, N. M., 88, 89
Hurd, Y., 362
Hurdle, D., 234
Hurley, D., 111
Hurley, R., 34
Hurrelmann, K., 84
Hurst, J., 242
Hurt, H., 25, 57, 63, 301
Hurt, T., 228
Hurtig, T., 351
Hurtig, T. M., 33
Hurtig-Wennlöf, A., 35
Husky, M., 351
Hussain, S., 89
Hussey, M., 24
Hussong, A., 8, 110, 144, 292, 352, 359, 360, 361
Hussong, A. M., 115
Huston, A., 161, 337
Huston, A. C., 158, 159
Hutchinson, M., 303
Hutt, S., 187
Hutteman, R., 211
Hutzell, K., 149
Huurre, T., 101
Huynh, V., 88, 227, 228, 259
Hwang, A., 326
Hwang, C., 213
Hwang, N., 184, 328
Hyde, J., 231, 232, 233, 299, 310, 377
Hyde, L., 352, 372
Hyeyoun, H., 271
Hymel, S., 145, 149, 382
Hysing, M., 119, 382, 383

I

Iacono, W., 101, 301, 333, 359
Iacono, W. G., 108, 109, 114, 136
Ialongo, N., 227, 352
Iannotti, R. J., 35
Ibañez, G., 332
Icenogle, G., 2, 9, 17, 47, 54, 57, 62, 63, 64, 84, 245, 246, 301
Ichien, N., 65, 247
Iedema, J., 223
Iida, M., 228
Ikramullah, E., 297
Im, M., 160, 332
Imai-Matsumura, K., 45
Infurna, F., 102, 274
Infurna, F. J., 274
Inhelder, B., 9
Inoff-Germain, G., 353
Insabella, G., 114
Insel, C., 35, 51, 54
Institute of Medicine, 35, 62, 74, 230, 356, 363, 380
Ioannidis, K., 31
Ioverno, S., 311
Ipp, L., 356
Irdam, G., 149
Ireland, M., 37
Irvin, M., 149
Irvine, C., 48
Irwin, C. E., Jr., 37
Irwin, K., 173
Irwin, L., 53
Irwin, M., 29
Isakson, K., 161
Iselin, A. M., 86
Isensee, B., 35, 195
Ispa-Landa, S., 166
Ivanova, K., 114, 279, 282, 304
Ivers, R., 63
Iwamoto, D., 164, 357
Izenstark, D., 191

J

Jaccard, J., 302, 318
Jack, F., 46
Jackson, C., 204, 300
Jackson, D., 47
Jackson, J., 227, 277
Jackson, J. S., 33
Jackson, K., 201, 273, 333
Jackson, K. M., 33, 100, 161
Jackson, L., 193
Jackson, T., 39
Jackson-Newsom, J., 103
Jacobs, J., 4, 188, 189
Jacobs, J. E., 95, 214
Jacobsen, W., 174
Jacobson, K., 109
Jacobson, R., 253

Jacobs-Quadrel, M., 62
Jacobus, J., 362
Jacoby-Senghor, D., 337
Jacques-Tiura, A., 92
Jadva, V., 119
Jaffe, P., 309
Jaffee, S., 319
Jaffee, S. R., 32
Jager, J., 210, 241, 356
Jagers, R., 226
Jaggers, J., 351
Jaggers, J. W., 92
Jahromi, L., 227
Jain, S., 291
Jain, U., 383
Jalanko, E., 316
Jalbrzikowski, M., 53
Jamal, F., 321
James, S., 115
James, W., 310
James-Burdumy, S., 363
Jamieson, J., 190, 202, 203, 328, 383
Jamieson, P., 199
Jamal, F., 321
Jang, B. J., 85
Jang, S., 261
Jang, Y., 187
Janikian, M., 149
Jank, W., 311
Janosz, M., 145, 214, 344
Jansen, B., 63
Jansen, B. R. J., 245
Jansen, K., 372
Jansen, M., 248
Janssen, I., 28
Janssen, S., 46
Janssen, T., 201, 362
Janssens, A., 110
Jaramillo, J., 228
Jaramillo, N., 321
Jarcho, J., 247, 248, 275
Jarcho, J. M., 103, 264
Jarrett, R., 191
Järvelin, M.-R., 360
Jarvis, P., 161
Jaser, S., 383
Jason, L., 363
Jayaram, L., 186
Jayawickreme, E., 190
Jelic, M., 199
Jemal, A., 34
Jemmott, J., III, 303
Jemmott, L., 303
Jen, S., 231
Jenkins, L., 277
Jenner, E., 321
Jenner, L., 321
Jenness, J., 147
Jenness, J. L., 56, 381
Jenni, O. G., 28
Jennings, J., 165

Jennings, W., 374
Jensen, A., 111
Jensen, A. C., 108, 111, 198
Jensen, L., 249
Jensen, L. A., 241
Jensen, M., 90, 225
Jensen, R., 334
Jensen, T., 91, 107
Jensen-Campbell, L., 280
Jeon, S., 117
Jessop, N., 191
Jessor, R., 352, 361
Jessor, S., 352
Jewell, J., 138
Jewett, R., 187
Jeynes, W., 114, 166
Ji, J., 31, 372
Ji, L., 106, 143, 270
Ji, X., 187
Jia, C., 24
Jia, M., 203
Jia, Y., 168, 234
Jiang, D., 287
Jiang, G., 339
Jiang, J., 192
Jiang, X., 360
Jiang, Y., 112, 113, 379
Jih, Y-R., 271
Jiménez, T., 174
Jin, R., 8
Jin, S., 140
Job, V., 244
Jobson, C., 361
Jodl, K., 117
Jodl, K. M., 111, 346
John, O., 212
Johnco, C., 204
Johnson, A., 276
Johnson, B., 77
Johnson, C., 51, 231
Johnson, D. W., 168
Johnson, J., 304, 311
Johnson, M., 314, 344, 345, 346, 347
Johnson, M. D., 268
Johnson, P., 314
Johnson, R., 357
Johnson, R. T., 168
Johnson, S., 170, 187, 190
Johnson, W., 109, 333, 359
Johnston, L., 184, 189, 349, 354, 355, 356, 357, 363, 374
Johnston, N. E., 53
Joiner, T., 271, 376
Joiner, T., Jr., 375, 382
Joiner, T. E., Jr., 381
Jolles, D., 46
Jolles, D. D., 47
Jomro, K., 136
Jones, A., 173
Jones, D., 19
Jones, D. C., 38

Jones, D. J., 88, 90
Jones, H., 363
Jones, J., 266, 363
Jones, J. D., 269
Jones, L., 149
Jones, M., 195, 197, 306, 310, 363
Jones, N., 56, 304
Jones, P. B., 53, 378
Jones, R., 9, 54, 295, 313
Jones, S., 226, 299, 303, 362
Jones, T., 352
Jones, V., 210
Jones Harden, B., 119
Jonkmann, K., 140
Jonsson, L., 205
Joos, C., 23, 26
Jordan, A., 150, 195, 196, 198, 199, 200, 299, 360
Jordan, C., 362
Jordán-Conde, Z., 218
Jorgensen, N., 248
Jose, P., 149, 277
Jose, P. E., 210
Jose, R., 138
Joseph, C., 231
Josephs, R., 190, 202, 203, 328
Joshi, S., 197
Josse, G., 58
Jouriles, E., 136
Joyner, K., 230, 289
Ju, D., 114
Ju, E., 184
Juang, L., 217, 228
Juarascio, A., 38
Judge, B., 378
Jung, J., 19, 195
Jungert, T., 149
Junkin, R., 183
Juonala, M., 35
Juras, R., 321
Jurinec, N., 202
Jurkovic, G., 332
Jussim, L., 169
Juul, A., 24
Juvonen, J., 32, 34, 133, 134, 135, 143, 144, 145, 146, 147, 149, 150, 165, 173, 187, 188, 233, 234, 327, 334
Juzang, I., 314

K

Kaciroti, N., 16
Kackar, H., 256
Kackar-Cam, H., 330
Kadosh, K., 56, 59, 209
Kaess, M., 50
Kaestle, C., 296, 298
Kågesten, A., 300, 321
Kahn, G., 273
Kahn, L. E., 43

Kahn, R., 269, 301
Kahneman, D., 45, 62, 66
Kail, R. V., 46, 47
Kakade, M., 370
Kakihara, F., 243
Kalakoski, V., 223
Kaliher, G., 277
Kalil, A., 328
Kalman, Z., 270
Kam, J., 247
Kambam, P., 245
Kamenetz, A., 84
Kamentz, D., 187
Kamkar-Parsi, K., 287
Kan, E., 90, 91
Kandel, D., 357, 358, 360
Kandler, C., 212
Kane, J., 357
Kang, C., 272
Kang, G., 247
Kang, H., 206
Kang, Y., 187
Kaniušonytė, G., 217
Kann, L., 311
Kannas, L., 161
Kanouse, E., 302
Kansky, J., 242
Kantomaa, M., 164
Kantor, L., 321
Kao, G., 145, 226, 338
Kapetanovic, S., 97
Kaplan, A., 38
Kaplan, J., 92
Kaplan, N., 268
Kaplan, R., 86, 88
Kaplan, S., 15
Kaplow, J., 187, 257
Kaplow, J. B., 258
Kaprio, J., 22, 23, 360, 382
Karageorge, J., 333
Karaman, N. G., 271
Karch, K. M., 164
Karpovsky, S., 270
Karre, J. K., 116
Karremans, J., 132, 141
Karremans, J. C., 132
Karriker-Jaffe, K., 143, 289, 290
Karsay, K., 198
Karver, M., 147
Karvonen, S., 101
Kashy, D., 275
Kata, A., 150
Kataoka, S., 363
Katz, A., 309
Katz, E., 196
Katz, J., 299
Katz, L. F., 89, 369
Katz, M., 82, 84
Katzman, D., 35
Katz-Wise, S., 231
Kaufman, C., 216

Kaufman, J., 174
Kaufman, T., 145, 147, 310
Kaufman-Parks, A., 291
Kawabata, Y., 143, 164
Kay, J., 337
Kayser, A. S., 27
Keane, S. P., 108
Keating, D., 5, 41, 44, 45, 46, 54, 256, 327
Keefe, G., 203
Keel, P. K., 36, 37, 38
Keenan, K., 37, 53
Keijsers, L., 12, 26, 96, 101, 103, 118, 137, 138, 161, 211, 222, 223, 242, 274, 374
Keizer, R., 241, 269
Kelada, L., 379
Kelch, R., 15
Kelleghan, A., 135
Keller, G., 383
Keller, M., 213, 252, 254, 270, 382
Keller, T., 89
Kelley, C., 149
Kelley, M., 225, 303
Kelley, W. M., 34
Kelly, A., 35
Kelly, B., 287, 298
Kelly, B. M., 92, 100, 133, 334
Kelly, S., 161
Kelsey, M., 321
Kempadoo, K., 357
Kendig, S. M., 88
Kendler, K., 351
Keniston, K., 73
Kennard, B., 382
Kenneavy, K., 198
Kennedy, D., 138
Kennedy, D. P., 138
Kennedy, T. M., 92
Kenny, S., 103
Kenyon, D. B., 81
Kerestes, R., 382
Kern, M., 190
Kernic, M., 115
Kerns, K., 266, 269, 291
Kernsmith, P., 205
Kerpelman, J., 302
Kerr, M., 33, 106, 107, 137, 186, 243, 288, 301, 382
Kerslake, J., 150
Kertes, D. A., 91, 311, 383
Keshavan, B., 26
Kessler, R., 8, 36, 351, 382
Kett, J., 11, 79, 82, 84
Kettrey, H., 310
Keyes, K., 189, 356, 357, 360
Keyes, K. M., 28, 29
Keyes, M. A., 136
Khalife, N., 164
Khalis, A., 203
Khan, S., 203

Khoddam, H., 92
Khoddam, R., 363
Khoo, A., 199
Khundrakpam, B., 51
Khurana, A., 25, 63, 150, 299, 301, 343, 360
Kiang, L., 99, 134, 224, 225, 226, 227, 242, 261, 327, 378
Kibler, J., 297
Kidd, S. A., 378
Kiefer, S., 141
Kiehl, K., 372
Kiehl, K. A., 59
Kiekens, G., 379
Kiesner, J., 142
Kieta, J., 374
Kiger, T. B., 336
Kilford, E., 55, 247
Kilford, E. J., 54
Kilgore, S., 167
Killen, J., 36, 37
Killen, M., 60, 61, 234
Killoren, S., 108, 137, 297, 303
Killoren, S. E., 107
Kilpatrick, D., 352
Kim, C. I., 37
Kim, D., 268
Kim, H., 289, 290, 310, 374
Kim, I. J., 30, 32
Kim, J., 137, 197, 225, 233, 234, 336, 361
Kim, J.-I., 326
Kim, M., 326
Kim, M. J., 85
Kim, R. W., 29
Kim, S., 100, 106, 150, 227, 332, 333
Kim, S-I., 326
Kim, S. Y., 115
Kim, T., 225, 255, 257
Kim, Y., 35, 195, 257
Kimonis, E., 365, 370
Kim-Spoon, J., 63, 87, 117, 147, 260, 261, 267, 269, 301
Kindermann, T., 335
King, E., 317
King, K., 226, 372
King, K. M., 92, 99
King, L., 164, 378
King, L. S., 15
King, M. D., 165
King, P., 258, 259, 260, 261
King, P. E., 261
King, R., 37, 242
King, R. B., 88, 101
King, S., 276
King, V., 92, 112, 113, 115, 116, 117
King-Casas, B., 63, 87, 117, 261
Kingsbury, A., 142
Kingsbury, M., 142
Kinney, D., 129

Kins, E., 242
Kipp, H., 372
Kirby, D., 288, 313, 321
Kircanski, K., 15, 381
Kirk, D., 91
Kirkpatrick, L., 268
Kirschenbaum, D. S., 35
Kishor, N., 311
Kistler, M., 215
Kitrossky, L., 165
Kiuru, N., 135, 138, 161, 334, 335
Kiviruusu, O., 101
Kivlighan, K., 142
Klahr, A., 101
Klasen, L., 58
Klassen, R., 325
Klauer, S., 65
Klausner, J., 314
Kleibeuker, S., 46
Kleibeuker, S. W., 47, 58
Klein, D., 351, 358, 362, 375,
    381, 382
Klein, H. W., 34
Klein, J., 158, 317
Klein, V., 303
Kleinepier, T., 90
Kleitman, S., 184
Kliewer, W., 261
Klimes-Dougan, B., 30, 144
Klimstra, T., 213, 222, 223, 241, 372
Klimstra, T. A., 100, 101
Kling, J., 89, 369
Klingberg, T., 47, 51
Klinoff, V. A., 297
Klodnick, V. V., 92
Kloep, M., 4
Klopack, E., 30
Kloska, D., 362
Kloska, D. D., 172
Klostermann, S., 351
Klump, K. L., 19, 36, 37, 38
Knafo, A., 243
Kne, L., 311
Knecht, A., 138
Knifsend, C., 133, 187, 188
Knight, C., 321
Knight, E., 311
Knight, G., 225, 253
Knight, G. P., 99, 106, 225–226
Knight, K., 344
Knight, R. T., 45
Knighton-Wisor, S., 243
Knoester, C., 106
Knoll, L., 63, 247
Knoll, L. J., 50, 59
Knopik, V. S., 16
Knoppick, H., 163
Knowles, A., 90, 91, 314
Knutson, B., 46
Ko, L., 224
Kobak, R., 263, 264, 266, 268

Koball, H., 112, 113
Kobeisy, A. N., 108
Koch, G., 22, 310
Koch, M., 381
Koch, T., 24
Kochel, K., 234
Kochel, K. P., 145
Kochenderfer-Ladd, B., 142, 145, 234
Kochendorfer, L., 269, 291
Koenig, B., 178
Koerner, S. S., 81
Koester, B., 199
Koff, E., 30
Kofler, M., 352
Kogachi, K., 135
Kogan, M., 189
Kogan, S., 228, 360
Kogan, S. M., 30
Kohen, D. E., 114
Kohler, J. K., 119
Kol, K., 332
Kolaric, G., 30
Kolbe, L., 35, 311
Kolburn Kowal, A., 303
Kolla, B., 29
Köller, O., 163, 171
Koller, S., 253
Kollerová, L., 149
Kolobe, T. H., 35
Költő, A., 285, 286
Komro, K., 363
Konarski, R., 129, 279, 281
Koning, I. M., 33
Konold, T., 148, 168
Konstabel, K., 35
Konty, K. J., 35
Koolschijn, P., 245
Koolschijn, P. C., 47, 48
Koot, H., 26, 118, 137, 151, 214, 219,
    221, 253, 254, 365, 366,
    368, 372
Koot, H. M., 26, 100
Kopish, M., 255
Kopf, M., 255
Kordic, T., 204
Korgaonkar, M. S., 51
Korhonen, T., 360
Kornbluh, M., 257
Kornienko, O., 134, 137, 225,
    228, 232
Korol, L., 87
Kosciw, J., 310
Kosinski, M., 213
Kosir, K., 202
Koss, K. J., 115
Kost, K., 315
Kosterman, R., 90, 136
Kotagal, S., 29
Kotchick, B., 117
Kotler, J., 365, 383
Kotov, R., 365, 381
Kottke, M., 313

Kouros, C. D., 241
Koutamanis, M., 202, 217
Kowal, A., 111
Kowal, A. K., 108
Kowaleski-Jones, L., 114
Kowaleski-Jones, P., 304
Koyanagi, A., 147, 379
Kracke, B., 33, 345
Krafft, C., 362
Kraft, M., 178
Krahé, B., 199, 254
Krahn, H., 74, 76
Kramer, J., 300
Kramer, L., 108, 111
Kramer, T., 379
Krauss, S., 217
Krawchuk, L., 325
Kreager, D., 138, 141, 279, 300, 304,
    313, 361, 373
Kreager, D. A., 140, 188
Kretsch, N., 30, 64, 136, 248
Kretschmer, T., 33, 275, 310, 373
Krettenauer, T., 252
Kriegsfeld, L. J., 27
Kriepe, R., 35
Kriston, L., 204
Kroff, S. L., 198
Kroger, J., 218, 223
Krohn, M., 89, 136
Krueger, F., 200
Krueger, R. F., 109
Krull, J. L., 29
Krumer-Nevo, M., 91
Kruse, A., 241
Kruse, M. I., 85
Krygsman, A., 147
Kubiszewski, V., 149
Kubitschek, W., 166
Kuczynski, L., 60
Kuehn, K., 147
Kugler, K., 300
Kuhlman, K., 29, 381
Kuhn, D., 41, 42, 43, 44, 45, 46,
    57, 382
Kuhn, E., 241
Kuhn, E. S., 96
Kuja-Halkola, R., 372
Kuklinski, M., 363
Kulin, H., 22
Kulis, S., 234
Kull, R., 310
Kumpfer, K. L., 120
Kumra, S., 362
Kuncel, N., 336
Kuncel, N. R., 336
Kunkel, D., 197
Kuo, C., 360
Kuo, S. I-C., 108
Kuo, Y-L., 324
Kuosmanen, T., 195
Kuperminc, G., 170, 332

Kupersmidt, J., 201
Kuppens, P., 117
Kuppens, S., 382
Kupper, L., 287, 289, 290
Kurdek, L., 116
Kurdziel, G., 164
Kurlychek, M., 77
Kurtz-Costes, B., 228, 235, 329,
    330, 332
Kushi, L. H., 35
Kuttler, A., 129, 130, 279
Kwok, O., 160
Kwon, D., 362
Kwon, J., 360
Kwon, J.-S., 25
Kwong, A., 377
Kyauk, C. K., 28
Kypri, K., 361

L

Laake, P., 48
Laceulle, O., 244
Lacey, K., 261
Lachman, M., 98
Lachman, P., 289, 290
Lacourse, E., 33, 305
Ladd, G., 141, 142, 143, 145,
    234, 372
Ladd, G. W., 145
Ladewski, B., 116
Laditka, J., 319
Laditka, S., 319
Ladores, S., 321
Ladouceur, C., 28, 56, 203, 375
Ladouceur, C. D., 28, 42, 101, 203
LaFleur, L., 96
Låftman, S. B., 167
La Greca, A., 129, 130, 150, 279, 383
La Greca, A. M., 119, 132, 382, 383
Lahat, A., 60
Lahey, B., 304, 353, 372
Lahiff, M., 297
Lai, B., 150
Lai, T., 145
Lai, X., 253
Laible, D., 276
Laird, R., 96, 101, 107, 144,
    240, 241
Laird, R. D., 96, 241, 270
Laitinen, J., 164
Laje, G., 376
Lakon, C., 138
Lalonde, F., 43
Lam, B., 199
Lam, C., 103, 122, 127, 186, 275
Lam, C. B., 103, 108, 122, 127, 275
Lam, T., 282
Lamb, M., 119, 213
Lambert, H. K., 92
Lambert, L., 361

Lambert, L. E., 160
Lambert, S., 92, 227
Lambert, S. F., 99
Lamborn, S., 114, 137, 225, 335
Lampard, A. M., 34
Landers-Potts, M., 352
Landess, J., 206
Landoll, R., 150
Lane, K. L., 173
Lang, D., 313, 314
Lang, F., 98
Langer, D. A., 382
Langer, L., 299
Langley, J., 212, 361
Långström, N., 368
Laninga-Wijnen, L., 140, 141, 334
Lansford, J., 97, 106, 107, 242, 244, 267, 291, 343, 360, 366
Lansford, J. E., 25, 92, 107, 115, 117, 210
Lansu, T., 132, 139, 140, 141
Lansu, T. A. M., 132
Lantagne, A., 280, 283, 284
Lanthier, R., 277
Lanza, S., 214, 299
Lanzi, R., 321
LaQuea, R., 200
Laraia, B. A., 35
Lara-Ruiz, J., 195
Lardier, D., 92, 93
Laris, B., 321
Larkby, C. A., 92
Larkin, M., 35
la Roi, C., 310
Larsen, B., 51, 52
Larsen, R., 215
Larson, J., 7, 126, 127, 128, 130, 131, 132, 277
Larson, M., 289
Larson, R., 2, 72, 73, 79, 84, 86, 122, 151, 185, 186, 187, 188, 191, 214, 238, 276, 278, 289, 291
Larson, R. W., 191
Larsson, H., 164, 351, 372
Latimer, L. A., 29
Latina, D., 148
Latorre-Martínez, P., 150
Latvala, A., 372
Latzman, N., 290
Lau, J., 247, 271
Laub, J., 371
Laube, C., 50, 51, 64
Lauckhardt, J., 88, 255
Lauharatanahirun, N., 63
Laurent, H., 267
Laursen, B., 29, 95, 96, 99, 101, 109, 138, 139, 151, 185, 217, 237, 238, 240, 241, 264, 270, 273, 276, 280, 288, 304, 329, 335
Laurson, K., 35, 195

Laut, D., 198
Lavagnino, L., 34
Lavell, C., 19, 266
Laviola, G., 204
Laviolette, S., 363
Laviolette, S. R., 361
Lawford, H., 222, 268
Lawford, H. L., 210
Lawler, M., 37, 38
Lawley, K., 202
Lawrence, D., 195
Lawrence, H., 379
Layne, C., 257
Layzer, C., 321
Layzer, J., 321
Le, V., 289
Leadbeater, B., 143, 149, 151, 168
Leaper, C., 232, 233, 310, 334
Leatherdale, S. T., 35
LeBlanc, M., 344
Leckie, G., 377
Leclerc, M., 231
Lee, A., 35
Lee, A. M., 29, 30
Lee, B., 261
Lee, C., 182
Lee, D., 86, 187, 261, 363
Lee, D. Hsieh, 261
Lee, F., 362
Lee, H., 147, 148, 149, 190, 202, 203, 328, 383
Lee, H. J., 37
Lee, J., 29, 87, 183, 184, 297, 299, 304, 344, 352, 363
Lee, J. M., 16
Lee, J. P., 225
Lee, J. S., 37
Lee, K., 56, 59, 350, 382
Lee, K. H., 55
Lee, K. S., 37
Lee, K. T. H., 363
Lee, L., 356
Lee, M., 184, 372
Lee, P., 22
Lee, R., 217, 226
Lee, R. M., 225
Lee, S., 65
Lee, S. S., 109, 110
Lee, S.-Y., 163
Lee, T., 202, 352
Lee, T.-H., 108
Lee, T. K., 118
Lee, T. M., 27
Lee, V., 116, 158, 177, 178, 337
Lee, W., 360
Lee, Y., 38
Leeder, E., 297
Leemis, R., 379
Leen-Feldner, E. W., 32
Leerkes, E., 226, 360
Leets, L., 60

Lefkowitz, E., 138, 240, 260, 300, 303, 304, 313, 361
Lefner, E., 350
Lehman, B., 143
Lehmann, R., 163
Lei, H., 204
Leibenluft, E., 100, 372
Leichtman Research Group, 192
Leichtweis, R., 379, 381
Leitenberg, H., 298
Lejuez, C., 38
Lejuez, C. W., 101, 269
LeMare, L., 144
Lemery-Chalfant, K., 29, 360
LeMoult, J., 378, 381
Lengua, L., 351
Lengua, L. J., 91, 244
Lenhart, A., 192, 202
Lennarz, H., 272
Lenroot, R., 58
Lenroot, R. K., 109
Lens, W., 326
Lenski, A., 325
Lenzi, M., 186, 202, 255, 361
Leon, G., 36
Leonard, G., 55, 248
Leonard, J., 178, 337
Leonard, K., 361
Leonard, P., 201
Leonard, S., 275
Lepage, R., 53
Leppälahti, S., 316
Leppert, J., 199
Lerch, J., 58
Lerner, J., 190, 335
Lerner, J. V., 191
Lerner, R., 2, 171, 187, 188, 190, 191, 244, 277, 335
Lerner, R. M., 161, 168, 244
Leshem, B., 92
Leslie, F., 357
Lessard, J., 361
Lessard, L., 135, 144, 311
Lessard, L. M., 34
Lester, L., 277
Leung, C., 60, 96, 97
Leung, C. W., 35
Leung, C. Y. Y., 96, 97
Leung, J., 247
Leung, J. T., 246
Leung, R., 138, 361
Leventhal, A., 363
Leventhal, T., 89, 90, 91, 92, 93, 112, 305
Leversen, I., 206
Levin, E., 335
Levin, M., 303, 310
Levine, J., 319
Levine, M., 19
Levine, P., 63
Levitt, J., 275, 277

Levitt, M., 275, 277
Levitt, S., 155
Levran, E., 283
Levy, S., 243
Lewin, K., 10
Lewin-Bizan, S., 190
Lewinsohn, P., 33, 289, 375, 379, 381, 382
Lewis, C., 357
Lewis, G., 31, 294, 363
Lewis, J., 51, 169
Lewis, K. S., 133
Lewis, M., 37, 240, 268, 361
Lewis, M. D., 25
Lewis, R., 227–228, 296, 298
Lewis, R. W., 363
Lewis, T., 311
Lewis-Smith, H., 39
Li, D., 145, 199, 242, 360
Li, G., 308, 356
Li, J., 103, 106, 107, 224, 227, 245, 339
Li, J. L., 109
Li, K., 65, 374
Li, L., 140
Li, M., 137
Li, P., 321
Li, R., 32
Li, S., 24, 204
Li, X., 137, 160, 199, 289
Li, Y., 161, 168, 188, 335, 357
Li, Z., 197, 245
Lian, Q., 32
Liang, B., 173
Liauw, I., 210
Lichenstein, P., 372
Lichtenfeld, S., 332
Lichtenstein, P., 164, 351, 372
Lichtwarck-Aschoff, A., 272
Lictenstein, P., 108
Liddle, H., 363
Lieberman, M., 211, 267, 270
Lieberman, M. D., 43, 55, 301
Liem, G., 328
Liew, J., 102
Light, R., 159
Lillard, A., 50
Lim, A., 195
Lim, C., 199, 382
Lim, K., 199, 362
Limber, S., 168
Lin, A., 66
Lin, H., 242
Lin, J., 228
Lin, W., 195
Lincoln, A., 89
Lindberg, L., 295, 296, 312, 315, 321
Lindberg, S., 233, 310
Lindemeier, L., 29
Lindenberg, S., 140, 141, 148, 248, 371

Lindenberger, U., 46
Linden-Carmichael, A., 299
Lindentthal, J., 263
Linder, G., 310
Lindquist, K., 248
Lindsay, M., 90–91
Lindstrom, J. S., 210
Lindstrom Johnson, S., 92, 168, 361
Ling, G., 168
Linton, S., 28, 195
Linton, S. J., 28, 195
Linver, M., 188
Linver, M. R., 114
Linzarini, A., 52
Lipperman-Kreda, S., 361
Lippold, M., 107, 120, 160, 242
Lippold, M. A., 96, 101
Lipsey, M., 374
Liptak, A., 77
Lister-Landman, K., 194
Liston, C., 51
Litalien, D., 277
Litrownik, A., 311
Litt, I., 195
Little, K., 109, 313, 381
Little, S. A., 160
Little, T., 143
Little, T. D., 99
Litwack, S., 139
Liu, C., 60, 147
Liu, D., 107, 214
Liu, G., 147
Liu, J., 60, 91, 96, 145, 242, 311, 360, 372
Liu, W., 291
Liu, X., 370
Liu, Y., 106, 117, 199
Liu, Z., 32
Liverpool, M., 165
Livingston, G., 112, 180, 229
Livingston, J., 310, 361
Livingston, M., 67, 361
Lizotte, A., 319
Lo, A. Y. H., 119
Lobel, A., 199
LoBraico, E., 242
Löckenhoff, C., 213
Lockhart, G., 38, 138
Lodder, G., 145, 275
Loeb, E., 136, 137, 269, 275, 374
Loeb, E. L., 242, 264, 349
Loeber, R., 136, 137, 365, 366, 367, 370, 372, 374
Loehlin, J. C., 109
Loftus, J., 287, 298
Logan, J., 379
Logis, H., 140, 141, 334
Logue, S., 247, 362
Lohman, B., 300, 360
Lohr, M., 319

Loiselle, R., 88, 90
Lollis, S., 144
Lombardi, D. A., 28
Lomniczi, A., 14, 16
Lonardo, R., 368
London, S. J., 360
Loney, B., 365
Long, E., 38, 138
Long, J., 76, 352, 358, 359
Long, J. D., 129
Longest, K., 184
Longmore, M., 280, 282, 291, 298, 299, 303, 368
Longmore, M. A., 280
Longo, G., 261
Lonka, K., 193
Loose, F., 235, 325
Looze, M. E., 232, 233
Lopez, A., 259
Lopez, C., 214, 352
Lopez, E., 136
Lopez-Duran, N., 381
Lopez-Larson, M., 48, 362
Lopez-Tello, G., 250
Lord, H., 137, 185
Lord, S. E., 160
Lorenz, F., 117, 227, 275
Lorenz, R., 64
Lorenzo-Blanco, E., 222, 228
Losoya, S., 102, 371, 375
Loth, K., 35
Loth, K. A., 38
Louden, L., 114
Lougheed, J. P., 9, 25
Loughlin, E. K., 187
Loughlin, G., 356
Loughlin, J., 187
Loughlin, S., 357
Loughran, T., 375
Loughran, T. A., 63, 86
Louis, K., 160
Loukas, A., 96, 160, 356
Loureiro, M., 363
Lourenco, F., 246
Lovato, C., 361, 363
Lovden, M., 46
Loveless, T., 167
Low, C., 270, 272, 292
Low, N., 294
Low, S., 138, 287, 291
Lowe, D., 321
Lowe, K., 332
Lowe, S., 277
Lowery, B., 370
Lowry, R., 299
Loya, J., 314
Lozada, F., 202
Lozano-Blasco, R., 150
Lozier, L., 372
Lu, L. H., 47

Lu, M., 204
Lu, T., 140
Lu, Y., 205, 361
Lu, Z., 168
Luan, S., 254
Lubienski, C., 166
Lubienski, S. T., 166
Lubman, D. I., 53
Luby, J., 353
Lucas, S., 162
Lucas-Thompson, R. G., 15, 115
Luce, K., 195
Luciana, M., 47, 54
Luciano, E., 288, 289
Luciano, E. C., 210
Lucier-Greer, M., 113
Ludden, A., 358
Luder, M., 299
Ludtke, O., 163, 325
Lüdtke, O., 140
Ludwig, J., 89, 368, 369
Luebbe, A., 106, 273, 382
Luengo Kanacri, B. P., 167
Lugtig, P., 352, 360
Luhmann, M., 213
Luking, K., 353
Lukkes, J. L., 15
Luman, M., 165
Luna, B., 51, 52, 53, 54, 245, 360
Lund, T. J., 90
Lundh, L., 148
Lundin Kvalem, I., 214, 215
Lundström, S., 372
Lunetti, C., 117, 244
Lunkenheimer, E., 89
Lunkenheimer, E. S., 115
Luo, F., 290
Luo, T., 134, 140, 142
Lussier, P., 372, 373
Luster, T., 311
Luta, G., 360
Luthar, S., 90, 102, 274, 325, 333, 334, 360, 382
Luthar, S. S., 90, 140, 187, 274
Lutz, A., 186, 334
Luyckx, K., 37, 38, 217, 221, 222, 223, 275, 379
Lydon-Staley, D., 64, 360
Lydon-Staley, D. M., 64, 360
Lynam, D., 33, 59, 301, 365, 372
Lynch, A. D., 92
Lynch, J., 145, 146
Lyndon, S., 150
Lynn, M., 275, 291
Lynne-Landsman, S., 352, 361
Lynne-Landsman, S. D., 32
Lyons-Ruth, K., 268
Lytle, L., 195
Lytle, L. A., 29

M

Ma, J., 34
Ma, M., 297
Ma, Y., 332
Maas, I., 135
Maas, M. K., 105
Määttä, S., 329
Maaz, K., 163
Mabbe, E., 96, 242
Mac Cárthaigh, S., 194
Maccoby, E., 103, 104, 108, 115, 116, 117
Macdonald, J., 109
MacDougall, J., 310
Macdowall, W., 296, 298
Mac Giollabhui, N., 381
Maciejewski, D., 26, 214
Maciejewski, D. F., 26
Mackey, A., 337
Mackillop, J., 360
MacLehose, R. F., 34
MacLellan, S., 65
Macleod, J., 294
Macmillan, R., 336
MacMurray, J., 304
MacPhail, C., 313
MacPherson, L., 164
Madan, A., 92
Madan Morris, A., 291
Madden, M., 202
Madden, P. A., 114
Madden-Derdich, D., 275
Madigan, S., 198, 205
Madjar, N., 129
Madkour, A., 297, 300, 301, 302
Madkour, A. S., 297, 300, 301
Madon, S., 12, 169
Madsen, S., 263, 264, 266, 287
Madsen, S. D., 74
Maeir, A., 165
Maes, H., 351
Maes, J., 214
Maes, M., 145, 275, 353
Mäestu, J., 35
Mager, W., 374
Maggs, J., 30, 184, 349, 362, 372
Magis-Weinberg, L., 53, 63, 247
Magnussen, C., 35
Magnusson, B., 299
Magnusson, D., 33
Magnusson, J., 285, 286
Magson, N., 204
Maheux, A., 204
Mahler, A., 91, 372
Mahoney, J., 137, 173, 185, 186, 188, 189, 190
Mahoney, J. L., 187
Maïano, C., 214
Maimon, D., 92
Main, M., 268

Majeno, A., 227
Mak, H. W., 105
Makara, K. A., 129
Makaruk, K., 149
Makel, M. C., 163
Makino, K., 317
Malachuk, O., 338
Malamut, S., 134, 135, 140, 142
Malanchuk, O., 327, 346
Malcolm, L. R., 297
Maldonado-Molina, M., 374
Malek, M., 165
Mali, L., 134, 135
Mali, L. V., 92, 100
Malin, H., 210
Malinauskienė, O., 217
Malley, P., 74, 75, 184, 189, 349,
   354, 355, 356, 357, 362,
   363, 374
Malley Olsen, E., 311
Malloy, L. C., 77
Malone, P., 371, 374
Manago, A., 202
Manasse, S., 38
Mancini, J. A., 113
Mandara, J., 106, 216, 225
Mandl, R., 245
Mangino, A., 60
Manke, B., 109
Manley, D., 377
Manlove, J., 119, 297, 313, 314, 319
Manly, J., 291
Mann, F., 64, 212, 372
Mann, F. D., 63, 136
Mannering, A., 120
Mannheim, K., 10
Manning, W., 280, 282, 291, 298,
   299, 303, 368
Manning, W. D., 280
Mansukhani, M., 29
Manzoni, O., 362
Marbell, K., 332
Marceau, K., 16, 33, 100
March, J., 382
Marchand, A., 228, 327, 338
Marchante, M., 150
Marcia, J., 221
Marcoen, A., 43
Marcus, D., 365
Marcus, S., 8, 382
Marczak, M., 99
Marecek, J., 134
Mareĝek, R., 55
Margola, D., 331
Margolin, G., 92, 101, 114, 276
Marin, B., 288
Mariner, C., 319
Marion, D., 151, 335
Markey, C., 200
Markey, P., 200
Markiewicz, D., 287

Markovic, A., 50
Markowitz, A. J., 114
Markowitz, L., 314
Marks, A., 226
Marks, H. M., 173
Marks, J., 35, 138
Markstrom, C., 5, 76, 78, 79, 81,
   224, 227
Markus, H., 209
Marold, D., 212
Marques, M., 37, 38
Marquet, M., 277
Marrero, M., 107, 240, 241
Marroquin, Y., 333
Marsee, I., 115
Marsee, M. A., 241, 270
Marsh, A., 372
Marsh, H., 147, 162, 163, 183, 184,
   214, 215, 328, 332
Marsh, H. W., 163
Marsh, P., 140, 241, 268, 269
Marshal, M., 310
Marshal, M. P., 310
Marshall, J., 119
Marshall, L., 303
Marshall, S., 204, 217
Marshall, S. W., 67
Marshall, W., 18, 21
Marsiglia, F., 226, 234
Marston, E., 266
Marti, C. N., 35
Martin, A., 91, 168, 328
Martin, C., 141, 310
Martin, C. L., 232
Martin, D., 301
Martin, G., 203, 271, 376, 379
Martin, J., 104, 315, 316
Martin, M., 6, 96, 104, 115, 227,
   245, 361
Martin, M. J., 95, 115, 267
Martin, N. C., 150
Martin, P., 227–228
Martin, R., 51, 178
Martin, R. E., 54
Martin, S., 287, 289, 290
Martin, S. B., 35
Martinez, A., 333
Martínez, M., 96, 249
Martínez, M. L., 96
Martinez-Ferrer, B., 150, 289, 351
Martinez-Fuentes, S., 226
Martino, S., 197, 302
Martins, S., 360
Martin-Santos, R., 362
Martin-Storey, A., 149, 227, 233,
   290, 310
Martyniuk, U., 198, 299
Martz, M., 362
Martz, M. E., 172
Marucci-Wellman, H., 28
Marusak, H., 242

Marx, R., 310
Masarik, A., 361
Masarik, A. S., 110
Maslowsky, J., 28, 29, 54, 184, 349,
   351, 356
Mason, S. M., 37
Mason, W., 137, 217, 351, 360
Mason, W. A., 33
Mason-Singh, A., 8
Masselink, M., 217
Massoglia, M., 374
Masten, A., 76, 282, 352
Masten, A. S., 213
Masten, C., 211, 228, 248, 267
Masten, C. L., 43, 53, 56
Masten, S. V., 67
Master, A., 347
Masters, S., 234
Mastro, S., 19, 266
Mastrotheodoros, S., 103
Masucci, M., 257
Mata, J., 252
Matas, L., 266
Mateos-Pérez, E., 205
Mathews, C., 311
Mathias, J., 289, 290
Mathieson, L. C., 144
Matjasko, J., 6, 186, 187
Matsuba, M., 253
Matsui, M., 50
Mattes, E., 300
Matthews, T., 92, 107
Matthys, W., 109
Mattingly, M. J., 88
Matusko, N., 33
Maughan, B., 33, 352, 365
Maulana, R., 334
Mauras, C., 243
Maxwell, E. C., 48
Mayberry, M., 178
Mayer, K., 311
Mayers, R., 258
Mayes, L., 142, 266
Mayeux, L., 141, 288
Maynard, R., 318, 319
Mayo, N., 363
Mays, D., 187, 360
Mazza, G. L., 99
Mazzardis, S., 186, 202
Mazzareillo, A., 341
Mazzarella, E., 59, 247
Mazzer, K., 28, 195
Mazziotta, J. C., 43
Mazzone, A., 149
McAdams, T., 352
McAdams, T. A., 103
McAnally, H., 200
McArthur, B. A., 114
McAuley, E., 195
McBride, C., 302

McBride Murry, V., 302, 304
McCabe, K., 187
McCabe, M., 36
McCabe, M. P., 38
McCabe, S., 355, 356
McCallum, D., 334
McCarley, K., 37
McCarthy, W. J., 361
McCarty, C., 351
McCauley Ohannessian, C., 101
McClean, S. A., 199
McClelland, S., 294, 295, 299
McClintock, M., 15, 294
McClung, G., 381
McClure, E., 100
McClure, S., 245
McClure-Tone, E., 378
McConnachie, A., 119
McConnell, K., 361
McConnell, M., 311
McCord, J., 137
McCormick, C. M., 15
McCormick, E., 12, 54, 56
McCormick, M., 66, 92
McCormick, M. J., 66
McCormick, S., 29
McCrae, R., 212, 213
McCreath, H., 227
McCreath, H. E., 29
McCurdy, A., 230, 309
McDade, T., 291
McDaniel, B., 61, 106, 238, 250,
   251, 252, 253, 254, 255, 273
McDermott, E., 134, 226, 228
McDonald, J., 297
McDonald, K., 143
McDonough-Caplan, H., 351
McElhaney, K., 7, 140, 142, 237,
   239, 240, 241, 264, 266,
   268, 269
McElwain, A., 302
McFarland, C., 241, 268
McFarland, F., 140, 269
McGee, E. O., 169
McGee, R., 213
McGill, R., 225
McGill, R. K., 234
McGinley, M., 138
McGloin, J., 138, 247
McGovern, P., 363
McGrady, P. B., 170
McGue, M., 101, 108, 109, 114, 136,
   301, 333, 359
McGuigan, K., 363
McGuire, S., 109
McHale, S., 99, 102, 103, 108, 111,
   122, 127, 134, 159, 173, 186,
   188, 225, 226, 232, 233,
   234, 275, 278, 291
McHale, S. M., 101, 103, 107, 108,
   122, 127, 233, 234, 275

McIntosh, A., 248
McIsaac, C., 7, 279, 281, 282, 283, 284, 285, 287, 288, 289
McKay, B., 160
McKellar, S., 327, 338
McKenney, K., 283
McKenney, S., 234
McKenny, M., 226
McKernan, C. J., 15
McKinney, K., 32
McKinnon, B., 368
McKone, K., 19, 31
McKone, K. M., 23
McLachlan, K., 77
McLanahan, S., 116, 291, 337
McLaughlin, B., 174
McLaughlin, K., 92, 147, 351, 360, 381, 382
McLaughlin, K. A., 56, 92, 231
McLean, K., 223, 276
McLean, R., 242
McLean, S. A., 36, 37, 38
McLeod, D., 187
Mcleoud, J., 300, 301
McLeroy, K., 303
McLoyd, V., 86, 88, 226, 336
McLoyd, V. C., 184
McMahon, R., 365
McMahon, S., 261
McMahon, S. D., 173
McMahon, T., 334
McMorris, B., 301, 310, 379
McMorris, B. J., 85
McNaughton Reyes, H., 290, 291
McNaughton Reyes, H. L., 291
McNealy, K., 53, 267
McNeely, C., 296
McNelles, L., 270, 273
McNulty, J., 313
McNulty, T., 91, 304, 370
McPhie, M. L., 35
McQuade, J., 142
McQuillan, G., 314
McRae, C., 115
McRee, A., 296
McRee, A-L., 118, 349
McRitchie, S., 195
McRoy, R. G., 119
McShane, L., 46
Mead, M., 11, 126
Meade, C., 304
Meadows, S., 377
Meadows-Oliver, M., 319
Meca, A., 222, 225, 228
Mechammic, M., 99
Mednick, S., 309, 372
Meece, D., 190
Meeks Gardner, J., 199
Meerkerk, G., 203
Meerkerk, G.-J., 203
Meesters, C., 378

Meeus, W., 12, 26, 90, 100, 101, 118, 120, 211, 213, 214, 219, 220, 221, 222, 223, 241, 242, 271, 273, 275, 276, 282, 291, 296, 351, 368, 374, 382
Meeus, W. H., 132
Meeus, W. H. J., 26, 100, 101, 102, 128
Mega, C., 324
Mehari, K., 146
Mehari, K. R., 92
Mehta, C., 127, 133, 134
Mehus, C., 379
Meier, A., 186, 299
Meijer, S., 296
Meisel, S., 144, 361
Meisel, S. N., 244
Mejia, Y., 99, 226
Mejia, Y. C., 226
Melanson, S., 335
Melas, P., 357
Melby, J., 337
Melching, J., 241
Melde, C., 136
Meldrum, R., 188
Melis, M., 362
Melkevik, O., 214
Mello, S., 187, 326
Mello, Z., 228
Mellor, R., 313
Meltzer, L. J., 146
Meltzoff, A., 327, 347
Memmert, D., 45
Memmott, M., 115
Memmott-Elison, M., 206, 242, 244, 254
Menachemi, N., 66
Menaghan, E., 304
Mendelson, T., 169
Mendez, J., 321
Mendle, J., 19, 22, 23, 24, 25, 30, 31, 33, 300, 301, 304, 381, 382
Mendoza, R., 378
Menezes, I., 256
Meng, X., 24
Mennecke, B., 218
Menning, C. L., 116
Menon, M., 234
Mensah, F. K., 23
Menzer, M., 145
Menzies, L., 51
Mercado, P., 357
Mercer, C., 296, 298
Mercer, D., 363
Mercer, N., 220, 374
Merchant, J. S., 43
Merchant, M., 383
Mereish, E., 274, 310
Merikangas, K., 8, 29, 350, 351, 362, 375, 376, 377

Merikangas, K. R., 351
Merkas, M., 103
Merlo, J., 145, 146
Mermelstein, R. J., 376
Merrick, M., 291
Merrick, S., 268
Merrill, B., 193
Merrin, G., 143, 310
Merskin, D., 29
Merten, D., 141
Meruelo, A., 362
Mervielde, I., 212
Merz, E. C., 87, 168
Merz, J., 365, 372
Mesch, G., 133
Messersmith, E., 173, 180, 182, 183, 184, 344, 349
Meter, D., 136, 149, 192, 193
Metz, G. A. S., 47
Metzger, A., 60, 254, 255, 258
Metzler, C., 147
Meuss, W., 137
Meuwese, R., 49, 142, 247, 254
Meyer, A., 157
Meyer, H., 51
Meyer, I., 310
Meyer, R., 225
Meyers, J., 360
Mezulis, A., 273, 377, 378, 379
Michael, A., 346
Michaud, P., 299
Michl, L., 381
Michou, A., 326
Mickus, M., 277
Middlestadt, S., 35
Midgley, C., 160, 161, 325
Miech, R., 349, 354, 355, 356, 357
Miernicki, M., 144, 270
Miernicki, M. E., 55
Miettunen, J., 360
Mikami, A., 202, 203, 204, 326
Miklikowska, M., 87, 167, 254
Mikulich-Gilbertson, S., 362
Mikuška, J., 200
Milam, A., 261, 361
Milbrath, C., 282
Milburn, M., 339
Miles, B., 120
Miles, J., 358
Milfont, T. L., 210
Milich, R., 374
Milkie, M. A., 103
Miller, A., 204, 379, 381
Miller, B., 163, 164, 303
Miller, B. A., 100
Miller, C., 111, 234, 381
Miller, D., 331
Miller, D. I., 48
Miller, E., 289, 291, 376
Miller, G., 92, 227
Miller, G. E., 92

Miller, J., 311, 337
Miller, K., 276, 303, 304
Miller, L., 258
Miller, N., 79, 84
Miller, S., 289, 374
Miller, T., 360
Miller, W., 296, 298, 313
Miller-Cotto, D., 225
Miller-Johnson, S., 58
Miller-Tejada, S., 225
Milligan, C., 311
Milliren, C. E., 91
Millner, A., 53
Mills, B., 63
Mills, C., 212, 330
Mills, K., 63, 194, 269, 372
Mills, K. L., 43, 49, 53, 54
Mills, M., 114, 304
Millsap, R., 282
Millsap, R. E., 33
Mills-Koonce, W., 230, 309
Millstein, S., 306
Millstein, S. G., 314
Milne, B., 373, 374
Milnitsky-Sapiro, C., 96
Milojevich, H., 371
Milojevich, H. M., 105
Miltimore, S., 375
Mimiaga, M., 231
Minas, J., 337
Minchin, J., 149
Minguez, M., 321
Minor, K., 167
Miranda-Chan, T., 89, 277
Miranda-Dominguez, O., 53
Mireles-Rios, R., 250, 314
Mirpuri, S., 225
Mischel, W., 35, 325
Mishali, M., 204
Mishkin, A., 193
Mishna, F., 149
Missotten, P., 277
Mistry, R., 361
Mistry, R. S., 118, 170
Mitchell, C., 216
Mitchell, E., 34, 35, 195
Mitchell, J., 195
Mitchell, K., 149, 205, 227, 296, 298
Mitchell, K. J., 195, 206
Miu, A., 144, 190, 197, 328, 373
Miyawaki, T., 50
Mizuno, K., 45
Mlawer, F., 141
Mobasser, A., 63, 269
Modecki, K., 57, 149, 187, 194, 372
Modecki, K. L., 63, 65
Modell, J., 71, 72, 73, 84
Modi, H., 32, 147
Modin, B., 167
Moe, S. G., 29

Moed, A., 102
Moffitt, T., 33, 92, 105, 108, 173, 212, 213, 217, 244, 319, 352, 365, 368, 370, 371, 372, 373, 374, 381
Moffitt, T. E., 92, 107
Mohanty, A., 56, 304
Mohr, P., 35, 138
Mohr-Jensen, C., 372
Moilanen, I., 351
Moilanen, K., 160, 244, 372
Molcho, M., 92, 357
Molgora, S., 331
Molina, B., 372
Molina, B. S. G., 164
Molina, G., 318
Mollborn, S., 194, 319
Mollen, C., 312
Möller, I., 199
Molloy, L., 279
Molloy, L. E., 129, 214
Molnar, B. E., 93
Moltisanti, A., 357
Monahan, K., 15, 64, 138, 142, 161, 183, 184, 195, 198, 246, 247, 248, 288, 299, 351, 372, 373, 374, 383
Monahan, K. C., 63, 92
Mond, J., 215, 216
Moneta, G., 188, 214
Monroe, S., 289, 382
Monshouwer, K., 352, 362
Monsour, A., 211
Montgomery, M., 279, 281, 283, 311
Monti, J., 32, 57, 147, 353, 381
Monti, M. M., 53
Montor, P. R., 46, 52
Montoro, J. Medina, 225
Montoya, J., 204
Moody, J., 279, 304
Moon, U., 193, 333
Moons, P., 37, 38
Moore, C., 141
Moore, E., 191
Moore, J., 261
Moore, J. P., 261
Moore, K., 298, 321
Moore, M., 174
Moore, M. R., 115
Moore, N., 306
Moore, S., 19, 29, 147, 300, 326
Moore, S. R., 30
Moore, T., 363
Moore, W., III, 248
Mora, M., 37, 198
Morales, L. S., 34
Morales-Chicas, J., 32, 165
Moran, P., 365
More, D., 202
Moreau, N., 285, 286
Moreno, M., 28, 203

Morgan, A., 92
Morgan, J., 56
Morgan, J. E., 110
Morgan, J. K., 101
Morgan, M., 196
Morgano, E., 135
Mori, C., 205
Mori, I., 338
Morin, A., 145, 214, 277, 325, 328
Morin, A. J. S., 163
Morisi, T., 181
Morisky, D., 298
Morris, A., 7, 61, 106, 238, 250, 251, 252, 253, 254, 255, 273
Morris, J., 190
Morris, M., 382
Morris, N., 20
Morris, Z., 327
Morrisey, M., 66
Morrison, D., 319
Morrison, K. M., 29, 195
Morrow, A., 343
Morrow, B., 312
Morrow, J., 37
Mortelmans, D., 117
Mortenson, E., 174
Mortimer, J., 86, 181, 182, 183, 184
Mory, M., 129
Moser, U., 170
Mosteller, F., 159
Motl, R., 195
Mott, A., 149
Mott, F., 304
Mott, F. L., 129
Motta-Mena, N. V., 27, 55
Motti-Stefanidi, F., 87, 99, 134
Mõttus, R., 212
Motz, R., 174
Moua, M., 225
Mounts, N., 137, 249, 335
Mounts, N. S., 116
Mouratidis, A., 326
Mouw, T., 134
Moya, J., 46
Mozley, M., 91
Mroczek, D., 244
Mroczkowski, A., 226, 338
Mrug, S., 91, 92, 279, 291, 362
Mucci, L., 290
Mueller, A., 135, 310, 380
Muenks, K., 324
Muhleman, D., 304
Mukherjee, P., 134
Mulder, M., 53
Mulgrew, K., 199
Mulhall, P., 337
Mulkeen, P., 276
Mullarkey, M., 202, 203
Mullen, M., 261
Muller, C., 135, 140, 187
Müller, C., 136

Müller, C. M., 247
Müller-Oehring, E., 362
Mulligan, R., 164
Mulsant, B., 376
Mulut, O., 187
Mulvey, E., 174, 246, 248, 365, 371, 372, 375
Mulvey, E. P., 63, 86
Mulvey, K., 149
Mulvey, K. L., 61, 234
Mumford, E., 289, 291
Mun, C., 360
Munafò, M., 363
Munakata, Y., 245
Munn-Chernoff, M., 351
Munniksma, A., 134
Muñoz, M., 19
Munson, S., 34
Murayama, K., 326, 332
Murchison, G., 231
Murdock, K., 202
Murdock, T., 160, 334
Murphy, B., 253
Murphy, L., 66
Murphy, R., 34, 35, 195
Murray, A. L., 164
Murray, D., 36
Murray, G., 164
Murray, H., 38
Murray, J., 136, 248
Murray, K., 243
Murray, S. B., 37, 38
Murray-Close, D., 142
Murre, J., 46
Murry, V., 106, 120, 227, 228
Murty, V., 51
Murty, V. P., 53
Musial, T., 247
Musselman, S. C., 53
Must, A., 22
Mustanski, B., 91, 311, 383
Mustanski, B. S., 23
Mustard, C., 89
Mustillo, S., 287
Musu-Gillette, L., 167
Mychasiuk, R., 47
Myers, J., 263
Myers, K., 317
Myers, M., 374
Myers, T., 92

N

Na, J., 203
Nadeem, E., 30, 338
Nader, P., 195
Nagaoka, J., 336
Nagata, J. M., 37, 38
Nagel, B., 362
Nagel, B. J., 48, 51

Nagengast, B., 163, 183, 214, 326, 328
Nagin, D., 365, 373
Nagoshi, J., 226
Nagy, G., 326, 336
Nagy, N., 325
Nahapetyan, L., 358
Nair, R. L., 100, 117
Nalipay, M., 242
Nangle, D., 265, 283
Nansel, T., 189
Napolitano, C. M., 170
Nappo, S., 361
Nardos, B., 47, 54
Narr, R., 136, 137, 374
Narr, R. K., 349
Nash, K., 182
Nasir, N., 327
Nasrallah, N., 362
National Campaign to Prevent Teen and Unplanned Pregnancy, 315
National Center for Education Statistics, 82, 153, 157, 174, 175, 176, 183, 339, 341, 343, 370
National Center for Health Statistics, 368
National Center for Juvenile Justice, 367, 368
National Commission on Social, Emotional, and Academic Development, 155
National Conference of State Legislatures, 118
National Research Council, 35, 62, 84, 182, 230
National Runaway Safeline, 118
Natsuaki, M., 23, 287, 289, 377
Natsuaki, M. N., 30
Neal, C., 324
Neal, C. W., 35
Neal, J., 140
Neblett, E., 140, 261
Neblett, E., Jr., 86
Needham, B., 34, 135
Neel, C., 118, 335
Neemann, J., 282
Negriff, S., 23, 30, 31, 32, 33, 352, 372
Negru-Subtirica, O., 221
Neiderhiser, J., 23, 111, 377
Neiderhiser, J. M., 108, 109
Neill, J., 174
Nejad, H., 328
Nelemans, S., 7, 161, 211, 214, 215, 219, 221, 222, 242
Nelis, S., 353
Nelson, C. A., 49
Nelson, E., 100, 247, 248, 275, 367, 378
Nelson, E. E., 53, 55, 103, 264

Nelson, I. A., 180
Nelson, J., 261, 267
Nelson, J. M., 261
Nelson, L., 66
Nelson, L. J., 74, 222, 260
Nelson, M., 51, 199
Nelson, S., 226, 358
Nelson, T., 116
Neppl, T., 275, 360
Neppl, T. K., 117
Nesbit, K. C., 35
Nesdale, D., 144, 266, 289
Nesi, J., 204, 280
Ness, A., 294
Neubauer, S. A., 129
Neuenschwander, M., 345
Neufeld, S., 31
Neumann, A., 214
Neumann, D., 327
Neumann, M., 163
Neumark-Sztainer, D., 34, 35, 36, 37, 38, 39, 198, 215, 216, 310
Nevell, A. M., 362
Neventsal, O., 165
Newbury, J., 92, 105, 173, 368
Newcomb, A., 273, 284
Newman, B., 8, 131
Newman, J., 199
Newman, K., 174, 369
Newman, P., 8, 131
Newsome, J., 372
Neyt, B., 6
Ng, F. F.-Y., 12
Ng, M., 382
Ng-Mak, D., 92
Ngo, V., 374
Nguyen, H., 247, 287
Nguyen, H. N. T., 36
Nguyen, J., 224
Nguyen, Q., 369
Niaura, R., 142, 360
Nic Gabhainn, S., 24
Nick, E., 150
Nickleach, D. C., 35
Nickodem, K., 187
Nicolson, N. A., 27
Nicotra, E., 142
Nie, Q., 199
Niederkrotenthaler, T., 381
Nielsen, J., 381
Nielson, M., 253
Nieuwenhuis, J., 90
Niggli, A., 325
Nikken, P., 38, 199
Nilsson, K. W., 199
Nishina, A., 108, 141, 145, 146, 147, 165, 169, 173, 225, 229
Niu, L., 140
Niwa, E. Y., 216
Nix, R., 242

Nixon, E., 37, 38
Noack, P., 328
Noah, A., 297
Noakes, M., 273
Noble, K. G., 51, 87, 168
Nock, M., 378, 379
Noftle, E., 214
Noguchi, K., 50
Nogué, S., 362
Nogueira Avelar e Silva, R., 300, 302
Noh, A., 326
Nolen-Hoeksema, S., 381
Noll, J., 311
Noll, J. G., 105
Nolle, K., 173
Noller, P., 276
Nomaguchi, K. M., 103
Noor, N., 37
Norberg, K., 363
Norman, R., 147
Norman, T., 247
Noroña, A. N., 110
Norona, J., 266, 283
North, E., 140
North, K., 146
Norton, E., 140
Norton, R., 63
Norwalk, K., 371
Nosko, A., 268
Noto, A., 361
Nottelmann, E., 353
Nottingham, K., 107
Novak, J., 290
Novilla, L., 299
Novilla, M., 299
Novoa, A., 227
Nucci, L., 60, 96
Nuñez, A., 176
Nurius, P., 209
Nurmi, J., 138, 223, 325, 329
Nurmi, J. E., 135, 138, 223, 334, 335, 376
Nurnberger, J., 300
Nusslock, R., 92
Nuttall, A., 299
Nydegger, L., 136
Nykiforuk, C., 363
Nylund-Gibson, K., 225, 229

O

Oakes, J., 161, 162
Oakley, D., 312
Oar, E., 204
Obeid, N., 36
Obeidallah, D., 33
Oberlander, S., 311
Oberle, E., 187
Oberski, D., 213
Obradovic, J., 352

Obradović, J., 76
Obront, E., 317
Obsuth, I., 268
Ocean, M., 89
Ochner, C., 39
Ochsner, K. N., 35, 51, 54
Odgers, C., 88, 92, 360
Odgers, C. L., 92, 202
Odudu, C., 107
OECD, 341, 342
Oelsner, J., 160
Oesterle, S., 351, 363
Oetting, E., 337
Oettinger, G., 184
Offer, S., 106
Office of Juvenile Justice and Delinquency Prevention, 367
Ofner, S., 314
Ogawa, J., 267
Ogbu, J., 133
Ogle, J. P., 36
Oh, H., 147, 379
Oh, S. M., 37
Oh, S. W., 37
Ohannessian, C., 100, 202, 215
Ohannessian, C. M., 102
Ohlson, B., 282
Oi, K., 326
Oi-yeung Lam, B., 184
Ojeda, M., 204, 205
Okado, Y., 372
Okazaki, S., 339
Okdie, B., 193
Okeke, N., 289
Okeke-Adeyanju, N., 329, 330, 332
Okonofua, J., 170
Olatokun, W., 204
Oldehinkel, A., 273, 275, 378
Oldehinkel, A. J., 217
Olfson, M., 376
Olino, T. M., 17, 32, 53, 54
Oliva, A., 107, 241, 242
Oliva, E., 358, 359
Oliver, B. R., 33
Olmstead, S., 283
Olmsted, M., 38
Olson, C., 200
Olson, K. R., 231
Olson, L., 344
Olsson, C., 109, 377, 381
Olszewski-Kubilius, P., 163
Olvera, N., 37
Oman, R., 303, 360
Omer, H., 204
Omey, E., 6
Onatsu, T., 325
O'Neil, S., 51
Onofrio, B., 304
Onofrio, B. M., 33, 114, 115
Oosterhoff, B., 60, 187, 254, 255, 257, 258

Opaleye, E., 361
Opara, I., 92
Op de Macks, Z. A., 27
Opdenakker, M., 334
Openshaw, A., 200
Oppenheimer, C., 382
Oppenheimer, C. W., 101, 106, 381
Oransky, M., 134
Orbell, S., 313
Orben, A., 193
Orchowski, L., 290
Orcutt, H., 352
Ordaz, S., 54, 87, 378, 381
Ordaz, S. J., 54
Orihuela, C. A., 91
Orlando, M., 362
Ormel, J., 244, 273, 357, 371, 378
Ormrod, R., 149
Orobio de Castro, B., 256, 327
Orpinas, P., 287, 289, 358
Orr, D., 295
Orr, M., 321
Ortega, F. B., 35
Orth, U., 213, 214, 216, 217, 288, 289
Ortiz, J., 352
Orue, I., 290
Osborne, M., 195
Osgerby, B., 73, 180
Osgood, D. W., 4, 102, 111, 129, 141, 181, 184, 188, 189, 214, 346, 349, 373, 374
Oshri, A., 360
Oslak, S., 37
Öslund, C., 199
Osmont, A., 52
Osswald, K., 248
Osterman, M., 315, 316
Oswald, T., 248
Osypuk, T., 89, 369
Osypuk, T. L., 89
Otsuki-Clutter, M., 106, 224, 226
Ott, M., 309, 321
Ott, M. A., 314
Otten, R., 360
Ou, S., 255
Oudekerk, B., 140
Oudekerk, B. A., 167
Ouellette, R., 170
Ouimet, M., 65
Ouimet, M. C., 65
Overbeek, G., 30, 109, 198, 203, 268, 286, 301, 303, 304
Overbye, K., 52, 56
Overgaauw, S., 58
Overpeck, M., 189
Owen, M., 267
Owens, A., 165
Owens, E., 318
Owens, S., 378
Owens, S. A., 379, 380
Owotomo, O., 54, 356

Oxford, M., 319
Oyserman, D., 338
Oz, A., 165
Ozbardakci, N., 105, 371
Ozcan, M., 184
Özdemir, M., 87, 107
Özdemir, S., 310
Ozdemir, S. B., 32
Özdemir, Y., 173
Ozer, E. J., 28, 316

P

Paasch, K., 167
Pabian, S., 150
Paceley, M., 231
Pacella, M., 136
Pachucki, M., 255
Paciello, M., 291
Paclopoulos, V., 134
Padgett, J., 216
Padilla, B., 217
Padilla, J., 108
Padilla Paredes, P., 378
Padilla-Walker, L., 96, 150, 192,
    195, 200, 204, 206, 242,
    244, 253, 254, 277, 324
Padilla-Walker, L. M., 80, 108,
    111, 253
Padilla-Walker, L. P., 118
Padmanabhan, A., 54, 245
Pagani, L., 145
Pagliaccio, D., 353
Paglisotti, T., 291
Pahl, K., 134, 225
Pahlke, E., 333
Paik, A., 305
Paikoff, R., 27, 29, 302, 320
Pain, E., 301
Paino, S., 378
Pál, J., 132
Paladino, M., 203
Palardy, G., 178
Palladino, G., 73
Pallesen, S., 194
Pallock, L., 114
Palma Zamora, J., 187
Palmer, A., 360
Palmer, C. A., 258
Palmer, M., 296, 298
Palmer, N., 310
Palmeroni, N., 37, 38
Palmgren, C., 62
Pan, Y., 147
Pancer, M., 257
Pancer, S., 256
Pancer, S. M., 256
Papadakis, A., 265
Papadakis, J. L., 27
Papadakis, S., 35
Papandonatos, G., 142

Papillo, A., 319
Parada, R., 147
Pardini, D., 136, 137, 365, 374
Parekh, J., 321
Parent, S., 109, 110, 362
Parente, M., 189, 190
Pariante, C. M., 107
Parides, M., 38
Park, A., 360, 361
Park, H., 60, 181, 182, 280, 281
Park, I., 227
Park, M., 225
Park, M. J., 37
Park, S., 25, 37, 148
Parke, R. D., 99
Parker, J., 142, 263, 270, 272,
    289, 292
Parker, K., 83, 85
Parker, K. F., 89
Parker, P., 135, 147, 163, 204, 217,
    242, 243, 277, 328, 336
Parker, W., 212
Parkes, A., 300, 301
Parkin, C. M., 60
Parks, M., 374
Parra, A., 241
Parra, G., 360
Parry, L., 115
Parsai, M., 226
Pas, E., 168
Pascal, S., 145
Pascarella, E., 223
Pasch, K., 136
Pasch, K. E., 29
Pasco Fearon, R., 372
Pasquali, E., 35
Passel, J., 85
Pastore, M., 186, 202
Pastorelli, C., 117, 167, 328,
    336, 337
Pasupathi, M., 107, 253
Patalay, P., 37
Patall, E., 328
Patchin, J., 204
Pate, R., 195
Patel, A., 317
Patel, M., 361
Patel, S., 149, 201
Paten, S., 381
Paternoster, R., 247, 344
Patrianakos, J., 63
Patrick, M., 299, 349, 354, 355,
    356, 357, 362
Patrick, M. E., 172
Pattarroyo, M., 222
Patterson, C. J., 119
Patterson, G., 137, 374
Patterson, G. R., 95
Patterson, M., 64
Patterson, M. W., 136
Pattiselanno, K., 273

Patton, D., 149, 201
Patton, F., 226
Patton, G., 321, 357, 374, 377
Patton, G. C., 23
Patwardhan, I., 360
Paul, E., 333
Paul, M., 55, 361
Paul, S., 372
Pauldine, M., 137
Pauletti, R., 231
Paulozzi, L., 174
Paulsen, D., 245
Paulson, J. F., 225
Paunesku, D., 326, 330
Paus, T., 26, 50, 55, 57, 248
Paxton, S., 37
Paxton, S. J., 36, 37, 38, 39, 199
Payne, A., 149
Payne, K., 280
Payne, P. A., 29
Paysnick, A. A., 88
Payton, A., 142, 204, 248
Peake, S., 59, 214
Peake, S. A., 43
Pearce, L., 111, 112, 261
Pearce, L. D., 260
Pearce, N., 191
Pearl, R., 141
Pearlman, D., 290
Pearman, F. A., II, 169
Pearson, C. M., 38
Pearson, J., 135, 187
Pearson, R., 377
Peck, S. C., 172
Peckins, M., 372
Pedersen, E., 358
Pedersen, E. R., 201
Pedersen, G., 246
Pedersen, N. L., 108
Pedersen, S., 129, 133, 144,
    278, 279
Pediatric Imaging, Neurocognition,
    and Genetics Study, 48,
    87, 168
Peebles, R., 195
Peeters, E., 202, 272
Peeters, M., 362
Peguero, A., 338, 344
Pekrun, R., 325, 332
Pelham, W., 372
Pelham, W. E., Jr., 164
Pellegrini, A., 278
Pellegrini, A. D., 129
Pellerin, L., 168
Pellis, S. M., 15
Pelphrey, K., 142
Peña Alampay, L., 168
Penelo, E., 37, 198
Peng, C.-Z., 164
Peniche, M., 90, 91
Penner, E., 77

Peper, J., 245, 362
Peper, J. S., 17, 25, 26, 48, 53,
    54, 55
Pepin, J., 233
Pepler, D., 279, 282, 283, 287
Pepper, M., 263
Pereira, B., 361
Perella, J., 173
Pérez, J., 96, 249
Perez-Brena, N., 225, 226
Perez-Brena, N. J., 99
Perez-Brumer, A., 231
Perez-Edgar, K., 103, 248
Perilla, J., 332
Perino, M., 56
Perino, M. T., 55
Perkins, D., 92, 311
Perkins, D. D., 186, 202
Perkins, S. A., 240, 250
Perlman, G., 381
Perreira, K., 224, 339
Perren, S., 147
Perrin, E., 34
Perrino, T., 202
Perry, A. A., 37
Perry, B., 138
Perry, C., 136, 358, 363
Perry, C. L., 36
Perry, D., 231
Perry, J., 194
Perry, R., 383
Perry, S., 191
Perry, T., 270
Persike, M., 271, 274
Persson, A., 186
Pervanidou, P., 14, 26
Peskin, M. F., 91
Pesko, M., 356
Peter, J., 38, 197, 199, 202,
    204, 274
Peters, J., 210, 301
Peters, S., 54, 100, 221, 222, 362
Petersen, A., 32, 33
Petersen, A. C., 216
Petersen, I., 366
Petersen, J., 310
Petersen, S. E., 46, 47, 53
Peterson, J. L., 134
Peterson, K., 314
Peterson, S., 360
Peterson-Badali, M., 241
Petraitis, J., 360
Petrie, C., 174
Petrie, T. A., 35
Petrovich, J., 37
Pettifor, A., 313
Pettigrew, J., 92, 168
Pettit, G., 59, 144, 190, 242, 267,
    291, 292, 303, 343, 360,
    366, 373
Pettit, G. S., 115, 116

Pettit, J., 375, 382
Peugh, J., 4, 35, 74
Peviani, K., 87, 261
Pevzner, E., 247
Pexman, P., 44
Peyser, H., 115
Pfeifer, J., 59, 63, 100, 209, 211, 214, 248, 267, 269
Pfeifer, J. H., 43, 53, 56
Phalet, K., 167, 170
Phan, J. M., 96
Phelps, E., 188, 190, 191
Philbin, J., 298
Philbrook, L. E., 29
Philips, K., 144
Phillips, M. L., 27
Phillips, P., 362
Phillipsen, L. C., 270
Phinney, J., 225
Piacentini, J., 382
Piaget, J., 9
Pianta, R., 326
Picariello, S., 222
Picci, G., 56
Piccoli, V., 150
Piccolo, L. R., 87, 168
Pickard, L., 321
Pickering, S. J., 47
Piehler, T., 137, 372
Piekarski, D., 25, 48
Piekarski, D. J., 25, 48
Pierce, J., 90, 255, 358
Piero, L., 92
Pietiläinen, K. H., 22
Pike, A., 109
Pike, G. B., 55
Pimentel, E., 182
Pimentel, P. S., 77
Pincham, H., 372
Pinderhughes, E., 119
Pine, D., 100, 275, 372, 378
Pine, D. S., 55, 103
Pinetta, B., 225
Pingault, J.-B., 164, 362
Pinquart, M., 103, 241
Pintrich, P., 328, 330
Piquero, A., 136, 366, 370, 371, 372, 374, 375
Piquero, A. R., 244
Piran, N., 310
Pirie, P., 363
Pirkis, J., 381
Piroddi, B., 149
Pitskel, N., 142
Pittard, W., 319
Pittet, I., 299
Pittman, J., 302
Plana-Ripoll, O., 350, 375
Plant, A., 204
Planty, M., 256
Plastin, K., 321

Pletnikov, M., 362
Plomin, R., 103, 114, 164, 372
Pluess, M., 110
Poels, K., 150
Pogarsky, G., 319
Pokinko, M., 361
Pokorny, S., 363
Polanin, J., 138
Polk, R., 227
Polk, W., 173
Pollack, H., 319
Pollak, S. D., 35, 53
Pollak, Y., 165
Pollard, M., 138, 310
Pollard, M. S., 138
Pomerantz, E., 12, 211, 241, 249, 326, 327, 329, 330, 332, 333, 334
Pomerantz, E. M., 106, 141
Ponce-Garcia, E., 92, 136
Pond, A. M., 111
Pong, S., 114, 338
Ponnet, K., 107, 117, 202, 205, 206, 272
Poorthuis, A., 7, 214, 215, 327
Pop, E., 221
Pope, D., 172
Pope, H., Jr., 36
Poropat, A., 325
Porta, G., 382
Porter, M., 140, 241, 268
Posner, M. I., 46
Potard, C., 149
Poteat, V., 274, 310
Potter, J., 216
Poulin, F., 129, 133, 137, 138, 139, 142, 147, 180, 187, 188, 274, 278, 279
Poulsen, C., 248
Poulton, R., 108, 217, 381
Pouwels, J., 141
Powell, W., 261
Power, J., 47, 54
Power, K., 191
Power, T., 215
Powers, A., 35, 51, 54, 62
Powers, J., 144, 311, 373
Power to Decide, 315
Pradhan, A. K., 65
Prado, G., 202
Pragg, B., 113
Pratt, M., 268
Pratt, M. W., 222
Prattini, R. J., 92
PrepScholar, 340
Prescott, T., 148
Presnell, K., 35
Price, A., 378
Price, C., 188, 321
Price, C. D., 35
Price, C. L., 162

Price, J., 292
Price, M., 173
Price, M. N., 299
Price, R., 375
Priebe, G., 195
Priess, H., 231, 232, 233
Prindiville, S., 214
Prins, S., 189
Prinstein, M., 132, 138, 140, 143, 144, 204, 227, 248, 279, 288, 296, 304, 308, 378, 379
Prinstein, M. J., 33, 132, 204, 248, 273, 280, 379, 380
Prinzie, P., 212, 243, 373
Pronk, R., 143
Pronk, T., 362
Propper, C., 164
Prossinger, H., 301
Prot, S., 199
Pryor, J., 277
Przepiorka, A., 204, 272
Przybylski, A., 193, 194
Przybylski, A. K., 193
Puhl, R., 229, 230, 311
Pulaski, S., 200
Pulkkinen, L., 23, 360
Pullman, A., 361
Pungello, E., 58
Purcell, A., 313
Purcell, K., 192, 202
Purdie, N., 328
Purtell, K., 86, 88
Purtell, K. M., 184
Purwono, U., 260
Putallaz, M., 163
Putnam, F., 311
Putnick, D., 241, 242
Pykett, A., 257
Pynoos, R., 257
Pyrooz, D. C., 136

Q

Qian, Z., 338
Qin, D., 134, 224
Qin, L., 141, 211, 249, 334
Qu, Y., 12, 65, 106, 247, 329, 330, 333
Quach, A., 360
Qualter, P., 34, 145, 275
Quandt, T., 150, 199
Quas, J. A., 105
Quatman, T., 327
Quayle, E., 205
Quillian, L., 134
Quinn, K., 136
Quinn, P. D., 155
Quinn, T., 373
Quintana, K., 202
Quintana, S. M., 225
Quintelier, E., 257

R

Raaijmakers, Q., 213, 222
Raat, H., 300, 302
Rabi, O., 165
Rabin, B., 383
Rabinak, C., 242
Raby, K., 267
Racine, M., 362
Racine, Y., 89
Racz, S., 100
Radmacher, K., 273, 274
Raes, F., 273, 378
Raffaelli, M., 191, 242, 270, 273, 276, 277, 302, 383
Raftery-Helmer, J., 332
Ragan, D., 136, 246
Ragsdale, B. L., 216
Rahal, D., 88
Rahkonen, O., 101
Raich, R. M., 37, 198
Raichle, M., 372
Raifman, J., 311
Raiford, J., 305
Raine, A., 27, 352, 365, 372
Raine-Bennett, T., 313
Rainie, L., 202
Raj, A., 290
Rakesh, D., 381
Raley, R., 282
Ralph, L., 317
Ralston, E., 137
Ram, N., 100, 214
Rambaran, J., 138, 334
Ramesh, S., 317
Ramey, C., 58
Ramey, H. L., 210
Ramirez, N., 181, 184
Ramos, J., 260
Ramsden, S., 58
Ramsey, M., 270
Randall, E., 187, 332
Randall, G., 137
Randel, J., 289
Rankin, L. A., 81
Ranney, J., 150
Ranney, M., 149
Rapee, R., 204
Raposa, E., 89
Raposa, E. B., 89
Rapuano, K. M., 34
Rarick, J., 227
Rasanen, M., 22
Rasberry, C., 147
Rasmussen, M., 363
Rastogi, R., 135
Rasumussen, E., 206
Ratelle, C., 333
Rathouz, P., 353
Rattan, A., 327
Raudenbusch, S., 91

Raudino, A., 267
Rauer, A., 291
Rauh, V., 51
Rauscher, K., 183
Ravanbakht, S., 34
Ravens-Sieberer, U., 145
Raver, C., 257
Ravitch, D., 154, 177
Rawana, J. S., 35
Ray, C., 118
Ray, J., 92, 365, 374
Read, J., 351
Reader, J., 311
Ready, D. D., 158
Ream, G., 303
Ream, R., 334
Rebellon, C., 324, 374
Rebellon, C. J., 180
Recchia, H., 107, 149
Recchia, H. E., 60, 253
Reckdenwald, A., 89
Reddy, R., 160
Redlich, A. D., 77
Reeb, B. T., 110
Reece, M., 296
Rees, H., 313
Rees, J., 35
Reese, E., 46
Reeslund, K., 383
Reeves, P., 287
Régner, I., 235, 325
Regnier, M., 256
Rehder, P., 230, 309
Rehkopf, D., 369
Reich, R., 357
Reich, S., 202, 270, 271, 272
Reid, A., 289
Reid, J. A., 63
Reid, R., 92, 93
Reid, V., 319
Reidy, D., 290
Reiersen, A., 164
Reiffman, A., 311
Reijneveld, S., 352, 357
Reijntjes, A., 211, 254
Reilly, D., 327
Reiner, S., 370
Reingle Gonzalez, J., 367
Reinhardt, L., 28, 203
Reis, H., 202, 203
Reisel, L., 343
Reiser, L., 30
Reisner, S., 231
Reiss, D., 23, 108, 109, 111, 116, 377
Reiter, E., 24
Reitz, E., 304
Reker, D., 248
Rekker, R., 118
Ren, Y., 379
Renard, J., 361, 363
Renaud, O., 210

Rende, R., 360
Rendell, P., 199
Reniers, R. L. E. P., 66
Rentfrow, P. J., 216
Repovš, G., 58
Reppucci, N., 89, 370
Resett, S., 150
Resko, S., 143, 361
Resnick, M., 296
Resnik, F., 150
Reuman, D., 162
Revenson, T., 331
Reyes, B. T., 108
Reyes, H., 289, 290, 310
Reyes, H. L. M., 146
Reyes, M., 328
Reyna, V., 63
Reyna, V. F., 66
Reynolds, A., 255
Reynolds, A. J., 160
Reynolds, B., 245
Reynolds, B. M., 32
Reynolds, J., 336
Reynolds, J. R., 170
Reynolds, L., 361
Rhew, I., 351, 363
Rhoades, H., 382
Rhodes, J., 88, 89, 160, 277, 339
Rhodes, J. E., 89
Ribar, D., 112
Ribeaud, D., 164
Ricciardelli, L. A., 38
Rice, C., 300
Rice, E., 204, 382
Rice, K., 276
Rice, L., 334
Rich, M., 204
Richard, P., 138
Richards, J. M., 101
Richards, M., 92, 122, 185, 214, 276, 278
Richards, M. H., 87, 91, 216
Richardson, B., 225
Richardson, C., 149
Richardson, E., 137
Richardson, F., 58
Richardson, J., 114
Richman, S. B., 106
Richmond, T. K., 91
Rickman, A., 2, 72, 73, 79, 84, 86
Rideout, V., 192, 193, 195
Riediger, M., 212
Rieffe, C., 142, 247, 254
Rieger, G., 230
Rieger, S., 217
Riegle-Crumb, C., 135
Rierdan, J., 30
Rigdon, J. L., 336
Riggs, K. J., 41
Riggs, L., 320
Riina, E., 91

Rijsdijk, F., 164, 352, 372
Riley, J., 25, 352
Riley, L., 108
Rinaldi, C., 273
Rincón, C., 289
Rind, B., 311
Rinehart, J., 314
Rinehart, P., 120
Ringwalt, C., 363
Rioux, C., 109, 110
Risch, S., 117
Rising, K., 361
Rissanen, A., 22
Ristikari, T., 351
Riva, P., 203
Rivara, F., 188
Rivas-Drake, D., 225, 227, 228
Rivenbark, J., 88
Rivera, W., 136
Rivers, S., 63
Rizzo, C., 290
Rizzo, J. A., 19
Roalf, D. R., 48
Roalson, L., 160
Robb, M., 192, 193
Robbins, C., 296
Robbins, M., 202
Robbins, S., 324
Roberts, A., 234
Roberts, A. L., 93
Roberts, B., 213, 214, 345
Roberts, B. W., 217
Roberts, D., 118, 180, 195, 198, 199, 200, 201, 326
Roberts, M., 227
Robertson, E., 372
Robertson, L., 200
Robins, G., 35, 138
Robins, R., 87, 92, 117, 143, 188, 212, 213, 214, 217, 225, 226, 227, 299, 339, 345, 357, 362, 372
Robins, R. W., 74, 92, 99, 117, 214, 217
Robinson, B., 230
Robinson, M., 168, 300
Robinson, N., 217
Robinson, T., 36
Robnett, R., 334
Roche, A., 22
Roche, K., 227, 249, 338
Roche, K. M., 92, 99, 100
Roche, L., 162
Rocque, M., 63, 244
Rodas, C., 115
Roded, A., 60, 97, 242
Rodenhizer-Stampfli, K., 290
Roderick, M., 336
Rodgers, J., 304
Rodgers, J. L., 33
Rodgers, K., 215

Rodgers, R. F., 36, 37, 38
Rodil, J., 228
Rodil, J. C., 225
Rodine, S., 303
Rodkin, P., 140, 141, 145
Rodrigues, H., 60
Rodriguez, A., 164
Rodriguez, A. X., 37
Rodriguez, C., 245
Rodriguez, G., 191
Rodriguez, N., 370
Rodriguez de Jesus, S., 99
Rodríguez De Jesús, S. A., 108
Rodríguez-Meirinhos, A., 107, 242
Roeder, K. M., 150
Roelofs, J., 378
Roelofs, K., 92
Roesch, S., 253
Roeser, R., 160, 161, 168, 169, 177, 178, 259, 260, 264, 326
Roeyers, H., 164
Rogers, A., 193, 201, 242
Rogers, C., 55, 108
Rogers, C. R., 108
Rogers, L., 228, 235
Rogers, M., 271, 376
Rogers-Sirin, L., 227
Rogowska, J., 362
Rohail, I., 271
Rohde, P., 35, 289, 375, 379, 381, 382
Rohlfing, T., 362
Rohrer, J., 213
Roisman, G., 267, 287, 352, 372, 373, 374
Rokkum, J., 195
Romanelli, M., 90–91
Romashkin, A., 29, 195
Rombouts, S. A. R. B., 46, 54, 245
Romeo, R., 9, 14, 15, 16, 17, 51
Romer, D., 25, 57, 63, 66, 150, 199, 299, 301, 314, 352, 360
Romero, C., 330
Romero, C. V., 95, 267
Romero, E., 91
Romero-Garcia, R., 53
Romm, K., 258
Rommelse, N., 372
Rommes, E., 30, 198
Romo, L., 250, 303, 314
Rompilla, D. B., 12
Ronconi, L., 324
Ronis, S., 307
Ronneberg, T., 28
Rood, L., 378
Rook, K., 277
Roosa, M., 228
Roosa, M. W., 33
Ros, A. M., 27
Rosario, M., 92, 234
Rose, A., 143, 263, 270, 273, 282

Rose, A. J., 273
Rose, C., 228
Rose, R., 22, 360, 382
Rose, R. J., 23
Rose-Krasnor, L., 142, 248
Rosen, A., 363
Rosen, D., 375
Rosen, L., 195, 361, 363
Rosen, M. L., 56
Rosenbaum, G., 66
Rosenbaum, J., 174, 305, 313
Rosenbaum, J. E., 336
Rosenberg, F., 214
Rosenberg, M., 195, 214
Rosenblum, G., 37
Rosenthal, D., 296
Rosenthal, G., 53
Rosenthal, S., 268, 300
Rosés, R., 37
Roseth, C. J., 168
Ross, A., 134
Ross, G., 63
Rossi, G., 255
Rosso, C., 48
Rostad, W., 290
Rote, W., 59, 96, 97, 264, 353, 358
Rote, W. M., 96, 97, 241
Roth, J., 15, 188
Rothbart, M. K., 46
Rothenberg, A., 360
Rothenberg, W., 97, 107, 244
Rothenberg, W. A., 25, 107, 115, 117
Rothman, A., 217
Rothman, E., 289, 290, 291
Rothman, E. F., 32
Rothmann, S., 194
Rounds, J., 212
Rouse, C., 337
Rousseau, A., 19, 199, 202
Roux, S., 45
Rowe, C., 363
Rowe, D., 109, 212, 304, 361
Rowe, H. L., 136
Rowe, R., 352, 365
Rowe, S., 266, 289
Rowhani-Rahbar, A., 188
Rowland, B., 67, 374
Rowley, S., 225, 227, 228, 329, 330, 332
Rowley, S. J., 88
Roy, A., 257
Roy, A. L., 92, 93
Rozek, C., 229
Ruback, R., 368
Ruberry, E. J., 43, 53
Rubin, D., 46
Rubin, K., 144, 243, 263, 276
Ruch, D., 381
Rucian, M., 46, 52
Ruck, M., 241, 256
Ruck, M. D., 60

Ruder, T., 376
Rudie, J. D., 53
Rudolph, J., 266, 289
Rudolph, K., 32, 57, 142, 144, 147, 148, 268, 353, 378, 381, 382
Rudolph, K. D., 46
Rudy, W., 175
Rueger, S., 277
Rueter, M., 101
Rufino, K., 368
Ruggeri, A., 254
Ruggero, C., 381
Ruggiero, A. R., 29
Ruhl, H., 269
Ruiz, J. R., 35
Ruiz Peláez, J. G., 299
Rulison, K., 141, 373
Rumberger, R., 178, 334, 343, 344
Runions, K., 149
Ruparel, K., 48
Rusby, J., 147
Rushlow, W., 363
Rusley, J., 311
Rusow, J., 204
Russell, J., 245
Russell, M., 88
Russell, M. A., 92, 360
Russell, S., 168, 231, 233, 299, 310, 311, 319, 333
Russell, S. T., 33, 103, 230, 330
Russotti, J., 334
Rust, J., 234
Ruth, G., 4, 188, 189
Rutherford, C., 189
Ruthig, J., 383
Rutland, A., 61
Rutter, M., 103
Ruttle, P. L., 23
Ryabov, I., 337
Ryan, A., 135, 138, 140, 142, 168, 334
Ryan, A. M., 141
Ryan, C., 233
Ryan, G., 174
Ryan, J., 119
Ryan, N., 277, 375, 383
Ryan, N. D., 27, 381
Ryan, R., 31, 242, 243, 303
Ryan, R. M., 23, 114
Ryan, S., 119, 313
Ryba, T., 188
Rydell, A., 372
Ryoo, J., 145
Ryu, S., 182

S

Saafir, A., 334
Saarento, S., 141
Sabbineni, A., 313
Sabiston, C., 361, 363

Sabiston, C. M., 187
Sabuwalla, Z., 382
Sacchet, M., 87, 381
Sachs, J., 159
Sackett, P., 336
Sackett, P. R., 336
Sacks, V., 321
Sadler, S., 161, 332
Saewyc, E., 230, 309, 311
Safa, M., 217
Sagar, K., 362
Sağkal, A., 173
Sagrestano, L., 29
Sagy, S., 91
Sahdra, B., 204, 277
Sainio, M., 148
Saint-Georges, Z., 144
Saint-Maurice, P., 35, 195
Sakai, J., 362
Sakhardande, A., 246
Sakhardande, A. L., 59
Sako, C., 52
Salafia, E., 38
Sala-Hamrick, K., 242
Salas-Wright, C., 367
Salazar, L. F., 314
Salcedo, A., 92
Saleem, F., 92
Sales, L., 275
Saletin, J. M., 28
Sallis, H., 377
Sally, I., 360
Salmela-Aro, K., 135, 138, 161, 193, 242, 243, 326, 330, 334, 335, 351
Salmivalli, C., 141, 144, 148
Salmon, D., 39
Saltzman, H., 298
Saltzman, L., 310
Salusky, I., 191
Salvatore, J., 266, 337
Salzano, S., 59, 247
Salzer Burks, V., 373
Salzinger, S., 92
Samant, S., 321
Samarova, V., 310
Sambrook, K. A., 56
Samdal, O., 206
Samek, D. R., 108, 136
Samela-Aro, K., 3
Sameroff, A., 346
Sampson, N., 382
Sampson, R., 91, 371
Sampson, R. J., 92
Samuel, R., 344
Sanchagrin, K., 305
Sánchez, B., 89, 226, 338
Sanchez, Z., 361
Sanchez-Armass, O., 383
Sánchez-Queija, I., 241
Sandahl, J., 167

Sandberg-Thoma, S. E., 85
Sanders, J., 317
Sanders, L., 114
Sanders, S., 164, 296
Sandfort, T., 233
Sandler, I., 116
Sandstrom, M., 141
Sanson, A., 258
Santelli, J., 295, 296, 311, 312, 313, 315, 321
Santesso, D., 248
Santiago, C., 92
Santiago, C. D., 27, 87
Santiago, D., 338
Santinello, M., 92, 186, 202, 255
Santo, J., 149
Santos, C., 140, 141, 228, 234
Santos, C. E., 232
Saporito, S., 167
Sargent, J., 197
Sargent, J. D., 34
Sarwer, D. B., 35
Sasabe, T., 45
Sasson, H., 150
Satterthwaite, T. D., 48, 58, 66
Sattler, P., 231
Saudino, K., 109
Sauer, J., 193
Saunders, B., 352
Saunders, J. F., 38
Saunders, M., 372
Savage, J., 360
Saval, K., 300, 301
Savani, K., 327
Savickaitė, R., 279, 310
Savin-Williams, R., 7, 230, 270, 285, 294, 295, 298, 299, 300, 301, 302, 303, 306, 308, 309, 311
Savin-Williams, R. C., 230, 231
Savitz-Romer, M., 173
Savolainen, J., 33, 299, 351, 353, 360
Sawalani, G., 143
Sawardekar, S., 51
Sawyer, A., 374
Sawyer, S., 357
Saxbe, D., 92
Saxbe, D. E., 23, 114
Saxon, J., 327
Saxton, E., 383
Sayal, K., 164
Sayre Smith, D., 233
Scalco, M., 138, 351, 360, 362
Scanlan, L., 188
Scanlan, T., 188
Scarapicchia, T., 187
Schachner, M., 217
Schacter, H., 144, 147, 149, 150
Schacter, H. L., 34, 147, 234
Schad, M., 140, 266, 269

Schaefer, D., 138, 188
Schaefer, D. R., 35
Schaible, L. M., 92
Schallert, D., 326
Scharf, M., 281
Scharkow, M., 150
Schebendach, J., 35
Scheepers, F., 372
Scheepers, P., 134
Scheer, J., 310
Scheier, L., 218
Schelar, E., 119
Schendel, D., 350, 375
Schenke, K., 363
Scheres, A., 63, 244
Scherf, K. S., 55, 56
Scherf, S., 27, 55
Schick, V., 296
Schiff, A., 28
Schiller, K., 135, 161
Schlaggar, B., 47, 53, 54
Schlaggar, B. L., 46, 47
Schlegel, A., 2, 70, 79
Schlomer, G., 302, 362
Schlomer, G. L., 110
Schmaal, L., 381
Schmeiser, C., 324
Schmid, C., 270
Schmid, K., 135
Schmid, S., 363
Schmidt, C., 28, 255
Schmidt, C. J., 90, 255
Schmidt, J., 217, 256, 330, 338, 341
Schmidt, N., 89, 369
Schmidt, N. M., 89
Schmiedek, F., 46
Schmiege, S., 321
Schmitt, M., 214
Schmitz, R., 118
Schmukle, S., 213
Schneider, B., 345
Schneiders, J., 27
Schnyder, I., 325
Schoeny, M., 302, 304, 363
Schofield, T., 188
Schofield, T. J., 99, 117
Scholte, R., 145, 203, 275
Scholte, R. H., 217
Schonert-Reichl, K., 187
Schoneveld, E., 141
Schooler, D., 197
Schoon, I., 336, 346
Schreier, H., 311
Schriber, R., 362
Schriber, R. A., 56
Schubert, C., 22, 365, 375
Schubert, C. A., 86
Schulenberg, J., 28, 29, 74, 75, 173,
      180, 182, 183, 184, 189,
      344, 349, 351, 354, 355,
      356, 357, 362

Schulenberg, J. E., 161, 172
Schuler, K., 381
Schullehner, J., 350, 375
Schultz, P., 327
Schulz, K. M., 17
Schuster, M., 249, 301, 302
Schuster, M. A., 34, 91
Schütte, K., 171
Schutz, R., 19
Schvey, N., 36
Schwab-Stone, M., 254
Schwartz, D., 92, 100, 133, 134,
      135, 140, 142, 334
Schwartz, J., 299, 367
Schwartz, J. A., 108
Schwartz, O., 99, 110
Schwartz, R., 77, 245
Schwartz, S., 89, 137, 222, 223,
      226, 357
Schwartz, S. E. O., 89
Schwartz, S. J., 225
Schwartz-Mette, R., 273, 379
Schwartz-Mette, R. A., 273
Schwarz, D., 312
Schweder, R., 76
Schweitzer, J., 245
Schweizer, T., 353
Scott, E., 57, 76, 77, 78, 245, 365, 374
Scott, H., 28, 203
Scott, J., 147, 363
Scott, J. T., 37
Scott, M., 115, 228, 314
Scottham, K., 225
Scott-Sheldon, L., 361
Scovill, L. C., 12
Scull, T., 201
Seaman, J., 324
Seamon, E., 92
Sears, H., 30
Seaton, E., 30, 165, 224, 225,
      227, 228
Sebastian, C., 56, 59, 209
Secker-Walker, R., 363
Secor-Turner, M., 301
Sederevicius, D., 52
Sedgh, G., 313, 315, 316, 318
Sedikides, C., 211
Seelam, R., 201
Seeley, J., 33, 289, 375, 379, 382
Seeman, T., 29, 88
Seena Fazel, F., 368
Seff, M., 99
Segalowitz, S., 248
Séguin, J., 362
Seguin, J. R., 109, 110
Segura, L., 174
Seider, S., 190
Seidlitz, J., 53
Seidman, E., 160, 224
Seiffge-Krenke, I., 43, 213, 241, 269,
      271, 274, 285, 299, 376

Sela, Y., 204
Selänne, H., 188
Sela-Shayovitz, R., 367
Selemon, L., 50
Seligman, M., 325
Sellers, R., 224, 225, 226, 227–228
Selman, R., 148
Selvaraj, S., 34
Sen, B., 66
Senra, C., 37
Senserrick, T., 63
Sentse, M., 107, 275, 373
Seo, D., 35
Seoane, G., 37
Serbin, L., 102
Serna, I., 161, 162
Serra Poirier, C., 108
Sesé, A., 215
Setoh, P., 211
Sexton, H., 319
Sexton, J. A., 48
Seymour, K., 164
Shachar-Shapira, L., 115, 291
Shackleton, N., 321
Shadish, W., Jr., 336
Shaffer, L., 266
Shalev, I., 33
Shanahan, L., 31, 102, 108, 111
Shanahan, M., 184
Shanahan, M. J., 75
Shane, J., 337
Shane, M. S., 59
Shannon, B., 372
Shannon, C., 314
Shannon, D., 226
Shannon, S., 140, 287
Shao, T., 60
Shapero, B., 381
Shapiro, L., 276
Shapka, J., 203, 327
Shariff, S., 150
Sharkey, J., 255, 361
Sharma, A., 109
Sharma, S., 383
Sharp, E., 324
Sharp, E. H., 180
Sharp, P., 54, 63
Sharp, W., 165
Sharpe, H., 37
Shattuck, A., 149
Shaver, K., 95
Shaver, P. R., 269
Shaw, D., 103, 108, 160, 352, 361, 372
Shaw, D. J., 55
Shaw, D. S., 53, 91, 381
Shaw, H., 34, 35, 39
Shaw, P., 58, 165
Shearer, L., 356
Shedler, J., 358
Sheeber, L., 56, 109, 117
Sheehan, H. C., 178

Sheeran, P., 313
Sheffield Morris, A., 92, 136
Sheftall, A., 381
Sheikh-Khalil, S., 333
Shek, D., 103
Shelton, J., 225
Shelton, J. N., 225
Shen, W., 336
Shen, Y., 103, 106, 227, 253, 333
Shepard, S., 253
Shepherd, K., 381
Shepperd, J., 273
Sher, K., 360, 361
Sheridan, M., 371
Sheridan, M. A., 56
Sherman, L., 142, 204, 247, 248
Sherman, L. E., 53
Sherman, M., 117
Sherman, R., 6, 297
Shernoff, D., 185, 338
Sherrill, J., 382
Sherrod, L., 88, 255
Sheshko, D., 339
Shi, H., 282
Shi, Y., 100
Shiffrin, N., 378
Shifrer, D., 187
Shih, J., 377
Shih, R., 201, 358
Shilo, G., 310
Shilton, T., 195
Shimizu, M., 29
Shin, H., 135, 138, 168, 334
Shin, J., 91, 92
Shin, W., 206
Shiner, R. L., 213
Shinohara, K., 214
Shipman, K., 240
Shirtcliff, E., 14, 16, 23, 365, 372
Shirtcliff, E. A., 46
Shiyko, M. P., 33
Shlay, J., 321
Shomaker, L., 283
Shope, J., 352, 361
Shope, J. T., 65
Shorey, R., 289
Shortt, J., 287, 291
Shoulberg, E., 142
Shoulberg, E. K., 111
Shoum, K., 325
Shteynberg, R. V., 77
Shu, J., 54
Shu, X., 275
Shuan, Y., 336
Shubert, J., 160, 353, 358
Shuey, E. A., 92
Shukla, K., 148, 168
Shulman, E., 9, 63, 69, 70, 77, 78,
      123, 244, 247, 331, 365, 372
Shulman, E. P., 9, 17, 54, 61, 63, 64,
      84, 244, 283

Shulman, S., 7, 115, 270, 281, 283, 291, 299
Shumer, D., 231
Shumow, L., 190, 256, 330, 337
Sibinga, E. M. S., 92
Sibley, M., 372
Sibley, M. H., 164
Siebenbruner, J., 300, 358, 359
Siegel, A., 12
Siegle, G., 56, 350, 375, 382
Siegle, G. J., 55
Siegler, R., 47
Siennick, S., 188, 300, 351, 372
Sieving, R., 301
Sigfusdottir, I., 90
Sigman, M., 303
Signorelli, N., 196
Sijtsema, J., 138, 248, 372
Sijtsma, K., 213
Silbereisen, R., 33, 84, 85, 241
Silbereisen, R. K., 85
Silk, J., 15, 28, 56, 102, 203, 304, 350, 375, 381, 382, 383
Silk, J. S., 27, 28, 53, 55, 92, 101, 136, 203
Silva, K., 9, 63, 65, 66, 123, 247
Silva, P., 22, 33, 212, 213, 319
Silva, S., 382
Silventoinen, K., 360
Silver, E., 184
Silver, R., 247
Silverberg, S., 99, 240
Silveri, M., 5, 47, 362
Silverman, J., 290
Silverman, W., 383
Silvers, J. A., 35, 51, 54
Silverthorn, N., 89
Sim, T. N., 128
Simmens, S., 111
Simmons, C., 114
Simmons, J., 99, 381
Simmons, J. G., 110
Simmons, R., 32, 143, 214
Simon, T., 289, 310
Simon, T. R., 174
Simon, V., 138, 205, 266, 282, 283, 288
Simone, M., 38, 138
Simons, L., 19, 30, 105, 116, 117, 140, 227, 287, 302, 304, 352, 371
Simons, L. G., 30, 106, 118
Simons, R., 19, 30, 32, 106, 117, 302, 304, 336, 371
Simons, R. L., 30, 106, 228
Simons-Morton, B., 65, 144, 173, 248, 351
Simons-Morton, B. G., 65
Simpkins, S., 138, 173, 186, 188, 189, 190
Simpkins, S. D., 35, 328
Simpson, A., 100

Simpson, D., 92
Simpson, E., 202
Simpson, J., 217, 267, 268
Sims, J., 90
Sinclair-McBride, K., 150
Singer, M., 173
Singer, S., 370
Singer, T., 54
Singh, M., 381
Singh, P., 149
Singh, S., 297, 313, 315, 316, 318
Sinyor, M., 381
Sippola, L., 278, 279, 284
Sirin, S., 227
Sisk, C., 9, 14, 15, 16, 17, 51
Sisk, C. L., 17
Sisk, L. M., 15
Sisson, S. B., 35
Sitka, A., 188
Sitnick, S., 352, 361
Sitnick, S. L., 53
Sittner, K., 361
Sittner, K. J., 362
Siu, A., 332
Sivertsen, B., 119, 382, 383
Sizer, M. A., 93
Sjöström, M., 35
Skalamera, J., 310
Skelton, J., 34
Skinner, A., 34
Skinner, B. F., 10
Skinner, E., 335, 383
Skinner, M., 363
Skinner, O., 228
Skinner, S., 318
Skinner, S. R., 300
Skoog, T., 32, 33, 301, 310
Skorikov, V. B., 345
Sladek, M., 383
Slater, A., 39, 198
Slavick, J., 302, 304
Slocum, L., 60, 174
Slomiak, S., 363
Slopen, N., 234
Slora, E., 22, 24
Slurske, W. S., 114
Sly, P., 147
Smahel, D., 204, 270
Smailes, E., 311
Small, P., 90
Small, R., 357
Small, S., 311
Smalls, C., 86, 88
Smeding, A., 235
Smetana, J., 42, 59, 60, 61, 96, 97, 106, 238, 241, 243, 250, 252, 256, 264, 275, 276
Smetana, J. G., 105
Smirnov, I., 135
Smith, A., 9, 48, 65, 192, 202, 247, 296

Smith, B., 160
Smith, C., 116, 268
Smith, D. G., 64
Smith, D. S., 234
Smith, E., 311, 330
Smith, E. P., 93
Smith, G., 334, 360
Smith, G. T., 38
Smith, J., 145, 158, 177, 178, 318
Smith, K., 276, 327
Smith, L., 147, 310, 379
Smith, M., 147, 190
Smith, M. A., 300
Smith, R., 226, 273
Smith, R. K., 226
Smith, R. L., 273
Smith, S., 135
Smith, T., 29, 190, 198
Smith-Bynum, M., 227
Smith Carter, J., 383
Smith-Darden, J., 205
Smokowski, P., 149
Smolak, L., 19
Smolen, A., 110, 381
Smoll, F., 19
Smollar, J., 241, 264
Snarney, J., 251
Snedker, K. A., 90
Sneider, J., 362
Snell, E., 27
Snow, D., 358
Snyder, A., 372
Snyder, A. R., 85
Snyder, F., 374
Snyder, H., 245, 353
Snyder, J., 108, 137
Soares, J. C., 34
Sobolewski, J. M., 115
Society for Adolescent Health and Medicine, 313
Soenens, B., 60, 96, 107, 240, 242, 275, 326
Sohoni, D., 167
Sokolik, E., 327
Solazzo, A., 308
Sole-Padulles, C., 46
Solis, J., 202
Soller, B., 138
Solmeyer, A. R., 107, 108
Solomon, R., 374
Solomon, S., 374
Somerville, L., 9, 54, 64, 65, 360
Somerville, L. H., 43, 52, 53, 54, 55, 56, 62, 247
Somerville, L. J., 53
Somsen, R., 42
Song, Q., 212
Song, X., 287, 358
Sonneville, K. R., 19, 37
Sonsteng-Person, M., 351

Sontag, L., 8, 150, 350, 353, 375, 376, 377, 381, 382
Sonuga-Barke, E., 164
Sorbring, E., 17, 54
Sorell, G., 279
Sorenson, A., 320
Sorhagen, N. S., 169
Sorkkila, M., 188
Sorrentino, R., 206
Sorsoli, C., 197
Soto, C., 212, 254
Soto, D., 228
Sotres-Alvarez, D., 146
Soukup, P., 149
South, S., 334
South, S. J., 92
Southam-Gerow, M. A., 382
Sowell, E. R., 47, 48, 51, 87
Spaans, J., 143
Sparks, H., 261
Sparks, S., 157
Spear, L., 5, 47, 51, 52, 362
Spear, L. P., 47
Specht, J., 213
Speekenbrink, M., 59, 63, 247
Spees, L., 339
Speizer, I., 321
Spencer, G., 290
Spencer, R., 89
Spencer, S., 133
Spengler, M., 213
Spicer, P., 216
Spiegler, O., 225
Spieker, S., 287, 319
Spielberg, J., 275
Spielberg, J. M., 53
Spielvogel, B., 88, 90
Spies Shapiro, L. A., 114
Spijkerman, R., 203
Spilker, A., 266
Spina, S., 274, 277
Spinelli, T., 150
Spinrad, T., 61, 106, 238, 250, 251, 252, 253, 254, 255, 273, 373
Spinrad, T. L., 102
Spitz, S., 100
Spitzer, B., 326
Spitznagel, E., 300
Spivey, L., 308
Spoth, R., 12, 137, 358, 360, 362
Spotts, E. L., 108
Spriggs, A., 287, 289, 290, 299
Spruijt-Metz, D. S., 35
Squeglia, L., 362
Srikanth, S., 35
Sroufe, A., 268
Sroufe, L., 266, 267
Staats, S., 271, 291
Stack, D., 102
Stack, S., 381
Stadtfeld, C., 132

Staff, J., 30, 173, 180, 181, 182, 183, 184, 344, 349, 362, 372
Stamp, F., 59
Stams, G.-J., 89
Stams, G. J. J. M., 89
Standish, A. R., 35
Stange, J., 381
Stanger-Hall, K., 321
Stanik, C. E., 108
Stanke, L., 187
Stanley, L., 361
Stanton-Salazar, R., 274, 277
Stanwood, N., 317
Stark, J. H., 35
Stark, T. H., 134
Stattin, H., 32, 33, 87, 106, 107, 137, 148, 186, 227, 243, 257, 268, 275, 288, 301, 329, 351, 382
St Clair, M., 115
St Clair, M. C., 378
Stearns, E., 134, 344
Steca, P., 328
Steeger, C. M., 242
Steele, C., 327
Steele, J., 196
Steele, J. S., 51
Steele, M., 116, 117
Stefansson, K., 171, 244
Stefansson, K. K., 244
Steffensmeier, D., 367
Steffes, J., 16, 24
Steger, M., 221
Steglich, C., 135, 138, 140, 273, 334
Steglich, C. E. G., 33
Stein, B. D., 376
Stein, G., 99, 225, 226, 227, 327
Stein, G. L., 99, 226
Stein, J., 30
Steinbeck, K. S., 26
Steinbeis, N., 52, 54
Steinberg, D., 205
Steinberg, E., 190
Steinberg, L., 2, 3, 7, 9, 12, 15, 17, 23, 25, 29, 42, 47, 48, 50, 54, 57, 59, 62, 63, 64, 65, 66, 69, 70, 71, 76, 77, 78, 84, 86, 90, 91, 92, 95, 98, 99, 102, 103, 105, 106, 108, 114, 120, 123, 128, 132, 136, 137, 138, 155, 156, 157, 161, 171, 172, 176, 183, 184, 188, 190, 195, 198, 210, 213, 237, 238, 240, 241, 244, 245, 246, 247, 248, 249, 250, 255, 283, 291, 301, 313, 314, 321, 331, 332, 333, 334, 335, 339, 340, 341, 349, 352, 362, 363, 365, 366, 370, 371, 372, 373, 374, 375, 376, 383
Steinberg, W., 98, 99
Steiner, R., 28, 147
Steinhausen, H., 372

Stepanyan, S. T., 30
Stephanou, K., 382
Stephens, C. M., 106
Stephens, L., 116
Stephens, N., 337
Stephenson, J., 7, 237, 239, 240, 264, 266, 268, 269
Stephenson, S., 361
Stepp, S. D., 37
Sterba, S., 379
Stern, J. A., 269
Sternberg, A., 360
Sternberg, M., 314
Sterrett-Hong, E., 92, 333
Sterzing, P., 145
Sterzing, P. R., 310
Stevens, G., 87, 140, 204, 357
Stevens, G. W. J. M., 232, 233
Stevens, J., 381
Stevens, M. C., 51, 53
Stevens, P., 338
Stevenson, A., 317
Stevenson, C. E., 58
Stevenson, D., 345
Stevenson, H., 339
Stevenson, J., 372
Stevenson, M., 63
Steward-Streng, N., 314
Stewart, A., 34, 35, 195
Stewart, E. A., 336
Stewart, E. B., 336
Stewart, J., 308
Stewart, S. M., 282
St. George, I., 22
Sticca, F., 147
Stice, E., 34, 35, 37, 38, 39, 377
Stigler, J., 339
Stillwell, D., 213
Stochl, J., 31
Stockdale, G., 299
Stockdale, L., 150, 193, 199, 201, 203, 204
Stocker, C., 217, 277
Stocker, C. M., 110
Stoddard, S., 92, 187, 255, 368
Stoddard, S. A., 90, 92, 255
Stok, F., 103, 106, 107, 245
Stoltz, S., 199
Stone, D., 290
Stone, J., 183, 378
Stone, L., 199, 378
Stoneman, Z., 118
Stoolmiller, M., 120, 201
Stormshak, E., 279, 351
Storvoll, E., 371
Story, M., 35, 36, 37, 39
Stotsky, M., 254
Stout, M., 174
Stouthamer-Loeber, M., 137, 212, 365, 367, 370, 372, 374
Stoycos, S., 92

Strang, N., 48, 65, 247
Strang, N. M., 53
Strange, J. P., 32
Strasburger, V., 195, 196, 199, 200
Strathdee, S., 310
Strausser, A., 201
Streit, C., 225–226, 253
Strenziok, M., 200
Striegel-Moore, R., 216
Stritzel, H., 116
Stroet, K., 334
Strohmeier, D., 149
Stroud, C., 383
Stroud, L., 142
Stroud, L. R., 55
Strough, J., 127, 133, 134, 273
Stuart, E., 359
Stuart, G., 289
Stuart, M., 145
Stucky, B., 143
Studer, F., 136
Å tulhofer, A., 198, 299, 303
Stumper, A., 32
Sturge-Apple, M., 245, 266
Sturge-Apple, M. L., 95, 267
Su, B., 379
Su, J., 360, 361
Su, Q., 32
Su, X., 106
Suárez, L., 92
Suárez-Orozco, C., 339
Suazo, C., 93
Subrahmanyam, K., 204, 270, 271
Subramanian, S. V., 91
Subramanyam, M., 291
Substance Abuse and Mental Health Services Administration, 357, 376
Suchert, V., 35, 195
Suchindran, C., 37, 143, 289, 290
Sue, S., 339
Sugden, K., 108, 381
Sugimura, K., 218, 222, 223
Sugimura, N., 191
Sugranyes, G., 46
Suicide Prevention Resource Center, 379
Suizzo, M., 333
Suleiman, A., 294, 304, 305
Sullivan, C., 138, 353, 372
Sullivan, E., 362
Sullivan, H. S., 264
Sullivan, L., 283, 296
Sullivan, P., 191
Sullivan, T., 92, 146, 157, 289, 290, 291
Sumner, R., 218
Sun, Q., 100
Sun, S., 87
Sun, W., 253

Sun, X., 291
Sun, Y., 23, 24, 114
Sunwolf, 60
Supple, A., 99, 225, 226, 227, 327, 360, 361
Supple, A. J., 99
Suris, J., 299
Suryanti, T., 260
Susman, E., 18, 23, 353, 372
Susman, E. J., 14, 23, 26, 30, 32, 33, 35, 100
Sutin, A., 35
Sutton, T., 30, 116, 140, 287, 302, 304
Sutu, A., 213
Suyemoto, K., 228
Suzuki, K., 199
Suzuki, M., 332
Svedin, C., 205
Svensson, R., 226
Swaim, R., 361
Swanson, S., 350, 375, 376
Swarr, A., 278
Swartzwelder, H., 362
Swearer, S., 145, 382
Sweet, L. H., 92
Sweeten, G., 289, 344, 366
Swendsen, J., 350, 351, 362, 375, 376, 377
Swenson, L., 143, 215, 216, 273
Swing, E., 199
Swinton, A., 329, 330
Syed, M., 213, 224, 226
Symons, K., 107, 206, 306
Syvertsen, A., 174, 181, 254, 258, 346
Szalacha, L. A., 216
Szapocznik, P., 226
Szatmari, P., 376
Sze, W., 32, 147
Szklo-Coxe, M., 29
Szkudlarek, H., 361
Szmukler, G., 37
Sznitman, G., 222
Sznitman, S., 314, 343
Szwedo, D., 202, 203, 204, 248, 269, 275, 277
Szwedo, D. E., 275

T

Taanila, A., 351
Taanila, A. M., 33
Tabler, J. L., 38
Tach, L., 113
Tackett, J., 64, 212, 254, 372
Tackett, J. L., 136
Taggart, T., 261
Taiarol, J., 143
Takács, K., 132
Takahashi, A., 120

Takash, H. M. S., 64, 84
Takezawa, M., 252
Talmud, I., 133
Talwar, V., 150
Tammelin, T., 164
Tamnes, C., 56
Tamnes, C. K., 48, 49, 52, 212
Tan, D., 60, 256
Tan, J., 269, 275
Tan, J. S., 242
Tanabe, J., 362
Tanaka, C., 50
Tanaka, M., 45
Tang, C. S., 29, 30
Tang, S., 46, 226, 319
Tang, X., 326, 330
Tanner, D., 153, 154
Tanner, J., 20, 21, 22, 24
Tanner-Smith, E. E., 31, 174
Tanofsky-Kraff, M., 36
Tanton, C., 296, 298
Tanyu, M., 89
Tapales, A., 363
Tapert, S., 362
Tarokh, L., 27, 28, 29, 50
Tartakovsky, E., 226
Tashjian, S., 88
Tashjian, S. M., 53
Tasker, F., 119
Taskinen, P., 171
Tate, J., 225
Tatnell, R., 379
Tavernier, R., 29, 223
Taylor, A., 108, 381
Taylor, B., 291
Taylor, C., 36, 37, 195
Taylor, J., 383
Taylor, K., 195, 290
Taylor, R., 118, 326
Taylor, R. D., 114
Taylor, S., 301
Taylor, Z., 92, 117
Taylor, Z. E., 92, 117
Taylor-Thompson, K., 57, 77, 245
Tchetgen, E. J., 89
Teachman, J., 167
Tebes, J., 358
Technow, J. R., 106
Tehranifar, P., 23
Tein, J., 360
Tein, J. Y., 33, 106, 116, 117
Tejada-Gallardo, C., 190
Tell, G. S., 119
Tellegen, A., 213, 352
Telzer, E., 12, 54, 55, 56, 63, 65, 67,
    144, 147, 148, 226, 247, 248,
    267, 270, 333, 339, 378
Telzer, E. H., 54, 55, 65, 100, 101,
    108, 301
Tement, S., 202
Temple, J., 198, 205, 289

Tenenbaum, H., 256
Teng, Z., 199
Teran, L., 318
ter Bogt, T., 138, 140, 204
ter Bogt, T. F., 132
ter Bogt, T. F. M., 128
Tercyak, K., 360
Terenzini, P., 223
Terpeluk, A., 289
Terracciano, A., 35, 212, 213
Terry, K., 338
Terry, M., 23
Terry, R., 229
Tervo-Clemmens, B., 53, 360
Terzian, M., 321
Teslovich, T., 53, 54
Tetzner, J., 163
Teurbe-Tolon, A., 150
Tevendale, H., 214, 215, 216
Tharp, A., 290
Thartori, E., 167
Thayer, R., 313
Thayer, S., 134, 137
Theokas, C., 88, 191, 277
Thieu, M., 46
Thijs, J., 163, 167
Thillay, A., 45
Thomaes, S., 7, 211, 214, 215,
    254, 327
Thomann, C., 228
Thomas, A., 25, 48, 105, 371
Thomas, A. W., 25, 48
Thomas, H., 147
Thomas, J., 279
Thomas, K., 60, 138, 247
Thomas, K. J., 136
Thomas, K. M., 56
Thomas, M., 58
Thomas, R., 164
Thomas, S. L., 162
Thomas, V., 206
Thomasius, R., 204
Thomason, M., 242
Thompson, C., 245
Thompson, E., 92, 146
Thompson, M., 115, 363
Thompson, N., 187
Thompson, P., 164
Thompson, T., 327
Thompson, T. L., 134
Thomson, E., 116
Thornberg, R., 149
Thornberry, T., 136, 319, 344
Thorne, A., 223, 276
Thornton, L., 92, 365, 374
Thorsen, M. L., 117
Thorsteinsson, E., 350, 375
Threlfall, J., 226
Thrul, J., 361
Thurner, S., 135
Tian, L., 382

Tianyi, Y., 227
Tienda, M., 291, 338
Tieu, T.-T., 222, 268
Tiggemann, M., 37, 198
Till, B., 381
Tilley, E. H., 110
Tillman, K. H., 282
Tilton-Weaver, L., 30, 81, 96, 106,
    110, 137, 241, 243
Timeo, S., 203
Timmerman, G., 310
Timmons, A., 276
Timmons, A. C., 101
Timpe, Z. C., 89
Timpson, N., 377
Tinney, F., Jr., 144, 248
Tippetts, A., 361
Tirado, L. M. U., 92, 117
Titzmann, P., 87, 217
Titzmann, P. F., 87, 134
Tobler, N., 363
Tobore, T., 356
Todorov, A., 360
Toenders, Y., 381
Tolan, P., 136, 215, 225, 228, 374
Tolma, E., 360
Tolman, D., 197, 294, 295, 299
Tolsma, J., 134
Tolson, J., 129, 138
Tolstrup, J., 361
Tomasi, D., 48
Tomasik, M., 84, 85
Tomasik, M. J., 85, 170
Tomek, S., 362
Tompsett, C., 92
Tompsett, C. J., 92
Tonev, S., 382
Toomey, R., 227, 233, 310
Toomey, T., 363
Topitzes, D., 93
Torgersen, S., 353
Torney-Purta, J., 145
Toro, C. A., 14, 16
Toro, P., 120
Toro, R. I., 99
Torquati, J., 29
Torrelles-Nadal, C., 190
Torres, S. A., 27, 87
Torres-Gomez, B., 119
Torsheim, T., 232, 233
Tortolero Emery, S., 91
Toste, J., 343
Toth, S., 291
Tottenham, N., 51, 53
Totura, C., 147
Tough, P., 157, 158
Toumbourou, J., 138, 361, 374, 377
Toumbourou, J. W., 67
Townsend, A., 218
Toyokawa, N., 99
Toyokawa, T., 99, 336

Trabjerg, B., 350, 375
Trainor, C. D., 32
Tran, A., 226
Tran, S., 242, 268
Tran, U. S., 381
Tran-Dubongco, M., 225
Trautwein, U., 140, 163, 217, 325,
    326, 336
Travers, L., 187, 332
Treboux, D., 268
Treitman, L., 205
Trejos-Castillo, E., 3
Trekels, J., 19, 198
Tremblay, R., 34, 305, 334, 344,
    362, 365, 366
Tremblay, R. E., 109
Trent, K., 318
Trevaskis, S., 144
Trevitt, J., 312
Trezsniewski, K., 217
Trickett, P., 31, 311, 372
Trickett, P. K., 23, 33
Trifan, T., 275
Trinder, J., 27
Trinh, S., 304
Trinh, S. L., 32
Trompeter, N., 150
Troop-Gordon, W., 32, 144, 147,
    150, 268
Trucco, E., 110, 138, 360
Trucco, E. M., 91
Trudeau, L., 12, 137
Truelove-Hill, M., 52
Truong-Vu, K.-P., 194
Trussell, J., 306
Trzesniewski, K., 213, 214, 217,
    329, 330
Tsai, K., 225, 226, 227
Tsai, K. M., 99, 101, 260
Tsai, Y., 336
Tschann, J., 316
Tse, W., 332
Tseng, W., 143, 164
Tsitsika, A., 149
Tsui, A., 312
Tsukayama, E., 155, 331
Tu, C., 106
Tu, K., 149
Tubman, J., 311
Tucker, C., 107, 186, 324
Tucker, C. J., 108, 180
Tucker, J., 138, 310, 358, 362
Tucker, J. S., 138, 201
Tucker-Drob, E., 64, 109, 212,
    372, 373
Tucker-Drob, E. M., 64, 109, 136
Tucker Smith, C., 273
Tugenberg, T., 89
Tulen, J., 92
Tunçalp, Ö., 321
Tung, I., 110

Turanovic, J., 147
Turbin, M., 361
Turbin, M. S., 352
Turel, O., 29, 195
Turiel, E., 60, 96, 97, 240, 242, 250
Turke, S., 321
Turkheimer, E., 31, 89, 109, 114, 301, 304
Turkle, S., 271
Turner, H., 149
Turner, J., 320
Turner, M., 351
Turner, P., 81
Turner, R., 145, 320
Turney, K., 111
Turok, D., 317
Tuval-Mashiach, R., 283
Twenge, J., 6, 181, 182, 203, 216, 271, 280, 281, 297, 376
Twigg, L., 204
Tyler, K., 118
Tynes, B., 195, 202, 227, 228
Tyrell, F., 282
Tyrka, A. R., 36
Tyson, D., 173, 332
Tyson, K., 133, 227
Tzavara, C., 149
Tzavela, E., 149
Tzoumakis, S., 372

U

Uchino, B., 292
Uckert, K., 247, 248
Udry, J., 20, 37, 289
Uematsu, A., 50
Ueno, K., 291
Uggen, C., 374
Ugueto, A., 382
Uhls, Y., 192
Umaña-Taylor, A., 108, 134, 224, 225, 226, 227, 228, 246, 248, 250
Umaña-Taylor, A. J., 99, 108, 225, 226, 248
Uncapher, M. R., 46
Underwood, M., 136, 143, 150, 192, 193, 202, 203
Unger, J., 138, 222, 226, 228, 318
Unger, J. B., 225
United Nations, 86, 124, 153
Upadhya, K., 313
Upadyaya, K., 193
Updegraff, K., 108, 134, 137, 141, 225, 226, 227, 228, 234, 275, 291
Updegraff, K. A., 99, 107, 108
Upton, R., 227
Urberg, K., 129, 138
Uribe Tirado, L. M., 25, 117, 167
Uriostegui, M., 92, 93

U.S. Census Bureau, 82, 85, 87, 112, 123, 280, 340
U.S. Department of Commerce, 181
U.S. Department of Education, 155, 156
Usher, E. L., 328
U.S. Senate Committee on the Judiciary, 192
Uy, J., 88

V

Vagi, K., 290
Vaillancourt, T., 37, 144, 147, 148, 290
Valdes, O., 329
Valencia, E., 115
Valencia-Agudo, F., 379
Valente, T., 138
Valido, A., 148
Valiente, C., 373
Valkenburg, P., 197, 202, 217, 274
Valkenburg, P. M., 202
Valle, G., 282
Valle, L., 291
Vallerand, R., 187
Vanable, P. A., 314
Van Acker, R., 141
van Aken, C., 275
van Aken, M., 30, 198, 246, 256, 301, 327, 360
van Aken, M. A., 61
Van Boekel, M., 187
Vancampfort, D., 147, 379
Van Cleemput, K., 150
van Dam, S., 59
Van Damme, J., 163
van de Bongardt, D., 300, 302, 303, 304
Vandebosch, H., 150
van de Groep, S., 254
Vandekar, S., 48
Vandell, D., 173, 185, 186, 188, 189, 190
Vandell, D. L., 363
van de Meer, E., 200
van den Akker, A., 243
Van den Akker, A. L., 212
Van Den Berg, D., 360
van den Berg, P., 198, 215, 216
van den Berg, Y., 139, 140, 141, 199
van den Berg, Y. H. M., 140
Vandenbergh, D., 136, 248
Vandenbergh, D. J., 362
van den Bos, E., 55
van den Bos, N., 211
van den Bos, W., 50, 51, 58, 64, 245, 271
Vandenbosch, L., 197, 198, 204
van den Broek, N., 141
van den Eijnden, R., 203, 204

van den Eijnden, R. J. J. M., 33
Van Den Noortgate, W., 110
van der Aa, N., 203
van der Aar, L., 58
Vanderbilt-Adriance, E., 381
Vanderbroek, L., 360
Van der Cruijsen, R., 100
van der Ende, J., 92, 365
Van der Giessen, D., 214
Van der Graaf, J., 242
Van der Graaff, J., 253, 254, 273, 291
van der Heide, D., 362
van der Lely, S., 28
van der Molen, M., 42, 244
van der Put, C., 343
van der Schaaf, M., 165
Vander Stoep, A., 115
van der Valk, I., 271, 291
van der Werf, M., 169
van de Schoot, R., 222, 223, 282
Van de Vaijver, F., 290
Vandevivere, E., 269
Van Dijk, E., 142, 247, 254, 271
van Dijk, M., 211
Van Doorn, M. D., 102
van Duijvenvoorde, A., 63, 245, 248
van Duijvenvoorde, A. C., 58
van Duijvenvoorde, A. C. K., 54, 55, 62
van Dulmen, M., 119
VanEseltine, M., 184
van Geel, M., 138, 144, 217, 338
Van Gelder, J.-L., 210
van Gelderen, L., 269
van Goethem, A., 256
Van Gool, E., 202, 272
Van Gundy, K., 324
Van Gundy, K. T., 180
Vanhalst, J., 145, 217, 273, 275
van Ham, M., 90, 92
van Harmelen, A-L., 31
Van Hoorn, J., 54, 55, 56, 132, 142, 143, 247, 254, 258
Van Houte, M., 338
Van Houtte, M., 306
Van Hulle, C., 304, 353
Van Hulle, C. A., 33
VanHuysse, J. L., 19
van IJzendoorn, M., 143
van Leeuwen, A., 357
van Leeuwen, K., 110, 117, 161, 242
Van Leijenhorst, L., 54, 63, 132, 245
van Lier, P., 26, 144, 151, 211, 214, 220, 273, 366, 368, 372, 373
van Lier, P. A. C., 26
van Lieshout, C., 145, 275
Van Lissa, C., 241
Van Lissa, C. J., 100
Van Meel, C., 54, 245
Vanmeter, J., 372

Van Noorden, T., 145
Vannucci, A., 102, 202, 215
Van Oosten, J., 204
van Os, J., 27
Van Ouytsel, J., 202, 205, 272
Van Petegem, S., 60, 222, 240, 242, 275
van Reijmersdal, E., 59
Van Rijsewijk, L., 273
Van Roekel, E., 145, 217, 275
Van Ryzin, M., 358
Van Ryzin, M. J., 38
VanSchyndel, S., 253
Vansteenkiste, M., 60, 96, 107, 240, 242, 326
van Tubergen, F., 135
van Velzen, L., 381
Van Wagenen, A., 310
Vanwesenbeeck, I., 296
van Zalk, M., 135, 382
van Zantvliet, P., 282
Vaquera, E., 226
Varga, S., 381
Vargas, I., 381
Vargas, R., 92
Varner, F., 225
Varner, F. A., 88
Varol, E., 52
Váša, F., 53
Vasey, M., 353, 365
Vasilenko, S., 289, 299, 300, 313
Vasilenko, S. A., 260, 261
Vasquez-Suson, K., 142
Vaughan, C., 377
Vaughan, E. B., 33
Vaughan, J., 260
Vaughn, M., 365, 367
Vaughn-Coaxum, R., 382
Vazsonyi, A., 3, 173, 200, 212, 361, 372
Vazsonyi, A. T., 107
Veblen-Mortenson, S., 363
Vedder, P., 138, 144, 217, 338
Veed, G. J., 138
Veenstra, R., 6, 114, 122, 127, 130, 135, 138, 140, 141, 145, 148, 244, 264, 273, 275, 279, 304, 310, 334, 371
Veits, G. M., 92
Velderman, M., 145
Velez, W., 175
Vélez-Grau, C., 90–91
Veliz, P., 356
Venables, P., 372
Venkatraman, V., 66
Verbakel, E., 282
Verhaest, D., 6
Verhagen, M., 109, 145, 275
Verheijen, G., 199
Verhoef, M., 33

Verhulst, F., 273, 275, 357, 365, 371, 378
Verkuyten, M., 163
Verma, S., 27
Vermeersch, H., 306
Vermulst, A., 203, 268
Vermunt, J. K., 100, 101
Vernon, L., 194
Véronneau, M., 135
Véronneau, M.-H., 334, 374
Veroude, K., 43
Verschueren, K., 110, 161, 163, 167, 170, 242
Verschueren, M., 37, 38, 222
Verstynen, T., 51, 52
Vértes, P. E., 53
Vesely, S., 303, 360
Vest, A., 188
Vest, A. E., 35, 187
Vetters, R., 231
Viau, A., 180, 187, 188
Vicary, J., 215
Victor, B., 205
Victor, E. C., 63
Victor, R., 252
Viding, E., 164
Vieno, A., 186, 202, 255
Vierling, A., 149
Vigen, T., 201
Vigfusdottir, T. H., 38
Vijayakumar, N., 52, 110, 269
Viken, R. J., 23
Vilhjalmsdottir, A., 90
Viljoen, J., 77
Villafuerte, S., 110, 360
Villalobos, M., 59, 60, 61, 96, 238, 250, 252, 256
Villalobos Solis, M., 276
Villani, V., 198
Villarreal, V., 140
Villatoro, A. P., 166
Villodas, M., 343
Vincent, G., 365
Viner, R., 321
Viner, R. M., 51
Visser, I., 63
Vitacco, M., 365, 372
Vitaro, F., 108, 109, 136, 144, 151, 273, 287, 300, 334, 362, 365, 366, 372, 373
Vitiello, B., 382
Vittinghoff, E., 37
Vivolo-Kantor, A., 311, 379
Vloet, T., 372
Voas, R., 361
Vogel, M., 92, 174
Vogelgesang, J., 150, 199
Volcevski-Kostas, D., 199
Volkow, N. D., 48

Vollebergh, W., 140, 141, 219, 221, 222, 223, 244, 276, 334, 352, 357, 362
Vollebergh, W. A. M., 33, 232, 233
Vollet, J., 143, 335
Vollrath, M. E., 212
Volpe, V., 227
Von Bank, H., 128, 132, 240
Vondracek, F. W., 345
von Eye, A., 190, 191
Von Polier, G., 372
Von Rhein, D., 165
Von Soest, T., 188, 214, 215
Voon, D., 379
Vorona, R. D., 29
Voss, J., 92
Vossen, H., 202, 217
Vossen, H. G. M., 202
Vrangalova, Z., 231, 299
Vrolijk, P., 241
Vuchinich, S., 243, 374
Vuolo, M., 181, 184
Vygotsky, L., 58

W

Waaktaar, T., 353
Waasdorp, T., 149, 150, 170
Wachs, S., 227
Waddell, J., 360
Wade, T. D., 38
Wadlington, W., 76
Wadman, R., 115
Wadsworth, M., 23, 26
Wadsworth, S., 33
Wadsworth, S. J., 30
Wagenaar, A., 361
Wagner, A., 46
Wagner, D., 374
Wagner, E., 311
Wagner, G., 212
Wagner, K., 382
Wagner, L., 269
Wainryb, C., 60, 107, 253, 257
Waite, E. B., 108
Waithaka, E., 333, 334, 337, 343
Waizenhofer, R., 103
Wake, M., 23
Wakefield, M., 357
Walasek, N., 55
Wald, M., 177
Waldron, M., 109, 300
Walhovd, K., 56
Walhovd, K. B., 212
Walker, A., 270, 272, 292
Walker, D., 55, 142, 361
Walker, E., 382
Walker, L., 252, 253
Walker, S., 296, 305
Walker Marciano, A., 289
Walkup, J., 382

Wall, M., 35, 37, 310, 360
Wall, M. W., 38
Wallace, J., 259
Wallace, S., 338
Waller, E., 273
Waller, E. M., 273
Wall Myers, T., 374
Walrave, M., 107, 202, 205, 206, 272
Walsh, B., 38
Walsh, E., 301
Walsh, S., 87, 299, 321, 368
Walsh, W., 205
Walters, E., 8
Walters, G., 108, 246
Walters, R., 10
Walton, G., 326, 330
Walton, M., 361, 368
Walts, K. K., 87
Wang, C., 138, 145, 352
Wang, D., 91, 92
Wang, E., 321
Wang, F., 6, 372, 373
Wang, F. L., 360
Wang, J., 35, 65, 141, 200, 212
Wang, K., 167, 204
Wang, L., 47, 92, 227, 360
Wang, M., 103, 141, 160, 173, 289, 327, 329, 330, 332, 333, 334
Wang, M. T., 103, 160, 172, 174, 343
Wang, M.-T., 108, 161, 168, 169, 326, 328, 329, 330
Wang, N., 247, 311
Wang, P., 195
Wang, Q., 12, 249, 326, 332
Wang, S., 160, 357, 363, 376
Wang, S.-C., 92
Wang, W., 310
Wang, X., 195
Wang, Y., 106, 115, 143, 165, 220, 226, 227, 228, 253, 314, 331, 332, 333, 382
Wångby-Lundh, M., 148
Wangqvist, M., 213
Wang-Schweig, M., 100
Wanner, B., 373
Warburton, W., 193, 199
Ward, E., 34
Ward, L., 197, 198, 294
Ward, L. M., 198, 230
Ware, A., 383
Wargo, J., 142
Warner, L., 304
Warner, S., 326
Warner, T., 91, 304
Warner, T. D., 91, 304
Warren, C., 311
Warren, J., 344
Warren, M., 32, 353, 358
Warren, M. P., 31
Warren, O., 361

Warren, R., 100
Wartberg, L., 204
Waschbusch, D. A., 164
Washbrook, E., 164
Washington, T., 149
Wasserman, A. M., 64
Wasserman, D., 339
Wasserman, R., 16, 22
Watanabe, Y., 45
Waterman, A., 222
Waters, A., 19, 266
Waters, E., 268
Waters, N. E., 46
Waters, P., 215
Waters, S., 277, 336
Watson, P., 376
Watson, R., 229, 230, 231, 311
Watson, R. J., 330
Watson-Thompson, J., 363
Watt, H., 327
Watt, T. T., 158
Watts, A., 363
Watts, E., 164
Watts, S., 91, 304
Way, N., 87, 134, 160, 168, 216, 224, 225, 226, 227, 228, 234, 235, 270, 273, 274, 338
Waylen, A., 294, 300, 301
Wearing, H., 47
Webb, H., 19, 266
Webb, H. J., 19
Webb, L., 92
Weber, E., 63
Weber, E. U., 62
Weber, J., 35, 54
Webster, D., 174, 369
Wechsberg, W., 305
Weddle, C., 165
Weeda, W. D., 62
Weeks, M., 142
Weeks, M. S., 275
Weeland, J., 109
Weerman, F., 138
Weersing, V., 382
Weesie, J., 138
Wegge, D., 150
Wegman, D., 183
Wegner, L., 311
Wehner, E., 283
Wei, E., 374
Wei, X., 106
Wei, Y., 23
Weich, S., 204
Weigard, A., 247
Weinberg, S., 235
Weinfield, N., 267, 268
Weinstein, J., 166
Weinstein, N., 193, 194
Weinstein, S. M., 376
Weiser, J., 245
Weiss, B., 374, 382

Weiss, C., 158, 159
Weisskirch, R., 205
Weisskirch, R. S., 243
Weissman, D., 87, 92, 362, 372
Weisz, J., 382, 383
Weisz, J. R., 382
Weithorn, C., 76
Weitkamp, K., 241
Weitzman, M., 356
Welborn, B. L., 55
Weldon, R. B., 66
Welk, G., 35, 195
Wellings, K., 296, 298
Wells, A., 161, 162
Wells, B., 6, 297
Wells, M., 195
Welner, K. G., 158
Welsh, D., 266, 283, 313
Wen, H., 363
Wen, M., 360
Wendelken, C., 46, 51
Weng, C., 227
Wentzel, K., 161, 333, 334
Werchon, D., 198
Werner, L., 242
Wertheim, E., 37
Wertheim, E. H., 199
Wertz, J., 105, 107, 173, 368
Wesche, R., 138, 300, 304, 361
Weseter, K., 173
West, B., 355, 356
West, M., 178, 337
West, S., 332
West, S. G., 160
Westenberg, M., 271
Westenberg, P. M., 54, 55, 63, 245
Weulen Kranenbarg, M., 210
Weybright, E., 288
Weymouth, B., 105, 242
Weyns, T., 167
Whalen, D. J., 381
Wheeler, L., 108, 226, 228, 282
Wheeler, L. A., 99
Wheldon, C., 229, 230
Whichard, C., 372
Whitaker, D., 303, 304
Whitaker, K. J., 46, 51, 53
Whitbeck, B., 361
White, C., 304
White, G., 112
White, H. R., 85, 136
White, L., 266
White, N., 46
White, R., 92, 168, 217, 225, 253
White, R. M., 117
White, R. M. B., 33, 92, 100, 106,
    168, 225–226
White, S., 92, 365
Whitehead, K. A., 224
Whitehouse, A., 147
Whiteman, S., 107, 108, 134, 233

Whiteman, S. D., 107, 108
Whitesell, N., 212, 215, 216
Whiteside, L., 368
Whiteside, T., 383
Whitsett, D., 117
Whittle, S., 53, 109, 110, 381, 382
Wichstrøm, L., 37, 214, 215,
    371, 377
Wickrama, K., 337, 352, 360
Wickrama, K. A. S., 35, 113, 118
Widaman, K., 92, 117, 214, 217, 225,
    241, 299, 339
Widaman, K. F., 23, 92, 110, 117
Widdowson, A., 63, 351
Widman, L., 140, 204, 248, 280,
    304, 308, 313
Widom, C., 311
Wieczorek, W., 351
Wieczorek, W. F., 91
Wiehler, A., 210
Wielgus, M., 379
Wierenga, L. M., 48
Wiers, R., 362
Wiersma, J., 288, 290
Wiesen-Martin, D., 108
Wiesner, M., 373, 374
Wigfield, A., 8, 214, 324
Wight, D., 300, 301
Wijtzes, A., 302
Wilbrecht, L., 25, 48
Wildes, J., 53
Wildes, J. E., 37
Wildsmith, E., 314
Wiley, A., 383
Wiley, D., 298
Wiley, S., 60, 174
Wilhelms, E. A., 66
Wilkinson, L., 187
Will, G., 144
Will, G.-J., 143
Willard, J., 12
Willems, Y., 103, 106, 107, 245
Williams, C., 363
Williams, D., 227
Williams, J., 225, 228
Williams, K., 267, 328
Williams, L., 299
Williams, M., 107
Williams, R., 134
Williams, S., 22
Williams, T., 328
Williams, W., 58, 336
Williamson, D., 383
Willing, J., 55, 361
Willis, D. S., 259
Willms, D., 305
Willoughby, B., 74, 115
Willoughby, T., 29, 192, 193, 199,
    206, 223, 248, 260, 261,
    352, 360, 379, 382
Willroth, E. C., 74

Wilson, C., 35, 138
Wilson, D., 352
Wilson, H., 309, 311
Wilson, J., 189, 374
Wilson, J. L., 195
Wilson, M., 60, 368
Wilson, S., 2, 72, 73, 79, 84, 86, 214
Wimberly, J. C., 362
Windle, M., 92, 288, 291, 373
Wingood, G., 313, 314
Wingrove, T., 77
Winsler, A., 29
Winston, C., 229
Winter, M., 362
Winter, T., 22
Wirz-Justice, A., 28
Wischnia, S., 327
Wiseman, R., 143
Wishard, A., 136
Wisnowski, J., 51
Witherspoon, D., 228
Witkiewitz, K., 365
Witkow, M., 135, 141, 169, 175, 224,
    225, 229, 327, 335, 338
Witkow, M. R., 229
Wittig, M. A., 224
Witvliet, M., 151
Wodzinski, A., 23, 26
Wodzinski, M., 361
Woertman, L., 282, 296
Woessner, M., 351
Wójcik, S., 149
Wolak, J., 205, 206
Wolchik, S., 116
Wold, B., 214, 217
Woldford-Clevenger, C., 289
Wolf, D. H., 48, 52
Wolf, L., 55, 247
Wolf, P., 362
Wolfe, D., 309
Wölfer, R., 134, 135, 225
Wolfers, J., 111
Wolff, J. M., 66
Wolfrum, S., 231
Wolfson, A., 29
Wolfson, A. R., 27, 28, 29
Wolfson, M., 363
Wolke, D., 147, 324
Womack, S., 60
Wong, I., 325
Wong, J. J., 33
Wong, S. S., 15
Woo, H. S., 226
Wood, D., 238, 332
Wood, G., 289, 291
Wood, J., 202
Wood, L., 195
Wood, P., 352
Wood, S. J., 66
Woodcock, A., 327
Woodhouse, S., 266, 268

Wooding, J., 183
Woods, H., 28, 145, 203
Woods, H. C., 28, 203
Woodward, L., 319
Woodward, M., 63
Woolard, J., 63, 77, 210, 244,
    245, 365
Woolley, M., 332
Woolnough, A., 184
Worden, J., 363
World Population Review, 314
Worrell, F., 228
Worthman, C., 5, 14, 31
Worthman, C. M., 48
Wouters, E., 117
Wouters, S., 163
Wray-Lake, L., 89, 160, 181, 187,
    253, 254, 255, 258, 277,
    334, 346, 353, 358
Wright, A., 261
Wright, B., 368
Wright, D., 361
Wright, M. F., 149, 227
Wright, P., 378
Wrzus, C., 212
Wu, C., 100
Wu, J., 191, 266, 379
Wu, P., 370
Wuerker, A., 372
Wuyts, D., 242
Wylie, L., 368
Wynn, P., 374
Wynn, S. R., 328

X

Xia, M., 275, 291
Xiao, L., 64
Xiao, Y., 90–91
Xie, W., 272
Xin, Z., 214
Xu, F., 314
Xu, J., 332
Xu, X., 303

Y

Yabko, B. A., 145
Yahner, J., 289, 290
Yamaguchi, R., 363
Yanagida, T., 149
Yang, B., 333
Yang, C., 59, 147, 193, 292, 373
Yang, J., 195, 324
Yang, L., 203
Yang, P., 145
Yang, R., 235
Yang, S., 60
Yang, W., 57
Yang, X., 289

Yang, Y., 270
Yang, Z., 321
Yap, M., 99
Yarger, R. S., 47
Yarkoni, T., 58
Yarnell, L., 136
Yasui, M., 225
Yasutake, S., 112
Yau, J., 96, 202, 271, 272
Ybarra, M., 148, 205
Ybarra, M. L., 195
Yeager, D., 147, 148, 149, 172, 190, 202, 203, 267, 326, 328, 330, 383
Yeager, D. S., 144, 214, 373
Yeh, F., 51, 52
Yen, I. H., 35
Yendork, J., 261
Yeo, G. H., 128
Yeo, L., 325
Yerkes, R., 325
Yetnikoff, L., 361
Yetter, A., 181, 184
Yeung, A., 215
Yeung, D. Y., 29, 30
Yeung Thompson, R., 149
Yi, R., 314
Yildiz, M., 92
Yip, T., 165, 220, 224, 225, 227, 228
Yisrael, D., 310
YMCA, 190
Yong, M., 351
Yoon, J., 143
Yoon, Y., 363
Yorgason, J., 277
Yoshikawa, H., 87, 117, 234
Yoskikawa, H., 168
Yotanyamaneewong, S., 25, 92, 107, 117
You, J., 379
Young, A., 310, 355
Young, B., 310

Young, H., 285, 286
Young, J., 140, 147, 339, 375, 382
Young, J. F., 106, 381
Young, V., 331
Youniss, J., 241, 256, 264
Younts, C., 368
Youssef, G., 109, 381
Yu, C., 160
Yu, J., 242
Yu, R., 90, 351, 368
Yu, T., 92, 110, 227, 228, 267
Yuan, A. S. V., 117
Yuan, M., 357
Yücel, M., 53, 362, 376, 381
Yuen, C., 54, 100, 241
Yuen, C. X., 100
Yun, H., 145
Yun, H.-Y., 142
Yurgelun-Todd, D., 362
Yurgelun-Todd, D. A., 48

Z

Zaban, L., 309
Zabin, L., 316, 318
Zach, M., 204
Zachrisson, H. D., 90
Zadow, C., 195
Zadow, C., 195
Zajac, K., 268
Zakin, D., 32
Zald, D., 353
Zaller, N., 361
Zamboanga, B., 222, 226
Zamboanga, B. L., 225
Zamboni, G., 200
Zametkin, A. J., 34
Zammit, S., 363
Zanolie, K., 42, 54, 245, 254
Zapert, K., 358
Zapolski, T., 227
Zarbatany, L., 138, 271

Zarrett, N., 173, 186, 188, 189, 190
Zaslavsky, A., 382
Zaslow, S., 231
Zaso, M., 361
Zavodny, M., 313
Zee, P. C., 28
Zeiders, K., 217, 225, 228, 253
Zeiders, K. H., 99, 108
Zelazny, J., 382
Zelazo, P. D., 50, 60
Zeldin, S., 93
Zelkowitz, R. L., 150
Zeman, J., 240
Zentner, M., 210
Zeringue, M., 96
Zervos, M., 231
Zervoulis, K., 234
Zettergren, P., 135, 151, 334
Zha, W., 359
Zhang, A., 167
Zhang, D., 147, 174, 372
Zhang, H., 199, 352
Zhang, J., 35, 38, 167, 289
Zhang, L., 270, 310, 311
Zhang, Q., 199
Zhang, W., 106, 143, 160, 240, 253, 270
Zhang, X., 141, 211, 334
Zhang, Y., 328
Zhang, Z., 65, 115, 308
Zhao, F., 195
Zhao, L., 51
Zhao, W., 35
Zhao, X., 135
Zhao, Y., 96
Zheng, A., 212
Zheng, H., 361
Zheng, L., 143
Zheng, Y., 164
Zhong, H., 367
Zhou, Q., 253
Zhou, R., 357
Zhu, J., 225, 379

Zhu, X., 339
Zick, C., 181
Zickuhr, K., 192, 202
Zimiles, H., 116
Zimmer-Gembeck, M., 7, 19, 57, 143, 147, 237, 238, 239, 240, 242, 266, 278, 289, 300, 310, 372
Zimmer-Gembeck, M. J., 19, 144
Zimmerman, G. M., 92
Zimmerman, L., 317
Zimmerman, M., 89, 92, 187, 255, 261, 314, 361, 368
Zimmerman, M. A., 89, 92
Zimmerman, R., 299
Zimmermann, F., 171
Zimmermann, G., 60, 222, 242
Zimring, F., 374
Ziol-Guest, K., 328
Zito, R., 304
Zito, R. C., 116
Zlotnik, A., 115, 291
Zohar, A., 212
Zohra, I., 353
Zolna, M., 317
Zolotor, A., 311
Zook, J., 334
Zoon, C. K., 34
Zoratto, F., 204
Zottoli, T. M., 77
Zubrick, S., 147
Zucker, R., 110, 351, 360, 362
Zuckerman, A., 334
Zuffiano, A., 336, 337
Žukauskienė, R., 217
Zurbriggen, E., 234
Zurcher, J., 193, 201
Zwaanswijk, W., 144, 217
Zweig, J., 289
Zweig, J. M., 290
Zwiers, M. P., 165
Zwir, I., 212
Zytynski, T., 363

Subject Index

A

abilities
  beliefs about, and achievement, 339
  and occupational choice, 345
ability grouping, 161–165
abortion, 315–317
abstinence-only sex education, **321**
abstract thinking, 42, 250, 256
academic achievement, **336**–344
  adolescent parenthood and, 319
  in alternatives to public schools, 166–167
  beliefs about success and failure and, 326–327
  bullying and, 147
  changes over time, 339–341
  discrimination and, 227
  early maturation and, 33
  electronic media use and, 193–194
  environmental influences on, 331–335
  ethnic differences in, 157, 337–339, 340
  ethnic stereotypes and, 327
  family influences on, 106, 166, 326, 331–334, 337
  fear of failure and, 325
  friends and, 173, 334–335
  in inner-city schools, 336
  intelligence and, 327–328
  mainstreaming and, 163
  measures of, 336
  motivation and, 325–326
  national trends, 339–341
  No Child Left Behind and, 154–155
  noncognitive factors in, 324–331
  peer attitudes toward, 135, 173
  peer influences on, 135, 173, 334–335
  school choice and, 166
  school size and, 158
  and self-esteem, 215, 217
  and self-image, 215
  socioeconomic status and, 88, 333, 336–337
  standards-based reform and, 156–157
  of students with learning disabilities, 163
  teacher expectations and, 168–170
  tracking and, 162
  transition to secondary school and, 159–160
  and underachievement, 325
  victimization and, 147
  work and, 173, 183–184
academic pressure, 325, 339
acculturation
  and academic achievement, 338
  and parent-adolescent conflict, 100, 250
  and sexual activity, 297
  and susceptibility to peer pressure, 248
achievement, 7, 322–347. *See also* academic achievement; occupational achievement
  as adolescent issue, 8, 323–324
  beliefs about success and failure and, 326–327
  cognitive changes and, 324
  definition of, 323
  disparities in, 336, 341
  environmental influences on, 331–335
  of identity, 221, 222, 223
  importance of, 323
  mastery vs. performance orientation toward, 326, 328
  motivation for, 325–326
  noncognitive factors in, 324–331
  puberty and, 324
  social role transitions and, 69, 324
achievement attributions, **329**
achievement motivation. *See* motivation
acne, 20
Adderall, 165
addiction
  to electronic media, 204
  Internet, 204
  to nicotine, 358, 362
  to social media, 202–203, 204
  susceptibility in adolescence, 361
ADHD (attention deficit/hyperactivity disorder), **164**–165, 372
adolescence
  anthropological perspectives on, 11
  boundaries of (*See* boundaries of adolescence)
  contexts of, 5–6
  definitions of, 2, 3
  elongation of, 70–71
  framework for studying, 4–8
  fundamental changes of, 4–5
  historical perspectives on, 11, 70–73
  invention of, 11, 71–73
  psychosocial development in, 7–8
  scientific study of, 11–12
  social map of, 131
  as social transition period, 69–70
  stereotypes about, 11–12, 95, 96
  theoretical perspectives on, 8–11
  transitions of, 3, 4–5
adolescence-limited offenders, **371**, 373–374
adolescent growth spurt, **17**–19
adolescent parenthood, 318–320
  consequences for children, 318–319
  fathers in, 320
  poverty and, 91, 318, 319
adolescent population
  changes in size of, 122–123
  cohorts, 123, 125
  distributions worldwide, 124
  by ethnicity, 87
  religious affiliation in, 260
adolescent pregnancy. *See* teen pregnancy
adolescent thinking. *See also* cognitive changes
  abstract, 42, 250, 256
  and achievement, 324
  age differences in values and priorities and, 63
  behavioral decision theory on, 62–63
  and cognitive autonomy, 250
  and decision-making abilities, 244–245
  egocentrism in, 43
  emotional and contextual influences on, 63–65
  and identity, 209, 210
  information-processing view of, 45–47
  and intimacy, 264
  about laws, civil liberties, and rights, 61
  logic and intuition in, 66
  moral, 251–253
  multidimensionality of, 43–44
  organization in, 47
  Piagetian view of, 44–45
  political, 255, 256–258
  about possibilities, 41–42
  prosocial, 52, 54, 253–256
  relativism in, 44
  religious, 258–261
  and risk taking, 62–67
  and self-conception, 210–212
  about sexuality, 295
  social, 59–61
  about social conventions, 60–61
  speed of, 46–47
  and susceptibility to influence, 246–249
  theoretical perspectives on, 44–47
  theory of mind in, 59–60
  about thinking, 42–43
adopted adolescents, 119
adrenal gland, 15
adrenarche, **15**
adult attachment interview, **268**
adulthood. *See* emerging adulthood; social redefinition; young adulthood
adult plasticity, **50**–51
adults. *See also* parent(s)/parenting
  attitudes toward adolescent sexuality, 294
  nonfamilial, relationships with, 277
  susceptibility to influence of, 246
advertising
  aimed at adolescents, 180
  alcohol and tobacco, 201, 353
  and body image, 198
affluent adolescents. *See also* socioeconomic status (SES)
  delinquency/juvenile offending by, 370
  parental pressure on, 325
  psychosocial moratorium for, 219
  psychosocial problems in, 90
  substance use by, 90, 360
  tracking and, 161
affluent neighborhoods
  and academic achievement, 336–337
  poor adolescents in, 89–90, 336
  psychosocial problems in, 90
  resource access in, 93
African American adolescents. *See* Black adolescents
African countries, 23
after-school programs. *See also* extracurricular activities; leisure time/activities
  for positive youth development, 190–191
  unstructured, 188–190
after-school work. *See* work, after-school
age-crime curve, **366**

age grading, **122,** 123, 133, 159
agency, **222**
age of majority, **70**
age of opportunity, 50–51
age segregation
   in cliques, 133
   in schools, 122, 123, 133, 159
   in society, 122
aggression, **365.** *See also* bullying;
      violence
   and antisocial peer groups,
      136–137
   in childhood, 365, 373
   as core personality trait, 213
   genetic and environmental
      influences on, 109
   and hostile attributional bias,
      144, 373
   instrumental, 150
   interventions for, 373
   moral disengagement and, 253
   parental psychological control
      and, 242
   and popularity, 140–141
   poverty and, 368
   proactive, 141
   reactive, 141
   and rejection, 142, 144
   relational (meanness), 143–145
   sex differences in, 232, 365
   television violence and, 200
   in unpopular adolescents, 144
   by victims, 147–148
   video gaming and, 199–200
agreeableness, 212
AIDS (acquired immune
      deficiency syndrome), **314**
alcohol abuse
   binge drinking, 354, 362
   consequences of, 359–360
   risk factors for, 360, 361
alcohol use. *See also* alcohol
      abuse; substance use
   arrests of girls for, 367
   brain effects of, and
      addiction, 362
   and dating violence, 289–290
   experimentation with, 355,
      357, 358
   as gateway, 357
   living arrangements and, 85
   in mass media, 200, 201
   messages about, 353
   prevalence and patterns of,
      354–355, 356
   prevention measures, 363
   and self-esteem, 217–218
   and sexual activity, 299
   as transitory behavior, 349, 350
alleles, **108**
androgens, **15,** 301–302
anger, expression of, 276

anhedonic, **353**
anorexia nervosa, **36**
anthropological perspectives
   on adolescence, 11
   on peer groups, 126
antidepressants, 382
antisocial behavior. *See also*
      behavior problems;
      specific types
   adolescence-limited, 371,
      373–374
   causes of, 352, 370–374
   childhood-onset, 364, 366,
      371–373
   chronic/life-course persistent,
      364–365, 371–373
   comorbidity with other
      problems, 351
   as conduct disorder, 364–365
   covert, 366
   as delinquency, 136
   discrimination and, 227
   early maturation and, 30
   early sexual activity and, 300
   family structure and, 112, 371
   friends and, 136–137, 138
   future orientation and, 210
   genetic influences on, 109,
      352, 372
   in girls, 367–368
   interventions for, 137, 373, 374
   as juvenile offending, 367–370
   moral disengagement and,
      253, 372
   overt, 366
   parenting and, 371, 374
   peer groups and, 136–137,
      138, 374
   peer pressure susceptibility
      and, 246–247, 374
   personality traits in, 222, 372
   poor neighborhoods and, 371
   and popularity, 140–141
   progression of, 366
   rates and trends of, 367–370
   sports participation and, 188
   as transitory problem, 349
   work and, 184
antisocial peer groups, 136
antisocial personality
      disorder, **364**
anxiety
   and achievement, 325
   breakups and, 289
   in childhood, 350, 375
   co-rumination and, 273, 378
   and intimacy, 264, 265, 266
   parental psychological control
      and, 242
   and rejection, 144
   sports and, 188
anxiety disorders, 350, 375, 382

anxious-avoidant attachment, **260**
anxious-resistant attachment, **260**
Asian/Asian American
      adolescents
   and academic achievement,
      157, 338–339
   and behavioral autonomy, 248
   behavioral autonomy
      expectations of, 249
   beliefs about achievement, 339
   dating by, 282
   and discrimination, 227, 228
   ethnic identity in, 224
   family structure of, 112
   parenting styles and, 106
   peer pressure susceptibility
      of, 248
   quality of friendships, 270
   self-esteem in, 216
   and sexual activity, 297
   substance use in, 357
   and suicide attempts, 379
   teacher expectations of, 170
   teen pregnancy in, 314
   in U.S. population, 87
   victimization of, 368
attachment, **266**
   in adolescence, 268–269
   and emotional autonomy, 239
   in infancy, 266–268
   in parent-adolescent
      relationships, 268–269
   and rejection sensitivity, 144
   in romantic relationships,
      281, 283
   to school, 165–166, 187–188
   theory of, 266–269
   types of, 266
attention, 45–46
attention deficit/hyperactivity
      disorder (ADHD),
      164–165, 372
authoritarian parenting, **104**
   and behavioral autonomy, 249
   and emotional autonomy, 243
   in ethnic minority families, 106
   after permissive parenting, 243
authoritarian thinking, 256
authoritative parenting, **104,**
      105–107
   and academic achievement,
      332–333
   and behavioral autonomy,
      248–249
   in divorced and remarried
      families, 116
   and emotional autonomy,
      242–243
   and identity, 222
   overview of, 106–107
   and prosocial behavior, 253
   and sexual activity, 302

authority, questioning of, 60
authority conflicts, **366**
autobiographical memory, **46**
autoerotic behavior, **296**
autonomy, **7,** 236–261
   as adolescent issue, 7, 237–239
   in authoritative parenting,
      106, 107
   behavioral (*See* behavioral
      autonomy)
   cognitive (*See* cognitive
      autonomy)
   emotional (*See* emotional
      autonomy)
   overview of, 237
   puberty and, 238
   social role transitions and, 69,
      238–239

B

baby boom, **82, 123**
baby boom generation,
      82, 123, 125
Bar (Bas) Mitzvah, **79**
basal metabolism rate, **33**
behavior. *See also specific types*
   and brain development, 57
   crowd membership and, 132
   friends' influence on, 138
   puberty and, 16–17, 25–33
   sex differences in, 231–232
behavioral autonomy, **239,**
      244–250
   decision-making abilities and,
      244–246
   expectations for, group
      differences in, 249–250
   and intimacy, 283
   susceptibility to influence and,
      246–249
behavioral decision theory,
      62–63
behavioral genetics, **108**
behaviorism, 10
behavior problems, 364–375.
      See also specific types
   childhood-onset, 350
   conduct disorder as, 364–365
   co-occurrence of, 352
   in early-maturing boys, 30–31
   in early-maturing girls, 33
   as externalizing disorders, 351
   future orientation and, 210
   genetic and environmental
      influences on, 352–353
   masculine orientation and, 234
   media portrayal of, 349
   parenting and, 371, 374
   religious involvement and, 261
   self-esteem and, 217–218
   transitory nature of, 349

unstructured leisure time
and, 190
video gaming and, 199, 200
work and, 184–185
beliefs
about abilities, and
achievement, 339
and academic achievement,
326–327
development of, 259
political, 257–258
religious, 258–261
"best friendships," 270
biculturalism, 225
Biden administration, 156
Big Brothers/Big Sisters
programs, 277
big fish–little pond effect, **163**
binge drinking, **354,** 362
binge eating disorder, **36**
biological transitions, 4–5, 13–39.
See also puberty
biosocial theories, **8–9**
biracial adolescents, 216,
228–229
birth control pills, 311, 313
birth rates, 86
bisexuality, 229. *See also*
LGBTQ youth
Black adolescents. *See also* ethnic
differences; ethnic
minority adolescents
and academic achievement,
157, 336, 338, 340
and "acting White," 133
cross-ethnic friendships of, 166
and crowds, 133
and discrimination,
226, 227, 228
eating disorders in, 36–37
and educational
attainment, 340
ethnic identity in, 224
families of, 106, 112
homeless, 118
as juvenile offenders, 370
obesity in, 34
parenting styles and, 106
peer pressure susceptibility
of, 248
poverty rates for, 112
religious involvement in,
260, 261
and romantic relationships, 282
school discipline and, 170
and school violence,
173, 174
self-esteem in, 216–217
and sexual activity, 297
stereotypes of, 370
substance use in, 357
and suicide attempts, 379

teacher expectations of,
169–170
teen pregnancy in, 314
tracking and, 161
transition to secondary
school, 161
in U.S. population, 87
body dissatisfaction
in boys, 37, 38–39
in girls, 18–19, 31–32, 37
prevalence and causes of,
37–38
body fat
as puberty trigger, 16
ratio of muscle to, 18–19
body hair, 20
body image, 19, 198–199
body mass index (BMI), **34**
boredom, at school, 172–173
boundaries of adolescence, 2–4
adolescents' views on, 81
brain development and, 3
legal, 76–78
in social redefinition, 76–78
boys. *See also* sex differences
ADHD in, 164
antisocial behavior/
delinquency in (*See*
antisocial behavior)
body dissatisfaction in, 37,
38–39, 199
cross-sex friendships and,
278–279, 281
cyberbullying by, 150
depression in, 376, 377–378
early- and late-maturing, 30–31
ethnic discrimination
toward, 227
first ejaculation in, 20, 30
first sexual experience, 297,
306–307
gender-role behavior in,
232–233, 234–235
growth spurt in, 18
identity development in, 222
intimacy in friendships,
273–274
intimacy in romantic
relationships,
281–282, 286
"jocks," 127, 187
meaning of sex to, 306
parental relationships of,
276, 303
peer rejection of, 142
popular, 141
pubertal timing in, 22, 24
reaction to first ejaculation, 30
risk taking in, 64
sexual activity in, 288, 297,
298, 301–302, 306
sexual maturation in, 19–21

sexual orientation in, 309
in sports, 187, 188
time spent with peers, 127
transition to secondary
school, 161
Boys and Girls Clubs of
America, 190
brain activity. *See* brain function
brain development, 47–57
in ADHD, 164–165
and behavior, 57
and boundaries of
adolescence, 3
and brain plasticity, 26, 50–51
in chronic antisocial
behavior, 372
and decision-making
abilities, 245
dual systems theories on, 9
functional changes in, 52–53
hormonal influence on, 16–17,
25, 48, 54
and intelligence, 57–59
Internet addiction and, 204
and intimacy, 264
and memory, 46
and peer pressure
susceptibility, 55, 248
poverty and, 87–88
rejection sensitivity and, 144
research methods, 47–48
and risk and reward behavior,
53–54, 62–67
and self-regulation, 9, 52–53
sex differences in, 48
and social brain, 54–56
socioeconomic status and, 337
structural changes in, 51–52
substance use and, 51, 361–363
synaptic formation and
pruning in, 49–50
violence and, 92
Brain Development Index, 58
brain function, **47**
changes in, 52–53
and depression, 381
in Instagram "likes," 204
overview of, 48–50
and peer pressure
susceptibility, 247
in rejection, 144, 267
substance use and, 361–363
brain imaging, 47–48
brain plasticity, **26, 50**–51, 362
"brains," 131, 133
brain size, 48
brain structure, **47**
changes in, 51–52
Internet addiction and, 204
media violence and, 200
and self-esteem, 214–215
breakups, 281, 289

breast development, 21
*Brown v. Board of Education
of Topeka,* 165
bulimia, **36**
bullying, 145–149. *See also*
relational aggression;
victimization
effects of exposure to, 145–146
in inner city schools, 157
interventions against, 148–149
of and by LGBTQ youth, 168
nature of, 145
online, 149–151
progression of, 366
rates and trends, 145, 146
responses to, 149
school climate and, 168
sexual, 310
traits of bullies, 145
by victims, 147–148
Bush administration, 154–155

C

callous-unemotional (CU) traits,
365, 372
casual sex, 299
Catholic schools, 166
causation, **196**
CBT (cognitive behavioral
therapy), 382
charter schools, **156**–157,
166–167
childbearing, teen. *See* adolescent
parenthood; teen
pregnancy
childhood
aggression in, 365, 373
antisocial behavior in, 364,
366, 371–373
anxiety in, 350, 375
depressed mood in, 376
friendships in, 264, 265
identity in, 209
image of parents in, 240, 241
interpersonal needs in, 264
moral reasoning in, 251
psychosocial problems
starting in, 350
sexuality in, 294
child protectionists, **72**
children
of adolescent mothers,
318–319
brain connectivity in, 53
thinking in, 41, 42, 43
Chinese American
adolescents, 333
chlamydia, **314**
cis-gender, 229
citizenship role, transition
into, 83

CIU (compulsive Internet use), 204
civic engagement, **254**–256
civil liberties, adolescent thinking about, 61
classroom climate, 167–174
 and bullying, 168
 mastery vs. performance orientation in, 328
 positive, characteristics of, 167–168
 of private vs. public schools, 167
 and school violence, 173–174
 and student engagement, 170–173
 teacher expectations and, 168–170
class size, 159
cliques, **127**–129, 133–139
 common interests in, 135–137
 vs. crowds, 128, 129
 popular, dynamics of, 141
 selection vs. socialization in, 137–139
 similarities of members, 133–135
 structural changes over time, 129–131
 and student engagement, 173
cofigurative cultures, **126**
cognitive autonomy, **239**, 250–261
 and moral development, 250–253
 and political thinking, 256–258
 and prosocial reasoning and behavior, 253–256
 and religion, 258–261
cognitive behavioral therapy (CBT), **382**
cognitive changes, 40–67. *See also* adolescent thinking; brain development; intelligence
 and achievement, 324
 by age 15, 47
 in attention, 45–46
 and autonomy, 238
 and cognitive autonomy, 250
 electronic media use and, 193
 and emotional autonomy, 241
 and identity, 209–210
 and intimacy, 264
 in memory, 46
 metacognition as, 42
 in organizational ability, 47
 overview of, 5, 41–44
 and peer group structure, 130
 and sexuality, 294–295
 social cognition as, 59–61
 in speed of thinking, 46–47

thinking about possibilities as, 41–42
cognitive development, Piagetian theory of, 9–10, 44–45
cognitive-developmental view, **44**
cognitive style, and depression, 381–382
cohorts, **78**
 adolescent population, 123, 125
collective efficacy, **91**
college-bound students, 175–176
 resources spent on, 176–177
college students. *See also* postsecondary education
 identity development in, 223
 religious involvement of, 260
 social distancing guidelines ignored by, 2, 61
comic books, 192
Common Core, **156**
communication
 on Internet (*See* social media)
 parent-adolescent (*See* parent-adolescent communication)
 in transition to romantic relationships, 283
community(ies). *See also* neighborhoods
 and academic achievement, 333–334
 leisure activity support by, 189, 190–191
 secondary schools' integration into, 178
 and social capital, 333–334
 and substance use risk, 361
community college students, goals of, 176
community service, 255–256
comorbid, **351**
comprehensive high school, **154**
comprehensive sex education, **321**
compulsive Internet use (CIU), **204**
concentration, leisure activities and, 185–186
concrete operations, **44**
condom use, 311, 312, 313, 314
conduct disorder, **364**–365
conflict
 authority, 366
 in friendships, 270, 271, 273, 276
 intergenerational, 10
 marital, 114–115
 parent-adolescent (*See* parent-adolescent conflict)
 resolution of, 271
 in romantic relationships, 283, 291
 sibling, 107, 277

connectedness. *See* attachment
conscientiousness, 212
consumers, adolescents as, 73, 180
continuous transitions, **83**
contraception, 311–314
conventional moral reasoning, **251**, 252
correlation, **196**
cortisol, **15**
co-rumination, **273**, 378
covert antisocial behavior, **366**
COVID-19 pandemic
 anxiety during, 376
 college education during, 61, 247
 impact on adolescents, 2
 and political thinking, 258
 risk-taking during, 2
 schools during, 2, 154, 156
 sedentary behavior during, 35
 social distancing guidelines ignored during, 2, 61
 young adults living at home during, 82, 85
"crews," 136
crime victims, adolescents as, 368–369
criminal behavior, **365**. *See also* juvenile offending
criminal defendants, adolescents as, 77
criminal justice system, **76**
critical thinking, **155**
cross-ethnic friendships, 166
cross-sectional study, **25**
cross-sex friendships, 278–279, 281
crowds, **127**–133
 changes in influence of, 130–131
 changes in structure of, 129–131
 vs. cliques, 128, 129
 map of, 131
 parents' influence on, 134
 as reference groups, 131–133
cultivation theory, **196**
cultural capital, **333**
cultural differences. *See also* ethnic differences; international comparisons; *specific groups*
 in behavioral autonomy expectations, 249–250
 in body dissatisfaction in girls, 38
 in bullying rates, 145
 in family's importance, 99, 123
 in family vs. peer socialization, 126

in parent-adolescent relationships, 96, 99, 102, 106
 in peer pressure susceptibility, 248
 in puberty onset reactions, 32
 in self-conceptions, 211
 in transition to adulthood, 80–85
custody, 115–116
CU (callous-unemotional) traits, 365, 372
cutting, 379
Cyberball (game), 266–267
cyberbullying, **149**–151
 of romantic partners, 289
 sexting as, 205

D

date rape, 288, **309**, 310
dating. *See also* romantic relationships
 age of onset, 282
 decline in, 280, 281
 patterns of, 282–283
 reasons for, 283–284
 violence in, 289–291
death penalty, 77
decision making
 behavioral decision theory on, 62–63
 changes in abilities of, 244–245
 development of, 62, 66, 244
 legal, 245–246
 logic and intuition in, 66
 occupational, 345
 peer pressure susceptibility and, 248
 and risky behavior, 62–63
de-idealization, 240–241
delayed phase preference, **27**–28
delay of gratification, **325**
delinquency, 136, **365**. *See also* antisocial behavior; juvenile offending
 causes of, 352, 370–374
 and early sexual activity, 301
 in poor neighborhoods, 91, 92
 on school days, 189
 self-reported rates of, 370
 sports participation and, 188
 work and, 184
dendrites, 48
depressed mood, 375, 376
depression. *See also* mental health problems
 breakups and, 289
 bullying and, 147
 causes of, 26–27, 381–382
 childhood anxiety and, 375

comorbidity with other
problems, 353, 375
co-rumination and, 273, 378
diagnostic criteria for, 376
diathesis-stress model of, 109,
381–382
discrimination and, 227
in early-maturing girls, 31, 32
emotionality traits in, 353
environmental influences
on, 382
false-self behavior and, 211–212
friends and, 138, 273
genetic influences on, 381
in girls, 377–378
hormones and, 382
in LGBTQ adolescents, 230
low self-esteem and, 217
nature of, 375–376
parental psychological control
and, 242
prevalence of, 375–376
puberty and, 26–27, 382
rejection and, 144
and self-injury, 379
sex differences in, 377–378
sexual activity and, 300
social media and,
202–204, 376
stress and, 377–378, 382
and suicide, 379
symptoms of, 375, 376
in transgender adolescents, 231
treatment of, 382
in unpopular adolescents, 144
video gaming and, 200
depressive disorder, 375, 376
depressive syndromes, 375, 376
desegregation, 165–166. *See also*
multiethnic schools
detachment, **239–240**
developing countries, adolescent
populations of, 86
developmental plasticity, **50–51**
developmental readiness
hypothesis, 32
developmental stages
adolescence as, invention of,
11, 71–73
emerging adulthood as, 11,
73–74
and interpersonal development,
264–265
midlife as, 76
developmental trajectories,
357–358
deviance, 352. *See also*
antisocial behavior
"deviancy training," 137
diathesis, 109
diathesis-stress model, **109, 381**
of depression, 109, 381–382

dieting, 35, 198
differential susceptibility
theory, **110**
diffusion tensor imaging
(DTI), **47**
discontinuous transitions, **83**
discrimination. *See also*
victimization
and achievement, 338
ethnic (*See* ethnic
discrimination)
against LGBTQ youth,
230, 310
disengagement. *See* moral
disengagement; student
engagement
dismissing adolescents, 268
disordered eating, **35–37**
disorganized attachment, **260**
distress, internalized, 38, 376
divided attention, **45**
divorce
custody, contact, and conflict
after, 115–116
and dating, 282
effects of, 113, 115
and grandparents, 277
marital conflict and,
114–115
prevalence of, 111
and sexual activity, 303–304
dopamine, **53, 361–362**
dropping out, 157, 184, 341–344
drug use. *See* substance use
dual systems theories, 9
dyscalculia, **163**
dysgraphia, **163**
dyslexia, **163**

E

early adolescence, **4**
cliques in, 129
crowds in, 130
dating in, 285
decision making in, 244, 245
divorce in, 114
ethnic identity in, 224
and intimacy, 265, 269, 274,
275, 276
moods in, 185
moral reasoning in, 251
parent-adolescent relationships
in, 100–101, 275
peer group structure in, 129
peer pressure susceptibility in,
246, 247
political thinking in, 256
romantic relationships in,
284, 285
school transitions and,
159–160

self-image in, 214
sex segregation in friendships
in, 278
sexual activity in (*See* early
sexual activity)
sibling relationships in,
107, 277
substance use in, 358
work in, 182
early maturation. *See also*
pubertal timing
and dating, 282, 287–288
and eating disorders, 38
psychosocial impacts of, 26,
30–33
and sexual activity, 301–302
and sexual harassment, 310
early sexual activity
and antisocial behavior, 300
early dating and, 288
household composition and,
303–304
and mental health, 300
parental influences on, 302,
303–304
peer influence on, 305
psychological profile of,
299–300
risk factors for, 297
"early starters," 4, 287–288
eating disorders, 35–39
contributing factors of,
37–39
disordered eating and,
35–37
mass media and, 198
risk of developing, 19
ecological perspective on human
development, **6**
education
during COVID-19 pandemic,
2, 61
postsecondary (*See*
postsecondary education)
secondary (*See* secondary
education)
educational achievement. *See*
academic achievement
educational attainment, **336**
college enrollment and
graduation rates, 175
ethnic differences in, 340
high school graduation
rates, 343
trends in, 340
and work and earnings, 177,
178, 336
"education focused," 4
education policy
alternatives to public school as,
156–157
encouraging college education,
176–177

historical, 153–154
No Child Left Behind,
154–156
social promotion as, 155, 344
standards-based reforms as,
156–157
egocentrism, **43**, 214
ejaculation, first, 20, 30
electronic cigarettes. *See* vaping
electronic media use, 191–206.
See also social media use;
text messaging; video
games/gaming
as addiction, 204
controversial content,
196–201
and cyberbullying,
149–151, 289
impacts of, 193–195
and mental health, 193,
194–195, 203
prevalence and frequency of,
192–193
as puberty trigger, 16
and sleep, 194–195
theories of, 195–196
elementary schools, secondary
schools compared to, 160
embarrassment, 55, 56
emergency contraception, 312
emerging adulthood, **4**. *See also*
young adulthood
historical perspectives on, 73,
82–83, 84
living with parents in, 85
non-universality of, 74
psychological well-being in,
74–76
as social invention, 11, 73–76
emotional autonomy, **239–243**
detachment and, 239–240
parenting practices and,
241–243
research on, 240–241
triggers of development, 241
emotional intelligence, **254**
emotionality, negative, 353
emotional problems. *See* mental
health problems
emotional reactivity
brain development and,
53–54
and risk taking, 63–65
romantic relationships and, 275
emotional states of others, 56
empathy, 155, 199, 253,
254, 271
employment. *See* occupation; work
"employment focused," 4
empty nest, 99
endocrine system, **14–15**.
See also hormones

environmental influences
    on academic achievement,
        331–335
    on depression, 382
    differential susceptibility
        to, 110
    on gender-role behavior, 232
    genetic influences interacting
        with, 108–110
    on homosexuality, 309
    on intelligence, 58–59
    on obesity, 35
    on personality, 212
    on psychological
        development, 8
    on pubertal timing, 22–25
    shared and nonshared, 108, 109
epiphysis, **18**
EPOCH (Engagement,
    Perseverance, Optimism,
    Connectedness, and
    Happiness) model, 190
Eriksonian theory of identity
    development, 9, 218
erotic fantasies, 296
ESM (experience sampling
    method), **185**–186
estrogens, **15,** 302
ethnic composition
    of social environment, and
        self-esteem, 216–217
    of U.S. population, 87
ethnic differences. *See also*
        specific groups
    in academic achievement, 157,
        337–339, 340
    in achievement self-
        handicapping, 326
    in adolescent parenthood, 318
    in behavioral autonomy
        expectations, 249–250
    in beliefs about intelligence, 327
    in body dissatisfaction in girls,
        19, 31–32
    in college enrollment, 175
    in eating disorders, 36–37
    in educational attainment, 340
    in family structure, 112
    in friendship quality, 270
    in homelessness, 118
    in obesity, 34
    in parenting, 106
    in peer pressure
        susceptibility, 248
    in poverty rate, 112
    in pubertal timing in girls, 22
    in religiosity, 260
    in romantic relationships,
        282, 283
    in school discipline, 170
    in school victimization, 173
    in self-esteem, 216–217

in sex differences in
    intimacy, 274
in sexual initiation age,
    297–298
in substance use, 357
in suicide attempt rate, 379
in teacher expectations,
    169–170
in teen pregnancy, 315
in violent crime
    victimization, 368
ethnic discrimination
    and academic achievement,
        338–339
    and Black adolescents, 224
    and ethnic identity, 224,
        227–228
    in juvenile justice system, 370
    parents' communication
        about, 226
    in school discipline, 170
ethnic identity, **224**–229
    development of, 224–226
    discrimination and, 224,
        227–228
    of immigrants, 224, 226
    of multiethnic adolescents,
        228–229
    and self-esteem, 216
ethnicity. *See also* ethnic
        differences; *specific groups*
    and academic achievement
        stereotypes, 327
    adolescent population by, 87
    and crowd membership, 133
ethnic minority adolescents.
        See also specific groups
    and academic achievement,
        106, 337–339
    discrimination and (*See* ethnic
        discrimination)
    ethnic identity in, 224–229
    in multiethnic schools, 165–166
    and No Child Left Behind, 155
    and obesity, 34
    parenting of, 106
    political behavior of, 257
    and poverty, 88
    self-esteem in, 216–217
    teacher expectations of,
        169–170
    tracking and, 161
    transition to adulthood,
        86–87
    transition to secondary
        school, 161
    and violent crime
        victimization, 368
ethnic segregation
    in peer groups and friendships,
        134–135
    in secondary schools, 165–166
ethnic socialization, **225**–226

ethnography, 141
European countries
    age of sexual initiation in,
        297–298
    pubertal timing in, 23, 24
    teen pregnancy rates in, 315
    evenings out, 188–189.
        See also dating
evidence-based practices, **374**
executive function, **52**
exit examinations, 156
experience sampling method
    (ESM), **185**–186
experimentation
    in identity development, 219,
        220, 221
    with risky/problem behavior,
        300–301
    with roles, 219
    with same-sex sexual
        activities, 308
    with substances, 218, 358, 361
extended-family relationships, 277
externalizing disorders, **351,**
        364–375. *See also*
        aggression; antisocial
        behavior; behavior
        problems; juvenile
        offending
    categories of, 364–366
    comorbidity of, 351–353
    conduct disorder as, 364–365
    prevention and treatment of,
        374–375
    stress and, 383
extracurricular activities, 6,
        186–188
    historical perspectives on, 180
    impacts of, 187–188
    participation patterns, 186
    positive youth development
        programs, 190–191
    school size and, 158
    sports, 186, 187–188
    and student engagement, 173
extraversion, 212

F

"Facebook depression," 203
facial expression recognition, 55–56
facial hair, 20
failure
    attributions for, 329
    beliefs about, 326–327
    fear of, 325
false-self behavior, **211**–212
familism, **99,** 253
family(ies), 6, 94–120. *See also*
        parent(s)/parenting
    and academic achievement,
        106, 166, 326, 331–334

and adolescence, overview of,
    6, 95
Black, 106, 112
changes in relations in
    adolescent years, 95–103
changes in structure of,
    111–120
conflict in (*See* parent-
    adolescent conflict)
divorce and, 111, 113–116
extended, 277
foster, 119–120
and genetic influences, 108–111
immigrant, 99–100, 338
importance in traditional
    cultures, 99, 123
importance to adolescents,
    99, 120
with lesbian or gay parents, 119
marital conflict in, 114–115
and mood, 185
needs and functions of, 99
and occupational choice, 346
in poverty, 92, 112–113, 117–118
and pubertal timing, 23
remarried/stepfamilies, 112,
    116–117
sibling differences within,
    110–111
sibling relationships, 107–108
single-parent, 111–112
socialization by, vs. peers, 126
supportive, 276–277
family-based interventions, 374
family capital, **343**
family roles, adult, transition
    into, 83
family structure. *See also* divorce;
        single-parent families
    changes in, 111–120
    and sexual activity, 303
family systems theory, **95**
family therapy, multisystemic, 374
Fast Track program, 373
fat. *See* body fat
fathers
    attachment to, 266
    de-idealization of, 240–241
    in divorce, 114, 116
    intimacy with, 275, 276
    midlife crisis in, 98
    relationship with, 102–103,
        114, 276
    in teen pregnancy and
        parenthood, 320
fear of failure, 325
fear of missing out (FOMO), **203**
feedback loop, **15**
    hormonal, 14–15
femininity, 233–235, 274, 377.
        See also gender-role
        behavior

finances/financial strain.
See also poverty
in adolescent years, 99
and autonomy, 237
stress effects of, 117–118
work and, 183
five-factor model, 212
FOMO (fear of missing out), **203**
formal operations, **44**
foster care, **119**–120
free speech, right to, 78
free time. *See* leisure time/activities
Freudian theory, 9
friendship(s). *See also* cliques;
peer relationships
and academic achievement,
173, 334–335
and antisocial behavior,
136–137, 138
and attitudes toward
school, 135
"best," 270
changes in nature of, 269–270
common interests in, 135–137
conflict in, 270, 271, 273, 276
cross-ethnic, 166
cross-sex, 278–279
display of intimacy in, 270–271
increase in quality of, 270
influence on behavior, 138
in interpersonal
development, 265
intimacy in, 263, 265, 270–271
jealousy in, 270
parents' role in choice of, 137
popularity and, 142
selection vs. socialization in,
137–139
sex differences in, 270
sex segregation in, 278
similarities of friends, 135–137
social media use and, 202, 203,
271–272
stability of, 138–139
and substance use, 138
time spent with friends, 122,
126–127
tracking and, 161
and transition to secondary
school, 161
unstructured leisure time with
friends, 189, 190
functional connectivity, **53**
functional magnetic resonance
imaging (fMRI), **47**
future orientation, **210**

G

gangs, **136**
gateway drugs, **357**
gender equality, 232, 233

gender fluidity, 229, 231
gender identity, **229**
gender intensification
hypothesis, **232**
gender-role behavior, **229**
and depression in girls, 377
development of, 231–232
and gender identity and sexual
orientation, 229–230
masculinity and femininity
and, 233–235
nonconformity to, 232–233, 234
socialization into, 232–233
generational dissonance, **99**–100
genetic influences, 108–111
on antisocial behavior, 109,
352, 372
on depression, 381
on divorce effects, 114
on early sexual activity,
303–304
on homosexuality, 309
interaction with environmental
influences, 108–110
on obesity, 35
on personality, 212
on pubertal timing, 16, 22–25
and sibling difference, 110–111
on substance abuse, 360
Gen X, 123, 125
Gen Y, 123
Gen Z, 123, 125
gifted students, **162**
girls. *See also* sex differences
ADHD in, 164
antisocial behavior in, 367
beliefs about, and
achievement, 327
body dissatisfaction in, 18–19,
31–32, 37, 198–199
cross-sex friendships and,
278–279, 281
cyberbullying by, 150
depression in, 376, 377–378
early-dating, 287–288
early-maturing, 26, 31–33
early sexual activity in, 300,
303–304
eating disorders in, 19, 35–39
ethnic discrimination
toward, 227
first sexual experience,
306–307
gender-role behavior in, 233,
234–235
growth spurt in, 18
homeless, 118
hormonal and social factors in
sexual activity, 302
identity development in, 222
intelligence of, beliefs
about, 327

intimacy in friendships,
272–274
intimacy in romantic
relationships,
281–282, 286
jealousy in friendships, 270
as juvenile offenders, 367–368
low self-esteem in, 270
meaning of sex to, 306–307
menarche in, 22, 23–24, 29–30
parental relationships of, 276,
303
popular, 141
pubertal timing in, 22, 23–24
reaction to menarche in, 29–30
relational aggression
(meanness) in, 143–145
same-sex sexual activity in, 308
self-esteem of, 215–216
sexual abuse of, 311
sexual activity in, 288, 297,
298, 300, 306–307
sexual harassment of, 310
sexual maturation in, 21–22
sexual orientation in, 309
suicide and suicide attempts in,
379–380
time spent with peers, 127
glands, **14**
gonadotropin-releasing hormone
(GnRH) neurons, **14**
gonads, **15**
gonorrhea, **314**
grades, 159, 336
grandparents, 277
gratification, delay of, 325
gray matter, 49–50
grit, 155
growth mindset, **327**, 330
growth spurt, adolescent, **17**–19
guns, 368, 369

H

Harlem Children's Zone, 157
height, 18
helplessness, learned, 327
herpes, **314**
high-ability students, placement
of, 162
high school. *See also*
secondary schools
comprehensive, 154
graduation rates, 343
hippocampus, 362
historical perspectives
on adolescence, 11, 70–73
on social redefinition, 82–83, 84
HIV (human immunodeficiency
syndrome), **314**
home alone. *See* self-care,
after school

home environment. *See also*
family(ies)
and academic achievement,
331–334
home leaving, 84–85. *See also*
living with parents
homeless adolescents, 118
homeschooling, 166
homosexual adolescents. *See*
LGBTQ youth
homosexuality, 230, 308–309
antecedents of, 309
attitudes toward, 308
and gender identity and gender-
role behavior, 229
prejudice against, 230, 285, 310
"hooking up," 297, 299
hormonal feedback loop, 14–15
hormones, **14**
biosocial theories on, 9
and brain development, 16–17,
25, 48, 54
and depression, 382
in emergence of sexuality, 301
HPG axis and, 15, 16
influence of, 16–17
levels and set point, 14–15
and mood, 26–27
set point, 14–15
sex, 15
and sexual activity, 301–302
stress, 15
hostile attributional bias, **144**, 373
household composition.
See family structure
housing, 85, 92
HPG (hypothalamic-pituitary-
gonadal) axis, 15, 16
human development, ecological
perspective on, **6**
human papillomavirus
(HPV), **314**
hyperactivity, 164–165
hypothalamus, **15**
hypothetical thinking, 42

I

iatrogenic effects, **137**
identity, **7,** 208–235
achievement of, 221, 222, 223
as adolescent issue, 7, 209–210
cognitive change and, 209–210
crowd membership and,
132–133
development over time,
222–223
Eriksonian theory of, 9, 218
ethnic (*See* ethnic identity)
gender, 229
and gender, 229–235 (*See also*
gender-role behavior)

vs. identity diffusion, 218
moral, 252
negative, 221
occupational, 345
personality dimensions and, 212–213
problems in developing, 220–221
psychosocial moratorium and, 219, 221, 222, 223
puberty and, 209
religiosity and, 260
research on, 221–223
role experimentation in, 219
and self-conception, 210–213
and self-esteem, 213–218
sense of, 210
and sexual orientation, 229–230
social roles and contexts and, 69, 210, 218–220
states of, 221–222, 223
identity crises, 218–221
and behavioral problems, 350
Erikson's theory on, 9, 218
in ethnic identity, 224
as social invention, 11
ways of resolving, 220
identity diffusion, **220**, 221
identity vs., **218**
problems in, 222
studies of, 223
identity foreclosure, 220-**221**, 222, 223
identity status, **221–222**
imaginary audience, **43**
imitation, 10, 132
immigrant adolescents
and academic achievement, 338
vs. Americans of same ethnicity, 226, 338
and behavioral autonomy, 250
cliques and friends of, 134
conflict with parents, 99–100
and discrimination, 227
and ethnic identity, 224, 226
and family obligations, 99, 338, 339
and postsecondary education, 175
substance use in, 357
transition to adulthood, 86–87
value of family to, 99
immigrant paradox, **226**, 338
impulsivity, 103, 164–165, 245, 360. *See also* self-regulation
inattention, 164–165, 360
independence, vs. autonomy, 237
indifferent parenting, **105**, 243

individuation, **240**
parenting practices and, 242, 243
process of, 241
indulgent parenting, **104**, 243
industrialization, 71–72, 153–154
infant attachment, 266–268
information-processing perspective, **45**–47
initiation ceremonies, **76**, 81–82
injuries, 188
inner cities. *See also* poor neighborhoods
education and schools in, 157–158, 161, 336
violent crime victimization in, 368
insecurity
of attachment, 266, 267
in interpersonal development, 265
Instagram, 202, 204
instrumental aggression, 150
intellectual development. *See* cognitive changes; intelligence
intelligence
beliefs about, and achievement, 327–328
brain development and, 57–59
culture and, 58–59
emotional, 254
environmental influences on, 58–59
ethnic and gender stereotypes of, 327
as fixed vs. malleable, 328, 339
genetic influences on, 109
individual differences in, 57–59
intelligence quotient (IQ), 58
intergenerational conflict, 10
intergenerational transmission of violence, **291**
internalizing disorders, **351**, 375–382. *See also* depression
causes of, 381–382
comorbidity of, 38, 351, 353
stress and, 377–378, 382, 383
treatment of, 382
internal working model, **260**
international comparisons. *See also* cultural differences
of academic achievement, 341
of age of sexual initiation, 297–298
of behavior problems, 353
of bullying rates, 145, 146
of pubertal timing, 23, 24
of religiosity, 259, 260
of secondary education enrollment, 153

of sex differences in self-esteem, 216
of teen childbearing, 315, 318
of teen pregnancy, 315
Internet addiction, **204**
Internet use. *See also* social media use
compulsive, 204
effects of, 195
for pornography, 196, 197, 198
prevalence and frequency of, 192–193
problematic, 204
interpersonal development
in adolescence, 265–266
attachment security and, 267, 268
Sullivan's theory of, 264–266, 281
interpersonal needs, 264–265
interpersonal therapy (IPT), **382**
intimacy, **7**, 262–292
as adolescent issue, 7, 263–264
attachment and, 266–269
changes in nature of friendship and, 269–270
cross-sex, 278–279, 281
display in friendships, 270–271
with extended family, 277
in friendships, 263, 265, 270–271
interpersonal development and, 264–266, 281
and LGBTQ youth, 285
in parent-adolescent relationship, 274–277
peers and, 274–277
and psychosocial development, 291–292
puberty and, 263–264
and romantic relationships, 281–283
sex differences in, 232, 272–274
sexuality and, 263, 265
social media use and, 271–272
social role transitions and, 70, 264
targets of, 274–278
theoretical perspectives on, 264–269
intrauterine devices (IUDs), 312
introspection, 43
intuition, 66
inventionists, **71**
IPT (interpersonal therapy), 382
IQ tests, 58, 336
irony, 44
IUDs (intrauterine devices), 312

J

jealousy, 270
Jewish adolescents, 217

jobs. *See* occupation; work
"jocks," 127, 131–132, 187
judicial bypass, **317**
junior high school, **159**. *See also* middle school
transition into, 159–160
justice system
criminal, 76
juvenile, 76
juvenile justice system, **76**
juvenile offending, **365**–366
adolescents' reports on, 370
female, 367–368
interventions for, 373, 374
juvenile justice system and, 76
progression to, 366
rates and trends in, 367
school infractions as, 170
selective and underreporting of, 370
street violence vs. school shootings, 369–370

K

KIPP, 157
kisspeptin, **16**

L

LARC (long-acting reversible contraception), 312
late adolescence, **4**
emotional autonomy in, 240, 241
ethnic identity in, 224
identity development in, 222
parental relationships in, 101, 275
peer group structure in, 129–130
political thinking in, 256, 257
romantic relationships in, 275, 283, 285, 286, 288
late bloomers, 287, 288
late maturation, 30–33, 282
Latinx adolescents. *See also* ethnic minority adolescents; immigrant adolescents; Mexican-American adolescents
and academic achievement, 157, 338, 340
and discrimination, 227, 228
eating disorders in, 36
and educational attainment, 340
ethnic identity in, 224
family structure of, 112
and gangs vs. "crews," 136
homeless, 118
obesity in, 34

parental relationships of, 100, 106
peer pressure susceptibility in, 248
poverty rates for, 112
quinceañera for, 79
religious involvement in, 260
and romantic relationships, 282
and school violence, 173
and self-esteem, 216
and sexual activity, 297
substance use in, 357
and suicide attempts, 379
teacher expectations of, 169–170
teen pregnancy in, 314
transition to college, 176
transition to secondary school, 161
in U.S. population, 87
laws
on abortion access, 317
adolescent thinking about, 61
on juvenile offending, 365
on sexting, 205–206
on substance use, 361, 363
learned helplessness, **327**
learning disabilities, **162**
students with, 162–164
learning theories, **10**
legal status
changes in, 76–78
decision-making abilities and, 245–246
inconsistencies in, 77–78, 81
leisure time/activities, 6, 185–191. *See also* electronic media use; extracurricular activities; sports
for adolescents, origin of, 180
and mood, 185–186
overview of, 180–181
participation patterns, 186
positive youth development programs, 190–191
screen time (*See* electronic media use)
self-care after school, 190
structured, 186–188
unstructured, 188–190
leptin, **16**, 24
lesbian and gay parents, 119
LGBTQ (lesbian, gay, bisexual, transgender, and questioning) youth, 229–231, **285**. *See also* homosexuality
gender-role behavior and, 229
homeless, 118
and identity, 229–230
and intimate relationships, 285

prejudice against, 230
transgender, 229, 230–231
victimization of, 168, 230, 231, 310–311
life-course-persistent offenders, **371–373**
light exposure, 16
"likes," and brain activity, 204
limbic system, **51**, 53–54
living arrangements
of adolescent parents, 319
of emerging adults, 85
living with parents
adolescent mothers and children, 319
attachment security and, 269
autonomy and, 237
in contemporary era, 84–85
in historical perspective, 82
and leaving home, 84–85
logical thinking, 66
loneliness, 275
long-acting reversible contraception (LARC), **312**
longitudinal study, **25**
long-term memory, **46**
low-achieving students
attribution and, 329
and dropping out, 343, 344
friends and, 334
as underachievers, 325
low-income families. *See* poor adolescents
low self-esteem
breakups and, 289
consequences of, 217–218
false-self behavior and, 211
in girls, 270
loyalty, in friendships, 269–270
lying
adolescents to parents, 97
parents to adolescents, 97

M

magnet schools, 166
Mahanoy Area School District v. Levy, 77–78
mainstreaming, **163**
marginality, of adolescents, 10
marijuana use. *See also* substance use
and brain development, 362–363
experimentation with, 356, 357, 358
as gateway, 357
prevalence and patterns of, 354, 355, 356–357
marital conflict, 114–115
between ex-spouses, 116

marriage
of adolescent mothers, 319, 320
age at, 70, 279–280
masculinity, 233–235, 274. *See also* gender-role behavior
mass media, 6. *See also* television
and body image, 19, 198–199
sexual content and messages in, 197–199
substance use in, 200–201
theories of influence of, 195–196
violence in, 199–200
mastery motivation, **326,** 328
masturbation, 20, 296
mathematics, 41–42, 157
maturation, early *versus* late, 30–33
maturational deviance hypothesis, 32
maturational imbalance theories, 9
maturity, in personality development, 212–213, 222
meanness, 141, 143. *See also* relational aggression
media. *See* mass media; television
media practice model, **196**
media use. *See* electronic media use; social media use
melatonin, **16,** 25, 27–28
memory, 46, 362
menarche, **22,** 23–24, 29–30
mental health
electronic media use and, 193, 194–195, 203
ethnic identity and, 225
obesity and, 34
of parents, 99
puberty and, 26
sexual activity and, 299–301
violence and, 92
mental health problems, 348–383. *See also* psychosocial problems; *specific types*
academic pressure and, 339
adolescence-onset, 26, 349–350
bullying and, 146–147
childhood-onset, 350
common factor underlying, 381
compulsive Internet use and, 204
co-occurrence of, 352
co-rumination and, 273, 378
in cyberbullying, 149, 150
differential susceptibility to, 109–110
discrimination and, 227, 228
divorce and, 114

early dating and, 287–288
in early-maturing girls, 31–33
and eating disorders, 35–39
in emerging adulthood, 74–76
and emotional autonomy, 242
false-self behavior and, 211–212
financial strain and, 117–118
gender-role nonconformity and, 233, 234
general principles of, 349–350
housing and, 92
as internalized distress, 38, 376
in LGBTQ youth, 230
marital conflict and, 115
at midlife, 98
parent-adolescent conflict and, 96
of parents, 99
prevalence and persistence of, 350
and rejection, 143–144, 289
and self-esteem, 214
in sexual abuse victims, 311
sexual activity and, 300
sibling relationships and, 108
social media and, 202–204, 376
in transgender adolescents, 231
as transitory, 349
victimization and, 146–147
mentalizing, **59**
mental states of others, understanding of, 56
mentoring, 88–89, 277
metacognition, **42**
methylphenidate (Ritalin), 165
Mexican-American adolescents. *See also* Latinx adolescents
academic achievement in, 332
ethnic identity in, 226
ethnicity of friends, 134
male, and intimacy, 274
parental relationships, 99, 332
and sexual activity, 297
middle adolescence, **4**
cliques in, 129, 133, 134
crowds in, 131
depression in, 376
ethnic identity in, 224
friendship changes in, 270
identity in, 222–223
parental relationships in, 100, 101, 275
peer group structure in, 129
peer pressure susceptibility in, 246, 247
popularity in, 141–142
romantic relationships in, 283, 285, 286
self-esteem in, 214
social responsibility in, 254

middle-class adolescents
    and academic achievement,
        336–337
    leisure activities of, 186
    and occupational choice, 346
    working, 184
middle school, **159**. *See also*
        secondary schools
    academic achievement
        trends, 340
    transition into, 159–160
    violence in, 173
midlife, 76, 98–99
midlife crisis, **98**
Millennials, 10, 123, 125
mind, theory of, **59**-60
minority adolescents. *See also*
        ethnic minority
        adolescents; *specific groups*
    and identity development, 224
    and self-esteem, 216–217
mixed-sex peer groups
    psychosocial effects of, 278
    transition to, 133–134
    transition to romantic
        relationships from, 283
mnemonic devices, 42, 47
molecular genetics, **108**
money management, 183
Monitoring the Future, **354**, 355
mood
    decline during adolescence,
        214, 376
    depressed, 375–376
    family and, 185
    hormones and, 26–27
    leisure activities and, 185–186
    in puberty, 26–27
    social media use and, 202–203
mood disorders, 375. *See also*
        depression
moral behavior, 252–253
moral development, 250–253
moral disengagement,
        145, **253**, 372
moral identity, 252
moral reasoning, 250–253
moratorium, psychosocial, 219,
        221, 222, 223
"morning after pill," 312
mothers
    adolescent, 318–320
    attachment to, 266
    de-idealization of, 240–241
    intimacy with, 266, 268, 275,
        276, 277
    midlife crisis in, 98
    relationship with, 29,
        102–103, 276
    as single parents, 112
    in talks about sex, 303
    "Tiger Mother," 106, 333

motivation
    and achievement, 325–326
    decline in transition to
        secondary school,
        159–160, 329–331
    in ethnic minority
        adolescents, 339
    leisure activities and, 185–186
    mastery vs. performance,
        326, 328
    and occupational choice, 346
movies, 197, 199
multidimensional model of racial
        identity, **227**-228
multidimensional thinking, 43–44
multiethnic, **228**
multiethnic adolescents, 228–229
multiethnic schools
    effects on students, 165–166
    peer groups in, 133
    violence in, 173
multisystemic family therapy, **374**
multitasking, 46
murder, 369–370
muscle, sex differences in, 18–19
music/music videos, 197, 200
myelination, **50**

N

National Assessment of
        Educational Progress
        (NAEP), **340**
National Runaway Safeline, 118
Native American adolescents
    and ethnic identity, 224
    poverty rates for, 112
    self-esteem in, 216
    substance use in, 357
    and suicide attempts, 379
    and transition to adulthood, 76
    in U.S. population, 87
negative emotionality, **353**
negative feedback seeking, 273
negative identity, **221**
neighborhoods, 89–93
    and academic achievement, 336
    affluent/middle-class, 90
    collective efficacy in, 91–92
    poor (*See* inner cities; poor
        neighborhoods)
    processes of influence,
        91–93
    resource access in, 93
    stressors in, 92
    and substance abuse risk, 361
    violence in, 92, 118, 368
"nerds," 131, 133
Neural Maturation Index, 52
neuroendocrine, **381**
neurons, **48**
neuroticism, 212. *See also* anxiety

neurotransmitters, **49**
new media, **191**. *See also*
        electronic media use;
        mass media
nicotine, 356, 358, 362
No Child Left Behind (NCLB)
        Act, 154–155
nonbinary gender identity, 229
noncognitive factors (in
        achievement), **324**-331
noncoital sexual activity, 296
non-college-bound adolescents,
        176–177
noncustodial parents, 117
nonshared environmental
        influences, **109**
non-suicidal self-injury
        (NSSI), **379**

O

Obama administration, 155–156
obesity, 34–35
    causes and consequences of,
        34–35
    electronic media use and, 195
    prevention and treatment of,
        35
    as puberty trigger, 16
observational learning, 10
occupation
    choice of, 346–347
    historical perspectives on, 84
    transition into, 83
occupational achievement,
        344–347
    influences on, 345–347
    occupational plans and,
        344–345
    work values and, 345–346
occupational attainment, **346**
occupational plateau, 98
openness, 212
oppositional-defiant disorder, **364**
optimism, in ethnic minority
        adolescents, 338–339
oral sex, 295, 296, 298
organismic theories, **9**-10
organization, in information
        processing, 47
ovaries, **15**
overt antisocial behavior, **366**
oxytocin, **378**

P

pandemic. *See* COVID-19
        pandemic
pansexual adolescents, 229
parent(s)/parenting
    and academic achievement,
        326, 332–333, 337

    and adolescence-limited
        offending, 374
    adolescents as, 318–320
    adolescents lying to, 97
    and antisocial behavior,
        371, 374
    and attachment security, 266,
        268, 269
    authoritarian (*See* authoritarian
        parenting)
    authoritative (*See* authoritative
        parenting)
    authority of, 58
    and behavioral autonomy,
        248–249
    conflict between parents,
        114–115
    consent for contraception, 313
    and contraceptive behavior, 313
    criticism by, 56, 325
    de-idealization of, 240–241
    divorce of (*See* divorce)
    electronic media use of, 195
    and emotional autonomy,
        241–243
    ethnic/cultural differences
        in, 106
    ethnic socialization, 225–226
    financial strain and, 99
    and friendships, 137
    good, basic principles of, 105
    harsh or neglectful, 92, 143
    and identity, 221, 222
    importance of, 241
    indifferent, 105, 243
    indulgent, 104, 243
    lesbian and gay, 119
    living with (*See* living
        with parents)
    lying to adolescents, 97
    mental health of, 99
    at midlife, 98–99
    and moral and prosocial
        development, 253
    noncustodial, 117
    and occupational choice, 346
    in poverty, 92, 112–113,
        117–118, 190
    psychological control in, 96, 242
    remarriage of, 112, 116–117
    school involvement by, 170,
        173, 332, 337
    and self-care after school, 190
    and self-esteem, 217
    separation from, 79
    and sexual activity, 302–304
    and sibling difference, 110–111
    styles of, 104–107
    and substance abuse risk, 360
    "survival guides" for, 12, 95
    susceptibility to influence
        of, 246

transition into role of, 83
and transition to secondary school, 161
parent-adolescent communication
about ethnic discrimination, 226
about sex, 302–303
parent-adolescent conflict, 95–97, 239
and early sexual activity, 302
fact vs. fiction about, 95, 96
in immigrant families, 99–100
vs. peer conflict, 276
puberty and, 25, 29, 100–102
parent-adolescent relationship
with adolescent mother, 319
adolescent thinking about, 60
attachment in, 268–269
in authoritative parenting, 105–107
balance of power in, 100
changes in adolescent years, 95–103
and chronic antisocial behavior, 371–372
detachment and, 239–240
distance in, 29
in and after divorce, 113–116
in early vs. late adolescence, 100–101
expectations and, 12, 332
and friend choice, 137
in immigrant families, 99–100
importance of, 241, 276, 277
in individuation process, 240
influence on adolescents, 103–108
and intimacy, 274–277
with LGBTQ youth, 230
marital conflict and, 115
midlife and, 98–99
parenting styles and, 104–107
and peer pressure susceptibility, 248–249
psychological control in, 96
puberty and, 25, 29, 100–102
sex differences in, 102–103
and sibling relationship, 107–108
in single-parent families, 111–112
supportive, 276–277
parental demandingness, **104**
parental monitoring
and adolescence-limited offending, 374
adolescents' reactions to, 243
in divorced homes, 115
effective, 107
of electronic media use, 150
in poor neighborhoods, 118
in self-care after school, 190
and sexual activity, 303–304

parental responsiveness, **104**
parochial schools, 166
PATHS (Promoting Alternative Thinking Strategies), 145
peer conflict, 270
peer exclusion. *See also* rejection
adolescent thinking about, 60
peer groups, 6, 121–151. *See also* cliques; crowds; peer relationships
and academic achievement, 135, 173, 334–335
antisocial, 136
and antisocial behavior, 136–137, 138, 374
bullying and victimization by (*See* bullying; victimization)
changes in adolescence, 126–127
in contemporary society, 122–126
"crews," 136
definition of, 122
ethnic segregation in, 134–135
and ethnic socialization, 225–226
ethnographic study of, 141
and extracurricular activities, 188, 189, 190
gangs, 136
importance in adolescence, 99
industrialization and, 123
map of, 131
mixed-sex, transition to, 133–134
nature of, 126–131
need for, 123–126
parents' role in choice of, 137
in poor neighborhoods, 92
popularity in, 139–151
rejection in, 139–151
relational aggression (meanness) in, 143–145
romantic relationships and, 129–130
selection vs. socialization in, 137–139
and sexual activity, 304–305
socialization by, 126
and student engagement, 173
and substance use, 360–361
time spent with, 122, 126–127
unstructured leisure time with, 189, 190
peer pressure
and antisocial behavior, 246–247, 374
brain development and, 55
crowds and, 132
and gender-role behavior, 232–233
and risk taking, 64–65, 247

and sexual activity, 304–305
susceptibility to, 246–249
peer rejection. *See* rejection
peer relationships. *See also* friendship(s); peer groups; romantic relationships
adolescent thinking about, 60
attachment security and, 267
changes in middle adolescence, 129
conflict in, 276
discrimination in, 227
early maturation and, 30–33
importance in adolescence, 99, 276, 277
and intimacy, 274–277
parent-adolescent relationship and, 276
puberty and, 25
and self-esteem, 217
and sibling relationships, 107
supportive, 276–277
peer victimization. *See* victimization
penis development, 20
perceived popularity, **139**
performance, 340–341.
See also achievement
school, 336
performance motivation, **326,** 328
permissive parenting. *See* indifferent parenting; indulgent parenting
personal fable, **43**
personality
dimensions of, 212–213
five-factor model of, 212
stability of, 212, 213
pessimism, discrimination and, 338–339
pheromones, **23**
physical appearance
media messages on, 19, 198–199
and self-esteem, 215, 216
and sexual attractiveness, 301–302
physical self-esteem, 215, 216
Piagetian theory of cognitive development, 9–10, 44–45
PISA results, 342
pituitary gland, **15**
"Plan B" (emergency contraception), 312
plasticity, **26, 50**–51, 362
platonic relationships, **265,** 279
political behavior, 257–258
political thinking, 255, 256–258
poor adolescents. *See also* socioeconomic status (SES)
and academic achievement, 333, 337

in affluent/middle-class neighborhoods, 89–90, 336
and antisocial behavior/ delinquency, 371
and dropping out, 343
and gangs, 136
lack of psychosocial moratorium for, 219
neighborhood influences on, 89–93
and No Child Left Behind, 154–155
parenting and, 92, 112–113, 117–118, 190
and sexual activity, 91, 304, 305
statistics on, 112
stressors of, 92
substance use by, 363
teacher expectations of, 169
and teen pregnancy and childbearing, 91, 318, 319
tracking and, 161
transition to adulthood, 86–88
transition to secondary school, 161
violence and, 92, 118, 368
and work, 184
poor neighborhoods, 89–93.
See also poor adolescents
collective efficacy in, 91–92
early and risky sexual activity in, 304, 305
education and schools in, 157–158, 161
home environments in, 92
resource access in, 93
stressors in, 92
violence in, 92, 118
popularity, 139–151
and academic achievement, 140
and aggression, 140–141
cyberbullying and, 149–151
determinants of, 139–142
dynamics of, 141–142
in early-maturing girls, 32
and meanness (relational aggression), 143–145
perceived, 139
social media and, 203
sociometric, 139
thinness and, 37
and unpopular adolescents, 144, 145
population. *See also* adolescent population
U.S., ethnic composition of, 87
pornography, Internet, 196, 197, 198
positive risk taking, **54**

positive youth development, **190**
    programs for, 190–191
possibilities, thinking about,
    41–42
possible selves, **209**
postconventional moral
    reasoning, **251**, 252
postfigurative cultures, **126**
postsecondary education,
    175–177. *See also*
    college students
    encouragement for all students,
        176–177
    enrollment and graduation
        rates, 175–176
    historical background of, 175
    and identity development, 223
    transition to, 176
poverty. *See also* poor
    adolescents; poor
    neighborhoods
    and brain development,
        87–88
    chronic, 117–118
    and families, 92, 112–113,
        117–118
    neighborhood influences in,
        90–91
    and parenting, 92, 113
    prevalence of, 112
    stressors of, 88
    and teen pregnancy and
        parenthood, 91
    and violence, 92
power imbalance, 100
precocity, 295, 297
preconventional moral reasoning,
    251, 252
prefigurative cultures, **126**
prefrontal cortex, **51**, 52, 54, 362
pregnancy. *See* teen pregnancy
preoccupied adolescents, 268
preoperational period, **44**
prescription drug abuse, 355
primary control strategies, **383**
principled moral reasoning, 251
principled thinking, 256–257
private schools, 166
proactive aggression, **141**
problem behavior. *See* behavior
    problems
problem behavior syndrome, **352**
Project DARE, 363
promiscuity, 295, 297
prosocial behavior, 52, 54, 99,
    250, 254
prosocial games, 199
prosocial reasoning, 253–256
protective factors, **361**
pseudomaturity, 287
psychological control, 96, **242**
psychopaths, **364–365**

psychosocial development, **7**
    intimacy and, 291–292
    issues of, 7–8
    puberty and, 25–33
    social redefinition and, 69–70
psychosocial moratorium, **219**,
    221, 222, 223
psychosocial problems, 8,
    348–383. *See also*
    behavior problems;
    mental health problems;
    specific types
    in affluent adolescents, 90
    childhood-onset, 350
    of children of adolescent
        mothers, 319
    in divorce, 114
    of gang members, 136
    general principles on, 349–350
    in LGBT youth, 230
    nature and covariation of,
        351–353
    peer groups/relationships
        and, 151
    rejection and, 143–144
    in sexual abuse victims, 311
    sexual activity and, 300
    stress and, 383
    in teen pregnancy, 316
    transitory, 349
    in victimization, 146–147
pubertal timing, 22–25
    age of menarche, 23–24
    influences on, 16, 22–25
    and psychological
        development, 25
    psychosocial impacts of, 30–33
    secular trend in, 23–24
    variations in, 22
puberty, **4**, 13–39. *See also*
    hormones
    and achievement, 324
    adolescent growth spurt in,
        17–19
    adolescents' reactions to, 29–30
    and behavior, 16–17, 25–33
    and depression, 26–27, 382
    and emotional autonomy,
        238, 241
    endocrine system and, 14–15
    and family relationships, 25,
        29, 100–102
    hormonal influence in, 16–17,
        301–302
    and identity, 209
    immediate impacts of, 26–29
    and intimacy, 263–264
    overview of, 4–5, 14–17
    peer relationships in, 25
    physical manifestations of, 14
    psychosocial impacts of, 25–33
    and self-esteem, 26

and sexuality/sexual activity,
    294–295
    sexual maturation in, 19–22
    sleep patterns in, 27–29
    somatic development in, 17–22
    as start of adolescence, 70–71
    tempo of, 22–25
    timing of onset (*See* pubertal
        timing)
    triggers of, 16
pubic hair, 20, 21
punishment, 10

Q

quinceañera, **79**

R

"Race to the Top" policy, 156
racial discrimination. *See* ethnic
    discrimination
racial socialization. *See* ethnic
    socialization
rape, 311
    date, 288, 309, 310
    statutory, 70
reactive aggression, **141**
reading, 157, 193
reaffiliation motive, **275**
rebellion, 96–97
recapitulation, theory of, 8–9
reference groups, **132**
reinforcement, 10, 132–133
rejection, 139–151. *See also*
    victimization
    brain activity in, 144, 267
    consequences of, 142, 143–145
    determinants of, 139–142
    insecure attachment and, 267
    negative feedback seeking
        and, 273
    peer, adolescent thinking
        about, 60
rejection sensitivity, 144, **260**,
    267, 270, 275, 289
relational aggression (meanness),
    143–145
relativism, 44
religiosity, 258–261
    and community service, 255
    definition of, 260
    and sexual activity, 300, 313
remarriage of parents, 112, 116–117
reminiscence bump, **46**, 223
resilience, 212, 213, **383**
response inhibition, **52**
responsibility
    after-school programs and, 191
    and agency, 222
    work and, 183

reverse causation, **196**
reward sensitivity
    brain development and, 53–54
    and decision-making abilities,
        244–245
    to "likes," 204
    and risk taking, 63
    substance use and, 362
rights, adolescent thinking
    about, 61
risk factors, **297**
risk taking
    brain development and, 53–54,
        62–67
    during COVID-19 pandemic, 2
    moral reasoning and, 253
    peer pressure and, 64–65, 247
    positive, 54
    reducing, 66–67
    sexting as, 205
risky sex, 311–321. *See also* teen
    pregnancy
    contraception and, 311–314
    parental communication about
        sex and, 303
    peer influence on, 304
    predictors of, 299
    sex education and, 320–321
    and STDs, 314
    virginity pledges and, 305
Ritalin (methylphenidate), 165
rite of passage, **5**
role experimentation, 219
romantic relationships, 279–291
    age of onset, 282, 287
    attachment in, 281, 283
    breakups of, 281, 289
    conflict in, 283, 291
    contextual factors in, 282
    dating patterns, 282–283
    decline in dating, 280, 281
    development of, 283–286
    early starters, 287–288
    emotional impacts of, 287–291
    historical perspective on,
        280–281
    and intimacy, 281–283
    late bloomers, 287, 288
    nature and significance of,
        281–282
    overview of, 279–281
    partner preferences in,
        285–286
    and peer group structure,
        129–130
    phases of, 284–285
    psychosocial impacts of, 288
    reasons for dating, 283–284
    same-sex, 285
    sex differences in, 285–286
    sexual pressure in, 288
    social media use and, 289

transition to, 283
violence in, 289–291
Roper v. Simmons, 77
routine activity theory, **188**–189

S

Safe Dates program, 310
same-sex attraction, 230,
    308–309. *See also*
    homosexuality
same-sex friendships
    in early adolescence, 278
    and intimacy, 274, 278, 279
    transition to mixed-sex groups,
        133–134
sandwich generation, 99
sarcasm, 43–44
scaffolding, **59**
scarification, **80**
Scholastic Assessment Test
    (SAT) scores, 329, 340
school(s), 6, 152–178. *See also*
    middle school; secondary
    schools
    age grading in, 122, 123, 133, 159
    during COVID-19 pandemic,
        2, 61
    discrimination in, 227, 228
    friends influencing attitude
        toward, 135
    starting time in, 28
    unhealthy foods in, 35
school attachment
    and ethnic composition of
        school, 165–166
    extracurricular activities and,
        187–188
    and location of school, 165
    and school violence, 174
school choice, 156–157, 166
school engagement. *See* student
    engagement
school environment. *See also*
    classroom climate
    and academic achievement, 331
    and dropping out, 344
    transition to secondary school
        and, 160
school performance, **336**.
    See also academic
    achievement
school reform. *See* education
    policy
school shootings, 174, 369–370
schools within schools, **158**
school violence, 173–174.
    See also bullying
school vouchers, 156, 157,
    166–167
sciences, 157
scrotum development, 20

secondary control strategies, **383**
secondary education, **153**
    age groupings in, 159
    alternative types of, 156–157
    comprehensive, 154
    dropping out of, 157
    enrollment proportions, 153
    historical background of,
        153–154
    in inner cities, 157–158
    No Child Left Behind and,
        154–156
    policies and reforms, 154–157
    school choice in, 156–157, 166
    time spent in, 153
secondary schools. *See also*
    middle school
    ability grouping in, 161–165
    and adolescent mothers,
        319, 320
    age groupings/grade
        configurations, 159
    alternatives to public, 156–157,
        166–167
    and bullying, 145
    classroom climate (*See*
        classroom climate)
    class size in, 159
    community service required by,
        255–256
    contraceptive use encouraged
        by, 313–314
    dropping out of, 157, 184,
        341–344
    elementary schools compared
        to, 160
    ethnic composition and,
        165–166
    good, characteristics of,
        177–178
    graduation rates, 343
    historical background, 153–154
    inner-city, 157–158, 161
    large vs. small, 158–159
    multiethnic (*See* multiethnic
        schools)
    and non-college-bound
        students, 176–177
    peer groups in (*See* peer
        groups)
    sexual harassment in, 310
    social organization of, 158–167
    student attachment to,
        165–166
    student engagement in
        (*See* student engagement)
    time spent in, 153
    tracking in, 161–165
    transition into, 159–160,
        329–331
    transition to college from, 176
secondary sex characteristics,
    19–22, 294

secular trend, **23**–24
secure attachment, **260**
security. *See also* insecurity
    of attachment, 266, 268, 269
    as need in interpersonal
        development, 264, 265
selective attention, **45**
selective serotonin reuptake
    inhibitors (SSRIs), **382**
self-care, after school, 190
self-conception(s), **210**
    differentiation of, 210–211
    false-self behavior and, 211–212
    organization and integration
        of, 211
    social media use and, 203
self-consciousness, **214**
self-control. *See* self-regulation
self-efficacy, **328**
self-esteem, **210**, 213–218
    breakups and, 289
    components of, 215
    crowd membership and, 132
    early maturation and, 31, 32
    ethnic differences in, 216–217
    ethnic identity and, 225
    extracurricular activities
        and, 187
    false-self behavior and, 211
    in girls, 215–216
    high, 217–218
    influences on, 217
    low (*See* low self-esteem)
    physical appearance and,
        215, 216
    puberty and, 26
    rejection and, 144
    relationship quality and,
        288, 289
    romantic relationships and,
        268, 288, 289
    and self-image, 214
    sex differences in, 215–216
    sexual activity and, 299
    social, 215
    stability of, 213–215
    and substance use, 363
    transition to secondary school
        and, 160
self-evaluations, 214
self-fulfilling prophecy, **95**, **169**
self-handicapping, 325–**326**
"selfies," 214
self-image, 25, 26, 214
self-image stability, **214**
self-injury, non-suicidal
    (NSSI), **379**
self-regulation
    and alcohol use, 362
    brain development and, 9, 52–53
    in chronic antisocial
        behavior, 372

improvements in, and decision-
    making abilities, 244–245
and peer pressure
    susceptibility, 248
and pubertal timing, 25
sensation seeking, **63**
    and antisocial behavior/
        delinquency, 373
    brain development and,
        63–64
    pubertal timing and, 25
    and substance abuse risk, 360
sensitivity
    rejection, 144
    reward (*See* reward sensitivity)
sensorimotor period, **44**
serotonin, **53**
service learning, **255**–256
set point, **15**
Seventeen magazine, 73
sex differences. *See also*
    boys; girls
    in achievement self-
        handicapping, 326
    in aggression, 232, 365
    in antisocial behavior/
        delinquency, 367
    in brain development, 48
    in cross-ethnic friendships, 165
    in cyberbullying, 150
    in depression, 377–378
    emphasis on, in social
        redefinition, 79
    in friendships, 270
    in gender-role nonconformity,
        232–233, 234
    in height, 18
    in intelligence beliefs, 327
    in intimacy, 232, 272–274,
        281–282
    in juvenile offending, 367
    in leisure activities, 180
    in maturity, 212–213, 222
    in meaning of sex, 305–307
    in muscle-to-fat ratio, 18–19
    in parent-adolescent
        relationship, 102–103
    in peer pressure susceptibility,
        246, 248
    physical, 231
    in prosocial reasoning and
        behavior, 254
    in psychosocial problems,
        351, 378
    in religiosity, 260
    in romantic relationships,
        285–286
    in self-esteem, 215–216
    in sexual activity, 296,
        297–298
    in substance use, 354
    in time spent with peers, 127

sex drive, 294
sex education, 320–321
    abstinence-only, 321
    comprehensive, 321
    timing of, 298
sex hormones, 15, 301, 302
sex roles. *See* gender-role behavior
sex segregation
    in cliques, 133–134
    in early adolescent
        friendships, 278
    in social redefinition
        processes, 79
sexting, **204**–206
"sextortion," 205
sexual abstention
    traits of abstainers, 300
    virginity pledges and, 305
sexual abuse, 311. *See also* rape
    of homeless adolescents, 118
sexual activity, 295–311
    abstention from, 300, 305
    casual, 299
    contextual factors in, 302
    and contraception use, 311–314
    and depression, 300
    early (*See* early sexual activity)
    first intercourse, 297–298,
        306–307
    hormonal influences on,
        301–302
    household composition and,
        303–304
    intercourse prevalence,
        296–297
    involuntary/unwanted, 288,
        298, 310, 311
    meaning of, sex differences in,
        305–307
    and mental health, 299–301
    noncoital, 296
    oral sex, 295, 296, 298
    parental communication about,
        302–303
    parental influence on,
        302–304
    peers and, 304–305
    pressure for, 288
    promiscuous, 295, 297
    research topics on, 294
    risky (*See* risky sex)
    same-sex, 308–309
    sex education and, 320–321
    sexting and, 204, 205
    sexual media content and, 198
    social role transitions and,
        70, 295
    spread of, 304
    stages of, 295–296
    substance use and, 299
    trends in, 298–299
    virginity pledges and, 305

sexual assault, 311. *See also* rape
sexual attraction, 294, 308
    same-sex, 308–309
sexual harassment, 310
    of early-maturing girls, 310
    in sexting, 205
sexual intercourse, 296–299.
        See also sexual activity
    first, 297–298, 306–307
    involuntary, 298, 311
    prevalence of, 296–297
    progression toward, 296
    trends in, 298–299
sexuality, **7**, 293–321. *See also*
        homosexuality; sexual
        activity
    as adolescent issue, 7–8,
        294–295
    in adolescents, adult attitudes
        toward, 294
    emergence of, 301–302
    and intimacy, 263, 265
sexually transmitted diseases
        (STDs), **314**
sexual maturation, 19–22.
        See also puberty
sexual media content,
        197–199
sexual-minority youth, **285**,
        310–311. *See also*
        LGBTQ youth
sexual objectification,
        in media, 198
sexual orientation, **229**, 308–309
    development of, 229–230, 309
    fluidity of, 229, 308
    and gender identity and gender-
        role behavior, 229–230
sexual socialization, **306**
shared environmental
        influences, **108**
sibling rivalry, **111**
siblings
    differences in, 110–111
    relationships with,
        107–108, 277
    and sexual activity, 304
single-parent families
    and early sexual activity,
        303–304
    parent-adolescent relationships
        in, 111–112
    and race and poverty, 112
    social support for children
        in, 114
    statistics on, 112
    violent crime victimization
        and, 368
sleep, 16, 27–29, 35, 194–195
sleeper effects, of divorce, 115
smartphone use, 192, 202.
        See also social media;
        text messaging

smoking. *See also* substance use
    consequences of, 358, 359–360
    dependence risk, 358
    as gateway, 357
    in mass media, 200–201
    prevalence and patterns of,
        354, 355, 356
    prevention measures, 201, 363
    reducing, 67
    risk factors for, 360, 361, 362
Snapchat, 202
social brain, 54–56
social capital, **167**, 333–334
social class. *See* socioeconomic
        status (SES)
social cognition, **59**–61
social competence
    attachment security and, 269
    cross-sex friendships and, 279
    interventions for, 145
    rejection and, 144
    social media use and, 271–272
    in unpopular adolescents, 144
social-competence training
        programs, 363
social context. *See also*
        environmental influences;
        social role changes;
        socioeconomic status
        (SES)
    and adolescent thinking, 60
    and identity, 218–220
    and occupational choice, 346
    and political thinking, 257
social control theory, **352**
social conventions, **60**–61
social distancing guidelines, 2
social exclusion. *See* rejection
social invention, adolescence as,
        11, 71–73
socialization
    ethnic, 225–226
    by family vs. peers, 126
    into gender-role behavior,
        232–233
    vs. selection, by peers,
        137–139
    and sex differences in
        intimacy, 274
    sexual, 306
socializing
    and academic achievement, 335
    on social media, 202–204
social learning theory, 10
social media use, 6, 201–206
    and body image, 198–199
    brain activity from "likes," 204
    compulsive, 202–203, 204
    cyberbullying, 149–151
    and depression, 202–204, 376
    and friendships, 202, 203,
        271–272

    and intimacy, 271–272
    problematic, 204
    reasons for, 201
    and romantic relationships, 289
    and self-esteem, 216
    sexting in, 204–206
    and socializing, 202–204
social networks. *See* peer groups
social promotion, **155**, **344**
social redefinition, **69**
social redefinition (transition to
        adulthood), 68–93
    adolescence as social invention
        and, 71–73
    adolescents' views of, 81
    boundaries of adolescence in,
        76–78
    in contemporary society,
        80–81, 83, 86–89
    elongation of adolescence and,
        70–71, 86
    emerging adulthood and,
        73–76
    in historic perspective,
        82–83, 84
    legal status changes in,
        76–78
    methods of easing problems of,
        88–89
    for minority adolescents,
        86–87
    neighborhood influences on,
        89–93
    overview of, 69–70
    for poor adolescents, 86–88
    process and practices of,
        78–80
    and religiosity, 260
    in traditional cultures, 81–82,
        83–84
    variations in, 80–85
social relationships. *See also*
        specific types
    and self-esteem, 217
social role changes, 68–93.
        See also social context;
        social redefinition
    and achievement, 69, 324
    and autonomy, 69, 238–239
    gender-based (*See* gender-role
        behavior)
    and identity, 69, 210,
        218–220
    and intimacy, 70, 264
    as marker of adulthood,
        80–81
    overview of, 5
    role experimentation and, 219
    and sexuality, 70, 295
social self-esteem, 215
social skills. *See* social
        competence
social status, subjective, **88**, 90

social support, **276**
  for adolescent mothers, 320
  adolescents' preferences for, 276–277
  for children in single-parent families, 114
  failure to seek, in low self-esteem, 217
  at school, importance of, 161
social transitions. *See* social redefinition; social role changes
societal changes
  and age segregation, 122
  and family life, 111–113
  speed of, 126
  and transition to adulthood, 86
society, adolescent thinking about, 61
socioeconomic status (SES). *See also* affluent adolescents; poor adolescents; poverty
  and academic achievement, 88, 333, 336–337
  and dropping out, 343
  and extracurricular activities, 186
  and obesity, 34
  and occupational choice, 346
  and political thinking, 257
  and sexual activity, 297
  and stress, 88, 92
  and substance use, 363
  and teen childbearing and parenthood, 91, 318, 319
  and tracking, 161
  and transition to adulthood, 86–87
sociological theories, **10**
sociometric popularity, **139**
somatic development, 17–22
  adolescent growth spurt, 17–19
  sexual maturation, 19–22
South Park (TV program), 43–44
speed of information processing, 46–47
"spillover effect," 187
spirituality, **260**
sports
  and cross-ethnic friendships, 165
  impact of, 187–188
  participation patterns, 186
  school size and, 158
spurious causation, **196**
SSRIs (selective serotonin reuptake inhibitors), 382
stability, self-image, 214
standardized testing, 155, 336
standards-based reform, **156**–157
status offense, **76, 365**
statutory rape, **70**

STDs (sexually transmitted diseases), 314
stepfamilies, 112, 116–117
stepfathers, 23
stereotypes
  of adolescents, 11–12, 95, 96
  in crowds, 128, 129
  of intelligence, 327
  of juvenile offenders, 370
stereotype threat, **327**
stimulant medications, 165
"storm and stress" period, 8, 12, 27, 213, 237
street violence, 92, 369
stress
  consequences of, 383
  coping strategies, 383
  and depression, 377–378, 382
  in divorce, 114
  and genetic susceptibility to mental health problems, 109–110
  in immigrant families, 99–100
  and mood, 376
  peer rejection and, 142
  in poor adolescents/neighborhoods, 92
  and pubertal timing, 23
  puberty and, 26
  reactivity, 15
  resilience to, 383
  socioeconomic status and, 88, 92
  vulnerability to, 15, 26
  work and, 183, 184
stress hormones, 15
student achievement. *See* academic achievement
student engagement, **171**
  bullying and, 147
  decline in transition to secondary school, 159–160, 329–331
  forms of, 171
  importance of, 170–173
  lack of, 171–173
  outside influences on, 173
  school size and, 158
  school transitions and, 159
subjective social status, **88, 90**
substance abuse, **351,** 353–363
  comorbidity with other problems, 351
  predictors and consequences of, 359–360
  prevention and treatment of, 363
  protective factors against, 361
  risk factors for, 360–361
substance use, 353–363. *See also* alcohol use; smoking
  by affluent adolescents, 90

  age of onset, 357, 358
  and brain development, 51, 361–363
  causes and consequences of, 358–361
  developmental trajectories of, 357–358
  early maturation and, 30, 31, 33
  experimentation with, 356, 357, 358
  friends/peer groups and, 138
  groups by usage pattern, 358–359
  heightened effects on adolescents, 362
  in media, 200–201
  messages about, 353
  prevalence and patterns of, 354–358
  prevention measures, 201, 363
  problematic (*See* substance abuse)
  and sexual activity, 299
  stress and, 383
  as transitory problem, 349, 350
  work and, 184
substance use disorder, 360
success. *See also* achievement
  attributions for, 329
  beliefs about, 326–327
  of immigrants, 338
suicidal ideation, **378**
  in transgender adolescents, 231
suicide, 378–381
suicide attempts, 378, 379
suicide contagion, **380**–381
Sullivan's theory of interpersonal development, 264–266, 281
"survival guides," 12, 95
"survival sex," 118
susceptibility to influence, changes in, 246–249
synapses, **49**
synaptic pruning, **49**–50

T

Tanner stages, **19**
teachers
  ability grouping by, 162
  authority of, 58
  and classroom climate, 168–170
  discrimination by, 228
  evaluation of, 156
  expectations of, 168–170
  in good secondary schools, 177–178

  middle and junior high school, beliefs of, 160
  performance orientation of, 326, 328, 330
  sexual harassment by, 310
  violence against, 173
teenager, **72**
teen pregnancy, 314–320. *See also* adolescent parenthood
  and abortion, 315–317
  causes of, 317–318
  contraceptive use and, 312, 313
  fathers in, 320
  poverty and, 91, 318
  rate of, 315–316
  sex education and, 321
  virginity pledges and, 305
television. *See also* mass media
  sexual content on, 197
  substance use on, 353
  viewing habits, 193
  violence on, 199, 200
testes, **15,** 20
testing, standardized, 155, 336
testosterone, 17, 27, 64, **301**
text messaging
  extent of, 192
  impacts of, 194
  sexting, 204–206
theory of mind, **59**–60
thinking. *See also* adolescent thinking
  critical, 155
  hypothetical, 42
  about thinking, 42–43
thinness
  cultural preference for, 32, 33, 36
  ideal of, in eating disorders, 38
  mass media on, 19, 36
  and popularity, 37
13 Reasons Why (Netflix series), 381
"Tiger Mother" parent, 106, 333
tracking, **161**–165
  and students at the extremes, 162–164
traditional cultures. *See also* cultural differences
  family's importance in, 99, 123
  social redefinition in, 81–82, 83–84
transgender, 229, **230**
transgender adolescents, 230–231
transition to adulthood. *See* social redefinition
trichomoniasis, **314**
Trump administration, 156, 166

U

unconventionality, 352
underachievers, **325**
unpopular adolescents, 144, 145
uses and gratifications
    approach, **196**

V

values
    familistic, 99, 253
    in moral reasoning, 252
    of parents, and academic
        achievement, 332
    and risk taking, 63
    in talks about sex, 303
    work, 345–346
vaping, 354, 355, 356, 357
victimization, 146–149. *See also*
        bullying
    cycle of, 144–145
    in dating violence, 289–290
    effects of, 146–147
    gender-role nonconformity and,
        233, 234
    of LGBTQ youth, 168, 230,
        231, 310
    rates and trends, 145, 146
    school size and, 158
    in school violence, 173, 174
    in sexting, 205
    sexual, 310–311
    in violent crime, 368–369

video games/gaming
    impacts of, 199, 200
    violence in, 199–200
violence. *See also* aggression;
        antisocial behavior
    and antisocial peer
        groups, 136
    dating, 289–291
    effects of exposure to, 92
    in girls, 367–368
    intergenerational transmission
        of, 291
    in media, 199–200
    in poor neighborhoods,
        92, 118, 368
    progression to, 366
    in schools, 173–174
    on television, 199, 200
    in video games, 199–200
virginity pledges, 305
voice changes, 20, 24
volunteering, 190–191,
        254–256
vouchers, 156, **157**, 166–167

W

Wechsler Adult Intelligence
        Scale (WAIS-III), 58
Wechsler Intelligence Scale for
        Children (WISC-IV), 58
weight gain, 18–19.
        See also obesity
weight loss efforts, 35, 198

White adolescents. *See also*
        ethnic differences
    academic achievement in, 157
    behavioral autonomy and, 249
    body dissatisfaction in,
        31–32
    cross-ethnic friendships of, 166
    and educational
        attainment, 340
    ethnic identity in, 224
    ethnicity of friends, 133
    in poverty, 88
    and school violence, 173
    self-esteem in, 216
    and sexual activity, 297
    substance use in, 357
    and suicide attempts, 379
    teacher expectations of, 170
    teen pregnancy in, 314
    tracking and, 161
    in U.S. population, 87
white matter, 50
withdrawal (contraceptive
        method), 311
withdrawnness, 144
women
    college enrollment of, 175
    objectification in media,
        197, 198
work
    in adult life (*See* occupation)
    after-school, 6, 181–185
    and academic
        achievement, 173

historical perspectives on,
        180, 181
    impact of, 182–185
    recent trends in, 181–182
working memory, **46**
work values, **345**–346

Y

Yerkes-Dodson law, **325**
YMCA, 190
young adulthood
    autonomy issues in,
        237–238, 240
    without college degree,
        176–177
    historical perspectives on, 73,
        82–83, 84
    identity development in,
        222–223
    living with parents in, 82, 85
    occupational development
        in, 345
    psychological well-being in,
        74–76
    social redefinition in, 78
    transition to (*See* social
        redefinition)
youth, **73**

Z

zero tolerance, **174**
zone of proximal development, **59**